Nineteenth-Century Literature Criticism

Topics Volume

Guide to Gale Literary Criticism Series

For criticism on	Consult these Gale series
Authors now living or who died after December 31, 1999	*CONTEMPORARY LITERARY CRITICISM (CLC)*
Authors who died between 1900 and 1999	*TWENTIETH-CENTURY LITERARY CRITICISM (TCLC)*
Authors who died between 1800 and 1899	*NINETEENTH-CENTURY LITERATURE CRITICISM (NCLC)*
Authors who died between 1400 and 1799	*LITERATURE CRITICISM FROM 1400 TO 1800 (LC)* *SHAKESPEAREAN CRITICISM (SC)*
Authors who died before 1400	*CLASSICAL AND MEDIEVAL LITERATURE CRITICISM (CMLC)*
Authors of books for children and young adults	*CHILDREN'S LITERATURE REVIEW (CLR)*
Dramatists	*DRAMA CRITICISM (DC)*
Poets	*POETRY CRITICISM (PC)*
Short story writers	*SHORT STORY CRITICISM (SSC)*
Black writers of the past two hundred years	*BLACK LITERATURE CRITICISM (BLC)* *BLACK LITERATURE CRITICISM SUPPLEMENT (BLCS)*
Hispanic writers of the late nineteenth and twentieth centuries	*HISPANIC LITERATURE CRITICISM (HLC)* *HISPANIC LITERATURE CRITICISM SUPPLEMENT (HLCS)*
Native North American writers and orators of the eighteenth, nineteenth, and twentieth centuries	*NATIVE NORTH AMERICAN LITERATURE (NNAL)*
Major authors from the Renaissance to the present	*WORLD LITERATURE CRITICISM, 1500 TO THE PRESENT (WLC)* *WORLD LITERATURE CRITICISM SUPPLEMENT (WLCS)*

ISSN 0732-1864

Volume 84

Nineteenth-Century Literature Criticism

Topics Volume

Excerpts from Criticism of Various
Topics in Nineteenth-Century Literature,
including Literary and Critical Movements,
Prominent Themes and Genres, Anniversary
Celebrations, and Surveys of National Literatures

Suzanne Dewsbury
Editor

Detroit
New York
San Francisco
London
Boston
Woodbridge, CT

STAFF

Janet Witalec, Lynn M. Spampinato, *Managing Editors, Literature Product*
Suzanne Dewsbury, *Editor*
Mark W. Scott, *Publisher, Literature Product*

Gianna Barberi, *Associate Editor*
Patti A. Tippett, Timothy J. White, *Technical Training Specialists*
Kathleen Lopez Nolan, *Managing Editor*
Susan M. Trosky, *Content Director*

Maria L. Franklin, *Permissions Manager*
Edna Hedblad, Kimberly F. Smilay, *Permissions Specialists*
Erin Bealmear, Sandy Gore, Keryl Stanley, *Permissions Assistants*

Victoria B. Cariappa, *Research Manager*
Tracie A. Richardson *Project Coordinator*
Andrew Guy Malonis, Barbara McNeil, Gary J. Oudersluys, Maureen Richards, Cheryl L. Warnock, *Research Specialists*
Tamara C. Nott, *Research Associate*
Scott Floyd, Timothy Lehnerer, Ron Morelli, *Research Assistants*

Dorothy Maki, *Manufacturing Manager*
Stacy Melson, *Buyer*

Mary Beth Trimper, *Manager, Composition and Electronic Prepress*
Evi Seoud, *Assistant Manager, Composition Purchasing and Electronic Prepress*
Carolyn Fischer, *Composition Specialist*

Randy Bassett, *Image Database Supervisor*
Robert Duncan, *Imaging Specialist*
Michael Logusz, *Graphic Artist*
Pamela A. Reed, *Imaging Coordinator*
Kelly A. Quin, *Imaging Editor*

Library of Congress Catalog Card Number
ISBN 0-7876-3260-0
ISSN 0732-1864
Printed in the United States of America

10 9 8 7 6 5 4 3 2 1

Contents

Preface vii

Acknowledgments xi

Preface

Since its inception in 1981, *Nineteeth-Century Literature Criticism* (*NCLC*) has been a valuable resource for students and librarians seeking critical commentary on writers of this transitional period in world history. Designated an "Outstanding Reference Source" by the American Library Association with the publication of is first volume, *NCLC* has since been purchased by over 6,000 school, public, and university libraries. The series has covered more than 300 authors representing 29 nationalities and over 17,000 titles. No other reference source has surveyed the critical reaction to nineteenth-century authors and literature as thoroughly as *NCLC*.

Scope of the Series

NCLC is designed to introduce students and advanced readers to the authors of the nineteenth century and to the most significant interpretations of these authors' works. The great poets, novelists, short story writers, playwrights, and philosophers of this period are frequently studied in high school and college literature courses. By organizing and reprinting commentary written on these authors, *NCLC* helps students develop valuable insight into literary history, promotes a better understanding of the texts, and sparks ideas for papers and assignments. Each entry in *NCLC* presents a comprehensive survey of an author's career or an individual work of literature and provides the user with a multiplicity of interpretations and assessments. Such variety allows students to pursue their own interests; furthermore, it fosters an awareness that literature is dynamic and responsive to may different opinions.

Every fourth volume of *NCLC* is devoted to literary topics that cannot be covered under the author approach used in the rest of the series. Such topics include literary movements, prominent themes in nineteenth-century literature, literary reaction to political and historical events, significant eras in literary history, prominent literary anniversaries, and the literatures of cultures that are often overlooked by English-speaking readers.

NCLC continues the survey of criticism of world literature begun by Gale's *Contemporary Literary Criticism* (*CLC*) and *Twentieth-Century Literary Criticism* (*TCLC*).

Organization of the Book

An *NCLC* entry consists of the following elements:

- The **Author Heading** cites the name under which the author most commonly wrote, followed by birth and death dates. Also located here are any name variations under which an author wrote, including transliterated forms for authors whose native languages use nonroman alphabets. If the author wrote consistently under a pseudonym, the pseudonym will be listed in the author heading and the author's actual name given in parenthesis on the first line of the biographical and critical information. Uncertain birth or death dates are indicated by question marks. Single-work entries are preceded by a heading that consists of the most common form of the title in English translation (if applicable) and the original date of composition.

- The **Introduction** contains background information that introduces the reader to the author, work, or topic that is the subject of the entry.

- A **Portrait of the Author** is included when available.

- The list of **Principal Works** is ordered chronologically by date of first publication and lists the most important works by the author. The genre and publication date of each work is given. In the case of foreign authors whose works have been translated into English, the list will focus primarily on twentieth-century translations, selecting those works most commonly considered the best by critics. Unless otherwise indicated, dramas are dated by first performance, not first publication. Lists of **Representative Works** by different authors appear with topic entries.

- Reprinted **Criticism** is arranged chronologically in each entry to provide a useful perspective on changes in critical evaluation over time. The critic's name and the date of composition or publication of the critical work are given at the beginning of each piece of criticism. Unsigned criticism is preceded by the title of the source in which it appeared. All titles by the author featured in the text are printed in boldface type. Footnotes are reprinted at the end of each essay or excerpt. In the case of excerpted criticism, only those footnotes that pertain to the excerpted texts are included. Criticism in topic entries is arranged chronologically under a variety of subheadings to facilitate the study of different aspects of the topic.

- A complete **Bibliographical Citation** of the original essay or book precedes each piece of criticism.

- Critical essays are prefaced by brief **Annotations** explicating each piece.

- An annotated bibliography of **Further Reading** appears at the end of each entry and suggests resources for additional study. In some cases, significant essays for which the editors could not obtain reprint rights are included here. Boxed material following the further reading list provides references to other biographical and critical sources on the author in series published by Gale.

Indexes

Each volume of *NCLC* contains a **Cumulative Author Index** listing all authors who have appeared in a wide variety of reference sources published by the Gale Group, including *NCLC*. A complete list of these sources is found facing the first page of the Author Index. The index also includes birth and death dates and cross references between pseudonyms and actual names.

A **Cumulative Nationality Index** lists all authors featured in *NCLC* by nationality, followed by the number of the *NCLC* volume in which their entry appears.

A **Cumulative Topic Index** lists the literary themes and topics treated in the series as well as in *Classical and Medieval Literature Criticism, Literature Criticism from 1400 to 1800, Twentieth-Century Literary Criticism,* and the *Contemporary Literary Criticism* Yearbook, which was discontinued in 1998.

An alphabetical **Title Index** accompanies each volume of *NCLC*, with the exception of the Topics volumes. Listings of titles by authors covered in the given volume are followed by the author's name and the corresponding page numbers where the titles are discussed. English translations of foreign titles and variations of titles are cross-referenced to the title under which a work was originally published. Titles of novels, dramas, nonfiction books, and poetry, short story, or essay collections are printed in italics, while individual poems, short stories, and essays are printed in roman type within quotation marks.

In response to numerous suggestions from librarians, Gale also produces an annual paperbound edition of the *NCLC* cumulative title index. This annual cumulation, which alphabetically lists all titles reviewed in the series, is available to all customers. Additional copies of this index are available upon request. Librarians and patrons will welcome this separate index; it saves shelf space, is easy to use, and is recyclable upon receipt of the next edition.

Citing *Nineteenth-Century Literature Criticism*

When writing papers, students who quote directly from any volume in the Literary Criticism Series may use the following general format to footnote reprinted criticism. The first example pertains to material drawn from periodicals, the second to material reprinted from books.

Kim McQuaid, "William Apes, Pequot: An Indian Reformer in the Jackson Era," *The New England Quarterly,* 50 (December 1977): 605-25; excerpted and reprinted in *Nineteenth-Century Literature Criticism,* vol. 73, ed. Janet Witalec (Farmington Hills, Mich.: The Gale Group, 1999), 3-4.

Richard Harter Fogle, *The Imagery of Keats and Shelley: A Comparative Study* (Archon Books, 1949), 211-51; excerpted and reprinted in *Nineteenth-Century Literature Criticism,* vol. 73, ed. Janet Witalec (Farmington Hills, Mich.: The Gale Group, 1999), 157-69.

Suggestions are Welcome

Readers who wish to suggest new features, topics, or authors to appear in future volumes, or who have other suggestions or comments are cordially invited to call, write, or fax the Managing Editor:

Managing Editor, Literary Criticism Series
The Gale Group
27500 Drake Road
Farmington Hills, MI 48331-3535
1-800-347-4253 (GALE)
Fax: 248-699-8054

Acknowledgments

The editors wish to thank the copyright holders of the excerpted criticism included in this volume and the permissions managers of many book and magazine publishing companies for assisting us in securing reproduction rights. We are also grateful to the staffs of the Detroit Public Library, the Library of Congress, the University of Detroit Mercy Library, Wayne State University Purdy/Kresge Library Complex, and the University of Michigan Libraries for making their resources available to us. Following is a list of the copyright holders who have granted us permission to reproduce material in this volume of *NCLC*. Every effort has been made to trace copyright, but if omissions have been made, please let us know.

Lyons, David. From *In the Interest of the Governed: A Study in Bentham's Philosophy of Utility and Law.* Clarendon Press, 1973. © Oxford University Press, 1973. Reproduced by permission of Oxford University Press.—Marshall, Peter. From "Human Nature and Anarchism" in *For Anarchism: History, Theory, and Practice.* Edited by David Goodway. Routledge, 1985. © Peter Marshall 1989. Reproduced by permission.—Morland, David. From *Demanding the Impossible? Human Nature and Politics in Nineteenth-Century Social Anarchism.* Cassell, 1997. © David Morland 1997. Reproduced by permission.—Narveson, Jan. From "Rights and Utilitarianism" in *New Essays on John Stuart Mill and Utilitarianism.* Wesley E. Cooper, Kai Nielson, Steven C. Patten, eds. Canadian Association for Publishing in Philosophy, 1979. © Canadian Association for Publishing in Philosophy, Guelph, Ontario, 1979. Reproduced by permission.—Narveson, Jan. From "Rights and Utilitarianism" in *New Essays on John Stuart Mill and Utilitarianism.* Wesley E. Cooper, Kai Nielson, Steven C. Patten, eds. Canadian Association for Publishing in Philosophy, 1979. © Canadian Association for Publishing in Philosophy, Guelph, Ontario, 1979. Reproduced by permission.—Oliver, H. From *The International Anarchist Movement in Late Victorian London.* Croon Helm, 1983. © 1983 H. Oliver. Reproduced by permission.—Patsouras, Louis. From *Jean Grave and the Anarchist Tradition in France.* Amherst, NY: Humanity Books, 1995. © 1995 by Louis Patsouras. Reproduced by permission.—Ritter, Alan. From *The Political Thought of Pierre-Joseph Proudhon.* Princeton University Press, 1969. Copyright © 1969 by Princeton University Press. All rights reserved. Reproduced by permission.—Rosen, Frederick. From *Jeremy Bentham and Representative Democracy: A Study of the 'Constitutional Code.'* Clarendon Press, 1983. © Frederick Rosen, 1983. Reproduced by permission of Oxford University Press.—Spitzer, Alan B. From *The Revolutionary Theories of Louis Auguste Blanqui.* Columbia University Press, 1957. Copyright © 1957 Columbia University Press, New York. © 1983 Alan Barrie Spitzer. Republished with permission of the Columbia University Press, 562 W. 113th St., New York, NY 10025.—Strasser, Mark. From *The Moral Philosophy of John Stuart Mill: Toward Modifications of Contemporary Utilitarianism.* Longwood Academic, 1991. © 1991 by Mark Philip Strasser. Reproduced by permission.—Thomas, D.A. Lloyd. From "Rights, Consequences, and Mill on Liberty" in *Of Liberty.* Edited by A. Phillips Griffiths. Cambridge University Press, 1983. © The Royal Institute of Philosophy 1983. Reproduced with the permission of Cambridge University Press.—Tomsich, John. From *A Genteel Endeavor: American Culture and Politics in the Gilded Age.* Stanford University Press, 1971. © 1971 by the Board of Trustees of the Leland Stanford Junior University. Reproduced by permission of the publishers, Stanford University Press.—Trachtenberg, Alan. From *The Incorporation of America: Culture and Society in the Gilded Age.* Hill and Wang, 1982. Copyright © 1982 by Alan Trachtenberg. All rights reserved. Reproduced by permission of Hill and Wang, a division of Farrar, Straus and Giroux, LLC.—West, Henry R. From "Mill's 'Proof' of the Principle of Utility" in *Limits on Utilitarianism.* Edited by Miller/Williams. University of Minnesota Press. Reproduced by permission of the publisher and the author.

PHOTOGRAPHS APPEARING IN *NCLC*, VOLUME 84, WERE RECEIVED FROM THE FOLLOWING SOURCES:

Blanqui, August (seated, reading letter), lithograph. Archive France/TAL/Archive Photos, Inc. Reproduced by permission.—Byrd, William (standing), painting. Archive Photos, Inc. Reproduced by permission.—Buntline, Ned, photograph. Archive Photos. Reproduced by permission.—Proudhon, Pierre Joseph, engraving. Archive Photos, Inc. Reproduced by permission.—Title page from Beadle and Adams' dime novel "The Deadwood Dick on Deck; or Calamity Jane, the Heroine of Whoop-Up" by E.L. Wheeler. The University of Michigan Library. Reproduced by permission.—Title page from Beadle's Dime N.Y. Library, "Texas Jack, The Prairie Rattler, or The Queen of the Rivers," 1884, wood engraving. Corbis Corporation. Reproduced by permission.—Title page from Beadle's Half Dime Library, "Dandy Rock, the Man from Texas," 1879, woodcut engraving. Corbis Corporation. Reproduced by permission.

Anarchism

INTRODUCTION

The doctrine of Philosophical Anarchism presents a theoretical framework for the construction of a society without government. Critics carefully distinguish anarchism from the related concept of anarchy, which simply denotes a society without rule, and from the sensationalistic outpouring of so-called anarchist activities of the late nineteenth century associated with a number of prominent political assassinations. As a social-political theory, anarchism is more broadly defined according to its philosophical justifications for anarchy as a practicable goal, coupled with a view of complete human freedom brought about by mutual aid, and its emphasis on individualism and the moral and rational perfectibility of humankind. Generally, anarchist thought of the late eighteenth and nineteenth centuries is critical of law, private property, and political authority, all of which it considers to be means of oppression. Overall, the anarchists forwarded a radically optimistic view of human nature that suggests that human beings, unrestrained by laws and governments, may form a society based on the principle of cooperation.

Philosophical Anarchism found its expression in the writings of several nineteenth-century European thinkers, particularly the French writer and polemicist Pierre-Joseph Proudhon. A significant portion of Proudhon's radical thought can be summed up in his dictum, "property is theft." In place of private property, Proudhon advocated an egalitarian distribution of wealth and power in his work *Du principe fédératif et de la nécessité de reconstituer le parti de la révolution* (1863; *The Federal Principle*). Basing his theory on the concepts of individual freedom and mutual aid, Proudhon championed the eradication of privately-owned property, which, he argued, exploits the labor of workers. Commentators observe, additionally, that despite apparent affinities between Proudhon's anarchism and the communist theories of Karl Marx, the analyses of society provided by both men differ significantly. Proudhon's ideas did, however, prove influential on the Russian theorists Mikhail Bakunin and Peter Kropotkin. Bakunin was largely in agreement with Proudhon's anarchist goals, although he proposed collectivism and violent revolution as necessary means to the development of Proudhon's mutualist society. Kropotkin likewise modified several of Proudhon's views in developing a theory that critics characterize as anarcho-socialism. In such works as *La Conquête du pain* (1892; *The Conquest of Bread*) and *Vzaimnaia pomoshch, kak faktor evoliutsii* (1902; *Mutual Aid: A Factor in Evolution*) Kropotkin presented a plan for a communist federation and analyzed the mechanisms of human cooperation that would factor into a free anarchist society.

Anarchist theory in England and North America followed a somewhat different line of development from that associated with continental European anarchism. Considered the principal theoretician of Reformist Anarchism, William Godwin published *An Enquiry Concerning Political Justice* in 1793, a work that outlines the essentials of classic anarchist thought and finds the source of evil in the subjugation of human free will to the arbitrary dictates of authority. According to Godwin's somewhat utopian vision of an anarchist society, advances in technology would result in a drastic reduction in work—perhaps to as little as one half hour per individual per day—with no loss in material comfort. Unlike Russian anarchists, who frequently proposed a collectivist solution to the problem of realizing an anarchist society, Godwin advocated individualism but criticized democratic practices that could curb individual liberty through the tyranny of majority rule. In the United States, Godwin's theories proved influential on the American anarchist Josiah Warren, whose ideas differ from his English predecessor in their emphasis on the free market system and the acceptability of private property as a means of expanding the material well-being of humanity.

REPRESENTATIVE WORKS

Mikhail Bakunin
Fédéralisme, Socialisme et Antithéologie[*Federalism, Socialism and Anti-theologism*] (philosophy) 1895

William Godwin
An Enquiry Concerning Political Justice, and its Influence on General Virtue and Happiness (socio-economics) 1793

Jean Grave
La Société mourante et l'anarchie [*The Dying Society and Anarchy*] (socio-economics) 1893

Peter Kropotkin
La Conquête du pain [*The Conquest of Bread*] (socio-economics) 1892
Vzaimnaia pomoshch, kak faktor evoliutsii [*Mutual Aid: A Factor in Evolution*] (socio-economics) 1902

Pierre-Joseph Proudhon
Qu'est-ce que la propriété [*What Is Property?*] (essay) 1840

Système des contradictions économiques [*System of Economic Contradictions*] (socio-economics) 1846
Du principe fédératif et de la nécessité de reconstituer le parti de la révolution [*The Federal Principle*] (socio-economics) 1863

Max Stirner
Der Einzige und sein Eigentum [*The Ego and His Own*] (philosophy) 1845

Josiah Warren
Equitable Commerce: A New Development of Principles as Substitutes for Laws and Governments, for the Harmonious Adjustment and Regulation of the Pecuniary, Intellectual, and Moral Intercourse of Mankind Proposed as Elements of a New Society (socio-economics) 1852

OVERVIEWS AND GENERAL STUDIES

Harold Barclay (essay date 1990)

SOURCE: "On the Nature of Anarchy," in *People Without Government: An Anthropology of Anarchy,* Kahn & Averill, 1990, pp. 15-33.

[*In the following essay, Barclay enumerates the differences between anarchy and anarchism, and goes on to define each in theoretical and practical terms.*]

On Anarchy and Anarchism

Our first task must be to clarify the meaning of anarchy in relation to a variety of different terms. Let us begin by considering anarchy and anarchism. These must be distinguished from one another, just as one distinguishes 'primitive communism' from Marxian communism. The latter is an elaborate sociological system, a philosophy of history and an idea for a future condition of society in which property is held in common. 'Primitive communism' refers to a type of economy, presumably found among 'archaic' or 'primitive' peoples, in which property is held in common. By property is to be understood the crucial resources and means of production of wealth. In fact, what is communally held in such societies is invariably land; tools, livestock, and many other kinds of resources (eg, fishing sites) are individually owned. In any case, Marxist theory does not identify primitive communism with the intended Marxist communism. One might say that implicitly it is held that the historical process involves a grand cycle where humans commence with primitive communism and ultimately return to communism at a higher level—which is somewhat reminiscent of the progressive-cyclic theory of Giambattista Vico.

As we distinguish between the two communisms, so we must also distinguish between anarchy and anarchism. An-

archy is the condition of society in which there is no ruler; government is absent. It is also most clearly associated with those societies which have been called 'archaic' and 'primitive', among other pejorative adjectives. Anarchism is the social political theory, developed in 19th century Europe, which incorporates the idea of anarchy, but does so as part of, and as a result of, a broader, self-conscious theory of values which makes human freedom and individuality paramount. Thus, in anarchist theory, the first premise is something which Josiah Warren called the sovereignty of the individual and from this it follows that government and state are oppressive of individual freedom and should be abolished. But, at the same time, the anarchist looks to the abolition of other institutions similarly interpreted as oppressive: the Church, the patriarchal family and any system which appears to enshrine 'irrational' authority. Anarchist theory is egalitarian and antihierarchical, as well as being decentralist. Discrimination based on 'race, colour, or creed' or sex are always anathema. Anarchists were probably the first advocates of women's liberation.

In place of the old system, anarchist theory advocates self regulation and voluntary co-operation. Social relations are to be carried out through free contractual agreements of mutual or equal benefit to all parties involved. For Proudhon 'mutualism' was a basic cornerstone of anarchy. His mutualist conception has an interesting similarity and concordance with the contemporary anthropological theory of Mauss and Levi-Strauss, since mutualism may be readily seen as reciprocity. To Levi-Strauss, reciprocity as a mutual exchange is the fundamental structural principle of society; it is a kind of 'category of thought', so fundamental as to be imbedded in the human mind. Pierre Clastres, following in the tradition of Levi-Strauss, argues that 'coercive power', that is, both state and government, are unreciprocal since a ruler receives more than a subject, so upsetting the balance of equity. Therefore, state and government are in opposition to the basic principles of social life: society is against the state. . . . Here I only wish to indicate that anarchist theory and anthropological theory do impinge upon one another.

In addition to mutualism, Proudhon and Bakunin, among others, also stressed the idea of federalism, designed to facilitate relations between increasingly larger and more widespread groups of people. The initial building blocks of the federalist plan are the local, 'face to face' groups, either of neighbours or persons with common occupational interests—in any case they have a common mutual interest in working with each other for one or more ends. Such groups form and concern themselves with achieving their specified goals. In order to facilitate these ends they 'federate' with other similar groups to form a regional federation and in turn regional federations join with others to form yet a broader federation. In each case the power invested in the organised group decreases as one ascends the different levels of integration. As Bakunin and others said, the system was to be 'built from the bottom up and not from the top down'. Each member of a federation has a right to withdraw if in disagreement with the majority's proposed action.

It is interesting to note here the similarity between anarchist federalism and the segmentary lineage system characteristic of many anarchic polities, especially in Africa. In both cases the sum is composed of segments and each segment of sub segments and so on. In both cases the most effective authority is in the smallest unit, decreasing directly as one ascends to broader levels of integration, so that at the 'top', the ultimate federation has little influence whatsoever. In both cases, as well, we have a technique for establishing a broad network which draws innumerable small groups into a large integrated whole. One major contrast between the two systems, however, is that federalism is based upon the co-operation between groups—the principle of mutualism or reciprocity—while for segmentary lineages the operative principle is opposition or conflict between groups of the same level.

Anarchist federalism should not be confused with the kind of 'confederacy' advocated by such men as John Calhoun and other early 19th century American political thinkers. Anarchists would be sympathetic to such a view only in that it proposes to strip central government of most of its authority, permitting member states to withdraw from the system if they see fit. However, from an anarchist point of view, Calhoun and his sympathisers were inconsistent, in that they were primarily concerned about maximizing the power of the several states within the Union. Had they been interested in the freedom of the individual unit members, they would also have recognised the legitimate right of the counties to withdraw from states, of towns to withdraw from counties and of individuals to withdraw from towns.[1]

Anarchism is in sum a complex theoretical orientation. It should not, however, be seen in any sense as a single monolithic conception, or a grand theoretical system to be compared, say, with Marxism. Anarchism, on the contrary, entails several related, but often distinct, points of view. And no anarchist theoretician has ever presented an integrated theoretical system. Yet all anarchist theory shares a common concern for the individual and freedom, opposition to the state and a desire to establish a system of voluntary co-operation. It is obvious that the sort of society envisioned by anarchists does not exist and, except for a few isolated and short lived attempts, has never existed. Nevertheless, we do have numerous examples of anarchy—societies without government and without the state.

Just as Marxist communists might not be thoroughly pleased with a functioning 'primitive communism', so we cannot expect anarchists to approve extant anarchic polities. It is obvious that many would be horrified by some of their characteristics. While these societies lack government, as we shall see, patriarchy often prevails; a kind of gerontocracy or domination by the old men is not uncommon; religious sanctions are rampant; children are invariably in a 'second class' position; women are rarely treated in any way equal to men. Indeed, there are invariably strong pressures to conform to group traditions. But since they are highly decentralised, lacking government and the state, they do exemplify anarchy. And thus we must look at such systems as examples of the application of anarchy.

It may be argued that to employ the term 'anarchy' for a major group of human societies is ethnocentric and confuses ideology with social classification. It is to take a highly emotionally charged word, one with a very clear ideological connotation, identified with Euro-American cultural traditions, and to apply it cross-culturally when those in the other cultures would clearly lack the ideology and values of the anarchist. Thus, not only is the word distorted, but so also is the meaning of those cultures.

But if this is true of the word 'anarchy', it applies equally to the use of such words as 'democratic', 'government', 'law', 'capitalist', 'communist' and a host of others employed daily by social scientists, yet derived from ordinary speech. Social science is full of terms in common usage which are applied to social contexts in other cultures. There are certainly dangers to such a procedure. It is easy to carry extraneous ideological baggage along with the term. On the other hand, if we cannot at all make such cross-cultural transfers, we are left with a proliferation of neologisms which become pure jargonese, enhancing obfuscation rather than clarification. There are, after all, *types* of social phenomena which occur throughout the world. Scientific understanding is not furthered by a kind of radical phenomenology which makes every cultural item, every individual perception, unique. I believe many anthropologists, in their own projection of personal and cultural values, have obstinately refused to apply the one truly clarifying term to those numerous societies which are without government and are, therefore, anarchies.

SOCIAL ORDER AND AUTHORITY

One of the universal characteristics of mankind, or of any species for that matter, is that it survives and thrives in the context of some kind of order. That is, humans have peace of mind where behaviour and events are on the whole predictable. We are animals of habit or animals of custom—traditionalists. Behaviour in human societies is, therefore, standardised and deviations are punished. A society by definition has order and structure and operates with regularised, relatively fixed modes of behaviour. The term 'society' implies that the component members are operating according to some 'rules of the game'. Such rules can be extremely vague and open to conflicting interpretations, or they may be very specific and explicit. In any case, there are guidelines without which we would be lost in a sea of *anomie*. Part of the problem of the modern world is that many of these guildelines have become so ambiguous that the level of general anxiety of the population increases. It is clear that where there is no structure, there is no order and there is no society. And, as the first lesson in any anthropology or sociology course points out, humans without society are not human. But another part of that first lesson is that there is an immense amount of variation within human society, including the amount and kind of structure and order.

Having said this, let me add that humankind often seeks a holiday from routine and structure. Max Gluckman pointed to what he called 'rituals of rebellion', which are periods in which the populace is expected to behave—within limits—in a manner counter to normal expectation. Thus there is the 'Mardi Gras', which is a traditional relaxing of behaviour before the commencement of the exacting observations of the Lenten season. We have Hallowe'en as a traditional time when children are permitted a short expression of rebellion against the adult community.

Victor Turner has suggested that there are two countercurrents in a society: one of structure and the other of *communitas* or antistructure. The latter expresses the spontaneous, the unplanned and the ecstatic, as a kind of reaction to the usual, predictable and structured. This in a way parallels Proudhon's view that authority and liberty operate as antinomies within any society, each acting so as to delimit the other. In terms of these polarities, anarchism as a social theory is allied with communitas and liberty. Like Thoreau, anarchists are critical of those elements within a culture which become so engrained as to be stultifying and superficial or empty rituals. They look with favour on the new and the untried. Perhaps Nietzsche's call to live dangerously has some relevance here.

On occasion, the anarchist sympathy for communitas has appeared to go to extremes. Thus Hippies, in their rejection of modern structures, sometimes reject every form of structure so as to enshrine dirt—the ultimate of disorder. But while, of all social theories, anarchism has more sympathy for communitas, it is still not opposed to structure, to order or to society. Indeed, Proudhon once wrote that liberty is the mother of order not the daughter. The issue for anarchists is not whether there should be structure or order, but what kind there should be and what its sources ought to be. The individual or group which has sufficient liberty to be self-regulating will have the highest degree of order; the imposition of order from above and outside induces resentment and rebellion where it does not encourage childlike dependence and impotence, and so becomes a force for disorder.

The relation of anarchy to power, authority, politics and political organisation is another misunderstood area. In human groups some manoeuvring for power characterises the relationship between individual members. The intensity and emphasis on the contest varies from one culture to another and from one individual to another. The cultural values of the Pygmies . . . and also of such Pueblo Indian groups as the Zuni and Hopi, play down attempts by individuals to stand in the forefront, although one cannot say that the desire to influence others is absent. And within every culture there is variation. Some people strive more than others; a few even opt out. Nevertheless, the contest for power manifests itself in some fashion within each human group.

Power means the ability to get others to do what you want them to do. Thus, someone who convinces ten others to follow orders has more power than someone who is able to get only one to obey. But this depends on all other things being equal, since, for example, someone who controls the one individual who knows how to use a nuclear detonating device can have more power than someone who controls the behaviour of a million ordinary men and women.

Power means influence—convincing others by logical argument, by the prestige of one's status or rank, by money or bribe. Or it means implied or overt threat of injury—either by physical or psychological means—and the ability to carry it out.

The contest for power is an important dynamic force in the social group—a major mechanism by which the group undergoes change over time. The 'push and pull' of members not only causes 'palace revolutions', that is, shifts in the personnel of the less powerful and the more powerful, but leads as well to changes in rules and values.

Ralf Dahrendorf, a German sociologist who is certainly no anarchist, presents a thesis in a way amenable to anarchist thought, particularly as an answer to Marx. Dahrendorf suggests that the conflict for power is central in a society; Marx was primarily concerned with one feature of the power complex, namely, economic power. This emphasis has meant that those who follow Marx devalue the non-economic dimensions of power. Consequently, we find the world full of peoples' democracies in which the oppression of ordinary people is no less than it was before the 'revolution'. Marxism in practice has tended to transfer the forces of power from the capitalist to the professional bureaucrat and military officer, primarily because it does not see that the central problem is the problem of power itself. The anarchist insists upon addressing this larger issue.

Neither anarchy nor anarchist theory deny power; on the contrary, in anarchist theory this is a central issue for all human societies and the limiting of power is a constant concern. Bakunin recognised the great human drive for power (Maximoff, 248ff). Anarchy is, after all, the condition in which there is the maximum diffusion of power, so that ideally it is equally distributed—in contrast to other political theories, such as Marxism, in which power is transferred from one social group (class) to another. It is, of course, true that much anarchist thinking regarding power has been muddled by 'utopian' dreaming of the ideal society where no-one infringes on anyone else. Godwin and Kropotkin, for example, believed that in the course of time the human race would evolve towards a condition where all were good to their fellows and did not try to take advantage. But other anarchists are not such optimists about human nature; if they were they would not be so worried about the uses and abuses of power.

Max Weber stressed the difference between power and authority. In any society, individual members recognise certain others as having authority within specified realms. Thus, in modern society, members accept as *legitimate* the right of certain individuals to carry and, where 'necessary', to employ firearms, in order to apprehend suspected law breakers. These policemen invariably wear special dress. Members of this society do not recognise as legitimate the use of force by others, such as gangsters. In both cases coercive force is employed. In the first the power is authority since it is seen as legitimate and right; but the second is not authority; it is the illegitimate use of power. Something of this kind of distinction can be identified in all societies. Yet a significant modification of Weber's terminology is in order. Most Canadians would eagerly subscribe to the notion that the power of the Ottawa government is legitimate, but some would only acquiesce to that power. The several generations of colonial rule of the Dutch in Indonesia, for example, commenced as a pure case of the imposition of brute and raw force. But with the passage of time it acquired a certain 'legitimation', so that the power became authority in Weber's terms. But it becomes legitimate power because the Indonesians learned to acquiesce: they grew accustomed to the situation and tacitly accepted it. Raymond Firth has noted that power acquires some kind of support from the governed either because of "routine apathy, inability to conceive of an alternative or acceptance of certain values regarded as unconditional" (123). Most authority commences as the raw power of the gangster and evolves into the 'legitimate' authority of tacit acquiescence. This is certainly the history of the nation state. Fried observes that legitimacy is the means by which ideology is blended with power. The function of legitimacy is "to explain and justify the existence of concentrated social power wielded by a portion of the community and to offer similar support to specific social orders, that is, specific ways of apportioning and directing the flow of social power" (Fried, 26).

No philosopher or social theorist accepts the legitimacy of 'raw' use of power and none rejects totally and completely any and all kinds of authority. Even the anarchist recognises that there is a place for legitimate authority. An anarchist conception of legitimate authority was long ago intimated by Proudhon: " . . . if man is born a sociable being, the authority of his father over him ceases on the day when his mind being formed and his education finished, he becomes the associate of his father. . . ." (n.d., 264). Later Bakunin wrote: "We recognise then, the absolute authority of science. . . . Outside of this only legitimate authority, legitimate because it is rational and is in harmony with human liberty, we declare all other authorities false, arbitrary and fatal" (Maximoff, 254).

Paul Goodman in *Drawing the Line* writes of natural coercion in which the infant is dependent upon his mother or the student upon the teacher—cases in which teaching is involved with the intent of increasing the independence of the one to attain the level of the other (1946). I don't know whether Fromm ever read Proudhon, Bakunin or the early Goodman, but certainly his view of the nature of authority closely parallels and further explicates that of his anarchist predecessors. Fromm distinguishes, as does Bakunin, between 'rational' and 'irrational' authority. Rational authority has its source in competence; it requires constant scrutiny and criticism and is always temporary. It is based upon the equality of the authority and the subject "which differ only with respect to the degree of knowledge or skill in a particular field". "The source of irrational authority, on the other hand, is always power over people"—either physical or mental power (9).

Stanley Milgram has said that people appear to believe that those in positions of authority, including politicians, are the most knowledgeable. But perhaps this is only wishful thinking in an attempt to justify their authorities. People delude themselves into thinking that through the electoral process they put those in office who are intellectually superior.

Modern society has many in authority who have earned rationally the right to authority, but it has many whose claim to authority is irrational and they are our politicians, judges and policemen. These the anarchist rejects, accepting only rational authority. Anarchists recognise that there are specialists, that is, authorities in various realms, who are accepted as such because of their expertise. Yet one can readily see the potential danger inherent even here, that those holding one form of authority may seek to extend their power so that rational authority is transformed into irrational authority.

Closely related to the concept of authority is that of leadership. Again, no one can deny that there are individuals who appear in every human group who stand out as influential persons for one reason or another. The anarchist movement has long accepted leaders within its own folds, even though it has remained suspicious of the general idea. Although group leadership is a universal of human social organisation, it is, at the same time, necessary to stress that leadership is conceived differently amongst different peoples. The Pygmies and Hopi of Arizona express an anarchist distrust of leaders, such that each individual seeks to avoid the leadership role, blending into the group as much as possible.

Since societies have order and structure and must deal with the problem of power, they are therefore involved in politics. When we use the word politics, we are concerned with power and its uses in a human group. Not only do all societies have politics, but they have political organisation or political systems—that is, standardised ways of dealing with power problems. Political organisation is not a synonym for government. Government is *one* form of political organisation. Politics may be handled in a variety of ways; government is just one of those ways. Thus it is clear that even anarchism as a theory does not deny or oppose politics or political organisation. It is, on the contrary, very political.

In the broadest sense politics can be applied to any kind of social group. That is, there may even be politics within the family—where clearly the distribution of power between father, mother, son and daughter is a major issue. A local club also has politics in a similar small-scale fashion. Ordinarily, however, when one speaks of politics or political organisation, one does not think of the internal affairs of the family. Political organisation applies more to 'public' affairs—relations which are territorial and cut across kinship groupings. Politics involves a substantial geographical area—a community, or at least an extensive neighbourhood. Yet even this kind of conceptualisation leads to ambiguity as to whether one is dealing with political or family affairs. We may have a confrontation between two groups related by kinship, but beyond the level of extended family (for example, two patrilineages), which would be considered at least as a quasi-public affair. Nevertheless, the terms of address employed and the atmosphere of the exchange will unmistakably be those of kinship.

SOCIAL SANCTIONS

Neither anarchy, nor anarchist theory in sum, is opposed to organisation, authority, politics, or political organisation. It is opposed to some forms of these things, especially to law, government and the state, to which terms we must now proceed.

Radcliffe-Brown proposed the term 'sanctions' to apply to the manner in which a social group reacts to the behaviour of any one of its members. Thus, a positive sanction is some form of expression of general approval. A soldier is given a medal; a scholar an honorary degree, or a student an award; mother kisses little junior for his good behaviour, or daddy gives him a piece of candy. A negative sanction is the reaction of the community against the behaviour of a member or members; it expresses disapproval. Thus, a soldier may be court martialled; a scholar fired or put in jail; a student failed in course work or ostracised by fellow students and the child slapped by his parent. It seems obvious that it is the negative sanctions which become most important in any society.

Sanctions may also be categorised as being 'diffuse', 'religious' or 'legal'. Here my interpretation deviates slightly from that of Radcliffe-Brown. Diffuse sanctions are those which are spontaneously applied by any one or more members of the community. Crucial to the conception of diffuse sanctions is the notion that their application is not confined to the holder of a specific social role. They may be imposed by anyone within a given age/sex grade or, occasionally, there may be no limit to who may initiate them. This is the meaning of diffuse: responsibility for and the right to impose the sanction is spread out over the community. Society *as a whole* has the power. There is no special elite which even claims a monopoly on the use of violence as a sanctioning device. Further, when and if sanctions are applied is variable, as is the intensity of the sanctions imposed.

Diffuse sanctions include gossip, name calling, arguing, fist fighting, killing and ostracism. Duelling and formal wrestling matches are less widespread forms. Inuit have ritualised song competitions in which two opponents try to outdo one another in insults before an audience which acts as judge. Diffuse sanctions may be resorted to by an individual or a group. And their effectiveness is enhanced as the entire community joins in participation in the sanctions. Vigilante style action and feuds are common forms of diffuse sanction which depend upon collective action.

In many societies, fines and other punishments are meted out by an assembly. Radcliffe-Brown calls these 'organised' sanctions. Yet they are still not 'legal' but have the character of diffuse sanctions, of a more formalised type, *if* the assembly has no authority to use force in executing its decisions. In such instances the assembly members act as mediators rather than judges and are successful to the extent that they can convince two disputing parties to come to some compromise.

Diffuse sanctions are a universal form of social regulation; if a social group has nothing else it will have various techniques which can readily be classified as diffuse sanctions.

Religious sanctions involve the supernatural. 'Black magic' may be performed against a person; one may be threatened with the eternal torment of hell, or encouraged with a positive religious sanction promising everlasting ecstasy in heaven. The Nuer leopard skin chief may get his will done by threatening to curse another. The Ojibwa Indians believed infractions of the rules led to the acquisition by supernatural means of specific kinds of diseases. Thus, religious sanctions may either have a human executor, as in the case of a curse which must be invoked, or be seen as automatic, as with the Ojibwa belief, or the idea that breaking out of the ten commandments commits one to hell fire. In another respect religious sanctions are either those which are intended to bring forth punishment in this life, or those which are for an after-life: physical versus ultimate spiritual punishment.

Legal sanctions involve all expressions of disapproval or approval of the behaviour of an individual wherein:

a: such expressions are specifically delegated to persons holding defined roles, one of the duties of which is the execution of these sanctions;

b: these individuals alone have the 'authority' to threaten use of violence and use it in order to carry out their job and;

c: punishments meted out in relation to the infraction are defined within certain limits and in relation to the 'crime'.

Policemen, justices of a court, jailers, executioners and lawmakers are examples of those who may enforce legal sanctions. In our society they collectively constitute a government. The state, through its agent the government, declares it has the monopoly on the use of violence against others within society, meaning that only certain agents of the state, for example, policemen, can take a person off the street and put him or her in jail. Only certain collectivities, that is, the courts, can determine guilt and assess a punishment in accord with what others, the lawmakers, have established as law. Finally the punishment connected with a legal sanction is fairly standardised and precise. A person found guilty of robbing a store will receive, say, a year to ten years in prison.

Legal sanctions are laws. Laws exist where one has specific social roles designed, or delegated, to enforce regulations by force of violence, if necessary and where punishment has certain defined limits and is not capricious. Law exists where you have government and the state; conversely, if you have a government you have law. Legal sanctions, and thus law and government, are not universal, but are characteristic of only some human societies—albeit the most complex ones. Such societies also, it should be borne in mind, retain a peripheral position for both diffuse and religious sanctions.

Malinowski suggested that the term 'law' should be applied loosely to cover all social rules which have the support of society (Malinowski, 9-59). Such usage, however, obscures the fundamental and important difference in the means by which different rules are enforced. Law and government are invariably associated with rule by an elite class, while governmentless societies are invariably egalitarian and classless. Hence, Malinowski's loose usage obfuscates the important difference concerning who, or what, enforces regulations.

It should be clear that any society characterised by the prevalence of legal sanctions can hardly be called anarchic. As we shall note in considering some of the case studies below, there are marginal examples. There is no clean-cut line between anarchy and government. The relation of anarchy to diffuse and religious sanctions, however, requires some further clarification. In the social theory of anarchism the idea of voluntary co-operation has been made the positive side of the coin of which abolition of government is the negative. Where the idea of voluntary co-operation is so critical to anarchist thought, it is important to consider it in relation to the nature of functioning anarchic polities, giving special attention to the employment of diffuse and religious sanctions.

Voluntary co-operation, like its antonym, coercion, is a highly ambiguous term. From one point of view nothing may be seen as purely voluntary and all acts as being in some way coerced. For one thing, it might be said that conscience, ego, id, 'the inner spirit' or what have you, are fully as coercive forces as the policeman, or as public ostracism. However, coercion may be best conceived as a relationship of command and obedience, wherein the commanding force is either human or supernatural, but is always external to the individual person. Ideally, for true voluntary co-operation to prevail, there must be no such forms of external coercion. Yet, in fact, even anarchists themselves accept the use of such coercive force and limit

voluntary co-operation. In their everyday activity, in their writings and in their own creation of anarchist communes and societies, anarchists use a variety of diffuse sanctions. Some have advocated and applied what are clearly legal sanctions.

It is sometimes difficult to distinguish the type of society envisioned by a Bakunin or Proudhon from a decentralised federal democracy. Towards the end of his life, Proudhon seems to have moved away from his advocacy of voluntary association, towards a sort of minimal state. " . . . .(I)t is scarcely likely", he writes in *Du Principe Federatif,* "however far the human race may progress in civilisation, morality, and wisdom, that all traces of government and authority will vanish" (20). For him anarchy has become an ideal type, an abstraction, which like the similar ideal types, democracy and monarchy, never exist in a pure form, but are mixtures of political systems. "In a free society, the role of the state or government is essentially that of legislating, instituting, creating, beginning, establishing; as little as possible should it be executing. . . . Once a beginning has been made (for some project) the machinery established, the state withdraws leaving the execution of the new task to local authorities and citizens" (45). Proudhon has become an advocate of a federal or confederal system, in which the role of the centre is reduced "to that of general initiation, or providing guarantees and supervising. . . . (T)he execution of its orders (are) subject to the approval of the federated governments and their responsible agents" (49). He cites the Swiss confederation with approval. "If I may express myself so", Proudhon had written in a letter of 1864, "anarchy is a form of government or constitution in which the principle of authority, police institutions, restrictive and repressive measures, bureaucracy, taxation, etc, are reduced to their simplest terms" (quoted in Buber, 43). We are left wondering if the elder Proudhon would now not feel more at home with such early American opponents of centralised government as John Taylor of Caroline or John Randolph of Roanoke, even John Calhoun.

Bakunin, who absorbed most of Proudhon's federalist ideas, presents a similar problem. In describing his idea of a federal system in the *Organisation of the International Brotherhood,* Bakunin makes some disconcerting statements: "The communal legislatures, however, will retain the right to deviate from provincial legislation on secondary but never on essential issues . . ." while the provincial parliament "will never interfere with the domestic administration of the communes, it will decide each commune's quota of the provincial and national taxation". There are to be courts and a national parliament as well. This national parliament "will have the task of establishing the *fundamental principles* that are to constitute the *national charter* and will be binding upon all provinces wishing to participate in the national pact". The national parliament "will negotiate alliances, make peace or war, and have the exclusive right to order (always for a predetermined period) the formation of a national army" (Lehning, 72-73). Bakunin's anarchy sounds like a decentralised federalist democracy. Yet a year after writing this document he seems to redeem himself for anarchy in an essay on *Federalisme, Socialisme et Antitheologisme:* "Just because a region has formed part of a State, even by voluntary accession, it by no means follows that it incurs any obligation to remain tied to it forever." "The right of free union and equally free secession comes first and foremost among all political rights" (Lehning, 96).

Kropotkin favourably described the early Medieval city commune as an anarchistic system, when, as we shall note below, it surely had a governmental structure. The same may be said concerning the 'anarchist collectives' established in the Ukraine in 1917 and later in some of those in Spain. Even such an individualist anarchist as Josiah Warren saw the need for organised militias. And most anarchists have legitimised military force to achieve their ends, or have considered it an unfortunate necessity. In a word, anarchists have sometimes been equivocal about legal sanctions, to say the least.

In focussing on highly centralised realms of coercion in modern society such as the state and the church, they have also tended to neglect the sometimes more oppressive force of such diffuse sanctions as gossip and ostracism. Nevertheless, there is an important difference between the coercion of the state and the coercion of diffuse sanctions, which may in part justify anarchist reliance on the latter while rejecting the former. In the state or government there is always a hierarchical and status difference between those who rule and those who are ruled. Even if it is a democracy, where we suppose that those who rule today are not rulers tomorrow, there are nevertheless differences in status. In a democratic system only a tiny minority will ever have the opportunity to rule and these are invariably drawn from an elite group. Differential status is not inherent in diffuse sanctions. Where a group or individual employs gossip or ostracism against another person, that person may freely use these same techniques. Where differential status is associated with diffuse sanctions, such as in the command position of the father over his son, we do have a form of coercion which begins to approach that of government. Yet still the father role has the quality of a rational authority and a young man may expect eventually to 'graduate' to a position of greater equality with his father, eventually achieving fatherhood himself. In no diffuse sanctions is there a vesting of the power to employ violence into the hands of a restricted group of commanders.

Anarchism as a social theory cannot, and I believe in actuality does not, reject all forms of coercion. While its advocates may wield the slogan of voluntary co-operation, it is recognised that this too has limits. For anarchists there is a tacit and, for many, an overt recognition of the legitimate use of some kind of force in some circumstances and this force is what anthropologists refer to as diffuse sanctions. Indeed, as psychologists have informed us and as Allen Ritter has lately reiterated, these sanctions are imperative for the development of personality. The growth of the in-

dividual's self image relies upon knowing what others think of his or her behaviour. At the same time, the operation of sanctions instills awareness of others and so builds community by building empathy (Ritter, 1980).

Concerning religious sanctions, anarchist theoreticians have generally looked upon religion as another oppressive system aimed at curbing the free expression of the individual. Michael Bakunin, especially, saw God and the state as two great interrelated tyrannical ogres which must be destroyed. All well-known anarchists at least opposed the church—religion being seen as an organised and hierarchical social structure. Even Tolstoy agreed in this, although his anarchism derived from his interpretation of a Christianity which stressed the literal acceptance of the teachings of the Sermon on the Mount.

The Catholic Worker Movement is a rather unusual development within American anarchism. Led by a convert to Catholicism, Dorothy Day, it professes both an adherence to the principles of pacifist anarchism and to the Roman Catholic Church—a kind of Catholic Tolstoyan movement. Few outside this movement have understood how anarchism, or for that matter any moderately libertarian doctrine, could be reconciled with Roman Catholicism and its dedication to an absolutist monarchy—the papacy—and to a rigid hierarchical structure.[2]

Most anarchists see any religion as an authoritarian system, but are all religious sanctions necessarily incompatible with anarchy? I think not. We must appreciate the distinction made above between those religious sanctions which require human mediation and those which are 'automatic'. A religious sanction which is least compatible with anarchy and takes on some of the character of a legal sanction, is one which can only be invoked by a specific individual as part of a formal office and where there is consensus that such a person has a legitimate monopoly on the power—ie, the authority—to impose sanctions. The priest is the best example of this. On the other hand, where the power to invoke religious sanctions is available to the many and not legitimately monopolised, we have a situation which parallels diffuse sanctions. A punishment which is believed to come directly from God or some other supernatural force, does not require human intervention and is more on the order of subjugation to natural occurrences such as storm and earthquake. Indeed, it is quite clear that punishment by one's conscience is a sanction of this order. Those religious sanctions which parallel diffuse sanctions, as well as those which require no human intermediary, do not seem incompatible with anarchy as we have here conceived it.

GOVERNMENT AND THE STATE

Conceptions of government and the state and the relationship between them are often confused. Marxists and some anarchists, including Bakunin, declare their opposition to the state and desire to replace what is called 'political' government with a government over 'things'. But this seems like playing with words and sloganeering. Any 'things' are going to be manipulated by people and will therefore be seen as in need of governing because people are involved. So it is still a government over people. Further, one cannot abolish the state and still have a government, since the latter is the institutional apparatus by which the state is maintained.

Nadel (1942, 69-70) has given three specific characteristics of the state and in doing so has also indicated the role of government in the state. First, the state is a territorial association. It claims 'sovereignty' over a given place in space and all those residing within that area are subject to, and must submit to, the institution of authority ruling or governing that territory, that is, the government.

While the state is a territorial entity, it is often an inter-tribal and inter-racial structure. The criteria for membership are determined by residence and by birth. Membership is ordinarily ascribed, although one may voluntarily apply to join if one immigrates and settles within the territory of the state.

The state has an apparatus of government and this is to some degree centralised. The government functions to execute existing laws, legislate new ones, maintain 'order', and arbitrate conflicts to the exclusion of other groups or individuals. It comprises specific individuals holding defined social roles or offices. Crucial to the definition of such roles is the claim to a monopoly of the legitimate use of violence within that territory. The part played by the different role holders in using violence may vary so that there can be a highly differentiated system or division of labour (cf the discussion of legal sanctions above). All are in any case part of a single integrated monopolistic institution. Such a situation differs, for example, from the role of the Inuit shaman who may threaten a victim with violence, since the shaman cannot claim a monopoly on its legitimate use.

The ruling group in any state tends to be a specialised and privileged body separated by its formation, status and organisation from the population as a whole. This group collectively monopolises political decision. In some polities it may constitute an entrenched and self-perpetuating class. In other more open systems such as a democracy, there is a greater circulation or regular turnover of membership of the ruling group, so that dynasties or other kinds of closed classes of rulers do not ordinarily occur. This, of course, contributes to the illusion of equality of power in a democracy and obscures the division between rulers and ruled.

Fundamental to both government and the state is the employment of violence to enforce the law. This may be variously viewed as either the imposition of the will of the ruling group, or as a device to maintain order, keep the peace and arbitrate internal conflicts. In fact states and governments fulfil all these functions by enforcing the law. It is theorists of the left and especially anarchists, how-

ever, who emphasise that the paramount and ultimate end of all law enforcement is to benefit the ruling interests, even though there may be positive side effects such as keeping the peace. They would further emphasise that the existence of the state is conducive of strife and conflict since as a system based upon the use of violence it thereby legitimises and incites it. The state is further predicated upon the assumption that some should be bosses giving orders while others should be subordinates—a situation which can only irk the subordinates and frustrate them and, thus, become yet another provocation of violence. Democratic systems may ameliorate this situation but they do not cure it. By their nature state and government discourage, if they do not outlaw, the natural voluntary co-operation amongst people, a point made by Benjamin Tucker and more recently in some detail by Taylor. Anarchist theory is therefore clearly opposed to Hobbes' thesis that without government society is nasty and brutish. Indeed, anarchists set Hobbes on his head and argue that the world would be more peaceful and amenable to co-operation if the state were removed. And, clearly, the anthropological record does not support Hobbes in any way. Stateless societies seem less violent and brutish than those with the state.

Above all, the state and government are organisations for war. No more efficient organisation for war has been developed. It is interesting and perhaps ironic that right-wing and anarchist theoreticians have converged in recognising the significance of violence to the life of the state. Machiavelli's practical guide to the operation of a state has disturbed many a naive believer in democracy, since the Italian politician recognises force and fraud as the obvious central mechanisms for the success of any state. Von Treitschke, the German historian whose greatest hero was Frederick the Great, observed that "without war no State could be. All those we know of arose through war and the protection of their members by armed force remains their primary and essential task. War, therefore, will endure to the end of history as long as there is a multiplicity of States . . . the blind worshipper of an eternal peace falls into the error of isolating the state, or dreams of one which is universal, which we have already seen to be at variance with reason" since a state always means one among states and thus opposed to others (38). "(S)ubmission is what the State primarily requires . . . its very essence is the accomplishment of its will" (14). "The State is no Academy of Arts, still less is it a Stock Exchange; it is Power. . . ." (242).

The pioneer British anthropologist, Edward B Tylor, wrote in his *Anthropology,* "A constitutional government whether called republic or kingdom, is an arrangement by which the nation governs itself by means of the machinery of a military despotism" (156).

Nietzsche, who contrary to popular opinion was no friend of the state, noted its predatory nature: "The State (is) unmorality organised . . . the will to war, to conquest and revenge. . . ." As a predator the state attempts to become larger and larger, ever expanding its sphere of influence and subjugation at the expense of other weaker states. It is true that in the course of time in this interstate struggle most states opt out of the conflict and resign themselves to becoming satellites of larger states, realising they cannot effectively compete. It is also true that the giant states may not always seek to gobble up weaker states, because they find it better for their own interests to keep such states as ostensibly independent entities. Thus, in the modern world, we have super powers which are in the midst of the struggle for expansion, carrying on the traditional predatory role of the state—the United States, Soviet Union, China, France, the United Kingdom (now marginally). There are innumerable satellite states of each of the big predators. There are those—usually known as 'Third-world' states—which may try small order predation against neighbouring states, but on the whole they keep their independent status and opt out of full conflict because they are buffers between, or pawns of, the big predators. Finally there are a few states such as Switzerland and until recently Lebanon which are perpetually neutral zones; the big predators do require such zones in which to operate, particularly for information gathering purposes.

CONCLUSION

The classification of sanctions discussed above may now be summarised in relation to political systems by means of the following diagram presented as a continuum with anarchy, where there is no government, at one end and archy, where the state and government clearly exist, at the other. Under anarchy only diffuse and certain supernatural sanctions are operative, while archy is characterised by the prevalence of legal sanctions. In the middle, between the two poles, there is a limbo which may be seen as a marginal form of anarchy or a rudimentary form of governmental or archic system. There are many anomalous cases of this kind. . . . Such entities may possibly be considered as transitional examples from anarchy to statism. As Lowie has said, states do not appear full blown out of the stateless condition; they too must evolve or develop and this takes time.

Notes

1. Proudhon's latterday ideas on federalism have recently been raised in connection with the discussion of the nature of Canadian federalism and thus of the Canadian nation (cf. Proudhon, 1979).

2. The *Catholic Worker* newspaper allowed the appointment of a priest as Church censor and Dorothy Day herself has said she would stop its publication immediately if so ordered by the Church.

George Crowder (essay date 1991)

SOURCE: "Three Sources of Anarchism," in *Classical Anarchism: The Political Thought of Godwin, Proudhon, Bakunin, and Kropotkin,* Clarendon Press, 1991, pp. 6-38.

[*In the following essay, Crowder illuminates three major sources of anarchist thought: the concept of the moral and rational perfectibility of man, Jean-Jacques Rousseau's critique of civilization, and the optimism of Enlightenment science.*]

The history of Western political thought contains many anti-authoritarian currents. The vision of a golden age without government is a favourite theme from Ovid to Rousseau, and those writers who have advocated release from the authority of Church and State are too numerous to mention.[1] Only in the wake of the Enlightenment and the French Revolution, however, does anarchism (along with the other great modern ideologies: liberalism, socialism, conservatism) emerge as a systematic political theory. As David Miller puts it, for inchoate defiance to crystallize into a reasoned challenge to the existing order and a determinate proposal for its replacement, 'such wholesale reconstruction needed to be thinkable'.[2] The practical example of the Revolution and the background beliefs of the intellectual climate from which it sprang made anarchism thinkable. In the new century the anarchist idea evolved into a distinctive, although multifaceted, theoretical and ideological tradition. In this [essay] I shall discuss three of the most important intellectual sources of that tradition. Sections 2 and 3 will deal with the influence on the anarchists of Rousseau and scientism respectively, sources that identify anarchism as preeminently a product of the Enlightenment and the Revolution. To begin with, however, I shall examine the most fundamental of all constituents of the anarchists' argument: their conception of freedom. To understand this idea, together with the notion of moral law from which it is inseparable, we should be prepared to follow a trail leading back to antiquity. Far from being rebels against all precedent, the classical anarchists are, in this respect at least, legitimate heirs to the mainstream of Western political thought.

1. FREEDOM AS MORAL SELF-DIRECTION

The freedom of the individual is widely assumed to be a leading ideal for the classical anarchists, but it has seldom been asked just what sort of freedom this is and why they value it so highly. A preliminary approach to the anarchist idea may be made by way of the familiar distinction between 'negative' and 'positive' liberty. Although doubt has now been cast on the validity of the distinction as a tool of analysis, it remains useful at least as a historical framework, a guide to the way freedom has been conceived by theorists in the past. In this way the contrast was memorably drawn by Isaiah Berlin in terms of two traditions: the negative, conceiving of freedom as the absence of (humanly removable) obstacles to the fulfilment of actual or potential desires (Hobbes, Locke, Constant, J. S. Mill, etc.); and the positive, insisting that real or truly valuable freedom is self-government in accordance with the 'real' will, the will of the true self, which may not be identical with actual wants (Plato, Rousseau, Kant, Fichte, Hegel, Marx, etc.).[3] The same distinction can be expressed in somewhat more precise terms as follows. In social and political discourse all freedom is the absence of constraints on action. Negative liberty is the absence of constraints on action willed by 'empirical' persons, meaning individuals as we find them, identified by all the desires they might (actually or potentially) have. Roughly speaking, I am negatively free if I am not prevented by human agency from doing whatever I might want to do. Positive liberty, on the other hand, is the absence of constraints on action willed by the 'true' or 'real' or 'authentic' self, or that part of the personality with which the individual is most closely identified.[4] What exactly is to be taken as authentic to one's personality is a question which has received many different answers, and corresponding to these are many different versions of positive liberty. I shall shortly come to one such answer, and to one such version of the positive idea.

So far as the issue has been raised at all, most commentators, including Berlin, have assumed that the anarchists conceive of freedom in the negative sense.[5] This assumption goes back to the heyday of the anarchist movement at the turn of the century. *The Times* in 1911 described the anarchists as claiming 'a right of rebellion on the part of the individual' that covers 'whatever the individual pleases to do', an opinion echoed by those more recent writers who picture classical anarchism as 'extreme individualism' or an extreme extension of liberalism.[6] The idea of negative liberty is in keeping with this sort of picture since it is commonly associated with the idea of a personal area of non-interference asserted against the State or one's neighbours—one of the ideals of classical liberalism. If anarchists are concerned above all with securing the right to do as one pleases, then it might seem reasonable to think of anarchism as an extreme development of classical liberalism, as a doctrine urging the expansion without restraint of spheres of personal independence.

If such a view were correct, it would be hard to reconcile the anarchists' commitment to freedom with their claim that they are providing an account of social order. If their ideal is the maximal expansion of individual freedom conceived simply as the absence of impediments to whatever the individual might please to do, there would seem good reason to endorse the vulgar association of anarchism with the advocacy of disorder.

Many of those who have taken the 'extreme individualist' line have been happy to make just such a connection. H. M. Hyndman, for example, described anarchism as 'individualism gone mad', and according to D. G. Ritchie anarchists 'carry out the principles of individualism to their logical conclusion—the destruction of all orderly society whatever'.[7] In fact, as we shall see, interpretations such as these egregiously misrepresent the general tendency of the classical anarchist tradition. Far from being ruthlessly individualistic or amoral, the anarchists are, without exception, highly moralistic in temper.

A more sophisticated reading of anarchist freedom has recently been given by Alan Ritter.[8] According to Ritter, the classical anarchist thinkers conceive of the free man as one who governs his own actions in accordance with a stringent critical rationality. This 'procedural' freedom 'specifies only the manner in which members of an anarchy must choose their acts and says nothing about the attributes their acts must have'. It follows that a free action, for the anarchists, may be one that is morally 'abominable'. Ritter concludes that the anarchists are therefore committed to placing restrictions on freedom, for which purpose they recommend 'public censure', the control of the individual by pressure of public opinion. At this point one may begin to wonder whether anarchism might not prove more suffocating than the State. It is this kind of picture that George Orwell has in mind when he accuses anarchism of harbouring a 'totalitarian tendency'. 'Public opinion,' he argues, 'because of the tremendous urge to conformity in gregarious animals, is less tolerant than any system of law.[9] Again, this reading of the anarchists departs radically from their real meaning. The anarchists are no less alive than Mill and Tocqueville to the possibility of the tyranny of opinion, and no less opposed to it.[10]

Both the crude 'negative liberty' interpretation and Ritter's more sophisticated reading fail to give a satisfying account of the relation between freedom and order in anarchist thought, and they do so because they fail to give a satisfactory analysis of anarchist freedom. The defect common to both is that the ideal of freedom they attribute to the anarchists is too open-ended. Classical anarchism is committed to untrammelled freedom, but the anarchists do not characterize the good society simply as one in which people act as they please, even if this is sanctioned by a strong rationality. Negative liberty and critical rationality do matter to the anarchists, but their thought cannot be explained in these terms alone. If it could be, there might be more justice in the allegation of disorder—unless, as on Ritter's view, one were prepared to see them as limiting freedom by public censure. Such speculations are irrelevant, however, once one has grasped certain crucial features of the anarchist conception of freedom that have generally been overlooked.

To begin with, the anarchist idea is not negative but positive.[11] The anarchists are most concerned to promote a freedom to act in accordance not with the empirical self but with the authentic self, with that part of my personality which identifies me most fundamentally. What meaning do they attach to the 'authentic' here? It has two elements. First, rationality. Authentic individuals are governed by a stringent, critical reason, such that they judge or act only for reasons that are 'their own' in a strong sense. (Thus far Ritter is a helpful guide, although he does not present the anarchist ideal of rationality as part of an ideal of authenticity.) Secondly (crucially omitted by Ritter), virtue. The authentic self is not only the rational but also the moral self: that part of the personality that wills morally right action. I am free, for the anarchists, to the extent that I conscientiously govern my actions in accordance with moral rules. The good society is a realm neither of chaos nor of competition nor of purely procedural reason, but a moral order in which freedom implies virtue as part of its meaning. Freedom in this sense need not be restricted on moral grounds, since it already entails obedience to moral rules by definition. I shall refer to this conception of freedom as 'moral self-direction'.

The moral rules which, according to the anarchists, must be followed by the free man are not merely his own subjective inventions or projections, or even those of mankind at large. If they were, that might leave room for divergence in the judgement and conduct of free men, and consequently the renewal of doubts about anarchist order. Although the classical anarchists might regard particular conventional moralities as subjective and divergent, they all hold that beyond convention there is an overarching moral law, 'immanent' (to use Proudhon's word) in the nature of things, that is objectively valid or 'true'. The anarchists subscribe (in Godwin's case only implicitly) to the ancient tradition of 'natural law'. Truly free men, by definition obedient to that law, will necessarily converge on the same universal norms.

As to exactly what sort of conduct is enjoined by the moral law, the anarchists give somewhat differing, although overlapping, accounts, and these tend to be fairly vague. (For reasons that will become clearer, they might reasonably argue that they are not yet in a position to be more precise.) Godwin is an avowed utilitarian who commends the pleasures of benevolence, while Proudhon rejects uncompensated assistance in favour of strict reciprocity. Both give a central place in the pictures they draw of the good society to images of reason controlling the passions, and to aspects of self-sufficiency. Bakunin and Kropotkin, on the other hand, are more open to the cultivation of the emotional side of human nature, especially the sentiments of sympathy and brotherhood. These they see as the basis for an interdependent and solidaristic community, although they differ over the criteria according to which such a community will distribute property. All four are agreed on one point, however, which is that moral self-direction is itself enjoined by the moral law, indeed is the highest value of all.

It might be objected that moral self-direction as thus conceived contains a conceptual difficulty: its rational and moral elements may pull apart. My reason, that is, may not invariably lead me to act rightly, may even suggest the opposite. The short analytical answer to this apparent difficulty is that it depends on a failure to give proper weight to the role played here by the notion of authenticity. So far as I am 'free', reasons 'I' find convincing, as the anarchists understand these terms, can never lead me away from substantive moral imperatives. This is because the 'I' here is not just an empirical (albeit rational) self, but the authentic self, which is conceived as partly *constituted* by a commitment to right action. Classical anarchist freedom is not simply Ritter's procedural freedom plus obedience to moral rules, the two juxtaposed, but the freedom of an authentic self in which reason and moral will are fused or in harmony. Reason, so far as it is authentic, will necessarily lead to right action.

To understand this more clearly requires some appreciation of the historical dimension of the idea of moral self-direction. Far from being peculiar to the anarchists, the notion can be traced back at least as far as the concept of 'self-mastery', the rule of the 'naturally better', that is to say, rational and right-willing, element of the personality over the 'worse', found in Plato.[12] There the sense of self-mastery as 'freedom' is only latent, but it becomes explicit in the work of a long line of successors: in the Stoics and other thinkers in the natural law tradition, in Spinoza, Locke, Rousseau, Kant, Hegel. I shall call this way of thinking about freedom the 'perfectionist' tradition.

According to this tradition, men are capable of achieving an authentic or perfected condition in which their nature or essence as human beings is fully realized. That authenticity or perfection consists in the full development of man's two distinctive faculties, his reason and his moral nature. The two are not merely contingently related but fused or harmonized. To be fully human is to be fully rational, which is necessarily to be virtuous. Perfected reason can only lead to the perfection of man's moral nature. Why should that be so? Underlying the perfectionist view is an assumption of ultimate harmony in the universe. Where reason is perfected it surely cannot, it is supposed, give equal sanction to two conflicting ends, since that would deny the evident nature of the universe as a rationally comprehensible whole. This, as Berlin has pointed out, is the assumption of 'the central Western tradition in ethics and politics', and its consequence is the belief 'that the ends of all rational beings must of necessity fit into a single universal, harmonious pattern'.[13] The human personality, which is an integral part of the universal order, must, when perfected, reflect the harmony of the universe at large. Since this perfection of the human personality involves the release of the authentic nature from that which is unauthentic or alien—the lower passions, ignorance, vice—it naturally suggests a conception of freedom. As Berlin puts it: 'when all men have been made rational, they will obey the rational laws of their own natures, which are one and the same in them all, and so be at once wholly law-abiding and wholly free'.[14]

This is the source of the basic anarchist conception of freedom. When the anarchists talk about the freedom they uphold as a social and political ideal, they are talking about the liberation not of an empirical, open-ended self, but of a perfected self which is in part constituted by ethical commitments sanctioned by reason. Such a view contrasts with the modern outlook introduced by thinkers like Machiavelli and Hobbes, according to which the individual's reason may well bring him into conflict with moral norms, since the whole notion of a human essence that mirrors the harmony of a universal order has been abandoned. Rationality, on this latter view, is entirely instrumental and open-ended, a picture that is now, for the most part, our own. But it was not the view of the anarchists. For them, in accordance with the earlier tradition, to be truly free is to realize one's nature as a human being, to be fully rational and, therefore, moral. The anarchists, moreover, are heirs to the perfectionist tradition in the form of argument they advance for the high value they place on freedom as moral self-direction. Man is free, his true potential realized, when that part of him that expresses his full humanity—that is closest to the divine or, in the secular version, furthest removed from the non-human—is released from bondage to his merely animal component. Freedom in this sense is valuable because equivalent to the perfecting of human nature; to deny such freedom is to deny man his status as a fully human being.

The idea of freedom as moral self-direction finds little favour with current philosophers and social theorists, but it was widespread among their counterparts of the nineteenth century. It was associated with philosophical positions as diverse as idealism and materialism, and with political ideologies of the right (Fichte and Hegel), of the centre (the British neo-Hegelians T. H. Green and Bosanquet), and of the left (Marx, for whom work rather than reason or morality is definitive of human authenticity). Uniting these disparate writers in their commitment to moral self-direction and cognate notions of positive freedom is their use of these concepts to criticize the ascendant doctrines and sensibility of *laissez-faire* liberalism.[15] The basic insight is trenchantly expressed by Hegel. The purely negative notion of liberty as the ability to do as we please is 'mere arbitrariness', the determination of the will by 'natural impulses', an idea that reveals 'an utter immaturity of thought' since it lacks any inkling of, among other things, 'right' and 'the ethical life'. True freedom is obedience to duty, 'the attainment of our essence, the winning of *positive* freedom'.[16] The freedom promised and, at least for some, delivered by the *laissez-faire* system is for Hegel and like-minded theorists not true freedom but mere 'licence', the enslavement of man by his lower, animal nature. The freedom worthy of humanity could only be created by a different social order—or at least, in the case of the British neo-Hegelians, by the energetic amelioration of the existing order.

This is the view of the anarchists. What the dominant classes call freedom is really servitude; the prospects for true freedom depend on the complete abolition of the bourgeois order. Neither their basic conception of freedom itself nor their use of it as the focus of a radical critique of *laissez-faire* liberalism makes the anarchists unique among nineteenth-century thinkers. What is distinctive in their thought is that while so many nineteenth-century positive libertarians seek the advancement of freedom through the expansion of the State—or at least, in the case of Marx, through the temporary harnessing of its power—the anarchists move in the opposite direction, toward the State's complete abolition.

This raises an interesting conceptual issue. It has often been argued, most famously by Berlin, that the general tendency in positive libertarians to promote the power of the State follows somehow from the nature of the positive idea itself.[17] The rationale of this tendency is said to look back to Rousseau's dictum in *The Social Contract* that the

individual who is forced to act in conformity with the General Will, which is identical with his own real will, is in effect 'forced to be free'. Berlin warns of the authoritarian implications of this. The way is opened for a blinkered or unscrupulous regime to represent its own ideals as the real will of the people, and so to justify oppression in the name of freedom. If this analysis were correct it would leave the anarchists in a position that is not merely unique among social critics of the nineteenth century but highly anomalous, since they would be upholding a libertarian ideology on the basis of a concept of freedom that is logically or naturally authoritarian.

In fact it has been repeatedly demonstrated that the positive idea is by no means logically or naturally authoritarian. One after another of Berlin's 'negative' liberals have been shown to possess (perhaps in addition to the negative idea) a positive conception of freedom.[18] My argument that the anarchists succeeded in founding a coherent non-authoritarian theory on a positive conception of freedom is therefore not as surprising as it might have been some years ago, although Berlin's influence in this area is still remarkably resilient. My further claim that the success of the anarchist argument in this connection implies the need to revise Berlin's thesis can also be seen as extending an argument the broad pattern of which is already familiar. What will be less familiar is the anarchists' largely successful use of positive freedom as the basis for a theory that is not merely liberal but thoroughly libertarian, involving not merely the limitation of government power but its wholesale rejection. The anarchist case also has its limits, however, and I shall try to indicate some of these by focusing on what remains of value in Berlin.

To summarize: the widespread assumption that classical anarchist thought is founded on a negative or open-ended conception of freedom is false and leads to a distortion of the anarchists' views, especially on the crucial question of social order. Rather, the anarchist idea is positive, more precisely 'perfectionist': the idea of moral self-direction. That such an idea could be the basis of a libertarian political theory suggests that the influential view of positive liberty as naturally authoritarian in tendency is mistaken.

2. THE ANARCHISTS AND ROUSSEAU

Writing in 1851, Proudhon refers to the 'authority' of Rousseau as having 'ruled us for almost a century'.[19] The ambiguity in the word 'authority' here points to a significant ambivalence. For Proudhon, and for the classical anarchist tradition as a whole, Rousseau is both authoritative and authoritarian, both starting point and adversary. Proudhon is inclined to emphasize the negative view, at times exhibiting a near-hysterical hatred of Rousseau: 'Never did a man unite to such a degree intellectual pride, aridity of soul, baseness of tastes, depravity of habits, ingratitude of heart: never did the eloquence of passion, the pretension of sensitiveness, the effrontery of paradox arouse such a fever of infatuation.'[20] Yet, elsewhere he calls Rousseau a 'great innovator' and 'the apostle of liberty and equality'.[21] Rousseau is an ambiguous figure for the other anarchists, too. Godwin, for example, although starting from a more sympathetic perspective, feels obliged to admit reservations. 'Rousseau,' he writes, 'notwithstanding his great genius, was full of weakness and prejudice.'[22]

The question of the precise relation between the anarchists and Rousseau is therefore a complicated one.[23] He is a figure of unique significance for the origins of anarchist thought, but it is difficult to capture concisely just what that significance is. Godwin and Proudhon in particular are vividly aware of him, engaging explicitly with his work in many places. This engagement amounts sometimes to positive influence, sometimes to negative reaction; the former tends to predominate in Godwin, the latter in Proudhon. There are several points in the thought of the anarchists where some degree of influence, either positive or negative, might plausibly be suspected, although it cannot be demonstrated conclusively. And aside altogether from questions of causal influence, a comparison of the anarchists with Rousseau reveals many illuminating affinities and contrasts. Explanatory illumination rather than pure historical enquiry will, indeed, be my main concern; it is this that makes the difficult task of unravelling and assessing these connections and parallels worthwhile. The full extent of the Rousseauian connection can emerge only through detailed textual comparison, and much of the evidence for this will be reserved for subsequent chapters dealing with individual anarchists, in particular Godwin and Proudhon. However, the broad pattern of the argument can be sketched in advance.

At its most general, Rousseau's significance for classical anarchism is tied to his embodiment, at the level of popular reputation, of certain aspects of the Enlightenment and the French Revolution. Beyond the many expressions of resistance to authority contained in Western thought, it was the Enlightenment and the Revolution that laid the foundations of the systematic social and political theory that became known as anarchism. In many ways Rousseau was not a representative Enlightenment thinker. His doubts about the value of reason and civilization, his sense of religion and community and his rejection of progress set him apart from the confidently rationalistic and cosmopolitan *philosophes*. On these issues the anarchists are very much closer to Rousseau's rivals than to him. He was, nevertheless, in some respects the most radical thinker of his age, and despite the peculiarities of his position he inevitably became associated in the public, and to some extent the anarchist, mind with that critical, iconoclastic side of the Enlightenment that challenged received tradition and established institutions.

In particular he was identified with the spectacular culmination of this broad movement of ideas, the French Revolution. That watershed, like the man held to have inspired it, is regarded by the anarchists with mixed feelings. On the one hand 'the myth of the revolution', as James Joll calls it, provides them with a precedent for wholesale social change: for the defeat of the entrenched interests of

the governing classes in the name of freedom and equality.[24] On the other hand the history of the revolution, its degeneration from popular uprising to Jacobin Terror and eventually Napoleonic dictatorship, strikes them as a tragic demonstration of how the quest for liberty and social justice can miscarry. The example of the revolution is always before them, as both inspiration and warning. The same is true of the revolutionary role of Rousseau. For Kropotkin, he is a more or less sympathetic figure in this regard, an exceptionally eloquent spokesman for equality and human rights. Equality in particular is a principle which, according to Kropotkin, Rousseau 'upheld . . . so passionately, so alluringly, so convincingly that his writings exerted a tremendous influence not only in France where the Revolution wrote on its banner "Liberty, Equality, Fraternity" but throughout Europe as well'.[25] Bakunin also sees Rousseau as having had a powerful effect on the Revolution, but judges this to be essentially malign. He links Rousseau with Robespierre and the perversion of the Revolution's ideals, calling him

> the falsest mind . . . of the last century . . . the real creator of modern reaction. To all appearances the most democratic writer of the eighteenth century, he bred within himself the pitiless despotism of the statesman. He was the prophet of the doctrinaire state, as Robespierre, his worthy and faithful disciple, tried to become its high priest.[26]

Again, however, it is worth noting that Bakunin had once seen Rousseau in a very different light. In 1843, while staying on the island of Saint Pierre where the *Reveries of the Solitary Walker* had been written, he refers to the place as 'Rousseau's island', and declares that in his faith in the eventual triumph of mankind over priests and tyrants he is at one with the 'immortal Rousseau'.[27]

At the level of general historical reputation, then, Rousseau gets a mixed reception from the anarchists, corresponding to the ambivalence they feel toward the revolution with which he was associated. But what about their response to his actual writings? Here, too, the story is far from straightforward. Most of Rousseau's main works were well known to Godwin and Proudhon, while Bakunin and Kropotkin, although giving little evidence of firsthand familiarity with the Rousseauian texts, at least knew of them through the writings of others, including Proudhon.[28] Various parts of Rousseau's many-sided output might be expected to have excited the sympathy of some or all of the anarchists. *La Nouvelle Héloïse* was among Godwin's favourite books, and both he and Proudhon would have found much to admire in the austere morality preached by the *Discourse on the Arts and Sciences* (*First Discourse*) and the *Letter to d'Alembert*. The young Bakunin, as just seen, seems to have been attracted by the *Reveries*. *Emile* contains, in the Savoyard Priest section, an account of natural law and conscientious self-direction that is somewhat congenial to anarchist views, while the scheme of natural education advocated in the rest of the book inspired Godwin's attempt to found a school in 1781 and in some degree anticipated the proposals put forward by Bakunin and Kropotkin for 'integral education'.[29] Yet the more significant effect Rousseau had on the anarchists is owed neither to his theory of education nor his romanticism. Ironically, the two works in which his influence is at its most direct and crucial are those which the anarchists purport to dislike most intensely: *The Social Contract* and the *Discourse on Inequality* (*Second Discourse*).

Of all Rousseau's works *The Social Contract* is the least loved by the anarchists. Godwin, after dealing sympathetically with the *Second Discourse* and *Emile,* remarks that 'in his writings expressly political, *Du Contrat Social and Considérations sur la Pologne,* the superiority of his genius seems to have deserted him'.[30] Proudhon and Bakunin are less restrained in describing *The Social Contract* as a 'monument of incurable misanthropy', 'a clever fraud', 'an absurd and, what is more, an evil fiction'.[31] The anarchists see the work as the representative text of the most influential secular line of justification of the State, the social contract tradition. To make matters worse, Rousseau's version of the contract is expressed in the very language of freedom that is so dear to the anarchists. Rousseau may pose as a defender of liberty, they say, but his real intentions are transparent. *The Social Contract* amounts to no more than an especially devious form of the basic argument against freedom found in all the contractarians: that freedom is pre-social and must be limited by government if men are to coexist in society.[32] As an interpretation of the treatment of freedom in *The Social Contract* this hardly does justice to the subtlety of Rousseau's position. Indeed it might be argued that Rousseau's blueprint is not far removed from the anarchists' own: that if every citizen is indivisibly a member of the sovereign, each governs himself and the contract creates not a State, separate from those it governs, but a self-governing community. That possibility the anarchists either do not appreciate or merely dismiss as sleight of hand.

Whether they are entirely fair in this is a matter I need not pursue. What is important for my purposes is that although they reject Rousseau's theory of the legitimate sovereign they do not dispute his starting point, the inviolability of moral self-direction. Indeed, they adopt it as their own.[33] Moreover, there is evidence, which will appear in its place, that one of their sources for this principle is *The Social Contract.* There Rousseau describes moral self-direction as 'the quality of man', invoking the perfectionist argument that the rule of the right-willing self over the rest of the personality is part of human perfection.[34] Rousseau's elevation of freedom in this sense to the status of supreme good was unprecedented. Spinoza and Locke had placed a high value on freedom, but no one before Rousseau went so far as to make it pre-eminent above all other values, or to insist that for a State to count as legitimate every member must literally prescribe the law to himself. The detested *Social Contract* is thus a possible source of that most fundamental of the anarchists' premises, the paramount value of moral self-direction.

The Social Contract contains much else that the anarchists would agree with. The inadequacy of representatives as

guardians of freedom, the difficulty for even the best-constituted legislature to discover the moral law and to translate it into positive law, the implication that existing States must be regarded as illegitimate, the tendency of even the best executive to degenerate because of the weaknesses of human nature—all these Rousseauian principles and observations are tenets of anarchism too. It is by no means obvious that the anarchists themselves saw Rousseau as their source for all of these ideas, but at least in the highly significant case of the argument against representation the authority of Rousseau is expressly cited by both Godwin and Proudhon.[35] In another respect, however, the anarchists are quite right to sense in *The Social Contract* an outlook inimical to their own. For there Rousseau looks to political institutions for the answer to all difficulties. Government is a source not only of happiness but of virtue itself, the one modern institution capable of shaping the best people. For the anarchists the truth is the exact opposite: government is capable only of evil; life in the State is in the most literal sense demoralizing. But if *The Social Contract* is in this respect so clearly antipathetic to anarchist thought, there is a quite different aspect of Rousseau from which they might seek support. That the realm of freedom is a 'natural' order outside the artificiality of the State is a proposition that might well be derived from the *Second Discourse.*

The *Discourse* is essentially a lament for lost authenticity. It describes a hypothetical evolution of man from his origins in a solitary, animal state of nature, through primitive association in which he is humanized by realizing his potential as a moral being, to the breakdown of primitive happiness and the emergence of troubled modernity. The condition of modern man, corrupt, discontented, driven to endless acquisition in order to satisfy his desire for admiration (*amour propre*), is contrasted with the virtuous and integrated life of primitive society, where *amour propre* had nothing to feed on. While the savage could satisfy his simple desires for himself, the accumulation of wealth made possible by improved agriculture has created sophisticated wants that can only be satisfied with the assistance of others. Where this is not forthcoming post-primitive man resorts to manipulation, deception, and eventually force.

The contrast is also to be understood in terms of freedom. While the primitive associate is free in the sense that he is governed by the authentic, moral part of his nature, the modern *civilisé* is 'dependent'. 'Dependence' in Rousseau's usage has two elements. In a purely descriptive sense it refers to reliance on others for assistance or direction, especially in production. But it also carries a normative connotation of lack of integrity and freedom. Reliance on others places a man at the mercy of others' arbitrary wills, preventing him from being governed solely by the moral law. Virtue is expelled from human relations and thus moral self-direction destroyed. The kind of social relation most characteristic of the post-primitive epoch is dependence in the economic sphere. Accumulation leads to inequality of wealth and to the creation of rival classes, each of which must enlist the assistance or compliance of the other in order to satisfy its increasingly sophisticated desires. Neither rich nor poor are free, because relations between them are governed by desire and need rather than by morality. The attempts of the poor to beg or extort a subsistence from the rich, and of the rich to keep the poor in subjection lead eventually to violence. Government is then instituted by the rich ostensibly as a solution to violence in the interests of all but in reality to serve their own purposes by maintaining the proprietory *status quo.* Global unhappiness, inauthenticity, and unfreedom are thus set permanently in place.

Rousseau's description of the primitive society is a potential source of inspiration for the anarchists, for here is a vision of a society which is at once fully human—virtuous and free—and without government. The *Nouvelle Héloïse* contains similar pictures in its descriptions of the model estate of Clarens and of peasant life in the Swiss Haut Valais. (The isolated rural simplicity depicted in *Émile* is also similar, but less truly social in character.) In all these cases the simplicity of quiet village and household life is seen as a protection against *amour propre,* hence a bulwark of moral self-direction. The model of the good life is what Judith Shklar has called Rousseau's notion of the 'Golden Age', one of two distinct and irreconcilable utopias he holds up for the edification of his corrupt and enslaved contemporaries.[36] The alternative ideal, that of 'Sparta', the virtuous republic evoked in the *First Discourse, The Social Contract* and elsewhere, is the better known. But although relatively neglected, the vision of the Golden Age is an important part of Rousseau's thought, and one that might have attracted the anarchists.

Rousseau's vision of stateless freedom is, however, spoiled for the anarchists by what they see as deep flaws. First, a tension runs through the *Second Discourse,* as it does through Rousseau's thought as a whole, between the idea that social life is necessary to the perfection of man's distinctively human nature and the suspicion that society itself lies at the root of man's present corruption and enslavement. On the one hand it is only when man associates that his life assumes the moral character distinctive of his humanity; on the other, association brings with it the emergence of *amour propre*—although this does not become damaging until developing material conditions give it the opportunity to flourish. Thus Proudhon sees Rousseau as having 'rigorously decided against society, while recognizing that there was no humanity outside of it'.[37] The anarchists for their part insist that society is both essential to human perfection and in itself natural and blameless. Only certain kinds of society are undesirable. To suppose that society itself is corrupting is a monstrous error, since it implies that people cannot coexist without being restrained from harming one another. To suppose this is as damaging to the cause of freedom as to accept that other slander against human nature, the doctrine of original sin. Proudhon writes: 'the ancients accused individual man; Rousseau accuses collective man: it is fundamentally the same proposition, and equally absurd.'[38]

A second aspect of Rousseau's treatment of society without government which the anarchists would have cause to dislike is the assertion that such a society is now irretrievably lost along with the simplicity of desire that characterized it. The implication is that a social order without government might be conceivable, but only under primitive conditions in which desires can be satisfied by austerely self-sufficient producers. The emergence of more sophisticated wants inevitably leads to social conflict, which can be contained only by the institution of government. The anarchists, however, are committed to arguing that statelessness is both desirable and possible under modern conditions. Yet in making that assertion they perhaps betray the extent to which Rousseau's vision remains at the back of their minds. This is most explicit in Godwin, who, in a long footnote devoted to Rousseau's 'general merits, as a moral and political writer', remarks that

> he has been subjected to continual ridicule for the extravagance of the proposition with which he began his literary career: that the savage state was the genuine and proper condition of man. It was however by a very slight mistake that he missed the opposite opinion which it is the business of the present enquiry to establish. He only substituted, as the topic of his eulogium, the period that preceded government and laws, instead of the period that may possibly follow upon their abolition.[39]

Rousseau's narrative locates a happy, virtuous, and free anarchy in the primitive past and presents it as irrevocably displaced by the misery and servitude of the modern regime of property secured by government. Godwin would accept relevantly similar categories but set them in a reversed chronology. There is also a trace of this in Proudhon, who in his unpublished notes on the *Second Discourse* reproaches Rousseau for 'relegating equality to an ideal condition'.[40] Bakunin and Kropotkin may similarly be read as reversing Rousseau's scheme of history. They take pains to reject his notion of a state of nature, Bakunin in particular attacking the implication that this was a realm of perfect freedom now lost with the advent of society.[41] In similar spirit, although without express reference to Rousseau, Bakunin writes that 'The light of humanity, which alone can light us and warm us, deliver us and exalt us, make us free, happy and brothers, stands never at the beginning of history but always at the end.'[42] Such a view might be held by any of the anarchists. Inequality and government, they suppose, are legacies of an irrational past which will be superseded by a desirable anarchy in the future.

A theme from the *Second Discourse* of especial significance for understanding the anarchists is Rousseau's description and analysis of the modern social and political predicament. The unprecedented radicalism of that message is best brought out by comparing it with the standard views of the classical republican tradition. Classical republicanism, with its roots in the politics of the Greek and Roman city-states and in the writings of Aristotle, Polybius, and the Roman historians, exerted a powerful influence on Rousseau, who admired its values of conscientious citizenship: the capacity to rule and be ruled in turn, to play one's part in the defence of the city, in general to place public before private interest.[43] Revived by Renaissance humanism, republicanism survived into the eighteenth century to become, in the hands of Rousseau among others, one of the main theoretical counterweights to the values of the burgeoning commercial culture.[44] A persistent concern of republicanism had always been that the good life of citizenship could be undermined by excessive concern for private material gain. While a certain level of wealth was desirable, indeed essential in order to ensure the leisure in which the virtues of the citizen could be cultivated, this must not lead to an overmastering preoccupation with 'luxury'. But hostility to luxury did not necessarily imply a hostility to inequality of wealth or social position as such. For many republican writers the only wholly desirable equality was *isonomia,* 'equal subjection to the *res publica*', or public authority.[45] Economic and social inequality were accepted with equanimity.

Although some classical republicans exhibit a concern that marked inequalities of wealth might lead to instability in relations between citizens, Rousseau takes the analysis of the effects of economic inequality, and opposition to that inequality, very much further. Imbalance of wealth is for him not merely a threat to social stability but the cause of a much more profound blight on modern life, the psychological malaise he describes in terms of corruption, unfreedom, and man's alienation from his true nature.[46] The level simplicity of primitive society was a period of wholeness, happiness, and freedom. It is only when the possibility of accumulation emerges that man begins his downward slide. Every relation of man-made inequality is an instance of dependence, of corruption and enslavement, but Rousseau's principal focus in the *Second Discourse* is on economic inequality; it is from this starting point that all else follows. Once trapped in the power relations of wealth and poverty, the whole life of post-primitive man becomes infected with self-interest and consequently vice, enslavement, and the feeling that he is living 'outside himself', separated from his authentic identity.

A similar pattern appears in all the anarchists: the analysis of modern society as a complex of power relations, the inherently evil character of all power, the linking of both the subservient and the dominant in a web of mutual dependence that alienates each from his true moral nature, the role of government in fixing the whole structure permanently in place. Rousseau's picture of a moral crisis so deep that it pervades the whole of society points the way to the anarchists' conviction that mere reform is inadequate if freedom and virtue are to be attained; nothing less than a total transformation of society is necessary. The anarchist insistence that freedom and virtue must be based not merely on political but on economic and social equality looks back to Rousseau's distinctive development of republicanism.

In the *Second Discourse* at least, Rousseau sees no hope of escape from the plight he describes. The primitive soci-

ety in which virtue was possible is now irretrievable. Nevertheless, embedded in the essay is a theme which, once separated from Rousseau's degenerative historical pattern, could give grounds for optimism. The modern sickness, though pervasive and profound, is not to be understood as the result of God's will or of features inherent in human nature. Man is not inherently evil but vulnerable to social influences that have led him to develop in unfortunate ways. The anarchists would agree. Where they differ from Rousseau is in their view of the fundamental nature of the present sickness, and consequently in their conception of its treatment and prognosis. For Rousseau, modern corruption is basically a sickness of the heart, the eclipse of the virtuous sentiments by the lower passions. The only way out is to renew contact with the pure conscience within—an all but hopeless task in the prevailing environment of decadence. The anarchists, on the other hand, see the problem, in terms more characteristic of the Enlightenment, as basically one of ignorance, the ascendancy of the passions over a still feeble but improvable reason. The State, with its attendant evils, is merely the product of an imperfectly evolved human rationality. Its eventual dissolution is assured if only we can expect the requisite improvements in human knowledge.

We can now see that although there are parallels and connections between the anarchists and Rousseau at many points, two areas of affinity are especially striking: the paramount commitment to freedom understood as moral self-direction, and the radical critique of modern 'civilized' society, which is pictured as destructive of moral self-direction. Indeed there is evidence, as will appear, that these two Rousseauian positions are not only paralleled by Godwin and Proudhon but received by them directly. Together they form a platform from which the anarchists develop their attack on the State. In addition, Rousseau's work offers the anarchists some cause for hope. On this point there is only limited evidence of positive influence, although Rousseau's picture of the primitive anarchy and his diagnosis of the present social sickness as man-made are suggestive of the anarchist vision of future statelessness. That vision, however, owes more to another source, to which I shall now turn.

3. SCIENTISM

The anarchists' sanguine view of the possibilities for moral and political progress through the growth of knowledge originated, like the critical phase of their case, in the Enlightenment. The spectacular advances of the natural sciences in the age of Newton had suggested that no problem was impenetrable to human reason, and the eighteenth century saw the beginning of the attempt to extend the triumphant empirical method to the study of man and society. Just as the physical sciences had unveiled the true principles of nature, so the social sciences, constructed on the same methodological model, would reveal the true principles of morals and politics. Rousseau was untypical of his age in his belief that man should seek moral truth through introspection. The anarchists are heirs to the mainstream of advanced eighteenth-century opinion when they look for moral guidance to modern empirical science.

'Scientism', the belief that the methods of empirical science provide a model appropriate to all fields of inquiry, is the chief support of the anarchists' optimism about the possibility of a non-coercive social order. This aspect of their thought has generally been overlooked in favour of their romanticism.[47] The cause of this neglect may be in part political, since it has served the purpose of those who have claimed the status of the sole 'scientific' form of socialism for Marxism. Similarly it may be wondered whether the attention received by the romantic strand in anarchism is not due in some degree to its providing a highly convenient peg on which to hang the change of lack of realism that has been foisted on anarchism from all sides. Certainly there is a romantic side to the anarchists; it is part of their mixed Rousseauian heritage. But there is also a strong scientific ambition, and it is this that I shall emphasize in order to restore it to its rightful prominence in classical anarchist thought. Compared with the influence of Rousseau, the influence of scientism on the anarchists is of a more general, imprecise nature, the transmission not so much of specific arguments traceable to particular works as of a general intellectual climate. That influence is nevertheless of great importance in forming the basic assumptions of the anarchists.

It should first be asked just what the classical anarchists believe science can reveal to us, what they take to be the object of scientific knowledge relevant to morals and politics. Here there is room for confusion, since the commitment of the anarchists to natural law might be thought antipathetic to scientism. In the eighteenth and nineteenth centuries, however, the line between natural law and the laws of nature was not always clearly drawn, and was sometimes crossed by social and political theorists seeking the normative implications of empirical observation or scientific sanction for normative claims.[48] For the anarchists, the concept of natural law served as a strong antidote to those theories—notably the social contract theories of Hobbes and, on some readings, Rousseau—which implied that there was no morality outside the State. The anarchists reply that the laws of governments are one thing, the moral law quite another. (As suggested above, Rousseau might be cited as authority for this latter view if one emphasizes the *Second Discourse* and the Savoyard Priest.) Drawing on the venerable tradition that reaches back to the Stoics, they conceive of morality as a species of truth inherent in the nature of the universe. Unlike the laws of governments, which merely serve the interests of the dominant, the moral law of nature is universal, eternal, and seamlessly harmonious (its injunctions never conflict with one another). As Herbert Read puts it, 'modern anarchism . . . is based on analogies derived from the simplicity and harmony of universal physical laws'.[49] To reject the laws of men and follow the law of nature is to abandon the realm of interest and conflict for that of truth and concord as reflected in the structure of the universe itself.

That structure can be variously conceived, and precisely how it is conceived will determine the means by which the content of the natural law can be known. In the medieval conception the universe is a hierarchy of essences created by God and governed by his laws. Natural law is that part of God's law accessible to human reason, which attains knowledge of the law through a priori reflection on the essences of things. The anarchists, however, conceive of natural law in the secularized and mechanical (but still partly normative) form in which it emerged from the Enlightenment. The universe is now the mechanism described by Newton, governed by the laws of physics. Man is part of that universe, and the laws that govern him, including the laws of morality, are to be known not by revelation or semi-mystical intuition or even reasoning a priori, but by investigating the sensible universe, which is the province of natural science. Thus Kropotkin, in his survey of the history of ethical thought, praises what he sees as the (admittedly imperfect) naturalism of the Stoics, leaving the medieval version of natural law largely out of the picture. The Stoics are linked directly to 'the modern natural-scientific school of ethics' that includes 'Bacon, Spinoza, Auguste Comte and Darwin'.[50]

The moral law must be derived from science rather than 'metaphysics'. But it must also be seen to express the eternal truths of nature, not mere contingency. With the exception of Godwin, the anarchists are hostile to utilitarianism, which they see as too narrowly focused on the contingent interests of individuals, the ethical expression, they believe, of unrestrained Anglo-Saxon individualism and commercialism.[51] Godwin saw it otherwise, as the expression of disinterested justice, moreover a theory of justice which relied solely on the materials of experience. Although the European anarchists give them no credit for it, the utilitarians were the initiators of the project of deriving ethical principles from the application of empirical scientific methodology. Hume's 'attempt to introduce the experimental method of reasoning into moral subjects' was the basically explanatory or descriptive beginning from which evolved Bentham's declaration that mankind's 'two sovereign masters, pain and pleasure . . . point out what we ought to do as well as what we shall do'.[52] To the alleged psychological truth that man's primitive motivation is his desire for pleasure and the avoidance of pain, was added the characteristic utilitarian axiom that only pleasure is desirable for its own sake: that pleasure is the only good. To judge the morally right course an agent must gauge the consequences, in terms of the pleasure and pain experienced by those affected, of the choices facing him. Moral judgement is not, as for Rousseau, a matter of simply knowing or feeling by immediate apprehension or sensation what one ought to do; it requires a process of reasoning, of weighing up the likely repercussions of the relevant actions. That process must be based on knowledge of the world, which is best obtained by scientific observation. The rise of utilitarianism is an important element in the intellectual background of Godwin. Although far from the consistent utilitarian he has often been painted, he was clearly much influenced by the scientific climate of the eighteenth century. This source of his thought ought not to be overlooked now merely because his utilitarianism has been over-emphasized in the past.[53]

The impact of the accelerating scientific revolution was felt still more powerfully by the Continental members of the anarchist tradition, who were influenced by streams of scientistic thought other than the utilitarian. This part of the intellectual ancestry of Proudhon and Bakunin began, perhaps, with the celebration of progress by Turgot and Condorcet. The former set out a historical scheme of advancing human rationality which anticipated Comte's, while the latter, writing contemporaneously with Godwin, predicted a rational amelioration of social and political institutions which would in turn lead to enhanced rationality. Condorcet's hopes are summed up in a passage that could have been written by Godwin or any of his anarchist successors: 'The time will come when the sun will shine only upon a world of free men who recognize no master except their reason, when tyrants and slaves, priests and their stupid or hypocritical tools, will no longer exist except in history or on the stage.'[54] It was after the turn of the eighteenth century, however, that this mood of rationalist optimism was combined with more explicit proposals for the role of science. As Kropotkin observes, the first half of the new century was a period of exhilarating advances in virtually every field of knowledge: 'in philosophy—positivism; in science—the theory of evolution . . . in sociology the socialism of its three great founders: Fourier, Saint-Simon, and Robert Owen, together with their followers'. But the most important development was 'in ethics—a free morality, not forced upon us from without, but resulting from the innate endowments of human nature'.[55] This was the scientific morality: a normative system that would not need to be enforced (the anarchists would add that it could not be enforced) because it perfectly reflected the fundamental, authentic moral will of man discovered through scientific investigation of his nature. The key figures in this broad movement of ideas were Saint-Simon, Comte, and Darwin.[56]

The anarchists refer less often to Saint-Simon than to his followers the Saint-Simonians, whom they dismiss, with some justification, as proponents of the *dirigiste* strain in socialist thought and as religious cranks.[57] Saint-Simon himself was a more substantial thinker, and a complex one. His views were hardly likely to appeal unproblematically to anarchist sympathies, since he was in no way committed to economic equality and he believed that the desirable society would be governed by an élite. But his conception of that élite and of its mode of government make him an anarchist precursor of real importance. Unlike the ruling classes of the past, whose authority was founded on military power, Saint-Simon's governors will be scientists and industrialists whose right to rule, reflecting the demands of a new technological age, will rest not on coercion but on a common recognition of their specialist knowledge: the application to man and society of the scientific or 'positive' method. Ordinary people will accept the directions of this technocracy as one would accept the

opinion of experts in other fields; hence, force will no longer be necessary to govern mankind and 'government' will become mere 'administration'. Proudhon takes up this point, quoting Saint-Simon's declaration that 'the human race . . . is destined to pass from the *governmental* or *military* rule to *administrative* or *industrial* rule, after it has made sufficient progress in the physical sciences and in industry'. He goes on to present himself as Saint-Simon's successor, his own economic analysis supplementing the latter's deduction of the 'negation of government' from the study of history and progress.[58]

Saint-Simon's positive approach was expanded and refined by his one-time assistant and follower Comte, who constructed a massively comprehensive 'positive philosophy' aiming at the unification of all the sciences, natural and social. Although they share similar reservations about the religious tendency of his later work, Bakunin and Kropotkin think very highly of Comte, like so many of their contemporaries regarding the positivist principle as the key to the future.[59] Kropotkin refers to Comte's 'flashes of genius', and Bakunin goes so far as to rate him 'after Hegel, the greatest philosopher of our century'.[60] Proudhon, on the other hand, seldom mentions him, and then usually for the purpose of brusque dismissal: 'the most pedantic of savants, the most shallow of all philosophers, the most insipid of socialists, the most unbearable of all writers'.[61] But this may be because he regards Comte as an unwelcome rival, for some of his own ideas, especially in the works of the 1840s, are very similar.[62] Proudhon's tripartite account of intellectual and social evolution, outlined in *La Création de l'ordre dans l'humanité* (1843), is almost certainly a renarration of Comte's 'law of the three stages', according to which human knowledge ascends from the 'theological' to the 'metaphysical' before reaching to 'positive' form of modern science.[63]

Comte made explicit a claim which had long been implied by European scientism but which had never been brought fully into the open: that the province of science included not only the question of why men act as they do but also that of how they ought to act. The culmination of Comte's positivism was the proposal of a truly scientific morality, a system of ethics that would be demonstrably true according to scientific method. In this he went further than his admirer J. S. Mill, who looked to the natural and social sciences to provide information that would help to guide moral improvement, but who maintained a careful distinction between assertions of fact, which were the business of science, and practical rules of 'art', the stuff of ethics.[64] But even Mill contributed, through his support for Comte's early work and his own hopes for the social sciences, to a climate of opinion in which the distinction between fact and value was submerged by a pervasive enthusiasm for the moral potential of science. Comte expressed one of the most powerful intellectual currents of the age when he argued that science would become not merely the servant of ethics but its master.

A scientific view of history indicates, according to Comte, that in proportion as society develops and man progresses, the self-regarding affections are restricted and the benevolent affections become stronger. On the principle that a scientific morality must accord with and even assist the inevitable course of social progress, the chief aim of positive morality must therefore be 'to make our sympathetic instincts preponderate as far as possible over the selfish instincts'.[65] This prescription appeals strongly to Kropotkin, and, together with the principle that ethics should be given a scientific grounding, it earns Comte his warm endorsement.[66] But Kropotkin also sees Comte as having been insufficiently rigorous when it came to applying his positivist principles to morals and politics, accusing him of abandoning naturalism at this point for metaphysical speculation and invention. What Comte lacked, he argues, was the biological knowledge that would have provided him with a fully naturalistic account of the moral sentiments. Fortunately such knowledge and such an account are now available in the work of Darwin. *The Descent of Man* becomes the basis of Kropotkin's own science of ethics. In successive works he sets out to show that modern evolutionary science implies a scheme of morals and politics. In this he is hardly alone among his contemporaries, but he turns against the prevailing current of Social Darwinism by characterizing the scientific morality and politics as altruistic and anarchistic.

Kropotkin's appeal to a permanent law underlying all evolution is perhaps better adapted to anarchist purposes than the historicist moral relativism of Comte or Marx. There may be more than a trace of the latter in the view sometimes found in the anarchists that institutions like the State and the Church were in some sense fitting for pre-modern forms of society. But time and again the anarchists return to the idea of eternal natural law. Beliefs in conflict with that law are explained as expressions of social forms that are not merely archaic but imperfectly human, antedating the emergence of man as a being capable of recognizing his capacity for self-directed virtue. Truly human morality has always required the recognition of man's capacity for moral self-direction, with all the implications which flow from that. If such recognition has been withheld at previous stages of social development, then man could not at that time have been fully humanized. The mission of modern science is therefore not merely to describe past conjunctions of intellectual and moral improvement, nor even to predict the nature of the moral system that will emerge out of contemporary social advance, although these are part of its task. In addition it must reveal the permanent moral order that has been concealed, by ignorance and conspiracy, hitherto. It is not the sociological aspect of Saint-Simon, Comte, and Darwin that is echoed most clearly by the anarchists, but their role as moralists. The climate of confidence in science assures the anarchists that the moral world is part of the natural, investigation of which will uncover the moral law itself. Once that law is revealed, man will be able to accept its guidance in just the same way that he recognizes the validity of the laws of nature demonstrated by natural scientists. In so doing he will be free: rationally and morally perfected and self-

directing. Government will then be unnecessary and will be dispensed with.

Where Rousseau almost despaired of the prospects for quietening the din of passions and opinions sufficiently to let the voice of conscience be heard, the anarchists share the widespread confidence of the high Enlightenment and the nineteenth century that intellectual and material improvement will lead to moral improvement. Moral conviction is principally a function of knowledge, and knowledge of the moral law lies along the same continuum as knowledge of the laws of physics; evidence for the one is of essentially the same kind and is similarly compelling as evidence for the other. By arguing for the eventual redundancy of government, the anarchists, as Berlin has noted, are doing no more than following out the logic of contemporary scientism—granting the further assumption that scientific knowledge of morality will be accessible to everyone, so that there will be no need for the Saint-Simonian expert.[67] Here, then, are the three principal of the anarchist argument: the perfectionist idea of rational and moral self-mastery, Rousseau's passionate critique of modern civilization, the scientistic optimism of the Enlightenment and the nineteenth century. Together these form much of the basis on which the anarchists build their distinctive theories.

Notes

1. The prehistory of anarchism is surveyed by G. Woodcock, *Anarchism: A History of Libertarian Ideas and Movements* (Harmondsworth, 1963), ch. 1.

2. D. Miller, *Anarchism* (London, 1984), 3.

3. I. Berlin, 'Two Concepts of Liberty', in *Four Essays on Liberty* (London, 1969).

4. This form of the distinction is developed more fully in G. Crowder, 'Negative and Positive Liberty', *Political Science* 40 (1988), 57-73.

5. Berlin, *Four Essays on Liberty*, xliv-xlv. But note that the 'negative liberty' Berlin attributes to the anarchists here is quite different from what he usually means by this term, and indeed is difficult to distinguish from what he calls positive liberty elsewhere. He gives the impression of stretching the negative category to fit his negative/liberal—positive/authoritarian pattern. Cf. ibid. 149, where the anarchists seem to be placed in the positive category, and his treatment of Bakunin, discussed in Ch. 4, s. 2 below. Other 'negative' readings of anarchist freedom include R. B. Fowler, 'The Anarchist Tradition of Political Thought', *Western Political Quarterly* 25 (1972), 738-52 at 745-7 (but cf. 750); and P. Thomas, *Karl Marx and the Anarchists* (London, 1980), 7-11.

6. *The Times,* 7 Jan. 1911. Among those who see the classical anarchists as extreme individualists see J. Bowle on 'rampant individualism' in Godwin: *Politics and Opinion in the 19th Century* (London, 1954), 140; and E. H. Carr's description of Bakunin

as 'the most complete individualist who ever lived': *Michael Bakunin* (London, 1937), 434-5. For the claim that classical anarchism is essentially an extreme form of liberalism see Fowler, 'The Anarchist Tradition of Political Thought', 745-7; and Thomas, *Karl Marx and the Anarchists,* 7-11.

7. H. M. Hyndman, *The Historical Basis of Socialism in England* (London, 1883); D. G. Ritchie, *Natural Rights* (London, 1894), 19.

8. A. Ritter, *Anarchism: A Theoretical Analysis* (Cambridge, 1980), ch. 1.

9. See G. Orwell, 'Politics *vs* Literature', in *Inside the Whale and Other Essays* (Harmondsworth, 1962), 132-3.

10. I agree with Ritter, however, that a demanding level of rationality is *part* of the anarchist conception of freedom (although see below for the question of how 'rationality' should be interpreted in this context). It might also be argued that the notion of 'communal individuality' that Ritter attributes to the anarchists as their primary goal is in some respects not far from what I shall identify as their idea of the desirable freedom.

11. On the question of whether classical anarchism is more properly described as an extension of liberalism or as a species of socialism, it is more difficult to reach a straightforward conclusion. My own view is that from a historical point of view classical anarchism belongs more properly within the socialist tradition (see M. Fleming, *The Anarchist Way to Socialism: Élisée Reclus and Nineteenth-Century European Anarchism* (London, 1979); G. D. H. Cole, *A History of Socialist Thought,* ii (London, 1954)), but that conceptually it shares a good deal of ground with liberalism, although this should not entail its misinterpretation as a doctrine of negative liberty.

12. *Republic,* 431.

13. Berlin, 'Two Concepts of Liberty', 154.

14. Ibid.

15. This is by no means true of *every* proponent of positive liberty, as shown by the example of J. S. Mill. For the positive idea in Mill see J. N. Gray, *Mill on Liberty: A Defence* (London, 1983); G. W. Smith, 'Mill on Freedom', in Z. Pelczynski and J. N. Gray (eds.), *Conceptions of Liberty in Political Philosophy* (London, 1984), 182-216.

16. *Philosophy of Right,* trans. T. M. Knox (London, 1952), paras. 15, 149, 149A. Hegel did not reject negative liberty entirely, since he also saw the market economy as having a liberating aspect. But he clearly believed that the positive freedom he commended was a more complete and valuable form of liberty.

17. Berlin sometimes seems to suggest that his thesis is purely historical—that it does no more than draw attention to the fact, which might have been otherwise, that the positive idea has been abused rather more than the negative: see, especially, the Introduction to *Four Essays on Liberty.* But he is surely saying more than this when the whole tendency of 'Two Concepts' is to link the allegation of historical abuse with an examination of conceptual features of positive liberty not shared by its negative counterpart.

18. For positive liberty in Mill see above, n. 15. The case of Locke is conceded by Berlin himself: 'Two Concepts', 147; see also J. Tully, 'Locke on Liberty', in Pelczynski and Gray, *Conceptions of Liberty,* 57-82. Constant is also a positive libertarian: see S. Holmes, *Benjamin Constant and the Making of Modern Liberalism* (New Haven, 1984).

19. *General Idea of the Revolution,* 120-1 (trans. A. Noland, in 'Proudhon and Rousseau', *Journal of the History of Ideas* 28 (1967), 33-54, at 36-7).

20. Ibid.

21. *Carnets,* ed. P. Haubtmann (Paris, 1960), no. 8, 26 Oct. 1850, cited by Noland, 'Proudhon and Rousseau', 35; *What is Property?* (Second Memoir), trans. B. Tucker (New York, 1970), 391.

22. *Enquiry concerning Political Justice, and its influence on Morals and Happiness,* 3rd edn., ed. I. Kramnick (Harmondsworth, 1976), v. xv. 497 note.

23. The literature occasionally refers to affinities between aspects of Rousseau and of anarchism, and to the influence of the former on the latter, but these connections have never to my knowledge been pursued very fully. In some cases these matters receive no more than a passing mention: see, e.g., A. Carter, *The Political Theory of Anarchism* (London, 1971), 1; D. Guérin, *Anarchism,* trans. M. Klopper (New York, 1970), p. xi; J. Plamenatz, *The English Utilitarians,* 2nd edn. (Oxford, 1958), 90. In others there are brief references to the presence in the anarchists of various Rousseauian themes, including: man's natural goodness and perfectibility, 'dependence', the opposition between 'nature' and repressive civilized convention (especially in education), the rejection of the liberal social contract, opposition to the 'overgrown' State. See, e.g., C. J. Friedrich, *Tradition and Authority* (London, 1972), 100; B. Goodwin, *Using Political Ideas,* 2nd edn. (Chichester, 1987), 123-5; J. Passmore, *The Perfectibility of Man* (London, 1970), 177-9; J. Joll, *The Anarchists,* 2nd edn. (London, 1979), 15-16; C. Pateman, *The Problem of Political Obligation* (Chichester, 1979); J. Plamenatz, *Democracy and Illusion* (London, 1973), 45-7. As we shall see, similar parallels and connections have also been noted between Rousseau and particular anarchists.

24. Joll, *The Anarchists,* 33-4.

25. *Ethics: Origin and Development,* trans. L. S. Friedland and J. R. Piroshnikoff (New York, 1924), 195. This apparently supersedes Kropotkin's earlier view that Rousseau had only a limited role as an inspirer of the Revolution and that Mably was a more important influence: *The Great French Revolution, 1789-1793,* trans. N. F. Dryhurst (London, 1909), 12.

26. *God and the State* (New York, 1970), 79. See also *Œuvres,* I. 263 for a reference to Rousseau and Robespierre as 'absolutist Jacobins'; similarly Proudhon, *General Idea of the Revolution,* 121-2.

27. Letter to Ruge, quoted by Carr, *Michael Bakunin,* 117, and by A. Kelly, *Mikhail Bakunin* (Oxford, 1982), 108.

28. Godwin's Rousseauian readings are listed below, Ch. 2, s. 1. For Proudhon's see Noland, 'Proudhon and Rousseau', 37, and P. Haubtmann, *Pierre-Joseph Proudhon: sa vie et sa pensée 1809-1849* (Paris, 1982), 250-1. The evidence concerning Bakunin and Kropotkin is sparse, but references to Rousseau are scattered throughout their writings: see below, Ch. 4, s. 1.

29. Godwin, *An Account of the Seminary, etc.* . . . in *Four Early Pamphlets,* ed. B. R. Pollin (Gainesville, Fla., 1966). Bakunin, 'L'Instruction intégrale', *Œuvres Complètes* (Paris, 1895-1913). v. 134-68; Kropotkin, *Fields, Factories and Workshops Tomorrow,* ed. C. Ward (London, 1974), ch. 4. Another anarchist educator influenced by Rousseau is Herbert Read: *Education Through Art,* 3rd edn. (London, 1961).

30. *Political Justice,* v. xv. 497 note.

31. Proudhon, *The General Idea of the Revolution in the Nineteenth Century,* trans. J. B. Robinson (London, 1923), 118, 119; Bakunin, *Œuvres,* i. 139-40.

32. See Bakunin, *Œuvres,* i. 139-40 (*The Political Philosophy of Bakunin: Scientific Anarchism,* ed. G. P. Maximoff (New York and London, 1953) 165-7).

33. Note that, as will appear in more detail later (see Ch. 2, s. 2 below), the anarchist conception of moral self-direction is by no means identical to Rousseau's. While Rousseau tends to stress the role of sentiment in human authenticity, the anarchists follow the usual line of the perfectionist tradition in assigning a dominant role to reason. (There is, nevertheless, a rationalist element in Rousseau, too: R. Derathé, *Jean-Jacques Rousseau et la science politique de son temps* (Paris, 1950).) But this is chiefly a difference of emphasis. Both the anarchist and Rousseauian conceptions of freedom are recognizably conceptions of moral self-direction, involving the claim that freedom implies conscientious obedience to an objective moral law, however that law is known. My argument is, in any case, not that the anarchists derive their basic concept of freedom directly from Rousseau (they derive it, more generally, from the perfectionist tradition at large), but that they share with Rousseau a conception of freedom which is recognizable as moral self-direction, and that Rousseau is at least one of the sources of their claim that freedom in that sense is inviolable.

34. *The Social Contract,* I. iv.

35. See below, Ch. 2, s. 3; Ch. 3, s. 4.

36. J. Shklar, *Men and Citizens, a Study of Rousseau's Social Theory* (Cambridge, 1969).

37. *Système des contradictions économiques, ou philosophie de la misère,* 2 vols. (Paris, 1923), i. 350. See similarly *General Idea of the Revolution,* 117.

38. *Contradictions économiques,* i. 350.

39. *Political Justice,* v. xv. 497 note.

40. Quoted by P. Haubtmann, *Pierre-Joseph Proudhon,* 250 (see also 315, n. 19).

41. Bakunin, *Œuvres,* i. 139-43 (Maximoff, *Political Philosophy of Bakunin,* 165-7), and see below, Ch. 4, s. 2. See also Kropotkin, *Mutual Aid: A Factor of Evolution* (Harmondsworth, 1939), 23-4, 75, 99, *Ethics: Origin and Development,* trans. L. B. Friedland and J. R. Piroshnikoff (New York, 1924), 78, *The State: its Historic Role,* trans. V. Richards (London, 1969), 12.

42. *God and the State* (New York, 1970), 21.

43. For the influence of classical republicanism on Rousseau see Shklar, *Men and Citizens;* and M. Viroli, *Jean-Jacques Rousseau and the 'Well-Ordered Society',* trans. D. Hanson (Cambridge, 1988).

44. Commerce and republicanism are, however, to some degree reconciled by the writers of the Scottish Enlightenment. See I. Hont and M. Ignatieff (eds.), *Wealth and Virtue: The Shaping of Political Economy in the Scottish Enlightenment* (Cambridge, 1983).

45. J. G. A. Pocock, *The Machiavellian Moment* (Princeton, NJ, 1975), 469.

46. For the embryonic theory of alienation in Rousseau see J. P. Plamenatz, *Karl Marx's Philosophy of Man* (Oxford, 1975); I. Mészáros, *Marx's Theory of Alienation,* 4th edn. (London, 1975).

47. A notable exception to this tendency is Marie Fleming, although she confines the scientific strand of anarchism to 'Bakunin's spiritual descendants', i.e., Reclus, Kropotkin, and their followers: *The Anarchist Way to Socialism,* 22.

48. Perhaps the clearest example of this tendency is provided by the Victorian social evolutionists: see J. W. Burrow, *Evolution and Society* (Cambridge, 1966), 263.

49. H. Read, 'The Philosophy of Anarchism', in *Anarchy and Order* (London, 1954), 43.

50. *Ethics,* 110.

51. The Continental anarchists all reject utilitarianism more or less explicitly. See Ritter, *Anarchism,* 115-16; and below, Ch. 3, n. 48, and Ch. 4, n. 18.

52. Hume, *A Treatise of Human Nature,* ed. L. A. Selby Bigge and P. H. Nidditch, 2nd edn. (Oxford, 1978), subtitle; Bentham, *Introduction to the Principles of Morals and Legislation* (London, 1970), 11.

53. See below, Ch. 2, s. 1.

54. Quoted in G. H. Sabine, *A History of Political Theory* (New York, 1937), 572.

55. *Ethics,* 250.

56. It is tempting to add the name of Marx, who was probably a greater influence on the European anarchists than any of them cares to admit. But the intellectual links between Marx and the anarchists are so obscured by political differences that the matter cannot be done justice here and is best left to one side. For a thorough treatment of this question from a Marxian point of view see Thomas, *Karl Marx and the Anarchists.* An account more sympathetic to the anarchist side of the dispute is given by R. Hoffman, 'Marx and Proudhon: A Reappraisal of Their Relationship', *The Historian,* 29 (1967), 409-30, and *Revolutionary Justice: The Social and Political Theory of Pierre-Joseph Proudhon* (Urbana, Illinois, 1972), ch. 4.

57. See, e.g., Bakunin, Maximoff, *Political Philosophy of Bakunin,* 278.

58. *General Idea of the Revolution,* 122-5.

59. For the general influence of Comte see W. M. Simon, *European Positivism in the Nineteenth Century* (Ithaca, NY, 1963).

60. Ibid. 48 note; *Œuvres,* iii. 331.

61. Quoted by Simon, *European Positivism* 142.

62. The evidence for and against seeing Comte as an important influence on Proudhon is reviewed by de Lubac, *The Un-Marxian Socialist: A Study of Proudhon,* trans. Canon R. E. Scantlebury (London, 1948), 236-9; Haubtmann, *Pierre-Joseph Proudhon,* 384-97.

63. Proudhon's 'Three great stages in the development of human knowledge' are, similarly, 'the Religious, the Philosophical and the Scientific': *De la création de l'ordre dans l'humanité* (Paris, 1927), 36-7, 39 (*Selected Writings of Pierre-Joseph Proudhon,* trans. E. Fraser, ed. S. Edwards (London, 1969), 239).

64. *A Systēm of Logic* (London, 1843), vi. See the final section, 'The Logic of Practice, or Art: Including Morality and Policy'.

65. *Auguste Comte and Positivism: The Essential Writings,* ed. G. Lenzer (New York, 1975), 337.

66. *Modern Science and Anarchism* (London, 1912), 18-19; *Ethics,* 48 and note.

67. Berlin, 'Two Concepts of Liberty', 148-9.

THE FRENCH ANARCHIST TRADITION

S. Y. Lu (essay date 1922)

SOURCE: "Proudhon's Theory of the State from the Standpoint of an Anarchist-Creative," in *The Political Theories of P. J. Proudhon,* M. R. Gray, Inc., 1922, pp. 95-121.

[*In the following essay, Lu studies the development of Proudhon's anarchist political theory.*]

As has already been said, Proudhon was the father of anarchism.[1] From 1840 to 1863, he repeatedly declared himself an anarchist.[2] In discussing his theory of anarchy, we may, for the sake of clearness, divide the work into three parts: (1) why he preferred anarchy to the other forms of government, (2) how it can be realized, and (3) what are its general characteristics.

I. WHY PROUDHON PREFERRED ANARCHY TO THE OTHER FORMS OF GOVERNMENT.

Society, he declares, is perpetually progressive.[3] Anarchy is the condition of existence for adult society. Hierarchy is the condition of existence for primitive society. There is an incessant growth in human society from hierarchy to anarchy.[4]

There are two chief differences between anarchy and all the other forms of government. First, anarchy is the rule of justice, while all the other governments are that of power. In the family, where authority is close to the heart of man, government is based upon birth; in the savage and barbaric society, upon patriarchy, or force; in a sacerdotal society, upon faith; in an aristocratic society, upon primogeniture or caste; in the system of Rousseau, upon chance or number. Birth, force, faith, primogeniture, chance and number are all equally unintelligible, with which we cannot reason but to which we can only submit. They are not principles but different modes through which the investiture of power is effected.[5]

Second, in anarchy, public action will be exercised by all the citizens individually, and independently of each other, while in all the other forms of government it becomes the exclusive practice of a selected few, that is, the few public functionaries elected by the people for this end. All the others are no longer associates of these public functionaries, but their subjects. It is this system which has been in vogue up to the present and which is called in turn theocracy, monarchy and obligarchy:—all these designations indicating one and the same thing, that is, the state of priests, dynasties, patricians or nobles.[6]

II. How Can Anarchy Be Realized.

Anarchy can be realized through (1) revolution of ideas,[7] (2) revolution of education,[8] (3) economic revolution,[9] (4) social revolution,[10] and (5) political revolution.[11]

Before discussing these topics, we may first consider what Proudhon's general idea of revolution was. Revolution, according to him, is extraordinary acceleration of movement in the continuous progress of humanity.[12] It must first be legitimate and must proceed directly from the anterior state. Second, it must be legal. It must support itself upon established right. Thirdly it must be pacific. It must be capable of developing itself freely on one hand and tolerating the existing ideas on the other.[13] Fourthly, it must be accomplished through progressive reform, instead of through violence.[14] Violence is useless and contradictory; useless because social problems can be easily solved by pacific means,[15] contradictory because violence is an appeal to force, to arbitrariness.[16] Fifthly, it must be universal. It will be ineffective if it is not contagious. In other words, it will fail in France if it is not rendered universal throughout the whole world.[17]

(1) REVOLUTION OF IDEAS.

Revolution is a French name for the new idea. There is a distinction between progress and revolution. When our ideas on any subject, material, intellectual or social, undergo a thorough change because of new observations, we call that movement of the mind revolution. If the ideas are simply extended or modified, there is only progress. Thus the system of Ptolemy was a step in astronomical progress, that of Copernicus was a revolution.[18] As soon as the idea is vulgarized, or popularized, the transformation of society will be accomplished, with or without the support of government.[19]

(2) EDUCATION.

In close connection with the revolution of ideas is education. Proudhon strongly attacked the old system of education. "Schools are the seminaries of the aristocrats," he said; "It is not for the people that the polytechnic school, the normal school, the law school, and the school of Saint-Cyr have been founded. It is mainly for maintaining and fortifying the distinction of classes between the bourgeoisie and the proletariat that they have come into existence."[20]

Proudhon, therefore, substituted his new idea for the old idea of education. First, education must be secular. It must be freed from ontological and religious speculations.[21] Second, education must be professional. By the obligation of apprenticeship, by coöperation with all the parts of the collective work, the division of labor will no longer be a cause of degradation for the working men; on the contrary it will become an instrument of education, and a pledge of security for them.[22] To separate education from apprenticeship, and what is more detestable still, to distinguish professional education from the real, useful, serious daily exercise of the profession, is to reproduce under another form the separation of powers, and the distinction of classes, the two most energetic instruments of governmental tyranny and of subordination of the workingmen.[23] Thirdly, education must be democratic. It must be the same for all the people.[24] Through the democratization of education, we shall arrive at a stage in which intellectual equality may be approached, if not completely realized.

(3) ECONOMIC REVOLUTION.

Economic anarchy is the chief cause of the existence of governmental institutions.[25] If economic forces are well organized, there would be no need of government. In the place of the feudal, military or governmental regime, we should establish the industrial regime.[26] How will the economic forces be organized? Proudhon's answer to this question is rather complicated, and sometimes contradictory. Broadly speaking, we may divide his economic reforms into three classes: (a) industrial, (b) commercial and (c) agricultural.

(a) Industrial reforms.

Proudhon knew perfectly well that the progress of society might be measured by the development of industry.[27] First, he urged the division of labor,[28] the equalizing of wages,[29] the complete subordination of capital to labor, and the identification of the workers with the capitalists.[30] Second, he urged the centralization of industry—centralization of the industries affecting natural resources (including mining, fishing, hunting and gathering of fruits), centralization of manufacturing industries, centralization of commercial industries, centralization of agricultural industries and centralization of science, literature and the arts. The organization in each of these five great categories should be democratic. Each should elect its own minister by relative or absolute majority. Each should form its own central administration and support it at its own expense.[31] Thirdly, he urged the organization of workingmen's societies (*Compagnies ouvrières*). Since a great number of workers are employed in the industries, it will be necessary for them to organize into different societies. These societies will be the real basis of the future industrial organizations. It is in them that Proudhon laid his hope for the future of the workingman.[32] Fourthly, he believed that each of these workingmen's societies should be autonomous. Each household, each workshop, each corporation should have its proper police, and should administer with exactitude its own affairs.[33] In other words, all the affairs of police, justice and administration would be managed by the workers.[34] Industrial organization would take the place of political government.[35]

(b) Commercial reforms.

There are two schools of socialism; one based on the theory of production and the other on that of exchange.

For the former the technique of production is the basis of society; in order to reform society, it is necessary for us to reform the technique of production. For the latter, the technique of exchange, instead of production, is the economic basis of society; in order to transform society, it is necessary to reform the technique of exchange. Proudhon belongs to the second school. He believes that the social problem is, fundamentally, a problem of correlation of credit and exchange.[36] He believes that the transformation of the mechanism of exchange would bring about the reformation of society. His plan for the reform of exchange is two-fold—(x) the abolition of interest and (y) the abolition of money.

(x) The abolition of interest.

In exchange, the basis of all value should be labor.[37] The price of the product should be made in terms of its real value, that is, the net expense incurred in the process of production. In this way, all the intermediary parasites will disappear. The banker will get from his creditors a remuneration corresponding to the cost of services which he has rendered to them, and nothing more. Such will be the case with the money-lender, the land-owner, and in general with all those who render services to other people. They will violate the law of reciprocity if they exact any excessive remuneration, passing beyond the cost which the rendition of the service may entail. In short, all the forms of usury should be abolished. There would be no discount for the money-lenders, no rent for the landlords, no interest or dividend for the stockholders.[38]

(y) The abolition of money.

In substitution for the old system of exchange, Proudhon is in favor of instituting a new system of exchange in which reciprocity and justice would be the guiding principles.[39] The intermediary of money would be abolished. We should use banknotes only. The buyer of a product, instead of paying his creditor in cash would meet his debt by a letter of exchange which the seller would immediately take to the bank. The bank would give him, in exchange for his letter, a bank-note in value equal to the amount inscribed upon the letter. With the bank-note the seller could then obtain such merchandise as he needed. Having in his hand a legal promise, redeemable at sight, he finds himself losing nothing by the suppression of money. The bank in all these operations would not run any risks, because the social paper (*papier social*) or the letter of exchange that he obtained from the seller, is secured by commodities.[40]

(c) Agricultural reforms.

In applying the principle of contractual justice, the small farmers would, by the payment of rent, gradually gain a right to a part of the property. Through the development of this process, the great land-owners would tend to disappear and the small farmers would become directly and without any intermediary, the proprietors of the land they cultivated. Proudhon considered this system preferable to the social project of nationalization or communizing of the soil, because it would fundamentally satisfy the desire "*propriétiste*" of the peasant.[41] In the organized republic, agriculture, formerly the work of the slave, would become the first of the fine arts for the people. They would pass their lives in innocence, free from all seductions of the ideal.[42]

The result of the economic revolution would be two-fold: (1) social and (2) political. Socially, there would be no strong and weak in the state. There would be no capitalists, but all producers.[43] Politically, the economic revolution would end in the disappearance of government within and the growth of international peace without. Within the state, the governmental system would tend to merge into the economic system.[44] The industrial regime would be substituted for the military or governmental regime.[45] There would be no courts, no law, no police.[46] Between the states all the agricultural, financial and industrial interests would become identical and solidified. The commercial market would be open to all. Its advantages would be the same for all the nations. There would be no need of diplomatic officers, nor national distinctions. The producers and consumers of the world would be merged into one another.[47]

(4) SOCIAL REVOLUTION.

Historically speaking, Proudhon asserts, society has undergone three stages of development. The first period was that of equality. All men were equal, socially as well as economically. They were all producers.

The second period was that of military conquest. As the result of war, those who were taken prisoners became the slaves of the conqueror. Society was then divided into two classes: (1) the privileged class composed of the priests and nobles, especially devoted to the altar and to the vocation of war, and (2) the slaves, servitors or serfs, charged with the care of the household, the providing of food, and the performing of those services which concern industry and production. The distinction between the privileged class and the slaves was based upon a double prejudice—cult and war. If we should abolish war and religion, we would abolish the distinction between these two classes.

The third period was that of economic exploitation, in which the bourgeoisie class was formed between the privileged class and the servile class. There grew up, consequently, a distinction in industry analogous to that of master and slave: on the one hand, we see the capitalists, proprietors, *entrepreneurs,* or bourgeoisie; on the other, we see the laborers or proletariat. While gradually ameliorating their economic conditions, the former serfs became merged into the laborers and formed a new class which we call by the generic name of plebeians. Notice, then, that the distinction between the bourgeoisie and the plebeian is no more rational and legitimate than the distinction between the master and the slave. It is based upon the no less arbitrary separation of labor and capital.[48]

The bourgeoisie may again be divided into three subdivisions: (1) those who live on the rent of their land and houses, on the interest of their capital and on the profits of their enterprises, (2) the small manufacturers, artisans, shopkeepers and farmers, and (3) the laborers, or employees whose income surpasses in some degree the average income of the people.[49] The first subdivision constitutes the capitalistic bourgeoisie; the second and the third the "*petite bourgeoisie*," or the "*classe moyenne*."[50] In another place we find that Proudhon divided French society into three classes instead of two: (1) the bourgeoisie, (2) the middle class, and (3) the proletariat.[51]

His attitude toward these three classes was inconsistent. In 1848-1849, he thought that the economic problem would be solved through the combined effort of the bourgeoisie and the proletariat.[52] Later on in 1851, he appealed especially to the bourgeoisie for the accomplishment of the revolution. Though the workingmen may be capable of realizing social readjustment and the reconstitution of property, they are incapable of managing great interests such as those of industry and commerce.[53] The bourgeoisie are, on the contrary, the most intrepid, the most skilful of revolutionaries.[54] It is upon the bourgeoisie alone that Proudhon laid his hope of the revolution. "The revolution holds its arms to you," said Proudhon; "save the people, save yourselves as your fathers have done by revolution."[55]

In 1852, however, he changed his mind. Not in the capitalistic bourgeoisie, but in the middle class, he saw the hope of the nation. The bourgeoisie who have endeavored to perpetually maintain the antiquated relation of labor and capital, deserve the criticism hitherto addressed to them. They are destined to disappear, for they have no plausible excuse for existence. The middle class, in whose bosom lives and moves the spirit of liberty, holds the hope of the future. Even though it is oppressed by the bourgeoisie insolence from above, and the proletarian jealousy from below, the middle class will nevertheless form the heart and the brain of the nation.[56]

As for the plebeians, or the workingmen, Proudhon generally entertained a very low opinion of them between 1840 and 1858.[57] First, the plebeians represented two of the lowest elements of society: (1) the former slaves, and (2) the degenerated men of the superior class. From the slaves, they derived a strain of cruelty or savagery. From the degenerate bourgeois among them, they have in their midst the element of baseness and of corruption.[58] Second, the plebeians are pitilessly ignorant. They are incapable of seeing further than their noses. They lack the spirit of originality, of initiative, and of revolt. What they want is the increase of their wages, the reduction of their working hours, and the diminution of the price of bread and rent.[59]

Having considered briefly the nature of the three social classes, we come now to the question of how Proudhon

was going to transform society. He strongly opposed the idea of class war. He claimed that his work was a plan of general conciliation, a project for the treaty of peace between the different classes.[60] He declared emphatically, "There is no greater crime in my eyes than the excitation to civil war."[61] Instead of an armed conflict of hostile classes, Proudhon would effect the abolition of economic classes. As mentioned above, his distinction between the bourgeoisie and the proletariat is based upon the distinction between labor and capital. If we abolish the distinction between labor and capital we also do away with the distinction between the bourgeoisie and the proletariat. There would then be no more capitalists and laborers; all would be producers,[62] all would be members of the middle class.[63]

(5) POLITICAL REVOLUTION.[64]

Political revolution is closely connected with economic revolution. The chief political reforms proposed by Proudhon were (a) the substitution of the industrial regime for the political regime; (b) the substitution of free contract for law; and (c) the organization of universal suffrage.

(a) [The substitution of the industrial regime for the political regime.]

We have discussed the first question in connection with the problem of economic revolution.[65] We may now consider the second and third questions.

(b) The substitution of free contract for law.

Before discussing Proudhon's theory of contract, a little attention given to his criticism of Rousseau's theory of social contract, would probably not be amiss.

First, the basic idea of Rousseau's contract as understood by Proudhon is individualistic. According to Rousseau, the individual by himself is good. But he is depraved by society. It is, therefore, desirable for him to abstain as much as possible from all relations with his fellow men. While thus remaining in his systematic isolation, all that he has to do is to form between him and his fellows a mutual agreement for the mutual protection of their persons and properties.[66] This, and this alone, is the aim of Rousseau's contract.

Second, Rousseau's theory is political instead of economic. He does not know economic principles. He neglects the fundamental elements of contract, and occupies himself with its secondary questions only. He thinks that he will gain all if he has established, by the simultaneous abdication of liberty, a power before which all will yield. As to work, exchange, the value and price of product, the mode of acquisition and transition of property, and a series of important economic questions, Rousseau has remained silent. He leaves all of them to the hazard of birth and speculation.[67]

Thirdly, Rousseau's social contract is neither an act of reciprocity between individuals nor even an act of society. Rousseau has neglected all the essential conditions of a free contract—the absolute liberty of the contractor, his direct and personal concern with the contract. The social contract for Rousseau is rather an act creating arbiters, chosen by the people. These arbiters are invested with power sufficient to carry out their judgment or desire.[68] "Where in your so-called contract do you provide for my rights and stipulate my duties?" Proudhon asked. "Without such provisions and stipulations your punishment for crime is an excess of power; your juristic state, flagrant usurpation; your policies, your judgment and your execution are all abusive acts."[69]

Fourthly, the chief aim of Rousseau's contract being the protection of persons and properties, his contract is, therefore, nothing other than a defensive and offensive alliance of those who possess property against those who do not. It is the coalition of the barons of property, of commerce and of industry against the disinherited proletariat. It is a pact of hatred, a monument of incurable misanthropy. It is the oath of social war which Rousseau presumptuously calls the social contract.[70] It is, finally, a dangerous fiction which tends to nothing less than the annihilation of liberty.[71]

Proudhon is, however, not an obstinate opponent, but an enthusiastic advocate, of contract. What he attacks is the contract creating arbiters, not the contract between free and independent men. According to him, the notion of contract should succeed that of government.[72] The regime of contract should be substituted for the regime of law. This would constitute the true government of man, the true sovereignty of the people, the true republic.[73]

In discussing Proudhon's theory of contract, we may, for the sake of convenience, divide his work into three parts: (x) How would the contract be drawn up? (y) what would be its fundamental principles? and (z) how would it be observed?

(x) How would the contract be drawn up?

The contract would be an act, by which two or several individuals would agree to organize for a fixed time the industrial power which we have called barter and exchange. In consequence the contractors would reciprocally guarantee to each other a certain amount of services, products, advantages, or duties which they are in the position of procuring from, or rendering to, each other.[74] The formula of the contract would be as follows: "Promise to respect the person, liberty and property of your brothers; promise never to take their product or possessions by violence, by fraud, by usury or by stock-jobbing; and above all, promise never to deceive in justice, in commerce or in any of your transactions."[75]

(y) What would be the fundamental principles of the free contract?

The fundamental principles of Proudhon's proposed free contract are fivefold. First, the idea of contract is exclusive of that of government, or of authority. Under the institution of authority, liberty and the well-being of the people would be greatly diminished.[76] Second, the contract cannot be perpetual. The idea of the communists that the contract is signed once for all eternity is absolutely wrong. It must be subject to revision.[77] Thirdly, the contract must be free. It must be freely debated, consented to and signed by all those who participate in the agreement.[78] It must be the expression of the free will of the social individual.[79] In short, it must be a free contract which tends to unite all the contracting groups.[80] Fourthly, the contract must be reciprocal. It must be an act by which those who have formed themselves into groups declare the identity and solidarity of their respective dignities and interests, and, therefore, assure to each other mutual guarantees.[81] Fifthly, the basis of the contract must be economic. It should be an economic rather than a political contract.[82]

So far we have discussed the main principles of contract. There is still one complicated question remaining to be considered—that is, whether the contract should be general or special. In respect to this question Proudhon's idea changed: (1) In favor of universal contract (1851) and (2) in favor of special contract (1858).

In 1851 Proudhon thought that the contract ought to embrace the universality of all the citizens, of all their interests, and of all their relationships. If any one man is excluded from the contract, or if any one interest in which any member of the nation is concerned, is omitted in the contract, the contract would be more or less special. It could not then be called social. The social contract ought to increase each citizen's liberty and well-being. If any one class of the people finds itself, by virtue of the contract, subdued and exploited by the other, the contract would become null and void. It would then be a fraud. It could then at any time, and with full right, be revoked and annulled by the people.[83]

In 1858, however, Proudhon changed his view. He then contended that the contract could not be general. It ought to be special. The idea of the communist that there should be only one contract for the whole of humanity and of all its affairs is entirely wrong. "One who engages himself in an association of this kind. . . ." said Proudhon, "is surrounded with numerous obstacles and is submitted to numerous burdens. He does not have any initiative."[84] Proudhon, therefore, believed that society could not engage all the actions of men by a general contract without destroying in itself all personality and liberty.[85]

(z) How would the contract be observed?

One who is constituted a member of society through the sentiment of justice which is immanent in his nature, is no longer the same as one who lives in a state of isolation. Without abandoning the rule of well-being, he will subordinate himself to what is just. Through the lapse of time justice would become for him a habit, a need, a second nature. In other words, it would become another egoism for him. He would discover in the observation of the contract a superior felicity.[86]

(c) The organization of universal suffrage.

Proudhon denounced the old system of universal suffrage as the estrangement of public conscience, the suicide of popular sovereignty, and the apostasy of revolution.[87]

In the first place, the majority of the people are unintelligent.[88] They are incapable of discerning at the first glance the merit and the honesty of candidates.[89] Very often the candidates are designated in advance. The worker nominates his employer; the domestic his master; the farmer his landlord; the soldier his general. If we would give the vote to the woman she would elect her husband. If we would give the children the vote, they would elect their father.[90] As long as people are uneducated, universal suffrage is not an organ of progress, but a drag-chain on liberty.[91] It is bound to violate the social will in its legitimate manifestations.[92] "Whoever preaches universal suffrage as the principle of order and certainty is a liar, a charlatan," said Proudhon. "Sovereignty without knowledge is blind."[93]

In the second place universal suffrage is contra-revolutionary. It is retrograding. Man has generally two instincts, the one for conservation, the other for progress. Each of these two instincts never acts except in the interests of the other. Thus each individual, judging everything from the point of view of his private interests, understands by progress the development of his private interests which are contrary to the collective interests. The result of universal suffrage will be general retrogression instead of general progression.[94]

In the third place, universal suffrage is the principle of political atheism. It is atomistic. The legislator, unable to make the people speak in a substantial unity, invites them to express their idea per capita. The surest way of making the people lie is to establish universal suffrage.[95]

In the fourth place, universal suffrage legalizes oppression. When the theorists of popular sovereignty claim that the remedy for the tyranny of power consists of the establishment of popular suffrage from which power will be drawn, they have turned like squirrels in their cage. From the moment the chief elements of power, that is, authority, property, and hierarchy, become fixed, the suffrage of the people becomes no more than the consent of the people to their oppression.[96]

In the fifth place, universal suffrage is a child's plan,[97] a true lottery. It neglects individual rights. "Over the principle," said Proudhon, "or the very essence of rights . . . over the organization of industrial forces, over my work, my subsistence, my life I denounce all presumptive authority, all indirect solutions. I wish to treat them directly, individually, for myself."[98]

In the sixth place, universal suffrage considers the sum total of the individuals, instead of society as a whole, as the sovereign. It confuses the generality of an opinion with the social idea, the action of a multitude with the action of society.[99]

In the seventh place, universal suffrage means the triumph of the minority. We may take the election of 1848 for example. In that election more than 400,000 citizens had the right to vote in the Department of the Seine. But only 300,000 participated in the election. About 100,000 were absent. Of the 300,000 votes, only thirteen candidates received more than one half of the votes cast. There were twenty-one candidates who were elected only by a relative majority of 144,000 to 104,000 votes. How could they be called the representatives of the people when they were elected by only a minority of them?[100]

Proudhon attacked not the principle, but only the old system, of universal suffrage. What he intended to do was not to abolish, but to reorganize it. In order to make universal suffrage intelligent, moral and democratic, it is necessary, he maintained, after organizing the balance of services and assuring, by free discussion, the independence of suffrage, to provide that the citizens vote by groups, according to their respective occupations, in conformity with the principle of collective force which is the basis of society and the state.[101] The candidates of the people would then represent positive interests. They would be the expression of organized labor. The people would have real representation and real elections.[102]

III. WHAT ARE THE GENERAL CHARACTERISTICS OF ANARCHISM?

Proudhon's theory of anarchy may be divided into four periods: (1) Anarchy vaguely defined (1840-1847), (2) anarchy, the real formula of the republic (1840-1850), (3) anarchy in its purest form (1851-1857), and (4) the anarchistic state (1858).

(1) ANARCHY VAGUELY DEFINED (1840-1847).

Proudhon constantly changed his idea, now lingering upon the ideas of governmentalism, and statism, and now endeavoring to abolish them completely. From 1840 to 1847 his thought was always vague and even superficial. First, he defined anarchy as the absence of master and sovereign.[103] Regarding questions of how to constitute the regulation of anarchy he was silent. Second, he fought against authority. "I labor to stir up the reason of individuals to insurrection against the reason of authorities," said he. "According to the law of the society of which I am a member, all the evils which afflict humanity arise from faith in external teachings and submission to authority.[104] Thirdly, he attacked government and the state. Government of man by man, under whatever name it may disguise itself, is the reign of will, of caprice and of oppression.[105] The state, whatever form it may assume, aristocratic or theocratic, monarchical or republican, as long as it is not the organ of a society of equals, will be for the people a hell and a damnation.[106]

(2) ANARCHY THE REAL FORMULA OF THE REPUBLIC (1848-1850).

From 1848 to 1850 Proudhon's idea became both negative and positive. Negatively he attacked authority,[107] government, the state[108] and capital. Government of man by man is slavery.[109] Its chief aim is to protect the rich against the poor.[110] The productivity of capital, which Christianity has condemned under the name of usury, is the true cause of poverty, the eternal obstacle to the establishment of the true republic.[111] Positively, he developed from the theory of anarchy the theory of the republic. In one place he considered anarchy as the real formula of the republic.[112] In another, he defined the republic as positive anarchy.[113]

The republic, as conceived by him in 1849, was not anarchy in its purest form, but direct popular government. "In the republic," he said, "all the citizens in doing what they desire and nothing more than they desire, will participate as directly in legislation and government as they participate in production and the circulation of wealth.[114] The republic is also another name for pure democracy. In pure democracy all the citizens ought to participate in the formation of the law, in the government of the state, in the exercise of public functions, in the discussion of the budget, in the nomination of the functionaries.[115] Thus in 1849 the republic meant for Proudhon direct government or pure democracy. It was opposed to monarchy as well as to democracy[116] in its sophisticated form, that is, democracy of the proletariat.[117]

No less important a fact we have to notice is the distinction between the governmental republic and the perfect republic, or the republic of anarchy. "In order to establish the republic, the last expression of the revolution, it is necessary to begin by the establishment of the governmental republic," said Proudhon.[118] What is meant by him here as the governmental republic is the republic in which the legislator and the magistrate act in conformity with the instinct and general tendencies of the people. What is meant by him as the real republic, or in other words, the most perfect form of the republic, is the government in which every citizen is legislator and magistrate.[119]

The main characteristics of the real republic are fivefold. First, the republic, or anarchy, is the affirmation of liberty—liberty not submitted to order as in a constitutional monarchy nor imprisoned in order as in the provisional government of 1848 but freed from all its obstacles, superstitions, prejudices, sophisms and authorities. Liberty, in the republic, is reciprocal. It is the mother rather than the son of order. All the opinions, all the attributes of the people are free. Everyone is king because he has full

power. He governs and he is governed.[120] Again, liberty in the republic is positive as well as negative. The liberty of religion, for example, is negative, but the liberty of free credit, of universal association or of integral education is positive.[121] Second, in the republic, the people would be autonomous. They would have no masters, no delegates, no representatives.[122] Each one of them would be legislator and magistrate.[123] There would be no other rights except those which have been guaranteed by the people, no other government than that of the people, no other justice than that of the people, no other functionaries than the people themselves. All is for the people, by the people.[124] Thirdly, the real republic means equality—the coordinated equality of functions and persons.[125] There would be no monopoly, no castes, no inequality of conditions.[126] Fourthly, the basis of the real republic would be economic. Its social constitution would be twofold: (1) The equilibrium of interests founded upon free contract,[127] and (2) the organization of economic forces. What Proudhon meant by economic forces here, included, in general, commerce, competition, money, machines, credit, property, collective power, division of labor, equality in transactions and the reciprocity of guarantees.[128] As a result of the economic revolution there would be no capital,[129] no state, no government,[130] no strong and no weak in society.[131] Fifthly, the state would be absorbed in society. By the cessation of authority, the suppression of governmental organs, the abolition of the impost, the simplification of the administration, and the organization of universal suffrage, there would be no other state than society itself.[132]

Between 1848 and 1850 Proudhon's idea went from a state of vagueness to a state of confusion. In 1840 he fearlessly attacked the government and the state, but he had no definite idea of what would be their substitutes. In 1840-1850 he began to have a general idea of what he meant by anarchy, but he confused anarchism with governmentalism. Professing himself a deadly enemy to government, he hesitated to eliminate it entirely. On one hand, he identified anarchy with the republic, or direct government. What he intended to abolish was not direct government, but all the other forms of government. On the other hand, he admitted that, through the necessity of things, there might exist a government which would be subordinate to the people.[133]

(3) THE UNIVERSAL REPUBLIC[134] OR ANARCHY IN ITS PUREST FORM (1851-1857).

In 1851 Proudhon's theory of anarchy reached the stage of definiteness and clearness. For the old political regime, the regime of law, of authority, of divine right, he desired to substitute the new economic regime, the regime of industry, of contract, and of human rights.[135] The chief characteristics of the new regime would be sevenfold. First, Proudhon denounced authority, or the absolute being. He would substitute for it the synthetic and positive idea of economics.[136] Second, he denied the state, the police and the public minister. As soon as society should become well organized, all of these would disappear.[137] There would be no state, no nation, no war. There would exist only a great harmonious humanity,[138] Thirdly, he denied all the forms of government. There would be no more monarchy, no more aristocracy, no more democracy. But the most significant of all is that Proudhon also denied direct government. "Direct or indirect, simple or composite," said he, "government of the people will be the juggling of the people. It is always the man who commands the man."[139] Fourthly, in anarchy, each citizen, each workshop, each corporation, each department would be sovereign. In consequence, each of them would act, directly and by itself, in the management of its respective interests and exercise in this regard the full power of sovereignty.[140] Each of them would have its own police, and administer its own affairs.[141] Fifthly, in anarchy the interests of the people would be harmonious. "The people are nothing more than the organic union of wills individually free and sovereign, which union could and ought to act in concert, but never be dissolved," said Proudhon. "It is in the harmony of interests that this union should be sought, not in a factitious centralization which, far from expressing the collective will, expresses the alienation of the particular wills.[142] Sixthly, in anarchy, the free contract would be substituted for law. The producer would treat with the consumer, the commune with the canton, the canton with the department, etc. It would be always the same interests which would be exchanged, adjusted, and balanced with each other to the infinite.[143] Seventhly, science, particularly the science of economics, instead of religion or authority, would be the general rule of society and the sovereign arbiter of the interests. The truth of science is universal. It knows no distinction between nations or races. It is the unity of mankind.[144]

To sum up, the new regime of anarchy would substitute industrial organization for government, contract for law, economic forces for political power, collective force for public power, industrial societies for standing armies, identity of interests for police, economic centralization for political centralization, and finally the classification and specializing of agricultural, industrial and commercial functions in place of the old class distinction between the nobles and the serfs or between the bourgeoisie and the plebeians.[145]

(4) ANARCHY AND THE STATE (1858).

In 1858, Proudhon changed his idea again. He now became more or less moderate. For the sake of clearness we may classify his work into two parts: (a) His criticism of the old regime, and (b) the establishment of the new regime.

(a) His criticism of the old regime.

Proudhon denounced authority, government and the state because they all protect capitalism against the proletariat.[146] He attacked monarchy, aristocracy and democracy. "Democracy," said he, "is simply a lie."[147]

(b) The establishment of the new regime—the republic.

In contrasting Proudhon's idea of 1858 with that of 1851, we see two great differences in the development of his thought. First, in 1851 Proudhon attacked authority and the state just as if they were two synonymous terms. In 1858, he differentiated the state from authority. It was authority, not the state, that he then attacked.[148] Second, in 1851, he thought that there should be no government, no state in anarchy. But in 1858, he strongly affirmed the function of the state in civilization. "The state," he said, "is the most energetic agent of civilization."[149] When he denied the state or government it was not the state or government of the new regime, but that of the old regime. In other words, he desired to create a new state and a new government in anarchy.

(x) The new state of anarchy.

The fundamental principles of the new state would be (1) the development of economic forces, the first of which would be the collective force, (2) the discovery of social power in the relation of all the forces of society to each other, (3) the idea of universal solidarity of humanitarian force, emerging now from the struggle between, and now from the harmony of, the states, (4) the balancing of economic or social forces, and (5) the elaboration of rights, the supreme expression of man and of society.[150] The aim of the new state would be to organize justice and make it effective. Justice is the law of the material, intellectual and moral world. It is the essential attribute, the principal function of the state. Its formula is equality.[151]

(y) The new government of anarchy—the real republic.[152]

The real republic is a government in which liberty and right would play the first role in opposition to all the other forms of government founded upon the preponderance of authority and the "reason of state." The more the action of liberty and right would be generalized, the more would the republic be perfected.[153] In order to establish the republican government in the true sense of the word, the following five conditions would be necessary:—(1) The definition of economic right, (2) the balance of economic forces, the formation of agricultural, industrial and commercial groups,[154] and the organization of the services of public utility (credit, discount, circulation and transportation, etc.) according to the principle of mutuality, of gratuity, or of net cost, (3) the creation of political guarantees, that is, liberty of press and of platform, liberty of meeting and of association, complete separation of justice and of government, (4) administrative decentralization, and resurrection of communal and provincial life, and (5) cessation of the state of war, demolition of fortresses and the abolition of the standing army. Under these five conditions the principle of authority would tend to disappear. The state, "the public thing," would rest upon an unshaken basis of right and liberty. Government in its true sense (that is, in its old sense of authority) would not exist. Society would be carried on by its liberal and balanced forces.[155]

Proudhon is confident about the triumph of the revolution.[156] Very often he indulged in the imagination of a revolutionary utopia. "Humanity," he said, "is, above all, passionate. What should be our lives when we have no prince to lead us to war, no priests to assist us in piety, no great personages to draw our admiration, no villains or paupers to excite our sensibility: when we could do what the philosopher Martin recommended in *Candide,* we could cultivate our gardens. The exploitation of the soil, formerly the work of the slave, would become the first of the fine arts as it is the first of the industries. We would pass our time in the calm of our lives and the serenity of our spirits.[157]

The development of Proudhon's political thought from 1840 to 1858 is clearly shown in the following summary:

(1) Anarchy chiefly negative (1840-1847)
    (a) Definition—anarchy, the absence of master, of sovereign.
    (b) Criticism against government and the state.
(2) Anarchy, the real formula of the republic (1848-1849)
    (a) Negative
        (x) Criticism against government
        (y) Criticism against the state
    (b) Positive
        (x) The republic—positive anarchy
        (y) The republic—direct government
        (z) The republic—pure democracy
(3) Universal republic, or anarchy in its purest from
    (a) Negative
        (x) No government (against direct government also)
        (y) No state
    (b) Positive
        (x) Economic organization for government
        (y) Contract for law
(4) Anarchy or the republic
    (a) Negative
        (x) Criticism against authority
        (y) Criticism against government
        (z) Criticism against the state
    (b) Positive
        (x) The state as distinct from authority still exists
        (y) Government in its true sense does not exist.

Notes

1. Maurice Lair, in "Annales des sciences politiques," 15 Sept. 1909, p. 588.

2. What is Property, p. 260 (1840). Letter of Dec. 14, 1849. "Confessions" ch. IX (1849). Letter of March 7, 1851. Idée Générale, p. 109 (1851).

3. Corresp. V, p. 249.

4. Mélange II, p. 9.

5. Idée Générale, p. 142. See also Chap. V, his criticism against the government.

6. Mélange III, p. 74.

7. Corresp. IV, p. 179.

8. Mélange I, p. 115.

9. *Ibid:* III, p. 48.

10. Justice VI, pp. 87-89.

11. Mélange III, p. 48.

12. *Ibid:* II, p. 19.

13. *Ibid:* I, p. 14. *Ibid:* II, pp. 19 and 210.

14. *Ibid:* II, p. 122. Justice II, p. 94. Corresp. II, pp. 194-200.

15. *Ibid:* I, p. 350.

16. Corresp. II, pp. 199-200. Proudhon admitted, however, the right of legal resistance. "Résistance legale, c'est-à-dire maintien, défense et conservation de la constitution et des droits qu'elle consacre." Mélange II, p. 68.

17. Idée Générale, p. 297.

18. Justice I, p. 67. What is Property, p. 55.

19. Corresp. IV, p. 149. See also Justice I, pp. 133-134.

20. Idée Générale, p. 291.

21. Justice II, p. 148.

22. Idée Générale, p. 235.

23. *Ibid:* p. 290.

24. Mélange I, p. 115.

25. Idée Générale, p. 297.

26. *Ibid:* p. 115.

27. Création de l'ordre, p. 242.

28. Mélange II, p. 23.

29. Proudhon's theory of wages underwent three stages of change: (1) equality of wages for all the workers regardless of their service (1840), (2) abolition of wages (1851) and (3) equal wages for equal service (1858). In 1840 he strongly advocated the equalizing of wages. "The limited quantity of available material proves," he said, "the necessity of dividing labor among the whole number of laborers. The capacity given to all for accomplishing a social task—that is, an equal task—and the impossibility of paying one laborer save in the products of another, justify the

equalizing of wages." (What is Property? p. 137.) In 1851, he urged the abolition of wages (Idée Générale, p. 297). He changed his idea again in 1858, and did not favor the equalizing of wages among all the workers because he believed that their services might not be equal. He advocated the determination of one's wages by what he produced. (Justice II, p. 385.)

30. Mélange III, p. 48.

31. *Ibid:* I, p. 71. Desjardin I, pp. 107-108.

32. Idée Générale, p. 232.

33. *Ibid:* p. 289.

34. *Ibid:* p. 297.

35. *Ibid:* p. 259. Confessions, p. 33. See also Desjardin I, p. 176.

36. Bouglé, p. 173.

37. Cont. Eco., I, pp. 92 and 97.

38. Mélange I, pp. 60-62 (See also Mélange II, p. 41-42).

39. Solution du Problème social, p. 93.

40. L'organization du crédit et de la circulation, pp. 111-131. Proudhon's theory of money and credit may be found in the sixth volume of his complete works and in the second volume of his "Économic Contradictions." For a brief view of his idea, see Marc Aucuy "Les Systèmes Socialistes d'échange," Paris, 1908, p. 137. Pareto "Systèmes Socialistes," II, pp. 267-280. Osgood "Scientific Anarchism," pp. 13-18. Mülberger, "P. J. Proudhon" pp. 87-88, 104-117, 129-138.

41. Idée Générale, pp. 217-226.

42. Justice II, p. 133.

43. Mélange II, p. 18. Mélange III, p. 48.

44. Idée Générale, p. 196.

45. *Ibid:* p, 297-298.

46. Cont. Eco. I, p. 208. See also Corresp. V, p. 66.

47. Idée Générale, pp. 297-298, 301-302.

48. Justice VI, pp. 87-89.

49. Justice II, pp. 6 and 159.

50. Capacité, p. 178.

51. Révolution Social, p. 135. See also Manuel du Spéculateur, p. 450.

52. Mélange III, p. 161.

53. Idée Générale, p. 235.

54. *Ibid:* p. 1.

55. *Ibid:* p. 3 (See also Mélange III, pp. 124, 161).

56. Révolution Sociale, p. 233.

57. Justice VI, pp. 86-125.

58. Justice, VI, p. 90.

59. *Ibid:* II, p. 13. *Ibid.,* III, pp. 8, 160. *Ibid.,* VI, pp. 91, 98. Corresp. V, pp. 57-58.

60. Justice Poursuivie, p. 244.

61. Corresp. VI, p. 381. See also Idée Générale, p. 181. Manuel du Spéculateur, p. 479. (For a general view about his philosophical theory of equilibrium vs. antagonism, see Mélange II, p. 74 and Mélange III, p. 16.)

62. Justice VI, p. 89. Mélange II, p. 138 (see also p. 74).

63. Révolution Social, p. 135. Manuel du Spéculateur, p. 450.

64. It must be legal and pacific (Mélange II, p. 125).

65. See above pp. 98-102.

66. Idée Générale, pp. 120-121.

67. *Ibid:* pp. 116-120, 122.

68. *Ibid:* pp. 118-19. See also Philosophie du Progrès, pp. 38-39. Idée Générale, p. 98.

69. Idée Générale, pp. 119-120.

70. *Ibid:* pp. 120-121.

71. *Ibid:* p. 124. (See also Osgood, p. 9.)

72. *Ibid:* p. 130.

73. Justice II, p. 527.

74. Idée Générale, pp. 116-117.

75. *Ibid:* p. 312.

76. *Ibid:* pp. 116-117, 236.

77. Justice II, p. 527.

78. Idée Générale, p. 118 (See also 116-117).

79. *Ibid:* p. 174.

80. *Ibid:* p. 236.

81. *Ibid:* p. 222.

82. Bouglé, pp. 244-245.

83. Idée Générale, pp. 117-118.

84. Justice II, pp. 527-528.

85. Fournière, p. 192.

86. Justice I, p. 222.

87. *Ibid:* II, pp. 4, 144.

88. What is Property, pp. 19-20.

89. Idée Générale, p. 145. See also Mülberger, "Studien . . . ," p. 33.

90. Justice VI, p. 105.

91. Mülberger "Studien . . . ," p. 44.

92. Desjardin II, p. 216. Proudhon's letter of Sept. 27, 1853.

93. Corresp. I, p. 275.

94. Mélange I, p. 15. See also Mülberger "Studien . . . ," pp. 18-21.

95. Mélange I, pp. 19-20. Solution du Problème Social, p. 62. See also Mülberger "Studien . . . ," p. 18.

96. Desjardin II, p. 223.

97. Idée Générale, p. 150.

98. *Ibid:* p. 146.

99. Corresp. V, pp. 266, 268.

100. Mélange I, p. 20.

101. Justice II, pp. 4, 128, 145.

102. Mélange I, p. 43.

103. Qu'est-ce que la propriété, premier mémoire, p. 216.

104. *Ibid:* deuxième mémorie, p. 354.

105. *Ibid:* premier mémoire, p. 30.

106. Cont. Eco., I, p. 267.

107. Mélange II, pp. 12-13.

108. Solution du Problème Social, p. 49. Mélange II, p. 14.

109. Diehl, pp. 110-11.

110. *Ibid:* pp. 107-108.

111. Mélange I, p. 184.

112. Mélange II, pp. 12-13.

113. Solution du Problème Social, p. 87.

114. *Ibid:* pp. 2 and 87.

115. *Ibid:* p. 61.

116. *Ibid:* p. 87.

117. *Ibid:* p. 61. See Ch. V for his criticism of democracy.

118. Mélange II, p. 205.

119. *Ibid:* I, p. 84.

120. Solution du Problème Social, p. 87. See also Mélange III, p. 59, Confessions, p. 27.

121. Mélange II, pp. 12-13; III, p. 147.

122. *Ibid:* II, pp. 12-13. Solution du Problème Social, p. 49.

123. *Ibid:* I, p. 84.

124. *Ibid:* pp. 115-116. *Ibid:* p. 84.

125. *Ibid:* p. 141.

126. *Ibid:* p. 115-116.

127. An Stelle der Gesetze solten freie Verträge treten, die von den Mitgliedern der einzelnen wirtschaftlichen Gruppen, Vereine, Gesellschaften, Korporationen, Assoziationen unter einander auf Grundlage des freie Austausches des Produkte und des unentgeltlichen Kredits geschlossen werden." Diehl, pp. 107-108.

128. Confessions, p. 166-167.

129. Mélange II, pp. 15, 17. "Capital and labor will be identified."

130. *Ibid:* II, p. 9. See also III, p. 50.

131. *Ibid:* II, pp. 15-17.

132. *Ibid:* III, p. 48.

133. *Ibid:* II, p. 67.

134. "L'institution gouvernementale abolie, remplacée par l'organisation économique, le problème de la république universelle est résolu. Idée Générale, p. 298.

135. Idée Générale, pp. 257-258.

136. Philosophie du Progrès, p. 48.

137. Idée Révolutionnaire, p. 91.

138. Diehl, pp. 115-116.

139. Idée Générale, p. 130.

140. *Ibid:* p. 292.

141. *Ibid:* p. 289.

142. *Ibid:* p. 292.

143. Idée Générale, pp. 283-284.

144. *Ibid:* pp. 297-300.

145. *Ibid:* p. 259. See also Philosophie du Progrès, p. 56.

146. Justice II, pp. 4 and 70. V, p. 184.

147. *Ibid:* II, pp. 115-116. (See also pp. 9-10.)

148. Justice V, pp. 183-184.

149. *Ibid:* p. 183.

150. *Ibid:* II, pp. 116-117.

151. *Ibid:* V, p. 64.

152. "The republic is organized according to the principle of economy and of right." Justice II, p. 132.

153. Justice V, pp. 178-179.

154. *Ibid:* II, pp. 120-121.

155. *Ibid:* V, p. 179.

156. Idée Générale, p. 9.

157. Justice II, p. 133.

Alan B. Spitzer (essay date 1957)

SOURCE: "The Life and Historical Role of Blanqui," in *The Revolutionary Theories of Louis Auguste Blanqui,* Columbia University Press, 1957, pp. 3-27.

[*In the following essay, Spitzer describes the life and evaluates the influence of the martyred anarchist and precursor of modern revolutionary socialism, Louis Auguste Blanqui.*]

The fact and idea of revolution have been crucial to French political history ever since 1789. Throughout the nineteenth century an articulate minority advocated the revolutionary solutions of political problems and actively fostered the resolution of ideological conflicts by physical violence. However, the great French theorists of fundamental social change, St. Simon, Fourier, Proudhon, Cabet, and their disciples, contributed a body of "socialist" ideology which repudiated the political revolutionism so eagerly espoused by the radical wing of the contemporary republican movement. The combination of revolutionism and socialist theory was a minority tendency among French radicals before 1870, and one to which few memorable figures were committed. There was, however, one socialist who not only advocated political revolution,[1] but whose career virtually embodied the revolutionary aspects of the history of nineteenth-century France. This was Louis Auguste Blanqui.

THE LIFE OF BLANQUI

Blanqui began his active political career in the conspiracy of the French Carbonari against the Restoration monarchy and concluded it as a spokesman for the socialist opposition to Gambetta's republican Opportunism. He received the first of many wounds in 1827, during street demonstrations against Charles X,[2] and died in 1881, immediately after speaking at a mass meeting for total amnesty of the Communards.[3] He spent forty of his seventy-six years in the prisons of all the regimes which governed France from 1830 through 1881. Blanqui faced every government as an implacable critic who was always ready to translate criticism into subversive political action. His star shone most brightly during those periods of social unrest and political violence which distinguished the history of nineteenth-century France, but on the day that "order" was restored Blanqui would take his stand among the partisans of *révolution à outrance,* an object of hatred and fear to the erstwhile revolutionaries who desired merely to consolidate what they had already won. Blanqui's commitment to a permanent revolution against all feudal, religious, and capitalist institutions condemned him to a role of perpetual opposition and guaranteed his political martyrdom, or impotence, depending upon one's point of view.

Blanqui was born at Puget-Théniers in the Alpes Maritimes on February 1, 1805. He was the second son of Dominique Blanqui, a former Girondist *conventionnel* and Napoleonic functionary whose job and security disappeared with the First Empire. The small income of the young and beautiful Mme Blanqui enabled the family to send their brilliant sons Adolphe and Louis Auguste to be educated in Paris. There Blanqui received a classical education and, after leaving the *lycée* laden with honors, supported himself as a private tutor while he undertook the study of both law and medicine.[4] As a young student he developed a passion for politics which involved him with the Carbonari. These early political years probably had a lasting influence on his ideas of revolutionary technique. His biographer, Geffroy, has observed:

> Blanqui, introduced to politics under the Restoration, assumed the habits of a conspirator of the Restoration period, and the Carbonarist cell became for him the ideal type of the secret society and of possible political opposition.[5]

He was one of the leaders of Paris student agitation during the last years of the Restoration, and was wounded three times during riots in 1827. He was in Paris, working as a parliamentary reporter for the liberal journal, the *Globe,* when the Revolution of July, 1830, began. When the Paris workers poured into the streets to destroy the Bourbon monarchy, Blanqui scornfully left his vacillating and legalistic employers at the office of the *Globe* and plunged into the maelstrom, brandishing a rifle and the tricolor.[6] For his part in the "three glorious days" of the Revolution he was later awarded the "Decoration of July" by Louis Philippe. This was the last award, aside from prison sentences, that he was ever to receive from the French government.

Almost immediately after the Revolution, Blanqui joined the radical opposition to the July Monarchy and soon aligned himself with a small minority of young republicans who demanded a complete social revolution which would free the poor from economic, as well as political, thralldom. Although Blanqui was not the only republican of the period to characterize the political struggle as a struggle between social classes, he seems to have formulated most precisely the vague revolutionary demands for social, or class, justice.

In 1832, he defended himself at the trial of the republican Société des Amis du Peuple in a speech which has been described as "the first socialist manifesto of this epoch."[7] When Blanqui was asked at this trial to give his profession, he made the famous reply: "Proletarian the class of thirty million Frenchmen who live by their labor and who are deprived of political rights."[8] The eloquent young firebrand was acquitted by the jury, but sentenced to one year in prison for his attempt, in the words of the court, "to trouble the public peace by arousing the contempt and hatred of the citizenry against several classes of people which he had variously described as the privileged rich or the *bourgeoisie.*"[9]

Upon his release from prison Blanqui plunged into the old Carbonarist atmosphere of clandestine organization which was revived as the Orleanist government severely curtailed freedom of association. He founded a secret revolutionary "Society of Families" in 1834, but his careful organization was shattered when he and the other leaders of the society were arrested in 1836 for the illegal possession of arms.[10]

When the amnesty of 1837 released him from prison Blanqui returned to Paris, for him the only possible arena of the class struggle. There, with the aid of two popular young republicans, Armand Barbès and Martin Bernard, he established another organization, "The Society of Seasons." Classic conspiratorial techniques were utilized to form a tightly disciplined and hierarchical organization. The small isolated cells of the rank and file received orders from subaltern leaders who themselves were unaware of the identity of the mysterious directors of the conspiracy. All of the conspirators were sworn to unquestioning obedience. From time to time the small individual groups assembled in the streets at the word of their immediate superiors without ever knowing which call was to be the signal for the real coup.

During the economic and political crisis of May, 1839, Blanqui decided to make his attempt. On the twelfth of May, the little band of students and workers formed in the streets, broke into arsenals and gunshops, and tried to carry the city's key positions. The Paris of workers and artisans which was expected to transform the insurrection into a revolution stood by silently and apathetically while government troops easily crushed the rising.[11] Blanqui evaded arrest for a few months but was finally captured, tried by the Chamber of Peers, and sentenced to death.[12] His sentence was commuted to deportation by Louis Philippe, and he was sent to join most of his comrades in the prison-fortress of Mont-Saint-Michel.

For nine years he lived the role for which he is probably best remembered—*L'Enfermé,* the imprisoned one, the suffering but uncompromising hostage of the conservative forces of five successive regimes. The little society of the political prisoner, with its hopeless defiance of a barbarous prison administration, its perpetual effort to preserve a shred of personal integrity under the most degrading conditions, and its bitter and self-consuming factional struggles, was isolated and politically ineffectual, but an object of widespread interest and sympathy.

Blanqui remained a prisoner, at Mont-Saint-Michel,[13] and then at Tours, until 1848, when the February Revolution released him and brought him hurrying to the center of the Paris stage. By this time the myth of Blanqui as the sinister incarnation of bloodthirsty anarchism was held not only by the good conservative families of France, but by most of his more moderate colleagues in the republican movement as well. Tocqueville's description of Blanqui at the rostrum of the National Assembly on May 15, 1848, is a fair picture of how this revolutionary appeared to the conservative politicians:

> It was then that I saw appear in his turn on the tribune a man whom I have never seen since, but the recollection of whom has always filled me with horror and disgust. He had wan, emaciated cheeks, white lips, a sickly wicked and repulsive expression, a dirty pallor, the appearance of a moldy corpse; he wore no visible linen; an old black frock coat tightly covered his lean withered limbs; he seemed to have passed his life in a sewer and to have just left it. I was told it was Blanqui.[14]

A considerably different idea of Blanqui was cherished by a small but devoted coterie of disciples. To them this small, ascetic, prematurely aged man had unstintingly given his health and freedom to an ideal, and received and expected no rewards but prison, hatred, and contumely. Many more objective observers were impressed by his apparently exclusive and selfless devotion to a cause and by the magnetism of his dedicated personality. Delvau, who had been Ledru-Rollin's secretary, in his *Historie de la Révolution de Février* described his personal impressions of Blanqui in 1848 as follows:

> At first sight Blanqui does not appear very attractive, but that is because suffering is not always very agree-

able to watch. One is disposed to obey him, but not to love him. He does not attract, he dominates. Blanqui replaces the physical strength that he lacks with a virility of the soul, which on certain occasions is all-powerful.[15]

As soon as he had arrived in Paris, Blanqui formed a club to organize the dissatisfaction of the extreme radicals with what they considered the potentially counterrevolutionary activity of the Provisional Government. Apparently Blanqui eschewed revolutionary conspiracy while attempting to force the government to the left by the pressure of speeches, journals, and mass demonstrations.[16] The provisional government, including its most radical members, repaid Blanqui's mistrust with fear and hatred. His growing influence was undermined by the publication of a document alleged to have been copied from a confession made by Blanqui which gave Louis Philippe's police information about the conspiracy of 1839.[17] The accusation has never been decisively proved or disproved, but the supporting testimony of Barbès, Blanqui's former fellow conspirator who had become his bitterest enemy, struck a sharp blow to his prestige among the Paris militants.[18]

The tensions among the disparate groups which had taken over the heritage of the July Monarchy were heightened as the attempts of the Provisional Government to establish order according to moderate middle-class principles were met by the street demonstrations and incendiary manifestoes of the Paris radicals. The continuous agitation bore fruit on May 15, when a mob invaded the precincts of the newly elected and quite conservative Constituent Assembly. What had begun as a demonstration for a revolutionary war against the Russian oppression of Poland became an attempt to overthrow the government. Blanqui was reluctantly involved in the inception of this movement, but did not join the mob when it made its way to the Hôtel de Ville to proclaim a revolutionary government.[19] Nevertheless, he was imprisoned along with most of the socialists and radical leaders after this improvised insurrection had been crushed by the bourgeois National Guard. Therefore he was unable to join the Paris workers in their last desperate attempt to achieve a social revolution in the bloody "June days" of 1848.

Throughout the next decade Blanqui languished in various republican and imperial prisons. There he read, lectured on political economy, and led his disciples in demonstrations against the prison authorities. A great deal of his energy was spent in factional clashes with fellow prisoners—disputes common to socialist politics. He was not entirely forgotten by the outside world for he managed to shock liberal opinion by condemnations of all of those republicans and moderate socialists, including Louis Blanc, who had in his opinion betrayed the workers in 1848. He emerged at this time as perhaps the first socialist "anti-participationist" who demands the absolute proletarian purity of his party.[20]

In 1859 Blanqui was released from prison and went straight to Paris to do battle with the Second Empire. By

Auguste Blanqui (1805–1881)

1861 he was back in jail, sentenced to four years for "conspiracy."[21] During this period he met and influenced a new generation of young intellectuals who had been imprisoned for various crimes against the security of the state. Some of them, "Blanquists of the second rank," admired him without accepting his complete domination. In this group were Clemenceau and Ranc, among others, who were to become the stalwarts of the Radical Socialist Party.[22] Other young militants subordinated themselves completely to the will of *le Vieux* and were the nucleus for a devoted revolutionary general staff after Blanqui escaped from a prison hospital in 1865.[23]

In these last years of the tottering Empire, Blanqui naturally did all that he could to hasten its collapse. From his refuge in Belgium he guided an expanding group of young Blanquists in the formation of a revolutionary organization along the old conspiratorial lines, equally divided among students and workers.[24] Many of Blanqui's lieutenants were to play important roles in the Commune of 1871. Eudes, Tridon, Ferré, Rigault, and other communard leaders began their revolutionary careers under the tutelage of *le Vieux,* the old master revolutionary. Blanqui slipped into Paris from time to time to direct the activities of his approximately two thousand adherents. In August, 1870, he was reluctantly compelled by the impatience of his enthusiastic disciples, and by the fear that his organization would melt away, to lead a premature assault on the tottering Second Empire.[25] Adventures of this nature have stamped him with the somewhat invidious label of "insurrectionist."

When the Empire did fall on September 4, 1870, power was immediately seized by the liberal politicians who were willing to accept a republic and eager to forestall a social revolution. They guided the country through its last hopeless writhings beneath the Prussian heel and handed it over to a National Assembly which was to arrange the surrender in approved constitutional fashion.

At first the Parisian radicals, including the Blanquists, had agreed to cooperate with the bourgeois government of National Defense in the face of the German menace. Blanqui, soon suspecting that the government preferred Prussian troops in Paris to armed French workers, began to attack the new administration on patriotic grounds in his newspaper *La Patrie en danger.* He had been raised in the peculiarly French atmosphere of leftist chauvinism which yearned for a war in the great revolutionary tradition, and whose main objection to conservative governments had been their relatively peaceful and internationalist outlook. When the news of the surrender of Metz impelled an angry crowd to seize the Hôtel de Ville on October 31, 1870, Blanqui followed it, and participated in the abortive attempt to set up a new government of revolutionary patriots. With this failure disappeared his last faint hope of inspiring Paris to fight a revolutionary war.[26]

Heartbroken and disgusted by the surrender to the Prussians, Blanqui left Paris in February, 1871, and retired to the country. There he was arrested for his part in the attempted coup of October, and hustled into secret confinement on March 17, the day before civil war broke out in Paris. The government of Versailles refused the offer of the Communards to exchange all of their hostages for Blanqui, who in the words of his archenemy, Thiers, "was worth an army corps."[27] The "mathematician of revolution" languished in a hidden prison while his followers fought their hopeless battle on the walls and in the streets of Paris.

For a few tragic months in 1871 the accumulated political bitterness of a century was distilled into the bloody struggle between the Paris of workers and radical intellectuals and the France of the middle class and the Catholic peasantry. The real nature of the Commune has been the subject of endless controversy. Its leaders were predominantly agitators and journalists of middle-class origin, its soldiers, as in the "days" of 1830 and 1848, were the workers. The ideology of the Commune was a mixture of neo-Jacobinism, Proudhonism, and Blanquism, and each of these loosely descriptive terms covers a multitude of political ideas.[28]

The role of the Blanquists in the Commune is known to have been significant, but is also somewhat obscure and subject to various interpretations. It is certain that the Blanquists contributed a great deal to the consolidation of the spontaneous rising that gave birth to the Commune. They became the consistent supporters of vigorous direct action against Versailles, and of many of the acts of violence which marred the dying days of the Commune. The Blanquists did not function as an organized political party and confessed to a sense of confusion and lack of direction which they felt the missing Blanqui would have supplied.

The Blanquists who did not perish in the final holocaust fled abroad, especially to London. There they were somewhat influenced by Marxism, and supported Marx and Engels in their struggle against the anarchists in the First International. However, the Blanquists' exclusive devotion to a program of immediate revolution alienated Marx from them. A fear of Blanquist domination of the International was probably one of Marx's motives for moving the headquarters of the organization to New York.[29]

While the Third Republic staggered through its first precarious years, Blanqui, the hero of a thousand battles for the republican ideal, remained behind the walls of a republican prison. In 1879 a campaign led by a group of young radicals resulted in Blanqui's election to the Chamber of Deputies by a Bordeaux constituency. The election was annulled by the Chamber which, at the same time, bowed to public opinion by giving him his liberty.[30] He became the editor of the newspaper *Ni Dieu Ni Maître,* and spent his last years stumping for a general amnesty of the Communards, and accusing the Opportunist republicans of a surrender to royalist and clerical forces. On December 27, 1880, he was felled by a stroke a few hours after speaking at a mass meeting in Paris. He died on January 1, 1881. His funeral was attended by a vast crowd of Parisian citizens, workers, and members of all leftist parties, for whom he had become the symbol of the long fight for socialism and for the Republic.[31]

After Blanqui's death his disciples tried to carry out his tradition in a "Blanquist" party, which eventually split over *Boulangisme* and was absorbed into the French Socialist Party.[32] Blanquism as the basis of a specific political party was dead, but its influence, direct and indirect, has been manifest in French leftist politics until today. As late as 1928 Albert Mathiez felt impelled to publish and refute Blanqui's previously unpublished critique of Robespierre, on the following grounds:

> Blanqui exercised a very important influence on the *avant-garde* of the French revolutionary parties during nearly a half-century from 1830 to 1880. Although of delicate health, he outlived all of his rivals from Barbès to Proudhon and Raspail, who could have counterbalanced his popularity. With the prestige of a martyr's halo, he became, after the Commune, a sort of patriarch whose judgments were oracles. He had fanatic disciples who extended his influence long after his death, until the coming of Jaurès began to push it little by little into the shadows. The violent hate that Blanqui bore Robespierre has thus imposed a decisive deviation on the attitudes that the socialists held toward the founder of French democracy. They had adored him until 1848. Blanqui taught them to detest him.[33]

The persistence of Blanqui's influence in the French socialist movement is reflected in the controversy over Blanquism which disturbed the French Communist party a few years ago.[34]

Although Blanqui was committed to a predominantly French, one might say parochial, brand of socialism and had relatively little contact with the international revolutionary community of his era, his influence did pass beyond the borders of his beloved France. In 1848 the German socialist Lassalle pasted Blanqui's "Manifesto to the People" upon the door of his prison cell.[35] Sixty-seven years later Mussolini took from this same proclamation the phrase "He who has steel, has bread," for the masthead of his paper *Il Popolo d'Italia.*[36]

The link between Blanquism and Russian Bolshevism was embodied by Peter Tkatchev, a nineteenth-century revolutionary who was studied and admired by Lenin. Tkatchev was one of the first to introduce the idea of a vanguard revolutionary party and of a revolutionary dictatorship into Russian socialism.[37] At Blanqui's funeral Tkatchev eulogized the Frenchman as a leader of the world revolutionary movement:

> To him, to his ideas, to his abnegation, to the clarity of his mind, to his clairvoyance, we owe in great measure the progress which daily manifests itself in the Russian revolutionary movement.
>
> Yes, it is he who has been our inspiration and our model in the great art of conspiracy. He is the uncontested chief who has filled us with revolutionary faith, the resolution to struggle, the scorn of suffering.[38]

The Meaning of the Life

Many subsequent radicals, while rejecting Blanqui's political tactics, have found in his dedicated career the embodiment of the struggle to realize the idea of the Great Revolution in the nineteenth century. Gustave Geffroy, the novelist and literary critic, who was a lifelong friend and journalistic collaborator of Clemenceau, wrote an impassioned tribute to Blanqui which is still the chief, albeit somewhat idealized, biography of the old revolutionary. He concluded this work with the observation: "Finally there is his life, which is itself a creation and his only doctrine—Blanqui was the political manifestation of the French Revolution in the nineteenth century."[39]

In 1885, Benoît Malon, the integral socialist and firm supporter of eclectic and humanitarian reformism, wrote that Blanqui, lacking the personal attraction of Barbès, Mazzini, Garibaldi, or Bakunin, surpassed them all by the extent of his knowledge, the power of his mind, and "by the unity of his life, without a ray of personal pleasure, a life of suffering and struggle, for the emancipation of humanity."[40]

In 1920, Stalin contrasted the proletarian leaders who were men of action but weak in theory with theorists such as Plekhanov and Kautsky who contributed nothing to revolutionary practice. Blanqui was among the former, one of the "leaders in times of storm, practical leaders, self-sacrificing and courageous, but who were weak in theory."[41]

The almost universal agreement that Blanqui's career was a monument of indefatigable revolutionary purpose has not extended to his significance in the history of the socialist movement or to the substance of his social and political theory. The few lines assigned to Blanqui in histories of socialist thought usually characterize him as a naïve activist whose social theories are completely expressed in his career of abortive insurrections, candle-lit conspiracies, and perennial imprisonments.[42] He is often described as an anarchist[43] or terrorist who thought of social progress only in terms of barricade and bomb.

There has always been a minority, however, which finds in Blanqui's life something more than a series of revolutionary anecdotes and in his writings an important prevision of modern revolutionary socialism. The triumph of the Bolshevist brand of socialism has considerably increased the interest in Blanqui as a theorist. Both friendly and hostile critics of Bolshevism and Blanquism have called attention to the similarities between Blanqui's faith in a compact, disciplined, insurrectionist organization and the Leninist concept of a Communist elite which will act as the "advance guard" of the proletariat, as well as their common proclamation of the necessity for a revolutionary dictatorship over the disarmed bourgeoisie.[44]

The increasing interest in the possible relationship between Blanquism and contemporary ideologies has sharpened the controversy over the precise nature of Blanquism, especially in France where there is a very strong sense of the continuity between contemporary politics and its historical antecedents. Just as the heritage of the French Revolution or of the Commune of 1871 is claimed by the various publicists of the French left, each of whom finds his party the true heir of the French revolutionary tradition, so Blanqui, the personification of that tradition throughout the nineteenth century is retroactively enlisted in the ranks of the various factions. French political groupings, from the Radical Socialists to the Stalinists, have found something in Blanqui which is a reflection of their own ideologies, which they consider characteristic of all that is praiseworthy in Blanquism. They all distinguish between Blanquist errors and the true inheritance which has been passed to them alone.

Some of Blanqui's greatest admirers have denied that he exhibited any theoretical capacity whatsoever. Georges Clemenceau, who was a Blanquist in his youth, described his old master as virtually a democratic saint,[45] but so completely a man of action as to be a total stranger to systematic thought.[46] The great Radical Socialist politician was proud of his association with the old revolutionary and identified himself and his party with Blanqui's struggle against the nineteenth-century monarchies. Yet when one considers Clemenceau's career it seems obvious that the man who came to be such an enemy of revolutionary socialism must be considered not the heir, but the antithesis

of Blanqui, unless the latter's expression of revolutionary and socialist values is completely discounted and only his qualities of leadership and disinterestedness are considered characteristic.

Benoît Malon, on the other hand, placed Blanquism in an essential relationship to late nineteenth-century socialism: "Blanqui's work gives us a sort of synthesis of Babouvist revolutionism and scientific socialism."[47] This viewpoint has been expressed even more strongly by some modern French historians and socialists. For example, Maurice Dommanget, the outstanding contemporary biographer of Blanqui, not only credits him with a valid and clearly formulated social theory, but sees in his writings a brilliant theoretical edifice which in many ways is a precursor of Marxism and actually is congruent with it in all essentials. Dommanget flatly states,

> the liaison between Babouvism and Bolshevism by way of revolutionary Marxism is realized, so to speak, through Blanquism. . . . Blanqui formulated, in nearly the same terms as Marx, the law of accumulation.[48]

The relation of Blanquist theory to Marxism has been the subject of continuous interpretation by Marxists ever since Marx himself in 1852 described Blanqui and his followers as "the real leaders of the proletarian party, the revolutionary communists."[49] Subsequently Blanquism has been the subject of rigorous criticism and moderate praise by Engels,[50] Lenin,[51] and Stalin, and of course of special interest to French Communists. In 1951 a Parisian Society of the Friends of Blanqui was formed which opened its proceedings with an address entitled "Some Aspects of Blanqui's Activity" by André Marty, at that time still one of the leaders of the French Communist party.[52] In this pamphlet Blanqui was given a position of considerable importance as a forerunner of modern Marxism-Leninism. Marty asserted that Blanqui's political role had been distorted by "bourgeois and social-democrat" historians who minimized his positive contributions and maximized his errors. Communists should realize that Blanqui is to be praised for his clear conception of the class struggle and its consequence, the bitter fight against the middle class, the instrument of capitalist domination of the workers. At the same time the two great Blanquist errors, the lack of interest in agitation for the workers' everyday economic demands, and the absence of any scientific conception of revolution, should be discussed as lessons for modern young revolutionaries and workers.

Marty himself was subsequently accused by the French Communist party of a lack of faith in the masses which has led him to attempt the substitution of "a narrow and sectarian Blanquist conception" for the Leninist-Stalinist idea of a party "immersed in the working class and the masses."[53]

Marty's political sins include an apparent scorn for mass propaganda efforts, such as the Stockholm peace petition; the heretical insistence that, in 1944, the Communists could have seized power in France; and "factionalist maneuvers" which are marked by covert demonstrations of hostility toward Maurice Thorez. An article in the January, 1953, issue of *Cahiers du Communisme,* the organ of the Central Committee of the French Communist party, attacked Marty's brochure on Blanqui as the theoretical manifestation of his opposition to the will of the party and to Leninist principles. According to the Communist historian Roger Garaudy, Marty has mistakenly credited Blanqui with a clear formulation of the class struggle; he has ignored Blanqui's essentially *petit bourgeois* economic ideas; and he has dismissed without sufficient criticism Blanqui's idealist interpretation of progress and historical development. Under the cover of Blanqui's well-deserved prestige he has attempted to smuggle "neo-Blanquist" errors of adventurism, nationalism, and factionalism into the organization.[54]

The very elements of Blanquism which modern Communists do praise, such as the insistence upon a vanguard organization of professional revolutionaries and a postrevolutionary dictatorship, are often characterized by anti-Bolsheviks as Leninist perversions of true Marxism. In K. J. Kenafick's work on Marx and Bakunin, which has a definite anarchist orientation, Leninism is defined as "Marxism plus Blanquism" and the present Russian dictatorship is described as essentially Blanquist: "for it is based on the conception of a 'vanguard party,' a party of ruthless and violent action, and this is a Blanquist, and not a Marxist conception."[55]

Max Eastman, in his *Marx and Lenin,* remarked that Lenin "corrected the error of Blanqui which was to trust all to the organization of revolutionists," but asserted that Lenin's insistence on centralized authority and military discipline in the party which leads the proletariat "smacks more of the tactics of Blanqui than of the philosophy of Marx."[56]

Communists have praised and anticommunists have criticized Blanqui's alleged uncompromising militancy and revolutionary authoritarianism. However, the image of Blanqui as activist and relentless conspirator is not the only one.[57] Many French socialists and republicans have interpreted his statements, especially those on education and universal suffrage, as fundamentally reformist. They argue that in the reactionary France of 1815-1871, a revolution was perhaps the only meaningful expression of political dissent for a sincere and selfless reformer. In a republic, even a bourgeois republic, which permitted freedom of speech, association, and the press, Blanqui would have eschewed conspiratorial techniques and carried on his fight through the press, the tribune, and the ballot box. The last two years of his life, in which he criticized the leaders of the Third Republic without attempting to overthrow its institutions are cited as evidence of his fundamentally reformist position. Therefore many parliamentarians and moderate reformers have accepted Blanqui's revolutionary career as a worthy contribution to the glorious French Republican tradition, while characterizing their own non-revolutionary position as a logical consequence of his ideas, applied in a different milieu.

In the *Encyclopédie Socialiste* of 1912, Compère-Morel affirmed Blanqui's revolutionism, but listed the bases of Blanquism as "*Liberté, Laïcité, Instruction:* These are the three ideas behind Blanqui's action. Communism will result from them quite naturally."[58] Social Democrats have quoted this analysis out of context to prove that Blanqui was essentially a democratic reformer whose primary commitment was to universal secular education.[59] One republican anticlerical went so far as to maintain that in his last hours Blanqui saw the reversal of his belief in the necessity of violent revolution and the imminent solution of *all* social problems by the application of the new anticlerical laws.[60]

Blanqui's fiery patriotism has often been cited as the truly French radical's answer to socialist pacifism or revolutionary internationalism. During the First World War especially, Blanqui's fierce anti-German polemics were exhumed and used to identify him as a spiritual forebear of Clemenceau's fighting nationalism, and as the antithesis of Marxian internationalism.[61] On the other hand, in at least one speech delivered during a period when French socialism was strongly internationalist and pacifist, the lesson of Blanqui's life was found to be "a call to the fight against religion, capitalism, and patriotism."[62]

It is apparent that the essential nature of Blanquism, which seems so obviously embodied in Blanqui's singularly unified political experience, has been interpreted according to various predispositions, each of which can be supported by some relevant quotation from Blanqui's writings. Therefore Blanqui can, to some extent, be placed in a correct historical perspective by an analysis of the total content of his expressed ideas, the premises from which they were derived, and the historical context in which they were formulated. An understanding must be sought, not in the so-called "Blanquism" of his disciples, nor solely in the dramatic events of his crowded political career, but in the text of his own writings and speeches as well.

Unfortunately, not everything that Blanqui wrote has been preserved. His published writings make up only a segment of his intellectual output and actually give an incomplete and distorted impression of his total viewpoint. The bulk of his salvaged unpublished manuscripts is bound in twenty volumes in the Paris Bibliothéque Nationale.[63] From this disorganized mass of notes, letters, and drafts for speeches and pamphlets, from fragments which have been collected in his published works, and from the speeches he made at his various trials, one can piece together the outline of a social and political philosophy.

This material demonstrated, first of all, that Blanqui, "the activist," was a self-conscious intellectual and omnivorous reader, interested in theoretical formulations of innumerable social, scientific, and philosophic problems. Among his notes are thousands of abstracts of books and periodical articles, often followed by his own comments. He read widely not only in contemporary political problems, but in the histories of every period, geographies, books on military science, collections of national population and economic statistics, philosophic treatises, and scientific articles of every description. His interests ranged from techniques for pressing grapes to the problem of the limits of the universe, and from the history of the early church fathers to the population statistics of Illinois.[64]

This extensive intellectual preparation was to furnish the material for Blanqui's discursive theorizing which usually took the form of trenchant but rather unsystematic polemics written to define and defend the role of revolutionary socialism in France. Some of these ideas are now commonplace and so directly related to action that they are not usually dignified with the label of "theory." Nevertheless a theory of action has as much instructive content as a carefully constructed Utopia, and a somewhat greater relevance to contemporary social movements.

Blanqui, the man of action *par excellence,* perfectly exemplified the fact that all political action, rational or irrational, is connected with certain ideas, unconscious or explicit, about reality, man, and society. Without an understanding of "Blanquist" theory, a full assessment of Blanqui's historical role in the socialist movement cannot be made.

1. See M. Ralea, *L'Idée de révolution dans les doctrines socialistes* (Paris: Jouve et Cie., 1923), p. 218: "Blanqui's primary importance rests in having transmitted the tactics of radical republicanism to socialism."

2. H. Castille, "L. A. Blanqui," *Portraits politiques et historiques au dix-neuvième siècle* (Paris: Ferdinand Sartorius, 1857), p. 9.

3. M. Dommanget, *Blanqui* (Paris: Librarie de l'Humanité, 1924), p. 44.

4. Blanqui's older brother, the conservative economist Adolphe Blanqui, wrote a touching account of this early period. J. A. Blanqui, "Souvenirs d'un etudiant sous la Restauration," *Revue de Paris* (Nov.-Dec., 1918), pp. 159-61.

5. G. Geffroy, *L'Enfermé* (Paris: Les Éditions G. Crès et Cie., 1926), I, 38. When the entire work cited is not a translation, the translation in the text is the author's.

6. For his own impression of these events, see pp. 132-33 below.

7. J. Tchernoff, *Le Parti républicain sous la Monarchie de Juillet* (Paris: A. Pedone, 1901), p. 261.

8. Société des Amis du Peuple, *Procès des Quinze* (Paris: Imprimerie de Auguste Mie, 1832), p. 3.

9. *Ibid.,* p. 148.

10. This organization was described in detail by the public prosecutor Mérilhou at Blanqui's trial in 1839, Cours des Pairs, *Affaire des 12 and 13 Mai, 1839* (Paris: Imprimerie Royale, 1839), pp. 9-30.

11. A book has been devoted to this effort: A. Zévaès, *Une Révolution manquée* (Paris: Éditions de la Nouvelle Revue Critique, 1933). See also M. Dommanget, "Auguste Blanqui et l'insurrection du 12 Mai 1839," *La Critique Sociale,* XI (March, 1934), 233-45.

12. *La Gazette des Tribunaux,* July 13-14, 1840.

13. F. Girard, *Histoire du Mont Saint-Michel* (Paris: Paul Permain et Cie., 1849); L. Noguès, *Une Condamnation de Mai 1839* (Paris: J. Bry Ainé, 1850).

14. A. de Tocqueville, *Recollections,* tr. A. T. de Mattos (New York: Columbia University Press, 1949), p. 130. Cf. V. Hugo, *Souvenirs personnels, 1848-1851,* ed. H. Guillemin (Paris: Gallimard, 1952), pp. 167-70.

15. A. Delvau, *Histoire de la Révolution de Février* (Paris: Garnier Frères, 1850), I, 318.

16. A very fine work on Blanqui's role in 1848 is: S. Wasserman, *Les Clubs de Barbès et de Blanqui* (Paris: Édouard Cornély et Cie., 1913).

17. This document was published by a certain Taschereau in *Revue Retrospective* (Paris: Paulin, 1848), pp. 3-10. It is often referred to as the "Taschereau Document."

18. A strong partisan of Blanqui has written a rather persuasive book mustering the evidence, although not the absolute proof, of Blanqui's complete innocence of the charge: M. Dommanget, *Une Drame politique en 1848* (Paris: Les Deux Sirènes, 1948). For the opposite point of view: J. F. Jeanjean, *Armand Barbès* (Paris: Édouard Cornély et Cie., 1909), I, 159-70.

19. For a more detailed account of these events, see pp. 150-52 below.

20. There is a very full account of this period, including several important documents, in M. Dommanget, *Auguste Blanqui à Belle-Ile* (Paris: Librairie du Travail, 1935).

21. *La Gazette des Tribunaux,* June 14, 1861.

22. A. Ranc, *Souvenirs—Correspondance 1831-1908* (Paris: Édouard Cornély et Cie., 1913), p. 27.

23. See Paul Lafargue's appreciation, "Auguste Blanqui—souvenirs personnel," in *La Révolution Française,* April 20, 1879. Lafargue wrote: "To Blanqui belongs the honor of having made the revolutionary education of a section of the youth of our generation."

24. C. Da Costa, *Les Blanquistes,* Vol. VI of *Histoires des partis socialistes en France* (Paris: Marcel Rivière, 1912), *passim.* Cf. M. Dommanget, "Les groupes Blanquistes de la fin du Second-Empire," *Revue Socialiste,* XLIV (Feb., 1951), 225-31.

25. Blanqui's own description of this event appeared in his journal *La Patrie en danger.* L. A. Blanqui, *La Patrie en danger* (Paris: A. Chevalier, 1871), pp.

49-61. Cf. A. Zévaès, *Auguste Blanqui* (Paris: Marcel Rivière, 1920), pp. 216-20.

26. M. Dommanget, *Blanqui, la Guerre de 1870-71 et la Commune* (Paris: Éditions Domat, 1947), pp. 70-84.

27. B. Flotte, *Blanqui et les otages en 1871* (Paris: Imprimerie Jeannette, 1885), p. 27.

28. Two relatively recent additions to the tremendous mass of literature on the Commune, which give well-reasoned but conflicting interpretations of its ideological composition are: E. S. Mason, *The Paris Commune* (New York: MacMillan Co., 1930), and F. Jellinek, *The Paris Commune of 1871* (London: Victor Gollanz Ltd., 1937).

29. F. Mehring, *Karl Marx* (New York: Covici-Friede, 1935), p. 511. This can only remain a conjecture, but the Blanquists would have been one of the strongest sections of an International purged of the anarchists if it had maintained its headquarters in London.

30. Geoffroy, *L'Enfermé,* II, 199.

31. *Ibid.,* II, 199.

32. Zévaès, *Auguste Blanqui,* pp. 232-46.

33. A. Mathiez, "Notes de Blanqui sur Robespierre," *Annales Historiques de la Révolution Française,* V (July-Aug., 1928), 305-6.

34. See p. 22 below.

35. A. Schirokauer, *Lassalle,* tr. Edan and Cedar Paul (London: George Allen and Unwin Ltd., 1931), p. 124.

36. G. Megaro, *Mussolini in the Making* (London: George Allen and Unwin Ltd., 1938), p. 324.

37. M. Karpovitch, "A Forerunner of Lenin, P. N. Tkatchev," *Review of Politics,* IV (July, 1944), pp. 336-50.

38. *Ni Dieu Ni Maître,* Jan. 9, 1881.

39. Geffroy, *L'Enfermé,* II, 218-20.

40. B. Malon, "Blanqui Socialiste," *Revue Socialiste,* II (July, 1885), 597.

41. J. Stalin, "Lenin as the Organizer and Leader of the Russian Communist Party," in Vol. I of V. I. Lenin, *Selected Works* (Moscow: Foreign Languages Publishing House, 1950), p. 34.

42. For examples of this point of view: M. Prelot, *L'Évolution politique du socialisme français, 1789-1934* (Paris: Éditions Spes, 1939), p. 42; J. Plamenatz, *The Revolutionary Movement in France, 1815-71* (London: Longmans, Green and Co., 1952), p. 45.

43. For example: D. Thomson, *Democracy in France* (London: Oxford University Press, 1946), p. 25. "Blanqui represents the simplest form of the revolutionary tradition, anti-parlimentarian and anarchist "

44. E. Mason, "Blanqui and Communism," *Political Science Quarterly,* XLIV (Dec., 1929), 498. R. W. Postgate, "The Prisoner," *Out of the Past* (London: The Labour Publishing Co. Ltd., 1922), p. 54.

45. Clemenceau wrote a brief eulogy of Blanqui in *Le Journal,* Nov. 27, 1896.

46. Sylvain Molinier described a conversation with Clemenceau in which he expressed this viewpoint. S. Molinier, *Blanqui* (Paris: Presses Universitaires de France, 1948), p. 69.

47. B. Malon, "Blanqui Socialiste," *Revue Socialiste,* II (July, 1885), 597.

48. M. Dommanget, *Auguste Blanqui à Belle-Ile,* pp. 7-11.

49. K. Marx, "The Eighteenth Brumaire of Louis Bonaparte," *Selected Works,* ed. V. Adoratsky (New York: International Publishers, 1939), II, 323.

50. For Engels's critique of Blanquism see his letter to *Der Volksstaat,* 1874, No. 73; "The Program of the Blanquist Fugitives from the Paris Commune," reprinted in K. Marx, *The Civil War in France* (Chicago: Charles H. Kerr and Co., 1934), pp. 133-44. There is also an interesting remark of Engels's to the effect that Russia was the only country in which a Blanquist conspiracy might succeed, in "A letter to Vera Zasulich, April 23, 1885," reprinted in Marx-Engels, *Selected Correspondence,* Vol. XXIX of *Marxist Library* (New York: International Publishers, 1942), p. 437.

51. For Lenin's distinction between Blanquism and Bolshevism see: V. I. Lenin, *On the Eve of October,* Vol. XIII of *Little Lenin Library* (New York: International Publishers, 1932), pp. 5, 41.

52. A. Marty, *Quelques Aspects de l'activité de Blanqui* (Paris: Société des Amis de Blanqui, 1951). This also appeared in: *Cahiers du Communisme,* April, 1951, pp. 389-415.

53. Le Bureau Politique du Parti Communiste Français, "Les problèmes de la politique du parti, et l'activité factionelle des camarades André Marty et Charles Tillon," *Cahiers du Communisme,* Oct., 1952, p. 951.

54. R. Garaudy, "Le Néo-blanquisme de contrebande et les positions antiléninistes d'André Marty," *Cahiers du Communisme,* Jan., 1953, pp. 38-50.

55. K. J. Kenafick, *Michael Bakunin and Karl Marx* (Melbourne: Hawthorn Press, 1948), pp. 276-77.

56. M. Eastman, *Marx and Lenin* (New York: Albert and Charles Boni, 1927), pp. 144-45.

57. A. Rosenberg, *Democracy and Socialism,* tr. G. Roben (New York: Alfred A. Knopf, 1939), p. 94: "Blanqui was neither a fomenter of insurrections, nor an adventurer. Instead he was the living conscience of French democracy."

58. C. Rappaport and Compère-Morel, *Un Peu d'histoire,* Vol. I of *Encyclopédie Socialiste,* ed. Compère-Morel (Paris: Aristide Quillet, 1912), p. 291.

59. Cf. F. Simon, *L. A. Blanqui en Anjou,* (Angers: Cooperative Imprimerie Angevine, 1939), pp. 51-54.

60. Sénés, "Blanqui," in *Provenceaux—Notes Biographiques* (Toulon, 1904), p. 146.

61. E.g., A. Callet "Un Grand patriote méconnu. Auguste Blanqui," *La Nouvelle Revue,* XXXV (May-June 1918), 111-18.

62. E. Albringues, *Discours anniversaire de Blanqui,* aux Jeunesse Socialiste Révolutionnaire, Groupe de Toulouse, Jan. 1, 1898 (Toulouse: Imprimerie Lagout et Sebille, 1898), p. 8.

63. Bibliothéque Nationale, Blanqui MSS, Nouvelles acquisitions françaises, 9578-9598. (Will henceforth be cited as Blanqui MSS, followed by Nouvelles acquisitions number, section, and page, e.g., Blanqui MSS, 9580 [part 2], p. 33).

64. This is attested by various fellow prisoners: Noguès, *Une Condamnation de Mai 1839,* p. 242; A. Scheurer-Kestner, *Souvenirs de jeunesse* (Paris: Bibliothèque—Charpentier, 1905), pp. 80-81.

Alan Ritter (essay date 1969)

SOURCE: "Proudhon as a Radical Critic of Established Institutions," in *The Political Thought of Pierre-Joseph Proudhon,* Princeton University Press, 1969, pp. 94-117.

[*In the following essay, Ritter examines Proudhon's critique of hierarchy, government, law, and political rule.*]

A critic qualifies as radical by carrying his assault on the status quo beyond its surface defects to their hidden sources. He grabs matters by the root, as Marx said, while others are content to prune their leaves and branches. Proudhon wants to grab by the root what he regards as the present world's most potent instruments of oppression: hierarchy and government.[1]

THE SOCIAL EVILS: DEFERENCE AND INEQUALITY

Proudhon's critique is usually examined from an economic angle. Most commentators have placed it in that long line of attacks on exploitation known as socialism. Yet this perspective obscures as much as it clarifies. For though Proudhon was indeed a vigorous opponent of exploitation, his strictures against it are an outgrowth of something more basic. He denounced exploitation because he saw in it the same disrespectful features that he condemned in other aspects of modern society. To fully understand the critical side of his theory it is therefore necessary to focus attention on its general premises, rather than on its application to economics.

Proudhon's opposition to existing social arrangements is inspired by Rousseau's similar onslaught in the *Discourse on Inequality.* Proudhon's only quarrel with Rousseau's critique is that it does not go far enough; his mistake "is not, cannot be in his negation of society: it consists in his not having carried his argument to the end."[2] Proudhon proposes to resume Rousseau's battle and press on to a complete victory.[3] He accepts his forebear's critical premises and draws out their extreme conclusions.

Both writers make the same practice the target of their attack: deference, the use of conventional standards of rank—mainly wealth, power, and prestige—to rate all members of society.[4] In Rousseau's words, which could just as well have been Proudhon's, when "a value came to be attached to public esteem," so that men "set a value on the opinion of the rest of the world," the first step "toward vice" was taken and "combinations fatal to innocence and happiness" resulted.[5] Where Proudhon differs from Rousseau is in being more explicit about the reasons why deference is bad. Unlike his forebear, he has precise norms with which to appraise it. Though he never formally judged deference by the rules of respect, his thought can be completed by considering the remarks he makes about it in the light of their critical implications.

The first rule of respect enjoins acceptance of the choices of others. A man who practices deference has little concern for the decisions made by those he ranks as poor, weak, and lowly. Thinking them unworthy of consideration, he tends to disregard their decisions, or perhaps impute false ones to them. Moreover, he will be just as mistaken about the aims of those he ranks highly. Thinking of them as strong, rich, or honored, he will tend to believe that they seek power, money, or prestige.

In the "Cours" Proudhon compares this deferential social outlook with the way an army's echelons regard one another. The soldier accepts military rank as his evaluative standard and hence tends to ignore the aims of his subordinates and misunderstand those of his superiors: it is not worthwhile to find out what the privates want, the generals' objective is obviously to command.[6] In society as a whole there is the same connection between judging others according to rank and misunderstanding their purposes. Choice can never be free where men view one another in a graded hierarchy.

Judged by the second rule of respect—enjoining freedom of action—deference appears as pernicious as when judged by the first. It is easily seen that one will be apt to hinder the execution of decisions which one misunderstands or denigrates. Hence, in a deferential society, the poor, unhonored, and weak will usually be kept from reaching their ends, while those highly ranked in these respects are allowed to attain theirs. Deference engenders "special perquisites, privileges, exemptions, favors, exceptions, all the violations of justice"—in short, oppression, including economic exploitation of the unprivileged.[7]

If respect is impossible in a deferential society, how do its members treat one another? Those who enjoy high esteem

Pierre-Joseph Proudhon (1809–1865)

can be said to respect others only "if by respect you mean the compliments, obeisances, and all the affectations of a puerile and Christian civility. Is it not the height of good breeding for a great lord to know how to say 'hello!' in as many different ways as there are rungs on the hierarchic ladder? M. Guizot calls this science of pretences respect. For us, men of the Revolution, it is insolence."[8] As for those who give deference, they are just as disrespectful as those who receive it. The only difference is that the highly esteemed are servile. To those at the bottom, with their "instinctive obedience," the rich, honored, and powerful "always seem to be thirty centimeters taller than other men."[9]

Having shown more fully than Rousseau why deference leads to injustice and oppression, Proudhon goes on to draw the critical conclusions his predecessor had avoided. The most obvious is that the practice of deference, being supremely immoral, ought to be abolished. Rousseau was kept from saying this by his belief that deference is due to social inequality.[10] By ascribing deference to this particular cause, he made its cure depend on the creation of a strictly egalitarian society. But he doubted the possibility, and feared the consequences of such a society. Hence, though he deplored deference as much as Proudhon, he did not want to eliminate it. It was to be maintained and only its worst symptoms alleviated.[11]

Proudhon agrees completely with Rousseau about the cause of deference and, consequently, about what is needed to abolish it. Deference, he says, arises from "the distinction of ranks. . . . As long as [a] society includes a mean and extremes, the distance remains the same between the poor and the rich, between the serf and the baron; there is no public happiness."[12] But he disagrees with Rousseau about the possibility and value of eliminating hierarchy. Hence, while he praises his predecessor for ascribing deference to inequality, he berates him for "relegating equality to the status of an ideal."[13] Such equivocation is inadmissible. Since inequality causes deference, and since deference is profoundly objectionable, inequality must be abolished.[14]

Proudhon even goes a step further. The existence of inequality presupposes application of a rule that tells how much wealth, power, and prestige each member of society should receive. Such a rule, indicating how goods should be allocated among members of society, is an obvious example of a principle of distributive justice. Hence, if inequality is to be abolished so must its underlying distributive principle. All rules of distributive justice must be eliminated.[15]

By assailing the venerable distributive principle, Proudhon introduced a radical element into his critique. Condemnation of hierarchy was itself a radical move, since hierarchy is a basic feature of all existing societies. But criticism of distributive justice went even further. For no thinker, however libertarian, had ever dared to question the view that some rules for allocating goods are indispensable for social life.

Proudhon's total opposition to distributive justice had curious results for his attitude toward those of his contemporaries who shared his hostility to inequality. Their view contrasted with his in that they did not oppose the principle of distributive justice, but simply wanted to apply it differently. Proudhon found himself objecting more strongly to these contemporaries than to the hierarchy that was their common enemy.

One kind of attack on inequality came from the liberals, who objected to the caste features of existing rank differences. What bothered them was that the prestige, power, or wealth a man enjoys is too often unrelated to the efforts he makes to obtain it. Instead, it devolves on him by virtue of some circumstance beyond his control, such as his birth. In this view inequality is perfectly legitimate, provided it arises for the right reasons. Liberals do not find fault with the principle of distribution *per se,* but only with the way it is actually applied.

Proudhon attacked the liberals repeatedly, on the ground that they would merely substitute one form of inequality for another. One of their arguments, used in Proudhon's day by the Saint-Simonians, criticizes the existing hierarchy as unfair to the claims of talent. But, as Proudhon points out, the application of the principle, to each according to his ability, rules out "both the fact of equality and the right to it." A hierarchy of talent is still a hierarchy. Hence "the evaluation of talents . . . is an offense against personal dignity."[16] Another liberal attack on inequality objects to its inadequate compensation of productive contribution. Proudhon opposes this position too. "Is it just that he who does more receives more?" No indeed! "All workers are equal; . . . the product of each is limited by the right of all."[17]

The other prevalent objection to the existing pattern of inequality came from the socialists, who criticized, not its neglect of personal achievement, but its frustration of basic human needs. They felt the unequal distribution of advantages kept too many people from enjoying a decent standard of living. This criticism of inequality could be no more acceptable to Proudhon than the other. It too finds nothing intrinsically wrong with ranking people and merely prescribes a different distributive rule. Hence Proudhon repeatedly attacks the two leading French spokesmen for this view, Louis Blanc and Etienne Cabet, who both defend the formula, to each according to his need. This maxim "accords less than equality: it preserves inequality."[18] Since needs vary, reward proportioned to them produces unequal distribution of income. The criterion of need must also cause substantial inequality of power. "Who will be the judge of need?" Each man cannot be his own judge, for unreconcilable disputes would arise. So decisions about needs "will be coercively enforced." But "that is slavery." Distribution according to need "leads to despotism."[19]

It is hard to see how Proudhon's attack on inequality could have been any more radical than this. His opposition is so fundamental that not one of its other critics is spared by his attack.[20]

The Political Evils: Government and Law

Anyone acquainted with Proudhon knows that he was an anarchist, a foe of all government; yet few are able to account coherently for his objections. The reason why this aspect of his thought remains obscure is that it is part of a whole anarchist realm of discourse which is itself ill understood. Some remarks on the unfamiliar context of Proudhon's anarchism may help in its analysis.

One of the premises of anarchism is simply that because government is coercive and violent, it must be evil. Such a view is rather common. Luther, for instance, described political rule as "the fastening of wild and savage beasts with chains and bands . . . so that they must needs keep peace outwardly against their will" and found fault with it for doing so.[21] Rousseau returns to Luther's picture of government as an enchainer and also criticizes it on this ground. But neither Rousseau, nor Luther, nor most of the other writers who use this argument, qualify as anarchists. This position requires additional ingredients.

One reason Rousseau does not move from criticizing government to recommending its destruction is that he has a high regard for one of its essential features, law-making. "It is to the law alone that men owe justice and liberty," he declares.[22] Behind this statement lies the familiar argument that laws, being general and applicable only to external behavior, are self-limiting and hence praiseworthy. For Rousseau, these merits of legal control outweigh the disadvantages of political coercion. Government is indeed an enchainment, but if men are chained by laws, their bondage is salutary. For this reason Rousseau recommends not the destruction of government but its legal legitimization.

Rousseau's position suggests that another ingredient of full-blooded anarchism is antipathy toward law. Such antipathy takes many forms; the most prevalent involves reversing the usual argument in praise of law by criticizing its generality and externality. Luther makes both of these reversals. He finds fault with law's generality on the ground that this makes it too crude for dealing with the particular cases it is supposed to regulate. General rules cannot be adapted to the changing conditions they are meant to control. He concludes, "the body politic cannot be felicitously governed by rules."[23] This argument is really an objection to all rule-making, not only to legislation. Luther also attacks law's externality. By doing so he raises an objection to specifically legal rules. His point is that since law can only regulate overt conduct, it can do nothing to correct the thoughts and feelings that are the source of evil-doing.

Though Luther is critical of both law and government, he does not qualify as a full-blooded anarchist any more than does Rousseau. His ideal is certainly the absence of all legal and political regulation. "By the Spirit and by faith all Christians are throughout inclined to do well . . . much more than any one can teach them with all the laws and need so far as they are concerned no commandments nor law."[24] But he is unwilling to transform this vision into a proposal to abolish law and government, because, though he thinks that they are bad, he also regards them as indispensable. Most men are not Christians and so cannot be freed from their coercive, crude, and external chains. If they were, being vicious, they would destroy each other.

Luther's insistence on the need for government suggests that still a third ingredient is required if anarchistic thinking is to count as unequivocal anarchism: the belief that government is unnecessary. This suggestion first appears in a developed form in the thought of William Godwin. So convinced was Godwin of society's aptitude for self-regulation that he thought law and government dispensable. His theory also contains anarchism's other two essentials: he condemns law as a procrustean bed, and government as unduly coercive.[25] By committing himself to all three of these positions, Godwin was able to take the step foreclosed to others: he could make a logically valid case for abolishing government and law.

This analysis shows what in Proudhon's critique of political rule bears most directly on his anarchism. The relevant points are his evaluation of government and law and his assessment of the need for them.

The starting point of his evaluation is Rousseauist, because he regards Rousseau's test for good government as compatible with the rules of respect. This test, as reformulated by Proudhon, is that "no one should obey a law unless he has consented to it himself."[26] For him as for Rousseau this belief leads immediately to a denunciation of every form of autocratic government. Since all autocracies force their subjects to obey regulations they have not consented to, all must be condemned.

His premise also leads to denunciation of representative government. Like Rousseau, but in greater detail, Proudhon criticizes this kind of regime on the ground that representatives cannot express the will of their constituents. In a passage recalling Rousseau's remark that Englishmen are free only during parliamentary elections, he writes, "All citizens of the Second Republic are eligible . . . to vote. . . . .. This moment of public political participation is short: forty-eight hours at the most for each election. . . .. The President and the Representatives, once elected, are the masters: everything else obeys. It is subject, governable and taxable, without abatement."[27]

One reason why citizens are powerless between elections is that a deputy cannot work for all who vote for him, even if he knows what they want, because their objectives change and conflict.[28] The deputy also has environmentally produced motives for ignoring the aims of his electors. Anticipating numerous critics of the French parliament as a closed arena, Proudhon remarks that no sooner is a candidate elected than he acquires a new perspective on politics, as a member of the legislature, that gradually isolates him from his constituents.[29]

In Proudhon's eyes, it is as doubtful that representatives will respond to the desires of the public during elections as well as during the intervals between elections. The tragic results of numerous French elections had convinced him that voters often choose a candidate who does not even profess to support their views.[30] Since French voters have learned to choose more shrewdly since Proudhon's day, this argument no longer carries as much weight. But a final objection to representative government is as valid now as when Proudhon raised it. Electors cannot choose candidates responsive to their wishes because their political judgment is warped by membership in a hierarchic society. Being divided into inferiors and superiors, people vote "from motives of servility or hatred."[31] The mental blinders imposed by inequality keep them from understanding either the aims of the candidates or their own true interests.

Rousseau had not tested constitutional governments with his standard. Proudhon tries to fill the gap. It is true, he admits, that constitutional regimes are less oppressive than autocratic ones.[32] But their superiority is only marginal, because they are unstable. They are usually swept away by civil war if they do not degenerate into naked dictatorships.[33] Those that avoid these outcomes have an equally dismal end. They become secret instruments of bourgeois domination. The bourgeoisie thinks constitutionalism is better than autocracy for maintaining the confidence so helpful in the quest for profit.[34] Hence, when it can do so, the bourgeoisie respects constitutional government's "legal forms, its juridical spirit, its reserved character, its parliamentary rituals."[35] Behind these trappings there lurks "a vast system of exploitation and intrigue, where politics is the counterpart of speculation, where taxation is but the payroll of a caste, and monopolized power the assistant to monopoly."[36]

Much of this critique sounds Marxian; but its theoretical basis is Proudhon's own. He calls constitutional government oppressive because it merely alleviates the symptoms of political illness while leaving their causes undisturbed. It accepts inequality as an unalterable fact, to be controlled, not removed. Then, in order to control inequality, government oppresses the upper strata to some degree, but the lower even more. By doing so government behaves disrespectfully, for in both cases it imposes regulations to which its subjects have not given their consent.[37]

Rousseau had criticized the representative, but not the democratic, aspect of representative democracy. Indeed, he had approved of the latter. Proudhon thinks he was mistaken in doing so. If an autocracy is unacceptable because it forces men to follow decisions that conflict with their own, then direct democracy is also unacceptable since it too must sometimes prevent its subjects from executing their own decisions. In a direct democracy it is usually only the minority who are repressed, while in an autocracy the choices of everyone except the ruling elite are often blocked. But this difference in the amount of disrespect in the two regimes does not warrant a more favorable judgment of democracy; there is no reason to prefer the oppression of a majority to that of an autocrat.[38]

In at least one way, Proudhon finds democracy worse than dictatorship. The repression that an autocrat can impose is limited by the illegitimacy of his status. His subjects obey him from fear of disobedience, not because they accept his title to rule. The legitimacy of democratic regimes, on the other hand, is widely accepted, at least in modern times. Hence democratic governments can repress their subjects more outrageously than can autocracies.[39]

This argument no doubt goes too far. Though the range of alternatives open to democratic rulers may be wider than that available to autocrats, this does not mean democratic rulers can do anything they please. There are repressive policies they cannot follow, like massacring the innocent, which autocrats sometimes carry out with impunity. But whatever the weakness of Proudhon's argument, it does point to democracy's unprecedented capacity to mobilize and reshape society, a capacity that has had fateful consequences in our own time.

The most obvious objection to Proudhon's entire critique of existing government challenges its excessively formal view of the political process. It can be argued that just as too formal an analysis of British government was responsible for the mistaken thesis that Parliament is all-powerful, so Proudhon's failure to consider extra-legal influence in assessing the power of rulers leads him to under-estimate their responsiveness to the wishes of the ruled.

The substance of this objection is undoubtedly correct. Proudhon takes no account of the informal pressures that even the most abject subjects exert on an autocrat. Nor does he consider the far more obvious influence of an electorate on its representatives. If he had done so, he could never have said that once in office deputies are exempt from all popular control.

But though the substance of the objection is correct—and it does reveal a shortcoming in Proudhon as a political analyst—it does not diminish his stature as a critic. His standard for judging governments would have required their condemnation even if he had been fully aware of the informal popular influence at work in them, because this influence only mitigates, and does not eliminate, disrespectful political coercion. Not even the most responsive government can dispense entirely with authority, "the right to command," no matter how elaborately it conceals this fact.[40] It is authority in this sense that Proudhon cannot abide. Thus the basis of his dislike for government is not a faulty analysis of the political process, but an exceedingly rigorous standard for judging it. As he said in 1848, explaining his vote against one of France's most democratic constitutions, "I voted against the Constitution, because it is a Constitution."[41] Any government, *ipso facto*, must be condemned.

In the final stage of his political critique, Proudhon turns the tables on Rousseau, by applying their common test of good government to his predecessor's scheme for an ideal one. Rousseau had sought a plan for political rule that would allow each citizen to execute his own decision whenever he obeyed the law. Had he found such a plan, Proudhon would surely have praised it, since it would have assured freedom of action. But he saw that Rousseau's attempt to design a respectful government was a failure and that his only accomplishment was to hide repression behind a libertarian mask. Hence he repeatedly criticizes Rousseau's ideal as "a theory destructive to liberty."[42]

The heart of Proudhon's objection to Rousseau is a denial of his claim that no coercion is inflicted by a properly constituted government when it forces a man to obey the law. Rousseau could say this because he used unusual conceptions of will and freedom. He thought of the will as having two parts, a particular or self-regarding part, and a part that is general or community-regarding. Freedom he conceived as the capacity for self-legislation, the ability to make and obey self-imposed laws. By distinguishing between self- and community-regarding will, and by conceiving of freedom as self-legislation, Rousseau laid a foundation for the view that liberty entails repression of will. If a man follows his self-regarding will when it con-

flicts with his community-regarding one, his action is not free. For when a self- and community-regarding will conflict, the action dictated by the self-regarding one cannot be made into a universally practicable action, i.e., a law. Consequently, if a man in such a situation is prevented by his government from following his self-regarding will, he is not constrained; rather, his opportunity to act freely is protected, for he retains the chance to follow his general will. Thus Rousseau's concept of the will as divided, and of liberty as self-legislation, serves as the theoretical basis for justifying coercion in the name of freedom.

Proudhon saw through this impressive bit of sophistry. The whole argument was nothing but an "enormous swindle,"[43] because a person kept from executing a selfish choice is in fact no less coerced than a person kept from executing a universalizable one. In neither case does government respect its subject's freedom of action, for in both it keeps him from doing what he wants to do.[44] Hence Rousseau's scheme of government does not succeed in eliminating disrespectful coercion. Rulers in his ideal state, as in any other, thwart achievement of their subjects' aims.

Why does Rousseau employ such peculiar and dangerous conceptions of will and freedom? Part of the explanation is his esteem for law. Since he regards legislation as highly desirable, he must deny it is coercive, for if obedience to law involves coercion, it cannot be desirable. His conceptions of freedom and will enable him to do this. If obedience to universally applicable decisions does not curtail my freedom of action, then neither does legal compulsion to obey them. Similarly, if my liberty to do as I please is not reduced when I am kept from executing selfish decisions, then a legal ban on executing them does not curb it either. Rousseau's definitions serve to protect his defense of law's value from the charge that legislation can be oppressive.

As an anarchist, Proudhon finds fault not only with the coercion justified by Rousseau's political ideal, but also with the basis of that justification: Rousseau's esteem for law. It is true that Proudhon frequently opposed law as a mere symptom of more basic malaise, rather than as something inherently inadmissible.[45] Implicit in this way of arguing is the thesis that if society and government were not defective in the ways already analyzed, law would not be objectionable either.

But Proudhon also has some basic criticisms of legislation. Law puts "external authority . . . in the place of citizens' immanent, inalienable, untransferable authority."[46] There are two things wrong with law's externality. First, its method of enforcement, coercion by identifiable external agents, violates the second rule of respect by preventing the execution of decisions. The need for coercive enforcement makes law just as authoritarian, in Proudhon's eyes, as more arbitrary means of political control. The object to which law applies contributes further to its immorality. Law applies to overt behavior, not inward thought. It ignores, or at most gives minor attention to choices and aims, being content for the most part to consider action's form and results. The first rule of respect, on the other hand, calls for accepting the internal preliminaries to action, the decisions and purposes that direct it. From the standpoint of respect, law is thus blind to the kind of motivation worthy of the highest consideration.

Proudhon objects to more than the immediately disrespectful features of law's externality. He also denounces the externally oriented frame of mind encouraged by legal institutions. A society where the rule of law is dominant nurtures the sort of personality which "is convinced that the more or less improper acts that it performs every day, from morning to night, are necessary and hence legitimate, and that there is consequently no such thing as swindling or theft, except in the cases defined by law."[47] What is described here is the legalistic point of view personified by Shylock, which equates virtue with a legal claim and the just man with the lawful one. It sanctions judging others by how law-abiding they are, rather than by the degree to which they follow inwardly affirmed moral principles. Such an attitude is totally at odds with Proudhonian morality, since the rules of respect are precisely the sorts of moral principles it repudiates.

Though Proudhon fiercely attacks law's externality, he does not criticize its other trait: its generality. This is not surprising, since his whole ethical theory assumes that morality is a matter of accepting and following general rules. So strongly does Proudhon favor a rule-keeping morality that he thinks "the true judge for every man is his own conscience, a fact that implies replacement of the system of courts and laws with a system of personal obligations and contracts, in other words, suppression of legal institutions."[48] On the surface, this statement may seem totally hostile to law. But it is also partial to a legalistic conception of morality that pictures conscience as a judge who decides which of several rules governing conduct and choice applies to a particular case. Having approved of general principles in the moral realm, Proudhon could hardly object to law on the ground that it used them. He quarreled with law only because it was external, not because it was general. General *moral* rules, being applicable to choice, are praiseworthy.

But though Proudhon does not condemn the generality of legal regulation, he does consider it. His point is that law cannot be general enough to avoid being arbitrary. "Laws in small number! . . . Why, that is impossible. Mustn't the government regulate all interests and judge all claims? Well, owing to the nature of society, interests are innumerable, their relations are variable and infinitely changeable: how can it possibly make few laws? How can they be simple?"[49] A complicated code of detailed laws, the only kind that can be effective, "sows disorder in men's minds, obscures the notion of justice and makes necessary a whole caste of interpreters to explain the system."[50] Laws must be so numerous, complicated, specific, changeable, so subject to twisted interpretation, so incomprehensible, that they must oppress. Only a rule that is "unchanging," "su-

premely intelligible," "the inviolable standard of all human actions," in short, as general as possible, is sanctioned by the ethics of respect.[51] Since law cannot have these attributes, it must be fundamentally condemned.

Proudhon's critique of law helps to explain his opposition to Rousseau's ideal state. He not only objected to the coercion justified by Rousseau's ideal; he did not think the benefit gained by justifying it was worth the price. Rousseau may perhaps have realized that the man who is kept from following his self-regarding will is, in a sense, just as constrained as the one kept from following his general will. But since self-regarding wills cannot be universalized, the cost of repressing them could not strike him as high, while the benefit of doing so seemed enormous. If some people were now and then kept from following their worthless particular wills, all would benefit immensely. For then everyone would follow the law. To Proudhon, on the other hand, who fundamentally disapproved of law, the cost of such repression seemed enormous, and its benefits negligible.

The first two ingredients in Proudhon's anarchism—his objections to government and law—ally to support a sweeping denunciation of rulership. His hostility toward political coercion prompts him to apply Rousseau's test of good government just as rigorously as its inventor had done. His opposition to law leads him to extend its application to areas from which Rousseau had excluded it and to detect coercion where Rousseau, with his admiration for law, had professed to see freedom. But all this criticism of government and legislation, however vigorous, would not support their abolition, unless Proudhon's theory contained anarchism's third essential: the belief that political rule is unnecessary.

Proudhon does indeed hold this belief, but in a rather sophisticated form, easier to defend than the dogmatic assertions that government is needless, made by anarchists like Tolstoy. The statements of Tolstoy, and writers like him, give whatever backing there is to anarchism's reputation as a naïve belief in government's easy dispensability.[52] Proudhon, of course, is more circumspect. His theory of political development kept him from thinking government easily dispensable, because it asserted that until his own time government had performed vital functions by building character, extirpating laziness, and so on. Even in his own day, its abolition could not seem easy to Proudhon; his reflections on human nature and society had convinced him that government continued to perform the valuable service of maintaining order and that, if it were abolished, some substitute would have to be found.

The question of the need for political rule thus depended on whether government was indispensable for the maintenance of order. Proudhon denied that it was. To begin with, government was certainly not a logical requisite for order, though as the expression "law and order" shows, the two are often equated in common usage. "*Order* is a genus, *government,* a species. In other words, there are several ways to conceive of order: what proof is there that order in society is of the sort its masters wish to assign to it?"[53] Nor could government be considered a causal requisite for order. Causal *necessity* does not exist, at least in human affairs, where innovation can occur.[54] As for the causal *connection* between government and order, it was proved tenuous by the not infrequent failure of political rule to control conflict.[55] Thus the need for government in civilized societies was extremely dubious, though ironclad proof of its dispensability depended on discovery of a suitable replacement. When this conclusion was added to Proudhon's denunciation of government, unmitigated anarchism resulted. Government was in most respects profoundly evil. Its one good effect could be achieved by some other means; hence it ought to be eliminated.

To many realists arrival at such a judgment would be a signal for re-examining first principles. Something must be wrong with values and analysis which imply that indispensable institutions like government and law, not to mention hierarchy, must be abolished. To other realists, these conclusions would suggest not revision, but withdrawal. Denunciation of the actual would not be diluted, but attempts to improve it would be abandoned. To Proudhon, however, as a true radical, these findings occasion no such second thoughts. Instead, they give impetus to further theorizing. Having proved to his satisfaction that hierarchy and political authority should be abolished, he presses on to discover new arrangements that will vindicate his case by making superior substitutes available. The obverse of his radical critique is a proposal for fundamental change.

Notes

1. Proudhon, of course, believed that religion was a third instrument of oppression. This should not be forgotten but bears only indirectly on his social and political ideas.

2. *Cont.,* I, 351.

3. "Rousseau has always struck me as misunderstanding the cause he wanted to defend and as getting entangled in baseless a priority, when he should have reasoned according to the nature of things." *Dim.,* p. 55.

4. Jean-Jacques Rousseau, *The Social Contract and Discourses,* trans., G. D. H. Cole (New York, 1950), p. 265. Cf. *Justice,* III, 174: "Generally, the consideration attached to a man . . . is proportional to his reputation, his fortune and his power. We are so made that we always suppose that noumena are proportional to phenomena, that appearance is proportional to reality." The contrast between reality and appearance (*être* and *paraître*) was also much emphasized by Rousseau, e.g., p. 247.

5. Rousseau, pp. 240-41, 270.

6. "Cours," 1-3 (30).

7. *Justice,* III, 174.

8. *Ibid.,* II, 383.

9. *Cap.,* p. 88.

10. Rousseau, p. 271.

11. Judith Shklar, "Rousseau's Images of Authority," *American Political Science Review,* LVIII, No. 4 (December 1964), p. 920.

12. *Avert.,* pp. 205-206.

13. Quoted in Pierre Haubtmann, "Pierre-Joseph Proudhon: sa vie et sa pensée" (unpublished thesis for the Doctorat d'Etat, Faculté des lettres et des sciences humaines de Paris, 1961), p. 282, annex 20.

14. Proudhon also condemns hierarchy for causing political oppression. This aspect of his social criticism is discussed in the next section of this chapter, where his critique of government is examined.

15. *Prop.,* p. 313; *I. G.,* p. 187; *Justice,* I, 453. Yves Simon is the only critic, so far as I know, who remarks on Proudhon's total hostility to distributive justice. See his "Note sur le fédéralisme proudhonien," *Esprit,* No. 55 (April 1937), p. 55.

16. *Justice,* 11, 72.

17. *Prop.,* pp. 221-22. Proudhon later reneged this criticism, as will become clear in due course.

18. "Résistance à la Révolution," reprinted in *I. G.,* p. 378.

19. *I. G.,* pp. 173-74; *Justice,* 11, 72.

20. The typology of anti-hierarchic arguments used here is suggested by Sanford Lakoff's *Equality in Political Philosophy* (Cambridge, Mass., 1964). Lakoff tries to fit Proudhon into his scheme somewhere on the borderline between the liberals and the socialists but senses that he does not fit well into the slot assigned him. The reason is that Proudhon does not belong anywhere on the map Lakoff has charted. He is off by himself on some exotic island where the principle of distributive justice is not accepted.

21. Martin Luther, *Martin Luther: Selections from His Writings,* ed., John Dillenberger (New York, 1961), p. 370.

22. Rousseau, p. 294, cf. Shklar, "Images," p. 922.

23. Luther, p. 331. This argument is ancient, going back to Plato, who, of course, used it for the perfection rather than the condemnation of government.

24. *Ibid.,* p. 269.

25. D. H. Munro, *Godwin's Moral Philosophy* (Oxford, 1953), pp. 129, 151.

26. *I. G.,* p. 267.

27. *I. G.,* p. 226, cf. *C. P.,* p. 283.

28. *Ibid.,* p. 210.

29. "A propos de Louis Blanc," reprinted in *I. G.,* p. 438; cf. *Carnets,* x, 52. Representative government

is "a perpetual abuse of power for the profit of the reigning caste and the interests of representative, against the interests of the represented."

30. *Sol.,* p. 48.

31. *Conf.,* p. 229.

32. *Conf.,* p. 221; but cf. *C. P.,* p. 377, where a constitution is called "a system at once wise, just and free." This enthusiasm is anomalous as Théodore Ruyssen shows in his introduction to *C. P.,* p. 123, but it also turns up in *Justice,* III, 277.

33. *Conf.,* pp. 223, 230.

34. *Justice,* III, 145.

35. *P. F.,* p. 304.

36. *Ibid.,* cf. *Conf.,* p. 227.

37. *P. F.,* pp. 245-47; *Conf.,* 217-18; *Carnets,* XI, p. 479: "Constitutional power is always arbitrary power, if not unstable power, lacking all character and morality. To produce balance it is unnecessary to create a device that imposes it: it suffices to put [social] forces into the kind of agreement that induces them to hold one another in equilibrium."

38. *I. G.,* pp. 208-16; *Cont.,* I, 340.

39. *Sol.,* p. 48.

40. *Justice,* II, 312; cf. *Corr.,* IV, 149: "Organization of any kind is equivalent to the suppression of liberty, so far as free persons are concerned."

41. *Conf.,* p. 215.

42. *I. G.,* p. 193.

43. *Justice,* III, 270.

44. *Ibid.,* II, 362; *P. F.,* 345.

45. *I. G.,* p. 204.

46. "Résistance à la Révolution," reprinted in *I. G.,* pp. 374, 378.

47. *Cap.,* p. 227; cf. *Cont.,* II, 219-20.

48. *Conf.,* p. 236.

49. *I. G.,* p. 205.

50. *Cont.,* I, 337.

51. *Justice,* I, 426.

52. Isaiah Berlin, "Tolstoy and Enlightenment," *Encounter,* XVI, No. 2 (February 1961), p. 38.

53. *I. G.,* p. 202.

54. *Justice,* III, 173.

55. *I. G.,* p. 302.

Louis Patsouras (essay date 1995)

SOURCE: "Road to Revolution," in *Jean Grave and the Anarchist Tradition in France,* The Caslon Company, 1995, pp. 79-89.

[*In the following excerpt, Patsouras investigates the theoretical views of the anarcho-communist Jean Grave.*]

The theoretical views of [Jean] Grave and anarchism in certain key areas—criticism of bourgeois society, revolution, and other related topics—are the focus of this section. More developed restatements are needed in order to better understand the anarchist position.

Grave's thought is greatly indebted to Proudhon, Bakunin, contemporary anarcho-communism (Kropotkin's and Elisée Reclus' influence is obvious), and to Marx(ism), especially in its view of the capitalist economic structure and primacy attached to class struggle. In fact, there are many similarities between anarcho-communism and Marxism and from a general theoretical perspective, the two are closely related. With respect to Grave's thought one cannot but be impressed by its rich familiarity with past utopian and socialist thinkers, the Enlightenment *philosophes* (Diderot was his favorite), the English Classical Economists, and contemporary sociology, economics, literature, and so forth. His erudition is reflected in such major works as *La Société au lendemain de la révolution* (1893), *La Société mourante et l'anarchie* (1893); *La Société future* (1895), *L'Individu et la société* (1897), and *Réformes révolution* (1910).

In *La Société mourante et l'anarchie* Grave postulated that anarchism's major struggle was against authority:

> Anarchy is the negation of authority. Authority, however, pretends to justify its existence by its necessary defense of existing social institutions: the family, religion, property, and so forth, and has thus created a complex of machinery to buttress its power and legitimacy. It has founded the law, the courts, legislative power, the executive, and so forth. In confronting this situation anarchism should attack all social prejudice, examine in depth all human understanding, and finally demonstrate that its conceptions conform to the physiological and psychological nature of man, while showing that the present social organization, established contrary to all logic and good sense, has brought about unstable and revolutionary-prone societies from the accumulated hatred of those oppressed by its arbitrary institutions.[1]

This multifaceted concept not only encompassed oppressive economic, social, political, and religious structures associated with class society, but also such concomitant cultural attitudes as patriotism and racism. Before examining authority in detail, we shall observe its relationship to scarcity and mutual aid.

Grave interlaced authority with the concept of scarcity when he argued that a parsimonious nature was an element in promoting social disharmony in certain social constructs. (Scarcity was a factor in the social thought of many other thinkers, including Marx/Engels and Jean-Paul Sartre, noted libertarian Marxist and Existentialist.) This problem for Grave and Marxism was not the critical one, however, in regarding social development because for revolutionary leftists, the class struggle was the key factor in history.[2]

The underlying factor for the destruction of authority was mutual aid, a sociobiological concept developed by Kropotkin, embodying something stronger than love, the need to cooperate for survival. In the evolution of animal life, he postulated that within species cooperation was more important than competition in the struggle for existence. As applied to the human condition, he saw mutual aid as its key element, which unfortunately was weakened by the advent of civilization and concomitant rise of class society and social oppression. In the present period the basic depository of mutual aid (although in vitiated form) resided in the working masses, while their rulers embodied authority through domination and exploitation. His hope was that the mutual-aid component in the life of the workers and peasants would so succeed in strengthening itself that the class struggle would intensify to the point where it would lead to their victory over the ruling groups. For Grave, this too was the expectation.[3]

According to Grave, the present general historical tendency was propitious for achieving anarchism through mutual aid. The masses had ameliorated their position from slavery to serfdom to civil freedom with extensive political rights under capitalism. These rights, now acquired, would be the weapons to bring about final emancipation and full realization of mutual aid for anarchism. In fact, the progressive advance of mutual aid has now so weakened authority that it only continues with the consent of the people themselves.[4] From a practical perspective mutual aid mandated that the individual's moral aversion to social injustice coalesce with that of others to liberate humanity from the chains of oppression. Grave's suggestions to combat state authority included evasion of military draft, refusal to pay taxes, joining unions and utopian colonies, and doing propaganda work which also involved criticism of bourgeois ideologues.[5] An example of the last was his rejection of Malthus' thesis in *Essay on Population* which asserted that the poor were responsible for their own misery; Grave saw this based on rank social prejudice and as a shallow attempt to justify the status quo.[6]

For Grave, the strengthening of mutual aid would necessarily propel the revolution forward. In fact, this was necessary because the human personality needed freedom and equality; lacking them it would not be at peace with itself, but engage in destructive individual and collective acts. Indeed, without the strengthening of mutual aid at the expense of authority greater disasters would engulf humanity. This line of thought is reminiscent of Christian millenerianism in which a small minority (for the anarchists, a small revolutionary elect; for the Christians, the pure remnant) knows the truth leading to the promised land.[7]

Grave's anthropological views should shed further light on the basic underlying assumptions of his thought. He postulated that man through evolution was progressing to a higher plane, in which as an active and creative agent he changed himself by altering his "conditions of life." At first, however, man was "more animal than man," signifying that his moral sense as yet was not fully developed.

Early man lived in associative groups of general equality, but competitive elements were stronger than those of solidarity. In time, as groups became larger, inequality arose due to differences in strength and intelligence. Yet he mentioned that some tribes did not develop "authority," indicating that before the advent of civilization there was equality and fraternity; this was at a later stage of human development than the earlier one when man was "more like an animal."[8] In viewing early man as cooperative and competitive—although the former element was dominant—he was aware of contradiction. In this schema, Grave synthesized the anthropological views of Bakunin and Kropotkin: from the former, he borrowed the competitive element, linking it to a deficient moral sense; from the latter he stressed the importance of mutual aid.[9]

The rise of organized authority, presumably with civilization, was tied by Grave to the development of private property which he considered the greatest bulwark of bourgeois society and the root cause of inequality and social misery. Like Proudhon, he regarded it as theft whose roots originated in early history when, as competition developed, the more ruthless were able to appropriate the labor of others.[10] To counter this inequality, Grave advanced the following arguments. First, man was basically equal in essential qualities and if differences existed in the matter of strength or intelligence, they were minimal.[11] Second, since it took eons to form the world's natural resources, they should be the equal birthright of all.[12] Third, because humanity is the recipient of the accumulated knowledge and achievements of past generations (present day technology and what has been built are thus a common heritage) and because there is more extensive labor division since the advent of large industry, making for ever greater interdependence in the processes of production, no one should profit from these realities; this despite the fact that some individuals are more intelligent than others.[13] These arguments of Grave (and Kropotkin) have both moral and rational components.

The institution of private property spawned the state and its different arms (bureaucracies, court systems, police, and armies, among others). The state itself was in the hands of elites, especially those controlling the larger segments of property (the bourgeoisie in the contemporary period); thus the state was not an impartial umpire between rich and poor. (This interpretation is also that of Marxism.) Indeed, the fall of the bourgeoisie would necessarily lead to the demise of the state.[14]

For Grave, religion completed the triad of authority. Anarchism, representing atheism, could not but be antithetical to a Christianity based on defending the master class, which rationalized social oppression by admonishing the poor to accept their difficult lot in life for future reward, thus reinforcing their feelings of passivity. Following general anthropological views, Grave situated the origins of religion in man's dependence on and fear of an incomprehensible nature and asserted that with increasing mastery of science, religion would disappear.

In rejecting traditional religion, Grave replaced it with a humanistic anarchist philosophy, which accepted the finality of individual death, but which did not succumb to the despair of the life-is-absurd syndrome. Life had its own validity without being tied to the supernatural. Indeed, every generation was of critical importance in the chain of life—both culturally and biologically.[15] (Grave is not entirely correct in viewing religion as a reactionary force. In the United States, for example, the Protestant Social Gospel was highly influenced by Walter Rauschenbusch, a fundamentalist and socialist).[16]

Grave's criticism of bourgeois society reached a fairly large audience. For instance, his most widely known work, *La Société mourante et l'anarchie* was translated into many languages, including English as *The Dying Society and Anarchy*. In this and other works he mentioned such obvious failings of the present society as chronic unemployment, armaments races between the great powers, war, colonialism and its corollary of racism, the parasitical military, civil, and other bureaucracies, the deadening effects of extensive labor division which reduced workers to be "machines of machines," the barbarous behavior of governments toward the labor movement, and the general social misery of the people as contrasted to the opulence and privileges of the rulers. For instance, a fuller statement of the last: for the governors there are "joys and abundance," for the masses there is "misery, privation, and anomie."[17] In this cruel and pitiless world, irony and paradox dominated. Every advance in mechanical invention enriched the bourgeoisie at the expense of the proletariat whose insecurity and misery would increase by further unemployment. Labor itself was reduced to a mere commodity in the market place which became the new arbiter of value.[18]

Before proceeding further, let us for the moment focus on one of the most important malignancies of bourgeois society which Grave commented on, racism. Is it not of interest to note that in Grave's *La Société mourante et l'anarchie* there is a chapter entitled "There Are No Inferior Races." Perceptively, Grave tied Western racism to colonialist exploitation of subject people and added that those who talk of "inferior races" wish to justify the crimes of the "superior races."[19]

In a world of deep socioeconomic division characterized by authority, a key Marxist concept to describe a basically limited and unfree human condition is "alienation," one that has been widely used in the last two centuries to explain man's tragic fate. Although many commentators use "alienation" to portray man's awareness of his finite existence, or the impossibility to approach the perfection and power of God, others use it to signify that man's full human potential is thwarted by an oppressive society. Certainly, when Rousseau in *Discourse on the Origins of Inequality* isolated the rise of private property as the cause of social oppression and general unhappiness, he was aware of the latter use of alienation. The brilliant German philosopher, Georg F. W. Hegel in various works (*The Phenomenology of the Mind,* for example) commented on the alienated human condition by contrasting the lord and slave. it was Marx, however, who in his *Economic and Philosophical Manuscripts* and *Capital,* among other works, systematically and concretely tied alienation to class oppression that inexorably pitted the proletariat against the bourgeoisie. He condemned capitalism for its alienating socioeconomic structures: it doomed the worker to be not only a mere "machine" in the capitalist mechanism, but "the more value he [worker] creates the more worthless he becomes." Also, he added that work is often so mechanical and repetitive, so difficult and arduous that one "feels himself to be freely active only in his animal functions—eating, drinking and procreating."[20]

Grave, no less than Marx, was aware of the many facets of alienation in describing workers as "machines of machines,"[21] who labored in an increasingly sophisticated technology under capitalist control, which was at once characterized by the twin tendencies of greater labor division and more unemployment.[22] That this alienation is an inherent part of bourgeois ideology is apparent thus: bourgeois political economists from Smith in the eighteenth century to Keynes in the twentieth have regarded the worker as a mere factor in the cost of production or in other words a commodity. Grave was not opposed to modern technology, but he insisted that it not be used by one segment of the community to exploit the other.[23] In Grave's literary work alienation is conspicuous; the example of Caragut in *La Grand famille* is the most noteworthy. To summarize with respect to alienation: both Grave and Marx advocated that for its abolition the present bourgeois society should be replaced by a socialist one of free, equal and creative individuals.[24]

Before exploring in greater detail Grave's views of the class struggle and revolution, in which he rejected voting and reform, it would be useful to briefly examine the larger historical context which influenced him. Grave was in the vanguard of a Parisian working class whose revolutionary experiences in 1789-94, 1830, 1848, and 1871 led it increasingly to prefer class struggle and revolution to fickle and uncertain social reform as portrayed by the representative parliamentarism of the Third Republic. Grave's antipathy to this republic was based on: (1) its domination by conservative bourgeois and aristocratic elites, who not only played the leading role in destroying the Paris Commune of 1871, but who opposed basic social reform; (2) its inheritance of a society sharply divided by classes—the farmers and workers, comprising more than eighty percent of the people, carried the heavy burden of sustaining the privileged groups. Because of these circumstances, social compromise in Grave's perspective was impossible. For him, therefore, only by waging an incessant class struggle would the working class, including independent artisans, with the aid of the peasantry, be able to overthrow the bourgeois and aristocratic oligarchs.

For Grave, following Bakunin and Marx, the class struggle was the principal historical engine to effect change, to overcome the power of the ruling classes—in the Middle Ages between the serfs and the nobility, while after the industrial revolution, between the bourgeoisie and the workers. The class struggle itself, involved in the multifarious elements of life, occurred at once in the economic, social, political and cultural spheres, but the economic one dominated the others for any dislocation in this area would exacerbate tensions in the others.[25]

The importance that Grave attached to the economic aspect resided in the fact that capitalism made for a state of interdependence in production in which any breakdown might shatter the entire mechanism. Grave's scenario in this respect is basically Marxian. Class antagonism was sharpened by economic crises thus: ever motivated by profit, capitalism had an inherent tendency to increase the use of labor-saving machinery, which in turn tended to depress wages and increase unemployment; even the use of colonies as outlets for goods could not for long delay this progression. Succeeding depressions would eliminate small enterprise, until finally the few wealthy capitalists would be overthrown by the proletarianized majority that would inaugurate socialism.[26]

In Grave's revolutionary model, like Marx's, the spearhead of the industrial workers would be aided by the majority of the peasantry. For Grave and other anarchists, the revolutionary potential of most of the peasantry resided in their being part of the exploited masses. Indeed, the anarchist program for the peasantry allowed for ownership of land directly used, although the ideal was to have voluntary collectivization.[27]

Grave and Marx also agreed that in the relationship between masses and leadership to effect revolution, although the first element was more important, the second was also essential in providing necessary direction. (Marx has been erroneously accused by many of overstressing leadership.) They disagreed, however, on the organizational structure of the two factors.[28] Disdaining formal organization, Grave envisaged leadership in his Bakuninist phase in the form of small, clandestine groups committing propaganda by deed, while in his reformist-revolutionary phase, he counseled militants to concentrate on education and propaganda. For Marx, however, the leaders of the workers' party would direct the revolution.[29]

In the actual revolutionary change, some fighting would occur between the revolutionaries and the bourgeoisie because Grave did not believe that any ruling class would voluntarily relinquish its privileges. Once in motion, the revolution would rapidly destroy state authority and its various appendages (the military, civil administration, and so forth) along with exploitative private property within a few months.[30]

Grave, well aware of the international implications of a proletarian-led revolution in France, replayed the model of the French Revolution when, on the one hand, he expected foreign bourgeois government intervention, but, on the other hand, hoped it would spark revolution throughout the world.[31]

The Gravian model of imminent revolution, opposed to any reform within a capitalist structure, regarded reform as inefficacious—as a dampening influence on the revolutionary temper of the people.[32] At the turn of the last century, Grave, however, rather cautiously at first, superimposed a layer of reformism on his pattern of imminent revolution, which over the years became significant. In agreement with many other socialists, including Marxists, Grave finally realized that capitalism would endure for a lengthy period of time since the expected revolution did not materialize. This was due to the basic apathy of the people themselves, who in large measure still supported the aspirations and assumptions of capitalism, and their habits of subservience imposed by economic insecurity. It was, however, still possible to effect piecemeal reform through the exertions of the majority for pressing socioeconomic needs. Grave postulated that although most people were literally ignorant as to the basic causes of social oppression, they could well understand the need for urgent and specific reform.[33]

With the postponement of revolution, what were Grave's ideas about the possible peaceful transition from capitalism to anarchism? He was acquainted with, but largely rejected, the Proudhonian mutualist vision which theorized a long period of evolutionary change from capitalism to anarchism through cooperatives. This was a basic difference between mutualists and anarcho-communists. Although Grave admitted that producers' cooperatives might bring about some economic amelioration, he was fearful that capitalist influences within them, especially the profit motive, might intensify with economic success. In this respect, he was not overly sanguine then concerning the fact that sections of the proletariat could resist the temptations of *embourgeoisement*. This view had affinity to Lenin's thesis (later modified) that proletarian consciousness did not go much beyond union activity. As for consumers' cooperatives, in a more optimistic vein, Grave saw their educating workers to defend their purchasing power, but he remained cautious, opining that they should always be motivated by the ideals of anarchism. In this analysis, he was not dogmatic, and even saw the remote possibility of producers' cooperatives becoming important institutions to achieve anarchism.[34]

Even after Grave became a "reformist," he did not view reform as an end in itself, but as a necessary and integral part of the revolutionary spirit that continued to operate even within the confines of democratic political structures. With respect, for example, to the most significant political reform in nineteenth-century Europe, universal male suffrage, he envisioned it, on the one hand, as a delaying tactic of the status quo to deflect the popular revolutionary temper, but, on the other hand, admitted to its usefulness as a mechanism for further reform, which at a critical juncture might lead to revolution. In fact, in *La Société future*, Grave argued that it was perfectly possible for social tensions to intensify from greater social equality due to reform, a pattern analagous to that in de Tocqueville's *Democracy in America*. In general, Grave still feared that while reform could expand both liberty and the general welfare, it also contained the seeds to further pacify the people by instilling a false consciousness with respect to the authoritarian nature of capitalism. This view is analagous to Marcuse's distinction between the "repressive tolerance" of democratic and class-ridden societies and the genuine tolerance of those based on equality. Ultimately, Grave's ambivalence to reform indicated his unrelenting hope for imminent revolution; in this vein, he was still, for example, against voting.[35]

Although Grave accepted the importance of reform, he partially rejected Proudhon's insistence in *De La capacité politique des classes ouvrières* for the proletariat to establish both a countersociety through cooperatives and a counterculture through newspapers and other informational organs to do battle with the bourgeoisie. Grave opposed Proudhonian countersociety, but actively engaged in the counterculture aspect through his newspaper work, theoretical speculations, and in participating to establish an anarchist school for children. Grave's interest in the formation of a proletarian counterculture has its counterpart in the communist movement: Antonio Gramsci, one of the founders of the Italian Communist Party and principal inspirer of contemporary Eurocommunism, advocated the creation of such mass proletarian institutions as workers' councils and the establishment of popularly based communist parties to engage the bourgeoisie in a protracted war of position by challenging their cultural hegemony.[36]

For Grave, sooner or later, the revolution would still erupt: at a certain critical juncture of events, one involving economic and other related crises (similar to the imminent revolutionary model), the workers would overthrow the bourgeoisie for socialism.[37] Since, Grave, however, had allowed for a lengthy period of reform before revolution, which presumably would have mitigated social bitterness, revolutionary violence would be minimal.[38]

From a general perspective concerning the immediacy of revolution, Grave and anarcho-communism were more hopeful than the Marxists and other socialists of the Second International. By the eighteen-eighties and nineties, Western European Marxists had basically rejected revolution for reformist politics, while Grave and his comrades maintained their purist revolutionary stance through electoral abstention. When the expected revolution, however, did not occur, Grave became pessimistic, and predicted in *La Société future,* for example, that it was generations away.[39]

The question arises why anarcho-communists like Grave were more revolutionary than the Marxists in such parties as the German Social Democratic Party and the French Unified Socialist Party? Individual temperament in a given sociohistorical environment undoubtedly played a role; the anarchists tended to be more idealistic and thus not willing to compromise. Grave, for example, as has been noted, may be regarded, at least during his younger years, as a "true believer." There is usually enough dissatisfaction in

most societies that individuals like Grave are not unknown.[40] At any rate this very utopianism and talk of revolution, added to the terrorism and crime of a few anarchists, led a distinguished Italian criminologist at the turn of the last century, Cesare Lombroso, to characterize anarchists as belonging to the criminal type—thus, their revolutionary bent.[41]

Although few in number, anarchists were more politically conscious and active than their counterparts in the other socialist groups, allowing for the widespread dissemination of their ideas. They were concentrated in urban areas and were in many occupations, although, as one commentator stated, they were often in occupations where one could often talk. A *Le Matin* article in 1894, partly based on a police report, had about five hundred anarchists in Paris in the early eighteen-nineties. Leading occupations and numbers included 10 journalists, 25 typographers, 17 tailors, 16 shoemakers, 15 mechanics, 12 hairdressers and barbers, 15 cabinetmakers, 10 bricklayers, 3 grocers, an architect, and an insurance agent. The same article estimated about eight thousand anarchists in France, of whom twenty-five hundred were in the Paris area, two thousand in Lyons, and one thousand in Marseilles. Jean Maitron, undoubtedly the foremost authority on French anarchism, was much more conservative as to the number of anarchists in France during the nineties: he calculated that there were only about one thousand active anarchists concentrated in about forty or so groups, supported by an inactive element of between five to ten thousand; and, if there were an anarchist party, it might have received about one hundred thousand votes. Grave's *Mouvement Liberataire* was very optimistic in estimating twenty thousand French anarchists in 1914.[42]

A brief postscript concerning Grave's later thought in which one can find a few aberrations. To begin with, he rejected the concept of class:

> Classes no longer exist. There are only people, many of whom are not capitalists, who in trying to survive do so very well in the society of today. Others, who live very poorly, nevertheless defend existing society. Others, who do not know any better, support it. Then, there is a group that wishes to do away with capitalism: it includes some members of the bourgeoisie.[43]

Too, his reformism became more pronounced. Change would come basically in piecemeal fashion in which shifting groups would temporarily merge to support specific reforms. Indeed, because society had made progress, advancing from slavery to serfdom to political freedom, the possibility of continued reform might occur without cataclysm. Thus, he emphasized the importance of speech and press freedoms to insure this.[44] To be sure, the anarchists, as a conscious minority, would have their usual important role as propagandists and as disinterested spokesmen for the ideals of humanism.[45] As for organization, he continued to unalterably oppose it.

For Grave, association was normal for man was a social animal; but if he once admitted any formal organization, man, like Sisyphus, would be doomed to climb forever the mountain of authority. Therefore, Grave still condemned the syndicalist position that society be organized through the various unions.[46] As for anarchism's future, he hoped that it would remain receptive to the exigencies and demands of a changing world.[47]

Notes

1. Grave, *La Société mourante* pp 1-2. Octave Mirbeau's preface hailed the work as a "masterpiece of logic full of enlightenment".

2. Cf *ibid*, pp 39-48, concerning scarcity, technology, and class oppression with the generally similar views of Jean Paul Sartre, *Critique de la raison dialectique* (Paris: Gallimard, 1960), I, 200ff. [this work was translated into English as *Critique of Dialectical Reason* (London: NLB, 1976), to be referred to in the future as *Critique*] and Marx, *Capital,* I, 91-92.

3. On mutual aid, see Jehan Le Vagre [Jean Grave], *La Révolution et l'autonomie selon la science* (Paris: A. Bataille, 1885), pp 5-11. The key work on mutual aid is by Peter Kropotkin, *Mutual Aid; A Factor in Evolution* (New York: Alfred A. Knopf, 1919), pp 1-10 are especially interesting.

4. Grave, *L'Anarchie; son but, ses moyens,* p 11ff. On the historical tendency comments, see Jean Grave, "Il n'y a pas plus de raison de se décourager que de s'illusioner," *Publications,* No. 28 (August 10, 1924), pp 4-14.

5. Grave, *L'Anarchie, son but, ses moyens,* pp 207-08; Grave, *La Société mourante,* pp 45-71; and Karl Marx, *Theses on Feurbach* in Lewis S. Feuer, ed. *Marx and Engels; Basic Writings in Politics and Philosophy* (Garden City, N.Y.: Anchor Books, 1959), pp 243-45.

6. Grave, *La Société future,* pp 19-20 and 46-49. Jean Grave, *Les Scientifiques* (Paris: Les Temps Nouveaux, 1913), pp 2ff.

7. Cf Grave, *L'Anarchie, son but, ses moyens,* pp 11-12, 17-18 and Grave, *L'Individu et la société,* pp 145-71 with Norman Cohen, *The Pursuit of the Millenium; Revolutionary Messianism in Medieval and Reformation Europe and Its Bearing on Modern Totalitarian Movements,* pp 272-306.

8. Grave, *L'Individu et la société,* pp 23-25.

9. Grave, *La Société mourante,* pp 44-47; Grave, *L'Individu et la société,* pp 23-25; Maximoff, *Bakunin,* p 94.

10. Grave, *La Société mourante,* pp 49ff. Other who regarded private property as the root cause of social misery, for example, are Rousseau and Winstanley.

11. *Ibid.,* p 51 and 58.

12. *Ibid.,* pp 50-51.

13. Grave, *L'Anarchie; son but, ses moyens,* p 7 and p 11.

14. Cf Grave, *La Société mourante,* pp 83ff and his *Réformes, révolution,* p 44 with Frederick Engels, *Socialism; Utopian and Scientific* (New York: International Publishers, 1935), pp 69ff. Both saw the state under bourgeois control.

15. On Grave and religion, see his *La Société mourante,* pp 43-44, 51, and 115-16; *L'Individu et la société,* pp 50-53, 260-74; *L'Anarchie, son but, ses moyens,* p 19. Erich Fromm, *Psychoanalysis and Religion,* pp 21ff stated that Christianity developed authoritarian attitudes when it became a state religion—obedience and submission are the hallmarks of this authoritarianism. Also, the teachings and life of Christ are seen as essentially humanistic, wherein "joy" not "sorrow" or "guilt" is stressed. Erich Fromm, *Escape from Freedom* (New York: Farrar and Rinehart, 1941), pp 10ff posits that Calvinistic predestination that emphasizes man's wickedness is basically authoritarian.

16. See, for example, Walter Rauschenbusch, *Christianity and the Social Crisis* (New York: Macmillan, 1914), pp 44-142.

17. Cf Grave, *L'Anarchie; son but, ses moyens,* pp 11-12 with Thorstein Veblen, *The Theory of the Leisure Class; An Economic Study of Institutions,* intro. C. Wright Mills (New York: A Mentor Book, 1957), pp 21ff—both see that power and wealth are exalted at the expense of poverty, weakness, and virtue.

18. Grave, *La Société mourante,* pp 56-59 and 126ff.

19. *Ibid.,* pp 183-97. On Gobineau, Chamberlain and the linkage of racism with slavery and imperialism, see Georg Lukacs, *La Destruction de la raison* (2 vols.; Paris: L'Arche, 1958), II, 233-74. Elisée Reclus was another pioneer in attacking racism—Fleming, *The Anarchist Way,* pp 48-50.

20. Erich Fromm, *Marx's Concept of Man; With a Translation from Marx's Economic and Philosophical Manuscripts,* by T. B. Bottomore (New York: Frederick Ungar, 1961), pp 93ff. The first manuscript titled *Alienated Labor,* pp 93-109 states that the worker, considered as a commodity of production under capitalism, despised his work for that very reason. The quotations are on page 97. On Hegel's progressive thought, see Jacques d'Hondt, *Hegel et son temps* (Paris: Editions Sociales, 1968). Also, see Erich Fromm (ed.), *Socialist Humanism; An International Symposium* (Garden City, N.Y.: Anchor Books, 1966), Part III: "On Alienation."

21. Cf Marx, *Alienated Labor* in Fromm's *Marx's Concept of Man* with Grave's *La Société au lendemain de la révolution,* p 113 in which the worker is seen as essentially being a robot.

22. See Grave, *La Société au lendemain de la révolution,* pp 108ff, and Grave, *L'Anarchie; son but, ses moyens,* pp 11ff and p 70.

23. Grave, *La Société au lendemain de la révolution,* p 113.

24. On Marx's basic egalitarianism, see Karl Marx, *Critique of the Gotha Programme: With Appendices by Marx, Engels, and Lenin,* ed. by C. P. Dutt (New York: International Publishers, 1938), pp 8ff and V. I. Lenin, *State and Revolution* (New York: International Publishers, 1932), pp 35ff.

25. On Gravian determinism (there are certain social "laws"), see Grave, *L'Anarchie; son but, ses moyens,* p 116. Grave's use of the term "people" indicated its broad nature—*ibid.,* p 139. On the general historical pattern discussed, see Grave, *La Société future,* pp 21-24.

26. Cf the revolutionary pattern of Karl Marx and Friedrich Engels, *Manifesto of the Communist Party* (New York: International Publishers, 1948), pp 9-21, with Grave, *La Société mourante,* pp 269ff and Grave, *L'Individu et la société,* pp 226-27 and pp 295-96. For a similar anarchist view, see Pierre Kropotkine, *L'Action anarchiste dans la révolution* (Paris: Les Temps Nouveaux, 1914), pp 2ff Fleming, *The Anarchist Way,* pp 187-93 saw the Marxian connection in Elisée Reclus' revolutionary pattern.

27. On Grave and the peasantry, see Grave *L'Anarchie; son but, ses moyens,* pp 307-24. Also, see Elisée Reclus, *A Mon frère le paysan* (Amiens: Editions de Germinal, 1905), pp 1-8; and Errico Malatesta, *Entre paysans* (Paris: Les Temps Nouveaux, 1901), pp 1-32. All three authors have similar views.

28. Grave, *L'Anarchie; son but, ses moyens,* p 37 and pp 193ff. Peter Kropotkin, *The Great French Revolution, 1789-1793* (New York: G. P. Putnam's Sons, 1909), pp 11-15 insisted that mass movements make revolution. On Marx and revolution by the masses, see Michael Harrinton, *Socialism* (New York: Saturday Review Press, 1972), pp 36ff.

29. On the role of a conscious revolutionary elite, see Jean Grave, *L'Entente pour l'action* (Paris: Les Temps Nouveaux, 1911), pp 11ff; Grave, *Réformes, révolution,* p 86; Grave, *L'Individu et la société,* pp 250ff; and Marx and Engels, *Manifesto of the Communist Party,* p 19.

30. Grave, *La Société future,* p 207; Grave, *La Société au lendemain de la révolution,* pp 14ff. On p 35, Grave even envisaged a transitory period (he does not specify the time frame) after the revolution in which anarchists do not hold power—probably other socialists hold it.

31. Grave, *L'Anarchie; son but, ses moyens,* p 14, pp 202-03. Grave, *La Société au lendemain de la révolution,* pp 14ff.

32. On Grave's advocacy of immediate revolution, see Grave, *L'Anarchie; son but, ses moyens* (1899), pp 107ff. For a Gravian blast against reformism, see Jean Grave, *Si J'avais à parler aux électeurs* (Paris: Les Temps Nouveaux, 1911), p 3.

33. Cf the Grave for immediate revolution in *L'Anarchie; son but, ses moyens* (1899), pp 107ff with the more patient one in *Réformes, révolution* (1910), p 40. There was not any exact year with reference to this change; for example, in *La Société future* (1895), pp 1-5, revolution would take generations. Generally, after 1900, Grave was more patient with respect to revolution. On the ignorance of the people as to the cause of their social misery, see Jean Grave, *La Panacée-Révolution* (Paris: Les Temps Nouveaux, 1898), p 14.

34. On Grave and cooperatives, see *Réformes, révolution,* pp 145-62; and A. D. Bancel, *Le Coopératisme devant les écoles sociales,* préface Jean Grave (Paris: Bibliothèque Artistique et Littéraire, 1897), pp i-iii. On Lenin's ideas concerning the tendency of workers to stay at the stage of mere union activity, see Thomas H. Hammond, *Lenin on Trade Unions and Revolution, 1893-1917* (New York: Columbia University Press, 1957), pp 17ff.

35. On pacification of the masses, see Grave, *L'Anarchie; son but; ses moyens,* p 136. Grave's view that social tensions increase with the approach of equality in *La Société future,* pp 1-5 is similar to that of Alexis de Tocqueville, *Republic of the United States of America and Its Political Institutions,* trans. Henry Reeves (2 vols. in 1; New York: A. S. Barnes, 1867), I, 9. This work is more well known as *Democracy in America.* Herbert Marcuse, "Repressive Tolerance" in Robert Paul Wolff, Barrington Moore Jr., and Herbert Marcuse, *A Critique of Pure Tolerance* (Boston: Beacon Press, 1965) pp 81-123.

36. Pierre-Joseph Proudhon, *De la Capacité politique des classes ouvrières* (Paris: Marcel Rivière, 1924). On Gramsci's life and ideas, see Guiseppe Fiori, *Antonio Gramsci; Life of a Revolutionary* (New York: Dutton, 1971). Also, see Quinton Hoare and Geoffrey Nowell Smith (editors and translators), *Selections from the Prison Notebooks of Antonio Gramsci* (New York: International Publishers, 1971), pp 228-45 on the great resiliency of Western capitalism which necessitated that revolutionaries adopt a more patient stance.

37. For an example of revolutionary violence, see Grave, *La Société au lendemain de la révolution,* p 18. On peaceful transition to socialism in Marx and Engels, see George Lichtheim, *Europe in the Twentieth Century,* (New York: Praeger, 1972), p 139.

38. This is implied in Grave's work during the last twenty years of his life. More on this later.

39. Grave, *La Société future,* pp 1-5.

40. On the mind set of the revolutionary fanatic and the socioeconomic background, see Eric Hoffer, *The True Believer; Thoughts on the Nature of Mass Movements* (New York: A Mentor Book, 1958), pp 51ff; Cohn, *The Pursuit of the Millenium,* pp

307-19. André Malraux's *La Condition humaine* (Paris: Gallimard, 1946) has an excellent example of the revolutionary fanatic—Tchen.

41. Cesare Lombroso, *Les Anarchistes* (Paris: Flammarion, 1896), pp 59ff saw anarchists as belonging to the criminal type.

42. *Le Matin,* "Contré l'anarchie," March 5, and 9, 1894; *HMA,* pp 115-24 and 432ff; *Mouvement libertaire,* p 287.

43. On Grave's attack, on *Capital,* see his "Le Capital de Karl Marx," *Publications,* No. 24 (Dec. 25, 1923), pp 8-15; and, "A Travers nos lectures," *ibid.,* No. 28 (Aug. 10, 1924), pp 15-16 on Marx. The quotation in the text is from p 15 of the first citation.

44. That peaceful reform may replace the revolutionary syndrome to achieve anarchism, see Grave, *Publications,* No. 7 (1921); pp 4-11.

45. *Ibid.*

46. *AM,* letter, Grave to Nettlau, July 24, 1934. Jean Grave, "Un monde qui ne différerait guère de l'autre," *Publications,* No. 90 (Dec., 1934), pp 3-6.

47. Jean Grave, "A propos d'une ânerie," *ibid.,* No. 54 (June 20, 1928), pp 3-6.

ANGLO-AMERICAN ANARCHISM

William Gary Kline (essay date 1987)

SOURCE: "The Birth of Individualist Anarchism," in *The Individualist Anarchists: A Critique of Liberalism,* University Press of America, 1987, pp. 1-34.

[*In the following excerpt, Kline discusses the American brand of individualist anarchism advocated by Josiah Warren and Stephen Pearl Andrews.*]

INTRODUCTION

Almost fifty years ago the last distinct vestiges of an entire radical American tradition disappeared with the death of Benjamin Tucker. Since that time the radical tradition which Tucker represented has been virtually lost in American history books. The reasons for this obscurity are manifold but two seem to predominate. The first reason is that American radicals have frequently been either neglected, or treated quite glibly and tendentiously. The second major reason is reflected in the neat, quiet manner in which this tradition was absorbed into the mainstream of traditional American thought. In turn, the reason for such absorption is to be found in the many fundamental assumptions shared by the mainstream and this radical tradition.

Tucker was the last major representative of a collection of thinkers and social activists known today as the Individualist Anarchists. Though in many ways they were a diverse collection, a bond existed between them at the core of their philosophies. They all desired a society without a government, based instead upon voluntary association. Indeed, many of these anarchists hoped, like their European cousins, to extirpate authority in all of its forms.

They were libertarians, then, absolutely distrustful of all authority and institutions and of hierarchy in general. Instead, they proposed to substitute such mechanisms as self-discipline, federalism, mutualism, and mutual aid. In the case of these Individualist Anarchists, the market would play a special part in bringing about justice and social harmony. But it will be argued here that the market is itself capable of a tyranny of sorts. Moreover, some anarchists proposed that social customs and mores be allowed to act upon individuals to an extent which might well have seriously threatened any meaningful autonomy.

These American anarchists were distinct from the European Socialist-anarchists not merely for their emphasis upon a market system. Although most of the Individualist Anarchists adamantly opposed such essential aspects of capitalism as rent, interest, and profits as distortions arising from state established privilege and monopolies, they were generally committed to the sanctity of private property. The Europeans, on the other hand, tended more toward communitarian forms of socialism.

Where the Communist-anarchists, such as Bakunin and Kropotkin, conceived of property primarily in terms of social relations (and thus manipulable), most of the American anarchists followed Locke in viewing it as an extension of the individual, and a guarantee of his liberty. After all, the liberal stalwart Adam Smith had not referred to capitalism in his *Wealth of Nations,* but rather to "the system of natural liberty."

The American anarchists also differed from the Europeans in their emphasis on individualism. Along with their devotion to private property, individualism provided the glue which would bind the Americans into a distinct group of anarchists. Worker struggles, relatively advanced in Europe, had given the anarchists of the continent an appreciation of solidarity, communitarian values, and direct action. Individualism in Europe was thought by many to be a threat not only to the solidarity requisite to the oppressed in their struggles for social justice, but also to the basic social bonds necessary for preserving order and culture: the result of individualism would be social dissolution and individual isolation.

By contrast, there was nothing pejorative in the term "individualism" as defined by the Americans. For them it expressed, above all else, the dignity and sovereignty of the individual. The term denoted the right of the individual to autonomy and self-direction, especially in a sphere of activity separate from the public realm where each person could cultivate his unique skills and characteristics. Since the individual was supreme, it followed that society should be secondary, arranged to accommodate the individual. Society had to rest on the consent of free individuals; it should have no other function than to enable the individual to pursue his own, chosen course and to protect him in this pursuit. If government had confined itself to protection of property and of individual liberty, as posited by Lockean liberalism, the American anarchists would not have objected to it. However, it seemed to them inevitably to overstep these bounds, and to create privilege, protect monopoly, and trample the rights it was supposed to secure.

The individualism of the Americans was predicated upon a belief that each individual would display rational economic conduct in a rational market system in order to maximize individual good; this conception, of course, was a familiar tenet of Adam Smith, among other classical political economists. The philosophy of the Individualist Anarchists, then, emphasized individual initiative and individual activity and interests, this latter measured principally in terms of material well-being (that is, private property).

The Individualist Anarchists have generally been presented as a stripe of radicals who fundamentally broke with the liberalism of their society. This has been the tenor of studies from Eunice Schuster's, *Native American Anarchism* to James Martin's, *Men Against the State* and William Reichert's, *Partisans of Freedom*. In the course of this essay it will be argued, however, that the Individualist Anarchists offered not a genuine critique of American society but, rather, an anomalous expression of the liberal tradition in the United States. If so, this provides more substance to the claim that "anarchism . . . had much deeper roots in the culture of this country than most people realize."[1]

It will be argued that they are distinguished in that they took liberal democratic theory much more seriously than most other Americans. No other group of American radicals gave such a central place in their philosophy to the concept of individualism. One need only philosophically un-pack the concept to understand what the Individualist Anarchists shared with traditional American thought: entailed are assumptions about human nature and human relations, property and liberty firmly grounded in classical liberal thought. The anarchists shared a belief in the essential rationality and goodness of the individual; in a set of natural individual rights, fully developed in the state of nature, the protection of which is the reason for society itself, as Locke argued. They believed in the basically contractual nature of society and in minimal government, which for the anarchist was no government; in a transcendental order of truth; and foremost, of course, in the absolute value and autonomy of the individual.

Individualism, as a basic theoretical stance, was incorporated into the philosphy of Hobbes. It was important in America as early as the Puritan period in the form of an assertion of the moral worth of each individual. Rogues Island, later known as Rhode Island, was initially the freest of the American colonies. Settlements without governments were founded there by those fleeing the religious and political authoritarianism of Puritan Massachusetts. Leading a politico-religious movement, Roger Williams, who bore some resemblance to the levellers of England,[2] founded in 1636 the settlement of Providence. Discussing the manner of operation of settlement, Williams said that "the masters of families have ordinarily met once a fortnight and consulted about our common peace, watch and plenty; and mutual consent have finished all matters of speed and pace."[3]

This respect for the rights and wishes of men was carried over into the relationship between the settlers and those they were to displace. Unlike the Massachusetts settlers who forcefully expropriated land from the Indians, the settlers of Rhode Island acquired land by purchase from the natives. Gaining titles to their lands eventually resulted in a kind of "feudal" system; land could not be acquired by homesteading, but rather had to be purchased or rented from the original claiments. This eventuated in oligopolistic rule.[4]

Roger Williams was assuredly a libertarian, but his contemporary, Anne Hutchinson, was, according to Murray Rothbard, the first explicit American anarchist. Like Williams, a religious leader, Hutchinson and her followers also fled Massachusetts and in 1638 founded the settlement of Portsmouth, Rhode Island. Their constitution of 1639 declared all male inhabitants equal before the law, the separation of Church and State, and the right of trial by jury for all accused. The anarchistic belief of Anne Hutchinson had origin in her theology. She thought salvation to be contained in the breast of every Christian; she therefore posited absolute religious freedom so that this guidance from within should not be obstructed. And if there must be absolute religious freedom, and if guidance comes from within each individual, what right, asked Hutchinson, does the government have to rule any individual at all?[5]

Meanwhile, in Plymouth, Roger Williams began to lose his libertarian temper as he aged. A group of Baptist Anarchists opposed themselves to him; led by Reverend Thomas Olney, this group included Roger's brother, Robert, John Field, William Harris, and John Throckmorton. These men circulated a petition claiming that the punishment of transgressors and the bearing of arms were anti-Christian acts. When Roger Williams denounced the petition, the anarchists rebelled but were put down by force. Yet the adherents of Baptist Anarchism increased until 1657, when Williams brought the four leaders into court. He achieved his purpose. Of the leaders, only William Harris persisted; he circulated petitions condemning all taxation, civil government, officials, legislative assemblies, punishments and prisons.[6] At about the time this movement in Rhode Island was collapsing, the would-be governor of another American colony began to grapple with a larger number of colonists with similar anarchistic bent.

In 1681, William Penn began his "Holy Experiment." Initially the Quaker colony waived all taxes to encourage settlement. However, Penn had planned eventually, as feudal landlord of the colony, designated by the Crown, to collect quitrents from the settlers. But "freedom and tax-less society had contaminated the colonists,"[7] and Penn found it impossible to exercise the perquisites of his authority. In 1684, William Penn went to England and government of the colony was lodged in the Council of Pennsylvania which had no focus of power and met infrequently; in effect, Pennsylvania was without government during this period of time.

In the period between 1684 and 1688, no funds were provided for a permanent bureaucracy. The people of the colony were pleased with the situation. Penn, alone it seems, was not satisfied with the conditions in his colony and he enlisted the assistance of an old Puritan soldier, John Blackwell, who he named governor of Pennsylvania. Within months, however, the tough old soldier was frustrated to the point of surrender, convinced by that time that the Quakers were the Devil's agents, defiant of every authority.[8]

The Quaker creed, argued George Keith, militates against any participation in government. Keith lead a group of Quakers who subscribed to this belief and though they were persecuted by the majority and their pamphlets banned, they were not much more extreme than most other Quakers. By 1692, King William was thoroughly disgusted with the pacifism and anarchy of Penn's colony and removed Penn, naming as governor Benjamin Fletcher. The King wanted to attack the French in Canada and had been unable to obtain suitable conditions in Pennsylvania.[9]

Taxation was still a serious problem from the viewpoint of the would-be governors of the colony: there was none. In 1693, the King got a bill passed to allow taxation, but collection was frustrated. So in 1694 William returned the colony to Penn. In 1695, the Council refused to consider a tax bill but the appointed governor, Markham, usurped this power and finally successfully instituted taxation among the Quakers.

To be sure, these were not highly conscious political movements based upon political speculation as in the case of the later Individualist Anarchists, but were religious movements grounded upon theology, the unique physical conditions of the New World, and the temper of settlers acquainted with intolerance, many of whom fled some kind of authoritarianism. They do, however, illustrate the fact that anarchistic tendencies were present in America in its earliest phase.

Benjamin Tucker once referred to Thomas Paine as the first American anarchist.[10] Certainly, the philosophy of Paine approximated Anarchism, but Tucker's assessment overlooks Paine's staunch advocacy of republicanism. Like the anarchists who were to arise in the United States in the 1840's and 1850's, Thomas Paine rejected all au-thority not based upon consent. Wrote Paine in *The Rights of Man:* "Every age and generation must be as free to act for itself, *in all* cases, as the ages and generation which preceded it."[11] He adhered to a theory of natural rights and denied that these rights could be alienated, nor, emphatically, could the rights of posterity.

"Every man is a proprietor in society, and draws on capital as a matter of right."[12] The structure of society, according to Paine, must harmonize with the natural rights of men: "The end of all political associations is the preservation of the natural and imprescriptible rights of man," said Paine "and these rights are Liberty, Property, Security and Resistance of Oppression."[13] Order, he taught, "has its origins in the principles of society and the natural constitution of man"[14] It follows from this that government is for the most part superfluous and, indeed, Paine adds that "society performs for itself almost everything which is ascribed to Government. . . . The instant formal Government is abolished, society begins to act: a general association takes place, and common interest produces common security."[15] Paine's conception of order and social harmony was intimately bound to his conception of progress. Like Proudhon after him, Paine felt that government diminishes as civilization progresses. Disorder is introduced as government deprives society of "its natural cohesion."[16] In any case, government should have no other object than *general* happiness, since for Paine, unlike the Individualist Anarchists, the culmination of his theory is society and not the individual.

Paine believed men to be naturally good and possessed of reason which might govern men successfully if not hampered. "Man, were he not corrupted by Governments, is naturally the friend of man, and . . . human nature is not of itself vicious."[17] He viewed Reason in almost evolutional terms; since "no man is prejudiced in favor of a thing knowing it to be wrong" one must conclude that "Reason, like time, will make its way, and prejudice will fall in a combat with interest."[18] Elsewhere Paine reiterates optimistically: "Reason and discussion will soon bring things right, however wrong they may begin."[19]

It is important to note the conception of Liberty posited by Paine. "Political Liberty consists in the power of doing whatever does not injure another. The exercise of the natural rights of every man, has no *other* limits than those which are necessary to secure to every other man the free exercise of the same rights."[20] This formulation bears striking resemblance to the "law of equal liberty" advocated by later American Anarchists and Herbert Spencer.

Paine even anticipated the faith in *Laissez faire* which was later to seize, among others, the Individualist Anarchists. "If commerce were permitted to act to the universal extent it is capable, it would extirpate the system of war, and produce a Revolution in the uncivilized state of Governments."[21] he wrote.

The elements of anarchist philosophy were indeed present before 1800 but Josiah Warren would become known as the father of American Anarchism, the first to propose Anarchism as a system based upon a philosophy of society. During the Jacksonian period a multitude of reform and intellectual movements, including attempts at fundamental economic reform and communities designed to replace the existing system, flourished and were tolerated. There arose religious communes, communities of property settlements such as those of Wilhelm Weitling and Etienne Cabet, Fourierite joint-stock phalanxes, and communities planned and under the guidance of enlightened philanthropists such as Robert Owen. It was out of this milieu and, more specifically, out of an experiment of this last type that Josiah Warren appeared.

Warren was born in 1798; the place of his birth, however, is unknown. Some early historians thought him the descendant of the General Warren of Revolutionary war fame, though this is today generally thought to be a spurious claim. In 1819 Warren moved West with his wife and settled in Cincinnati, Ohio where he earned a living as a musician and a teacher of music. His mind was disposed to experimentation and innovation and he invented, among other things, a lard-burning lamp which would probably have insured his fortune had Warren not, at his point, been influenced by Robert Owen; Warren determined to abandon the lamp business and follow Owen.

Robert Owen was an environmental determinist: he did not believe in free will, personal responsibility, praise and blame. It was his conviction that social systems are responsible for the character of their peoples. For a sum of 150,000 dollars Owen purchased 30,000 acres from a German Lutheran sect in Harmony, Indiana. The community was renamed New Harmony and Josiah Warren involved himself in its establishment. He helped to draft and approve the first constitution of New Harmony in February of 1826. Warren occupied himself as the leader of the community band. From this point Warren committed himself to a life of social experimentation.

JOSIAH WARREN, SOCIAL SCIENTIST

The inhabitants of New Harmony had confidently created a central organization, but a year and a half after its inception the community was seen to be a failure. Warren viewed New Harmony as an effort to harmonize the multitude of interests of the individuals involved, to establish a situation in which the various interests cooperate rather than conflict. The problem had been, as Warren identified it, that the individual was submerged under the community. He also felt that the elimination of individual property rights had diminished the sense of personal responsibility.[22] He concluded that "difference of opinion, tastes and purposes *increase* just in proportion to the demand for conformity."[23] Varying opinions were, thus, less and less tolerated.

Warren, however, retained some of the ideas he had absorbed from Owen. He adopted Owen's view that happiness is the proper goal of life and utility the measure of virtue. Like Owen, Josiah Warren believed in the possibility of Man's emancipation and that his happiness is conditioned by his social environment.[24] At the same time Warren believed that men produce their environment.[25] He embraced Owen's concern with determinism but attempted to combine with it a belief in free will and individual responsibility.

Warren subscribed to the labor theory of value of Adam Smith and he was especially attracted to Owen's labor exchange ideas, building relentlessly upon these for nearly fifty years following the New Harmony experiment. Warren immediately began developing an economic doctrine of cooperation employing a system of equal exchange of labor in the production of goods and services; exchange was to be upon an hour for hour basis facilitated by the use of labor notes.

His first social research using these economic ideas began on May 18, 1827. James Martin refers to Warren's Cincinnati Time Store as the first experiment in cooperative economy in modern times.[26] Upon opening the Time Store, Warren posted the prices he had paid for all of his goods and he added a seven percent charge for "contingent expenses," including shipping and overhead. For his services as a merchant, however, Warren asked only that the customer agree to give him a labor note promising to repay the storekeeper with an amount of labor in time equal to that expended by Warren in the transfer, or exchange, of merchandise.

Warren placed in his store two clocks, one whose hands would remain fixed wherever set and the other functioning in the ordinary fashion. Thus, when Warren began each transaction he would set the hands of the first clock at the time the exchange began; at the end of the exchange the time elapsed could be easily calculated by comparing the fixed hands with those of the ordinary clock.

Within three months Warren's store was a success and had made a significant impression on people of the area. At least three other stores arose based upon the same principles, two of which were located in Philadelphia.[27] Two doctors who had traded with Warren at his store began to offer their services on the same basis—labor in exchange for labor. Within one year the capacity of the Time Store was doubled to accommodate the increased volume of business. Warren continued to teach music but now upon the basis of the labor exchange used in his store.

According to Warren, demand is but a desire for a particular thing, regardless of ability to pay. In his Time Store he posted a paper with a list of demands of various people of the community and with offers of labor to exchange. Thus Warren facilitated a kind of market system for labor exchange. In addition, he listed commodities which he would exchange for labor.

In the course of his examination of the labor theory of value, Warren seized upon and inveighed against the conditions of wage labor with respect to women and children. Their wages he realized were kept artificially low. Warren followed this up with an investigation of the apprentice system and again concluded that the system was a means of intentionally and unnaturally restricting employment and production and services, an "obsolete barbarity"[28] designed to drive down wages and to thwart a cost-basis economy to the benefit of a few.

The popularity of Warren's store with the community encouraged him to expand it and insured him an adequate living. His labor for labor principle, as well, seemed to be catching on. By these standards a success, then, in May, 1830, Josiah Warren closed his Cincinnati Time Store satisfied that he had proven the practicability and virtues of his economic principles. Owen himself seems to have been impressed with Warren's experimentation. In 1832 he established his "Equitable Banks of Labor Exchange." Value was determined by the average quantity of labor spent in the production of a given commodity. Owen used only time as a measure of labor. Warren, on the other hand, who was the first to employ the labor theory of value in a Bank of Exchange, used time and repugnance, which he intended as a criterion for measuring the offensiveness or odiousness of a task or job. This latter concept he left rather inchoate, however, suggesting that he was but dimly aware of the degree to which advancing industrialization and division of labor were complicating any pure labor theory of value. Doubtless, Warren was confident that an unrestricted market could equitably assign values to labor and account for repugnance in its workings.

Between 1830 and 1831 Warren returned to the problem of apprenticeships and established schools in Ohio for teaching young men trades quickly to reduce the periods of apprenticeship; these appear to have been precursors of the contemporary trade schools.

In 1833 Warren established *The Peaceful Revolutionist,* the first anarchist paper anywhere. Warren is also distinguished by the fact that he established the first anarchist communities: Tuscarawas County, Ohio (1835-1837); "Utopia" in Clermont, Ohio (1847-1851); and "Modern Times" in Brentwood, Long Island (1850-1862). This last settlement lasted for twelve years and was the most successful of his colonies. Goods were exchanged using the medium of labor notes. The basic moral principle of "Modern Times" is said to have been the maxim: "Mind your business."[29] In fact, Warren's vision was a nation of small, autonomous communities. The principles of individuality and of mutual exchange based upon the labor theory of value were to provide the groundwork for these communities.

His observation of the variety of human differences manifested during the New Harmony experiment led Warren to abandon any hope of achieving economic equality; he assumed that different individuals would inevitably invest varying amounts of energy and time toward accomplishing the same goals.[30] Yet he believed that "enlightened self-interest" would supply the requisite motivational drive to make the system work and he proposed as a substitute for economic equality, equality of opportunity. He advocated equal access to land, raw materials, and credit. Individual differences would interact in free competition so as to produce an equitable society. The quest for equity Warren thought to be the highest human goal, and equity was always conceptualized in terms of the individual. In his Practical Details Warren wrote the following:

> Society must be so converted as to preserve the SOVEREIGNTY OF EVERY INDIVIDUAL inviolate. That it must avoid all combinations and connections of persons and interests, and all other arrangements which will not leave every individual at all times at liberty to dispose of his or her person, and time, and property in any manner in which his or her feelings or judgement may dictate, WITHOUT INVOLVING THE PERSONS OR INTERESTS OF OTHERS.[31]

For Warren, Liberty involved a recognition by every individual of the equal rights of every other to this own life, conscience, and property, but this latter only insofar as the individual produced or acquired it in fair exchange. In addition, he thought each should have a right to the tools and materials necessary to production. He denied that Liberty could be defined without negating it, asserting instead the right of the individual to make such a determination according to his own conscience.[32] Each individual should be free and each should accept the consequences of his own acts. In *Practical Details* he made this point by saying that each individual should be "a system within himself."[33] Warren felt that the "law of natural consequences," of cause and effect would produce a balance between the multiplicity of individual self-interests.

Many entrepreneurs and businessmen at this time were calling for less government interference. What they actually wanted is a question that will go unexamined here. In a sense, though, Warren wanted to extend to every individual the freedom exercised by the capitalists. Warren, like Proudhon, wanted to eliminate the "middle man" and the large, unearned profits, to mitigate the disparity in the distribution of wealth, and to halt the tendency of industrializing society to overwhelm the individual. To this end he rejected the democratic system and the combinations and integrations increasingly a part of modern society.[34]

In his labor-cost theory of value, indirectly received from Smith, in his labor exchange ideas and the proposal for a kind of mutual banking system—the borrower securing capital directly from the possessor, without interest—Warren anticipated Pierre-Joseph Proudhon. In addition to an entire school of anarchist thinkers, Warren influenced the advocate of women's rights, Frances Wright; a group of English anarchists who founded the London Confederation of Political Reformers in August of 1853; Robert Dale Owen; Henry George; and even John Stuart Mill, who credited Warren with influencing some of his own thought, especially with regard to his conception of individualism.[35] Warren's primary method of disseminating his doctrines was by means of his "Parlor Conversations." However, his ideas were set down in various writings, and the task remains to detail his thought based upon these writings.

EQUITABLE COMMERCE

Perhaps no phrase summarizes the thrust of Josiah Warren's philosophical effort as concisely as "equitable commerce." In 1852, one of the most significant of the written works of Warren was published, *Equitable Commerce: A New Development of Principles as Substitutes for Laws and Governments, for the Harmonious Adjustment and Regulation of the Pecuniary, Intellectual, and Moral Intercourse of Mankind Proposed as Elements of a New Society.* In his introduction he described the book as the culmination of twenty-five years of investigation and experimentation with a proposal for peaceful, yet fundamental, social change.

Warren's initial proposal is to identify the social problem. Society, he said, wants the following:

I. The proper, legitimate, and just reward of labor.

II. Security of person and property.

III. The greatest practicable amount of freedom to each individual.

IV. Economy in the production and uses of wealth.

V. To open the way for each individual to the possession of land, and all other natural wealth.

VI. To make the interests of all to cooperate with and assist each other, instead of clashing with and counteracting each other.

VII. To withdraw the elements of discord, of war, of distrust, and repulsion, and to establish a prevailing spirit of peace, order, and social sympathy.[36]

In the course of the book, then, Warren addressed himself to these issues and attempted to resolve each. He began by praising technology and its benefits for the workman; also, he applauded the doctrine of environmentalism for helping men better to understand themselves and society. However, these preliminaries were quickly discarded as Warren undertook examination of the concept of "Individuality" which is the underpinning of his entire philosophy.

It should here be recalled that one of the primary lessons Warren had drawn from his critique of the New Harmony experiment was the fact of the great variety and diversity constitutive of human life. This lesson was reflected in his conception of individuality. In a section of *Equitable Commerce* entitled "The Study of Individuality, or the Practice of Mentally Discriminating, Dividing, Separating, Disconnecting Persons, Things, and Events According to their Individual Peculiarities," Warren made the claim that individuality "pervades everything" and is "the life principle of society."[37] Nature, said Warren, produces diversity. "The surrounding atmosphere, the contact of various persons and circumstances, all contribute to make us more the *mirrors of passing* things than the possessors of any fixed character," he said.[38] For example, mood affects feelings and perceptions. Thus people may interpret differently any given written rule; though words comprise the primary means of our "intellectual commerce," "written laws, or rules, or institutions, or verbal precepts" are rendered ambiguous at least and usually arbitrary, liable to multifarious interpretations.[39]

Carrying an interesting idea with an element of validity ad absurdum, Warren argued that since language admits only of individual interpretations and cannot be made definite, positive human institutions cannot be based upon language because "to possess the interpreting power of verbal institutions is to possess UNLIMITED POWER!"[40] This flaw is an intrinsic element of all governments and such institutions. Thus "to require conformity in the appreciation of sentiments, or in the interpretation of language, or uniformity of thought, feeling, or action where there is no natural coincidence, is a fundamental error in human legislation."[41] Only disorder and enmity could arise where conformity is demanded of diversity.

Since individuality is a product of Nature, according to Warren, we must conclude that "out of the indestructibility or inalienability of this Individuality grows the ABSOLUTE RIGHT of its exercise or the absolute SOVEREIGNTY OF EVERY INDIVIDUAL."[42] Individuality, therefore, has primacy and is properly above "institutions based on language. Institutions thus become subordinate to our judgement and subject to our convenience." That is, individuality is a given and "we must conform our institutions to it!"[43]

For Warren, the principle of individuality is synonymous with his conception of progress, order, and harmony. "It is within everyone's experience," he wrote, "that when many things of any kind are heterogeneously mixed together, *separation, disconnection, division, Individuality* restores them to order, but no other process will do it."[44] He argued that this observation applies to all situations. "Every person is an individual, and therefore possesses the essential qualification for a leader",[45] but there must be a lead, or "directing power" whether a person or a thing. He was adamant also that responsibility for one's actions must rest with the individual; otherwise it is a hollow notion.[46] Individual responsibility is subverted, however, whenever it is deputed to the "phantom" known as the State. This violates the dictum against placing institutions above individuals.[47]

"Definiteness," he taught, can arise only out of individuality and the sovereignty of the individual is not possible under conditions of "close connections and combinations." Therefore, it is necessary to find

> modes by which all these connections and amalgamated interests can be Individualized, so that each can exercise his right of individuality *at his own cost,* without involving or counteracting others; then, that his cooperation must not be required in anything wherein *his own inclinations do not concur or harmonize with the object in view.*[48]

The true basis for a society is the opposite of connections, amalgamations, combinations, communism and their like.

Rather it is "FREEDOM to differ in all things, or the SOVER-EIGNTY OF EVERY INDIVIDUAL."[49] Social harmony, then, is conditional upon the commitment of every individual to respect the right, or liberty, of other individuals to differ.

Warren could hope for the realization of this social condition because he believed in the perfectibility of reason. Thus he was confident that "among a multitude of untried routes, only one of which is right, the more Liberty there is to differ and take different routes, the sooner will all come to a harmonious conclusion as the right one."[50] He concluded that "this is the only possible mode by which the harmonious result aimed at can be attained. Compulsion will never be harmonious."[51]

The process of individualization, then, had to be applied to the questions of concern to society as posited by Warren. Currently, price, noted the author of *Equitable Commerce,* is dependent upon want. As want increases, just so does price increase. *Value,* he thought, should not go into the determination of price, for value includes some measure of want. *Cost,* on the other hand, consists in a particular amount of labor used in the production of a given commodity, plus such contingent expenses as taxes, insurance, shipping and the like. In *True Civilization* Warren further clarified the concept of cost. He said there that it signifies

> the endurance of whatever is disagreeable Fatigue of mind or body is Cost. Responsibility which causes anxiety is Cost. To have our time or attention taken up against our preferences—to make a sacrifice of any kind—a feeling of mortification—painful suspense—fear—suffering or enduring anything against our inclinations, is here considered Cost.[52]

"Cost, then, is the only rational ground of price."[53] Essentially, what Warren advocated was that value and cost be individualized, or disconnected, in order to avoid the confusion and discord he perceived in the realm of commerce. This principle he extended to all forms of commerce. Intellectual commerce, conversation, or the "intercourse of mind with mind," he said, may be of great value but if the cost is nothing, no price should be laid upon it.[54] Additionally, "talents which cost nothing, are *natural wealth,* and should be accessible to all without price."[55] The same principle applied to the loan of money would dictate that the legitimate—"equitable"—compensation for the loan be "the cost of *labor in lending it and receiving it back again.*"[56] Equitable rent would include only the cost of wear and insurance, and the cost of making the contracts and receiving the rent. Herein lies the resolution of the first social problem identified by Warren: Cost being made the limit of price will insure that labor receives its just and equitable reward.

The principle of "cost-the-limit of price" would have this effect by placing the responsibility upon each to earn just so much as he consumes. It would lighten the burden of work in producing the needed goods for society by distributing that burden more equitably; it would reduce prices for goods; it would create security and obviate cupidity arising from insecurity, the "scramble for unlimited accu-

mulations of property, and all degradation and crime and the horrors of punishments arising from these causes!"[57]

With regard to the second social need, security of person and property, Warren denied that government could provide for this. Indeed, government is, for Warren, its antithesis: "security of person and property cannot consist in anything less than having the supreme government of himself and all his own interests; therefore, security cannot exist under any government whatever."[58] Where government exists, however, greater relative security is to be obtained in positions of political power, thus explaining the reason that a premium is placed upon their acquisition.

But "supreme government" must rest with each individual, or as Warren poses the issue in his work *True Civilization,* "SELF-SOVEREIGNTY is an instinct of every living organism" and as an instinct it cannot be alienated. Generally, a person may exercise "*supreme* power or absolute authority" in the sphere of his or her own person, property, time and responsibilities[59]—a formula reminiscent of that of John Stuart Mill, and equally vague. Self-sovereignty and the principle of equivalents will provide guidelines for determining when an action is invasive, he argued.[60] From its status as an instinct, the instinct of self-preservation, derives the absolute right of its exercise.[61] Government, however, cannot provide the security requisite to self-sovereignty.

In *Equitable Commerce* Warren expressed the belief that government exists primarily for the benefit of combination, a condition of which he disapproved. Eleven years later he ascribed to government the function of "intervention for the sake of non-intervention," or the use of force against force or invasiveness.[62] This he felt to be the only proper use of government and the only justification for the violation of individual sovereignty.

Coercive government should be responsible for the protection of persons and property from invasion, and it should have just so much force as to perform this function.[63] As an anarchist, Warren objected to any element of government which violated the liberties and self-sovereignty of the non-invasive individual. However, he had no objection to cooperating—in the form of "government" if that term were used—to protect against invasions of liberty. The only possible objection to a "government" with this limited function, he said, would be an objection to a misapplication of its power. By 1863 he had used this belief to justify a military "for the advantage of drill and systematic cooperation."[64] The term militia would probably be more descriptive of the military he invisioned since all action was to be placed upon a voluntary basis. "It will be asked, what could be accomplished by a military organization, if every individual were allowed to judge of the propriety of an order before he obeyed it? I answer," replied Warren, "that nothing could be accomplished that did not commend itself to men educated to understand, and trained to respect the rights of persons and property set forth in the 'Declaration of Independence.'"[65] This would provide a check on barbarities, theorized Warren. Further, Warren proposed a "Deliberative Council" as a kind of judiciary for rendering advice in cases of dispute, but not possessing coercive powers. If the advice were not followed and the dispute continued unresolved, he suggested that the matter then be put to the military "to act at its discretion; selecting that course which promises the least violence or disturbance."[66]

But who will decide when violence in resistance is necessary? Warren believed that in cases of blatant invasion, most would resist; in cases of less obvious invasion, resistance would occur in varying degrees. The important thing, according to Warren, is to insure that each individual has the freedom to judge of himself and to differ.

Warren was convinced that "this Modern Military, as a Government, will be necessary only in the transitionary stage of society from confusion and wanton violence to true order and mature civilization."[67] He optimistically envisioned a period of examination of the causes of avarice, crimes, wars and violence, poverty, etc. followed by peace and order: the discovery would be made that making value the basis of price results in disorders in the market, business uncertainties, inequitable rewards, poverty, greed and the other ills of society. Cost, the limit of price, alone, he thought, could provide for society the security of person and property it desires.

In his analysis of equitable commerce, Warren addressed himself to the issue of the "greatest practicable liberty." Warren equated Liberty with the Sovereignty of the Individual and claimed that "Liberty defined and limited by others is slavery!"[68] The Sovereignty of the Individual demands that each live and act "at his own cost," and this, according to Warren, is impossible "just in proportion as we or our interests are UNITED *or combined with others.*"[69] On the contrary, he claimed that "the only ground upon which man can know liberty, is that of *disconnection, disunion, individuality.*"[70] Warren claimed at this point, that government arose out of a necessity for some third party to arbitrate in a society filled with the discord of united interests, a self defeating measure which further jeopardizes Liberty.

Warren notes that the desire for human "Sympathy," "Harmony" or "Unity" is indeed one of the strongest of all human needs and he hoped to accommodate these by providing the space for each person to move in without disturbing others. However, his proscription upon combination stood. He decried communism for the often overlooked flaw intrinsic to it—the attempt to achieve harmony by combination. Harmony can only be realized in the *"freedom to differ in all things* where difference is possible."[71] Warren was confident that "enlightened and regulated self-interest" would give rise to the desired harmony and "universal sympathy."[72] Education in the principles of anarchy would provide the enlightenment necessary to achieve such harmony.

The cost principle was the cornerstone of Warren's system and the focus for any education into that new system.

Such "continuous convulsions" as reflected by the Civil War were viewed by Warren as the products of a system unjust to labor; "the whole of what is called civilization rests upon labor, and . . . it is everywhere prostrate—starving—groaning, and imploringly lifting up its hands in silent agony for help. . . ."[73] He compared the functioning of the value principle to cannibalism[74] and he designated the government and money as the two oppressors. But his conception of government was limited to its overt coersive functions and he failed to discuss such elements of power as symbolism, socialization, the State as idea, and other related forms.

Warren relied on the cost principle to obviate the search for harmony in union. The cost principle was said by Warren to render competition harmless and a regulating and adjusting power. Competition, he reasoned, would not drive work below equivalents because the comparative cost in labor for any given product would be established by public opinion; and anyone could leave an occupation that did not suit them—by talent or wage criteria—until all occupations were equalized. Also, it was through competition that Warren expected the cost system, by virtue of its natural superiority, to replace the system as it existed in the Nineteenth Century. The cost principle would make natural wealth accessible to all; and all would have an interest in helping another begin a business with the awareness that products would then be had at cost.[75] Since losses and waste would become part of the price, each would have an interest in minimizing cost.[76] Thus there would arise cooperation without combination; with this Warren claimed to have "solved the great problem of the individual good harmonized with the public good!"[77]

The problems with which Warren concerned himself were those of the expanding middle class of the Jacksonian period. Many Jacksonian Democrats were making the same sorts of demands, that privilege and monopoly no longer be sanctioned, that equal access to the system be granted to all. Walt Whitman argued that the only necessary function of government is the prevention of anyone from infringing on the rights of any other. William Leggett demanded that government confine itself to "equal protection."[78] John Vethake and Theodore Sedgwick, Jr. inveighed against the monopolies and Stephen Simpson blamed the laws for creating privileges and robbing labor of its reward. "The mischief," complained Andrew Jackson, "springs from the power which the moneyed interest derives from a paper currency which they are able to control. . . ."[79] Langdon Byllesby demanded that labor receive its full product and have control over it, that exchange be based upon reciprocity (equal quantities of labor), that interest be abolished, and that no one consume without exact compensation. Warren went beyond calls to disconnect the political and economic spheres; he proclaimed the complete superfluity of the political sphere.

Many proponents of laissez faire assumed the continuance of the state, however, and expected it to have a subtly pro-business orientation which would sanction, if not encourage, combinations and trusts, collusion, growth of corporations, and the like. Stephen Pearl Andrews foresaw this culminating in the laissez faire doctrine of a plutocracy which was only another species of authoritarianism. Warren and his supporters, on the other hand, believed that if government were abolished and the struts upholding privilege and monopoly thus eliminated, trusts, combinations, and collusion would soon wither in a free market competition. With access to the market free and open to all, voluntary and cooperative associations would proliferate to supply goods and services on a cost-basis. Without government regulations, subsidies, patents, and so forth, profit-oriented entities could not extract unearned value from consumers, nor could they successfully compete with producers and suppliers operating on a cost-basis.

Warren's demands, then, were within the spirit of the times. His proposed solutions, however, his extreme emphasis on individualism, and his rejection of government placed him outside the mainstream of Jacksonian Democrats. Central proposals of his thought—cost the limit of price and labor for labor exchange—were soon outdated. The Civil War period saw a series of major legislation (the National Bank Act of 1863, subsidies for railroads, contract labor laws) heralding a system of government partisanship rather than laissez-faire. The idea that politics and economics could be separated became positively anachronistic. (Charles Beard has called this the period of the "Second American Revolution.") The war hastened industrialization and technology, scientific farming and the growth of cities. The role of labor was altered as relations between employer and employee were de-personalized, economic insecurities increased and labor unions began to develop. The Republican Party and big business, with its Captains of Industry (Vanderbilt, Rockefeller, Carnegie and Gould) were wedded. Yet Warren remained convinced that he had discovered the essential elements of a program to bring harmony to American society; and in the mid-fifties this claim was accepted by a former Fourierite named Stephen Pearl Andrews, who was later to popularize Warren's social research and transmit his ideas to future Individualist Anarchists.

STEPHEN PEARL ANDREWS AND THE SCIENCE OF SOCIETY

The man whom Henry Appleton, American anarchist, called "the intellectual giant of America" and English anarchist Henry Seymour proclaimed "the most intellectual man on this planet" early displayed a proficiency in languages and went on to learn thirty-two of them while studying philology. Not surprisingly, he also earned a reputation as a brilliant orator. Born in Massachusetts in 1812, Stephen Pearl Andrews could claim to be of solid New England stock. When only 19 years of age, Andrews moved with an older brother to Louisiana and took up the study of law. Over the next several years he taught at Louisiana State University, introduced the first system of shorthand from England to America, translated the laws and constitution of Texas into Spanish at the request of

that state's legislature, developed a language which he intended to be used for global communication, and practiced law in New Orleans. In 1839 he began practicing law in Galveston, but four years later when his efforts to conspire against slavery became known he was forced to flee for his life just minutes ahead of a violent mob. Thus, in his first thirty years, Andrews had experienced and achieved more than most manage in a lifetime. But at this point, his contributions were just beginning.

During the 1840's Andrews came under the influence of Fourierism and of the Swedish mystic, Emanuel Swedenborg. However, in a speech before the New York Mechanics Institute in 1850, Andrews professed his belief that the formula of Fourier, that "destinies are proportioned to attractions" meant that a social system should be organized so as to give each individual the power to "choose and vary his own destiny or condition and pursuits in life, untrammelled by social restrictions . . . so that every man may be a law unto himself, paramount to all other human laws, the sole judge for himself of the divine law and of the requisitions of his own individual nature and organization."[80] Shortly prior to that year Andrews had met Warren and found the philosophy of the social experimenter to be a completion of the tendencies of his own philosophy.

Like Warren, Andrews perceived the essential law of nature to be the manifold diversity of life. He thought all that threatens this diversity stifles life and results in social unrest, crime, war, and the like. The goal, he taught, is not to attempt to limit diversity and human individuality, but to establish social relations so as to put them on a just basis.

Andrews became acquainted with the philosophy of Comte through his American exponent, Henry Edger, and by 1857 had absorbed many of the tenets of positivism into his own philosophy. Andrews was also among the first Americans to discover Marx and the first to publish his *Communist Manifesto* in the U.S. In 1869 Andrews helped to found the First International, but his flirtation with Marxism was short-lived and mostly based on a spiritual kinship rather than on principles. In his *Basic Outline of Universology* published in 1872, Andrews attempted to mesh what he considered to be the scientific approach of Warren with the metaphysical approach of Comte. He still considered Fourier an important early pioneer in this attempted synthesis.[81]

In the post-Civil War period Andrews was active in the feminist movement. He was at that time closely associated with Victoria Woodhull, often writing speeches for her stressing the intimate relationship between the sexual bondage of women and the political and economic bondage obtaining in society.

By 1877, Andrews' increasingly syncretistic philosophy could scarcely be identified as a form of anarchism. During the railroad strike in that year he called for "the forced transfer of all railroads, magnetic telegraphs, and great public works to the government, with the laborers paid fixed and equitable prices, as government employees."[82] In addition, he envisioned "the organization of great government work-shops, or organized government colonization, or other similar enterprises, and the honest effort that government shall become the social providence of all the people."[83]

Andrews thought that by the Twenty-first Century a single governmental unit would exist for all the world and that all people would speak the same language and share the same religion. This would be the result of a conflict between plutocracy and the "politarchy" of state socialism. Andrews had come to believe that government, if manipulated by social scientists, might be an effective agent for the social reforms he wanted to see. From this condition of world order anarchism would eventuate as government control was discarded "to relegate the management of all human affairs to the pure, unorganized, unregulated spontaneity of the people themselves."[84] Though not abandoning the anarchist principle, Andrews had come to the unorthodox conclusion that it would be realized through a strange dialectical conflict between two competing notions of the state idea, one capitalist and the other socialist. In the hands of system-builders like himself, the state might even help bring about this utopian stage of society.

Andrews' principal contribution to Individualist Anarchism, however, was his lucid elaboration of the thought of Warren. Andrews must be credited with passing this philosophy to the Individualist Anarchists that were to proliferate in the 1880's. *The Science of Society* commences with a declaration, in the manner of Warren, of the supremacy of the individual. Protestantism, Democracy, and Socialism, proclaimed Andrews, are the growing expressions of that supremacy. For him, Protestantism represents the demand for "emancipation of the individual from ecclesiastical bondage."[85] DeMaistre, after all, had dubbed individualism political Protestantism in 1820. As Protestantism reflected a rejection of religious absolutism, Democracy expressed a demand for emancipation from political absolutism and Socialism a demand for emancipation from economic bondage, or absolutism. (This last is in stark contrast to the interpretation of socialism given by George Fitzhugh in his Sociology of the South appearing in the same year as Andrews' work, 1854. Fitzhugh thought the growth of socialism signified a desire—perhaps unconscious—for slavery.)

Individuality, wrote Andrews, is the generic principle from which the doctrine of the sovereignty of the individual is derived. No two things or events in the universe are exactly the same. Taught Andrews: "Infinite diversity is the universal law."[86] This fact "mocks at all human attempts to make laws, or constitutions, or governmental institutions of any sort, which shall work justly and harmoniously amidst the unforeseen contingencies of the future."[87]

Men must choose between despotism and revolution argued Andrews. Despotism is successful in proportion as it "denaturalizes mankind." Revolution, however, explodes the unnatural bonds of institutions. Institutions are made by man, Individuality by God, according to Andrews, and, thus, it could not be alienated. Each person was for Andrews a microcosm, "an image or reflection of God."[88] It followed that to the extent that conformity is demanded of Individuality disorder would increase.

In *Love, Marriage and Divorce, and the Sovereignty of the Individual: A Discussion Between Henry James, Horace Greely and Stephen Pearl Andrews* (1889), Andrews labelled Greeley a conservative. There are two theories of government, declared Andrews: one that views Man as essentially irresponsible and incapable of self-government, the theory adhered to by Greeley; and the second theory asserting that Man is potentially capable of governing himself, lack of practice being the only obstacle to realization of this potential."[89]

One facet of Andrews' anarchism resembled the colonial religious anarchism of Anne Hutchinson: he argued that Protestantism posits the individual as the ultimate and highest authority to interpret God's laws. He concluded that "in religious affairs the end must be that every man shall be his own sect."[90]

Majoritarian rule, Andrews claimed, is antithetical to democracy, the assertion "that every individual is of right free and equal, that is, that every individual is of right free from the governing control of every other and all others."[91] Democracy, then, "is identical with the no-government doctrine."[92] He asserted that democracy is inconsonant with the existing order and would remain so until the demand of socialism, that labor receive its just reward, be realized.

Andrews thought governments originate from a need to "restrain encroachments" and "to manage the combined interests of mankind."[93] Coercive government for the first purpose is clearly unnecessary, however, if, as Andrews claimed, "a clear scientific perception of the point at which encroachment begins" can be formulated.[94] For Andrews, the rule that governs this is derived from the principle of equity: "every individual is the rightful Sovereign over his own conduct in all things, whenever, and just so far as, the consequences of his conduct can be assumed by himself."[95] Yet this rule could be made practicable only after changes in the "commercial, ethical, and social spheres."[96] Andrews dismissed the second purpose occasioning the rise of government since it obviously contradicts the principle of individuality; union, connection, etc. inevitably introduce into society the disorder which government is meant to eliminate or mitigate. According to Andrews, the goal is to disconnect, individualize, separate, all this after the fashion of Josiah Warren.

Andrews considered the cost principle to be the primary mechanism by which this could be accomplished and the second part of *The Science of Society* is devoted to expatiation of this principle. His discussion opens with a condemnation of prior political economy: It has failed, Andrews asserted, because "it treats wealth as if it were an abstract thing having interests of its own, apart from the well-being of the laborers who produce it."[97] He thought that the scientific method alone could place social relations on an equitable basis; and toward a scientific resolution of this goal Andrews adopted the five major principles of Warren's program: Individuality, the sovereignty of the Individual, cost the limit of price, a circulating medium founded on the cost of labor, and adaptation of the supply to demand.

Andrews recognized cooperation and economies of scale as beneficial and worth preserving. To this end he distinguished between combination and cooperation:

> By Combinations are meant partnership interests and community of property or administration, such as confuse, in any degree, or obliterate the lines of Individuality in the ownership or use of property.
>
> By Co-operation, or co-operative relations, is meant such an arrangement of the property and industrial interests of the different Individuals of the community, that each, in pursuing his own pleasure or benefit, contributes incidentally to the pleasure or benefit of the others.[98]

His description of cooperation, then, paralleled the principle represented by Adam Smith's "invisible hand." The interests were to be individual and the pursuit by self-interested, acquisitive individuals would, in theory, lead to their mutual benefit.

However, cooperation can be achieved only by a scientific restructuring of society, taught Andrews, and the new structure of society must be predicated upon the exchange of equivalents in all forms of commerce. Wrote Andrews: "Simple equity is this, that so much of your labor as I take and apply to my benefit, so much of my labor ought I to give you to be applied to your benefit."[99] Exchanges might have been reduced to simple exchanges of equal hours of labor were it not for the additional complexity introduced by the necessity for measuring the repugnance of various labors. "Equity," Andrews claimed, "is the equality of burdens."[100] Each individual must determine the extent to which his labor is a burden. He would then reflect his determination of repugnance through the medium of the labor note. Under the Cost Principle the "more ordinary and menial kinds of labor will be usually paid best" due to the repugnance entailed in such labor.

The labor note would make "every man his own banker."[101] It would be a circulating medium and a means of credit as well; and it would represent a definite amount of labor or property. If the subjective measure of repugnance determined by an individual for a given type of labor were greater than that determined by most other individuals in that type of labor, the expression of this fact in labor notes would have the result of making them less competitive with the labor notes of those enjoying their work more. It would also indicate that the individual should consider another, less onerous type of labor. In any case, cost would

not and should not reflect the value of the labor or good to the purchaser, but only the amount of labor time and a determination of repugnance. Competition would force cost to its minimum.

Andrews' analysis of the results of the existing condition of commerce may be summarized as follows: (a) It nurtures falsehood and hypocrisy in trade. (b) It increases the disparity of wealth. (c) The quest for profits results in trade for the sake of trading and the concomitant of this is an increasing number of non-producers who must be supported by labor. (d) Labor is demeaned. (e) Supply cannot be "scientifically" adjusted to the demand. (f) Competition becomes "desperate and destructive" when a determination of value is included in the cost; unemployment results. (g) In addition to this, the Value Principle transforms machinery into a weapon against labor rather than a blessing.[102]

Andrews argued that a system of commerce founded upon the Cost Principle would provide for "Attractive Industry," a concept elaborated by Fourier: each individual would have the opportunity to seek his occupation "according to his natural bias or genius" resulting in the most efficient and advantageous "employment of all human powers."

The Cost Principle, claimed Andrews, would render competition harmless. Under this principle competition would "operate at the point of *superiority of performance* in the respective functions of each member of society, and will, therefore, be purely beneficent in its results." On the other hand, wrote Andrews, "in the existing social order it is chiefly destructive, because it operates upon the point of *insuring security of condition* or the means of existence."[103] That is, competition manifests itself primarily in struggles for jobs or job security.

Andrews noted that in our society overproduction merely signifies a condition in which the worker cannot afford to purchase the available goods. But the cost principle was perceived by Andrews as the mechanism by which price would be adjusted scientifically to accord with actual demand.

One might assume that Andrews' philosophy implies the ideal of a society of individual, self-employed workers. This, however, is not the case. Wrote Andrews: "the relation of employer and employed is stigmatized daily as vicious in itself, and the ideal is entertained of each individual being employed as to be his own 'boss' and to work solely for himself. No such arrangement is either desirable or feasible."[104] Indeed, Andrews approved of both economies of scale and the wage system. He claimed to have "no sympathies with aimless and fruitless struggles, the recrimination of different classes in society, not with merely anarchical and destructive onslaughts upon existing institutions"[105] Change was to be a gradual and peaceful substitution of the new for the old.

Andrews thought that all people are subject to refinement and that if the laborer enjoyed the full results of his own labor in immediate products or equivalents of cost, *two hours of labor a day* would be ample to supply the ordinary wants of the individual—that is, to bring his condition up to the average standard of comfort—even without the benefits of labor-saving machinery, or the economies of the large scale.[106]

This would leave time for each individual to develop his mind, pursue hobbies and amusements, store up wealth for illness and old age, and the like.

To the charge that the Cost Principle makes no provision for the poor and unfortunate, Andrews replied that "mutual benevolence can only exist after all the requirements of equity have been complied with, and that can only be by first knowing what the requirements of equity really are."[107] That is, where justice ends, only there does benevolence begin:

> First do justice and extinguish the pauperism, crime, and disease which grow out of relations of injustice, and cease to fear that the spontaneous benevolence of humanity will not be amply adequate to provide for the sparsely scattered instances of misfortune which may ever remain as an incentive to the healthy action of that affection.[108]

Andrews saw the world becoming more integrated, national boundaries dissolving, pacifism growing. He thought a day would come when military forces would be unnecessary. Patriotism would be transformed into philanthropy and each individual would become "his own nation" at peace with every other.[109] The functions of government and its bureaucracy would become obsolete and disappear. Andrews believed the increasing unpopularity of politics adumbrated this. In the place of government, the "excellence of achievement" would rule. "Those who have the most power to impress themselves upon the community in which they live, will govern in larger, and those who have less will govern in smaller spheres," giving rise to a natural hierarchy where each individual is "a sovereign having sovereigns for subjects" . . . who might transfer loyalties at will.[110]

One author has referred to Andrews as a "utopistic system-building type of social scientist" in the French tradition. It does appear that he had greater affinity to the followers of Fourier and Comte than to most political economists. Andrews was certainly a visionary; yet his ideal had a force of persuasion and Andrews, himself, the impact of a prophet among a small but growing number of equally inspired disciples.

Notes

1. William O. Reichert, *Partisans of Freedom* (Bowling Green, Ohio: Bowling Green University Popular Press, 1976), pp. 196-197.

2. Murray N. Rothbard, "Individualist Anarchism in the United States," *Libertarian Analysis* vol. 1, no. 1 (New York: Winter 1970): p. 15.

3. Ibid.

4. Ibid.

5. Ibid.

6. Ibid., p. 19.

7. Ibid., p. 20.

8. Ibid., p. 22-24.

9. Ibid., p. 26

10. Benjamin Tucker, "On Picket Duty," *Liberty* vol. 5, no. 16 (10 March 1888): p. 1.

11. Thomas Paine, *The Essential Thomas Paine* (New York: The New American Library, 1969), p. 128.

12. Ibid., p. 151.

13. Ibid., p. 186.

14. Ibid., p. 228.

15. Ibid., p. 228-29.

16. Ibid., p. 230.

17. Ibid., p. 264.

18. Ibid., p. 227.

19. Ibid., p. 281.

20. Ibid.

21. Ibid., p. 267.

22. James J. Martin, *Men Against the State* (DeKalb, Illinois: Adrian Allen Associates, 1953), p. 9.

23. Ibid., p. 10.

24. Eunice M. Schuster, *Native American Anarchism* (Northampton, Mass.: Dept. of History of Smith College, 1932), p. 95.

25. Ibid., p. 100.

26. Martin, p. 13.

27. John R. Commons and Associates, *History of Labor in the United States* (New York: The Macmillan Co., 1936), vol. 1: p. 99.

28. Martin, p. 21.

29. Rudolf Rocker, *Pioneers of American Freedom* (Los Angeles: Rocker Publications Committee, 1949), p. 64.

30. Martin, p. 13.

31. Martin, p. 14.

32. Schuster, p. 101.

33. Ibid., p. 102.

34. Martin, p. 99.

35. Martin, p. 67.

36. Josiah Warren, *Equitable Commerce* (New York: Burt Franklin, 1852), p. 13. (Hereafter referred to as *Commerce.*)

37. Ibid., p. 15.

38. Ibid., p. 37.

39. Ibid., pp. 18-19.

40. Ibid., p. 52.

41. Ibid., p. 19.

42. Ibid., p. 18.

43. Ibid., pp. 19.

44. Ibid., p. 20.

45. Ibid., p. 35.

46. Ibid., p. 23.

47. Ibid., p. 27.

48. Ibid., p. 24.

49. Ibid., p. 26..

50. Ibid.

51. Ibid.

52. Josiah Warren, *True Civilization* (New York: Burt Franklin, 1967), p. 74. (Hereafter referred to as *Civilization*.)

53. Warren, *Commerce,* p. 43.

54. Ibid., p. 44.

55. Ibid., p. 45.

56. Ibid., p. 46.

57. Warren, *Civilization,* p. 83.

58. Warren, *Commerce,* p. 50.

59. Warren, *Civilization,* p. 14.

60. Ibid., pp. 178-79.

61. Ibid., p. 10.

62. Ibid., p. 12.

63. Ibid., p. 15.

64. Ibid.

65. Ibid., p. 18.

66. Ibid., pp. 29-31.

67. Ibid., p. 33.

68. Warren, *Commerce,* p. 56.

69. Ibid., p. 57.

70. Ibid.

71. Warren, *Civilization,* p. 146.

72. Ibid., p. 148.

73. Ibid., p. 69.

74. Ibid., p. 70, 73, 95.

75. Warren, *Commerce,* p. 93.

76. Ibid., p. 77.

77. Ibid.

78. Joseph L. Blau, *Social Theories of Jacksonian Democracy* (New York: The Bobbs-Merrill Co., 1954), pp. 74-75.

79. Ibid., p. 17.

80. Commons., p. 517.

81. Martin, p. 158.

82. Commons., p. 159.

83. Ibid., p. 160.

84. Ibid., p. 165.

85. Stephen Pearl Andrews, *The Science of Society—No. 1* (New York: T. L. Nichols, 1854), p. 15.

86. Ibid., p. 19.

87. Ibid., p. 19-20.

88. Ibid., p. 21.

89. Martin, p. 155.

90. Ibid., p. 40.

91. Ibid., p. 38.

92. Ibid., p. 39.

93. Ibid., p. 43.

94. Ibid., p. 44.

95. Ibid., p. 63.

96. Ibid., p. 44.

97. Stephen Pearl Andrews, *The Science of Society—No. 2* (New York: T. L. Nichols, 1854), p. 13.

98. Ibid., p. 48.

99. Ibid., p. 53.

100. Ibid., p. 55.

101. Ibid., p. 63.

102. Ibid., p. 120-31.

103. Ibid., p. 164.

104. Ibid., p. 209.

105. Ibid., p. 68.

106. Ibid., p. 137.

107. Ibid., p. 146.

108. Ibid., p. 148.

109. Ibid., p. 48.

110. Ibid., p. 54.

ANARCHISM: INCIDENTS AND ISSUES

H. Oliver (essay date 1983)

SOURCE: "The Era of Propaganda by Deed II: 1894-7," in *The International Anarchist Movement in Late Victorian London,* Croom Helm, 1983, 99-119.

[*In the following essay, Oliver details several prominent anarchist incidents of the 1890s, including the event that inspired Joseph Conrad's novel,* The Secret Agent.]

THE GREENWICH PARK EXPLOSION

The sole outrage that occurred in London, a bomb explosion outside the Greenwich Observatory in February 1894, killed the man carrying the bomb. It is probably best known because Conrad based his novel *The Secret Agent* on it. In his "author's note" to the novel, Conrad said that the subject came to him "in the shape of a few words uttered by a friend in a casual conversation about anarchists or rather anarchist activities". His friend told him that the man carrying the bomb "was half an idiot" but "these were absolutely the only words that passed between us". Conrad was sure that if his friend once his life had seen "the back of an anarchist", that must have been the whole extent of his connection with "the underworld".[1] He admitted about a week later that he had read "the rather summary recollections of an Assistant Commissioner of Police" and also that suggestions for certain passages "came from various sources".[2] Two authorities on Conrad, Professors Norman Sherry (in his *Conrad's Western World,* published in 1971) and Ian Watt (in *Conrad: The Secret Agent,* published in 1973) have carefully studied Conrad's sources and the question of how much he knew about the Greenwich Park explosion. Both emphasised the importance of Conrad's friendship with Ford Madox Ford, who was closely connected with the anarchist journal the *Torch,* published by the children of W. M. Rossetti. Ford's sister, Juliet Hueffer, lived with the family. In his reminiscences, Ford said that both he and Conrad knew "a great many of the Goodge Street group (meaning the Ossulston Street office of the *Torch*). Ford also provided Conrad with anarchist literature and introductions. But, as Professor Sherry knew, Ford's memoirs are very unreliable. As was recently shown, Ford positively took pride in doctoring them, claiming that he had "for facts the most profound contempt".[3] And Conrad visited W. M. Rossetti's house between the start of 1903 and August 1904, when only Helen Rossetti (then Helen Angeli), one of the two sisters who ran the *Torch,* lived there. Whatever she may have told Conrad about the Greenwich Park explosion must have been anarchist hearsay, because at the time when it happened, both Rossetti sisters were in Italy and the *Torch* was in suspense (see Ch. 6). Helen Angeli is however likely to have given Conrad a good deal of information about London anarchists in general.

Professor Sherry pointed out that in November 1906 Conrad wrote to Sir Algernon Methuen saying that the novel was based on inside knowledge. But in 1923 he denied all inside knowledge when he wrote to Ambrose Barker, who had sent him a pamphlet on the subject.[4] Sherry commented that it looked as if Barker had stumbled on one of Conrad's sources and that Conrad's denial arose from a desire to conceal the sources he had used.[5] However, on the basis of Conrad's denial, Professor Watt thought that it should be assumed that Conrad's main informant was Ford. He also believed that "there is also some evidence to show that the CID was directly involved in the affair through a secret agent pretending to be an anarchist" and mentioned David Nicoll's allegation that in the Walsall case Coulon

had started an anarchist journal on behalf of the police.[6] Conrad's denials have in the meanwhile been blown sky high in Dr Paul Avrich's study of Conrad's "Professor", published in 1977.[7] Avrich has demonstrated that "the Professor" in *The Secret Agent* was based on a passage in the 13 January 1885 issue of a Chicago paper called the *Alarm,* edited by the "Haymarket martyr" A. R. Parsons. (This paper appeared, disguised as *The Gong,* in the novel among the "obscure newspapers" in the window of Conrad's "secret agent's" shop.) As Dr Avrich says, Conrad "always tried to conceal the extent of the research he undertook for this novel". In fact his data for it came "from a whole array of London newspapers, police reports, and anarchist periodicals and pamphlets". It seems worthwhile to reconsider Conrad's main plot in this novel in the light of firmer evidence than Ford's and Helen Angeli's recollections. In the novel, a "secret agent", Verloc, employed by the Russian embassy, was responsible for making his half-witted brother-in-law, Stevie, take the bomb to Greenwich Park, where he stumbled and was blown to pieces. Stevie is represented as so much looking up to and trusting Verloc that he would do anything for him.

What actually happened in February 1894 was reported in the press and at the inquest on Martial Bourdin. The press reported that a man had blown himself up when he was carrying a bomb on the 16th. The date is important because on 12 February Emile Henry had been arrested in Paris for throwing a bomb in the café of the Hotel Terminus, in the evening, when a number of people were listening to the orchestra. One person was killed and Henry was immediately arrested. It was alleged that there was reason to believe that he got the ingredients and material for the bomb in London, where several bombs thrown in Paris were made.[8] Martial Bourdin was brother of the tailor Henri (mentioned by Mrs Wilson in 1884) and brother-in-law of H. B. Samuels. He was a ladies' tailor. But the news of the explosion was conveyed to Scotland Yard not by telegram but by letter. An inspector was fined £4 for this mistake.[9] This detail was reported in *The Times* but seems to have been overlooked by all later commentators. Sherry positively says that the police officers got in touch with Scotland Yard by telegraph. However, this delay explains why no searches of suspects or of the Autonomie club were made immediately. (Bourdin was a member of the French section of the club.) And Robert Anderson, the assistant police commissioner, testified later that during that afternoon in February 1894, when he was told that Bourdin had left his Soho shop with a bomb in his pocket, it was impossible to track him. All he could do was to send out officers in every direction to watch persons and places he might be likely to attack. The Greenwich Park Observatory was "the very last place" the police would have thought of watching.[10] Since railway stations would obviously be watched, to put the police off the scent Bourdin went by tram (as was shown at the inquest). But Conrad's Stevie went to Maze Hill station, perhaps on the basis of earlier press reports alleging that Bourdin went by train. Conrad's admitted interest in Anderson's memoirs seems to have been mainly because they alleged that the

Home Secretary was kept in the dark. This became the germ of the sub-plot of *The Secret Agent*.

Hard evidence about Martial Bourdin emerged at the inquest. His brother Henri (who would not take the oath) said that Martial came to London from Paris about seven years ago (i.e. about 1887), had then visited the Continent once or twice, and about 18 months ago went to America for five months. (An Autonomie club member said that he then travelled first class.) Before returning to England, Martial went back to France.[11] On this evidence, his latest visit to France was in 1892 or 1893, when Ravachol had become a cult figure. Martial was 26 or 27 when he died and so was born in 1867 or 1868. Though work had been scarce, he did not seem short of money and had about £40 on him when he went to America. His landlord, Ernest Delbecque (former treasurer of Louise Michel's school), who also refused to take the oath, testified that Martial had lent him £20 before he went to America. Martial had a furnished room and his meals at Delbecque's house, 30 Fitzroy Street.[12] It was also said that Martial at one time had adopted the pseudonym of J. Allder, and that in Paris he was connected with a society known as the "Needles", because all members were tailors. He was so prominent in these circles that in 1884 he was sentenced to two months in prison for trying to arrange a meeting in a public thoroughfare.[13] If this was true, he seems to have belonged to a group called "L'Aiguille", founded in June 1882 by some tailors, which became increasingly anarchist. It seems to have been the same "important" group of some 60 anarchist working tailors in the 2nd *arrondissement* which figured in a Paris press report on anarchist groups in May 1892.[14]

There was striking agreement about Martial's character. His brother said that he was "very quiet and reserved" and kept his private affairs to himself.[15] His brother-in-law Samuels, in the memorial piece he published in *Commonweal* on 10 March 1894, extolled Martial's tenacity of purpose but said that he lacked affection because he was "too much wrapped up in the movement". Anarchist leaders in London confirmed that Martial was a "secretive, self-centred man" (though this too may have come from Samuels). An Autonomie club member was reported as saying that Martial "acted on his own initiative" and was always so completely convinced that his opinions were right that he aired them on every possible occasion. This seems to be corroborated by the 1884 incident in Paris. He was "eminently an individual man", working for himself without the help of others.[16] Ted Leggatt, reporting in the *Star*, gave a quite different impression (noted by Sherry). He said that Bourdin was a bit of a simpleton.[17] But this is unconvincing. To say nothing of his friendship with Nicoll, Leggatt did not speak French, was not an individualist, and would not have gone to meetings of the Autonomie club's French section. Leggatt's opinion, however, clearly played a part in Conrad's portrayal of Stevie. Samuels added, in an interview he gave to the *Morning Leader*, that Martial's hobby was collecting anarchist literature—as a boy he had been fascinated by the enthusiasm of the anar-

chists. He had not (as was alleged) given lectures on explosives at the Autonomie club but had always gone to parties and balls. Samuels was right. At Martial's workshop quantities of anarchist literature were found. On his person were two admission cards to a masked ball in aid of the "Revolutionary Party".[18] He was also found to have had a sizeable sum of money—£12 in gold and £1 is silver. And there was evidence of visits to Paris and America, as well as an Autonomie club membership card, identity card, and recipes for the preparation of explosives that he had "copied from a book in the British Museum". These recipes were handed in a sealed packet to the Coroner by the chief government explosives expert, Colonel Vivian Majendie.[19] The press reported on explosives concealed in pieces of furniture at Bourdin's lodgings as well as photographs of public characters and beautiful women.

At the inquest the tram timekeeper said that Bourdin's overcoat was undone all the way up and looked as if there was something in the left-hand pocket. A park labourer said that he was carrying a small brown paper parcel, walking very fast in the direction of the zigzag path leading to the Observatory. Colonel Majendie's evidence showed that because Bourdin's left hand and arm were so badly injured, the bomb must have been in his hand and not in his pocket. If it had exploded in his pocket, it would have blown his clothes to bits, but they were not torn. Since no brown paper was found at the scene, he believed that it must have been left between the place where it was noticed and the spot where Bourdin was found. Otherwise he would have expected to have found charred bits of it in the wounds. He judged that Bourdin must have been standing facing the Observatory holding the bomb about 46 yards from the Observatory wall. He could not have stumbled or his legs would have been wounded and the gravel would have been disturbed. The explosive used "was not one of the authorised explosives within the meaning of the act" (the Explosive Substances Act of 1883). Possession of it constituted a felony. In the public interest and with the jury's approval, the Coroner declined to name the explosive. Bourdin had in his pocket a glass bottle in a metal cover, containing sulphuric acid. Asked if the explosive might have ignited accidentally, Majendie said he had "perfect confidence" that Bourdin must have taken out as much sulphuric acid from the bottle as was necessary to prepare the bomb and then replaced it in his pocket. Through "some mischance or miscalculation or some clumsy bungling", the explosion occurred prematurely. Majendie was sure that Bourdin had intended to attack the Observatory.[20] (Prestige buildings were anarchist targets in other cases.)

The Home Office managed to prevent the funeral from being turned into an anarchist demonstration. There was only one funeral coach. In it were Henri Bourdin, Samuels, Dr Fauset Macdonald, and an unnamed French friend. There was so much hostility from the crowd waiting for the cortège in Fitzroy Square that six young men had to be taken into custody. The mob broke a window in the Autonomie club. In fact, English hostility to the anarchist stereotype, to which this incident contributed so much, was increasing. And the individualist anarchist Henry Seymour cancelled a lecture he was to give at the Autonomie club in order to dissociate himself from the "suicidal and unnecessary" anarchist-communist tactics.[21]

Majendie's evidence completely disposed of the theory that Bourdin had stumbled. Unfortunately one very important question, wholly outside the scope of the inquest, can never now be answered. Did Bourdin intend to attack the Observatory when he went to Greenwich Park, or did he want to fox the police by setting off via the park to another place so as to get the bomb to France? Did he then impromptu think of attacking the Observatory when he saw it? Samuels himself, in his memorial article, said that Bourdin undertook to carry "dangerous explosive compounds to a secluded spot" to test a new weapon of destruction that would have provided the "revolutionary army" with a weapon against those who consigned "so many innocent lives to destitution and despair". This was repeated later, but at second hand. In any case, it throws no light on Bourdin's destination if he had meant to go on somewhere else. And Nettlau explicitly said that Samuels was "absolutely outside the game" because no one entrusted any risky action to such a known blabber.[22] Nor does it fit Bourdin's character to have confided in anyone else, let alone Samuels. Nettlau thought that Bourdin intended to hand over the bomb in the park near the Thames to someone who would have taken it straight to France. Some local anarchists believed that he would have caught the next train for Dover and Calais to continue Henry's exploits. Bourdin's visits to France, his personal knowledge of Henry through the Autonomie club, the money found on him, and his membership of the Paris "L'Aiguille" group make this possible. London anarchists likewise reported that he had said he intended to go to Paris, that it was well known that he had had the bomb several days before his death, and that he left London "with the intention of imitating Vaillant and Henry in Paris".[23] The fact that both the French and English police believed that the Greenwich Park incident was part of a plot that had close connections with outrages on the Continent[24] means nothing, because they had an *idée fixe* about anarchist plots. As Sherry noted, Samuels too suspected that the incident was "the commencement of an extensive plot".[25]

After the delay caused by the letter instead of a telegram, the metropolitan police searched Bourdin's lodgings, the Autonomie club, and the house of a French electrical engineer in Marylebone said to have been a close friend of Bourdin. At the Autonomie they found a virulent circular printed in London on blood-red paper headed "Death to Carnot", and at the house in Marylebone portraits of Ravachol and Vaillant, French circulars, a leaflet called "Vengeance is a Duty", and a "Dynamiter's Manifesto" which advocated wholesale destruction of the bourgeoisie. Another leaflet urged the murder of judges and jurors. French newspapers found included *La Révolte* and the *Père Peinard*. Their dates coincided with the French outrages.[26]

There the matter might have rested but for David Nicoll, who started a second *Anarchist* in Sheffield in March 1894. First in this, and later in two pamphlets called *The Greenwich Mystery* (published in Sheffield in 1897)[27] and *The Greenwich Mystery: Letters from the Dead* (published in London in 1898), as well as in the Jubilee number of *Commonweal* (which he also published in London), Nicoll wrote a version of the incident that was in essence a rerun of his Walsall scenario. (As Quail explains, the reason why the first pamphlet did not appear until 1897 was that Nicoll's resentment was probably fanned in 1896, when the new Home Secretary rejected appeals for amnesty for the Walsall prisoners.) This time, in Nicoll's final version, Samuels and Dr Macdonald were the police agents, Coulon came in marginally, but Samuels was the chief villain. Samuels, Nicoll alleged, known and trusted by Bourdin (who was represented as out of work and facing starvation) offered Bourdin £13 to carry "a small parcel" to a mysterious comrade. Samuels then went with him to Charing Cross to give him courage, and "doubtless" suggested that he should attack the Observatory. (Samuels said in the *Morning Leader* on 17 February that he met Bourdin, but they had parted after walking 20-30 yards together. On 21 February the paper said that Bourdin was followed by a "French" spy.) Macdonald came in as the subsidiary because Samuels had "stolen" sulphuric acid chlorate of potash, and the explosives" Bourdin had used from his surgery in such quantities that Macdonald must have noticed the loss. Sulphuric acid and chlorate of potash are legitimately used by doctors, but they do not account for the recipes copied in the British Museum and could not alone have caused such an explosion. Nicoll must have read Majendie's evidence (published in the *Morning Leader,* on which he relied), but he maintained that the explosion was caused by a fall or accidental leakage, and that Bourdin was "the dupe of a gang of scoundrels hired by the police."[28] Since Nicoll did not read *The Times,* he buttressed his account by alleging that Inspector Melville might have identified the body by 8 p.m. on the same day. He might have raided the houses of suspects the same evening, because the Greenwich police "doubtless" telegraphed at once. Although Nicoll had proclaimed his story from the housetops, "the police took their time" so giving Samuels, Macdonald, and Coulon 24 hours' notice, and had raided instead the places where they knew no "conspirators" could be found. Nicoll finally alleged that Macdonald (with another man) had come to Sheffield to try to persuade him to make no disclosures, but soon afterwards Macdonald left England never to return. The implication was that he had skipped the country.

Nicoll described Bourdin as "a quiet harmless fellow", sitting at Samuels's foot and "looking into his eyes with loving trust" (at the Autonomie club at Christmas 1893).[29] Sherry noted that Conrad had read this and made full use of it, but does not seem to have known what those closer to Bourdin thought of him, or Nicoll's motivation in smearing Samuels. (In Nicoll's version, the police agents had injured a man "who had done his best, poor as he is, for those who toil and suffer".[30]) Nicoll chiefly supported his allegations by a letter by L. S. Bevington included in *Letters for the Dead.* She said that Bourdin was "told" to take a new compound for experiment and he hit on Epping Forest, but Samuels persuaded him to go to Greenwich instead: "Mrs Samuels, whom I used to see very often at the time, told me".[31] She said that before Samuels was suspected, he too had boldly related this. But such second-hand testimony is virtually worthless in the face of what is known of Samuels's boasting, of Bourdin's true character, of Nettlau's statement that no one would have trusted him, and of Mrs Bevington's bias as a comrade. She was besides already so seriously ill that on 3 May 1894 she told Nettlau that she was not well enough to go to see him.[32] She died in December 1895.

That Nicoll's version mainly sprang from his hatred of Samuels (as his supplanter as editor of *Commonweal*) and from his "police-plot" mania is evident. But mainly thanks to Conrad's novel, Nicoll's has become the "received" version of the Greenwich Park explosion. Quail too, though he believed that Nicoll's resentment "was probably fanned by isolation, poverty, and the failure of the Walsall prisoners campaign", substantially accepted Nicoll's account. He said that the police were "lackadaisical" and that Samuels was seen with Bourdin in Whitehall, although he admitted that "evidence" that Samuels was a police spy was "circumstantial". Sherry noted that there was no proof whatsoever that Samuels went with Bourdin to Charing Cross.[33] It seems relevant to add that there is no sign that Samuels ever received any police payment—he was in any case wholly mistrusted by them. Unlike Coulon after the Walsall affair, Samuels neither moved to a better house nor was able to drop his tailoring. It was still more telling that he remained on friendly terms with Martial's brother. In a letter dated 28 June 1894, he told Nettlau that "Bourdin" (i.e. Henri) had a copy of a "Revue" he could lend Nettlau.[34] It is hard to believe that they would have been on these terms if Samuels was a double agent who had sent Henri's brother to his death. There is an addendum to Nicoll's version. In 1897 Nettlau wrote to Nicoll protesting about the attacks on Macdonald and saying that Nicoll's pamphleteering was as crazy as Coulon's. When he had posted the letter, he ran into Nicoll in Hyde Park on 1 May and, after hearing Nettlau's explanations, Nicoll, though not convinced, was friendly and reasonable—until he returned to find Nettlau's letter.[35] Hence the Jubilee *Commonweal* issue (when Macdonald was in Australia).[36] Because Macdonald could not defend himself, Kropotkin took the matter up, after Mme Kropotkin and Nettlau had unsuccessfully tried to persuade Nicoll to withdraw his allegations. Kropotkin wrote a retraction for Nicoll to sign and sent a covering note to Nettlau ending "Nicoll must be *compelled* to *sign* a retraction and beaten if he does not".[37] *Freedom*'s protest, when Nicoll did not sign, appeared in its June-July 1897 supplement. It had been circulated to members of the group as well as Mrs Wilson (who had by then retired for family reasons). The protest announced that the group had read "with the deepest indignation" the insinuations made by Nicoll against "our friend Dr Fauset Macdonald" and also against Dr Nettlau, well known "for

his honesty and purity of character". Because these "wicked insinuations" were the worst of libels, they dissociated themselves entirely from Nicoll until he withdrew them (without reserve and publicly".

Allegations that Samuels was handing out explosives were made mainly in press reports in 1894.[38] Without giving a precise date, Nettlau says that he did take some chemicals from Macdonald's dispensary and that Macdonald then complained to the *Commonweal* group.[39] Whether this is true or not, the last time Edgware Road appeared as *Commonweal*'s address was in the issue of 10 March 1894. The April issue was published at 18 Glengall Road (Samuels's house). This may indicate that the Edgware Road lease had expired. On checking his stores, Macdonald may have found some missing and blamed Samuels because of current talk. At all events, the complaint was discussed at Sidmouth Mews in the spring of 1894. John Turner took it seriously, suspecting Samuels of some link with the police, but others thought it much more improper that he had made three guineas from his press interview, and that taking the chemicals was just showing off. At this point Mrs Samuels appeared and made such a scene that the meeting had to break up. Both Samuels walked out for ever. He was already on a war footing with his wife. Nettlau added: "I was there that evening and did not take these grounds for suspicion seriously, just because I knew how little Samuels was worth".[40] Samuels told Nettlau on 28 June that he had earned a rest and on no account would work again with "laggards and liars".[41] This seems to be the reason why he joined the ILP in 1895. His last number of *Commonweal* appeared on 12 May 1894. It is not certain how it was started again after a suspension. The July issue of *Freedom* shows that Joseph Pressburg was now the editor. Cantwell was the printer, but he was taken into custody on 30 June, which explains why no new issue appeared until August.

Cantwell's arrest and trial happened at a most unfortunate time. On 24 June the French President, Sadi-Carnot, was mortally stabbed by an Italian, Santo Caserio, because he had refused to pardon Vaillant. Caserio had no known connection with the London groups, but the "Death to Carnot" leaflet found at the Autonomie club after the Greenwich explosion must have been widely distributed. On 30 June, when the then Prince and Princess of Wales were to open Tower Bridge, Cantwell and the Christian individualist anarchist Carl T. Quinn held an open-air meeting near the bridge, where they sold an "Address to the Army" pamphlet and another on "Why Vaillant Threw the Bomb". At their trial on 1 August they were accused of trying to persuade others to murder members of the royal family and politicians who were coming to open the bridge. But a number of those who were at Tower Bridge said they did not hear the words Cantwell and Quinn were alleged to have used or see them distribute pamphlets. They said there was an organised band of interruptors in the crowd. Search of Sidmouth Mews produced a manuscript of courses in chemistry, but it was not written in Cantwell's handwriting, Cantwell had letters on him showing that

Commonweal was on its last legs and said that the army pamphlet was not set up in its office but was a cast made long ago. The Vaillant pamphlet did not contain his opinions; he had never advocated throwing bombs. Quinn, who denied incitement to murder, argued that while he was a Christian the law was not. But Mr Justice Lawrance found both guilty, and each got six months' hard labour.[42] This seems to have been the only sentence not in accordance with a Home Office statement of 1894, that it was no offence to be an anarchist. It was one if anarchists attempted "to enforce their views by crime".[43]

PÈRE PEINARD COMES TO LONDON

In France two more bomb outrages occurred in February 1894, before Carnot was assassinated. There was therefore some concern in official quarters when it was known that *Le Père Peinard,* edited by Emile Pouget (which had been suppressed in France) intended to set up in London. Pouget, who made use of biting caricature and slang, had also published an anarchists' almanac. The one for 1893 included a portrait of Ravachol and a new song about him. Robert Anderson said that when the customs searched some deal cases addressed to E. Boiteaux, a pseudonym of Pouget's, they found printing blocks, copies of the paper, and other anarchist literature. But in the opinion of the law officer (Sir Godfrey Lushington), so far as he could understand the paper, there was nothing in the number handed to him to justify interfering with it. He thought later issues should be watched.[44] This explains why Pouget was able to bring out eight numbers of a London edition from October 1894 until 1895. Pouget, of provincial bourgeois origins, had a disturbed youth and then had had to earn a living in a Paris shop, where he edited an anti-militarist journal for a textile union. In 1883, after a meeting of unemployed, he and Louise Michel had pillaged a bakery and were sent to prison. From 1889 he edited the *Père Peinard* on the model of the French Revolutionary *Père Duchêne*. He escaped arrest when it was suppressed by coming to England via Algeria.[45] He took a floor in a building in London not far from the Angel and was adept at disguising brochures he issued. The first, called "Il n'est pas mort", was sent to the Home Office by the police in September 1894 but was minuted "nothing to be done at present. Lay by."[46]

Maitron noted how much Pouget's London visit influenced him because he saw the gains made by workers through the trade unions.[47] In October 1894 the *Père Peinard* pointed out how much anarchists had to gain by infiltrating the unions and propagating their ideas. The November issue said that the Chicago anarchists had understood that a general strike "is an open door" to a great upheaval. When Pouget returned to Paris in November 1896, he continued to issue anarcho-syndicalist, i.e. revolutionary syndicalist propaganda.

FOUR FOREIGN ANARCHISTS ARRESTED

In France terrorism continued. On 4 April 1894 a bomb thrown in the Foyot restaurant cost the French writer Lau-

rent Tailhade one of his eyes. The French were thus gratified by the arrest in London on the same day of Théodule Meunier, who had been wanted since 1892 for the bombs thrown at the Cafe Véry and the Lobau barracks. He was arrested by Melville at Victoria station just as the train was about to start for Queenborough, Isle of Sheppey. He resisted and was helped by a German, John Ricken. When both appeared at Bow Street on 5 April, R. W. Burnie, who had defended Mowbray in 1892 defended Meunier. An excellent carpenter, Meunier had been denounced in France by two women, one his mistress. Burnie denied that there was anything to identify the prisoner with Meunier, but the judge decided otherwise.[48] The identification was likely to be right because a detailed description of him had been published in the French press on 28 June. Meunier was easily recognisable, if only because he was small and slightly deformed. He was extradited and condemned to perpetual forced labour in Cayenne. The English anarchist press regarded his extradition as a miscarriage of justice.

On 14 April Francis Polti, and on the 22nd Guiseppe Farnara were arrested, both implicated in manufacturing bombs. Polti, described as a "traveller", aged 18, was caught in Farringdon Road with a bomb wrapped in brown paper. It seems to have been identical with Bourdin's bomb—an iron cylinder fitted with two caps screwed down. Polti was described as an individualist and as a great friend of Martial Bourdin's. He disappeared from his Soho haunts after Bourdin's death. Liquids in bottles, many letters, and quantities of anarchist literature were found at his lodgings. Farnara was arrested because Polti talked. A mechanic, aged 44, he had anarchist literature in his pockets and in his room in Clerkenwell. He said that he employed Polti to order material from ironmongers for the manufacture of bombs. A good deal of information about both men was published in the *Standard* on 23 April, before the trial. The Home Office believed that this must come from the police.[49] Among other things, Polti alleged that Farnara was responsible for the bomb used by Bourdin and had handed Bourdin the money found on him.

At the trial (before Mr Justice Hawkins) on 3 and 4 May a copy-book in Polti's handwriting was produced. It expressed sympathy for Emile Henry. Polti was determined to avenge Vaillant's death, and so he had decided to sacrifice his life. An Italian witness said that Polti had told him that anarchists were "very nearly done on the Continent" and they were going to start in London very soon. Farnara caused a sensation by saying that if he had the money, he would have taken the bomb to France or Italy. Since he had no money, he meant to throw it at the "Royal Exchange". He meant the Stock Exchange. He wanted to do this because England was the richest country and there would be more rich people together at the exchange than anywhere else. If he did not escape, he would have blown up a good number of bourgeois and capitalists and could only be executed. Italians did not ask English people to go to Italy every year, but they went with the money made by English workers. "For us there are no frontiers. The *bour-*

geois are the same all the world over."[50] In the language of the day, the judge could find no extenuating circumstances "for the foul, abominable" design. Polti was sentenced to ten years and Farnara to 20 years' imprisonment—twice as long as the longest Walsall sentence. With exemplary moral courage Seymour, on behalf of the SDF, sent a resolution to the Home Office protesting against these sentences as "atrocious and inhuman and more criminal than the foolish acts of the Anarchists themselves". He made it clear that the SDF disavowed any sympathy with anarchism or its methods.[51]

The chief interest of the last of these cases involving Continental anarchists in London is that it showed that English law insisted on proof. On 31 May 1894 Melville and a party of police searched the Chelsea lodgings of a German cabinet maker, Fritz Brall, who had come to London in 1893. A member of the Autonomie club, still not rebuilt, Brall had made a moonlight flit from Soho because of complaints about noise. Among others who had visited him was John Ricken, who had tried to prevent Meunier's arrest. The police found apparatus for making counterfeit coin, chemicals and recipes, a photograph of Vaillant, and a Bourdin memorial card. They also found anarchist papers and a copy of what seems to have been Most's *Revolutionäre Kriegswissenchaft,* accurately described as "The Scientific Revolutionary Warfare and Dynamite Guide". There were minute instructions for preparing explosives and for the conduct of those making war on society. Brall said he was not an anarchist and had only gone to the Autonomie club so as to dance with his wife. He was let off because the government analyst said that he did not have enough fulminate of mercury to be dangerous.[52]

In November a bomb was aimed at the house of Mr Justice Hawkins. All it did was to slightly damage another house in the same street. The culprit was never found but Majendie said that the explosive used was picric acid, which was almost invariably used by French anarchists.[53] Pouget's London *Père Peinard* noticed that the English anarchists did not like fireworks and said that it was not in their interest to excite the ferocity of the establishment.[54]

INFLAMMATORY LEAFLETS

In 1894 quantities of violent French and Italian leaflets were forwarded to the Home Office. Some purported to be printed abroad but were in fact printed in London. More and more French and Italian refugees were leaving their countries as their domestic laws were tightened up. Many of the French ones slipped over to avoid a celebrated trial of thirty anarchists, and in September 1894 the Italian government dissolved all socialist, anarchist, and labour organisations. Anderson said that "an enormous quantity" of such leaflets were issued.[55] They illustrate the outlook of the *enragés* of the movement but, as is shown by the "Death to Carnot" leaflet found at the Autonomie club, they were part of the London scene. Among them was a ferocious pamphlet called "Résolution et révolution" (a corruption of *Evolution et révolution*). This warned the

wife of the new French President, Mme Casimir-Périer, that her husband's execution, like Carnot's, would be very sudden. The President was told that they wanted his skin too, while waiting for those of his accomplices and successors. An Italian leaflet signed "La Libera Iniziativa" (free initiative) announced a terrible vendetta for Pallas, Ravachol, Henry, and others. It ended "Death to the Bourgeois Society! Long live anarchy!" Possibly the most violent one was written in Italian. It urged sons to rebel against parents, students against masters, workers against the hierarchy, soldiers against officers. It outdid Bakunin in wanting, if it could not get freedom, "infinite and manifold destruction until universal ruin chokes the planet."

ANGIOLILLO

In 1896 a bomb was thrown at a Corpus Christi procession in Barcelona. It did not kill the officials at the head of the procession but some of the humbler people at the tail. It might have been an accident in timing the explosion, but there was no proof that it was thrown by an anarchist. The reactionary government of Antonio Cánovas del Castillo ordered anarchists, republicans, socialists, free-thinkers, and even Catalan separatists to be rounded up. In Montjuich prison many of the 400 detainees were tortured so severely that they died before the trial in May 1897. News of the atrocities soon reached France. The first article, describing a month in a Spanish prison, appeared there on 15 October 1896. Georges Clemenceau and others spoke at a protest meeting.[56] In London at a mass meeting reported in *Freedom*'s January 1897 supplement, its editor Joseph Pressburg (now calling himself Perry) reported on all the facts collected by the daily press. In May a Spanish atrocities committee, with Perry as secretary, included delegates from the Humanitarian League, the Fabian Society, the ILP, SDF, and *Freedom* group. It decided to hold a protest meeting in Trafalgar Square, which passed a resolution expressing horror and indignation and calling for an enquiry.[57] Protest meetings held in numerous other European countries seemed to have some effect. Only 8 of the accused were sentenced to death, but 26 were condemned to prison sentences and 61 were transported to the deadly climate of Rio de Oro. When, therefore, Cánovas was shot dead by Michele Angiolillo on 8 August 1897, it seemed a classical case of revenge. Even Señora Cánovas forgave him because she knew his "great heart".[58] Angiolillo was tried by a military court. Before he was garrotted on 20 August, he had time to write a trial speech, which was smuggled into France. In September *Freedom* printed it. In it, Angiolillo said he had noticed everywhere the hardness of heart and contempt for human lives among the rich and those who governed. He had learned that "in the classic land of the Inquisition, the race of torturers was not dead".

Angiolillo was born in Foggia (Apulia) in June 1871. He was educated at a technical institute and had first been attracted to anarchism while doing military service. After that he worked as a printer, but in April 1895 escaped a prison sentence for an anti-government manifesto by going first to Marseilles and then to Barcelona. There, in late

1895-6, he worked as a printer on a paper run by a Spanish anarchist journalist, F. Tarrida del Mármol. He was said to have left Barcelona a few days before the Corpus Christi bomb and then returned to Marseilles, but he was expelled from France and went to Brussels. There he again worked as a printer. He left Brussels in April 1896.[59] *Freedom*'s memorial issue said that between then and his return to Spain, "the united police of Europe" had failed to discover what he was doing.

In 1908 a French journal, the *Revue hispanique,* published an article by Rafael Salillas on Angiolillo's execution.[60] He reproduced a record made in 1896 by the Spanish journalist and writer José Nakens, who published a Madrid paper. Because of the assassination of Cánovas, Nakens wrote an account of three visits Angiolillo paid him. The second visit occurred during the second fortnight of July ("la segunda quincena de julio de 1897"). Angiolillo then said he knew Nakens's newspaper and had read his book. Nakens gave him a signed and inscribed copy. When Angiolillo returned three days later, he told Nakens that he had come to Madrid to murder Cánovas. He intended to avenge the Montjuich prisoners, but did not claim to have seen any of them. He wanted to imitate Caserio. On 8 August Nakens read an account of the assassination and feared that the inscribed copy of his book might incriminate him. Next day he sent an account of Angiolillo's visits to a friend to publish if necessary. The point of this record is that it pinpoints Angiolillo's return to Spain, a date that was confirmed by a report from Madrid published in *The Times* on 10 August saying that Angiolillo had returned to Spain "last month".

The Times on 2 August reported the arrival of 28 Montjuich prisoners at Euston on 28 July. They had come to take refuge in England. A mass meeting in Trafalgar square was arranged by the atrocities committee on 22 August. One of the men who had been tortured, Francisco Gana, was there and described the horrible cruelties inflicted on him.[61] By then Angiolillo had been executed. But the American anarchist Emma Goldman, who was in the United States at the time, categorically said that in Trafalgar Square Angiolillo saw "with his own eyes" the results of the atrocities when the Spaniards "opened their shirts and showed the horrible scars or burned flesh. Angiolillo saw, and the effect surpassed a thousand theories".[62] This must of itself cast doubt on her saying that in England Angiolillo had got a job as a compositor "and immediately became the friend of all his colleagues". No article by him appeared in any anarchist journal, although these journals often published articles by compositors. If he had even helped as a compositor, this would have been bound to be mentioned by a contemporary witness because of Angiolillo's status as a "martyr". An intriguing press report by the correspondent of *Le Temps* in London, published by the Spanish paper *Epoca* on 16 August, said that anarchists saw him in London in the Fitzroy Square region, but he had no recommendations or letters and was suspected of being a police agent. But Goldman had started the ball rolling. In 1937 Tom Bell (Mary Turner's brother-in-law)

wrote to a Los Angeles paper saying that he had known Angiolillo in London.[63] It is conceivable that he did—he was in London in 1896. But an account so long after the event is suspect. Rudolf Rocker's son Firmin (not even born at the time), in an interview in New York City in February 1972, said that Angiolillo was so much upset at a meeting in his father's flat, where he saw one of the victims, that he "at once left for Spain on a mission of reprisal".[64] This could only be a confused account of Gana's visit to Rocker's flat, which is on record.[65]

Two Home Office memoranda on the surveillance of anarchists in London are revealing, and they also refer to Angiolillo. The first, dated 1902, refers to a note from the Italian ambassador suggesting that Italian police should be put in touch with Scotland Yard. It mentioned that "the spy" referred to had become notorious some years ago by "publicly eulogising" Angiolillo. But the metropolitan police commissioner thought that any such arrangements would make things worse. The police had to rely on informers for what went on at secret meetings when important matters were discussed. Unless informers could trust the way information would be used, they would not come forward "through dread of vengeance" by their comrades. The second, dated 1903, recorded the belief that Angiolillo "was denounced in Paris by his Anarchist confrères as a police spy, came over to London where his reputation followed him, and made his life so unendurable" that he was impelled to assassinate Cánovas. It mentioned similar instances, and concluded that, while there was no proof that Angiolillo's action was "caused by the desperate plight of being abandoned by authorities and denounced by former friends and comrades", this was "in a high degree" probable.[66] It was at least indisputable that at the end of the mass meeting in Trafalgar Square on 20 August 1897, arranged by the Spanish atrocities committee which included representatives of "almost every shade of social and democratic opinion", Gana and "a prominent English Anarchist" were mobbed, hissed, and loudly hooted.[67] Public hostility to anarchist outrages was such that the police had to protect the "prominent English Anarchist" and Gana had to escape in a passing cab.

Notes

1. Conrad, *The Secret Agent* (Dent, London, 1923), pp. ix-x.

2. Ibid., pp. xi and xiii.

3. *Times Literary Supplement,* 13 Feb. 1981, p. 171.

4. N. Sherry, *Conrad's Western World* (Cambridge UP, Cambridge, 1971), p. 228.

5. Ibid., p. 229.

6. I. Watt (ed.), *Conrad, The Secret Agent: A Casebook* (Macmillan, London, 1973), pp. 222-3, 231, and 234.

7. "Conrad's Anarchist Professor: An Undiscovered Source", *Labor History,* vol. 18, no. 3 (Summer 1977).

8. *Morning Leader,* 17 Feb. 1894; The Times, 23 Feb. 1894.

9. *The Times,* 22 Feb. 1894.

10. R. Anderson, *The Lighter Side of My Official Life* (Hodder and Stoughton, London, 1910), p. 176.

11. *The Times,* 27 Feb. 1894.

12. Ibid., 27 Feb. 1894.

13. Morning Leader, 19 Feb. 1894.

14. Maitron, 1975, vol. 1, p. 125; French press report on anarchist groups dated 5 May 1892.

15. *Morning Leader,* 17 Feb. 1894.

16. Ibid.

17. Cited by Sherry, *Conrad's Western World,* p. 314.

18. *Morning Leader,* 17 Feb. 1894 and inquest report of chief constable in *The Times,* 20 Feb. 1894.

19. *Kentish and Deptford Observer,* 23 Feb. 1894.

20. Ibid. for the fullest account of Majendie's evidence.

21. *The Times,* 22 and 24 Feb. 1894.

22. Nettlau, *1886-1914,* 3, Ch. 5, fo. 106.

23. *Morning Leader,* 19 Feb. 1894.

24. See *Police Chronicle and Guardian,* 17 Feb. 1894.

25. Sherry, *Conrad's Western World,* p. 243.

26. *The Times,* 23 Feb. 1894.

27. The full title is *"Commonweal", The Greenwich Mystery.* It is reproduced in an appendix to Sherry's *Conrad's Western World.*

28. Nicoll, *Greenwich Mystery* (Nicoll, Sheffield, 1897), p. 16.

29. Ibid., p. 12.

30. Nicoll, *Letters from the Dead* (Nicoll, London, 1898), inside front cover.

31. Ibid., pp. 3-4 (misquoted as "Mr Samuels" by Quail, p. 168).

32. L. S. Bevington to Nettlau, 3 May 1894, (IISH).

33. Sherry, *Conrad's Western World,* p. 243.

34. Samuels to Nettlau, 28 June 1894 (IISH).

35. Nettlau, 1886-1914, 3, Ch. 5, fo. 121n 195.

36. He is listed among "practitioners resident abroad" in the 1897 medical directory, indicating that he was abroad from the end of 1896.

37. Quail, p. 209, referring to "Nettlau Collection".

38. Ibid., p. 178. Quail reports that Nicoll said that Samuels had handed out potassium picrate, the charge in Bourdin's bomb. It has been seen that the explosive used was not disclosed.

39. Nettlau, *1886-1914,* 3, Ch. 5, fo. 106. Quail (p. 179n 119) interprets the date as 22 May.

40. Nettlau, *1886-1914,* 3, Ch. 5, fo. 107.

41. Samuels to Nettlau, 28 June 1894 (IISH).

42. *The Times,* 3 July and 1 Aug. 1894.

43. HO144/545 A55/176/31.

44. HOA55/684 (dated 2 Mar. 1894).

45. Dict. MOF, vol. 14, pp. 299-301 (which says that Pouget came to the 1881 London congress).

46. HOA55/684/11, 25 Sept. 1894. The first of these brochures was printed by the *Torch* press.

47. Maitron, 1975, vol. 1, p. 296.

48. *The Times,* 5 May 1894.

49. HO144,259 A55,860.

50. *Standard,* 24 Apr. 1894.

51. HOA55/860/3.

52. *The Times,* 2 and 19 June 1894.

53. Ibid., 4 and 6 Nov. 1894.

54. *Le Père Peinard* (London), Nov. 1894.

55. HOA55/684/4 and 11.

56. See F. Tarrida del Mármol, *Les Inquisiteurs d'Espagne* (Stock, Paris, 1897).

57. *Freedom,* June-July 1897; *The Times,* 31 May 1897.

58. *The Times,* 14 Aug. 1897.

59. Andreucci and Detti; *The Times,* 11 Aug. 1897; *Freedom,* Sept. 1897.

60. R. Salillas, "Una Página histórica fotografada: La Ejecución de Angiolillo", *Revue hispanique,* vol. 19 (1908), pp. 135-8.

61. *The Times,* 23 Aug. 1897.

62. E. Goldman, *Anarchism and Other Essays* (Mother Earth Publishing Association, New York, 1911), pp. 101-3. Sheila Price drew my attention to this at an early stage in my research for this book.

63. P. Avrich, *An American Anarchist* (Princeton UP, Princeton, 1978), p. 114.

64. Ibid.

65. In a letter from V. de Cleyre of 3 Aug. 1897, cited ibid. p. 114n.

66. HO144/545 A55,176/44 and A55,176/51.

67. *The Times,* 23 Aug. 1897.

Peter Marshall (essay date 1985)

SOURCE: "Human Nature and Anarchism," in *For Anarchism: History, Theory, and Practice,* edited by David Goodway, Routledge, 1985, pp. 127-49.

[*In the following essay, Marshall considers the anarchist theories of William Godwin, Max Stirner, and Peter Kropotkin, and offers his own critique of the concept of human nature.*]

Critics of anarchism, indeed of any attempt to expand freedom, have repeatedly fallen back on the tired argument that it is against 'human nature'. The conventional wisdom amongst historians of political thought is that anarchists have an optimistic view of human beings as being naturally good and that it is only the state that produces evil in people. Abolish the state, they believe anarchists assert, and society will achieve a condition of perfect harmony. Convinced of the need for political authority, they argue that in reality the opposite would occur; without the state, society would collapse into the Hobbesian nightmare of violent disorder and permanent war. To criticize anarchism, it becomes enough to assert that is just a 'puerile Utopia'.[1] 'Human nature' is thus depicted as a nasty fellow blocking our path to a free society and any further improvement.

The concept of human nature is undoubtedly a powerful weapon. It is appealed to as if it has its own invincible weight. On the one hand, it is given the force of logic so that like 2+2=4 it only has to be asserted to be self-evidently true. On the other, it is presented as an empirical reality. Traditional Christian moralists who asserted that we are irredeemably fallen in original sin with depraved and corrupt natures were given a pseudo-scientific gloss by the Social Darwinists of the last century who maintained that in the struggle for survival only the most powerful and cunning survive. In our own century, psychoanalysts have given their own version of original sin by arguing that we are in the grip of irrational and unconscious forces or driven by the will to power. In their attempt to trace the biological roots of capitalist society, the sociobiologists have argued more recently that human beings are naturally aggressive, genetically selfish, and overwhelmed by a territorial imperative.

The corollary of these arguments is that a society of violent, property-owning egoists seeking power and wealth is natural and that political authority in the shape of the state and law is necessary to curb human excesses. Any alternative model of society which might suggest that human beings are capable of governing themselves and of leading peaceful and productive lives without external coercion is dismissed as hopelessly naïve, implausible, and utopian. The anarchist vision of a free society is therefore said to be not only an impossibility but a self-deluding fantasy.

I would like to argue, however, that while classic anarchist thinkers, such as William Godwin, Max Stirner, and Peter Kropotkin, share common assumptions about the possibility of a free society, they do not have a common view of human nature. I also hope to show that their views of human nature are not so naïve or optimistic as is usually alleged. Finally, I would like to present my criticism of the very notion of human nature and offer a plausible view of the limits and possibilities of human beings which embraces the anarchist ideal of a free society. Libertarians clearly have to explain why the violence, oppression, and exploitation which have characterized so much of the past need not continue in the future. They also have to show how the increasing power of states in modern industrial societies throughout the world can be not only checked but actually dissolved. An account of human behaviour is needed which can explain the horrors of Auschwitz and Hiroshima and which can envisage the reign of peace, justice, and freedom.

HUMAN NATURE AND CLASSICAL ANARCHIST THEORY

If we look at the views of human nature put forward by the three nineteenth-century anarchist thinkers, William Godwin, Max Stirner, and Peter Kropotkin, we find some profound and often incompatible differences. Godwin was the most consistent and logical. In his *Enquiry Concerning Political Justice* (1793), Godwin firmly based his ethics and politics on a clear view of human nature. He believed in universal determinism; that is to say, both human nature as well as external nature are governed by necessary and universal laws. Within this broad philosophical framework, Godwin then asserted that the 'characters of men originate in external circumstances'.[2] The effects of heredity are therefore minimal (there are no innate ideas or instincts): we are almost entirely the products of our environment. We are not born either virtuous or vicious, benevolent or selfish, but become so according to our upbringing and education.

But while Godwin argues that human nature is malleable, he also believes that it possesses certain characteristics. In the first place, we are both unique individuals and social beings. Godwin certainly valued personal autonomy and made the corner-stone of his anarchism the Dissenters' 'right to private judgement'.[3] He insisted that to be truly happy we must not forfeit our individuality by becoming dependent on others or losing ourselves in the mass. But it is wrong to categorize him as an individualist who did not take into account the social dimension of human life. He repeatedly stressed that we are social beings, that we are made for society, and that society brings out our best sympathies and abilities. Indeed, he saw no tension between autonomy and community, since 'the love of liberty obviously leads to a sentiment of union, and a disposition to sympathize in the concerns of others'. In a free and equal society, Godwin believed that we would become both more social and more individual.

Godwin also thought that we are rational beings who can recognize truth and act accordingly. As potentially rational, we are voluntary beings, capable of consciously directing our actions. It is through reason that Godwin reconciled his belief in determinism and in human choice: while every action is determined by a motive, reason enables us to choose what motive to act upon. The will is therefore 'the last act of the understanding'.[4] Since we are both rational and voluntary beings, Godwin inferred that we are also progressive. Godwin's view of the 'perfectibility of man', as he called it, was based on the proposition that our voluntary actions originate in our opinions and that it is the nature of truth to triumph over error. He made his case in the form of a syllogism:

Sound reasoning and truth, when adequately communicated, must always be victorious over error: Sound reasoning and truth are capable of being so communicated: Truth is omnipotent: The vices and moral weakness of man are not invincible: Man is perfectible, or in other words susceptible of perpetual improvement.[5]

If vice is nothing more than ignorance and our opinions determine our actions, then education and enlightenment will enable us to become virtuous and free. Thus while we may be products of our circumstances, we can think critically about them and are able to change them. We are therefore to a large extent the creators of our own destiny.

Godwin has often been dismissed as a naïve visionary because he believed that human beings are rational and progressive in this way. In fact, his position is far from naïve. As a historian, he was only too well aware that from one point of view history is 'little else than a record of crimes'.[6] He knew from first hand the power of evil and the weight of coercive institutions. Yet Godwin discerned in the past clear signs of social and intellectual progress and saw no reason why the process should not continue in the future, although he warned that improvement would be inevitably gradual and often interrupted.

Again, it is difficult to sustain the charge that Godwin was too rational. He may have felt with John Stuart Mill that truth should be left alone to fight its own battles—he based his eloquent defence of the freedom of thought and expression on the belief—but he was fully informed of the force of prejudice. The fate of his own work and the political reaction in Britain after the French Revolution proved a daily remainder of the fragility of truth. It is true that Godwin argued that people usually do what they think is right. But while there is clearly on some occasions a gap between thought and action, it is quite plausible to say that we cannot be really convinced of the desirability of an object without desiring it.

Finally, Godwin cannot be accused of dismissing the power of the emotions. He maintained that 'passion is inseparable from reason' and that virtue cannot be 'strenuously espoused' without it being 'ardently loved'.[7] Indeed, reason is not an independent principle, and from a practical point of view is 'merely a comparison and balancing of different feelings'.[8] It is a subtle position which cannot easily be dismissed. In the final analysis, however, Godwin held firm to his view that human beings are potentially rational and that it is to the development of our reason that we are to look for the improvement in our social condition.

Godwin's view of human nature and social change placed him in a difficult dilemma. On the one hand, he stressed how opinions are shaped by economic and political circumstances, especially in the form of government. On the other, he was committed to education and enlightenment as the principal means of reform. It followed for Godwin that, since government is founded in opinion, all that is

William Godwin (1756–1836)

necessary to dissolve the foundation of government is to change public opinion. This meant, however, that he was left with the contradiction that human beings cannot become wholly rational as long as governments exist and yet governments will exist as long as human beings remain irrational.

Although Stirner like Godwin came to similar anarchist conclusions about the dissolution of the state and political authority, their views of human nature could not have been more disparate. Stirner was an out-and-out egoist. Where Godwin thought that human beings are capable of reason, benevolence, and solidarity, Stirner did not believe that such ideals were possible. Where Godwin claimed that the rational person would be benevolent, Stirner maintained the very opposite and asserted that human beings could only act in a self-interested way. There is no place for Godwin's calm reason and universal benevolence in Stirner's scheme of things: man (the word is appropriate, not sexist in this context) is driven by selfish instincts, and the self is his most valuable possession.

As the title of his principal work *The Ego and Its Own* (1845) implies, Stirner maintains that each individual is unique and the ego the sole arbitrator. His position may best be understood in the context of the left-Hegelian critique of religion that developed in Germany in the 1840s. Opposing Hegel's philosophical idealism which saw history as the unfurling of Spirit, the left-Hegelians argued that religion was a form of alienation in which the believer projected certain of his own desirable qualities on to a transcendent deity. Man is not created in God's image, but God is created in man's ideal image. To overcome this alienation, they argued that it was necessary to 'reappropriate' the human essence and to realize that the ideal qualities attributed to God are human qualities, partially realized at present but capable of being fully realized in a transformed society. The critique of religion thus became a radical call for reform.

Stirner went even further in his critique. Where the left-Hegelian Feuerbach argued that, instead of worshipping God, we should try to realize the human essence, Stirner declared that this kind of humanism was merely religion in disguise. Since the concept of human essence is merely an abstract thought, it cannot be an independent standard by which we measure our actions. It remains, like the concept of the people, nothing more than a 'spook'.[9]

In metaphysical terms, Stirner is not strictly a solipsist in believing that the ego is the only reality, but he does hold that the ego is the highest level of reality.

In his psychology, he believes in psychological egoism. The self is a unity acting from a self-seeking will: '*I am everything to myself and I do everything on my account.*'[10] The apparent altruist is an unconscious, involuntary egoist. Even love is a type of egoism: I love 'because love makes *me* happy, I love because loving is natural to me, because it pleases me'.[11] Stirner thus anticipates Freud in his stress on the force of the desires to influence reason, and Adler in his description of the will as the highest faculty of the ego.

In his ethics, Stirner believes that self-interest is the sole good. There are no eternal moral truths and no values to be discovered in nature. There are no natural rights, no social rights, no historical rights. Right is merely might: 'What you have the *power* to be you have the *right* to.'[12] The dominant morality will therefore be the values of the most powerful. The individual has no obligation to law or morality; his only interest is the free satisfaction of his needs. The conscious egoist is thus beyond all good and evil:

> Away, then, with every concern that is not altogether my concern! You think at least the 'good cause' must be my concern? What's good, what's bad? Why, I myself am my concern, and I am neither good nor bad. Neither has meaning for me.
>
> The divine is God's concern; the human, man's. My concern is neither the divine nor the human, not the true, good, just, free, etc., but solely what is *mine,* and it is not a general one, but is—unique, as I am unique.
>
> Nothing is more to me than myself![13]

Indeed, Stirner goes so far as to place one's 'ownness' above the value of freedom, since it is easier to be oneself than be free:

one becomes free from much, not from everything. . . . .'Freedom lives only in the realm of dreams!' Ownness, on the contrary, is my whole being and existence, it is I myself. I am free from what I am *rid* of, owner of what I have in my *power* or what I *control.* My own I am at all times and under all circumstances, if I know how to have myself and do not throw myself away on others.[14]

With this stress on the primacy of the ego, Stirner goes on to develop a view of freedom which calls not merely for an absence of constraint, but for the ability to act out of a truly free choice of the uncircumscribed individual: 'I am my *own* only when I am master of myself.'[15] On these grounds, he proceeds to demolish all those doctrines which demand the subordination of the interests in the individual to such mental fictions and abstractions as God, Humanity, Law, State, and Church.

Given his account of human nature, Stirner, no less than Hobbes, sees society as a war of all against all. As each individual tries to satisfy his desires he inevitably comes into conflict with others. But while Stirner's view of human nature as selfish, passionate, and power-seeking is close to that of Hobbes, they come to opposite conclusions. Where Hobbes called for an all-powerful state resting on the sword to enforce its laws to curb the unruly passions of humanity, Stirner believed that it is possible and desirable to form a spontaneous union of egoists. Moreover, he did not think that a long period of preparation and enlightenment would be necessary as Godwin suggests. People simply have to recognize what they are: 'Your nature is, once for all, a human one; you are human natures, human beings. But, just because you already are so, you do not still need to become so.'[16]

The reason why the state and even formal institutions of society can be done away with is because we are more or less equal in power and ability. It is enough for people to become fully egoist to end the unequal distribution of power which produced a hierarchical society with servants and masters. In the 'war of each against all', force might be necessary to redistribute wealth, but Stirner goes beyond any revolution which seeks to make new institutions in his final celebration of individual self-assertion and rebellion:

> Now, as my object is not the overthrow of an established order but my elevation above it, my purpose and deed are not a political and social but (as directed toward myself and my ownness alone) an *egoistic* purpose and deed.
>
> The revolution commands one to make *arrangements,* the insurrection demands that he *rise or exalt himself.*[17]

In fact, Stirner celebrates the will to power not over others but rather over oneself. If all withdrew into their own uniqueness social conflict would be diminished and not exacerbated: 'As unique you have nothing in common with the other any longer, and therefore nothing divisive or hostile either.'[18] He therefore believed it was possible to form loose associations or spontaneous unions with other egoists. Human beings might therefore be fundamentally selfish, but it is possible to appeal to their selfishness for them to make contractual agreements among themselves to avoid violence and conflict and to pursue their selfish interests. In the final analysis, it seems little different from Adam Smith's enlightened self-interest.

With Godwin and Stirner we thus have two diametrically opposed views of human nature, but a common faith in the desirability and possibility of a free society without government. They both look to some form of enlightenment to change human conduct. But where Godwin felt human beings are capable of reason and benevolence and looked to education to improve their lot, Stirner felt human beings are irredeemably selfish and merely called on them to follow their interests in a clear-sighted way.

The problem with Stirner's position is that, given his view of human beings as self-seeking egoists, it is difficult to imagine that in a free society they would not grasp for power and resort to violence to settle disputes. Without the sanction of moral obligation or threat of force, there is no reason to expect that agreements would be binding. If such agreements were only kept out of prudence, then it would seem pointless making them in the first place. Again, to say that, because they have a substantial equality, a truce would emerge in the struggle for power seems unlikely. It was precisely because people have roughly equal talents that Hobbes felt there would be a war of all against all outside the restriction of the laws.

Like Hobbes's, Stirner's model of human nature would seem to reflect the alienated subjectivity of capitalist society. He applied the assumptions of capitalist economics to every aspect of human existence and reproduced in everyday life what is most vicious in capitalist institutions. As such his view differs little from that of Adam Smith (whose *Wealth of Nations* he translated into German) or the contemporary apologist of *laissez-faire* capitalism, Murray Rothbard.

In the final analysis, however, Stirner is not entirely consistent in his doctrine of amoral egoism. The consistent egoist would presumably keep quiet and pursue his own interest with complete disregard for others. Yet by recommending that everyone should become an egoist, he implies a moral ground. Stirner may reject all objective values, but he celebrates some values, even if they are only egoistic ones. His aggressive nihilism would therefore seem to imply a moral position after all.[19]

Kropotkin at the end of the nineteenth century proposed a very different model of human nature. On the one hand, he rejected what he called Stirner's 'superficial negation of morality'.[20] On the other, he echoed Godwin in his scientific view of nature as governed by necessary laws, his stress on man as a social being, and his recognition that change will often be gradual. What was new was his confidence in the creativity and virtue of people living in simple societies, his desire to give a scientific grounding to his anarchist conclusions, and his overall evolutionary perspective.

Kropotkin's approach to nature and 'man' (as he called the human species in the linguistic habit of his day) was rigorously scientific. As a professional geographer and explorer, the subjective and windy imaginations of Stirner were anathema to him. He came to realize, he tells us, that anarchism is

> part of a philosophy, natural and social, which must be developed in a quite different way from the metaphysical or dialectical methods which have been employed in sciences dealing with men. I saw it must be treated by the same methods as natural sciences . . . on the solid basis of induction applied to human institutions.[21]

In *Modern Science and Anarchism* (1901), he went further to argue that the movement of both natural and social science was in the direction of the anarchist ideal.

Kropotkin developed his views in the context of Darwin's theory of evolution. The theory had come to be used by Social Darwinists to give pseudo-scientific support to capitalism, racism, and imperialism. Since there is allegedly a struggle for survival in society as well in nature, they argued that it is right and inevitable that the fittest should survive and rule, whether it be a class, a race, or a nation. T. H. Huxley, Darwin's bulldog, presented moreover the animal world as a perpetual 'gladiator's show' and the life of primitive man as a 'continuous free fight'. Kropotkin threw himself into the controversy to offer an alternative interpretation of the evolutionary process.

It was his contention that there is more evidence in nature of co-operation within species than of competition. In his book *Mutual Aid* (1902), he suggested with a rich array of data taken from the life of animals and the development of human society that biological and social progress is best fostered by the practice of mutual aid:

> we maintain that under *any* circumstances sociability is the greatest advantage in the struggle for life. Those species which willingly or unwillingly abandon it are doomed to decay; while those animals which know best how to combine have the greatest chance of survival and of further evolution.[22]

Kropotkin made clear that the struggle for survival which takes place is a struggle *against* adverse circumstances rather than *between* individuals of the same species. Where the Social Darwinists argued that the struggle between individuals leads to the survival of the fittest, Kropotkin asserted that the unit of competition is the species as a whole and that the species which has the greatest degree of co-operation and support between its members will be the most likely to flourish. Mutual aid within the species thus represents 'the principal factor, the principal active agency in that which we may call evolution'.[23]

Kropotkin does not hesitate to apply these observations of the animal world to human society. He maintains that society is a natural phenomenon existing anterior to the appearance of humanity, and humanity is naturally adapted to live in society without artificial regulations. Humanity is and always has been a social species. Kropotkin draws on the findings of anthropology to argue that in traditional societies human beings have always lived in clans and tribes in which customs and taboos ensured co-operation and mutual aid. He concludes from his historical studies that mutual aid reached its apogee in the communal life of the medieval cities. Even the appearance of coercive institutions and the state has not eradicated voluntary co-operation. According to Kropotkin, evolutionary theory, if properly understood, will demonstrate the possibility of anarchism rather than justify the capitalist system. Anarchism as a social philosophy is therefore not against but in keeping with evolving human nature.

Kropotkin not only argues that this is an accurate and true description of nature and the human species, but sees it as providing the ground for morality. 'Nature', he writes in his posthumous *Ethics* (1924),

> has thus to be recognized as the *first ethical teacher of man*. The social instinct, innate in men as well as in all the social animals,—this is the origin of all ethical conceptions and all the subsequent development of morality.[24]

Human beings are therefore naturally moral. Moreover, by living in society they develop their inherent sense of justice so that it comes to operate like a habit. As a result, we are morally progressive, and our primitive instinct of solidarity will become more refined and comprehensive as civilization develops.

Kropotkin thus presents man as a social being, and suggests that the most important factor in his development has been voluntary co-operation and mutual aid. But for all his respect for the sociability of traditional societies, Kropotkin does not reject the gains of civilization and culture. Humans like other animals need their basic needs satisfied, but they are also creative and imaginative beings. Indeed, our intellect and moral sense are primarily called forth by society. In *The Conquest of Bread* (1906), Kropotkin's principal criticism of the unequal distribution of property was that it does not give the necessary leisure for all to develop full human personalities:

> Man is not a being whose exclusive purpose in life is eating, drinking, and providing a shelter for himself. As soon as his material wants are satisfied, other needs, which generally speaking may be described as of an artistic nature, will thrust themselves forward. These needs are of the greatest variety; they vary with each and every individual, and the more society is civilized, the more will individuality be developed, and the more will desires be varied.[25]

In the development of civilization in a free society, human beings would not only be able to evolve the full range of their artistic and intellectual abilities but become more truly social and individual. For this reason work would be made attractive and meaningful, fulfilling and not degrading the workers as at present. The incentive to work would be moral rather than material—the conscious satisfaction of contributing to the general well-being. And once bread was secured, leisure to develop the full human potential would be the supreme aim.

Kropotkin's anarchism is thus, like Godwin's, firmly based on a clear view of human nature. Mutual aid is a principal factor in natural and human evolution. There is a moral principle in nature which ensures that human beings have a sense of justice. We are naturally social, co-operative, and moral. But while society is a natural phenomenon, the state with its coercive institutions is an artificial and malignant growth.

If co-operation is natural, Kropotkin of course is left with the problem of explaining existing inequalities and egoism. To overcome this, he implies that human beings developed a secondary drive of self-assertion which led them to seek power and to dominate and exploit their fellows. Again, while he recognized the influence of economic arrangements on political institutions, his account of the origin of the state by which a minority combined military and judicial privileges suggests that political power was initially more important than economic power.

Nevertheless, Kropotkin remained confident that the dispossessed majority would destroy the new coercive institutions, and develop their natural propensity to help each other. If political authority were removed with all other artificial restrictions, Kropotkin was convinced that human beings would act socially, that is to say, in accordance with their social nature. However distant, he believed that a free society would eventually be realized as the natural outcome of human evolution.

HUMAN NATURE, PHILOSOPHY, AND HISTORY

While I share some of the assumptions of these three classic anarchist thinkers, my own philosophical starting-point is somewhat different. I have little sympathy for Stirner's egoism and consider his account of human motivation to be simply false. Godwin's view of human beings as potentially rational, voluntary, and progressive is attractive, but it is ultimately based on the belief in the omnipotence of universal truth which is difficult to maintain. Kropotkin's evolutionary perspective is important, but his ethical naturalism is untenable. There are no values to be discovered in nature; all values are human creations.

It is my view that we should abandon the use of the term 'human nature' since it implies that there is a fixed essence within us which requires certain conditions to express itself, or some inherent force which directs us outside the influence of history or culture.

Sweeping assertions about human nature are notoriously suspect. They are often disguised definitions—as in the statement 'all men are wild beasts'—and as such cannot be verified, proved, or disproved by appealing to any evidence. In addition, they usually contain a confused mixture of fact and value, a description of how people are and how they should be. The statement that 'human beings are naturally aggressive' is posed as a factual statement—'all beings are actually aggressive'—but it also implies the value that we should all be aggressive. This becomes even more evident in statements like 'pacifism is unnatural'.

Clearly facts are relevant to values, for to understand what we are helps us to decide what we can and should do. But what counts as a fact invariably depends on a prior theory and value. Ethnologists and psychologists are notorious for projecting human values into nature and then claiming that they have observed them as hard and certain 'facts'. They extend, for instance, ideas of domination and hierarchy into the natural world of non-human biological relationships, but such ideas are the product of the socially conditioned human mind. Thus 'man' is depicted as a 'naked ape' driven by a 'territorial imperative' and prey to geese-like 'aggression'. Science can help us to understand society and culture, but it is well to remember that so-called 'objective' science is also shaped and influenced by them.

In the circumstances, it would perhaps seem a good idea to go beyond the whole 'fact/value', 'is/ought' debate and to recognize that there is no unbridgeable gap between normative and prescriptive statements. Viewed dialectically, 'what could be' and 'what should be' are inseparable parts of 'what is', since the former contain the moral and practical potential of the latter.

The trouble with most views about 'human nature', particularly the ones put forward by psychoanalysts and sociobiologists, are that they have an uncanny similarity with the world view of the class to which the thinkers belong. In the West, the view of the dominant class is that human beings are fundamentally selfish, competitive, and aggressive. Yet this view is historically limited to the rise of capitalism and the nation state, and takes no account of either the organic and co-operative behaviour of traditional societies or even the mutual aid practised in the Middle Ages. The possessive individualism of the West is a comparatively recent development. The ruling class and their ideological apologists try to persuade us that certain human traits like self-interest and possessiveness which are historical and temporary are in fact existential and permanent.

Another difficulty with the concept of human nature is that for an assertion about human nature to be true it has to be true of all those beings classified as human. If counter-examples of human behaviour can be discerned in the findings of anthropology and history, then such statements are not universally valid. They should therefore be qualified by certain conditions; for instance, it can only be said that in certain capitalist societies human beings are possessive. Alternatively, such statements should be interpreted as only carrying the weak sense of meaning that people, or even most people, normally behave in particular ways. If this is the case, then it is easy for libertarians to argue that even if most people have been aggressive in the past, or even if most people are selfish today, it does not follow that they always will be, or that changed conditions will not bring about different behaviour. It then becomes possible to point to different societies in time and place (drawing on anthropology and history as Kropotkin and more recently Murray Bookchin have done) to show that self-interest and hierarchy are not universal and that it is possible to create a society different from the models held up by those in power. Rather than offering a single model of humanity, a knowledge of history and anthropology would suggest that human behaviour is systematically unpredictable.

I would take the argument further, however, and suggest that it is quite misleading to talk of the collective abstraction 'Man'; there are only men and women, human beings. Human beings are social animals but they also have an irreducible uniqueness of their own. The human species is too diffuse to talk about an underlying fixed essence which society and culture are designed to express. Since 'human nature' is such an ambiguous and misleading term it would seem a good idea to abandon its use altogether.

This is not to suggest that there are no characteristics which are peculiarly human. We are a species which has developed during millions of years of biological evolution. With other species, we share the fundamental instincts of hunger and sex. Without the satisfaction of the former, we would not survive as individuals, and without the latter, our species would die out. I would also agree with Marx that we are fundamentally social beings: we are all born into a set of social relationships. But unlike other species we have emerged from the natural world to become thinking beings—*Homo sapiens*. The human mind is uniquely capable of conceptual thought, symbolic communication, and self-consciousness. We are therefore the product of an evolutionary process which has gone in the direction of increasing complexity, consciousness, and individuality.

Beyond biological evolution, we have entered in the last million years a phase of cultural evolution, in which our accumulated experience is handed down from generation to generation. The result is that while we share biological needs with other animals the manner in which they are expressed and satisfied is determined culturally and socially. In addition, human society itself has created new needs, such as the need for productive work, loving relations, and a meaningful relationship with the world.

Although we do not have a 'human nature' as a fixed essence, we are born with a certain evolving range of perceptual, conceptual, and linguistic powers. These innate capacities, which form a central part of human consciousness, enable us to think, to communicate, and to create. In the case of language, for instance, we are born with an ability to understand and use language. It not only enables us to interpret the world we find ourselves in but provides the basis of personal identity and social freedom. The advantage of this position is that it avoids the reductionism both of the rationalist, who maintains that we are born with innate ideas, and of the empiricist, who argues that we are blank sheets at birth.

The innate powers or capacities are not fixed however, but open. They may be innately determined but are also shaped by experience. The tired debate of the relative importance of heredity and environment, nature versus nurture, over-looks that the fact that neither are constant variables. From the moment a human being is conceived, heredity and environment interact on each other, and later experience is always interpreted according to earlier experience. Even varieties in height, for instance, used to depend on environmental factors like diet and health, and only recently have become largely genetically determined.

It follows that the way in which our innate capacities are expressed will depend on the circumstances we are born into. Our circumstances act as a series of limits and pressures upon us. But our circumstances, like everything else in the universe, are in a state of flux. In addition, since we are conscious beings, we are capable not only of adapting to our circumstances but of creating new ones. By changing our circumstances, we change ourselves. We are both the products and agents of history. Human society is thus not built on an unchanging bedrock of 'human nature', or on some fixed biological foundation, but develops dialectically and can be consciously shaped to express and satisfy our needs.

There are of course existential limits to our human condition: we long for immortality, yet we are born to die; we search for absolute knowledge, yet remain in doubt. Again, we do not choose our parents: we are born into a particular body in a particular time and place. But how we respond to our existential predicament is not predetermined or fixed.

It is our consciousness which sets us free. Because consciousness is intentional, we can become aware of and understand the influences at work on us. We can then choose which influences we want to check or develop, which motives we wish to act upon. Between ourselves and the world, there is a gap in which we can say 'no'. We are not foregone conclusions: we can refuse to be the type that our mentors and leaders would like us to be.

Therein lies our freedom, the area of conscious choice. We are free to come to terms with our existential and social condition and to take up our past and to launch ourselves into a future of our own making. We have all been conditioned into dependence and obedience. We can choose, as Sartre suggests, not to choose and so become like a stone. We can be fearful of freedom and avoid the responsibility it entails. Nevertheless, in the end we are all responsible to a large degree for our individual lives, for our social arrangements and for nature itself.

This position may be called a kind of soft determinism. It recognizes that there are causes which influence us, but it sees all causes as incomplete and open-ended. Such causes dispose but do not determine.[26] It sees knowledge as inseparable from freedom and defines freedom both as the release from external restraint and as the ability to realize one's innate capacities. Like plants, human beings realize their potential according to their environment; but unlike plants, they can change the environment they find themselves in.

It also offers the possibility of elaborating a case for anarchism, as Noam Chomsky has hinted, based on the self-regulation of the innate intellectual and creative abilities of the human mind.[27] It is a kind of self-regulation which does not require coercive institutions or political authority; indeed, it is positively harmed by them. It sees freedom as the unique condition under which human consciousness and happiness can develop and grow. It is a liberty, as Bakunin observed, which implies

> the full development of all the material, intellectual and moral capacities latent in everyone; the liberty which knows no other restrictions but those set by the laws of our own nature, consequently there are, properly speaking, no restrictions, since these laws are not imposed upon us by any legislator from outside, alongside, or above ourselves. These laws are subjective, inherent in ourselves; they constitute the very basis of our being.[28]

Moreover, it is not only the mind but also our emotional and sexual drives which regulate themselves when not interfered with by artificial restrictions imposed by coercive institutions. As Wilhelm Reich argued; 'The vital energies, under natural conditions, regulate themselves spontaneously, without compulsive duty or compulsive morality.'[29] The traditional conflict between reason and desire is not inevitable but a result of our social arrangements. Since the body and mind are two aspects of the whole person, and the whole person is self-regulating, only in a free society of self-governing individuals would people be able realize their full potential as social and creative beings.

To be self-regulating and autonomous individuals does not mean that we are floating atoms unconnected to each other. We are shaped by the whole and can only realize our individuality through others. To become truly individual, we must become fully social. This apparent paradox becomes less problematic when compared to Arthur Koestler's description of biological and social individuals as 'holons'— 'self-regulating systems which display both the autonomous properties of wholes and the dependent properties of parts'.[30] They have a dual tendency to assert their individuality as autonomous wholes and to function as an integrated part of a larger evolving whole.

As for the controversy about whether we are 'naturally' good or bad, selfish or benevolent, gentle or aggressive, I consider the search for one irreducible quality to be as absurd and reductionist as looking for a human essence. We have innate tendencies for both types of behaviour; it is our circumstances which encourage or check them. While our present authoritarian and hierarchical society encourages egoism, competition, and aggression, there is good reason to think that a free society without authority and coercion would encourage our benevolent and sympathetic tendencies. Instead of universalizing what we find in our own society, we should recognize that it is an exception rather than the norm. The present ideology, which identifies progress with growth and competition, defines happiness with consumption, and confuses having with being, is historically unique.

Anthropology shows that there have been many gentle societies where human beings have no wish to kill or dominate each other. The very disparate societies of the Arapesh of New Guinea, the Lepchas of Sikkim in the Himalayas, and the pygmies of the Ituri rain forest in the Congo offer striking examples. There is a wealth of data to demonstrate that for the greater part of history human beings have lived co-operatively and peacefully without rulers. These societies vary from small groups of hunter-gatherers like the Eskimos and Bushmen, to the Tiv gardeners, who number over a million in Nigeria. Even amongst agricultural societies, which can create a surplus for a ruling class and often have governments, there have been a number of highly decentralized federations. The Berbers, throughout the Middle East, and the Kabyles in Algeria, manage themselves through autonomous village councils. Again, the Santals, over three million of whom dwell in eastern India, decided their affairs in free and open meetings with the village headman merely being the voice of the consensus.

The anarchy of these traditional societies without rulers does not necessarily mean that they are free in the modern sense of offering a wide range of choices to the individual. They are often characterized by sexism and ageism, with power conferred on men and elders. In place of laws, there are also strong sanctions to reform the wrongdoer and to make the dissenting individual conform. These can be religious sanctions, such as the threat of supernatural punishment, and social ones, particularly in the form of ostracism, ridicule, and gossip. The force of habit and custom is also very strong, and can perpetuate ignorance, intolerance, and prejudice. Nevertheless, these societies show that human beings have lived and can live without coercive institutions and authoritarian leaders and rulers.[31]

In recent history, there have moreover been several self-conscious attempts to realize on a large scale a commonwealth which contains age-old patterns of co-operation with a modern desire for personal freedom. The self-managing districts in the Paris Commune remain an inspiration. The peasants in the Ukraine during the early days of the Russian Revolution formed anarchist communes. The greatest experiment so far was during the Spanish Revolution, when peasants in Aragon and Valencia and workers in Barcelona organized themselves in communes and councils and fought the civil war against Franco on anarchist lines. The fact that the revolution failed, largely due to external factors, does not alter the case that the anarchist ideal was partially realized and shown to be practicable.

The present direction of history would seem to be towards more centralized, militarized, and authoritarian states, but the dying breed of indigenous anarchies can tell us much about how to organize society without rulers. They show that the nation-state is only a recent cancer on the body politic. Above all they remind us of the important truth that liberty is the mother and not the daughter of order. While no self-conscious anarchist society as yet exists, the great social experiments in the last hundred years show that it is an ever-present possibility and an ineradicable

part of human potential. A free society is in the realm of objective possibilities. There is no pre-ordained pattern to history, no iron law of capitalist development, no straight railroad which we have to follow. Although it is always made on prior circumstances, history is what we make it; and the future, as the past, can be either authoritarian or libertarian depending on our choices and actions.

Towards a Free and Ecological Society

Having exposed the myth of human nature as some fixed essence and sketched an alternative view of human limits and possibilities, I would like consider some moral implications. While nature does not preclude the possibility of freedom and autonomy, it is difficult to ground an objective ethics in a philosophy of nature as Kropotkin and now Murray Bookchin have attempted.[32] In the first place, such an attempt overlooks the logical fallacy of maintaining that, because something *is,* it follows that it *ought* to be. A study of aggression in geese may or may not illuminate aggression in men; it does not tell us whether aggression is good or bad. There are no moral values to be discovered or revealed in nature. Stirner is right in stressing that it is human beings that create values. We tend to read into nature what we want to find. Kropotkin's and Bookchin's strategy, like that of the Social Darwinists and their contemporary counterparts, the sociobiologists, makes this fundamental error.

Nevertheless, I would argue that it is important to keep an evolutionary perspective which recognizes that human beings have changed in the past and are likely to continue to do so in the future. It reminds us that we are one species amongst others, and that there is a difference only in degree and not in kind between us and other animals. We are a part not only of human society, but of a wider community of all living beings. We have no God-given prerogative to become managers of the cosmic process or the lords of creation.

More important still, we should develop an ecological perspective which sees humanity as an inseparable part of the living web of nature, recognizes that our survival depends on the survival of our habitat, and sees different species as intrinsically valuable members in a non-hierarchical world. The integrity of the whole and the integrity of the part are mutually dependent. This is not to say that we should appeal to mere expediency to stop humans despoiling the earth. Nor does it imply that all organisms are equal citizens in a biospheric democracy.[33]

Contrary to biocentric ethics, I would argue that all organisms are not of equal worth. They do not possess equal 'rights' which entitle them to identical treatment. Not only are rights purely human conventions, but such reasoning would put human beings and rhinos on the same level as the AIDS virus or smallpox. But while the utilitarian calculus can lead to abhorrent conclusions, and the language of rights is ambiguous and confused, I believe on the ground of the ability to feel—to suffer pain or enjoy happiness—that there should be equal consideration of different species.[34] The degree of consciousness may have a side constraint in our deliberations. While both are capable of suffering, it would be reasonable to conclude that the interests of a child are more important than the interests of a slug, since one is more conscious than the other. But even if we make this decision, we should also bear in mind the wider principles of the sanctity of life and the vitality of evolution and recognize that there is a place in the world for slugs as well as children.

While it is misleading to transpose observations about the natural world to human society, it is nevertheless salutary to be reminded of the ecological principle that the more variety there is in nature the greater the overall vitality. It offers a model of unity in diversity, difference with equality, change and equilibrium in a non-hierarchical framework. Applied to society, the principle suggests that the health of a free society might be measured by the amount of individuality it could tolerate and parasites it could support. Again, ecology presents the earth as a self-regulating and evolving system which reflects the self-regulating and evolving capacity of human beings.

We have evolved to be uniquely conscious and creative beings, and as such we have a responsibility for the world. We are rational and moral agents. We are in a position to participate in natural evolution and help realize the evolutionary trend towards greater complexity, consciousness, and individuality. We should go beyond Kropotkin, who was still committed to the nineteenth-century notion of 'industrial progress' as a 'conquest over nature', and develop Godwin's notion of stewardship of the good things of the world.[35] We should act not as conquerors but as stewards of the planet. It may be too arrogant and ambitious to try to 'free' nature itself by developing its potential, as Bookchin has suggested, but, by our intervention into the natural processes of evolution, we can certainly foster diversity, diminish suffering, and encourage latent life forms.[36] It is worth stressing that this is a moral and social problem, not to be confused with the fashionable misanthropy or vague calls for universal love which permeate sections of the Green movement.

How do we create a free society which is ecologically sound? I believe that such a desirable state of affairs is likely to be brought about gradually and peacefully. I do not agree with Godwin that a period of education and enlightenment must precede the dissolution of government, but share Kropotkin's confidence in the ability of ordinary people to shape their own lives and govern themselves. The resort to violence to transform society, however, which has been a minor but significant trend in the anarchist tradition, is inevitably self-defeating. As the major revolutions this century—the Russian, the Chinese, the Cuban—have only too vividly demonstrated, it is impossible to use authoritarian means to realize libertarian ends. The means have to be the same as the ends, or the ends themselves become distorted. The process and goal must be one. Although there is a possibility, there is no certainty that a free society will ever be achieved. If it is to be realized, then it will only be through our conscious choice and through persuasion and example.

I hope by now that I have persuaded that nasty fellow 'human nature' to step aside and to question his very existence! I have also tried to make clear that anarchism is not a puerile dream based on an unduly optimistic or simple view of what it is to be human. It not only expresses a central part of human experience but reflects the organic processes of nature itself. It offers a plausible ideal for the post-industrial age to come. I therefore see no bar within our make-up to prevent the creation of a society which will free us from psychological dependence and economic want and enable us all to develop in harmony with nature the full potential of our being.

Notes

1. For a recent version of this view, see Leszek Kolakowski's review of David Miller, *Anarchism* (London: Dent, 1984), in the *Times Literary Supplement,* January 4 1985, p. 3. Miller himself is not guilty of such an oversimplification (op. cit., p. 76).

2. William Godwin, *Enquiry Concerning Political Justice,* ed. Isaac Kramnick (Harmondsworth: Pelican, 1976; reprint of 3rd edn, 1798), book I, chapter iv.

3. *The Anarchist Writings of William Godwin,* ed. Peter Marshall (London: Freedom Press, 1986), pp. 172–3. See also my *William Godwin* (New Haven, Conn., and London: Yale University Press, 1984), pp. 112–13, 400.

4. Godwin, *Political Justice,* op. cit., p. 349.

5. *The Anarchist Writings of William Godwin,* op. cit., p. 61.

6. Godwin, *Political Justice,* op. cit., p. 83.

7. *The Anarchist Writings of William Godwin,* op. cit., p. 29.

8. Ibid., p. 51.

9. Max Stirner, *The Ego and Its Own,* trans. Steven T. Byington (London: Rebel Press, 1982; reprint of 1963 edn), pp. 39–43.

10. Ibid., p. 162.

11. Ibid., p. 291.

12. Ibid., p. 189.

13. Ibid., p. 5.

14. Ibid., p. 157.

15. Ibid., p. 169.

16. Ibid., p. 332.

17. Ibid., p. 316.

18. Ibid., p. 209.

19. Cf. John P. Clark, *Max Stirner's Egoism* (London: Freedom Press, 1976), p. 53.

20. Peter Kropotkin, *Ethics: Origin and Development,* ed. N. Lebedev (Dorchester: Prism Press, n.d.; reprint of 1924 edn), p. 338.

21. Quoted by George Woodcock, *Anarchism: A History of Libertarian Ideas and Movements* (Harmondsworth: Penguin, 1983), p. 184.

22. Kropotkin, *Mutual Aid: A Factor of Evolution* (London: Heinemann, 1919; reprint of 1902 edn), pp. 49-50.

23. Kropotkin, *Ethics,* op. cit., p. 45.

24. Ibid., p. 45.

25. Kropotkin, *The Conquest of Bread* (London: Elephant Editions, 1985; reprint of 1913 edn), p. 108.

26. Cf. Mary Midgley, *Beast and Man: The Roots of Human Nature* (London: Methuen, 1980), p. 64.

27. In an interview with Paul Barker published in *New Society,* 2 April 1981, Chomsky argued that the 'libertarian left should have a vested interest in innateness'. I would not, however, go so far as Chomsky, who believes in a well-defined biological concept of human nature which is independent of social and historical conditions. He does not hesitate to consider the faculty of language as part of human nature and maintains that in such domains 'we can begin to formulate a significant concept of "human nature", in its intellectual and cognitive aspects' (*Language and Responsibility* (New York: Pantheon Books, 1979), p. 77). Cf. Carlos P. Otero, 'Introduction to Chomsky's social theory', in Noam Chomsky, *Radical Priorities,* ed. C. P. Otero (Montréal: Black Rose Books, 1981), pp. 26-8. Where Chomsky claims that there is no inconsistency in believing that the 'essential attributes of human nature give man the opportunity to create social conditions and social forms to maximize the possibilities for freedom, diversity, and individual self-realization' (*For Reasons of State* (New York: Pantheon Books 1973), pp. 395-6). His stress on human nature as an underlying innate structure undermines a creative and open-ended view of human intelligence and action.

28. Bakunin, 'The Paris Commune and the idea of the state', in *Bakunin on Anarchy,* ed. Sam Dolgoff (London: Allen & Unwin, 1973), pp. 261-2, and cited by Noam Chomsky in the *New York Review of Books,* 21 May 1970. Chomsky compares in his note 11 Bakunin's remark on the laws of individual nature with the approach to creative thought in his own works *Cartesian Linguistics* (New York: Harper & Row, 1966) and *Language and Mind* (New York: Harcourt, 1968). In an interview with Graham Baugh, a version of which appeared in *Open Road* (Summer, 1984), Chomsky acknowledges, however, that 'one cannot simply deduce social or political consequences from any insights into language'. He adds that while one may hope to be able 'to show that structures of authority and control limit and distort intrinsic human capacities and needs, and to lay a theoretical basis for a social theory that eventuates in practical ideas as to how to overcome them', there are 'huge gaps' in any such argument.

29. Wilhelm Reich, *The Function of the Orgasm* (New York: Noonday Press, 1942), p. xix, quoted by Charles Rycroft, *Reich* (London: Fontana, 1971), p. 40.

30. Arthur Koestler, *The Ghost in the Machine* (Chicago: Regnery, 1967), p. 341. Cf. Clark, *Egoism,* op. cit., p. 98.

31. See Harold Barclay, *People without Government: An Anthropology of Anarchism* (London: Kahn & Averill with Cienfuegos Press, 1982), especially chapter 8.

32. See Kropotkin, *Mutual Aid,* op. cit.; and *Ethics,* op. cit.; Bookchin, *The Ecology of Freedom: The Emergence and Dissolution of Hierarchy* (Palo Alto, Calif.: Cheshire Books, 1982); and 'Thinking ecologically: a dialectical approach', *Our Generation,* 18, 2 (Spring/Summer 1987). While Bookchin's contribution to social ecology has been profound and stimulating, his attempt to ground an 'objective ethics' in nature not only assumes a rational pattern and order in nature but tends to undermine the moral spontaneity and creativity of human beings. Again, his view that human society is a 'second nature' derived from 'first nature' made self-conscious, and his dialectic in which 'what could be' is contained in 'what is' seems unduly deterministic and Hegelian. Finally, he argues that 'human nature' does exist, even though he suggests that it consists of 'proclivities and potentialities that become increasingly defined by the instillation of social needs' (*Ecology of Freedom,* op. cit., p. 114). Such a loose definition hardly adds up to the notion of a 'human nature' as usually defined.

33. For this view, see Bill Devall and George Sessions, *Deep Ecology* (Salt Lake City: Peregrine Smith Books, 1985), p. 67.

34. Cf. Peter Singer, *Animal Liberation: Towards an End to Man's Inhumanity to Animals* (London: Paladin, 1977), p. 22.

35. Kropotkin, *Mutual Aid,* op. cit., p. 221; *The Anarchist Writings of William Godwin,* op. cit., pp. 130, 133.

36. Bookchin, 'Thinking ecologically', op. cit., p. 36. See also his article 'Social ecology versus "deep ecology" ', *Green Perspectives,* 4-5 (Summer 1987), p. 21.

David Morland (essay date 1997)

SOURCE: "Kropotkin: Mutual Aid and Anarchy," in *De-*

manding the Impossible? Human Nature and Politics in Nineteenth-Century Social Anarchism, Cassell, 1997, pp. 125-79.

[*In the following excerpt, Morland analyzes Kropotkin's theory of anarchism.*]

Of all the classical anarchists it is perhaps Kropotkin who corresponds most closely to informed perceptions of anarchism. Martin Miller, for example, has described him 'as the world's leading anarchist theoretician.'[1] Certainly, when compared to Proudhon and Bakunin, there are fewer doubts associated with the standing or status of Kropotkin as an anarchist. Nevertheless, doubts persist and there are strong grounds for contesting the consistency of Kropotkin's anarchist ideology. Although all three social anarchists under review endorse a conception of human nature that is comprised of both sociability and egoism, the emphasis on egoism in Proudhon and Bakunin, and its associated difficulties, renders it on occasion truly problematical to conceive of either as truly anarchist. Seemingly, Kropotkin's writings constitute a watershed in the development of anarchist ideology. Upon initial inspection, Kropotkin does not seem to suffer from the problems that arise from the emphasis on egoism that permeates the works of Proudhon and Bakunin. And whereas both Proudhon and Bakunin have evinced very telling critiques against the state, Kropotkin develops a significantly more positive and constructive aspect of social and political thought. Kropotkin is unlike Bakunin in that there is no accent upon the urge to destruction nor on violence. Although Kropotkin may see violence as necessary, it is to be employed very sparingly. The significant fact is that it was, as Woodcock argues, 'the positive, constructive aspect of anarchism' that appealed to him.[2] It is here that Kropotkin begins to forge a new identity for anarchism; and the hallmark of this anarchism is the synthesis which it undergoes with communism. It is this which, purportedly, distinguishes Kropotkin from his predecessors. Distribution of goods and services according to need, rather than according to labour performed, separates Kropotkin from both Proudhon's mutualism and Bakunin's collectivism. At least, that is how it is usually seen. It is my contention that Kropotkin is closer to his predecessors, and their failings, than is traditionally thought.

KROPOTKIN'S ANARCHIST VISION

. . . What did Kropotkin's vision of a new social order entail? The first thing worth noting is that Kropotkin's anarchist future is closely associated to his conception of human nature. In common with his predecessors, Kropotkin builds the possibility of anarchism on a specific conception of human nature. Like all ideologies, anarchism carries an outline of how it would like to see society develop—whether it cares to admit this or not. In Kropotkin's works this vision is presented in two distinct stages. The first conveys his thinking as to why it is necessary to discuss such images in the first instance. Once this is concluded, Kropotkin embarks on the second step of the pro-

cess, revealing the details of that vision. This section of the chapter is concerned to adumbrate the arguments presented by Kropotkin as he proceeds to develop his vision of an anarchist future, whilst the following section examines his specific vision in greater detail.

To begin with Kropotkin was not only convinced that anarchism would be the next stage in the evolutionary process, he was also persuaded that contemplations of future society are an integral part of the revolutionary process itself. He writes in Emile Pouget's and Emile Pataud's *Syndicalism and the Co-operative Commonwealth* (1913):

> It is often said that plans ought not to be drawn up for a future society. . . . On the other hand, it is necessary to have a clear idea of the actual concrete results that our communist, collectivist or other aspirations might have on society. For this purpose we must picture to ourselves these various institutions at work. Where do we want to get to by means of the Revolution? We need to know this. There must, therefore, be books which will enable the mass of the people to form for themselves a more or less exact idea of what it is they desire to see realised in a new future.[3]

Given the requirements of ideological argument, Kropotkin is obliged to portray a vision of how society ought to be, regardless of the detail elaborated. Kropotkin appears to be cognizant of this prerequisite himself. Writing in his *Modern Science and Anarchism,* he proclaims that no revolutionary

> struggle can be successful if it is unconscious, if it has no definite and concrete aim. No destruction of existing things is possible if men have not already settled for themselves, during the struggles leading to the destruction, and during the period of destruction itself, what is going to take the place of that which is destroyed. Even a theoretical criticism of what exists is not possible without one picturing to oneself a more or less exact image of that which he desires to see in its place. Consciously or unconsciously, the *ideal,* the conception of something better, always grows in the mind of whoever criticises existing institutions.[4]

An image of a better society is an inherent part of any ideology. Ideologies are proprietary bodies of thought that each contain a vision of a better future that derives from a critique of contemporary society. They are both descriptive and prescriptive. Both present and future tenses exist in parallel in ideological argument.

Almost inevitably then, Kropotkin engages in a form of speculative sociology, constructing a vista of anarchy that encourages the development of the revolutionary process itself. The question that has to be resolved is to what extent does Kropotkin's examination of the possible uncover the fine detail of the future? Some, such as Woodcock, argue that Kropotkin offers little more than a general framework for overcoming the problems of contemporary society.[5] Others, such as Miller, contend that 'Kropotkin was not afraid to be specific about the kind of society he would like to see after a revolution.'[6] I side with the latter interpretation. There are three texts in particular which support it: Kropotkin's first major essay in politics, *Must We Oc-*

cupy Ourselves with an Examination of the Ideal of a Future System? (1873); *Fields, Factories and Workshops* (1899); and *The Conquest of Bread* (1892). From the outset of his first political tract, Kropotkin is keen to answer the question of his essay title in the affirmative. He believes that one should think about the ideal of a future system; for if one is afraid to contemplate that ideal it is most unlikely that it will be established in practice. Nevertheless, he does not consider himself to be furnishing a detailed scheme that will correspond to the society of the future; rather he is simply producing 'an outline of this future system in the most general terms.'[7] He considers himself unable to do more than this for epistemological reasons. In an argument that shares more with Herbert Read than Malatesta, Kropotkin asserts that 'there does not even exist now that mind which comprehends all the future moral ideas of mankind. Consequently, any contemporary idea will be a manifestation of present-day conceptions of morality, a manifestation which will be impossible, because before it is realised, in its totality, new conceptions of justice will be created and *begin to be realised.*'[8]

To my mind Kropotkin underplays the specificity of his argument here, for the text reflects a concentration on detail that is possibly only surpassed in *The Conquest of Bread* and *Fields, Factories and Workshops*. In many respects Kropotkin's wider ideological concerns are prefaced in his 1873 essay. It is not long, for example, before Kropotkin warns his audience that assigning functions and power to a government or state will lead nowhere. No matter how responsive and dynamic that body proves to be, the danger is that 'the group of individuals to whom society cedes its rights would always be the power, separate from society, trying to broaden its influence, its interference in the business of each separate individual. And the wider the circle of activity of this government, the greater the danger of enslavement of society, the greater the likelihood that the government would stop being the expression of the interests and desires of the majority.'[9] The consistency of such statements with his conception of human nature is plainly visible. Moreover, these dangers cannot be prevented by way of checks and balances. Liberalism holds little attraction for Kropotkin. The state cannot be rendered acceptable by tinkering and fine tuning; it has to be abolished. Radical action is a prerequisite for remedying social injustices because the inconveniences of the state 'lie in the most basic conception of the institution, in its very essence, and so cannot be eliminated by any measures such as limitations, control, and so on as long as the very essence of the institution continues to exist.'[10]

One of the first measures to be taken in reaching the objective of an anarchist society is the expropriation of capital. This is designed to promote equality in rights to work. Additionally, expropriation occurs within a federal framework, which was favoured by Kropotkin as a means of organizing society. Kropotkin is seemingly under the influence of Proudhon here, especially as he goes on to say that products will be exchanged between artels on the ba-

sis of labour receipts.[11] But Kropotkin suffers from the same types of problems that beset the earlier anarchist. For instance, there is no mention here of who or what is to attempt to broker an agreement concerning 'necessary measures.' This is a little surprising in light of Kropotkin's own admission that there are likely to be problems of exchange in that society. Anticipating the possible causes of such disputes, Kropotkin reasons that the farmers of one commune might value their ten hours of labour at ten measures of wheat, whereas the farmers of another commune believe that their ten hours of work is equal to eleven measures of wheat. Obviously, other communes would prefer to exchange their products with the first set of farmers, and this in itself will probably lead to problems and 'even quarrels.'[12]

One possible solution ventured by Kropotkin is that of the committee, which is responsible for issuing labour notes. Committees are an important tool in Kropotkin's assessment of how to realize the goals elaborated in this document. They are involved in many organizational tasks, including the division of land, the allocation of housing and the economy. Their economic remit is quite broad, covering the appraisal of cargo transportation and the responsibility for purchasing provisions at the market.[13] Apparently, economic or trade disputes would be settled by committees, comprised of elected representatives. As with Proudhon, the resolution of difficulties is accomplished by means of majoritarianism. The writing was on the wall, so to speak, when Kropotkin referred to 'the interests and desires of the majority' when considering how government constantly strives to extend the tentacles of its power and influence.[14] And when situated within the context of the committee Kropotkin's apparent solution sounds increasingly like the foundations for authoritarian centralism, operating through a planned economy, rather than the free production he talks of in other places. Suspicions of the imposition of a majoritarian culture are corroborated upon recognition that the condition of equality in labour dictates 'that everyone should be compelled to earn his livelihood through his own labour.'[15] A better, or perhaps this should be worse, example of Kropotkin's indebtedness to Bakunin could not be found. If individuals wish to live in and partake of the benefits offered by life in community then they have to labour. Although free to choose an occupation, everyone must comply with the assignment received from the artel. Whilst individuals may wish to prosecute their own private ends, they are free to do so only after they perform what is deemed to be socially useful as decreed by the majority of society.[16] In the tradition of Bakuninian collectivism, Kropotkin constructs a labour proviso that is at odds with the declared aims of a free society.

Perhaps this residue of collectivism is necessary to counteract the free-rider problem, a not infrequent objection levelled at utopias. Consider, Kropotkin asks, a person who does no work and is compelled to steal in order to live. Once apprehended 'an autonomous communal court will deal with him—by itself or through elected representatives.' There is no need of government, for 'in all its own internal affairs the *obshchina* [a Russian peasant commune], just as now, is and will be able to be in command without creating a government.'[17] If, Kropotkin continues, one commune were to seize the land of another commune on which to feed its own cattle then there are mechanisms for settling the dispute. Both communes are likely to belong to the same agricultural union or federation; hence it is obvious to Kropotkin 'that the *offended obshchina* has to appeal with the complaint to its own union of agricultural *obshchiny*.'[18] The elected representatives of the *obshchiny* would resolve the altercation. Once again the spirit of Proudhon radiates through Kropotkin's vision of future society, and just as equally through his rather vague description of the remit of the representatives. Reticence compels a conclusion in favour of majority voting, a judgment not out of line with the remainder of the work. The question that has to be asked now, is whether such a judgment casts a mould into which his later political writings were confined? On the specific subject of majoritarianism an unequivocal answer cannot be tendered. David Miller, for instance, accepts that Kropotkin depends on majority decisions to determine socially useful work, but remarks that 'this is not mentioned later, and one must take it that he is relying on a universal consensus.'[19] But why assume that? There is no hard evidence, to my mind, that can be cited in favour of that conclusion, and what intimations Kropotkin does make in later works suggest the opposite. The problem is real and relevant. For whilst it might present itself as little more than speculative semantics, anarchists, as Woodcock and Avakumovic hold, do not accept majority decisions.[20]

There are potentially more serious objections to be levelled at Kropotkin's work, one of which emanates from the adoption of committees into his revolutionary society. Seen as part of his whole ideology, the introduction of committees would constitute a major difficulty for Kropotkin, creating a fundamental inconsistency between his conception of human nature and his programme of revolutionary action. The committee cannot be regarded in any way as a solution to the problems of social organization, it can act only as an irritant. In this respect, the position Kropotkin held in 1873 was abandoned in his later works, notably *The Conquest of Bread,* in which his conception of human nature served as a warning that committees and other organs of officialism breed egoism in individuals.[21] Evolution of Kropotkin's economic argument resulted in the development of his theory of anarchist-communism, a brand of anarchist theory distinct from both Proudhon and Bakunin. The employment of labour notes in his 1873 essay bears a striking resemblance to Proudhon's economic theory. But in formulating a mechanism of distribution according to deed rather than need Kropotkin placed himself quite squarely in the collectivist camp of Bakunin. This was to change, or so it is told, as Kropotkin worked out a new basis for the economic organization of anarchist society.

Cahm, for example, relates how Kropotkin began to explore anarchist theory in depth in the late 1870s. The re-

examination, she holds, was stimulated principally by Elisée Reclus and Paul Brousse in a debate at the Congress of the Jura Federation at Fribourg in 1878, during which Brousse edged toward communism as opposed to collectivism.[22] By 1879 Kropotkin appears to have been partially persuaded. At the Congress of the Jura Federation at La Chaux-de-Fonds in 1879 Kropotkin made a speech entitled *The Anarchist Idea from the Viewpoint of Its Practical Realisation.* In it he seemingly adopted a compromise position, adhering to a collectivist standpoint on property, but expressing that anarchist-communism was to be the final aim of the revolution.[23] By the time of the 1880 congress, held in the same location, Kropotkin had jettisoned collectivism in favour of communism. In a speech given at the congress and published in *Le Révolté* on 17 October 1880, Kropotkin remarks how the collectivist stance on property can be nothing more than a transitory stage in the revolution rather than the pinnacle of the revolution itself. This shift in position was to be the launching-pad from which Kropotkin was to expand his theory of anarchist-communism that was expressed fully in *The Conquest of Bread.*

The principal objection against collectivism is that it inferred the existence of collective property, which as a result might give rise to the prospect of competition. 'Collectivists,' argues Kropotkin, 'begin by proclaiming a revolutionary principle—the abolition of private property—and then they deny it, no sooner than proclaimed, by upholding an organisation of production and consumption which originated in private property.'[24] Fundamentally, this criticism contained two separate but related points: the remuneration of labour and distribution according to work done rather than need. Neither Proudhon nor Bakunin foresaw the problems associated with collectivism, whereas Kropotkin purports to surmount both of these obstacles. The introduction of labour cheques will, for Kropotkin, result in the peasants withholding their produce. 'We must offer to the peasant in exchange for his toil not worthless paper-money, but the manufactured articles of which he stands in immediate need.'[25] An integral part of the problem is that the labour theory of value subscribed to by the collectivists glosses over a number of potential pitfalls. Principal among these are three areas of obvious concern to any anarchist society. First, it is exceedingly difficult to rationalize individual contributions in what is effectively a collective enterprise. Thus Kropotkin attacks Proudhon for asserting that the value and quantity of work necessary to produce an object are proportional. Rejecting the labour theory of value, Kropotkin denies that the exchange value of commodities necessarily corresponds to the labour required to produce them.[26] Secondly, maintenance of the wages system and differential rewards corresponding to different types of work will inevitably create social stratification. Thirdly, social division will furnish the kind of environment in which egoism thrives.[27]

All three objections listed here reside under the broader umbrella of Kropotkin's belief that society's wealth is a common inheritance. 'There is not even a thought, or an invention,' Kropotkin states, 'which is not common property, born of the past and the present.'[28] All inventions of mind and labour depend on the discoveries of the past and the assistance of others in the present. Accordingly, it is unjust of anyone to appropriate part of the whole and claim it for themselves. Thus, 'the means of production being the collective work of humanity, the product should be the collective property of the race. Individual appropriation is neither just nor serviceable. All belongs to all. All things are for all men, since all men have need of them, since all men have worked in the measure of their strength to produce them, and since it is not possible to evaluate every one's part in the production of the world's wealth.'[29] In recognition of the interdependency of industry and manufacturing one should, Kropotkin claims, abandon the collectivist position 'that payment proportionate to the hours of labour rendered by each would be an ideal arrangement, or even a step in the right direction.' As far as Kropotkin is concerned, 'the Collectivist ideal appears to us untenable in a society which considers the instruments of labour as a common inheritance.'[30] The formula for the distribution of social goods has undoubtedly been altered to that which is commensurate with human need rather than deed. Or has it? One would expect that it had, but a closer examination of the texts reveals that Kropotkin may have retained a remnant of collectivism in his theory of anarchist-communism that was present in his 1873 essay. That residue is the labour proviso.

If Kropotkin had entirely discarded any notion of compulsory labour, then he would have stood apart from both Proudhon and Bakunin. Initially, one is led to believe that the transformation of the collectivist formula is complete. Kropotkin himself attempts to buttress the revision by declaring without hesitation that an anarchist-communist society is 'a society that recognises the absolute liberty of the individual, that does not admit of any authority, and makes use of no compulsion to drive men to work.'[31] If by this Kropotkin means that people will not be compelled to engage in wage-labour then there is really nothing to worry about. But this does not seem to be Kropotkin's meaning. Whilst he makes clear, in both *The Conquest for Bread* and *The Place of Anarchism in Socialistic Evolution,* that anarchist-communism entails the free consumption of goods, so long as they are abundant, because everyone has the right to live, access to these goods is conditional upon performing socially useful labour.[32] In the very same two texts Kropotkin transgresses the essential barrier between his putative anarchist-communism and the collectivism of previous writers. 'All is for all!' he declares in the chapter entitled 'Our Riches' in *The Conquest of Bread,* immediately before delivering a collectivist left hook. 'If the man and woman bear their fair share of work, they have a right to their fair share of all that is produced by all, and that share is enough to secure them well-being.'[33] And in 'Expropriation', in the same text, Kropotkin confirms that the resident of an anarchist society 'knows that after a few hours of productive toil he will have a right to all the pleasures that civilisation procures.'[34] *The Place of Anarchism in Socialistic Evolution* contains an identical message. 'All

belongs to everyone! And provided each man and woman contributes his and her fair share of labour for the production of necessary objects, they have a right to share in all that is produced by everybody.'[35]

These are not documents only relevant to the contemporary Russian populist struggle, as might be said about Kropotkin's first political essay of 1873. *The Conquest of Bread* was first published in 1892, although it originated as a series of articles that first appeared in 1886 when Kropotkin was at the apogee of his revolutionary journalism. And *The Place of Anarchism in Socialistic Evolution,* first published in 1886, was originally delivered as a lecture in Paris on 28 February 1886, shortly after Kropotkin's release from Clairvaux prison.[36] The gap between these works and Kropotkin's original essay is at the very least thirteen years, but arguably more, given the publication date of *The Conquest of Bread.* Sufficient time, one would think, to allow for the expression of an evolution of thought, and a clear three or four years since Kropotkin last defended the vestiges of his collectivism at the Jura Federation congresses in the early 1880s.

Any difference that existed between Kropotkin and the collectivists was quashed by the restatement of the fundamental collectivist demand, that the enjoyment of social privileges requires work. Kropotkin may not be requesting remuneration proportionate to labour, as the collectivists enjoin under a wages system, but it is undoubtedly remuneration of social privileges for the contribution of labour. The charge of collectivism is given further credence by Kropotkin's treatment of the land question. The subject was of immense significance to the Russian populists, simply because of the demographic imbalance between peasants and proletarians in favour of the former. In light of that, Kropotkin drew up a series of measures to be implemented after the revolution in Russia. The following steps he thought it imperative to undertake:

> The land should be declared the property of all, of the whole Russian people.
>
> Every village and countryside settlement should receive the use of those lands which they now control.
>
> All the lands taken by the whole countryside or by separate peasants of the village or countryside should become the possession of this village or countryside.
>
> All the landowner's lands which are lying fallow should become the possession of the former peasants of this landowner.
>
> All the lands bought by separate peasants for themselves should become the possession of the whole community of the village where such peasants are registered.[37]

It seems that whilst the land is to be the common property of all it is to be held in collective possession of local villages or communes. In essence this is a position not too far removed from Proudhon, and one that Kropotkin generally adheres to in his later writings. In *Modern Science and Anarchism,* Kropotkin again talks of the people regaining 'possession of the land and of all that is required for producing all sorts of necessaries of life' in a future society.[38] Elaboration of detail is rather thin in the aforesaid text, in what amounts to a rather vague antecedent of a more concrete argument in *Words of a Rebel*. To be sure, Kropotkin's standpoint is not unambiguous. In the essay 'Expropriation,' for example, Kropotkin consolidates the position he initially took up in his first political essay of 1873, referring to the 'collective possession' of the land. A few pages later he enunciates that whilst the individual holding of the land would remain, the social revolution 'would expropriate all land that was not cultivated by the hands of those who at present possess the land.' Seemingly, there would exist a 'communist cultivation' alongside peasant proprietors.[39]

The above reflects a similar argument advanced in a previous essay, 'Representative Government,' but contrasts somewhat with what Kropotkin has to say in 'The Paris Commune.'[40] Here Kropotkin appears to return to the argument of Proudhon. The people, he argues, will take possession 'of the whole of social wealth', whilst simultaneously establishing 'their rights of usufruct immediately.'[41] Bafflement arises because of the nature of the usufructuary relationship to the land. As Proudhon makes clear, rights of usufruct establish only rights of use and possession, not of proprietorship. Kropotkin, then, conflates notions of possession with ideas of proprietorship. Hence it is not entirely clear what he intends to happen to the land. Individual ownership by peasants stands firmly at odds with the idea of collective possession and use. Either one assumes that Kropotkin has retreated from his earlier outlook and permits the existence of individual ownership, or that peasants retain individual possession of their holdings whilst becoming subject to collective ownership by the village or commune. The only other alternative available is that individual proprietors enjoy the privilege of proprietorship on condition that they pool their resources and produce under the aegis of the free organization, production and consumption that is the hallmark of anarchist-communism. Either way, individual ownership seems a peculiar concession to grant. Not only does it undermine the process and standing of common or collective ownership, it is also bound to lead, like differential rewards for workers, to the recrudescence of egoism.

THE POLITICS OF ANARCHY

It is at this juncture that an investigation of the finer details of Kropotkin's conception of anarchy is called for. It is important to do this for two reasons. First, it allows an assessment of the extent to which his vision of anarchist society corresponds to his conception of human nature. And, secondly, it will provide a basis from which to analyse the consistency of Kropotkin's anarchist ideology. Much of Kropotkin's earlier and some of his later writings bear witness to the vacillating influence of both Proudhon and Bakunin. However, it is Rousseau who seems closest to equipping Kropotkin with a foundation for his conception of anarchist society. Before illustrating the margins of Rousseau's influence, it is worth noting that Kropotkin ac-

cepts the Marxist idea that the political regime 'is always an expression of the *economic* regime which exists at the heart of society.'[42] Absorption of this mode of analysis has obvious consequences for Kropotkin's own theories; for if his own economic arguments exude mechanisms of compulsion or coercion then that might well be reflected in the political territory of his anarchist ideology. As means influence ends so the economic base of Kropotkin's ideology will influence his anarchist politics.

To determine whether that is true it is first necessary to sketch out the details of the society Kropotkin upholds as his ideal. That society is reached through a revolution, and the task of the revolution, as Kropotkin sees it, is to establish an environment in which everyone 'may live by working freely, without being forced to sell his work and his liberty to others who accumulate wealth by the labour of their serfs.'[43] Communism, then, embodies 'the conquest of perfect liberty by the individual, by free agreement, association, and absolute free federation.'[44] Put differently, anarchist-communism is built upon a commitment to abolish authority. At times Kropotkin approaches this subject rather blithely, insisting on one occasion that anarchism 'works to destroy authority in all its aspects.'[45] At other times Kropotkin's attitude is more conservative. Thus in *Modern Science and Anarchism* authority is only partially rejected. Here it is only centralized authority that Kropotkin objects to, not authority *per so*.[46]

Authority bears a moral capacity, in that authority is a reflection of accepted moral norms within anarchy, that is fundamental in most of what Kropotkin says about revolutionary society. Kropotkin outlines how anarchism is impregnated with moral feeling in his *Anarchist Morality*. In 'proclaiming ourselves anarchists we proclaim beforehand that we disavow any way of treating others in which we should not like them to treat us; that we will no longer tolerate the inequality that has allowed some among us to use their strength, their cunning or their ability after a fashion in which it would annoy us to have such qualities used against ourselves. Equality in all things, the synonym of equity, this is anarchism in very deed.'[47] Morality plays a multi-faceted role in Kropotkin's anarchism. First, it underpins the prescriptive element of his ideology. By fabricating an argument that links morality to human nature, Kropotkin establishes the necessity of revolution if individuals are to enjoy freedom. Morals improve or decline as the social environment improves or declines. The resurgence of mutual aid, for Kropotkin, will lead to a betterment of human morality. Severing the sinews of authority, by ushering in a social revolution, engenders a climate in which mutual aid and sociability can flourish. Because morality is essential to the well-being of society and to freedom, anarchist society enshrines certain moral rules. Absence of moral rules and obligations would, for Kropotkin, render the functioning of society impossible.[48] Morality, then, fulfils an important role in prescribing how individuals ought to behave toward one another, as well as providing a basis for the more formal agreements that individuals might enter into. Kropotkin's vision of anarchy, as expounded in *Modern Science and Anarchism,* embraces 'a society in which all the mutual relations of its members are regulated, not by laws, not by authorities, whether self-imposed or elected, but by mutual agreements between the members of that society, and by a sum of social customs and habits.'[49] No actions are to be imposed upon individuals as in bourgeois society. Individuals are free to enter into contracts that are fair and self-imposed.

Outside personal agreements and contracts, the freedom of the commune is best maintained through a federal structure. Local communities and villages need to marry themselves together under a federation in order to sustain relations with their neighbouring urban centres and organize themselves around these centres. The partnership between urban and rural is not balanced in favour of the former. As Kropotkin notes in his essay 'The Commune,' the

> centre will not be able to establish an intrusive preponderance of its own over the communes in its environment. Thanks to the infinite variety of the needs of industry and commerce, all inhabited places have already several centres [to] which they are attached, and as their needs develop, they will enter into relations with further places that can satisfy new needs. Our needs are in fact so various, and they emerge with such rapidity, that soon a single federation will not be sufficient to satisfy them all. The Commune will then feel the need to contract other alliances, to enter into other federations.[50]

Relations between and within communes are consistent and commensurate with the principle of federalism. For if, as Kropotkin ponders in 'The Paris Commune,' 'we concede to the free initiative of the communes the task of coming to an understanding between themselves on enterprises that concern several cities at once, how can we refuse this same initiative to the groups of which a Commune is composed? A government within the Commune has no more right to exist than a government over the Commune.'[51]

After countenancing the desirability of revolution and having served as the framework for personal and collective behaviour and action, it would be surprising if morality did not permeate Kropotkin's critique of contemporary society. In this third role of morality in Kropotkin's anarchism, the influence of Rousseau is visibly obvious. This is not to say that Kropotkin considers Rousseau to have been an anarchist; it is simply to suggest that Kropotkin shares some of the concerns of Rousseau and seems to invoke the spirit of Rousseau when formulating his vision of anarchy. Rousseau's *First Discourse,* for example, underscores Kropotkin's critique of the excesses of greed and luxury in his *An Appeal to the Young* (1885).[52] But the resemblance to Rousseau does not end there. In attempting to mitigate the passions resident in humankind, Kropotkin insists, like Rousseau, that anarchists 'take men as they are.'[53] And in an analogy of Rousseau's fusion of liberty and law in the general will, Kropotkin proceeds to argue that society should be arranged 'so that each man may see his interest bound up with the interests of the others';[54]

only then will evil passions be subjugated. Like Rousseau, Kropotkin wants to create a community of self-governing individuals whose morality is fully developed and given practical expression in mutual agreements and free contracts. To Kropotkin's mind anarchism represents 'the ideal of a society where each governs himself according to his own will (which is evidently a result of the social influences borne by each).'[55] Human morality, as expressed through mutual aid and sociability, manifests itself in its most developed form in anarchist-communism. Anarchism's strength is that it understands human nature. Hence anarchist-communism, as explained by Kropotkin in *Anarchism: Its Philosophy and Ideal,* transpires to be 'the best basis for individual development and freedom . . . that which represents the full expansion of man's faculties, the superior development of what is original in him, the greatest fruitfulness of intelligence, feeling and will,'[56] Anarchy is not a utopian ideology. Rather it is the tendency of modern social development and the realization of human nature.[57]

AN ASSESSMENT OF KROPOTKIN'S ANARCHISM

Without doubt Kropotkin is a compassionate and persuasive writer, who is often held to be both systematic and clear. That may be a rather charitable assessment, but it should be said that in comparison to Proudhon and Bakunin, Kropotkin stands proud as a paragon of clarity and coherence. He was, moreover, fully cognizant of the charge that anarchists are little more than romantic dreamers, a charge levelled recently by George Woodcock among others.[58] Kropotkin responded to the criticism that anarchists are romantic dreamers by exhibiting a measure of realism that not only contradicts Woodcock's concomitant allegation that the anarchist was the proprietor of an especially benign account of human nature, but is seldom found in other anarchist writings.[59] Thus Kropotkin's reflection that people 'will not turn into anarchists by a sudden transformation; yet we know that on the one hand the insanity of governments, their ambitions, their bankruptcies, and on the other hand the incessant propaganda of ideas will result in great disturbances of equilibrium. At such a time we must act.'[60] Even amidst his realism, then, Kropotkin exercises a cautious optimism that the revolutionary opportunity will present itself.

But on what grounds does he base his optimism? Why will people revolt? And why, as David Miller has questioned, should we accept that it is anarchism that will evolve out of capitalism rather than some other form of social organization?[61] According to Miller there are two possible answers within Kropotkin's writings. The first is that Kropotkin has a theory of moral progress; and the second, that he has also a theory of technological progress. For Miller, Kropotkin's moral ideas flow from human characteristics, like sympathy, that are 'unchanging' but become refined with the passage of history. And as 'anarchist principles are the fullest development of these moral ideas, anarchy is the final outcome of history.'[62] Likewise, technological progress has steadily created a situation in which individuals are increasingly dependent upon one another, rendering obsolete the view that individuals can succeed on their own. Anarchist-communism is the society best suited to enhance these technological developments.

Ultimately, Miller's responses have to be discarded. Before doing so, however, a few comments should be made. The first thing of note is that what Miller says here about Kropotkin's supposed theory of moral progress elicits a tension with what he says later about egoism. At one point Miller argues that Kropotkin regarded egotism as a perversion of capitalist society to be corrected by altruism in the long run.[63] The problem, for Miller, is that such a view invokes the contextualist account of human nature inherent in Kropotkin's writings. As such, human nature may respond to the environment in which it is situated, for humans are adaptable, but in itself human nature is incapable of determining the course of historical events. There is no assumption of an 'unchanging' human nature in Kropotkin's conception of human nature. Nor does he afford a notion of human nature that is capable of self-improvement. Human nature may recover from a prolonged bout of egoism, but the context within which human nature finds itself is integral to the process of convalescence. Altruism and sociability may resume their predominance at the expense of egoism, but human nature cannot accomplish this through some mystical self-ameliorating dynamic. If altruism and mutual aid are to be the benchmarks of future society that can only come about by way of a conscious, deliberate effort on the part of the people themselves to change history. The progression of human morality and human history is a matter of human will, ably assisted by education.

Miller's identification of a theory of technological progress is more defensible, but again encounters the difficulty discharged by the argument of non-determinism. Kropotkin's enthusiastic predictions of imminent revolution were, as noted above, inspired partly by the revolutionary climate and partly, as Miller has indicated, by a favourable assessment of technological progress. Whether this was displayed in agriculture or science matters little; what is important is that Kropotkin, as Marshall observes, shared in the nineteenth century's positivistic faith in science to bring about progress.[64] In that sense, Miller's notion of a theory of technological progress rings true. Kropotkin did place great stock in the idea that the evidence of history illustrated the coming of anarchism. The vehicle of this progress, though, is not so much the technological advancement that Kropotkin sees around him, but the tendencies present in historical development. Improvements in science and agriculture, and an optimism animated by the potential ability to change through education, amount to little more than fuel in the tank of the vehicle of history in which anarchy is a passenger. Kropotkin's objective, as Marshall informs us, was 'to demonstrate that anarchism represents existing tendencies in society towards political liberty and economic equality.' Furthermore, he endeavoured to show that 'the conclusions of anarchism could be scientifically verified.'[65]

None of the above, however, detracts from the fundamental difficulty that envelops Kropotkin's ideological narrative. In denying that anarchism is nothing but a utopian dream Kropotkin is forced to rely on an argument that placed anarchy as the outcome of existing social and historical tendencies. The state, he believed, had reached its apogee; its future progress was downhill towards disintegration. The social revolution loomed large on the horizon. History was not acting alone, however. Human nature was supporting its progress in the direction of a brighter future. But none of this can be guaranteed. History is not amenable to scientific laws of inevitability, it is a matter of human will. Thus, if Kropotkin's analysis is wrong (and history to date vindicates such a judgment), if it is simply an expression of faith rather than fact, then perhaps Kropotkin's anarchism should be considered utopian rather than scientific.

To complement his conception of human nature, as encapsulated in the concept of mutual aid, Kropotkin enunciates a vision of the good life characterized by voluntary agreements and free access, so long as one labours, to the produce of society. His brand of federal politics and free communism, set out in *The Conquest of Bread,* is consistent with his conception of human nature as expounded in his work *Mutual Aid.* The relationship between his conception of human nature and the philosophical basis of his conception of history is somewhat less satisfactory. The twin pillars of his conception of human nature, sociability and egoism, are mirrored in the dominating trends that he identifies in history: liberty and authority. But when viewed in conjunction with his philosophy of history, the contextualist element of his notion of human nature precludes any guarantee that history will evolve in a given direction. As there is no certainty that a social revolution will occur, so there is no certainty that the forces of liberty will triumph over the forces of authority. The contextualist dimension of his conception of human nature is a hurdle that history cannot cross without the assistance of human will. Capitalism, 'that bane of present society' is a 'stumbling-block in the path of intellectual and moral progress.'[66] History cannot be conceived as a unilinear development for the better, for Kropotkin.[67] Neither human morality nor human nature are bound to develop in a given direction. Which way they travel is a matter of human will. If history were perceived to be on a unilinear path of progression, then Kropotkin would have tremendous difficulty in explaining the rise of the modern state. It is because of the collapse of the medieval guilds, because history may proceed in a retrograde manner, that egoism vanquished sociability and the capitalist state secured its predominance at the expense of the medieval city-state. Kropotkin is no Hegelian idealist, but there is an admixture of ideas and material circumstances that combine to explain his philosophy of history. But, given the lack of historical determinism in Kropotkin, it is surprising that one does not discover a heavier emphasis on the role of the revolutionary in disseminating ideas. Undoubtedly, Kropotkin did support such activity, but his vocal backing of such measures is rather quiet at times. It would seem as if Kropotkin is actually caught in two minds about this, a reflection perhaps of his dualistic approach to the driving forces of history.

Traditionally, those who have relied on human will as the initiator of social revolutions, such as Bakunin, have placed great stock in the necessity of revolutionary groups and organizations in the promotion of a revolutionary consciousness. Hence the importance, to Bakunin, of secret societies and the International Brotherhood. One may argue that such thinkers have to emphasize the importance of revolutionary groups and organizations because they do not rest easy in the arms of historical destiny. Kropotkin is in a similar position. His philosophy of history disqualifies the leisurely inevitability of historical determinism. Yet he offers only qualified support for revolutionary minorities and revolutionary actions like 'propaganda by the deed.' It is not that he deliberately underestimates the prominence of ideas in the making of revolutions; the acquisition of a revolutionary consciousness in the masses reflects the fact that, for Kropotkin, a social revolution is a revolution in the minds of men as much as anything else. Rather it is that his conception of human nature warns him against investing too much authority in such organizations. Just as the perpetuity of egoism dictates caution in trusting individuals with power, so the contextualist dimension of his conception of human nature reinforces the necessity of prudence. The everlastingness of egoism, combined with a milieu that might unleash that capacity for self-assertion, shepherds Kropotkin away from the dangers of revolutionary minorities and their organizations as much as it forewarns him of the potential pitfalls of the dictatorship of the proletariat. Both the permanent and contextualist components of his understanding of human nature counsel against unqualified support for such institutions. Consequently, Kropotkin hovers in a state of limbo. Precluded from the comforts of historical determinism by his philosophy of history, his assumptions concerning human nature prevent him from bestowing too much optimism in revolutionary organizations and activity. Even if a successful revolution were to materialize, Kropotkin's problems do not disappear. To be sure, the new environment would favour the development of human morality and the consolidation of mutual aid. However, together with the contextualist conception of human nature there stands that which is permanent or given. Egoism and self-assertion survive in anarchy as sociability and mutual aid endures in capitalism. Neither can be truly eradicated. Just as Kropotkin has to assume a will to revolution so he infers a will to power. It is because of this that the dangers of the Marxist 'dictatorship of the proletariat' are of constant concern to the anarchist.

In light of the fact that altruism or mutual aid is the glue that holds Kropotkin's anarchist society together, one has to ask whether it is up to the job? On its own it is patently not capable of this task. Support is required by way of social rules and moral coercion. Acknowledging that conflict will arise both within and between communes, because of the presence of egoism, Kropotkin was forced to concede that measures of social disapproval, ostracism and public opinion would have to be employed to curtail anti-social behaviour.[68] And that in itself raises the spectre of authoritarianism. As Marshall remarks, 'Kropotkin thinks that it is right for public opinion to oblige all people to do manual work and he believes it justifiable to use force against inveterate monopolisers. There are authoritarian elements here which cannot be dismissed.'[69] The evidence is not hard to find. In discussing the problems of free riders in *The Conquest of Bread,* Kropotkin suggests that besides ostracism other workers could threaten to withdraw contracts, and if the recipient of these threats finds this to his dislike then he may leave. 'This is,' writes Kropotkin, 'what would be done in a communal society in order to turn away sluggards if they become too numerous.'[70] Evidently, as the collectivist prerequisite of labour entails compulsion so too do the excesses of egoism and self-assertion. Increasingly, the distinction between Kropotkin's two competing historical trends is beginning to look a bit thin.

Of course it could be asked why any form of compulsion or coercion is necessary in the first place? Is it not that Kropotkin has latently acknowledged that his concept of mutual aid may not be as strong as he paints it? This at any rate is the line of reasoning prosecuted by Avrich. In his *Anarchist Portraits,* Avrich accepts that Kropotkin's theory of mutual aid was 'a valuable corrective' to the arguments of the neo-Malthusians and social Darwinists. 'But,' he continues, 'Kropotkin erred in the opposite direction. He took insufficient account of the naked violence that dominates the life of most animals, from insects and fish to reptiles and mammals. He underestimated the widespread brutality in nature, the persecution of the weak by the strong, among humans as well as among animals.'[71] Although Avrich may have a point, it seems that his argument would be fairer if construed in a slightly different manner. It is not correct to say that Kropotkin underestimated the extent of the evolutionary struggle, nor that 'he underrated the urge to power in many and the willingness of the mass of people to follow charismatic leaders.' Rather it is that the concept of the struggle was considered less relevant in the formulation of his ideological narrative. This is not to say that Kropotkin completely disaccommodates the notions of struggle and egoism. Indeed, a refusal to recognize the importance of these concepts would have left his ideological programme of action open to the gate-crashing tendencies of the revolutionary avant-garde party and the centralized communist state. It is simply that mutual aid and sociability were given preference over egoism and self-assertion, for mutual aid and sociability are the bedrock of his anarchist society.

To understand why compulsion and coercion are a necessary feature of Kropotkin's anarchist society, a more subtle analysis of his concept of mutual aid is called for. As part of an ideological armoury employed by Kropotkin to defend his vision of how things are now and how they could be in the future, mutual aid, as representative of his conception of human nature, does a reasonably good job. But it may not do all that Kropotkin would like it to do. For instance, citing mutual aid as a relevant factor in the struggle for existence between a species and its environment does much to justify the weight that Kropotkin attaches to the concept. However, that does not preclude a rival interpretation in which egoism or self-assertion is the chief motivating factor in the existence of struggle within a species. Essentially, Kropotkin's mutual-aid thesis is a concerted defence against the neo-Hobbesian view of competitive egoism. And that really is about the limit of its explanatory powers. As Cahm has noted, Kropotkin knew that his theory of mutual aid, considered as only one factor in the process of evolution, could not in itself account for the development of evolution.[72] Moreover, as David Miller has remarked, the evidence that Kropotkin cites in support of it 'does nothing to prove that species and groups are more likely to survive the more they practise it; it would be equally compatible with the view that there is an optimum level of mutual aid, above which a species' or group's chances of survival are lessened.'[73] Even in the example of mutual aid that has the most bearing on the possibility of anarchist-communism, that of mutual aid in social institutions, Kropotkin's argument may not be as comprehensive as first appears. Mutual aid, as represented in the medieval guild and city-state, is an important element in Kropotkin's ideological tale about how such institutions established precedents that predict the feasibility of an anarchist society. As such Kropotkin is full of praise for what was achieved in these institutions at this time. Nevertheless he was honest enough to admit that they were not without their own problems. Thus, there are 'conflicts' and 'internal struggles,' 'bloodshed' and 'reprisals.'[74] Precious little is said, however, about their inherent inegalitarianism, and no mention is made of the fact that the medieval guilds were at the same time religious brotherhoods. Their camaraderie and practices of mutual aid, then, could have been inspired by religion as much as human nature. The upshot of this is that Kropotkin is requesting that mutual aid play a role that it cannot fulfil. The obligations imposed on Kropotkin's account of human nature by the remainder of his ideological narrative are too heavy for it to bear. Mutual aid, and therefore human nature, cannot determine the course of historical development because Kropotkin's philosophy of history forbids it. Furthermore, mutual aid is unable, in the final analysis, to guarantee the smooth functioning and well-being of any future anarchist society, because there is a parallel feature of Kropotkin's conception of human nature, namely egoism, that constantly undermines its good intentions.

Notes

1. M.A. Miller, *Kropotkin,* (University of Chicago Press, Chicago, 1976) p. vi.

2. G. Woodcock, *Anarchism: A History of Libertarian Ideas and Movements,* (Penguin, Harmondsworth, 1975) pp. 171-2.

3. Quoted in Cahm, *op. cit.,* p. 65.

4. Kropotkin, *MSA,* pp. 43–4. Emphasis in original. However, Kropotkin tempers this argument further

into the text. 'It is impossible', he writes, 'to legislate for *the future*. All we can do is to vaguely guess its essential tendencies and clear the road for it.' (Ibid., pp. 87–8.)

5. Woodcock, *Anarchism,* p. 190. It should be noted that in the biography of Kropotkin that Woodcock wrote with Avakumovic, he does acknowledge that whilst Kropotkin's *The Conquest of Bread* does not outline 'an exhaustive plan of the future' it does offer 'a somewhat elaborate sketch of the free society of the future and the anarchist answer to various social problems.' See Woodcock and Avakumovic, *op. cit.,* p. 314.

6. D. Miller, *Social Justice,* p. 236. Miller's judgment is echoed in his later work *Anarchism,* (Dent, London, 1984), p. 8, in which he argues that anarchists are not averse to elaborating 'models of the kind of society that they want to see.'

7. Kropotkin, *Fugitive Writings,* p. 32.

8. Ibid.

9. Kropotkin, 'Must We Occupy Ourselves with an Examination of the Ideal of a Future System?' in *Fugitive Writings,* p. 16.

10. Ibid., p. 25.

11. Ibid., p. 29. As Ward acknowledges, Kropotkin's theory of federalism is similar to those espoused by Proudhon and Bakunin. See C. Ward, 'Kropotkin's Federalism,' *The Raven,* 5, 4, (1992) p. 328.

12. Kropotkin, 'Must We Occupy Ourselves with an Examination of the Ideal of a Future System?' in *Fugitive Writings,* p. 31.

13. See ibid., pp. 29, 34 and 35.

14. See p. 155 above.

15. Ibid., p. 16.

16. Ibid., pp. 19 and 16.

17. Ibid., p. 26.

18. Ibid.

19. D. Miller, *Social Justice,* p. 237.

20. Woodcock and Avakumovic, *op. cit.,* p. 362. It should be noted that this is a contentious point. Some anarchists find democratic decision-making the only realistic solution. See, for example, M. Bookchin, *Social Anarchism or Lifestyle Anarchism: An Unbridgeable Chasm,* (AK Press, Edinburgh, 1995) pp. 17-18.

21. See Kropotkin, *The Conquest of Bread,* p. 93.

22. The congress took place on 3-5 August 1878. For a description of the events and debate see Cahm *op. cit.,* pp. 44-9. According to Cahm the first exposé of anarchist-communism was delivered by Reclus at Lausanne in March 1876.

23. Two slightly differing versions of this speech are provided by Cahm, *op. cit.,* p. 49 and M. Miller,

Kropotkin pp. 141-2. The congress at La Chaux-de-Fonds was held on 12 October 1879.

24. Kropotkin, *The Conquest of Bread*, pp. 162-3.

25. Ibid., p. 84.

26. Kropotkin's argument is to be found in *MSA*, p. 76.

27. These problems have been outlined by David Miller in 'The Negelected (II): Kropotkin,' p. 325. All three, however, are subsumed within Kropotkin's general position, in *The Conquest of Bread* and elsewhere, that social wealth is a common inheritance. Whilst Miller recognizes the overarching importance of Kropotkin's argument on social wealth, he fails to address in any detail the contextualist perspective of Kropotkin's conception of human nature.

28. Kropotkin, *The Conquest of Bread*, pp. 28-9.

29. Ibid., p. 33.

30. Both citations are drawn from ibid., p. 46.

31. Ibid., p. 143.

32. For details of the right to life as the basis for the free distribution of goods, see ibid., pp. 42-3. When goods are scarce preference is given to children and the aged. See Kropotkin, *The Place of Anarchism in Socialistic Evolution*, pp. 7-8.

33. Kropotkin, *The Conquest of Bread*, p. 34.

34. Ibid., p. 61.

35. Kropotkin, *The Place of Anarchism in Socialistic Evolution*, p. 6.

36. Confirmation of the date of the Paris address can be had from M. Miller, *Kropotkin*, p. 165. The lecture was first published in *Le Révolté* between 28 March and 9 May 1886. Again Miller provides the source of information at p. 298, n. 24.

37. Kropotkin, 'Must We Occupy Ourselves with an Examination of the Ideal of a Future System?' in *Fugitive Writings*, p. 33.

38. Kropotkin, *MSA*, p. 64.

39. The details of these arguments may be found in Kropotkin, *Words of a Rebel*, pp. 211, 214, 215 and 220. Kropotkin also emphasizes that industrial plant will be returned to the community. See ibid., p. 219.

40. See P. Kropotkin, 'Representative Government.' in *Words of a Rebel*, p. 143.

41. P. Kropotkin, 'The Paris Commune,' in *Words of a Rebel*, p. 99. Cf. also ibid., p. 101. For details of Proudhon's argument on usufructuary, see P-J. Proudhon, *What is Property? An Inquiry into the Principle of Right and of Government*, (William Reeves, London, n.d.) pp. 98-9.

42. Acceptance of the base-superstructure paradigm is to be found in Kropotkin, *Words of a Rebel*, p. 118. Assimilation of the same model is evident in *The Conquest of Bread*, p. 54.

43. Kropotkin, *Words of a Rebel*, p. 208.

44. Kropotkin, 'Anarchism: Its Philosophy and Ideal,' in *Fugitive Writings*, p. 111.

45. Ibid., p. 115.

46. Kropotkin, *MSA*, p. 5.

47. Kropotkin, 'Anarchist Morality,' in *Fugitive Writings*, p. 142.

48. Kropotkin, *Words of a Rebel*, p. 30; *The Place of Anarchism in Socialistic Evolution*, p. 12.

49. Kropotkin, *MSA*, p. 45. Somewhat akin to Proudhon, Kropotkin talks of free contracts between individuals and groups in his *The Conquest of Bread*, p. 50.

50. Kropotkin, *Words of a Rebel*, p. 87.

51. Ibid., p. 97.

52. P. Kropotkin, 'An Appeal to the Young,' in Baldwin, *op. cit., passim*.

53. Kropotkin, *The Place of Anarchism in Socialistic Evolution*, p. 16.

54. Ibid. Cf. Kropotkin, *Fugitive Writings*, p. 114.

55. Kropotkin, 'Anarchism: Its Philosophy and Ideal,' in *Fugitive Writings*, p. 106. Parentheses in the original. Such thoughts are obviously inconsistent with what he has to say in *Ethics*. See the discussion at pp. 138-9 above.

56. Kropotkin, 'Anarchism: Its Philosophy and Ideal', in *Fugitive Writings*, p. 119.

57. Kropotkin, *MSA*, p. 46.

58. Woodcock, in particular, indicts Kropotkin's *Words of a Rebel*. See his 'Introduction' to that text, p. 13. For Kropotkin's appreciation of the accusation of romanticism, see *Fugitive Writings*, p. 114.

59. For details of Woodcock's opinion of Kropotkin's supposedly kind appraisal of human nature, see Woodcock, *Anarchism*, p. 206.

60. Kropotkin, *Words of a Rebel*, p. 219.

61. D. Miller, *Social Justice*, p. 211.

62. Ibid.

63. Ibid., p. 246.

64. Marshall, *Demanding the Impossible*, p. 318.

65. Ibid., p. 336. There are numerous examples of Kropotkin's belief that anarchism would be the outcome of existing historical tendencies, two of which are to be found in *The Conquest of Bread*, p. 45, and in P. Kropotkin, *Fields, Factories and Workshops Tomorrow*, (Freedom Press, London, 1985) p. 26.

66. Kropotkin, *The Conquest of Bread*, p. 117.

67. See his comments in *The State*, p. 59. The closing pages of this text provide good reasons for thinking

that Kropotkin believed that the two competing trends of historical development are forever in opposition.

68. For an extensive and informed survey of the degree to which anarchism is dependent upon notions of public censure, see A. Ritter, *Anarchism: A Theoretical Analysis,* (Cambridge University Press, Cambridge, 1980).

69. Marshall, *op. cit.,* p. 338.

70. Kropotkin, *The Conquest of Bread,* p. 154.

71. Avrich, *Anarchist Portraits,* p. 75.

72. Cahm, *op. cit.,* p. 5.

73. D. Miller, 'The Negelected (II): Kropotkin,' p. 337.

74. For an appraisal of Kropotkin's treatment of the medieval guilds and city-state, see Avrich, *op. cit.,* pp. 76-7 from whom these citations are drawn.

FURTHER READING

Criticism

Adán, José Peréz. *Reformist Anarchism 1800-1936: A Study of the Feasibility of Anarchism.* Braunton: Merlin Books, Ltd.: 1992, 242 p.

Examines the philosophical theory and political solutions postulated by the Reformist Anarchists—William Godwin, Josiah Warren, Stephen P. Andrews, and others.

Ehrenberg, John. *Proudhon and His Age.* Atlantic Highlands, N. J.: Humanities Press International, Inc., 1996, 184 p.

Studies Proudhon's thought in regard to capitalism and its effects on the *petite bourgeoisie* of mid nineteenth-century France.

Guérin, Daniel. "Marxism and Anarchism." In *For Anarchism: History, Theory, and Practice*, edited by David Goodway, pp. 109-26. London: Routledge, 1989.

Discusses the ideological conflict between the thought of Marx/Engels and the anarchist theorizing of Proudhon, Bakunin, and others.

Hyams, Edward. *Pierre-Joseph Proudhon: His Revolutionary Life, Mind and Works.* New York: Taplinger Publishing Company, 1979, 304 p.

Critical biography of Proudhon and his relation to socialist thought of the nineteenth century.

Scrivener, Michael Henry. *Radical Shelley: The Philosophical Anarchism and Utopian Thought of Percy Bysshe Shelley.* Princeton, N. J.: Princeton University Press, 1982, 354 p.

Analysis of Shelley as an anarchist poet influenced by William Godwin.

Thomas, Paul. *Karl Marx and the Anarchists.* London: Routledge & Kegan Paul, 1980, 406 p.

Explores Marx's disputes with the anarchist theorists Proudhon, Stirner, and Bakunin as a means of better understanding Marxist thought.

Varias, Alexander. *Paris and the Anarchists: Aesthetes and Subversives During the Fin de Siècle.* New York: St. Martin's Press, 1996, 208 p.

Investigates the diversity of anarchist convictions and activities among Parisian artists, poets, and critics of the 1890s.

Dime Novels

INTRODUCTION

In its broadest sense, the term *dime novel* refers to all cheap, mass-produced pulp fiction published from approximately 1830 until the first decade of the twentieth century, and includes literary newspapers, weekly magazines, and pocket-size paperback books. However, scholars use the term most often to refer to the small paperback fictional novels popular in the second half of the nineteenth century that sold at newsstands for five to twenty-five cents. Specifically, the term emerged from the Dime Novel Library first published in 1860 by the New York firm Beadle and Adams, comprised of Irwin P. Beadle, Erastus F. Beadle, and Robert Adams. Until the firm's demise at the turn of the century, Beadle and Adams and their competitors published hundreds of thousands of these small books, with an estimated worldwide readership in the millions.

Dime novels consist of formulaic stories of adventure and action, usually ranging from twenty-five to thirty-five thousand words. Initially, they were aimed at the entire family and featured reproductions of classic works of fiction; novels about the old frontiers of New York, Pennsylvania, Ohio, and Kentucky; romances; war stories; and sea tales. However, by the 1870s publishers were facing stiff competition in a saturated market, sparked by the immense success enjoyed by Beadle and Adams. Writers began to target new audiences: young boys with pocket change and the working class. Dime novels became increasingly violent and gory, and featured sensational descriptions, urban settings, and gaudy cover art. Detectives, cowboys and courageous boys became the favored characters. Scholars and critics argue that the decline in the quality of the fiction, the lurid cover art, and the resulting debates about the moral influence of the novels on youth led to the demise of the literary form by about 1900. The novels, often printed in serialized newspapers and magazines, were also popular in England and France.

Dime novels revolutionized popular culture and the literary world in the nineteenth century. They emerged from a unique set of historical circumstances. Mandatory education laws in most states produced an increasingly literate population, particularly among the working class. The introduction of the steam printing press and other technological innovations created a cheap means of printing large volumes of material. The expansion of the railroad and the proliferation of the newsstand established a means of distributing literature across the country. The working class and former Civil War soldiers were a ready market. However, the first popular literary form of the nineteenth century was not the paperback book but the literary newspaper. In the United States, the post office gave preferential treatment to the transportation of newspapers; at times it was cheaper to send a newspaper than a letter. Initially, literary publications serialized existing stories which they directly plagiarized or altered slightly. Out of this success, publishers such as Maturin Murray Ballou began publishing small novels for twenty-five cents. However, it was not until 1860 that Beadle and Adams revolutionized the printing market by offering a new standardized literary form. That year the newly established printing house published *Malaeska; The Indian Wife of the White Hunter* by Ann S. Stephens, a well known and highly regarded author. Every month initially and then every two weeks, Beadle published a new volume in the series, soon earning an immense following. Many of these first novels did not constitute a new literary style. *Malaeska*, for example, had first appeared in the *Ladies Home Journal* in the 1830s. Revolutionary aspects of this novel included its packaging, price, and distribution at newsstands. The books were manufactured in a smaller size and uniform shape with pale orange covers and included cover art and illustrations. In addition, in 1860 Beadle launched an innovative advertising campaign to publicize the release of the novel *Seth Jones; or the Captive of the Frontier* by Edward S. Ellis. The publishing firm covered cities with posters and ads asking "Who is Seth Jones?" before the novel went on sale, thus piquing the curiosity of the public. The novel achieved record sales, and Ellis went on to become one of the most popular juvenile fiction writers of the century.

Initially, these novels were written by well-known authors of the period. Popular authors such as Ellis, Metta V. Victor, Prentiss Ingraham, and Ned Buntline published numerous volumes throughout their careers. Increasingly, newspaper reporters were lured into the industry, motivated by the opportunity to earn between seventy-five and one hundred dollars for seven to ten days' work. Publishers also sought authors with personal experience in the West and on the frontier who could bring factual detail and local color to their books; two-thirds of all Beadle's publications were set on the frontier. Such authors as Louisa May Alcott and Bret Harte wrote stories published in dime novels, and Mark Twain read them as research and inspiration for his writing.

The stories written by these middle-class writers reflected the strong moral values of the Victorian age, a moral standard which publishers promoted. In addition, the novels were nationalistic and patriotic, advocating a new social order in which people—or at least white males—were judged by their character and accomplishments rather than their social class. This ideology was particularly apparent in Westerns, in which the heroes always won and the villains were always brutally punished, in which women were presented as chaste and modest and whites were characterized as superior to members of all other races.

Soon after they emerged, however, the subject matter of many dime novels became more and more sensational, sparking heated controversy over their effect on the morality of readers. Social reformers such as Anthony Comstock led campaigns to ban the books and public librarians initiated programs to discourage youth from reading them. In numerous highly publicized trials, defense attorneys attributed murders and robberies to the influence of dime novels. As the century progressed, the public fervor over the destructive nature of the novels corresponded to the increase in violence and sensationalism in the novels as well as the publishers' attempts to capitalize on the youth market. On the other hand, influential leaders downplayed the potential harm. Abraham Lincoln, for instance, was reputed to have praised Victor's novel about slave life entitled *Maum Guinea and Her Plantation Children* (1860). Into the twentieth century, reviewers called for a revision in this negative thinking, recalling their own happy youths spent reading dime novels, and arguing that they had suffered no personal adverse effects. Many of the essayists of the 1920s argued that although dime novels were lurid, they only led to the downfall of youth already predestined for a life of crime. Modern scholars are focusing increasingly on the pervasiveness of the media, the revolutionary nature of the format, and the massive influence the literary movement had on popular culture. Philip Durham writes that the genre "has had a tremendous influence on our social, cultural, political, and economic life."

REPRESENTATIVE WORKS

Albert W. Aiken
> *Richard Talbot of Cinnabar; or, The Brothers of the Red Hand* (novel) 1880

Joseph E. Badger Jr.
> *The Prairie Ranch; or, The Young Cattle Herders* (novel) 1899

Ned Buntline [pseudonym of E. Z. C. Judson]
> *The Black Avenger of the Spanish Main; or, The Fiend of Blood. A Thrilling Story of Buccaneer Times* (novel) 1847
> *Stella Delorme; or, the Comanche's Dream* (novel) 1860
> *Old Nick of the Swamp* (novel) 1868
> *The Terror of the Coast* (novel) 1872

Edward S. Ellis
> *Seth Jones; or the Captives of the Frontier* (novel) 1860
> *The Huge Hunter; or the Steam Man of the Prairies* (novel) 1882

Pauline Hopkins
> *Winona: A Tale of Negro Life in the South and Southwest* (novel) 1902

Prentiss Ingraham
> *Buffalo Bill, from Boyhood to Manhood. Deeds of Daring, Scenes of Thrilling Peril, and Romantic Incidents in the Early Life of W. F. Cody, the Monarch of Bordermen* (novel) 1878

Harry Oavendish
> *The Privateer's Cruise, and the Bride of Pomfret Hall* (novel) 1860

Ann S. Stephens
> *Malaeska; The Indian Wife of the White Hunter* (novel) 1860

Metta V. Victor
> *Maum Guinea and Her Plantation Children* (novel) 1860

Edward L. Wheeler
> *Deadwood Dick, the Prince of the Road; or, The Black Rider of the Black Hills* (novel) 1877
> *Deadwood Dick on Deck; or, Calamity Jane, the Heroine of Whoop-Up. A Story of Dakota* (novel) 1878
> *Solid Sam, the Boy Road-Agent; or, The Branded Brows. A Tale of Wild Wyoming.* (novel) 1880

OVERVIEWS AND GENERAL STUDIES

Charles M. Harvey (essay date 1907)

SOURCE: "The Dime Novel in American Life," in *The Atlantic Monthly,* July, 1907, pp. 37-45.

[*In the following essay, Harvey recounts the development of the dime novel in America.*]

I

Are not more crimes perpetrated these days in the name of the dime novels than Madame Roland ever imagined were committed in the name of liberty? It looks that way. Nearly every sort of misdemeanor into which the fantastic element enters, from train robbery to house-burning, is laid to them.

But these offending books must be only base counterfeits of the originals of their name. When the average American of fifty years of age or upward hears about dime novels he thinks of Beadle's. They were the first and the best of their order. Although nearly all of them bubbled over with thrills, they were not of a character to provoke breaches of the peace. For a few years they had a great run, incited many imitations, all of a lower grade; and at length, after suffering a gradual deterioration in quality, dropped out under the competition. Many of Beadle's original novels deserved the social and financial conquests which they won.

What boy of the sixties can ever forget Beadle's novels! To the average youngster of that time the advent of each of those books seemed to be an event of world consequence. The day which gave him his first glimpse of each of them set itself apart forever from the roll of common days. How the boys swarmed into and through stores and newsstands to buy copies as they came hot from the press! And the fortunate ones who got there before the supply gave out—how triumphantly they carried them off to the rendezvous, where eager groups awaited their arrival! What silver-tongued orator of any age or land ever had such sympathetic and enthusiastic audiences as did the happy youths at those trysting-places, who were detailed to read those wild deeds of forest, prairie, and mountain!

And how those heroes and heroines and their allies, their enemies and their doings, cling to the memory across the gulf of years! The writer of this article has a far more vivid picture of some of the red and white paladins whom he met in Beadle's pages than he has of any of Red Cloud's, Spotted Tail's, or Black Kettle's fierce raiders, whom he saw at unpleasantly close range, or of the white warriors who alternately defeated them and were defeated by them, in the irruptions into Kansas, Nebraska, the Dakotas, and Wyoming, in the later sixties and early seventies. Through Beadle's hypnotic spell,—

> Bliss was it in that dawn to be alive,
> But to be young was very heaven.

Soon after the middle of the nineteenth century the Beadles began selling ten cent books, each a complete work in its field. They comprised manuals of games of many kinds, family medicine, etiquette, letter-writing, dreams, cookery, prose and poetical quotations, and so on. Most of these attained such a sale that the publication of little books on American adventure suggested itself.

Irwin P. Beadle, his brother Erastus F. Beadle, and Robert Adams were the founders of the Beadle publications. Orville J. Victor was the editor. Beadle's dime novels, issued once in each month at first, but much oftener subsequently, made their appearance in 1860. Many Americans who were old enough to read at that time remember 1860 better from that circumstance than they do because it was the year of Lincoln's election and the secession of South Carolina.

These little books ranged from 25,000 to 30,000 words, or about a third of the average bound novel of today. Conveniently shaped for the pocket, they promptly became an inseparable part of the outfit of the boy (and to some extent of the girl also) of the period. Their paper covers were salmon-colored. And they were just as free from yellowness on the inside as they were on the outside.

Orville J. Victor organized victory for the house of Beadle. He selected some writers of ability and standing to con-

tribute to his series. He discovered other writers who made reputations in higher fields of literature afterward. He invented a few writers who quickly "made good." Rules of possibility, morality, and action in the narrative were laid down by him, which all writers had to observe. Mr. Victor himself, who, at the age of eighty, is today not only alive but also mentally and physically alert, had done some good journalistic and literary work before the first of Beadle's novels was issued. He had edited two or three papers, was a leading contributor to *Graham's Magazine*, a well known periodical of the days just before the Civil War, and had written some short biographies of Paul Jones, Israel Putnam, and other American heroes.

A contributor to the *North American Review*, writing a little over forty years ago in that periodical, said this:—

> A young friend of ours was recently suffering from that most harassing of complaints, convalescence, of which the remedy consists in copious draughts of amusement, prescribed by the patient. Literature was imperatively called for, and administered in the shape of Sir Walter Scott's novels. These did very well for a day or two, when, the convalescence running into satiety of the most malignant type, a new remedy was demanded, and the clamor de profundis arose: 'I wish I had a dime novel.' The coveted medicament was obtained, and at once took vigorous hold of the system.

That was a typical boy of the sixties. There were millions like him, as well as many thousands of girls, back in the spacious times of Abraham Lincoln.

Malaeska, the Indian Wife of the White Hunter, by Mrs. Ann S. Stephens, published in the summer of 1860, was the first of Beadle's dime novels. Although forgotten long since, Mrs. Stephens was as well known to the literary world of that year as Edith Wharton or Mrs. Deland is to that of 1907, and she was much better known to the social world than is either of these writers.

Like many greater novelists of the olden day,—Scott, Cooper, and others,—Mrs. Stephens began her chapters with a poetical quotation; but she departed from most of her contemporaries and predecessors in rejecting the "happy ending." The time of the tale, the eighteenth century, saw a large part of the country east of the Alleghenies still in possession of the red man. After her father killed her white husband, Malaeska carried their child to her father-in-law Danforth in New York City (a town which was more familiar with sights of the blanket Indian then than Tahlequah or Pawhuska is today), was prevented by Danforth from revealing her relationship, and went back alone to her tribe. Years afterward she returned, met her son just as he was about to be wedded, told him of his Indian blood, and in the general catastrophe he killed himself and she died.

The plot was crude, but there was action in it. Editor Victor always insisted on action in his stories. In Malaeska herself there was some vitality. A little of the aroma of the forest swept through the book's pages. Mrs. Stephens received $250 for the story; but the compensation for these tales usually ranged from $100 to $150.

Harry Cavendish's *Privateer Cruise,* Mrs. Metta V. Victor's *Backwoods Bride,* and Col. A. J. H. Duganne's *Massasoit's Daughter* were a few of the best known of the earlier Beadle's. Mrs. Victor was the wife of the editor of the series, and she had won some reputation as a writer before she appeared in this company. She wrote half a score of stories for the Beadles. By far the most popular of them all was *Maum Guinea and Her Plantation Children.*

Maum Guinea was a tale of slave life, and appeared in the early part of the Civil War. It was spirited and pathetic, and had a good deal of "local color;" its sales exceeded 100,000 copies, and it was translated into several languages. "It is as absorbing as *Uncle Tom's Cabin,*" was the judgment which Lincoln was said to have passed on it. The New York *Tribune,* the New York *Evening Post,* and other prominent papers in that day of large deeds, when newspaper space was valuable, gave some space to Mrs. Victor's story.

One day in the fall of 1860 a bustling youth of twenty crossed from the wilds of New Jersey, entered the office at 141 William Street, New York, and laid a manuscript on the desk of Editor Victor. It was a great moment in the annals of the house of Beadle. The boy was Edward S. Ellis. The manuscript told the adventures of *Seth Jones, or the Captive of the Frontier,* the most successful novel which ever bore the Beadle imprint.

A few years later Dr. Ellis, who is alive today, graduated from the 10-cent into the $1.50 class of fiction writers, and he has also, in the past fifth of a century, written histories and educational works, some of which have been very popular. His juveniles, many of which have been translated into several languages, exceed in number the sixty-seven years of his life. His readers, diffused through America, Europe, Asia, Africa, and the islands of the sea, won't allow him to stop. As a writer of Indian tales he easily holds the world's long-distance record.

"How de do? How de do? Ain't frightened, I hope. it's nobody but me, Seth Jones of New Hampshire."

As read today, these words, for thousands of Americans, will rouse recollections which will turn time's flight backward several decades. This salutation was Seth Jones's introduction to Alfred Haverland (and likewise to the reader of the story) at Haverland's clearing in the wilderness of Western New York near the close of the eighteenth century. They may also serve to recall, faintly at least, the woodcut picture on the cover of the book, of a stalwart bearded man garbed in fringed hunting shirt, fringed breeches, and coonskin cap, and armed with rifle, powder-horn, and knife. Today, costume, armament, and picture would strike the observer as archaic; but on the scale of their time all were adequate.

Seth, who had been a scout among the Green Mountain boys under Ethan Allen in the war of the Revolution a few

years earlier, and who was fully equipped in the tricks of the fighting frontiersman's trade, told Haverland that the Indians of the vicinity were about to go on the war-path again, and his warning was immediately verified by the capture of Haverland's sixteen-year-old daughter Ina, and by the burning of Haverland's house just as the latter and his wife had fled from it to seek refuge at a white settlement twenty miles away. Just at this moment Evarard Graham, a sweetheart of Ina, turned up, and, under Seth's leadership, joined in the cautious pursuit of the Indians and their captive. After some wonderful, though not inherently impossible, adventures, lasting several days, Ina was recovered, and she and her rescuers reached the settlement and safety.

About this time it was divulged that Seth Jones was a myth, that his real name was Eugene Morton, and that his uncouth garb and language were a mask which he assumed in searching the frontier for his affianced, Mary Haverland, sister of the backwoodsman in the tale, from whom he had become separated during the Revolutionary War. He discovered her soon after he met Alfred at the clearing; but he postponed revealing himself until the clouds rolled by. There was a double wedding—Ina and Graham, Mary and Morton—with a fiddler and revelry as accompaniments. And then—

> Slumber, with the exception of the sentinels at the block house, fell upon the village. Perhaps the Indians had no wish to break in upon such a happy settlement, for they made no demonstration through the night. Sweetly and peacefully they all slept. Sweetly and peacefully they entered on life's duties on the morrow. And sweetly and peacefully these happy settlers ascended and went down the hillside of life.

Believing that this tale could be made a "best seller," the counting-room rose to the occasion with Napoleonic audacity. One morning the residents of most of the big towns of the United States found staring at them from gutters and dead walls the words, "Seth Jones," which were followed a week afterward by "Who's Seth Jones?" The book's appearance on the newsstands in immense stacks a few days later answered that query. This booming and the plaudits of its readers quickly exhausted several editions, and sent the sales ultimately up to more than 600,000 copies, in half a dozen languages.

The Civil War, which started about three quarters of a year after the advent of Beadle's novels, opened a new and vast market for them. In their leisure moments the soldiers craved cheap and exciting reading. Beadle bundled it like bales of hay and sent it to them in carloads. And, in their rate of increase, the carloads kept step with the expanding armies.

Mrs. Stephens, Col. Duganne, Mrs. Victor, Mrs. Mary A. Denison (who wrote *Chip, the Cave Child,* and a few other novels for this series) and Dr. Ellis, fairly represented the Beadle contributors when the corps was at its best estate. Of all the persons connected with these publications in their great days, only Ellis, Mrs. Denison, and Editor Victor are alive today.

Prosperity killed Beadle. He would have done better had he done worse. The streams of money which flowed to him made 141 William Street seem, to some envious persons, like a branch of Secretary Chase's United States Treasury. Rivals sprang up in New York, Boston, Chicago, and other places, who pandered to passions which Beadle shunned. These soon began to take away many of his patrons, and with the hope of regaining his ascendency he lowered the tone of his publications. It was vain. The days of his supremacy never returned.

The blow which hit Beadle first and hardest came from his own household. "Over there is a man," said Erastus F. Beadle, the head of the firm, one day, to one of his leading contributors, "who will be content with his routine work forever." He referred to George Munro, who was a book-keeper for the house. The original partners had by that time been reduced in number by the withdrawal of Irwin P. Beadle, leaving in the concern Erastus F. Beadle and Robert Adams. Less than a year after Beadle passed this judgment, Munro stepped out, hunted up Irwin P. Beadle, and the two began publishing Munro's "Ten Cent Novels." That was in 1866. With the Munro competition began the decline and fall of the house of Beadle.

Munro's novels won a large patronage from the start, and in connection with these he drifted into other fields of publication, establishing the *Fireside Companion* in 1867, and beginning the "Seaside Library" in 1877. The latter contained the work of many foreign writers of ability. At the time of his death in 1896 Munro had amassed a fortune of ten million dollars.

Beadle's pocket-form publications were changed into the large folio page "Beadle's Dime Library" in 1876, and the name Beadle and Adams still figures on dime and half-dime publications issued by N. J. Ivers and Company, New York. But the glory of the house of Beadle vanished when the pocket-form tales passed on.

II

By the close of the seventies several sorts of "dime," "half-dime," and "nickel" novels appeared, the Indian eventually dropping out as the reservation corraled him, and the cowboy, the detective, and the train robber taking his place. At length the dime novel—a term applied to all the cheap fiction indiscriminately—became an atrocity. Many are published today in the United States, and almost as many like them in quality and scope are printed in England.

Not all the dime novels, though, even of today, deserve this epithet. Between some of them and some of the bound novels the only recognizable difference is the difference between ten cents and $1.50.

Of the writers of the "dimes" and the "half-dimes" of the past third of a century the best were Thomas C. Harbaugh,

Albert W. Aiken, Edward L. Wheeler, Joseph W. Badger, Jr., and Col. Prentiss Ingraham. There are whole "libraries" of Buffalo Bill "dimes," but Ingraham wrote most of them. Bill himself is credited with the authorship of about a dozen of them. Among them is *Death Trailer, the Chief of the Scouts, or Life and Love in a Frontier Fort.* As Colonel Cody had seen something of life, and possibly of love, at frontier posts, the reader would presume that this book would be the "real thing." It starts out briskly, as most of the "dimes" did:—

> Mingling with the rumble of wheels and the rattle of hoofs upon the stone road, came the clear notes of a bugle, piercing the deepest recesses of the chaparrals, and floating far off over the prairie until the sound died away upon the evening air. Suddenly out of a dense piece of timber dashed a horseman, well mounted, and wearing the uniform of an officer of the cavalry of the United States army.

Dime novel horses never trot or walk,—they always gallop. The officer who dashed out of the timber was Col. Hugh Decatur, the place was Texas, near the Rio Grande, and the colonel, with his daughter Helen and an escort of four dragoons, was on the way to Nebraska, where he was to take command of a military post. After a breathless succession of encounters with Cortina's Mexican guerrillas, road agents, renegade jayhawkers, and villains of a promiscuous and desperate order of villainy,—in which regulators, avengers of different kinds, British noblemen, and other titled personages figure, and in which daylight is let into many sorts of mysteries,—the end came at Castle Glyndon, in England, where Helen became Lady Radcliffe.

Injun Dick, Detective, or Tracked from the Rockies to New York, is a typical tale by Aiken, who was probably the most skillful, and nearly the most prolific, of writers of detective stories.

"You have seen your last sunrise, as I am going to shoot."

Thus the story opened. There was no preface. In dime novels deeds and not words talk. Scene: A mining camp on the Bear River, in southwestern Colorado. Personages: Dick Talbot, hero of a score of Aiken's tales; Joe Bowers, another Aiken favorite; Limber Bee, and Limber's wife, Alethea, "about twenty-five, tall and queenly, with the most magnificent hair, and eyes black as the raven's wing." Limber, drunk as usual, and insanely jealous of Talbot, was to be the executioner, and Talbot the victim.

"You have been trying to separate me from my wife, the peerless Alethea, and you must die."

Right here Joe Bowers's frying-pan, loaded with flapjacks, hit Limber in the face; he went down under the blow; the bullet intended for Talbot flew wide of the mark, and Talbot sprang upon him and held him down until he begged for mercy. Alethea, angry at Talbot for sparing Limber, revenged herself subsequently on both by running away with a mysterious stranger, who assassinated Limber, and by making off with Talbot's, Bowers's, and Limber's gold, hidden in their cabin. Tracked across the continent, the stranger, who turned out to be Malachi Everest, a notorious burglar, was encountered red-handed in robbing a safe in New York, and killed by Talbot.

Aiken had a record of one story a week for a long time. When pressed, Wheeler and Badger often equaled this gait. Some of the dime-novel writers had several aliases. Col. Thomas C. Harbaugh wrote under his own name and those of Capt. Howard Holmes and Maj. A. F. Grant (in the "Old Cap. Collier" series). Though retired from the dime providing business, Col. Harbaugh is an active contributor today to literary papers in Chicago and other places.

The most prolific, however, of all the dime novelists was Col. Prentiss Ingraham, who wrote more than six hundred cheap stories in all, besides many plays and poems. One of his "dimes," forty thousand words, was written on a "rush" order in twenty-four hours, and that was before the popularization of the typewriter. It has been mentioned here that Ingraham wrote most of the Buffalo Bill stories. Ingraham had been an officer in the Confederate army, and afterward served under Juarez in Mexico, in the Austrian army against Prussia, in Crete against Turkey, and in part of the Cuban war of 1868-78 against Spain; and he had traveled widely in Europe, Asia, and Africa. He led a far more adventurous life than Buffalo Bill, and more adventurous than did the hero of almost any of his own tales. In *A Rolling Stone,* one of Beadle's books, his friend William R. Eyster, a well-known dime novelist, told some of the story of Ingraham's life. In the past quarter of a century the average compensation to Aiken, Ingraham, and their associates was $150 for writing "dimes," and $100 for "half-dimes."

III

What did the dime novel stand for? What influence did it have on the minds of its readers? What forces did it represent in the evolution of American society?

The aim of the original dime novel was to give, in cheap and wholesome form, a picture of American wild life. At the time when it began to be published, 1860, less than fifteen years had passed since the country's boundary had been pushed from the Sabine, the Red, and the Arkansas rivers, and the Rocky Mountains, onward to the Pacific. In that decade and a half we had gained Texas, Oregon, New Mexico, and California, and had enlarged the national area to an extent equal to that of the entire territory east of the Mississippi. A real frontier in 1860 along the line of the Missouri and the Arkansas, with thousands of fighting Indians beyond that line, and some of them east of it, gave the reader an ardent concern in the adventures in *Malaeska, Seth Jones, Massasoit,* and other tales which told of life when the frontier was in New York, Massachusetts, and Pennsylvania. These tales had both contemporaneousness and vitality.

As editor I sought the best work of the best writers in that particular field of fiction," said Mr. Victor a few years ago to the author of this article. "All was up to an excellent standard of literary merit. The detective and love story came later, when rank competition on the ten-cent trade made it seem necessary to introduce these elements. Almost without exception the original dime novels were good. Their moral was high. All were clean and instructive.

This judgment by the man who shaped these little books will be accepted by most persons who remember them in their best days. Ethically they were uplifting. The hard drinkers, and the grotesquely profane and picturesquely depraved persons who take leading rôles in many of the dime novels of recent times were inexorably shut out from their progenitors of Beadle's days.

These tales incited a love of reading among the youth of the country. Though making no pretensions to be historical novels, they often dealt with historical personages. Many of the boys and girls who encountered Pontiac, Boone, the renegade Girty, Mad Anthony, Kenton, and Black Hawk in their pages were incited to find out something more about those characters and their times, and thus they were introduced to much of the nation's story and geography. Manliness and womanliness among the readers were cultivated by these little books, not by homilies, but by example. It can be truthfully said that the taste and tone of the life of the generation which grew up with these tales were improved by them.

No age limit was set up among Beadle's readers. Lincoln was one of them. So was Seward, and Henry Wilson of Massachusetts. Report of a later day had it that Toombs—who, however, as an officer of the Confederacy, was on the wrong side to find them accessible in their early days—was a devourer of these tales when he could get at them. "The man," said Zachariah Chandler, "who does not enjoy *Onomoo, the Huron,* has no right to live."

One at least of Beadle's tales registered itself in the politics of the time. *Maum Guinea,* Mrs. Victor's slavery tale, which issued at a critical moment in the Civil War, and which, republished in London (all Beadle's novels were republished in London until 1866), circulated by the tens of thousands in England, had a powerful influence in aid of the Union cause at a time when a large part of the people of that country favored the recognition of the independence of the Southern Confederacy. Mr. Victor's own "Address to the English People," issued at the same time, and in connection with the London edition of the novels, was widely distributed in England, and helped to overcome the sentiment which was clamoring for the breaking of the blockade and the purchase of Southern cotton for Lancashire's idle mills.

"My dear fellow," said Henry Ward Beecher to Mr. Victor afterward, "your little book and Mrs. Victor's novel were a telling series of shots in the right spot." This is testimony which counts. Beecher was a special commissioner from

Lincoln to England in 1863, to counteract the hostility to the Union cause in the Palmerston cabinet and among the aristocracy.

The very small claim which the black man ever had upon the dime novelists ended with Appomattox and emancipation; but the red man had a far longer and more prosperous career. While Red Cloud, Black Kettle, and their compatriots ravaged the frontier, the Indian tales had an easy ascendancy. The annihilation of Colonel Fetterman and one hundred of his troops near Fort Phil Kearney in 1866, and the slaughter of Custer and two hundred and fifty of his men on the Little Big Horn in 1876, sold forest and prairie stories by millions of copies. But that was near the end of the Indian's service for the fictionists. The campaign against Chief Joseph and the Nez Percés in 1877, and the rounding up of Geronimo and the Apaches in 1886, shut up the last of the descendants of King Philip and Pontiac on the reservations, and the novelists had to turn to other fields for material. Before Sitting Bull's ghost-dance irruption at Pine Ridge in 1890, the cowboy and detective tales had supplanted the Indian story in the popular favor.

For a few years the Santa Fé trader and the cowboy ran a flourishing career among the dime novelists. Soon after the Mexican war Capt. Mayne Reid, one of the heroes of that conflict, began his tales of the Southwest—*Rifle Rangers, Scalp Hunters, Captain of the Rifles,* and the rest of them,—some of which told of bloody deeds along the Santa Fé trail, and a few of which were reprinted among Beadle and Adams's "dimes" and "half-dimes." Like most of the early cowboy tales, these stories had Indians among their leading characters, intermixed with "Greasers."

The alien white ingredient in these tales injected an element of variety which the youthful reader appreciated. Reid had seen the Mexican at close range. He knew enough of the Mexican language to make his imprecations and objurgations—his "Sacre-e-s" and "Carambas"—sound real. This delighted the boy readers, and set the fashion in profanity which later writers in this field followed. Reid, J. E. Badger, Oll Coomes, P. S. Warne, and others, who told of the wild riders of the plains, red, yellow, and white, made every foot of ground between the Missouri and the Sierra Nevadas, and the Arkansas and the Rio Grande, familiar to dime novel readers.

More than a quarter of a century ago, however, the Atchison, Topeka and Santa Fé railway ended the days of the old trail and its story tellers. Between the railroads which transported the cattle from the ranges to the stockyards, and the barbed wire fences of the settlers who are abolishing the ranges, the cowboy as a picturesque feature of the Western landscape has passed out, and the dime novel will know him no more. This leaves the detective in possession of the stage.

In certain directions the detective tale has attractions for writers and readers beyond those offered by the average Indian story. The white "bad man" is more versatile in his badness than is his red or yellow counterpart. His field of activities is far wider. For the past half century the Indian's operations have been shut in between the Missouri and the Sierra Nevada Mountains, but the white crook's ravages have covered the whole landscape between the two oceans. Aiken's *Black Hoods of the Shasta* made life exhilarating in the neighborhood of the Golden Gate, but in most of his most popular tales the action centred in New York. In Boston, St. Louis, Philadelphia, New Orleans, St. Paul, and other towns, the Vidocqs of Harold Payne, William H. Manning, Edward Willett, J. W. Osbon, and others cut their Gordian knots.

Calling the roll of the items in the vast output of Wheeler, Ingraham, Aiken, and their associates, it would seem that there could not be enough truth in the United States to last them. No complaint of this sort, however, was ever made by any of their constituents. In their pages the reader encountered life in all tints of shade and brightness. His imagination was kindled. He was incited to do things; and commonly the things which he wanted to do were heroic.

There were no problems in any of the dime novels, old or new, not even in *Maum Guinea.* Duganne's *Massasoit* appeared before psychology was invented. If a paragraph or two of Arthur Dimmesdale's soul torture had strayed into any of Beadle's novels, the whole series would have been ruined. The things which were done in those little books were physical, and they were told in language that made pictures in the mind. There were no verbal puzzles in any of them, like those which James or Meredith impose. Long ago James said novelists ought to make their readers do a share of the work. Capt. Mark Wilton, Major S. S. Hall, Dr. Frank Powell, and their coworkers believed that their duty to their readers was to entertain them.

Between the writer and his constituents there was a bond of affection which incited him to make them glad to be alive. In the mind of every healthy boy there is romance. For that boy's entertainment the producer of dime fiction strewed romance through farm, mining camp, and city street. Out of his surroundings, however sordid, the boy was lifted. He became, to himself, the centre of the universe. At the particular spot on the globe on which he stood all the parallels and the meridians converged. In no more intense a degree than this did exaltation ever come to the Count of Monte Cristo;—the world was his. What was Edmond Dantes's paltry twenty million dollars to the vast treasures, physical and spiritual, spread out by Osbon before "Plucky Paul, the Boy Prospector," and his tens of thousands or hundreds of thousands of readers?

And the boy got all of this without any prefaces. The action began right in the first line. No little Peterkin ever needed to ask any Old Kaspar what this was all about. The battles with Indians and "Greasers," the capture of road agents and bank burglars, and the retribution which hit the villain who attempted to cheat the girl out of her patrimony, told their story in language so plain that the wayfaring man, though a fool, never made any mistake in grasping it.

From Beadle's days onward most of the dime tales have been American. Names, scenes, atmosphere, are familiar. In reading them the American boy's soul soared and sang. This is why the average youth who found *Rob Roy* and *Ivanhoe* dull was immensely entertained by Ellis's *Bill Biddon,* or Leon Lewis's *Daredeath Dick, King of the Cowboys.*

Were these things all illusions? Many of them were, yet they were pleasing illusions. Illusions jolt us every day, which the dime novelists never touch, and which we would not want to read about. Some of us might like occasionally to see time's clock turned back to the days when the world was young enough and rich enough to have illusions that make us glad.

Was everything that the dime necromancers told us melodrama? Much of it unquestionably was. But an age which has seen a nation rise from Balboa's isthmus at the wave of a Prospero wand from Washington; which has recently looked on while a people in the Caribbean committed suicide; which is watching Nome's argonauts, up under the Pole Star, rival the glories of the Comstock under the reign of Mackay, Flood, and O'Brien; and which held its breath in November, 1906, while Roosevelt and Croker, like Castor and Pollux, rushed to rescue the nation from a New York editor who had built up an army in a night, has no right to object to melodrama in fiction.

Christine Bold (essay date 1996)

SOURCE: "Malaeska's Revenge; or, The Dime Novel Tradition in Popular Fiction," in *Wanted Dead or Alive: The American West in Popular Culture,* edited by Richard Aquila, University of Illinois Press, 1996, pp. 21-42.

[*In the essay below, Bold examines the role of dime novels, pulp fiction, and the commodification of literature in transforming views about the West.*]

Read collectively dime novels and their descendants tell the story of the frontier West's commodification in popular literature. This process was mediated by changing historical circumstances and individual authorial contributions, from the first intersection of mass literature and westward movement in the mid-nineteenth century to the "nostalgic remorse" for the frontier West of late twentieth-century capitalist culture.[1] Early and late, however, the commercial frameworks within which cheap Westerns were produced left their imprint on this fiction's format, formulaic action, narrative voice, and reception.

The mass production of American cheap fiction took off in the 1830s as part of the explosion in America's market economy.[2] The commodification of literature was facilitated by a huge increase in urban population, the spread of literacy, and rapid advances in transportation, industrialization, and print technology. The newly invented rotary press and the fanning out of a railroad network made pos-

sible, for the first time, fast, voluminous production of low-priced literature and transcontinental distribution to a mass audience. The new technology also dictated the appropriate form of this reading material. Story papers' large folio sheets with serials set in cramped columns of diminutive typeface, few illustrations, and a very low price—three to six cents per issue—were the result of a narrow calculation about how to attract and hold the largest audience as cheaply as possible. The meshing of cheap literature with a range of commercial interests and pressures was established.

With the beginning of the dime novel, these developments bore down on—and were refined in—Western fiction, the dominant genre of adventure story in the dime format.[3] Irwin and Erastus Beadle and Robert Adams began dime novels in 1860 when they produced uniformly packaged series of complete, predominantly American novels in compact pamphlets priced at five or ten cents. The Beadles' major innovation was gearing their marketing strategies to the period's trends: the portable format suited escalating rail travel; the distinctive cover designs, uniform for each series and "library," and the increasingly lurid illustrations made effective displays at the recently developed newsstands; and the very low price for stories of 35,000 and 70,000 words ("A DOLLAR BOOK FOR A DIME!!" the publicity blared) was affordable even for the poorer industrial workers and immigrants. These mass publishers attempted to regulate not only production, advertising, and distribution but writing as well. Beadle and Adams regimented authors' production mainly in terms of quantity, speed, length, and fixed payment rates, supplying only general instructions on content. The results were massively successful; before they folded in 1898 Beadle and Adams published 3,158 separate titles and sold copies in the millions. By 1879 W. H. Bishop could declare that dime novel literature was "the greatest literary movement, in bulk, of the age, and worthy of very serious consideration for its character." He concluded, "the phenomenon of its existence cannot be overlooked."[4]

A host of imitators sprang up. The most successful were Frank Tousey, George Munro, Norman Munro, and Street and Smith (the last transferring from the story paper to the dime novel field late, in 1889, but immediately becoming the Beadles' main rival and surviving as pulp magazine and comic book publishers until 1950). These later publishers extended the network of commercial pressures bearing down on cheap fiction by introducing advertising and cutting prices to produce competitive "nickel novels"; furthermore, by narrowing the output to juvenile fiction and by supervising their writers much more closely, they systematized the production line more rigorously than Beadle and Adams had. Dime publishers came to commodify authors, denying them decision-making powers: by 1896 Ormond Smith dictated character, plots, and scenes to the author who was ostensibly "inventing" Frank Merriwell.[5] Writers in dime and nickel stables lost their individualized signatures, too. Publishers and editors shunted authors around from one house pseudonym to another; at Street

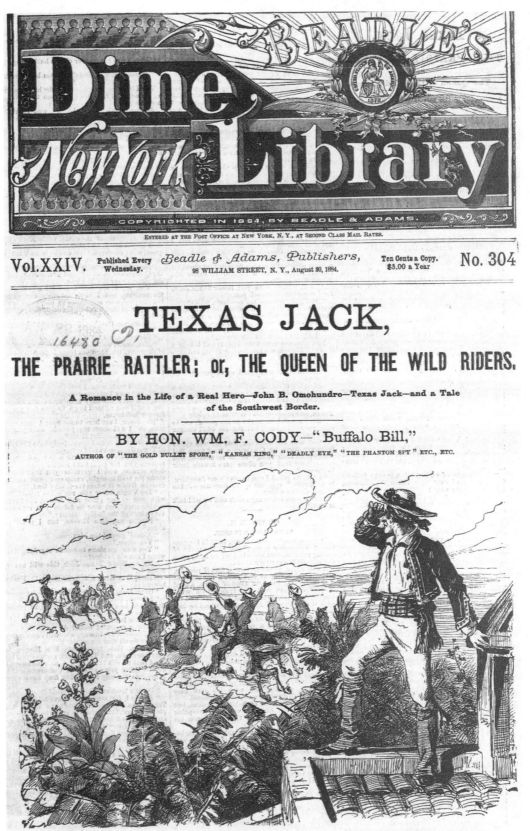

BEADLE'S
Dime New York Library

COPYRIGHTED IN 1864, BY BEADLE & ADAMS.

ENTERED AT THE POST OFFICE AT NEW YORK, N. Y., AT SECOND CLASS MAIL RATES.

Vol. XXIV. | Published Every Wednesday. | *Beadle & Adams, Publishers,* 98 WILLIAM STREET, N. Y., August 20, 1884. | Ten Cents a Copy. $5.00 a Year | **No. 304**

TEXAS JACK,

THE PRAIRIE RATTLER; or, THE QUEEN OF THE WILD RIDERS.

A Romance in the Life of a Real Hero—John B. Omohundro—Texas Jack—and a Tale of the Southwest Border.

BY HON. WM. F. CODY—"Buffalo Bill,"

AUTHOR OF "THE GOLD BULLET SPORT," "KANSAS KING," "DEADLY EYE," "THE PHANTOM SPY" ETC., ETC.

"YES, IT IS MY LOVELY RENA THAT IS COMING BACK TO ME. AND BY HER SIDE RIDES THAT PRINCE OF TEXANS, WHOM MEN CALL THE THUNDERBOLT.

and Smith multiauthored series under one trademark name came to be the rule.

This emphasis on standardization left direct and indirect textual imprints on dime novel Westerns. The conservatism of the Western's fictional formula can be explained in a number of ways: by the political conservatism of frontier society that is represented—to however mediated a degree—in these adventure stories, by the slowness with which large-scale popular tastes change, or by the imitative tendencies of individual authors. Nonetheless, publishing calculations clearly encouraged caution and the reproduction of proven successes. Typical of the mass publishers' shrewd commercial strategies is Erastus Beadle's choice of the first dime novel: *Malaeska: The Indian Wife of the White Hunter*, by Ann S. Stephens, which was reprinted from its serialization in the *The Ladies' Companion* of 1839 to appear as number 1 of Beadle's Dime Novels in June 1860. Not only did Erastus Beadle begin with a proven bestseller, but he grafted an example of sentimental or women's fiction—the most popular genre of the mid-nineteenth century—onto a new format and new publicity that exploited public interest in the westward movement. *Malaeska* is a decidedly woman-centered frontier narrative. Set in the early wilderness of the Hudson Valley, the story traces the fate of a Native American woman who is left widowed by the death of her white soldier husband, robbed of their son by her aristocratic in-laws in New York City, forced to witness his suicide when his Native American heritage is revealed to him years later, and finally killed by her own grief on her boy's grave. That this is a distinctively female, as well as Native American, experience is suggested by the narrator's comment on Malaeska's self-sacrifice: "It was her woman's destiny, not the more certain because of her savage origin. Civilization does not always reverse this mournful picture of womanly self-abnegation."[6]

Although *Malaeska* sold at least a half-million copies in its dime format, its plot did not become the dominant formula for Western dime novels. Later in 1860 Edward S. Ellis, a young schoolmaster, brought to the Beadles a wilderness adventure with clear sales potential. *Seth Jones; or, The Captives of the Frontier* tells the frontier story from a perspective different from *Malaeska*'s, focusing on a white hunter who saves various white captives from the Mohawks in a series of melodramatic adventures in the wilderness of western New York State. Orville J. Victor, Beadle's editor, called *Seth Jones* "the perfect Dime Novel."[7] Publishing it as number 8 of Beadle's Dime Novels, the firm puffed it with a massive advertising campaign in which newspaper advertisements, billboards, and handbills carried the tantalizing question "Who is Seth Jones?" followed by lithographs of a coonskin-capped hunter declaring, "I am Seth Jones." The public response was even more massive than that to *Malaeska*, and the story of male heroism became entrenched as the dominant dime novel formula.

This paradigm shift, from a centrally female to emphatically male Western, carries cultural and political reso-

nances. In direct contrast to *Malaeska, Seth Jones* and its imitators articulated the West in the optimistic, patriarchal terms of Manifest Destiny then in the ascendancy in public rhetoric. Whereas *Malaeska* to a degree exposed the human cost of the western movement, the male-centered dime novel drew on the same fund of triumphant images and nationalistic narratives as did newspapers and politicians. At the same time the Beadles' preference for the Ellis version of frontier adventure can be read as one beachhead in the attack on women's sentimental, religious culture. Jane Tompkins has tracked brilliantly how men seized the public imagination in the post-Civil War Western and into the twentieth century. It may be that what Tompkins names "the deauthorization of women" profited from an early, explicitly commercial boost.[8]

Although *Seth Jones* was a new story, it strongly resembled an earlier series of bestsellers—James Fenimore Cooper's Leatherstocking Tales (1823-41)—in terms of plot, setting, character types, and the representation of social roles.[9] Like Cooper, Ellis chose an attack by "savage" Native Americans on a family of white settlers as the framework for his plot and an avuncular, Indian-slaying hunter as their rescuer. If Ellis's disposition of gender and race is recognizably conventional, his configuration of class is modified. Whereas Cooper's backwoodsman, Natty Bumppo, is unfit for the romantic role because he lacks social standing, Seth Jones casts off his hunter's disguise at the end of the tale to reveal himself as a young, aristocratic easterner suited to marry the white heroine whom he has saved from captivity. Both authors play out European social hierarchies in the American wilderness, but Ellis's frontier hero transcends class stratifications in a way that Cooper's does not. This sunny, optimistic ending erases the tension between East and West evident in Cooper: a shift of register with particular symbolic power in a time of national strife. Ellis's adaptation of Cooper also serves patriotic nationalism by simplifying the ethics of white settlement: demonizing the Native Americans justifies white conquest, and the elision of backwoodsman and aristocrat harmonizes competing economic interests. (By 1868 an obvious imitation of *Seth Jones* had made this message explicit. Percy St. John characterizes white frontier settlers thus: "Never weary, never conquered, they advanced still onward toward the setting sun, laying first the foundations of home and then of empire.")[10]

This version of the frontier adventure, appropriating the wilderness for the glorification of white men rescuing white women and killing Native Americans, held sway thereafter in the Beadle production line and its imitators. Over time a combination of publishers, editors, and authors adapted the scenes, character types, and political rhetoric in response to changing historical circumstances, but the familiar narrative line of the formula survived. This strategy of innovation contained within repetition is perceptible in the development of heroic types in dime and nickel Westerns. The imperative to produce a hero transcending class and region remained paramount, but as the figure was inserted into different cultural environments, his specific lineaments changed: the hunter gave way to the scout, the cowboy, the outlaw, the frontier detective, and the freelance law-enforcer. In different accents these heroic types voiced their commitment to a certain brand of democracy and nationalism.

Buffalo Bill extended the Western hero's range, both fictively and commercially. Bill Cody was working as a buffalo hunter and scout for the Western army when he was discovered in 1869 by E. Z. C. Judson, a prolific popular author, entrepreneur, and sometime political activist better known by his most famous pseudonym, Ned Buntline. Buntline recognized Cody's commercial potential. He wrote him up as a heroic scout, Sioux fighter, freelance law-enforcer, and rescuer of captive maidens, first in *Buffalo Bill, the King of Border Men!* (which was serialized in Street and Smith's story paper *New York Weekly* of 1869-70) and then in dime novels; Buntline also briefly put Cody on the New York stage.

When Prentiss Ingraham took over authorship of Buffalo Bill stories in 1879, the figure became more violent, slaughtering scores of Native Americans in defense of whole communities instead of picking off single attackers in the style of Seth Jones, and more flamboyant, dressing in rich, elaborate costumes. In Ingraham's formulation the violent plainsman's gentlemanly demeanor and exotic appearance endowed Buffalo Bill with the marks of gentility necessary to the romantic hero. Ingraham also worked the figure up as nationalist icon: anticipating the Turner thesis by fifteen years, Ingraham depicted Buffalo Bill as "a barrier between civilization and savagery, risking his own life to save the lives of others."[11] When Cody began to star in his own Wild West show from 1883, he extended his dime novel persona into the historical and political arena by incorporating America's imperialist ventures into his act, while Ingraham continued to produce melodramatic dime and nickel fiction as tie-ins to the performances.[12] Gradually a commercial constellation emerged around the imperialist frontier hero. . . .

Overlapping this development was the construction of another version of the dime novel hero. Edward Wheeler promoted the popularity of the Western outlaw when he introduced Deadwood Dick in the first number of Beadle's Half Dime Library in 1877. Deadwood Dick is the familiar amalgam of savagery, culture, nationalism, and individualism but inflected in a new direction. An easterner, Deadwood Dick has been forced to flee west under threat of imprisonment through the depredations of a pair of eastern financiers. Disguising himself in a black costume and mask, Dick gathers a hardy band around him and undertakes a series of violent adventures whose ethical status is ambiguous. On the one hand, the reader is told that Dick has abandoned himself to illegal pursuits; on the other, Dick is repeatedly shown rescuing innocent, genteel easterners, dispatching villains who are more often crooked businessmen than savage Native Americans, and becoming entangled in a number of romantic attachments. These melodramatic adventures play out class interests more ex-

plicitly than earlier dime novels, partly because the site of the action is the frontier boomtown rather than the sparsely settled wilderness. Dick frequently opposes "purse-proud aristocrats," who are clearly censured by the democratic narrative voice: in *Deadwood Dick's Device or, The Sign of the Double Cross* (1879), the scheming Howells are "a leading family, both financially and socially—for Leadville, mind you, has its social world as well as its Eastern sister cities, formed out of that class whom fortune has smiled upon. And surrounded by great superfluity of style, pomp and splendor, they set themselves up as the 'superior class,' ye gods!"[13] But the social bandit's alignment with the laboring classes does not extend to political activists: "on a visit to Chicago soon after the Haymarket Riots of 1886, Deadwood Dick, Jr., denounces the anarchists who are on trial because they are an undesirable foreign element. He declares that all the accused persons deserved to be hanged."[14] A number of dime publishing firms capitalized on the popularity of the outlaw hero by developing entire libraries devoted to increasingly sensational tales of actual and fictional bandits. As the thrills became more exaggerated, the explicit sociopolitical commentary waned.

In the early twentieth century this sensationalizing of outlaws drew the wrath of some concerned citizenry and public bodies. One cultural institution in particular acted on this outcry against dime and nickel publishers: the office of the postmaster general determined what material could be sent through the mail and at what rates. This office, perhaps in response to concerns over worker unrest and rising socialism, censored inflammatory outlaw stories from 1883 through the turn of the century by refusing mailing privileges.[15] In response dime publishers turned to moralistic adventure stories, fastening particularly on the heroic cowboy.

The cowboy had emerged gradually as a cultural hero; partly through the intercession of dime fiction, his image shifted over the 1880s from hell-raiser to half-wild, half-cultured frontier hero and democratic individualist who could function equally adroitly on the open range and in the frontier town.[16] The decisive gentrification of the cowboy occurred beyond the dime novel genre, in the fiction of Owen Wister, the political rhetoric of Theodore Roosevelt, and the art of Frederic Remington.[17] That development was reincorporated, in turn, into the juvenile nickel Westerns of the twentieth century, which transformed the gentlemanly cowboy into a clean-cut boy. Frank Tousey's *Wild West Weekly,* a series about a gang of boys in the West (again led by a displaced easterner) that began in 1902, was the most popular version of this formula. In 1904 Street and Smith produced a close imitation, *Young Rough Riders Weekly* (later, *Rough Rider Weekly*), authored under the house pseudonym "Ned Taylor." These stories played on associations with Teddy Roosevelt, who was beginning his second term as president when the series began: the leader of this gang of boys is Ted Strong, an easterner who inherits two ranches in the Dakotas and one in Texas, and each gang member wears "a neatly-fitting khaki uniform such as those worn by the

Ned Buntline (pseudonym of E. Z. C. Judson) (1823–1886)

his punishment is a stark dehumanization: catching Tony in an assassination attempt, the hero first cuts a cross into his forehead and then returns him to his master with a letter pinned to his breast. Red Ralph the sailor later carves anchors into the servant's cheeks, and the heroine finally scalds him white.)

Variations to these flat caricatures appear, but ultimately they seem contained by the heroic imperative. For example, when Deadwood Dick defends the land rights of a peaceful Crow Indian in *Deadwood Dick's Claim; or, The Fairy Face of Faro Flats* (1884), the point is more the extent of the hero's protective powers than American Indians' rights. Wheeler also produced a series of female figures who transcend the passive gentility of the typical dime novel heroine: Hurricane Nell, Wild Edna, Rowdy Kate, and most famously, Calamity Jane, who figures briefly as Dick's wife but more regularly as his sidekick in the Deadwood Dick series.[19] These women adopt masculine attire, display prowess on horseback and in gunplay, and often save the hero from fatal danger. Ultimately, however, their ostensible power is negated: either the masculine role is only a stage in a woman's maturation toward adult domesticity, or her masculinized behavior results in her death, or (as in the case of Calamity Jane, who has lost her chastity) she leads a kind of living death, forever branded a degenerate and outcast from respectable society. In lip service to women's changing social roles in the early twentieth century, Stella, Ted's companion in *Rough Rider Weekly,* is empowered in gradual, limited ways: she initiates and conducts her own adventures, and her western costume is practical yet feminine; ultimately, however, she depends on Ted for her safety. With these stereotypes the fictional narratives entrenched a disposition of gender and race that was reflected in the demographics of the publishing houses, where white men predominated in all professional roles.

However simplistic the dime—and nickel—novel formula, the embedding of topical references in the narratives and their responsiveness to changing cultural climates suggest that these melodramas were offered as prisms through which to view current affairs. Implicitly and explicitly the frontier wilderness came to be aligned with modern society, to the extent that the dime Western could be read, in Daryl Jones's words, "as a vehicle for addressing social problems associated with urbanization and industrialization."[20] Public discourse and cheap fiction symbiotically supported a vibrant, optimistic political rhetoric that characterized the Far West as site of national, economic, and personal regeneration. On a number of fronts dime and nickel Westerns seem to support the dominant rhetoric of the era by mimicking and extending it into frontier melodrama.

Complicating the easy alignment of text to sociopolitical arena, however, is the author-reader relationship. Inscribed in these formulaic Westerns are authorial voices that attempt to circumvent the regulation of the marketplace by insisting on their individual contributions to narrative pro-

Rough Riders during the Spanish-American War."[18] Although the standard captivity-and-rescue ritual survives, the action is modernized and heavily influenced by marketplace issues: battles revolve around corporate trust busting, the regulation of property rights, technological advancement, and sporting competitions, not the killing of Native Americans. Ted Strong's pervasive influence functions primarily to eradicate the wildness from the West.

What these shifts and turns in dime fiction share is the location of power in the white hero. In the dime and nickel Western white women and all nonwhite figures are relegated to providing the occasion for the excitement but are permitted no agency in its momentum or consequences. White women are typically passive victims saved by the hero's courage and wilderness skills; Native Americans, the threatening savages whom he destroys; Mexicans, the lustful degenerates whom he drives off; and blacks, the comic childlike incompetents whom he protects. (The most extreme reification of an African American occurs in Buntline's *Red Ralph, The River Rover; or, The Brother's Revenge* [1870]. The black figure, Tony, is servant to the aristocratic villain. Repeatedly doing his master's bidding,

duction and by recovering an oral relationship with their readers. The details of both mass-publishing history and textual developments suggest that, ultimately, these voices were circumscribed by the culture industry. Nevertheless, they can be read as limited but significant challenges to the powerful institutions of cultural production, as signs that the fictional West was not completely homogenized by commerce.[21]

Some Beadle and Adams authors forged a facsimile of a storyteller's relationship with their audience by talking to their readers about the commercial paraphernalia of the dime novel. Buntline, for example, mounted a running commentary on his place in the production line, as well as a defense of his populist politics, within his repetitive dime tales of captivity, chase, and rescue on the frontier. In a typical acknowledgment of the competitive commercialism of his task, he ended a stirring frontier tale with "I hope you feel as if you had got your money's worth."[22]

Edward Ellis and Prentiss Ingraham implicated authors, characters, and readers in self-conscious codes, conventions, and sign systems, thus moving the fiction closer to an acknowledgment of its status in the publishing field. In Ellis the narrative commentary is supplemented by characters simultaneously enacting and discussing the formulaic plots: series characters typically cite by title their appearances in earlier publications, and they explicitly acknowledge their participation in ritualistic, somewhat predictable action. Ingraham's fiction insists that the production and decipherment of codes are at the heart of Western adventure. In *Buffalo Bill's Redskin Ruse; or, Texas Jack's Death-Shot* (1895), for example, characters spend much time translating secret messages, "reading signs" on trails, devising "talking papers" (as maps are called), and interpreting key clues on clothing and bodies, all the while identifying their adventures as types of games.

Edward Wheeler's characters emphasized the constructedness of the formula further by becoming independent of their author to the extent that they wrote their own plots, devised their own identities, and fought their own publishing battles. For example, just at the time that Street and Smith marketed an imitation of the Deadwood Dick Series, Wheeler had his hero declare, "I see that counterfeits are being shoved on the market—that is, sham Deadwood Dicks. We have one here in Eureka. . . . I wish to meet this chap and learn where he obtained the right to use my copyrighted handle?"[23] The voice that recognizes the rules of the marketplace and the systematic interchange between producer and the consumer now belonged to the characters. The shift in rhetorical power is a textual illustration of the diminution of authorial power, just around the time when authors were losing more of their autonomy in the publishing hierarchy.

As dime publishers became more interventionist, these authorial gestures disappeared from the text. In Street and Smith juvenile nickel series an editorial voice at the end of the story comments on the construction of the fiction, en-

courages readers to distribute it for financial rewards, and in time, invites the audience to participate in its composition. The most emphatic example of this process occurred in the letters pages of *Rough Rider Weekly,* significantly revolving around the social construction of gender. In response to conflicting advice from readers about whether Ted Strong should marry Stella, the editor threw open the author's study and invited in all the readers: "So you think Ted and Stella should marry? What do the rest of our readers think about it? . . . There are two sides to this question, and we should like to have it decided by our readers."[24] The fiction thus became an overt bargaining tool between publisher and public; the only role left to the author was to carry out the audience's demands.

The question of how all these textual signals—of topicality, authorial presence, and reader power—were received by readers is linked to the equally knotty question of who constituted the massive new audience for dime and nickel Westerns.[25] The Beadles avowedly aimed at a large and diverse audience, attempting to transcend class division in audience as well as hero; they announced in 1860 that they "hoped to reach all classes, old and young, male and female."[26] They advertised dime novels in the nationally influential *New York Tribune,* and some of their publications were reviewed (favorably) in the highbrow *North American Review.* The Civil War produced a captive audience of soldiers, who were highly responsive to the sensational adventure that some publishers became adept at producing. Later, industrialization, urbanization, and economic calculations seem to have delivered the working classes as the main audience for cheap fiction. Frederick Whittaker specifically enumerated the audience: "The readers of the dimes are farmers, mechanics, workwomen, drummers, boys in shops and factories"; extrapolating from this and other evidence, Michael Denning has averred that "the bulk of the audience of dime novels were workers—craftworkers, factory operatives, domestic servants and domestic workers."[27] Retrospectively commentators tended to style dime novels as "part of the youth of many of us" (this from an editorial in the *New York Sun* in 1900). In fact, however, it was only toward the end of Beadle and Adams's life and throughout Street and Smith's dime career that a specifically juvenile audience was targeted. Within these reading groups for dime novels, more males than females seem to have been attracted to Westerns, and readers developed different interpretive strategies according to their level of investment as "Committed, Regular, or Casual" readers.[28] Hypothetical reconstructions of these readers' responses to authorial and narrative signs suggest that working-class readers, at least, read dime fiction in ideologically charged ways, not as simple escapism dissociated from their daily lives. Piecing together evidence from a patchwork of autobiographies, diaries, and reports by social reformers, Michael Denning has argued that workers read cheap novels allegorically or typologically, interpreting a range of scenarios as microcosms of their social world. Thus, especially at times of industrial agitation and strikes in the late nineteenth century, workers could read the triumph of labor in stories of western outlaws, such as Wheeler's *Deadwood Dick, The Prince of the Road; or, The Black Rider of the Black Hills* (1877). One way of understanding the authorial gestures toward the commercial constructedness of the work is as invitations to what John Fiske labels a "producerly reading":

> the producerly text has the accessibility of a readerly one . . . but it also has the openness of the writerly. . . . It offers itself up to popular production; it exposes, however reluctantly, the vulnerabilities, limitations, and weaknesses of its preferred meanings; it contains, while attempting to repress them, voices that contradict the ones it prefers; it has loose ends that escape its control, its meanings exceed its own power to discipline them, its gaps are wide enough for whole new texts to be produced in them.[29]

Both empirical evidence and theorized hypothesis suggest, then, that the audience of dime and nickel Westerns was not undifferentiatedly passive. Some readers could respond to textual hints and ambiguities according to their own agendas, contributing their own meanings to the complex multiple authorship of these cheap forms.

In their ritualistic adventures of attacks, captivity, and pursuit, dime novels encode a West where nationalism and commerce intersect regeneratively. The market operates visibly on the manufacture of the dime novel as product, on the textual representation of the West—which develops from untamed wilderness to site of business opportunities—and on the narrative voices that deliver those images. Within this representational space a hierarchy of gender and race is formulaically inscribed. Distributed by the millions, this version of the West could claim a democratic voice on many levels.

The pulp magazines and comics that succeeded dime and nickel novels display similar strategies, although potentially to different rhetorical effect. The production process became slicker and more intense as the technological and commercial environment heated up, distribution increased exponentially, and certain narrative features became increasingly exaggerated. Encoded within these changes, however, is a familiar story of white male supremacy impelled by a democratic ethos that conflates nationalism and commerce.

Partly because of the postal restrictions on series of complete novels, pulp magazines took over from dime novels after World War I, bringing with them a new format and different editorial methods.[30] These weekly and monthly magazines were miscellanies of short and long fiction with various features like quizzes, letters pages, and factual articles, printed on cheap pulp paper and selling for ten or fifteen cents. Pulps were invented in 1896, but they reached the height of their popularity only once they began to specialize after 1919: Street and Smith were first with this innovation, with their all-Western *Western Story Magazine*. Within the Western genre further subdivision (into, for example, romance Westerns—*Ranch Romances, Romantic Range*—and adventure Westerns—*Ace-High Western Stories, Double Action Western*) enabled publish-

ers to target specific audiences. This precision was important because of the attempts to raise advertising revenue; advertisers wanted assurance that notice of their products was reaching appropriate audiences. The run of pulp authors was slotted into this regulated scheme, with uniform payment rates—two cents and, later, one cent per word—and manuscript lengths—5,000 words for a story, 30,000 words for a novelette, and 60,000 words for a serial. The reigning climate was imitation and reproduction, the editorial consensus being that "if there is one trait that the pulpwood reader has it is his predilection for sameness."[31] The pulps died as a popular form around 1950, partly because of competition from the more seductive media of television and cinema and from the boom in slick magazines and paperback books when paper quotas ended after World War II. In at least one pulp editor's opinion, however, pulps suffered also because the automation of production became too oppressive for the writers, artists, and editors involved in their making.[32]

By and large pulp magazines recycled the formulaic narratives and character types of the twentieth-century nickel novels, dispensing with the juvenile emphasis and adding some violence and sex to the action. For example, when Street and Smith turned *Wild West Weekly* into the pulp magazine *Wild West* in 1927, the lead story simply took the characters from the nickel novel and turned them into mature young men, enlarging the scope of their violent action and romantic entanglements. Although the subgenre of the romance Western seems to privilege women figures, by endowing them with economic power (typically portraying them as ranch owners) and positioning them in the center of the adventurous action, the female sphere is ultimately limited in familiar ways. In "Hearts and Saddles," by J. Edward Leithead—the lead story of *Ranch Romances* for July 1931—the heroine is contained by the essentialist marks of femininity; Sally Kerrigan is "a very pretty girl in overalls and brass-studded buzzard-wing chaps, a gray curled-brim sombrero drawn low on her head. Unless one looked closely, noting the wholly feminine cast of brown features and the soft, well rounded contours of a girlish form, she might be mistaken for a rider of the opposite sex."[33] It is not surprising that, despite her contribution to the vanquishing of rustlers, the crises of the cattle drive, and the hard work of the ranch, Sally Kerrigan ends the tale in the hero's arms, "her eyes . . . shining in proclamation of surrender."[34] Figures from minority cultures within America continue to function as appendages to the white male hero, too. Occasionally a more distinctive narrative emerged from the mass, from a "star" writer who succeeded in parlaying his or her work into paperback book format. The pulp fiction of Zane Grey and Frederick Faust (better known by one of his twenty pseudonyms, Max Brand), for example, has marked characteristics. Both authors worked up the Western's mythological associations, shaping familiar adventures into an archetypal pattern of separation-initiation-return; Grey emphasized sexual thrills and lavish scenic descriptions; and Brand came to reverse the dominant trend, turning from the Virginian type of romantic hero to the Leatherstocking type of extrasocietal loner. Ultimately, however, these variations seem primarily structural, not challenging the ideological limits of the pulp formula.

The diminution of the authorial voice continues in the textual dynamics of the pulp magazines, with the further impression that readers, too, are being articulated as component parts of a commercial scheme run for the benefit of the publishers. Generally the stories lack even the limited individuation of the dime narrative voices, although occasional stars like Grey and Brand sustained characteristic accents in their work. Story functioned as product in this format more explicitly than ever; in the words of one pulp editor, "Serials are nothing more than sales promotion efforts."[35] The power of the editorial voice was institutionalized in departments such as "The Round-Up" in Street and Smith's *Western Story Magazine* and "The Wranglers' Corner" in the same firm's *Wild West,* where editors orchestrated characters' responses to readers' letters in a facsimile of direct contact. Authors, particularly star authors, were intermittently given a voice in this conversation, but it was heavily mediated by editorial invention and the injunction that authors are "just common folks, same as you and me."[36] This device served not only to induce community identification in the reader but to gauge and manipulate audience response for financial profit. As part of this rhetoric, in 1924 readers of Street and Smith's *Western Story Magazine* were enlisted in the effort to drum up advertising revenue: "We know you read the advertisements in our magazines, and that you can help us prove it to the advertisers."[37] In a final sign of commodification, when the latter-day pulp *Far West* was launched in 1978, the readers' responses were limited to a multiple choice questionnaire that explicitly controlled the range of responses available to them. The implication is that publisher-editors were attempting the ultimate rationalization of labor, incorporating authors and readers as component parts of their smoothly operating machine. Given Henry Steeger's judgment that "pulps were the principal entertainment vehicle for millions of Americans," the circulation of such traditional images of the West and the attempt to reify their readers potentially marked a large sector of American cultural life.[38]

The genre that finally linked the written Western to the movie and television version was the comic.[39] According to Maurice Horn, "the birth of the comics as a distinct medium"—as strips with sequential narrative, continuing characters, speech balloons, onomatopoeia, and frame-enclosed pictures—occurred in 1896, with the panel *Yellow Kid* by Richard Outcault in Joseph Pulitzer's Sunday supplement to the *New York World.*[40] By the early years of the twentieth century comic strips were a regular feature in daily newspapers, too. Over time these strips expanded from juvenile to adult forms; from about 1929 many privileged adventure action over comedy; and from the early 1920s, they increasingly imitated the "syntax" of movies with much cross-fertilization of content between comics and animated cartoons. American comic books took off in the 1930s, first with reprinted comic strips, and then with original material, mainly addressed to young readers. Since World War II the development of comic strips and books has been intermittent, with periods of censorship, decline, and renewed innovation, especially from underground "comix."

The economics of comic production were distinct from dime and pulp calculations because strips were controlled by a syndicate distribution system that rationalized production and centralized control more fiercely than any publishing house. There is diverse evidence of syndicate editors seizing the creative initiative from artists and authors. For example, Joseph Patterson, founder of the Tribune-News Syndicate, "often took average artists, suggested titles, changed characters and outlined themes, to create classic comics."[41] Especially after the consolidations of the 1930s, syndicates also managed energetic cross-fertilization among the entertainment media. In the 1970s the Field Newspaper Syndicate developed features and continuities on the basis of quasi-scientific planning and polling, including canvassing newsagents' responses to new titles. Audiences were massive: in 1938 a Gallup survey stated that 63 percent of adults read daily comics and 73 percent of adults read Sunday comics.[42]

Strips devoted to the Wild West appeared in the late 1920s, and flurries of humorous and adventure Western stories occurred throughout the 1930s, 1940s, and 1950s, both in newspaper strips and in comic books. By 1965 comic Westerns kept pace with developments in the cinematic Western with such irreverent anti-Western comics as *Tumbleweeds.* The hand of the syndicate is evident in these developments. The Tribune-News Syndicate initiated many Western titles; *Texas Slim,* for example, which ran from 1925 to 1928 and then from 1940 to 1958, arose in response to Patterson's request for a humorous Western. The comic strip *Bronc Peeler,* drawn by Fred Harman from the early 1930s, was transformed into *Red Ryder* by New York entrepreneur Stephen Slesinger, who then parlayed the figure into movie serials, comic books, novels, radio shows, and advertising. With the Lone Ranger the commercial diversification operated in the opposite direction. Beginning life as a radio serial in 1933, the figure's massive success led editors at King Features to initiate Lone Ranger comic strips and comic books, which survived until the 1970s; there was also highly successful marketing of Lone Ranger guns, Lone Ranger costumes, Lone Ranger books, and Lone Ranger movie serials. . . . There were comic strips of Zane Grey's novels and of screen cowboys such as Tom Mix and Gene Autry.

The narratives of these Western comics remain recognizably formulaic. The following summary of *Broncho Bill* (begun by Harry O'Neill for United Features in the late 1920s as *Young Buffalo Bill,* later *Buckaroo Bill*) suggests their debt to the dime and nickel formulas of an earlier era: "The stories in *Broncho Bill* came to center around the activities of a Bill-led group of youthful vigilantes calling themselves the Rangers, sort of gun-toting boy scouts. O'Neill's idea of suspense was to have some innocent, a hapless infant or a golden-haired little girl, about to fall over a cliff or be eaten by a grizzly bear."[43] The positioning of Native American sidekicks—speaking, at least in *Bronc Peeler* and *The Lone Ranger,* the most ludicrous "You Betchum!" patois—is familiar, too. Some suggestive exceptions to the formula appeared, however; the protagonist of *White Boy* (from 1933) was raised among Native Americans, and *Ghost Rider* (from 1950) was a supernatural Western. Moreover, the graphic articulation of comics served, in time, to heighten the sensationalism of both violence and voyeuristic sex. Even more resonantly than earlier forms, the comics speak to the political world; they not only incorporate topical references (during the World Wars, for example), but the strips' position within newspapers links them to cultural events, however dissociated their fantasy world may seem. Western comics survive to an extent today, although, as with movie Westerns, they are no longer the dominant genre; perhaps their heritage is most strongly imprinted in the individualistic "superheroes" such as Superman and Spiderman.

Within this matrix of production authors' and artists' choices and roles were heavily determined by the syndicate machine. When entrepreneurial forces took over Fred Harman's comic strip, for example, the artist was turned into an economically productive celebrity: "Harman appeared in the ads along with his characters. 'Fred Harman, famous cowboy artist who draws the popular NEA newspaper cartoon RED RYDER COMIC STRIP, was a sure 'nough Colorado cowboy before hittin' the trail to New York City. Fred helped Daisy design this genuine Western-style saddle carbine an' hopes you get your RED RYDER CARBINE right away!'"[44] The Daisy Manufacturing Company (a maker of BB guns) also conducted competitions, with the artist as first prize: "SEE Fred Harman DRAW his famous Cartoon Strip." In a familiar ironic juncture Harman was puffed as the originary talent just at the time when his strip was being scripted by a number of ghost artists. Most syndicate employees enjoyed less exposure than this, being shuffled from strip to strip as market forces dictated.

Despite all these structural similarities between comic narratives and modes of production and those of earlier mass-produced Westerns, readers' responses may have made different meanings out of comics. Martin Barker's nuanced reading of non-Western comic books suggests that an increasingly sophisticated and knowing rhetoric—on the cover, in the editorial matter, and within the strips themselves—plays with the slippage between fantasy and reality and with self-reflexive commentary in ways much more complex than, though still recognizably related to, the rhetoric of dime novels. Barker reads these socially embedded signals as offering readers a "contract" involving resistance to authority (adult authority, in the case of juvenile audiences); working with a more textual interpretation, Horn argues that "if the medium is the message, then the message of the comics, with their flouting of the rules of traditional art and of civilized language, can only be subversion."[45] This hypothesis can be extrapolated to Western comics. As early as 1939 the comic strip *Little Joe*

emphatically parodied the genre's reliance on racial stereotypes. Utah, the old frontiersman, seeks to cheat "an Injun" out of his fine horses in exchange for what Utah believes is a defunct automobile:

> UTAH: Howdy! Right nice pair o' hosses you got thar—care to sell?
>
> "INJUN": Ugh! No sellum!
>
> UTAH: Ah—I see you like-um automobile—nice car—swap cheap! Have look-see anyway—
>
> "INJUN": Ugh! Heap fine smell buggy!
>
> UTAH [*sotto voce*]: Heh! Heh! Look at him! Them simple red men is all suckers fer bright paint—jest watch me git him—[to "Injun"] Done! I git th' hosses! You git th' car . . . all even—no backin' out! (Heh! Heh! Jest wait'll th' illiterate cuss tries drivin' it!)
>
> "INJUN": Ugh! [driving off in car] Yes—a very snappy job—superb lines—abundant power—much improved over the model I had while in college—nice to have met you—adios!
>
> [Utah collapses in astonishment, mouth agape.][46]

Marvel Comics' *Kid Colt Outlaw* plays up the parody of its "BLAM! WHUMP! WHAM!" action with pointed editorial comments: Kid Colt's "Deadly Double" is a "Wild and Wooly Western Masterpiece! . . . Lettered by: Al Kurzrok . . . Villain Booed by: Sagebrush Irv."[47] Such reminders of comics' artifice and their melodramatic absurdities proliferate throughout the recognizably formulaic tale of robbery, vengeance, and justice. These textual gestures can be interpreted as inviting a resistant reading of the plot, thereby undermining the narratives of law and order. Such subversion is, of course, significantly contained by the syndicate machine producing and profiting from these publications. Nevertheless, at the rhetorical level comics offer readers the opportunity to challenge the codes and hierarchies of the Western genre (and the society that it represents). The comics' pronounced foregrounding of parody is largely foreign to the pulp magazines and promises more subversion than the "producerly readings" or space for contestation opened up by the dime novels.

Evidence that these subversive gestures in comics are matched by readerly resistance, expressed as critical distance, comes in the reading practices of the comic audience most studied to date: children. Working from various case studies, Barker identifies "children's handling of the 'hidden curriculum' of adult power" in their reactions to weekly comics.[48] Reflecting more personally on his son's response to 1950s comics, Robert Warshow speculated that the boy's fascination with the publishing house, the staff, and the drafting processes indicated a specific strategy on the part of the juvenile reader: "I think that Paul's desire to put himself directly in touch with the processes by which the comic books are produced may be the expression of a fundamental detachment which helps to protect him from them; the comic books are not a 'universe' to him, but simply objects produced for his entertainment."[49] Again, a critical leap is required to extrapolate from this evidence specifically to Western comics. Nevertheless, the potential is clearly there for comic readers to construct a West of the imagination more self-consciously parodic or knowingly limited than any mere plot summary might suggest.

In this chapter I have tried to read the frames of production and reception that mediate narratives of the Wild West in dime, nickel, pulp, and comic publications. The image of the West that results is shifting and, to a degree, fractured. On the one hand, at the level of textual representation, the West of the majority of cheap fiction seems unremittingly masculinist, racist, and nationalistic, whether represented as savage wilderness, vanguard of American civilization, wellspring of imperialist energy, limitless playing field, home of entrepreneurial capitalism, or a de-historicized, moralistic environment that legitimizes violence and, later, sexual titillation. Yet the reading of this simple triumphalism is complicated by the contradictory voices that emerge as part of the commodification process. The most dynamic developments in the fictional formula seem to occur in the nineteenth and early twentieth centuries, when dime and nickel Westerns adapted their lineaments to changing cultural and political climates, partly by incorporating the market economy into their fictional action. Thereafter, repetitions in plot, character, setting, and language saturate the fictive material. At the same time, however, editorial gestures to readers become more knowing and sophisticated; whereas the formulaic fiction petrifies in the later twentieth century, the rhetorical devices framing that fiction become increasingly suggestive, offering readers various kinds of resistance to the heroic narratives. Audiences of different classes and periods seem to have followed their own agendas, their interpretations sometimes running counter to and sometimes colluding with the manifest story lines and the commercial paraphernalia. The "meanings" of mass-produced Western fiction can be read as the product of all these forces in contention and collusion with one another, contested terrain playing out a range of economic, national, and personal interests.

Notes

1. Umberto Eco, *Travels in Hyperreality,* trans. William Weaver (London, 1987), 10.

2. I address this period at greater length in Bold, "Popular Forms I," in *The Columbia History of the American Novel,* ed. Emory Elliott, 285-305 (New York, 1991). Sources include Mary Noel, *Villains Galore: The Heyday of the Popular Story Weekly* (New York, 1954); Madeleine B. Stern, ed., *Publishers for Mass Entertainment in Nineteenth Century America* (Boston, 1980); and Jane Tompkins, *Sensational Designs: The Cultural Work of American Fiction, 1790-1860* (New York, 1985).

3. The proportion of dime novels devoted to western topics is documented in Philip Durham, "Introduction," *"Seth Jones," Edward S. Ellis and "Deadwood Dick on Deck," Edward L. Wheeler: Dime Novels* (New York, 1966): "approximately three-fourths of the [Beadle and Adams] dime

novels deal with the various forms, problems, and attitudes of life on the frontier, and . . . more than half are concerned with life in the trans-Mississippi West" (ix). The details of dime novel production and formulas are drawn from Christine Bold, *Selling the Wild West: Popular Western Fiction 1860 to 1960* (Bloomington, Ind., 1987); Michael Denning, *Mechanic Accents: Dime Novels and Working Class Culture in America* (London, 1987); Albert Johannsen, *The House of Beadle and Adams and Its Dime and Nickel Novels: The Story of a Vanished Literature,* 2 vols., supplement (Norman, Okla., 1950, 1962); Daryl Jones, *The Dime Novel Western* (Bowling Green, Ohio, 1978); Quentin Reynolds, *The Fiction Factory; or, From Pulp Row to Quality Street: The Story of 100 Years of Publishing at Street and Smith* (New York, 1955); and Madeleine Stern, *Publishers for Mass Entertainment.*

4. W. H. Bishop, "Story-Paper Literature," *The Atlantic Monthly,* September 1879, 383.

5. Reynolds, *Fiction Factory,* 88-89.

6. Ann S. Stephens, *Malaeska: The Indian Wife of the White Hunter,* Beadle's Dime Novels no. 1 (New York, 1860 [1839]), 57.

7. Henry Nash Smith, *Virgin Land: The American West as Symbol and Myth* (Cambridge, Mass., 1950), 93.

8. Jane Tompkins, *West of Everything: The Inner Life of Westerns* (New York, 1992), 42.

9. For more information, see John Cawelti, *Adventure, Mystery, and Romance: Formula Stories as Art and Popular Culture* (Chicago, 1976); and Smith, *Virgin Land.*

10. Jones, *Dime Novel Western,* 22.

11. Prentiss Ingraham, *Buffalo Bill, from Boyhood to Manhood. Deeds of Daring, Scenes of Thrilling Peril, and Romantic Incidents in the Early Life of W. F. Cody, the Monarch of Bordermen.* Beadle's Boy's Library of Sport, Story, and Adventure no. 2 (New York, 1878), 2.

12. Christine Bold, "The Rough Riders at Home and Abroad: Cody, Roosevelt, Remington, and the Imperialist Hero," *Canadian Review of American Studies* 18 (Fall 1987): 324-30; Richard Slotkin, "The 'Wild West,' " in *Buffalo Bill and the Wild West,* 27-44 (Brooklyn, 1981).

13. Jones, *Dime Novel Western,* 84-87.

14. Smith, *Virgin Land,* 101.

15. Bold, *Selling the Wild West,* 6-7; Jones, *Dime Novel Western,* 79.

16. Warren French, "The Cowboy in the Dime Novel," *Studies in English* 30 (1951): 219-34.

17. G. Edward White, *The Eastern Establishment and the Western Experience: The West of Frederic Remington, Theodore Roosevelt, and Owen Wister* (New Haven, Conn., 1968).

18. Ned Taylor, "The Young Rough Riders in the Rockies; or, a Fight in Midair," *Young Rough Riders Weekly* no. 38 (1905), 1.

19. For further information about dime novel heroines, see Smith, *Virgin Land,* 112-20.

20. Jones, *Dime Novel Western,* 127. Various articles in *Reckless Ralph's Dime Novel Round-Up* (1931-; retitled *Dime Novel Round-Up* in 1953) document examples of topical references.

21. I develop this argument in much greater detail in Bold, *Selling the Wild West.*

22. Ned Buntline, *The White Wizard; or, The Great Prophet of the Seminoles,* Beadle's Dime Library 2, no. 16 (New York, 1879 [1858]), 32.

23. Edward L. Wheeler, *The Phantom Miner; or, Deadwood Dick's Bonanza* (Cleveland, 1899 [1878]), 17.

24. "A Chat with You," *Rough Rider Weekly* no. 140 (1906), 30.

25. That this audience was new and massive is confirmed by Smith, *Virgin Land,* 91, and Jones, *Dime Novel Western,* 8, 14.

26. Johannsen, *House of Beadle and Adams,* 1:9.

27. Frederick Whittaker, "Reply," *New York Tribune,* March 16, 1884, 8; Michael Denning, *Mechanic Accents,* 27.

28. Martin Barker, *Comics: Ideology, Power, and the Critics* (New York, 1989), 51.

29. John Fiske, *Understanding Popular Culture* (Boston, 1989), 104.

30. These details of pulp magazine production are drawn from Bold, *Selling the Wild West;* John A. Dinan, *The Pulp Western: A Popular History of the Western Fiction Magazine in America,* I. O. Evans Studies in the Philosophy and Criticism of Literature, no. 2. (San Bernardino, Calif., 1983); Tony Goodstone, ed., *The Pulps: Fifty Years of American Popular Culture* (New York, 1970); Ron Goulart, *Cheap Thrills: An Informal History of the Pulp Magazines* (New Rochelle, N.Y., 1972); Frank Gruber, *The Pulp Jungle* (Los Angeles, 1967); and Harold Brainerd Hersey, *Pulpwood Editor: The Fabulous World of the Thriller Magazines Revealed by a Veteran Editor and Publisher* (New York, 1937; reprint, Westport, Conn., 1974).

31. Hersey, *Pulpwood Editor,* 2.

32. Daisy Bacon, "The Golden Age of the Iron Maiden," *The Roundup,* April 1975, 7-9.

33. J. Edward Leithead, "Hearts and Saddles," *Ranch Romances,* July 1931, 169.

34. Ibid., 215.

35. Hersey, *Pulpwood Editor,* 23.

36. "The Round-Up," *Western Story Magazine,* October 27, 1927, 135.

37. "A Chat with You," *The Popular Magazine,* February 1905, n.p.

38. Goodstone, *Pulps,* v.

39. Information about comics is drawn from Barker, *Comics;* Herb Galewitz, *Great Comics* (New York, 1972); Goulart, *Cheap Thrills;* and Maurice Horn, ed., *The World Encyclopedia of Comics,* 2 vols. (New York, 1976).

40. Horn, *World Encyclopedia of Comics,* 1:10-11.

41. Richard Marschall, "A History of Newspaper Syndication," in *World Encyclopedia of Comics,* ed. Horn, 2:726.

42. Galewitz, *Great Comics,* vii.

43. Goulart, *The Adventurous Decade* (New Rochelle, N.Y., 1975), 184.

44. Goulart, *Adventurous Decade,* 187.

45. Barker, *Comics,* 61; Horn, *World Encyclopedia of Comics,* 1:50.

46. Galewitz, *Great Comics,* 244.

47. Gary Friedrich, Werner Roth, and Herb Trimpe, "The Deadly Double," *Kid Colt Outlaw,* August 1978, 1.

48. Barker, *Comics,* 86.

49. Robert Warshow, *The Immediate Experience: Movies, Comics, Theater, and Other Aspects of Popular Culture* (Garden City, N.Y., 1962), 87.

Paul J. Erickson (essay date 1998)

SOURCE: "Judging Books by Their Covers: Format, the Implied Reader, and the 'Degeneration' of the Dime Novel," in *Nineteenth-Century American Literature and Culture,* Vol. 12, No. 3, September, 1998, pp. 247-63.

[*In the essay below, Erickson argues that the transformation of the distribution and packaging of dime novels—rather than fundamental changes in the content of the stories—led to their decline.*]

[The Beadle publications] are without exception unobjectionable morally, whatever fault be found with their literary style and composition. They do not even obscurely pander to vice or excite the passions.

—William Everett, 1864 (qtd. in Nye 203)

The dreadful damage wrought to-day in every city, town, and village of these United States by the horrible and hideous stuff set weekly before the boys and girls of America by the villainous sheets which pander greedily and viciously to the natural taste of young readers for excitement, the irreparable wrong done by these vile publications, is hidden from no one.

—Brander Matthews, 1883 (qtd. in Denning 9)

The saffron-backed Dime Novels of the late Mr. Beadle, ill-famed among the ignorant who are unaware of their ultra-Puritan purity, . . . began to appear in the early years of the Civil War; and when I was a boy in a dismal boarding school at Sing Sing, in the winters of 1861-1863, I reveled in their thrilling and innocuous record of innocent and imminent danger.

—Brander Matthews, 1923 (qtd. in Denning 9)

The above quotes, from prominent arbiters of nineteenth-century American taste, illustrate the drastically fluctuating fortunes of the signature popular fiction phenomenon of the century, the dime novel. The New York firm of Beadle and Adams published the first dime novel, *Malaeska; the Indian Wife of the White Hunter* by Mrs. Ann Stephens in June, 1860. In October of that year, Beadle's first rival in the ten-cent fiction series field began publication. By 1864, the prestigious *North American Review,* having taken notice of these short books with their salmon-colored paper covers, stated that over five million Beadle and Adams dime novels were in circulation, and by the late 1870s, hundreds of competing cheap fiction series flooded the market. Yet by 1896 the Beadle firm had disappeared, and their main competitor, George Munro, had died, leaving behind an estate of $10 million. The last true dime novel series, Street and Smith's "New Buffalo Bill Weekly," stopped publication in 1912. In 1922, examples from a collection of 1400 Western dime novels donated to the New York Public Library were put on display to illustrate the history of the dead genre.

Such books were especially well-suited to being put on display, for the dime novel industry was a pioneer in many aspects of book production and design: including the use of cover illustrations and colored pictures, the variation in size of different series, and the production of books to be sold at newsstands. These innovations played a crucial role in the creation of a "literary marketplace," the entrance of books into the burgeoning consumer culture of late-nineteenth-century America. As Russel Nye has written, "Beadle and Adams's contribution to publishing was one of merchandising, not content. They organized production, standardized the product, and did some shrewd guessing about the nature and extent of the market" (201). Thus the dime novel can be situated within the larger context of the literary market in nineteenth-century America, which saw the creation of different types of textual presentation, such as different styles of binding and illustration, that could be applied to the same texts in order to reach different segments of the market, strategies with which any contemporary book buyer will be abundantly familiar. Like almost all other consumer goods, due to changes in population patterns, improvements in transportation, and the development of new retail outlets, books were made available to the American public in a multitude of new ways in the years after the Civil War.

Such changes in format and distribution, however, were not viewed as morally neutral by many cultural critics. Increasing concerns about the character of the urban street and its denizens made newsstands suspect, and the popularity of publications such as the *Police Gazette* heightened the attention paid by at least some concerned citizens to the physical appearance of reading materials, just as the signature bindings of "quality" fiction houses such as Ticknor and Fields became automatic signifiers of acceptability. As the tireless reformer Anthony Comstock noted, "We assimilate what we read. The pages of printed matter become our companions" (ix). This vision of the connection between books as material objects and their moral impact fed logically into Comstock's attacks in the 1880s on dime novels. Ever concerned with what people consume and where they do it, Comstock was aware of the combined attractions of the format and price of these novels, and stridently condemned these "series of new snares of fascinating construction, small and tempting in price" (21).

Comstock did not separate his assault on what the books looked like from what the books said, despite the fact that many of the stories published in the nickel broadsheets he so despised had been published earlier in family magazines or more traditional "dime novels." The generally accepted narrative of the decline and disappearance of the dime novel is one of gradual degradation, a descent into sensationalism provoked by increased competition from other media, until the dime novel, a decadent parody of its former greatness, breathed its last. But this account ignores the extent of the practices of textual recycling that went on within the industry; the same novels were reprinted again and again, often with different titles and in different formats. Since the rise of the dime novel was not due to an innovation in textual content—Mrs. Stephens's *Malaeska* had initially been published in the *Ladies' Home Companion* in 1839—but to innovations in format and distribution, it is possible that the *decline* in the reputation of the genre was caused, at least in part, by changes in packaging and distribution, and the changes in readership which they implied, rather than by changes in the texts themselves.

Using editions of two dime novels—*Stella Delorme; or, the Comanche's Dream* and *Old Nick of the Swamp*—by Ned Buntline, one of the genre's most famous practitioners, each published first in the 1860s and then reprinted 40 years later, this article will examine the physical changes in these books *as books,* as well as implied changes in distribution and readership, to argue that the shift in the cultural perception of the dime novel was not due solely to a cheapening of their stories. Format and distribution—what books look like and how readers get them—assist in both constructing and instructing an audience. Readers take cues not just from the text, but from its physical appearance and from the environment in which it is acquired. Likewise, non-readers of texts often take cues on how to evaluate texts from what books look like and from whom they perceive the intended readership to be. Everett Williams and Brander Matthews made the statements at the beginning of this article, generally speaking, about the same *texts,* but not about the same *books.* This shift in the views held by representatives of "high" culture is in large part, I argue, a response to the readership of the texts, which is in turn constructed (and engendered) by the format of the novels and the ways in which they were sold and distributed. Thus, we can see, as D. F. McKenzie and other scholars in the expanding field of the "history of the book" have pointed out, the importance of the physical reality of books in creating their meaning, at times independent of the words which their pages bear.[1]

The stories in these Ned Buntline dime novels did not become any more sensational or offensive over 40 years of recycling, although their references to the Texas Revolution and wild Comanches probably became less familiar. What changed for these books, as for almost all printed materials in the nineteenth century, was how they were published, how much they cost, where they were purchased, and, most importantly, the readers who were constructed by and inferred from these three elements. Thus, these examples of dime novel Westerns bear out McKenzie's claim that, "Meanings are not therefore inherent but are constructed by successive interpretative acts by those who write, design, and print books and by those who buy and read them" (18). Yet to McKenzie's crucial analysis of the status of the "text as an *unstable* physical form" can be added an examination of how the physical form of books is read by people (such as cultural critics or concerned parents) who don't read the books, the cultural signals emitted by specific formats, and the extent to which texts remain stable (although not in meaning) while the format is altered. As McKenzie notes, "every book tells a story quite apart from that recounted by its text," but, as the changing responses to the dime novel show, that story is not told only to the readers of the text (8).

Ned Buntline was one of nineteenth-century America's more picaresque figures. After a stint in the Navy and a journalistic career which brought him mixed success, Buntline became a star of the popular fiction industry with the 1848 publication of *The Mysteries and Miseries of New York.* Following a period of political involvement in the early 1850s, when he was instrumental in founding the nativist Know-Nothing Party, Buntline signed a contract with a story paper, *The New York Mercury,* in 1858 which would eventually lead him to fame as a dime novelist and, ultimately, as the "discoverer" of Buffalo Bill Cody. Although Buntline got his start in fiction writing sea stories, he quickly adapted his skills to the changing demands of the market, and began producing Westerns, the genre with which he is today most often identified. Two of Buntline's western-themed novels that were recycled by the dime novel industry were *Stella Delorme; or, the Comanche's Dream* and *Old Nick of the Swamp,* which both draw on the same fragments of central Texas history for their plots. *Stella Delorme* first appeared in book form in 1860, published by Frederic A. Brady (it appeared in serial form in *The New York Mercury* in 1859). The example I was able to examine (in the Center for American History, University of Texas at Austin) no longer has its original cover (nor any of the ads that may have been included), but it most likely had a cheap board cover and sold for 25 cents. It was slightly larger than a typical dime novel, had 72 pages, and contained five illustrations. The story takes place during the Texas Republic, when a young Comanche

chief, Lagona, has a vision of a beautiful white girl about to be killed by Lipan Apaches. He rescues the girl, who turns out to be Stella Delorme, daughter of a wealthy Texas planter. Stella is rescued several times by Lagona, who demands her hand in marriage, but is refused by her father and the head of the local Texas Rangers, Major Ben McCullough. After attempting to take Stella from her home by force, Lagona asks Mr. Delorme to take him in, educate him, and teach him the ways of the white man. After his education, Lagona leaves the Delormes, only to return with a gang of Galveston criminals, and kidnap poor Stella once again. She is rescued from the Comanches by Major McCullough, only to be recaptured by Lagona yet again. At the end, Lagona realizes that the woman he loves will never love him and returns her, unharmed, to her father before killing himself, and Stella is married to her white fiancé.

Old Nick of the Swamp; or, The Bravo's Vengeance was first published in 1868 as No. 100 in George Munro & Co.'s "Munro's Ten Cent Novels" series. The title page states that the story is "By an Old Hunter," and Buntline's name appears nowhere on the book; given Buntline's marketability, this implies that he most likely was officially under contract to another firm at the time and wrote the novel for Munro on the side. This novel is a typical example of the early dime novel: 96 pages long, covered in pale orange paper, in the "traditional" dime novel size (6.25″ × 4″). The cover bears the series name, the title, and an illustration of an Indian with a tomahawk seemingly growing out of the ground behind a grizzled backwoodsman, evidently Old Nick, bearing a rifle. . . . The incident in the illustration does not take place anywhere in the novel, but it did allow for the inclusion of both an Indian and a trapper as well as their weapons of choice.

The plot of *Old Nick* is fairly similar to that of *Stella Delorme.* Set during the Texas Revolution, the novel contains more scenes of graphic violence than did *Stella,* and the wartime setting offers many more opportunities to insult and kill Mexicans, who are always "greasers" or "yaller-bellies." Ben Long, a frontier scout, and Adrian Leland, known as "The Bravo," visit their friend Old Nick, a hermit backwoodsman who lives in the middle of a swamp in central Texas. While visiting, they are told that Inez Montero, the daughter of a prominent Texas merchant, has been kidnapped by raiding Comanches with the aid of Juan Fernandez, Señor Montero's jealous Mexican clerk. With the help of the Lipan Apaches, the only friendly Indians in Texas, the Bravo, Ben, and Old Nick track the Comanches, steal Inez from the middle of the camp, and flee toward home. They are forced to take refuge in an abandoned farmstead, and the Comanches, by this time joined by Mexicans, lay siege to the farm. Old Nick, reprising Davy Crockett's role at the Alamo, leaves for San Antonio to get help, which arrives just in time in the form of Captain Jack Hays and his Texas Rangers. A general slaughter commences, Juan Fernandez is found hiding on the field of battle behind a dead horse, Texas prevails, and the Bravo and Inez are married.

Although Erastus Beadle claimed that his strategy for dealing with rivals who published trashier novels was to "kill a few more Indians than we used to," both of these novels were republished exactly, without a single additional Indian being killed (qtd. in Pearson 99). *Stella Delorme*, under various titles, was published five times by Beadle and Adams, first in the "American Tales" series in 1869, then in 1874 as one of the early issues of "Frank Starr's American Novels" after the series switched to a slightly larger format. This series, in 1874, also introduced "illuminated covers" to the market. The announcement accompanying this change in the series' format claimed that the new format offered, "A Twenty-five cent book for ten cents! . . . [the series] will embrace a considerable number of novels hitherto not accessible to readers, or only to be had in more expensive shape" (qtd. in Johannsen 1: 154-56). Thus, the Beadle firm concealed the extent to which the texts in the series were not only recycled, but recycled from other cheap-fiction series in the Beadle catalog. The novel was released again in 1877 as No. 23 in "Starr's New York Library";[2] the price for novels in all of these various formats was ten cents. *Stella* was reissued yet again as No. 1038 in "Beadle's Dime Library" in July, 1900 (the copy examined for this paper), after Beadle and Adams had been taken over by M. J. Ivers. All of these various editions were identical textually, and were in fact printed from the same stereotype plates.[3]

Since other dime novel publishers have not received as much scholarly attention as has Beadle and Adams, it is impossible to say how many times, if any, *Old Nick of the Swamp* was republished by Munro. The 1908 edition was issued by M. J. Ivers in the "Beadle's Frontier Library" series, a series name that was never used by Beadle and which included many novels, such as *Old Nick*, which Beadle never published. This edition was printed on very cheap wood-pulp paper, stapled instead of sewn, with the cover glued on—a clear example of cutting corners in production in order to keep costs down. The primary differences are the title page, of course, which bears the new publisher's information but also carries Buntline's name as the author, and the cover, which is a garishly colored illustration (a style introduced in 1895) of an Indian on horseback who has just been shot. Another crucial difference is in price—the 1868 edition sold for a dime, while the 1908 edition sold for a nickel, which in the early twentieth century evidently did not generate enough revenue, as the Ivers firm went out of business later that year.

These two novels by Ned Buntline provide us with examples of dime novels that were recycled, not merely having their *texts* reprinted, but being reprinted from the identical stereotype plates. So why is the standard account of the dime novel Western, even according to the most astute students of the genre, one of degeneration? Writing of dime novel heroines, Henry Nash Smith wrote that these characters "took a distinct turn for the worse, no doubt corrupted by the general increase of sensationalism," and that "these changes in the characters reveal a progressive deterioration in the Western story as a genre" (Smith 115,

119). Edmund Pearson writes that Munro's competition forced Beadle to "cheapen the tone of his own books and deal more or less in blood and thunder" (Pearson 85-86). Even the encyclopedic Albert Johannsen writes, "With the introduction of the broadleaves, the type of story gradually changed and deteriorated . . ." (Johannsen 1:59). There is no question that some dime novel series did grow more sensational with time, and the introduction of new genres, especially the urban detective stories that roared onto the scene in the 1880s, might have allowed for the inclusion of more salacious material. What is striking about the products of an industry that produced stories in such profusion is not how much they changed but how little. The imperative to save money by reissuing the same story in different forms under different titles seems to have at least balanced, if not outweighed, the desire to keep up with the Joneses by spicing up the stories.

As these two novels suggest, even if the stories were newly-written, dime novel authors worked so quickly and according to such established formulae that different stories by the same author cannot help but closely resemble each other. Buntline wrote these two stories almost ten years apart: *Stella Delorme* before dime novels as such even existed, and *Old Nick* well into the era of fierce competition for the dime novel audience, when standards were supposed to be slipping. Yet save for a slight increase in violence in the later story, the two are almost identical, and the later novel contains more moralizing and less cursing. These similarities should not be surprising in a genre for which the conditions of production have often been compared to automatic writing, a comparison that seems apt if we are to believe Buntline's claim that he once wrote a 610-page novel in 62 hours. The various reprints of these novels roughly correspond with the dates of the three quotations from Williams and Matthews at the beginning of this article, yet we can see that at least in these two instances, the texts printed in 1877, 1900, and 1908 do not differ at all from their 1860 or 1868 predecessors. The differences in these responses to dime novels at these times can be attributed to a complex nexus of factors including the format in which they appeared, how they were distributed, how they promoted themselves, and who read them.

In answer to the question "Who read these dime novels?" Johannsen answers: "We ourselves read them. . . . But we were in good company, for they were also read by bankers and bootblacks, clergymen and clerks . . . in fact by almost everyone except schoolma'ams, pedants, and the illiterate" (Johannsen 1:9). Indeed, the readership that is implied and, I would argue, constructed by the advertisements in the early Beadle publications supports this claim. An ad on the inside cover of the 1868 *Old Nick* for the next number, *The Gamecock of the Santee*, states that, "The novel is recommended to every class of readers, and they will find it both interesting and amusing." In 1863, in response to criticism of their products on moral grounds, Beadle and Adams ran an ad listing the merits of their dime novels. Two items from the list are:

5. Beadle's Dime Novels are particularly adapted to the Houses and Firesides of America, and may safely be placed in the hands of young as well as old.

6. Beadle's Dime Novels are good, pure, and reliable. . . . [They] are adapted to all classes, readable at all times, fit for all places. (qtd. in Johannsen 1: 45-46)

This appeal to the entire family is also clear in the other kinds of publications advertised in the early dime novels. The back cover of the 1868 Munro *Old Nick* lists dime novels for sale, as well as song books and French and German grammars. Beadle and Adams included similar books in their lists, as well as books of dialogues, letter-writers, the "Dime Elocutionist," the "Housewife's Manual," "Beadle's Base-ball Player" and the "Dime National Tax Law." In contrast, the 1900 *Stella Delorme* contains six pages of ads, almost entirely for other dime novel or adventure series, all aimed at young readers. The 1908 *Old Nick*, produced in the last days of the Ivers firm, contains sloppily produced ads for a book of "Standard Dialogues for Young Folks," "Beadle's Frontier Series," and "Beadle's Boys Library."

The readership of dime novels was implied in other ways as well. As more forms of inexpensive reading material came on the market, publishers understandably began to target publications for specific audiences. While the early story papers and dime novels had been targeted at a broad readership, as the advertisements mentioned above illustrate, in the 1870s various series began to be associated with specific readers. In 1877, several months after Beadle and Adams published the first number of the "Dime Library," a series of reprints of "quality" literature that aimed for the adult market, they also began "Beadle's Half-Dime Library" which was the first series *targeted* specifically to boys, although many of its numbers appeared in other series that were not "boys" series. That same year Beadle introduced the "Fireside Library," which consisted mostly of romances and seems to have been intended for girls. The fact that both series cost a nickel, instead of a dime, shows that publishers such as Beadle and Adams were aware that juveniles and working-class readers made up a large part of their readership and were trying to make their books more accessible to people with little disposable income. W. H. Bishop, writing in the *Atlantic* in 1879, expressed the predominant view of dime novels at the time, saying that they were "written almost exclusively for the use of the lower classes of society." He described the traffic at an urban newsstand on publication day, saying that "a middle-aged woman . . . a shop girl . . . [and] a servant" stopped by to buy dime novels, "but with them, before them, and after them come boys. . . . The most ardent class of patron . . . are boys" (qtd. in Denning 29-30).

It may be no coincidence that in the 1870s, when the bulk of readership was considered to consist of boys, and when advertising for them became more directly focused on attracting boys as consumers, dime novels began to be seen as dangerous influences on young people. As soon as they came to be seen as age-specific reading material, instead of shared family pleasures, these books could be used to explain the perennially awful behavior of children. The indefatigable Anthony Comstock wrote, in *Traps for the Young,* that a young man he arrested for obscenity in Massachusetts maintained his cool up to the moment of the discovery of a stack of nickel weeklies in his room: "When these were discovered, he . . . said with great feeling, 'There! that's what has cursed me! That has brought me to this!'" (28-29). At the time, story papers were at the height of their popularity and circulated to hundreds of thousands of American homes. They were almost identical in format to the broadsheet dime novels, but contained a wide variety of stories, making them the reading material of choice for families who could only afford one periodical. The crucial differences from the broadsheet dime novels, however, were that the story papers were delivered into the home instead of bought at newsstands, and were marketed to the entire family instead of to boys. The fact that these weekly story papers contained material almost identical to the adventure tales appearing in the dime novels makes the questions of distribution and readership crucial to understanding how dime novels were perceived.

The answer to the question "Who read these dime novels?" seems to be that everyone read them, but that they were *associated* with young readers, especially boys; as Comstock claimed, "Boys read these stories almost incessantly after once a taste is acquired" (24). A more difficult question to answer, and one that is much less often asked, is how did the boys get them? The early dime novels appear to have been sent largely through the mail. Since the first American postal laws in 1792, postal rates were structured to allow for the easy and inexpensive access of all Americans to information that was deemed essential to the functioning of a democracy. This, of course, meant newspapers, while books were seen less as conveyors of information or vessels of national culture than as items of merchandise.[4] Newspapers were favored to such an extent—in the early 19th century, postage on a newspaper going an unlimited distance was 1.5 cents, while postage on a one-page letter going over 450 miles was 25 cents—that people began to write letters in the margin space in newspapers to save money (Fuller 111). Richard Kielbowicz makes the valuable distinction between "books" and "book-material," for publishers discovered that they could send "books" through the mail at much cheaper rates if they didn't look like books (133). In the 1830s and 40s story papers began to appear, which merely serialized books in newspaper format, taking advantage of the low rates. Publications such as *Brother Jonathan* and the *New World* started printing gigantic issues, some measuring four feet by seven feet and weighing over a pound, while still mailing them for 1.5 cents. In 1852, the rate for periodicals, which had been different from newspapers (the distinction depended on frequency, format, and content), was made the same as the newspaper rate. Not only did this provide further incentives for publishers to disguise books as periodicals or newspapers, it lowered the prices that people expected to pay for reading matter. The early dime novels were paid for in advance, and then mailed out, most often with the postage to be paid by the recipient; this was the primary

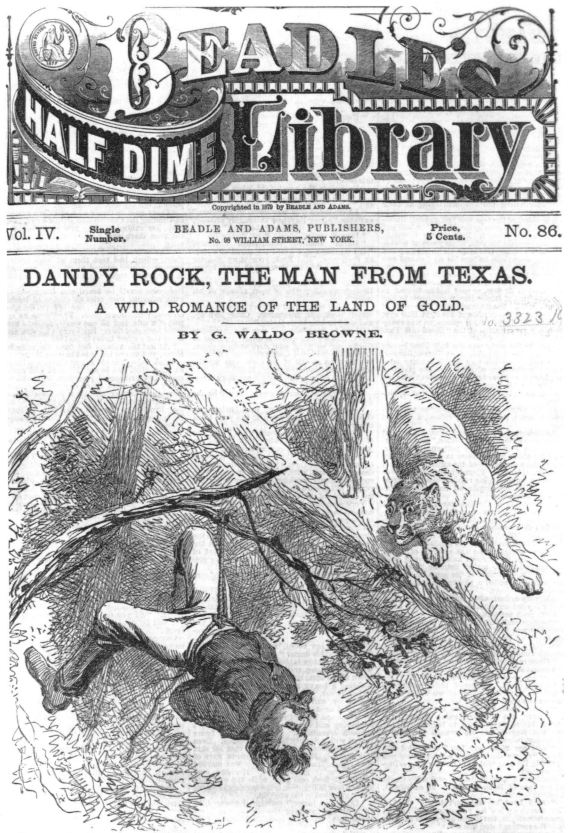

BEADLE'S Half Dime Library

Copyrighted in 1879 by BEADLE AND ADAMS.

Vol. IV.   Single Number.   BEADLE AND ADAMS, PUBLISHERS, No. 98 WILLIAM STREET, NEW YORK.   Price, 5 Cents.   No. 86.

DANDY ROCK, THE MAN FROM TEXAS.

A WILD ROMANCE OF THE LAND OF GOLD.

BY G. WALDO BROWNE.

Five, ten, fifteen minutes wore away, and still the cougar had not left his perch, neither had the gleaming eyes left for even a moment their prey.

mode of paying second-class postage well into the 1870s. George Munro, instead of using the Beadle trademark image of a dime on the title page, used an image of a ten-cent postage stamp, cementing the connection between price and distribution. This method of distribution seems to have changed quite soon, however, especially with the appearance of the American News Company in 1864, which served as sales agent for all Beadle publications. Beadle dime novels were still available through the mail, but the ANC had a standing order of 60,000 for each number that they in turn distributed to booksellers and news-dealers nationwide.

This did not lessen the importance of postal rates, however, since an 1861 ruling had allowed agents to receive periodicals at the same rates as individual subscribers. So large shipments of dime novels could be sent to "subscribers," i.e., news agents, who then sold them at their newsstands. Publishers still had to ensure that their products looked like periodical literature in order to qualify for the lower rates. Dime novel publishers engaged in a continual game of cat and mouse with the Postal Service, which accounts for many of the changes in dime novel format. In 1885, the Postal Service issued a definition of mail that would qualify for the lower second-class rate, stating that it must "be published at stated intervals—four times a year at least—to issue from a known office of publication, possess a legitimate subscription list, and have no bindings of board or cloth" (Fuller 133). This requirement of "stated intervals" made reprints an even more attractive option to publishers, since it is much easier to actually issue something at regular intervals if no writers are involved. The Postal Service's new definition of second-class mail enabled most dime novel publishers to sneak traditional dime novels through at the lower rate, but with the advent of broadsheet, or quarto, publications such as Beadle's "Half-Dime Library"—which looked like newspapers—the issue was made somewhat moot. In 1890, however, the Postal Service excluded the "dime libraries," which were mostly pirated reprints, from second-class rates, claiming that they were not "periodicals" and that most were sold on newsstands anyway. But even though the mail continued to serve as a vital distribution channel for dime novels, the way in which actual readers acquired them changed drastically, and with significant results.[5]

This shift from mail distribution to newsstand sales worked to change both the readership of the dime novels and the cultural perception of their value. Once dime novels were readily available at newsstands, instead of through the mail, they became more accessible to young readers who were impatient with their money and whose parents kept a closer eye on the mail than they did on their sons. In the 1870s, when the price dropped to a nickel, dime novels became accessible to an even broader range of low-income and young readers. The lower price, combined with the change in format to broadsheets, made dime novels look more like less reputable forms of reading, such as the *Police Gazette,* which was reflected in how they were perceived. Anthony Comstock made this connection manifest

at the opening of his chapter dealing with dime novels in *Traps for the Young,* which begins, "And it came to pass that as Satan went to and fro upon the earth, watching his traps and rejoicing over his numerous victims, he found room for improvement in some of his schemes" (20). Satan finds that the daily and weekly press

> were too high-priced for children, and too cumbersome to be conveniently hid from the parent's eye or carried in the boy's pocket. So he resolved to make another trap for boys and girls especially. He also resolved to make the most of these vile illustrated weekly papers, by lining the news-stands and shop windows along the pathway of the children from home to school and church. . . . (20)

The appearance of colored cover illustrations in 1874 provides additional evidence for the shift from consumers buying direct from the publisher through the mail to buying at newsstands or bookstores. Colored covers only make sense if readers can both see the cover at the point of purchase and compare it to the competitors' (presumably uncolored) products. The use of cover illustrations increased the similarity these novels bore to more suspicious forms of literature, since the illustrations became more lurid as competition increased. William Graham Sumner, in an 1880 diatribe entitled "What Our Boys Are Reading," wrote that the new novels targeted at boys, *to judge by the pictures,* are always worse than the old" (Sumner 367, italics mine). The two quotations from Brander Matthews at the beginning of this article illustrate this distinction. In his later quotation, he is nostalgic for the "saffron-backed Dime Novels," while in 1883 he condemned the "villainous sheets" for their corruption of the young; he clearly considered the two formats to represent different kinds of texts. As these two novels illustrate, the distinction between the two was not one of subject matter, but of format and readership. Suddenly they were the chosen distraction for hordes of boys, especially, in William Graham Sumner's words, of the "idle and vicious boys in great cities" where newsstands proliferated, instead of shared family reading material (367). As Sumner notes, these novels, which he finds "indescribably vulgar," "can be easily obtained and easily concealed, and it is a question for parents and teachers how this is to be done" (369, 377). By 1880, the changes in distribution and format discussed above were firmly in place, and were clearly working to change Sumner's, and many others', view of dime novels' salubrity.

The many recollections of dime novel reading assembled by Edmund Pearson in his 1929 book *Dime Novels* constitute a wonderful body of anecdotal information about the genre, especially about its reputation, since the questions he asked of his acquaintances about their juvenile reading habits seem to have been focused on the issue of whether or not dime novels were forbidden by the respondents' parents. The responses highlight the connection between reputation and format and distribution. Pearson recounts a story included by famed dime novelist Edward S. Ellis in a new introduction to *Seth Jones* about Ellis's involvement with his church Sunday School. Ellis presented the Sunday

School superintendent with a finely bound volume, asking if he thought it suitable for inclusion in the church library. When the superintendent told Ellis that he found the book morally upright and eminently appropriate, Ellis informed him that it was merely one of his own dime novels that he had had rebound, with the closing admonition: "The good brethren who gave that vicious French novel a prominent place in the Sunday-school library would have revolted at the proposal to put this little story beside it, for the reason that it has a paper cover, [and] is of a salmon color . . ." (qtd. in Pearson 103). George Ade observed of the later quarto format publications that, "One reason for the enduring popularity of the nickel library was that it could be spread open inside of a school geography and entirely concealed from any teacher who did not approach from the rear" (qtd. in Pearson 239). Many of Pearson's respondents mentioned that the size and thinness of the quarto format novels made them perfect for hiding within more respectable reading material, both at home and at school, illustrating that Sumner's fears were not entirely without basis. Frank O'Brien told Pearson that his parents destroyed his cache of "Jack Harkaway" novels, but approved of the "Frank Nelson" stories: "The principal difference was, I think, that [the Frank Nelson stories] came in book form, and therefore parents thought it was O.K." (qtd. in Pearson 249).

It is telling that almost all of Pearson's sources seem to recall dime novels as being forbidden, or at least disapproved of, and that none recall receiving them through the mail. Those men who did confess to having read dime novels said that they either bought them at newsstands or bookshops or found them in attics, barns, and outhouses. Even more importantly, several of these men remember their families receiving story papers through the mail, and that they were considered acceptable reading, despite the fact that they contained many stories that either had appeared or would appear as dime novels and nickel weeklies. Many of his sources also distinguish between dime novels and the nickel libraries, saying that the latter were much more disreputable—again, the primary difference being price and format—while some respondents seem aware that the dime novels, the nickel libraries, and the story papers were really all the same in terms of content. The editor Marc Connelly noted that:

> Dime novels did not circulate in my set. However, our parents referred to the nickel weeklies we read as 'dime novels.' I spent a good part of my ninth, tenth, and eleventh years explaining the difference, but it never did much good. Occasionally I found myself in possession of a real dime novel; I believe my acquaintance with Nick Carter and his faithful Chick, came exclusively through that high-priced medium. It was a pleasant acquaintance, but (could it have been the difference in price?) they never fascinated me as did those two detectives of the five cent libraries, 'Old' and 'Young King Brady.' (qtd. in Pearson 240)

These recollections of youthful reading offer clues to the ways in which the format, price, and means of acquisition of books conditioned the responses of both readers and non-readers (parents) to these books. When viewed through the prism of the values and strictures of late nineteenth-century American bourgeois culture, these factors combine to produce both a class-biased response to the later dime novels and a nostalgic longing for the earlier, "purer" examples of the genre. Many came to believe that the cheap format meant more lurid stories, and thus, even as the texts themselves did not change, felt that the genre was going downhill. This view has been internalized by many contemporary scholars, who frequently invoke this narrative of degeneration when discussing the dime novel in its later stages without acknowledging the relative *textual* stability of the genre.

While it is impossible to generalize from two examples, these two dime novels provide evidence that leads to a fuller view of the "decline" of the genre. Instead of attributing the increasing cultural suspicion of dime novels to a decline in quality of the texts, changes in format, price, and distribution may play significant roles in how this fiction was perceived. Factors such as these are beginning to play a more prominent role in literary and cultural studies of nineteenth-century America more generally, but they are often only taken into account as an afterthought. It is by now a commonplace when analyzing any contemporary media that "the medium is the message." Nevertheless many scholars of the nineteenth century still tend to ignore that the medium through which a text is presented is an essential element of that text's message. No different from readers today, nineteenth-century Americans did not judge books without their covers. The case of the dime novel and its fluctuating reputation is an example of the extent to which "material literacy" was expanding along with textual literacy in nineteenth-century American society in ways that were crucial to the reception of texts on the part of readers and non-readers alike.

Notes

1. See McKenzie. In Buntline's case, this analysis is complicated by the racial content of the two novels, as well as Buntline's well-known role as one of the founders of the Know-Nothing Party. The novels examined for this paper are two frontier-themed novels, both set in central Texas during the years of the Texas Republic. Buntline's politics combine with the Texas setting to offer representations of Indians and Mexicans that would be of crucial importance in the ways in which the books were recycled and repackaged, especially with regard to their cover art. This held true for the industry in general, as is indicated by Erastus Beadle's answer in 1884 to a reporter's question about how Beadle and Adams dealt with rivals who published trashier novels: "Oh, we had to kill a few more Indians than we used to; we held our own against them" (qtd. in Pearson 99).

2. This 1877 edition appeared in the new quarto format that had been introduced a month earlier with the "Fireside Library" series. This format was roughly 12″ × 9″, and consisted of no more than 8 stapled leaves, making for a very thin text block, which looked a great deal like a newspaper. The name of

"Starr's New York Library" was changed to "Beadle's Dime Library" after No. 26, but the first 26 numbers were reissued, printed from the same plates but with a new heading inserted. According to Johannsen, some numbers were issued with the new series name heading simply pasted over the previous heading, yet another type of physical recycling engaged in by Beadle, this time to get rid of excess stock.

3. Not only did Beadle use the same plates for its reprintings in the same series, but the 1900 edition of *Stella Delorme* was printed from the same plates as the 1860 Brady edition, which itself may well have been printed from the same plates used when the story appeared in the *Mercury* in 1859. The plates appear to have been saved in columns instead of pages; the columns were split up and spliced together differently depending on the size of the pages being printed. This fact underlines the extent to which Beadle, and their competitors, mastered the art of textual recycling within the corporation—not only were books recycled *textually,* but the physical plates from which the books were printed were made with such eventual recycling in mind. This outlook was not limited to plates of text, as the front page of the 1900 edition bears one of the illustrations that was in the 1860 edition, but with the Indians in the background effaced and a different caption.

This same physical recycling of plates occurred in the case of Munro's *Old Nick of the Swamp* as well. The 1908 Ivers edition was printed from the same plates as the 1868 Munro edition, although two pages evidently had to have new plates made, as the line endings differ and the type is much clearer.

4. As Richard John notes, "Prior to 1851, postal regulations excluded books from the mail altogether; even after this date, postal officers regarded their transmission as an unusual event" (39). The prohibition, dating from 1799, on the mailing of packets weighing more than three pounds effectively barred packages of books from the mail. According to Richard Kielbowicz, however, some postmasters were willing to accept books for mailing, although, in the absence of any explicit policy, they were able to charge exorbitant rates if they so desired (133). Books were not admitted without restriction to the mail until the New Deal, and then only by Presidential order.

5. The 1900 edition of *Stella Delorme* shows how completely newsstand sales had taken over. The back page of the broadsheet is an advertisement listing 190 numbers of "Beadle's Dime Library," stating that they are for sale "by all newsdealers, ten cents per copy, or sent by mail on receipt of twelve cents each. Beadle and Adams, Publishers, 98 William Street, New York." But Beadle and Adams had gone out of business and moved out of 98 William Street in 1896, when M. J. Ivers, located at

379 Pearl Street, bought out their stock. Nevertheless, Ivers continued to cling to the efforts to present the Dime Library as a periodical for postal purposes; the heading states that the broadsheet is "Entered as Second Class Matter at the New York, N.Y., Post Office."

Works Cited

Buntline, Ned, [Judson, Edward Zane Carroll]. *Old Nick of the Swamp; or, The Bravo's Vengeance.* New York: George Munro & Co., 1868.

———. *Old Nick of the Swamp.* New York: M. J. Ivers & Co., 1908.

———. *The Red Warrior; or, Stella Delorme's Comanche Lover.* New York: M. J. Ivers & Co., 1900.

———. *Stella Delorme; or, The Comanche's Dream.* New York: Frederick A. Brady, 1860.

Comstock, Anthony. *Traps for the Young.* New York: Funk & Wagnalls, 1884.

Denning, Michael. *Mechanic Accents: Dime Novels and Working Class Culture in America.* New York: Verso, 1987.

Fuller, Wayne. *The American Mail: Enlarger of the Common Life.* Chicago: U of Chicago P, 1972.

Johannsen, Albert. *The House of Beadle and Adams and its Dime and Nickel Novels.* 2 vols. Norman: U of Oklahoma P, 1950.

John, Richard. *Spreading the News: The American Postal System from Franklin to Morse.* Cambridge, Massachusetts: Harvard UP, 1995.

Kielbowicz, Richard. *News in the Mail: The Press, Post Office, and Public Information, 1700-1860s.* Westport: Greenwood P, 1989.

McKenzie, D. F. "What's Past is Prologue," The Bibliographic Society Centenary Lecture (July 14, 1992). N.p.: Hearthstone P, 1993.

Nye, Russel. *The Unembarrassed Muse: The Popular Arts in America.* New York: Dial P, 1970.

Pearson, Edmund Lester. *Dime Novels; or, Following an Old Trail in Popular Literature.* Boston: Little, Brown, & Co., 1929.

Smith, Henry Nash. *Virgin Land: The American West as Symbol and Myth.* Cambridge, Massachusetts: Harvard UP, 1970.

Sumner, William Graham. "What our Boys are Reading." in *Earth-hunger and Other Essays.* New Haven: Yale UP, 1913.

POPULAR CHARACTERS

Warren French (essay date 1951)

SOURCE: "The Cowboy in the Dime Novel," in *Studies in English,* Vol. XXX, 1951, pp. 219-34.

[*In the following essay, French traces the role of the cowboy character in the dime novel, revealing the character's emerging importance in the works of four novelists.*]

Sentimentalists are poor prophets. In his nostalgic tribute to the old dime novel, Charles Harvey wrote in the *Atlantic Monthly* in 1907:

> More than a quarter of a century ago . . . the Atchison, Topeka, and Santa Fe ended the days of the old trail and its story tellers. Between the railroads which transported the cattle from the ranges to the stockyards, and the barbed wire fences of the settlers who are abolishing the ranges, the cowboy as a picturesque feature of the Western landscape has passed out, and the dime novel will know him no more.[1]

Harvey was wrong; it was the dime novel, not the cowboy, which was doomed. The stereotype of the noble, fearless cowboy is today firmly rooted in American literature. The advent of television has confirmed the hypothesis, suggested by the motion pictures and numerous western magazines, that purveyors of popular entertainment are agreed that the epic hero of the new world came riding out of the West.[2]

How did the now seemingly immortal cowboy arrive at his present eminence? Since "dime novel" lingers in literary fancy as a blanket term for all the cheap, paper-backed publications of the nineteenth century, one may assume that the contents of these old thrillers were much akin to those of contemporary formula fiction about the West and that the cowboy, like Athena, sprang forth full-grown and armed for the good fight. Yet an examination of the "dime novels"[3] themselves, as may be made in the representative collection preserved by the University of Texas, proves that the nineteenth century cowboy was not himself a stereotyped figure, but a man interpreted from several viewpoints who evolved, largely as a result of outside influences, into the current stereotype. The purpose of this article is to describe the evolution of the fictional cowboy through an analysis of the works of four representative writers.

The cowboy was not the central figure in early Western fiction. The Indian scout, the prairie guide, the road agent, and the buffalo hunter were more interesting than the ranch hand to Newton M. Curtis, Edward Ellis, "Ned Buntline," and "Buckskin Sam" Hall, early exponents of the Western tradition. Buffalo Bill, Kit Carson, Bigfoot Wallace, and the James Boys loom large in the old hierarchy, but one must wade through many pages of microscopic print before finding a work that can legitimately be called "cowboy" fiction. The cowboy one does find has not been adequately interpreted by analysts like Douglas Branch, who, although he wrote the most comprehensive work about the cowboy in fiction, formulated some erroneous generalizations about his subject.

Branch first assumed that "the greatest of the dime novel cowboys is Young Wild West,"[4] although, strictly speaking, Young Wild West is not a dime novel hero at all. This prototype of the modern fictional cowboy did not make his appearance until 1902, whereas the traditional "dime novel" had expired in 1899, when the firm of Beadle and Adams, responsible for originating this lightly regarded art form, closed its doors.

Since Branch had chosen Young Wild West as exemplary of the dime novel cowboy, he was led to the further generalization that "in the dime novel, if not in the American monthly magazines, the cowboy was nature's nobleman."[5] He errs here in confusing two periods. The magazine articles adversely critical of the cowboy appeared in the eighteen-seventies and eighties; by 1886 a writer for *Harper's Monthly* was prepared to admit, "the *morale* of the entire range and ranch cattle business of the United States now compares favorably with that of other large enterprises."[6] Young Wild West and his kind were a product of the twentieth century, who emerged after Owen Wister had stabilized the picture of the cowboy in *The Virginian*.[7] Many changes took place during the intervening years. The range cattle industry still existed when the unfavorable articles appeared, but had become a romantic legend by the time Young Wild West galloped into print.[8] As often, there is a difference between writers' attitudes toward something existent and something recalled.

Actually the cowboy had a short life as hero (or, as will be shown, villain) in the dime novel. Although forerunners of the dime novel had appeared as early as 1838, when improvements in printing methods rendered feasible the large-scale production of inexpensive books, the cowboy did not receive more than passing mention in these publications until 1885.[9] Although Cooper's *The Prairie* was a story of the plains, the frontier of popular literature was, until 1860, Cooper's old New York frontier; Edward Ellis moved the frontier to Illinois, but romance still lagged behind reality. It was not until Beadle and Adams' Half Dime and New York Dime Libraries, designed to appeal to juvenile readers, were launched in 1878 that the cowboy came into his own. Even then tales of the Southwest were less common than detective and sea stories. Not until Buffalo Bill brought his famous Wild West show to New York in 1883 and "Col." Prentiss Ingraham began to immortalize the dashing scout did the exploitation of the cowboy begin.[10] Cody probably had a greater effect upon the American imagination than any other showman.

When the cowboy did appear, he was not the same person we expect to find in contemporary romances; nor was he alike in all dime novels. There is no typical dime novel. Each author approached his subject matter consistent with his own predilections and prejudices, not in a way characteristic of the dime novel as an entity. Even a generalization like Henry Nash Smith's "Whatever may be the merits of the dime novel cowboy . . . he apparently had nothing to do with cattle"[11] is an over-simplification, because one of the first writers to be concerned with the cowboy, Joseph Badger, Jr., attempted to portray life on the ranch realistically.

Charles Harvey made another unfounded generalization when he wrote that "there were no problems in any of the dime novels, old or new."[12] Although dime novelists generally ignored social issues, Capt. Frederick Whittaker, as will be shown in the discussion of his works, used the paper-backed publications as platforms from which to expound political doctrines commonly absent from adventure fiction.

Only four of the Beadle and Adams staff wrote enough about the cowboy to provide a body of work in which distinctive qualities may be discerned. The different and contradictory approaches of these four illustrate the evolution of the concept of the cowboy. Joseph E. Badger, Jr., the earliest, wrote with restraint, good humor, and an attempt at realism. Capt. Frederick Whittaker joined the Eastern journals in launching a vicious attack upon the ranch hand. "Col." Prentiss Ingraham based his creations upon real persons (members of Buffalo Bill's troupe), whom he attempted to develop into counterparts of the heroic figures of early nineteenth-century romance. William G. Patten, the junior member of the group, was one of the first to depict the cowboy as a moral superman and to suggest the transformation of the unassuming herdsman into the singing Lothario who is heroic by virtue of his special position as a free agent in a regimented world.

Badger wrote several hundred novels for the dime serials, only a few of them about cowboys. Practically nothing is known about Badger's life, but in a probably apocryphal biography written by one of his fellow workers he is described as having been an outlaw on the Texas border.[13] If he had been a wayward youth, he began his career appropriately by writing novels like *Gospel George; or, Fiery Fred, the Outlaw* (1879), about gamblers and road agents. Later he came over to the side of the law and in the bulk of his works described the adventures of omniscient sleuths in works like *Masked Mark, the Mounted Detective* (1885). When he discovered the literary potentialities of the cowboy, he was one of the first to use authentic western scenery in his novels. Into *Laughing Leo; or, Spread Eagle Sam's Dandy Pard,* which is nothing but an extended conversation about a lost heir, he incorporates credible descriptions of a cattle stampede and a round-up characteristic of the "stock ranges of Montana and Wyoming"[14] about which he was writing. A passage like the following was not then the cliché it has since become:

> It was the season of the "Fall round-up," and this was the concluding day of that arduous task.
>
> For two weeks past masters and men had been working hard, gathering in the scattered "bands" of cattle, marking, branding, culling out for market such as had been left over from the earlier drive.
>
> According to custom, every ranch within miles and miles had been represented, all working together, chosen riders from each ranch taking turns in "cutting out" stock bearing their respective brands, until the last bunch was attended to. Then the unbranded slice—the Mavericks without marks—were put up at auction, the proceeds to revert to the Stock-growers' 'Association,' and the cattle themselves to be caught, thrown, marked, and seared with hot irons.[15]

One of the unusual features of his work is his attempt to satirize the conventional treatment of the romantic hero and villain. His villains are often attractive persons, while his heroes and heroines are the victims of their bad tempers and rash actions rather than of nefarious intrigues. *Rob Roy Ranch; or, The Imps of the Panhandle,* a tale of Texas in the days of the settlement of the Llano Estacado, is typical of his work. One accustomed to formula western fiction is sure that Fergus Cameron, a young Scotsman, who is "gay, laughing, light-hearted under any and all circumstances,"[16] will turn out to be a misunderstood hero, while his morose rival, Hal, will be exposed as a blackguard. The assumption is wrong; the roles are reversed. The further revelation that the villain operates outside the law because he is "stealing to get enough money to live an honest life without working"[17] is also disconcerting; most dime novel wrongdoers have less inviting motives.

One is equally sure that the gallant young cowboy called "The Prairie Kid" in *The Cowboy Chief's Sure Shot; or, Hard Knox, the Rogue Rancher,* will turn out to be a wronged hero, while the vicious-tempered and spiteful vigilante, Hard Knox, will be proved a masquerading rascal, especially since Badger indicates that his sympathies are with the "Kid." The young man, however, proves to be a rustler, while Knox is established as being just what he seemed to be—a mean-tempered and maladjusted vigilante attempting to bring law and order to a wayward community. Preceptors of youth might shudder at the morality of this fable, but the story is more spontaneous and convincing than most of its genre. Badger taught geography, not ethics.

The best of his western works is *The Prairie Ranch; or, The Young Cattle Herders,* which is distinguished by the author's use of the kind of restrained realism and gentle satire usually associated with the work of Andy Adams. Badger proposed in this work, published in 1884, to give Eastern boys an account of Texas ranch life, without, like many of his contemporaries, writing down to his audience. There are no heroes, villains, romances, hair-breadth escapes, or improbable feats of horsemanship in the novel. Although Badger calls a tornado a "Norther,"[18] he presents, through his account of a young New Yorker's introduction to a relative's ranch, information about such western institutions as the "Californian" saddle, the *rodeo* (used here to mean the round-up on the ranch, not a public riding and roping contest), the Longhorn, the coyote, and the trail drive. The only concession to romantic convention is the inclusion of an incident in which the boy mistakes the ranch-owner's visiting brother for a road-agent. Here Badger satirizes rather than inflames the workings of the romantic imagination.

The restraint and veracity of Badger's work set him apart from his contemporaries, but his work proves that at least one novelist attempted to launch a popular western fiction in which he would describe the West as he found it, not as he or his readers would like to imagine it was.

While Badger was sympathetic toward the cowboy, another Beadle writer, Capt. Frederick Whittaker, an ex-

Union army officer, was markedly hostile. He considered the cowboy as a vulgar reversion to primitive man and thought of the West as a lawless and uncultured twilight zone somewhere beyond the fringe of civilization. There is no evidence that Whittaker ever visited the West; but a dime novel writer did not need first-hand knowledge of his settings.[19]

Whittaker's antipathy toward the West is manifest in two of his earliest books, *The Death Head's Rangers, a Tale of the Lone Star State*, and *The Texan Sport; or, The Boy Mustang Hunter*, in which he uses the Spanish term *vaqueros* when speaking of cowboys.[20] Both novels contain anachronisms. When soldiers gather in Kentucky to come to Texas in 1836, ". . . every man's got one of Curnel Colt's six shooters, . . ."[21] although the revolvers were first manufactured in 1838.[22] A group of French fugitives prepare to sally forth on the plains wearing "silver, arrow-proof hauberks" and other accouterments of the medieval knight.[23] In both books Whittaker contrasts savage, drunken Kentuckians and sadistic Texans unfavorably with gentle, grouse-hunting Englishmen and cultured, chivalrous Frenchmen. He depicts one of the Texans exacting revenge by horribly torturing a foe before shooting his brains out, while, in contrast, "the Frenchman," the author comments, "was one of those chivalrous tender-hearted men, of whom, thank God, there are some left, whose souls revolt at cruelty and revenge."[24] At the end of *The Texan Sport*, when the young mustang-hunter has been converted from his wild ways and has abandoned a jealous rancher's daughter for a wholesome French heiress, all abandon Texas and move to New Orleans to enter society. Even one of the old Texas rangers was redeemed and became a "respectable member of society."[25]

The author's condescending attitude is most noticeable in his cowboy novels, Apparently the earliest of these is a short libel entitled *Parson Jim, King of the Cowboys*, which depicts the regeneration of corrupt and uncouth Colorado by a young consumptive from Boston. The descriptive passages in this novel dispel the notion that all dime novels glorified the cowboy. Whittaker's concept of Western manhood is revealed in a passage which describes what happens just after the young consumptive arrives in Muleville, Colorado. He is at the hotel when a distraught native rushes in shouting:

> "The cowboys are coming! Git to hidin'! Thar on a tear."

> The warning seemed to be perfectly understood by all but young Arthur. . . . The judge turned pale, and the whole crowd rushed wildly for the back yard, where they disappeared.

> Up to the door of the Metropolitan Hotel dashed a score of mounted men, on small wiry horses, covered with foam and dirt, and James Arthur, for the first time in his life, saw the spectacle so familiar to the citizens of Muleville—"cowboys on a tear". . . . All wore red silk sashes, garnished with knives and pistols. . . . These men all seemed crazy with excitement or drink, and were firing recklessly all round them into the windows of the houses, as if careless what damage they did.[26]

Arthur is beaten by the cowboys, but regains his health and outwits his depraved foes. He is hired by a young Eastern girl, whose ranch Whittaker holds up as an example to the West. His description of Queen's Ranch shows that Whittaker approved the establishment because it was conducted in accordance with Eastern standards:

> The Queen's Ranch was remarkable in Colorado for more things than one. It was the richest in the state, the only one run by a lady, the only one where they tried to breed thoroughbred horses and cattle exclusively, getting rid of all other stock, and the only one where there was a civilized house, a garden, wheeled vehicles, roads and a grand piano. . . . The hostess of the establishment went so far as to indulge in pocket handkerchiefs and little napkins. . . . She wore a Worth costume of wine-colored velvet and satin and seemed much out of place in the rough life of a cattle ranch.[27]

Whittaker appears to have been the only writer concerned about the supply of grand pianos and little napkins in Colorado. No lover of untamed nature was he. While the mistress of the Queen's Ranch is listening to a singer who will make her "forget that [she is] on a cattle ranch," her cowboys are outside beating each other with long whips.[28] Whittaker preferred life in the great indoors.

The author had more on his mind than denouncing the cowboy; he was also concerned about the abuse of privilege by the wealthy and powerful. The central action of *Parson Jim* revolves around a contested election in which the tyrannical cattle ranchers are seeking to impose their will upon the less dynamic members of the community. Whittaker believed the cowboys might be redeemed if they followed the lead of James Arthur. His Boston cowboy thus harangues the oppressed Westerners:

If you'll follow where I lead, we'll show the ranchers that the cowboy is king of Colorado and that all the wealth a man can acquire will not make him our master. It is the old battle between the people and the rich few, who shall be masters. I stand on the side of the people, and I say that the cowboy, and not the rancher, is the true king of Colorado. We have all heard a good deal of our cattle kings, simply because they are rich men. They go to Europe and live in wealth, while the cowboys take care of their cattle and work for a bare pittance. I think all this can be changed. We have the votes and can rule if we will.[29]

Even if the reader ignores the question of which was politically more liberal, the East or the West, he may find that this speech sounds suspicious. It would ring more true in Union Square than in the Colorado Hills. Whether or not one accepts Whittaker's moral that the West will redeem itself by becoming like the East, one must admit that such assaults upon the prerogatives of the privileged class discredit the notion that there are no social ideas in the dime novels.

Whittaker's attitude toward the cowboy is shown again in *Top Notch Tom, the Cowboy Outlaw; or, The Satanstown Election*, which has virtually the same plot as *Parson Jim*, but a Texas rather than a Colorado setting. At the beginning of the novel a Scottish bartender shouts, "Bats, laddies, bats! The cowboys are coomin'."[30] An old resident says disgustedly, as the town arms: "'A caowboy will be a caowboy, anyway ye can fix him, and ye can't no more keep him from goin' on a tear when he gets paid off than ye can get a steer to stop bellerin' when he feels the hot iron at round-up time.'"[31] Satanstown, Texas, is to Whittaker much like Muleville, Colorado. His description of it shows his concept of the West: "When Satanstown was not 'on a drunk,' it was a pretty quiet place; for half the inhabitants were getting over the last debauch, and the only noise that disturbs the silence is the occasional howl of a gentleman who is being kept in a back room by his friends, on account of a fancy he had that the house was full of snakes."[32] He also charges that in the West women were not allowed to "mess in affairs,"[33] although women were frequently civic leaders there and first gained equal suffrage in the plains states.[34]

In the most biased of his novels, *The Texas Tramp; or, Solid Sol, the Yankee Hercules,* an 1890 production, Whittaker extended his accusations to include Southerners as well as Westerners. This novel begins with a description of a group of cattlemen gathered "in front of the apology for a dwelling which was dignified with the title of ranch-house," lamenting the fall of the Confederacy and hating the Yankees.[35]

Into this scene of despair walks Solid Sol, a New Hampshire hobo, who eventually sets things right. Although hated at first by the embittered Southerners and brutal cowboys, Sol establishes himself by rescuing a ranch-owner from marauding Mexicans and Indians, spanking a recalcitrant cowboy, and beating up Geronimo, the notorious Apache chief. All the while he lectures the ex-Confederates, chastising them for their bad manners and inefficient ranch management and holding up Yankee manners and efficiency as an ideal. His preachments are finally effective, for Whittaker informs us at the end of the book: "In a place where it had been the boast of the inhabitants that they had 'driven out every Yankee who had ever entered Texas,' Northern men became as numerous as men born in the state, and the result had been that Mesquite Country [*sic*] had become noted as the richest in the South."[36]

Whittaker compounded an apparent ignorance of the West with a provincial bias and native bad temper to produce the moral that only Easterners could make the plains barbarians acceptable members of American society. He exemplified an attitude toward the cowboy which made even "Buckskin Sam" Hall, a native Westerner who never wrote a distinctly "cowboy" novel, include in one of his tales of the Army in the West a digression objecting to the malicious criticism of the cowboys and placing the blame for their misbehavior on the townsmen Whittaker defended. He wrote in *The Brazos Tiger:*

> . . . These so-called cowboys have been greatly traduced by the American press; for, as a class, they are

noble, brave, and fearless men, liberal to a fault, tender-hearted, and devoted to each other. In fact, few men can be found, who lead a roaming life in Nature's garden, who will not divide their little all with anyone in need. Fewer still would desert a friend, or take advantage of an enemy.

> If, when they reach a town, they are poisoned with "Prussic Acid bugjuice," until they become insane, and use the weapons they are obliged to carry too freely—more in sport than otherwise—it is the fault of the town that permits the sale of the vile poison, more than of the poor fellows whose protracted privation and continuous watchfulness by day and night, naturally cause them to take advantage of a day's rest to have a free and easy "jamboree."[37]

Hall's panegyric contains the germ of the attitude which was to result finally in the ennoblement of the cowboy. "Nature's garden" is a favorite concept of the cultural primitivists who see in a natural order a benevolent norm for man's conduct and who find man at his best when he lives close to unspoiled nature. Hall's lead was followed by writers like Prentiss Ingraham and William Patten in their glorification of the cowboy. It appears likely that the legend of the noble cowboy arose, at least in part, as a reply to Eastern attacks upon the West and that the combined effect of the writings of the attackers and defenders of the cowboy precluded a continuation of the kind of realistic treatments Joseph Badger, Jr., had written. One might even ponder whether literary sensationalism is so much the result of public demand as of the efforts of opinionated writers to attract attention to themselves.

One of the defenders who initiated the literary legend of the heroic cowboy was the self-styled "Colonel" Prentiss Ingraham, who is reputed to have written more dime novels than any other man.[38] He is best known as the writer of more than a hundred tales about the exploits of Buffalo Bill. His writing of these stories led him to the writing of cowboy novels, but his contribution to the literature of the range was incidental to his other interests. He did not attempt to present a valid picture of the West; cattle are hardly ever mentioned in his works. He treated the cowboy in the same way he treated the pirate, the detective, the Confederate soldier, and a variety of other heroes. He was not interested in proving that the cowboy was "nature's nobleman," but that he was cut from the same cloth as heroic figures in other professions in other parts of the world. "Blood will tell" was his basic concept.

He made one important contribution to the development of the literature of the cattle kingdom—the establishment of one unusually gifted cowboy as the hero of a series of related tales. The device of making one man the central figure in a succession of novels was an old one among dime novel writers, but Ingraham was the first to take a cowboy—Buck Taylor, a member of Buffalo Bill's troupe—and build a series of stories around him. Ingraham may have used a real person, not only because he was interested in publicizing Cody's touring company, but also because, like his father, Joseph Holt Ingraham, a prolific novelist of an earlier period, he was obsessed with the notion that the writer of romances should try to persuade his readers that he was writing biography rather than fiction.

The Taylor series of six related novels began with *Buck Taylor, King of the Cowboys,* published in 1887, but did not flower until 1891, when in a series of long tales—*Buck Taylor, the Saddle King; The Lasso King's League;* and *The Cowboy Clan*—Ingraham suggested the way in which a real person, familiar to many of his readers, could be developed into a romantic hero engaged in seemingly ceaseless warfare against one especially durable criminal band. To prove that Taylor was no ordinary person, Ingraham wrote in the first book about the cowboy: "It was no easy task to load that long rifle on the back of a wild horse, but Buck managed it, and turning in his saddle, again sent a bullet flying toward his pursuers."[39] Another feat earned Buck his title "King of the Cowboys": the eighteen-year-old youth rode on five different horses in succession, wearing five different costumes, and made a group of bloodthirsty Indians, who were besieging a group of Texas Rangers, believe that he was a rescue party.[40] In a later book, Ingraham described Buck in more detail: "He was a person over six feet in height by several inches, with a slender form, but athletic, broad shoulders, and the very *beau ideal* of a Texas cowboy. . . . His face was one to remember when once seen, beardless, youthful, yet full of character and fearlessness, amounting to reckless daring."[41]

According to Ingraham, the cowboy tended cattle only so long as he had nothing else to do. One of the Taylor novels begins with this deceptively realistic description: "Cattle and horses by the hundreds were asleep upon the prairie, or grazing upon the rich grass, while about them the cowboy sentinels rode to keep them from straying, either whistling or singing to soothe the dumb beasts."[42] But as far as the reader knows the cattle stay asleep through the exciting events that follow. The cowboy's important tasks are rescuing distressed damsels, penetrating the disguises of the wicked and meting out punishment to rogues who might have stepped right out of the pages of Scott, Cooper, or Ingraham's own father. The rustler, the range war, the struggle between farmer and fence-cutter made no impression upon "Col." Ingraham. He did not need to study ranch life, for he had a stock of dramatic situations left over from his earlier novels about buccaneers and soldiers. A conversation from one of the Taylor novels illustrates Ingraham's concept of a dilemma. Buck speaks to one of his cohorts:

> "There are Indians in the timber to the right and left of us and we must dash through."
>
> "Why not go back, pard?"
>
> "Because there are Indians following on our trail."[43]

Ingraham was not concerned with the cowboy as a son of nature; he depicted him as the inheritor of the Medieval tradition of knight-errantry. His concept of the cowboy is apparent from this passage:

> They were proud to be called "Texas Cowboys," and knew the country perfectly. They could follow a trail as well as an Indian, ride even better, throw a lasso unerringly, and shoot straight to dead center every time. A reckless lot of men they were, light-hearted, utterly fearless, generous, noble in the treatment of a friend or a fallen foe, and though feared by evildoers and redskins, they were admired and respected by the soldiers and people of the settlements.[44]

The evolution of the cowboy from a subordinate figure in tales of Western adventure to the central figure in a distinctive literary genre was virtually completed by William G. Patten, one of the glibbest of the Beadle authors. It is ironic that the cowboy should have won his long fight to replace the scout and road agent as the principal exemplar of Western life after the days of the long trail had passed; but it is often only after the representatives of a type, like the ante-bellum planter or the New York Indian, have disappeared that a stereotype can be formed which may be exploited without caution. Patten wrote with the lack of restraint and with the talent for oversimplification necessary for the creation of a myth. No one's heroes have endured more excruciating trials or made more remarkable recoveries than his. Patten speeded up the pace of the stories. Always a man of action, the cowboy in Patten's works became a dynamic stampede-stopper, rounder-up of rustlers, and even cattle-herder. Patten's cowboys apparently never ate or slept, although they sometimes made love. While most previous literary cowboys had been laconic, his were incessantly talkative. Most of his stories are told largely through dialogues, as are many Western stories today. Whereas Badger's cowboys had been morally unpredictable, Whittaker's morally depraved, Ingraham's moral according to a transplanted code, Patten's were symbols of Western morality and Western loyalty. Typical of Patten's concept of the cowboy is Hustler Harry:

> . . . a man at least six feet tall and "built from the ground up." Not a thick-set, ox-like figure, but one which combined great strength and manly grace; a form which filled the rough cowboy costume until the clothes fitted as if cut by a metropolitan tailor. Every limb was rounded and muscular, yet not overburdened and cumbersome. The head was well-poised on a perfect neck, the wide-brimmed sombrero being set jauntily on the side of his brown, curly mass of hair. His features were round and clear-cut, as if chiseled from marble, but the square, full lower jaw, denoted a determined, unswerving nature. His eyes were blue and filled with half-mirthful yet wholly unfathomable light. . . . No weapons were in sight on the belt or in the pocket of this independent cowboy, for cowboy he appeared to be.[45]

He was not only a cowboy, but a paragon of virtue, who belied all the vile rumors that had been circulated about uncouth, gun-carrying Westerners. He did not even drink. "I hope you won't think me uncivil, but I don't touch ther stuff," he tells a well-wisher who has offered him whiskey.[46] He was, furthermore, the spokesman for a new philosophy about cowboy life. He was not a cowboy because of a sense of duty, but because he loved the free life. Harry spoke for most of Patten's cowboys when he said to an admirer:

> "Fact is, if I war rollin' in yaller wealth, I never cu'd give up the range. Just one whiff of ther trail, one beller

from the hurd, one rattle of long horns sets my blood
ter bilin' and seethin' like I was set fair onto a red-hot
furnace and 'er nigger fireman shovin' pitch-pine an'
rosin fer all he war wu'th."[47]

Patten also advocated the notion that the cowboy is "nature's nobleman." In *Wild Vulcan,* an incredible compound
of Gothic claptrap and prairie romance, he thus describes
his hero:

> Standing in the full glow of the fire, Prairie Paul ran
> his eye over the encampment in a critical manner. He
> was a tall, frank-faced, manly-appearing youth of
> twenty, and was dressed in an unusually neat-appearing
> suit of fringed buckskin, but wore long-legged cowboy
> boots minus the high heels. . . . His face was *smooth-
> shaved,* and the dark eyes which peered from beneath
> the brim of the *sombrero* were keen and piercing. His
> long curling hair fell upon his shoulders. In truth, Prai-
> rie Paul looked decidedly picturesque and handsome as
> he stood in the full glow of the firelight, glancing
> keenly around at the encampment, and it was not
> strange that Nida's heart felt a little thrill as she
> watched him. Perfect grace and strength were blended
> in his fine figure. He was one of those grand creations
> of the mountains and the plains, a young nobleman of
> nature.[48]

Patten's most noteworthy contribution to cowboy literature
was neither Hustler Harry nor Prairie Paul, but Cowboy
Chris, "the *beau ideal* of a rough and ready cowboy, such
a person as would make an excellent friend or a very unpleasant enemy."[49] Chris did not appear in the Beadle series until 1897, shortly before they disappeared from the
newsstands, but he made up quickly for lost time. Several
dozen of his adventures were published during the last
years of the once famous publications. While the stories
themselves are but carbon copies of Patten's earlier tales,
they represent a step forward in the development of the
cowboy-hero, because Chris, unlike his predecessors, did
not settle down at the end of one adventure, but, like the
heroes of the recent radio and motion picture cowboy serials, resolved the situation so that another might settle
down while he himself remained free to take on new challenges. At the end of *Cowboy Chris, the Vengeance Volunteer,* for example, Chris surrenders the heroine to another
and says to one of his companions, "somewhat sadly,"
"Come away and leave them together. They are happy."[50]

With Chris, we arrive at the modern concept of the heroic
cowboy; he is the link that unites the original dime novels
with the pulp Western fiction and "horse operas" of today.
It is not surprising to find that his creator ended his career
writing the Frank Merriwell stories.[51] Patten was the maker
of the commercially durable heroes who could entrance
the unsophisticated through volume after volume. His characters are the archetype of a modern myth. Badger had
suggested that the cowboy might be treated realistically;
Whittaker had treated him as a blight upon society; Prentiss Ingraham had shown that the members of a Wild West
troupe might be re-incarnations of the knights of old. It
was Patten who transformed the cowboy into "nature's
nobleman," and at the same time returned to authentically
Western problems to provide the bases for his plots.[52]

I do not mean to suggest that these four writers exhausted
the possible varieties of the early cowboy novel, but I do
believe that they represent the main steps in the evolution
of the concept of the cowboy. One might speak of Badger's cowboys or of Whittaker's cowboys, but not of a
common type to be found in the works of all these writers.
The cowboy we know as a literary stereotype evolved
through a series of stages, and his evolution is reflected in
the dime novels. The works of Owen Wister, Andy Adams,
and Emerson Hough, as well as others credited with the
advancement of cowboy fiction, appear less isolated when
they are viewed against the background of the lowly "dime
novels" in which the cowboy hero fought his way into existence and prominence.

Notes

1. Charles M. Harvey, "The Dime Novel in American
   Life," *Atlantic Monthly,* C (July, 1907), 44.

2. See Walter P. Webb, *The Great Plains* (New York,
   1931), pp. 464-470, 491-496, for an account of the
   popularity and appeal of the cowboy hero.

3. Even this generic label is inaccurate; many "dime
   novels" sold for prices ranging from five to
   twenty-five cents. The true "dime novels" were
   salmon-colored, paper-covered booklets published
   by the firm of Beadle and Adams in the 1860's;
   subsequently, the title was applied to publications,
   of varying formats, produced by a number of
   competing firms.

4. Douglas Branch, *The Cowboy and his Interpreters*
   (New York, 1926), p. 185.

5. *Ibid.,* p. 191.

6. Joseph Nimmo, Jr., "American Cowboys," *Harper's
   Magazine,* LXXIII (1886), 884. Nimmo's article
   contains a résumé of contemporary opinions about
   the cowboy. The unfavorable articles are discussed
   by Henry Nash Smith in *Virgin Land* (Cambridge,
   1950), p. 109.

7. Wister believed that in his novel he was writing the
   cowboy's epitaph. In his introduction to the novel,
   he wrote, "But [the cowboy] will never come again.
   He rides in his historic yesterday. You will no more
   see him gallop out of the unchanging silence than
   you will see Columbus on the unchanging sea come
   sailing from Palos with his caravels." (Owen Wister,
   The Virginian [New York, 1902], p. viii.)

8. Webb. *op. cit.,* p. 240, suggests 1885 as the best
   date for marking the end of the range cattle industry.

9. In an early novel about ranch life by W. H.
   Bushnell, *The Hermit of the Colorado Hills* (New
   York, [1864]), the cowboy was not even mentioned
   by that name; he was still called *vaquero* or simply
   "herdsman."

10. Richard J. Walsh, *The Making of Buffalo Bill*
    (Indianapolis, [1928]), p. 222.

11. Smith, *op. cit.,* p. 111.

12. Harvey, *op. cit.*, p. 44.

13. A. H. Post, *Roving Joe: The History of a Young "Border Ruffian,"* Beadle's Boys' Library of Sport, Story and Adventure, No. 7 (New York, 1882). The Beadle writers took turns eulogizing one another's colorful careers in this "realistic" serial.

14. Joseph E. Badger, Jr., *Laughing Leo; or, Spread Eagle Sam's Dandy Pard,* New York Dime Library, No. 433 (New York, 1887), p. 6.

15. *Ibid.*, p. 3. This description of the round-up may be compared with the discussion in Webb, *op. cit.*, pp. 255-259.

16. Badger, *Rob Roy Ranch; or, The Imps of the Panhandle,* New York Dime Library, No. 409 (New York, 1886), p. 2.

17. *Ibid.*, p. 3.

18. Badger, *The Prairie Ranch; or, The Young Cattle Herders,* Beadle's Boys' Library of Sport, Story and Adventure, No. 8 (New York, 1899), p. 21. This copy is a reprint of an 1884 publication. Many dime novels were re-printed several times, sometimes with new titles.

19. Gelett Burgess, "Confessions of a Dime Novelist," *Bookman,* XV (1902), 532, relates that Eugene Sawyer, creator of Nick Carter, based all of his New York stories on impressions gained during one four-hour visit to the city.

20. Frederick Whittaker, *The Texan Sport; or, The Boy Mustang Hunter,* Beadle's Pocket Library, No. 465 (New York, 1872), p. 27.

21. Whittaker, *The Death's Head Rangers, A Tale of the Lone Star State,* Beadle's Dime Novels, n.s, No. 95 (New York, 1872), p. 24.

22. Webb. *op. cit.*, p. 171.

23. Whittaker, *The Texan Sport,* p. 51.

24. *Ibid.*, p. 89.

25. *Ibid.*, p. 93.

26. Whittaker, *Parson Jim, King of the Cowboys; or, The Gentle Sheperd's Big "Clean Out,"* New York Dime Library, No. 215 (New York, 1882), p. 3.

27. *Ibid.*, p. 8. Whittaker predicted many of the improvements which were made in cattle breeding, but not necessarily the way in which they were brought about.

28. *Ibid.*, p. 8.

29. *Ibid.*, p. 19.

30. Whittaker, *Top Notch Tom, the Cowboy Outlaw,* New York Dime Library, No. 303 (New York, 1884), p. 3. The "bats" are baseball bats which the Texans used for defense rather than recreation.

31. *Ibid.*, p. 3.

32. *Ibid.*, p. 2.

33. *Ibid.*, p. 15.

34. Webb, *op. cit.*, pp. 504-506.

35. Whittaker, *The Texas Tramp; or, Solid Sol, the Yankee Hercules,* New York Dime Library, No. 609 (New York, 1890), p. 2.

36. *Ibid.*, p. 30.

37. Sam S. Hall, *The Brazos Tiger; or, The Minute Men of Fort Belknap,* New York Dime Library, No. 212 (New York, 1882), p. 2.

38. E. S. Jenks, "Dime Novel Makers," *Bookman,* XX (1904), 112. Elaborations upon this statement can be found in any biographical account of Ingraham. He was best known of the dime novel writers and is mentioned in almost every work concerning the genre. He posed as a former officer of the Confederate Army, although War Department records show that he never rose above the enlisted ranks.

39. Prentiss Ingraham, *Buck Taylor, King of the Cowboys; or, The Raiders and the Rangers,* Beadle's Half Dime Library, No. 497 (New York, 1887), p. 5.

40. *Ibid.*, p. 8.

41. Ingraham, *Buck Taylor, the Saddle King; or, The Lasso Rangers' League,* New York Dime Library, No. 649 (New York, 1891), p. 2.

42. Ingraham, *Buck Taylor, The Comanche Captive; or, Buckskin Sam to the Rescue,* Beadle's Half Dime Library, No. 737 (New York, 1891), p. 2. The Buckskin Sam of the sub-title is Sam Hall, the dime novelist; not only did dime novelists sometimes become characters in the work, but also various characters, especially Buffalo Bill, were sometimes represented as the authors.

43. Ingraham, *Buck Taylor, the Saddle King,* p. 4. Although Ingraham was writing of the plains, he was addicted to forest scenes, another indication that he was adapting the conventions of an older fiction rather than contriving new ones adapted to his purported settings.

44. Ingraham, *The Cowboy Clan; or, The Tigress of Texas,* New York Dime Library, No. 658 (New York, 1891), p. 7. If we substitute "lists" for "lasso-throwing" and "Turks" for "red-skins" the resemblance to the Medieval knight is striking.

45. William G. Patten, *Hustler Harry, the Cowboy Sport; or, Daring Dan Shark's General Delivery,* New York Dime Library, No. 545 (New York, 1889), p. 3.

46. *Ibid.*, p. 3.

47. *Ibid.*, p. 4.

48. Patten, *Wild Vulcan, the Lone Range Rider; or, The Rustlers of the Bad Land,* Beadle's Half Dime Library, No. 682 (New York, 1890), p. 4.

49. Wilder, William West [pseud.], *Cowboy Chris, the Desert Centaur; or, Hawkers for the Human Hawk,* Half Dime Library, No. 1066 (New York 1897), p. 2.

50. Patten, *Cowboy Chris, the Vengeance Volunteer,* Half Dime Library, No. 1075 (New York, 1898), p. 16.

51. Edmund Pearson, *Dime Novels; or, Following an Old Trail in Popular Literature* (Boston, 1929), pp. 216-217.

52. One of Patten's works, *Nobby Nat, the Tenderfoot Detective; or, The Girl Rancher's Rough Rustle,* Beadle's Half Dime Library, No. 820 (New York, 1893), for example, is based upon the war between the cattlemen and the farmers over fencing the range.

Daryl E. Jones (essay date 1973)

SOURCE: "Clenched Teeth and Curses: Revenge and the Dime Novel Outlaw Hero," in *Journal of Popular Culture,* Vol. VII, No. 3, Winter, 1973, pp. 652-65.

[*In the essay below, Jones explores the development of the outlaw hero in dime novels, arguing that the character emerged from the cultural context of the times.*]

Among the select brotherhood of Western heroes who live eternally in the popular imagination, one figure is strangely prominent—a man clad wholly in black, seated astride a black horse. Characteristically, his fist is raised in defiance, his teeth are clenched, and from the shadow obscuring the top half of his face two black, magnetic eyes are smoldering. He is, of course, the noble outlaw, Robin Hood in New World guise, a synthesis of timeless human desires and the unique combination of forces operating upon the development of popular American fiction in the last half of the nineteenth century.

Inasmuch as the dime novel was the age's most widely read form of fiction, it is not surprising that the noble outlaw made his debut in one of these pulp thrillers. He did so on October 15, 1877, when the House of Beadle and Adams released Edward L. Wheeler's *Deadwood Dick, the Prince of the Road; or, The Black Rider of the Black Hills.*[1] Intelligent, handsome, and chivalrous, Deadwood Dick gunned and galloped his way into the hearts of the reading public. So popular did the black-clad road agent become, in fact, that soon no profit-minded publishing firm was without its own dashing lawbreaker. Moreover, these outlaws were not exclusively the products of imagination; in the desperate search for new material, dime novelists often turned to historical accounts of actual Western badmen, a practice which spawned countless novels sensationalizing the notorious careers of such desperadoes as Jesse and Frank James, the Younger brothers, the Daltons, Rube Burrows, Joaquin Murieta, Tiburcio Vasquez, and Butch Cassidy and the Sundance Kid. Nevertheless, whether purely fictional or modeled after a legendary figure, the dime novel outlaw hero exhibited extraordinary appeal; by the 1890s, one series which printed a high percentage of outlaw stories, Street & Smith's Log Cabin Library, boasted a weekly circulation of 25,000 to 30,000 copies, and other outlaw series were equally popular.[2]

This popularity may be explained in part by the manner in which the stereotyped outlaw hero embodied certain cultural values and satisfied, through his conventionalized role in the dime novel Western formula, the socio-psychological needs of the reading public. In one sense, of course, the outlaw was simply a reincarnated archetype, a nineteenth century American manifestation of the devil-may-care European rogue or highwayman traditionally prominent in popular fiction. In another sense, however, he was the unique product of a specific cultural context—a cultural context which, through a complex interplay of several aesthetic and cultural dynamics, fostered the development of those character types most responsive to its own social imperatives and psychological preoccupations.[3]

The nineteenth century, despite its expressed optimism and faith in progress, was an age preoccupied by all of the problems which inevitably accompany rapid social change. It was an age of industrialization, urbanization, class polarization, and control of society by big business and the international agricultural market. It was an age in which new values seemingly threatened established morality. Above all, it was an age in which the average individual found his freedoms severely abridged by gargantuan social and economic forces. Totally subject to these forces, powerless to effect any real change in his life, the common man could still escape into the pages of a pulp thriller and become, if only temporarily, a self-reliant Western hero eminently free in a fantasy realm where every problem had a swift and clear-cut solution. Thus, the astounding popularity of the outlaw hero may be explained in part by his capacity for resolving in fantasy the otherwise insoluble cultural conflicts of the age.

One such conflict in particular played a crucial role in the development and consequent popularity of the outlaw hero: namely, the ambivalent American attitude toward law and the legal system. While most citizens professed belief in the value of law as a positive, organic force which served to build freedom into society, they felt that the legal system was largely unresponsive to the needs of the average individual. Undoubtedly, the intricacies of the judicial process contributed to this notion. More importantly, however, the majority of Americans suspected a nefarious association between law and special privilege. In an age of increasing class polarization, of growing antagonism between labor and capital, it seemed that unscrupulous members of the upper class were exploiting the intricacies of the legal system as a means of furthering their own interests while simultaneously denying the fundamental democratic rights of the majority. By the last half of the nineteenth century such sentiments were sufficiently widespread as to constitute a general antipathy toward law and the legal system. In addition to harboring a natural distaste for artificial restraints, the average individual doubted the ethics of pettifogging lawyers, regarded courtroom procedure as mere chicanery, and looked upon law itself as a tool employed by a vast conspiracy of the rich to subjugate and exploit the poor. In sum, the average American could no longer see a connection between moral and civil law.[4] Too often there seemed to be a wide and unsettling disparity between that ideal justice which *ought* to prevail in the application of law and that lesser justice which, in fact, *did* prevail.

This concern for the meaning and value of law had long been a central theme of the Western. "There are regions," observes Natty Bumppo in *The Prairie* (1827),

> where the law is so busy as to say, In this fashion shall you live, in that fashion shall you die, and in such another fashion shall you take leave of the world, to be sent before the judgment-seat of the Lord! A wicked and troublesome meddling is that, with the business of One who has not made his creatures to be herded like oxen, and driven from field to field as their stupid and selfish keepers may judge of their need and wants. A miserable land must that be, where they fetter the mind as well as the body, and where the creatures of God, being born children, are kept so by the wicked inventions of men who would take upon themselves the office of the great Governor of all![5]

Natty speaks from bitter experience, for he had come into conflict with the law a short time before. In *The Pioneers* (1823), the novel commonly credited with providing the Western's characteristic setting, character, and themes, Cooper brings the anarchic world of the wilderness personified by Natty Bumppo into conflict with the ordered, law-governed society personified by Judge Marmaduke Temple. Natty, schooled in Nature but untutored in the ways of the law, lives an upstanding life regulated solely by his own personal moral code. In contrast, Judge Temple lives by the maxim that "Society cannot exist without wholesome restraints." These opposing philosophies clash when Natty kills a deer out of season; accordingly, he is charged with a violation of the game laws and brought before the bench. But when asked whether or not he is guilty, the old trapper resolutely replies, "I may say not guilty with a clear conscience . . . for there's no guilt in doing what's right. . . ."[6]

These same words might have been spoken by any one of the stereotyped Western heroes who attained popularity more than forty years later in the dime novel. Whether trapper, plainsman, cowboy, or outlaw, each of these popular heroes was, like Natty, characterized by his asocial status and his intuitive recognition of the disparity between that which was merely legal and that which was morally just. But this similarity between the venerable trapper and his pulp successors should not be construed simply as a naive and unimaginative attempt by second-rate writers to follow an old trail blazed by Cooper. Instead, dime novelists recognized in the disparity between morality and legality a sure-fire method for creating popular heroes; specifically, it offered them a magic formula whereby they

might synthesize in the person of a single fictional character the two ostensibly irreconcilable traits which the reading public most highly prized and most often demanded of those it would venerate: virtue and rebelliousness. On the one hand, public demand had always existed for a standard hero who, guided by his own unerring sense of right and wrong, would lead the forces of good into battle against evil. On the other hand, in an age in which socioeconomic forces suppressed individual freedoms, public demand also existed for a hero who would reject any and all forms of artificial restraint, especially law. The dime novel Western hero satisfied both of these demands; wholeheartedly engaged in fighting villainy, he sometimes found it necessary to subvert the law in the interests of a higher justice.

The introduction of heroes who occasionally acted without regard to the law touched off an ascending spiral of rebelliousness in the dime novel. Evolving through respective incarnations as trapper, plainsman, cowboy, and outlaw, the Western hero progressively abandoned traditional social and legal codes of behavior in favor of sensationalism and absolute self-reliance.[7] In one sense the outlaw hero was merely the culmination of this trend; in another sense, however, he was a unique figure whose characterization posed a singular problem for dime novelists. While previous Western heroes had either acted in the absence of law or, on occasion, bypassed legal formalities in an attempt to exact a more nearly perfect justice than that which an imperfect legal system could ever hope to realize, never before had a Western hero openly opposed the law; never before had a Western hero reacted against societal restraint so violently as to waylay stages and rob banks. How then might this new and virulent strain of rebelliousness be reconciled with the hero's traditional virtue? And how might the outlaw hero be differentiated from that mob of ordinary badmen who, in league with the forces of evil, also opposed the law?

Dime novelists attacked the problem in two ways. First, they masked the bandit hero's questionable behavior with a thin veneer of respectability, always emphasizing his social polish, courtly manners, and chivalrous conduct toward friend and foe alike, particularly women. Second, and more importantly, they provided him with a justification for his rebelliousness. Though his heart was as true as steel, they explained, he had been unjustly persecuted and driven outside the law. Thereafter, a good but dangerously embittered man, he lived solely for revenge.

Once instituted, the theme of persecution and justifiable revenge rapidly assumed the nature of a formal plot convention in the outlaw story. Indeed, so pervasive did it become, and so familiar to readers, that authors merely needed to refer to "a thin smile" or "eyes glowing like coals" in order to supply all necessary character motivation. Of genuine significance, however, is the manner in which dime novelists tailored the timeworn theme of persecution and revenge to their own cultural context, consciously transforming it into a narrative convention which enabled them to instill in the outlaw hero that quality most responsible for his appeal—the violent but morally justifiable rejection of all forms of restraint, especially the law.

One of the more prolific writers on the staff of Beadle and Adams was a flamboyant Philadelphian who wore a Stetson hat, saluted strangers as "Pard," and billed himself "Edward L. Wheeler. Sensational Novelist."[8] Acquaintances thought Wheeler somewhat odd, but no one could dispute his knowledge of the writing business, for it was his pen that produced one of the most popular fictional heroes of the age: Deadwood Dick, the Black Rider of the Black Hills. Galloping through a series of adventures in more than thirty novels, the dashing Prince of the Road embodies all of the attributes of preceding Western heroes. A deadly shot and skilled equestrian, a master in the art of disguise, he cleverly evades pursuit or tracks down villains—tasks facilitated by a guaranteed income of five thousand dollars a year from his own gold mine. Forever young, handsome, and chivalrous, Deadwood Dick brings a blush to the cheeks of the beautiful and yearning women who abound in the novels; usually he resists their awkward advances, but he does marry three times and father two children. Each time, however, his wife's unfaithfulness or death shatters his domestic bliss, banishing him once again to a rootless life roaming the hills with his two valiant sidekicks, Calamity Jane and Old Avalanche, the Indian fighter.

In the first novel of the series, *Deadwood Dick, the Prince of the Road; or, The Black Rider of the Black Hills,* Wheeler begins to define the outlaw hero in terms of persecution and revenge, a theme he would return to in later novels, consciously developing and refining it as a narrative convention. When first introduced to the reader, Deadwood Dick is already a road agent. Though he spends considerable time eluding those who would claim the price on his head, he is actually in hot pursuit of Alexander and Clarence Filmore, two crafty malefactors who, we are given to understand, figure prominently in the outlaw's mysterious past. As the novel nears its conclusion, Deadwood Dick captures the villains and spirits them off to his mountain stronghold. Preparations are made for a hanging, and Deadwood Dick's loyal followers only await a signal from their captain before hoisting the two Filmores into eternity. But that signal is long in coming, for the outlaw chieftain must first justify the deed to all present, including the reader. Flinging aside his black mask and addressing the crowd, Deadwood Dick reveals that his real name is Edward Harris; an orphan, he had been taken in and raised by the kindly Harris family. But this home was soon denied to him, for the scheming Filmores successfully managed the "accidental" deaths of his foster parents. Then, as executor of the Harris estate, the elder Filmore swindled Edward and his lovely sister out of their share of the family wealth. Moreover, he foully mistreated them. "Finding that this kind of life was unbearable," the outlaw explains, "I appealed to our neighbors and even the courts for protection, but my enemy was a man of great influence, and after many vain attempts, I found that I

could not obtain a hearing; that nothing remained for me to do but to fight my own way. And I did fight it." Taking his sister with him, Deadwood Dick continues, he escaped from the Filmores, but not until he had first gone to his father's safe and "purloined a sum of money sufficient to defray our expenses." Though the money was rightfully his, its theft branded him a criminal in the eyes of the law. As a result, the outlaw concludes, "The Hills have been my haunt ever since. . . . Now, I am inclined to be merciful to only those who have been merciful to me. . . . Boys, string 'em up!"[9]

Insofar as it is embodied in the plot of this, the first of the Deadwood Dick stories, the theme of persecution and revenge manifests itself primarily through a relationship between individuals: the Filmores persecute Deadwood Dick and he takes revenge upon them. But the theme also has an obvious social dimension in that Deadwood Dick's justification for taking the law into his own hands rests on society's refusal to take a stand against the social evil which the Filmores represent. Were it not for the unresponsiveness of the legal system and the inaction of the public, Deadwood Dick contends, he would not have been forced to act on his own. And had he not been forced to act on his own he would not have become involved in that chain of events which ultimately deprived him of his rightful place in the community. Through a kind of emotional transference, then, Deadwood Dick comes to resent not merely those villainous individuals who actually precipitated his problems but the whole of society as well.

This anti-social sentiment assumes much wider scope in subsequent Deadwood Dick novels, largely as a result of a significant refinement made by Wheeler in the manner in which he implemented conventional persecution and revenge. Whereas he had instituted the convention in the original Deadwood Dick story primarily to justify Deadwood Dick's attack upon specific individuals, he utilized it in later novels to create stock situations which would afford the outlaw an opportunity to justifiably attack society in general. Usually Wheeler employed one or the other of two situations, each of which placed society in the role of oppressor and Deadwood Dick in the role of misunderstood defender of virtue. In the first, Deadwood Dick attempts to aid a party in distress but finds himself repeatedly hampered by an ignorant populace. This, of course, provokes the outlaw's wrath. In the second situation, Deadwood Dick renounces his life on the road and strives to become a law-abiding member of the community; invariably, however, he is persecuted by an unforgiving public and driven back into the hills where he broods over his unjust treatment and swears vengeance.

By depicting Deadwood Dick's encounters with society in terms of conventional persecution and revenge, Wheeler gained two artistic advantages. First, it allowed him to employ the community as a foil against which to define in the noble outlaw an essential trait common to all Western heroes: namely that he is a man possessed of superior powers of moral perception.[10] Inasmuch as the Western hero is able to detect the presence of evil when the general public is not, he takes it upon himself to protect the community by acting swiftly—even if this entails subverting those social and legal codes which the public holds most dear. Unlike other Western heroes, however, the outlaw hero does not merely subvert these codes; he violates them outright, and since the public remains unaware of the need for prompt and decisive action it inevitably misinterprets such violations. Hence, the outlaw hero incurs the animosity of the very community he is striving to protect—a bitter irony which, in turn, transforms his previously latent disdain for the credulous public into overt enmity. By depicting the outlaw's encounters with society in terms of conventional persecution and revenge, then, Wheeler dramatized that tension which exists between the alienated individual and the community, between insight and credulity, and between morality and legality. It is from this tension that the central ambivalence of the outlaw hero arises; he is at the same time a paragon of virtue and a confirmed rebel, a public servant and an expendable martyr.

A second advantage stemmed from Wheeler's use of conventional persecution and revenge. Deadwood Dick's banishment from the community affords him an opportunity to vent his righteous indignation in the form of bitter social criticism. Throughout the Deadwood Dick saga, the outlaw's attacks focus essentially upon the same three interrelated issues which he initially raised in his justification for lynching the Filmores: first, the stolidity of a citizenry that either cannot or will not distinguish between good and evil and which, through its inaction, consequently furthers the spread of evil; second, the iniquity of a social system which sanctions the exploitation of the common man by an unscrupulous ruling class; and, finally, the fundamental injustice of a legal system which, while it permits those of wealth and influence to perpetrate the most heinous crimes, at the same time severely punishes the common man for the least indiscretion.

The artistic advantages which Wheeler gained by defining the outlaw's relationship to the community in terms of conventional persecution and revenge become apparent in two consecutive stories which relate Deadwood Dick's encounters with the citizens of the bustling boom town of Leadville, Colorado. In each of these tales, Deadwood Dick is portrayed as both a misunderstood protector of the people and an outspoken social critic. In *Deadwood Dick in Leadville; or, A Strange Stroke for Liberty,* the outlaw holds up a stage but takes great pains to assure the passengers that he means them no harm: "These mountain districts are infested with ruffianly bands of road-agents and outlaws, who prey not only upon one another, but upon all who come within their reach, often resorting to the most fiendish torture to extort money. It does me proud to claim that Deadwood Dick and his followers are in no way allied to such gangs." Instead, maintains the outlaw chief, he is "a protective agent for the people." Though he waylays stages and deprives the passengers of their money, he does so only to prevent the unscrupulous Captain Hawk from

getting his hands on it when he halts the stage farther down the road. After the passengers have arrived safely in Leadville, Deadwood Dick explains, he will see to it that their money is returned. In spite of this valuable service, Deadwood Dick and his men are nevertheless ostracized by a society which refuses to make a distinction between good and bad outlaws. Still, it is of little consequence, notes the outlaw proudly: "Let the world regard us as it will—we care not. We are a band, to a man, who hate the world and everything worldly. . . ." And as for the citizens themselves, he continues, unable to repress a bitter laugh: "The people—well! . . . they would smite me down, were I to do them each and every one a blessing. They have a grudge against me which only my death can appease."[11]

Though Deadwood Dick is persecuted by a community which fails to recognize that he is acting in its best interest, it is nevertheless apparent that such individual action is necessary. Lamentably, Leadville's legal system is clearly unresponsive to the needs of the people—so much so, in fact, that a number of citizens have, "in defiance of the law, set themselves up as adjusters of their own wrongs. . . . Almost to a spirit of insubordination has this thing amounted to among those who plead for justice without receiving it, and hence came the organization known as the Regulators and Adjusters, making Leadville the possessor of two laws—a law of the State and a law of the people."[12]

In essence, the remainder of the novel contrasts the relative effectiveness of each of these forms of law. On the one hand, the law of the State is plainly inept. When Noel Farnsworth complains to the town sheriff that his sister has been abducted, the genial but incapable lawman throws up his hands in resignation. After a moment's hesitation, he feebly suggests the Farnsworth offer an ample reward in hopes that his sister will be returned unharmed. Then too, Ralph Gardner, the miscreant who has engineered the abduction, repeatedly uses his influence as "one of the richest men in Leadville" to bend the law in his favor, even invoking it in his defense when caught cheating at cards. And on still another occasion, Beautiful Bill, an inaptly named town bully who refers to himself as "a respected and law abidin' citizen," harasses the cowed citizenry. But the officers of the law are afraid to oppose him, so "Justice let him alone." On the other hand, the law of the people is not without its failings either. Too many of Leadville's citizens glory "in taking human life, whether in self-defense, in justice, or cold-handed." Blinded by mob psychology, manipulated by those "ruffianly and villainous characters . . . who literally 'boss' the town," the enraged populace is not only ineffective but potentially dangerous as well. At last, in a revealing scene which follows the capture of the notorious road agent Captain Hawk, the two alternative forms of law come into direct conflict:

> An instant trial was ordered by the people, and though the sheriff should have waited the slow motion of the law, by rights, he could not resist without running the risk of having his own life taken by the mob. . . . Ac-

cordingly a jury was selected, and the case was brought up, with a prominent lawyer as prosecutor. . . . A young pettifogger undertook the defense, but after he had spoken a few words, the crowd grew so excited, and revolvers were displayed in such profusion, that he wisely took a seat. A verdict of 'guilty' soon followed—the jury not leaving their seats.[13]

On the following morning, just as the sun edges up over the horizon, Captain Hawk is hanged.

Against this backdrop of confusion, coercion, and iniquity, Deadwood Dick stands out as a cool and incorruptible enforcer of true justice. Guided solely by his own infallible sense of right and wrong, unrestricted by legal impedimenta, he is the defender of unarmed virtue, the champion of the down-trodden. And yet he is not free; he is an exile, a lonely and homeless man untiringly persecuted by the very community for which he fights. Confiding to Calamity Jane his grim conviction that the "justice grabbers . . . will never get over their antipathy toward me, until they see me dangling in mid-air beneath a tree-limb," Deadwood Dick resolves to surrender to the people and pay his debt to society. However, he has an ulterior motive, and therefore extracts from Calamity Jane a promise that she will cut him down immediately after he is hanged and, if possible, resuscitate him. "After that," he explains, "I am not afraid of them, for they cannot hang a man but once, and that satisfies the law for all previous misdemeanors. I have but to hang, and then I can laugh at them all, for I shall be a free man—free to go where, or do whatsoever I choose." Accordingly, Deadwood Dick rides into Leadville and surrenders himself to mob justice. Permitted a few last words before being hanged, the Prince of the Road defends his notorious past in such a way as to implicitly contrast the true justice he has enforced with that lesser justice exacted by the law:

> Some of you may say that my life as a road-agent has been highly criminal. I don't agree with you on that score, for where I have tapped you, I have done so in a gentlemanly manner, and have, as a rule, circulated the spoils among poor and needy families. . . . I have aided a few ruffianly characters in getting a grand send-off, to be sure, but they were the worst of human brutes, and feared neither God nor man, and whose lives were a curse to the country and a discredit to the name of man. . . . Therefore, in balancing my accounts, I have not much to regret. But the law has seen fit to regard me as a ferocious criminal, and not wishing to offend the law—the great, majestic law—I do deliver myself up to be lynched from the nearest limb of the nearest tree.[14]

Moments later, "in the name of the law," Deadwood Dick makes his exit at the end of a rope.

It proved to be a brief exit, however, and when Deadwood Dick appeared in the next number of Beadle's Half Dime Library he was eminently free. As he explained in a later novel, "while I hung and paid my debt to nature and justice, I came back to life a free man whom no law in the universe could molest for past offenses."[15] Yet his days of freedom were numbered. Resurrecting his hero in *Dead-*

wood Dick's Device; or, The Sign of the Double Cross, Wheeler again constructed his story in terms of conventional persecution and revenge.

The plot involves Deadwood Dick's efforts to maintain ownership of a mine which he has inherited upon the death of a friendly miner. The Howells, the miner's avaricious family, resent Deadwood Dick's acquisition of the property and use all of their vast wealth and power to wrest it from him. It is clearly a class struggle, for Wheeler intrusively describes the Howells as "a leading family, both financially and socially—for Leadville, mind you, has its social world as well as its Eastern sister cities, formed out of that class whom fortune has smiled upon. And surrounded by a great superfluity of style, pomp and splendor, they set themselves up as the 'superior class,' ye gods!"[16] Using their influence, the Howells prejudice the citizens against Deadwood Dick, and soon the servile sheriff makes a rash attempt to arrest him. Cornered, his vehement protest that he is "lawfully a free man" ignored, Deadwood Dick regretfully guns down the sheriff's men and effects his escape—but not before he utters a fearful proclamation: "To-night I have been forced again into crime, and am an outlaw, by the decree of the people. Let them look out, for I will not stop now, but they shall learn to fear my name as an omen of death."[17]

Characteristically, Deadwood Dick's oath of vengeance is justified on the grounds that he has been unjustly persecuted by a society which, lacking his own "keen sense of perception," too often honors its enemies and maligns its benefactors. As he declares in a rare moment of self-revelation:

> I despise a man who is proud of himself, his name, or any worldly possession. No! I am not proud of the name of Deadwood Dick—I should be a contemptible sinner were I. It is not a name to be proud of, for there are many stains upon it, never to be washed out; yet, outlaw, road-agent, dare-devil though I have been, and am now, I have been driven on, step by step, by a people who have no mercy—who refuse to let me alone, after I had hanged and thus paid the penalty of crime. So that, though my future prospects may not be pleasant to reflect upon, I have the consolation of knowing that no man was ever paid nature's debt by my agency, who was not at heart a ruffian and villain, and whose death was not a relief to the community, and a favor to every honest man.[18]

And again, when asked if he must always live such a "wild, strange life," the noble outlaw fiercely replies, "Always! . . . I am an outcast, and as such I have only to remain. Society or the public at large refuse [sic] to receive me. They are everlasting enemies. . . . They curse me, and drive me about, and I have no choice except between this life and death." Reflecting upon Deadwood Dick's blighted life, Old Avalanche mutters, "He's bin treated like as ef he war sum dishonorable coyote, an' ef he ain't got cause fer revenge, I don't know myself."[19] Calamity Jane heartily agrees, and together they join Deadwood Dick in a campaign of terror against the citizens of Leadville.

Throughout the remainder of the Deadwood Dick saga, Wheeler again and again utilized conventional persecution and revenge as a means of creating stock situations which afforded the invincible Prince of the Road an opportunity to justifiably defy the law in order to defend the downtrodden and, in the process, bring swift justice to a society in which affluent evil-doers further their own ends by duping the public and manipulating the hopelessly ineffective legal system. In *Deadwood Dick on Deck; or, Calamity Jane, the Heroine of Whoop-Up. A Story of Dakota,* the outlaw hero comes to the aid of an honest miner who feels, "that very few men are so poor but what they can stand firm for their rights"; if there were more men in the country like him, we are told, "there would, undoubtedly, be a change for the better, when every man would, in a greater or lesser degree, have an independence, and not be ground down under the heel of the master of money."[20] In *Deadwood Dick of Deadwood; or, The Picked Party,* the outlaw chief cooperates with a detective to topple the corrupt business empire of a "purse-proud aristocrat" who lives by the maxim that "wealth is omnipotent." For his efforts, however, Deadwood Dick is sentenced to death by a drunken judge, and it is only because of Calamity Jane's quick thinking that he manages to escape.[21] On another occasion, while defending the rights of a peaceful Crown Indian whose lands have been usurped in *Deadwood Dick's Claim; or, The Fairy Face of Faro Flats,* the noble outlaw threatens to kill Philander Pilgrim, the local attorney and editor of the town newspaper. "A man is liable to arrest, sir, for uttering a threat!" exclaims the attorney. "Good Blackstone," the outlaw chuckles, "but it don't answer here. If you have ever heard of me you will know that I am the man who has found it right, necessary, and convenient to defy arrest."[22] Always defiant, the prince of outlaws continues to lead the forces of good into battle against evil until, in *Deadwood Dick's Dust; or, The Chained Hand. A Strange Story of the Mines, Being the 35th and Ending Number of the Great 'Deadwood Dick' Series,* he is killed while successfully destroying a town whose citizens have appropriated his own tract of land and lynched Calamity Jane.[23] Thus, ironically, the valiant hero who has spent his life defending the rights of others in the end loses it in defense of his own.

During the eight years that Wheeler concentrated his efforts primarily on the Deadwood Dick series, he penned a number of other novels which also illustrate his awareness of the fact that the noble outlaw's source of popular appeal lay in his justifiable rebellion against society. In these tales Wheeler consistently implemented the narrative convention of persecution and revenge to explain his hero's death as a social being and rebirth as a free individual immune to law. Fred Brayton, formerly a detective, and hero of *A No. 1, the Dashing Toll-Taker; or, the Schoolmarm o' Sassafras,* takes to the road as a result of a false conviction of murder.[24] In *Solid Sam, The Boy Road-Agent; or, The Branded Brows. A Tale of Wild Wyoming,* Solid Sam turns to a life of crime because a band of ruffians has appropriated his gold mine. Though he plans to waylay them individually and collect the gold which is rightfully his, he finds this impossible and instead demands that the citizens of Placer City restore his gold and pay him protection money. When they refuse, the outlaw and his men "justifiably" reduce the town to a "series of heaps of smoking ashes and charred embers, to tell of the vengeance of Solid Sam."[25] One of the clearest examples of the noble outlaw's vindication occurs in *Apollo Bill, the Trail Tornade; or, Rowdy Kate from Right-Bower. A Story of the Mines.* Approaching the problem laterally, Wheeler explains that "circumstances have been chronicled of a brave and gallant man, with a spice of nobility in his heart, who has taken to the profession of stage robbery, more on account of some secret life trouble, than taste for the business itself." Soon Wheeler reveals the "secret life trouble" that has caused law-abiding citizen Bill Blake to be reborn as the dashing Apollo Bill. His home and family, it seems, were destroyed by a roving gang of border ruffians. Swearing an oath of vengeance, Blake set out to track down the murderers; in the process, however, he accidentally shot and killed an innocent man. Pursued thereafter by the untiring

> minions of the law . . . hunted down to the last resort, he rallied around him a band of fellows and took to the mountains. They were discovered in their first retreat and branded road-agents ere they had earned the right to such a calling. Assailed by despondency and anger at this injustice, Apollo Bill fled to this fastness and organized his men into what is known as Apollo Bill's road-agents.[26]

Like so many other fictional outlaws, Apollo Bill has been falsely accused by a society ignorant of the nature of true justice; he is given no choice but to rebel.

On the basis of these tales and those in the Deadwood Dick saga, it is possible to outline the structure of persecution and revenge as a narrative convention. Essentially, it may be divided into three separate phases. In the first, a good man unjustly persecuted by one or more evil individuals discovers that the legal system can neither protect him nor punish his oppressors—a fact usually attributed to the villain's ability to use wealth and influence either to manipulate the law itself or to corrupt those involved in the slow and complex judicial process. On occasion, though, the hero simply refuses to entrust his fate to a jury composed of citizens who lack his own moral insight. In the second phase, the hero undertakes individual action to avenge his wrongs but, through a fatal misstep, breaks the law and becomes a social outcast. In some instances, the hero does not himself break the law; rather, he is framed by the villain. In the final phase, the outlaw's hatred for the evil individuals who initially persecuted him changes to hatred for society in general. This hatred invariably finds expression in violent action against the community; implicit at all times, however, is the fundamental assumption that such chastisement is merely part of the hero's paternalistic duty as protector of the people and enforcer of true justice.

Although Edward L. Wheeler was the first dime novelist to employ the timeworn theme of persecution and revenge as a means of creating a Western hero capable of responding to the social and psychological imperatives of the

Copyright 1878–1885, by Beadle & Adams. Entered at Post Office, New York N Y., as second class matter. Mar. 15, 1899

No. 15   THE ARTHUR WESTBROOK CO.
Cleveland, Ohio   Vol. II

DEADWOOD DICK ON DECK;

Or, CALAMITY JANE, The Heroine of Whoop-Up.

By E. L. Wheeler.

CALAMITY JANE.

nineteenth century, he was by no means the last. Other dime novelists followed his lead, and conventional persecution and revenge soon became a standard device in the outlaw story. Moreover, although originally formulated as a means of fashioning fictional outlaws, conventional persecution and revenge also played a profound role in the development and popularization of legends about actual Western badmen. Seizing upon those few facts which were germane to the convention, and shamelessly altering those that were not, dime novelists portrayed famous outlaws of the West as victims of an oppressive social system—a practice which influenced the legends of men like Jesse and Frank James, Bob Ford, and Joaquin Murieta.

But whether used to create fictional outlaws or implemented as a means of transforming actual Western badmen into misunderstood rebels, the narrative convention of persecution and revenge enabled dime novelists to provide the American public with heroes who possessed a capacity for resolving in fantasy the otherwise insoluble cultural conflicts of the age. In essence, the outlaw hero served two interrelated cultural needs. On the one hand, he was a projection of the widespread American preoccupation with the meaning and value of law. As a good man victimized by the unsettling disparity between that which was morally just and that which was strictly legal, the outlaw hero won a kind of immunity from restraint. Thereafter, guided solely by his own infallible sense of right and wrong, he could resolve that disparity between moral and civil law by taking swift and decisive individual action which insured the execution of true justice. On the other hand, the outlaw hero was a projection of the average American's growing alienation in a modern society characterized by industrialism, materialism, class polarization, and the suppression of individual freedoms by a rigid socioeconomic structure. Eminently free, the invincible outlaw hero was a man who would not, in Edward L. Wheeler's words, "be ground down under the heel of the master of money." Neither would he stand idly by in an age of apparent moral decline; inevitably, he punished the wicked and triumphed over evil. And if, like an angel of wrath from *Revelation,* he sometimes found it necessary to purify an entire society with thunder and pillars of fire, then this too was just.

Notes

1. Beadle's Half Dime Library, No. 1 (Oct. 15, 1877).
2. William A. Settle, Jr., *Jesse James Was His Name: or, Fact and Fiction Concerning the Careers of the Notorious James Brothers of Missouri* (Columbia: Univ. of Missouri Press, 1966), p. 189, and Quentin Reynolds, *The Fiction Factory; or, From Pulp Row to Quality Street* (New York: Random House, 1955), pp. 115-16.
3. For an invaluable discussion of popular art forms and their relationship to the cultural context, see John G. Cawelti, *The Six-Gun Mystique* (Bowling Green, Ohio: Bowling Green Univ. Popular Press, 1971).
4. The growing disparity between civil and moral law culminated formally in the Supreme Court's momentous decision in the Girard Will Case of 1844. For a fuller discussion of this and other aspects of the popular attitude toward law in the nineteenth century, see "The Legal Mentality," Book Two of Perry Miller's indispensable study, *The Life of the Mind in America, from the Revolution to the Civil War* (New York: Harcourt, Brace, 1965).
5. James Fenimore Cooper, *The Prairie* (1827; rpt. New York: Rinehart, 1950), pp. 402-03.
6. Cooper, *The Pioneers* (1823; rpt. New York: Washington Square, 1962), pp. 352, 334.
7. Henry Nash Smith, *Virgin Land: The American West as Symbol and Myth* (1950; rpt. New York: Vintage-Knopf, n.d.), p. 134.
8. Albert Johannsen, *The House of Beadle and Adams* (Norman: Univ. of Oklahoma Press, 1950), II, 296.
9. Beadle's Half Dime Library, No. 1 (Oct. 15, 1877), p. 13.
10. For an interesting discussion of the Western hero's superior moral perception, see James K. Folsom, *The American Western Novel* (New Haven, Conn.: College & University Press, 1966), pp. 136-37.
11. Beadle's Half Dime Library, No. 100 (June 24, 1879; rpt. Deadwood Dick Library, No. 23, Mar. 15, 1899), pp. 5, 16.
12. p. 7.
13. p. 26.
14. pp. 30-31.
15. *Deadwood Dick's Dream; or, The Rivals of the Road. A Mining Tale of Tombstone,* Beadle's Half Dime Library, No. 195 (Apr. 19, 1881), p. 8.
16. Beadle's Half Dime Library, No. 104 (July 22, 1879; rpt. Deadwood Dick Library, No. 21, Mar. 15, 1899), p. 5.
17. p. 8.
18. p. 23.
19. pp. 23, 25.
20. Beadle's Half Dime Library, No. 73 (Dec. 17, 1878; rpt. Deadwood Dick Library, No. 15, Mar. 15, 1899), p. 9.
21. Beadle's Half Dime Library, No. 156 (July 20, 1880; rpt. Deadwood Dick Library, No. 17, Mar. 15, 1899), pp. 9, 12, 30-31.
22. Beadle's Half Dime Library, No. 362 (July 1, 1884) p. 3.
23. Beadle's Half Dime Library, No. 430 (Oct. 20, 1885), p. 14.
24. Beadle's Half Dime Library, No. 299 (Apr. 17, 1883; rpt. *The Detective Road-Agent; or, The Miners of Sassafras City,* Deadwood Dick Library, No. 63, Mar. 15, 1899).
25. Beadle's Half Dime Library, No. 141 (Apr. 6, 1880; rpt. Deadwood Dick Library, No. 32, Mar. 15, 1899), p. 31.

26. Beadle's Half Dime Library, No. 236 (Jan. 31, 1882; rpt. *Dick Drew, the Miner's Son; or, Apollo Bill, the Road-Agent,* Deadwood Dick Library, No. 48, Mar. 15, 1899), pp. 4-5, 17.

MAJOR FIGURES AND INFLUENCES

Ralph Admari (essay date 1933)

SOURCE: "Ballou, the Father of the Dime Novel," in *The American Book Collector*, September-October, 1933, pp. 121-29.

[In the essay below, Admari provides an overview of publisher, writer, and editor Maturin Murray Ballou's career and his contribution to American literature and periodicals in the nineteenth century.]

In the years to come when the popular literature of the United States shall have been thoroughly explored many disputes will arise as to whom should go the credit for having brought about the dime novel. As early as 1872, Frederic Hudson in his remarkable history of Journalism stated that Park Benjamin, who was responsible for the first sensational weekly or story paper (1839) and the first cheap book (12½¢) paper binding same year, was the father of cheap literature. This was more than five years before the dime novel became an important function in the cultural advance of the masses. The Englishman, Bracebridge Hemyng, author of the enduring Jack Harkaway (1869) introduced the action minus description and sacrificed everything to the story itself. Another claimant, Norman L. Munro publisher, was the first to issue crude blood and thunder stories for children about 1875. But the one to whom all now give most of the laurels is Erastus F. Beadle who issued the name of a series from which the dime novel got its name, *Beadle's Dime Novels* (1860). Still another is Orville J. Victor, editor for the House of Beadle, who is credited with having given the idea of the dime paper books to Beadle. This article is concerned only with Maturin Murray Ballou who solidified cheap literature and periodicals at a time when European domination threatened our cultural progress.[1]

Ballou was born in Boston, 1820, and was the youngest child of Hosea Ballou, the leading minister of New England. In those early days most of the Ballou family were so concerned with religion that they issued magazines, pamphlets and books on the absorbing subject. Naturally young Maturin grew up in a publishing environment that was to develop into one of the most powerful figures in the world of cheap literature. Young Ballou was sent to Harvard but did not graduate due to ill-health, a curse that followed him all his life. To cure himself he took to travelling and this brought on a subtle disease, wanderitis,

which he never got out of his system. From the time he left Harvard to his death he could be found in some remote spot of the world. During the interim when he stayed at home he accomplished so much that it is a mystery how he did it.

His literary career started at the age of eighteen when he wrote editorials for the famous Boston family story paper, *The Olive Branch.* To this paper he contributed sketches, poems and short stories. After leaving Harvard he got a job in the Boston Customs house but kept up his literary efforts. When he was twenty-five, Frederick Gleason, another youthful writer, got him to publish three novels (*Fanny Campbell, Red Ruppert, The Naval Officer*) all of which achieved sensational successes, the first selling 80,000 copies within a few months. Together with Gleason they continued this series of books by hiring J. H. Ingraham, Mrs. Ann Stephens and Justin Jones (Harry Hazel) to write novelettes for them. This was the first series of sensational stories ever issued in America. They were started by Gleason in 1844 and were called shilling novelettes because that was a coin famous in the 30's and 40's when the dime was unknown. A shilling was valued at 12½¢ or half a quarter and by some was called a York shilling, a derisive term, to show that it came from New York. The sizes of these paper books were 8½ x 5 inches; they contained fifty pages and were illustrated, in most cases, by a lurid hand-colored wood cut. In the latter part of 1846 the novels were increased in size to 9½ x 6 and 25¢ in price, and contained one hundred pages or more.

When Ballou joined hands with Gleason in 1845, they established a unique company known as the United States Publishing Co., whose purpose was to spread their publications all over the United States, having various dealers and publishers as agents in the various large cities. This was really the first attempt to distribute books scientifically over the United States. They had agencies in New York, Buffalo, Philadelphia, St. Louis, Cincinnati, Baltimore, New Orleans, and Detroit. The New York agent was Samuel French, who is still in business today publishing his plays without interruption.

Deciding to branch out more the two youngsters put out in January 24, 1846, the family paper *Flag of Our Union,* which became within a year, under the editorial genius of Ballou, the most powerful story paper of the period. Although it had strong competitors, in *Boston Notions, Olive Branch* and the famed *New World,* a New York mammoth paper that claimed the largest size of sheet ever printed, it soon crowded them off the map. The "Flag" kept this lead until New York, ever jealous of its Hub rival, began coming out with stiffer opposition, such as the *New York Ledger* (1851), and *New York Weekly* (1855). The "Flag" declined when the New York story papers took all its writers away, luring them with juicier contracts. The "Flag" went through various changes, at first it was a mammoth four-page paper[2] the size of a double bed when unfolded. In the 50's it was reduced in size, but its pages increased to eight, until finally it merely imitated the papers then being issued, going out in January 1, 1871, when it merged with the *American Union.*

Not content with this step Ballou got hold of one Robert Carter who later became known to the world as Frank Leslie, a young Englishman who had just landed from London and they conspired together to put out the first illustrated weekly in America. This was in May, 1851; it was called *Gleason's Pictorial Drawing Room Companion* as Gleason had put up the "dough." It was a frank imitation of the *London Illustrated News* which had taught Frank Leslie all he knew about publishing.

The firm which was called Gleason's Publishing Hall, grew prosperous steadily but all due to Ballou's guiding hand. Gleason had done very little except to put up money for the first two ventures. By the time 1854 rolled in Ballou was determined to have no entangling alliances. In November of that year he forced Gleason out by an old trick in publishing, that is he threatened Gleason with two rival weeklies unless he sold out his half to Ballou. It was a low foul but Gleason swallowed his defeat and walked off leaving the business to Ballou. The next year, January, the name of the "Pictorial" was changed to *Ballou's Pictorial.* The same month he launched what turned out to be the first all fiction monthly ever issued in the United States. It was *Ballou's Dollar Monthly* and it was widely advertised as the cheapest magazine in the world. This was a quarto affair of a hundred pages. It contained mostly short stories, an article or two, some illustrations, and editorial comment.

Continuing his experiments Ballou placed on sale a series entitled *The Weekly Novelette,* containing part of a special story reprinted from his magazines. Each part consisted of one-fifth of the story. It was completed in five issues, each part being four cents, the complete novel costing twenty cents. The size of the weekly paper was 9″ × 12″ inches and it contained sixteen pages. There had been attempts in this fashion before but only popular authors like Charles Dickens, Alexandre Dumas and Victor Hugo had been considered. This attempt started April, 1857, was a pioneer one so far as native sensational literature was concerned. There was a kind of dignity with Ballou's efforts to corral the popular literature in Boston. So long as he hung on and kept fighting the New York publishers, Boston really put out the best paper books. In fact the Hub city did not yield its lead until the Civil War. Then New York emerged triumphant and has never lost its eminence. Had Ballou held on to his most important authors the tale might have been different, for he was constantly seeking new and fresher talent and the eyes of the literary world were on Boston in those days. True to form Ballou had never deviated one iota from one principle of his early days as editor and publisher. This was that no article other than American be printed in his pages. Look over his papers and you will see how closely he stuck to this resolution. There is not a single article or sketch composed by foreign brains, in any one of his papers. When we consider that all New England was a second-hand England, Ballou's achievement is too heroic to be talked about calmly.

Nor was this great revolt due to any puritanical effort to overcome old world culture. It simply meant that the Democratic elements, the worker, the common housewife and the lad and girl (the latter after the Civil War) demanded their fiction based on rough adventure and homely love. These elements had been submerged since the Revolution. The fact is that except for an occasional bawdy ballad or poem the lower classes never found their articulate artists in the New World until the newspapers became established, and such early great humorists as George W. Arnold, Seba Smith and others came along with the great Jackson administration.

In 1857 the publications of Ballou, which now dominated the field, had the following circulations: *Flag of Our Union,* 80,000 weekly; *Dollar Magazine,* 100,000 monthly; the *Pictorial,* 140,000 weekly.[3] Thus with a few half-baked ideas, two youths, starting in 1844, had by 1857 established a great publishing house and made fortunes for all those associated with them. But Ballou, whose initiative and progressive spirit had advanced the firm to its domination of cheap publications, really did more than merely make money. He had, without being aware of it, literally crushed foreign domination of proletarian culture here. The masses after Ballou's advent sought for its hero and heroine in fiction in their native land and demanded a vigorous, racy literature containing the breath of the New World. This was a peculiar country in many ways. Where the snobs in Europe had dominated the culture of their respective countries and demanded easy mushy fiction and poetry, the American, free, independent and aware that he was just a sweating worker, sought a literature that had a different breath from old world decayed art. Nationalism was beginning to come to the fore in literature as well as in politics.

In various years Ballou had gathered under his banner the most formidable group of sensational and popular writers ever assembled in the publishing field. The sensational writers were Sylvanus Cobb, Jr., H. W. Herbert (Frank Forester), Justin B. Jones (Harry Hazel), Dr. J. H. Robinson, J. H. Ingraham, A. J. H. Duganne, Harry Hazleton, E. C. Z. Judson (Ned Buntline), and Edward S. Ellis. The writers of the more restrained type were William T. Adams (Oliver Optic), Horatio Alger, Jr., Park Benjamin, Mrs. Ann S. Stephens, Mrs. L. H. Sigourney, Rev. F. W. Holland, T. S. Arthur, who inflicted our literature with that midsummer's nightmare, *Ten Nights in a Barroom,* and Thomas Bullfinch whose *Fables From Antiquity,* published in the "Pictorial" are still used in our schools. The Carey sisters contributed most of their poetry to his periodicals. Ballou also wrote for the periodicals under his pseudonym Lieutenant Murray, composing various stories of the west and of the sea, and historical romances.

It is obvious to all who read about his life that giving this sickly man credit for having changed the course of native literature is no exaggeration. Ballou contributed the following services to native literature:

> 1. He was the first to give more than one *nom-de-plume* to a popular writer of fiction, Sylvanus Cobb, Jr.[4]

2. He was the first to employ native talent exclusively for stories, articles, poetry, and illustrations.

3. He was the first to build up a popular publishing house that lasted long enough to influence others in the same direction.

4. He was the first editor to formulate an editorial policy as regards construction of stories, type of plots, mostly having to do with the frontier as a background.

5. He established the first illustrated weekly[5] and the first "all fiction" magazine and contributed largely to the success of the first series of American blood and thunder tales of the west and early frontier, which had been started by Gleason.

6. He was the first editor-publisher to write blood and thunder tales (under his *nom-de-plume* Lieutenant Murray).

7. He was the first to actually encourage his writers and to take an interest in them, to pay fair prices, and to consistently use their efforts.

At the time Ballou came on the scene in 1845, the various editors of the country looked to Europe to fill up their columns. Whatever was published by an American was hidden in some corner and apologized for. *The Brother Jonathan,* the first sensational story paper (1839) stated that American writers were few and far between and whatever there were of them were incompetent. A. Gallenga, famous Italian exile, visiting this country in the 30's and 40's, stated that American ideas were swiped from English books that came over in batches. In other words our culture was secondhand; it had no dignity; it was cheap, vulgar, because it camped on the doorstep of another culture, older and thoroughly its own. Every time a ship came in from Europe there would follow a mad scramble by every tin-horn publisher to get the first English book and magazine and republish it as its own. It was shameful. While American writers walked from editor to editor with seedy clothes and while Poe and Emerson bitterly railed at the American bourgeoisie for its European culture, the country had not backbone enough to overthrow the shackles of foreign thought. We had won political freedom but that was all. At this time, about 1830, a new audience was being born for the public schools became a power in the land and about fifteen years later this audience demanded a new deal.

Ballou changed everything like magic. As an editor he might be compared with Mencken although unlike Mencken he took absolutely no interest in politics. This was of vast importance to his success for this neutrality brought him readers who also felt as he did. This red herring of politics had strung a line of corpses in its path.[6]

When he took hold of popular publishing it was in the hands of half-wits, charlatans and other lice. The conservative magazines published the efforts of only those un-American authors such as Hawthorne, Mellville, Longfellow, Whittier, Lowell and others who lickspittled to everything outside of America. Harper's Magazine, Putnam's, Graham's, all grabbed foreign illustrations and discouraged the boisterous native artist who came to their

doors. After Ballou's debut it was a different story. As early as 1847 William T. Porter, editor of *Spirit of the Times,* decided not to reprint foreign articles. Ballou had been making a success of his policy to print only American stories and material. The other editors began joining the bandwagon one after another. Only the conservative magazines stuck up their noses to the masses. In fact he became a model for other young hopefuls, one of them, his writer Jones (Harry Hazel), quitting him and starting a new paper, *Harry Hazel's Yankee Blade,* which lasted to 1895. This new spirit in popular literature reached its climax when the House of Beadle in June, 1860, issued a ten-cent novel, the series of which would employ exclusively American talent. Then came the flood.

The times needed a stern one-track mind like that of Ballou. He had only one love, publishing and writing sensational books and issuing like periodicals. The environment in which he was born, surrounded by God-fearing parents and brothers—puritanical but austerely just and honest, while not calculated to develop a humorous, happy lad nevertheless gave him qualities of mind and intellectual independence that were vital for the pioneer work he accomplished alone and unaided. No mamma's boy could have kept his goal, under such trying times, as Ballou had done. His work was heroic as much so as any general had accomplished in the Revolution and more so because it was spiritual and aimed at hidden enemies. There was something grave, thoughtful about his face. He never smiled. It was the face of a man who had known all of life and was now resigned to living it peacefully and without great rumpus. Ballou loved work for the sake of it. He was not only a publisher, editor and writer, but he was a traveler, lecturer, playwright, builder, and journalist. However he could make mistakes too, for on December 27, 1859, he put out a new mammoth paper, *The Welcome Guest,* which lasted a very short time. This failure seems to have hit him hard for two years after 1861 he sold his great publishing house to Elliot, Thomes & Talbot, which firm continued his publications but were content to imitate other rivals, putting out, in November 10, 1863, the first of a series of dime novels competing with those of Beadle.

Ballou was not through with publishing. Unable to get periodicals out of his blood he decided on a new venture, a daily newspaper. He established the famous *Boston Globe* March 4, 1872. This proved a costly undertaking and ruined him for in seventeen months he and his backers lost $300,000 when he relinquished control to Taylor. One reason for the failure was Ballou's dislike of politics. It was a notorious fact that whenever a political controversy came up he would ignore it. Instead he actually printed an editorial on Jute and Jute making or How Palm Trees sway gently 'neath the moon! Not that Ballou was a coward but politics left him cold. He hated the breed. He could get away with periodicals and magazines but newspapers, even in those days, demanded dirt and political squabbles.

How was Ballou as a man? Very little is known about him. He was too retiring, too austere. There is no doubt that his soul was crushed in early youth by the stern up-bringing imparted by his religious parents. Perhaps his search for health was also a seeking for certain elements in his soul, dormant all his life. He was essentially a business man, not an artist, though now and then there were flashes in his work which show that if he had been encouraged in early youth he might have contributed something personal to literature. He was a passionate lover of liberty, in the real sense. The Anglo-Saxon ideal of personal liberty was a part of his soul. His controversial editorials or books are on this subject, liberty for all. He championed the negro and the Cuban, and wrote a book on Cuba in 1854, and was one of the pioneers believing in the liberation of Cuba from Spanish domination. One of the finest pieces of poetry he wrote was on Cuba.[7] He was a hard worker when illness did not interfere. He lectured, he wrote plays, and he built hotels, but his attempts out of his real life work were all failures. From the time he quit the field where he had made a marvelous success hard luck dogged him. So he became a wanderer. He wrote, under his own name, many books on the lands he visited. He died, almost without making a ripple in his former world, in Cairo, Egypt, March 27, 1895. He had lived to see the declining fortunes of the dime novel which was being edged aside by the pulpwood magazines coming into favor under the guiding hands of William R. Hearst and Frank A. Munsey and which he had anticipated more than forty years before. He died just a year before the debut of Frank Merriwell, saga of American literature.

In his writings Ballou never showed his real soul. It is hard to judge the man from them. They are so colorless and dull. In one of his travel books, *The Pearl of India*, 1894, he tells about the Indians of Ceylon and outlying places but in the whole book fails to mention a single fact about their life under the British. It is an aimless childish book. Why he chose to ignore the people is a mystery. In the other books of travel he commits the same crime. His sensational writings are as dull as his travel books. They were written in his early youth from 1844 to 1858, but they were influenced by the times. It was an era when the most independent of them frankly imitated the pioneer of Indian stories, James Fenimore Cooper. This chap who had struck on a brilliant idea but who had spoiled it by vulgarly imitating Scott, so much so that every character in his books is a fifth-rate Englishman, completely dominated American fiction until the dime novelists came along to overthrow his influence. Why did Ballou give up writing fiction? One good reasons that may be advanced is that in youth a man is more or less free from family shackles and his ideals are mostly radical. Public Opinion leaves him cold. Most of these early or pre-dime-novelists wrote their sensational fiction until they either married of settled down. Then remorse would come. Nearly every one of them felt that they had written naughty books and so they forgot completely about their early careers. In the case of the youthful fire-eater, J. H. Ingraham, who had written at least one hundred books of sensational fiction before 1855, his son relates that when he J. H., had become a minister in Mississippi his wife influenced him to spend a large

fortune buying up his old books and burning them. Judson (Ned Buntline) frankly confessed to Venable, one of the first of the radical historians, that he had written nothing but trash. If you will note the cases of the two, they had only recently been married.

When Ballou took over the publishing house in 1854 he got slightly highbrow and arranged with Samuel French of New York to take over his blood and thunder paper books. At the same time he harped more than ever that his publications were so piously pure that even a church mouse could read them without blushing. This idiotic course did not get him many readers. As he got older he became more conservative and naturally other young publishers, not so finicky as he, began taking away his best writers. Beadle took Harry Hazleton, Edward S. Ellis, and A. J. H. Duganne; Bonner of the *New York Ledger*, grabbed Dr. J. H. Robinson and Sylvanus Cobb, Jr. (by taking away the latter, 1856, Bonner practically scuttled the House of Ballou for Cobb was the most popular writer of fiction before the Civil War, writing more than two hundred novels, all of them immensely successful) and Street of *New York Weekly* pirated Ned Buntline.

Ballou's influence therefore came in his early youth. His pioneer work in the cheap publishing field cannot be dimmed by his later mistakes. He gave the worker, the farmer and the humble housewife something they never had before, books and magazines written and published solely for their benefit and pleasure. In doing this he accomplished a vast step in art and culture in the United States and for this service he deserves a monument, next to Whitman.

The following is a list of all published books written by Ballou. Those issued under his pseudonym Lieutenant Murray are marked L. M., those not so marked were issued under his own name. Where no place of publication is mentioned Boston is meant. Dates signify when book was first issued except otherwise specified. Ballou's novels received many changes in titles when rival publishers got hold of them; in fact he himself was guilty of the same offense. For instance he published the *Sea Witch*, 1855, later reprinted 1859 as *Sea Lark; Turkish Spies* becomes *Turkish Slave*; Evert H. Long takes *The Naval Officer* and reprints it as *Captain Lovell* (1860) as a dime novel; *Fanny Campbell* is disguised as the *Pirate Queen* and so on.

Red Rupert, The American Bucanier by L. M., 1845, paper.

Fanny Campbell, the Female Pirate Captain, by L. M., 1845, paper.

The Naval Officer or The Pirate's Cave by L. M. 1845, paper.

The Child of the Sea or the Smuggler of Colonial Times (together with another short novel, The Love Test) by L. M. 1846, paper.

The Spanish Musketeer by L. M. 1847, paper.

The Gipsey or the Robbers of Naples by L. M. 1847, paper.

The Adventurers or The Wreck in the Indian Ocean by L. M. 1848, paper.

The Circassian Slave by L. M. 1851, paper.

The Heart's Secret or The Fortunes of a Soldier by L. M. 1852, paper.

Biography of the Reverend Hosea Ballou, 1852, cloth.

History of Cuba, 1854, cloth.

The Magician of Naples: A Tale of Fortune's Freaks and Fancies by L. M. New York, 1854, paper.

The Duke's Prize: A Story of Art and Heart in Florence. New York, (by L. M.), 1854, paper.

The Sea Witch or The Africa Quadroon by L. M. New York, 1855, paper.

The Turkish Spies: A True History of the Russo-Turkish War by L. M. Baltimore, 1855, paper.

The Greek Adventurer or The Soldier and The Spy by L. M. New York, 1856, paper.

The Arkansas Ranger or Dingle, the Backwoodsman, by L. M. 1858, paper, (reprint first edition not known).

Miralda or The Justice of Tacon (a play), 1858, paper.

The Cabin Boy or Life on the Wing by L. M. 1858, paper.

Roderick the Rover or The Spirit of the Wave by L. M. New York, 1858, paper.

The Outlaw or The Female Bandit. A Story of the Robbers of the Apennines. New York, 1859, paper.

A Treasury of Thought, An Encyclopedia of Quotations. Edited by Ballou, 1875, cloth.

Notable Thoughts About Women, edited by Ballou, 1882, cloth.

Pearls of Thought, edited by Ballou, 1884, cloth.

Due West or Round the World in Ten Months, 1884, cloth.

Due South or Cuba, Past and Present, 1885, cloth.

Edge-Tools of Speech, edited by Ballou, 1886, cloth.

Due North or Glimpses of Scandinavia and Russia, 1887, cloth.

Genius in Sunshine and Shadow, 1887, cloth.

Under the Southern Cross or Travels in Australasia, 1888, cloth.

The New Eldorado. A Summer Journey in Alaska, 1889, cloth.

Footprints of Travel or Journeyings in Many Lands, 1889, cloth.

The Dog Detective and His Young Master by L. M. New York, 1889, paper, (Reprint, no first edition available.).

Aztec Land, 1890, cloth.

Equatorial Africa, 1892, cloth.

The Story of Malta, 1893, cloth.

The Pearl of India, 1894, cloth.

The above list is as complete as possible considering that Ballou's earlier works, being contemporary with those of Poe, are almost impossible to get. The age in which both Ballou and Poe wrote was careless of paper books. They were destroyed upon being read hence the vast prices that Poe's first editions bring. Poe in his time was considered a sensational writer and his books were printed as such. He had the same complex that all the sensational writers of his period held to their breasts, shame of their craft. When Poe sent several of his poems to Ballou to be printed in the *Flag of Our Union* he felt that he had bandied with a lot of cheap hacks, yet he was one himself and it wasn't until Europe discovered him that his genius was appreciated here.

Again speaking of this complex, which seemed abundant only in the psychology of the American artist in the early years, Ballou never even let any one know what he had done in his youth. He never mentioned his connections with cheap paper books and periodicals in his last books. Anyone looking over the bibliography of his works would be forced to believe that they were the work of two men. This shame seemed peculiar only to the native artists. By some illogical process, deeply imbedded in the past, the artist came to feel that creation of literature for the masses was a deplorable and sinful task. Their idea seemed to be to get the money and get the hell out of such literature as fast as they became independent. It never occurred to any one of them that the mob, against whom Poe shot his bitter targets and who practically supported him when his more intelligent confreres ignored him, could appreciate a masterpiece as much as the highbrow public had appreciated the works of Shakespeare during the Elizabethan era.

Not so with the English and French popular writers like Dumas, Marryat, Hugo, Sue, Dickens (the latter is a dime novelist of the extravagant type), Charles Knight (editor, author, publisher and conceded to be father of cheap literature in England) and others, who not only wrote for the washerwoman, coal miner, and the servant but who actually felt proud of their niche in life. Most of them wrote memoirs about their early struggles, their first hack novels, and gloried in them. Thus many of them wrote masterpieces that even a Shakespeare might well envy.

Notes

1. In *Living Authors of America* by Thomas Powell, (an English scholar), published in 1850, the following statement is made; "The salvation of America lies in the possession of Republican Literature. The literature of England is slowly sapping the foundations of her institutions. England does all her thinking. . . . Nay, even worse, she openly discourages them in their attempt, and tacitly confesses that it is hopeless to compete with the writers of England and France." This statement was made when Poe (an American writer in a begrudging way) Bryant, Longfellow, Melville, Hawthorne, Lowell, Irving and many others had already become famous abroad. In fact more credit

2. When *Brother Jonathan* was issued, 1839, it was a large mammoth sheet so large that it had to be folded up half a dozen times before it could be conveniently carried under the arm. This craze for jumbo papers lasted til about 1860, when paper became very expensive, the size as a result growing smaller and smaller. A rough estimate of these papers amounts to about 200 different kinds issued in two decades. Some wit claimed that one of the causes of the Civil War was due to these papers which were used in place of cotton as bed sheets.

3. It must be remembered that in pre-Civil-War times a circulation of 100,000 was sensational. In proportion it tallied with the million circulation of today. A paper of that much circulation in those days was an institution of power and influence.

4. For more details about this prolific writer see "Memoir of Sylvanus Cobb, Jr.", by Ella W. Cobb.

5. The illustrated magazine had long been established here. As early as 1845, two monthlies were started, the *N. Y. Illustrated Magazine,* and the *Pictorial World.* Both soon gave up the ghost. Another came out the first week of January, 1846, and was issued fort-nightly about every 12 days. It was a folio of 16 pages and a frank imitation of the *Illustrated London News.* It was called *Hewet's Excelsior and N. Y. Illustrated Times,* edited by Charles Fenno Hoffman. However these early pioneers added nothing to cheap periodicals. Their attempts were doomed from the first issue.

6. Antonio Gallenga in *Episodes of My Second Life* shrewdly notes this phenomenon in American art. He states that our intellectuals were too interested in politics to pay attention to art. Too much democracy allowed room for nothing else but political talk. Thus every editor whatever his views, published his newspapers, weeklies and magazines from the standpoint of some political party. Before Ballou's time editors and publishers were not interested in developing a genuine American literature but were devoted, heart and soul, in some dubious cause to advance their interests either in their state or in Washington. Ballou was therefore an innovator. He excluded from his papers everything of a controversial nature, making them strictly literary magazines.

7.   Queen of the Antilles (1851)Bright
Gem of the Ocean, the Antilles' queen,
The fairest, the richest the tropics have seen,
With shores softly fanned by the trade winds, so free.
And sweet zephyrs breathing o'er upland and lea.
Alas! that with beauties so lavishly blessed,
The homes of thy children should be so oppressed.

So nearly thou liest in the Caribee sea,
To the rock-bound shores of the land of the free,
That thy children look hopeful, its influence feel,
While they frown at the yoke of distant Castile.
Then gird thee for freedom, ay, gird for the fight,
Thy lone star has risen, may God bless the right!

Gregory M. Pfitzer (essay date 1994)

SOURCE: "'Iron Dudes and White Savages in Camelot': The Influence of Dime-Novel Sensationalism on Twain's *A Connecticut Yankee in King Arthur's Court*," in *American Literary Realism, 1870-1910,* Vol. 27, No. 1, Fall, 1994, pp. 42-58.

[In the essay below, Pfitzer argues that Twain transformed the formulaic components of dime novels into a master-piece of literature.]

In the summer of 1884, Mark Twain was enjoying a rare moment of self-satisfaction. Having just finished writing the *Adventures of Huckleberry Finn* after long delays, he was hard at work on a sequel which by contrast seemed to be writing itself—a western novel tentatively entitled *Huck Finn and Tom Sawyer among the Indians.*[1] Fulfilling Huck's promise to "light out for the Territory" at the conclusion of *Huck Finn,* Twain sends his rambunctious hero out West to experience life among "the Injuns."[2] In preparation for this relocation of Huck from the soggy river-banks of the Midwest to dusty prairies of the frontier, Twain devoted the early part of the summer of 1884 to reading every "western adventure" on which he could lay his hands. Part of his strategy was to pester his business agent, Charles Webster, for any books he could find on the subject. "Dear Charley," Twain wrote in June, "Send to me, right away, a book by Lieut Col Dodge U.S.A., [and] . . . several other personal narratives of life & adventure out yonder on the Plains & in the Mountains, if you can run across them, especially life among the Indians. . . . I mean to take Huck Finn out there."[3] By mid-summer the "Injun books" had arrived, and shortly thereafter, according to Walter Blair, the first eight-and-a-half chapters of the novel were completed.[4] Writing nearly 240 double-spaced manuscript pages in less than two weeks, the normally guarded Twain was confident enough about his progress to announce to his close friend William Dean Howells that a "new story (Huck Finn and Tom Sawyer among the Indians 40 or 50 years ago)" was well under way.[5]

But then, mysteriously, Twain's "tank" ran dry, and he suddenly stopped work on the western novel. Offering no explanation to either his editor or Howells, he simply abandoned the project altogether, dismissing the season as a complete loss from a literary point of view. "This is the first summer which I have lost," he wrote dejectedly to Webster in early September. "I haven't a paragraph to show for my 3-months' working session. And Twain's rejection was complete; he never wrote an additional line of text for the aborted novel. The manuscript remained buried amidst his private papers until it was published merely as a curiosity piece nearly six decades after his death.[6]

What caused this change in attitude on the part of Twain toward *Huck Finn and Tom Sawyer among the Indians?* Various theories have been offered through the years to explain the abandonment. His first biographer, Albert Bigelow Paine, believed that Twain simply lost interest in the story, as he had in the case of dozens of other unfinished works.[7] Walter Blair argues that Twain may have sensed he was borrowing too liberally from the western sources his agent had supplied and that the attendant loss of originality was too much of a sacrifice for him to make.[8] And Wayne Kime has recently echoed the contention of others (including Blair) that Twain had painted himself into a literary corner of sorts by allowing themes of adolescent infatuation and love to spill over (indiscreetly by Victorian standards) into a discussion of mature sexual relationships and even sexual violence.[9] To this list of intrinsic reasons as to why Twain abandoned *Among the Indians,* we might add yet another more extrinsic cause: Twain's acute understanding of the literary marketplace for western novels in the 1880s. Having spent the summer of 1884 working on his western tale, Twain seems to have sensed, correctly perhaps, that the market for such works was becoming saturated. As late as the early 1870s, when Twain completed his western travelogue *Roughing It* (1872), it was still possible to say something personal and original about the American West.[10] By the mid-1880s, however, so many Americans had either experienced the West firsthand or absorbed its themes through mass-produced narratives, that it became a nearly insurmountable task to write anything about the region without falling into highly prescribed, formulaic modes of literary expression. Indeed, by the 1880s, the western "motif" had become so conventionalized that it began to parody itself in melodramatic comic operas like Buffalo Bill's Wild West show and in hundreds of quickly written western dime-novels in which "endless repetitions" of plot, themes and stock characters contributed to a perversion of form and function. Originality in the dime-novel market had become increasingly a matter of distortion and sensationalism.[11]

Examples of the deleterious effects of these tendencies were everywhere available to Twain, but perhaps nowhere more glaringly than in the career of his acquaintance, the dime-novelist Edward S. Ellis. A New Jersey school teacher turned writer, Ellis was one of the most popular novelists of his day; his careful novel *Seth Jones* (1860) sold over four hundred thousand copies and helped to create the initial demand for western narratives.[12] But steadily over the 1870s and 1880s, Ellis's novels demonstrated not only a certain hurriedness of presentation, but a growing dependence on sensational violence and death as well. Murder, rape, and brutal assault became standard plot devices for Ellis, who seemed to view them as necessary for securing readers in an increasingly competitive market-

place. In his controversial novel *The Huge Hunter; or the Steam Man of the Prairies* (1882), for instance, Ellis altered a prosaic earlier story about eastern fortune seekers looking for gold out West by introducing a cast of bizarre characters who act out unusual dramas in a theatre of the grotesque and the absurd. The central hero of the novel is a perverse Natty Bumppo figure named Baldy Bicknell, whose strange appellation derives from his having survived a scalping by the Indians. A horribly disfigured reminder of the savagery of the West, Baldy must wear a hat at all times lest he be exposed to the sweltering western sun or the equally blistering taunts of relentlessly critical western miners. Baldy's sidekick is a young, hunchbacked and fatherless boy, the ingenious inventor Johnny Brainerd, who is incapable of participating in the hard physical work of "winning the West" because of his deformities, but who tries (with mixed results) to lend his technological expertise to the effort. Johnny is the creator of a still more curious travelling companion, an enormous iron robot dubbed the "Steam Man of the Prairies," who marches across the plains intimidating Indians and expediting the work of mining. In their disturbing travels, these motley adventurers participate in the slaughter of animals, the mutilation of human bodies, and mass death by scalding, all in the pursuit of pecuniary gain.[13]

While works such as *The Huge Hunter* remained popular with audiences throughout the 1880s, their excesses did not go unnoticed. Ellis was one of many dime novelists assailed by parents and various public watchdogs who viewed highly sensationalist works as corrupting to the morals of American youth. A highly publicized court case in which a fourteen-year-old murderer of children blamed his violent nature on reading Beadle's western dime novels, for instance, sparked a campaign by prominent figures against the publisher.[14] In an article entitled "What Our Boys Are Reading," William Graham Sumner argued that the literary material of dime-novels "is either intensely stupid, or spiced to the highest degree with sensation." Family values were ignored, while boys were taught to respond only to the "indescribably vulgar" impulses of "physical pain and lack of money."[15] In *Childhood in Literature and Art,* Horace Scudder declared that "[a]nyone who has been compelled to make the acquaintance of this literature must have observed how little parents and guardians figure in it, and how completely children are separated from their elders. The most popular books for the young are those which represent boys and girl as seeking their fortune, working out their own schemes, driving railway trains and steamboats it may be. . . ."[16] And violent western novels remained a particular target of the disgruntled, self-proclaimed moralist Anthony Comstock, who noted in *Traps for the Young* that adventure stories of the prairies encouraged children to "run away from respectable homes . . . to seek their fortune[s]" in the West, where they inevitably degenerated into "boy-bandits" and "little villains."[17]

Twain may have felt particularly vulnerable to this line of criticism as he sketched his tale of western adventure in the summer of 1884. Gary Scharnhorst and others have noted that long before the writing of *Among the Indians,* Twain had been linked in the popular mind to the excesses of writers like Horatio Alger, Jr., with whom he shared a mutual interest in the themes of abandoned or orphaned boys and a common attachment to the cult of sentimentality.[18] Twain's association with so-called "juvenile" writers was strengthened by the publication of the *Adventures of Huckleberry Finn,* a novel viewed by those who condemned it in Boston as "no better in tone than the dime novels which flood the blood-and-thunder reading population."[19] Compounding problems for Twain in this regard was his well-publicized reputation as an avid reader of dime-novels. To the disgust of his wife and others, Twain often entertained his children with recitations from such books and studied their reactions in preparation for the planning of his own works. A process of literary adaptation was evident in 1881, for instance, when Twain asked James Osgood to send him several of his company's dime-novel sea stories, including "Tom Cringle's Log," "Green Hand," "Sailor's Sweetheart," and "The Cruise of the Midge." Although ostensibly for his children, these "juvenile" novels encouraged Twain to begin writing a never-completed "Tom and Huck" story "concerning an elaborate boys' naval battle on rafts in the river."[20] Additionally, the overstated melodrama of the maritime scenes in many of these nautical dime novels also found a place in completed works like *The Adventures of Huckleberry Finn,* in which Twain's reliance on sensationalized steamboat accidents caused some critics to wonder at the sophistication of his literary preparation and sourcework.[21]

In the summer of 1884, Twain may well have been reading dime-novels again in preparation for the writing of *Among the Indians,* since the completed chapters of the partial novel share a great deal in common with the sensationalist novels produced in record numbers throughout the 1880s. Twain's piece begins innocently enough when a hopelessly romantic Tom Sawyer persuades a reluctant Huck and a suspicious Jim to journey in search of "Cooperesque" Indians out on the western plains and to partake in whatever related "adventures" might materialize along the way. The rag-tag trio stumble along the Oregon trail in blissful ignorance of the "rules of the road," until they meet and befriend the family of Old Man Mills, with whose daughter, Peggy, they fall simultaneously in love. But the tone of *Among the Indians* suddenly changes in the third chapter when Indians murder all the males in the Mills caravan and take Jim and two of the Mills daughters (including Peggy) as captives to the heart of the Indian territory. The discovery by Huck and Tom of the Mills brothers "laying dead—tomahawked and scalped," each with as many as "twenty-five arrows sticking in him," divests them quickly of their preconceptions of Indians as "noble savages," and the boys spend the remainder of the fast-paced and increasingly violent novel in pursuit of these treacherous kidnappers. In this work, the boys are accompanied by Peggy's fiancé, Brace Johnson, whose arrival on the plains several days after the grizzly murders signals an escalation of the sensational and violent themes

to which Huck and Jim are subjected. Brace not only exposes Huck to death by starvation, gunshot wound and drowning, he also introduces the themes of mature love and violent sexuality into the innocent, prepubescent worlds of Huck and Tom. It is Brace, that is, who by definition of his relationship with Peggy, destroys Huck and Tom's adolescent hopes for playful love-making with her; and it is Brace whose insinuations of the possible rape of Peggy by the Indians awakens the boys to the potential of violence and perversity in mature sexual relationships.[22]

Even *The Adventures of Huckleberry Finn,* with its frank treatment of the injustices of slavery and its gruesome handling of the alcohol-induced death of "Pap" Finn, did not come close to matching the macabre sensationalism of these early chapters of *Among the Indians.* Clearly, by the summer of 1884, Twain was drifting dangerously close to the brutal excesses of Ellis's dime-novel format, and the uncompleted chapters of the narrative demanded some form of violent resolution. Recycled heroes like Huck, Tom and Jim, in short, did not lend themselves very well to this new, more "fatal environment of the West," and even the resourceful Twain could not protect them from the dreadful implications of the rape of Peggy Mills to which all plot lines in the final written chapter were pointing.[23] And the seeming inevitability of such a barbarous conclusion may explain why, after a summer of work on *Among the Indians,* Twain abandoned the novel. Concerned about the violent implications of the story he was writing and sensitive to the charges of extremism being raised against western dime-novelists, he wisely repressed the piece. Twain was not afraid to experiment with controversial writing techniques, but he was generally unwilling to publish any but the most conventional of products of these efforts. In this, as in many literary matters, Twain trusted his own good instincts, since too close an association with the potentially insidious influence of the dime-novel tradition almost certainly would have affected his literary reputation in the way it had those of Ellis and others.[24]

In addition, Twain's notebooks from the mid-1880s indicate that he was being distracted by several new ideas of a less controversial nature. In his journal for 1885, for instance, he described a story "wherein the pantaletted little children talked the stilted big-word sentimental hifalutin of Walter Scott's heroes & other & older novels."[25] Shortly thereafter, he read Sir Thomas Malory's *Morte d'Arthur,* which inspired him to consider elaborating on his Walter Scott theme: "Dream of being a knight errant in armor in the middle ages," he wrote in his now much-quoted shorthand. "Have the notions and habits of thought of the present day mixed with the necessities of that. No pockets in the armor. . . . Iron gets red hot in the sun—leaks in the rain, gets white with frost and freezes me solid in winter. . . . Can't dress or undress myself. Always getting struck by lightning. Fall down, can't get up."[26] These comical remarks became the inspiration for *A Connecticut Yankee in King Arthur's Court,* the work that engaged Twain for the next five years and seemingly deflected forever his interest in the Huck and Tom story, *Among the Indians.*[27]

Yet to paraphase Twain himself, reports of his novel's death may "have been greatly exaggerated." Not in the habit of giving up on anything he had written if he could make some literary or monetary use of it, Twain frequently resurrected "dead" fragments, reshaping and recontextualizing them to fit new circumstances. In these matters, alterations were often made by Twain in accordance with the perceived needs of his readers and his own shifting priorities as an author. In the case of *Huck Finn and Tom Sawyer among the Indians,* Twain made eventual use of his western research and manuscript by dramatically adjusting both the setting and the thematic trajectory of the story. If the market for western adventure stories seemed too saturated for Twain's purposes or if it required too many literary concessions of a sort Twain was unwilling to make, that is, he might nonetheless transfer its hackneyed themes and characters to other, more fertile literary grounds—in this case, the Arthurian England of *A Connecticut Yankee in King Arthur's Court.* As T. Jackson Lears and others have demonstrated, Twain was an "antimodernist" in philosophical outlook and was therefore obsessed with the medieval world as a setting for literary speculations about human development. The middle ages served as a point of reference, a lodestone for consideration by disenchanted Victorians of "where it had all gone wrong."[28] For Twain, as for the wizard Merlin in his new novel, travelling backward in time helped clarify America's place on the historical continuum; it highlighted the causal relations between a "golden" past and a jaded present. In this sense, the spirit and even the subject matter of Twain's older, aborted western novel may have informed his new medieval one in highly significant ways. The disturbingly violent qualities of the American West had their roots, Twain believed, in the decline of the human condition since the time of knights and round tables.

On the surface, of course, a novel set in sixth century England would appear to owe little literary debt to a nineteenth-century adventure tale undertaken by Huck, Tom, and Jim in the American West. But as Richard Slotkin and others have pointed out, there are a considerable number of western elements in *A Connecticut Yankee.*[29] When Twain's disoriented time-travelling hero, Hank Morgan, lands in the sixth century, for instance, he describes his surroundings in the only vocabulary available to him for the description of the unusual and the bizarre—that of the American West. Morgan identifies the primitive residents of Camelot as "white Indians" and "modified savages" who hold "powwows" and slink "stealthily" around sabotaging the work of western civilization.[30] Men in King Arthur's kingdom are, in Morgan's words, "a sort of polished-up court of Comanches," while the typical woman is a "squaw" who is "ready at the dropping of a hat to desert to the buck with the biggest string of scalps at his belt" (138). The knights of the round table are depicted as iron-clad "cowboys," who spend their days "on the trail" in search of adventure and mischief (136). And ultimately these transplanted cowboys and Indians will submit only to the brutally violent and vindictive "law of the West." Hence, Hank Morgan becomes a lariat-slinging cowhand,

Slim Jim, who must lasso knights and gun down dissenters in dramatic "high-noon" fashion in order to maintain his reputation as top gun of Camelot. In addition, he subdues the "red" hordes of the kingdom by using six-shooters and gatling guns in ways strikingly similar to those recorded in the western campaigns against the Indians (357). And, revealingly, the fate of these Arthurian cowboys and Indians is the same as that of their western analogues on the American frontier—they refuse to submit to technologies packaged as tools of "progress," so they must die pathetically in a desperate and hopeless attack against them.

Read in this fashion, the last scene of *A Connecticut Yankee* is particularly significant, since it becomes a kind of Custer's Last Stand in which the Indian nation achieves a temporary victory but is ultimately defeated.[31] As Hank Morgan is surrounded by massive numbers of knight-cowboys and peasant-Indians, he receives the fatal news that "there would be no reinforcements" and instantly understands that "this is the last stand of the chivalry of England" (396). In an impassioned speech paraphrasing General Sherman's remarks regarding good Indians and dead Indians, Morgan tells his small circle of supporters that the impending war "will be brief—the briefest in history. Also the most destructive to life, considered from the standpoint of proportion of casualties to numbers engaged." In this war of absolute attrition, Morgan proclaims: "We know what is before us. While one of these men remains alive, our task is not finished, the war is not ended. We will kill them all" (396). Substitute Indian nation for English nation, and you have a neat paraphrase of the U.S. Army attitude toward the Indians of the American West. In this final symbolic standoff, Hank Morgan manages to kill many of the sixth-century Indians who encircle him, but ultimately he becomes the ironic victim of his own genocidal successes. Surrounded by lifeless warriors, he has no means of escape; like Custer, he is entombed behind a "solid wall of dead" (403).

If *A Connecticut Yankee* is a variant of the westernized adventure tale, then it should not be surprising to find in its pages the violence and sensationalism of the dime-novel format as well. By the 1880s, the American West may have become too stale and predictable a locale for the meaningful presentation of extraordinary themes; but medieval England provided new, fresh ground for such literary demonstrations. While genteel Americans like Sumner, Scudder and Comstock preferred to think of the American West as a region capable of reform, that is, nearly everyone was willing to believe that the medieval world was a shockingly crude and inescapably brutal place.[32] Hence for Twain it was an easy transition from the dime-novel massacre and rape scenes in *Among the Indians* to the scenes of torture and death in *A Connecticut Yankee,* especially those involving enslavement, persecution in dungeons, and death by "the rack" at the hands of "white savages." Huck and Hank, alliterative counterparts, share a similar revulsion for the excesses of the savage people they seek to control, and both try to employ superstition and melodramatic suspense to accomplish their goals. Both novels adopt standard literary devices common to conventional-ized western novels as well, including frontier romances, horse stealing, picaresque journeying, and "codes" of proper behavior. And for Twain, the transition from the American West to Arthurian England was made easier by the prodigious research notes he had accumulated in the process of writing *Among the Indians.* Transposing west-ern themes onto medieval landscapes may have been as simple a matter as shifting one stack of notes on his crowded desk over to another and shuffling the two to-gether.[33]

Among the pieces Twain may have resurrected from his pile of western material was Ellis's *The Huge Hunter.* There is a good deal of evidence internal to both Ellis's novel and Twain's *A Connecticut Yankee* to suggest at least a shared community of ideas between the two au-thors, if not a direct literary relationship. One obvious par-allel is the central theme common to both works—the transplanting of advanced technology from one era into the anachronistic time frame of another. The Steam Man is described by Ellis as "a singular apparition," a "gigantic man" of such "colossal proportions" that it could "scarcely" be "dreamed of at that day, by the most imaginative phi-losophers" (108). The closest analogy nineteenth-century viewers of this giant "Titan" can employ to describe the Steam Man is the railroad, a symbol with powerful meta-phoric significance for the culture. Spouting "a black vol-ume of smoke" and cinders from its head and shrieking "with the sharp screech of the locomotive whistle" (108) as it moved, the Steam Man was "a sort of peregrinating locomotive," Ellis writes, which could carry a wagon be-hind it "as smoothly as if running upon a railroad" (109). The robot has anthropomorphic qualities as well: a face of iron painted black with "a pair of fearful eyes, and a tre-mendous grinning mouth"; a chest of "aldermanic propor-tions" with a large knapsack arrangement over the shoul-ders and back for the transfer of energy from the "bowels" and "capacious abdomen of the giant"; and a reserve cham-ber for the build up of excess steam, which gave him a "seething" appearance, as if "ready to explode with the tremendous power pent up in its vitals" (113 . . .).

This precise mechanical description of the Steam Man re-flected Ellis's awareness of the technological maturity of his readers and suggested his recognition of their interests in the dynamics of machine operation. Twain was intrigued by mechanical matters as well; indeed, his tastes in this re-gard were perhaps more grandiose and farfetched than even Ellis's. In the case of *A Connecticut Yankee,* techno-logical achievement was both cause and effect, serving as both the central thematic inspiration for the novel and its intended method of production. In this connection, the well-known story of Twain's disastrous involvement with the Paige typesetting machine during the writing of *A Connecticut Yankee* is significant.[34] Having invested over two hundred thousand dollars on Paige's machine during the late 1880s—a machine being built in the same Colt Arms factory where Twain's fictional "Connecticut Yan-kee" is employed—Twain intended to conflate the progress

of his novel with that of Paige's invention. "I want to fin-ish the day the machine finishes," Twain wrote, once again too hopefully. After an unsuccessful attempt to typeset (of all pieces!) the unfinished manuscript of *Among the Indi-ans,* Twain grew despondent about the machine's success. The typesetter ultimately proved "impossibly delicate and temperamental," Justin Kaplan wrote, "having been con-ceived . . . as an organism rather than a machine." A "magnificent creature" with a "gargantuan appetite," Paige's "creature," like Ellis's Steam Man, occasionally worked "with all the ease and celerity that it could have done if really human" (112); but it was also at times a "cunning devil," as Twain put it, which evinced uncontrol-lable and corrupting power.[35] The Paige typesetter was a real equivalent to Ellis's "demon of the darkness," "a di-vil, broke loose" (108), whose "ear-splitting" screech was "hideous enough to set a man crazy" (112).

The theme of technology run amuck is central to *A Con-necticut Yankee,* and Twain derived considerable comedic effect from depicting the sometimes silly human reactions to machine failures. The same playfulness is evident in El-lis's descriptions of the impact of technology on Irishman Mickey McSquizzle, a hypersensitive miner who is filled with "superstitious awe" when he first sees the Steam Man. Wondering aloud whether he is "shlaping or dhram-ing" and shying instinctively away from the machine "as the timid steed does at first sight of the locomotive," Mickey declares: "I'm so frightened entirely that I don't know who I am myself" (108). As a representative of the natural over the mechanistic, Mickey has but one feeble defense against the obdurate machine—ridicule. Adopting this old-fashioned and sentimental (even medieval) atti-tude toward machinery, Mickey shares much in common both with Ellis's "red savages" and Boss Morgan's "white savages," groups that respond with initial but shortlived contempt to the new technologies introduced into their "natural" landscapes. "The savages sat as motionless as statues upon their horses," Ellis notes of their first encoun-ter with the Steam Man, until, recognizing too late the ma-chine's awesome power, they were forced to run "as though all the legions of darkness were after them." With Twain-like wit, Ellis muses that it was just a matter of time before these savages "would have tumbled off their horses and died, for they were bearing almost all the fright, terror and horror that can possibly be concentrated into a single person" (113).

This terrifying side of technology had its obvious advan-tages to the harbingers of machinery—the "Connecticut Yankees" in both works—who are able to use this fear as leverage for what they want. Ellis's Connecticut Yankee, Ethan, is the first to be shaken from the superstitious fears associated with the Steam Man. When he and his compan-ion Mickey first hear the terrifying shriek of the robot, which "like some agonized giant came home to them across the plains," they "both looked around, as if about to flee in terror." But in the case of Ethan, "the curiosity of the Yankee restrained him. His practical eye saw that what-ever it might be, it was a human contrivance, and there could be nothing supernatural about it." As the machine approached still closer, "Mickey sprung a half dozen feet backward, and would have run off at full speed down the ravine, had not Ethan Hopkins caught his arm." Immediately familiarizing himself with the internal mechanisms of the creation, Ethan reveals that he had dreamed of manufacturing just such a steam man himself once, inspired by the engineering achievements of the inventors at none other than "the Colt's pistol factory" in Hartford, Boss Morgan's employer at the outset of *A Connecticut Yankee* (108). It is Ethan who immediately recognizes how useful such a machine could be in the West, and who insists that it remain "terra incognita" to the Indians— "clothed with a terror such as no array of enemies could wear" and such that they would "keep at a goodly distance from it entirely" (113). Boss Morgan also understands the powerful force of technology on his subjects in Camelot. This "Yankee of Yankees," who is a self-described pragmatist ("nearly barren of sentiment"), determines to "boss" the sixth century, where he will be "the best-educated man in the kingdom by a matter of thirteen hundred years" (50).

In addition, Boss Morgan bears a remarkable physical as well as symbolic resemblance to the Steam Man. Donning a suit of armor in accordance with the impractical dress code of the ruling elite in Camelot, Morgan is hideously uncomfortable as an "iron dude" of the realm (119). But he continues to wear the torturous outfit, because, like Ellis's Steam Man, it gives him a certain stature and intimidating presence. Lighting his pipe in an effort to distract the bugs that fly mercilessly about his helmet (with tobacco of the sort "the Indians use" we are told), Morgan startles those around him in the same manner as Ellis's iron terror of the prairies. "When the first blast of smoke shot out through the bars of my helmet, all those people broke for the woods," Morgan records, and one, like Ellis's Indians, "went over backwards and struck the ground with a dull thud" (131-32). Instantly recognizing that his constituents are filled with superstitions about this "fire-belching dragon," Morgan gains an advantage by telling them it "was only a bit of enchantment which would do harm to none but my enemies" (131). When he is attacked subsequently by a large group of threatened but headstrong knights and squires, he imitates the Steam Man by spouting "a column of white smoke through the bars" of his helmet, compelling them to "go to pieces and scatter!" (133). And this superstitious air must be preserved, Morgan recognizes, even if it means creating a sideshow atmosphere. Reflecting some of the sensationalism of the dime-novel format, Twain's Morgan becomes a ringmaster of a circus of freaks and misfits whom he manipulates for his own private gain. In this way, he is reminiscent of Ellis's Baldy Bicknell, who urges Johnny Brainerd to make money with the Steam Man by marketing him as "Barnum . . . did . . . his Woolly Horse" (113).

That Twain made use of Ellis's themes seems even more clear when we consider the common moral message that emerges from the two pieces. Boss Morgan's effort to push technology in the sixth century leads to disaster, since the people are not ready for his innovations. Power, especially technological power, still clearly corrupts. Having developed a railroad, a telephone, a telegraph, and a line of steamboats that puff up and down the Thames, Morgan is discouraged to find that they are viewed consistently as objects of fear. In Ellis's fictional world, the nineteenth century seems no better prepared to embrace new inventions than Twain's savages, despite a smug public belief to the contrary. Noting that Robert Fulton's steamboat created "a consternation and terror" when it first ascended the Hudson ("many believing that it was the harbinger of the final destruction of the world"), Ellis editorialized: "Of course, at this late day, no such excitement can be created by any human invention." Yet Johnny Brainerd's Steam Man was too futuristic even for a nation of self-proclaimed tinkerers to accept. "[T]he sight of a creature speeding over the country, impelled by steam, and bearing a grotesque resemblance to a gigantic man, could not but startle all who should see it for the first time," (112) Ellis wrote. And such suspicions were held not merely by the Mickey McSquizzles or by the Plains Indians, but by men of the western world like Baldy Bicknell as well. Like the discouraged Twain, jaded by the failure of his Paige typesetter, Baldy anticipates the tragic disappointment of machine technologies. "[T]hese new-fangled things generally do well at first," Bicknell notes, "and then, afore yer know it, they bu'st all to blazes" (112).

Machines are dangerous, both Twain and Ellis imply, because they lead to false feelings of security and power. In *A Connecticut Yankee,* Boss Morgan is certain that his sixth-century subjects need only have exposure to technology in order to be converted to its benefits. Throughout the novel he daydreams about the empire he will establish by putting operations like mining "on a scientific basis" (102), training "iron and steel missionaries" (101), and establishing himself as President. Comforting as these visions of a machine metropolis are, however, they distract Hank Morgan from the real dangers swirling all around him. Toward the end of *A Connecticut Yankee,* as he and his compatriots are being surrounded by enemies of the realm, the Boss sees "a row of black dots" appear along a ridge and correctly speculates that they are "human heads." But Morgan quickly rejects the image (with disastrous consequences), arguing that "it mightn't be anything at all" since "you can't depend on your eyes when your imagination is out of focus" (401). Johnny Brainerd of *The Huge Hunter* also has delusionary empire-building visions and experiences the dangers of overindulgence in this regard. While riding atop the Steam Man and imagining the creation of a "steam" animal world, with steam horses, steam birds and other animal contraptions, Johnny is thrown "with violence" from his invention, "falling directly between the legs of the monster, which seemed to stand perfectly motionless like the intelligent elephant that is fearful of stirring a limb, lest he might crush his master lying beneath him" (112). The fatalistic aspects of flirtations with creationism of this circus variety appear again, when, in the midst of another technological reverie, Johnny endangers his companions by failing to notice a band of Indians that has surrounded them. Like the whalers in Melville's *Moby-Dick* who allow themselves to descend into "Cartesian vortices" while daydreaming at sea, Johnny slips into "a reverie" and becomes "totally oblivious to whatever was passing around him." As "a drowsiness began stealing over him," Johnny imagines he sees "the black shadows of wolves" (which are actually encircling Indians); but like Hank Morgan, he discounts the vision because "he was sure it was only a phantom of his brain" (120). It is the hubris and negligence of both Johnny and Hank that ultimately leads to the downfall of their respective technological kingdoms.

In the final scene of *A Connecticut Yankee* already alluded to, the catastrophic nature of rushed technology becomes painfully evident. Trapped in a cave by "white Indians" and "cowboy knights," Morgan and a small gang of supporters imagine themselves safe. "They won't drop any rocks down on us," (388) Morgan notes naively from within the comforting walls of his symbolic maternal womb. But shortly thereafter, Morgan is forced to blow up his "noble civilisation-factories" and to precipitate the "Gatling gun" mass destruction of his kingdom's knights. In the process, once living, breathing and easily manipulated human beings are fused into an inhuman, anonymous and impenetrable steel barrier. "Of course, we could not count the dead," Morgan notes, "because they did not exist as individuals, but merely as homogeneous protoplasm, with alloys of iron and buttons" (396). In an early scene in Ellis's dime-novel, the heroes are also trapped in a cave by Indians and remain "penned up for the better part of two days, by which time they had slain so many of their enemies that the remaining ones were glad to withdraw" (117). They manage to escape, only to be trapped again by the same Indians, who entomb them in a valley by sealing off the only entrance with a wall of boulders. So "thoroughly imprisoned that no human aid could ever extricate him," the Steam Man must be sacrificed. Johnny, who has gotten his fellows in this mess, conceives a plan to stoke the Steam Man full of logs and to rush him at the wall the Indians have created. In a scene of destruction hauntingly anticipatory of Twain's Battle of the Sand-Belt, Ellis describes the gruesome clash of technological and savage worlds. "The next moment it [the Steam Man] struck the bowlders with a terrific crash, . . . among the thunderstruck Indians [and] exploded its boiler! The shock of the explosion was like the bursting of an immense bomb-shell, the steam man being thrown into thousands of fragments, that scattered death and destruction in every direction. Falling in the very center of the crouching Indians, it could but make a terrible destruction of life, while those who escaped unharmed, were besides themselves with consternation" (120).

In the end, Ellis's story is slightly more hopeful than Twain's. Baldy, Ethan, Mickey and Johnny do escape the Indians and do get to keep the gold that the Steam man has helped them procure. Twain's Boss Morgan escapes in a manner of speaking, too, since he wakes up again in the

nineteenth century in time to tell his tale of medieval woe, but he remains a man out of step with his culture by virtue of his time-travelling exploits. To the extent that both works are morality plays, *The Huge Hunter* and *A Connecticut Yankee* convey similar anti-modernist messages as well: namely, that the world is not really ready for technology, especially technology used for monetary gain; that Nature, whether described in the cloudy, romantic atmosphere of medieval Camelot or the dusty, frolicsome climate of the American West, must prevail over would-be technological conquerors; and that the premature introduction of machinery is always disastrous. While in production, Johnny's Steam Man must be hidden from view to avoid attracting attention, and it is transported to the West in a crate that serves as a metaphoric womb for the unlucky and unlovable creature. "Stripped of all its bandages" and placed in the fetal position for the purposes of packaging, the Steam man "had a grotesque and fearful look . . . in all its naked majesty" (112). Liberated prematurely from this protective encasing, the Steam Man, like some misunderstood Frankenstein monster, is unable to gain acceptance in the western world and must be destroyed. In *A Connecticut Yankee,* the iron-suited, technologically-driven Hank Morgan also finds it impossible to function in a pre-industrial age. Characterizing himself as "a creature out of a remote unborn age" (409), the Boss admits to being an anachronism, an ill-fated technological prophet born too soon to be appreciated by pretechnological societies.

So what do these equivalences between Twain and Ellis imply about Twain's scholarship in the 1880s? In the first place, they suggest that Twain had not completely abandoned his partial novel *Among the Indians* in the summer of 1884, but rather reworked it in the service of a larger and more impressive piece of fiction. Read as an example of literary cross-fertilization, *A Connecticut Yankee* calls attention to Twain's astute awareness of the vicissitudes of the literary marketplace both in America and abroad and to his keen abilities to restretch used and fatigued ideas over new frames to create lively and impressive narratives. In the second place, these overlaps suggest that Twain had not completely rejected the tropes, character-types and emplotments of the dime-novel format. In the process of writing *A Connecticut Yankee,* that is, Twain created a literary masterpiece by reviving hackneyed western dime-novel formulas and employing them in a new and richly complex historical setting. And in the third and most important place, these equivalences demonstrate Twain's ability to turn frustrations over disappointments in his own life (in this case about the Paige typesetting machine) into literary successes. At the time of its publication, Twain feared that *A Connecticut Yankee* would be attacked as too sensational by the critics who had dismantled the works of Ellis and others, and he downplayed his expectations for the novel.[36] But after re-reading the text years later, Twain was struck by the value of the project. "Yesterday I read 'A Connecticut Yankee at King Arthur's Court' for the first time in more than 30 years," he wrote his daughter Clara in the spring of 1910, and "I am prodigiously pleased with it.

. . ."[37] The same sentiment has been expressed by thousands of readers over the last century who have found in its pages indications of a sophisticated and creatively satiric literary mind struggling to control (but not to kill) its preoccupations with scandalously theatrical and potentially corrupting western dime-novel influences.

Notes

1. Mark Twain, *Huck Finn and Tom Sawyer among the Indians,* in Walter Blair, ed., *Mark Twain's Hannibal, Huck & Tom* (Berkeley, CA: Univ. of California Press, 1969), pp. 92-140.

2. Mark Twain, *Adventures of Huckleberry Finn,* ed. by Walter Blair and Victor Fischer (Berkeley: Univ. of California Press, 1988), p. 362.

3. Samuel C. Webster, ed., *Mark Twain, Business Man* (Boston: Little, Brown, 1946), pp. 264-65.

4. Blair's contention that the manuscript was completed by the summer of 1884 has been challenged by some scholars who argue that portions of the fragment were composed as late as 1889. For a complete review of this debate, see "Appendix B," in *Hannibal, Huck & Tom,* pp. 372-74. See also, Maria Ornella Marotti, *The Duplicating Imagination: Twain and the Twain Papers* (Penn State Univ. Press, 1990) and Howard G. Baetzhold, "The Course of Composition of *A Connecticut Yankee:* A Reinterpretation," *American Literature,* 33 (May 1961), 195-214.

5. Henry N. Smith and William M. Gibson, eds., *Mark Twain-Howells Letters* (Cambridge, MA: Harvard Univ. Press, 1960), II, 496.

6. Mark Twain to Charles Webster, 1 Sept 1884, in *Mark Twain's Letters to His Publishers, 1867-1894,* ed. Hamlin Hill (Berkeley: Univ. of California Press, 1967), p. 179.

7. Albert Bigelow Paine, *Mark Twain: A Biography* (New York: Harper Brothers Publishers, 1912), pp. 899, 1680.

8. Walter Blair, "The Reasons Mark Twain Did Not Finish his Story," *Life* (20 December 1968), p. 50A.

9. Wayne R. Kime, "Huck Among the Indians: Mark Twain and Richard Irving Dodge's *The Plains of the Great West and Their Inhabitants,*" *Western American Literature,* 24 (1990), 321-33.

10. Twain himself was known to have read and admired such works as Keim's *Sheridan's Troopers on the Borders* (1870), Custer's *My Life on the Plains* (1874), and Richard Irving Dodge's *The Plains of the Great West and Their Inhabitants* (1877).

11. Henry Nash Smith, *Virgin Land: The American West as Symbol and Myth* (Cambridge, MA: Harvard Univ. Press, 1950), pp. 92, 119. See also Russel B. Nye, *The Unembarrassed Muse: The Popular Arts in America* (New York: The Dial Press, 1970), pp. 200-215.

12. For more on Ellis and his place in the western dime-novel tradition, see Albert Johannsen, *The House of Beadle and Adams and Its Dime and Nickel Novels: The Story of a Vanished Literature* (Norman: Univ. of Oklahoma Press, 1950), II, 93-96.

13. Edward S. Ellis, *The Huge Hunter; or the Steam Man of the Prairies* (New York: Beadle and Adams, 1868; 1882 half-dime edition). Although first published in the late 1860s, the work did not become nationally popular until mass-produced in the tens of thousands by Beadle and Adams in the "half-dime" edition of 1882 cited in this paper. All subsequent references to this text will be given in parentheses.

14. J. N. Makris, *Boston Murders* (New York: Duell, Sloane, and Pearce, 1948), pp. 8-9, as cited in Albert Stone, Jr., *The Innocent Eye: Childhood in Mark Twain's Imagination* (Archon Books, 1970), p. 101.

15. William Graham Sumner, "What Our Boys Are Reading," *Scribner's Monthly* (March 1878), as cited in Stone, *The Innocent Eye,* pp. 103-04.

16. Horace Elisha Scudder, *Childhood in Literature and Art* (1895) as cited in Stone, *The Innocent Eye,* pp. 105-08.

17. Anthony Comstock, *Traps for the Young* (Cambridge: The Belknap Press of Harvard Univ. Press, 1967), pp. 32-33.

18. Gary Scharnhorst with Jack Bales, *The Lost Life of Horatio Alger, Jr.* (Bloomington: Indiana Univ. Press, 1985), pp. 106-118.

19. Arthur L. Vogelback, "The Publication and Reception of *Huckleberry Finn* in America," *American Literature,* 11 (Nov. 1939), 260-272. See also "The Banning of Huckleberry Finn," in *Critics on Mark Twain: Readings in Literary Criticism,* ed. by David B. Kesterson (Coral Gables, Florida: Univ. of Miami Press, 1973), p. 17.

20. Mark Twain to James R. Osgood, 23 May 1881 in the Mark Twain Papers, as cited in Stone, *The Innocent Eye,* p. 161.

21. Many critics believe Twain intended *Tom Sawyer, The Adventures of Huckleberry Finn* and *Among the Indians* as nothing more than extended dime-novels, "fast-paced narrative[s] meant mostly for boys"; see Stone, *The Innocent Eye,* p. 177.

22. Stone refers to Brace Johnson as "pure dime-novel stereotype" in *ibid,* p. 125. See also Blair, *Hannibal, Huck & Tom,* pp. 84-7.

23. Richard Slotkin, *The Fatal Environment: The Myth of the Frontier in the Age of Industrialization, 1800-1890* (New York: Atheneum Press, 1985), p. 521.

24. Blair concurs; see *Hannibal, Huck & Tom,* p. 84.

25. Notebook 18, pp. 21, 31 in *The Mark Twain Papers,* as cited in Stone, *The Innocent Eye,* p. 162.

26. Notebook 18, *The Mark Twain Papers,* p. 11.

27. Walter Blair, "An Unpublished Tale by Mark Twain," *Life* (20 December 1968); insert, n.p.

28. T. J. Jackson Lears, *No Place of Grace: Antimodernism and the Transformation of American Culture, 1880-1920* (New York: Pantheon Books, 1981), pp. 164-166, 168.

29. Slotkin, *The Fatal Environment,* pp. 516-30. See also Kirsten Powell, "Cowboy Knights and Prairie Madonnas: American Illustrations of the Plains and Pre-Raphaelite Art," *Great Plains Quarterly* 5 (Winter 1985), pp. 41, 42-43, 50-52.

30. Mark Twain, *A Connecticut Yankee in King Arthur's Court* (New York: Penguin Books, paperback edition, 1984), pp. 53, 125, 317, 402. All subsequent references to this text will be given in parentheses.

31. Justin Kaplan, "Introduction," in *ibid,* p. 22.

32. Lears, *No Place of Grace,* pp. xv-xx.

33. For more on Twain's chaotic filing system and unique working habits, see William Dean Howells, *My Mark Twain* (New York: Harper & Brothers Publishers, 1910).

34. For Twain's own version of these events, see "The Machine Episode," in *Mark Twain's Autobiography,* ed. Albert Bigelow Paine (New York: Harper & Brothers Publishers, 1924), II, 70-78.

35. Justin Kaplan, *Mark Twain and His World* (New York: Simon and Schuster, 1974), pp. 141, 148. See also "The Yankee and the Machine," in Justin Kaplan, *Mr. Clemens and Mark Twain* (New York: Simon and Schuster, 1966), pp. 280-311.

36. In some instances, particularly in the British press, such attacks did occur. See especially "Mark Twain's Camelot," *Spectator,* 64 (5 April 1890), p. 484; and James Ashcroft Noble, "Review of *Connecticut Yankee,*" *Academy* (London), 37 (22 February 1890), 130.

37. Clara Clemens, *My Father Mark Twain* (New York, 1931), p. 289, as cited in John B. Hoben, "Mark Twain's *A Connecticut Yankee:* A Genetic Study," *American Literature,* 18 (1946), 197.

SOCIO-POLITICAL CONCERNS

Daryl E. Jones (essay date 1970)

SOURCE: "Blood 'n Thunder: Virgins, Villains, and Violence in the Dime Novel Western," in *Journal of Popular Culture,* Vol. IV, No. 2, Fall, 1970, pp. 507-17.

[*In the following essay, Jones considers the relationship between sex and violence in dime novels, concluding that the genre promoted traditional American values even as it "provid[ed] mass purgation through vicarious participation in fictional violence."*]

The plethora of violence is probably the most notable characteristic of the dime novel western. Certainly this was the case in the nineteenth century, for numerous clergymen, teachers, and moralists, angrily pointing out the deleterious effects of super-abundant bloodshed on the young minds of America, severely denounced the "lurid yellow-backed novels" as the bane of the age. "Instructors in some of the schools," wrote W. H. Bishop in 1879, "report that every third boy reads such literature, and that he is the hardest to deal with. It is in him to resist something, to dare something, in his own modest way. Prevented from engaging in hand-to-hand conflicts with howling savages, he can yet, if circumstances be favorable, break his teacher's watch-chain."[1] Whether or not the dime novel's numerous beatings, scalpings, and cold blooded murders had a pernicious effect upon the morals of America remains a matter of question. However, violence undoubtedly contributed to the widespread popularity of pulp literature.

Always a necessary ingredient of melodrama, violence was often exploited by dime novelists as a means of endowing their simple plots with fast action and sensational events. Readers were thrilled when the trapper's unerring flintlock sent a bullet hundreds of yards to bring down a diabolical savage only seconds before he could deprive the heroine of her silken tresses. More importantly, though, violence was, and continues to be, popular because it has traditionally been the ultimate expression of individual freedom. By resorting to violence, the western hero was able to act quickly in times of crisis; he could invoke individual justice without recourse to confusing legal and political apparatus. Furthermore, whether trapper, plainsman, cowboy, or noble outlaw, the anarchic western hero found violence the most immediately satisfying method of rebelling against the artificial restraints of organized society. In pulp fiction, this violent rebellion was usually painted as being self-righteous and motivated purely by a desire to rectify, or avenge, the blind injustice of society. In *Solid Sam, The Boy Road-Agent; or, The Branded Brows. A Tale of Wild Wyoming,* Solid Sam has turned to a life of crime because a group of ruffians has appropriated his gold mine. He plans to waylay them individually and collect the gold which is rightfully his. Finding this impossible, the hero instead demands that the innocent citizens of Placer City restore his fortune and pay him protection money. When they refuse, the noble outlaw strikes a devastating blow against organized society. He and his cohorts "justifiably" reduce the town to a "series of heaps of smoking ashes and charred embers, to tell of the vengeance of Solid Sam."[2]

With the exception of war—fighting Indians, Mexicans, thugs, etc.—violence in the dime novel western is always explained as being motivated by revenge. In the case of female characters who resort to violence, the desire for vengeance is born of sexual dishonor. The dime novel western abounds with aggressive women who thirst for the blood of the men who ruined them. On the other hand, the vengeance of male characters has usually been invoked by the deprivation of power and wealth. Solid Sam, it will be remembered, first became involved in crime while searching for the border ruffians who had appropriated his gold mine. In a great many cases, however, the deprivation of power and wealth is symbolized in sexual terms. In the classic situation, two suitors compete for the hand of a blushing maiden who will inherit a great fortune from her powerful and prestigious father. The suitor who fails to win her, of course, feels that he has been deprived of enormous wealth. Therefore, he seeks to avenge this injustice either by murdering his competitor, or by kidnapping the heroine and forcing his will upon her. However, the struggle for the heroine and the power and wealth which she represents is basically a sexual struggle. Subsequent violence and death—the villain's revenge, or the hero's violent attempt to save the heroine—is thus portrayed as the direct result of sexual conflict. An investigation, first of the nineteenth century concept of the relationship between sex and violence as reflected in the sentimental novel, and then of the manner in which the dime novel reflected this concept, provides a satisfactory explanation for the high incidence of sexually motivated violence in the dime novel western.

II

In colonial America, the general scarcity of women eventually led society to place a high value on both the individual woman and the institution of marriage. Because of her rarity, the woman came to be regarded as a possession of great value. Accordingly, sentimental fiction identified her with other valuable possessions. Heroines often stood in a position to inherit great wealth or an immense estate. Thus, when a suitor won the hand of the heroine, he also won worldly success. In a society conditioned by Puritanism, however, wealth was a manifestation of innate virtue; it indicated that one was numbered among God's elect. It was necessary, therefore, that heroines be as virtuous as they were wealthy. In fiction, they were remote, untouchable, and unbearably fragile before marriage; after marriage they became doting mothers through a process of immaculate conception. At no time during courtship or marriage was a sexual relationship acknowledged, for sex was, in the Puritan mind, the tool of Satan. Instead, love was purely romantic, a matter of blushing cheeks and palpitating hearts.

As a symbol of worldly success and innate virtue, the heroine of the sentimental novel was constantly under attack by agents of evil—the vile seducers. In its most typical form, the plot of the sentimental novel dealt with the struggle between two suitors for the hand of the virtuous heroine. One of the suitors, the hero, offers pure romantic love. The other suitor is a villain who, since Puritan society fostered the belief that sin was primarily sexual in na-

ture; is motivated by lust and greed. When it is remembered that the heroine was a symbol of both worldly success and innate virtue, the implications of the plot may be discerned. The competition between a good suitor and a villainous suitor for the hand of the heroine is basically symbolic, in sexual terms, of the larger struggle for material success, and the even greater struggle between good and evil. Thus, the sentimental novel established the villain as a specifically sexual symbol of universal evil who, by attempting to seduce the heroine, was striving to overcome the power of good in the world. It was necessary, then, that the villain be destroyed. Similarly, if the heroine allowed herself to be seduced, she inevitably died, usually in childbirth, or simply by dwindling away under the pangs of an unbearable guilt. Heroines were spotlessly innocent; if they were anything less, they received the "wages of sin." Thus, in the sentimental novel, sex and death were inextricably related.[3]

It is not surprising that popular American fiction of the eighteenth and early nineteenth centuries betrayed a penchant for associating sex and death. In a Christian society which had traditionally regarded primordial sin as sexual sin, it was not an unnatural reaction. Had not Eve succumbed? And, had not mankind been punished by pain and death? Therefore, literature that implied a link between sex and death served a morally didactic purpose; it sternly warned of the danger inherent in sexual license. Fallen women were inevitably deserted and left to bear the physical and spiritual consequences alone. Sexual sin was the ultimate sin, and would thereby invoke the ultimate punishment—death and damnation. This concept dominated the sentimental novel, and it was later to have a powerful effect on the dime novel.

During the nineteenth century, however, the industrial revolution threatened the established concept of the American woman as the guardian of virtue. The shortage of labor caused the woman to forsake her traditional place in the home, and to assume a position in the national economy. This was popularly regarded as a threat both to woman's femininity, and to the institution of marriage. In the home, the woman was isolated from the temptations of the outside world; her virtue could be kept sacred. In the working world, however, the woman would be deprived not only of her femininity, but of her virtue as well. Quite possibly, she might even begin to assume traditional male prerogatives, including sexual license. Such thoughts gave rise to widespread anxiety. As David Brion Davis explains in *Homicide in American Fiction, 1798-1860: A Study in Social Values,* "the transformation in woman's economic and social position was accompanied by psychological tension, reflected in fiction by the heightened association between sex and death."[4] Thus, as a reaction against rapid social change and the accompanying fear about the decline of established morality, popular fiction of the nineteenth century reaffirmed traditional moral concepts. Heroines became incredibly genteel, and fallen women and their vile seducers were inevitably destroyed.

III

The dime novel western continued this pre-existent response to the fears which accompanied woman's integration into the national economy. It rigidified the standards of female characters and reaffirmed the sanctity of marriage. From 1860 to 1880, dime novel females showed little development beyond the genteel heroine as she had existed in the sentimental tradition for nearly a hundred years. Despite a changing world, they remained symbols of the ideal woman, delicate damsels whose ultrafemininity betrayed itself through a marked capacity for fainting in moments of emotional crisis. In adventure stories these moments were numerous, for plots based almost entirely upon capture and pursuit naturally abounded with villains who persistently strove to kidnap or seduce the virtuous heroine.

By employing the typical plot of the sentimental novel, the dime novel western continued to symbolize the universal struggle between good and evil in specifically sexual terms, although admittedly in a less overt form than the ordinary seduction novel. However, because of the anxiety surrounding the changing status of women in the nineteenth century, this struggle assumed an additional dimension and greater intensity. The villain, traditionally a symbol of sexual evil, easily became associated in the popular mind with the sexual threat which women were facing in the working world. As a result, sexual assault is implicit in the activity of dime novel western villains. In Edward S. Ellis's *Brimstone Jake; or, The Robbers of Dead Wood Valley,* a band of "roughs" captures a wagon train. Lola Moulton, the genteel heroine, "was in a terrible state of mind. She felt that her life was in danger, and even more than that might befall her." In the same novel, Job Jahnes, an evil Dutch miner, attempts to force his attentions upon another heroine, the plain but pleasant Annette: "His face wore a determined look, and there was an ominous gleam in his usually stolid eye . . . Job Jahnes came up to her and laid his heavy hand on her shoulder . . . encircling his brawny arms about the girl, he held her as in a vise and began kissing her in a most affectionate manner, despite all her womanly struggles to the contrary."[5] At this moment, however, the traditional trapper, Grill Devereaux, comes to the aid of the frightened girl.

Similar incidents abound in the dime novel western, and the villain is inevitably punished with death. When it is considered that the villain is a symbol of sexual evil, and that he always meets a violent death, a possible explanation for the high incidence of violence in pulp fiction becomes apparent. The hero, by resorting to violence and killing the villain, could not only assert his individualism in its ultimate violent form, but in addition, be personally responsible for eliminating evil in the world—evil which threatened everyone, but especially women, in an age of sweeping social change. Much of the popularity of the dime novel western, then, may be ascribed to the psychological gratification it provided the reader. In an age of anxiety and doubt, pulp literature offered a fantasy realm where, without exception, good was triumphant and evil was punished. Additionally, by identifying with the hero, the reader could vicariously participate in the hero's violent act, thereby aiding the elimination of evil from society.

The dime novel western also reflected popular fears about woman's declining morality and decreasing femininity through its portrayal of fallen women. Inevitably, unchaste women are paid the wages of sin; however, whereas the sentimental novel heroine died as a result of childbirth or guilt, the fallen woman of the dime novel meets her end in a more sensational manner. In general, she either becomes a revenge-crazed tigress who first kills her seducer and then herself, or, a vengeful Amazon who, stripped of her feminine nature, suffers a kind of living death.

Both varieties of ruined women appear in Edward L. Wheeler's *Deadwood Dick's Ward; or, The Black Hills Jazebel,* a story which clearly illustrates the sexual motivation of much of the violence in the dime novel western. As the tale opens, Wheeler introduces Girard Athol and his daughter Kate. Girard, a cripple, is searching for his wife, Kate's mother, who had married him only for his money, and then departed with his gold savings. In the meantime, he has learned that she resides in the area under the name of Madame Cheviot, for she has illegally remarried, and plans to marry for a third time in the near future.[6]

Kate, Girard's daughter, is the typical dime novel Amazon; she wears men's clothes, handles ruffians with ease, and is known by the alliterating nickname "Kentucky Kit," a standard attribute of masculine dime novel characters. As we suspect, she is a fallen woman, for her father describes her as a genuine "blue-grass widow," and Ned Harris, better known as the delightful rogue Deadwood Dick, can see that the young lady has "a secret under all her bright and smiling exterior." With her virtue she has also lost her femininity; instead of being shy and retiring, she is decidedly bold. Discovering Ned Harris asleep in the grass, she steals a kiss, thinking "I'll bet he's a reg'lar 'masher,' too, as they say out East. Anyhow, it wouldn't take long for him to 'mash' me, if he's as good as he looks." When Ned awakes, she disregards his "bold, unwavering eye" and declares that she trusts him, "though you are the first I have placed confidence in, for many a year." Eventually, she becomes Ned's "ward" and lives under the same roof with him, despite his fear of public opinion.[7]

In the meantime, the evil Madame Cheviot has learned of the proximity of Girard Athol and Kentucky Kit, and accordingly hires Bloody Bill and Black Bob to dispose of them along with the ever dangerous Deadwood Dick. The two ruffians fail, however, and during the wedding ceremony between Madame Cheviot and a wealthy rancher, Kentucky Kit shoots her mother. But the wicked woman is only wounded. Attempting to conduct the wedding again several days later, she is again foiled, for her husband, the hunchbacked Girard Athol, arrives on the scene shouting "my time has come for vengeance. It is too late to mend your ways, for Jezebel! you shall die ere you do any further deviltry." With a demonic laugh, the betrayed husband plunges a dagger into her bosom and escapes.[8]

However, a sub-plot involving another fallen woman has been taking place simultaneously. Millicent Raymond, who has been seduced by the traditional villain Ralph Randall, begs him to marry her: "What assurance have I that you will fulfill your promise, to me, sir, after dyeing my soul, with sin, to satisfy your will?" Randall replies that she must rob her father and dispose of Deadwood Dick. She explains that she will comply with his wishes, for she is presumably pregnant, and would rather face "the inevitable result of a few months to come" with a husband. However, she also gives him a stern warning: ". . . if you refuse to marry me, I'll send you to one of the most horrible deaths that my ingenuity can devise. You shall find that Millicent Raymond is yet able to right her wrongs, or to kill her betrayer and avenge them."[9] Shortly thereafter, Randall betrays signs of growing affection for Kentucky Kit, and Millicent responds instantly. She kills Kentucky Kit and then herself. Wheeler does allow both the villainous Randall and the crazed hunchback Girard Athol to escape death, but only because they must live on to terrorize a subsequent novel.[10]

Thus, all of the violence in the novel is either motivated by, or described within a symbolic framework of sex. Girard Athol kills Madame Cheviot because she has stolen his gold, but the deprivation of power and wealth is, as usual, symbolized by her sexual betrayal. Even more directly, the deaths of the fallen women, Madame Cheviot, Millicent Raymond, and Kentucky Kit, are motivated by sexual dishonor. In the fantasy realm of the dime novel western, then, the "wages of sin" concept is invariably reaffirmed. The belief that sin was inevitably punished, and that evil would eventually destroy itself, was no doubt a very comforting thought for the ordinary reader.

The presence of a different type of Amazon heroine in dime novels written after 1880, however, suggests a further dimension of the traditional theme of sexually motivated violence. This type of Amazon is best represented by Calamity Jane, the loyal companion of Deadwood Dick. In Edward L. Wheeler's *Deadwood Dick on Deck; or, Calamity Jane, the Heroine of Whoop-Up. A Story of Dakota,* Jane dresses in men's clothes, does trick riding, and smokes a cigar. Beneath her masculine exterior, however, she possesses "a form both graceful and womanly," and a face that is "peculiarly handsome and attractive, though upon it were lines drawn by the unmistakable hand of dissipation and hard usage, lines never to be erased from a face that in innocent childhood had been a pretty one."[11] Like other Amazons, Calamity Jane is a fallen woman; her lack of femininity is simply a manifestation of her lack of virtue. However, unlike Kentucky Kit, Calamity Jane is not condemned to death. Instead, she assumes all of the characteristics of the stereotyped noble outlaw, including a justification for her anti-social behavior. Strangely enough,

that justification is sexual dishonor, a crime for which she holds society as a whole responsible. In the character of Calamity Jane, then, the traditional theme of sexually motivated violence has taken a further step, for she is regarded simply as the product of a society which tolerates the existence of evil—an evil which is, as usual, symbolized in sexual terms. It is no longer personal sin but social sin that has led her to ruin. As a result, she attains a kind of martyrdom. Not only does her face bear "lines drawn by the unmistakable hand of dissipation and hard usage," but in addition, her prospects for marriage have been shattered: ". . . life here in the Hills has—well, has ruined her prospects, one might say, for she has grown reckless in act and rough in language."[12] As a fallen woman, she is fit only to marry another tainted soul: Deadwood Dick. The ambivalent character of Calamity Jane, then, offered the reader a dual catharsis. On the one hand, the reader could vicariously participate in her justifiable rebellion against an evil society. On the other hand, the reader's traditional moral values were reaffirmed; deprived of her femininity, Calamity Jane endured a kind of living death.

Thus, several factors contributed to the high incidence of violence in the dime novel western. Although much of it can no doubt be attributed to the fast action and sensationalism required of adventure stories, aggressive acts are often an expression of individual rebellion against the restraints of civilization. In addition, deliberate aggression is often rationalized by attributing to it motives of revenge for past injustice. Drawing from the tradition of the sentimental novel, the dime novel western depicted injustice as an aspect of universal evil, that amorphous malignant principle which attained form in the popular imagination only when cast into a framework of sexual symbolism. During the nineteenth century, an age of sweeping social change, declining morality, and the liberation of women, this sexual symbolism was charged with an additional emotional intensity. In response to the resultant widespread anxiety, the dime novel western reaffirmed traditional moral values while simultaneously providing mass purgation through vicarious participation in fictional violence.

Notes

1. W. H. Bishop, "Story Paper Literature," *The Atlantic Monthly,* XLIV (Sept., 1879), 385.

2. The Deadwood Dick Library, No. 32 (1900), p. 31.

3. David Brion Davis, *Homicide in American Fiction, 1798-1860: A Study in Social Values* (Ithaca, N.Y., 1957), p. 171.

4. Davis, p. 148. For a fuller discussion of the relationship between sex and violence in American fiction before 1860, see chapters VI-VIII, pp. 147-236.

5. Captain L. C. Carleton [Edward S. Ellis], *Brimstone Jake; or, The Robbers of Dead Wood Valley,* Beadle's Frontier Series, No. 44 (1908), pp. 77, 72.

6. The Deadwood Dick Library, No. 41 (1900).

7. pp. 5, 10.

8. p. 28.

9. p. 17.

10. p. 29.

11. *Seth Jones by Edward S. Ellis and Deadwood Dick on Deck by Edward L. Wheeler: Dime Novels* (Popular American Fiction edition), ed. Philip Durham (New York, 1966), pp. 104-105.

12. p. 131.

Michael Denning (essay date 1987)

SOURCE: "'The Unknown Public': Dime Novels and Working Class Readers," in *Mechanic Accents: Dime Novels and Working-Class Culture in America,* Verso, 1987, pp. 27-46.

[*In the following essay, Denning argues that dime novels constituted the primary reading material of the working class and that the books were specifically created by the middle class for workers.*]

Who read these stories and what did they think of them? Though this question is now central to the study of popular culture, it remains a difficult and elusive one. In part, this is because of sketchy and uncertain evidence. Even when one can determine who the readers were, it is very difficult to determine how they interpreted their reading. But the difficulty also lies in the reluctance of cultural historians of the United States to use class categories to describe and analyze the reading public. As a result, they often end up with a simple dichotomy between the few and the many, the discriminating and the mass, the elite and the popular. However, the place of dime novels in American culture depends not only on the industrial character of their production but on the class character of their reading public. Thus, this chapter will attempt to characterize the readers of dime novels by exploring the relations between popular fiction and its working class audience.[1]

The question of who read dime novels becomes two questions in the context of the relation between popular fiction and working class culture. One begins from the artifacts: who were the audience of dime novels, story papers, and cheap libraries? The other begins from the reading public: what did working class people read in the late nineteenth century? My argument is that these two questions converge: that the bulk of the audience of dime novels were workers—craftworkers, factory operatives, domestic servants, and domestic workers—and that the bulk of workers' reading was sensational fiction.

Recent accounts of the readers of dime novels by literary critics and cultural historians tend to be rather vague. In his book on dime novel westerns, Daryl Jones (1978, 14) writes only that 'though dime novelists aimed their stories at a predominantly working-class audience, the appeal of the genre in fact pervaded the entire culture. Dime novels

provided a source of entertainment and diversion for any individual of any social class who sought relief from the anxieties of the age.' Mary Noel (1954, 290-291), on the other hand, sees the story paper audience as 'middle class and American'. 'Whether or not the lowest economic group read the story papers must remain in doubt'—and she doubts it. Nina Baym (1984, 47), in an examination of antebellum reviews of fiction, concludes that 'in novel criticism, the audience seems to be divided into two groups, correlated loosely with presumed class membership. First, and more numerous, were ordinary or "mere" novel readers looking for pleasure and reading for story; second, there was a small group of cultivated, discreet, intelligent, educated, tasteful, thoughtful readers who wanted something more than, but not incompatible with (reviewers hoped), the tastes of the ordinary reader.' But Baym misses a third group only occasionally mentioned in the reviews she cites: the readers of cheap literature. Far more adequate than either the nostalgic image of a single 'American' reading public or the split between the few and the many is the picture sketched by Henry Nash Smith (1978, 8-9). He invokes the terminology of 'brows', noting an important distinction between:

> . . . the work of the new women novelists and yet another kind of fiction that proliferated during the 1840s—crude adventure stories represented by Tom Sawyer's favorite, *The Black Avenger of the Spanish Main; or, The Fiend of Blood. A Thrilling Story of Buccaneer Times,* by 'Ned Buntline' (E. Z. C. Judson), published in 1847. For want of a more elegant terminology I shall call the sentimental fiction of Warner and Cummins, together with the system of values embodied in it, 'middlebrow', and Ned Buntline's work 'lowbrow'. In such a scheme, Hawthorne and Melville evidently must be categorized as 'highbrow'. Although not enough evidence has been accumulated to support confident statements about the sizes of these segments of the mid-nineteenth century reading public, it appears that the total sales of lowbrow fiction were the largest—especially after the Beadle & Adams dime novels began to appear in 1860; but a few best-selling middlebrow titles far outstripped any individual lowbrow items in circulation.

But Smith argues that the relation between 'brow levels' and social and economic classes is obscure: 'The notorious vagueness of class lines in the United States precludes any close linkage between brow levels and the actual social structure.'[2] A closer look at the nineteenth-century sources can make the relation between brows—a twentieth-century concept—and classes clearer.

Smith's picture of antebellum fiction readers is very similar to George Woodberry's survey of the fiction-reading public in 1891. Woodberry, a leading genteel literary critic, identified a three-tier public: the readers of 'pure literature', interested in the art of fiction proper; the readers of the popular success novels; and the readers of 'the literature of the "Unknown Public", addressing itself to thousands of readers, whose authors were quite unknown, their subjects and methods strange, and that was all "written for money"—"the whole complexion of the thing is of a different world"' (Ickstadt 1979, 93). Woodberry echoes Edward Everett's (1860, 488) early comment that the story paper was the first attempt to reach the 'Unknown Public'. Indeed the 'Unknown Public' was one of a variety of epithets contemporaries used for the dime novel audience: the 'great people', the 'million', the 'submerged tenth'. The slogan of Beadle and Adams was 'Books for the Million!'. In his defense of the dime novel, Frederick Whittaker (1884, 8) speaks of 'the "great people" to whom the papers are constantly appealing. The readers of the dimes are farmers, mechanics, workwomen, drummers, boys in shops and factories, and a great many people who are so much appalled by the abuse of the daily press that they do not confess what they have been reading.' Dime novelist Eugene Sawyer, on the other hand, maintained: 'It is not, however, only the "submerged tenth" who reads cheap stories. I have been in bookshops and seen bankers and capitalists gravely paying their nickels for the same tales as their elevator boys read' (Burgess 1902, 532). Despite Sawyer's somewhat self-justifying assertion, W. H. Bishop (1879, 389) expressed the nineteenth-century consensus when he wrote in the *Atlantic* that the story papers and cheap libraries were 'written almost exclusively for the use of the lower classes of society.'

Nevertheless, more exact delineations of the audience are hard to find. The publishers themselves left little evidence more specific than Beadle's 'books for the million'. A bookseller noted that 'the people who buy the "libraries" are the people who take in the *New York Ledger*, . . . utterly unknown to bookstores.'[3] In 1871, the *New York Weekly* explicitly linked publishing stories about women sewing machine operators with seeking them as an audience:

> Every sewing machine girl in the United States should not only read *Bertha Bascomb, the Sewing Machine Girl,* but should make it her especial business to see that everybody else reads it. The story is designed to benefit the working girl, and therefore every working girl in our broad land should constitute herself an agent for its distribution. Everybody will be better for reading this great story; and we confidently look for an addition of at least one hundred thousand extra readers to swell our already unprecedented circulation (Noel 1954, 278).

Moreover, one can assume that some part of the audience was made up of immigrants and ethnics, particularly Irish and Germans, since publishers issued series like Ten Cent Irish Novels and George Munro's Die Deutsche Library. There were, however, no dime novels aimed at Blacks; and I have not found evidence of any Black readership.[4] The audience clearly was predominantly young. W. H. Bishop (1879, 384) describes 'the traffic on publication days':

> A middle-aged woman, with a shawl over her head and half a peck of potatoes in a basket, stops in for one; a shop-girl on her way home from work; a servant from one of the good houses in the side streets. . . . But with them, before them, and after them come boys. . . . The most ardent class of patron . . . are boys.

Nevertheless, except for the story papers and libraries explicitly aimed at boys and girls, this could not be called 'children's literature'. When William Wallace Cook (1912, 35) began writing dime fiction, he was criticized by the editor for writing for too young an audience: 'I hope you have not made the hero too juvenile, as this would be a serious fault. The stories in the Ten-Cent Library are not read by boys alone but usually by young men, and in no case should the hero be a kid.' Thus the 'people', the 'unknown public', the 'million', the audience of dime novels and story papers seems to be predominantly young, 'lowbrow', and internally divided by gender. It includes, depending on one's rhetoric, the 'producing classes' or the 'lower classes', encompassing German and Irish immigrants and ethnics but excluding Blacks and Chinese immigrants and ethnics.

If we turn to the other question—what did nineteenth-century working-class people read?—a complementary picture emerges from recent studies of literacy and from the two basic types of contemporary accounts of workers' reading; those of observers and reformers of working-class life, and those of workers in autobiographies and memoirs.[5] First, the success of the dime novel industry was in large part a result of the high levels of literacy among American workers. This was spurred not only by the availability of cheap reading matter but by the development of the 'common school' of universal primary education for whites in the years between 1830 and 1850. In their detailed examination of literacy in the nineteenth-century United States, Lee Soltow and Edward Stevens (1981, 51) find that there are three major reductions in illiteracy: 'the first following a decade of intense social reform, including common school reform (1850-1859), the second (more modest) appearing in the decade following the Civil War, when a number of states enacted compulsory education laws (1870-1879), and the third appearing in the decade following the passage of compulsory school attendance laws in most states and their enforcement in some (1880-1889).' Though the 1840 Census found that 97% of white adults over 21 in the Northeast, and 91% in the Northwest, were literate, this was based on a minimum standard of literacy. Soltow and Stevens, using a stricter standard and working from army enlistment files, find that 89% of northern artisans and 76% of northern farmers and laborers were literate in the period between 1830 and 1895 (52). 'Farmers and laborers, who were the two groups exhibiting the highest rates of illiteracy between 1799 and 1829, underwent rapid declines [in rates of illiteracy] . . . by the end of the century' (54). Indeed by 1870, just before the emergence of the cheap libraries, there were similar literacy rates among native-born and foreign-born men (though foreign-born women were substantially more illiterate than native-born women until 1890) (199). Together, common-school literacy and the fiction factory provided the conditions for written narratives to become a significant part of working-class amusement.

Indeed, one of the earliest observers of working-class reading, the Presbyterian minister James Alexander (1839, 66), who published two books about and for workers in 1838 and 1839, called attention to the new story papers:

The demand for this merely entertaining literature is evinced by the character of the large weekly newspapers, and low-priced magazines, which circulate most among operatives. I need not name these; our cities abound in them. The newspapers to which I allude are commonly issued on Saturday, and their immense sheet gives occupation to many a poor reader for the whole of Sunday. Now you will observe, that a large part of the outer form of these publications is frequently taken up with just that kind of reading which is fitted to make a sound mind sick, and a feeble mind crazy. Tales upon tales of love, of horror, of madness, and these often the effusions of the most unpractised and contemptible scribblers, who rejoice in this channel for venting their inanities, succeed one another week after week, and are the chief reading of persons whom I could name, for year after year.

Forty years later, the Unitarian minister Jonathan Baxter Harrison (1880, 167-171) noted in his 'Study of a New England Factory Town' that:

> The young people of the mills generally read the story papers, published (most of them) in New York City, and devoted to interminably 'continued' narratives, of which there are always three or four in process of publication in each paper.

I will look later at Harrison's characterization of the stories and his assessment of their effects in what is perhaps the most extensive observer's account of working class reading. For now, we should note his account of the mill workers' reading of story papers, his sense that they were young people's reading, and his assumption that his middle class audience would be unaware of their content. He goes on to observe that 'many hundreds of the older operatives, especially foreigners, of two or three nationalities, were reading a paper which is devoted to the liberation of the working-people of America. . . . This paper has a large circulation among operatives, miners and city mechanics, in nearly all parts of the country. . . . It always contains two or three serial stories by popular writers, which are designed to "float" the heavier articles devoted to the propagation of the doctrines of the agitators.' Finally he discusses a local labor-reform newspaper. The term 'newspaper' implied a wide variety of reading matter in the nineteenth century, so when 'newspapers' are said to be the principal reading matter of workers (e.g. Harvey 1974, 107), this may describe papers that consisted mainly of sensational fiction.

A decade later, the *Atlantic Monthly* published another series of articles on working class life. Lillie B. Chace Wyman (1888-1889, 607-608), in her 'Studies of Factory Life', finds a reading room started by mill operatives and patronized by immigrant men. The reading material was mainly newspapers. The few books, she writes, 'on examination, proved to be largely such as people are willing to give away, because they are of no interest to anybody.'

Another observer who notes newspaper reading is Emile Levasseur (1900, 393-435) of the French *Académie des Sciences Morales et Politiques,* who writes of the 1890s, 'the workman reads the newspaper as everyone else does

in America. . . . Daily papers cost 1 and 2 cents, weekly papers, 5 cents, as a rule. There is no doubt that the enormous development of the American newspaper in the last forty years has been due in part to the laboring classes.' He bases his conclusions not only on observation but on the federal and state government investigations of workers' budgets which show a high proportion of families making some expenditure for newspapers and books: a recent study of these budgets shows that in 1889, in ten northeastern states, 89.5 percent of native American working-class families and 87 percent of Irish-born working-class families had significant expenditures for newspapers and books (Modell 1978, 214).

An illuminating account of women's reading is given by Jennie Croly, a middle class patron and supporter of young working women. In testimony before the Senate Committee on Education and Labor in 1883, she said, in response to a question about working girls' recreation:

> In the first place, such girls do not care much about sitting down to read. If they have half a day of spare time they want to get out of doors, they want air . . . as for reading, they want something very different from what they have in their daily lives, and so they run to the story papers that contain flashy stories; that tell about the fine ladies and how many dresses they have, and that tell about the worst murders and the most exciting incidents that they can get. And I do not blame them for it. They are crazy for something that is outside of themselves, and which will make them forget the hard facts of their daily lives (U.S. Senate, Committee on Education and Labor, 2: 613-614).

Other observers also note story paper reading, usually in passing. An example from early in the period is the Englishman James D. Burn (1865, 34), who notes the wide circulation of the *New York Ledger,* a paper 'solely occupied by light literature', and, in criticizing the boarding-house life that marks American working-class life, says that it encourages women to 'pass away the time by lounging over sensational literature' (6-7). At the end of the nineteenth century, Walter Wyckoff (1898a, 179-180), in his experiment with life as a transient casual laborer, finds an Irish logger, on a rainy day, 'reading a worn paper copy of one of the Duchess's novels, which is the only book that I have so far seen in camp.' He notes that 'most of the men here can read, but to not one of them is reading a resource.'

These accounts by observers of working-class reading need to be read skeptically, however, because all stand within a class conflict over the 'reform' of working-class reading, a conflict I will turn to in the next chapter [of *Mechanic Accents*]. Thus one will find advocates of reform stressing the sensational and immoral character of working-class reading, while defenders of the working class will often cite examples of independent 'literary' and 'self-improving' reading.

As we turn to workers' memoirs and autobiographies, similar qualifications apply. Most people, when recalling books that influenced them, will recall literary and political readings more often than sensational fiction, particularly given the general disdain in which it is held: as dime novelist Frederick Whittaker (1884, 8) wrote, dime novels were read by 'a great many people who are so much appalled by the abuse of the daily press that they do not confess what they have been reading.' Furthermore, cheap stories are part of the texture of everyday life; they are not *events* that the autobiographer will tend to narrate. Nevertheless, one does find some accounts of reading sensational fiction in workers' autobiographies.

Some of the earliest accounts of workers' reading are in some ways the most exceptional: those of the Lowell mill girls. Drawn from the New England countryside, they were formed within a genteel Congregationalist culture, and the paternalism of the boarding-house system reinforced this culture. They also preceded the development of mass cheap literature, so their reading was almost entirely within the genteel literary system. So the reading cited by Lucy Larcom and Harriet Robinson includes the English poets and essayists, the literary reviews like *North American Review* and *Blackwood's,* the new women's magazines like *Godey's Ladies Book* and *Graham's Magazine,* and the Christian newspapers: the source for this reading is the circulating library. Harriet Robinson (1898, 57) writes:

> Novels were not very popular with us, as we inclined more to historical writings and to poetry. But such books as *Charlotte Temple, Eliza Wharton, Maria Monk, The Arabian Nights, The Mysteries of Udolpho, Abellino, the Bravo of Venice,* or *The Castle of Otranto* [this list includes popular Gothic and domestic novels], were sometimes taken from the circulating library, read with delight, and secretly lent from one young girl to another.

When she reflects on the mill girls of the present (1898), she writes that 'public libraries are provided, and they have more leisure to read than the mill-girls of forty years ago. But they do not seem to know how to improve it. Their leisure only gives them the more time to be idle in; more time to waste in the streets, or in reading cheap novels and stories' (122). Lucy Larcom has a somewhat less censorious attitude; after detailing at length her reading in the English poets, she writes: 'And we were as fond of good story-books as any girls that live in these days of overflowing libraries.' Nevertheless after saying that she 'devoured a great many romances', she adds, 'there are so many books of fiction written nowadays, I do not see how the young people who try to read one tenth of them have any brains left for every-day use.' She herself had at least one encounter with the new story papers when she tells of reading Dickens's *Old Curiosity Shop* in a Philadelphia weekly paper.[6]

The most detailed accounts for later in the century are found in the series of short life stories published in *The Independent* between 1902 and 1906, and in the autobiographies of Rose Cohen, Abraham Bisno, and Dorothy Richardson. *The Independent,* a reform magazine, published a series of life stories of 'undistinguished Americans' in order to 'typify the life of the average worker in some particular vocation, and to make each story the genuine experience of a real person' (Katzman and Tuttle 1982, xi). In these testimonies, some written and some the result of interviews, one finds several references to reading. Sadie Frowne, a Polish immigrant and New York garment worker in a sweatshop, says, 'I can read quite well in English now and I look at the newspapers every day. I can read English books, too, sometimes. The last one that I read was *A Mad Marriage* by Charlotte Brame [an English novelist whose works were a staple of the story papers and romance libraries; the original 'Bertha M. Clay']. She's a grand writer and makes things just like real to you. You feel as if you were the poor girl yourself going to get married to a rich duke' (Katzman and Tuttle 1982, 56). A similar sentiment is expressed by a tailoress who does given-out work: 'What chance I get I read something light, like *The Fatal Wedding.* It is one of the best things I've had yet. *The Earl's Secret* is another good one. . . . Sometimes I wonder how it would seem if I should have the luck that you read about in the novels—get rich all of a sudden and have your fine house and carriage as some of the girls have that I used to go with. I don't know as I would feel much better' (Stein and Taft 1971, 110).

Rose Cohen (1918), a Russian Jewish immigrant of the 1880s, tells of her early reading in her autobiography. It begins with her reading novels in Yiddish to her mother, novels that were rented from soda water stand keepers for five cents, never more than one a week: 'Mother always listened reluctantly, as if she felt it were a weakness to be so interested. Sometimes she would rise suddenly during the most interesting part and go away into the dark kitchen. But soon I would catch her listening from the doorway. And I lived now in a wonderful world. One time I was a beautiful countess living unhappily in a palace, another time I was a beggar's daughter singing in the street' (187-191). This account ends with her reading a Yiddish translation of *David Copperfield.* A later key moment is her first book read in English, a love story whose name she does not remember: 'I felt so proud that I could read an English book that I carried it about with me in the street. I took it along to the shop. I became quite vain' (249). This leads her to join the free library at the Educational Alliance, and to attempt, unsuccessfully at first, to read Shakespeare (252-254). But throughout her life story, changes in reading mark changes in life and sources of conflict: her father did not 'take kindly' to her reading, fearing that the reading of Gentile books would take her away from Judaism.

Abraham Bisno (1967, 49-50), a Russian Jewish immigrant and garment worker, gives an account of the place of cheap stories in his autobiography that is not dissimilar to that of Rose Cohen:

> At fifteen [1881] I began to learn to read. Both in Jewish and in English. I learned English from signs and from advertisements I looked at during the slack period of the trade. Jewish I learned when there was no work and a man who peddled Jewish stories loaned them out

weekly to me for five cents a week. He persuaded me to learn to read these stories because they were great romances. An agent of a Jewish newspaper got me to subscribe to a weekly paper. In those years I was very ignorant. I practically knew nothing of what was happening in the United States, and outside of my work and family experiences knew very little. The Jewish stories I read opened my eyes to new worlds. A man named Shomer wrote a great many Jewish romances copied from the French with a change only of names and habits from the French to the Jewish. He wrote a great many of them and I would read three or four a week, absorb their contents enthusiastically and eagerly.

The stories went like this: a poor girl, but very beautiful, fell in love with a rich young man, whose parents would not permit a marriage. Tragedy would follow. The boy would talk of suicide, the girl was miserable, until something happened where the girl was found to really be a heiress, the family smiled on her, they married and lived happily ever after. In a great many of them, there was an intriguing character who would cause either the boy or girl to distrust the other by false tale-bearing. He would be found out in his lies, and the differences were patched up again. Some tales of adventure and enterprise, but most of them about romantic love, the difficulties besetting the path of love, the difficulties ensuing, marriage, and everlasting happiness. But for me these were great finds. When there was no work I read them day and night and would tell about them to any who would listen.

Bisno's autobiography, which was never published during his life, is unusually frank and detailed in its depiction of everyday life; and his voracious reading of sensational fiction for its introduction to 'new worlds' is, I suggest, a typical experience. It is worth noting not only the physical resemblance between the dime novels and these Yiddish *shundromanen* of the 1880s, but the deep similarity of plots: the story Bisno recounts is very close to those written by Laura Jean Libbey. This similarity of plots, together with the absence of an international copyright agreement until 1891, made for a kind of 'world literature' as sensational novels were translated back and forth from English, French, German and Yiddish, translated not to be faithful to the 'original', but, as in the case of Shomer, to be adapted to local names, geography and customs. Moreover, that Bisno seems to have read more romances than tales of adventure or enterprise should make us realize that although cheap stories were clearly marked and marketed by the gender of the implied reader, this did not exclude significant cross-reading.

A somewhat different perspective emerges from Dorothy Richardson's *The Long Day: The Story of a New York Working Girl*. Because Richardson, of whom little is known, had a middle-class background, the story that emerges is less one of the development of her own reading than of the confrontation in the paper box factory between her genteel reading culture and the sensational reading of her workmates. She is asked, 'Don't you never read no story-books?'; but her 'confession of an omnivorous appetite for all sorts of story-books' leads not to a point of contact but to the great gap in the sorts of stories they read. She is told the story of *Little Rosebud's Lovers*, a novel by

Laura Jean Libbey that I will examine in chapter ten, and hears of the merits of the stories of Charlotte Brame, Charles Garvice, and Effie Adelaide Rowlands, all mainstays of the story papers and the cheap libraries. When she recounts her reading, 'the names of a dozen or more of the simple, every-day classics that the school-boy and -girl are supposed to have read' [Dickens, *Little Women, Gulliver's Travels*], her workmates have never heard of them. 'They were equally ignorant of the existence of the conventional Sunday-school romance . . . and similar goody-goody writers for goody-goody girls; their only remarks being that their titles didn't sound interesting' (Richardson 1905, 75-86). Richardson concludes that:

> The literary tastes of my workmates at the box-factory [are] typical of other factories and other workshops, and also of the department store. A certain downtown section of New York City is monopolized by the publishers and binders of 'yellow-backs', which are turned out in bales and cartloads daily. Girls fed on such mental trash are bound to have distorted and false views of everything (299-300).

Richardson's dramatic account of the gap between herself and her workmates is a striking example of the class character of a divided reading public.

There are also passing references to the reading of sensational fiction in the autobiographies of labor leaders. Terence Powderly (1940, 15) recalls 'having read love stories in the old *New York Ledger*, and James J. Davis (1922, 75) writes of his siblings that 'we were fluent readers, much better readers than our parents, but we had no books. We took the *Youth's Companion*, and it was the biggest thing in our lives. Every week we were at the postoffice when the *Companion* was due. We could hardly wait, we were so eager to see what happened next in the "continued" story.' But the reading that figures in most autobiographies is, not surprisingly, either tokens of self-improvement and self-culture or signs of the development of political and labor consciousness.

These testimonies to the reading of sensational fiction illuminate not only the audience of dime novels but the circumstances under which the reading of popular fiction took place, the situation of reading. This can tell something of the place of cheap stories in working-class culture, and indeed give the critic and historian some idea of how they ought be read and interpreted now. There were three main sites of reading: at home, at work, and while traveling. If these seem to exhaust all the possibilities, let me note first some sites where sensational fiction does *not* seem to have been read (though proving the absence of something is clearly less certain than establishing its presence): at school where little fiction was read; at religious institutions (here we must recall the wide range and circulation of Sunday School fiction); at saloons where evidence of reading seems limited to commercial or political newspapers; and at other sites of cultural and leisure activities such as sporting events, theatrical productions, and holiday picnics and parades.

The rise of railroad and streetcar travel both for commuting to work and for leisure gave a new place and opportunity for light, entertaining reading. As the distance between residential neighborhoods and factory districts grew in the late nineteenth century, more time was spent commuting, and cheap reading matter accompanied the journey: at the end of the century, Emile Levasseur observed workers reading newspapers on the New York streetcars. J. S. Ogilvie, a New York publisher who often reprinted serials that had appeared in Street & Smith's *New York Weekly,* became, according to one historian of cheap book publishing, 'the largest "purveyor" of "Railroad Literature" in the country' in the 1880s with ten and fifteen cent novels (Shove 1937, 95). Frank Leslie also aimed his cheap books, particularly *Frank Leslie's Home Library of Standard Works by the Most Celebrated Authors,* at railway consumption: 'Nearly every book bearing the Leslie imprint was in the class of cheap railroad literature and was handled by the American News Company. Through that company's system, and with the development of railroads throughout the country, cheap popular books could be retailed at newsstands, station kiosks, and on the trains themselves, where train boys included books among the wares they offered. . . . Leslie was keenly alive to the need for appropriate reading matter for the masses of people enjoying train travel in the 1870s' (Stern 1980, 184-6).

Nevertheless, if one considers the European experience of railway reading, the evidence is not so clear-cut. If in Britain, as Tony Davies (1983, 49) has remarked, 'the production of cheap fiction from the 1840s onward has two social destinations: the family home and the railway, corresponding perhaps to "respectable" and "disreputable" conceptions of the popular classes', in the United States the home was the key social destination. 'Railroad literature' does not appear to be as developed a category in American publishing as in England and France; there are few dime novel series or cheap libraries that have the word in the title.[7] Moreover Wolfgang Schivelbusch (1979, 69) has argued that 'a glance at the offerings of the English and French railway bookstalls shows that the reading public is almost exclusively bourgeois. An English survey of 1851 shows that, in contrast to the supply of trashy mass literature in the regular bookstores, the railway bookstalls and lending libraries in London carry highly respectable nonfiction, fiction, travel guides, etc.' It is still somewhat unclear whether, in the US, railway literature means cheap reprints of genteel and polite fiction for middle-class travellers or dime novels. However, the culture of the railroad is deeply inscribed in the dime novel, whether as the technical force that makes mass distribution possible, as the mode of transportation that encourages reading, or as the subject of innumerable novels themselves.

Most reading of sensational fiction, however, was probably done in the household. The story papers figure this in their titles, invoking the family as in *Family Story Paper* or the home and hearth as in the *Fireside Companion.* Their weekly publication schedules were aimed at Sunday reading, the only day off for workers, and one of the main reasons for the decline of the story papers toward the end of the century was the emergence of the Sunday newspaper.

There seems to have been, in this period before broadcasting, much reading aloud in the family: the decline in reading aloud is one of the major changes in leisure habits that the Lynds found in comparing the 1920s to the 1890s. The story papers themselves encouraged reading aloud (Noel 1954, 292). And in a context where children often had a greater grasp of English than their parents, the account Rose Cohen gives of reading aloud to her mother while her mother worked in the home is probably not atypical.

The serialized narratives were probably read intermittently, with installments missed and less exciting narratives forgotten. In Germany, popular narratives—*colporteur* novels—were sold in installments door to door; thus Ronald Fullerton (1977) is able to show, by looking at sales figures, that relatively few novels were read in their entirety. Ironically, the historian who is often working from incomplete collections of the story papers may experience the stories in a way closer to that of the original readers than if the complete run were available. Fullerton also suggests that the popularity of serialized and installment novels was based not only on the price (indeed sometimes it was more expensive to buy all the installments of a novel than to buy the novel as a whole) but on the fact that story papers and pamphlet-sized novels were less intimidating in sheer size to someone with rudimentary reading skills than a full volume, let alone a three-volume novel.

Fiction reading was also part of the culture of the workplace. It was a way to relieve boredom; so one finds accounts of reading filling dead times, as when the original Beadle's dime novels found an audience among Civil War soldiers (Kaser 1984) or when William Wyckoff finds the logger reading a dime novel during a rainy day in a logging camp. Reading was a part of factory lunch breaks (see, for example, Lang 1948, 22). And it filled times of unemployment: Bisno says that he read 'during the slack periods of the trade' and 'when there was no work'. But there was also reading on the job itself. Lucy Larcom (1889, 175-6) tells of how, despite regulations against books in the mill, she and others pasted clippings from the weekly papers at their work places. Herbert Gutman (1976, 36) points out that 'Samuel Gompers recollected that New York City cigarmakers paid a fellow craftsman to read a newspaper to them while they worked.' And James Alexander (1838, 225-226), an evangelical minister addressing the 'American mechanic' in the late 1830s, writes:

> Reading aloud . . . besides being a useful accomplishment, is highly advantageous to the health, and is recommended by the best physicians, as a preservative of the lungs. All this may be gained without any self-denial, by the custom of reading the papers, or other entertaining publications, during the intervals of labour. This is an advantage possessed by mechanics whose operations are sedentary and indoors; and this, I suppose, will go far to account for the fact, that learned men have so frequently proceeded from the shops of tailors and shoemakers.

One can conclude from this that in certain trades the practice was fairly widespread.[8]

The place of dime novels in working-class culture can also be inferred from the place of dime novels in labor newspapers. The labor papers often carried serialized fiction that resembled dime novels in title and subject matter. In contrast to the burgeoning star system of the story papers where the names of Sylvanus Cobb, Ned Buntline, or E. D. E. N. Southworth sold thousands of copies, the stories in labor papers often appeared without an author's name; however, this may be because the stories were pirated. Indeed the *New York Weekly* once accused Patrick Ford's *Irish World* of stealing a poem and illustration from them, an offense compounded by Ford's characterization of them as 'sensational' and 'trashy' (*New York Weekly* 10 April 1876, 4). But often the labor papers promoted the cheap stories, as when the *Labor Leader* recommended a serial running in Norman Munro's *Family Story Paper,* or used them as promotions, as when the *National Labor Tribune* offered dime novels as a bonus for readers who brought in new subscribers.

The place given to sensational fiction in two labor newspapers, the *Workingman's Advocate,* a national weekly 'devoted to the interests of the producing classes', and the *Labor Leader,* a Boston weekly that was close to the Knights of Labor, indicates a complex range of responses by the organizers and leaders of working-class culture and politics to this new commercial cultural form. The two papers not only published dime fiction, particularly of the workingman hero genre, but also published critiques of dime novels and examples of an alternative, 'serious' working-class fiction.

Throughout the 1860s, each issue of the *Workingman's Advocate* would lead the left columns of the front page with a poem and a short tale. Occasionally these tales might be continued over a few issues but none were of novel length. They were not introduced in any way, and often were anonymous contributions. They were basically sketches, exemplary romantic or pathetic incidents. In late 1866, however, the *Workingman's Advocate* editorialized about 'Cheap Literature':

> Every friend of progress and civilization insists upon reading matter being furnished to the people at the lowest possible price. It is by this means that agitation is continued and that knowledge is disseminated.
>
> But there are certain dangers to be guarded against, which result from the very fact that reading matter can be furnished at such a low price. It has brought before the public an immense mass of stuff, which so far from being valuable is enervating and distorts the minds of all those who are in the habit of reading such books. Take for example the ten cent novel: is there anything in one of them that deserves to be remembered? Is there a single picture of human character there that will furnish rational entertainment or thought? Nothing of the kind. A startling picture on the title page is the most attractive feature about the concern and is what sells the book.
>
> Then take the mass of weeklies and monthlies with their doleful stories, their fierce and bloody narratives, their low wit and comic pictures and, not unfrequently, their downright ribaldry; and consider to what extent

these foul publications circulate and you will form some conception of the baleful influence which they exert upon the youth of the country, male and female.

> We are far from advising against novel reading in the abstract, though certainly it may be carried to a dangerous extent. But we do say that the promiscuous reading of the yellow and the red-backed literature, which load the shelves of our bookstores, are not doing less in the work of ruin than the rum-shop or the house of ill-fame ('Cheap Literature' 1866, 2).

This condemnation of dime novels and story papers is in many ways not too far from those of the genteel critics I will look at in the next chapter. It does avoid the extremes of the genteel critics—that dime novels are meaningless opiates or are read literally and acted out—because it does not attack the readers of dimes, nor cheap reading generally, just the sensational stories themselves. Nevertheless, the cheap stories are doing the 'work of ruin', demoralizing the people and distorting their minds.[9]

However, this editorial was by no means the end of the issue for the *Workingman's Advocate.* Though I have not found any further explicit editorial statements on cheap literature, the shifts in the stories they themselves published is revealing. Soon after the editorial, they announced a series of stories to be published under the title 'Tales of the Borders' which would be a superior alternative to the yellow-back novels. However, a survey of the short tales published shows them to be neither particularly different from their earlier sketches nor from sensational fiction generally, and they were published without much ado, either in terms of introductory comments or bold headlining. This changed with the announcement of a labor story, Martin Foran's *The Other Side,* which was serialized with prominent attention between September 28, 1872 and March 29, 1873, much longer than any previous story. Foran wrote a lengthy preface (1872), published before the story itself began, which 'explains the circumstances under which, and the objects for which' this 'Trades' Union story' was written.

Foran, an organizer and leader of the International Cooper's Union, opens by asserting that 'if the laboring class could be made a *reading* class, their social and political advancement and amelioration would be rapid and certain. . . . The men most to be feared by labor, are not its open and avowed enemies, but those of its own ranks, *who do not, will not read.*' Thus for Foran, a central question for the workers movement becomes 'how are we to make the toilers in our fields, workshops and factories, toilers in the vast realm of mind—readers as well as workers?' One answer is to turn to the novel: 'We have long noticed the popular taste among the masses high and low, for fiction—novel-reading. An inherent love for fiction seems implanted in the many, especially in those whose educational advantages were limited, or at least did not include a classical training, and in contemplating this patent fact, we were led to think that much of interest and benefit to labor could be conveyed to the popular mind through this medium.' This explicit overall project for an alternative fiction from the point of view of the laboring classes is also sparked by Foran's immediate desire to respond to the popular anti-labor novel of Charles Reade, *Put Yourself in His Place.* Foran then apologizes for any shortcomings by admitting that he is 'not . . . a novel-wright or story writer by trade', and that *The Other Side* 'was not written with the sole design of amusing and pleasing those who might read it. The design of the author was didactic and defensory'.

Foran's novel was serialized prominently over the next six months, but, precisely because he was a union leader not a 'novel-wright', it was a unique intervention. However, immediately after *The Other Side* was completed, another short novel was serialized: *Reuben Dalton's Career; or, A Struggle for the Right. A Story for Workingmen* (C). This was the first of a series of novels written for the *Workingman's Advocate* between 1873 and 1876 by Weldon Cobb Jr., a novel-wright by trade, indeed a prolific writer of dime novels for Beadle & Adams, Street & Smith, and the Chicago-based Nickel Library. Most of Cobb's serials for the *Workingman's Advocate* were not explicitly 'stories for workingmen', but were standard sensational fare: *The Fatal Prescription, Under a Spell,* and *A Bold Game* are some of the titles.[10]

The *Labor Leader* also regularly published serial fiction, alternating between stories reprinted from other sources and stories written 'for the *Leader*'. In choosing reprints as in commissioning stories, the *Leader* favored romances of working-class life, particularly the workingman hero genre that I will examine in chapter nine. So they reprinted Charles Bellamy's *The Breton Mills: A Romance of New England Life* (BE) (with an advertisement that commended its portrayal of working-class life, despite its author's distaste for labor politics), and published the work of 'Seyek', their own pseudonymous dime novelist, which included *Ella Inness, A Romance of the Big Lockout; or, How the Knight Won the Prize* (Sa) and *John Behman's Experience; or, A Chapter from the Life of a Union Carpenter* (Sb). Indeed, Frank K. Foster, the editor of the *Labor Leader* and a leading figure in the International Typographical Union, the Knights of Labor, and the early American Federation of Labor, himself turned to fiction late in his career; in 1901 he published *The Evolution of a Trade Unionist,* an autobiography cast as a didactic novel.[11]

So, if the cases of the *Workingman's Advocate* and the *Labor Leader* are at all representative, working-class intellectuals had an ambivalent attitude toward cheap stories. There was a deep suspicion of the commercial culture and of its popularity: as a Detroit Knight of Labor, testifying before the Senate committee investigating the relations between labor and capital, said, long hours made workers 'incapable of doing anything requiring thought . . . They will read trashy novels, or go to a variety theater or a dance, but nothing beyond amusements' (Fink 1983, 10). But there were also attempts to use it, both opportunistically, to sell newspapers, and politically, to encourage cheap stories from the workingman's point of view. The attempts to create an alternative fiction were rare and rela-

tively unsuccessful, in part because the authors of this political fiction were not fiction writers by craft;[12] and, though some professional 'novel-wrights' were sympathetic to the workers movement and wrote cheap stories from 'the other side', most were still dependent on the factory-like production and standardization of the dime novel industry.

What then is the relation of dime novels to working-class culture? The evidence suggests that the bulk of the dime novel audience were young workers, often of Irish or German ethnicity, in the cities and mill towns of the North and West; and, that dime novels and story papers made up most of their reading matter. On the other hand, the dime novel was certainly not the self-creation of these craftworkers, factory operatives, laborers, and servants; it was a commercial product of a burgeoning industry employing relatively educated professionals—writers who also worked as journalists, teachers, or clerks. Nor were dime novels limited to working class readers; they were read by clerks, shopkeepers, local professionals, small farmers and their families. Should they, then, be seen as part of a wide and inclusive 'middle-class culture'?

I think not; and a brief look at two central terms in the nineteenth-century rhetoric of class—'producing classes' and 'middle class'—suggests why not. Neither term refers to a specific class in the nineteenth-century American class structure; rather, both invoke class alliances which had unstable rhetorical and actual existence. 'Producing classes' invoked the union of craftworkers, operatives and laborers with, in the phrase of the Knights of Labor, 'the professional man, the clerk, and the shopkeeper' (Couvares 1984, 74), as well as the small farmer. 'Middle class', on the other hand, invoked a common world shared by manufacturers, bankers, large merchants, and the professional, clerk, shopkeeper, and small farmer.

This distinction is important in understanding the dime novel's public. As a cultural form, dime novels were *not* part of the popular culture of the 'middle class'. The magazines were the key literary form in that cultural universe; its metaphoric centers were the 'self-made' entrepreneur and the 'domestic' household. The dime novels were part of the popular culture of the 'producing classes', a plebian culture whose metaphoric centers of gravity were the 'honest mechanic' and the virtuous 'working-girl'. Indeed, this is how they were seen in that 'middle-class discourse and practice that sought to reform the culture and reading of the 'lower classes', to which I turn in the next chapter.

Notes

1. Since concepts of class are widely debated and have different meanings in different theoretical vocabularies, let me outline my use of the concepts drawn from the Marxist tradition. First, I follow Erik Olin Wright's (1985) discussion of class analysis, where he distinguishes between the analysis of *class structure,* 'the structure of social relations into which individuals (or, in some cases, families) enter which determine their class interests',

and of *class formation,* 'the formation of organized collectivities within that class structure on the basis of interests shaped by that class structure' (9-10). 'Classes,' he argues, 'have a structural existence which is irreducible to the kinds of collective organizations which develop historically (class formations), the class ideologies held by individuals and organizations (class consciousness) or the forms of conflict engaged in by individuals as class members or by class organizations (class struggle), and that such class structures impose basic constraints on these other elements in the concept of class' (28).

Second, one must also distinguish between at least two levels of abstraction in class analysis: the analysis of modes of production where classes are seen as 'pure types of social relations of production, each embodying a distinctive mechanism of exploitation' (10), and the analysis of specific social formations, where one rarely finds pure classes but rather fractions of classes, and alliances between classes as the result of specific historical combinations of distinct modes of production, uneven economic development, and the legacy of earlier class struggles. (On levels of abstraction in class analysis, see also Katznelson, 1981, chapter 8.) At the first, 'higher' level of abstraction, my study assumes that the United States between the 1840s and 1890s (particularly the north and mid west, the centers of dime novel production and reception) was fundamentally organized by the capitalist mode of production; its 'basic' or 'fundamental' classes were capitalists and workers; other classes were, in Wright's term, 'contradictory class locations', or, in Wolff and Resnick's (1982; 1986) term, 'subsumed classes'. However, most of my study is pitched at the second, 'lower' level of abstraction. Here I draw particularly on the analysis of the transformation of American class structures in Gordon, Edwards, and Reich, 1982; on the histories of the working classes by the 'new' labor historians—Gutman, Montgomery, Couvares, Ewen, Fink, Kessler-Harris, Laurie, Levine, Peiss, Rosenzweig, Ross, and Wilentz, among others—which focus on the class fractions and class alliances among the popular or subaltern classes; and, for the history of the dominant classes, on the work of Batzell, Bledstein, Halttunen, Pessen, Wallace, Warner. On middle-class formation, see the excellent essay by Blumin, 1985. In general, by the working classes, I include craftworkers, factory operatives, common laborers, domestic servants, and their families; by the capitalist classes, I mean manufacturers, large merchants, bankers and financiers, the patrician elite and their families. The contradictory class locations include small shopkeepers, small professionals, master artisans and clerks: I will examine later their relation to the rhetoric of the 'producing classes' and

the 'middle classes'. David Montgomery's (1967, 29-30) interpretation of the 1870 census concludes that:

> Of the 12.9 million people in all occupations, only 1.1 million (8.6 per cent) can be listed as nonagricultural employers, corporate officials, and self-employed producers or professionals. Thus the business and professional elites, old and new, totaled less than one tenth of the nation's economically active population. . . . 67 per cent of the productively engaged Americans were dependent for a livelihood upon employment by others. Industrial manual workers, or what would now be called 'blue collar labor' . . . numbered just over 3.5 million souls, or 27.4 per cent of the gainfully employed.

> Agriculture accounted for 52.9 per cent of the gainfully employed: 24.2 per cent were farmers, planters and independent operators; 28.7 per cent were agricultural wage earners. Domestic servants made up 8 per cent of the gainfully employed; white collar workers—clerks and salespeople—3 per cent.

My work is *not* a contribution to the history of 'class structure' in the United States, but rather to the history of 'class formation' in the United States. As Katznelson (1981, 207) writes, 'Class society exists even where it is not signified; but how and why it is signified in particular ways in particular places and times is the study of class formation.' In particular, my study is meant as a contribution to the history of 'class consciousness', or what I would prefer to call the *rhetoric of class,* the words, metaphors, and narratives by which people figure social cleavages. The ideological struggles to define social cleavages are determined by the existing class structure but they also play a part in the formation of class organizations and in class struggles. (Przeworski, 1985 and Therborn, 1980 are perhaps the best theoretical discussions of the ideological constitution of classes.)

2. The evidence of collectors and enthusiasts is even vaguer; they tend to stress the 'respectable' people who read dime novels and Albert Johannsen's list is characteristic: 'bankers and bootblacks . . . lawyers and lawbreakers . . . working girls and girls of leisure, President Lincoln and President Wilson' (Johannsen, 1950, 1:9). Edward Pearson, in his early book on dime novels, has a chapter devoted to readers' reminiscences; but the correspondents to whom he sent his questionnaire are largely established professionals: editors, librarians, professors. In the middle class homes of their childhood, dime novels were often prohibited and usually read by children on the sly; indeed this

image has become part of the commonsense knowledge about dime novels.

3. Quoted in Shove, 1937, 19. This assessment raises the question of the readership of the *New York Ledger*, an issue worth considering. For anyone who wishes to argue for an overlapping rather than discontinuous reading public in nineteenth century America, the *Ledger* is a key journal. It attained the highest circulation of any magazine or story paper by reaching a cross-class, 'popular' audience with stories, poems, and articles by leading writers and intellectuals including Edward Everett, Henry Ward Beecher, George Bancroft, Henry Wadsworth Longfellow, Harriet Beecher Stowe, and Fanny Fern. Thus, Mary Noel, focusing primarily on the *Ledger*, concludes that the story papers had a largely middle class audience. And, in her study of antebellum responses to fiction, Nina Baym (1984, 18) includes the *Ledger* in the same discursive universe as the major middle-class magazines, from *Godey's* to *Harper's, Graham's* to the *Atlantic*.

This, I would argue, is misleading. Far from being a representative journal, the *Ledger* achieved its wide circulation by uniquely straddling the boundary between the two worlds of genteel and sensational culture. It was the most respectable story paper, the least respectable magazine. Indeed, when appealing to advertisers, it claimed to be the 'leading high-class illustrated family weekly paper in America' (*N. W. Ayer & Sons American Newspaper Annual*, 1892, 1403.) Its genteel contributors came to it not because they felt it was part of their culture but because Bonner paid so well. When Bonner convinced Edward Everett, the former president of Harvard, to write fifty-two weekly columns in 1858 and 1859 in return for a substantial contribution to the Mt. Vernon fund, which was preserving Washington's home (and with which Everett was involved), E. L. Godkin, then a correspondent for the London *Daily News*, summed up the response of the genteel culture, and marked the gap between it and the *Ledger*:

The great topic of the quidnuncs for the last few days has been Edward Everett's extraordinary undertaking to write for the New York *Ledger*, a two-penny weekly magazine, circulating nearly three hundred thousand copies. . . . It is filled with tales of the 'Demon Cabman', the 'Maiden's Revenge', the 'Tyrant's Vault', and a great variety of 'mysteries' and 'revelations'; and, in short, barring its general decency of language, belongs to as low and coarse an order of literature as any publication in the world. The proprietor [Robert Bonner] was four or five years ago a journeyman printer, but by lavish use of puffery in aid of this periodical has amassed a large fortune, *a la* Barnum. . . . To the astonishment of the whole Union the ex-ambassador, ex-secretary of state, ex-president of Harvard University, ex-editor of the 'Greek Reader', the

scholar, the exquisite, the one aristocrat of the 'universal Yankee nation', has accepted the proposal. . . . If you knew the sensation which this incident has caused here amongst genteel people, you would hardly expect me to add a line to my letter after reciting it (Ogden, 1907, 1:179-180).

On the other hand, though Everett (1860) himself accepted Bonner's proposal with 'great misgivings', he concludes his series of articles with a peroration of the *Ledger*, beginning with an awed account of visiting the story paper's production plant, remarking on its circulation of four hundred thousand, and concluding with an invocation of its readers:

It has simply aimed to be an entertaining and instructive Family newspaper, designed, in the first instance, to meet the wants of what is called, in a very sensible and striking paper in Dickens' Household Words, . . . the 'Unknown Public'. The New York 'Ledger' is the first attempt in this country, on a large scale, to address *that* public; and the brilliant success, which has attended it thus far, is a strong confirmation of the truth . . . that the time is coming when 'the readers, who rank by millions, will be the readers who give the widest reputations, who return the richest rewards, and who will therefore command the services of the best writers of the time' (488).

4. As noted above, William Wells Brown's *Clotelle* was published in dime novel format during the Civil War, part of Redpath's abolitionist attempt to reach Union soldiers. There is some evidence that one of Beadle's authors was Black (see entry for Philip S. Warne in Johannsen, 1950, 2:289), and Victoria Earle Matthews may have written for the story papers (see Penn, 1891, 375-6). However, most fiction by black writers was published in Black newspapers and journals; the Black Periodical Fiction Project, headed by Henry-Louis Gates, has not found a Black equivalent of dime novels. For a discussion of the relation between dime novel conventions and early Afro-American fiction, and of the Afro-American fiction reading public in the late nineteenth century, see Carby, 1987.

5. The history of readers and the reading public is very undeveloped for the United States; the unsatisfactory typology of the 'brows' dominates most literary and cultural history, and as Henry Nash Smith pointed out, this has not been adequately articulated with social class. Kaser, 1984 is one of the few studies of nineteenth century American reading, and it confirms the importance of dime novel reading by soldiers in the Civil War. However, accounts of the British, French, German, and Russian reading publics offer suggestive parallels. In England, one finds a similar explosion of cheap stories—the 'penny dreadfuls' and weekly newspapers—in the 1830s and 1840s. Richard Altick (1957, 83) argues that 'it was principally from among skilled workers,

small shopkeepers, clerks, and the better grade of domestic servants that the new mass audience for printed matter was recruited during the first half of the century.' The staple of this cheap printed matter was sensational fiction, but it is important to note that this was a shift in reading matter. The first cheap reading matter for artisans was radical political journalism, and the desire to read was often connected to working class political activity and self-improvement. The fiction industry picked up a reading public after the failure and abandonment of political aspirations, particularly of Chartism (L. James, 1963, 25). By the end of the century, reading had spread throughout the working class. A recent examination of a U.S. Department of Labor study of British workers in 1889 and 1890 finds:

> almost all [families] had family members who were literate. At least 80 percent of those interviewed in every industry bought books and newspapers. These proportions apply to both laborers and the highly skilled in textiles, although in heavy industry the unskilled were less likely to read and spent smaller sums on books. . . . This extensive, but limited taste for reading is confirmed by Lady Bell's interviews of Middlesborough workers around 1900. Of 200 families she interviewed, only 15 percent did not care to read or had no reading member. Yet most chose just newspapers and light novels. . . . The literary world of most workers therefore mixed sports, crime, and general news with romantic or sensationalist fiction (Lees, 1979, 183).

On the British reading public, see Altick, 1957; L. James, 1963; Leavis, 1932; Mitchell, 1981; Neuberg, 1977; Webb, 1955. On the French popular reading public in the early nineteenth century, see Allen 1981; 1983.

German workers had similar reading tastes. The equivalent of the dime novel in Germany was the 'colporteur novel' of the 1870s and 1880s which was sold in installments and combined cheap prices with sensational fiction (Fullerton, 1977; 1979). See also Steinberg, 1976.

Brooks, 1985 offers an excellent history of both the Russian reading public and sensational fiction, the 'literature of the *lubok*', in the late nineteenth and early twentieth century, with suggestive cross-national comparisons.

In the United States, the research that is closest to a history of the reading public is the sociological studies of reading in the library science of the 1920s to 1940s, work exemplified by that of Douglas Waples. (For a history and overview of this work see Karetzky, 1982; Steinberg, 1972; see also Waples and Tyler, 1931; Waples, Berelson and Bradshaw, 1940.) A small part of this work focused on factory workers (see Gray and Munroe, 1930, 81-91; Ormsbee, 1927, 75-95; Rasche, 1937) and, though the period studied is the 1920s, it is suggestive for our purposes. A number of conclusions were drawn from the surveys carried out. First of all, newspapers were by far the most common reading matter of young workers (all of the surveys were primarily focused on young adult workers), followed by fiction magazines, the 'pulps'. Newspapers were read largely for sports, crime news and fashion, and the fiction magazines carried 'sensational' and 'salacious' stories. There was clear gender division in the reading of pulps, with the striking exception of *True Story,* Macfadden's innovative pulp of the 1920s which carried stories said to be true and written by readers; it was read by men and women alike. The gap between middle class reading and working class reading in the 1920s can be gauged by Hazel Grant Ormsbee's comment on finding that *True Story* was far and away the most read magazine by young working class women: 'Even though it may be found on all the street corner news stands, and indeed at almost every stand where magazines are sold, its name is probably not even known to the many persons who are familiar with most of the magazines in the second class [i.e., the middlebrow magazines like *Saturday Evening Post* and *Ladies' Home Journal*]' (Ormsbee, 1927, 80). There was also a close connection between reading and the movies: movie magazines and the novels that movies were based on were both common reading. The conclusions of these studies are summed up by Gray and Munroe: 'the quality of some of the material read is very good. On the other hand, there is a surprisingly large amount of reading of cheap, sensational material. . . . In fact, the need of elevating the reading interests and tastes of young workers presents a very grave problem' (Gray and Munroe, 1930, 89). This desire to 'reform' workers' reading has roots in the era of the dime novel.

A second general conclusion developed out of Douglas Waples' comparisons of people's expressed subject interest with their actual reading. He found that there was 'almost no correlation between the workers' expressed reading interests and what they read in the newspapers and similarly little relation between these interests and their magazine reading.' Waples concluded that the most important determinant of what is read is accessibility, particularly in the case of workers who read mainly newspapers (Karetzky, 1982, 99). This reading research of the 1920s and 1930s does offer some important insights and data, though it is marred by the condescension and moralism of the researchers and by the complete distrust of fiction in general and sensational fiction in particular. Another product of the 1920s sociological imagination, Helen and Robert Lynd's *Middletown,* is particularly interesting because, while confirming the general observations of the reading researchers for the 1920s, finding important cleavages in reading material by class and gender in Middletown, it compares workers' reading of the 1920s with that of the 1890s. The Lynds find three major changes: the general decline of the workers' self-improving reading culture that was manifested in the independent Workingmen's Library, which has disappeared by the 1920s; the increase in public library circulation which has replaced 'buying of cheap paper-covered books in the nineties and the reading of books from the meager Sunday School libraries'; and the slackening of attentiveness to reading: 'more things are skimmed today but there is less of the satisfaction of "a good evening of reading". There appears to be considerably less reading aloud by the entire family' (Lynd and Lynd, 1929, 229-242).

6. Larcom, 1889, 244, 105-106, 190. See for details, 99-106, 226-247. 'Libraries' here refers to the various series of cheap novels that appeared after the *Lakeside Library* of 1875.

7. Neither Beadle & Adams nor Street & Smith seem to have ever used the word 'railroad' or 'railway' in a series or story paper title, and the only instance mentioned in the histories of publishing, Shove, 1937 and Stern, 1980, is the American reprints of the English Routledge *Railway Library.*

8. Indeed there is a struggle over a similar sort of reading at the workplace by Cuban tobacco workers in the 1860s. As Ambrosio Fornet (1975) writes, 'the proletariat found in Reading—in "the enthusiasm to hear things read", as an editorial writer in *El Siglo* put it—the era's most democratic and effective form of cultural diffusion.' It began in 1865 in the large tobacco factory of El Figaro, with each worker contributing time to make up for the working time lost by the reader. 'From there,' Fornet goes on, 'readings sprang up in other workshops in Havana. . . . Wherever sedentary group work was carried out, the idea found supporters.' Readings included newspapers, histories and novels. The first struggles over reading had to do with owners wanting to select and approve the material to be read, but the campaign against reading escalated and by May, 1866 the political governor issued a decree that prohibited 'the distraction of workers in tobacco factories, workshops or any other establishment by the reading of books or periodicals, or by discussions unrelated to the work being carried out by these same workers'.

9. For an account of a similar reaction to commercial fiction by the German Social Democrats, see Trommler, 1983, 64-67.

10. Little is known of Weldon Cobb's life. I suspect that his serials written for the *Workingman's Advocate* preceded his success in the commercial story papers

and cheap libraries; perhaps they brought him to the attention of the fiction entrepreneurs. For the biographical data that exists, see Johannsen, 1950, 2:56; and Johannsen, 1959, 43. Unfortunately, Johannsen has no record of Cobb's connection to the *Workingman's Advocate.*

11. I am indebted to Joseph DePlasco for calling my attention to Foster and to the fiction in the *Labor Leader.*

12. Another example of this kind of labor fiction is the novel of Knights of Labor organizer T. Fulton Gantt, *Breaking the Chains,* which was found and has been edited and republished by Mary Grimes, 1986.

FURTHER READING

Criticism

Anglo, Michael. "Gothic Foundations." In *Penny Dreadfuls and Other Victorian Horrors*, pp. 11-29. London: Jupiter Books, 1977.

Surveys the subject matter of early dime novels and explores the genre's roots in Gothic fiction and in the social conditions of early nineteenth-century England.

Hoppenstand, Gary. "Introduction: The Missing Detective." In *The Dime Novel Detective*, edited by Gary Hoppenstand, pp. 3-4. Bowling Green, Ohio: Bowling Green University Popular Press, 1982.

Argues that through analysis of dime novels a new type of detective character, the "Avenger Detective," emerges.

Johannsen, Albert. "Authors, Artists, and Readers." In *The House of Beadle and Adams and Its Dime and Nickel Novels: The Story of a Vanished Literature*, pp. 7-11. Norman: University of Oklahoma Press, 1950.

Examines the identities of the authors and illustrators of dime novels.

Kent, Thomas L. "The Formal Conventions of the Dime Novel." *Journal of Popular Culture* 16, No. 1 (Summer 1982): 37-47.

Examines the common literary devices and structures found throughout dime novels.

Noel, Mary. "Dime Novels." *American Heritage: The Magazine of History* VII, No. 2 (February 1956): 50-5, 112-13.

Suggests reasons for the immense popularity of dime novels.

Pearson, Edmund Lester. "With, Ho! Such Bugs and Goblins." In *Books in Black or Red*, pp. 129-39. New York: Macmillan Company, 1923.

Examines the causes of public outrage against dime novels, arguing that the outcry was unwarranted.

Schulte-Sasse, Jochen. "Can the Disempowered Read Mass-Produced Narrative in Their Own Voice?" *Cultural Critique*, No. 10 (Fall 1988): 171-99.

Reexamines Michael Denning's scholarship on dime novels and class ideology.

Thompson, Charles Willis. "That Maligned Innocent, the Dime Novel." *New York Times Book Review* (3 November 1929): 2.

States that contrary to public opinion, the original dime novels adhere to a strong moral order.

West, Mark I. "Not to Be Circulated: The Response of Children's Librarians to Dime Novels and Series Books." *Children's Literature Association Quarterly* 10, No. 3 (Fall 1985): 137-39.

Describes the campaigns of nineteenth-century public librarians to prevent children from reading dime novels.

The Gilded Age

INTRODUCTION

Remembered as an era in American history characterized by great prosperity and industrial growth, the three decades following the Civil War have often been referred to as "The Gilded Age," so called in part because of the 1873 novel by Mark Twain and Charles Dudley Warner entitled *The Gilded Age.* The satirical novel, written in just a few months and intended as a caricature of the era, describes what the authors viewed as the greed and hypocrisy of American society and the folly of countless numbers of ordinary citizens who firmly believed that some magical scheme would lead them to riches. As articulated by Twain and Warner, the term "Gilded Age" refers primarily to the middle-class experience of the time, an experience typified by what author Thorstein Veblen called "conspicuous consumption"—of dress, home décor, and all material goods which were considered signs of "good taste." Along with the increased aestheticism of the age, and perhaps in direct response to it, developed more self-conscious literary criticism and realism.

The Gilded Age was characterized most significantly by the rapid industrialization that transformed the country from a primarily rural and agriculturally-based republic whose citizens for the most part shared a belief in God, into an industrial and urbanized nation whose values were changing rapidly due, in part, to increased wealth and to the ramifications of Charles Darwin's theory of evolution. Oil magnate John D. Rockefeller and steel tycoon Andrew Carnegie—both of whom virtually monopolized their respective industries—symbolized both the "self-made man" and the spirit of acquisition that dominated the late nineteenth century. This "spirit" is what Twain and Warner criticized in *The Gilded Age,* drawing attention to the artificial standards of taste attributed to the growing American bourgeoisie. As individual income levels increased due to such factors as improved communications resulting from the introduction of the telephone, technological innovations such as electricity, and rapid transportation via the new transcontinental railroads, many individuals—the "new rich"—could afford to indulge in finer clothing (which had become cheaper and more accessible), home decorations (which were mass-produced), and leisure activities that would previously have been considered impractical. The steam engine, the railroads, and the industrial boom following the Civil War years produced the country's first moguls and monopolies and created a collective dream both at home and abroad of self-made fortunes and streets "lined with gold."

But all that glittered was not gold. Economic change came unpredictably. In 1873-78, 1883-85, and again in 1893-97, the nation experienced serious economic depressions. African-Americans, betrayed by the false promises of Reconstruction, were subjugated in new and more subtle ways. Black Americans in the South were subject to Jim Crow laws (legal segregation sanctioned by the Supreme Court). These laws were often enforced with violent methods involving torture and lynchings. The North, too, was not entirely committed to racial equality: blacks there were typically relegated to subservient and subordinate roles. Critic James H. Dormon, studying the "coon song craze" of the late nineteenth century, has found that these immensely popular songs, which depicted stereotypical caricatures of black Americans, reflected the nationwide feeling that blacks should be held in subordinate and segregated positions in society. According to Dormon, these songs rationalized white America's perception of blacks not only as silly buffoons, but also as dangers to the existing social structure. Black Americans were not the only ones to suffer hardships during this period; many farmers lost their holdings as railroads and new machinery lowered their crop prices. Cities became crowded with immigrants eager to succeed but whose only real opportunity was to provide an endless supply of cheap labor. In short, the chasm between rich and poor seemed greater and more visible than ever.

The development of literature at the time reflects this division. Both "low-brow" and "high-brow" forms thrived, and so did artistic snobbery. For the first time in American history, art received critical attention for art's sake. Largely due to the support and example of William Dean Howells, one of the most influential writers of the late nineteenth century, authors like Samuel Clemens (Mark Twain), Stephen Crane, and Henry James turned their attention to realistically depicting human behavior and social experience. Crane and Twain often went further in focusing on a new and more "realistic" subject matter—the experience of those who were not part of the middle class that so defined the standards of their age. The era also saw the emergence of regional literature, typified by the New England fiction of Sarah Orne Jewett and the vernacular dialect in Joel Chandler Harris's Uncle Remus stories and George Washington Cable's Creole tales. Several critics have suggested that this type of literature flourished during the latter part of the nineteenth century in part because these "local colorists" sought to preserve these distinctive modes of life before they were swallowed up by industrialization.

America experienced an industrial revolution later than England but more rapidly. The concentrated shift from homogenous, rural populations to diversified, urban ones created crowding and poverty, yet the industrial elites enjoyed a new wealth and urbane lifestyle that allowed for increased cultivation of the arts. Advances in machinery and transportation destroyed the old dream of agrarian self-sufficiency yet allowed for the mass production and accessibility of both necessities and luxuries. It was a time of great division, as well as a time of significant instability and anxiety, as many saw and lamented the replacement of religious and moral values with materialistic ones. Critic Paulette D. Kilmer, examining the "rags-to-riches" model in late nineteenth-century literature, has suggested that a great portion of Gilded Age literature is still closely tied to religious values. In these tales, as Kilmer has stated, a young protagonist often aids a wealthy benefactor, whose gratitude in turn enables the youngster to rise to the middle class. The tales offer evidence of benevolence—rather than a "quick fix"—as the source of a young man's success. Howells, though, beginning with the novel *The Rise of Silas Lapham* (1885) and continuing with the novel *A Hazard of New Fortunes* (1890), addressed what he saw as the dangerous relationship between the economic growth of the United States and the corresponding decline of moral values under capitalism.

Modern critics have continued to debate this perception of the era. While many stress the negative influences of politics, industry, and technology on the society as a whole, others object to the emphasis on greed and corruption so often connected with the era, and instead focus on the dramatic and rapid transformation of the entire nation.

REPRESENTATIVE WORKS

Horatio Alger, Jr.
  Ragged Dick [*Street Life in New York with the Boot Blacks*] (novel) 1868

Edward Bellamy
  Looking Backward: 2000-1887 (novel) 1888

George Washington Cable
  The Grandissimes: A Story of Creole Life (novel) 1880

Abraham Cahan
  Yekl, A Tale of the New York Ghetto (short story) 1896
  The Imported Bridegroom and Other Stories of the New York Ghetto (short stories) 1898

Andrew Carnegie
  The Gospel of Wealth (essay) 1889

Stephen Crane
  Maggie: A Girl of the Streets (novel) 1893

Theodore Dreiser
  Sister Carrie (novel) 1900

Paul Laurence Dunbar
  Majors and Minors (poetry) 1895

Henry George
  Progress and Poverty (nonfiction) 1879

Charlotte Perkins Gilman
  The Yellow Wall-Paper (short story) 1892
  Women and Economics (nonfiction) 1899

Joel Chandler Harris
  Uncle Remus: His Songs and His Sayings (short stories) 1881

William Dean Howells
  The Rise of Silas Lapham (novel) 1885
  A Hazard of New Fortunes (novel) 1890

Henry James
  Daisy Miller: A Study (novella) 1879
  The Portrait of a Lady (novel) 1881
  The Bostonians: A Novel (novel) 1886
  The Golden Bowl (novel) 1904

Sarah Orne Jewett
  The Country of the Pointed Firs (novel) 1896

Mark Twain
  The Gilded Age: A Tale of Today (novel) 1873
  Adventures of Huckleberry Finn (novel) 1884
  Pudd'nhead Wilson: A Tale (novel) 1894

Thorstein Veblen
  The Theory of the Leisure Class (nonfiction) 1899

Charles Dudley Warner [with Mark Twain]
  The Gilded Age: A Tale of Today (novel) 1873

*With Charles Dudley Warner.

POPULAR THEMES

John Tomsich (essay date 1971)

SOURCE: "Exit Religion," in *A Genteel Endeavor: American Culture and Politics in the Gilded Age*, Stanford University Press, 1971, pp. 167-85.

[*In the following essay, Tomsich discusses the "genteel" authors of the Gilded Age, whose religious faith faded with the influence of evolutionary theory and gave way to a sometimes fatalistic moralism.*]

For all their disillusionment with the real world, the genteel authors were never much interested in turning toward the supernatural for solace. They were sentimentally nostalgic about the religious certainty of past generations, but they cared only that much. Religion was always just an appurtenance of the comfortable and cultured world in which the genteel group moved. In youth they had had their brush with orthodoxy, but later they found it irrelevant. In maturity they forgot it and rested easy in the superiority of their own religious liberalism. They occasionally worried over religious issues, but their worries were mainly personal, not social. At best religion offered private reassurance and meaning.

For all of the group but [Charles Eliot Norton, an authority on late medieval literature and architecture], the origins of genteel religion were synonymous with anti-Puritanism. In *The Story of a Bad Boy,* [poet, novelist, and short story writer Thomas Bailey Aldrich] gave a typical view of the dreary New England Sabbath.[1] Stoddard, always more antagonistic toward the Puritan spirit than Aldrich, recalled that in his early life at Hingham, Massachusetts, his relatives and their friends actually looked forward to dying. It seemed to be "the most laudable industry of the time," he remarked.[2] Stoddard carried his attitude over into literature; both he and [poet and playwright George Henry Boker] avoided religious themes in their poetry. Boker undoubtedly agreed when Stoddard said that from an early age he "could never endure religious verse. . . ."[3] Aldrich felt the same way. He described George Washington Cable as "speckled all over with the most offensive piety. He drools religion. . . ."[4]

In his courting days in the early 1860's, Aldrich expressed a simple faith in the love of God and a piousness that was not shared by his friends.[5] But he, like they, had already moved beyond a belief in preachers, forms, or creeds.[6] They agreed that the way man lived was more important than what he believed.[7] Aldrich called his religion the "New Faith." Praising [critic Edmund Clarence] Stedman's book on the widely known liberal pastor O. B. Frothingham, he said Frothingham's church was the only one worth attending and declared he would join it if he lived in New York.[8]

Genteel religion had little theology. Stoddard confessed to Stedman's mother in 1867 that he had not been a "bit of a Christian" for years.[9] He and Boker called their beliefs "the new religion" and were smug about its superiority over the older "prejudices."[10] Boker had acquired a hearty contempt for orthodox religion when he attended Princeton from 1838 to 1842. The restrictiveness of the conservative Presbyterians who controlled the school pushed him in the opposite direction, and he became a convinced rationalist. Among his favorite writers were Condorcet, Voltaire, Juvenal, Boccaccio, and Rabelais.[11] Once his adolescent inquiry had exhausted itself, Boker was uninterested in religion. He praised the pantheism of Stoddard's poetry, but probably only for the irritation it caused the orthodox.[12] Theology figured in his long sonnet sequence only as an obstacle.[13]

[Bayard] Taylor's religion was less negative in intent, but he, too, had little theology. He always believed that nature showed evidence of some "informing and directing Will";

Darwin did not shake him from that.[14] He did not believe, at first, in the Unitarian doctrine that Christ was a man.[15] In time his Unitarianism became more evident, and in his last and major works it was marked. After the Civil War as Taylor searched for the middle way, he thought the question of religion transcended all others in importance. "Merely *negative* argument will not answer;" he wrote, "very few human souls can accept it, and then through their own inherent power, lift themselves upon *positive* ground." He even conceded the usefulness of orthodoxy; "nine-tenths of the morality we have (such as it is—but we cannot spare it) comes through that doctrine."[16]

Taylor's tolerance of orthodoxy was undoubtedly backtracking, but it never threatened his liberal religious principles. In *The Masque of the Gods,* the first of three religious plays he wrote in the last decade of his life, Taylor presented a naturalistic explanation for religion. Men have torn the mask from the face of the gods, he maintained, "to find the mock of the face of Man." But the gods were not just men's creations; they were also dim perceptions of some unknown and supreme God, whom Taylor called "A Voice From Space." Influenced by nineteenth-century evolutionary theories, Taylor saw a progressive development in religion through historical time. He believed that Christ was the highest manifestation of the religious spirit yet to appear, the only begotten son of the true God. But he added that Christ himself was not perfect and would be superseded in time. The play ended on the confident note "that in some riper time Thy perfect Truth shall come." The Christian religion would give way to the "*over*christian."[17]

In 1874 Taylor published a second religious drama, *The Prophet.*[18] Some controversy attended this play because of its obvious criticism of the Mormons, which Taylor minimized publicly but admitted privately.[19] The crisis of the play presents the institution of plural marriage as a tragedy. In an attempt to resist it, the Prophet's wife, a good and pure creature, searches her Bible in vain.[20] Mrs. Taylor's notes to the play reinforce a point that the play itself makes clear: Taylor's attack on religious literalism applied as well to orthodox Protestants as to Mormons.[21]

Prince Deukalion (1878) was Taylor's *magnum opus.* The play derives from classical mythology. Deukalion, the human representative of Prometheus, longs for the return of Prometheus's spirit to earth. In Act I, set in A.D. 300, man rejects nature. Christianity has replaced beauty, grace, and joy with "atoning pain and crowned repentance."[22] In Act II, set in the time of Dante, the slight cheer Deukalion finds in Dante's "scarcely self-confessed ambition" to be a poet is overshadowed by the apathy of his world.[23] Not until the romantic period of the nineteenth century, the setting for Act III, does man again exult in nature. He finds joy in the world, pride in the mind, strength to forget the ill and to work for the good, freedom to seek dreams, and patience to find truth and eternal beauty.

Yet the nineteenth century suffers from two inhibiting influences. One is dogmatic religion with its inherited passivity and otherworldliness, and the other is science.[24] In his play Taylor forces science to concede that the absence of proof is no deterrent to a belief in the doctrine of immortality. The hope of eternal life, he says in closing his play, is no "unproven solace" but

> Proven by its need!—
> By fates so large no fortune can fulfill;
> By wrong no earthly justice can atone;
> By promises of love that keep love pure;
> And all rich instincts, powerless of aim,
> Save chance, and time, and aspiration wed
> To freer forces, follow! By the trust
> Of the chilled Good that at life's very end
> Puts forth a root, and feels its blossom sure!
> Yea, by the law!—since every being holds
> Its final purpose in the primal cell,
> And here the radiant destiny o'erflows
> Its visible bounds, enlarges what it took
> From sources past discovery, and predicts
> No end, or, if an end, the end of all![25]

Taylor's *Prince Deukalion* closes on a very strong note of positive religion. We *must* have immortality, Taylor wrote in 1877, a year before his death. "If there is no future for me, a Devil, and not a God, governs the universe."[26]

Like Taylor, Aldrich was troubled about religion and especially about immortality. While editor of the *Atlantic* in the 1880's, he enforced a moratorium on religious questions. He rejected or asked authors to revise manuscripts that would have offended readers with traditional religious views.[27] He discouraged religious speculation on insoluble questions. It was useless to ponder whether God was good, he wrote to Horace Scudder in 1882.[28] He agreed with Tennyson's statement that "there lies more faith in honest doubt, believe me, than in half the creeds." Tennyson had "summed up the whole matter" to his satisfaction, and it needed no repeating.[29] Always regretful that the conviction of New England had disappeared, Aldrich envied his grandfather's "unquestioning faith." "He used to read a big Bible covered with rough green baize," Aldrich wrote, "and believed every word he read, even the typographical errors."[30] Even Stoddard, for all his hatred of the Puritans, thought old-time religion had been a comfort to the people and wished that "such hope, such certainty, such rest be ours."[31]

But Aldrich and Stoddard agreed that almost all religious belief was conjectural. The frontier at which Taylor's religion halted, the doctrine of the immortality of the soul, gave them pause, but did not deter either man. Aldrich frankly admitted that nothing could be known about "the other side of death,"[32] and when his son became fatally ill in 1903, his doubts were strengthened.[33] The death of a friend in 1899 depressed Stoddard similarly. "God rest his soul, if he has a soul, and there be a God," he wrote.[34] The disillusionment they felt when faced with the possibility that there was no God and no immortality was summed up by Aldrich:

> Valor, love, undoubting trust,
> Patience, and fidelity

> Lie beneath this carven stone.
> If the end of these be dust,
> And their doom oblivion,
> *Then is Life a mockery.*[35]

Almost every figure in the genteel group was willing at least to toy with the idea that life was indeed a mockery—every one, that is, except [*Century* editor Richard Watson] Gilder. Youngest of all the group, he exemplified the final attempt of genteel culture to resuscitate traditional religious views. Gilder's poems, his editorials in the *Century,* and his letters frequently lapsed into a vapid optimism that was as much softheaded as softhearted. He himself admitted as much and explained it as an inheritance from his "ancestral orthodox religionist strain." He thought that the Methodist Episcopalianism of his father and the Huguenot strain in his mother's religious background had given him a certain complacency. "Untoward events surely cut me, depress me," he wrote in 1909, "but a spirit of fatalism—an appreciation or apparent discernment in events of a benevolent fate—has done much to keep me from despair, even from overanxiety."[36] Gilder's confidence was founded in his belief in the existence of a fundamental law that manifested the divine plan. Throughout his life he clung tenaciously to that belief although he considered himself a religious liberal. In 1894 he wrote to Helen Keller that he was a Christian only in the broad sense that did not depend upon the "obfuscations of theology." Nevertheless, perhaps theology had "its uses, like the equator and other respectables."[37]

Gilder believed that God himself did not change, but that man's perceptions of Him did. He hoped that what men saw as a "Mysterious Force" in ancient times had been replaced by a "friendlier plan."[38] Interpreting the evolution of religion in what he thought was a Darwinistic fashion, Gilder argued in the *Century* that it was nobler to think of God as coherent and logical than as capricious.[39] Gilder recognized that Darwin could be read differently. Even in the midst of joy, as Gilder declared in one of his poems, reflections on the cosmos were depressing.

> The awful void of space wherein our earth,
> An atom in the unending whirl of stars,
> Circles, all helpless, to a nameless doom;
> The swift, indifferent marshalling of fate
> Whereby the world moves on, rewarding vice
> And punishing angelic innocence
> As't were the crime of crimes; the brute, dull, slow
> Persistence in the stifled mind of man
> Of forces that drive all his being back
> Into the slime; the silent cruelty
> Of nature, that doth crush the unseen soul
> Hidden within its sensitive shell of flesh;
> The anguish and the sorrow of all time,
> These are forever with me. . . . .[40]

But Gilder hastened to conclude his poem by recalling his mother's face, which reassured him that the right must reign somewhere. The sentimentality of his conclusion makes suspect the "unescapable anguish" which, in another of his poems, he declared was the lot of mankind.[41]

Gilder repeatedly blamed scholars for his momentary doubts. They wearied him, he complained in "The Doubter"; they "hurt and bruised" his soul and confused his brain.[42] He decided to salvage his soul and his sanity by stifling his doubts on one fundamental issue—the divinity of Christ.[43] The pragmatic habit of mind increasingly appealed to Gilder as his convictions about the fundamental moral law wavered. Without ever explicitly denying the existence of such a law, he turned to speaking of the uses of religion. He suppressed his skepticism about the divinity of Christ by contending that Christ gave to existence a "reason sane."[44] Like Taylor, he asserted that Christianity could never be discarded because it provided an "aid to moral effort which no mere system of ethics, however evolved, claims to supply."[45] To think of Christ as a mere human being was for Gilder "the blackest thought the human brain may harbor."[46]

Gilder tried especially hard to discover a justification for the doctrine of immortality. In looking to the life principle itself for some basis for this belief, he seemed to reach toward philosophical idealism. But his justifications, unlike Royce's, were not rational; he felt that the heart could see where the mind could not. Because the human heart cried out, "Naught is but life," Gilder concluded that the force of its declaration implied there was truth in the feeling. Where reason could offer nothing, the heart maintained that life was immortal.[47] From this suggestion of immortality, Gilder did not deduce the traditional Christian heaven. From the nature of life exemplified on earth, Gilder felt that pain and suffering were inherent in it. Wherever there was life, on earth or beyond it, there would be pain. "For in all worlds," he wrote, "there is no Life without a pang, and can be naught." Adhering to the transcendental naturalism that characterized his discussion of the life principle, he avoided traditional theological explanations of evil. Pain was a simple fact of the human condition. Men, being what they were, could not comprehend happiness without sadness. The latter was the "eternal cost" of the former.[48]

There was neither joy nor conviction in Gilder's affirmations. They did not console him or save him from drifting into a passive agnosticism like that of his friends. He resisted more earnestly than they, but in 1905 he confessed that, despite all he had written, "if put on the rack of categorical questioning I fear I would prove a sad enough 'agnostic.'" His particular dilemma was that the "old leaven" of his fathers lurked in his mind and his heart. The New England cosmology went deep, and Gilder admitted that he could not help thinking "in and with" its symbols.[49]

The other genteel poets discovered their symbols elsewhere. The natural life, not the supernatural, attracted them. Yet even nature, once an avenue to the divine, had lost its ability to comfort. Stoddard and Taylor, like Stedman, agreed that Wordsworth's vision of the brotherhood of man and nature aptly described only immature life. Stoddard was impressed with Wordsworth's "Ode on Inti-

mations of Immortality." He sketched his own childhood delight in nature: "The gush of feelings, pure and undefiled, / The deep and rapturous gladness. / The nameless sadness, / The vision that overpowered the visionary child." In adulthood, too, his life was "blent" with nature's. "The soul of man detects and sympathizes / With its old shapes of matter, long outworn; / And matter, too, to new sensations born, / Detects the soul of man with spiritual purposes."[50] But in 1870, disregarding the fact that he had written a good deal of it, Stoddard complained that he did not like nature verse. "God made the country—well, what of it? . . . I am not a bird, or a fish, as far as I know, and I want to see men, houses, streets, and I want fresh newspapers and books, old and new. I want the feel of the pavement under my feet, and sight of the multitudinous life of cities before my eyes."[51]

Nevertheless, Stoddard did not stop praising nature and criticizing city life after 1870.[52] His early objections to Calvinist theology remained with him all his life in the form of a pantheistic identification of God and nature. Despite his strong religious skepticism, he never quite shook off the belief that nature was a source of truth and morals and an object of beauty.[53] But Stoddard knew, as Stedman had written in *The Nature and Elements of Poetry,* that nature did not participate sympathetically in human sentiment and passion. The belief that it did was only a "pathetic fallacy," said Stedman, using Ruskin's term. The poet must see that "the chances of life seem much at haphazard. . . . Rain still falls upon the just and the unjust. . . . The natural law appears the wind of destiny. Man, in his conflicts with the elements, with tyranny, with superstition, with society, most of all with his own passions, is still frequently overthrown. It *seems* as if the good are not necessarily rewarded except by their own virtue, or, if self-respecting, except by their own pride, holding to the last; the evil are not cast down, unless by their own self-contempt, and the very evil flourish without conscience or remorse. . . . Thus Nature, in her drama, has no temporary pity, no regret."[54]

Toward the end of his life Stedman expressed this view in a rather striking image from the animal world. On one occasion he pictured nature as a lioness who batters man playfully at first, but "soon shows she means business" and smashes him. The lioness is as little concerned with her victim as the blacksmith at the anvil, or the potter at the wheel. Nature—"so resolute, so implacable, the unnatural Mother"—cared only for the species, not the individual.[55] But man did have some sort of a "true and spiritual rapport" with Nature, and therefore it was "just as well" that some should cling to the belief in a sympathetic universe. The force of emotion dictated it, and feeling was perhaps truer and deeper than thought.[56]

Stedman and his friends, though they occasionally voiced romantic complaints about life in the city, were city men at heart. Their experience had not prepared them to see rural and small-town America as places of emotional impoverishment, a conception that dominated American literature after 1910, but neither had it prepared them to write the traditional romantic praise for nature that is sometimes evident in their poetry. There, where metaphors suggesting peacefulness, unselfishness, and creativity are repeatedly invoked, nature figures as little more than a refuge from the city. Even when the genteel group elaborated its myth of a pure and homogeneous rural populace in pre-Jacksonian days, it confined the potency of nature to the past.

American religion did assimilate the Darwinian concept of evolution and survive, but for the genteel poets, at least, the romantic view of nature could not. The loss was crucial for them because in their own intellectual development nature had assumed many of the traditional functions of religion. Stoddard, for one, could no longer be reassured. Faced with the fact that man was a transient being, Stoddard came to believe that nature, far from being a repository for certitudes, was just as transient as man himself.[57] Obsessed with this belief, Stoddard devoted poem after poem to the prospect of death. "For what was Earth but the great tomb of men, / And suns and planets but sepulchral urns / Filled with the awful ashes of the Past?"[58]

If Stoddard's gloom was especially acute, he was not alone in it. All the genteel poets clung to romanticism without the support they once had had in nature. The eighteenth century had found comfort in the fact that nature, even if cold and mechanical, was unchanging by virtue of the eternal laws that controlled it. But the genteel poets followed the romantics of the early nineteenth century in seeking to humanize the mechanical universe by projecting human passions into it. From their success, Stoddard in particular reaped bitter fruit. He had made nature human, but as a consequence, he had made it mortal. Nature now, like men, suffered under the sentence of death; the cycle of the seasons lost its dignity. The order of nature was evidence of truth, yes, but of the truth that there was only one truth—death. The very unification of nature and man achieved by romanticism bred new alienation.

For as Stoddard's age enforced clarity of vision upon him he knew that the differences, not the similarities, between men and nature were what counted. Stoddard had preached the rich and full life; he had meant the individual life. From birth he had been temperamentally unable—although he tried repeatedly—to understand that a general law possessed dignity precisely because it was general and spared no individual. That Stoddard agonized over death, and nature did not, was all that mattered. For consolation he turned to Stoicism. He found in Marcus Aurelius an awareness that human life was "worthless" and the entire universe nothing more than "ebb and flow."[59] Ironically, the romantic rebel came to advise men to retire into themselves to find "the seat of all tranquility." Rest, not emotional intensity, was Stoddard's final goal in life. Deliberately, he put behind him the activity of his youth, and turned instead to "the good ordering of the mind."[60]

Although Aldrich and Boker were free of Stoddard's funereal tone, the transience of existence suggested to them

also that whatever meaning tradition had brought to life had largely vanished. In a world of constant and undefined change, certainties were few. The gods were vague, they believed, and the purposes of existence entirely conjectural. Furthermore, if one believed that no new knowledge would show the way to truth—and certainly the new science had not done so—one necessarily became pessimistic. As man matured, it was his portion to suffer this disillusionment. As Aldrich wrote to a friend in 1904, "When one is young, one doesn't know any better than to be happy."[61] Forty years earlier, too, he had been convinced that knowing human nature meant knowing sorrowful things.[62] Stoddard summed the matter up in *The King's Bell* by permitting the bell of happiness to ring only at the hour of death. The King declares:

> Happy, alas, who's happy here on earth?
> Why man is wretched from his very birth.
> Frail as a flower's his hold on life, none know
> Whether the human bud will fade or flow;
> For hours on hours his lips are sealed in sleep,
> And when at last he wakes—it is to weep.[63]

Aldrich was well aware of the doubt and pessimism that marked the end of the nineteenth century.[64] But neither he nor his friends would have permitted any mere historical explanation for their pessimism. They would have insisted that it transcended time and place. Against the cosmic optimism that Royce attempted to revive in their day, they maintained that however good human life might be, there was profound sorrow in human existence. They were conservative enough to believe that the conditions that made for progress or retrogression did not touch that fact. Elizabeth Stoddard, who was more extreme in her sentiments that her husband's friends, was also more candid. Her analysis was simple. "Oh my God," she wrote to Stedman, "what an awful blunder life is, worse than a crime."[65]

Neither extreme of genteel religious thinking, the attempt of Taylor and Gilder to prop up the traditional idealism nor the decline of Stoddard and his circle into an emasculating pessimism upon finding nature indifferent to them, made any contribution to the theological controversies of the 1880's and 1890's. The genteel group had little contact with the Social Gospel movement to turn Protestantism from a religion of personal and private concern into a religion of moderate social action. Although reformers like Washington Gladden, Richard Ely, and Theodore T. Munger occasionally wrote for the *Century,* the religious liberalism of genteel culture remained within the economically and socially conservative Unitarian church.[66]

Charles Eliot Norton, always his own man, is an exception here, too. A rationalist by training and conviction, Norton was never tempted by emotional or intuitive appeals for the preservation of traditional religion. But neither did he permit his own doubts to interfere with what he regarded as the self-evident obligations of men toward one another. Uninterested in what interested the genteel poets, nature, and interested in what did not interest them, science, Norton was able to relinquish the one and base his hopes for the future on the other.

In the middle of the nineteenth century Norton's social and political ideas rested on a belief in a fundamental moral law. But Norton did not look to nature for evidence of the fundamental law. In fact, he pointedly distinguished the sphere of nature, where the laws of scientific determinism held, from the sphere of man, which was free and self-determined. Norton never explored the source and nature of the moral law and the manner in which men perceived it. The topic would have struck him as too metaphysical, and, like his friends, he had a prejudice against abstract philosophy. He preferred a philosophy like Santayana's that turned "speculative inquiry to moral ends—in other words to the uses of life."[67] Yet he rejected William James's pragmatism. Norton apparently misread James, for he thought pragmatism worth "just about as much as the systems of metaphysical speculation which have preceded it. . . ."[68] He did not understand that for all James's efforts to legitimitize the will to believe, James was no more interested in theology for its own sake than he was. Both men searched for a morality that could be founded only in human experience.

Norton was reared as a Unitarian. His father was a famous minister of the pre-War period and a fierce opponent of Emerson. Charles was no lover of Transcendentalism either; he dismissed it as a lot of muddled thinking. But by 1867 he was willing to say of Unitarianism what Emerson had said thirty years before, that the Unitarian protest against dogma and creed had nearly done its work and was in danger itself of "hardening" into a church. "The deepest religious thought," Norton wrote, "the wisest religious life is outside of Unitarianism at present, is not to be found, indeed, within the limit of any churches." Any conformity of doctrine whatsoever, he thought, must be abandoned. "We must have a free Church, to which all who are seeking the highest and best they know, and are trying to express their highest convictions in life, may come and be welcomed on equal terms, whether they call themselves Unitarians or Trinitarians, Christians or unbelievers."[69]

What Norton had in mind was a kind of moral society. If men were to have "utter freedom of individual opinion," common ideas could not be the basis for organization because no creed was broad enough for any two men. He admitted that his ideas were open to the charge that they failed to distinguish between religion and morality. And he admitted that religious and moral duties were "often indistinguishable." But he thought that religion was a "matter of absolute requirements; morals is a science and practice of the higher expediency."[70]

Norton's notion of moral expediency was not meant to conflict with the idea of a fundamental moral law. It simply restated his conviction that morality must devote itself to social concerns. Norton's free church would be a loose fellowship of all men for developing the religious character of the community and for "inspiring and regulating active efforts for the improvement of man." It would apply the spirit of religion to the difficulties of society. Its work would be "practical humanity."[71]

In another sense, Norton meant something revolutionary by moral expediency. Until the end of the nineteenth century Norton was unable to free himself from the typical Victorian and genteel belief that morality depended on organized religion. His arguments for a free church questioned it, certainly, but in 1875 he thought that the liberality of his own ideas would be a danger to America if widespread. Unlike England, where the aristocracy afforded "a fixed standard in the midst of the fluctuations of personal convictions or popular emotions," America had to rely upon extragovernmental organizations like the church for social order.[72] Yet in 1869 Norton had written to Ruskin that if a man in America were persecuted for atheism, he should "feel bound to declare myself on his side." The question of the existence of God had to be regarded as an open one, he felt, "and as one *which had no intrinsic relation with moral character.* I believe an Atheist may be as good, as enlightened, as unselfish, and may conduct his whole life from motives as pure, and under sanctions as strong as a Theist."[73] In 1897 Norton finally made himself clear. Casting aside all nostalgia for the past, he declared that "the loss of religious faith among the most civilized portion of the race is a step from childishness toward maturity." He had no fear for the morality of the race. "Our morals seem to me the result and expression of the *secular experience of mankind.* As such they have a solid foundation."[74]

When Norton spoke of morals as the "higher expediency" he meant that they ought to be calculated by means of liberal rationalism. He defended Bentham's utilitarian system against the attacks of Sir Henry Maine. He believed that Bentham's utility principle had to be weighed against customs ideas, and motives, but, granted that, he would apply it not only to laws but to morals as well. He admitted that there were difficulties in determining the objective happiness of a people, but insisted that utilitarianism was the best way. There was no such thing as "*absolute*" morality, he wrote in 1875.

What had happened to the fundamental moral law? During the Civil War, Norton had been certain that man was subject to "the purposes of God in the creation of the world." He had denied the Positivistic assumption that social laws could be discovered that would explain man's actions. Man was a "higher power" than the nature that surrounded him. Free men's actions were the stuff of history; although men were subject to "moral connections," they were not bound by scientific causation.[75] But as Norton lost all interest in religion and grew increasingly worried about the state of civilization in America, he turned to science as his only hope for the future. By 1878 he wrote that "the thought of any who have any capacity for thought" was moving toward Positivism.[76] When he had rejected guesses about the beginning and end of existence as "altogether futile," he was ready (in 1902) to assert that human thought and action were explainable. "If we could collect enough knowledge," he wrote, "our faculties, as they at present exist, would be sufficient to enable us to account, i believe, for what is now inexplicable to us in human conduct."[77]

In the 1880's Norton had been depressed because "the whole view of human existence which the world has held up to this time seems to be changing, and the new view is not yet clearly outlined. . . ." But he felt that although man would have fewer "glowing illusions" about himself, he would be more independent because of it.[78] He granted that the substitution of natural motives for supernatural ones would cause "considerable damage" to popular morality, but he thought eventually a "better order" would replace the "chaotic" and "unstable" civilization of the times.[79]

In explaining the radical transformation in his own views, Norton, like the genteel poets, gave major credit to Darwin. Darwin's recognition that nature was "clumsy, wasteful, blundering, low and horribly cruel" led Norton to believe that the moral process was no better.[80] "You expect less of men when you look at them not as a little lower than the angels, but as a little higher than the anthropoid apes."[81] He expected no comfort from a dead theology, but he was uneasy with the new cosmology.[82] Unlike the genteel poets, Norton seems genuinely to have wanted to accept life at it was. He could not always, however, resist the current pessimism. "The universe is unintelligible," he wrote in 1906. "We have no faculties for even forming rational theories concerning its nature, its origin or its purpose. Our words—'purpose,' for instance, have no significance in regard to it. Why should we, little atoms on a little atom, hope to account for our existence?"[83] He took grim comfort in recognizing "how absolutely insignificant and unimportant a part of the universe . . . is any individual life." In the teeth of the fact, he yet asserted that the aim of a good man should be "to make the best of himself for the service of others."[84] The sanctions for morality had collapsed, but men's needs allowed no argument.

Norton had been reared with deep respect for the New England tradition of public service. He was totally incapable of protesting the "despotism of citizenship" that so distressed the genteel poets. Although he would have substituted *Moral* for *Christian* he continued to believe, as Gilder put it in a speech in 1906, that whatever men "may believe or disbelieve in the realm of theology, [they] cannot doubt that bad citizenship is non-Christian."[85]

As a consequence, however, of relinquishing his belief in a fundamental moral law, Norton became all the more concerned with the immediate facts of American society, particularly American culture. In 1879 he wrote to an English friend that he felt "half starved" in America, but that he could be of more service there than in England.[86] By that time he had virtually given up any hope of improving American political or economic life, and he concentrated his efforts on raising the level of American culture. He thought that endeavor particularly important because he believed that culture was "the only real test of the spiritual qualities of a race, and the standard by which ultimately its share in the progress of humanity must be measured."[87] And in America more than elsewhere the arts were needed,

"for nowhere in the civilized world are the practical concerns of life more engrossing; nowhere are the conditions of life more prosaic; nowhere is the poetic spirit less evident, and the love of beauty less diffused. The concern for beauty, as the highest end of work, and as the noblest expression of life, hardly exists among us, and forms no part of our character as a nation."[88] Norton emphasized that the tradition of culture had never been more than "weak" and "limited" in America.[89] But the decline of even that limited tradition after the Civil War led Norton to write to Ruskin that he wanted his Harvard students to realize that "we have in our days nothing to say, that silence befits us, that the arts of beauty are not for us to practice;—and seeing this to resolve so to live that another generation may begin to be happier than we."[90]

Norton did not doubt that the passage of time had made for some progress, but he questioned "whether the increase in knowledge and mastery of nature is to be counted as true progress. . . . Is there a moral advance at all in proportion to the material?"[91] He admitted that prosperity had made physical comfort more widespread but he felt that Americans tended to confuse the "free gift of nature" and the benefits of increased knowledge with personal talent and capacity. They claimed a "sense of mastery over the world and fate" that was not only optimistic, but fatalistic.[92]

And the spread of democracy, when added to prosperity, threatened to lower the moral standards of the republic "to the level of those whose moral sense is in their trowsers." Democracy did work, to be sure, but "ignobly, ignorantly, brutally," as well as in better ways.[93] In the short run, Norton did not hope for more, because he was deeply distrustful of democracy itself. When Cleveland's message on the Venezuelan boundary dispute was issued, Norton voiced his contempt for it in the course of a general broadside against democracy. "It is the rise of the uncivilized," he wrote to Leslie Stephen, "whom no school education can suffice to provide with intelligence and reason."[94] The American public was "becoming less open to any teaching but that of its own experience. The scorn of wisdom, the rejection of authority, are part and parcel of the process of development of the democracy. . . . It seems to me not unlikely that for a considerable time to come there will be an increase of lawlessness and of public folly."[95]

Technology and democracy had combined to widen the gulf between present and past, but Norton worried that no past was left at all.[96] It was the appalling newness of the modern world that overwhelmed him. It was no wonder, he thought, that the great majority of Americans were shallow, trivial, and materialistic. Too many Americans had come up in too short a time from the "lower orders of society" that were wholly oppressed, ignorant and servile.[97] Economic opportunity, as well as political and economic institutions, propelled the immigrant up the social ladder too rapidly for the good of the nation. Americans never got to feel the advantages and restraints of civilization, Norton complained; their virtues were not the civic virtues.

Norton did not look to the American educational system to remedy the shortcomings of American society. He believed it was only a fallacy to think that the schools could educate anyone; they could only give instruction. Without proper influence in the home and community, Norton expected the schools to do little.[98] He did approve of efforts to include cultural, as well as intellectual and moral, education within the curriculum.[99] He worried, despite his Positivism, that American education gave undue emphasis to mathematics and the physical sciences.[100]

Norton never stopped hoping that science might provide a direction for the future. Nevertheless, it is quite clear that the world of science, as it was developing in his day, repelled him. When a friend of his died in 1897, Norton wrote to E. L. Godkin, the editor of the *Nation*, that he considered himself "the solitary representative of a generation more interesting, and I cannot but think of far better breeding both intellectually and morally than that which takes it place. We have able and good men left, and perhaps they will do as good service as their predecessors, but they lack the breadth and charm of the elder generation. The old men represented the humanities, the young men stand for science so-called."[101] What Norton respected as science was the science of a man like John Stuart Mill, a man of wide reading and sensibility. He was notably unsympathetic to the professionalism that was establishing itself in American universities near the end of the century, whether that professionalism operated in science or in literature. He was frank to state his preference for the "old-fashioned literary culture" of the mid-nineteenth century.[102] He anticipated that posterity would look back to that time "as we look back to pre-Revolutionary times, as presenting a picture of delightful simplicity of manners and innocence of living."[103]

Unable by temperament to be enthusiastic about the Positivism to which he was intellectually committed, Norton nevertheless avoided the typical genteel extremes of self-pity and hypocrisy. Because he recognized and admitted the evisceration of the intellectual structure of genteel culture, he was left in the end with little to do but advocate the gentle civilizer, manners. He acknowledged the difficulty even of that limited endeavor, and could never have agreed with Gilder that gentility might cure not only the superficial ills of society, but its deeper evils.[104] Gilder, of course, continued to believe, or continued to wish to believe, in a fundamental moral law, whereas Norton did not. Without that reassuring frame, the enterprise of civilizing men could only be a hollow endeavor. Gentility, bereft of religion, could do little but amble to its own defense. Whatever vigor it once possessed, it finally forgot. There was no need to force genteel culture out of history; by 1910 it had no real resources left to contest the sentence of retirement.

Notes

1. Aldrich, *Prose Works*, V, 66-70.

2. Stoddard, *Recollections*, p. 6.

3. *Ibid.*, pp. 32-33.

4. To Woodberry, March 5, 1893, HLH.

5. To Lillian Aldrich, Oct. 21, 1863, Oct. 28, 1963, April 4, 1863, Aug. 4, 1864, and Aug. 5, 1864, HLH.

6. To Lillian Aldrich, Aug. 17, 1864, HLH. See also Stoddard, *Songs of Summer*, p. 104; Aldrich, *Poems*, pp. 55-56.

7. Aldrich, *Poems*, pp. 881-89; Stoddard, *Poems*, pp. 382-85.

8. To Stedman, Nov. 16, 1876, CUL.

9. To Mrs. Kinney, May 23, 1867, CUL.

10. Boker to Stoddard, Aug. 12, 1850, PUL.

11. Bradley, pp. 15-17.

12. Boker to Stoddard, March 3, 1869, NYPL. See Stoddard, *Poems*, pp. 288-90.

13. Boker, *Sonnets, passim.*

14. Taylor, *At Home*, I, 216-17.

15. Taylor, *Lands of the Saracen*, pp. 84-85.

16. Schultz, pp. 140-41.

17. Taylor, *Dramatic Works*, pp. 173, 183, 188-89.

18. *Ibid.*, pp. 1-164.

19. Hansen-Taylor and Scudder, II, 635, 664-65.

20. Taylor considered this the key to his play; Taylor to Marie Taylor, Dec. 4, 1874, HLH.

21. Mrs. Taylor's notes to the play make it clear that Taylor's major argument was directed at religious literalism; *Dramatic Works*, pp. 323-45.

22. Taylor, *Dramatic Works*, pp. 203, 210, 220.

23. *Ibid.*, pp. 227, 230, 233-35, 250.

24. *Ibid.*, pp. 267, 274, 268-69, 286-87.

25. *Ibid.*, pp. 287, 299.

26. Hansen-Taylor and Scudder, II, 716-17.

27. To Richard Grant White, Sept. 14, 1883, HLH.

28. June 19, 1882, HLH.

29. To "Dear Sir," May 7, 1886, YCAL.

30. To William Dean Howells, May 12, 1902, HLH.

31. Stoddard, *Poems*, pp. 91-92.

32. Aldrich, *Poems*, pp. 19-21, 404.

33. To Francis Bartlett, Feb. 23, 1903, HLH.

34. To Alexander V. Stout Anthony, May 1, 1899, HLH.

35. Aldrich, *Poems*, p. 378.

36. Rosamond Gilder, p. 476; see also pp. 436-37.

37. *Ibid.*, p. 356.

38. Gilder, *Poems*, pp. 247-49.

39. *The Century*, II (1882), 790-92.

40. Gilder, *Poems,* p. 265.

41. *Ibid.,* pp. 247-49.

42. *Ibid.,* p. 245.

43. *Ibid.,* pp. 177-79.

44. *Ibid.*

45. *The Century,* III (1882-83), 460-62.

46. Gilder, *Poems,* pp. 239-42.

47. *Ibid.,* pp. 68-69.

48. *Ibid.,* pp. 181-85; Rosamond Gilder, pp. 423-24.

49. Rosamond Gilder, p. 425.

50. Stoddard, *Songs of Summer,* pp. 56-79.

51. To Stedman, June 15, 1870, CUL.

52. See his later praise of nature in *Poems,* pp. 302-4, 317-18, 492-94.

53. *Ibid.,* pp. 492-94.

54. Stedman, *Nature and Elements,* pp. 102-3.

55. Stedman and Gould, II, 584.

56. *Ibid.,* 581.

57. The following discussion of Stoddard's concept of transience is based on *Songs of Summer,* pp. 5, 7, 20, 30, 40, 45, 48, 56, 87-88, 91, 116, 117, 145-46; *Poems,* pp. 18, 42-44, 48, 305-6, 306-7, 311, 315-16, 319, 323-34, 336-51, 491, 498; *Lion's Cub,* 32-34.

58. "The Dead Master," *Poems,* p. 491.

59. Stoddard, "The Morals of Marcus Aurelius," in *Lion's Cub,* pp. 27-32.

60. *Poems,* pp. 392-93; See also pp. 390-91, 395-96.

61. To Francis Bartlett, Jan. 2, 1904, HLH.

62. To Lillian, (1863), HLH.

63. Stoddard, *Poems,* pp. 191-92. Aldrich spoke of sleep as a rest from that "sweet bitter world we know by day"; *Poems,* p. 394.

64. *Prose Works,* VII, 99.

65. N.d., CUL.

66. *The Century,* IV (1883), 633-34; V (1883-84), 784-85; IX (1885-86), 51-59, 737-49; XVII (1889-90), 89-90, 938-40.

67. Norton and Howe, II, 356.

68. *Ibid.,* 412. Norton's letters to William James in HLH were all written after 1900; they are friendly, but skeptical of all philosophy.

69. Norton and Howe, I, 294-96.

70. "Religious Liberty," *North American Review,* CIV (1867), 586-97.

71. "The Church and Religion," *North American Review,* CVI (1868), 376-96.

72. Norton and Howe, II, 53-54.

73. To John Ruskin, Oct. 8, 1869, HLH. Italics mine.

74. Norton and Howe, II, 248-49. Italics mine.

75. "Goldwin Smith," *North American Review,* XCIX (1864), 523-39; *Nation,* I (1865), 407-9.

76. To George E. Woodberry, Sept. 27, 1878, HLH.

77. To J. B. Harrison, Nov. 17, 1902, HLH.

78. Norton and Howe, II, 182-83.

79. *Ibid.,* 347.

80. *Ibid.,* 335-36.

81. *Ibid.,* 167-68.

82. *Ibid.,* 304-5.

83. To Samuel Gray Ward, Nov. 20, 1906, HLH.

84. To J. B. Harrison, Nov. 17, 1902, HLH.

85. "On Citizenship," Address to Presbyterian Social Union of Philadelphia, Feb. 26, 1906, NYPL.

86. Norton and Howe, II, 91-92.

87. *Forum,* VII (1889), 30-40, 89.

88. Norton and Howe, II, 8-9.

89. *Ibid.,* 401.

90. Feb. 10, 1874, HLH. The passage is omitted from Norton and Howe II, 34. In 1905 Norton wrote that he had been reluctant to join the American Academy of Arts and Letters because he thought the situation of American art and the nature of the national character would prevent the Academy from being of real service. To Robert Underwood Johnson, Nov. 14, 1905, LAAAL.

91. Norton and Howe, II, 297-98.

92. "Some Aspects of Civilization in America," *Forum,* XX (1896), 641-51.

93. Norton and Howe, II, 165-66.

94. *Ibid.,* 236-37.

95. *Ibid.,* 243-44.

96. To Samuel Gray Ward, March 3, 1904, HLH.

97. To J. B. Harrison, March 13, 1894, HLH.

98. "Some Aspects of Civilization in America," *Forum,* XX (1896), pp. 641-51.

99. "Educational Value of the History of the Fine Arts," *Educational Review,* IX (1895), 343-48.

100. "Education at the Great English Public Schools," *Nation,* I (1865), 149-50.

101. Jan. 3, 1897, HLH.

102. Norton and Howe, II, 401.

103. "Waste," *Nation,* II (1866), 301-2.

104. *The Century,* XXXVI (1899), 322-23.

Heinz Ickstadt (essay date 1983)

SOURCE: "Concepts of Society and the Practice of Fiction—Symbolic Responses to the Experience of Change in

Late Nineteenth Century America," in *Impressions of a Gilded Age: The American Fin de Siecle*, edited by Marc Chenetier and Rob Kroes, Amerika Institut, Universiteit van Amsterdam, 1983, pp. 77-95.

[*In the following essay, Ickstadt argues that in response to the increasing fragmentation of American society in the Gilded Age, many authors attempted to create a sense of community through utopian symbolism.*]

What has fascinated me for quite some time is the obvious affinity between the aesthetic, the moral, and the social imagination in late 19th century America. The proliferation of literary utopias comes to mind immediately, of course, but is only one of many factors—towards the end of the century one of diminishing importance at that. Howells's defence of realism was an argument for the novel's and the writer's social function, and his concern for the right shape of fiction cannot be separated from an implied ideal of conduct and from his passionate reflection on the right shape of society. On the other hand, practical reformers as well as social theorists not only tried their hand at fiction at times (Henry Demarest Lloyd's occasional satiric fables and utopian sketches are a case in point), they imagined the new society, as it was slowly taking shape about them, in terms of creation and aesthetic consummation, of life achieving the perfection of art.

We find, therefore, a surprising continuity between the different areas of social and symbolic action, and of social and aesthetic conceptualisation—a continuity at least partially explained by a growing desire for social coherence that arose from the pressures and disruptions of the new urban-industrial experience. This need for social cohesion is evident in the tremendous energy invested by all groups and classes in the organisation of their social and economic lives (in the foundation of clubs, unions, cooperative associations). It is evident in the effort of an intellectual elite to break out of its cultured seclusion and to offset the centrifugal pull of a society—increasingly divided along lines of class, language, culture—by descending into the lower regions of the chaotically expanding cities. It is further evident, on the symbolic level of narrative actions, in the advancement of the frontiers of society—i.e. of an area civilised by communication and self-control—into the new urban wilderness; and, finally, in the development of a philosophy of organic society—of a social order created, maintained and controlled by cooperation and communicative interaction.

These different elements were occasionally made conscious as a general consensus through the creation and interpretation of a number of public symbols of which the White City of the Columbian Exposition in Chicago in 1893 was by far the most important. It not only took hold of the popular imagination to a degree now hard to comprehend (for some it seemed nothing less than the "Heavenly City" come to earth), it also became the organising image of many tracts and novels of reform, entered, in fact, common rhetoric as a ready symbol of urban optimism and faith in the creative potential of the social body.[1]

If seen with quasi-Veblenesque detachment, the White City, of course, gave no reason for such idealisation. Clearly the product of an alliance between business and the arts, it seemed only a special instance of what Veblen, some years later, was to call "conspicuous consumption" since, under the conditions of a quasi-feudal rule of money, culture was the mere adornment of the rich and economically powerful. But even if this was a correct assessment of its ultimate function in the social process, as a fact of consciousness the White City meant much more: Set against the Black City of uncontrolled industrial expansion, ugliness, poverty, crime, immigrant violence, political corruption, it was seen as a prefigurative image of a new and still evolving urban order in which the general public, shocked by social conflict into an awareness of change and crisis, eagerly if controversially tried to recognise and redefine itself.

In the last instance, the White City visibly embodied an ideology of civilisation whose diverse and conflicting interpretations revolved around a dominant binary structure—that of the "savage" and the "civilised." Against the architectural evidence of "rampant individualism," of "chaos incident to rapid growth," Daniel Burnham—the architect of the White City—had set the neo-classical values of design, order and balance: aesthetic categories which can be easily translated into terms of moral and social hierarchy. As a metaphor of moral order the White City describes an inner space of controlled, of civilised experience—centred in Will, surveyed by Reason, organised by Memory and Foresight into temporal coherence. Outside this closed system of time, character and conduct, life is a moral wilderness, anarchic and incoherent, governed by chance, instinct, selfishness—an aimless and idle drifting from moment to isolated moment. Moral is not, of course, identical with social hierarchy (in fact, it is an ideological weapon that may be turned upwards as well as down) but the White City, seen as it was by some as a "flower of civilization" implied a perspective of genteel Social Darwinism that looked at lower-class life down along an evolutionary scale as to the animal or the barbaric.

However, there were also much more radical interpretations which made the "dream city" a symbol of social unity and cooperation to be achieved by an extension of order—the integration of chaos into design. In this context, Frederic Law Olmstead's transformation of South Chicago's swamps into the garden landscape of the exposition grounds became the quasi-archetypal image of the civilising process itself—of civilisation as reform. Jane Addams's and Graham Taylor's descent into the abyss of city life "to be swallowed and digested, to disappear into the bulk of the people" were therefore highly symbolic acts of personal and social regeneration. Their settlement on moral and social frontiers, Hull House and the Chicago Commons, were outposts of civilisation in a wilderness that, if it was dangerous, also promised the excitement of a more spontaneous and deeper life. But most important, Hull House and the Commons established a middle ground of communication between classes and ethnic groups that symbolically anticipated the future urban-industrial democracy.

For Addams, as for many others, the White City was not an escape into utopian fantasy but an image for action: It implied a commitment to an idea of society, at once urban and communal, whose outlines were already visible but that still had to be collectively created. To them the experience of the city was a deeply ambivalent one, yet it also raised their curiosity about the future:

> Merely mingling with the crowd [thus an early contributor to the *American Journal of Sociology*] that passes along the thoroughfares gives a man a different idea of his personality. He feels both less and greater than when alone . . . He has caught a glimpse of a larger self realized in the activities of those about him. He recognizes the city as . . . a spiritual unity, a unity not yet complete, but growing, enlarging, and striving for the realization of an adjusted order in which all men share.[2]

In what follows I shall concentrate on two questions mainly: How does the experience of the aesthetic, moral and social chaos of the new urban-industrial reality change the conceptualisation of society? For this I shall discuss, however briefly, social concepts and ideals of Henry Demarest Lloyd, Charles Horton Cooley and the early George Herbert Mead. My second question will then deal with fiction proper: How is the idea of social order symbolically enacted in the novel, and how does the experience of discontinuity and change enter into its symbolisation of social order? Here I shall concentrate on *A Hazard of New Fortunes* and, as part of an argument by contrast, on *The Golden Bowl* and *Sister Carrie*.

I

There are good reasons why any discussion of social thought at the turn of the century should begin with Henry D. Lloyd. The rhetoric of anti-laissez-faire communalism, of the social self, the cooperative commonwealth, the religion of solidarity is, of course, as much Bellamy's and Gronlund's as it is his. But he, more than anyone else, establishes the link between utopianism and reform on the one hand and between reform and academic social theory on the other—between, in short, an earlier concentration on utopian plans and images and a later preoccupation with action, process, function, consciousness.

Lloyd's only piece of utopian fiction, "No Mean City" explores the symbolic implications of the Columbian Exposition in terms of practical reform and of the coming social order. The sketch describes the gradual reconstruction of society by the civic impulse of the cultured few which then spreads among "the people as when the Middle Ages built the great Cathedrals." Once the decision to rebuild the White City not in fake plaster but in marble has been made, public opinion, united in a spirit of fraternity and cooperation and acting strictly on principles of reasonableness and practicality, implements one urban reform after another until it is at last confronted with the biggest problem of them all—that of labour and the unemployed. Funded by the city and guided by scientific expertise, the unemployed are allowed to start their own cooperative commonwealth (No Mean City) which is so successful that the dominant economic system is competed out of existence, and the Black City, under pressure from the municipal model of the White City on the one hand and the economic model of No Mean City on the other, becomes obsolete, at last, and is torn down. (Afterwards, "the soil of the city had to be plowed and disinfected, and sown with aromatic plants for many years before it was sweet again.")[3]

Lloyd uses a number of motifs from Bellamy, Howells, Olerich, and Donnelly[4] but insists that his story was no mere utopian fantasy since all reforms suggested had been already put into practice in Europe and Australia. Nevertheless—for whatever reason—he never published it. Unlike Bellamy, for whom the detailed elaboration of the utopian image gradually replaced its actual fulfillment, Lloyd concentrated his utopian fervour on the reforming act itself. To become spiritually one with evolution, to shape and mould what was still in the process of unfolding, not nostalgically to withdraw into dreams of past or future but to act in the living present—this he argued to a point almost of obsession: "Cheap prophets foretell the reconstruction of society. But it is *now* going on. While we dream of Utopia, Altruria is organizing under our hands." And again: ". . . if a better order is to succeed that in which we live, the new must *now* be growing within the old . . ."[5]

Two things may seem somewhat puzzling here: First, if Lloyd is completely committed to acting within what he believed to be the evolutionary process, he is also completely open as to aims and ends beyond the general principles of brotherhood and cooperation. This contradiction—if it is one—is also visible in his experimental politics of shifting strategies, of fighting battles of reform at different fronts, with different allies. Second, since the new and better order was organically growing within and out of the old, action would seem unnecessary—unless Nature needed Man in order to fulfill itself.

And indeed, combining contemporary theories of progress and evolution with an Aristotelian metaphysics of teleology, Lloyd talks about reform in terms of a mimetic theory of art (as, by the way, did Jane Addams):[6] the social act was a creative act, its product, society, a second nature and therefore organism as well as artefact. Evolution provided the mere material conditions; then Man, the Creator, tentatively, experimentally, tried to model out of an as yet unfinished social life its innate perfect form: "The whole theory of true reform"—he jotted down in 1888—"is to set free the inward perfect principle within the individual and society, to use Aristotle's words . . ."[7] And some years later he writes even more explicitly:

> Art is nature consciously creating itself, and all our arts are anticipations. We paint, model and make music in

the constantly defeated, constantly renewed attempt to become the masters of life. The innermost inspiration of the artist . . . is to seize more life and, make it better. Their rivalry is to personify the 'principle of perfection' which Plato saw at work in the nature of things. Realism is the demand, never silent since art began, that art be brave and take each day the one step along the shortening path that separates the picture from the reality . . . Already long at work among us, though few have the faith or the eyes to see it, is the art of arts, the art social colouring, modelling, harmonising mankind into living pictures, statues, songs and temples.[8]

The ideal social order as a work of art in which the People collectively and individually created and realised themselves—this, of course, was a transcendent image that belonged to sacred history. And yet, for Lloyd, it also was painfully and tantalisingly immanent and secular. It seemed a possible reality because it was already in existence—as an enlightened idea of humanity, as an idea of democracy, as a store of shared beliefs and principles. At the same time, Lloyd was very much aware that even what he had assumed as an ideally given, had yet to be converted into public will: "We thought to proclaim the 'new Industrial Republic' but are set to a much more elemental task—to create a people who want it." Shaping the new social order became thus synonymous with creating a popular faith, a new collective spirit. His appeal to workingmen to organise was not so much a drive toward an institutional foundation of the coming order as a call to the people to unite in recognition of their common lives, interests and mutual relations: "Man, the animal, becomes Man, the citizen, only to the extent that he unites with his fellows. The greater the number of his associations, as in family, state, church, club, labor-union, political party, the more of a man he is."[9] Organisation, association, communication all anticipated a future unity of consciousness—and this most clearly in the "free talk of free men and women in which human powers play at their best and human intercourse reaches at its highest—the outflowing conversation, unofficial and unabashed, of congenial people seeking the truth in each other and in the world about them of the partnership of men in the creative power."[10]

In passages like these Lloyd seems close to those early American sociologists who conceived of society exclusively in terms of consciousness and communication[11]—as a psychological or mental space, organised by discourse, explored and extended by a method of "sympathetic introspection." This at least was Charles Horton Cooley's conception of the social order whose organic unity was the symbolic expression of the organic unity of mind. Not only was the individual self constitutionally connected with the larger social whole—"Self and society are twin-born . . . ," ". . . the closer we look, the more apparent it is that separateness is an illusion of the eye and community the inner truth"[12]—the self was a mirror-image of the social order. Self-awareness meant social awareness, and to extend one's self to assume the place of the other—"to understand (always by introspection) children, idiots, criminals, rich and poor, conservative and radical—any phase of human nature . . ."[13]—was to fully realise one's

role and function within a network of social relations and, at the same time, symbolically to anticipate the social wholeness that, in fact, was still to be achieved.

Communication, for Cooley, was therefore a means to connect oneself with other people's lives; to realise that "human nature . . . (was) very much the same in those we reckon sinners as in ourselves."[14] At the same time, communication was a moral discipline, an instrument of self-control by which our latent animal nature could be sublimated and transformed into the spirit of family and neighbourhood. Communication, in short, was the central organising principle on which the social order functioned and through which it expressed itself from the level of simple discourse to the collective creation and interpretation of signs, from dialogue and group discussion to the complex processes of interaction in the larger social unit. To be successful it presupposed a mutual recognition of equality among participants and a "certain underlying likeness of nature" (common religious and moral convictions, common traditions, shared experience). It was therefore most complete in the simpler, more intimate, more cooperative relations of primary groups—the family, the playgroup of children, the neighbourhood. Cooley was fascinated by communities of "life and action" such as these who were the "springs of life," not only for the individual but for the social institutions—and he very clearly associated them with a more organic, essentially pre-urban phase of social life in earlier nineteenth-century America. George Herbert Mead, his friend and colleague, took the process of communication out of such immediate contexts and analysed it extensively as the central social act around which society ideally revolved—collectively created and controlled by the free and constantly renewed consent of all of its participants.

". . . the self does not project itself into the other. The others and the self rise in the social act together."[15] Dialogue is thus the very structure of the self—even when we talk to ourselves we talk to an internalised other. In assuming the role of an other and in addressing himself in the role of an other the self "arises in experience." Mead frequently compares this process to the complex interactions of a game. There, each player takes on the roles of all the other players and their collective attitude, in turn, controls and influences his own responding action. This communal attitude—this "generalized other"—functions as an authority of norm that arises in the interaction of the group as a mutual expectation of right behaviour. Thus, the creation of self is identical with the control of self, and self-control social control and as such the very basis of the social process. By entering into the perspective of the other and by assuming toward himself the attitude of the collective whole, each individual creates his own self in the image of the communal order. Nevertheless, he reconstructs the world from his own perspective, so that the community as such is the ensemble of the individual perspectives of all of its members.[16]

It is interesting that Mead treats the problem of society and self within the larger context of how to respond to the impact of evolutionary change, of how to "incorporate the methods of change into the order of society itself."[17] This, with different emphasis and a greater sense of urgency, had also been Lloyd's problem. It was definitely of central importance to Cooley who developed his concept of an organic social order explicitly against an overwhelming experience of social discontinuity, and who thought the main task of his generation was to extend the moral and social coherence of the primary groups across the chasms and disruptions of the new urban-industrial environment.

Mead's theory of communication quite similarly grew out of an effort to find a more flexible response to ongoing change, to work order out of the very flow of experience. In an early essay on the value of the working hypothesis in social reform he advised social workers to move with the evolutionary process, to make use of "actual human relationships," of "the social organization that is going on."[18] Order, for him, never meant structure but process, adjustment to changing situations, integration of new elements through communicative interaction that would steadily increase social coherence and rational consensus. Even though, for Mead, the process of communication was primarily a sociological model, an ideal type—it also rested on his evolutionary faith in the coming of a rational and harmonious world order (a faith he shared with Cooley, Lloyd, Howells, Dewey and a host of others). Like Cooley he was aware of the vast "spiritual distances," the "distances in space and time, and the barriers of language and social status" that worked against the spirit of community; and like Cooley, he expected help from yet more extensive communication—from the newspaper but even more so from the realistic novel.[19]

Perhaps this is not really surprising—bridges leading from this kind of social theory to literature are indeed numerous. Not only is Mead's model of the social act conceived in terms of drama, his model of communal order as an organisation of individual perspectives bears definite resemblance to the order of the novel—just as Cooley's method of exploring the conscious and unconscious relations of the social body by "sympathetic introspection" very much resembles the method of the novelist. The novel was able to anticipate on the symbolic level what was still to be achieved by evolutionary process and by communicative interaction. The distances and barriers that divided and obstructed its social space could, after all, be crossed if not, perhaps, by the protagonists then by the reader who, by entering into the lives of others and thus becoming a social self, advanced, however minimally, the gradual fulfillment of the social order.

II

It seems therefore possible to rephrase Howells's theory of realism in terms of a theory of communication. To be sure, it was the business of the novelist to make people "understand the real world through its faithful effigy of it" but also "to arrange a perspective . . . with everything in its proper relation and proportion to everything else."[20] To represent reality (i.e. "*Life* as one has *seen* and *known* and *felt* it") was to reveal in the experience of it an innate 'perfect principle' (to use Lloyd's phrase again)—a principle that Howells variously identified as shared tradition, as shared ideal of conduct, or as belief in human nature "that . . . is the same under all masks and disguises that modern conditions have put upon it."[21] The very experience of reality is thus based on common faith and confirmed by consensus. It is a consensus established *in* the novel through conversation and debate, and *by* the novel in the act of reading which was to help people know themselves and one another better, so that they might all be "humbled and strengthened with a sense of their fraternity."[22]

Much like Cooley, Howells conceived of the coming social order as an extension of primary group cohesion—of the family, of "good society"—across empty urban space.[23] In stretching the conventions of the novel of manners to include material that threatened, or defied even, the social and moral order that this genre ideally implied, his novels analyse society on the conditions of community. They should, therefore, be read as symbolic representations of the body politic whose organic unity is tested, even disrupted by experience, yet always symbolically reasserted.

In all of Howells's novels social space is dominant, life enacted in the interior—in offices, living rooms, salons—where people come together in work or conversation. In *A Hazard of New Fortunes,* however, that space still has to be created and then maintained against the pressures of the city. Its protagonists are homeless, transitional—immigrants from overseas and from all regions of America. The Marches who in their search for an apartment explore the expanding metropolis from Broadway to the Bowery, experience it as picturesque yet shapeless, an offence to the senses and a moral outrage in its display of social misery. The city appears to them as a moral wilderness, as a natural space of lawless elemental and economic forces. Walking through it, crossing its social geography on the elevated roads, they perceive it as a frantic panorama of shifting images, constantly in motion and forcing into motion, its blind energy visibly embodied in the power of the locomotive.

Against this knowledge of the city—but never removed from it—the protagonists establish networks of social interaction: the various family circles, Mrs. Horn's salon, the small transitional community at Mrs. Leighton's boarding house. This inner space of communication, for Howells, always has ideal implications. Where it works democracy is experienced in the free exchange of opinions, right conduct affirmed or redefined in rational discourse, experience reflected in dialogue. When conversation deteriorates or collapses, a deeper crisis is always indicated—many of his novels are centred in such catastrophes of communication.

In *A Hazard of New Fortunes* crisis develops around the publication of a literary magazine. Edited by a man of culture, managed by a jovial businessman, financed by Big Capital and with representatives of different social classes and political opinions in its employ, its organisation symbolically reproduces the body politic in miniature. The question of who runs the magazine and how independent culture can be from the capital that keeps it going, is evidently a crucial one. When put to the test of communication, the cooperative commonwealth of *Every Other Week* collapses. The dinner, which is to bring all members of the group together in the house of Capital, erupts in discord when conversation touches on the question of labour and of social justice. The general disorder of the social state, evident in the chaos of the city but also working its way into the inner social sphere, can no longer be controlled by polite and rational discourse. Passion and selfishness explode in the violence of daughter against father, of father against son, and climactically in the street-car strike in which competitive society reveals its inner state of civil war.

Whether the collapse of order may be the beginning of its regeneration, is very cautiously explored in the novel's last section. The senseless death of Coonrod Dryfoos reunites the symbolic society of *Every Other Week* in sympathy and mourning. However, if there is a moral universe at all, it has to be set into motion, willed into action. Coonrod's death is clearly *not* a sacrificial one. By interpreting mere accident as sacrifice, some members of the group project a myth of atonement and redemption that transcends self-interest and enlarges the individual perspective to include the position of the other.

While conflict and disruption still continue on the macrolevel, communication and community are restored on the symbolic: Dryfoos, representing the new plutocracy, takes himself out of the social body altogether. Lindau, his anarchist opponent, has to die as an agent of the revolution but his rhetoric is integrated into accepted speech (by March and others) as evidence of a changed social consciousness.

It is entirely possible, of course, to call this and the moderate happy ending of the novel an example of Howells's lack of nerve and of his readiness to make his peace with the conventions of romance. There is, however, more to it. These signals to the reader are in themselves symbolic actions that indicate surviving faith in history and communication. *AHNF* is a novel saturated with the shattering experience of change—of traditions, cultural identities repressed or destroyed in the pursuit of money—and it abounds with a genuine feeling of horror at the moral and human cost involved. Yet while at the beginning, the Marches still viewed the city from an aesthetic distance, they progressively come to see themselves as part of it and in discovering their own complicity become agents of social integration. By projecting themselves sympathetically, sentimentally even, into the selves of others, they create a sense of coherence that is repeated on another level of symbolic action as a reconstruction of community. The novel traces the connection between economy and moral consciousness by giving account of a proliferating, so-

cially destructive individualism; and by symbolically enacting a growth of social sense, it plays with the idea of possible reversal. The book thus presents a reality in flux, suspended between possibilities. In a sense, it reproduces its own field of communication in which it acts as an influence that may help shape a common reality still in the making.

III

It should be noted that it is the selfish who leave the city while the socially conscious choose to stay. Howells was committed to the city's evolving order but the made his symbolic investments in its future against encroaching doubts and against an overwhelming sense of loss. There was no question that the past was irrevocable and he always managed, however mechanically at times, to reassert his faith in humanity's progressive future,[24] but he found it increasingly difficult to trace continuities in the immediate present. This sense of crisis, this being at once hopeful and groping in the dark, going on "to we know not what"[25] he shared with many others. "It is as if each one should sit down to invent a language for himself . . . ," Cooley complained. "That great traditions should rapidly go to pieces may be a necessary phase of evolution and a disguised blessing, but the present effect is largely distraction and demoralization."[26]

To create community within such spiritual and organisational emptiness one had to improve and to extend communication. Bringing representatives of all groups and classes together in communicative interaction so that each participant could realise his function within the whole—this was Jane Addams's strategy at Hull House.[27] It was still based on face-to-face-relationships as was Mead's model of the social process where consensus was created through "living human relations"[28] in analogy to game, conversation, drama. The real difficulty, however, was to expand communication into ever larger units and yet keep it democratic, interactive: "Communication must be full and quick in order to give that promptness in the give-and-take of suggestions upon which moral unity depends. Gesture and speech ensure this in the face-to-face group; but only the recent marvellous improvement of communicative machinery makes a free mind on a great scale even conceivable. If there is no means of working thought and sentiment into a whole by reciprocation, the unity of the group cannot be other than inert and unhuman." (Cooley)[29] Whatever their occasional doubts and misgivings, both Cooley and Mead were sure that technology would finally save and guarantee community: "The pressure upon the inventor will not cease until the isolation of man within society has passed." (Mead)[30]

The whole argument is obviously self-defeating. In 1896 Henry D. Lloyd had been convinced that modern business had made the cooperative commonwealth a physical fact; now it had only to be turned into a moral fact (i.e. into a fact of consciousness).[31] Thirty years later, John Dewey noted that "we have the physical tools of communication as never before. The thoughts and aspirations congruous with them are not communicated . . ."[32] Evidently, whatever progress in the organisation and unification of society had been made, it had not realised its own ideal implications. Communication cannot by itself create community unless it is already there to be communicated.

For Lloyd community and the Communal had implied an ideal of cooperative conduct, a mystique of brotherhood and solidarity, and he invested it with the aura of the religious and the sacred. Even though this aura survived to some extent in Jane Addams's, Dewey's and Mead's ritualistic concept of Industrial Democracy,[33] it wore thin fast by the heavy secular and ideological use made of it in the cause of patriotism, nationalism, racism. And finally, when Cooley and Mead talk about organising society by means of a new technology of communication they are hard to keep separate, at times, from sociologists such as Edward A. Ross, for whom communication was a form of social engineering, of controlling the "gropings of a vast collective life"[34] by handing down models of character and conduct for collective imitation. Here normative projection of the coming social order merges easily with the description of what is already there—the urban order as a given social fact: a huge environment of heterogeneous elements isolated in their individual aspiration and mobility, yet held together by "unconscious forms of cooperation"—such as advertisement, fashion, public opinion and the media; in short, an order entirely conceived of and described in terms of mass.[35]

IV

It was against this growing evidence of mass and mass culture that James projected his religion of art and manners. Perhaps he did this nowhere more explicitly than in *The Golden Bowl*—a novel which presents a most complete, if also a most constricted image of the "blessed community."[36] Not only are its protagonists lifted from a state of moral imperfection to aesthetic consummation, they themselves "work" their transformation in a complex game of intense communicative interaction. By observing and interpreting their shifting relation to each other they create order in the process of reflection. "Reading it"—thus Quentin Anderson—"is like playing a game in which we are always shuffling the same elements."[37] "Arrangement," "re-arrangement," "symmetry," "design," "scheme" are keywords in the book: Fanny Assingham arranges the marriage of Prince Amerigo with Maggie Verver and leaves Maggie's father out of the arrangement; in order to create a "perfect symmetry" Maggie then arranges the marriage of her father to Charlotte Stant (Amerigo's former lover), Charlotte and the Prince drift into an arrangement that leaves Maggie out. Until Maggie, in turn, counters deception with a subtle strategy of re-arrangement that forces their relation back into its original symmetry.

Arrangement-re-arrangement, plot and counter-plot follow each other at increasingly higher levels of subtlety and consciousness until reflexion seems magically to create the situation that it has anticipated. Like players in a game whose rules are known to all, the protagonists act by responding to the attitude of the opponent who, in his turn, responds to the action of the other player. By her correct interpretation of gestures, actions, situations ("the most intricate interpretation of signs") Maggie is able to lead Charlotte by anticipating her. When Maggie concludes from Charlotte's behaviour that the Prince has not told her that Maggie knows of their betrayal, she can act on the assumption that Amerigo has submitted to her strategy. She now tells Charlotte that she has never thought of her "but as beautiful, wonderful and good." Thus confronted with Maggie's ideal image of her, Charlotte chooses to act in accordance with her better self and an accepted standard of behaviour. Her submission makes her an equal partner in a game in which each participant gains in value by acknowledging "the general duty of magnificence."

To reassemble the broken pieces of their love, or friendship, all three have silently agreed to spare the Father (who thus, by his mere presence, enforces the authority of rule), and without this precondition, that the weights of their relationship be changed "without disturbing the equilibrium," playing the game would be impossible. (". . . how it would have torn them to pieces, if they had so much as suffered its suppressed relations to peep out of their eyes").[38] Their communication is therefore only partially a verbal one—and conversation for the most part elliptical. Meaning is observed and felt in gesture, or the unfinished sentence, and then acknowledged in the short, yet semantically loaded phrase "I see." Thus acting in a play whose text is written in the very process of performance, they grow in consciousness, "work," "make," create themselves in and through the reflexion of the other. So that in the final consummation of achieved consensus they can mutually appreciate themselves—as much as they are appreciated by the auctorial voice—as "priceless" works of art.

James's version of the blessed community (in which the erring 'selfish self' is redeemed in the creation of the social), though conceived against the vulgarly democratic and addressing itself to an audience of an enlightened few, shows a metaphorical and structural kinship with the ideal communities of Lloyd and Cooley. (To Mead's it seems remarkably close in the dramatic conception of the social process). They share the neo-classicist ideal of balance and proportion that links aesthetic order to an ideal of conduct and of social equilibrium—and they all attempt to reconcile an apriori sense of order with the experience of change: to work order out of change, out of the very movement of experience. Of course, with Lloyd, art fulfills itself in social process—whereas, with James, society reaches perfection only in Art. However, not even he confined the image of the blessed community to the sanctum of the Beautiful but saw it work its way back into society ("through contact and communication")[39] as a model of conduct, a saving ideal of personal and social perfection. The lectures and essays written in connection with his trip to the United States in 1904 respond to what he took to be a growing need within the culture to restore—through an economy of manners—the massive violation of form, order and restraint that had been brought about by an economy of waste.[40]

That this ideal of manners, in *The Golden Bowl,* could be enacted only in atrophied seclusion from a contaminating world of history and public life, enters the consciousness of the protagonists themselves as a vague sense of their own unreality: "as if we were sitting about on divans, with pigtails, smoking opium and seeing visions."

Placed in this context, *The Golden Bowl* seems to have been provoked into existence—in the mysterious dialectics of literary history—by *Sister Carrie* which is in every way its exact counter-image. Rejecting the restrictions of the moral order and its interior landscapes of garden and salon, Dreiser establishes the city as the new reality—the Black City as the only city, as absolute fact of the experience. His heroine never even tries to control the experiential flow (is constitutionally unable, in other words, ever to become a 'self' in Mead's or Cooley's sense), only drifts in it, reacting to external stimulus, is swallowed by the material and sensual presence of the city. Interior social space is important only as it confines the individual's mobility. The street is city space, its order that of chance, its freedom the energy and anonymity of the crowd. Communicative interaction hardly matters here—yet signs proliferate, it is the things that speak.

But even Dreiser feels compelled to submit the flow of experience and the disruptive rhythms of the city to a higher metaphysics of natural and economic order; and he ties his protagonists on the wheel of Spencerian evolution that carries them upward toward Spirit and downward to the animal stage. Culture, in this context, is merely social status and a semblance of refinement—it has lost all implications of relation and community. Having transcended the materiality of the desired objects, Carrie is confronted with the emptiness of her desires. Isolated in the city, carried upward by the strength of her illusion, united with her fellow-beings only by common acts of acquisition and consumption, she represents indeed the new urban order—an order, however, that in its dynamic freedom and spiritual emptiness to James and Howells, for different reasons, seemed the embodiment of the Profane.

Notes

1. On the Chicago exposition of 1893 see John Cawelti, "America on Display: The World's Fairs of 1876, 1893, 1933," in F. C. Jaher, ed., *The Age of Industrialism in America,* New York, 1968, pp. 317-363; also H. Ickstadt, "Öffentliche Fiktion und bürgerliches Leben—der amerikanische Roman der Jahrhundertwende als kommunikatives System," in Christadler/Lenz, eds., *Amerikastudien—Theorie, Geschichte, interpretatorische Praxis,* Stuttgart, 1977, pp. 223-247. As to the relation of its symbolism to social reform see Graham Taylor, *Pioneering on Social Frontiers,* Chicago, 1930, esp.

p. 3: "In building its 'White City' Chicago rose above itself, above all it had ever been and above [all] it would become until it had time to grow the gradual realization of its future." Dalziel Duncan, *Culture and Democracy,* Bedminster, 1965, explores the relation of architecture and social thought in Chicago.

2. Howard B. Woolston, "The Urban Habit of Mind," *American Journal of Sociology,* 17, 1911/12, p. 614. Robert Park rendered this new urban feeling in more abstract terms: "The social problem is fundamentally a city problem. It is a problem of achieving in the freedom of the city a social order and a social control equivalent to that which grew up naturally in the family, the clan, and the tribe." "The City as a Social Laboratory," in Robert Park, *On Social Control and Collective Behavior,* Chicago, 1967, p. 4. See also Paul Boyer, *Urban Masses and Moral Order in America, 1820-1920,* Cambridge, Mass., 1978, esp. parts three and four.

3. Lecture of Nov. 1893, The H. D. Lloyd Papers, Wisconsin State Historical Society, Mfm. Reel 22: "Articles—Addresses, 1892-95," item 126. On Lloyd see Caro Lloyd, *H.D. Lloyd,* New York, 1912, 2 vls. and Chester McArthur Destler, *Henry Demarest Lloyd and the Empire of Reform,* Philadelphia, 1963.

4. See Henry Olerich, *A Cityless and a Countryless World* (1893) and Ignatius Donnelly, *The Golden Bottle* (1892), also the last chapter of William T. Stead's *If Christ came to Chicago!,* London, 1894.

5. "Autobiographical Notes," H.D. Lloyd Papers, Reel 22, Item 150.

6. "The chief characteristic of art lies in freeing the individual from a sense of separation and isolation in his emotional experience and has usually been accomplished through painting, writing, singing; but this does not make it in the least impossible that it is now being tried . . . in terms of life itself." Quoted in C. Lasch, ed. *The Social Thought of Jane Addams,* New York, 1965, p. 188.

7. Quoted in David W. Noble, "The Religion of Progress in America, 1890-1914," *Social Research,* 22, 1955, pp. 425 f.

8. H.D. Lloyd, *Man, the Social Creator,* (eds. Jane Addams/Anne Withington), New York, 1906, pp. 276 f.

9. "Why Workingmen Should Organize," H.D. Lloyd Papers, Reel 21, Nov. 10, 1891.

10. *Man, the Social Creator,* p. 39.

11. Charles Horton Cooley, "Social Consciousness ," *The American Journal of Sociology,* 12, 1906/07, pp. 675-687; "The Process of Social Change," *Political Science Quarterly,* 12, 1897, pp. 63-81; *Human Nature & the Social Order* (1902), New York: Schocken Books, 1964; *Social Organization* (1909),

New York: Schocken Books, 1962. On Cooley see the fine introductions of Philip Rieff to the Schocken re-edition of Cooley's major theoretical works; also David Noble, "The Religion of Progress . . . ," and *The Paradox of Progressive Thought, 1890-1917,* Chicago, 1970. On the tendency in late 19th-century American social thought to talk about society 'transcendentally,' i.e. only in terms of consciousness, see R. Jackson Wilson, *In Quest of Community,* New York, 1968, esp. chapter 1.

12. *Social Organization,* pp. 5 and 9.

13. *Ibid.,* p. 7.

14. *Ibid.,* p. 15.

15. George Herbert Mead, "The Objective Reality of Perspectives," in *The Philosophy of the Present,* Chicago, 1932, p. 169.

16. "It is then such a coincidence of the perspective of the individual organism with the pattern of the whole act in which it is so involved that the organism can act within it, that constitutes the objectivity of the perspective." *Ibid.,* p. 174 f.; also *Mind, Self & Society,* Chicago, 1972, pp. 308 f. On Mead see Habermas, *Theorie des kommunikativen Handelns,* Frankfurt, 1981, vol. 2, pp. 7-169.

17. Mead, *Movements of Thought in the Nineteenth Century,* Chicago, 1936, pp. 361 f.

18. "What is the function of reflective consciousness in its attempt to direct conduct? The common answer is that we carry in thought the world as it should be, and fashion our conduct to bring this about. . . . if this implies a 'vision given on the mount' which represents in detail what is to be, we are utterly incapable of conceiving it. And every attempt to direct conduct by a fixed idea of the world of the future must be, not only a failure, but also pernicious . . . Reflective consciousness does not then carry us on to the world that is to be, but puts our own thought and endeavor into the very process of evolution, and evolution within consciousness that has become reflective has the advantage over other evolution in that the form does not tend to perpetuate himself as he is, but identifies himself with the process of development." "The Working Hypothesis in Social Reform", *American Journal of Sociology,* 5, 1899/1900, p. 371; also see his review of Jane Addams's *The Newer Ideals of Peace* in *AJS,* 13, 1907, pp. 121-128.

19. "The Genesis of the Self and Social Control," *International Journal of Ethics,* 35, 1924/25, p. 276.

20. "Novel-Writing and Novel-Reading," in Gibson, ed., *Howells and James: A Double Billing,* New York Public Library, 1958.

21. "Concerning a Council of Perfection," *Literature,* April 7, 1899, p. 290.

22. "Editor's Study, Sept. 1887," *Harper's,* 75, 1887, p. 639.

23. Cf. his "Equality as the Basis of Good Society," *Century,* 51, 1895, pp. 67 ff. and "Who Are Our Brethren?," *Ibid.,* pp. 932-36.

24. "Certain hopes of truer and better conditions on which my heart was fixed twenty years ago are not less dear, and they are by no means touched with despair, though they have not yet found the fulfilment which I would then have prophesied for them. Events have not wholly played them false; events have not halted, though they have marched with a slowness that might affect a younger observer as marking time . . . ," Preface to the 1909 edition of *A Hazard of New Fortunes.*

25. Cooley, *Social Organization,* p. 170.

26. *Ibid.,* p. 352.

27. Jane Addams, *Twenty Years at Hull House;* also Daniel T. Rogers, *The Work Ethic in Industrial America, 1850-1920,* Chicago, 1978, p. 82 f. and Ickstadt, "The Descent into the Abyss: Die literarische Entdeckung des sozialen Untergrunds in der amerikanischen Literatur des späten 19. Js.," *Amerikastudien,* 26, 3/4, 1981, pp. 260-269.

28. Review of Jane Addams's *The Newer Ideals . . . loc. cit.*

29. *Social Organization,* p. 54.

30. "Every invention that brings men closer together, so that they realize their interdependence, and increase their shared experience which makes it more possible for them to put themselves in each other's places, every form of communication which enable them to participate in each other's minds, brings us nearer to this goal. While we marvel at the new inventions which enable us to pass into the experiences of others, we perhaps fail to realize the unrecognized, unconscious pressure of the isolated individual in modern society. The isolated man is the one who belongs to a whole that he yet fails to realize. We have become bound up in a vast society, all of which is essential to the existence of each one, but we are without the shared experience which this should entail. The pressure upon the inventor will not ease until the isolation of man within society has passed." "The Nature of Aesthetic Experience," *International Journal of Ethics,* 36, 1925/26, p. 389.

31. Cf. Noble, "The Religion of Progress", *loc. cit.,* p. 424.

32. John Dewey, *The Public and Its Problems,* New York, 1927, p. 142.

33. "It has been the inspiration of universal religions, of political democracy, and later of industrial democracy to bring something of the universal achievement, of the solemn festival, of common delight into the isolated and dreary activities which all together make possible the blessed community, the state, the cooperative society, and all those

meanings which we vaguely call social and spiritual." G. H. Mead, "The Nature of Aesthetic Experience," *loc. cit.,* p. 384; see also O. L. Triggs, "Democratic Art," *Forum,* 26, 1898/99, pp. 66-79.

34. Edward Albion Ross, *Social Control: A Survey of the Foundations of Order* (1901), London, 1969, p. 269.

35. Robert Park, "The City: Suggestions for the Investigation of Human Behavior in the City Environment," *American Journal of Sociology,* 20, 1915, pp. 577-612.

36. On the relation of *The Golden Bowl* to genteel neo-classicism see my "Offentliche Fiktion und bürgerliches Leben . . .", *Loc. cit.*

37. *The Imperial Self,* New York, 1971, p. 186.

38. Penguin Modern Classics, p. 543.

39. *The Question of Our Speech,* Boston, 1905, p. 17.

40. "Manners are above all . . . an economy; the sacrifice of them has always in the long run to be made up, just as the breakages and all dilapidations have to be paid for at the end of the tenancy of a house carelessly occupied . . . By an excess of misuse moreover a house is fatally disfigured—rendered, that is, unfavorable to life; in which case we become liable for the total ruin: to the infinite dismay of those members of the community . . . to whom the vision of such waste is a vision of barbarism." Quoted in Peter Buitenhuis, "Henry James and American Culture," in R. B. Browne, *Challenges in American Culture,* Bowling Green, 1970, p. 207; also see the last chapter of *The American Scene* for a very similar argument.

Paulette D. Kilmer (essay date 1996)

SOURCE: "News and Fiction: Prescriptions for Living," in *The Fear of Sinking: The American Success Formula in the Gilded Age,* University of Tennessee Press, 1996, pp. 1-7.

[In the essay below, Kilmer discusses the popularity of the "rags-to-riches" success formula during the Gilded Age, suggesting that news items as well as bardic tales featuring these types of formulaic plots often served as reminders to readers that "honor, public esteem, and fidelity could not be bought."]

Such opening phrases as "Once upon a time" or, in a newspaper, "The following story comes well authenticated from Trenton, Tennessee," alerted nineteenth-century readers to expect an outrageous sequence of events, followed by a moral. Editors of the time often launched bizarre reports with declarations of their veracity. For example, in October 1883, the *Alexandria (Louisiana) Town Talk* assured readers that trustworthy folks in Tennessee had witnessed the following train of events:

> A young man, long past maturity, had no beard at all. Then one day he noticed a lump on his neck a few inches beneath his chin. The unsightly wen resembled a large walnut. He asked the doctor to remove it. As the doctor made the incision, a matted, spongy substance popped out. The wad was a "closely matted and coiled mass of hair." It seems that the beard, which should have been spread over the young man's face, had concentrated in this one spot and grown beneath the skin. The hair was removed, and the opening soon healed, and the strange development became unnoticeable.[1]

Henry Nash Smith explains in *The Virgin Land* that such narrative codes point to a plane of reality where concepts and emotions fuse to form symbolic images.[2] Parables fascinate readers by posing plausible explanations that make the improbable incident sound factual. Their plots appeal to the reservoir of archetypes upon which each member of a community draws in interpreting messages. The cited news item generated conversations as well as guffaws; Sunday scientists and poets may have debated whether that freakish lump could have formed. Men with no beards or light beards may have felt comforted.

Such tales articulate affective truths rather than physical realities, however. The imagery resonates within the heart. Like a fairy tale, such a story works through symbolism. Indeed, the strange phenomenon reinforces the moral of Alger's rags-to-riches tales: be satisfied with middle-class affluence. The figures in the story represent values. For instance, the mature lad might be the nation and the lack of a beard the blindness of the population concerning wealth. The matted lump could be monopoly, covetousness, or the unhealthy acquisition of physical treasures. The physician may represent the bard, editor, minister, or other seer who lances the canker by cutting through the facade of unwise preoccupation with social climbing. The scar's final healing, of course, is the inner peace that awaits the community once no one hoards power or money and everyone avoids vice (and, in consequence, everyone ascends to the middle class).

This news account resembles a fairy tale in a number of striking ways. The central character has no name. The location could be Anywhere, U.S.A. The protagonist struggles and then proves himself worthy by having the wen removed. The doctor plays the role of the benefactor. The implicit moral—"the opening soon healed, and the strange development became unnoticeable"—promises redemption to those who lance the boils festering on their souls.

Sometimes, of course, false hopes and phony piety blind people. Mark Twain and Charles Dudley Warner coined the phrase "The Gilded Age" to describe the hypocrisy of their day, which was rooted in unrealistic expectations. Their novel, *The Gilded Age* (1872), satirizes the scramble for political renown, industrial power, and economic advancement through speculation. To Twain and Warner, the Gilded Age sparkled with a patina of noble values that glittered in speeches but crumbled when citizens took action. Many historians have agreed with the novelists. Certainly the historical record contains examples of greed. The Robber Barons, for example, gained prestige and aristocratic status through unscrupulous ploys more despicable than the chicanery of petty thieves.

The disparity between the Robber Barons and ordinary citizens has stimulated economic analyses of the forces of production in a capitalist society. For example, in *Mechanic Accents,* Michael Denning viewed the dime novels produced between 1840 and 1893 as helping to maintain class lines by blinding workers to their social immobility and by encouraging their unrealistic hopes of rising through diligence.[3] His "Unknown Public"—the million anonymous immigrant laborers and farmers, mostly Irish and German—bought the ten-cent thrillers. During the Gilded Age, Christine Bold concluded in a related study, the publishing industry discovered the money-making potential of formulas and forced writers to utilize predetermined plot lines, stunting their artistic development.[4]

For the first time in history, cheap paper and fast presses made it possible to write down what in earlier times would have been spoken or sung. By creating a mass market for stories, the publishing industry's innovations led to an increase in the number of a new variety of strolling minstrels. When stories became commodities to be bought and sold in a market, writers found new economic and occupational niches. The demand for entertaining reading enabled hundreds of authors to work independently as producers of cliff-hangers (serials composed of episodes that end suspensefully), paperbacks, feature articles, and news briefs.

The proliferation of magazines and books concerned both those who equated reading with spiritual well-being and those who denounced popular bards as mouthpieces of the devil. Popular culture became enmeshed in this argument over the social role of reading as the arena in which the desire to acquire wealth might be reconciled with the need to feel pure in spirit. Some ministers preached to the populace through cheap fiction. Like citizens, many preachers assumed making too much money incited ruthless behavior and obscured the futility of seeking fulfillment in owning things.

Editors hired cultural bards because plots containing the success archetype satisfied a demand in the marketplace. Nevertheless, although the writers lived on their earnings, they did not consider their work merely a means of paying bills. Interviews with them indicate many took pride in their ability to please readers who sought escape from drudgery and disappointment in eagerly awaited installments detailing a modern Cinderella's quest for happiness in a wicked world.

While both readers and writers shared in the struggle to survive financially, factors other than economic ones fu-

eled public interest in the rags-to-riches paradigm. For instance, changing technology, which multiplied the mechanical dangers the public faced daily, made the success prototype a refuge from modernity. This was especially true because the process of invention enticed individuals to acquire material possessions. Innovation was viewed ambivalently, as both creator and destroyer. Each wave of technological advancement exposed citizens to new threats, as well as to new pleasures and sources of wonder. Often, euphoria over time saved, money earned, or physical barriers surmounted repressed recognition of the anxiety introduced into the community by the new technology. The timeless Cinderella paradigm recalled a safe day when elves rather than machines made shoes and when frogs taught rude princesses lessons in decorum. The popular plots reassured those who felt overwhelmed by the stresses of everyday life. In fantasy, they briefly attained the success that often eluded them in the real world.

Frequently, progress intensified the misery of the poor, even while raising their standard of living. The urban Cinderella tales inspired optimism amid ugliness. Sunny plots about lucky folks who vanquished villainy, overcame their troubles with grit, and thereby earned the respect of kind strangers, provided a sanctuary for desperate people trapped in poverty. Like mystic chants, plots repeated a cherished archetype that promised better times ahead—times when justice would prevail against perfidy and the deserving would live happily ever after, secure in the knowledge the wicked had danced to death in flaming shoes or—in Victorian parlance—been annihilated by Demon Rum or Tempter Tobacco.

Before journalists were expected to be objective, reporters as well as fiction artisans exposed the sins of Demon Rum and invoked the magical power of words to redress social injustices. The Corliss Engine did not dethrone Cinderella. The ability to transform raw materials into such wonders as refrigerated railroad cars, bicycles, and ice-cream bricks did not relieve humans of their need for narrative closure. Indeed, the world remains a blank stage until the players codify their experiences in scenarios. Language provides the means of understanding life. For the throngs of anonymous readers, writers recycled ancient archetypes and myths that had sustained people for centuries. The story, and not the facts, prevails; because, without a narrative frame, societies collapse.

Past, present, and future coalesce in the web of archetypes implanted in cultural myths that bind society. A primary set of plot lines, distilled from centuries of exposure to the Cinderella tale, evolved around the notion that, without honor, money was worthless. Alger's adventures retold that tale from a male perspective and illustrated the effects of changing technology on individuals as well as on progress. Indeed, authors employed technology to update the ancient art of balladry. They sang the ballads people longed to hear. But, instead of lutes, they stroked typewriters. Instead of congregating in marketplaces to listen to a strolling bard, people read modern versions in new formats (news, serials, mysteries, adventures, romances, and horse operas) that recast proven values and symbols in modern guises recognizable to even the most obtuse spectator.

The new technology enabled writers to skip back and forth between the very separate worlds of traditional oratory and contemporary print. The hybrid was not always beautiful, but, in the age of the useful and the practical, it gave believers a bit of whimsy, a corner of fantasy, a dose of imagination. This was allowed only because it improved the reader's character or brought her or him one step closer to passing through the eye of the needle—that is, to laying up treasures both in heaven and on earth.[5]

The formula for balancing the desire for material goods with the need for spiritual well-being evolved as a part of the success archetype. The bardic tales combined elements from novels and fairy tales into a new form, a hybrid that conveyed archetypes to reinforce values. Writers adapted bardic tales to genres that appealed to the multitudes: dime thrillers, mysteries, domestic fantasies, romances, and idea novels. In *The American Myth of Success: From Horatio Alger to Norman Vincent Peale,* Richard Weiss observes, "Their writings reflect the craving for stability in a society in the throes of transformation."[6] Regardless of the format, these updated fairy tales denounced money as the root of all evil and illustrated how excessive wealth drove youths into billiard parlors, theaters, and race tracks.

The success paradigm helped people to negotiate reality by providing interpretations of what it meant to be rich. Popular bards cautioned that no one was truly rich without the love and esteem of family, peers, and colleagues. Gold could not replace fidelity.

Soon, however, the presence of thousands of wealthy families challenged the folk wisdom concerning amassing material goods. Steel mogul Andrew Carnegie and the Reverend Russell Conwell suggested prosperous individuals might attain salvation by serving as exemplars of success. Such individuals, by sagely investing the fortunes entrusted to them by God, could help the poor lift themselves up by their bootstraps. The meaning of the Cinderella paradigm fluctuated to accommodate progress. People sought to maintain their spiritual health amid massive upheavals in their understanding of the world. The rags-to-riches formula guaranteed constancy; but, to see that the success archetype continued to function as a viable link between past and present, the popular bards employed modern images in explicating it.

John G. Cawelti, author of *Adventure, Mystery, and Romance: Formula Stories as Art and Popular Culture,* and other scholars have demonstrated the cultural significance of formula writing. James D. Hart, in *The Popular Book: A History of America's Literary Taste,* and Frank Luther Mott, in *Golden Multitudes: The Story of Best Sellers in the United States,* trace the history of writing for the multitudes.[7]

Feminist scholars have made significant contributions to our understanding of such writing. By adjusting standards to reflect crucial historical contingencies, Jane Tompkins, in *Sensational Designs: The Cultural Work of American Fiction, 1790-1860,* enlarges the traditional literary canon to include romance writers. Her imaginative work proves it can be profitable to evaluate narratives using criteria other than those associated with literary masterpieces. Mary Kelley has studied the private diaries and papers of a dozen popular women writers to probe the social role of romances. Her analysis in *Private Woman, Public Stage: Literary Domesticity in Nineteenth-Century America* reveals the human side of these often-neglected creators of best sellers about women's struggles to provide happy homes for their children.[8]

Although some critics consider potboilers to be inferior works of literature, the analysis reported here demonstrates the bardic tales belong in the category of popular culture rather than in that of timeless classics. The essential differences between bardic tales and novels arise from the authors' and the readers' purposes. Popular bards breathe new life into the shared wisdom of the community, wisdom contained in the traditional formulas that impel individuals to aspire to serve forces larger than themselves and, concomitantly, to affirm their membership in society. Novelists, on the other hand, give readers a highly personalized, unique view of the human condition that provides intellectual stimulation and aesthetic pleasure.

Readers of all ages have found, and still find, intellectual satisfaction in novels and emotional grounding in formula tales. In the twentieth century, these bardic tales have inspired radio, television, and motion picture dramas. In the nineteenth century, children encountered the success archetype in several arenas. Their parents read to them from the Bible and from magazines that repeated popular plots. Their teachers taught them to recite from *McGuffey's Readers,* which reiterated the same values codified in the success archetype: thrift, perseverance, loyalty, integrity, honor. Aphorisms warned that money, unless invested honorably, corrodes one's soul. Rhymed exercises extolled diligent workers who surmounted obstacles and ultimately earned the respect of their neighbors, as well as modest remuneration. At church, ministers preached about the folly of squandering heavenly treasures to acquire objects. Some pupils won Sunday-school books given as prizes at picnics and socials. Others checked out volumes with character-building plots from the church library.

In fact, the Cinderella paradigm appealed so strongly to the popular bards that many of them recast their own life stories to fit the same imaginative formula they had written and rewritten so many times for publishers. Perhaps the power of this cultural icon—the image of a hard-working protagonist who deserves to succeed—seduced the writers so completely they could not see their own experiences except in ways that fit the cherished paradigm. They emphasized personal incidents that conformed to the same hallowed pattern their readers had found amusing and fulfilling for decades.

During the Gilded Age, newspapers, biographies, and cliff-hangers repeatedly echoed that same pattern, which promised good would prevail over evil. Editors deified community leaders, turning them into personifications of the success archetype. Obituaries and retirement stories praised diligent citizens who attained middle-class respectability but were too honest to make a fortune through speculating or profiting from the misery of others.

Reporters cast disaster accounts in the language of the pluck-and-luck myth. Fires served as almighty levelers. The rich and the poor suffered together. Money vanished. Only faith endured. Moreover, those endowed with integrity stood the test of the loss, while those pampered by a lifestyle of ease or sloth sank into oblivion. Devastation strengthened the true-hearted, who transformed their sorrow into opportunity. Individuals as well as towns arose from the ashes stronger than ever, according to editorials. Bardic tales similarly depicted fires and other tragedies as painful but invigorating chances to discover the inner strength that would revitalize a protagonist's life.

In addition to framing disaster accounts in terms of the archetypes that reinforced social mores, reporters reminded readers of the tension between materialism and spirituality. Stories about the sad consequences of spoiling sons and daughters underscored the pernicious effect of money on families. Both newspapers and publishing houses deplored the foolishness and decadence of the rich. Treasures of the heart, editors warned readers to remember, endured long after gold had lost its luster. Both bardic tales and news items pointed out that honor, public esteem, and fidelity could not be bought. The bards gradually reinterpreted paradigms to preserve traditional values.

Notes

1. *Alexandria (La.) Town Talk,* 3 Oct. 1883, 2:3. The notice carries no headline.

2. Henry Nash Smith, *The Virgin Land: The American West as Symbol and Myth* (Cambridge, Mass.: Harvard Univ. Press, 1950), xi.

3. Michael Denning, *Mechanic Accents: Dime Novels and the Working Class Culture in America* (New York: Verso, 1987).

4. Christine Bold, "The Voice of the Fiction Factory in Dime and Pulp Westerns," *Journal of American Studies* 17 (Apr. 1983): 29-46.

5. Lewis Atherton, in *Main Street on the Middle Border* (Chicago: Quadrangle, 1954), describes the late 19th century as the age of the useful and practical.

6. Richard Weiss, *The American Myth of Success: From Horatio Alger to Norman Vincent Peale* (New York: Basic Books, 1969), 11.

7. John G. Cawelti, *Adventure, Mystery and Romance: Formula Stories as Art and Popular Culture* (Chicago: Univ. of Chicago Press, 1976); James D. Hart, *The Popular Book: A History of America's Literary Taste* (New York: Oxford Univ. Press, 1950); Frank Luther Mott, *Golden Multitudes: The Story of Best Sellers in the United States* (New York: Macmillan, 1947).

8. Jane Tompkins, *Sensational Designs: The Cultural Work of American Fiction, 1790-1860* (New York: Oxford Univ. Press, 1985), esp. chap. 7, "Is It Any Good? The Institutionalization of Literary Value," 186-201; and Mary Kelley, *Private Woman, Public Stage: Literary Domesticity in 19th-Century America* (New York: Oxford, 1984).

REALISM

Robert Falk (essay date 1970)

SOURCE: "The Writers' Search for Reality," in *The Gilded Age:Revised and Enlarged Edition*, edited by H. Wayne Morgan, Syracuse University Press, 1970, pp. 223-37.

[*In the following essay, Falk characterizes the Gilded Age as a time of great literary change, largely due to a break from Romanticism and a movement toward increased realism.*]

The serious writers of any age are in search of reality, the real thing, the genuine article valid for their time. What make the difference between literary movements and periods are the special historical characteristics of the age and the particular literary form which embodies that reality and contemporaneity. In the Gilded Age literature increasingly expressed a vision of reality in the novel form, as distinguished from the "romance" of Cooper, Hawthorne, and Melville. The decades following 1865 were a blend of the old and the new. The older established writers of the mid-century—Longfellow, Whittier, Lowell, Bryant, Holmes, and Hawthorne—were still powerful spokesmen of romanticism. Their voices merged with those of younger writers beginning to be heard. Of the early realists in fiction, three indelibly stamped the Gilded Age: Howells, Mark Twain, and Henry James. Hawthorne's influence was strong in the early work of both Howells and James. Melville, by a strange and ironic commentary on the critical taste of the period, was relatively unknown. Poetry during the postwar decades was derivative, except for Emily Dickinson and Whitman, both of whom had to wait for the critical understanding of later generations. After 1890, a younger group of writers began to express in fiction a different and stronger variety of realism called naturalism which drew upon French and Russian fiction, native agrarian protest, and Populist ideas. Literature combined the inherited tendencies of romantic thought and expression with the newer methods of realism. This combination was further altered by the naturalistic mode of the nineties in the work of Hamlin Garland, Stephen Crane, and Frank Norris.[1]

Twentieth-century critics have emphasized the negative and corruptive factors of politics and society during The Gilded Age. It is difficult now to avoid certain of the preconceptions about that period of American culture which emerged during the 1920's and 1930's in the historical writings of Charles Beard, V. L. Parrington, Van Wyck Brooks, and others. These men saw the age as the source of economic and cultural disparities adversely affecting their own time. Rugged individualism, the "gospel of wealth," the railroad barons and oil magnates, corrupt politicians, the uncontrolled exploitation of the material resources of the nation, the survival of the fittest were the elements they used to castigate the decades after the Civil War. Historians dismissed morals and manners as "genteel" and "innocent," neo-Puritan in the general refusal to admit the facts of life. *Victorian* became a word to devaluate the taste and manners of The Gilded Age. To George Santayana "The Genteel Tradition" meant that American life then was characterized by a decadent Calvinism, merging with transcendental idealism and a kind of wishful idealism at odds with the pragmatic and materialistic forces of the nineteenth century. Others, like Edith Wharton in her novel *The Age of Innocence* (1920), dramatized the period's effeminate culture and hypocritical high-mindedness. She pictured the 1870's and 1880's as an orthodoxy of factitious purity and false delicacy which shielded wives and daughters from the reigning vulgarity and bad taste. Much of this pejorative criticism needs revaluation. We have proceeded far enough beyond the Menckenism of the twenties and the Marxianism of the thirties to see that some of this flagellation was motivated by the need to disparage the Gilded Age to justify the deficiencies of those later decades. We should go beyond the negative implications of such historical tags as "The Gilded Age," "The Genteel Tradition," and "The Age of Innocence."[2]

Such phrases have only limited validity in accounting for the climate of ideas which helped produce Henry James, Howells, Mark Twain, Henry Adams, and Stephen Crane. Like all men of exceptional gifts they were both of their age and apart from it. James, the most truly original and talented artist of the period, was an American Victorian despite his distrust of much of the American scene and his rediscovery of Europe as a source of value. Howells, old-maidish and conservative to a later generation, was a literary radical in his own time. Henry Adams felt alienated from the politics of the Grant administration, yet he was clearly a product of the intellectual milieu in which positivism, science, and evolution were leading doctrines. The ideas of such original minds as William James, Chauncey Wright, John Fiske, and Charles Peirce were closely woven with the cultural texture of that generation. In short, the literary and intellectual accomplishments of the period were a subtle mingling of new ideas and ways of expression with the public tone and flavor of that much-belittled era of history.

Seeming to have exhausted the possibilities for analysis of Henry James and Mark Twain, criticism has recently turned to lesser writers such as Howells, John W. DeForest, Bret Harte, George W. Cable, and Edward Bellamy. These men had distinguished careers and popular followings, and it would be inappropriate to reassess the period without estimating their accomplishments. Talented and now neglected writers of regional fiction such as Edward Eggleston, Constance Fenimore Woolson, Joel Chandler Harris, Hamlin Garland, and Sarah Orne Jewett were also important. If we include those writers of the 1890's such as Harold Frederic, Stephen Crane, and Frank Norris the literary portrait of the age takes on still larger proportions.

Influential editors directed flourishing literary periodicals. Howells of the *Atlantic Monthly,* R. W. Gilder of the *Century,* G. W. Curtis of *Harper's Weekly,* and J. G. Holland of *Scribner's* were all tastemakers charged by later critics with perpetuating the canons of propriety. The literary essay was an art, and men like T. W. Higginson, Thomas Bailey Aldrich, and H. H. Boyesen carried on the tradition of Lowell and O. W. Holmes. Criticism was slow to develop from conventional book reviews and provincial judgments, but in the hands of James, Howells, and a few liberal-minded men such as Thomas Perry, W. C. Brownell, and E. C. Stedman, it emerged as a literary genre, independent of didacticism. The best of this criticism helped to provide a rationale for the novel of realism.[3]

Popular and sentimental fiction also flourished, a sign of the generally low level of taste among the juvenile or somewhat-arrested-adult readers of boy-books, dime novels, romance, and the kind of fiction once described by Henry James as depending on "a 'happy ending,' on a distribution at the last of prizes, pensions, husbands, wives, babies, millions, appended paragraphs, and cheerful remarks." There were "good" and "bad" boy or girl stories. Frances H. Burnett's *Little Lord Fauntleroy* was a best seller, making a snob-appeal to the American worship of titles. "Juveniles" varied in juvenility from *Tom Sawyer,* a book for adults about boys, to George Peck's *The Story of a Bad Boy and his Pa* and Harriet Stone's *The Five Little Peppers and How They Grew.* Foreign imports such as Stevenson's *Treasure Island,* Blackmore's *Lorna Doone,* Anna Sewell's *Black Beauty,* and Madame Spyri's *Heidi* all found eager readers, along with the adventure novels of Ouida, Rider Haggard, Marie Corelli, and Jules Verne. Native writers indulged in sermonizing and sensation, chivalry and romance, tears and laughter, westerns, and dime novels. The Reverend E. P. Roe struck a new vein of popularity in *Barriers Burned Away,* inspired by the great Chicago fire of 1871. Lew Wallace's *Ben Hur* established a vogue for historical romance in the nineties shared by F. Marion Crawford and others. Edward Westcott's *David Harum* made bad grammar and "hoss-sense" a highly lucrative product and a patriotic fashion for thousands of native readers in the 1890's.

But the most enduring juveniles of them all were the boy-success novels of Horatio Alger. They reflected a taste for mawkish sentiment, faith in hard work, no smoking, and obedience to elders as sure ways of acquiring a fortune. Alger wrote with incredible speed, turning out 109 books between 1868 and 1898, averaging about 50,000 words each and marketed at from ten cents to $1.50 Young readers apparently could not get enough of Alger's painting of the rainbow possibilities of wealth amid degradation and poverty. But farm boys were less impressed by his moralizing than by his fascinating and realistic details of street life in New York.

The Alger books were not merely an adolescent form of the gospel of wealth or a juvenile ethic of acquisitiveness. This interpretation of their historical role is a tempting, but easily exaggerated thesis. For the Alger hero, wealth and success were rewards for duty, patience, and resignation. But the emphasis upon luck and pluck placed the formula more clearly in the traditions of Protestant piety and romantic melodrama. Alger's own evangelical background combined with the popular romance of the period to produce his money-and-happiness endings. These rewards were not the result of struggle and competition, but gifts of providence, chance, virtue, and good fortune.[4]

To many later observers the Gilded Age was a "golden age" of business. The illusion of ever-increasing fortunes was a powerful incentive to divert attention from harsher realities. American innocence, for one thing, was too often mistaken for a virtue, while European experience was considered corrupt. It was flattering to regard the evolutionary philosophy of Darwin and Herbert Spencer as leading upward to infinite progress and development, particularly in material things. Not until later did critical spirits recognize that Social Darwinism contained the seeds of uncontrolled individualism and the worship of strength over equality and humanity. The inequities of a rising urban and industrial civilization were obscured in the general optimism and meliorism. National pride and nativism led to an unwarranted complacency with the dogmas of democracy. It was enough for patriotic spirits that the nation, a century before, had professed in political documents that all men were created equal. Obvious indications to the contrary were dismissed as exceptional; all would be well in the end. There was a western frontier, still waiting to be exploited, a place where men were men, out of the reach of oppressive institutions of church or state. The nation was unconcerned by approaching middle age with its responsibilities and troubling problems.

Such was the general mood in 1870. But it was not the whole story. It established the socio-cultural background for the paradoxical character of Victorian realism. Literary and intellectual life, however, contained a direction and a purpose of its own. What was meant by realism in the fiction of that period? What did the best writers intend to accomplish? What theories and methods did they follow? In the major authors of the time, the disparate and often contradictory forces of the age formed a center which we can regard as the essence of literary realism.[5]

Realism as a literary phenomenon formed in the late 1860's as a protest against mid-century romantic attitudes and conventions. During the 1870's it was in a transitional and experimental stage, and by 1880, there was an authentic movement of realism in the novel; that decade produced the most characteristic writing of the period. After 1890 a different climate of ideas altered the character of realistic fiction when a new and younger generation, sometimes influenced by darker, deterministic philosophies, explored the naturalistic mode. But the gradual beginnings of realism around 1870 may be seen in the early stories of Henry James, in Howells' Italian sketches, De Forest's best novels, especially *Miss Ravenel's Conversion from Secession to Loyalty* (1868), Twain's *Innocents Abroad*, and Bret Harte's *Tales of the Argonauts*. A time of hesitation, the seventies was a decade of nationalism, and a merging of lingering romantic attitudes with newer realities. Henry James described the tone as "a romantic vision of the real." The mood was one of hope and anticipation of the coming dispensation combined with considerable innocence about its form and nature. A spirit of progress, based in part on the lure of material improvement, helped America move on from the tragedy of war. Walt Whitman expressed this somewhat vague idealism: "All goes onward and outward, nothing collapses." Whitman was one of the few who sensed the dangers of materialistic expansion and the neglect of other ideals. The public mind in 1870 was impatient of restraints, unwilling to brood over the human condition. Three factors mainly preserved the illusion of effortless growth: mid-century idealism, positivistic science and evolution, and the buoyant optimism of an expanding nation.

William Dean Howells succeeded in 1871 to the editor's chair of the *Atlantic Monthly,* the leading national literary periodical.[6] In this influential position, he was responsible for the persistence of certain earlier attitudes, but he was also sensitive to the fresh current of realism and contemporaneity apparent in the contributions he accepted for the magazine. His own fiction was at first a blend of "romance" with deft strokes of what he called "real life." Howells was still a decade away from writing convincing studies of manners and social analysis, but his style was flexible and carried the conviction of a genuine artist who could skillfully record authentic dialogue and convincing characters.

The *Atlantic* in the 1870's moved cautiously away from classical moorings toward the fascinating and untried waters of Darwinian controversy, adding the word *science* to its subtitle in 1868. *Appleton's Journal,* edited by E. L. Youmans, the *North American Review,* the *Popular Science Monthly,* and other periodicals discussed new ideas emanating from Darwin, Spencer, Huxley, Tyndall, and Mill. Chauncey Wright, John W. Draper, John Fiske, and other spokesmen of the new science brought positivism and evolution to support a teleological compromise between religious orthodoxy and a naturalistic explanation of man's origin. Instead of God, they substituted the preexistence in the mind of moral reason and self-consciousness. William James urged that emotional and semiconscious states of mind were active elements of reality, emphasizing the validity of desire, feeling, love, aspiration and habit. From the concept of the spontaneous variation of species which William James derived from Darwinian thought, variations from the norm came about mysteriously. But once appearing, they could be evaluated in the direction of useful and valuable ends, thus supporting a conventional ethical system.

Such pragmatic relativism affected fiction, especially in the handling of character. The mind was no longer a static and unitary fact, but was changing and complex, subject to environmental conditions. The brave hero and the virtuous heroine of romantic fiction and literary tradition gave way to the ambiguous and the complex personality—Howells' young women with pretty faces and neurotic psyches, James's highly sensitive individuals, or De Forest's scheming coquettes.

The naturalistic implications of the new science were temporarily suspended in postwar idealism. Nervous critics complained that the novels of James and Howells lacked old-fashioned passion and were too ironic and analytical, too "realistic." Daisy Miller was an outrage on American womanhood; Howells failed to create "noble" women. While there was still a reluctance to grapple with the more violent aspects of human perversity among the lower orders of society, there were important chinks in the façade of what Howells called "the large, cheerful average of health and success in America." Strokes of non-genteel dialect, hill-country speech, and anti-romantic views appeared in the work of such local colorists as Sarah Orne Jewett, Mary E. Freeman, and Constance Fenimore Woolson. Greater fidelity of language and verisimilitude informed the pages of Joel Chandler Harris and George Washington Cable in their sketches of Negroes and Creoles. In tentative ways realism entered select eastern circles and periodicals, where it mingled with tears and laughter, regional eccentricities, humor and sentiment.

In the West and on the middle border, a new and stronger literature of realism heralded a fresh beginning for an indigenous American literary style.[7] Mark Twain and Bret Harte opened this campaign during the late 1860's with *The Celebrated Jumping Frog of Calaveras County* and *Condensed Novels.* The tall tale, a special western kind of humor laced with exaggeration, laughter, and crudity characterized Twain's early writing. *Innocents Abroad* (1868) deflated romantic pretensions and struck a blow at romantic sentiment, flattering the American middlebrow tourist by looking at the Old World with a "show me—I'm from Missouri" attitude. Bret Harte imitated Dickens, Cooper, the Brontës, Dumas, with near-parody and burlesque. In 1870 *The Luck of Roaring Camp and Other Stories* gave its author tremendous and immediate popularity. Harte mingled romantic and realistic elements in a paradoxical way which typified the era's transitional character. His stories were melodramatic and the philosophy behind them meretricious. His people were burlesque variations of the real thing, his style elegant and precious. But in skillful juxtaposition of East and West, in "fine" writing about de-

graded scenes and frontier scamps, in humor mixed with condescension, and in realism compounded with romance, Harte's volume summarized the 1870's. His Dickensian contrasts of frontier types, card sharks, and prostitutes possessing heroic traits of idealism and self-sacrifice, struck a responsive chord typical of the reigning social and cultural nexus.

Sentiment, artifice, decorum, and gentility, which editors and readers in polite eastern circles accepted, were affronted by the weapons of a frontier psychology bent on puncturing romance, effeminacy, and prudishness. The horse sense, misspellings, and earthy humor in the work of Mark Twain, Bret Harte, Bill Nye, and Artemus Ward were not quite realism, but were a powerful antidote to lingering romanticism. Harte parodied Whittier's "Maud Muller"; Mark Twain burlesqued Franklin's earnestness, Cooper's noble scouts and savages, and rebuked the culture-seekers. Yet in many ways even the most intransigent of these iconoclasts belonged to the genteel tradition. Rarely did they overstep the bounds of propriety in relations between the sexes. A generation which could be shocked by Whitman's "indecency" preferred Tom Sawyer's harmless flirtations with Becky Thatcher, or the conventional courtships of popular fiction. If Bret Harte went somewhat further in "The Luck of Roaring Camp," it was overlooked or else disguised by the delicacy of his style. And Henry James's hinted adulteries in *The American* and *The Portrait of a Lady* went almost unnoticed, partly because of the readers' innocence, and partly because James concealed them behind the "fig-leaf" ambiguity of his impeccable prose.

The fiction of Howells and James chiefly revealed the gradual formation of a theory and, more importantly, a method of realism in literature. During the seventies their work was tentative and experimental, but showed a gradually evolving esthetic of the novel considerably in advance of critical theory. They had much in common, despite strong individual differences. They agreed that the writer's first responsibility was to illuminate character. Both were conscious of the need to describe an evolving American type. Almost simultaneously they discovered the *jeune fille,* the innocent but unconventional "heiress of all the ages," whose self-conscious Americanism and pretty face were significantly revealing in a European situation. She was a product of national and regional conditions and the most interesting phenomenon of the novel of realism. Henry James developed the international possibilities of the young American woman in all her complexity—"shocking" independence of manner, idealism, pride, and democratic instincts. Howells treated the type in a variety of domestic situations. His Kitty Ellison (*A Chance Acquaintance,* 1873) was cut from the same cloth as James's Mary Garland (*Roderick Hudson,* 1875) or Euphemia de Mauves or Daisy Miller or Isabel Archer.

Howells differed from James in the importance he attached to the transatlantic novel as a vehicle of realism. He mainly stayed at home. "At my age," he wrote his father in 1876, "one loses a great deal of indefineable, essential something, by living out of one's country, and I'm afraid to risk it." He stood with American nativism, and his fiction was the story of the commonplace, of "poor Real life."

The real dramatic encounter, for both novelists, was always between two or three persons—in short, "romance," but romance controlled and delimited by a firm sense of stern realities. Their novels frequently left heroines in unresolved dilemmas. James especially preferred the inconclusive ending with a near-tragic, or at least a strong renunciatory gesture. Howells, sensitive to the growing scientism of the age, mingled love of New England country inns and picturesque surroundings with shrewd and subtle observation of the moods and whims of Puritan maidens who titillated, but did not quite offend, his lady readers.

As editor and critic, Howells was outspoken in championing truth, actuality, verisimilitude, and fidelity to real human motives. He admired the realists who stressed commonplace events—Trollope, Jane Austen, George Eliot, Turgenev. He praised the honesty of Mark Twain, De Forest, and Bret Harte, but disapproved of Dickens' theatricality and Zola's "bad French morality." He avoided "the fetid explosions of the divorce trials" and overemphasis upon the master passion. His early realism was moderate, and he once said that he would never write a novel his own daughters could not read without embarrassment.

After 1880, when he had resigned from the *Atlantic* editorship, Howells revealed a growing awareness of social and economic facts. He became a Christian socialist with strong sympathies for the working man, and admired Tolstoy's humanitarianism. Later critics charged him with old-maidish propensities, but Howells consciously avoided the sensational and abnormal in his reaction against the high drama and bold adventure of the mid-century romantic novel. Reticence remained part of his conscious creed of realism. He rested the theoretical case squarely on faithfulness to the common, average, middle-class experience of his time.[8]

Henry James's relation to realistic fiction diverged from that of Howells. Beginning in the 1870's at about the same point as his friend and contemporary, he rapidly moved toward the French school of Balzac, Flaubert, and Maupassant.[9] Early European travel and exposure to the richer civilizations and traditions of the Old World saved him from some of the parochialism which affected Howells and other native novelists. In many reviews and essays of the seventies and early eighties, James worked out a wholly original and nearly impressionistic position in the conflicting debates between realism and idealism, or between didacticism and art-for-art's-sake, romance and reality, Anglo-Saxon decency and French license, and other literary dialectics. He admired the serious view of art and the technique in Daudet, Goncourt, and Balzac, while drawing back from "the rags, bad smells, and unclean furniture of the Gallic mind." He praised and practiced Anglo-Saxon wholesomeness and idealism, but his artistic sense and cosmopolitan taste rebelled at the too-insistent didacticism of George Eliot.

The best European models guided James in the 1870's. He was flexible, subtle, discriminating in searching for a literary synthesis to satisfy his own sense of morality and idealism without violating honesty and realism. Like his generation, James was not ready for a naturalistic approach to life or fiction. Temperamentally, he could not accept it even in his late years when it had prevailed. His realism was the modified creed of Turgenev or Daudet, and his critical theories were influenced by the impressionism of Sainte-Beuve and ~~Edmond Scherer~~.

James was a novelist of the highest stature in the great tradition of world literature, admired for experimental methods and an international point of view. Yet he shared the era's esthetic experiments along with some of its Victorian reticences and proprieties. He converted and transcended the limitations of the age through a steady preoccupation with the psychological springs of conduct, an unlimited respect for the potential of the human mind to survive against conventional attitudes and social tyrannies. In his vast curiosity over the techniques of fiction, the subtle, verbal solution to intellectual conflicts, and a strong carry-over into a more scientific age of certain transcendental and idealistic strains of thought, James was the leading realist of fiction during the 1870's. In *Roderick Hudson, The American,* and *Daisy Miller* he explored the theme of international contrast. In Isabel Archer, heroine of *The Portrait of a Lady,* he outlined the young American woman as a generic and symbolic figure of the time. He painted her not in the easy black-and-white contrast of romantic fiction, but in realistic and psychological colors which underlined her complexity.

The Portrait of a Lady (1881), one of his best long novels, marked the culmination of his early international phase. It was a tragedy of manners in a series of portraits, the heroine unifying the whole. The conception was derived from Turgenev, "the beautiful genius," who with George Eliot, contended for the mastery of James's artistic conscience in this novel. It was his first full-length experiment with the method which became his special contribution to the novel form, the use of a central consciousness as an angle of narration to provide dramatic suspense and psychological complexity. Character was his supreme interest, revealed not through action or plot, but through depth and perspective as in a portrait in oils. Isabel Archer filled the center of the canvas, surrounded by satellites arranged in varying attitudes of love, admiration, friendly counsel, or hostility. Deterministic forces entered the situation to compromise her destiny. But the interplay of character and circumstance, equally distributed, produced the dramatic qualities of this externally unexciting story.

The 1880's brought "The Triumph of Realism" in the novel. Howells' *A Modern Instance* (1882) and *The Rise of Silas Lapham* (1885) were his masterpieces. Mark Twain wrote *Huckleberry Finn* (1885) and *A Connecticut Yankee in King Arthur's Court* (1889), the former his most sustained work of fiction. There the romancer and poet, the social critic, the humorist, cynic, realist, satirist, and the rich narrator of the American past were all suffused in the imaginative strength of the style and point of view, restricted to the mind and accent of a young narrator-hero. In the eighties James lived in England, produced two purely American novels, *Washington Square* (1880) and *The Bostonians* (1885), and turned out many skillful short stories and a collection of fine critical essays, *Partial Portraits* (1888).

These three major writers had reached a peak in their productive lives. Each in a different way found the moment propitious for fiction. Some of the earlier hesitations and uncertainties of the seventies coalesced to produce a coherence of thought and an atmosphere of literary ripeness. The earlier idealism had mellowed and blended into a more pragmatic tone. Intellectual America seemed more settled after nervous apprehension over Darwinism and evolution had quieted down. A new synthesis of conflicting ideas came into sight. The self-conscious nationalism of the earlier decade gave way to a new confidence. The quest for reality was deepened, but not yet darkened by the industrial conflicts and social upheavals of the nineties. Realism became less talked about and more successfully practiced in the mid-eighties.

In adapting the methods of the English novel of manners to the American scene and by applying his keen sense of emerging national types, Howells made his finest contribution to realistic fiction. Character was still his primary interest, but a growing concern for social problems gave his work in the middle 1880's range and a new depth. In *A Modern Instance* a steady accumulation of circumstantial detail and environmental forces were marshaled to break up the marriage of Bartley Hubbard and his wife, Marcia Gaylord. The story's naturalistic, even deterministic direction, however, was somewhat weakened by a certain quality of ethical righteousness at odds with the main plot. Howells was more successful in integrating idealism with reality and circumstances in *The Rise of Silas Lapham* by placing within the main character a conflict of mind and a combination of moral weakness and social conscience. Silas Lapham was the first self-made businessman to be handled with psychological complexity against a detailed background. It was a muted but convincing portrait, drawn with a mixture of satire and sympathy after the manner of Jane Austen and with touches which recalled Balzac. From Europe, James described Howells as "the great American naturalist," but warned against a tendency toward certain "romantic phantoms and factitious glosses" in his novels. Howells called James the shaper of a new fiction, derived from Hawthorne and the milder realism of George Eliot and Daudet, rather than that of Zola.

James's own fiction failed to show significant technical advances beyond *The Portrait of a Lady*. His work in the eighties moved toward the social fiction of Balzac and Zola, but his true forte was not to be the novel of sociology or determinism. *Washington Square* and *The Bostonians* applied realistic methods to the American scene, but were not his best work. James failed to find in native conditions a coherence or tradition which did justice to his gift for psychological writing. Both novels were concerned with the realism of spectacle and documentary detail, containing multiple characters and descriptions of places and social conditions. Neither was favorably reviewed, and discouragement over their reception turned James away from the American scene. He omitted them from a later collected edition. Indignation in Boston over the brilliant satire on feminine suffragists and bluestockings in *The Bostonians* affected his own evaluation of the novel, and he turned to an English setting in his next long work, *The Princess Casamassima* (1886). This account of London underground socialists and anarchists and his next work about the London world of the theater and of politics, *The Tragic Muse* (1889), completed the cycle of his long novels of social significance. Their enduring qualities lay in skillful psychological portraiture rather than representation of sociological phenomena and naturalistic documentation. Hyacinth Robinson and Miriam Rooth were rounded literary portraits whose destinies were partially controlled by the different worlds that shaped them.

Mark Twain's relation to the Gilded Age has baffled criticism ever since 1920, when Van Wyck Brooks developed his "genius-thwarted-by-commercialism-and-Puritanism" thesis in *The Ordeal of Mark Twain* (1920).[10] Brooks's denigration of the culture which blunted Mark Twain's idealism and turned his satire into crude humor and vulgarity was echoed by later critics and blended with Marxist criticism of the 1930's. Mark Twain was typical of the age whose name he coined. He mirrored its puzzling contradictions and cross-currents, and shared Colonel Sellers' dream of sudden wealth. Money was the theme of many of his stories, but unlike Horatio Alger's his endings were often bitter. He was defensive about art, Europe, age, tradition, culture, and bookishness; yet he was one of the era's most cosmopolitan travelers. He possessed broad humanitarian sympathies and reformist tendencies, but condemned the human race as selfish, cynical, brutal, and deterministic. He was full of ribaldry and profanity,[11] yet he was one of the most sensitive and "exquisite" of men. He detested "novels, poetry, and theology," but defended the authenticity of local color and regional fiction which could be written only by a man who had years of "unconscious absorption" and prepared himself to report the soul of a nation, its life, speech, and thought.

He was not at home in philosophy or in theoretical criticism; his standards were reality, fact, verisimilitude. He did not write from any conscious theory of the novel. Mark Twain was a conscious literary artist, not a spontaneous genius, but he did not believe in schools or doctrinaire definitions of realism. His was a special blend of realism, born of experience and frontier skepticism, schooled by such hard disciplines as the printing office of a newspaper or the pilot house of a Mississippi steamboat. Travel

Mark Twain (Samuel Langhorne Clemens) (1835–1910)

made him conscious of personal limitations and threw him back upon the main affirmation of his life, faith in individual dignity and worth. In two books of the early 1880's, *Life on the Mississippi* and *Huckleberry Finn,* Twain achieved an equilibrium of the varying elements of his nature and talents.[12] It was not the middle zone between romance and naturalism sought by Howells, nor the special "ideal reality" of James, but a balance between the youthful, frontier humorist and the aging misanthropist of the 1890's. In these books he successfully expressed his strain of idealism and love of accurate dialects and local places and people. He could not hold the balance long. *A Connecticut Yankee,* for all its brilliance and bitter satire, exhibited less of the control and sustained writing skill that marked the two earlier masterpieces.[13]

Mark Twain belongs to world literature but he was a village iconoclast with the gift of laughter and a strain of eternal youth and innocence which have especially endeared him to Americans. In his one undoubted literary masterpiece, *Huckleberry Finn,* he raised the rural American past to the level of myth and gave a symbolic quality to the Mississippi River and the Midwest frontier. Miraculously, and seemingly without a conscious theory of fiction, he explored the dramatic potential of a narrating center by endowing the vernacular hero with a conflict between his natural idealism and the hereditary training of the established slave culture of prewar America. Huck thus

symbolized the nation's tragic divisions. Mark Twain was also the source of a genuine American idiom in which native humor, dialect, and speech rhythms created a literary style free of British mannerism. He remained part of the Gilded Age, but transformed its commonplace experience and even adolescent emotion into enduring literature. Youth and innocence helped shape his mind, but a powerful presentiment of reality and truth marked his genius.

In the late 1880's, literature began to reflect social and cultural changes. Civil unrest and labor strife increased, signaling intensified class conflict. The great popularity of Edward Bellamy's *Looking Backward* (1887) testified to growing concern over an unbalanced economy. Collectivist protest, which novelists had disregarded as unfit for genteel consumption, entered into the mainstream of realism around 1890 in the works of Howells, Hamlin Garland, and Stephen Crane. Deeply affected by the "civic murder" of the Chicago anarchists convicted after the Haymarket affair in Chicago in 1886 and strengthened by his reading of Tolstoy, Howells changed his private stance from passive humanitarianism to active protest. In *A Hazard of New Fortunes* (1890), *A Traveler from Altruria* (1894), and other novels he displayed a highly developed social conscience in behalf of the working class. His personal philosophy veered sharply in the direction of government control of key industries such as utilities. Garland's *Main Travelled Roads* (1891) voiced the silent suffering of agrarian life, made poignant by the first-hand experience of his family in Wisconsin and the Dakotas. And Stephen Crane, in *Maggie, A Girl of the Streets* (1893), reported with the dispassionate pen of a journalist and the irony of an artist how poverty and drunkenness drove the daughter of a Bowery family in lower New York to prostitution and suicide.

The naturalistic mode in fiction was in its early phase during the nineties, but its concern with social problems of the lower orders of society and its economic determinism dominated fiction well into the next century. Frank Norris' *McTeague* (1899) was the first full-blown naturalistic novel in America, using some of Zola's methods in a San Francisco setting. *McTeague* and *The Octopus* (1901) embodied Norris' special combination of Populist folklore, violence, and melodrama. His powerful prose style, a mingling of scientific documentation and the excessive use of reiterated symbols of natural forces, gave his writing its special quality and identified it with the 1890's. The decade was deeply divided between the new realism of economic protest and a resurgence of romantic interest in brute strength and Darwinian muscle. Norris had lofty notions of the novel as a pulpit from which to preach Truth to The People, and to demonstrate "whole congeries of forces, social tendencies, and race impulses." He felt it should contain violence, vast scenic effects, murder, bloodshed and "variations from the type of normal life" which he associated with the realism of Howells and his followers.[14]

War, poverty, shipwreck, and violence also provided the material for much of Stephen Crane's writing. As a journalist and reporter for a newspaper syndicate, Crane reported two wars, traveled much of the world, and wrote of first-hand experience in a distinctive style beyond reportage. Crane believed in immediacy of experience for the writer, yet paradoxically his masterpiece, *The Red Badge of Courage* (1895), was about a war he never saw. This account of a raw recruit facing battle conditions in the Civil War was a brilliant imaginative reconstruction of war scenes and a profound study in the psychology of cowardice, fear, and bravery. But Crane's technical accomplishments, impressionistic style, and symbolic devices were equally innovative. Myth and metaphor contributed largely to the meaning of *The Red Badge*. The story has suggested to some critics a search for self-identity by a young knight questing through perilous adventures for a holy grail of ancient myth. Much of this mythic ritual was contained in imagery with religious undertones and symbolic colors, and in abstract landscapes and allegorical figures. Like Mark Twain in *Huckleberry Finn,* Crane discovered much of the meaning and ironic complexity of his novel in careful handling of the limited point of view of his young and innocent hero.[15]

In this same decade Henry James turned to writing plays for the London theatre, an experience which taught him new techniques for fiction. In *What Maisie Knew, The Turn of the Screw,* and *The Sacred Fount,* all written in the late 1890's, he used a limited angle of narration to gain dramatic irony and suspense. Only after 1900 did he theorize about a "center of consciousness" in the prefaces to his novels. Both Mark Twain and Stephen Crane followed the course he charted in using a controlled center of narration, to be the single most important discovery of the twentieth-century novel.

The search for reality, begun in the 1870's with the mild and tentative realism of local-color writers and the early travel fiction of Howells and Mark Twain, gradually evolved into the complex novel of psychological and sociological significance during the eighties and nineties. This evolution brought new insights and methods that made *Huckleberry Finn, The Red Badge of Courage,* and the late major novels of Henry James masterpieces of American fiction, and placed them among the great novels in the English language.

Notes

1. Among recent works see: Larzer Ziff, *The American 1890's: The Life and Times of a Lost Generation* (New York: Viking Press, 1966); Warner Berthoff, *The Ferment of Realism: American Literature, 1884-1919* (New York: Free Press, 1965); Jay Martin, *Harvests of Change: American Literature, 1865-1914* (New York: Prentice-Hall, 1967); Everett Carter, *Howells and the Age of Realism* (Philadelphia: J. B. Lippincott, 1954).

2. In 1922 James M. Barrie warned younger critics: "Don't forget to speak scornfully of the Victorian age. There will be a time for meekness when you seek to better it." See "Courage," *Rectorial Addresses, St. Andrews,* May 3, 1922.

3. Sinclair Lewis was amusing but unfair in saying later that criticism in the Gilded Age was "a chill and insignificant activity pursued by jealous spinsters, ex-baseball reporters, and acid professors." *Why Sinclair Lewis Got the Nobel Prize* (New York, 1930), 20.

4. Frank Luther Mott, *Golden Multitudes* (New York: Macmillan, 1947), estimates the total sale of Alger books at about 16 million copies, but figures are debatable; see also Frank Gruber, *Horatio Alger, Jr.: A Biography and Bibliography* (Los Angeles: Grover Jones, 1961); and John W. Tebbel, *From Rags to Riches: Horatio Alger, Jr. and the American Dream* (New York: Macmillan, 1963).

5. Robert Falk, *The Victorian Mode in American Fiction, 1865-1885* (East Lansing: Michigan State University Press, 1965).

6. The literature on Howells is abundant, but see especially: E. H. Cady's two-volume biography, *The Road to Realism* (Syracuse: Syracuse University Press, 1956), and *The Realist at War* (Syracuse: Syracuse University Press, 1958); H. N. Smith and W. M. Gibson, eds., *The Correspondence of Samuel L. Clemens and William Dean Howells, 1872-1901,* 2 vols. (Cambridge: Harvard University Press, 1960); George N. Bennett, *William Dean Howells: The Development of a Novelist* (Norman: University of Oklahoma Press, 1959); Clara M. Kirk, *William Dean Howells: Traveller From Altruria, 1889-1894* (New Brunswick: Rutgers University Press, 1962); Robert L. Hough, *The Quiet Rebel: William Dean Howells as Social Commentator* (Lincoln: University of Nebraska Press, 1959); and Kermit Vanderbilt, *The Achievement of William Dean Howells* (Princeton: Princeton University Press, 1968).

7. Martin, *Harvests of Change,* covers regional literature well. Jean Holloway, *Hamlin Garland: A Biography* (Austin: University of Texas Press, 1960), goes beyond its title. See also William Randel, *Edward Eggleston* (New York: Twayne, 1963); Clyde E. Henson, *Joseph Kirkland* (New York: Twayne, 1962); James F. Light, *John William De Forest* (New York: Twayne, 1965).

8. See Carter, *Howells and the Age of Realism;* and Clara Marburg Kirk, *W. D. Howells and Art in His Time* (New Brunswick: Rutgers University Press, 1965).

9. The literature on James is enormous, and the first three volumes of Leon Edel's biography of James are indispensable. F. O. Matthiessen, *Henry James: The Major Phase* (New York: Oxford University Press, 1944), and the same author's *The James Family* (New York: Knopf, 1947), are useful. Percy Lubbock, ed., *Letters of Henry James,* 2 vols. (New York: Scribner's, 1920), contains primary material.

10. Justin Kaplan, *Mr. Clemens and Mark Twain: A Biography* (New York: Simon and Schuster, 1966), is an excellent biography. Louis J. Budd, *Mark Twain: Social Philosopher* (Bloomington: Indiana University Press, 1962), analyzes Clemens' attitude toward various public issues. Gladys C. Bellamy, *Mark Twain as a Literary Artist* (Norman: University of Oklahoma Press, 1950), is an excellent book. The old authorized life by Albert Bigelow Paine, *Mark Twain: A Biography*, 3 vols. (New York: Harper, 1912), is pedestrian but has valuable raw material. The most perceptive personal account in many ways remains William Dean Howells, *My Mark Twain* (New York: Harper, 1910).

11. In 1877 he wrote Howells: "Delicacy—a sad false delicacy—robs literature of the two best things among its belongings. Family circle narrative and obscene stories." A. B. Paine, ed., *Mark Twain's Letters,* 2 vols. (New York: Harper, 1917), I, 310.

12. See Walter Blair, *Mark Twain and Huck Finn* (Berkeley and Los Angeles: University of California Press, 1950).

13. See Henry Nash Smith, *Mark Twain's Fable of Progress: Political and Economic Ideas in 'A Connecticut Yankee'* (New Brunswick: Rutgers University Press, 1964); and the same author's *Mark Twain: The Development of a Writer* (Cambridge: Harvard University Press, 1962).

14. See Lars Ahnebrink, *The Beginnings of Naturalism in American Fiction* (Cambridge: Harvard University Press, 1950), for background. Franklin Walker, *Frank Norris: A Biography* (New York: Doubleday, Doran, 1932), remains the standard biography, but is outdated and thin. Warren French, *Frank Norris* (New York: Twayne, 1962), is a good brief account. Ernest Marchand, *Frank Norris: A Study* (Stanford: Stanford University Press, 1942), is still useful. So is Donald Pizer, *The Novels of Frank Norris* (Bloomington: Indiana University Press, 1966).

15. The newest biography is R. W. Stallman, *Stephen Crane: A Biography* (New York: Braziller, 1968). Lillian Gilkes, *Cora Crane* (Bloomington: Indiana University Press, 1960), is important. R. W. Stallman and Lillian Gilkes, eds., *Stephen Crane: Letters* (New York: New York University Press, 1960), is a basic primary source. See also: Donald B. Gibson, *The Fiction of Stephen Crane* (Carbondale: Southern Illinois University Press, 1968); Eric Salomon, *Stephen Crane: From Parody to Realism* (Cambridge: Harvard University Press, 1966).

Alan Trachtenberg (essay date 1982)

SOURCE: "Fictions of the Real," in *The Incorporation of America: Culture and Society in the Gilded Age*, Hill and Wang, 1982, pp. 182-207.

[*In the essay below, Trachtenberg follows the development of Realism during the Gilded Age as a reaction against the sentimentalism of earlier romances and dime novels.*]

I

"Realism," complained Hamilton Wright Mabie, erstwhile critic for the *Christian Union,* seemed bent on "crowding the world of fiction with commonplace people, whom one could positively avoid coming into contact with in real life; people without native sweetness or strength, without acquired culture or accomplishments, without the touch of the ideal which makes the commonplace significant and worthy of study." In such chiding remarks, the voices of gentility insisted on their view of art: on one side, "culture," "sweetness," "the ideal"; on the other, crowds of "commonplace people," with a broad hint of city streets and slums. Fiction, the critic implies, should display the good taste of gentlefolk; it should "avoid" vulgarity by the simple device of refusing to recognize it. Like the refined gentry, art should protect itself from common life, should concern itself with "ideal" characters, pure thoughts, and noble emotions.

Although gentility had strengthened its hold on institutions of education and art, publishing and philanthropy, nevertheless critics and editors frequently took a defensive tone, challenged as much by new currents of art and literature as by vulgar politics and business. "Realism" seemed such a threat, the term naming not so much a single consistent movement as a tendency among some painters and writers to depict contemporary life without moralistic condescension. Of course, the threats seem relatively timid now compared to the rise of modernist experiment and innovation in the arts which reached New York from Europe early in the twentieth century. In painting, for example, convention still held strong. Artists took their typical subjects from the familiar academic modes of landscape, genre, and allegory, excluding signs of contemporary conflict and disturbance. Fashionable salon art favored scenes of leisure, of polite ease amid comfortable surroundings; a passive enjoyment of sunshine and beaches, of rich interiors, of rural scenes glazed with nostalgia, struck the most frequent note. To be sure, exceptions appeared: John Ferguson Weir's industrial interiors in the 1870's, Thomas Pollock Anshutz's remarkable picture of lounging workers in "Ironworkers: Noontime" (1882), and Robert Kohler's dramatic "The Strike" (1886). But not until the "Ash Can School" at the turn of the century would a concerted movement appear to depict city life in its daily unheroic scenes.

In the works of the two most prominent realists of the period, Winslow Homer and Thomas Eakins, a greater range of subject matter and a more strenuous original vision did appear as striking exceptions. Homer's variety of subject was perhaps the most extensive among established easel painters, embracing figures intent in work or sport: fishermen and women mending nets, seamen battling roiling high waters, huntsmen tracking their prey, country children at chores and games. Homer's canvases seem free of thematic concerns, certainly of moral judgments, idealizations, or simple interpretations, but they often hint at philosophical reflections on man's vulnerable condition in nature and the consequently enduring value of activity, of play as much as labor. Eakins's work was often even more overtly athletic, isolating single figures—boxers, wrestlers, rowers—as lonely performers of skill and endurance. Eakins's pictures disclose a world scrutinized in fine detail, with exacting analytical rigor. As a teacher as well as an artist, he insisted on studying anatomy directly from human models, and defied the prudery of art schools in his native Philadelphia in employing nude models. He participated as a nude subject in the photographer Eadweard Muybridge's experiments in recording the human figure in motion at the University of Pennsylvania in the 1890's.

Eakins's unflinching acceptance of the body, encouraged by his friendship with the older Walt Whitman, troubled his relations with the established art world. His famous "The Gross Clinic" (1875) was consigned to the medical section of the Centennial Exposition in Philadelphia in 1876, excluded from the fine-arts exhibition because of the daring of its subject: the eminent surgeon Samuel Gross performing an operation while lecturing to a class. The canvas showed in detail an incision into a living body, and portrayed a range of responses in the audience, from fascination to horror. The picture also manifested Eakins's affinity with science, with its objectivity and rules of analysis: qualities he strived to achieve in his own art. Increasingly, Eakins turned to portraiture and the study of character; many of his canvases of performers, doctors, writers, businessmen, and their wives seem themselves surgical incisions, pictures of inward strain, disappointment, loneliness. Honesty of report, faithfulness to the act of seeing, refusal to idealize, disciplined accuracy: these features epitomized Eakins's realism, his break with the strictures of gentility, and his kinship with the rising rebellious spirit of the age.

II

The "realist feels in every nerve the equality of things and the unity of men," wrote William Dean Howells in the late 1880's. As for the complaints of genteel critics, he observed that "the aristocratic spirit," having lost its place of honor, now sheltered itself in aestheticism: "The pride of caste is becoming the pride of taste; but, as before, it is averse to the mass of men; it consents to know them only in some conventionalized and artificial guise." By contrast, "democracy in literature is the reverse of all this. It wishes to know and to tell the truth." Realists want to know the world as it really is, to create a world of fiction congruent with "real life." Thus, the literary battle lines were drawn, in Howells's mind, on a distinct political terrain. Realism represented nothing less than the extension of democracy into the precincts of fiction.

Howells launched monthly polemics against the aristocratic spirit from his seat in the "Editor's Study" of *Harper's Monthly* in the late 1880's and 1890's, a steady flow of reviews and screeds in defense of a fiction of the real. The target was not difficult to fix, but he well understood the superior resources of the enemy. Public taste, he complained, remained in vassalage to false values, preferring easy pleasures of shallow "romance" to the more exacting demands of the real. As he sensed defeat, his tone grew bitter and resigned. "By far the greatest number of people in the world," he lamented in 1899, "even the civilized world, are people of weak and childish imagination, pleased with gross fables, fond of prodigies, heroes, heroines, portents and impracticalities, without self-knowledge, and without the wish for it." The public imagination seemed to resist the healthier doses of reality, the general reader remaining a "spoiled child" spurning instruction. "I suppose we shall have to wait," Howells conceded sadly in a *New York Times* interview with Stephen Crane in 1894.

Howells waged a battle on behalf of literary principles he had begun to practice in his novels of the 1880's, fictions in which he wished not only to open his pages to the real but also to persuade his readers that reading was a moral exercise, a serious exertion of civic faculties. "The novelist has a grave duty to his reader," he wrote, a duty of no small consequence to the republic. In this regard, Howells's campaign for realism resembled other campaigns for culture, for public enlightenment and elevation, for a restored middle ground. The "real" his touchstone of value, "false" became his deepest term of disdain, directed especially against those "innutritious" novels "that merely tickle our prejudices and lull our judgment, or that coddle our sensibilities, or pamper our gross appetites for the marvelous . . . clog the soul with unwholesome vapors of all kinds." As fearful of "barbarism" (from the unmentionable worlds of dime fiction and sordid adventure) as he was contemptuous of arrested aesthetic sensibilities (in genteel sentimental romance), Howells takes his place among the legions of nervous intellectuals seeking a role for themselves and a sense of control in what he named at the turn of the century "our deeply incorporated civilization." But if, under the banner of realism, he stands within those ranks, the banner itself marked a difference; while it may have clad him in a certain insulating virtue of its own, it also tempted him perilously close to the edge of his middle-class convictions and values. As a doctrine, realism gave Howells a stand on an imagined middle ground. In literary practice, however, it often caused that ground to shift under his feet.

Realism served Howells less as a doctrine and more as a conviction of rectitude. As he told Stephen Crane in 1894, realism was a corrective to faulty vision, a way of disclosing what is really *there*. The realist novel is "made for the benefit of people who have no true use of their eyes." Its aim is "to picture the daily life in the most exact terms possible, with an absolute and clear sense of proportion." True fiction "adjusts the proportions," "preserves the balances," and thus "lessons are to be taught and reforms won. When people are introduced to each other they will see the resemblances, and won't want to fight so badly."

Seeing, picturing, recognizing: these represent realism's mode of reconciliation, the seriousness and gravity of its service to the republic.

Howells had arrived at his commitment to the healing powers of realism in the course of the troubled 1880's. In that decade, he moved from Boston and his post as chief editor of the prestigious *Atlantic Monthly,* to New York and eventually to the editorship of *Harper's Monthly.* The move corresponded to a shift in his own fiction, away from the courtship romances and polite travel narratives he had mastered in the 1870's, toward the novel of social realism in *A Modern Instance* (1882), *The Rise of Silas Lapham* (1885), *The Minister's Charge* (1887), *Annie Kilburn* (1889), and *A Hazard of New Fortunes* (1890). The change in residence and mode of fiction truly marked a major turn of Howells. As a young aspiring writer in rural Ohio before the Civil War, he had learned through self-education to adulate both the Republican Party and the high literary culture of New England, of Emerson, Lowell, and Longfellow. Rewarded with the position of consul in Venice for his campaign biography of Lincoln, he missed serving in the Civil War but gained enough of a reputation by his travel writings to return to a highly prized job on the staff of the *Atlantic,* tapped by the elder Brahmins as their adopted Western son. Even after his move to New York, Howells continued to cherish the Boston ideal. In its day, he wrote at the end of the century, Boston held together "a group of authors as we shall hardly see here again for hundreds of years." Moreover, "there was such regard for them and their calling, not only in good society, but among the extremely well-read people of the whole intelligent city, as hardly another community has shown."

Boston nourished a belief in the seriousness of literature, in the elevating influence of fine writing and reading, which remained a deep assumption of Howells's realism and a frequent theme of conversation within his novels. "I wonder what the average literature of non-cultivated people is," says the young Corey to his father, the old Boston Brahmin, in *The Rise of Silas Lapham.* The question concerns the young man's growing acquaintance with the Laphams, a country family newly rich on the weight of their father's success as a paint manufacturer. Living now in Boston, they seek acceptance in "society," and their unpolished ways, their lack of cultivation, and their conspicuous wealth pose a problem for the cultivated elite. "I don't suppose that we who have the habit of reading, and at least a nodding acquaintance with literature," replies the father, "can imagine the bestial darkness of the great mass of people—even people whose houses are rich and whose linen is purple and fine." The son agrees but ventures the opinion that the Laphams are nevertheless "intelligent people. They are very quick, and they are shrewd and sensible." "I have no doubt that some of the Sioux are so," Bromfield Corey retorts. "But that is not saying they are civilized. All civilization comes through literature now, especially in our country. A Greek got his civilization by talking and looking, and in some measure a Parisian may still do it. But we, who live remote from history and monuments, we must read or we must barbarize."

The elder Corey's words find echoes in Howells's own defense of literature: we must read or we must barbarize. But realism proposes a kind of reading, a way of seeing, which will mollify Corey's too stringent judgments; it will propose a more balanced view in which Silas Lapham's basic moral soundness will appear in true proportion to his country roughness and *arriviste* vulgarity (itself a result of a misplaced desire, on behalf of his daughters, to "rise" in Boston society). Throughout the novel, dialogue and action disclose how false readings misprepare people for real predicaments, the daily plights of normal existence, just as they prejudge inner character by social appearance.

In its narration, *Silas Lapham* asserts itself as the very model of the kind of reading and seeing the world needs badly: a pedagogy as well as a story. In this process of pointing to itself as an example of the realism missing from the human relations it portrays, the novel relies on the good Reverend Sewall, another Brahmin, intimate of the Coreys, yet also a sympathetic adviser to the Laphams. Sewall instructs the reader as well as his friends to beware of the false lessons of sentimental fiction. For the most part, he explains, novelists have had a "noxious" influence, fastening onto love and marriage "in a monstrous disproportion," praising self-sacrifice even when inappropriate. Considering their influence now that fiction forms "the whole intellectual experience of more people" than does religion, "novelists might be the greatest help to us if they painted life as it is, and human feelings in their true proportion and relation." For this they must overcome their abhorrence of the commonplace—"that light, impalpable, aerial essence which they've never got into their confounded books yet," exclaims yet another clear-eyed character. "The novelist who could interpret the commonplace feelings of commonplace people would have the answer to 'the riddle of the painful earth' on his tongue"—as Sewall attempts to interpret Lapham to the Coreys; as the novel itself attempts to interpret the entire Corey-Lapham world and all its misunderstandings, small and large.

The high value of reading, then, in the high culture of Boston, provided a key component in Howells's restorative realism. But the notion of reading as a corrective seeing, a true perspective, implied additional assumptions, not always in rapport with each other. When Howells insisted that "realism is nothing more and nothing less than the truthful treatment of material," it was partly to quiet alarms that realism held in store a revolution in letters, morals, and possibly society, hinted at by Flaubert in *Madame Bovary.* But "truthful treatment" does link Howells's realism with that of European writers in one significant regard. Appearing first in France in the 1830's, the term "realism" came to signify a general rejection in the arts of academic models, a defiance of the standards of symmetry and harmony on behalf of firsthand experience, direct observation of the visible world. In literature, its effects showed especially in the novel, in its "complete emancipation," in Eric Auerbach's words, from the neoclassical doctrine of "levels of style" according to which "everyday practical reality" and lower-class people "could find a place in literature only within the frame of a low or inter-mediate kind of style, that is to say, as either grotesquely comic or pleasant, light, colorful, and elegant entertain-ment." Thus, continues Auerbach, realism came to mean "the serious treatment of every reality, the rise of more ex-tensive and socially inferior human groups to the position of subject matter for problematic-existential representa-tion." In short, realism freed the "low" from the hold of the "high," permitting rough-edged slang-speaking charac-ters like Silas Lapham to be taken seriously as having genuine problems and true consciousness.

"But let fiction cease to lie about life," demanded How-ells. "Let it portray men and women as they are, actuated by the motives and the passions in the measure we all know." Moreover, "let it speak the dialect, the language, that most Americans know—the language of unaffected people everywhere." Howells well understood that simply to allow characters low on the social scale to speak with the same freedom as what he dubbed "grammatical char-acters" constituted a kind of revolution, an overturning of those ingrained conventions which still guided popular novels. Moreover, because those conventions of linguistic representation worked hand in hand with the ever-present convention of the romantic-courtship plot, freedom of speech alone implied a radical change in the status of that plot, if not a complete elimination of it. Thus, Sewall's at-tack on the "monstrous disproportion" of the courtship-marriage plot served also to justify a novel about Silas Lapham's mundane "rise" in the first place.

A discourse of the "low," in dialect and vernacular speech, had already found a place in American writing, in the Southwestern humorous tales published in the East before the Civil War, in "local color" stories which had begun to appear in the 1850's and broadened into a major current in the postwar decades, and even in very popular sentimental romances such as Susan Warner's *The Wide, Wide World* (1850). But by and large, the low remained low, subordi-nated by plot and other devices of social designation to what can be called a discourse of respectability—a mode of writing which takes as its own the speech and social perspective of its "grammatical characters": a subordina-tion found in varying degrees in Bret Harte's California mining-camp stories and poems, James Whitcomb Riley's Indian Hoosier poems, the Uncle Remus tales of Joel Chandler Harris, George Washington Cable's Creole sto-ries, Mary Murfree's treatment of rural Southern whites, the New England regional fictions of Mary Wilkins and Sarah Orne Jewett. With few exceptions, dialect either ap-peared within a grammatical framework or otherwise made clear it was intended for a grammatically proper reader. This placement of speech in such a way that it is unmis-takably recognized as "low," as culturally inferior to the *writing* of the narrator, owed as much to economics as to the social attitudes of writers (most of them middle or up-per class in origins), an effect of prudential considerations in a literary marketplace controlled largely by major East-ern periodicals like *Atlantic, Century,* and *Harper's.* In the 1880's, the monthlies had evolved a remarkable authority

over the production of fiction. Realism suited their pur-poses of reaching a national audience as long as it was tempered to accord with the predominant Protestant moral-ity they assumed among their readers. For the privilege of publication and payment, regional writers were expected to present *themselves* at least, even if not their characters, as standing within that morality, that national discourse of propriety.

Not until Mark Twain's *Adventures of Huckleberry Finn* (1884), told entirely in the vernacular voice of an illiterate outcaste boy of the Mississippi valley, did the linguistic freedom implicit in realism come to fruition in America. From the outset, Mark Twain had circumvented the jour-nals and the respectable publishing houses often (like *At-lantic* and *Harper's* and *Scribner's*) tied directly to the journals, by publishing his books on a subscription basis, sold door-to-door by traveling agents, reaching a nonliter-ary audience almost as large as that of dime novels and story papers sold at newsstands. Stamped thus with the onus of popularity, less an "author" than an entertainer, a personality, a "humorist," Mark Twain began his career outside the circle of respectability, and soon found a be-grudging genteel acceptance. In the linguistic experiment of *Huckleberry Finn,* he found a freedom for the realistic telling of tales of insanity, murder, thievery, betrayal, feud-ing and lynching, and brutalities of racism without prece-dent in American fiction: without precedent, and unique until the appearance in 1900 of Theodore Dreiser, who in *Sister Carrie* and later novels would abandon respectabil-ity altogether, along with the very notion of "high" and "low," romantic plots, and the entire apparatus of recon-ciliation that lay at the heart of Howells's enterprise.

In 1895, Howells defended the growing use of dialect as indicating "the wider diffusion of the impulse to get the whole of American life into our fiction." *Huck Finn* and *Sister Carrie* suggest that getting "into" fiction entailed more than the deft inclusion of vernacular speech. How-ells, who rarely employed dialect, confined the vernacular to dialogue: his narratives remained securely within the discourse of respectability, as in *Silas Lapham,* with the important modification that Silas is allowed a major, not merely a comic or incidental role, a role, moreover, which serves to correct the social, moral, and *literary* perspective of grammatical characters like Bromfield Corey and the reader. For it is clear from the narrator's own ease of dis-course that he addresses the Coreys among his readers, not the Silas Laphams, who are not yet presumed to have de-veloped a taste for serious fiction. Howells remains, then, within the circle, attempting to revise its vision from within.

And this posture, of standing within, of staking his risks on the middle ground, involved Howells in what has ap-peared to later critics as a fatal flaw in his realism: his per-mitting respectability to censor his observations and in-sights. This reservation, however, mislocates the contradiction. In fact, Howells revised the notion of real-ism to fit his own role, the role of fashioning serious fiction as an anodyne for the rifts he observed in the social fabric, the growing tensions between old and new ways of life. "Fidelity to experience and probability of motive" represented to Howells fidelity to the true underlying shape of American experience. Realism will always find "consolation and delight" in "real life" because, Howells believed, real life, in America at least, was at bottom truly governed by a moral universe. Neither callousness nor dishonesty led him in 1886, the year of the Haymarket crisis whose outcome would so agitate his convictions as to make of him a Christian socialist and in the 1890's a utopian novelist, to write: "In a land where journeymen carpenters and plumbers strike for four dollars a day the sum of hunger and cold is certainly very small, and the wrong from class to class is also inappreciable. We invite our novelists, therefore, to concern themselves with the more smiling aspects of life, which are the more American." What was "peculiarly American," he continued, was "the large, cheerful average of health and success and happy life."

The contradiction in his notion of realism may be found rather in his fictions: not in his beliefs but in his practices. The Reverend Sewall holds that fiction, however paradoxical, should be *true,* that novels should paint life "as it is." Howells himself stressed perspective, balanced and proportioned seeing; that is, *picture.* Picture implies the making of a form, and also the closure of an event: that is, it implies *plot.* By Howells's notion of "real life," balance, proportion, picture, and plot inhere in reality itself: all a matter of proper seeing. Yet, seeing is not, for him, description alone; realism is "false to itself" when it "maps life instead of picturing it." A true-to-life picture, then, will seem credible because life itself contains that picture, that form, that symmetry of plot.

So goes the theory. In practice, in his novels of the 1880's especially, Howells frequently felt he needed to force his picture into its proportions and balances even if by acts of arbitrary plotting, by transparent devices of romance such as the Corey-Lapham marriage, and Silas's quite unbusinesslike renunciation of the opportunity to revenge himself against a former crooked partner and make a handsome pile of money in the bargain: a renunciation which wins him the admiration of the Coreys as having in the end "behaved very well—like a gentleman." The denouement entails destruction of a scapegoat, the crooked partner Rogers, as indeed, in *A Modern Instance* and *A Hazard of New Fortunes,* acts of violence—the killing of Bartley and of Conrad Dreyfus—serve as punishments or sacrifices essential to the balance and proportion of the picture, of the plot. Moreover, the romantic-courtship element, which Howells never entirely abandoned, serves the same end by another course, the reverse of violence and murder: the regenerative powers of the good woman, of emotional and domestic love. For the sake of the moral order he assumed realism would disclose, it was essential that characters reap their just rewards, that good come to the good and bad to the bad—even at the cost of plausibility. Too often Howells contrived devices—chance encounters, changes

of heart, sacrificial acts—to ensure a relatively benign outcome, if not exactly a happy ending, then at least a morally pleasing one. Thus, Howells resorted often to "romance" to preserve the moral assurances of his "realism."

Realism, then, brings Howells to the point where, in spite of himself, his fictions of the real disclose the unresolved gaps and rifts within the traditional world view he wishes to maintain, to correct and discipline. That outlook no longer possessed the resources of self-renewal, of creative accommodation to the new shape of its world. Resorting to romance, Howells conceded, without acknowledgment, the fundament of illusion on which his realism rested: the illusion and romance of "America" itself.

For Howells, realism and America were always interchangeable terms, the one informing and assuring the other of that ultimate coming-out-all-right which held together the middle-class Protestant view. In response to Matthew Arnold's remark that America lacked "distinction," Howells respectfully if illogically replied that "somehow, the idea that we call America has realized itself so far that we already have identification rather than distinction." This means: "Such beauty and such grandeur as we have is common beauty, common grandeur, or the beauty and grandeur in which the quality of solidarity so prevails that neither distinguishes itself to the disadvantage of anything else." Howells remarks improbably that America invites "the artist to the study and the appreciation of the common, and to the portrayal in every art of those finer and higher aspects which unite rather than sever mankind, if he would thrive in our new order of things." As solidarity, as order, as higher and finer aspects which unite, "America" is thus America's own romance—what Melville would call in another connection, in the same troubled days at the end of the 1880's, "the symmetry of form attainable in pure fiction."

III

"My mother called them all *lies,*" Penelope Lapham says to Tom Corey about novels. "'They're certainly fictions,' said Corey, smiling." But fictions, in the best of cases, Howells would add, are also true. His campaign for realism had on one important side the high motive of establishing precisely this, the authority and legitimacy of serious fiction as a serious enterprise. Realism held within itself a defense of literature: a defense as much against the idealists' claim that art belonged to a "higher" sphere, as against traditional moral scruples, like Mrs. Lapham's, against novels and novel reading.

Like James, Howells was especially vexed by the apparent anomaly of serious literature, fictions with truth-telling claims, in a culture ruled by business values, by images of success and failure. The role of reading in *Silas Lapham,* of journalism in *A Modern Instance,* of the founding of a new periodical of letters, arts, and opinion in *A Hazard of New Fortunes,* embodied that concern; the novels can be taken as examinations of the predicament of serious writing as well as pedagogies of serious reading.

A critical predicament, central in *A Hazard of New Fortunes,* was the changed economic situation of the writer as a social type, a vocational category. Until the Civil War, Howells explained in an essay at the end of the century, "The Man of Letters as a Man of Business," few writers could hope for economic independence from literary income alone. Now, because of "the prosperity of the magazines," it is possible for writers to "live prettily enough," chiefly by sale of serial publications to journals. Still, the man of letters retains a "low grade among business men." This is because "literature is still an infant industry," book publication making "nothing like the return to the author the magazine makes." Also, even among "the highest class" of magazine readers, the "love of pure literature," as opposed to opinion, science, travel, and so on, has been "growing less and less," hardly strong enough "to justify the best business talent in devoting itself" to letters. For those seeking financial success, writing remains a poor investment of time and effort, though indeed storytelling is now a recognized trade, occasionally lucrative for those willing to produce "the sort of fiction which corresponds in literature to the circus and the variety theatre." Even the best-known serious writers often earn less than "a rising young physician," a fact "humiliating to an author in the presence of a nation of business men like ours."

The humiliation points to the mixed feelings rampant in Howells's essay. At the outset he had established as a basic premise the bizarre anomaly of art in a world of business. The artist knows "there is something false and vulgar" in the practice of selling art, something obscenely wrong in the conception of artworks as commodities, in the poet's use of his emotions, for example, "to pay his provision bills." "The work which cannot be truly priced in money cannot be truly paid in money." Yet there is no doubt that "Literature is Business as well as Art, and almost as soon." As things stand, in fact, "business is the only human solidarity; we are all bound together with that chain, whatever interests and tastes and principles separate us." The reference to circus-like fiction, however, cuts across the image of a solidarity of writers, for it implies that the artist is also perforce an entrepreneur and entertainer, a competitor. Even though "literature has no objective value really, but only a subjective value," authors have become "largely matters of fashion, like this style of bonnet, or that shape of gown."

In the shape of competition, serious writers preserve the subjective value, while circus-like writers produce the commodities, like sentimental romances and what Henry James excluded from "legitimate fiction" altogether, the dime novel or "sensation novel." The competitive scene, as James described it in "The Question of Opportunities" (1898), was "subdivided as a chessboard, with each little square confessing only to its own *kind* of accessibility." With "divisions and boundaries," he wrote, increasing stratification of readerships by social class, by level and interest, "the very force of conditions" compelled American writers to react against the possibility of any single literary mode, "any taste or tone," establishing itself as the "general" fashion, by staking out individual claims. If the process continued, he foresaw, "we may get individual publics positively more sifted and evolved than anywhere else, shoals of fish rising for more delicate bait." It was this that Howells faced with misgiving: further fragmentation of the social world and further diminishment of both the earning power and the cultural influence of that "pure" and serious writing on which a restored middle ground, a revived America, depended. And so his double-fronted campaign, against the "gross fables," prodigies and marvels of the popular, and for novels of enlightenment and instruction, of reflective consciousness. Unless novels tend "to make the race better and kinder," he wrote, they cannot be "regarded as serious"; they are "lower than the rudest crafts that feed and house and clothe, for except they do this office they are idle; and they cannot do this except from and through the truth." The function is both practical and religious: "Let all the hidden things be brought into the sun, and let every day be the day of judgment. If the sermon cannot any longer serve this end, let the novel do it." His defense of the realist novel is a defense, then, of civilized mind itself: "I confess that I should suspect an unreality, an insincerity in a mature and educated person whom I found liking an unreal, an insincere novel."

Yet, "in the actual conditions," Howells concludes his essay on "The Man of Letters as a Man of Business," the artist is "anomalous," no better than an amusement for the "classes," unknown and unregarded among the "masses": "the common people do not hear him gladly or hear him at all." Howells brings to a close this essay of complaint with a remarkable unexpected image—unexpected, yet once announced, a perfectly apt figure of speech.

In the end, the writer is "an artist merely, and is allied to the great mass of wage-earners who are paid for the labor they have put into the thing done . . . who live by doing and making a thing, and not by marketing a thing after some other man has done it or made it." In the last analysis, the author "is merely a working-man, and is under the rule that governs the working-man's life," the rule that he must earn his bread by the sweat of his brow. "I wish that I could make all my fellow-artists realize," he writes, "that economically they are the same as mechanics, farmers, day-laborers." The solidarity of business, which had assumed each individual writer to be an entrepreneur competing with his goods in the market, now appears as a solidarity of labor, a solidarity, moreover, which figures forth a broad community of producers strikingly like that of the antebellum free-labor doctrine, the revived America of Populism, of Bellamy's "Nationalism," of Christian socialism. "It ought to be our glory that we produce something," Howells exults, and "we ought to feel the tie that binds us to all the toilers of the shop and field, not as a galling chain, but as a mystic bond also uniting us to Him who works hitherto and evermore." The bond is nothing less than sacral America itself, now a distant hope of incarnation rather than an immediate prospect: "Perhaps the artist of the future will see in the flesh the accomplishment of that human equality of which the instinct has been divinely planted in the human soul."

Thus, the artist of the real is the artist of "America", a figure which not surprisingly submerges the competitiveness out of which realism had defined its own zealous mission against the degradations of circus and variety-house fiction. If the market-place has made wage workers out of artists, against the grain of their essentially subjective work, then the solidarity of producers ought to dissolve the competition, reattach the artist to the sacred body of the nation, at least as a future prospect. Certainly a compelling image, nevertheless it evades the very insight it embodies. For the burden of Howells's essay is that the artist *must* be a businessman in a business world, must sell his wares not as a wage slave but as an independent entrepreneur, directly into a competitive market. This is precisely the goal of Howells's realism: to take a competitive stance among competing modes, and yet insist on it as the only true mode, the only serious fiction. Thus, Howells's realism bears the mark of the very competition it condemns as alien to art and the instinct of equality.

And while Howells's own condemnation raged most angrily against the best sellers of the age, sentimental romances like *Ben-Hur, Little Lord Fauntleroy, Trilby,* his reference to circuses and "gross fables" also excluded the story-paper fiction which represented the reading of perhaps the majority of urban Americans. Published as pamphlets in mass quantities, without even the pretense of qualifying as "book," as belonging to culture, such fiction represented one of the most ephemeral commodities of the era. Dime fiction was indeed the product of proletarian labor—hundreds of authors working anonymously in factory-like quarters in New York, reported Edward Bok of the *Ladies' Home Journal* in 1892. Such a writer "turns into a veritable machine," paid at piece rates by the story or the word. As early as 1864, the *North American Review* took notice of their sales, "almost unprecedented in the annals of booksellers," obtaining "greater popularity than any other series of works of fiction published in America." Writing in Howells's *Atlantic Monthly* in 1879, novelist W. H. Bishop called "story-paper literature" the "greatest literary movement, in bulk, of the age, and worthy of every serious consideration for itself." It was a phenomenon, Bishop urged on his polite readers, which "cannot be overlooked."

Precisely because of its conditions of production, its popularity, its serving no other objective ends than the sale of quickly consumable commodities of entertainment and distraction, dime fiction was not susceptible to formal literary criticism; its producers did not enjoy "careers" subject to critical reception and the honor of reviews. They were Howells's lowest order of literary producers: the undisguised hacks. And their product thus raised the deepest, most unsettling fears among respectable critics: that for the young readers of such sensational and fantastic fiction, the line between fiction and real life might indeed be entirely obliterated. Ranging from the evangelical rhetoric of Anthony Comstock's *Traps for the Young* (1883), to newspaper and journal editorials and commentary, the commonest fear was that young people would take the "pernicious

stories of the 'dime novel' class" as models for themselves. According to Comstock, crusader for the Suppression of Vice, "these stories . . . disparage honest toil and make real life a drudge and a burden. What young man will serve an apprenticeship, working early and late, if his mind is filled with the idea that sudden wealth may be acquired by following the hero of the story?"

Editorial writers often described youngsters shooting themselves or others "during a period of mental aberration caused by reading dime novels." The fear was not only of random aberrant violence. In 1878, *Scribner's Monthly* worried about the "effects on society" of fiction so outrageously antisocial: "stories about hunting, Indian warfare, California desperado life, pirates, wild sea adventure, horrors (torture and snake stories), gamblers, practical jokes, the life of vagabond boys, and the wild behavior of dissipated boys in great cities." The magazine worried especially about the social effects of typical characterizations of authority: "all teachers, of course, are sneaks and blackguards"; "fathers and sons are natural enemies"; vagabond life is "interesting and enticing," while "respectable home life . . . is not depicted at all." Held up to admiration are "low people who live by their wits . . . heroes and heroines of bar-rooms, concert saloons, variety theatres, and negro minstrel troupes." The police are "all stupid louts," and the law not to be minded. It is impossible "that so much corruption should be afloat and not exert some influence."

Less moralistic, less fearful of personal disasters following an afternoon immersed in a tale of lurid adventure, Bishop viewed the story papers from a perspective similar to Howells's realism. The worst aspect of this fiction is its implausibility. "The admiration grows," he writes, "for the craving which can swallow, without misgiving, so grand a tissue of extravagances, inaneness, contradictions, and want of probability." Villains display "no redeeming traits," and the good are always good. Characters are "never exhibited attending to the ordinary duties of existence." To be sure, there are elements of genuine popularity: living persons and current events frequently appear, as well as "a great many poor people." Indeed, "the capitalist is occasionally abused." But, "though written almost exclusively for the use of the lower classes of society, the story papers are not accurate pictures of their life." Their fault lies, in short, in their not being realist novels.

More benign than other critics, Bishop also proposes a program of reform. All things considered, he writes, the story papers "are not an unmixed blessing." They "reward virtue and punish vice." "They encourage a chivalrous devotion to woman." And, most of all, they represent among the masses a "taste for reading" which, "however perverted, is connected with something noble, with an interest outside of the small domain of self." With their popularity, their profound hold on their vast audiences, perhaps story-paper fiction "offers a solution to the problem of how the literature of the masses is to be improved." Certainly, Bishop argues, "the enormous extent of this imaginative craving" will demand objects of satisfaction. "Lack of culture is a continuous childhood," he explains, and most of the present audience "is not reflective." But an improved popular literature may hold the key to an improved culture.

Dime novels consisted of a baffling melange of storytelling devices, overlapping plots, hidden identities, disguises, long-lost heirs. Violence was rife: fistfights, knifings, shootings, acts of treachery, cowardice, and bravery. Bishop is probably correct in supposing an absence of "misgiving" among their readers. They were read rapidly, probably with a rising pulse beat. What lay behind the appeal of such fictions of the unreal remained obscure, inaccessible at least to literary reformers and intellectuals like Howells. Embracing dime fiction along with sentimental romance under the same heading of "injurious" literature, Howells described it as "the emptiest dissipation," a kind of "opium-eating" drugging the brain and leaving the reader "weaker and crazier for the debauch," in "dumb and passive need." His own imagery of excoriation grew more extreme at the height of his campaign for realism in the late 1880's, depicting fictions "which imagine a world where the sins of sense are unvisited by the penalties which follow, swift or slow, but inexorably sure, in the real world," as "deadly poison: these do kill." Such pervasive appetite for poison, for opium, could only imply a state of barbarism. It is a "palpable error," he insisted, "to regard civilization as inclusive of all the members of a civilized community." Many still "live in a state of more or less evident savagery with respect to their habits, their morals, and the propensities . . . Many more yet are savage in their tastes, as they show by the decoration of their houses and persons, and by their choice of books and picture."

Obviously, it is not to these savage Americans Howells addressed his essays in *Harper's* or his novels. Howells's language of contempt indicates his abandonment of the popular. Whatever the reasons, the story papers expressed to him a mass consciousness at profound odds with realism, with culture itself. They stood as "low" to "high," and thus challenged Howells and others to their task of defining a level, a stratum of their own, a Central Park of the imagination, where civilized acts might be performed in the "light of common day" upon a greensward of measured vistas and balanced views: a communal spectacle of a revived Republic. It was for Howells as for Olmsted a matter of "civilization" or "savagery": we read, or we barbarize.

The virtually Manichaean antithesis of the alternatives arose from the depth of Howells's investment in the concept of America, of republican equality and solidarity. Fully capable of discerning how untenable the concept was fast becoming in the face of a rigidifying class structure and open class strife—how fragile the supporting moral universe seemed to be against social injustice and mechanization—he nevertheless persisted in his belief. "I'm not in a very good mood with 'America' myself," he wrote to Henry James in 1888.

It seems to be the most grotesquely illogical thing under the sun; and I suppose I love it less because it won't let me love it more. I should hardly like to trust pen and ink with all the audacity of my social ideas; but after fifty years of optimistic content with "civilization" and its ability to come out all right in the end, I now abhor it, and feel that it is coming out all wrong in the end, unless it bases itself anew on a real equality. Meantime I wear a fur-lined overcoat, and live in all the luxury my money can buy.

Blaming the word "America" as "illogical," Howells could only pass off his own illogicality with a self-deprecatory remark, burying his abhorrence in the persisting faith that the old America might yet "base itself anew on a real equality." Herein lay his desperate hope for a fiction of the real.

IV

"The symmetry of form attainable in pure fiction cannot so readily be achieved in a narration essentially having less to do with fable than with fact. Truth uncompromisingly told will always have its ragged edges." So wrote Herman Melville in *Billy Budd, Sailor,* the tale he called an "inside narrative," unfinished and unpublished at his death in 1891. Melville had endured the Gilded Age in virtual silence, unknown, unread, a ghost of the past performing a daily round of chores at the New York Custom House. It seems unlikely he attended to Howells's campaign for realism, but in these two sentences from his final tale the chief dilemma of a fiction of the real comes powerfully to the fore.

Howells proved unable or unwilling to accept the raggedness of "truth uncompromisingly told," retreating always into the symmetry of a fiction he held "pure," including the illogical fiction of "America." To be sure, the strains and tensions and the violence of his age make their way into his novels. Indeed, in the fictions of Howells, James, Mark Twain, in the regional stories of Kate Chopin, Mary Wilkins, E. W. Howe, Hamlin Garland, in the new "naturalism" of Crane and Frank Norris and Dreiser in the 1890's, a ragged picture does emerge, of lost hopes, hypocrisy, narrowed and constricted lives, grinding frustrations of poverty and isolation. The report is relieved, especially in the regional fiction, by acts of courage, a surviving residue of older ways, rural customs and habits and speech. But the major picture included a keen lament for the passing of an older, more secure and reliable way of life, one based on ingrained assumptions about the possibilities of freedom. The discovery of social constraints, of the incursions of history on the idyll of Huck and Jim on their raft, or of vile manipulation on Isabel Archer's belief (in James's *Portrait of a Lady*) in a perfect freedom of choice and self-determination, tainted much of the fiction of the age with sorrow, bitterness, cynicism. In worlds of greed and plotting, James's heroes and heroines learn what their author himself insisted in his writings on fiction: that experience is always social, that freedom only manifests itself within human relations. On the whole, realism portrayed the old American credo of a community of autonomous natural beings as a sad illusion. Howells's problems in arriving at satisfactory conclusions to his novels, like Mark Twain's last-minute resort to romantic plot at the end of *Adventures of Huckleberry Finn,* reflect the intellectual difficulty of absorbing that lesson, of creating fictions of fact rather than fable.

Under Howells's tutelage, writers embraced more unsettling contemporary fact than the audiences of respectable literature had been accustomed to reading. Yet fact consistently battled with fable in his own works, and in the end Howells narrowed his range, addressing an imaginary audience, a "literary elect" who might serve as a saving remnant against the future when the solidarity of writer and reader might be realized. "I believe," he confessed in a lecture in 1899, "that it is far from these nervous centres that the author finds his closest, truest, liveliest appreciation. For my part I like to think of my stories, if they are so blest, as befriending the loneliness of outlying farms, dull villages, distant exile."

From his own internal exile within the nervous city, Herman Melville had his say in the privacy of his cryptic tale of Billy Budd, without a hope of reaching living readers, high or low or middle.

Written late in the 1880's, *Billy Budd* turns to an event more than a generation earlier, the Somers Mutiny of 1842, in which a member of Melville's family joined the tribunal in sentencing to death a young offender against the ship's military discipline. Set "in the time before steamships," before the harsh industrial conflicts in the years in which Melville wrote, the tale bristles with personal implication for the aging writer whose family had thirty years earlier worried for his sanity. But the story of the "fated" Billy, a common sailor consigned to death by a possibly deranged captain during the naval wars between revolutionary France and counterrevolutionary England, also reflects on the turbulence of Melville's own times. The tale is set amid a turbulence which Melville is at pains to describe as not so much an external threat of French victory over England, "a Power then all but the sole free conservative one of the Old World," but an internal one of "insurrection" in the British fleet. Just months before the events, British sailors had rebelled at Spithead and Nore, signaling their mutiny by running up the royal flag "with the union and cross wiped out," thus "transmuting the flag of founded law and freedom defined, into the enemy's red meteor of unbridled and unbounded revolt." Growing out of "reasonable discontent" over "glaring abuses," the revolt flamed into an "irrational combustion," a "distempering irruption of contagious fever." It was a time, like the days and months following the summer of 1877, or Haymarket in 1886, when the red banner terrified established authority, portending even further unbounding revolt. Officers at sea felt compelled "to stand with drawn swords behind the men working the guns."

The similarities of historical moment—of mass unrest and challenges to authority, of issues brought to law and settled by authorized force—resound too insistently to be ignored. Certainly, this is not to say that Melville intended his tale to serve as an explicit commentary on the current events of his own declining years. Free of any direct allusion to contemporary affairs, the narrative does speak of the Great Mutiny at Nore as similar to "some other events in every age befalling states everywhere, including America," but it seems likely that Melville has in mind the Civil War, which elsewhere he had described as a mutiny against the Republic. Moreover, to what extent does the tale even concern itself with its own larger historical moment? True, Billy's story begins with an act—his impressment in the open sea—pointedly described as an example of abuse not redressed by the settlement at Nore. Snatched from the *Rights-of-Man,* a homeward-bound merchant ship named in honor of Thomas Paine, Billy is coerced into the King's service aboard the outward-bound HMS *Bellipotent,* a 74-gun warrior ship rushing to join the royal fleet awaiting battle with the French. The "inside narrative," writes Melville, will have "little concernment" with the actual maneuvers of the ship, but surely the revolutionary moment, and especially Britain's fear of the Red Flag, will contribute in no small way to Billy's end. The larger history will fade imperceptibly but nonetheless decisively into the drama of Billy, Claggart, and Starry Vere.

What concern us, then, are not so much the parallels between the represented history of the tale and that of Melville's America, but the reflection on history itself, on the impingement of an outside on an inside narrative. The tale recounts an act, a doubled act within an outside history: Billy's killing of Claggart, Vere's killing of Billy. It also recounts a continuing act of interpretation.

Billy Budd, the "Handsome Sailor," seems the incarnation of a "natural" goodness, the corporeal form of an otherworldly innocence. And Claggart, the "master-at-arms," seems a predestined opposite and foe, demonism incarnate as human malice, envy, and spite. In Claggart lurked some element of unmotivated evil the narrator cannot explain except by evoking, if only figuratively, the "mystery of iniquity" of the old Calvinist doctrine. Claggart seemed by nature "bad," while Billy "had none of that intuitive knowledge of the bad which in natures not good or incompletely so foreruns experience." Are Billy and Claggart, then, moral types, fables fallen into a world of fact? When Billy strikes out in speechless rage at Claggart's false accusation that the young sailor had plotted mutiny, and kills his superior officer at one blow, Captain Vere grasps instantly the fatal conjunction of fable and fact. "Struck dead by an angel of God! Yet the angel must hang!" He must hang, moreover, and hang at once, as Vere would argue before his own disbelieving officers, precisely because of those angelic features which arouse so powerful a current of sympathy. Vere had witnessed the false accusation and the deadly blow with rising fatherly feelings. But then, momentarily "eclipsed" by emotion, he emerged from his spell "with quite another aspect." "The father in him . . . was replaced by the military disciplinarian."

Did Vere act precipitously? After all, as members of the drumhead court themselves argued, Billy might have been held over in chains until a regular court might be convened. There is no doubt that Vere acts in a state of extreme distress. But what does his condition signify? Just as Vere performs an act of interpretation on Billy and Claggart, so the reader is constrained to interpret Vere, who indeed proves a more intractable case of ambiguity. "Who in the rainbow can draw the line where the violet tint ends and the orange tint begins?" asks the narrator. "Distinctly we see the difference of the colors, but where exactly does the one first blendingly enter into the other? So with sanity and insanity." The case is left to the reader: whether Vere must be considered insane or not "everyone must determine for himself by such light as this narrative may afford." Was it insanity, or guilt, or some stoic sense of impersonal tragedy which drove Vere, at the moment of his own death after a successful battle with the French ship the *Athée,* to murmur "words inexplicable to his attendant: 'Billy Budd, Billy Budd'"? Does the narrative finally afford sufficient light to clarify Vere's condition, or to make his final words explicable?

The narrative cloaks all questions of motive, of meaning, in a cunning uncertainty. Only the outside narrative, the chronicle of mere events, remains incontrovertible. Everything inside seems equivocal, murky, elusive. And it is precisely the encroaching sense of the inside world's ultimate obscurity which would have brought discomfort and protest from those among Melville's readers still faithful to inherited notions of an America, a city on a hill, in which reason and nature might achieve a perfect harmony. Such believers would fiercely reject Vere's instant condemnation of Billy. To hang an angel for performing his Father's work: what more violent desecration of the harmony once implied by the "rights of man" and by popular Christian belief?

Vere meets these objections without flinching. What springs to our attention in the following passage is not only a grim justification but its basis in a distinction of realms uncommon in popular American political thought:

> How can we adjudge to summary and shameful death a fellow creature innocent before God, and whom we feel to be so?—Does that state it aright? You sign sad assent. Well, I too feel that, the full force of that. It is Nature. But do these buttons that we wear attest that our allegiance is to Nature? No, to the King. Though the ocean, which is inviolate Nature primeval, though this be the element where we move and have our being as sailors, yet as the King's officers lies our duty in a sphere correspondingly natural? So little is that true, that in receiving our commissions we in the most important regards ceased to be natural free agents . . . Our vowed responsibility is in this: That however pitilessly that law may operate in many instances, we nevertheless adhere to it and administer it.

Not "nature" but "king" defines duty, not natural reason or natural law but the *state,* the arbitrary power whose authority, signified by the officers' buttons, runs like the King's yarn throughout the society. Finally, it is the irreconcilability of Nature and King which seals Billy's fate: the fate of "fable" in a world of "fact."

Billy would have had a home in the old imagined America of a natural law supporting a naturally reasonable society. But once impressed on the *Bellipotent,* he left behind all familiar meanings and unambiguous relations. The force which tore him from the haven of the *Rights-of-Man* represented the hard facts of warfare, class conflict, malice, intrigue, unrelenting law: in short, *history.* Meanings no longer secure, motives hidden at impenetrable depths, the very name Billy Budd "inexplicable": just so, his story in the end lies twisted and perverted in "official" accounts in the press. Moreover, neither the death of Billy nor that of Vere discloses any ultimate meaning, any symmetry of form. As Michael Rogin has argued cogently about this very political tale, the state no longer promises redemption. "Lying between two guns, as nipped in the vice of fate," Billy lies a victim of an order which, in the face of his utter innocence, cannot justify itself except by evoking "order" itself, form and symmetry for their own sake. And is not Vere himself also caught in that same nipping vice?

Of course, Melville writes about an earlier era, a distant event. But still, *Billy Budd* invites us to take it as Melville's final, undelivered message to his countrymen and fellow writers. In the light of the narrative, the historical world can no longer be mistaken as hospitable to the American fable of a *natural* innocence and solidarity. History discloses itself as the realm of power, the laws and iron weapons of the state set against the receding utopia of the "rights of man." Not in nature but in the King's yarn lay the hidden meaning of the law. So much is clear from the buttons on Vere's coat, and from the sight of Billy hanging from the yard-arm. But so much, in treating of narratives inside larger events, remains unclear. Melville's message thus includes a severe commentary on interpretation itself, on the ways of knowing and judging behavior. Melville's message, translated freely, argues not only that the state must be seen as distinct from "nature," grounded in power and social interest, but also that the process of seeing and knowing must be freed from "fable," from utopian wish. To perceive their new world, Melville implies, Americans must reckon with ragged edges, the cunning currents and deceits of history.

There is an even deeper message in Billy's fate. Just as the state no longer grounds itself in natural reason, neither does it even claim to represent a shared community of interest. That community known in the tale as "the ship's populace" finds itself utterly separate from the ruling state, subordinate to it, coerced by external law, the apparatus of the master-at-arms and his unholy crew of enforcers and spies. The populace is free only to obey or disobey, accept or rebel. Rewards and punishments remain wholly material: ultimately, life and death. There is no hint of redemption, of self-fulfillment in obedience. What survives in the tale, then, is not the power of the guns or of the coercive yardarm, but "Billy in the Darbies," the concluding ballad, a "rude utterance" from an "artless *poetic* temperament," testifying in "low" art to the separate and enduringly compassionate vision of "the ship's populace." Under the strict governance of the state, yet distinct from it in a very profound way, the sailors appear in Melville's narrative as a community of work and play in which a mutual predicament fostered a law of its own, a social law of sympathy and compassion. Billy Budd is their hero, the human image of their own precarious history. Only the poem at the end renders the name explicable.

Works Cited

There are several good introductions to realism as a movement in European and American fiction, including F. W. J. Hemmings, ed., *The Age of Realism* (Pelican Book, 1974) and Damian Grant, *Realism* (London, 1970). For a useful collection of documents, see George J. Becker, ed., *Documents of Modern Literary Realism* (Princeton, 1963). The classic study of the concept of "reality" in relation to literary convention is Eric Auerbach, *Mimesis: The Representation of Reality in Western Literature* (Princeton, 1953). And the major Marxist discussion, which sees realism as the essential mode of the novel, is Georg Lukacs, *Studies in European Realism* (London, 1950), a discussion continued as a polemic against literary modernism in *The Meaning of Contemporary Realism* (London, 1962). Other useful general discussions include Harry Levin, "What Is Realism?" in *Comparative Literature* (1951), and Rene Wellek, "The Concept of Realism in Literary Scholarship," in *Concepts of Criticism* (New Haven, 1963).

For a superb study of realism in European (chiefly French) painting, and of its cultural setting, see Linda Nochlin, *Realism* (Middlesex, England, 1971). See also Axel von Saldern, *Triumph of Realism* (New York, 1967). For an excellent and incisive general survey, see the relevant chapters in Joshua C. Taylor, *The Fine Arts in America* (Chicago, 1979); also Oliver Larkin, *Art and Life in America* (New York, 1949). Patricia Hills, *The Painters' America: Rural and Urban Life, 1810-1910* (New York, 1974), contains valuable discussions of industrial and urban themes. A standard brief work on Winslow Homer is Lloyd Goodrich, *Winslow Homer* (New York, 1944). See also John Wilmerding's excellent monograph, *Winslow Homer* (New York, 1972). For a study of Thomas Eakins, see Lloyd Goodrich, *Thomas Eakins, His Life and Work* (New York, 1933).

Although left incomplete at his death in 1929, Vol. Three of Vernon L. Parrington's *Main Currents of American Thought* (New York, 1927, 1930), "The Beginnings of Critical Realism in America," remains the most comprehensive treatment of the social and political ideas informing literary realism in America. For a briefer general introduction, see Jay Martin, *Harvests of Change: American Literature, 1865-1914* (New York, 1967). Bernard Bowron's essay, "American Realism," in *Comparative Literature* (1951), remains the best brief discussion of features distinctive to American writing. Warner Berthoff, in *The Ferment of Realism: American*

Literature 1884-1919 (New York, 1965), offers a comprehensive and intelligent survey of writers and ideas, as does Larzer Ziff in *The American 1890s* (New York, 1966). The opening chapter of Alfred Kazin, *On Native Grounds* (New York, 1942), is also relevant.

On the literary culture of the post-Civil War years, see Henry Nash Smith, "The Scribbling Women and the Cosmic Success Story," *Critical Inquiry* (September 1974), 47-70, and *Democracy and the Novel* (New York, 1978). The chapter on Howells in the latter work is especially instructive. Smith's concern is largely with the demands of the literary marketplace on the serious efforts of Howells, Mark Twain, and Henry James. For discussions of the marketplace itself, see William Charvat (Matthew J. Bruccoli, ed.), *The Profession of Authorship in America 1800-1870* (Columbus, Ohio, 1968), especially chap. 14 and 15. On best sellers, the standard works are James D. Hart, *The Popular Book* (Berkeley, 1961); Frank Luther Mott, *Golden Multitudes* (New York, 1947); and Donald Sheehan, *This Was Publishing: A Chronicle of the Book Trade in the Gilded Age* (Bloomington, 1952). For Howells's own critical writings, consult the useful selection in Edwin H. Cady, ed., *W. D. Howells as Critic* (London, 1973). See also Everett Carter's valuable discussion in *Howells and the Age of Realism* (1954). For biographical studies of Howells, see Edwin Cady's two volumes, *The Road to Realism* (Syracuse, 1956) and *The Realist at War* (Syracuse, 1958), and Kenneth S. Lynn's *William Dean Howells: An American Life* (New York, 1971). On the political meanings of *Billy Budd,* see Michael Rogin's forthcoming book on Melville.

AESTHETICISM

Robert R. Roberts (essay date 1970)

SOURCE: "Popular Culture and Public Taste" in *The Gilded Age: Revised and Enlarged Edition,* edited by H. Wayne Morgan, Syracuse University Press, 1970, pp. 275-88.

[*In the following essay, Roberts reflects on the Gilded Age as an era of popular aesthetic interest, wherein high and low-brow culture interacted to create a distinctly American fiction, journalism, theatre, lyric, and decor.*]

Popular culture in the hectic and colorful era that followed the Civil War encompassed diverse media. The daily newspaper, enriched with wire service news, the mass revival meeting, the Chautauqua lecture, and the traveling theater troupe all reflected American ideas and aspirations. Publicly accepted painting, sculpture, literature, music, and theatrical entertainment reflected social values. Audiences listened patiently while the actor Joseph Jefferson, the revivalist Dwight Moody, and the lecturer Russell Conwell each said something that touched national tastes.

The traditional values of Western Europe flavored this culture, whatever its variations of style or scope. Though covered with Victorian moralism and propriety, popular novels followed the eighteenth-century English precepts. Charles Dickens was very likely the "world's most popular author," and belonged both to "art" and to the popular culture of America.[1]

The arts were a major part of American life. George Makepeace Towle, a traveler returned to America from England, heard "boys in the street singing and whistling Mozart and Rossini, and hand organs grinding out the arias from *Faust* and *Lucrezia Borgia.*" Towle was also impressed by the lively American theater, including "more performances of Shakespeare in America . . . than . . . in England" and "tragedy, fine old comedy and the 'free and easy' burlesque."[2] Even in the cheap story-papers, authors of accepted stature appeared with the storytellers. Classical actors and actresses such as Edwin Booth and Sarah Bernhardt were immensely popular. The Gilbert and Sullivan musicals were immediate hits. In the theaters Shakespeare preceded *East Lynne.* Samuel Smiles or Mrs. E. D. E. N. Southworth might outsell Thomas Hardy or the Brontë sisters, but the classics were on the same lists and programs. The traditional culture of the Western world, albeit sometimes in diluted forms, held sway in America, in a healthy mingling of popular and classical taste. One opera house in a middle-sized American town in the 1880's offered the best from the classic tradition in music and drama.

The total society did not acclaim great art, or wholesome popular arts without exception. These years saw the rise of mass magazines and newspapers, and changes in the theater and other forms of entertainment that produced an increasing gap between popular culture and higher standards. Such artists as Albert Ryder and George Inness had a small audience at best. Surviving Brahmins like the Adams brothers believed the American people patronized only shoddy lectures and tasteless magazines. Pre-Civil War monuments such as Longfellow and Emerson lived into the postwar decades and did not find them good. But there was little of the spirit of "épater le bourgeois." The coterie artist and the self-conscious rebel against middle-class values were not dominant. This familiar schism had yet to appear in the Gilded Age.

Traditional and popular culture mingled, and was derivative—England naturally contributed most heavily to American public culture. The common name for the prevailing moral view was "Victorian," obviously not a native product. The most popular style of middle-class architecture was called the "Queen Anne." The arbiter of this building style and of home decoration and landscaping was Charles Locke Eastlake, Englishman and disciple of Ruskin and William Morris.

English standards cast the longest shadow in literature, especially the novel. More copies of Dickens were sold in the 1880's than in the 1860's, and his influence was strong.[3] Thackeray, Anthony Trollope, George Eliot, Jane Austen, and the Brontës regularly appeared on American publishing lists. Good reading was more readily available than at any prior time, and the press and magazines reached huge audiences.

English standards did not apply only in quality literature. The most celebrated novel of the sensational-romantic school, *East Lynne,* was by a Londoner, Mrs. Henry Wood. A second Englishwoman, Mary Elizabeth Braddon, contributed the "preposterously successful melodrama," *Lady Audley's Secret.* A third English lady romancer used the unusual pen name of Ouida, and wrote tales like *Under Two Flags* and *A Dog of Flanders.* The American reading public was not alone in its thirst for melodrama and romance. As literacy increased and, particularly, as more women received education, adventures and romances appealed to readers in Chicago or Manchester or New York or London.

Change and uneven development characterized most activities. The press remained from the 1850's to the 1880's a domain for personal journalism. In the early 1880's the American theater entered a new phase, the "Golden Age of the Road." Equally significant changes took place in minstrelsy and the Chautauqua movement. Popular culture defied exact classification, but generally, culture in the 1870's resembled that of the 1850's; the 1880's were the years of greatest transition.

Changes in architectural design and construction illustrated basic problems in developing a national cultural style. Building in the postwar years obviously continued earlier traditions, but new design in the Gilded Age was not always derivative. The era reveled in color and often mistook display for innovation. As in other sectors of life, a new building style suited for the factory or mass urban housing was slow to emerge. But the overt thrust of this newly rich society was toward an enlarging middle class. The Italianate brownstone in wealthy city areas, and the detached single-family dwelling on a spacious lot were two of the period's best developments. Large windows, high ceilings, decoration, and special functions for each house level provided both comfort and spaciousness.

Exceptional men produced the landmarks of architecture. Richard Morris Hunt designed residences for millionaires based on the chateaux of the French renaissance and a high style. His imaginative and splendid mansions, such as the Vanderbilt house on Fifth Avenue, or the even more successful Ochre Court at Newport, deserve to be remembered.[4] The firm of McKim, Mead and White, did noteworthy work—town houses built for Henry Villard and his friends, "the greatest private residence[s] ever erected in Manhattan."[5] Henry Hobson Richardson's churches, public buildings, and business structures were distinguished and utilitarian. But his most successful domestic design reflected the reigning Queen Anne style.[6] These leaders and such firms as Burnham and Root, or Adler and Sullivan in the Chicago school of business building, were ample evidence of a vital architecture.

Few people could afford distinctiveness in a family dwelling, however, and these men did not redirect the national tone.[7] The three principal influences on mass building all preceded the war: the Gothic revival, mansard roof, and Italianate style. The Gothic had heavily influenced public buildings, churches, and college architecture. But the translation of a traditional Gothic into "Carpenter Gothic" was well under way. This included "steep gables and pointed windows; sometimes they were sheathed with vertical boarding instead of the familiar horizontal clapboard." Decorative matter called gingerbread filled out these designs. Though the whipsaw might occasionally mar a plan, this ornamentation was basically healthy, and belonged with the "vigorous and pleasurable folk arts."[8]

The continuity of taste and style were also obvious in interior decoration. The prints of Currier and Ives, dating from the 1830's, continued to dominate a large national market, and in time became collectors' items.[9] The sculptor John Rogers was a folk hero of sorts, pleasing many people with an honest craftsmanship and understandable subject matter. His first popular work was "The Checker Players," in 1859, and he became "not only a household name but a household ornament."[10]

The novel also reflected this basic continuity. People who emerged in the 1850's continued to write best sellers. Mrs. Mary J. Holmes, described a trifle cruelly, if accurately, as "that prolific favorite of the unthinking," was a case in point.[11] Her publishing career began in the 1850's and continued into the 1880's at roughly the rate of a novel a year. Her protagonists were paragons of perfection, physically and morally, and her villains were monsters of evil. The story's outcome was never long in doubt, and her books belonged in the sentimental-moralistic school of writing. Publishers and booksellers had long recognized the market for such writing and welcomed successful lady authors.[12] The sentimental-moralistic novel was a staple of the weekly story-papers and the publishers' lists.

Mrs. E. D. E. N. Southworth was the queen of what Nathaniel Hawthorne called that "d———d mob of scribbling women." She was easily the "most popular authoress in the annals of American publishing" no mean achievement in a field where ladies have excelled.[13]

Mrs. Southworth generally set her stories in Virginia or Maryland. Occasionally a craggy mountain pass might defy the facts of geography, but usually a fine old plantation served as the background for a romantic tale. Handsome heroes of slim and graceful carriage, and pure and lovely heroines won through to true love in spite of fearsome villainies, ancient curses, and assorted tribulations. In *The Malediction; or The Widows of Widowville,* a mysterious stranger with patrician features learned that a noble plantation house, rising above the Chesapeake Bay, was the home of a beautiful heiress, prevented from marrying by an old family curse of a peculiar but unknown type.[14] Who could resist a situation fraught with such peril and promise? Obviously not the reading public of the Gilded Age who continued to buy Mrs. Southworth's books for over sixty years. Her works still sold in considerable numbers when she died in 1899.

The novel with more sensational elements like violence, a hint of sexuality, or exposures of vice in high places, was also popular. The English best sellers, *East Lynne* and *Lady Audley's Secret,* followed this formula. There were numerous practitioners of this style, including Sylvanus Cobb, Jr., and Charles Reade. Cobb began publishing in the cheap story-paper, the *New York Ledger,* in 1856 and was still active in 1885. The more "cultivated and genteel" readers disdained Cobb, but he had a contract for thirty years at $50 per week with the *Ledger.*[15] Reade was also a perennially popular author whose sensational tales appeared on publishers' lists from the 1860's to the 1880's. In *Griffith Gaunt* (1886), and *A Terrible Temptation* (1871), he proved that exposés of vice and sin in high society appealed strongly to the moralistic middle class.

The religious novel had its seed-time before the Civil War and blossomed in the following generation. The persistence of these novels was easy to understand. These were years of challenge and trial for churches, particularly traditional Protestant denominations. Orthodox theologies subjected to liberalizing influences in the prewar decades, now abruptly faced new scientific thought, especially Darwinian evolution. No other topic occupied more time in pulpit discourse or space in the religious press, and this interest carried over to the reading public. The churches' ideals and social programs were being severely tested by the social and economic problems of an urban-industrial growth of nearly frightening proportions. The faith of the fathers and traditional values were sorely tried; people grasped for reassurance in a happy and logical fictional world. This was the case in the three major religious best sellers, Augusta Jane Evans' *St. Elmo* (1859), Elizabeth Stuart Phelps's *The Gates Ajar* (1868), and the Reverend E. P. Roe's *Barriers Burned Away* (1872). In *St. Elmo* a beautiful and brilliant girl convinced St. Elmo to turn from atheism to the ministry. *The Gates Ajar* ignored theological problems and vanquished doubt by describing the beauties of a worldly sort of heaven. And in *Barriers Burned Away* the great Chicago fire and spiritual truths combined in a "sure-fire" formula. These books led publishers' lists throughout the late nineteenth century, testifying to the appeal of simple faith in a complex age.

In the 1880's, one of the major popular novels in American history appeared. In *Ben Hur,* General Lew Wallace combined the appeal of religion, the glamor of a historical setting in the Roman Empire, and sheer melodrama. The book had an immense vogue among people in all walks of life, and became a popular touring stage play.[16] Combining action with purpose, glorifying individualism, and reaffirming the religious verities, "A Tale of the Christ" inevitably appealed to Americans.

In varieties of style the self-help and success theme, with a strong admixture of inspiration, dominated most popular writings. The theme was still emphasized early in childhood through the widely used McGuffey readers. These school readers conveyed the well-known lessons of honesty, industry, obedience, thrift, piety, punctuality, and similar virtues.[17] Fame and fortune would follow strict adherence to these rules of living. The popular Horatio Alger books reinforced this doctrine. The young hero found that a life of virtue and the luck to save the daughter of a rich man from drowning could lead to worldly success. The role of chance loomed large in these success stories, but the American lad with enough gumption to seize that opportunity was firmly in the tradition of self-help and individualism.

By the late 1880's two famous essays had reinforced the gospel of uplift and success. The first was Russell Conwell's *Acres of Diamonds*. This Philadelphia minister insisted that a man could find wealth in his own backyard if he but looked, and that it was every man's duty to acquire riches. The second was Andrew Carnegie's celebration of competitive individualism in selecting those best fitted to prosper—and the obligations of wealth—in *The Gospel of Wealth*. These works suited the dominant middle class, and reflected the ideas of a nation engaged in building an industrial economy. But such tastes were not peculiar to that age or to America. Englishmen were buying Samuel Smiles in as great numbers, and the uplift theme had always been an American favorite.

The public also read and listened to boisterous humorists. Their techniques were not new. The grotesque exaggerations of the Davy Crockett story, the rural parody of the style and manners of "city folk," and the artful mishandling of the English language were all inherited from an earlier time. But there was an increasing consciousness of the peculiar traits of regions and localities. Economic forces were driving the nation toward nationalism, and this produced an audience for writers and lecturers who portrayed unique and disappearing types of American life. The Yankee, the midwestern "hayseed," the rough and ready westerner, and southern types found a public for their brands of humor.

The leaders of this school of humorists included David Ross Locke (Petroleum V. Nasby), Charles Farrar Brown (Artemus Ward), and Henry Wheeler Shaw (Josh Billings). As "hayseeds" or other simpletons, they poked fun at customs and conventions. Josh Billings wrote in his *Farmer's Allminax*, "Most people repent ov their sins bi thanking God they aint so wicked as their nabors."[18] Artemus Ward got off his share of quotable remarks: "I tell you, feller citizens, it would have been ten dollars in Jeff Davis' pockets if he had never been born." And "Old George Washington's fort was not to hev any public man of the present day ressemble him in eny alarmin extent."[19]

The sale of their books testified to popular appeal. Billings' *Farmer's Allminax* sold 90,000 copies in its first edition in 1869, and in ten years subsequent versions sold as many as 127,000 copies, and never less than 50,000.[20] These writers served up a pungent humor based on strong characterizations, parody, and broad social satire. In an age of colorful individuals, folk figures did not take a back seat to business barons or political leaders.

Major innovations in magazine publishing came in the 1890's. But in newspaper printing, the 1880's produced a major change, the fall of great editors and personal journalism to syndicates. New business methods, increased costs, lower prices, the demands of advertising, and the need for mass distribution diminished the personal note and encouraged the rise of the news merchant.

The changes that would be called "yellow journalism" had not yet occurred. Sensationalism, the comics, and other attributes of modern newspapers were not overly noticeable in the newspapers of the 1870's and were just beginning in the 1880's. An upstate New York farmer continued, after Greeley's death, to subscribe to the *Tribune* in the belief that Horace was still responsible for its contents.[21] Technical changes occurred rapidly. The telegraph and cable, press associations, expensive new machinery, labor unions, and advertising revenue transformed newspapers from personal organs to a big business. These changes in communication and distribution widened and deepened the content of every major newspaper. The feature article on politics or diplomacy was common, as were special departments and correspondents for social and artistic questions.

In magazine publishing, these were years of "boom."[22] The number of journals increased from 700 in 1865 to some 3,300 in 1885, and circulation figures rose.[23] There was also a major trend toward more dependence on advertising, and in the early 1880's advertising "demonstrated its value and established its place in the general magazine."[24]

Among magazines, the cheap story-papers which held sway before the Civil War continued to attract readers. The *New York Weekly,* the *New York Ledger,* and Frank Leslie's *Chimney Corner* purveyed fiction, poetry, essays, joke columns, and advice columns to a variety of readers. The *Ledger* and *Weekly* claimed a circulation of over 300,000, and the other shorter-lived story-papers had circulation figures in the thousands for a few years. Publishers of these competitive enterprises naturally tried to give the middle class what it wanted. The moral tone was smugly proper. Publishers assured readers that their particular publication was a family paper which the innocent daughters of the household could read safely.[25]

Fiction was the bulk of the material in these papers, largely serialized versions of romantic or historical novels of famous authors. If the publisher was not fortunate enough to have a popular writer under contract, imitators produced remarkably similar tales. Interspersed in the fiction was poetry of the pre-Civil War style and manner, never the unconventional barbarities of a Walt Whitman. There might also be something from Dickens or another noted English author, and for patriotism and inspiration, historical sketches of the Founding Fathers or essays by Horace Greeley or Henry Ward Beecher. There were also regular columns on "Advice to Young Women."

The subheading of the *New York Ledger* proudly announced that it was "Devoted to Choice Literature Romance The News and Commerce." Neither "The News" nor "Commerce" were much in evidence; stories, essays, advice columns, poems, and proper jokes made up the bulk of story-papers. The content reflected the desire for sentimental fiction and the triumph of the accepted values, which might be expected in any popular writing. There was also a taste for uplifting essays and poetic sentiments. An issue of *Frank Leslie's Popular Monthly,* contained a travel article, a sketch of a successful businessman, an episode in a continuing novel, and a poem beginning with the verse:

> Would I could send my spirit o'er the deep,
> > Would I could wing it like a bird to thee,
> To commune with thy thoughts, to fill thy sleep
> > With these unwearying words of melody,
> > > Brother, come home.

The "Entertainment Column" might have a coy joke: "Said the sailor to his sweetheart: 'I know that ladies care little about nautical matters, but if you had your choice of a ship, what kind would you prefer?' She cast down her eyes, blushed, and whispered: 'a little smack.'"[26]

Though not so widely read as story-papers, the actual leaders of the magazine world were the genteel aristocrats, *Harper's Weekly* or *Monthly, Atlantic, Galaxy,* and *Scribner's*. Some of these, notably the Harper publications, were popular; all reflected middle-class tastes and ideas. These were journals of "miscellany and opinion,"[27] and the dutiful reader ploughed through heavy prose. The upper middle-class reader had time for reading, and a stern sense of the duty of being informed. An article on "The Development of the Steamship, and the Liverpool Exhibition of 1886," complete with diagrams of hulls, super-structures, and engines, was thirty pages long, followed by a scientific article on the "Forests of North America." But perhaps many readers hurried on to "Marse Archie's Flight," a dialect Civil War story, or the last chapter of a long novel of New York family life.[28]

The journals reflected the era's great interest in scientific matters. Economics was another prominent subject. And almost any issue had an article on the evolutionary hypothesis and its significance for religion. *Harper's Weekly* described itself as "A Journal of Civilization." This whole group of periodicals ranged from popular fiction to foreign news, humor, travel, literary essays, editorials, and economic and scientific subjects, with excellent illustrations. Taken as a whole, they were an excellent mirror of the informed mind.

But Americans did not spend their evenings and Sundays solely in reading. They heard lectures, attended the theater, went to curiosity museums and circuses, and participated in self-improvement classes at Chautauqua institutes. They sought escape from reality, the confident proclamation of the "old truths" in a Moody revival meeting, or inspiration at a Chautauqua. They also attended that new phenomenon, organized, big-league baseball.

No revival team compared in popularity to Dwight L. Moody and Ira D. Sankey. Moody in 1875 was "the rising young tycoon of the revival trade as Andrew Carnegie was of the steel trade or John D. Rockefeller of oil."[29] He coupled businesslike methods with the old-fashioned gospel, and his success was enormous. Ira D. Sankey directed the music and contributed stirring solo renditions of popular hymns, many composed by the partners. But Moody was the driving force in this revival movement of the 1870's and 1880's. He used committees to prepare the way, asked for cooperation of the various denominations, made the act of conversion simple and businesslike, and preached in popular language. No learned theological discourse or flowery rhetoric ever marred the simple plea to "take Christ now." There were ties between Moody and popular writing. Magazines and novels were building a taste for "sentiment and make-believe," and the successful revivalist "would have to speak the new commoner's tongue."[30] Moody the lay preacher appealed to the same broad audience that read the story-papers and Mrs. E. D. E. N. Southworth. He was a remarkable combination of a revolution in techniques and a lag in values which characterized so much of popular culture. His methods were modern but the message consisted of forceful repetitions of the "old truths."

There were many other famous preachers, some conservative, a few liberal. Some argued that Christianity should be applied to social problems; others preached on sin and salvation. But one man symbolized the middle-class pulpit, Henry Ward Beecher. Although not a typical preacher, he spoke with tremendous authority from the Plymouth Congregational Church in Brooklyn, New York, and from his editorial position on the *Independent*. He rejected the theology of his Calvinist forebears, influenced in so doing by his father, Lyman Beecher. He preferred a doctrine of love and an ethic of individualism modified by the demands of brotherhood. His sermons were dazzling dramatic displays, more remarkable for emotional appeal than serious content. One notable admirer, Samuel L. Clemens, wrote of the Beecher style: "He went marching up and down the stage waving his arms in the air, hurling sarcasms this way and that, discharging rockets of poetry, and exploding mines of eloquence, halting now and then to stamp his foot three times in succession to emphasize a point."[31]

In 1872, Beecher was accused of seducing the wife of a close friend and co-worker, and the ensuing scandal, aired at two church councils and public trial, was a national sensation. In an era when sexual fidelity was considered an essential bulwark of public welfare, the affair created unique concern and sensation. As much as any other event, it raised serious questions about the prevailing mores in the realm of "private versus public conduct, the function of the evangelical church, and the place of women in the social order."[32]

The Chautauqua movement was significant. The later Chautauqua involved commercialization and led to some degradation of its educational content as entertainment supplanted most of the educational programs.[33] The original program was a summer session on the shores of Lake Chautauqua, New York, begun as a Sunday School Teachers Assembly by Lewis Miller, an Ohio manufacturer, and the Reverend (later Bishop) John H. Vincent of the Methodist church. Both the content and the number of such institutes expanded rapidly. Permanent Chautauquas were founded in Ohio, Michigan, Iowa, and eventually in the Willamette Valley at Gladstone, Oregon. The original Chautauqua added a Literary and Scientific Circle, a School of Theology, and a College of Liberal Arts with authority to grant a bachelor's degree. Eminent educators, ministers, and lecturers, eventually including six presidents of the United States, contributed or sold their services. The most prominent educator and a figure in the Chautauqua was William Rainey Harper, later president of the University of Chicago. But the champion lecturer was surely the Reverend Russell Conwell, who delivered "Acres of Diamonds," over 5,000 times.

The self-improvement drive and the success-through-knowledge theme demonstrated again that Americans eagerly sought the available learning. This phenomenon, the free library movement, the prosperity of the book publishing industry, and the magazine boom, all indicated a thirst for knowledge and desire for culture. This search customarily led to the reaffirmation of the values rooted in experience. The benefits of private property, the beauties of competition, and the stewardship of wealth were main themes of Chautauqua lectures on social and economic subjects. But popular institutions of a society never purvey ideas contrary to accepted values. The lonely prophet, perceptive intellectual, or sensitive artist will confront a society with its failures and injustices. Culture-heroes will not.

Of course, the public was not solely interested in uplift or education. The era witnessed the rise of spectator sports, the modern circus, minstrelsy, and a "golden age" of the theater. As people moved to cities and worked in factories, organized recreation and spectator events replaced rural games and entertainments. For these spectacles, on the playing field or on the stage, the audiences were large and enthusiastic. The first mammoth three-ring circus under "three acres" of tent, and the nation's foremost opera house, the historic Metropolitan, both opened in New York City in 1883.

Three developments shaped the theater: the dominance of the "road"; the vogue for light musicals and scenic spectacles, including the scantily attired female form; and the popularity and decline of minstrelsy. A remarkable number of road stars were available. Richard Mansfield; James O'Neill, assigned to permanent stardom in the role of Edmund Dantes in Dumas's *The Count of Monte Cristo;* Edwin Booth, the supreme Shakespearian; Mary Anderson; the brilliant Italian stars, Tammaso Salvini and Adelaide Ristori; Mme. Modjeska; Joseph Jefferson in *Rip Van Winkle;* Henry Irving and Ellen Terry; the Divine Sarah herself; or, near the end of the era, Eleanora Duse. A rich and varied fare went to millions of Americans in these years. *East Lynne* played on Saturday nights, but Shakespeare and Dumas, Racine, and later G. B. Shaw and Ibsen were available. By 1893 this "golden age of the road" was drawing to a close. The development of theatrical syndicates foretold the rise of a new kind of theater that would culminate in the "star" system.[34]

The taste for lighter theatrical fare also increased, particularly in major cities. This vogue originated in the success of a melodrama called *The Black Crook,* which included a Parisian ballet sequence, the most expensive and daring show Americans had seen as of 1866. Nor could the thunderous denunciations of clergymen and angry moralists stop the trend. *The Black Crook* ran for sixteen months and broke all box-office records. It was often revived and, naturally, was followed by a number of similar shows.[35] *The Black Crook* may have set a precedent for sexual material on stage.[36]

The sprightly, melodic works of Gilbert and Sullivan were major hits after the first American production in 1878. The authors even opened the *Pirates of Penzance* in New York City. This was partly to prevent the work from being pirated by American producers.[37] This taste for *opera bouffe* helped several works by Offenbach to succeed in America in spite of the usual charge of "French indecencies"—or perhaps because of it.

Lighter theatrical fare included vaudeville, created by Tony Pastor. His Opera House in New York City became the Tony Pastor Music Hall, the "cathedral of Vaudeville." Such immortal show-business figures as the four Cohans, Weber and Fields, Harrigan and Hart, Pat Rooney, Gus Williams, Eddy Foy, and many others appeared there.[38] Pastor also founded the touring vaudeville show in 1878. The vigor and exuberance of vaudeville theater, the variety and fast pace of the acts, made vaudeville beloved to several generations.

The third major trend in show business was the rise and decline of minstrelsy. The minstrel show dated back to the between-acts numbers of black-face performers in the prewar era, especially one Thomas Rice, famed for his "Jump Jim Crow" number. The stock Negro character of the stage bore little resemblance to any actual person. The authentic minstrel company evolved to include end men, jokes, and songs, and had its heyday from 1850 to 1870. Competition to form ever bigger and more elaborate shows soon reduced the quality of performances. This and increasing expenses, and competition with vaudeville, burlesque, and musical comedy sent minstrelsy into a long decline which ended the form in the 1920's.[39]

The success of the minstrel show casts light on the public attitude toward racial minorities. The Negro was portrayed on stage, in dialect stories, and in illustrations as a comic fellow, "ludicrously inept," often putting on "airs . . . above his true station in life." But he was happy and good-natured, perhaps gifted at singing or dancing, but never a "person of consequence or dignity."[40] Racial distinctions were taken as obvious and inescapable. Those concerned about minority groups acted from paternalistic motives, not from a sense of the legitimate dignity and worth of all men.

Other racial stereotypes were equally bald. The Jew was often a shadowy and alien figure, somehow enmeshed in international finance; or he was clannish and unassimilable. The Indian was first portrayed as a dangerous enemy, then as nature's nobleman going down to defeat bravely, and then as a romantic figure in Helen Hunt Jackson's *Ramona*. The stage Irishman was also a stock figure. The following definition appeared in the "entertainment" column of a popular monthly:

> An Irish Discussion—A contractor who was building a tunnel on a certain railroad observed one morning that the face of a member of his gang was disfigured with bruises and plasters. "Hallo, Jimmy," said he, "what have you been doin?"—"Not varey mush, sorr" answered Jimmy. "I was jist down at Bill Mulligan's last night, sorr, an' him an' me had a bit of a discooshen wid sticks."[41]

Though it was not so much P. T. Barnum as his partners who created the modern circus, "the greatest show on earth," he remains the symbol of this achievement. The growth of the circus was tied to the growth of railroads and centers of population adequate to support it. The gigantic circus was part of an age of great enterprises, from spanning a continent with iron rails to building a multimillion-dollar business empire. P. T. Barnum belonged among the empire-builders.[42]

Ballads reinforced the accepted values. The moralistic note was detectable in "Always Take Mother's Advice." The sentimental-religious theme pervaded "Flowers from an Angel Mother's Grave."[43] Respectability dominated "In the Gloaming." Sheer nostalgia filled "Down by the Old Mill Stream," or the most popular sentimental ballad of the era, "Silver Threads Among the Gold."[44]

A lusty love of life prompted many popular songs. The "greatest of all drinking songs," the "honest and earthy" "Little Brown Jug" was published in 1869.[45] The famous ballad celebrating a prostitute betrayed by her man, the classic "Franky and Johnny," came from the 1880's.[46] The celebration of individual heroics was evident in the popularity of the song "Jim Fisk." The well-known antics of this scoundrel of high finance made him a strangely sympathetic figure, and the truth was distorted to help in this ballad:

I'll sing of a man who's now dead in his grave,
as good man as ever was born.
Jim Fisk he was call'd, and his money he gave,
to the outcast, the poor and forlorn.
We all know he lov'd both women and wine,
but his heart it was right I am sure.
Though he lived like a prince in his palace so fine,
Yet he never went back on the poor.[47]

Americans were sentimental and moralistic, but could celebrate the earthier side of life.

The technology and sense of rapid change that pervaded economics, politics, and diplomacy also shaped popular culture. Newspapers and magazines revised methods and appeals. Chautauqua was commercialized and standardized. Revivalism took on business methods. Minstrelsy could not survive new competition. These changes testify to the most important development in popular tastes—the trend toward a national culture. The localism and regionalism of an earlier age could not survive the theatrical syndicate, national magazines, wire service news, or touring Chautauquas.

But in ideas the continuity of the Gilded Age and the pre-Civil War years deserved notice. Sentimentalization of human relationships was the dominant tone. The death of loved ones, the family, and romantic love were all powerful themes through the Civil War and into the postwar years. Popular works clung to older values and beliefs. The insistent celebration of these virtues of an earlier America revealed an awareness of and resistance to the forces that were transforming the nation.

But in spite of these continuities there was a characteristic quality to the Gilded Age. The period ended as the 1880's closed. The transformation of the publishing industry, the rise of theatrical syndicates, the passing of the "golden age of the road," the decline of minstrelsy, the disappearance of the cheap story-papers, all marked the change. Something would be lost, perhaps best described as the folk element, which endured into an industrial age from an earlier America. Another casualty of the more highly organized society was the uninhibited individualism, which for all its unfortunate results, lent a colorful and fascinating quality to this era. That sense of assurance and abundant optimism which, though a substantial part of the American character in all periods, was at a high point in the Gilded Age, began to decline.

These losses were bound to occur as the technology of an industrial society advanced, and mass markets for art and entertainment were both possible and necessary. Artists and entertainers, or their promoters and managers, probably should have anticipated the change. But there is legitimate nostalgia for a time when the individual seemed significant. A bold editor could display his personality in his paper. A colorful preacher could become a national figure. And every housewife could hope to be a famous writer with her latest romantic tale. And all of this they did with a firm belief in the triumph of their cause and surpassing faith in the imperviousness of their moral armor.

Notes

1. Frank L. Mott, *Golden Multitudes* (New York: Macmillan, 1947), p. 85.

2. Russell Lynes, *The Tastemakers* (New York: Harper Bros., 1947), pp. 65-66.

3. Mott, *Golden Multitudes,* p. 87.

4. Two excellent photographs of Ochre Court can be seen in Wayne Andrews, *Architecture in America, A Photographic History from the Colonial Period to the Present* (New York: Atheneum, 1960), p. 109.

5. Wayne Andrews, *Architecture, Ambition, and Americans* (New York: Harper Bros., 1947), p. 186.

6. Wayne Andrews, *Architecture in America,* p. 83.

7. Lewis Mumford, *Sticks and Stones,* 2nd revised edition (New York: Dover, 1955), p. 105.

8. Maas, *The Gingerbread Age,* pp. 63-66.

9. Morton Cronin, "Currier and Ives: A Content Analysis," *American Quarterly,* 4 (Winter 1952), 317-30.

10. Lynes, *The Tastemakers,* p. 70.

11. Mott, *Golden Multitudes,* p. 125.

12. James D. Hart, *The Popular Book* (New York: Oxford University Press, 1950), p. 97.

13. Mott, *Golden Multitudes,* p. 136.

14. *New York Ledger,* Jan. 4, 1868.

15. Hart, *The Popular Book,* pp. 99-100.

16. *Ibid.*

17. Harvey C. Minnich, *William Holmes McGuffey and His Readers* (New York: American Book, 1936), pp. 40, 89-90.

18. Harry F. Harrison as told to Karl Detzer, *Culture Under Canvas* (New York: Hastings House, 1958), p. xiii.

19. Hart, *The Popular Book,* p. 145; Harrison, *Culture Under Canvas,* p. xiv.

20. Hart, *The Popular Book,* pp. 145-46.

21. James M. Lee, *History of American Journalism* (New York, 1923), p. 352.

22. Mott, *History of American Magazines,* III, 5.

23. *Ibid.,* pp. 5-9.

24. *Ibid.,* p. 10.

25. *New York Ledger,* March 14, 1885.

26. *Frank Leslie's Popular Monthly,* 9 (June, 1880), 702; *ibid.,* 17 (June, 1884), 759.

27. Mott, *History of American Magazines,* III, 42.

28. *Scribner's Magazine,* May, 1887.

29. William G. McLoughlin, *Modern Revivalism: Charles Grandison Finney to Billy Graham* (New York: Ronald Press, 1959), p. 216.

30. Bernard A. Weisberger, *They Gathered at the River* (Boston: Little, Brown, 1958), pp. 172-73.

31. See Justin Kaplan, *Mr. Clemens and Mark Twain: A Biography* (New York: Simon and Shuster, 1966), p. 24.

32. Shaplen, *Free Love and Heavenly Sinners,* p. 5.

33. Victoria and Robert Ormond Case, *We Called It Culture* (New York: Doubleday, 1948), pp. 20-21.

34. See Lloyd Morris, *Curtain Time* (New York: Random House, 1953).

35. *Ibid.,* p. 231.

36. David Ewen, *Panorama of American Popular Music* (Englewood Cliffs, N.J.: Prentice-Hall, 1957), p. 81.

37. Morris, *Curtain Time,* p. 235.

38. Ewen, *Panorama of American Popular Music,* pp. 86-87.

39. Carl Wittke, *Tambo and Bones* (Durham, N.C.: Duke University Press, 1930), pp. 38-86.

40. Cronin, "Currier and Ives," 317-30.

41. *Frank Leslie's Popular Monthly,* 2 (Nov., 1876), 639.

42. See Irving Wallace, *The Fabulous Showman* (New York: Knopf, 1959).

43. Written, it might be noted, by a "hard-drinking" ventriloquist named Harry Kennedy. Sigmund Spaeth, *A History of Popular Music* (New York: Random House, 1948), p. 219.

44. Edward B. Marks, as told to Abbot J. Liebling, *They All Sang* (New York, 1934), pp. 43-49; Spaeth, *A History of Popular Music,* p. 196.

45. Spaeth, *A History of Popular Music,* p. 173.

46. *Ibid.,* p. 207.

47. David Ewen, ed., *Songs of America, A Cavalcade of Popular Songs* (Chicago: Ziff-Davis, 1947), p. 146.

Reginald Twigg (essay date 1992)

SOURCE: "Aestheticizing the Home: Textual Strategies of Taste, Self-Identity, and Bourgeois Hegemony in America's 'Gilded Age,'" in *Text and Performance Quarterly,* Vol. 12, No. 1, January, 1992, pp. 1-20.

[*In the following essay, Twigg argues that, in the Gilded Age, middle-class Americans sought to express their individuality, while conforming to the aesthetic ideal, through "tasteful" home decoration, which was documented in the various decorating texts popular among all levels of society.*]

A vital function of texts, if viewed in relation to their performers, is to define, or more importantly, to perform the self. American "new historicists" such as Gillian Brown, Alan Trachtenberg, John Kasson, Joy Kasson, and Jackson Lears have explored the degree to which literature, sculpture, and other aesthetic texts function as sites in which cultural conceptions of self are negotiated and performed.[1] These scholars observe that, particularly during the late nineteenth century, Americans engaged metonymic strategies of identity construction through performative engagement with texts. The tendency of the period was to define, to enact, or to perform the self through identification with the perceived coherence and stability aesthetic texts provided. New historicism has cleared the way for questions central to performance studies in particular and communication studies in general: namely, in specific historical periods, how do people perform self through engagement with aesthetic texts?

In historical periods of dramatic transformation, aesthetic phenomena provide a sense of comfort and stability both by offering escape from the turmoil of everyday life and by re-presenting or redefining the conditions of life (Lears 98). Especially during periods of crisis, aesthetic texts acquire greater significance precisely because they provide the illusion of stability perceived to be lacking in society. Yet, the metonymic stability of aesthetic texts contains residues of the very conflicts, contradictions, and instabilities they seek to transcend. The late nineteenth century provides a vital context in which to understand the process of self performance through aesthetic texts. Two substantial justifications for this focus come to mind. First, the process of modernization and its reaction, antimodernism, provide a context in which to view not only the nineteenth century but the present as well: "Antimodernism was a complex blend of accommodation and protest which tells us a great deal about the beginnings of present-day values and attitudes" (Lears xv). Second, the transformation of American social life by industrialization and the emergent power of the corporation produced enormous instability and anxiety: "Economic incorporation wrenched American society from its moorings of familiar values . . . [and] the process proceeded by contradiction and conflict" (Trachtenberg 7).

Within this historical context, the home was a perceived source of stability, especially after the realization of its aesthetic potential at the Philadelphia Centennial Exposition in 1876. As Mary E. W. Sherwood pointed out in *Harper's* in 1882, "nothing can be more orderly, more harmonious, than a modern New York house which has blossomed out in this fine summer of perfected art [at the Exposition]" (681). For Sherwood and her contemporaries, the home provided the sense of order and harmony in a society increasingly fragmented, disorderly, and unharmonious. In fact, if modernization threatened societal or cultural anomie, the home would provide the last bulwark of protection. Sherwood continues: "The present achievement of American art, promising and full of interest as it is, is remote from that which should properly signalize the de-

cay of a great nation. . . . If we are advancing toward decay, we are certainly barricading our fort against its insidious footsteps with many a strong mahogany plank, and much 'heart of oak'" (690). Offering shelter from cultural and societal turbulence, the renaissance of home decoration in the late nineteenth century should be viewed as a textual strategy to which Americans turned to provide coherent and stable representations of self. Decorating texts functioned as sites for performing and authenticating the Victorian bourgeois self. Yet, the relationship between interior decoration and the homeowner was not a passive one. Rather, self performance through decoration implicates the self in an immediately constitutive, interactive (even transformative) process. Hence when Sherwood proclaims that "there are, perhaps, no two words more frequently on the lips of the present generation than these two: internal decoration" (680), she is, perhaps unconsciously, calling attention to the performative value of decoration.

By uncovering the relationships between interior decoration and self construction, we can begin to see how aesthetic texts function as sites of struggle and contestation over individual and social identity. Furthermore, we can begin to understand how texts such as interior decoration function as strategies for encompassing cultural crises. Interior decorating texts attempted to counteract social instability through the practice of cultural hegemony. But, although Victorian decorating texts functioned to maintain the hegemony of the bourgeoisie, the image of stability they provided was illusory. The strategy of performing self through the metonymy of texts ultimately reproduced, rather than ameliorated, the emptiness and alienation brought about by modernization. In order to reach a fuller understanding of the complex relationship between interior decoration as a textual strategy and cultural hegemony, I shall first consider the role of the Victorian aesthetic as a strategy of self performance through authentication; second, examine the role of decorating texts in shaping bourgeois hegemony; third, explore decorating texts as transformative strategies of self construction; and, finally, clarify the implications of display in the home as self performance.

THE GILDED AGE AND THE SEARCH FOR AUTHENTICITY

Mark Twain and C. D. Warner term late nineteenth-century America the "Gilded Age" in their satirical novel of the same name. While Twain and Warner's story survives as an insightful critique of their historical period, their greatest insight lies precisely in the term in which they encapsulate the times. *Gilding* connotes many things. For Twain and Warner, the term evokes a dazzling age of individualism, economic prosperity, and technological revolution. More importantly, *gilding* meant an overlay, making something *appear* better than it is. Hence, the term "Gilded Age" suggests a social function for art and aesthetic texts in Victorian America: they provide a lustre which covers up or overlays deeper social and cultural anxiety.

As historian John Kasson notes, maintaining the proper appearances was vital to Victorians (6). Victorian culture required people, particularly the bourgeoisie, to put on the appearances of stability and refinement. The Victorian emphasis on appearances functioned as a way of obviating or encompassing deeper cultural and social anxieties brought about by rapid economic, technological, and aesthetic transformation. Aesthetic texts in general, and decorating texts in particular, then, are best conceived as strategies; for the appearance of order and harmony that they provide functions metonymically to offset perceived crisis in other aspects of social life.[2] The function of decorating texts as strategies for performing or authenticating self is best understood as a response to the growing sense of emptiness and alienation that characterize the Victorian era.

In his provocative 1936 essay, "The Work of Art in the Age of Mechanical Reproduction," German critical theorist Walter Benjamin observes that by the late nineteenth century art had lost its "aura" or its "authenticity" when industrial technology made art reproducible (221). Traditionally, Benjamin argues, art was assessed by its cult value, that is, the degree to which art conveyed deeply sensual, as well as intellectual and emotional impressions. Traditional aesthetic experiences were profoundly moving, truly religious in nature. Art's value of authenticity, its "aura," came from its embeddedness in tradition; aesthetic experiences were deeply contextualized, thus stable and extremely powerful. However, claims Benjamin, "the technique of [technological] reproduction detaches the reproduced object from the domain of tradition. By making many reproductions it substitutes a plurality of copies for a unique existence. And in permitting the reproduction to meet the beholder or listener in his own particular situation, it reactivates the object reproduced" (221). When emergent technology made art reproducible and capable of mass-distribution, exchange value and exhibition value replaced religious or ritual value. Art became, in the Gilded Age, a commodity to be possessed and displayed. Without the anchor of traditions, art became a "weightless," that is, decontextualized, expression whose value came from suitability for exhibition and its status as a possession. The weightlessness of art in the Gilded Age, the age of mechanical reproduction, is well-illustrated in Mark Twain's declaration that Leonardo's "Last Supper" had become "the picture from which all engravings and all copies have been made for three centuries" (John Kasson 213).

The importance of Benjamin's argument goes beyond its explanation of the transformation of art in the Gilded Age. Not only had art lost its authenticity in the late nineteenth century; so did the Victorian sense of self. Mechanical reproduction had uprooted American culture from its traditions and hence its stability. However, the sources of anxiety about the self were varied and highly complex. For my purposes, two important elements of social transformation merit discussion. First, advanced technology and the dominance of the Enlightenment values of rationality and science began to undermine the traditional institutions upon which stable self-identity rested. As Lears argues, nineteenth-century culture had become increasingly rationalized, due to the declining authority of traditional institutions, religion for example, and the emergent hegemony of technological and scientific thinking. With the declining authority of cultural traditions came a growing sense that life in the Gilded Age had become empty and alienating, that is, inauthentic. As Lears explains, the inauthenticity of Victorian bourgeois life took its form in the feeling of weightlessness of individual identity: "For many, individual identities began to seem fragmented, diffuse, perhaps even unreal. A weightless culture of material comfort and spiritual blandness was breeding weightless persons who longed for intense experience to give some definition, some distinct outline and substance to their vaporous lives" (32).

Second, when shaken from its traditional moorings, Victorian art was transformed into a textual rather than a sensual experience. Art had become, by the turn of the century, a matter of "taste" requiring disciplined spectatorship (Joy Kasson 24-25). Since the value of art in the Gilded Age came from its exhibitional qualities, taste emerged as a practice of spectatorship—the practice of disciplining and training one to view and appreciate art "properly." At one level, the specialized knowledge of art and the inculcated sense of appreciation that comprised taste were attempts to restore art's authenticity by reviving, at least textually, its traditions. If the actual *context* in which art was properly to be experienced had vanished, taste provided a *textual* reconstruction of art's cult value. However, at another level, the textual reconstruction of art's aura further distanced the viewer from the art object precisely because art became a discrete object of appreciation, a text. In an age where traditional sources of self-identity were withering away, taste provided the illusion of restoration of authenticity, albeit only in textual form.

The emergence of taste as a textual strategy of authentication has substantial implications for understanding the performative value of aesthetic texts. Taste, particularly in the nineteenth century, was intimately tied to social class because it required "cultural capital," that is, the means to "understand" as well as to own art (Bourdieu 164). Taste constructs self-identity in part through class identification. The disciplined spectatorship or "pure gaze" that defines artistic taste in the nineteenth century, observes Pierre Bourdieu, "implies a break with the ordinary attitude towards the world which, as such, is a social break" (175). Exercising artistic taste establishes the self as a member of an elite class; it affiliates, that is, socially links, the individual with an exclusive class. Bourdieu elaborates: "The naive exhibitionism of 'conspicuous consumption,' which seeks distinction in the crude display of ill-mastered luxury, is nothing compared to the unique capacity of the pure gaze, a quasi-creative power which sets the aesthete [apart] from the common herd by a radical difference which seems to be inscribed in 'persons'" (175). In the anxiety over the loss of authenticity in art, taste emerged as a powerful strategy of textual reconstruction, and, in the process, redefined artistic experience and appreciation along class lines. Taste provided the illusion of stable identity through the exclusions of disciplined spectatorship. In essence, taste transformed self-identity by investing it with social distinction.

As a consequence, taste constructs bourgeois class identity as transcendent: taste was the ability to transcend the common, brutal experience of the body. For this reason, textual reconstruction reappropriated the aesthetic: it removed aesthetic experience from the sensual domain and located it in the textual. The human body became inscribed with class identity. Bourdieu notes that "rejecting the 'human' clearly means rejecting what is generic, i.e. *common,* 'easy', and immediately accessible, starting with everything that reduces the aesthetic animal to pure and simple animality, to palpable pleasure or sensual desire" (175-176). The refinement of artistic taste, while operating as a strategy to provide a stable identity for the bourgeois subject, functioned simultaneously as a form of social control. Contained in the disciplining of the pure gaze was the fear of class conflict; at stake in bourgeois individual and class identity was the very legitimacy of bourgeois class positions. In a period of social instability, as the Gilded Age was, points of opposition pose major threats to the dominant order, not to mention the dominant class (Lears 28-31). Implicitly, taste was a strategy of containment for the bourgeoisie: disciplining the body, particularly that of the working classes, was crucial in maintaining the dominance of the ruling class.

The body, argues John Fiske, is a site of class opposition. Bodily expressions undermine the authority of class distinction because they make social status appear relative and arbitrary, that is, something arbitrarily imposed on that which is common to all. The body as source of expression threatens the social order: "The pleasures of the individual body constituted a threat to the body politic. Such a threat becomes particularly terrifying when the pleasures are indulged in to excess, that is, when they exceed the norms proposed as proper and natural by those with social control, when they escape social discipline, and, thus, when allied with class interests, acquire a radical or subversive potential" (75). The Victorian bourgeoisie were concerned with the textualization of art not only because it created social distinction but also because it enforced the social order. As Fiske concludes, "excessive pleasures always threaten social control, but when these pleasures are those of subordinated groups (whether the subordination is by class, gender, race, or whatever) the threat is particularly stark, and disciplinary, if not repressive, action is almost inevitable" (75). Textualization, or separation of art from bodily experience, enabled control of disorder. Taste functioned not only to erect class boundaries but also to control opposition to the dominant social order.

The textualization of art also functioned to displace social anxieties. Stephen Greenblatt speculates that social conflicts "circulate" through aesthetic forms (8). By his view, aesthetic texts are never autonomous spheres outside of society; rather, they function as sites where social conflicts are defined and negotiated. Social anxieties, consequently, emerge in aesthetic texts in different forms, usually to be resolved by the texts themselves. Social anxieties are displaced into aesthetic texts precisely because such texts appeared to be strategies of resolution. It is a popular myth, for example, that Victorians were repressed, stuffy people, displaying, as Peter Gay puts it, a "lust to conceal" (440). However, the anxieties Victorians so readily concealed from daily practice circulated somewhat freely in the scientific and aesthetic texts of the time (Foucault 4). According to Gay, anxieties, particularly the loss of sensual experience, were displaced into furniture design:

> Furniture and furnishings provided sensual cues and combined to cater to all the senses at once. They caressed the eye with polished wood and the intricate traceries of Turkish rugs; the ear with yearning melodies sounded on the piano or by companionable voices; the palate with melting candy and succulent grapes; the sense of smell with flowers and sachets and the aroma of food; the touch—always touch—with the surfaces of objects skillfully carved, woven, knitted. To sink into the embrace of a well-upholstered chair was to pamper one's musculature, to regress in the service of the body. (439)

As Gay's discussion suggests, furniture design was a vital textual strategy; for it attempted to authenticate the self by providing an illusory amelioration of the tensions between textual and sensual experiences. It becomes evident in this passage that a significant source of alienation in the Gilded Age was the very strategy intended to reconcile it. Textual reconstruction of aesthetic experience had alienated the bourgeoisie from sensual experience, thus contributing to their feeling of "weightlessness."

The "Gilded Age" suggests an overlay, a term that explains the social function of Victorian aesthetic texts. In many respects, aesthetic texts responded to the anxiety of weightlessness in social life through displacement, providing the illusion of reconciliation. As the rest of the essay will illustrate, the underlying problem of the Victorian aesthetic is that it ultimately reproduced the anxieties which it sought to redress. Aesthetic texts in general, and most significantly decorating texts, sought to redress the general loss of authenticity by covering it up.

INTERIOR DECORATION AS A HEGEMONIC STRATEGY

Decoration's significance stemmed primarily from its function as a *representation* of self, an image of self through which the bourgeoisie expressed and performed self to the public. George Sheldon, in his monumental treatise on the well-decorated home, *Artistic Houses,* published in 1883, declared that "the interior of the house of a professional man of scholarly pursuits, cultivated tastes, and wealth sufficient to gratify both, is at least the proximate expression of his experience and convictions" (87). Moreover, Victorians believed that "the house was also the environment that taught the young and sustained them in later years . . ." (Lewis, Turner and McQuillin 18). Of all sources of aesthetic experience, the home was most prevalent. Harriet Spofford in *Art Decoration Applied to Furniture,* 1878, wrote: "Its study is as important, in some respects, as the study of politics; for the private home is at the foundation of the public state, subtle and unimagined influences moulding the men who mould the state" (Lewis et al. 18). Decoration's performative function, as these passages suggest, lies in its exhibition value, its ability not only as a representation to display the self, but also as a representation to inculcate the dominant culture's important values. Specifically, decorating texts of the Gilded Age attempted to restore a sense of authenticity to the bourgeois conception of self by constructing class "affiliations" and legitimating, in the process, the exploitative and oppressive ideology and practice of colonialism. Hence, the function of decorating texts as strategies of identity construction can only be understood by positioning them historically in colonialism, a highly complex practice that constructs class identity by constructing and demonizing the Other.

"Affiliations," as Edward Said defines the term in *The World, the Text, and the Critic,* are those ties formed "by social and political conviction, economic and historical circumstances, voluntary effort and willed deliberation" (25). Affiliations construct self-identity by linking it with a social class. Because they establish boundaries of inclusion and exclusion around social ties, affiliations are political: affiliations hold social classes together and give them their power. The ability to set boundaries of taste is a source of substantial political power. Said carefully elaborates taste's political function:

> [c]ulture is a system of discriminations and evaluations—perhaps mainly aesthetic, as Lionel Trilling has said, but no less tyrannical for that—for a particular class in the State able to identify with it; and it also means that culture is a system of exclusions legislated from above but enacted throughout its polity, by which such things as anarchy, disorder, irrationality, inferiority, bad taste, and immorality are identified, then deposited outside the culture and kept there by the power of the State and its institutions. (*The World* 11)

Taste is a specific social practice through which class distinction and domination are maintained. However, class domination does not necessarily operate through force. More subtly, affiliations maintain class dominance, or, as Antonio Gramsci defines the process, class "hegemony" through "intellectual and moral leadership" (Hoare and Smith 57). If this leadership of the dominant class is effective, its hegemony is maintained without resorting to force, making taste vital politically; for taste can provide legitimacy for the dominance of the ruling class through ideology, that is, representations of reality in which the dominant social order appears "natural." Given the strategic importance of the home in Victorian culture, decoration's role in the process of defining and maintaining affiliations was central.

In the latter half of the nineteenth century, decorating texts of all kinds circulated among all levels of American society. Perhaps the most significant of these texts was George

Sheldon's *Artistic Houses Being a Series of Interior Views of a Number of the Most Beautiful and Celebrated Homes in the United States* because it documented in careful detail the contents of America's most "tasteful" homes and defined the parameters of tasteful decoration. Nearly all of the homeowners featured were prominent business, social, and government leaders—America's most elite. Throughout Sheldon's book are declarations of the class status one must enjoy in order to decorate tastefully, frequently equating such homes with those of European monarchs. As Arnold Lewis, James Turner, and Steven McQuillin point out, Sheldon's book served a vital purpose in an age where social status was becoming increasingly more important: "In the 1880s, both outside observers of the wealthy and those who saw themselves as inside guardians of 'society' began to be more systematic and explicit in their defining of categories, producing extensive lists of families and individuals. The lists, among their other functions, help define Sheldon's homeowners" (6). *Artistic Houses* defined class affiliations of the time because it made decorating taste the encompassing term for class identity. William H. Vanderbilt's house is a poignant illustration. Upon the completion of his two-million-dollar mansion in 1883 (a phenomenal amount for a house at that time), he commissioned a four-volume study to provide a detailed photojournalistic tour of his house and its belongings. That same year, *Artistic Houses* was released, devoting more photographs and descriptive space to Vanderbilt's house than to any other. It is no coincidence that Vanderbilt was admitted to the *Social Register* shortly after these two prominent publications featured his house (Lewis et al. 10). So vital to his social status was the presentation of his home that Vanderbilt hired a "taste consultant" whose sole task was to collect valuable decorative items, arrange them tastefully, and instruct Vanderbilt on these decorative objects (Lewis et al. 18). Vanderbilt's obsession with the appearance of his home demonstrates the vital function of decoration in strengthening class affiliations.

Implicit in decorating texts was the concern, particularly among the American bourgeoisie, that traditional sources of class identity had lost their authority.[3] The rationalization of American culture in the nineteenth century meant that traditional definitions of class identity—namely the claim that class distinctions were ordained by God—no longer held authority; yet the need to define self-identity through class remained strong. Decorating texts were important strategies through which Victorians could recapture the authority of class distinctions. For example, decorating texts tended to refer to the well-appointed homes of the wealthy as "palaces," a term that connotes the homes of royalty (Sherwood 686). Similarly, describing the home of the department store magnate Marshall Field, *Artistic Houses* referred to its owner as "the most widely known of Chicago's merchant princes . . ." (43). The terms used to describe the wealthy and their homes indicate that decorating texts subtly reconstructed class boundaries by shifting the sources of elite status onto secular practices such as success in business and government.

More importantly, since simple strategic use of vocabulary could not, by itself, lend authority to Victorian class distinctions, decorating texts constructed an ideology in which the source of social status was taste rather than traditional family ties. Through a textual reconstruction of traditions, decorating texts very subtly reconfigured the source of class identity as the ability to display art objects and appreciate them "properly." In many ways, these texts *reappropriated* historical traditions in secular terms, thus providing authority for class distinctions. By doing so, decorating texts established affiliations consistent with the needs of the Gilded Age's dominant class. Witness, for example, Mary E. W. Sherwood's careful alignments between contemporary and traditional styles, as well as her redefining of class as an issue of taste: "Then came the great Philadelphia Exposition, with its pretty Eastlake house from England, with its stuffs of all nations, with its orderly cataloguing of the good things of past and present, picking out for us what had been worthy in the reign of the tasteful Stuarts, whatever was magnificent in the day of stately Elizabeth, whatever of good (and there was much) in the reign of Queen Anne, also what could be curiously sifted from the luxury of Louis XIV and XV" (681). By implication, Sherwood's account of the Exposition suggests that the fundamental terms of class had not changed; rather, rationalization re-articulated the source of its authority as the possession of taste. Hence, decorating texts functioned strategically to define class identity and its attendant power relations on secular terms when religious justifications had lost their authority. Decorating texts could maintain class affiliations under the illusion of democratic equality; for when the law recognized, on the surface, no class boundaries, making boundaries themselves appear elusive, decorating texts marked a shift in class affiliations away from direct expressions, such as the law, and into the more subtle arena of "culture." The shift of domination into the realm of culture does not diffuse its power. On the contrary, as suggested earlier, taste's subtlety is its power because it constructs an ideology in which social distinctions are legitimated rather than forced. The power of decorating texts, then, lay in their illusion of intellectual and moral leadership, that is, the extent to which they maintained the hegemony of the ruling class.

The hegemonic function of decorating texts is further elaborated when viewed in the light of the ideological practice of colonialism. Though affiliations can explain how culture in the Gilded Age consolidated the power of the ruling class, we need to look further to understand how affiliations were strategies of self performance. In an age characterized as "weightless," texts could function as sources of stability, especially when they constructed clear conceptions of self. Abdul JanMohamed explains: "The dominant pattern of relations that controls the text within the colonialist context is determined by economic and political imperatives and changes, such as the development of slavery, that are external to the discursive field itself. . . . a field of diverse yet interchangeable oppositions between white and black, good and evil, superiority and inferiority, civilization and savagery, intelligence and emo-

tion, rationality and sensuality, self and Other, subject and object" (63). As a strategy of self performance, colonialism enacts self by constructing Otherness as inferior: the clearer the opposition between self and Other becomes, the more stable self-identity becomes (Burke 138-139). Victorian taste in general, and decorating texts in particular, attempted to stabilize self-identity precisely through the field of oppositions colonialist ideology provided. As JanMohamed's passage suggests, colonialism is ideological to the degree that it is articulated in discursive practice. That is, texts are the crucial sites where distinction is negotiated and acted upon. Consequently, we cannot understand colonizing texts as purely exploitative; rather, they are part of a complex cultural practice of identity construction.

Victorian decorating texts incorporated colonizing themes on several levels for different purposes. Initially, these themes attempted to stablize self-identity by counterposing it to the exotic Other, a strategy that was subtly articulated. Sherwood in 1882, for example, noted that the rage was "exotic" decoration motifs (681). *Artistic Houses* catalogued numerous rooms of Middle-Eastern or Far-Eastern influence. Charles Eastlake, in *Hints on Household Taste*, confessed a certain affection for "Oriental" carpets (108). The appeal of exotic objects lay in their ability as representations to make the exotic Other appear to be present, at least metonymically. By completing the self-Other, superior-inferior dialectic, decorating texts provided the illusion of stable self-identity. The bourgeoisie could exhibit their "superiority" by "tastefully" representing the objects of Other cultures as part of their own cultural capital. Colonialist ideology consolidated political power along with a stable sense of self because these texts defined the Other as inferior: the Other "lacked" taste as well as the economic means to satisfy it. As an illustration, *Artistic Houses* featured a description of a reception room decorated in a Chinese motif. The homeowner could not translate the "curious inscriptions in Chinese" because of "the prevailing ignorance of the great majority of our imported Chinamen. . . . unlike his neighbors, John Chinaman in America is seldom acquainted with the letters of his own language, to say nothing of interpreting them to foreigners" (27). In the process of completing the self-Other dialectic, decorating texts such as *Artistic Houses* commodified the colonized Other, thus inscribing in the colonized the status of inferiority by denying them their own subjectivity. The conscious and unconscious racism in these texts was a vital source of their strategic power; for they could confirm a stable self-identity by counterposing it to the "racially inferior" Other they constructed.

Much of colonialism's ideological power was derived from other discourses circulating in late nineteenth-century America. Most significant among these discourses was social Darwinism because it provided a "rational" or scientific justification for the social inequalities underlying colonialism. Rhetorically, social Darwinism was a secular counterpart to traditional notions of class identity, thus providing great appeal in an age marked by secular thought. By the latter decades of the nineteenth century many social theorists, anthropologists, and scientists claimed that the upper classes were "naturally" more fit to lead because society, like nature, was predicated on evolution. As historian Richard Hofstadter points out, scientific and social discourses naturalized social inequality by resting it on the assumption that "nature would provide that the best competitors in a competitive situation would win, and that this process would lead to continuing improvement" (6). Social Darwinists judged society from an evolutionary perspective that held social inequalities as evidence of different stages in social evolution. Decorating texts became vital markers of "advanced" civilization; for social Darwinism constructed taste as the highest stage of human development.

If taste was the marker of advanced civilization, the home was its proximate expression. Andrew Carnegie, writing in 1889, centrally located the home in social evolution: "The contrast between the palace of the millionaire and the cottage of the laborer with us today measures the change which has come with civilization" (123). Given the vital importance of the home as a symbol of social evolution, Carnegie admonished his readers that "this change, however, is not to be deplored, but welcomed as highly beneficial. It is well, nay, essential, for the progress of the race that the houses of some should be homes for all that is highest and best in literature and the arts, and for all the refinements of civilization, rather than that none should be so. Much better this great irregularity than universal squalor" (123). Decorating taste, from Carnegie's perspective, provided the source of leadership in society, making those with tastefully decorated homes most fit to lead. Decorating texts suggested that taste entitled upper-class Americans to plunder the art objects of Other cultures because such plunder was constructed as in the interests of everybody: plunder allowed the elite to perfect taste (the highest stage in social evolution), as well as to "uplift" the colonized through its leadership. Consequently, we cannot ignore the degree to which decorating texts legitimated colonialist practice and its attendant construction of the colonized Other as "inferior" in order to confirm the class status of the bourgeoisie. The Gilded Age was rife with the consequences of colonialist ideology, suggesting that the search for self-identity and its performance were accomplished at the expense of the colonized.[4]

Decorating texts functioned as strategies of self performance through the practice of cultural hegemony. While they were attempts to provide an authentic sense of self by defining it in the larger context of social class, decorating texts legitimated larger material practices of social inequality. By generating clear, allegedly "natural" sources of social inequality, the bourgeoisie of the Gilded Age could provide clearer conceptions of self. Decorating texts strategically positioned the upper class individual in the highest site of social hierarchy. However, the stability of self-identity contained in these texts was achieved at the expense of the Other they constructed. In the name of taste, these texts consciously and unconsciously trans-

formed both the Other's person and art into commodities for consumption. This transformation functioned to affirm the subjectivity of the bourgeois self by empowering it with the ability to objectify the Other. Thus, decorating texts, as strategies of textual reconstruction, reconfigured social relations in the process. Contained in the illusion of stability provided by affiliations and colonialist ideology, however, was a deeper feeling of weightlessness that decorating texts failed to address. Consequently, while the affiliations decorating texts constructed solidified class stability on one level, the strategies upon which this stability was built ultimately proved to be a symptom of the crisis in self-identity during the Gilded Age. The following discussion elaborates on the failure of decorating texts to restore the feeling of authenticity in Victorian America.

DECORATING TEXTS AND THE CRISIS OF
SELF-IDENTITY

While decorating texts functioned to stablize self-identity by constructing class affiliations, they operated, at a different level, as the very source of individual identity. Since the Gilded Age was an era where the traditional sources of self definition had lost their authority, or, in Benjamin's terms, their "aura," the decoration of one's home, as a practice, could restore, on the surface, an authentic sense of self. Art's transformation from cult value to exhibition value was mirrored in Victorian culture's ideology of self. Like art, individual identity was determined by its exhibition value, the ability to put on the proper appearances. If the self was defined by what it exhibited, then Americans in the Gilded Age literally defined the self through performance. Conceiving the Victorian self as a performance thus provides a poignant illustration of Twain and Warner's term, the "Gilded Age;" for it suggests that one's exhibited or performed identity was an overlay, a covering. However, since the Victorian self was something to be performed, specifically through the specialization and cushioning of private space, the textual strategy of its performance, decorating, contributed to the emptiness and alienation Americans of the time began to experience precisely because it was an overlay.

The nineteenth-century art historian and philosopher John Ruskin proclaimed that in the Gilded Age "taste is not only a part and an index of morality;—it is the *only* morality. . . . Tell me what you like, and I'll tell you what you are" (in John Kasson 169). To American Victorians, this statement was not to be taken lightly, for the home was viewed by decorating advisors as the purest expression of one's self-identity. Citing Ruskin, Sheldon in *Artistic Houses* declared: "I would have, then, our ordinary dwelling-houses built to last, and built to be lovely; as rich and full of pleasantness as may be, within and without, and with such differences as might suit and express each man's character and occupation, and partly his history" (43). In many respects, the home stood in a metonymic relationship to the individual. The collections of objects under the broad term "taste" summed up, through representation, an individual's identity. The nineteenth-century tendency to define individuals according to attributes or properties they possessed had profound implications for the conceptualization of the home. Human presence was subordinated to what the home said about it. For example, Clarence Cook, writing in 1881, pointed to the parlor as *the* representation of the self. Accordingly, this "room ought to represent the culture of the family,—what is their taste, what feeling they have for art, it should represent themselves, and not other people; and the troublesome fact is, that it will and must represent them, whether its owners would let it or not" (48-49).

Given the importance of their homes as representations of the self, Victorians lavished inordinate amounts of effort and money to furnish them. According to John Kasson, rooms were decorated primarily according to two strategies. First, furnishings were highly specialized, including gentlemen's armchairs, ladies' chairs, reception chairs, multitudes of rockers, and various sofas, settees, and lounges (174). Specialization reflected the increased tendency to isolate social functions, such that each item of furniture became connected to a specific social practice (chairs for reading, tables for leaving calling cards, for example). Specialization further fragmented the individual precisely because it splintered one's daily activities into series of practices often linked to specific material objects, resulting in a tendency for self performance and, consequently, self-identity to be inseparable from material possessions. Ultimately, specialization, as a textual strategy designed to provide coherence to the Victorian sense of self, undermined its own strategic value because it splintered the home into a collection of specialized objects designed for specific purposes. To the degree that Victorian self performance was tied to the objects in the home, decorative specialization contributed to the fragmentation it was intended to alleviate, thus surfacing the very anxieties it was intended to cover over.

While specialization directly reflected the transformation of social life into specialized tasks, another strategy, "cushioning," offered protection from the alienation this transformation caused (John Kasson 174). By using a plethora of decorated fabrics, Victorians transformed parlors into "virtual cocoons of gentility" (John Kasson 175). Cushioning provided a displacement of the safety of the womb into the public rooms of the house. More than this, however, cushioning represented a deeper anxiety about the tensions between the public and private self. The inevitable feelings of emptiness in a public sphere governed by appearances could at least be negotiated or compensated in the public spaces of the home. In *Artistic Houses,* a depiction of a drawing room provides a good example. Every surface, including the wall hangings and the fireplace, is draped in fabric, creating the impression of a soft, warm, enveloping space (Sheldon 60-64). In its extreme, though, the strategy of cushioning had similar effects to gilding in that they both cover up—making objects appear better than they are. The comfort in public spaces such decoration sought to create was itself an illusion, making the room itself as much an appearance as social performance

itself. Within the metonymy of decoration, the irony is that it attempted to give meaning to a vacuous self precisely through the strategy that rendered it problematic—putting on appearances. In this case decoration dealt with one displacement through another.

Cushioning and specialization, as strategies of self performance, functioned simultaneously to recapitulate American gender roles. When the specialization of American culture began to stratify social life into separate "spheres," it simultaneously reappropriated social roles as functions of these spheres. There was, as Gillian Brown notes, a redefining of domestic space, the home, in gendered terms, relegating women to the private sphere: "Domestic ideology with its discourse of personal life proliferates alongside this economic development [the market economy] which removed women from the public realm of production and redirected men to work arenas increasingly subject to market contingencies" (3). The market economy of the nineteenth century recapitulated the public sphere as man's space, and the domestic sphere as woman's. As Brown suggests, the reappropriating of women's roles into the domestic sphere further disempowered women politically. Moreover, representing the home as the cushioned safe-haven from the turbulence of social life suggested that the role of women was to maintain the comfort and emotional stability of men and children in the home. Joy Kasson observes that "increasingly, by the end of the nineteenth century, the family was defined as the proper sphere for women of the genteel classes, and the home had become a bastion of emotional retreat from a competitive, commercial culture" (3). Thus, constructing the home as the comfortable retreat from the anxieties of the market while simultaneously positioning women in the home removed women from the primary sources of political power. However, the removal of women from the public sphere reflected a deeper anxiety—namely the fear of women's empowerment. While decorating texts located women in the home, women were seeking greater representation in the workplace, politics, and public life in general (Joy Kasson 3). Decoration and decorating texts functioned strategically to construct an ideology that defined women's "ideal" place as in the home. Yet the ideology they constructed was itself an overlay: it attempted to cover up the deeper fear of women breaking from traditionally-defined sex roles.

Decorating the home became an important social practice because it was an instantiation of larger social changes. The segregating of space within the home mirrored the ideological division of city space into districts.[5] The metonymic relationship between home and individual reveals the extent to which Victorians sought authentic expressions of self through both material possessions and the refinement such possessions allegedly cultivated. However, as a representation of self, decoration was just as much an appearance—expressed through art, rather than conduct—as the social roles one assumed in public. For decoration was the process of covering up, making the ornamental interiors of middle class houses provide the illusion of coherent self-identity when social life became fragmented and weightless. In the end, decoration not only could not alleviate the anxieties of modern culture,[6] it reproduced them through displacements doomed to the same fragmentation they sought to mask.

THE DOMESTIC MUSEUM AND ITS IMPLICATIONS

Though museums had existed since the late eighteenth century, it was not until the 1860s that they became well-funded public institutions (Lewis et al. 23). As a social practice museums were predicated on the social function of display. Museums were strategies of textual reconstruction in which Americans attempted to restore the authenticity of art, as well as experience, by reconstructing contextualizing traditions. Since, as Benjamin contends, art's aura, authority, and authenticity came from its embeddedness in tradition, museums were attempts to restore these characteristics by careful ordering of objects. Creating from disparate objects of plunder the illusion of order was a vital strategy of self performance—one that functioned through the metonymy of orderly display. The emergent popularity of museums coincided with the transformation of the home into a domestic museum. John Kasson writes that a central function of decoration was to provide "the artful display of objects of cultural attainment and personal association. These objects included a piano or parlor organ, well-stocked bookcases, homemade artworks such as needlepoint and painted china, and personal collections of photographs, engravings, and souvenirs of travel, exhibited on walls, parlor tables, étagères, hanging shelves, mantelpieces, and art corners." Accordingly, Kasson observes, "the parlor became a kind of 'memory palace' of culture, a miniature museum thick with meaning, an artful declaration of its owners' sensibility" (175-6). The parlor was also an important stage for oral performance of speeches and literature (*The Art of Conversing* 27). In the semi-public performances of the parlor one could perfect his or her public image through such performance, thus assigning a directly performative function for this space. Conceiving of the home as a museum, more than any other decorating practice, was the most visible attempt to perform self through the perceived coherence, tradition, and order of exhibition. Yet, like the other decorating strategies, domesticating the museum was doomed to failure because it performed self through the display of objects. At best, the exhibition of objects functioned to overlay or stand in place of self but it could not address the underlying sources of anxiety. In fact, as this discussion illustrates, the strategic use of the museum reproduced the weightlessness of Victorian culture it was intended to alleviate.

As the domestic museum became a prominent social practice, decorating advisors increasingly demanded that patrons fill their homes with "authentic" art—art that had tradition or that which was original, not copied. Mass produced items were condemned as mere imitations, as Charles Eastlake warned in 1881: "The moment a carved or sculptured surface begins to *shine,* it loses interest. But

machine-made ornament, invested with an artificial lustre, is an artistic enormity which should be universally discouraged" (85). Applied ornament violated these notions of authenticity because it was a covering, a veneer over the real: "Even if it were carved out of solid wood, it would be very objectionable in design; but this trash is only lightly *glued* to the frame which it is supposed to adorn, and may indeed frequently be removed with infinite advantage to the general effect" (Eastlake 59). When fine finishing materials were in demand, prices went up, forcing many to resort to "faux finishes" or disguising cheaper materials to make them look better—a practice Eastlake, among others, condemned as trickery: "At the present time, when both marble and oak are beyond the reach of ordinary incomes, the usual practice is to cover the walls with a paper stained and varnished in imitation of marble. This is, perhaps, a more excusable sham than others to which I have alluded; but still it is a sham, and ought therefore to be condemned" (52). As Eastlake's declaration reveals, the search for authentic finishes made class distinctions based upon the prices certain materials commanded, suggesting that one's class affiliations were the basis of a truly aesthetic environment.

The domestic museum, however, was more than an expression of genuine materials: the objects themselves had to be genuine. In most cases, writers on decoration celebrated art objects for their embeddedness in history as the true criterion for authenticity. *Artistic Houses* praised tradition in a mantel ornament: "Another interesting historic curiosity is the head of the yellow-pine figurehead of General Jackson, which once adorned the bow of the United States frigate Constitution in Boston Harbor, but which, during the intense political excitement of 1835, was sawed off by a zealous young druggist of that city, who had rowed out to the frigate and climbed up her chain-cable during the night of Cimmerian darkness." *Artistic Houses* praises its display: "Mr. Dickerson has honored this relic with a place on the mantel of his spacious and well-lighted billiard-room" (85). Describing a guest room, *Artistic Houses* continues, "even the facing of the fireplace is of old blue Dutch tiles brought over by the colonists; and the corner cupboard extending to the ceiling, with the small glass panes of its doors and the old blue china behind them—how interesting a souvenir of the good old days it is!" (51). The attempts the Victorians made in search of authentic art reflected an obsessive search for lost traditions. Items that have history or tradition have an aura of authenticity. *Artistic Houses* praises the items of one dining room: "Some exquisite Sèvres porcelains glisten from a wallcabinet close by, and near them are two lofty candelabra once belonging to the first Napoleon, and afterward to the French embassy at Rome" (151). These passages reveal the extent to which historical artifacts are an integral part of the Victorian domicile. They invoke an experience tied to the past conceived as the "good old days."

Possessing such artifacts was only part of their status; one also had to display them appropriately. For this reason, many collectors built new houses in the latter decades of the nineteenth century to display items properly—a trend reflected in the fact that nearly all Eastern American cities had commissioned new metropolitan museums (Lewis et al. 22-23). One such house, notes *Artistic Houses,* was constructed as a display case for the art treasures its owner ransacked Europe and Asia collecting (a reminder of the colonizing nature of art collection): "Instead of building for them [art objects] a distinct and lofty gallery, the owner has constructed a series of apartments called cabinets, that not only open into each other, but are integral parts of the house itself" (149). The result blurs the boundaries between house and museum: "He seems to have had no desire to keep his family away from his pictures, and certainly any visitor once inside the building finds himself immediately within sight of the chef-d'oeuvres of the Gibson collection, and would be at a loss to say just where the 'gallery' began and just where it ended" (149). During this period, the "proper" artistic home was transformed into a display case for art objects. And, as the passages admit, it is very difficult to determine if people actually lived in such houses. The distance between art object and self was reduced to such a degree that the former could perform for the latter. By breaking down the distance between art and its owner, the domestic museum made it possible for the perceived stability of art's exhibition to stand for, and thus perform the self.

Both the concern for "genuine" artifacts and careful arrangement of them points to the subtle social and psychological dimensions of the domestic museum. In many ways, the domestic museum was an attempt to provide meaning in the form of order and authenticity for a confused and fragmented culture. In his essay, "The Museum's Furnace," Eugenio Donato argues that collections of artifacts functioned to provide meaning to experience by locating it in a larger, seemingly coherent history (220). Museums functioned to provide stable realities grounded in some sense of tradition. By tying objects to what was perceived as "real" history, Victorians were attempting to verify the authenticity of their own existence—attempting to locate themselves as part of a larger historical space—a space whose coherence and meaning could specifically define and position the self.

Unfortunately, as Donato observes, the coherence the domestic museum provided was illusory. Initially, the arrangement and collection of objects, regardless of the system under which they were organized, were arbitrary arrangements of objects stripped from their historical contexts. As such, the objects themselves were merely fragments of other cultures being appropriated to provide meaning for a culture that itself was fragmented. The problem of the museum, then, was precisely the problem of representation:

> The set of objects the Museum displays is sustained only by the fiction that they somehow constitute a coherent representational universe. The fiction is that a repeated metonymic displacement of fragment for totality, object to label, series of objects to series of labels, can still produce a representation which is some-

how adequate to a nonlinguistic universe. Such a fiction is the result of an uncritical belief in the notion that ordering and classifying, that is to say, the spatial juxtaposition of fragments, can produce a representational understanding of the world. (Donato 223)

Victorians transformed their homes into museums in an attempt to provide meaning for the past, which, in some ways, could provide meaning for the present. For historical objects only had value to the extent that they had meaning. Throughout the rhetoric of decorating texts is the search for meaning in objects. As a result, culture, as an umbrella term for knowledge, sensitivity, and a stage in social evolution, suggests a deeper anxiety in Victorian culture: the concern that modernization had alienated the individual from reality. Thus, stripping objects of their meanings in many ways denies their claim to reality. As Donato concludes, "should the fiction disappear, there is nothing left of the *Museum* but 'bric-a-brac,' a heap of meaningless and valueless fragments of objects which are incapable of substituting themselves either metonymically for the original objects or metaphorically for their representations" (223).

The domestic museum, thus conceived, was a strategy for coping with the anxieties of modern culture. Concerned that the schism between public and private life had created a vacuum for the individual, Victorians turned to domesticating the museum in order to provide through representations a unity that modern life had forever banished from them. As they intersect with gender and race, class distinctions informed aesthetic questions in the Gilded Age. Consequently, the very strategies of aestheticization—particularly strategies of decoration—were attempts to provide a lustre to mask deeper anxieties and concerns that were themselves products of the capitalist economy. The bourgeois aesthetic of the home reproduced the fragmented and hollow nature of the Victorian self precisely because it was a mask—an overlay. Hence the very strategy for alleviating the cultural crisis of the era was itself conducive to the crisis, rendering the hegemony of the Victorian bourgeoisie unstable. The instability of bourgeois hegemony, the crisis to which this study continually refers, was a "crisis of cultural authority" (Lears 5) because the bases upon which class distinctions were built were themselves fictions built upon collections of material possessions. Beneath the gilded mask of decoration was the deeper anxiety over the inauthenticity of Victorian experience, the crisis of cultural authority. Donato provides both an explanation of the failure of the domestic museum as a textual strategy of self performance and the general failure of decorating texts as sources of stability in Victorian culture: "spatially and temporally detached from their origin and function, they [artifacts] signify only by arbitrary and derived associations. The series in which the individual pieces and fragments are displayed is also arbitrary and incapable of investing the particular object with anything but irrelevant fabulations" (224).

CONCLUSION

We can begin to see how the various social, economic, and cultural forces began to merge in the discourses on interior decoration. Exploitative social inequality was intimately tied to the consumption of art. Textual reconstruction, social affiliations, colonialism, specialization, cushioning, and domesticating the museum gave the practice of interior decoration and its attendant texts rhetorical and performative power. Through the authority of taste, the wealthy of the Gilded Age were able to solidify their class positions and thereby maintain their exploitative relations of production. Through decorating texts the ideological practice of colonialism, defined and legitimated by social Darwinism and its accompanying discourses, rhetorically masked the interests of the wealthy. For deeper examination reveals that decorating texts simultaneously attempted to provide stable self-identity and justify the enormous exploitation of the colonized as in the interests of society in general. If taste, through its disciplining of the body, failed to keep the colonized and other oppressed classes quiescent, it provided an ideological justification for violent forms of repression. Since taste constructed the colonized as inferior, irrational, or immoral, as decorating texts implicitly did, it provided sanction for repression in the name of preserving order. For these reasons, interior decoration was central to the production of capitalist ideology. Capitalist ideology can operate, as this study indicates, to legitimate the position of the wealthy and therefore maintain oppressive relations of production.

More than this, however, the hegemony of the wealthy was an unstable one. The fragmented nature of the bourgeois individual thus generated a crisis of cultural authority. Anxiety over the growing sense of emptiness in bourgeois social life rendered problematic the leadership ability of the dominant class. For the shifting definitions of "taste" reflected the arbitrariness such distinctions themselves had. In many ways, decoration was a strategy to address the emptiness of the individual—to provide the illusion of wholeness and authenticity to offset, or cover-up, the weightlessness of Victorian self-identity. As a result, decoration and its attendant discourses reproduced the crisis of cultural authority precisely because they operated metonymically, transforming self-identity through its performative interaction with aesthetic objects. As strategies of self performance, decorating texts failed to restore a solid sense of self, for beneath the fictitious unity of decorating texts lay a disparate collection of objects; beneath the fiction of stability, a fragmented, alienated self.

Notes

1. "New historicism" is a contested term of late but is generally used to describe studies that attempt to show how texts in specific historical periods circulate social values and conflicts—how texts attempt to negotiate cultural crises. The term is most readily associated with Stephen Greenblatt. For a discussion of the circulatory functions of texts, see Greenblatt, 1-14. See also Simon During.

2. For the purposes of this study, text and textualization shall be used to designate cultural artifacts transformed into objects of appreciation or exhibition. Textualization is a process by which

aesthetic objects are appropriated as objects in relation to an owner. It need be noted that textualization refers to a necessary connection between object and owner (subject), an interaction, an engagement that subtly transforms both object and subject. Though decorating "text" refers to books and articles on decoration, it should be remembered that the relationship between the reader/owner and the texts themselves is textual. That is, readers/owners engage such texts in ways similar to the way they engage aesthetic objects and decoration itself through the auspices of "taste."

3. Peter Stallybrass and Allon White argue that most attempts to transgress class boundaries in the eighteenth and nineteenth centuries reflected a desire of the bourgeoisie both to erect and transgress class boundaries. However, as they point out, attempts to transgress class boundaries did not change the fundamental terms of class society. Similarly, the present study contends that the secularization of nineteenth-century culture did not change the essential terms of class distinction. Rather, the nineteenth century transformed the justifications for distinctions from religious to secular sources. For a relevant discussion, see Stallybrass & White, esp. chs. 3, 4, 5.

4. Richard Drinnon provides a detailed history of some of the more brutal practices of American colonialism, such as the American seizure of the Philippines during the Spanish-American War. He points out that a standard practice of American Imperialism of the late nineteenth century was to bring back "natives" to display in museums, circuses, amusement parks, and expositions. After his capture, for example, Geronimo was put on display in full "Indian" garb at the St. Louis World's Fair in 1904. For a more complete discussion, see *Facing West,* Ch. 22. Sander Gilman provides a fascinating and frightening discussion of the nineteenth-century practice of putting colonized people "on display" in his article "Black Bodies, White Bodies."

5. Although the functional separation of public, semipublic, and private spaces was centuries old by the nineteenth century, the ideological separation became more significant as a site of struggle, particularly over the meaning of gender identity. In the nineteenth century, spheres came to connote political segregation so that women and other colonized groups were removed ideologically from the sources of political power. For more comprehensive discussions of this ideological struggle, see Gillian Brown and Joy Kasson.

6. The term "modern culture" best represents the culture of the late nineteenth century because, as Jackson Lears suggests, the modern condition which Americans now inhabit began in the Gilded Age. For an excellent discussion of the roots of our

contemporary historical period, as well as reactions against it, see Lears, chs. 1, 3.

Works Cited

The Art of Conversing. Boston, 1845.

Benjamin, Walter. "The Work of Art in the Age of Mechanical Reproduction." Trans. Harry Zohn. *Illuminations.* Ed. Hannah Arendt. New York: Schocken, 1969. 217-251.

Bourdieu, Pierre. "The Aristocracy of Culture." *Media, Culture, and Society: A Critical Reader.* Eds. Richard Collins et al. Beverly Hills, CA: Sage Press, 1986. 164-193.

Brown, Gillian. *Domestic Individualism: Imagining Self in Nineteenth-Century America.* Berkeley: U of California P, 1990.

Burke, Kenneth. "Linguistic Approach to Problems of Education." *Modern Philosophies and Education.* Ed. N. B. Henry. Chicago: U of Chicago P, 1955. 259-303.

Carnegie, Andrew. "The Gospel of Wealth." *Words that Made American History Since the Civil War.* Ed. Richard N. Current et al. Vol. 2. 3rd ed. Boston: Little, Brown, & Co., 1962. 123-133.

Cook, Clarence. *The House Beautiful.* New York, 1878.

Donato, Eugenio. "The Museum's Furnace: Notes toward a Contextual Reading of *Bouvard and Pecuchet.*" *Textual Strategies: in Post-Structuralist Criticism.* Ed. Josue Harari. Ithaca: Cornell UP, 1979. 213-238.

Drinnon, Richard. *Facing West: The Metaphysics of Indian-Hating and Empire Building.* Minneapolis: U of Minnesota P, 1985.

During, Simon. "New Historicism." *Text and Performance Quarterly* 11 (1991): 171-189.

Eastlake, Charles L. *Hints on Household Taste.* 1881. Introd. John Gloag. New York: Dover, 1969.

Fiske, John. *Understanding Popular Culture.* Boston: Unwin Hyman, 1989.

Foucault, Michel. *The History of Sexuality Volume I: An Introduction.* Trans. R. Hurley. New York: Vintage Books, 1980.

Gay, Peter. *The Bourgeois Experience Victoria to Freud: Education of the Senses.* New York: Oxford UP, 1984.

Gilman, Sander. "Black Bodies, White Bodies: Toward an Iconography of Female Sexuality in Late Nineteenth-Century Art, Medicine, and Literature." *Critical Inquiry* 12 (1985): 204-242.

Greenblatt, Stephen. "Towards a Poetics of Culture." *The New Historicism.* Ed. H. Aram Veeser. New York: Routledge, 1989. 1-14.

Hoare, Quinton, and Geoffrey N. Smith, eds. and trans. *Selections from the Prison Notebooks of Antonio Gramsci.* New York: International Publishers, 1971.

Hofstadter, Richard. *Social Darwinism in American Thought.* New York: George Braziller, Inc., 1959.

JanMohamed, Abdul R. "The Economy of Manichean Allegory: The Function of Racial Difference in Colonialist Literature." *Critical Inquiry* 12 (1985): 59-87.

Kasson, John. *Rudeness & Civility: Manners in Nineteenth-Century Urban America.* New York: Hill & Wang, 1990.

Kasson, Joy. *Marble Queens and Captives: Women in Nineteenth-Century American Sculpture.* New Haven: Yale UP, 1990.

Lears, Jackson. *No Place of Grace.* New York: Pantheon, 1983.

Lewis, Arnold, James Turner, and Steven McQuillin. *The Opulent Interiors of the Gilded Age.* New York: Dover Publications, Inc., 1987.

Maass, John. *The Victorian Home in America.* New York: Hawthorne Books, Inc., 1970.

Mercer, Colin. "A Poverty of Desire: Pleasure and Popular Politics." *Formations of Pleasure.* Ed. Formations. Philadelphia: Open UP, 1983. 50-68.

Morgan, H. Wayne, *The Gilded Age.* Syracuse, NY: Syracuse UP, 1970.

Mumford, Lewis. *Sticks and Stones.* New York: Dover Publications, Inc., 1955.

Said, Edward W. "Representing the Colonized: Anthropology's Interlocutors." *Critical Inquiry* 15 (1989): 205-225.

———. *The World, the Text, and the Critic.* Cambridge, MA: Harvard UP, 1983.

Sheldon, George. *Artistic Houses Being a Series of Interior Views of the Most Beautiful and Celebrated Homes in the United States.* New York, 1883/1884.

Sherwood, Mary E. W. "Certain New York Houses." *Harper's New Monthly Magazine* 65 (1882): 680-690.

Stallybrass, Peter, and Allon White. *The Politics and Poetics of Transgression.* Ithaca, NY: Cornell UP, 1987.

Trachtenberg, Alan. *The Incorporation of America: Culture and Society in the Gilded Age.* New York: Hill and Wang, 1982.

SOCIO-POLITICAL CONCERNS

James H. Dormon (essay date 1985)

SOURCE: "Ethnic Stereotyping in American Popular Culture: The Depiction of American Ethnics in the Cartoon

Periodicals of the Gilded Age," in *Amerikastudien/ American Studies*, Vol. 30, No. 4, 1985, pp. 489-507.

[*In the excerpt below, Dormon surveys the use of ethnic stereotypes in American cartoon periodicals of the Gilded Age. He argues that they express increasing levels of fear and ethnocentrism in response to immigration.*]

Images of ethnic minorities in the United States have long been subjects of the popular media and the performing arts, and have provided a rich store of American humor, primarily in the form of caricature presentation. Afro-Americans, for example, began to appear prominently on the stage as early as the 1820s in the phenomenally popular act developed by Thomas Dartmouth ("Jim Crow") Rice, who sought and found an unlimited fund of high hilarity in "Jumping Jim Crow," ultimately producing a full-blown stage black caricature that sustained his career for two decades and spawned countless imitators along the way.[1] The minstrel tradition that flowed out of his enormous success continued to perpetuate caricature blacks as staples of the "blackface art," even as it continued to influence white attitudes toward blacks by way of the developing stereotype.[2] Similarly, German-American ethnics came to appear in burlesque and vaudeville (usually in the form of the ubiquitous "Dutch" act) precisely with the advent of these popular genres. Jews began appearing in vaudeville "Hebrew" acts as early as 1880, and became a staple item by 1890; so much so that few vaudeville bills for over a decade failed to include "Hebrew" material.[3] The stage Irish-American was even older, and though the image was more complex in the particulars of its development than were the stereotypes of American blacks and Jews, stage Irish were to be among the longest-lived of all ethnic stage caricatures.[4] Other American ethnics would appear later on the stage, and of course on radio and film and in the electronic media, but that is a part of another story.

With the advent of the popular cartoon periodicals of the 1880s, it was likely inevitable that ethnic minorities would come to serve as graphic sources of humor. By this time the ascribed peculiarities and vagaries of at least some of the ethnic population had come to be known qualities; part of the collective consciousness of the period, and the new magazines quickly came to feature ethnic caricature as a staple item. The continued arrival of countless new immigrant/ethnics perpetuated the ethnic as a source of material for the caricature cartoonist, even as the popular concern with the "New Immigration" insured a continuing interest in all matters pertaining to the newcomers. While the older periodical publications that featured illustrations—*Frank Leslie's Illustrated Magazine* as well as Leslie's *Budget of Fun,* or even *Harper's Weekly,* for example—occasionally looked to the ascribed characteristics of ethnics for material, cartoons became the primary feature of several new publications of the 1880s. In 1883, John Ames Mitchell and Edward S. Martin launched *Life Magazine,* designed to be a sophisticated humorous monthly featuring cartoons; shortly thereafter *Puck* and

Judge began publishing, and each of them offered periodic collections of cartoons under separate cover: Respectively, *Puck's Library* and *Judge's Library.* The cartoonists whose work sustained such magazines quickly discovered America's endemic fascination with the ascribed foibles of her ethnics and made caricature the mainstay of their material, even as C. Jay Taylor's "Taylor Made Girl" and Charles Dana Gibson's "Gibson Girl" provided popular versions of ideal Anglo-American femininity (though both Taylor and Gibson turned to ethnic material as well in their work).[5] Designed to appeal to a large middle-class audience, priced to sell at ten cents an issue, these new serial publications envisioned their purpose as, in the words of the *Judge's Library* mast-head, "A paper for the family and fireside. Satirical without being malicious, and humorous without being vulgar."[6]

The best of the artist/cartoonists who provided the material for such publications sold their work to any and all, and the most successful of them—Eugene Zimmerman (who worked under the pen name "Zim"), for example, or Edward Windsor Kemble, or Frederick Burr Opper, or Louis Dalrymple—were represented prominently in the pages of all three of the periodicals featuring cartoons. And the popularity of the publications grew apace. By 1901, *Judge's Library* claimed a subscription list of 114,000, and newsstand sales far in excess of this number. The editor also claimed his paper to be "the finest and most popular of all the American humorous weeklies" though the continuing competition of *Puck* and *Life* argued for the ongoing popularity of all three.[7] It is notable that *Judge* also stated as policy the determination to remain "ever scrupulous to keep within the bounds of modesty and good taste."[8]

The continuing popular fascination and delight with ethnic material, however, had already produced such a flood of ethnic cartoons as to suggest the policy of publishing entire issues devoted almost exclusively to a single ethnic group, usually with a cover illustration featuring the group of the month. The April, 1890, number of *Judge's Library,* for example, was entitled "Our Friend. The Hebrew." It consisted of some twenty cartoons depicting Jews as avaricious, grasping petit-bourgeoises, obsessed with material acquisition. Another number of the magazine, "Irish Aristocracy," was devoted to Irish-American types, uniformly portrayed as stupid, illiterate, feisty, drunken laborers or policemen (or their wives); the most familiar of the Irish-American caricatures that had prevailed for half a century on the stage.[9] *Judge's* had already published a black-oriented issue in 1888 entitled "Black and Tan"; another one followed in 1892 under the title "All About our Colored Brethren—coons"; a third issue in 1902 appeared as "Melon Time."[10] Blacks were revealed on all three covers (and in numberless individual cartoons) to be of two basic types: the rural, lazy, ignorant, watermelon-loving, chicken-stealing buffoon, or the dandified urban "Coon," with his silly pretensions to white middle-class lifestyle, his garish costume, and his outlandish, malapropistic misuse of the English language. He too, however loved watermelon and stole chickens, and was only superficially different from his country cousins. The fact that he carried a straight razor to all social functions suggests another ascribed characteristic of the ethnic culture, one with some potential for threat to bourgeois white society. Uniformly, however, the razor was wielded against other blacks, not whites. These were, after all, humor magazines.[11]

Caricature versions of American Blacks, Jewish-Americans, German-Americans, and Irish-Americans were, then, the standard fare of the cartoon periodicals of the late nineteenth century. But as the New Immigration continued to provide material for the caricature artists, the use of such augmented material increased accordingly. Having established the popularity of ethnic cartoon caricature, the publishers readily saw the potential in offering entire issues devoted to the full panorama of ethnic America, as in the 1890s issues of *Judge's Library* entitled respectively "All Sorts" and "Mugs" . . . [12] Such images as these were, through prior stereotyping, instantly recognizable as to ethnic type, and conveyed the fundamental features of the caricatures, group by group. The March issue of *Judge's* was entitled simply "Mixed." The lead cartoon was headed "A Cosmopolitan Locality".[13] The action of the cartoon features one "Jorelman," identified as "a new arrival from Hoboken," having come to Harlem "to get into better society," as the caption suggests. "Jorelman," the Scandinavian type, is greeted by his neighbors on the morning of his first day in his new locale: "Th' top o' th' mar-rnin' t' yez!"—"Gloodee mlorning!"—"Wie gehts'?"—"Mawnin' boss!"—"Sella banan for br-r-reakfasta?" Here was the full panoply of ghetto immigrant types as popularly perceived. A similar cover theme appeared in a later number of *Puck* entitled "Mixed Pickles," the cover illustration for which depicted a pickle jar containing ethnic Irish, Chinese, German ("Dutch"), Hebrew, and Afro-American: All in what was by then standard caricature from.[14] There can be no doubt that these images had come to be pervasive in the popular culture of the period. They were a part of a mentality.

In subtle ways, however, certain of these images were transformed in the decade of the 1890s, taking on a kind of malignancy previously missing (or understated) in what were essentially benign (if assuredly demeaning) stereotypes. The cartoon representations of the Irish constitutes a case in point. While "Paddy" in earlier popular incarnations was feisty, oafish, and surely given to alcoholic overindulgence, he was depicted as fundamentally decent, and while amusing in his foibles he was a good-hearted, hardworking bloke, be it as a laborer, bartender, or (increasingly) a policeman. The 1890s saw the image turn darker, the caricature becoming wholly unappealing, animalistic, even threatening to bourgeois society. Irish laborers became lazy parasites, as in "A Full-Blooded Irish Setter" . . . [15] The Irish policeman emerged as a petty criminal, extorting favors from those he is hired to protect (often enough immigrants themselves). In "Sunday Morning in Cincinnati," . . . for example, Officer Reagan, selectively enforcing a new Sunday closing ordinance,

speaks: "Pass me out a baloony sassage, Dutchy, or, be hivins! Oi'll infoorce th' ixcise law."[16] This is not the Paddy of old: it is a thoroughly disagreeable, predatory figure.

But the Irish were to undergo yet another transformation by way of popular image: They were to become animals, or at least not fully human. "A Sensitive Animal" . . . is a case in point. Here "Mr. Jayrick" points to the creature in the cage and explains to his companion: "This, my dear, is a Borneo gorilla. He looks nearly as intelligent as an Irish voter, doesn't he?" The "gorilla" replies: "Yez Yankee Shnake! Oi'll tek a fall out av yez if Oi lose me job."[17] This figure too constitutes a threat to white middle-class society: The potentially dangerous animal is free. And there are other threatening forms represented by the Irish beast. In "A Sweeping Count" . . . the inspector entering the hut of the Irish-American Muldoon inquires "How many have you in your family, Mrs. Muldoon?" To which she replies "Tin, sur; counting ther ould man an' ther pigs."[18] Here, of course, people are equated with pigs, and there are only three pigs. Notable as well are the facial characteristics of the "ould mon": hardly good old Paddy this. Such a family constituted a real threat to American society—at least to the society of those who mattered. This cartoon, incidentally, appears in the very issue of *Judge's* that assured its readership that it would remain "in good taste."

If the Gilded Age saw the image of Irish-Americans undergo a pronounced change toward malignant caricature, other immigrant groups made their initial appearances in the popular cartoon literature in essentially malignant forms. The Chinese, for example, began appearing frequently, and in the form of a wholly unappealing caricature—ugly, menacing, malevolent—from the beginning.[19] The familiar "Heathen Chinee," as Bret Harte had designated him, had appeared in the popular press and in popular literature prior to the 1890s, but he was now to become another stock figure in cartoon graphics. *Judge's* devoted a full issue to "A Trip to Chinatown" in 1893, opening with a four-part sequence headed "The Cute Celestial and the Hoodwinked Hounds: or How Ah There got There." . . . [20] The bone attached to "Ah There's" pigtail attracts the stray dogs to the family laundry, for dinner as it were, with the group. The ascribed manner of dress and appearance are by 1893 established (and instantly recognizable.) The humorous "switch" in the cartoon lies in the matter of the fate of the dogs. But the message is clear: The subhuman Chinese eat little dogs! They also eat rats, as evidenced by a second Chinese issue of *Judge's Library* entitled "Rough on Rats". . . . [21] Again, the facial expression is noteworthy, as are the long fingernails and exotic attire. The point is, of course, that this creature is surely not "American"; not one of *us*. He eats dogs and rats and birds' nests and even chicken roost straw, as in "A Mongolian Delicacy" . . . in which "Un Hung" (the name is significant) advises his mistress that the old straw will "Makee belly good sloup."[22] Ultimately he is *not* really human, and the popular image suggested that the Chinese actually evolved from the catfish, as suggested by the cartoon entitled "From Catfish to Que". . . . [23] Ascriptively, the Chinese resembled catfish, even to teach other. In "The Lost Found" . . . a typical Zimmerman illustration, "Ah Flue" exclaims upon hooking a river catfish "By th' gleat whitee dlagon! It is my blother Hop Wink flom Plekin."[24] This identification of the Chinese with river scavengers clearly suggests the dehumanization of the Chinese by way of the popular media.

But not only were the Chinese deemed subhuman in the cartoon images of the day: They were also dangerous. They routinely used and distributed opium, for example, and the Chinese opium den was a common theme of Chinese-American ascription, as in the cartoon entitled "The Paper Terror Must Go!". . . . In this richly detailed drawing, "Hunk Wink" demands that "Chung" eject "dlat Melican man" from the premises of the den because "Cigallet spoilly oplyum smell."[25] Or as a more direct threat, less subtly expressed, the Chinese were collectively a deadly disease: "The Asiatic Collar-er". . . . [26] Here the iconography of ascribed qualities are communicated directly and with unmistakable intent: The laundry, the que, the animalistic face with the inscrutable, malevolent expression. This creature is to be feared. He is at best an untouchable. Even among the Irish (at least in the cartoon version of reality) he is an anathema, as suggested by "An Episode of the North River". . . . Brogan, drowning, is offered a Chinese que (with the Chinese person still attached) as a life-line, but he declines, declaiming "Sorra th' day thot Oi laves a Choinaman save me loife. Let me sink, Ronan."[27] Once again the intent is clear: The Chinese are not acceptable. They must go. But even following passage of the Chinese Exclusion Act (of 1882; strengthened and extended in 1892) they were still feared; distrusted; likely to avoid the exclusion process, as in "Pat's View". . . . Pat observes: "Look at th' hathen comin' through th' earth. Begor! I knew, if they passed a law t' kape thim yeller divils out av th' counthry, they'd git in some way."[28] The Yellow Peril persisted, despite the law.

There was one other American ethnic group whose appearance in the cartoon periodicals marked a completely new departure in graphic image making. The Native American, whose ascriptive qualities had been part of American mythology and lore (and popular culture as well) since the initial trans-Atlantic contact gave Europeans the opportunity to assess the Amerindians, now in the 1890s began to appear in caricature form. And there can be no doubt as to the nature of the Indian type, as represented by the cartoonists of the day. He was a predatory, violent, evil, creature, given to atrocity and murder at the slightest provocation (though at the same time so ignoble and degraded as to be comic), as, for example, in "Livingston De Peyster's Death-Knell". . . . [29] Here "Man-Afraid-of-His-Shadow," attempting to smoke De Peyster's hiking-stick, speaks to his tomahawk-brandishing squaw: "Big heap poor smoke! No hole—no draw. Plunk him, Wanita!" Another captive paleface is offered "An Unaccepted Reprieve" . . . from the stake; unaccepted because the song the Indian requests

as a condition of reprieve—"White Wings"—is more than the captive is willing to provide.[30] (The song was apparently so popular—and so often performed—as to warrant death at the stake before singing it again.) But the Indian image is consistent: He is a creature who routinely burns others at the stake. Similarly, "The Obliging Prospector" . . . offers a murderous Indian a stick of dynamite in response to the demand for food; then comments after the explosion: "Whoop! That's better'n quarrelin' with him."[31] The supertitle of the two-part cartoon set "Is this a Foeman Worthy of Our Steel?" is particularly revealing.[32] The central Indian figure in the first frame has killed the family dog (lying in the right foreground) and now demands food of a frontier white woman. He is instead chased off by "Little Johnny," who exclaims "Th' dago didn't think ther wuz a *man* 'round the house, did he, marm?" Finally, in the realistic illustration entitled "Not a Merry Xmas" . . . artist Edward Kemble provides no suggestion of mirth whatever; rather, he has a frontier farm maiden awaiting an awful fate at the hands of a murderous Indian who has dispatched her lover and entered her home, pretending to be her "Joris." There can be no question as to the artist's meaning here: Indians are simply murderers, cold-blooded killers without morals or conscience, little if any better than animals.[33]

There remains now but to try to answer the difficult questions: Why these images? And why their continuing popularity? In truth there is no acceptable way of documenting the motivation for cartoonists who assigned ascriptive qualities and characteristics to their subjects, nor is there any accounting for the psychic needs of audiences who presumably recognized and found satisfaction and even humor in those images. About all that may be assumed for certain is that the stereotypes were identifiable; that the very basis of their humor usually turned on their instant identifiability through prior ascription. Hence, they represented to the beholder a form of reality. It is in the assumption of at least a grain of truth in the caricatures, in the recognition that these *are* in fact versions of reality, that the essence of cartoon caricature lies. The stereotype they represent *is* in effect the caricature, and vice-versa.

But might there not be something more to the popular fascination with such ethnic caricatures; something lying deeper in the social psychology of the phenomenon; something that provides an element of emotional fulfillment, both individually and collectively, of what might be deemed "rationalization needs"? I would like to suggest, at least tentatively, that the answer would have to be yes. Take the case of the Indian stereotype, for example: Might the pervasive image of this murderous, cowardly, ignoble predator not suggest the need to eliminate the threat; to rid the realm of this troublesome nuisance by straight-forward policies calculated to achieve that end? And had the nation not in fact developed such a policy: The combination of Indian wars, tribal manipulation through allotments in severalty, and the economic assault of the railroads crossing Indian territory, relentlessly diminishing both total population and cultural integration? Had the Indian "threat" not been eliminated by the 1890s with the reduction of the to- tal Native American population to under 200,000 widely scattered and thoroughly demoralized individuals?[34] Do the cartoon images not provide rationalization and justification for American "Indian" policy in the Gilded Age?

Similarly, the "Heathen Chinese" menace, as reified by the repeated image and fixed indelibly in the popular imagina- tion and popular culture, surely represented a threat that had to be undermined at whatever cost; an end that the na- tional government had now endeavored to accomplish by way of Chinese exclusion. The Golden Door had to be closed to this potential danger, no matter the American promise of hospitality to the wretched of the earth. The Chinese were not human; there was simply no way that these creatures could be accommodated in the American mainstream. And the cartoon images underscored this no- tion in subliminal ways, again providing fulfillment of col- lective rationalization needs.

The case of the Irish-Americans appears to be more prob- lematic: Few if any of the American-Anglo bourgeoisie se- riously considered *eliminating* even so undesirable an ele- ment as the Irish (as portrayed in the cartoons and other popular media). Yet it is clear that the lot of the average Irish immigrant had not improved greatly since the mid- nineteenth century, and in some respects had grown worse. Poverty was still the condition of the majority of the first- generation Irish-Americans; moreover, they were routinely relegated to the dirty and dangerous forms of work. As the old adage had it, not only was there no street paved with gold for the Irish in America: The street was not even paved, and what was more, the Irish were supposed to pave it—literally so in many cases. Or they were to build railroads (both above and below ground), under the most difficult and dangerous circumstances—the "sandhogs" were mostly Irish-Americans—and if the American dream of status elevation had been denied the Irish, there must be a reason. The *system* cannot fail; any failure must be charged to the inadequacies of the ethnic population itself; and more surely so in that this was ostensibly a *white* eth- nic population. Hence the need to dehumanize the Irish, to render them loutish, vulgar, ugly, feisty inebriates, pre- cisely as the cartoon artists of the day portrayed them. As George Tindall has observed, "Dominant peoples repeat- edly assign ugly traits to those they bring into subjec- tion."[35] Assuredly the Irish immigrants constituted a subju- gated population. Continuing negative ascription in the popular media served to justify continuing subjugation; to provide ongoing rationalization for what had been and still was. If we are to assume any credibility for the Theory of Cognitive Dissonance, and I would think that we must, the subliminal messages of the ethnic cartoons provided a mechanism whereby discordant realities might be shaped into acceptably harmonious forms of emotional response.

As regards Blacks, Jews, and the other popular cartoon figures, doubtless there were some subtle differences in the case of each, and each would have to be considered at greater length by way of looking at other factors. Ulti-

mately, however, I would argue that the acceptance of the caricature-as-stereotype-as-reality lay in the psychic needs of middle-class white America to *believe* in the image as real, and to argue thereby for immigration restriction and/or subordination (or elimination) of ethnic minorities. At the very least, the popularity of the cartoon images of ethnics suggests a concern bordering on fascination with such "other" kinds of people as were then coming to be perceived as a national social problem. The cartoon im- ages reveal a state of social tension, even as they find hu- mor in the situations and peoples they represent. In this sense, the ethnic cartoons, like the popular stage and popu- lar literature, argued for the continuing domination of the culture and society by its existing hegemonic structure, and the ultimate need to create images to support them in that determination. They argued for a WASP America at the time that WASP America seemed most threatened by its ethnic blight. . . .

Notes

1. On Rice and the development of the caricature stage Black, see Robert C. Toll, *Blacking Up! The Minstrel Show in Nineteenth-Century America* (New York: Oxford Univ. Press, 1974), pp. 27-28; James H. Dormon, "The Strange Career of Jim Crow Rice (with Apologies to Professor Woodward)," *Journal of Social History,* 3 (Winter 1969), 111-122.

2. Toll, *Blacking Up,* passim.

3. On the ethnic comic stage tradition, see Paul A. Distler, "The Rise and Fall of the Racial Comics in American Vaudeville," Diss. Tulane Univ. 1963, passim; Distler, "Ethnic Comedy in Vaudeville and Burlesque," in *American Popular Entertainment: Papers and Proceedings of the Conference on the History of American Popular Entertainment,* ed. Myron Matlaw (Westport, CT: Greenwood Press, 1979), pp. 33-42; Robert M. Dell, "The Representation of the Immigrant on the New York Stage, 1881-1916," Diss. New York Univ. 1960, passim. For a collection of contemporary "Hebrew" stage material, see Thomas Joseph Carey, *Hebrew Yarns and Dialect Humor* (New York: The Popular Publishing Co., 1900).

4. The complexity of the Irish-American stage characterization is the subject of D. T. Knobel, "Vocabulary of Ethnic Perception: Content Analysis of the American Stage Irishman, 1820-1860," *Journal of American Studies,* 15 (April 1981), 45-71.

5. See William Murrell, *A History of American Graphic Humor, 1865-1938* (New York: Published for the Whitney Museum of American Art by the Macmillan Co., 1938), pp. 93, 189, passim.

6. *Judge's Library,* November 1887, n.p. (Hereafter cited as *Judge's*). I have used this periodical most extensively for purposes of illustration, largely because of the superior quality of reproduction possible from its well-preserved pages. In no sense,

however, did the cartoons differ in content from journal to journal.

7. *Judge's,* February 1901, n.p.

8. *Judge's,* September 1901, n.p.

9. *Judge's,* April 1890; February 1890; Knobel, "Stage Irishman," passim.

10. *Judge's,* July 1888; June 1892; August 1902 (all unpaginated).

11. The subject of Afro-American stereotyping in popular culture is a large one, and outside the purview of the present paper (in other than this brief summary form). I have undertaken the matter in a larger work now in progress.

12. *Judge's,* December 1894; May 1897.

13. *Judge's,* March 1892, n.p.

14. *Puck,* December 1897, n.p.

15. *Judge's,* March 1897, n.p.

16. *Judge's,* January 1896, n.p.

17. Ibid.

18. *Judge's,* September 1901, n.p.

19. The popular image of the Chinese-American had been wholly negative from the advent of Chinese immigration. See Stuart C. Miller, *The Unwelcome Immigrant: The American Image of the Chinese, 1785-1882* (Berkeley: Univ. of California Press, 1969).

20. *Judge's,* September 1893, n.p.

21. *Judge's,* April 1901, n.p.

22. *Judge's,* March 1892, n.p.

23. *Judge's,* September 1893, n.p. Such "evolution" drawings were enormously popular in the period: Irish policemen, for example, evolve from whiskey bottles; Jews from the three balls of the pawn-shop logo. The phenomenon presumably reflects popular fascination with Darwinian matters. See *Life,* 25 June 1891, p. 404; *Judge's,* February 1897, n.p.

24. Ibid.

25. *Judge's,* September 1893, p. 25.

26. Ibid., p. 11.

27. *Judge's,* March 1898, n.p.

28. *Judge's,* March 1897, n.p.

29. *Judge's,* April 1894, n.p.

30. Ibid.

31. *Judge's,* July 1897, n.p.

32. *Judge's,* April 1894, n.p.

33. *Life,* December 1894, p. 14.

34. On the effects of the Indian wars and allotment acts, see Wilcomb E. Washburn, *The Indian in America* (New York: Harper and Row, 1975), pp. 202-208, 236-249; Alvin M. Josephy, Jr., *The Patriot Chiefs: A Chronicle of American Indian Resistance* (New York: Viking Press, 1969), pp. 341-343. See also Sean D. Cashman, *America in the Gilded Age: From the Death of Lincoln to the Rise of Theodore Roosevelt* (New York: New York Press, 1984), pp. 274-275. The best single work on the white perception of the "Indian" population is Robert F. Berkhofer, Jr., *The White Man's Indian: Images of the American Indian from Columbus to the Present* (New York: Knopf, 1978). Berkhofer also treats the policies that flowed out of such image-making. See especially pp. 96-102, 166-175.

35. George B. Tindall, *America: A Narrative History* (New York: Norton, 1984), I, 100.

James H. Dormon (essay date 1988)

SOURCE: "Shaping the Popular Image of Post-Reconstruction American Blacks: The 'Coon Song' Phenomenon of the Gilded Age," in *American Quarterly,* Vol. 40, No 4, December, 1988, pp. 450-71.

[*In the following essay, Dormon examines the popularity during the Gilded Age of 'coon songs' (songs about, and many times by, black Americans). Dormon suggests that the songs disseminated racist images and language in order to justify continued segregation and discrimination.*]

On the occasion of the celebrated "Conference on the History of American Popular Entertainment" in 1977, the performer-scholar Max Morath noted, with reference to the "coon song craze" of the 1890s, that the phenomenon "right now resides exactly where it should—on the back shelves of the pop museum collecting dust. it's a sociological curiosity and nothing more."[1] While one might well sympathize with the liberality of Mr. Morath's sentiment in his consignment of a major pop culture phenomenon to the dustbin of long dead, distasteful exotica, it has become clear that few contemporary students of American culture accept the implication that because racist phenomena are distasteful they are no longer important. It may even be said that the ongoing reassessment of the meaning of the coon song "craze" (of which this essay is a part) would suggest that the national fascination with coon songs between *circa* 1890 and 1910 underlay a major shift in white perception of blacks; a shift whereby existing stereotypes came to be either confirmed or embellished and indelibly encoded as part of the semiotic system of the period.[2]

The stereotyping of black Americans in the popular culture did not, of course, begin with coon songs. The British music halls of the eighteenth century occasionally introduced comic black figures, some of which were exported to Colonial America where, through the process of "ascription," a set of assumptions about black characters would come to be accepted as a form of reality.[3] Incidentally, the first English ballad opera to be published in

America, Andrew Barton's *The Disappointment; or the Force of Credulity* [1767], featured a black character—notably, he was called "Raccoon"—who sang a version of what would become our own "Yankee Doodle."[4] Within two years a second black character role—that of "Mungo" in Isaac Bickerstaff's *The Padlock*—afforded a rather different image of blacks: that of the suffering slave.[5]

It was not until the late 1820s, however, that a true stereotype began to develop on the American stage: the comic rustic song and dance figure introduced by Thomas Dartmouth Rice in the form of the character known as "Jim Crow."[6] Rice's enormous success with the Jim Crow character quickly gave rise to several imitators, including George Washington Dixon and Bob Farrel, both of whom claimed to have created a second major black stage figure: the ubiquitous "Zip Coon," who was to be rendered immortal by way of the song bearing his name sung to the tune of "Turkey in the Straw."[7] Zip Coon also introduced another dimension of black stage caricature: the character of the black dandy, sporting his flashy attire and projecting a slick, urbane persona, (this, of course, within the overall demeanor of the ignorant black buffoon mimicking the manners of sophisticated white folks). In essence, Jim Crow and Zip Coon provided the outlines of the two dominant caricatures that would become fixed in the popular imagination by way of the minstrel show, thus providing the two fully developed stereotypes of Afro-Americans that came to prevail by the outbreak of the American Civil War.[8]

While this essay is not the place for a detailed examination of the minstrel tradition, it is important to emphasize that the minstrel black was represented as an essentially unthreatening figure. He (or, less frequently, she) was unquestionably ignorant (though not always stupid: the minstrel blacks could be wily and even sage), maladroit, and outlandish in his misuses of the forms and substance of white culture. While they were normally portrayed as happy-go-lucky dancing, singing, joking buffoons, they were above all either humorous or pathetic. In either case they were *safe* figures. And as the accepted version of what was commonly perceived to be the "real" American black (accepted as such at least by the enchanted white audiences of the day), they stood as personifications of a type of humanity not to be taken seriously. Above all, implicitly at least, they were not to be afforded any form of equality in a social order ultimately based in a system of race relations shaped by chattel slavery. The minstrel black was a living adjunct of the proslavery argument and functioned as such until emancipation so drastically altered the foundation of the existing order.[9]

So much, then, for the antecedents. What of the "coon songs" of the post-reconstruction era? While their provenance is as yet not entirely clear, one clue to their advent lies in an essentially new etymological departure: the pervasive use of the word "coon" as a designation for "Afro-American." It was a usage that came into the language with such speed and such immutability as to constitute a

linguistic coup. American blacks had long been popularly associated with the raccoon, but the association was largely by way of the ascribed affection of blacks for the amiable and tasty little beasts. By ascription, blacks loved hunting, trapping, and eating raccoons. Moreover, the minstrel figure "Zip Coon" (as noted) had come to be symbolically identified with blacks in general. Nonetheless, the term "coon" as a nominative designation for "black" did not come into widespread use until the early 1880s.[10] Rather, it would appear that the usage was introduced and rendered pervasive by way of the songs that came to be called "coon songs," even as, reciprocally, blacks became "coons."

The first coon song, if indeed such a "first" can be established—surely an early prototype at least—appeared in 1880 with the publication of J. P. Skelly's "The Dandy Coon's Parade."[11] The second (or another prototype) may have been a number called "The Coons are on Parade," the lyrics of which describe in circumspect Victorian restraint what would within a decade become the orgiastic "coon balls" of the fully developed coon song phenomenon.[12] The year 1883 saw publication of J. S. Putnam's "New Coon in Town," which also achieved a measure of popularity. The lyrics featured the latest incarnation of the black dandy of the minstrel show tradition:

> There's a bran new coon in town,
> He came de other day,
> A reg'lar la-de-dah,
> Dat's what de girls all say.[13]

Sam Lucas's "Coon's Salvation Army" of 1884 employed another theme closely associated with the older minstrel tradition: The black as chicken-and-watermelon-thief. In describing a large black social convocation, Lucas's lyrics observe:

> De melon patch am safe today,
> No Coons am dar in sight,
> De chickens dey may roost in peace
> Wid in der coops tonight.[14]

The same year saw the publication of William Dressler's "Coon Schottische," placing the black participants in the said "Schottische" in a ludicrous version of the popular white dance form.[15] It is notable that Sam Lucas, author of what was by modern standards the most racially offensive of these early coon songs, was himself black. The term "coon" had by then taken on its accepted secondary meaning. "Coon" clearly and unmistakably meant "black" in the vernacular of Gilded Age America. Coon *songs* were thus songs about, and often enough *by*, blacks; they were songs that featured in their lyrics the ascriptive qualities associated with black life and character. Moreover, by the mid 1880s the coon song phenomenon was well on its way to becoming a national fad, a veritable "craze" as it was so often described.

There can be no doubt, then, that something in this formula appealed enormously to the American public, and coon songs proliferated in music hall and vaudeville performances and in sheet music form. Over six hundred of them were published during the decade of the 1890s, and the more successful efforts sold in the millions of copies. To take but a single example, Fred Fisher's "If the Man in the Moon were a Coon" sold over three million copies in sheet music form, and this was not exceptional. One song publisher aptly described his latest sheet music collection ("May Irwin's New Coon Song Hits") as "All the Rage in the Rage of Coon Songs." But perhaps most compelling of all in suggesting the dimension of the fad was a remark in 1899 by another publisher who chose to tout his newest song with the promise "This is *Not a Coon Song.*"[16]

The question, however, remains: *why* did these songs become so popular as to constitute a national craze that lasted fully a decade? And what does their popularity suggest about the mentality and the social psychology of the era? In pursuit of answers, it might be useful at this juncture to delve a bit further into the songs themselves, and their place in the history of American popular music.

Almost without exception coon songs were calculated to be hilariously funny. Overwhelmingly they were based in caricature. Over time they also came to share another notable quality. They tended to feature syncopated rhythmic structures—"catchy" rhythms—formerly associated with minstrel material but also with performance styles characteristic of black American folk music. The degree of syncopation varied from song to song, but the syncopated style was a constant in the coon song genre, and was perceived (correctly) to be a form of "black music," hence identified with black life.[17] The rhythmic structure suggests that the music originated as *dance* music, offered in a form essentially new to whites, though of course not to blacks, and this rhythmic dimension of the music was clearly a part of its appeal. Appearing initially in the form of two-steps, cakewalks, or even marches (the parade theme was common), the coon song featured appealing, foot-tapping, time-clapping rhythms accompanying the ostensibly funny descriptive lyrics.[18] This was in a word *happy* music, despite the grossly offensive lyrics as judged by modern sensibilities.

Moreover, the coon song craze occurred at precisely the same time as the popular music business reached its fullest development to date; indeed, the songs provided impetus to that development. This was the age of "Tin Pan Alley," and coon songs lent themselves to the development of the vaudeville and burlesque stage, providing entertainers not only with the songs but also with ample "coon" comedy material as well. Both soon became staples of the music hall stage, performed by whites primarily, but with some important exceptions.[19] In some respects, the coon song phenomenon may be viewed as yet another phase in the history of black caricature on the American stage, as vaudeville came to replace minstrelsy as the dominant form of popular theater in the United States.

All of these factors were doubtless important in accounting for the popularity of the coon songs in the 1890s. But the *dimensions* of the fad would suggest that the response was a manifestation of something that lay buried more deeply in the collective psyche of white bourgeois America, something that found expression in the popular response to these songs. In 1896, at the time that the coon songs were at the peak of their popularity, the comedy song and dance team of Bert Williams and George Walker opened at Koster and Bail's Music hall in New York, advertised as the "Two Real Coons." The variety critic for the New York *Dramatic Mirror* reviewed the show favorably, observing (within the context of the *realism* of the performers) that "the common every-day Nigger has only to open his mouth to bring laughs."[20] It was a significant comment, particularly so in that Williams and Walker were, of course, blacks *who performed in blackface,* thus maintaining the older minstrel blackface persona. They were blacks playing whites playing blacks, but were nonetheless accepted by the *Dramatic Mirror* critic as projecting a form of *reality,* the reality of the ludicrous "coon."

Eleven years later, in December of 1907, in a rather apologetic article entitled "The Stage Negro," *Variety* magazine noted that successful entertainers and producers must offer the public what the public wants—in this instance comic stage caricatures of black Americans and black American life. To do so, the account continued, they must also "give the public what the public will *recognize*"[21] (emphasis mine). That is to say, the features of the stage character, or those suggested by the song lyrics, must be features recognizable by the audiences. In the language of semiotics, they must be the features that had come to be accepted collectively as constituting the *signified* black; the features that had to be suggested, even by black performers playing black caricatures, or by the song lyrics evoking black types. The caricature, in order to be acceptable and effective, had to fit within the stereotype, which was itself essentially a codified cluster of signs. In this manner the caricature *became* the stereotype; the stereotype the caricature. Consequently, analysis of the features of blacks as portrayed in the coon songs provides us with a description of that which was accepted as the "real coon" in the vernacular—the codified Black. So what were the primary features of the "reality" as projected in the songs?

In order to synthesize the caricature/stereotype I have examined the lyrics of approximately one hundred of the most popular coon songs, whenever possible in the original sheet music (thus rendering it possible to combine the visual images of the sheet music covers with the lyrics that evoked the visuals). I have then established categories of the particular features emphasized in the lyrics such that a reasonably accurate count might be made of the repetitions of each feature, thus rendering generalization somewhat less impressionistic than might otherwise be the case. I have also quoted liberally from the lyrics for purposes of illustration. On the basis of this analysis, the primary features of American blacks and black American life are portrayed in the songs that follow.

First, there were clear similarities between the "coon" of the coon song and the minstrel blacks. There were still two fundamental types, with some variants between male and female.[22] But what of the *differences* between the minstrel "darky" of yore and the new "coon?" While they were in some cases differences of degree and emphasis, they were nonetheless significant and surely revealing. In the songs, for example, blacks began to appear as not only ignorant and indolent, but also devoid of honesty or personal honor, given to drunkenness and gambling, utterly without ambition, sensuous, libidinous, even lascivious. "Coons" were, in addition to all of these things, razor-wielding savages, routinely attacking one another at the slightest provocation as a normal function of their uninhibited social lives. The razor—the flashing steel straight razor—became in the songs the dominant symbol of black violence, while the "coon" himself became that which was signified by this terrible weapon. The subliminal message was clear and clearly part of the connotative code: Blacks are potentially dangerous; they must be controlled and subordinated by whatever means necessary.[23] They must also be segregated; set apart, for it was also clear in the evidence of the coon songs that they wanted to be white—to break down the most important barrier of all—the boundary separating "us" from "them."

Consider the following examples: By way of continuity with the older minstrel image, coon songs naturally featured the watermelon- and chicken-loving rural buffoon. "My Watermelon Boy," by Malcolm Williams begins:

> He's a common nigger of a very common kind . . .
> And he loves a melon from the heart right to the rind.

qualities which only endear him all the more to his sweetheart, who

> . . . loves to see him roll up his eyes,
> When watermelon that boy does spy,
> No coon can win me, no use to try,
> Cause I love my watermelon boy.[24]

As for chickens, "coons" crave them too, as in Elmer Bowman's "I've Got Chicken on the Brain":

> There's coons 'round town, they ain't hard to find,
> Would rather have a poke chop than have their right mind;
> But I likes my chicken, and I likes 'em fried. . . .[25]

Watermelons, chickens, pork chops—all familiar enough—but also razors. Williams and Walker provided the full panoply of post-minstrel black semiosis in their song entitled "The Coon's Trade Mark":

> As certain and sure as Holy Writ,
> And not a coon's exempt from it,
> Four things you'll always find together,
> Regardless of condition of sun and moon—
> A watermelon, a razor, a chicken and a coon![26]

A second major carry over from the older tradition that provided a slight switch (by way of emphasis) may be found in the pervasive suggestion in the songs that blacks were indolent and unambitious, devoid of the work ethic or internalized bourgeois values. They made their livings and gained their subsistence either by gambling or, more often, by stealing. Virtually *all* "coons" stole chickens and watermelons, of course; this was perhaps the single most enjoyable and profitable enterprise they shared. But the presumption is that they had also stolen whatever else they happened to possess. In "Any Rags," for example (the comparison with Horatio Alger's *Ragged Dick*—the archetypal bourgeois success story—is irresistible), it is claimed of the protagonist:

> He stole all his furniture, he stole his wife,
> If he'd steal from his friend he'd steal yer life.[27]

But if "coons" did not make their way in the world by stealing—if they acquired anything in the way of personal fortune by some other means—it was inevitably by gambling or hustling, and the gambler/hustler coon figures prominently in the song lyrics. In Nathan Bivins's "Gimme Ma Money," for instance, the narrator relates his tale:

> Last night I went to a big Crap game,
> How dem coons did gamble wuz a sin and a shame.
> . . .

But he joins the game and wins, proclaiming by way of justification

> I'm gambling for my Sadie,
> Cause she's my lady,
> I'm hustling coon, . . . dat's just what I am.[28]

As was the case here, the gambler/hustler frequently became involved in the trade in order to support a female friend in decent style. Indeed, the ladies in coon songs tend to be fairly avaricious, hardhearted sorts. In "I'm Always Glad to See You When You'll Buy," the story line reveals a prime example:

> A coon once had a ladyfriend,
> A black gal from Kentucky.
> His money she would help him spend,
> Whenever he was lucky.
> But when dis colored man was broke, she'd shake him mighty soon.
> She seemed to think it was a joke to tantalize dis coon.[29]

On the other hand, the "honey" in such a relationship could provide financial benefits too. In "I've just received a Telegram from Baby," a down-on-his-luck gambler finds himself jailed for disorderly conduct. His "honey," however, sends him money to make bail, so that:

> Next day, just at noon-time, he was singing songs in coon-time,

and he was back with his lady friend by evening.[30]

When the gambler/hustler was in the money, however, he knew how to spend it. Despite the misleading title, the song "I've Got Money Locked up in a Vault" is concerned with a successful gambler who hires poor blacks (designated "coons" in the lyrics) to shine his shoes, to fetch and carry, and to serve as his bodyguard. He boasts of his success:

> I've got money now to throw to the birds,
> I buy my chickens by the herds—[31]

There is, of course, nothing resembling thrift or frugality in lifestyle when the gambler coon is on a successful roll. "When a Nigger Makes a Hundred," observed one song title, "Ninety-nine Goes on His Back"; that is, he will spend it all on flashy clothes. In the domestic scenario that constitutes the body of the lyrics, the hustler, down on his luck and broke (having blown his bankroll), is spurned by his "honey":

> I had lots of coons but for your sake
> I gave them all the sack,
> Now you haven't got a dollar, its no wonder that I holler,
> If a nigger makes a hundred, ninety-nine goes on his back.[32]

And in the most famous episode involving the profligate gambler and his impatient "honey," the latter cries out in total exasperation:

> Rufus Rastus Johnson Brown
> What you goin' to do when the rent comes 'round?
> What you goin' to say, how you goin' to pay;
> You'll never have a bit of sense till judgment day,
> You know, I know, rent means dough,
> Landlord's goin' to put us out in the snow
> Rufus Rastus Johnson Brown,
> What you goin' to do when the rent comes 'round?[33]

Other coon songs posited the whole spectrum of ascribed qualities associated with the coon stereotype. Possibly the most revealing of these full-dress portraits in caricature was Will Heehan's "Every Race has a Flag but the Coon." In this fullscale exercise in ethno/racial ascription, Heehan has the leader of the "Blackville Club," a social-marching organization, bemoaning the lack of an emblem under which to march in club outings. To meet this perceived need, he suggests a flag that would serve all blacks:

> Just take a flannel shirt and paint it red,
> Then draw a chicken on it, with two poker-dice for eyes,
> An have it wav-in' razors 'round its head;
> To make it quaint, you've got to paint
> A possum with a pork chop in its teeth;
> To give it tone, a big ham-bone
> You sketch upon a banjo underneath,
> And be sure not to skip just a policy slip,
> Have it marked four-eleven-forty-four.

This is a flag to inspire pride in any "coon," Heehan suggests—one wholly representative of the "race."[34]

Lurking always near the surface of the ascribed character of black Americans was their sensuous nature and the un-restrained quality of their sexuality. What has come to be known in our time as the "living together arrangement"—the "honey" relationship in the coon songs—was commonly believed to be the typical form of black domesticity, as opposed to marriage and the nuclear family of the white norm. Such would naturally be the case with a people who knew only temporary sexual relationships, shifting and ephemeral, responding to the momentary requirements of their unrestrained libidos. The common designation for this feature of black character was "hot." A "Red Hot Coon," for example, features a "honey" proclaiming the virtues of her paramour:

> . . . he spends all his money on me—
> Dat's right, I'se his Lady you see;
> He am my honey ba—by.[35]

And from the male viewpoint, "De Swellest Ladies' Coon in Town" boasts (with reference to his prowess with females):

> . . . dey all know dat I'm a hot potato,
> Wid a razor, playing cards, or shooting dice.[36]

It bears repeating that black song writers and performers contributed their share to a primary feature of the "coon" image. Williams and Walker appeared in 1899 in an important all-black show called "Senegambian Carnival," with book and lyrics by Paul Lawrence Dunbar; music by Will Marion Cook. The hit song of the show was a number performed by George Walker entitled "The Hottest Coon in Dixie," a song that gained national exposure through a large sheet music sale.[37] The song, of course, featured the "hot coon" theme, this time provided by a group of black writers and performers who clearly represented the finest talent the period could offer.

Perhaps the best known of all coon songs, and surely the most controversial (in that it was the work of a black songwriter), was Ernest Hogan's "All Coons Look Alike to Me," the message of which was clear:

> All coons look alike to me
> I've got another beau, you see
> And he's just as good to me as you, Nig! ever tried to be.
> He spends his money free . . .
> So I don't like you no-how.
> All coons look alike to me.[38]

Clearly the love lives of these exotic, sensuous people were marked by considerable turbulence, and relationships were often anguished and normally short-lived. In "No Coon can come too Black for Me," a lascivious lady proclaims her taste for black lovers:

> No Coon can come too Black for me,
> I cert'ny love those dark men's 'ciety. . . . [39]

But the turbulent relationships often gave rise to domestic strife. "You're alright but you don't get in," insisted one offended lady:

> Better jus go back to where you have been,
> You comes a rollin' home 'bout half past four . . .

and this was simply not acceptable.[40] Normally, however, the anguish was also short-lived. There were always new conquests to be made, always another "honey" to be had, and even more than one at a time. The "Mormon Coon" was especially well-endowed with ladies:

> I've got a big brunette, and a blonde to pet,
> I've got 'em short, fat, thin, and tall,
> I've got a Cuban gal, and a Zulu Pal,
> They come in bunches when I call. . . . [41]

Despite the superficially good-natured quality of the lyrics, "The Mormon Coon" hints at a darker theme, one of several such dangerous topics potentially threatening to white society. This polygamous "coon" claims a *white* woman (or perhaps even two) among his conquests. The threat of miscegenation had long represented the ultimate threat to the white ruling order, and most especially so in the matter of the black male/white female version of race mixing. And here we find a libidinous black boasting of his prowess with "blondes" as well as a variety of brunettes. The threat is palpable, albeit hidden beneath the veneer of the comical coon character.

A second threat, similarly disguised in the songs' comic mode, was the threat of violence. We have already noted the razor/signifier as a manifestation of potential black violence, and the razor was unquestionably the key symbolic element transcending the comic veneer to evoke the pervasive threat. In "Leave Your Razors at the Door," one "big burly nigger by de name of Brown,"

> Gave a rag-time reception in dis here town.
> All his friends and relations with their blades came down
> For to mingle in de grand sasshay. . . . [42]

In that the razor was the inevitable adjunct of any social occasion, it was clearly recognized that "blades" and "sasshays" were part of the same function: black social life and black violence were inextricable. In truth, this particular affair was exceptional in that all the razors were confiscated by the doorman, who then absconded with the collected steel, necessitating the revellers' fighting barehanded. But far more typical was the ball scene in the song "Ma Angeline," which describes the inevitable brawl:

> Razzers got a flyin', Nigs and wenches cryin'
> Guns an' buns an' coons flew in de air . . . ,
> De Niggers dey wer' slashin',
> Steel dey wer 'a clashin',
> Coons were scrapin' all aroun de floor."[43]

Although black violence lay somewhere near the surface of virtually every episode or event described in coon songs, notably, the violence was uniformly perpetrated by blacks on blacks. Whites were never directly involved. To involve whites would eliminate the comic veneer altogether, and one simply did not write or perform comic songs about race riots. The black threat remained a subliminal threat, and "coons" remained hilariously funny.

But there were still other coded messages in the songs, messages that were transmitted and subliminally recorded. The "toughest" and "meanest" coon—the "bully coon"—was another stock figure prominent among the characters about whom coon songs were written. "I'm the Toughest, Toughest Coon" is typical of the sub-genre:

> I'm the toughest, toughest coon that walks the street;
> You may search the wide, wide world, my equal never meet;
> I got a razor in my boot, I got a gun with which to shoot,
> I'm the toughest, toughest coon that walks the street.[44]

Another case in point: "De Blue Gum Nigger":

> I'se a blue gum nigger
> You don't want to fool wid me,
> I'se as bad a nigger as a nigger man can be.[45]

And yet another (this one by another black songwriter, Edward Furber, with music by Bert Williams): "He's Up Against the Real Thing Now":

> A real bad coon once came to town, ev'ry body he met he'd knock down;
> At last he came across a coon bad as himself,
> Says he 'You may be warm, but I'se pretty hot myself . . .
> Den dis coon pulled a gun, and aimed it at his head;
> An de bad man, he threw up both his hands and said,
> I'm up against the real thing now,
> I'm up against the real thing now,
> I carved dem in de East, and I shot dem in de West,
> But I'm up against the real thing now.[46]

For all this carving, slashing, shooting, and other forms of mayhem the "coon" was prone to committing, and for all the implied danger of this sort of potential and actual violence, perhaps the single most threatening feature of the new ascriptive "coon" stereotype was the implied threat to the hallowed racial caste system protected in the past by slavery and now, in the early 1890s, devoid of clear sanction in law. This most threatening of all themes—threatening at least in its encoded subliminal message—was the theme of the black who wants to become white.

The "passing" phenomenon is, of course, an old theme in American literature and lore (and in reality as well). Not surprisingly, it became part of the subliminal message of many coon songs. Ernest Hogan's "No More Will I Ever be Your Baby," for example, is the lament of a spurned lover whose "honey" has hit on a policy number and gone "high-toned." She moves "up-town," and her estranged lover observes:

> She wants all the nigs to let her alone,
> She looks on them with a frown . . .
> She won't have anything to do with coons any more

. . .

She says she's got money and she's goin' to pass for white.

Her parting words to him are perfectly to the point:

No more will I ever be your baby . . .
Kase [sic] you're too black.[47]

Her lighter color and newfound fortune presumably enable her to pass. But the passing theme takes yet other forms in the coon songs. "Got Your Habits On," for example, suggests that *education* gives blacks pretensions with regard to the established racial order:

And when dey learn how to read and write,
Why most of dem niggers just think they're white.[48]

Money, too, produces dangerous pretensions in blacks. Andrew Sterling's "I've Got a White Man Working for Me" offers perhaps the ultimate in black pretensions to forms of power normally associated only with whites. In this scenario, a "coon" gets a little money and hires a white man to work for him shoveling coal. A group of other blacks gathers to watch the bizarre phenomenon, and the "coon" boasts:

I've got a white man working for me,
I'm going to keep him busy you see,
Don't care what it costs,
I'll stand all the loss,
It's worth twice the money for to be a boss . . .
Don't you dare to talk 'bout the white 'bove the black,
I've got a white man working for me.[49]

Not only do they want the status of whites, then; they also want the power associated with white status. In that power and whiteness are so clearly related, however, a common motif of the coon songs was the transmutation theme. This theme occurs in several forms, one of which concerns the presumed relationship between whiteness and the moon. In "Only a Little Yaller Coon," for instance, one black baby appears to lighten in color when exposed to moonlight. A group of "darkies" gathers to witness this intriguing spectacle:

And dey rolled dere eyes to heaben and declared he would be white,
When his skin changed at the full-ness ob de moon.[50]

Alas, he does not turn completely white—only "yellow"—and that is not sufficient to allow him to "pass." Similarly, the inordinately popular (even by coon song standards) "If the Man in the Moon were a Coon"—advertised as "the Biggest 'Hit' in 20 Years"—suggested that should this phenomenon come to pass, the man in the moon coon would first turn white; he would blanch out to match his luminous surroundings. Then he would extinguish the light of the moon so that the earthbound blacks could safely proceed, under cover of the dark night, to steal chickens (in that "chicken is a coon's delight").[51]

Perhaps the fullest development of the black-who-would-be-white theme appeared in another best-selling song entitled simply "Coon! Coon! Coon!" Touted as "The Most Successful Song Hit of 1901," it was another lament of a spurned lover, this one cast off because of his excessively dark complexion:

Though its not my color, I'm feeling mighty blue;
I've got a lot of trouble, I'll tell it all to you;
I'm cert'nly clean disgusted with life and that's a fact,
Because my hair is wooly and because my color's black.

To remedy the situation, he takes extreme measures:

I had my face enameled, I had my hair made straight;
I dressed up like a white man, and cert'nly did look great. . . .

He then proceeds to stroll through the park, where he is spotted by two doves who observe him closely, then croon in unison: "Coo-oo-oo-oo-oo-oon." Devastated, he sings the chorus:

Coon! Coon! Coon!
I wish my color would fade:
Coon! Coon! Coon!
I'd like a different shade.
Coon! Coon! Coon! Morning, night, and noon.
I wish I was a white man!
'Stead of a Coon! Coon! Coon![52]

Although this theme was pervasive in the songs, it should be noted that rarely if ever, except in dream sequences, did blacks ever actually *become* white: They only aspired to do so (though the aspiration itself would surely have been disturbing to whites). But the song that most accurately described the actual racial ordering of the day was doubtless the Bob Cole/Billy Johnson number entitled "No Coons Allowed":

No coons allowed,—no coons allowed,
This place is meant for white folks. . . . [53]

Cole and Johnson, both black, had experienced hard reality.

In yet another song—a variant form of "coon song" sometimes termed a "coon lament"—the message was equally clear. The song was a sentimental ballad out of the minstrel tradition entitled "Stay in your Own Back Yard." The lyrics tell of a small black child who is rejected by the white children with whom she tries to play. Her mother speaks:

Now honey, you stay in yo' own back yard,
Doan min' what dem white chiles do;
What show yo' suppose dey's a gwine to gib
A black little coon like yo'?
So stay on dis side ob de high boahd fence,
An honey, doan cry so hard,
Go out an' play, jes as much as yo' please,
But stay in yo' own back yard. . . . [54]

Here, in effect, was the answer to all suggestions that the racial order might be changed: "stay in your own back yard." It constituted a pop music affirmation of Jim Crow segregation, the institutionalized system of race relations then in the process of enactment in the states of the South.

In the larger sense, then, it would appear that the coon song phenomenon manifested a sociopsychological response to the need for addressing the "race question" so central and so troubling to the times. In order to pursue the matter further, however, we must abandon the relatively well-marked course afforded by traditional historical documentation and sail into the largely uncharted waters of interpretation. To begin this effort we might go back to the music historian Sam Dennison, compiler of a major collection of material relating to the black image in popular song, who refers to "the sea of musical invective" that inundated the late nineteenth-century popular media. Dennison concludes that "songs about the black were more brutally insulting than at any time following the advent of minstrelsy."[55] The imagery of the coon songs, he suggests further, was based in "a peculiarly American form of misoxeny"; that is, in a thoroughgoing unfamiliarity with "real" blacks, and the acceptance of stereotypes developed out of racial prejudice. With none of these conclusions have I any fundamental disagreement. But I would like to advance the argument beyond this point.

It was the black historian Rayford W. Logan who once referred to the period of the late nineteenth and early twentieth centuries as the "nadir" of black fortunes in American history. Following the Civil War and emancipation, the country faced the necessity of reestablishing a system of race relations—a new social order in reality—in which the "place" of black Americans was to be determined and institutionalized within the larger culture. During this time of trial and uncertainty the black population suffered the brunt of rampant violence and intimidation, most of it directed against any sign of black pretension to civil and social equality or the exercise of political power.[56] Violence and oppression were simply part of the readjustment process, deemed imperative by those who would maintain the caste orientation of American race relations. The wartime promise of a more equitable order proved empty. Ultimately the fate of the black population was left to be determined by southern whites.

In the South, the white Redeemers (having assumed control of the mechanics of state government in the 1880s) were by 1890 on the verge of a solution to their "Race Problem." The solution was to involve the subordination, disfranchisement, and ultimately the legal segregation of blacks by way of the Jim Crow laws. Black subordination would be enforced by law where possible, and by way of violence and intimidation where law proved inadequate. Violent forms of intimidation, including physical and psychological abuse—the notorious "bulldozing" tactics of the post-Reconstruction South—included lynching where extreme measures were deemed necessary, and lynching, sometimes preceded by unspeakably grisly forms of torture, grew ever more commonplace as the nineteenth century closed. Such violence was an accepted concomitant of black subordination, perpetrated usually in the interest of demonstrating the certain result of any violation of "place" (by whatever means) on the part of blacks.[57]

Outside the South, the new order of southern race relations had by the 1890s come to be generally accepted. While the old "radical" Republicans had held out for black civil and political rights throughout Reconstruction, their energies had perceptibly flagged by 1890, and the reigning attitude in the North and West was one quite willing to accept Jim Crow as the basis of the new southern social system. Besides, relatively few northern and western whites had ever been truly committed to the concept of black equality, and had clearly manifested their racism (and even their negrophobia) throughout the antebellum years and beyond.[58] The immense popularity of the "coon" image nationwide merely reflected the ongoing commitment to racist assumptions that underlay the system of American apartheid in which blacks were maintained in subordinate and subservient roles.

In order to justify the realities of the new order, the dominant whites had to find serviceable forms of rationalization to quell the psychic disturbance known to social psychology as "cognitive dissonance."[59] This they were quick to do. They found ample justification, for example, in the New Anthropology, in Social Darwinism (and in Biological Darwinism as well), and in the sort of "racial radicalism" (the term is that of Joel Williamson) represented by Charles Carroll's *The Negro a Beast* (1900) and Thomas Dixon's *The Leopard's Spots* (1902).[60] The white mentality adjusted readily to such blandishments. The segregation of blacks, black subordination and subservience, enforced when necessary by violence and murder, were found to be justifiable, indeed right.

It is within this historical context that the ultimate explanation of the coon song craze must be sought. And to guide the quest, one must make choices among the various interpretive models available to the cultural historian; either that, or attempt to create an all-encompassing eclectic model that subsumes all variables. The problem with this latter approach, tempting as it may be to those of us who lack absolute commitment to (and faith in) any one of the several alternatives, is that, as anthropologist Clifford Geertz has observed, eclecticism is "self-defeating"; not, he insists, "because there is only one direction in which to move, but because there are so many. . . ."[61] We must choose that model of cultural process which lends itself most persuasively to the analysis of the specific case at hand, he says. And I have been convinced by the arguments of Geertz and others who perceive the need to sort out the "structures of signification"; those "piled up structures of inference and implication that are part of any symbolic act."[62] The coon song phenomenon, I contend, was ultimately a manifestation of a complex code of signification central to the entire racial discourse of late nineteenth-century America.

As a symbol-system, the coon songs constituted a multilayered set of meanings and images, at times shifting and even contradictory in its implications. There can be no doubt, however, of certain of its primary dimensions. As heretofore noted, all of the songs' lyrics suggested the qualities ascribed to blacks by their authors—collectively, the signified "coon." And if the complex of symbols operating at the conscious, cognitive level were to be construed as a symbolic statement, the songs themselves may be said to have constituted a form of rhetoric encompassing a true *ideology,* that is, a belief system reflecting the social needs of bourgeois America. As such they provided, in the way of all ideologies, "matrices for the creation of collective conscience" and ultimately the "interworking" of social reality and rhetoric (in Geertz's terminology).[63] It is at the point of this juncture of social reality and ideological commitment that one must seek the ultimate meaning of the coon song phenomenon.

The coon song craze in its full frenzy was a manifestation of a peculiar form of the will to believe—to believe in the signified "coon" as represented in the songs—as a necessary sociopsychological mechanism for justifying segregation and subordination. The process of symbolic formulation was doubtless complex: recall that the signified creatures who constitute the subjects of the coon songs often comprised unlikely combinations of qualities which, taken to their extreme forms, would suggest the characters of both "Stepin' Fetchit" and "Sportin' Life." It was by fulfilling the need for rationalizations on the part of the dominant population that the coon songs gained and maintained their inordinate popularity. Over and over the dominant themes were repeated and reiterated until the variant images were rendered indelible, at least in their primary forms. Blacks were not only the simple-minded comic buffoons of the minstrel tradition; they were also potentially dangerous. They were dangerous not only in the way that animals are dangerous if allowed to roam unrestrained, but dangerous as well to white bourgeois culture itself. They constituted a threat to the American social order. For this reason, they *had to be* controlled and subordinated by whatever means, so the coon songs signalled. The songs also argued, implicitly at least, for coercion, for lynching if necessary, to maintain control and the domination of white over black. Such was their connoted message (Roland Barthes has referred to such connotation as *"what-goes-without-saying,"* suggesting that it often masks "ideological abuse.")[64] And the songs argued far more effectively than did the rationalist racial effusions of the Carrolls and the Dixons. They did so because they spoke through symbols directly to their listeners, without need for cognition or analysis. The coon songs were as popular as they were because they provided psychic balms by way of justifying the unjustifiable to white Americans who were as delighted with "coons" as they were determined to believe in them.

Yet the ironies abound. In their very willingness to participate in the coon song phenomenon, black performers and song writers were able to profit commercially and to produce, among other things, an entirely new black musical theater based, at least in part, in authentically black musical materials.[65] Certain lyrics of the songs influenced the development of the black blues tradition that may be said to have culminated with Bessie Smith in the 1920s (one thinks of the unforgettable "Gimme a Pig's Foot"). Moreover, the tremendous popularity of the songs provided the means whereby ragtime as a musical genre in its own right gained an element of acceptance by whites who in the past were unaware of and unconcerned with black culture. Though ragtime had to overcome the stigma of its origins, the popularity of the coon songs cleared the way for its acceptance, and ultimately its popularity.[66] Finally, the ragtime genre, the roots of which lay in black folk music, provided the necessary bridge to the popular performance style that came to be called "jazz" in the early twentieth century. The coon song craze thus contributed to the development of America's only truly endemic musical form, even as the sentimental ballad associated with the minstrel tradition provided material for Al Jolson and the other blackface performers of the same period. Later still, film and the electronic media would feature entertainers of the Amos and Andy variety who served to perpetuate the "coon" character as a function of ethnic semiosis long after the sociopsychological need for the "coon" had ceased to exist in white America. By then whites had moved into a comfortable acceptance of the new racial order based in American apartheid, and the laughable "coon" was nothing more than a happy reminder of how right the system was.

Notes

1. Max Morath, "The Vocal and Theatrical Music of Bert Williams and His Associates" in *American Popular Entertainment,* ed. Myron Matlow (Westport, Conn., 1979), 112.

2. The ongoing assessment would include such recent works as follow: J. Stanley Lemons, "Black Stereotypes as Reflected in Popular Culture, 1880-1920," *American Quarterly* 29 (Spring 1977): 102-16; Janet Brown, "The 'Coon-Singer' and the 'Coon-Song:' A Case Study of the Performance-Character Relationship," *Journal of American Culture* 7 (Spring/Summer 1984): 1-8; Berndt Ostendorf, *Black Literature in White America* (Sussex, 1982); and especially Sam Dennison, *Scandalize My Name: Black Imagery in American Popular Music* (N.Y., 1982). The Dennison work constitutes a major compilation of black imagery in popular song from the mid-eighteenth through the mid-twentieth century, and provides the essential foundation for anyone examining the subject.

3. Dennison, *Black Imagery,* 7; James H. Dormon, "The Strange Career of Jim Crow Rice (With Apologies to Professor Woodward)," *Journal of Social History* 3 (Winter 1970): 109-22. On the matter of ethnic ascription (and other theoretical notions), see Frederick Barth, ed., *Ethnic Groups and Boundaries: The Social Organization of Culture Difference* (Boston, 1969), 12-18; James H. Dormon, "Ethnic Groups and 'Ethnicity:' Some Theoretical

Considerations," *Journal of Ethnic Studies* 7 (Winter 1980): 23-36.

4. Dennison, *Black Imagery,* 8. Dennison notes that "Andrew Barton" was possibly a pseudonym of Thomas Forrest.

5. Ibid., 9; Dormon, "Jim Crow Rice," 113-14.

6. On the appearance of the new caricature see Dennison, 36-58.

7. "Zip Coon" was published in several editions, the best known of which was probably that of Atwill's Music Saloon (N.Y., [1835]).

8. Dennison, *Black Imagery,* 87-156; Robert C. Toll, *Blacking Up; The Minstrel Show in Nineteenth Century America* (N.Y., 1974). On the development of black stereotypes in American popular culture, see Joseph Boskin, *Sambo: The Rise and Demise of an American Jester* (New York, 1986). William F. Stowe and David Grimsted have made a strong case for the multidimensionality of the traditional minstrel figure. See Stowe and Grimsted, "White-Black Humor," *Journal of Ethnic Studies* 2 (Summner 1975): 82.

9. Ibid.; Dormon, "Jim Crow Rice," 120-22.

10. *A Dictionary of American English on Historical Principles,* s.v. "coon"; locates the earliest reference to "coon" as "A Negro. Often contemptuous . . ." in 1887. *Dictionary of American Slang,* s.v. "coon"; lists same date, 1887, as earliest reference.

11. J. P. Skelly, "The Dandy Coon's Parade" (N.Y., 1880). Dennison claims this to be the first of the songs to use "the term 'coon' to signify black." *Black Imagery,* 281.

12. Louis Bodecker, "The Coons are on Parade" (Chicago, 1882); cited in Dennison, *Black Imagery,* 282.

13. J. S. Putnam, "New Coon in Town" (Cleveland and Chicago, 1883.)

14. Sam Lucas, "The Coon's Salvation Army" (Boston, 1884).

15. William Dressler, "The Coon Schottische" (Cleveland and Chicago, 1884).

16. "May Irwin's New Coon Song Hits," (N.Y., [1896 or 1897]); George M. Cohan, "San Francisco Sadie" (N.Y., 1899). For additional material on the popularity of coon songs see David Ewen, *American Popular Songs: From the Revolutionary War to the Present* (N.Y., 1966), 164; Edward B. Marks, *They All Sang: From Tony Pastor to Rudy Vallee* (N.Y., 1934), 91-92; Russell B. Nye, *The Unembarrassed Muse: The Popular Arts in America* (N.Y., 1970), 317. Although the center of popular music production and distribution was clearly in the urban Northeast, the popularity of the coon songs was national in scope. The "coon" routine invaded the vaudeville houses and music halls of all parts of the

country, and coon songs were available in sheet music form nationwide.

17. See Eileen Southern, *The Music of Black Americans: A History* (N.Y., 1971), 314; Robert C. Toll, *On with the Show: The First Century of Show Business in America* (N.Y., 1976), 118; Brown, "Coon-Singer," 2.

18. *Etude Magazine* in 1898 associated the rhythms of the then emergent ragtime style with the "rhythmic features of the popular 'coon song.'" The article continues "It has a powerfully stimulating effect, setting the nerves and muscles tingling with excitement. Its esthetic element is the same as that in the monotonous, recurring rhythmic chant of barbarous races." The lyrics are normally, we are informed, "decidedly vulgar, so that its present great favor is somewhat to be deplored." Quoted in William J. Schafer and Johannes Reidel, *The Art of Ragtime: Form and Meaning of an Original Black American Art* (Baton Rouge, 1973), xix.

19. Ibid., 29. Schafer and Reidel refer to the "popular rage" for coon songs on the stage and in the music halls of the 1890s, while David A. Jasen and Trebor Jay Tichenor write that coon songs "became a craze" in 1896 and "remained standard fare in vaudeville and musical revues throughout the early 1900s." See Jasen and Tichenor, *Rags and Ragtime. A Musical History* (N.Y., 1978), 12.

20. *Dramatic Mirror* (N.Y., [1896]), quoted in Toll, *Show,* 124.

21. "The Stage Negro," *Variety,* 14 Dec. 1907, 53. Ironically, the reference was to *blacks* performing blackface roles.

22. On the old stereotype and its sociopsychological functions, see Dennison, *Black Imagery,* 101-10; Dormon, "Jim Crow Rice," 120-22; and Toll, *Blacking Up,* 75-79. Brown suggests that the "coon" type was an extension of the "classical fool." Brown, "Coon-Singer," 2.

23. For an analogue of the razor/signifier-black/signified equation, see William Boelhower, "Describing the Italian-American Self: Type-Scene and Encyclopedia," *In Their Own Words* 2 (Winter 1984): 37-48. My thanks to Professor Werner Sollors for guiding me to this important article.

24. Malcolm Williams, "My Watermelon Boy" (N.Y., 1899).

25. "I've Got Chicken on the Brain," words by Elmer Bowman; music by Al Johns (N.Y., 1899).

26. Bert Williams and George Walker, "The Coon's Trade Mark" n.p., n.d., quoted in Lemons, "Black Stereotypes," 107. Williams and Walker were not only performers of "coon" material but prolific writers of the material as well.

27. Thomas S. Allen, "Any Rags" (Boston, 1902); cited in Dennison, *Black Imagery,* 367-68.

28. Nathan Bivins, "Gimme Ma Money" (N.Y., 1898); cited in Dennison, 364.

29. "I'm Always Glad to See You When You'll Buy," words by George Totten Smith; music by A. B. Sloan (N.Y., 1899).

30. "I've Just Received a Telegram from Baby," words by Will A. Heehan; music by Harry von Tilzer (N.Y., 1899). Von Tilzer was, of course, author of such period standards as "Wait Till the Sun Shines, Nellie" (1905); "I Want a Girl, Just Like the Girl (that Married Dear Old Dad)" (1910); and "In the Evening by the Moonlight" (1912). His coon song phase produced one of the most popular of that genre, too: "What You Goin' to do When the Rent Comes 'Round?" (See below, note 33).

31. Irving Jones, "I've Got Money Locked up in a Vault"; revised by Bert Williams and George Walker (N.Y., 1899).

32. "When a Nigger Makes a Hundred . . ." words by Charles A. Wilson; music by Leo E. Berliner (N.Y., 1899).

33. Harry von Tilzer and Andrew B. Sterling, "What You Goin' to do when the Rent Comes 'Round?" (N.Y., n.d.).

34. Will A. Heehan and J. Fredrick Helf, "Every Race has a Flag but the Coon" (N.Y., 1901). The combination "four-eleven-forty-four" was in the lore of the numbers game believed to have a near-mystical promise of a big win, or at least such was reputedly the case among black players. Heehan and Helf later composed a second song based on the flag theme, apparently responding to protests over the assertion that American blacks had no emblem. They called it "The Emblem of an Independent Coon" (N.Y., [1902]), and designed it as a patriotic riposte to their own earlier effusion. The song featured musical quotations from "Hail, Columbia," "Marching through Georgia," "The Star-Spangled Banner," and Ernest Hogan's "All Coons Look Alike to Me." The lyrics read, in part:

> Some folks say the coons have got no emblem,They forget Abe Lincoln mighty soon.
> Remember, he unfurled the Stars and Stripes to all the world,
> As the emblem of an independent coon.
> . . .
> No coons should be neglected 'cause no other race it bars;
> For ev'ry man on earth, of ev'ry shade and birth,
> Is welcomed and protected 'neath the noble Stripes and Stars. . . .

35. Lu Senareus, "A Red Hot Coon" (N.Y., 1899).

36. Harry von Tilzer, "De Swellest Ladie's Coon in Town" (N.Y., 1897). It is tempting to conclude from the popularity of the "coon" material that white audiences subliminally envied the carefree, uninhibited, unrestrained "coon," and especially so during an era of Victorian restraint. White entertainers relished the "coon" role, even as whites had obviously enjoyed blacking up for minstrel shows. But whether or not white envy of black "freedom" lay behind the coon craze, it is clear that whites saw the unrestrained, lascivious "coon" as fundamentally lacking in the requisite forms of civility and intelligence to be conceded equality within the hegemonic social order.

37. "The Hottest Coon in Dixie," quoted in Henry T. Sampson, *Blacks in Blackface: A Source Book on Early Black Musical Shows* (Metuchen, N.J., 1980), 79.

38. Ernest Hogan, "All Coons Look Alike to Me" (N.Y., 1896). The song became controversial when, near the end of the century, some blacks began to condemn it as demeaning and refused to perform it. But despite the controversy, the song was deemed to be a gem of ragtime piano composition. See Lemons, "Black Stereotypes," 107.

39. Elmer Bowman, "No Coon Can Come too Black for Me" in *New Darkey Songs of the Era* (N.Y., 1899).

40. Jess Danzig, "You're Alright but you Don't Get In," in ibid., n.p.

41. "The Mormon Coon," words by Raymond A. Browne; music by Henry Clay Smith (N.Y., 1905), cited in Dennison, *Black Imagery,* 357.

42. "Leave Your Razors at the Door," words by Dave Reed, Jr.; music by Charles B. Ward (n.d., [ca. 1900]).

43. Charles S. O'Brien, "Ma Angeline" (N.Y., 1896).

44. "I'm the Toughest, Toughest Coon," words by Carl Stowe; music by L. Mauran Bloodgood (Boston, 1904), cited in Dennison, *Black Imagery,* 375.

45. A. B. Sloane, "De Blue Gum Nigger" (N.Y., 1899).

46. "He's Up Against the Real Thing Now," words by Edward Furber; music by Bert Williams, in *Ragtime Folio #2* (N.Y., n.d.).

47. Ernest Hogan, "No More Will I Ever Be Your Baby" (n.p., [ca. 1897]).

48. John Queen, "Got Your Habits On" (Chicago, 1899).

49. Andrew Sterling, "I've Got a White Man Working for Me" (N.Y., 1899).

50. Charles Shackford, "Only a Little Yaller Coon" (N.Y., 1896).

51. Fred Fisher, "If the Man in the Moon were a Coon" (Chicago, 1905). The "Coon-Moon" rhyme lent itself to many other coon-moon associations; for example Jake Cline's "The Coon from the Moon," which opens "I'm a Nigger, I'm a Coon, and I fell down from the Moon/Don't You Know . . ." (N.Y., 1894).

52. "Coon! Coon! Coon!" words by Gene Jefferson; music by Leo Friedman (N.Y., 1901). On the extraordinary popularity of the song, see Ewen, *Popular Songs,* 73.

53. Bob Cole and Billy Johnson, "No Coons Allowed!" (N.Y., 1899).

54. "Stay in Your Own Back Yard," words by Karl Kennett; music by Lyn Udall (N.Y., 1899).

55. Dennison, *Black Imagery,* 423-24. Joel Williamson, whose work represents the most important recent consideration of race relations in the period, echoes Dennison in noting that the late nineteenth and early twentieth centuries were "marked by a racist rhetoric never equalled in virulence in America. . . ." Joel Williamson, *The Crucible of Race: Black-White Relations in the American South Since Emancipation* (N.Y., 1984), 311-12.

56. See Rayford W. Logan, *The Negro in American Life and Thought: The Nadir, 1877-1901* (N.Y., 1954).

57. There were at least 1,665 lynchings in the United States between 1890 and 1900. Most of the victims were black. See Sig Synnestvedt, *The White Response to Black Emancipation* (N.Y., 1972), 56. The historical literature pertaining to black intimidation, depoliticization, subordination, and segregation is immense, commencing with C. Vann Woodward's seminal works: *Origins of the New South, 1877-1913* (Baton Rouge, 1951), and *The Strange Career of Jim Crow* (N.Y., 1955). Joel Williamson has provided the most recent version of the story in *Crucible of Race,* cited above. On the process of black disfranchisement, see especially J. Morgan Kousser, *The Shaping of Southern Politics: Suffrage Restriction and the Establishment of the One-Party South, 1890-1910* (New Haven, 1974). On the segregation process, see John W. Cell, *The Highest Stage of White Supremacy: The Origins of Segregation in South Africa and the American South* (N.Y. and London, 1982), 82-191.

58. On northern racial attitudes and the ultimate capitulation to southern Jim Crow see Williamson, *Crucible of Race,* 339-41. See also Idus A. Newby, *Jim Crow's Defense: Anti-Negro Thought in America* (Baton Rouge, 1965) for a good discussion of the pervasive racism in the nation at large by the end of the nineteenth century.

59. Gunnar Myrdal, *An American Dilemma: The Negro Problem and Modern Democracy* (N.Y., 1944), 1:106. For a good brief discussion of cognitive dissonance, see Harry C. Triandis, *Attitude and Attitude Change* (N.Y., 1971), 78-84.

60. Charles Carroll, *The Negro a Beast; or, in the Image of God* (St. Louis, 1900); Thomas Dixon Jr., *The Leopard's Spots: A Romance of the White Man's Burden* (N.Y., 1902). Dixon was also the author of a second bestseller, *The Clansman* (N.Y., 1905), which provided the story line for the controversial film,

Birth of a Nation in 1915. The subject of racial attitudes and ideologies in the late nineteenth-century United States has attracted a considerable scholarly interest. Representative works include Newby, *Jim Crow's Defense;* August Meir, *Negro Thought in America, 1880-1915: Racial Ideologies in the Age of Booker T. Washington* (Ann Arbor, 1968); Lawrence J. Friedman, *The White Savage: Racial Fantasies in the Postbellum South* (Englewood Cliffs, N.J., 1970); John S. Haller, Jr., *Outcasts From Evolution: Scientific Attitudes of Racial Inferiority, 1859-1900* (Urbana, Ill., 1971); George M. Frederickson, *The Black Image in the White Mind: The Debate on Afro-American Character and Destiny, 1817-1914* (N.Y., 1971); Bruce Clayton, *The Savage Ideal: Intolerance and Intellectual Leadership in the South, 1890-1914* (Baltimore, 1972); Barbara J. Fields, "Ideology and Race in American History," in *Region, Race, and Reconstruction: Essays in Honor of C. Vann Woodward,* eds. J. Morgan Kousser and James M. McPherson (N.Y., 1982), 143-77; Williamson, *The Crucible of Race.*

61. Clifford Geertz, "Thick Description: Toward an Interpretive Theory of Culture," in *The Interpretation of Cultures* (N.Y., 1973), 5.

62. Ibid., 7, 9.

63. Clifford Geertz, "Ideology as a Cultural System," in *The Interpretation of Cultures,* 213, 220.

64. Roland Barthes, *Mythologies,* trans. Annette Lavers (N.Y., 1974), 9. Italics in the original. The phrase is from the "Preface" to the 1970 edition, which opens with the announcement that the book "has a double theoretical framework: On the one hand, an ideological critique bearing on the language of so-called mass-culture; on the other, a first attempt to analyze semiologically the mechanics of this language." The same might be said of my efforts to assess the meaning of the Coon Song Phenomenon.

65. See, e.g., Ann Charters, "Negro Folk Elements in Classic Ragtime," *Ethnomusicology* 5 (Sept. 1961): 174-83.

66. On the origins of ragtime and its popular reception, see Jasen and Tichenor, *Rags and Ragtime,* and Schafer and Riedel, *Art of Ragtime.*

Mary W. Blanchard (essay date 1996)

SOURCE: "The Soldier and the Aesthete: Homosexuality and Popular Culture in Gilded Age America," in *Journal of American Studies*, Vol. 30, No. 1, April, 1996, pp. 25-46.

[In the following excerpt, Blanchard argues that with the increased aestheticism of the Gilded Age came a more open acceptance of homosexuality and alternative definitions of manhood.]

The aftermath of civil strife, note some historians, can change perceptions of gender. Particularly for males, the effect of exhaustive internal wars and the ensuing collapse of the warrior ideal relegates the soldier/hero to a marginal iconological status. Linda L. Carroll has persuasively argued, for instance, that, following the Italian wars, one finds the "damaged" images of males in Renaissance art: bowed heads, display of stomach, presentation of buttocks. In fact, male weakness and "effeminacy" can, notes Linda Dowling, follow on the military collapse of any collective state. Arthur N. Gilbert argues, in contrast, that historically in wartime, male weakness in the form of "sodomites" was rigorously persecuted. From 1749 until 1792, for instance, there was only one execution for sodomy in France, while, during the Napoleonic Wars, the period of 1803-14, seven men were executed. Such analysis suggests that, in the aftermath of civil wars, cultural attitudes toward effeminate or homosexual men shifted from suppression or persecution during martial crisis to one of latitude and perhaps tolerance in periods following the breakdown of the military collective.[1]

The aftermath of America's Civil War, the decades of the 1870s and 1880s, provides a testing ground to examine attitudes toward the soldier/hero and toward the effeminate male in a time of social and cultural disarray. At this time, an art "craze," the Aesthetic Movement, captured popular culture. Aestheticism, seen in the eighteenth century as a "sensibility," had, by the nineteenth century, an institutional base and a social reform ideology. Influenced by the English reformers, John Ruskin, William Morris and the pre-Raphaelite painters, American aestheticism centered around the tasteful pursuit of the decorative arts. But the umbrella philosophy insisted that one should live for art and beauty, that one should create an aesthetic social environment. Indeed, the site for aestheticism was the domestic sphere, alien to the political or military discourse of the Civil War years. Aestheticism entered middle-class culture through the influence of the English handicrafts at the Philadelphia Centennial in 1876, through the burgeoning of art societies, art journals, and industrial art schools at this time, through "cluttered" high Victorian decor which was considered "artistic," and through the mantra of the word "artistic" which saturated the popular media—from general advice on decoration to the rhetoric in trade journals and sophisticated publications. By using the Aesthetic Movement as a framing device, this essay examines cultural attitudes toward both the soldier and the aesthete to explore the emergence of "male weakness" and feminine or homosexual figures in Gilded Age America.[2]

I

In the 1870s and 1880s, the rise of the new male, self-stylized aesthete patterned after Oscar Wilde was, of course, in dialectical relationship to the more persistent and visible ideal in American culture, the man as soldier. This older, more static model, emerging from the republican hero as the freedom fighter and from the more recent soldier/citizen of the Civil War, was symbolically overlaid on other cultural heroes of the Reconstruction years. For the vigor, aggressiveness, tenacity, and "manliness" of the soldier/hero was attached as well, note historians, to the ethos of the assertive entrepreneur, to the bravado of the frontier warrior, and even to the commitment of the Populist rebel or the union agitator. This military metaphor was evident in the model of the "soldierly" industrial worker confronted by competition from new international markets, and evident, too, in the ideology underlying the rise of competitive team sports in the late nineteenth century. Even social reformers formulated their ideology of the "moral equivalent of war," the Salvation Army, for instance, in terms of the prevailing template of the "manly soldier."[3]

Yet, during the 1870s and 1880s, the aftermath of the Civil War, a certain war-weariness induced some Americans to seek alternate modes of self-definition, as new formats, aesthetic style for one, competed with older categories like the "manly" soldier to define masculinity. For the acceptance of Aestheticism and the male aesthete was symptomatic of a culture that no longer celebrated the soldier's victory, but instead aestheticized death and divorced "manliness" from warfare. For many, this shifted concepts of masculinity and subjectivity from the Civil War battlefield to the aesthetic parlor. Only a cataclysm as profound as a war between brother and brother could have temporarily suppressed the visibility and continuity of the soldier/hero in a culture formed from a revolutionary war ethos. Never entirely disappearing as a cultural value, "soldierly" manhood, nonetheless, was a contested model during the Aesthetic years. Aestheticism could not have been a popular movement without the Civil War, for, during the 1870s and 1880s, for some men, the ahistorical "escape" from the memory of Civil War armies and battles allowed scope for the new forms of artistic endeavors and gender experimentation so prevalent in the culture at large and so intimate to popular Aestheticism in America.[4]

Little needs to be recounted of the Civil War itself and the innumerable casualties that ensued. These ravages were precipitated by the new age of the rifle, a modern weapon of carnage used in combination with the old-age war manoeuvre of tactical assaults. "It was thought to be a great thing to charge a battery of artillery or an earthwork lined with infantry," recalled one soldier. "We were very lavish of blood in those days." In the end, more than 620,000 American men died and the United States began the painful process of Reconstruction, and the less visible, but crucial, drift toward Aestheticism.[5]

If the Philadelphia Centennial of 1876 was the catalyst for the Aesthetic Movement, the fair's themes signaled a perceptible emasculation of the valoric soldier/hero model and a negation of the war itself. Cataloging our "first century of national existence," the *Illustrated History of the Centennial Exhibition,* for instance, stressed "the noble arts of peace," with no mention of any war experience, although the Civil War had barely ended. This omission was deliberate policy, for no paintings of war scenes were allowed in the officially sponsored art exhibition. The most visible icon of male strength at the fair was not the warrior from the battlefield but the modern steam engine. The great Corliss engine was praised as "an athlete of steel and iron," but this male force was controlled by a woman, Miss Emma Allison, known for "the neatness of her dress and the perfection of cleanliness in both engine and engineroom." Perhaps symbolically, the most popular exhibit was, not an emblem of forceful nationhood, but a shrunken relic of the war, "Old Abe," the decrepit eagle mascot of a Wisconsin Civil War regiment.[6]

Other mass spectacles in the 1870s and 1880s suppressed the model soldier/hero as well. In her study of parades, Mary Ryan notes that women were the Goddess/heroes at civic events, while the "dashing citizen-soldier" of the war years was no more, replaced by older veterans or reluctant National Guard units "ordered to parade by their commanders." In 1885, Ulysses Grant wrote his *Personal Memoirs of U. S. Grant* (which sold 300,000 copies in the first two weeks after publication), an evocation to war that downplayed male heroism, revealing the womanly sentiment of compassion. Grant suffered personally over the death of his soldiers and of their animals. "I was always glad when a battle was over," the author admitted, a reflection of a culture wearied and uncertain over the memory of death on the battlefield.[7]

As Grant made amends for his military role by refusing to valorize warfare and death, so did the progeny of other Civil War generals. Most striking was the penance of William T. Sherman's son, Tom. Tom Sherman graduated from law school intending a career in law. But influenced by his Catholic mother, Tom Sherman was instead ordained a Jesuit priest. In 1891 at General Sherman's death, Father Sherman began his proselytizing in the "army of Christ." Like a "field commander addressing his troops," Father Sherman founded in 1901 the Catholic Truth Society of Chicago dedicated to converting Protestants, but ended his life with a complete mental breakdown, committed to asylums and often violently disruptive. At the hospital, Sherman always wore his military cloak when sitting in his wheelchair, and when offered Communion he murmured to his nurses, "It is too late, it is too late." Perhaps Tom Sherman's exile into a "sterile" parody of militarism and into spirituality and hysteria, the theaters of the Victorian woman, exemplified the profound dislocation some Americans felt in the post war years over the memory of the war's atrocities.[8]

Intellectuals, too, shared an ambivalence over national bloodletting. Henry James never served in the Civil War, but he perpetuated a life-long guilt over war, "this abyss of blood and darkness." Even Oliver Wendell Holmes, Jr. who, in 1862, spoke contemptuously of the "soft" and "sentimental" attitude toward war had, by 1884, admitted that war was "horrible and dull." By 1895, as the Aesthetic decades ended, Holmes would endorse the blind faith of the soldier-fighter, but there was a metaphoric quality to this ephemeral warrior who served more as a standard-bearer of the agnostic human condition than as a model for masculine aggression. Indeed, Holmes could not bear to read anything about the Civil War in later years, just as William Dean Howells retreated into his imaginary literary world of genteel society by the 1870s and 1880s. Howells never volunteered for the war, but exiled himself with a consulship at Venice from 1861 to 1865. On his return in the 1870s, Howells ignored war themes, concerning himself with the "minor ailments of middle-class life . . . sentimental infatuation and snobbish intolerance." Perhaps Howells himself is the real voice of one character in *The Rise of Silas Lapham* who discussed the "deathrate" of the Civil War: "Ah, nobody *feels* that anything happened . . . it's really a great deal less vivid than some scenes in a novel."[9]

Artists, too, dealt with death as a fictional issue. In the shadow of the war in the mid-1860s, the American pre-Raphaelite painters portrayed death as non-violent and gentle, an illusion of serenity. These artists chose diminutive still lifes, often of a single dead bird. Death was miniaturized, rendered frail and inconsequential through the corpse of a small titmouse in John Henry Hill's "Black Capped Titmouse," c. 1866, or the soft repose of the common Blue Jay in John William Hill's "The Blue Jay," c. 1865. The landscape painters, too, shifted their emphasis after the war. Where once artists at mid-century painted scenes of judgment and prophecy, like Thomas Cole in his "After the Deluge," by the 1870s painters focused on "bombastic, theatrical" landscapes like Albert Bierstadt's "Mount Corcoran," on subjective, symbolic interpretations like Albert Pinkham Ryder's "Jonah," or on New Testament subjects, the life of the human Christ. Nature was no longer virile and judgmental, but was mystical and kind like the now-feminized, gentle Jesus. Even the theological overtones of Frederic Church's landscape scenes gave way to the more aesthetic George Inness who "quickened [art] with imagination original in tone and feeling." Henry James articulated in 1873 what artists knew, and Americans sensed: There was a "thinness of American life," James noted, "Our silent past, our deafening present, the constant pressure about us of unlovely conditions, are . . . void of all that nourishes and prompts and inspires the artist."[10]

Such ennui provoked passivity and ambiguity towards violence and masculinity. In the 1870s and 1880s, American art critics censured gore and violence as pictorial themes "eloquent of mental and physical degradation," and, indeed, most American artists showing in the French salons favored dramatic expression over barbarous violence. Even the portrait painters, men like Thomas Eakins, William Merritt Chase, and John Singer Sargent, created elusive nonthreatening figures, treating gender ambivalently, as multi-faceted and tenable, a direct result of the dislocation James perceived in the post war years.[11] Sculpture, as well, evaded a realist celebration of military triumph in commemorative pieces. In public monuments, the Civil War conflict was often viewed in archetypal themes, of brother versus brother or the symbolic images of peace. Even local monuments, a common soldier on a simple pedestal, were executed in a uniform, standardized vernacular, mimicked by both North and South.[12] Although the Civil War was often seen at the time as an apocalyptic vision or as a testing of male supremacy, in Augustus Saint-Gaudens monument to General William Sherman's victory over the Confederacy, the sculptor elevated the statuesque female as Peace, a female who deflated masculinity by leading the passive general seated docilely on his horse. Conceived in 1877, Saint-Gaudens' design underplayed Sherman as military conqueror by his idealized figure. Henry James, however, perceived the incongruity of the warrior being led by a "beautiful American girl." "And I confess to a lapse of satisfaction," James mused, "in the presence of this interweaving—the result doubtless of a sharp suspicion of all attempts, however glittering and golden, to confound destroyers with benefactors."[13]

II

If the soldier/hero was upstaged by a "beautiful American girl," such ambivalence suggested the need for new models. Although the quest for a "man of character" had evolved since the early nineteenth century, E. Anthony Rotundo posits three ideals of middle-class manhood throughout the nineteenth century: the Masculine Achiever, the Christian Gentleman, and the Masculine Primitive. Forgotten in this surmise is the rise of the aesthete during the aftermath of the war years, a model personified by Oscar Wilde, the "Apostle of Aestheticism," during his 1882 lecture tour in America. Wilde was asked to lecture on aestheticism and house decoration to publicize Gilbert and Sullivan's new production, "Patience," a spoof of the Aesthetic Movement which was touring America at the time. Wilde criss-crossed the country for a year, lecturing in the West, in California, in the South, in Canada, and throughout the Northeast, speaking to audiences of many thousands. His speeches were printed in all the major newspapers, and Wilde traveled like a celebrity in a special train replete with a huge banner on the side of his special car. Advance agents marketed the Apostle of Aestheticism, and Wilde conformed to this image by dressing in "feminized" attire: lace cuffs, open shirt, velvet knickers and coat, long hair, and shaven, painted face.[14]

If noticed by cultural historians at all, Wilde plays a marginal role as outre, perceived as amoral, if not immoral, and aestheticism itself has been targeted as an idiosyncratic or elite venture. Unnoticed in this appraisal is the ramification of Wilde's perceived homosexuality by Americans at large, for Wilde was targeted as an "invert" through the staccato descriptions of his effeminacy by the press, for the charge of effeminacy was the usual nineteenth century caricature of male homosexuality. There was an awareness among the public and among the new breed of aggressive journalists at the time of Wilde's visit that, in fact, there was a viable, "invert" culture, a "school of gilded youths eager to embrace his peculiar tenets," noted the *Brooklyn Daily Eagle*. Wilde, indeed, often mirrored these very groups.[15]

For the popular media to refer to a "school of gilded youths" suggests that the urban homosexual world so diffusely detailed in police and sociologists reports at the time was, in fact, commonly acknowledged in straight society. Gilbert and Sullivan's "Patience" was popularly noted as "one long joke about Oscar Wilde's tastes," evidence that outsiders were cognizant of Wilde's particular "school." But the scientific knowledge of insiders was more impressive. In 1889, a Dr. G. Frank Lydston reported that "there is in every community of any size a colony of male sexual perverts . . . known to each other . . . likely to congregate together . . . [and] characterized by effeminacy of voice, dress, and manner." Jacob Riis, reporter for the New York *Evening Sun*, admitted a "demi-world" of "perverts" who had saloons protected by the police. On the Bowery, beer gardens, known picturesquely as The Slide or Walhalla Hall, catered to this demi-world with elaborate dances. George Chauncey has catalogued a complex culture among "fairies" and "queers" in lower New York at this time, a culture intersecting with the uptown middle-class men who frequented these downtown haunts. Paresis Hall, No. 392 Bowery, was "the place where [these] fancy gentlemen go," acknowledged one New York State Report. And "they act effeminately; most of them are painted and powdered," cautioned this investigator. To protest these intruding eyes, a splinter group in Paresis Hall formed a "little club, the Cercle Hermaphroditos . . . to unite for defense," evidence of the cohesion and loyalty of the homosexual subculture in Wilde's day. "We care to admit only extreme types—such as like to doll themselves up in feminine finery," ran the manifesto, a sympathetic echo of the "womanish" Wilde who appeared uptown in lace cuffs, with penciled eyebrows and flowing hair. Nearby Philadelphia, too, was "as rife . . . as any city in the east," and, again, one reporter mimicked the profile of Wilde by noting the faces of "these creatures" as "clean shaven and highly decorated with cosmetics."[16]

The curiosities of this known culture extended to the widespread reports of the meeting between Wilde and Walt Whitman on 18 January 1882, in Camden, New Jersey. Richard Ellmann tells us that one informant declared that Wilde boasted that the poet had made no effort to conceal his homosexuality from Wilde at this time. "The kiss of Walt Whitman is still on my lips," Wilde recalled, and reporters carefully documented each gesture of the two poets at this meeting, evidence that the straight public was perhaps both curious about and privy to the male coding of the invert world. The *Newark Daily Advertiser* was typical of the extended and descriptive coverage: Whitman, interviewed later, admitted that the two poets retired upstairs to a private third floor den where, after finishing a bottle of wine, "we had a jolly good time . . . a very happy time together . . . I saw him behind the scenes." Pregnant perhaps was the ensuing note: "We came up here, where we could be on 'thee' and 'thou' terms. One of the first things I said was that I should call him 'Oscar.' " This frank and bold intimacy was reciprocated by a physical gesture. "I like that so much," he [Wilde] answered, laying his hand on my knee." Possibly the reporters were exposing more than a rote narrative, for Whitman later played a womanly role by making Wilde "a big glass of milk punch." The *Washington Post* emphasized the unmanly aspect of this gesture: "Then they took some more milk punch and dreamed of faint lilies." On 1 March 1882, Wilde wrote to the venerable old poet, addressing Whitman as "My Dear Dear Walt," testimony to a male bonding that was perhaps seen as part of the larger subculture of emerging male eroticism.[17]

The inference of these reports is ambiguous, but the association of "young men" with the Apostle of Aestheticism was pronounced. An odd account of Wilde's visit to the New York Stock Exchange accented the homoerotic nature of the adulation, linking Wilde to "telegraph" and "messenger" boys. Telegraph boys were an integral part of a male prostitution ring uncovered in "The London Scandal on Cleveland Street," a scandal duly reported in the *New York Times* in November 1889. In the 1880s, descriptions of the New York Stock Exchange emphasized an undercurrent of physical playfulness and suppressed homoeroticism. At the Exchange, for instance, fraternal rituals included "Bacchic dances to the entrancing music of Italian organ-grinders, tremendous attempts at Graeco-Roman wrestling, exasperating 'tug-of-war' contests," and a Christmas Carnival with same-sex dancing. . . . Reporters covering Oscar Wilde's visit to the Exchange noted this physical interaction. "The jostling [was] severe," mentioned *Harper's New Monthly Magazine*, "The sunflower knight finds it difficult to keep his aesthetic legs." Wilde "looked his sweetest," reported the *Washington Post*, coding Wilde as the homosexual persona with "a form suggestive of corsets . . . flowing tresses . . . fresh from the oil jar, and rainbow stockings tucked into dapper knee-breeches." "About 1,000 messenger boys crowded close around the aesthete" on the street, observed this writer. Wilde was rushed inside the Stock Exchange:

> The hoodlums followed . . . The very bad little boys made the hallways and galleries of the Exchange ring with their enthusiasm . . . There arose a great shout which was a tempest, compared with the hootings and cries of the messenger boys . . . The crowds grew bigger and the cries grew louder. A hundred brokers stood at the foot of the main stairway ready for a concerted rush whereby to get Oscar upon the "floor."

If the implication of a gang rape was suggested ("the very bad little boys . . . a hundred brokers . . . a concerted rush"), the finale was a disappointment as, with Wilde "charging down a back stair," "the brokers were sadly disappointed, so were the messenger boys."[18]

Wilde's connection to street boys was not confined to this incident at the Stock Exchange. The male sports journal, the *National Police Gazette,* published an illustration of Wilde leading his following of "newsboys and bootblacks, that precocious set," indicating a knowledgeable sophistication among its readers concerning the "precocious set". . . . Certainly these implications were as telling as a later report of Wilde "permeating society even to its lower strata." Indeed, Wilde's influence permeated all of popular culture, for men throughout the country impersonated Wilde—from publicity-seeking journalists in Denver to young dandies at the Milwaukee Stock Exchange dressed in Wildean attire. Even a grocer in St. Louis declared himself to be Wilde in person. On 6 January 1882, at the time of Wilde's arrival, the *Jerseyman* (Morristown) reported on a man cross-dressing "in a black silk dress" and on the "adoption" of a newsboy by a Senator David Davis. "It is said of Senator Davis that he is constantly doing that sort of thing," added the *Jerseyman,* suggesting that the pederastic overtones of Wilde's conduct was a popular concept both to report on and to generate a homosexual response in the public at large.[19]

This "adoption" of a newsboy during Wilde's visit was a seemingly open act and one apparently sanctioned by the culture at large, for there was no censure in the *Jerseyman* report over Senator Davis's actions. For example, Charles Warren Stoddard, a California poet and secretary to Mark Twain lived openly in San Francisco at this time with a young boy named O'Connor. The boy's mother accepted this arrangement and helped Stoddard in his efforts on behalf of her son. Although Stoddard sent his work to Whitman to "get in among people not afraid of instincts," Stoddard's male household was a model of bourgeois domesticity and apparently approved, for Henry Adams, the genteel New Englander, sent the couple three "Persian pillows" to decorate their parlor.[20]

Such open cohesion between the "lower strata" of boys and middle-class domesticity mirrored efforts by reformers like Charles Loring Brace, founder of the New York Children's Aid Society, who, like Wilde, was a guru among the city's street children. Though Brace's relationship to homeless boys was activated by his reformist impulses, Brace often confessed to a "powerful attraction" toward the boys in his Newsboys' Lodging House. Associated with Brace's boy charities was Horatio Alger, Jr., who had in 1866 been accused of the "revolting crime of unnatural familarity with *boys,*" and who was instrumental, as Michael Moon argues, in "gentrifying" the concept of the "dangerous" lower-class boy to one of "gentle" middle-class idealism. Alger's Tattered Tom series, followed by the successful Ragged Dick stories, allied success in the Victorian marketplace with a rags to riches narrative that valorized male domestic partnership and bourgeois values. In reality, in the 1870s, a viable subculture of some estimated 6,000 hobos with their "prushuns," homeless boys of ten to fifteen, existed. That homeless boys could be sanitized into domesticity in acceptable middle-class success narratives indicated that the Wildean pederastic innuendos in 1882 were part of a larger literature of acceptable and muted boy love.[21]

In addition, the tone of levity in the accounts of Wilde's veiled homoerotic escapade at the Exchange in publications as conservative as *Harper's New Monthly Magazine* and the *Washington Post* suggests that the figure of the aesthete was viewed with tolerant good humor by the public at large. Such levity suggests, as well, that there was a sympathetic cohesion between the aesthete model and the middle-class itself, and, indeed, Wilde's lectures on the decorative arts were popular and prestigious events throughout the country. That Wilde, the guru of aestheticism and suspect invert, should present himself as arbiter of middle-class taste was reflected in the stage decorations for his lecture tour, decorations that made Wilde a symbolic icon of both Victorian domesticity and aesthetic, homosexual proclivities.

Indeed, the merging of the domestic and the aesthetic was evident in the artistic parlors which were created on stage for Wilde's lectures in cities from Salt Lake City to Boston. In Denver, for instance, the stage setting was "art decorations of the interior miniature house . . . [with] elegant and genuine Turkish upholstery . . . plush and raw silk curtains . . . with walls and pillars of . . . artistic beauty," while, in Milwaukee, the stage walls "were covered with wonderful and fearfully proportioned dados and eastlakes, and great storks standing knee-deep in "yaliery-greenery" . . . [with] wide Moorish doors with portieres of green material."[22]

III

If Wilde was popularly associated with a domestic aestheticism, this only reflected other examples in a culture that was redefining gender, a culture ambivalent, yet creative, in its attempt to reconstitute and defuse the warrior ethic. An unusual example of the merging of feminine and masculine taste was the celebrated interior of the Seventh Regiment Armory. Founded in 1812, the Seventh Regiment's historic record included defense of Washington during the Civil War and protection of the city during the violent riots of the nineteenth century. Many members were from socially prominent families in New York, and the construction of a new armory building in 1879 included contributions from William Astor, A. J. Stewart, and William J. Vanderbilt, as well as from banks and insurance companies. In 1879, A New Armory Fair which raised $140,000 was opened by President Rutherford B. Hayes, testimony to the importance of the Regiment, and testimony to the building itself as a national symbol of the ideals of masculinity and war.

Completed in 1880, the interior design was commissioned to the aesthetic decorators, Associated Artists, with Stanford White as consultant architect. Certainly the themes of the Veteran's Room, the public meeting area, centered around martial triumph, for the "chronological record of warring nations, and of war weapons" was the motif of a frieze on canvas which encircled the room. However, the execution displayed no emblems of the United States, no eagle or American flag. Rather a mythological rendering of twenty cultures and twenty battles transposed the reality of modern warfare into a distant, exotic and nearly fictional experience. . . . One chronicler noted the frieze as a "charming record" of national ornamentation, "the sharp zig-zags of the savages, the eccentricities of the Chinese . . . the many and labyrinthian convolutions of the Moorish, and Byzantine scroll-work."[23]

Interior detail, as well, transposed this masculine space into an ornamented, feminized arena. The textured blue-gray paper was stenciled in a silver and copper chain-link pattern which accented the iron-squared panels in the oak of the wainscotting. This juxtaposition of a chain-link theme in both oak and in shimmering wall coverings diluted the symbolism of bounded military strength as it revealed that aesthetic considerations dominated over military themes: noted one appreciative critic, "the links of copper and of silver color . . . [are] dancing and sparkling over all the surface of the walls." A further rendering of the chain-link pattern extended into the plush velvet and embroidered curtains which covered recessed stained glass windows in the north wall. This chain-link motif, undulating and sumptuous in the folds of the heavy velvet drape, was as fanciful and unreal as was the contrived patina of reddish glaze on the wood paneling which simulated rust on ancient iron walls. Supporting columns were wrapped with a simulacra of the pliable chain-links, patined, as well, to look like rusted medieval artifacts, and fancifully taut "as if giant had pulled home its twines and giants driven the spikes which hold it". . . . A belt of carved work on the wainscot, "tangles of old Saxon or Celtic tracery," jewelled stained glass. . . . and "a weird conception" above the mantel, "a red-tongued dragon . . . with the eagle making clutch at him,". . . . prompted William C. Brownell, the critic, to caution that the symbolism of the ornamentation evoked, not the virile soldier/hero, but "must be set down as phantasmagorical . . . the peculiar temptations of exotics, the temptation to fantastic efflorescence . . . [with] weak and pale tints."[24]

As these details conjured a theatrical setting of suggested medieval jousts or of a pre-modern Celtic past, or of unmanly "weak and pale tints," the balcony structure in the north-west corner evoked the Moorish echoes so popular in domestic aesthetic decoration and in the stage sets for Wilde. Stanford White, given the problem of an asymmetrical tower alcove, wanted to plumb out the space. But the final solution was Louis Comfort Tiffany's design, the replica of an enclosed harem space on a latticed balcony, where the stained glass window was copied from the "pattern of a harem". . . . That the commemoration of a distinguished fighting National Guard unit should include the exotic, artificial mimicry of an Oriental harem retreat suggests how permeable were the boundaries between the real and imagined world under aesthetic dictates. The Veterans Room decor implied, too, that domestic and public interior space could draw on the same aesthetic idioms and artistic applications, rendering a neutrality between the passive feminine sphere and male marketplace. Perhaps it was this acclaimed artistic showpiece that revealed how deeply the emergence of "male weakness" exemplified in the aesthetic life and in the visiting Wilde, and its connections to female domestic aestheticism, had captivated popular imagery during the Aesthetic decades. This aesthetic quest skirted the boundaries of female space and of female forms as it provided space for testing "male weakness" as a cultural asset in a post-war society.[25]

IV

Thus the aesthetic ideology filled the vacuum of historical time and space opened up by the suppression of Civil War carnage and the suppression of the soldier/hero model. As some Americans escaped the psychological effects of the Civil War by accepting an Aesthetic Movement so alien to the bravado of the war years, they accepted too, with the suppression of the Civil War soldier/hero model, the possibility of other definitions of manhood. For the acceptance of invert Wilde was a possible option. In the 1870s and 1880s, the aesthetic ideology suggested new ways to define both manhood and to define Victorian culture itself.

It was this final fear, that culture itself would be as feminine and "weak" as the homosexual Wilde which triggered in part the return to a realism based on the historic Teddy Roosevelt as the masculine icon and the return of virility and war as part of the American ethos. Certainly the imperialist plunge at this time (all the American colonies—Hawaii, the Philippines, Guam, Puerto Rico, the Guantanamo base and the Canal Zone—were obtained between 1898 and 1903) intensified the profile of the soldier/hero as it diminished the role of the aesthete in middle-class culture. Medical authorities were no longer tolerant of the invert in a Wildean model as homosexuality was now labeled as abnormal and decadent. Wilde was castigated as a sodomite at his 1895 trial in London, while the popular media in America neither reported on his trial nor on any of his subsequent plays. Perhaps harking back to the earlier rhetoric of classical republicanism from the Revolutionary era, spokesmen now mirrored the medical authorities by using effeminacy and the invert to scapegoat perceived enemies: for revolutionaries, an effete England; for physicians, threats to the ideal of normalcy; and for imperialists, the weaker and "decadent" Orientals.

For, if the example promulgated by Wilde prevailed, the male citizen, now an effete and "weak" decorator of domestic space, would produce an ineffective and degenerate nation, a nation in which culture was spawned from the hothouse aesthetic environment. Indeed, Wilde would publicly praise J. K. Huysmans's *A Rebours,* a detailed account of an aesthete's deliberate degeneracy into a "strange and extravagant" life amid a domestic suffocation of artificial and luxurious decor: "abnormal indulgences, unnatural pleasures . . . impotence was not far off."[26]

Writing from jail, Wilde, however, understood the compelling importance of the new martial tropes associated with pain and death. Words, warned Wilde defiantly, were "as the fire or knife that makes the delicate flesh burn or bleed." The aesthetic life of the invert was like the soldier/hero's parley with death, a flirtation with "the evil things of life . . . like feasting with panthers." "I used to feel as a snake-charmer," Wilde revealed, lured by "the brightest of gilded snakes, their poison was. . . . part of their perfection." Wilde admitted he once longed to die, but understood now that nothing was meaningless "and suffering least of all." "I am far more of an individual than I ever was," he affirmed.[27]

Wilde's words were lost to an American audience that now discarded the Aesthetic Movement and the ideals of living for art and beauty. If Wilde had, at one point, tentatively incorporated the "male weakness" of aesthetic style into the ethos of middle-class domesticity, he could not, by 1900 at his death, integrate the passion of the soldier/hero into his dying attempts to resuscitate his aesthetic and "weak" self. George Chauncey has charted the evolution of homosexual style in the early twentieth century into the lower and blue collar cultural milieu, a milieu vibrant and open—but one divorced from the middle-class compatibility of the Aesthetic Movement, and one divorced from the acclaimed and light-hearted Wilde who graced Gilded Age America.[28]

Notes

1. Linda L. Carroll, "Who's on Top? Gender as Societal Power of Configuration in Italian Renaissance Drama," *Sixteenth Century Journal,* 20 (Winter 1989), 531-32; Linda Dowling, *Hellenism and Homosexuality in Victorian Oxford* (Ithaca: Cornell University Press, 1994), 149; Arthur N. Gilbert, "Sexual Deviance and Disaster during the Napoleonic Wars," *Albion,* 9 (1977), 98-113.

2. Doreen Bolger Burke et al, eds., *In Pursuit of Beauty: Americans and the Aesthetic Movement* (New York: Metropolitan Museum of Art, Rizzoli, 1986); Roger B. Stein, *John Ruskin and Aesthetic Thought in America, 1840-1900* (Cambridge: Harvard University Press, 1967), 240-54.

3. On the rise of corporate America on the template of a military bureaucracy (multiunit enterprises, hierarchical administration), see Alfred D. Chandler, Jr., *The Visible Hand: The Managerial Revolution in American Business* (Cambridge: Harvard University Press, 1977). On the "soldier aristocrats" as frontier heroes, see Richard Slotkin, *The Fatal Environment: The Myth of the Frontier in the Age of Industrialization* (Middletown, CT: Wesleyan University Press, 1986). On the "manliness" of the Populists, see Nina Silber, *The Romance of Reunion: Northerners and the South, 1865-1900* (Chapel Hill: University of North Carolina Press, 1993), 99-101. On the "militant pragmatism" of the American worker, see Alan Dawley, *Class and Community: The Industrial Revolution in Lynn* (Cambridge: Harvard University Press, 1976), 173-93. On the equation of athletics and war, see E. Anthony Rotundo, *American Manhood: Transformations in Masculinity from the Revolution to the Modern Era* (New York: Basic Books, 1993), 240; Richard Collier, *The General Next to God: The Story of William Booth and the Salvation Army* (New York: E. P. Dutton & Co., Inc., 1965), 80-6, 164-75; William James, "The Moral Equivalent of War," in William James, *Essays on Faith and Morals* (New York: World Publishing, 1972), 311-29.

4. On the suppression of personal expression in wartime, see Edmund Wilson, *Patriotic Gore:*

Studies in the Literature of the American Civil War (Boston: Northeastern University Press, 1962), 487.

5. On the dislocation of the returning veteran, see Henry Adams, *The Education of Henry Adams* (Boston: Houghton Mifflin Co., 1973), 238. On the blurring of historical memory after the Civil War, see Michael Kammen, *Mystic Chords of Memory: The Transformation of Tradition in American Culture* (New York: Alfred A. Knopf, 1991), 93-113, esp. 105, 108-09, 117, 119, 128-29, 141.

6. James D. McCabe, *The Illustrated History of the Centennial Exhibition* (Philadelphia: National Publishing Co., 1876), 3, 125; G. Kurt Piehler, *Remembering War the American Way* (Washington: Smithsonian Institution Press, 1995), 74; Dee A. Brown, *The Year of the Century: 1876* (New York: Charles Scribner's Sons, 1966), 130, 132; John Maass, *The Glorious Enterprise: The Centennial Exhibition of 1876 and H. J. Schwarzmann, Architect-in-Chief* (Watkins Glen, NY: American Life Foundation, 1973), 122. On the decline in Navy power after the Civil War, see William Pierce Randel, *Centennial: American Life in 1876* (Philadelphia: Chilton Book Co., 1969), 159.

7. Mary Ryan, "The American Parade," in Lynn Hunt, ed., *The New Cultural History* (Berkeley: University of California Press, 1989), 149; "Jefferson Davis and His Book," *American Pottery and Glassware Reporter* 5 (1881), 18. On the failure to valorize the inventor of the "Monitor," see John Ericsson, *Contributions to the Centennial Exhibition* (New York: printed for the author at "the Nation" press, 1876), III. On the "dread and heart-ache" of the Civil War veteran, see Marietta Holley, *Samantha at the Centennial* (Hartford: American Publishing Company, 1887), 517; Edmund Wilson, *Patriotic Gore* (New York: Oxford University Press, 1962), 152-58; Ulysses S. Grant, *Memoirs and Selected Letters: Personal Memoirs of U. S. Grant, Selected Letters 1839-1865* (New York: Library of America, 1990), 348.

8. Edmund Wilson notes of Sherman's widow, Ellen: "Her son's dedication to the priesthood was perhaps the price paid by his father for the reckless elation of his March to the Sea." Wilson, ibid., 210, 208-18. On "untrustworthiness" in men after the Civil War, see "The Sense of Honor in Americans," *North American Review* 149 (1889), 207. On the failure of moral reform after the Civil War, see Ronald S. Walters, *American Reformers, 1815-1860* (New York: Hill and Wang, 1978), x.

9. Lutz, ibid., 249-50; George M. Fredrickson, *The Inner Civil War: Northern Intellectuals and the Crisis of the Union* (New York: Harper & Row, 1965), 86, 194-95, 217-38. On Holmes, see Charles Royster, *The Destructive War: William Tecumseh Sherman, Stonewall Jackson, and the Americans* (New York: Alfred A. Knopf, 1991), 280-85;

Wilson, ibid., 743-96; T. J. Jackson Lears, *No Place of Grace: Antimodernism and the Transformation of American Culture, 1880-1920* (New York: Pantheon Books, 1981), 23-24; William Dean Howells, *The Rise of Silas Lapham* (New York: Library of America, 1982), 1046. On the "distancing, if not expunging of the *working* war" in Civil War photography, see Alan Trachtenberg, "Albums of War: On Reading Civil War Photographs," in Philip Fisher, ed., *The New American Studies* (Berkeley: University of California Press, 1991), 287-319.

10. Linda S. Ferber and William H. Gerdts, *The New Path: Ruskin and the American Pre-Raphaelites* (New York: Schocken Books, Inc., 1985), 50-51. On Frederic Church's Hudson River School as "alien . . . defunct or moribund," see Clarence Cook, "Art in America in 1883," *Princeton Review* (January-May 1883), 312. On Elihu Vedder and John La Farge as the new artists with a "psychology in color . . . [and] the language of the soul," see "Fifty Years of American Art, 1828-1878," *Harper's New Monthly Magazine,* 59 (June to November 1879), 495; Alan Gowans, "Painting and Sculpture," in Wendell D. Garrett et al, *The Nineteenth Century: Arts in America* (New York: Charles Scribner's Sons, 1969), 235, 238; Elizabeth Brown, *Albert Pinkham Ryder* (Washington, D.C.: National Museum of American Art, Smithsonian Institution, 1990); Lois Marie Fink, interview with author, 23 May 1990, Smithsonian National Museum of Art; Lois Marie Fink, *American Art at the Nineteenth-Century Salons* (New York: Cambridge University Press, 1990), 163, 164, 211; Wilson, ibid., 49, 68, 69, 91, 96.

11. On Chase's portrait of Whistler as controversial, see Ronald G. Pisano, *William Merritt Chase* (Seattle: University of Washington, 1983), 81. On the multiplicity, divergence, and anti-enclosure of Eakins, Sargent (and Henry James) as well as the sexual ambivalence of Sargent and James as due to their lack of participation in the Civil War, see David M. Lubin, *Act of Betrayal: Eakins, Sargent, James* (New Haven: Yale University Press, 1985), 14-21; Elizabeth Johns, *Thomas Eakins: The Heroism of Modern Life* (Princeton: Princeton University Press, 1983), esp. 144-69.

12. Brooklyn Museum, *The American Renaissance, 1876-1917* (New York: Pantheon Books, 1979), 42-43; Alan Gowans, "Painting and Sculpture," in Wendell D. Garrett et al, *The Arts of America: The Nineteenth Century* (New York: Charles Scribner's Sons, 1969), 264-65; Kirk Savage, "The Politics of Memory, Black Emancipation and the Civil War Monument," in John R. Gillis, ed., *Commemorations: The Politics of National Identity* (Princeton: Princeton University Press, 1994), 127-49. G. Kurt Piehler notes that Civil War battlefields weren't preserved until the late nineteenth century: Piehler, ibid., 66-69.

13. On the Civil War as an apocalyptic vision, see Royster, ibid., and Russell F. Weigley, "War as Apocalypse in Nineteenth-Century America," *Reviews in American History,* 20 (September 1992), 326-30. On male supremacy in wartime, see William Divale and Marvin Harris, "Population, Warfare, and the Male Supremacist Complex," *American Anthropologist,* 78 (1976), 521-38. By 1898, Civil War veterans would protest the choice of a female figure as "Victory" because it lacked "martial character." See Phieler, ibid., 83; Martha Banta, *Imaging American Women: Idea and Ideals in Cultural History* (New York: Columbia University Press, 1987), 481; John Wilmerding, *American Views: Essays on American Art* (Princeton: Princeton University Press, 1991), 273-75.

14. Roberta A. Park, "Biological Thought: Athletics and the Formation of a 'Man of Character,': 1830-1900," in J. A. Mangan and James Walvin, eds., *Manliness and Morality: Middle-Class Masculinity in Britain and America, 1800-1940* (New York: St. Martin's Press, 1987), 7-35; E. Anthony Rotundo, "Learning about Manhood: Gender Ideals and the Middle-Class Family in Nineteenth-Century America," in Mangan and Walvin, ibid., 35-51; Lloyd Lewis and Henry Justin Smith, *Oscar Wilde Discovers America, 1882* (New York: Benjamin Blom, 1936).

15. Roger B. Stein, "Artifact as Ideology: The Aesthetic Movement in Its American Cultural Context," in Burke, ibid., 26; *Brooklyn Daily Eagle.* 3 Jan. 1882, p. 2. On the institutionalization of "manly" love in the nineteenth century, see Jeffrey Richards, "'Passing the Love of Women': Manly Love and Victorian Society," in Mangan and Walvin, ibid., 92-123. On homoerotic tendencies in straight men, see Martin Bauml Duberman, *About Time: Exploring the Gay Past* (New York, 1986), 43-45. On Wilde as the leader of a homosexual subculture in London, see Jonathan Dollimore, "Different Desires: Subjectivity and Transgression in Wilde and Gide," *Genders,* 2 (Summer 1988), 34.

16. On the view that nineteenth century Americans "who were wholly heterosexual were obsessed with homosexuality," see Dr. Hendrik M. Ruitenbeek, *Homosexuality and Creative Genius* (New York: Astor-Honor, Inc., 1967), 134-35; Jonathan Katz, *Gay/Lesbian Almanac* (New York: Harper & Row, 1983), 213, 219, 221, 235; Jonathan Katz, *Gay American History: Lesbians and Gay Men in the U.S.A.* (New York: Harper Colophon Books, 1987), 47, 368; George Chauncey, Jr., "Negotiating the Boundaries of Masculinity: Gay Identities and Culture in the Early Twentieth Century," paper presented 9 December 1989, conference on "Constructing Masculinities," Rutgers Center for Historical Analysis. On the nineteenth century homosexual culture at City Hall and in Battery Park (and the "silences" over the term sodomite), see Michael Lynch, "Silent Sodom," paper presented 5 November 1989, American Studies Association International Convention, Toronto.

17. Richard Ellmann, "Oscar Meets Walt," *New York Review,* 3 Dec. 1987, 44. "Wilde and Whitman," *Newark Daily Advertiser,* 20 Jan. 1882, 1. Ellman, *Oscar Wilde,* 166-72. *Washington Post,* 21 Jan. 1882, 2; Oscar Wilde to Walt Whitman, from New York, 1 Mar. 1882, Feinberg/Whitman Collection, Manuscript Division, Library of Congress. For a critique of Whitman, see "Walt Whitman's Poems," *Littell's Living Age,* 13 (Jan.-Mar. 1876), 91-102. On Whitman as a homosexual ("the scandalous suppression or bigoted interpretation of Whitman's homosexuality"), see Katz, *History,* 337. On Whitman's disavowal of his homosexuality to John Addington Symonds, see Katz, *History,* 337-57. On Whitman as a homosexual and American man of letters, Ruitenbeek, ibid., 120-40. On perceived connections between Whitman and the "peculiarly hot-house atmosphere of Mr. Rossetti," see Robert Moore Limpus, *American Criticism of British Decadence, 1880-1900* (Chicago: University of Chicago Libraries, 1939), 71. On Wilde's homosexuality: at Portora Royal School in Ireland, see Woodcock, ibid., 24; at Oxford, see Richard Pine, *Oscar Wilde* (Dublin: Gill and Macmillan, 1983), 19; as claimed by Robert Ross in 1886, see Percy Colson, "Oscar Wilde and the Problem of Sexual Inversion," in The Marquess of Queensberry, *Oscar Wilde and the Black Douglas* (New York: Folcroft Library Editions, 1977), 167; as a bisexual, see Martin Fido, *Oscar Wilde* (New York: Viking Press, 1973), 41. On Whitman's homoeroticism as a reflection of acceptable same-sex love in the nineteenth century, see David S. Reynolds, *Walt Whitman's America: A Cultural Biography* (New York: Alfred A. Knopf, 1995), 391-403.

18. On the Cleveland Street scandal, see Katz, *Almanac,* 215-16; Hyde, ibid., 123-27; Ed Cohen, *Talk on the Wilde Side: Toward a Genealogy of a Discourse on Male Sexuality* (New York: Routledge, 1993), 121-35; "Dancing in Stock Exchange," *Harper's New Monthly Magazine,* 71 (18 Nov. 1885), 844; "Oscar Wilde in Wall Street," *Washington Post,* 20 Sept. 1882, p. 2.

19. On incidents of impersonation, see "Oscar Field, How the Managing Editor of the Tribune Palmed Himself Off as Oscar Wilde," *Denver Republican,* 17 Apr. 1882, 1; on a bum's impersonation of Wilde, "Oscar Wilde's Renaissance," *National Police Gazette,* 11 March 1882, 7; on a St. Louis grocer's impersonation of Wilde, *New Orleans Times Picayune,* 28 June 1882, 2; on impersonations of Wilde in Milwaukee, "Rich Revelations, What May Be Expected When Milwaukee Men Don Oscar Wilde Attire," *Milwaukee Sentinel,* 5 March 1882, 7; *National Police Gazette,* 21 Jan. 1882, 10; *National Police Gazette,* 11 March 1882, 7; *Jerseyman* (Morristown), 6 Jan. 1882, 2.

20. John Crowley, "Charles Warren Stoddard: Locating Desire," paper presented 5 November 1989, American Studies Association International Meeting, Toronto.

21. Michael Moon, "'The Gentle Boy from the Dangerous Classes:' Pederasty, Domesticity, and Capitalism in Horatio Alger," in Fisher, ibid., 260-87; Vern L. Bullough, *Sexual Variance in Society and History* (New York: John Wiley & Sons, 1976), 611; Katz, *History,* 33; Brian Harrison, "Underneath the Victorians," *Victorian Studies,* 10 (Mar. 1987), 239. On the "high proportion of deviates" among lower-class emigrant groups to America, see Bullough, ibid., 607.

22. *Salt Lake Tribune,* 5 March 1882, 6; *Milwaukee Sentinel,* 5 March 1882, 6; *Milwaukee Sentinel,* 6 March 1882, 5; *Boston Evening Transcript,* 14 Jan. 1882, 6; "Oscar Wilde's Talk," (*Denver*) *Tribune,* 16 Apr. 1882, 12; *Newark Daily News,* 10 Jan. 1882, 3; *Brooklyn Daily Eagle,* 4 Jan. 1882, 2; *Independent,* 7 Sept. 1882, 25.

23. *The Veteran's Room, Seventh Regiment, N.G.S., N.Y. Armory* (New York: "Privately printed," 1881), 17.

24. *The Veteran's Room,* 13, 18; William C. Brownell, "The Seventh Regiment Armory," *Scribner's Monthly,* 22 (July 1881), 374-75, 378; Burke, ibid., 125-27.

25. Lisa Weilbacker, "The Decoration of the Veterans' Room by Louis Comfort Tiffany with Associated Artists," paper presented 21 November 1992, Victorian Society in America Fall Symposium, New York; Lisa Weilbacker, interview by author, 28 January 1993 and 1 February 1994.

26. J. K. Huysmans, *Against the Grain* (*A Rebours*) (1884; rept. New York: Three Sirens Press, 1931; Dover Publications, Inc., 1969), 7.

27. Limpus, ibid., 84-5; Terry L. Chapman, "'An Oscar Wilde Type': 'The Abominable Crime of Buggery' in Western Canada, 1890-1920," *Criminal Justice History,* 4 (1983), 97-118; Oscar Wilde, "De Profundis," in *Complete Works,* ibid., 755, 808, 788.

28. George Chauncey, *Gay New York: Gender, Urban Culture, and the Making of the Gay Male World, 1890-1940* (New York: Basic Books, 1994).

Stacy A. Cordery (essay date 1996)

SOURCE: "Women in Industrializing America," in *The Gilded Age: Essays on the Origins of Modern America,* edited by Charles W. Calhoun, Scholarly Resources, Inc., 1996, pp. 111-35.

[In the excerpt below, Cordery enumerates the limitations placed on women by the domestic ideologies of the Gilded Age and shows how, in spite of these, many women were influential activists.]

Women were 48 percent of the population during the Gilded Age.[1] Rather than attempting to describe the condition of women of every class, race, ethnicity, religion, and region (among the many categories possible), this essay focuses on how the origins of modern America affected women. As a near majority of the populace, women could not help being touched in tangible ways by the tensions that arose as the nineteenth century gave way to the twentieth. The determining context of Gilded Age America was the acceleration of industrialization. This process recast the ideology of woman's "separate sphere" and shaped the urban experience of migrants and immigrants. During this period, women's political campaigns, and above all the push for women's rights begun in 1848, gathered adherents and credibility. In addition, the continuing associational movement, the breakdown of the separate sphere, the increasing numbers of women in the labor force, and the westward movement affected the lives of middle- and working-class women. Many important trends evident during the Gilded Age presaged the emergence of the "new woman" of the Progressive Era.

The "typical" woman of the Gilded Age was white, middle class (broadly defined), Protestant, native born, married, and living in a small town. She was likely to be better educated than her mother and also likely to have fewer children.[2] The received wisdom about her sexuality saw her as "passionless," and the patriarchal society gave her little active control over her medical health or reproductive system.[3] She was assumed—and she assumed herself to be—morally superior to her husband and closer to God. Her husband as likely as not worked away from the home. She rarely stepped into the public sphere, confining her daily actions to the home. If she was among the small but increasing number of women who did move into public life, she did so within the supportive context of church-related or secular women's associations. Her causes ranged from the bold demand for suffrage to the popular temperance crusade, with myriad reforms in between. If she was a member of a woman's club, her children were probably grown or she had servants or she was unmarried or widowed. Her late nineteenth-century ideas about women and men were based on the "asexual nature of women and their concomitant moral superiority."[4] This dual ideology, stressing gender differences, fueled growing feminist demands among middle-class women, both white and black.[5]

Industrialization, which had begun in the United States approximately forty years before the Civil War, continued in the postwar decades to change the lives of middle-class women and reconfigure their households. The man's workplace moved out of the home and took the man with it—out of the middle-class woman's day. Instead of participating in his livelihood, she was confined to the domestic sphere, forbidden by social custom to appear in public without her husband or a chaperone (her father's representative if she was unmarried). As industrialization made deeper inroads into American society, middle-class men counted their worth in dollars and affirmed their masculinity by participating in men's rituals such as politics, fraternal associations, and sports—and both their masculine and their economic credentials were validated in the figure of the pious, pure, domestic, submissive, and leisured wife. Historian Barbara Welter termed this conception of women "the cult of true womanhood."[6]

With some exceptions, nineteenth-century Americans, both men and women, believed that a woman should be confined to the home. Her separate sphere—the domestic, female sphere—entailed certain tasks and responsibilities. She was the model wife and mother, and her highest calling was to bear and raise children. On her shoulders devolved the responsibility for rearing not only polite and well-mannered children but also children well-schooled in the precepts of Christianity. As the man returned home from the ruthless, amoral, competitive, materialistic world of work and politics—his sphere—she stood by him, gently questioning his morals or his religious habits only when they slipped from the ideal. She was to provide "a haven in a heartless world" for her besieged husband.[7] On the one hand, the social dictates of the cult of true womanhood put men and women in conflicting roles and defined the normal female life as one lived at home as a wife and mother in the company of women friends leading similar lives. On the other hand, they provided a safe, secure, and empowering space—a "female world of love and ritual"—from which women could set forth to ameliorate society's ills.[8] Nursing the spiritual and physical health of her immediate family had its analogy in serving the needs of strangers. Of course, these accepted notions of women in the nineteenth century applied most forcefully to white, middle-class women. Whether or not the notion trickled down to the working class or gained currency in all ethnic and racial communities is debatable. Even as the Gilded Age dawned, the idea of the "true woman" in her separate sphere was belied by increasing numbers of working women and those white and black middle-class women who were venturing out of the home and into the political realm.

Ironically, industrialization provided the impetus both for the creation of the separate sphere and for the effort by middle-class women to break out of it. Industrialization changed the way women worked within the home, supplying time-saving domestic appliances and often giving them greater leisure. It also created jobs outside the home for more and more women. By the turn of the century, one in seven women was employed. Most were single and fending for themselves. Some married women worked in remunerative jobs to supplement their husbands' insufficient incomes. The industrial work force dwelt in cities, and the squalor, disease, and wretched living conditions among the working poor created many social ills that middle-class women determined they should try to correct.

White and black women since the colonial era had formed organizations to provide charitable relief, but these associations multiplied during the Gilded Age as the industrializing cities filled with immigrants and rural Americans. Many nineteenth-century women's relief organizations be-

gan as study clubs—themselves a continuation of an earlier movement for women's self-improvement—but branched out to render relief to the poor, to provide assistance for immigrants, or to care for orphans and "wayward women." Reform groups used a voluntary work force to raise money, petition local and state governments, visit the objects of their charity, teach lessons in moral uplift, and make the larger community aware of the plight of the less fortunate. As they did so, they pushed against the customary boundary of the woman's sphere.

By far, the most popular women's association of the nineteenth century was the Women's Christian Temperance Union (WCTU). Founded in 1873 as a single-issue association, it soon became inextricably linked with the ideas and goals of its most prominent member and, by 1879, its president, Frances Willard. Her slogan was "Do Everything," and the women who flocked to join pursued various avenues of reform. The WCTU was managed locally and had chapters in every state. Claiming over 175,000 members by 1900, it was the largest women's organization in existence. The WCTU quickly moved past its early efforts at curtailing men's use of alcohol. From praying in saloons, the WCTU went on to run newspapers, own businesses, pay temperance speakers to preach the evils of alcohol, and care for the children of alcoholics. If nothing else, the WCTU demonstrated to women the effectiveness of their actions when organized—even across class and racial lines.[9] The leading African-American spokeswoman in the temperance fight was Frances Harper. She served as Superintendent of Colored Work in the WCTU, but labored hard, particularly in the South, to prevent white women from blaming the bulk of alcohol abuse on African-American men. While Willard welcomed black women to the WCTU, she did not run an organization free of racism. African-American women were not represented among the upper echelons of WCTU management, for example, nor were black delegates treated equally at regional or national meetings. Prominent African Americans such as Ida B. Wells and Josephine St. Pierre Ruffin supported the cause of temperance but deplored the overt racism of most of the WCTU women.

In the late 1870s, Willard converted to the cause of suffrage because she believed that the women's vote would bring about restrictions on alcohol that would help in her goal of home protection. As she threw the considerable weight of the WCTU into the suffrage fray, her support did not immediately garner votes for women. It did, however, introduce many other women to the suffrage idea from a friendly source. After Willard's death in 1898, the WCTU backed away from its militant prosuffrage position and focused again on the eradication of alcohol use.

While other groups had fewer members than the WCTU, their benefits and agendas could be just as multifaceted. Historian Anne Firor Scott credits club women with "inventing Progressivism" in the 1880s. In that decade, increasing numbers of women's clubs began "municipal housekeeping," or putting their piety, purity, and domesticity to work in the world around them. Literary and study club members became aware of the unsavory conditions of their towns and cities, usually through some unexpected personal experience. They communicated their shock, horror, and sadness at the conditions of their cities to their colleagues and then set to work. Scott's breakdown of the many types of municipal housekeeping is eye-opening. In the category of education, women engaged in political activity, promoted curricular innovations such as parent education, vacation schools, and special education for disabled children, and created structural innovations such as visiting nurses, vocational guidance, libraries, and school sanitation. Under the category of public health, women called for regulation of the water and milk supplies, pure food and drug legislation, sanitary garbage-disposal legislation, dental clinics, hospitals, well-baby clinics, school lunch programs, and public baths and laundries. Women combatted social evils by lobbying to close brothels, by setting up detention homes for delinquent girls, and by supporting vice commissions and scientific studies of prostitution and venereal disease. The category of recreation included pushing for legislation to regulate motion pictures and dance halls, and the building of playgrounds, gymnasiums, concert halls, and working-girls' clubs. Women's associations sponsored similar reforms in the categories of housing, social service, corrections, public safety, civic improvement, and assimilation of the races. The breadth of women's clubs' activities evinced the grassroots nature of the work. The General Federation of Women's Clubs (GFWC), founded in 1890, was the umbrella organization for white women's clubs, and it was the job of the GFWC to disseminate information and assistance on these seemingly countless programs.[10]

Separate female institutions boosted women's self-esteem, turned them into expert parliamentarians, introduced them to a wider world, put them at their ease in public places, and provided them with invigorating and supportive circles of friends and coworkers. For many women, club work became their career. Anna J. H. Pennybacker, a white, middle-class southern widow with a normal-school education, supported her three children in part from the profits of some rental houses but primarily from paid lectures to women's organizations all across the United States. They were her network of friends—colleagues upon whom she called for everything from emotional support to financial donations for the Belgian orphans during World War I. She founded three women's clubs, was a member of at least eight throughout her life (she often belonged to more than one at a time), and held various elected positions in them. She was president of the Texas Federation of Women's Clubs, the GFWC, and the Chautauqua Woman's Club. Her dedication to organized womanhood, as she called it, was lifelong, and she was not atypical.

In the Gilded Age, sometimes called the nadir for African Americans, middle-class black women labored in a racist society that denied them access to politics, the legal system, and governmental support. Because they were accustomed to depending upon their own initiative, it is possible that a larger percentage of black women engaged in associational work more frequently than did white women.[11] Like their white counterparts, black women had been organizing benevolent societies, often church-related, since the colonial era, and the acceleration of industrialization with its accompanying social ills generated more associations. Middle-class African-American women combined the bourgeois ideologies of the separate sphere and the cult of true womanhood with other qualities prized by the African-American community: intelligence, racial consciousness, an emphasis on education, self-confidence, and outspokenness.[12] These qualities stood women in good stead as racial slurs and attacks on their femininity from whites grew more shrill and were published in "respectable" journals. For Gilded Age black women, race and gender could not be divided. In part, the too-often invisible charitable work that women pursued was a rebuke to racist critics.[13]

African-American women moved from study clubs to municipal housekeeping, just as white club women did. The Art and Study Club of Moline, Illinois, visited the sick and clothed the poor. The Adelphi Club of St. Paul, Minnesota, distributed food, called on the ill in the hospital, and supported a South Carolina kindergarten and a local orphanage. African-American women elsewhere organized or managed homes for the elderly, juvenile delinquents, working women, unwed mothers, and orphans. They started hospitals and public health clinics. They created employment services and programs to train kindergarten teachers and librarians, thus, as historian Stephanie Shaw points out, turning club work into community development.[14] Black women's clubs engaged in municipal housekeeping to provide the sort of social services that the white power structure denied to African Americans, particularly in the South.

Many women's clubs took advantage of networking possibilities by joining an umbrella association. The Colored Women's League was the first to organize in 1892. Three years later, the National Federation of Afro-American Women formed. In 1896 both groups combined their resources to create the National Association of Colored Women (NACW), which provided assistance on the state and local level for various women's clubs' projects. Mary Church Terrell became its first president. "Lifting as We Climb" was the motto of the NACW. It made reference to "racial uplift," always a major goal of black club women.

Another important result of women's participation in voluntary associations was their heightened political acumen. Women learned to voice their demands in front of hostile audiences and to articulate critical rebuttals. Women in associations governed themselves, kept minutes, elected officers, presided over meetings, wrote out platforms, managed finances, and lobbied male politicians. Speaking about the seven years her club spent in preparation and study before tackling the prevailing social problems, the president of the Chicago Women's Club believed that "no one acquainted with the difficulty of managing large interests by means of a body of untrained women, without business habits or parliamentary experience, can feel that these years of preparation and education were wasted. It is my firm conviction that without this preliminary training we should never have attained that steadiness of purpose and that broad habit of looking at all sides of a question which has made us a power in the community."[15] They gained a sense of pride and increased self-esteem, even as they pushed against the behavioral codes that mainstream society prescribed for them.

All of the clubs taught women about the male political system. The increasing membership and rapidly multiplying types of women's associations were two hallmarks of the era. In the Gilded Age, the older, natural-rights justification for suffrage gave way to an ideology that embraced differences between women and men. Women redefined their sphere by emphasizing the transcendent piety and purity of "true womanhood." Most late nineteenth-century women who ventured out of their sphere did so under the banner of moral superiority. Society could hardly chastise women who were simply taking care of widows and orphans. From there it was a short step to the late Gilded Age notion of women becoming more overtly political. The Texas Federation of Women's Clubs noted in January 1901 that "while it is not the desire of Texas club women to 'get into politics,' there are matters to the furtherance of which the Federation stands pledged, that can only be consummated by legislation."[16]

If politics is defined as "any action, formal or informal, taken to affect the course or behavior of government or the community," then women of the nineteenth century—black and white, native-born and immigrant—engaged in a full spectrum of political activities.[17] In traditional politics, women supported men's activities. They made the food for the party gatherings. They sewed the political banners. In some cases, they participated in political parades dressed as the Goddess of Liberty or Columbia. Nevertheless, they could not vote. Legal and ideological constraints kept women from exercising their full franchise, and the push for women's suffrage claimed only a few proponents in the Gilded Age.[18] Giving women the vote and allowing them to occupy elected positions was the proposed reform that most directly challenged the era's gendered notion of politics. Women who appropriated the privileges of the man's sphere would not only cause social disaster—because they would not be at home to care for their families—but they would lose their position of moral superiority as they stepped down into the morass of chicanery that was politics. Furthermore, voting was a man's privilege. Ever since the passage of the Fifteenth Amendment in 1870, which gave the ballot to black men, all women understood that what kept them from the polls was only their sex. The vast majority of Americans quite happily maintained a masculine body politic. Nevertheless, some intrepid women carried on the fight begun at the first women's rights conference at Seneca Falls, New York, in 1848.

The Declaration of Sentiments, adopted by the two hundred and fifty women and forty men at Seneca Falls, became the platform of the nineteenth-century women's rights movement. Suffrage was the most radical reform in a host of demands concerning education, religion, property rights, and marriage and divorce laws. While all of these reforms would find advocates, suffrage became linked with Elizabeth Cady Stanton and Susan B. Anthony. These two friends had begun to push against the woman's sphere before the Civil War when they joined the ranks of the abolitionists. In 1869, however, Stanton, Anthony, and others criticized the Fifteenth Amendment and the Republican party, which sponsored it, because it excluded women. That year, they founded the National Woman Suffrage Association (NWSA). NWSA members felt passionately about suffrage—even to the point of adopting the racist argument that many white women were more fit to vote than many black men enfranchised by the Fifteenth Amendment. The NWSA worked throughout the Gilded Age to convince Americans of the need for a federal constitutional amendment for women's suffrage. Even though agitating for the vote was controversial and demanded of its crusaders the bravery to stand untroubled in the storm of public criticism, Stanton and Anthony faced competition from a rival organization. Created the year before the NWSA, the American Woman Suffrage Association (AWSA) believed it best not to fight passage of the Fifteenth Amendment, agreeing with Frederick Douglass that it was "the Negro's hour." The AWSA's strategy was to do battle state by state, by convincing legislators to insert the word "women" into or remove the word "men" from their suffrage laws. Throughout the Gilded Age these two associations fought each other for scarce members, financial backers, and support from male politicians.[19]

While the AWSA generally limited its concern to getting the vote, the NWSA called for several reforms. In 1892, Stanton attempted to explain the interconnectedness of the reforms to members of the House Judiciary Committee, stating that "the strongest reason why we ask for woman a voice in the government under which she lives; in the religion she is asked to believe; equality in social life, where she is the chief factor; a place in the trades and professions, where she may earn her bread, is because of her birthright to self-sovereignty; because, as an individual, she must rely on herself. No matter how much women prefer to lean, to be protected and supported, nor how much men desire to have them do so, they must make the voyage of life alone, and for safety in an emergency they must know something of the laws of navigation."[20] Even though the AWSA and the NWSA did not share the same strategy, they did pursue the same main goal. In 1890 the two organizations merged, becoming the National American Woman Suffrage Association (NAWSA). Stanton and Anthony were the first two presidents. The impetus for the merger came from the repeated failures of either organization to gain real progress toward the vote; from the (by then) enlarged sphere of middle-class women who had been participating in many social reforms; and from the grudging acknowledgment among a few more men and women that the vote for women would not destroy the family but might instead purify the immoral political realm. Caught up in the fervor of professionalism sweeping the country, and to accommodate fairly former members of the old organizations, the NAWSA formalized its procedures. It adopted the AWSA strategy of a state-by-state ballot referendum. Although the reformed NAWSA garnered additional members in the last decade of the nineteenth century, it failed to convince the majority of Americans to eschew their firm antisuffrage sentiments.

Neither the AWSA, the NWSA, nor the NAWSA could boast any real success in the Gilded Age. Eight states held referenda on women's suffrage, but none passed. The two states that did allow women to vote, Utah and Wyoming, did so for reasons having little to do with the suffragists. Utah gave women the vote to conserve its Mormon hegemony as more "gentiles" moved in, and Wyoming hoped to encourage families to settle in its desolate and sparsely populated territory. While wary of the ballot, state legislators were more receptive to the other demands in the women's-rights pantheon. By the close of the century, several states had passed laws to end women's "civil death" upon marriage. Thanks to suffragists and other reformers, many states allowed married women to own and dispose of property, to initiate lawsuits, to enter into legal contracts, and to keep their own earnings and distribute them as they wanted. In some states women were given guardianship over their children in the wake of a divorce. Although the long struggle for the vote would not be won nationwide until 1920, these by-products of the suffrage battle were great victories in their own right.

Along with club work and suffrage, middle-class women turned to another area of reform during the Gilded Age. To share in the misfortunes of the inner-city work force and to put their Christian beliefs into action, a number of women—often college educated and unmarried—lived among the poor in settlement houses. American cities were notorious for crime, disease, unhygienic living conditions, unsafe workplaces, and unscrupulous employers who would take advantage of the newly arrived. Amidst the noise and filth, women created a safe environment that was for them an alternative to standard family life. For the people they served, settlement houses were partly training schools and partly recreation centers. Settlement workers tried in multiple ways to make life better: they set up libraries; health clinics; kindergartens; night schools; classes in English, nutrition, politics, art, music, and vocational training; boys and girls' clubs; and penny savings banks.

The most famous settlement house was Hull House, founded in 1889 by Jane Addams and her partner, Ellen Gates Starr. Patterned on Toynbee Hall in London, England, this Chicago institution became itself the model for others to follow. Originally intending to uplift local working-class immigrants, the women associated with Hull House worked with the city and state government to lobby for antisweatshop legislation, an eight-hour work day, and a minimum wage. Hull House had its own women's club and men's club, gymnasium, public bath and kitchen, and labor museum. Trade unions held meetings at Hull House.

Addams and the women who lived and worked with her— Mary Rozet Smith, Florence Kelley, Julia Lathrop, Alice Hamilton, Grace Abbott—simultaneously sought to meet the needs of their neighbors and to weaken the power of the corrupt political bosses.[21] With different levels of success, hundreds of settlement houses opened across the United States. Janie Porter Barrett, a graduate of Hampton Institute, founded the Locust Street Settlement House in Hampton, Virginia, in the 1890s. This home for African Americans grew from her own charitable and informal instruction of young women at her residence. Barrett taught household management and job training skills for preparation both as wives and workers. Lillian Wald, a public-health nurse, began living among poor immigrants in New York in 1893. Her Henry Street Settlement House was established in 1895 to care for the medical, vocational, and social needs of her neighbors. Like Hull House, Henry Street became a bastion of civic reform. It offered safe playgrounds for children, campaigned to eradicate tuberculosis, and sponsored scholarships for needy boys and girls. Women such as Eleanor Roosevelt and Amelia Earhart worked for short periods in settlement houses and considered their time there formative and enlightening.

The effect of industrialization on working-class women had little to do with voluntary action and reformulating the boundaries of the separate sphere. Females provided labor to fuel industrialization. Women comprised 14 percent of the total work force in 1870 and 16 percent in 1890. At the same time, the percentage of all women who worked outside the home steadily increased throughout the Gilded Age: 15 percent in 1870, 16 percent in 1880, 19 percent in 1890, and 21 percent in 1900. The typical female worker was young, urban, single, and either an immigrant or the daughter of immigrants, who lived at home with her family. Her work was temporary—just until she married. The job she was most likely to hold was that of domestic servant.[22] Her labor in the homes of middle-class women allowed the latter more leisure to do their voluntary work. By definition, female wage workers contradicted the dominant social ideology of the cult of true womanhood. Middle-class reformers, physicians, ministers, and editors warned women that they would "unfit themselves" for marriage and motherhood if they continued in the work force. Yet, most women worked not because they wanted to but because family economics demanded it.

The only consistent exceptions seem to be women who were self-employed and some farmers' daughters. The former found their precarious independence usually better than being a wife, or better than being only a wife.[23] Farmers' daughters craved the independence and excitement of a city job, but the extent to which their salary was necessary for the family's survival is unclear. Wages for women were consistently lower than those for men and, in fact, provided barely enough for an individual to live on. The average cost of living for a self-supporting female worker was estimated to be $5.51 per week, but the average wage was $5.68 per week. Employers viewed women as temporary workers who labored for "pin money," not a wage necessary to support a family. Therefore, not only public sentiment but also the inequitable wage system placed laboring women in a difficult position.[24]

Prostitutes constituted a category unto themselves. While women's reform associations certainly censured this job choice, prostitutes frequently made a better wage than other working women, and, depending upon their situation, often enjoyed preferable working conditions. Female brothel owners could make great sums of money, but few prostitutes could acquire the necessary capital to open and run their own establishment. Married women sometimes engaged in prostitution, with or without the knowledge of their husbands, to add to the family's income. A few women were forced into it by bosses or family members. By far, the largest number of women who became prostitutes lived alone or suffered from chronically low wages, or both. Most did not stay in the field long and professed the same desire to be married and have children as other women.[25]

Domestic workers could be cooks, maids, laundresses, and nannies, in any combination. Married women and single women, immigrants, daughters of immigrants, native-born blacks, and native-born whites all worked as domestics. Numerically, foreign-born women held the most domestic positions, even though native-born white women were the most sought after by employers. Native-born servants dominated in the countryside, as did immigrants in the cities and African Americans in the South. In urban California, Mexican-American women who worked were usually domestics. Most domestics were "live-in" servants who received room and board for their work, along with a small wage. Employers preferred live-ins for various reasons, not the least of which was the round-the-clock surveillance. Daughters of immigrants and native-born servants more often lived with their employers than did African-American domestics. As the century progressed and more white women moved into factory and office work—two remunerative avenues closed to black women—African Americans led the trend to servants living outside the home. Living away more easily accommodated a married servant, and racism also played a role in black domestics living elsewhere. Many upper- and middle-class white women thought that the model of their own lives would uplift and assimilate poor immigrant servants, but for black women, that was not considered a realistic goal.

The relations between female employers and their domestic servants could be uncomfortable and fraught with tension. Domestics complained of being on call twenty-four hours a day and scrutinized at every task. They hated the tedious labor and the inherent inequality between themselves and the mistress. The job was lonely, as families usually employed just one domestic. She had no close friend nearby, nor even a sympathetic ear. If the employer was much older than the domestic, a maternal relationship might exist. This could be fulfilling for both women, or, especially if the employer was prejudiced, it could result in condescension and domineering treatment. For their part, employers complained about maids who broke and stole household goods, who wanted too much time off or were ill too frequently, and who were ignorant, lazy, forgetful, noisy, or rude. Conflict between Protestant employers and Catholic employees added to the mutual mistrust.[26]

In the urban South, nearly five times as many married black women as white women worked outside the home. Most of these wives were domestics. They were often forced into wage labor because of their husbands' low incomes. The majority of single, black female workers were domestics, too. In rural communities, African-American women in the South labored also in the cotton and rice fields, jobs that had been forced on them since slavery. Because white women would not work in someone else's fields, this backbreaking labor was reserved in the postbellum South for African Americans. Very few black women worked in factories, but their numbers increased as the century wore on. Almost none worked in white-collar jobs such as clerk and saleswoman. One of the major differences between black and white women workers was the support received at home. Black communities—although they might have glorified the domestic ideal of womanhood—conceded that economic necessity forced wives into the work force, and hence were less critical of women who worked after marriage.

Although native-born white women in early textile factories such as those in Lowell, Massachusetts, had constituted the first industrial laborers in America, by the Gilded Age the majority of the female industrial work force was comprised of foreign-born women or their American-born daughters. In immigrant communities wives and mothers took in boarders, but daughters went away from the home to work. Industry was not wide open for women. Instead, jobs were clustered in garment factories (in the manufacture both of cloth and clothing), laundries, carpet factories, tobacco factories, canneries, meat-packing plants, candy factories, and book-binderies. These jobs were extensions of "women's work" in the home. Because most women in industry were young, unskilled, and unmarried, bosses considered them temporary hires and paid them far less than they paid male laborers. The female work force was usually tractable—a result of the expected docile nature of women and also of the general exclusion of women from labor unions whose male members perceived women's labor as a threat to their own employment. Industrial jobs had the benefit of a shorter workday than domestic service (usually ten hours or longer at the beginning of the Gilded Age and eight by the turn of the century). Factory work, however, could be dangerous, unhealthy, difficult, boring, and cyclical. Industries had no safety codes as the Gilded Age dawned and no regulations regarding breaks, vacations, retirement, workers' compensation, injury pay or time off, or sexual harassment. In the 1890s, often because of the efforts of female reformers, factory codes began to improve working conditions.

Working women did express their unhappiness with the system of labor in the United States; when they went on strike, however, their protests were tailored to the local situation. Women's strikes in the Gilded Age were rarely successful. Most trade unions were closed to them, and so they did not have the benefit of male support and sheer numbers. Men did not welcome women into trade unions because they believed that the lower-paid women's work force would displace them or force wages down. Unskilled women worked the machines that had initially put skilled male workers on the unemployment lines, and thus the introduction of women into a field often heralded a new, and unwelcome, era for an industry and for the men who had previously worked it alone. Leonara Barry led the recruitment drive on behalf of the Knights of Labor from her position as the organization's general investigator of women's work, and by the early 1880s union membership was 10 percent female. Before the decade was over, though, the Knights had lost its strength and membership declined drastically. The next major trade union to arise was the American Federation of Labor, which was hostile to women. Some female workers organized their own associations, more mutual-aid societies than unions. Many women participated in work stoppages such as the wave of strikes in the garment industry in the 1880s.[27] In the late Gilded Age the push for protective legislation began and would bear fruit in the Progressive Era, helped along by the many female reformers in the Woman's Trade Union League (founded in 1903).

Native-born white women rarely worked in factories. Instead, they took the less stressful, but hardly better paying, clerical, teaching, and sales jobs.[28] These three fields had belonged exclusively to men, but as the Gilded Age progressed, public sentiment held that women's morals and futures would not be unduly damaged by jobs in offices and stores. Consequently, working-class and middle-class women moved with alacrity into cleaner and less physically demanding jobs such as bookkeeper, typist, stenographer, and copyist.

The Gilded Age witnessed a significant increase in college-educated women. Both coeducational and women's colleges had existed before the Civil War, but more colleges opened their doors to women in the postbellum years, including Bryn Mawr, Radcliffe, and Mount Holyoke. Although opponents of women's education, particularly scientists, warned that women's brains were too small to handle the work without compromising their reproductive systems, many women took the risk. Upon graduation, they married at a lower rate than the rest of the female population. This could have resulted from the empowering taste of the homosocial circle or the liberating dose of the life of the mind that women experienced at college, or it could have to do with the shortage of men in the wake of the Civil War. Certainly it was nearly impossible for a woman in the Gilded Age to have children and a husband along with a career. Seventy-five percent of all women who earned doctoral degrees between 1877 and 1924 remained single.[29]

Many college-educated women chose to enter the few professional careers open to women in the Gilded Age. Nursing and teaching were predominantly women's fields by the mid-Gilded Age. Also in this era, some institutions began to graduate women physicians and attorneys. By the turn of the century, several medical schools across the North and Midwest admitted women, and female doctors began to practice in women's hospitals, in clinics, and from their own offices. It was relatively easier to pursue a career in medicine than in law because of the obvious differences in men's and women's bodies. Sentiment existed for women to tend to ailing women, infants, and children, just as they had always done, and the move toward professionalism in the Gilded Age assisted the entrance of women into medicine and law. One decade into the twentieth century, there were nine thousand women physicians but only fifteen hundred female lawyers in the United States. Myra Bradwell was the first woman to seek admittance to the bar. When she initially applied for a license to practice in 1869, the Illinois State Supreme Court turned her down. The U.S. Supreme Court also found against her, but on technical grounds, and the Illinois legislature allowed her to practice. In 1879, Belva Lockwood was admitted to practice before the Supreme Court. Inroads into the legal system continued but at a snail's pace.

Science remained closed to women and the ministry nearly so. No female scientist held a job in industry, and few denominations allowed women to seek ordination. Most women in science were professors in women's colleges. Teaching in college became a viable option after the Civil War as more and more institutions of higher learning opened their doors to female students. The percentage of female college students increased throughout the Gilded Age and the Progressive Era, but the number of female college professors did not rise correspondingly. To have a career in the Gilded Age, most women had to forego marriage and children and face an uncertain financial future at the very least. Probably most women also risked the displeasure of their families because of their unusual life choice as well as the loss of a peer group. This latter was one reason that Hull House and other settlements attracted so many like-minded college-educated women. There, their aspirations found a receptive audience.

As industrialization, immigration, and urbanization caused a population increase in the East, the Homestead Acts and the lure of quick riches drew a number of Americans to the West. The experience of women in the West is difficult to characterize. Some single women took advantage of the free or inexpensive land given out by the U.S. government and established their own homesteads. Others went west as prostitutes or dance hall entertainers, and many led a peripatetic life following the mining camps. Some single women sought employment in the wide open West rather than in the crowded Eastern cities. Religion played a role in settling the frontier, as zeal led female missionaries and nuns to Christianize and care for the western families. Most women who made the journey toward the Pacific Ocean did so as wives, sometimes willingly and sometimes unwillingly accompanying their farmer, rancher, miner, or businessman husbands. For most women the journey was arduous, even after the railways crossed the plains and brought the trappings of eastern civilization closer. Women worried about Indian attacks, disease, the lack of doctors, the difficulty of keeping their homes clean, the dearth of formal educational opportunities in the West, and the relatives they left behind.

In the most rural areas, women did not inhabit a separate sphere. As the family began the process of building and planting, women's labor in the fields and the barns was crucial to the family's survival. The doctrine of separate spheres, if it was part of the intellectual construct of western women and men, was at least more flexible as they shared work. A 1901 editorial from the journal *The Independent* asserted that "there is nothing essentially masculine about outdoor employment. There is in running a reaper nothing more to weaken femininity than in running a sewing machine. To drive a team of horses in a hay field will no more unsex a woman than driving a fast team in a city park. To be compelled to drudge is as demoralizing in the kitchen as it is in the garden—no more, no less."[30]

Rather than being simply "gentle tamers" of the Wild West and its men, women helped to build community structures as they had done in the East. They founded and belonged to women's clubs and to women's auxiliaries of farm and ranch societies, such as the Women's Christian Temperance Union, the Populist party, the Grange, and the Farmers Alliance. Western women dedicated themselves to municipal housekeeping in the latter part of the Gilded Age. They established orphanages, Sunday schools, libraries, museums, and other institutions. In western states and territories, many women enjoyed the vote—even as their eastern sisters fought for it. School board elections were first opened to women in the West, and by 1870 in Wyoming and Utah women held the full elective franchise. While the initial impetus for giving women the vote in Utah probably did not come from women, female members of the Church of Jesus Christ of Latter-Day Saints took advantage of it, publishing their own suffrage newspaper and pushing to extend the vote to women elsewhere in the West.[31]

Native American women did not internalize the cult of true womanhood. Few had heard of it. The ones who had were usually exposed to white Christian missionary women who were trying to convert this people religiously and culturally. Gilded Age Anglo-Americans continued to marginalize Native Americans. The U.S. government's Indian policies consigned them to reservations, where women and men suffered terrible upheaval and ignominy. A facile generalization about the lives of Native American women is bound to be erroneous in its particulars, but, broadly speaking, Indian women did not live within a separate female sphere. More likely, men and women shared work or performed tasks that the writers of the separate sphere prescriptive literature would not have recognzied as "women's work." Native American women were agricultural as well as domestic workers. They were not significantly touched by industrialization, immigration, or urbanization,

except for the very few women whose home-industry products (baskets, pottery, or cloth) were sold to wealthy white women and the ever fewer women who worked as domestics (usually on the East Coast). Many Native American women were able to escape unhappy or abusive marriages with greater ease than the white majority, and in some tribes, women enjoyed a higher status because of their religious or medical skills or because of their longevity. It is possible that the ongoing pressure to assimilate into white culture robbed these women of their more nearly equal status in their communities, for by the end of the Gilded Age a larger number of white missionaries and others who believed in the cultural hegemony of European Americans sought to make Native Americans conform to the dictates of white society.[32]

Native Americans, however, were but distant figures for most middle- and working-class Americans. Politicians and editors proclaimed the might of industry, while immigrants and native-born Americans moved to the cities to seek a better future. Industry, with its promise of prosperity and progress, irrevocably altered the lives of women. Factories were the main attraction for immigrants to make the long journey to the United States, and, although many more men migrated, the women who did underwent the jarring cultural shock of discovering American social norms. Working-class women took in boarders, laundry, and piecework, while their daughters went off to factories. Labor in industry opened up for women during the Gilded Age, even though unions did not. The difficult jobs women performed belied the contemporary notion that they were fragile and domestic. Still, working-class life was an uphill struggle. Tenements, corrupt politicians, and unsanitary living conditions spurred middle-class women to their sisters' aid, but only infrequently did middle- and working-class women form partnerships in the business of cleaning up the slums and factories. More often, middle-class women pursued municipal housekeeping in voluntary associations drawn from their own social group, while they promoted the assimilation of their white domestic helpers as individuals. Women's associations and suffrage organizations provided the key for middle-class women to unlock the bonds of the cult of true womanhood, as did settlement houses, college education, and entry into professions.

As the Gilded Age ended and the Progressive Era dawned, middle-class club members and suffragists continued to ameliorate the troubles of women and children, the traditional objects of their concern. They began to appeal more and more frequently for direct governmental intervention and secured legislation on topics as broad ranging as the environment, sanitation, juvenile courts, historic preservation, education, pure food and drugs, and crime. Women such as Carrie Chapman Catt, who early in her life began work in the field of suffrage, continued the battle, finally gaining the vote for all women in 1920. The first generation of college-educated women opened the doors for others who followed in their footsteps seeking personal satisfaction in medical, legal, and governmental careers. African-American women persevered in the staggering task of "lifting as they climbed," educating whites and fighting stereotypes. The genteel activism in black women's clubs paved the way for better treatment by local and state politicians, at least in the North. Reform efforts had demonstrated the ability of women not only to survive but also to prosper outside their "proper" sphere. As a nurturing arena for action and a justification for excursions into public space, the separate sphere had buoyed women, but by the end of the Gilded Age its constraints had become obvious, its boundaries a liability. The "new woman" of the Progressive Era—educated, informed, and more free of the separate sphere—was clearly the legacy of Gilded Age activists on all fronts.

Notes

1. *Historical Statistics of the United States: Colonial Times to 1970* (Washington, DC, 1975), 6. These figures are taken from the 1890 census.

2. "The average number [of children] born to a white woman surviving to menopause fell from 7.04 in 1800, to 6.14 in 1840, to 4.24 in 1880, and finally to 3.56 in 1900." Daniel Scott Smith, "Family Limitation, Sexual Control, and Domestic Feminism in Victorian America," in *Clio's Consciousness Raised,* ed. Mary Hartman and Lois Banner (New York, 1974), 122.

3. The literature on women's sexuality in the Gilded Age is vast. See, for example, Nancy F. Cott, "Passionlessness: An Interpretation of Victorian Sexual Ideology, 1790-1850," *Signs* 4 (Winter 1978): 219-36; Carl Degler, *At Odds: Women and the Family in America from the Revolution to the Present* (New York, 1980); and John D'Emilio and Estelle B. Freedman, *Intimate Matters: A History of Sexuality in America* (New York, 1988).

4. William G. Shade, " 'A Mental Passion': Female Sexuality in Victorian America," *International Journal of Women's Studies* 1 (January/February 1978): 21. Shade cites Eliza Farnham, Antoinette Brown Blackwell, and Isabella Beecher Hooker as examples of late nineteenth-century feminists whose writings are based on a recognition of the differences between men and women, rather than on the earlier nineteenth-century beliefs of feminists such as Elizabeth Cady Stanton and Margaret Fuller, who contended that men and women, despite a few biological differences, were equal.

5. See Shirley J. Carlson, "Black Ideals of Womanhood in the Late Victorian Era," *Journal of Negro History* 77 (Spring 1992): 61-73. Carlson holds that "the ideal black woman embodied the genteel behavior of the 'cult of true womanhood.' . . . In addition, as an *African American,* her thoughts and actions exemplified the attributes valued by her own race and community" (p. 61, emphasis in text).

6. Barbara Welter, "The Cult of True Womanhood, 1820-1860," in *Dimity Convictions: The American Woman in the Nineteenth Century* (Athens, OH,

1976), 21-41. This article was first published in 1966. One of the most enduring historiographical debates in nineteenth-century women's history concerns this concept and whether the woman's homosocial sphere limited her power and influence or provided a powerful base of support from which she could pursue her social reforms. Welter and Gerda Lerner ("The Lady and the Mill Girl: Changes in the Status of Women in the Age of Jackson," *Mid-Continental American Studies Journal* 10 [Spring 1965]: 5-15) favor the former position, while the following historians argue some permutation on the latter: Carroll Smith-Rosenberg, "The Female World of Love and Ritual," *Signs* 1 (Autumn 1975): 1-29; Nancy Cott, *The Bonds of Womanhood: Woman's Sphere in New England, 1778-1835* (New Haven, CT, 1975); and Estelle B. Freedman, "Separatism as Strategy: Female Institution Building and American Feminism, 1870-1930," *Feminist Studies* 5 (Fall 1979): 512-29. For the most recent scholarship on the separate sphere see *Gendered Domains: Rethinking Public and Private in Women's History,* ed. Dorothy O. Helly and Susan M. Reverby (Ithaca, NY, 1992).

7. The phrase is Christopher Lasch's from *Haven in a Heartless World: The Family Besieged* (New York, 1977).

8. The phrase is from Carroll Smith-Rosenberg, "The Female World," p. 1.

9. On the WCTU see Frances Willard, *Glimpses of Fifty Years: The Autobiography of an American Woman* (Chicago, 1889); Barbara Leslie Epstein, *The Politics of Domesticity: Women, Evangelism, and Temperance in Nineteenth-Century America* (Middletown, CT, 1981); Ruth Bordin, *Woman and Temperance: The Quest for Power and Liberty, 1873-1900* (Philadelphia, 1981); idem, *Frances Willard: A Biography* (Chapel Hill, NC, 1986); and Suzanne M. Marilley, "Frances Willard and the Feminism of Fear," *Feminist Studies* 19 (Spring 1993): 123-46. For African-American women in the temperance movement see Patricia A. Schecter, "Temperance Work in the Nineteenth Century," *Black Women in America: An Historical Encyclopedia,* 2 vols., ed. Darlene Clark Hine (Brooklyn, NY, 1993), 2:1154-56.

10. The categories of municipal housekeeping are drawn from Anne Firor Scott, *Natural Allies: Women's Associations in American History* (Chicago, 1991), 184-89.

11. Idem, "Most Invisible of All: Black Women's Voluntary Associations," *Journal of Southern History* 56 (February 1990): 3-22.

12. Carlson, "Black Ideals of Womanhood," 61-62. For an understanding of how Christian ideals and the black churches have historically influenced the work of club women see Evelyn Brooks Higginbotham,

Righteous Discontent: The Woman's Movement in the Black Baptist Church, 1880-1920 (Cambridge, MA, 1993).

13. On the issue of the indivisibility of race and gender consult Else Barkley Brown, "Womanist Consciousness: Maggie Lena Walker and the Independent Order of St. Luke," in *Unequal Sisters: A Multi-Cultural Reader in U. S. Women's History,* ed. Vicki L. Ruiz and Ellen Carol DuBois (New York, 1994), 268-83.

14. On the myriad activities of African-American women see Stephanie J. Shaw, "Black Club Women and the Creation of the National Association of Colored Women," *Journal of Women's History* 3 (Fall 1991): 10-25 (the specific examples cited come from pp. 17 and 18); Kathleen C. Berkeley, " 'Colored Ladies Also Contributed': Black Women's Activities from Benevolence to Social Welfare, 1866-1896," in *The Web of Southern Social Relations: Women, Families, and Education,* ed. Walter J. Fraser, Jr., R. Frank Saunders, Jr., and Jon L. Wakelyn (Athens, GA, 1985), 181-203; Scott, "Most Invisible of All," especially p. 16; and Linda Gordon, "Black and White Visions of Welfare: Women's Welfare Activism, 1890-1945," *Journal of American History* 78 (September 1991): 559-90.

15. Although almost all historians of women's clubs make this point, see particularly Karen J. Blair, *The Clubwoman as Feminist: True Womanhood Redefined, 1868-1914* (New York, 1980); Scott, *Natural Allies;* and Lori D. Ginzberg, *Women and the Work of Benevolence: Morality, Politics, and Class in the Nineteenth-Century United States* (New Haven, CT, 1990). The quote is from Scott's book, 221-22.

16. Mary Y. Terrell, president of the Texas Federation of Women's Clubs, to the membership ("Dear Club Friends"), January 7, 1901, in the Anna J. H. Pennybacker Collection, Center for American History, University of Texas at Austin. The goals of the Texas Federation of Women's Clubs were the creation of a state library commission, a law prohibiting the killing of game and song birds, industrial education for women, and legislation controlling "the sale of that deadly drug Cocaine."

17. Paula Baker, "The Domestication of Politics: Women and American Political Society, 1780-1920," *American Historical Review* 89 (June 1984): 620-47. The quote is from p. 622. See also Michael McGerr, "Political Style and Women's Power, 1830-1930," *Journal of American History* 77 (December 1990): 864-85; and Baker, *The Moral Frameworks of Public Life: Gender, Politics, and the State in Rural New York, 1870-1930* (New York, 1991).

18. The list of women's participation in traditional politics comes from McGerr, "Political Style and Women's Power," 867. See also Mary Ryan, *Women in Public: Between Banners and Ballots, 1825-1880* (Baltimore, 1990).

19. On suffrage see Eleanor Flexnor, *Century of Struggle: The Woman's Rights Movement in the United States* (Cambridge, MA, 1975); Ellen Carol DuBois, *Feminism and Suffrage: The Emergence of an Independent Women's Movement in America, 1848-1869* (Ithaca, NY, 1978); Israel Kugler, *From Ladies to Women: The Organized Struggle for Woman's Rights in the Reconstruction Era* (New York, 1987); and Aileen S. Kraditor, *The Ideas of the Woman Suffrage Movement, 1890-1920* (New York, 1981).

20. Elizabeth Cady Stanton, "Solitude of Self," speech given before the House Judiciary Committee and the National American Woman Suffrage Association convention in 1892, in *Feminism: The Essential Historical Writings,* ed. Miriam Schneir (New York, 1972), 158.

21. On Hull House see Jane Addams, *Twenty Years at Hull House* (1910; reprint ed., Urbana, IL, 1990); Mary L. Bryan and Allen F. Davis, eds., *One Hundred Years at Hull House* (Bloomington, IN, 1990); and Davis, *American Heroine; The Life and Legend of Jane Addams* (New York, 1973).

22. The information in this paragraph is taken from Lynn Y. Weiner, *From Working Girl to Working Mother: The Female Labor Force in the United States, 1820-1980* (Chapel Hill, NC: 1985), 4-5. See also Alice Kessler-Harris, *Out to Work: A History of Wage-Earning Women in the United States* (New York, 1982); and Joanne J. Meyerowitz, *Women Adrift: Independent Wage Earners in Chicago, 1880-1930* (Urbana, IL, 1988).

23. For a study of self-employed women that broaches the idea that some women preferred their independence to marriage see Wendy Gamber, "A Precarious Independence: Milliners and Dressmakers in Boston, 1860-1890," *Journal of Women's History* 4 (September 1992): 60-88. Gamber found that there were 994 self-employed women in Boston in 1890.

24. Weiner, *From Working Girl to Working Mother,* 25.

25. Timothy J. Gilfoyle, *City of Eros: New York City, Prostitution, and the Commercialization of Sex, 1790-1920* (New York, 1992); Anne M. Butler, *Daughters of Joy, Sisters of Misery: Prostitutes in the American West, 1865-1890* (Urbana, IL, 1985).

26. Consult Fay E. Dudden, *Serving Women: Household Service in Nineteenth-Century America* (Middletown, CT, 1983); and David M. Katzman, *Seven Days a Week: Women and Domestic Service in Industrializing America* (New York, 1978).

27. For an example of women's essential role in a Knights of Labor-sponsored strike, see Susan Levine, *Labor's True Woman: Carpet Weavers, Industrialization, and Labor Reform in the Gilded Age* (Philadelphia, 1984).

28. Weiner, *From Working Girl to Working Mother,* 27-28.

29. Barbara J. Harris, *Beyond Her Sphere: Women and the Professions in American History* (Westport, CT, 1978), 101. See also Mary R. Walsh, *Doctors Wanted, No Women Need Apply: Sexual Barriers in the Medical Profession, 1835-1975* (New Haven, CT, 1977); and Gloria Moldow, *Women Doctors in Gilded Age Washington: Race, Gender, and Professionalism* (Chicago, 1987).

30. *The Independent,* July 18, 1901.

31. The information on western women comes from *The Women's West,* ed., Susan Armitage and Elizabeth Jameson (Norman, OK, 1987), particularly Elizabeth Jameson, "Women as Workers, Women as Civilizers: True Womanhood in the American West," 145-64, and Nancy Grey Osterud, " 'She Helped Me Hay It as Good as a Man': Relations among Women and Men in an Agricultural Community," 87-97, in *"To Toil the Livelong Day": America's Women at Work, 1780-1980,* ed. Carol Groneman and Mary Beth Norton (Ithaca, NY, 1987).

32. See Joan M. Jensen, "Native American Women and Agriculture: A Seneca Case Study," in *Unequal Sisters,* 70-84; and Glenda Riley, *Inventing the American Woman: A Perspective on Women's History* (Arlington Heights, IL, 1986), 142 and 175-76. . . .

Edmund J. Danziger, Jr. (essay date 1996)

SOURCE: "Native American Resistance and Accommodation During the Late Nineteenth Century," in *The Gilded Age: Essays on the Origins of Modern America*, edited by Charles W. Calhoun, Scholarly Resources, Inc., 1996, pp. 163-84.

[*In this excerpt, Danziger describes the struggles of Native Americans in the face of post-Civil War white migrations westward that forced Indian accommodation to reservation life.*]

> Long ago the Arapahoes had a fine country of their own. The white man came to see them, and the Indians gave him buffalo meat and a horse to ride on, and they told him the country was big enough for the white man and the Arapahoes, too.
>
> After a while the white men found gold in our country. They took the gold and pushed the Indian from his home. I thought Washington would make it all right. I am an old man now. I have been waiting many years for Washington to give us our rights.
>
> —Little Raven, Arapaho [Vanderwerth, *Indian Oratory* (p. 144)]

> If the Great Spirit had desired me to be a white man he would have made me so in the first place. He put in your heart certain wishes and plans, in my heart he put other and different desires. Each man is good in his sight. It is not necessary for eagles to be crows. Now we are poor but we are free. No white man controls our footsteps. If we must die we die defending our rights.
>
> —Sitting Bull, Sioux [Armstrong, *I Have Spoken* (p. 112)]

> I know that my race must change. We can not hold our own with the white men as we are. We only ask an even chance to live as other men live. We ask to be recognized as men. We ask that the same law shall work alike on all men. . . . Whenever the white man treats the Indians as they treat each other, then we will have no more wars. We shall all be alike—brothers of one father and one mother, with one sky above us and one country around us, and one government for all.
>
> —Chief Joseph, Nez Percé [Moquin and Van Doren, *Great Documents* (p. 251)]

Unbridled greed, exploitation of natural resources, enormous business profits, bloody racial conflict, cultural repression, and despair characterized the three decades following the Civil War when the American West was transformed. U.S. citizens and their families surged like a tidal wave across the Great Plains and beyond, homesteading farms, exterminating millions of buffalo and replacing them with herds of white-faced cattle, digging gold and silver from the mountainsides, and binding the Mississippi Valley to the West Coast with iron rails. These momentous events overwhelmed some aboriginal peoples. "When the buffalo went away," remarked the aged Crow, Chief Plenty-Coups, "the hearts of my people fell to the ground, and they could not lift them up again."[1] Other leaders, such as Sitting Bull and Chief Joseph, fought on, either militarily or using accommodation strategies. Their story is the subject of this essay, which also examines how federal Indian policymakers tried to improve conditions among displaced Native peoples. Sadly, by the 1890s the reservation scene suggested the unfulfilled hopes of both aboriginal leaders and altruistic "Friends of the Indian."

Post-Civil War America alarmed Native peoples of the trans-Mississippi West, many of whom maintained their nomadic and seminomadic hunter-gatherer life-styles. The U.S. Census Bureau estimated in 1870 that of the 383,712 Indians, 234,740 still freely roamed the western territories and states. Most nomads lived in Alaska (70,000), Arizona (27,700), Nevada (16,220), Montana (19,330), Dakota Territory (26,320), and in present-day Oklahoma (34,400).[2] What threatened their world was the rapid influx of pioneers with eyes fixed on aboriginal lands suitable for farming, ranching, lumbering, mining, town sites, and railroad rights-of-way. Settlers expected federal Indian Office agents and U.S. Army troops to support their countrymen by cajoling or forcing Native inhabitants off most of the land. At this point the often cordial relations between Indians and newcomers, referred to by Little Raven, turned sour and then bloody as many Indian families and their leaders tenaciously fought to save their homelands.

When confronted with "Indian trouble," federal policymakers usually believed that they had no choice but to remove Native impediments to the nation's expansion. Congress's initial strategy was to dispatch peace commissioners, including Civil War hero William T. Sherman, in hopes of concentrating nomadic tribes in either present-day South Dakota or Oklahoma, away from the major overland trails and railroad routes. Kiowa, Comanche, Kiowa-Apache, Cheyenne, Arapaho, and Sioux leaders negotiated a series of treaties in the mid-1860s that promised to restore peace and pledged the Natives to make way for white settlers. Neither side, however, listened carefully and respectfully to the views of the other, nor were the Indians convinced about the need to alter their traditional ways of life.[3] At the Medicine Lodge Treaty Council in October 1867, for example, Comanche Chief Ten Bears asserted:

> You said that you wanted to put us upon a reservation, to build us houses and to make us Medicine lodges [schools and churches]. I do not want them.
>
> I was born upon the prairie, where the wind blew free, and there was nothing to break the light of the sun. I was born where there were no enclosures, and where everything drew a free breath. I want to die there, and not within walls. I know every stream and every wood between the Rio Grande and the Arkansas. I have hunted and lived over that country. I lived like my fathers before me, and like them, I lived happily.[4]

With many Indians holding this kind of attitude, sporadic fighting thus persisted across the Plains and beyond the Rockies.

Crazy Horse, Sitting Bull, Geronimo, Cochise, Chief Joseph—their names resounded down through the decades and became symbols of Indian determination to control their hunting grounds and retain established ways of life. Their struggle with U.S. military forces during the late nineteenth century comprises one of the best-known chapters in American history.

Triggered by white encroachment on Indian lands, cultural differences, and the federal government's determination to use force if necessary to concentrate the tribes on small reservations, the Indian wars lasted well into the 1870s. U.S. soldiers, conditioned by formal warfare on eastern Civil War battlefields, had difficulty coping with the semi-arid western terrain and the martial skills of elusive, unorthodox fighters who often had no permanent villages to attack or crops to destroy. To elude the blue coats, hostiles sometimes found sanctuary and sustenance among peaceful fellow tribesmen living on reservations under the jurisdiction of civilian Indian agents. Yet time was on the Army's side as railroads crisscrossed the West, more and more settlers appropriated Indian resources, and buffalo—the Plains Indians' staff of life—were slaughtered by the millions. Individualistic Native societies also had difficulty uniting as tribes or forming intertribal alliances against the white invaders with their superior numbers, Indian scouts, railroads, telegraph lines, and mass-produced tools of war.[5]

Until the collapse of armed resistance, the Natives, who had much at stake, fought back stubbornly and often brilliantly, considering the odds. On the southern Plains, for example, reservation life galled the Kiowas, Comanches, Southern Cheyennes, and Southern Arapahoes. Farming failed to feed the warriors' families, Washington sent inadequate supplementary rations, whiskey hucksters sowed discontent, and whites nibbled at the edges of Native lands and slaughtered the buffalo for their hides, leaving the carcasses to rot. These circumstances provoked aboriginal peoples, who hungered for the old ways and were willing to fight rather than endure more reservation life. Kiowa Chief Satanta spoke for many when he said that "I love the land and the buffalo and will not part with it. . . . I have heard that you intend to settle us on a reservation near the mountains. I don't want to settle. I love to roam over the prairies. There I feel free and happy, but when we settle down we grow pale and die."[6] Partly out of desperation, the tribes sent hunting/raiding parties into Texas, Kansas, and Nebraska. Led by Satanta and other recalcitrant warrior-buffalo hunters, the southern Plains tribes fought against Washington's concentration policy for nearly a decade. The largest outbreak of hostilities was the Red River War of 1874-75. The Indians, finally overpowered, surrendered their weapons and horses and saw their leaders shipped off to prison in Florida.[7] Peace returned to the Plains south of the Platte River but at great cost to the aboriginal inhabitants.

Meanwhile, in the Southwest, reservation life together with further land losses drove many Apaches to take to the warpath rather than surrender their freedom and homeland. "This is the country of the Chiricahua Apaches," Chief Cochise once asserted. He continued:

> This is the country where the Chiricahua Apaches belong. The mountains and the valleys, the days and the nights belong to the Chiricahua Apaches. It was so from the memory of the oldest man, and that memory comes from the oldest man ahead of him. There was none but the Indian here and the land was filled with food. The Indians could make a living for themselves. The men with steel came and tried to take it from us and we defeated them. Now the Americans—and none is more treacherous than the Americans, and none more arrogant. The Americans think they are better than other men. They make their own laws and say those laws must be obeyed. Why?[8]

Led by Cochise, Victorio, Nana, and Geronimo, the Apaches fought intermittently until the mid-1880s, but their fate was similar to that of the southern Plains tribes: military power forever broken and leaders imprisoned.[9] The Apaches thus resigned themselves to reservation life as had their Navajo and Pueblo neighbors.

The story repeated itself with some variations in the Pacific Northwest and on the northern Plains, where reservation conditions, slipshod federal management, and charismatic Native leaders encouraged some groups to resist militarily. On the California-Oregon border, for instance, the Modocs refused to share a reservation with the Klamaths, and under Captain Jack the Modocs kept escaping back to their former home at Tule Lake. Following a brief war in 1872, Washington removed the tribe to the Quapaw Agency in Oklahoma. The Modocs' exile lasted until 1909.[10] In another example, the refusal of some Nez Percés to settle on the Lapwai reservation and their subsequent 1,300-mile flight toward Canada is well chronicled. Following Chief Joseph's surrender in 1877, his people were also held as prisoners of war in Oklahoma.[11] Joseph's famous surrender speech (to General Nelson A. Miles in Montana's Bear Paw Mountains) and subsequent remarks to American audiences and policymakers reflected the Indians' frustration as wards of the government.

> I have heard talk and talk, but nothing is done. Good words do not last long unless they amount to something. Words do not pay for my dead people. They do not pay for my country, now overrun by white men. . . . Good words will not give my people good health and stop them from dying. Good words will not get my people a home where they can live in peace and take care of themselves. I am tired of talk that comes to nothing. . . . You might as well expect the rivers to run backwards as that any man who was born a free man should be contented when penned up and denied liberty to go where he pleases.[12]

Many Sioux and northern Cheyennes also resisted being penned up on reservations that were poorly managed, ill suited to agriculture, and constantly encroached upon by land-hungry whites. Under the leadership of Red Cloud, Crazy Horse, Sitting Bull, and others, they fought for their freedom and their hunting grounds. First the white man promised "that the buffalo country should be left to us forever," Sitting Bull claimed. "Now they threaten to take that away from us. My brothers, shall we submit or shall we say to them: 'First kill me before you take possession of my Fatherland.'"[13] Not until 1877 did peace return to the northern Plains, and with the Indian barrier breached, white settlers quickly spread across the grasslands.[14]

The Indian wars, sparked by Washington's determination to concentrate all Native peoples on restricted reservations, were full of significance. They opened vast natural resources to non-Natives, although the cost was high. Between 1866 and 1891 regular U.S. troops fought 1,065 "actions" with Indians, and the War Department kept an average of 16,000 officers and men on active duty.[15] Concerns about the frontier Indian danger had been an integral part of the nation's story since its founding a century earlier. Now the country faced an equally perplexing problem: what role should former warriors and their families play in American society? From their perspective, the Sioux, Nez Percés, Modocs, Apaches, and other tribes— militarily humbled and stripped of their livelihoods—must have wondered, too, about their future as Uncle Sam's wards. The answers came quickly. Once gathered onto reservations, America's Native peoples found themselves caught up in a new struggle for their children, for their identities, and for their souls.

Mark Twain astutely observed that "soap and education are not as sudden as a massacre, but they are more deadly in the long run."[16] During the late 1870s, U.S. Indian policymakers set as their goal the cleansing and Americanization of "savage" reservation residents in preparation for their integration into mainstream society. Advocates of "civilizing" the Indians obviously believe that aboriginal peoples were capable of learning the English language and of adopting an alternative, superior mode of life if they

were brought under the influence of honest and capable Indian agents, Christian missionaries, farmers, and teachers. To "allow them to drag along year after year . . . in their old superstitions, laziness, and filth . . . would be a lasting disgrace to our government," wrote Commissioner of Indian Affairs Hiram Price, but to transform the Indians into self-sufficient and productive citizens would be "a crown of glory to any nation."[17]

Assimilation of Native Americans into the dominant society required specific strategies in the judgment of Washington officials and humanitarian reformers. These included the promotion of Indian self-sufficiency through farming and stock raising, the formal education of their young, the allotment of Indian land in severalty, and the conferring of U.S. citizenship on Indians who had abandoned traditional ways.[18] How to deal with America's aboriginal people, President Rutherford B. Hayes confided to his diary, "is a problem which for nearly three centuries has remained almost unsolved. . . . Let all our dealings with the Red man be characterized by justice and good faith, and let there be the most liberal provision for his physical wants, for education in its widest sense, and for religious instruction and training. To do this will cost money, but like all money well expended it is wise economy."[19] With the western Indians peaceful and concentrated on secluded and often infertile reservations, the time had come to test fully these techniques

By 1890 the Office of Indian Affairs supervised fifty-eight agencies scattered from New York to California. Washington charged each federal agent, who was responsible for one or more reservations, with destroying tribal customs and beliefs, replacing them with mainstream American life-styles and values, and encouraging Indian integration into the dominant society. At that point reservations (dubbed "virtual open-air prisons" by historian Donald J. Berthrong) would no longer be necessary. Agents' specific responsibilities included: administering agency as well as tribal moneys and property; controlling the chiefs; fostering farming by the men and instructing the women in household skills; safeguarding the health of the inhabitants; aggressively restricting Indian dress, language, and other "vicious habits"; advancing Christianity; and educating children. The agency staff (usually a clerk, farmer, medical doctor, blacksmith, and one or more teachers) also played key roles in this Americanization process.[20]

Two of the agents' biggest challenges were educating Indian youth and maintaining law and order. Considered "as bright and teachable as average white children of the same ages," Native youngsters were the key to Washington's "civilization" program. Congress therefore took back control of Indian education from Christian missionaries and between 1877 and 1900 created its own educational system and increased the level of annual funding from $20,000 to $1,364,368.[21] More than 20,000 Indians attended an elaborate federal school system by the close of the century. English was the language of instruction, and teachers emphasized the vocational application of knowledge. As with adults, this meant farming plus a knowledge of common trades for the boys and domestic arts for the females. Native self-sufficiency and Americanization remained the government's objectives.[22]

To make sure that reservation economic development and cultural change took place in an orderly environment, Congress in 1878 authorized experimental police units to fill the power vacuum created by the withdrawal of military troops from the West and the weakened authority of tribal chiefs. The system proved so successful that within three years it operated on forty-nine reservations and included 84 commissioned officers and 786 noncommissioned officers and privates.[23] To the Indian Office, a disciplined and well-trained police force also served as a "perpetual educator" for fellow Natives who would walk the white man's road. "Indian police became more than law enforcers," Berthrong noted; "they slaughtered issue beefs, returned truants to boarding schools, carried messages for agents, took tribal censuses, and built roads and agency buildings."[24] The courts of Indian offenses, established by the Interior Department in the early 1880s, formed another weapon in the federal government's acculturation arsenal. Soon, ninety-three Native judges staffed courts at twenty-eight agencies. They heard cases against Indians charged with theft, destruction of property, drunkenness, and trafficking in intoxicating liquors. The courts also enforced Indian Office rules that forbade various practices of medicine men, polygamy, and the sun, scalp, and war dances.[25]

Tribal sovereignty came under attack in the late 1800s as did traditional Indian customs, languages, and political structures. After 1871 the U.S. Congress legislated policies and programs, with or without Indian consultation. No longer would the government negotiate treaties with Native political groups. Tribal sovereignty, implied by earlier treaties, seemed inappropriate for the 1870s. Indians had become wards of the government. Congress also enacted the Major Crimes Act in 1885, which made Indians who committed certain infractions on reservations subject to federal government jurisdiction rather than tribal authority. The U.S. Supreme Court upheld the act's constitutionality in *United States v. Kagama.*[26] In another case the Court determined that the Fourteenth Amendment did not give U.S. citizenship to Native persons born on reservations.[27]

As vulnerable subject peoples hemmed in on reservations, Indians ironically suffered at times at the hands of the very persons charged with protecting them. Historian Francis Paul Prucha concluded that the "Indian service, upon which rested much of the responsibility for solving the 'Indian problem' of the post-Civil War decades, was itself a large part of the problem."[28] Opportunities for fraud corrupted many federal agents who were paid meager salaries yet annually handled large amounts of Indian money, annuity goods, and farm equipment "in isolated areas away from civilized restraints and comforts." Agents also supervised the leasing of reservation lands and negotiated contracts for agency improvements. Sioux Chief Red Cloud

once asked an audience in New York City, "I wish to know why Commissioners are sent out to us who do nothing but rob us and get the riches of this world away from us! I was brought up among the traders, and those who came out there in the early times treated me well and I had a good time with them. . . . But, by and by, the Great Father sent out a different kind of men; men who cheated and drank whiskey; men who were so bad that the Great Father could not keep them at home and so sent them out there. . . . I want to have men sent out to my people whom we know and can trust."[29]

Reform proposals were many but the results modest. Three times the House of Representatives approved transfer of the Indian Office from the Interior Department, where the spoils system governed appointments, to the War Department, but the bills got no further. Ulysses S. Grant's administration tried to improve Indian Office field operations by using inspectors and replacing political patronage appointees with more honest and competent agents nominated by religious denominations. The latter experiment failed miserably. Not enough qualified Christian men wished to become Indian agents, patronage pressures emanating from Congress and the White House undermined the process, and interdenominational competition degenerated into "flagrant bigotry," according to Prucha. Also ineffective was the Board of Indian Commissioners, a group of Christian philanthropists appointed to advise the government on Native affairs and serve as a watchdog over the Indian service. Hayes's secretary of the interior, Carl Schurz, reformed Indian Office operations and purged it of many dishonest officials, but the service did not fully eradicate the political spoils system until the next century.[30]

The reservation environment, as overseen by federal Indian agents, elicited mixed responses from Natives of the prairies, plains, mountains, and deserts of the West. Their eastern cousins, introduced to reservations earlier in the century, felt much the same way. Historian Arrell M. Gibson claimed that for many American Indians the reservation "matched, and in some cases exceeded, the somber 'Trail of Tears' for needless, agonizing want, unthinkable suffering, and personal and group decline to the brink of destruction."[31]

Reservation factionalism sprang from these mixed responses. Indian agents of the period quickly and conveniently categorized bands or tribal factions as "progressive" or "traditional," yet historian David Rich Lewis cautions that communities contained many interest groups that were sometimes in flux because of the variety of issues they faced. Furthermore, individuals, as Lewis discovered in his study of northern Ute leader William Wash, "frequently transcend the bounds of static factional categories."[32] Nevertheless, a few of the popular options available to reservation individuals and groups after the Civil War should be discussed, albeit with caution.

Some aboriginal leaders and their followers, believing that further military resistance was foolish, abandoned hope of ever restoring traditional life-styles and pragmatically tried to make the best of reservation life. They took up farming, sent their children to school, attended church services, adopted "citizen's dress," cooperated with the local Indian agent, and generally tried to walk the white man's road. The rural isolation of most reservations limited work opportunities, but by the turn of the century the U.S. Census Bureau calculated that 60 percent of Native American males able to hold jobs were "gainfully employed." Nearly 90 percent of the women, on the other hand, remained at home.[33]

For those willing to adjust to the white man's expectations, reservations offered chances for economic self-sufficiency. Most were in farming. Historian Donald L. Parman argues that prior to allotment restrictions in the 1880s and the decline of Indian agriculture (discussed below), "many Indians were making the adjustments necessary for successful agriculture. . . . On thirty-three unallotted reservations, eighteen increased the acreage under cultivation over 10 percent annually and thirteen raised production levels over 10 percent." Although nearly three-fourths of the Indian men worked as farmers or farmhands in 1910, other opportunities existed within reservation boundaries. Some contracted to carry supplies for the agency or, as noted above, worked as Indian police and judges.[34]

Others found off-reservation jobs. Most notable were Native performers who toured with the Wild West shows. Buffalo Bill hired between seventy-five and one hundred Indians during the 1880s, for example. They thrilled audiences in the United States and Europe and in return saw new sights, savored the appreciative crowds, and earned a livelihood. Less dramatic were the traveling medicine shows and their Native employees. Aboriginal dances and crafts attracted large crowds who were then sold a variety of quack medicines. In the late nineteenth century, thirty troupes of the Kickapoo Medicine Company, each employing ten or more Indians, traveled American roads. Indian scouts (often Apaches, Pawnees, Osages, and Delawares) employed by the U.S. Army also traveled for a living. Less glamorous was the hard work performed off-reservation by western Indians who hired out to local ranchers, for instance, and by Chippewa Indians of northern Michigan, Wisconsin, and Minnesota who worked in white towns, lumber camps, sawmills, and mines, and for railroad companies.[35]

Among the Natives who stayed closer to home, the old ways of life still beckoned, and many disregarded Indian Office prohibitions to keep such customs alive: courtship practices and polygamy, clan ceremonies, and sacred rituals such as the sun dance. Reservation residents also used two mind-altering drugs, alcohol and peyote, which Washington had forbidden.[36] These Natives massively resisted Washington's Americanization program. Parents withheld their children from government schools and their cooperation from officials who would change other aspects of the old ways. In some cases, the government seemed to ask the impossible. Farming, for example, ran counter to hunter-warrior traditions; furthermore, reservation lands often were semiarid or, in the north, had too short a growing season. When favorable agricultural conditions prevailed, the poverty-stricken Indians frequently lacked the equipment, livestock, and seeds to farm profitably. Constant white encroachment on Native lands also hurt the chances for economic self-sufficiency. Perhaps the most subversive force was the Indians' distrust, based on bitter experience, of the supposedly superior American way of life.[37] In 1875 an aged Navajo chief explained why he would not send his people's children to the agency school: "I do not believe in the white man or his ways. . . . The white man makes our young men drunk. He steals away our daughters. He takes away their hearts with sweet drinks and clothes. He is a wolf."[38]

Reservation living conditions in the late 1800s also prompted widespread despair and drunkenness and a leadership crisis. "Our men had fought hard against our enemies, holding them back from our beautiful country by their bravery," lamented Pretty-Shield, a Crow medicine woman. "But now, with everything else going wrong, we began to be whipped by weak foolishness. Our men, our leaders, began to drink the white man's whisky, letting it do their thinking. . . . Our wise-ones became fools. . . . But what else was there for us to do? . . . Our old men used to be different; even our children were different when the buffalo were here."[39] In 1881, when Sitting Bull ended his Canadian exile and surrendered to the commander at Fort Buford in Dakota Territory, he spoke with disdain about reservation life and Indian accommodationists, stating that "I do not wish to be shut up in a corral. It is bad for young men to be fed by an agent. It makes them lazy and drunken. All agency Indians I have seen were worthless. They are neither red warriors nor white farmers. They are neither wolf nor dog. But my followers are weary of cold and hunger. They wish to see their brothers and their old home, therefore I bow my head."[40]

Amid such resignation and despair on the reservations, Indian messiahs emerged offering some hope. Most influential was the Paiute Wovoka, who preached the Ghost Dance religion. It assured Indians that if they practiced the ritual Ghost Dance and behaved properly, their white antagonists would disappear and the old days would return—including the buffalo. Ghost Dancers would also be reunited with their ancestors. Washington's resolve to overcome such religious resistance to reservation acculturation plans climaxed with the notorious clash between federal troops and Sioux Ghost Dancers at Wounded Knee in South Dakota in 1890.[41] But more subtle, and far more devastating in the long run to Uncle Sam's wards, were federal Indian policy changes in the 1880s.

These changes resulted in part from the advocacy of the Women's National Indian Association of Philadelphia, the National Indian Defense Association, the Indian Rights Association, and other reform organizations established in the late nineteenth century and known collectively as

"Friends of the Indian." Building on the reform traditions of Christianity and the antebellum era, these groups shared a belief that past federal Indian programs had failed miserably. Beginning in 1883 their representatives convened annually, along with professional educators and government officials, at Lake Mohonk, New York, to discuss Indian affairs and promote reform efforts.[42] The Indian was clearly not being prepared for American citizenship by his reservation—"that hot-bed of barbarism," as Commissioner of Indian Affairs John H. Oberly called it, "in which many noxious social and political weeds grow rankly."[43] Instead, Natives, demoralized by dependence on the government dole, remained communal in their thinking and followed too many of the old ways. To save the aborigines, the reservation system must be dismantled. The Indian Rights Association urged Congress to provide the "three foundation stones" that Natives must have to become industrious and self-sufficient members of American society: education, a protected individual title to land, and U.S. citizenship.[44]

Native education greatly needed reform. In 1880, Congress appropriated a mere $75,000 to support aboriginal schools, and the Indian Office reported that only fifteen of its sixty-six agencies could adequately educated their children.[45] Reformers saw the greatest obstacle to their goals in the overpowering influence of the children's families to whom the youngsters returned each day and relapsed "into their former moral and mental stupor."[46] During the 1880s and 1890s, Friends of the Indian encouraged the building of more boarding schools on reservations as a partial solution to these problems. Here, the children learned academic subjects as well as "industrial training." For the boys, this included instruction in farming, stock raising, and gardening, plus such trades as carpentry, masonry, and blacksmithing. Girls learned competencies appropriate to their domains: the kitchen and dining room, dormitory, laundry room, and sewing room. The on-reservation boarding facility, like the day school, was still subject to strong reservation influences, particularly the pervasive Indian languages and the proximity of the children's parents.[47]

To improve education, that is, to detribalize the children and prepare them for integration into American life, Friends of the Indian involved students with two off-reservation institutions. In 1879, Richard Henry Pratt started a boarding school on an experimental basis in Carlisle, Pennsylvania. The school drew its first eighty-four students, a mixture of boys and girls, from the Rosebud and Pine Ridge Agencies in Dakota Territory.[48] By the mid-1890s, Carlisle enrolled 769 pupils whose education was similar to that offered by reservation residential schools except that students were under tighter discipline and totally cut off form home influences for years at a time. English was the only language of instruction.[49] So successful was the Carlisle experiment in the eyes of white reformers that the Indian Office created eighteen similar institutions by 1895. The number of Indians enrolled in nonreservation boarding schools that year was 4,673.[50]

Beginning in 1890, Commissioner of Indian Affairs Thomas J. Morgan advocated a second off-reservation educational experience. He observed how effective public schools were at "Americanizing our foreign population" and hoped that these institutions might do the same for Native children. Thus, he began contracting with selected school districts.[51] Within five years 487 children attended public schools in California, Oregon, Washington, Utah, Nebraska, Oklahoma, Wisconsin, and Michigan. By 1895 the Indian Office educational network had thus grown to include 19 off-reservation boarding schools, 75 reservation boarding schools, 110 reservation day schools, and 62 institutions (operated by churches or secular groups) with whom the government contracted. That year Congress appropriated $2,060,695 for Indian education. In the 1890s, Washington also required that all Indian children attend school and placed Indian Office educational personnel under Civil Service Act provisions.[52]

It is hard to generalize about Indian response to these educational reforms. Certainly many learned English and some of the ways of American society, including job skills. However, the lack of employment opportunity on their home reservations, to which most Indian students returned, meant that a large percentage "simply returned to camp life," as Berthrong has noted. Luther Standing Bear, a Sioux who attended Carlisle, took a different view of these relapses:

> According to the white man, the Indian, choosing to return to his tribal manners and dress, "goes back to the blanket." True, but "going back to the blanket" is the factor that has saved him from, or at least stayed, his final destruction. Had the Indian been as completely subdued in spirit as he was in body he would have perished within the century of his subjection. But it is the unquenchable spirit that has saved him—his clinging to Indian ways, Indian thought, and tradition, that has kept him and is keeping him today. The white man's ways were not his ways and many of the things that he has tried to adopt have proven disastrous and to his utter shame. . . . many an Indian has accomplished his own personal salvation by "going back to the blanket."[53]

No comprehensive studies exist about the lives of boarding school graduates, yet scholars agree that young Indian men and women who returned to their home reservations often ended up working for the paternalistic Bureau of Indian Affairs in menial capacities. Instead of converting their families and friends to Christian civilization, which the off-reservation boarding school system expected to happen, large numbers of graduates reverted to their community's lifeways.[54]

Besides education, reformers saw a second means for assimilating Indians into national life in the granting of land in severalty, that is, individual possession rather than tribal ownership. Throughout the 1880s, Friends of the Indian thus advocated an allotment program to break up reservation land holdings into individual family tracts. Indian farmers would learn how to compete in a market economy alongside their white neighbors. Allotment would also weaken tribal ties. Severalty was not a new program; the

Indian Office had applied it to selected tribes with mixed results.[55] Massachusetts Senator Henry L. Dawes, chair of the Senate Committee on Indian Affairs and a leading light at the Lake Mohonk conferences, led the lobbying effort for a general Indian allotment act. Not only reformers but also the railroads, white settlers, and other entrepreneurs favored severalty legislation because over sixty million acres of surplus reservation lands would be for sale following allotment.[56]

Success came in 1887. The Dawes Act provided 160-acre allotments to reservation families plus all the "rights, privileges, and immunities" of other U.S. citizens. Following a quarter-century trust period, Washington would issue fee-simple titles to the new owners.[57] According to historian Frederick E. Hoxie, the Dawes Act "was the first piece of legislation intended for the general regulation of Indian affairs to be passed in half a century, and it remained the keystone of federal action until 1934, when the Indian Reorganization Act replaced it. . . . [S]upporters of the Dawes Act hailed it as the 'Indians' Magna Carta.'"[58] This sense of satisfaction seemed justified. Communal reservations, so long an impediment to the acculturation process, were soon dismantled by allotment, which reformer Merrill E. Gates described as "a mighty pulverizing engine for breaking up the tribal mass."[59]

Understandably, Indians were less sanguine about the prospects of allotment. In the past, a paternalistic federal government rarely sought Native input into policy decisions, which usually led to more Indian land loss and removals. Delaware Chief Charles Journeycake shared this perspective with the Indian Defense Association in 1886: "We have been broken up and moved six times. We have been despoiled of our property. We thought when we moved across the Missouri River and had paid for our homes in Kansas we were safe. But in a few years the white man wanted our country. We had good farms. Built comfortable houses and big barns. We had schools for our children and churches, where we listened to the same gospel the white man listens to. The white man came into our country from Missouri. And drove our cattle and horses away." As for the prospects of allotment farming following the Dawes Act, Shoshone Chief Washakie made this pronouncement to Indian Office officials: "God damn a potato!"[60]

From the Indian perspective, the paternalistic allotment program "hung like a millstone" around their necks. The aboriginal land base had shrunk from 139 million acres to 34,287,336 acres by 1934, when Washington abandoned the program. Native communities lost not only "surplus" lands but also many individual allotments. Farmers lacked proper training and access to credit because they could not use their allotments as collateral. In 1888, Congress appropriated only $30,000 for Indian farm machinery, livestock, seeds, and other agricultural assistance. Fledgling Native farmers, under these circumstances, often leased or sold their lands rather than compete with non-Indian neighbors. Some land sales occurred without Native approval. The amount of Indian farm-land in the eleven major states where reservation land had been allotted declined from 3.1 to 2.4 million acres between 1910 and 1930. As they became an increasingly landless minority, aboriginal peoples' dependence on the federal government was perpetuated rather than eliminated.[61]

Nevertheless, Friends of the Indian persisted after 1887 in opening "surplus" Native land to non-Native settlers. "The greatest danger hanging over the Indian race," Schurz had warned in 1881, "arises from the fact that, with their large and valuable territorial possessions which are lying waste, they stand in the way of what is commonly called 'the development of the country.'"[62] During the 1890s, Congress abolished tribal governments in the Indian Territory, forced allotment upon the Natives there, thus opening the area to white settlement, and paved the way for Oklahoma statehood.[63]

To the north the Great Sioux reservation was reduced radically in 1889, triggering a tragic reaction. Here, as well as elsewhere in the West, thousands of Indians were prompted by the reservation ordeal, and even more by land loss, to join the messianic Ghost Dance movement. Once the Indians were a happy people, recalled the Paiute prophet Wovoka; then the white man came. "He dug up the bones of our mother, the earth. He tore her bosom with steel. He built big trails and put iron horses on them. He fought you and beat you, and put you in barren places where a horned toad would die. He said you must stay there; you must not go hunt in the mountains."[64] Chief Red Cloud revealed something of the Sioux's despair and why they reached out to the Ghost Dance for salvation:

> We had no newspapers, and no one to speak for us. We had no redress. Our rations were again reduced. You who eat three times each day, and see your children well and happy around you, can't understand what starving Indians feel. We were faint with hunger and maddened by despair. We held our dying children, and felt their little bodies tremble as their souls went out and left only a dead weight in our hands. . . . There was no hope on earth, and God seemed to have forgotten us. Some one had again been talking of the Son of God, and said He had come. The people did not know; they did not care. They snatched at the hope. They screamed like crazy men to Him for mercy. They caught at the promises they heard He had made.

The white men were frightened and called for soldiers. Indian provocation and resistance once again led to confrontation and bloodshed—this time at Wounded Knee, with the deaths of over two hundred Sioux men, women, and children.[65]

To summarize the post-Civil War era: as eastern Indians coped peacefully with reservation life, the western tribes battled fiercely to safeguard their homelands and traditional ways. Chiefs such as Sitting Bull, Joseph, and Geronimo became legends, but the consequences of 1,065 military engagements with U.S. troops meant that defeated Native nations would be confined to reservations, where altruistic Friends of the Indian tried to "civilize" and assimilate Indian wards through a battery of programs, including farming instruction, formal education of the young, and the allotment of aboriginal holdings. Some Natives accepted these initiatives, believing they had no choice but to walk the white man's road. Others continued to resist, militarily and in other more subtle but equally determined ways, as the Ghost Dancers showed in 1890.

At the turn of the century, America's 267,905 Indians, not including Native groups living in Alaska, had made their initial adjustment to life on widely scattered reservations. In 1899 the Indian Office had vital statistics for 187,319 of its wards and claimed that 13 percent resided in permanent homes, 28 percent spoke English for everyday purposes, and 23 percent could read. Schools enrolled 23,615 students.[66]

Aboriginal peoples were not thriving, but at least Indian adaptability and fortitude enabled them to survive the transition and establish permanent homes on restricted land bases. Native peoples had forged a new set of relationships with whites on and off the reservations by 1900. No longer free-wheeling nomads who controlled vast resources, the Indians led lives that revolved around island communities.

Non-Indian Americans who surrounded the reservations assumed that their neighbors would soon vanish into the dominant society; so, too, did Washington policymakers. A century later we realize how wrong they were. Native Americans, employing resistance and accommodation strategies and with help from generations of new leaders, have regained much numerical, cultural, and political strength.[67] Geronimo and Sitting Bull would be pleased.

Notes

1. Frank Linderman, *Pretty-Shield: Medicine Woman of the Crows* (1932; reprint ed., New York, 1972), 248.

2. "Census of 1870," in U.S. Bureau of the Census, *Report on Indians Taxed and Indians Not Taxed in the United States (Except Alaska) at the Eleventh Census: 1890*, 25 vols. (Washington, DC, 1894), 7:21-22. Other Indians were peacefully settled on reservations or at Indian agencies in the eastern states or the western states of Arkansas, California, Iowa, Kansas, Missouri, Nebraska, Nevada, Oregon, and Texas.

3. Thomas W. Dunlay, "Fire and Sword: Ambiguity and the Plains War," in Philip Weeks, ed., *The American Indian Experience: A Profile, 1524 to the Present* (Arlington Heights, IL, 1988), 137-39; William T. Hagan, "United States Indian Policies, 1860-1900," in William C. Sturtevant, ed., *Handbook of North American Indians*. 15 vols., vol. 4, *History of Indian-White Relations*, ed. Wilcomb E. Washburn (Washington, DC, 1988), 52-53. Hagan notes that the peace commissioners were much more successful in moving to Oklahoma the prairie tribes of eastern Nebraska and Kansas. These included the Sauk and Fox, Potawatomis, Osages, Iowas, Pawnees, and the Poncas.

4. Quoted in W. C. Vanderwerth, ed., *Indian Oratory: Famous Speeches by Noted Indian Chieftains* (Norman, OK, 1971), 161.

5. Robert M. Utley, "Indian-United States Military Situation, 1848-1891," in Washburn, *Handbook*, 170-73; Hagan, "United States Indian Policies," 55; idem, "How the West Was Lost," in Frederick E. Hoxie, ed., *Indians in American History: An Introduction* (Arlington Heights, IL, 1988), 181-84; Dunlay, "Fire and Sword," 140-51; Philip Weeks, *Farewell, My Nation: The American Indian and the United States, 1820-1890* (Arlington Heights, IL, 1990), 160-91.

6. Quoted in Virginia Irving Armstrong, comp., *I Have Spoken: American History through the Voices of the Indians* (Chicago, 1971), 86.

7. *Annual Report of the Commissioner of Indian Affairs to the Secretary of the Interior, 1873* (Washington, DC, National Cash Register Microfiche Edition, 1969), 200 (hereafter cited as ARCIA); ARCIA, 1874, 10-11; Francis Paul Prucha, *The Great Father: The United States Government and the American Indians*, 2 vols. (Lincoln, NE, 1984), 1:535-36; Arrell M. Gibson, *The American Indian: Prehistory to the Present* (Lexington, MA, 1980), 408-12; Weeks, *Farewell*, 160-69.

8. Quoted in Armstrong, *I Have Spoken*, 87-88.

9. Prucha, *Great Father*, 1:539; Hagan, "How the West Was Lost," 187-89; Gibson, *American Indian*, 418-22; Utley, "Indian-United States Military Situation," 178-80.

10. ARCIA, 1871, 297-309; ARCIA, 1873, 12-14; Gibson, *American Indian*, 351, 417-19.

11. Prucha, *Great Father*, 1:541-42, 574-77; Gibson, *American Indian*, 419.

12. Quoted in Armstrong, *I Have Spoken*, 116.

13. Quoted in T. C. McLuhan, ed., *Touch the Earth: A Self-Portrait of Indian Existence* (New York, 1971), 90.

14. ARCIA, 1873, 5-6; ARCIA, 1874, 6-8; ARCIA, 1875, 6-9; ARCIA, 1876, xiv-xv; Utley, "Indian-United States Military Situation," 174-76.

15. U.S. Bureau of the Census, *Report on Indians Taxed*, 7:637, 643.

16. Quoted in James Axtell, *The Invasion Within: The Conquest of Cultures in Colonial North America* (New York, 1985), 329.

17. "Annual Report," October 24, 1881, in Wilcomb E. Washburn, ed., *The American Indian and the United States: A Documentary History*, 4 vols. (New York, 1973), 1:300.

18. Carl Schurz, "Present Aspects of the Indian Problem," in Francis Paul Prucha, ed., *Americanizing the American Indians: Writings by the "Friends of the Indian," 1880-1900* (Cambridge,

MA, 1973), 14; "Report of Commissioner of Indian Affairs J. Q. Smith," October 30, 1876, in Washburn, *Documentary History,* 1:217; "Report of Commissioner of Indian Affairs Hiram Price," October 24, 1881, ibid., 300-301; Gibson, *American Indian,* 428; Prucha, *Great Father,* 1:593-94; Weeks, *Farewell,* 217-18.

19. T. Harry Williams, ed., *Hayes: The Diary of a President, 1875-1881* (New York, 1964), 148.

20. "Report of Commissioner of Indian Affairs Edward P. Smith," November 1, 1875, in Washburn, *Documentary History,* 1:210-11; Gibson, *American Indian,* 429-31; Prucha, *Great Father,* 2:645; Donald J. Berthrong, "Nineteenth-Century United States Government Agencies," in Washburn, *Handbook,* 261-63; idem. "The Bitter Years: Western Indian Reservation Life," in Weeks, *American Indian Experience,* 155; ARCIA, 1890, cxxix.

21. U.S. Bureau of the Census, *Report on Indians Taxed,* 7:74; David Wallace Adams, "From Bullets to Boarding Schools: The Educational Assault on the American Indian Identity," in Weeks, *American Indian Experience,* 220-21; Brian W. Dippie, *The Vanishing American: White Attitudes and U.S. Indian Policy* (Middletown, CT, 1982), 112; "Report of Commissioner E. A. Hayt," November 1, 1879, in Washburn, *Documentary History,* 1:249. For a discussion of Christian mission schools among the Indians see Prucha, *Great Father,* 1:141, 146-48, 597, and 2:693-94, 707-11.

22. Hagan, "United States Indian Policies, 1860-1900," 58-59; Prucha, *Great Father,* 2:689, 692-93; Gibson, *American Indian,* 431-32; Adams, "Bullets to Boarding Schools," 220-21.

23. ARCIA, 1873, 4-5; "Report of Hiram Price," October 10, 1882, in Washburn, *Documentary History,* 1:336-37; "Report of Price," 1881, in ibid., 1:307.

24. "Report of Price," 1881, in Washburn, *Documentary History,* 1:307; *Report on Indians Taxed,* 7:76; Berthrong, "Bitter Years," 158.

25. "Report of Hiram Price," October 10, 1883, in Washburn, *Documentary History,* 1:348-49; "Report of Commissioner of Indian Affairs T. J. Morgan," September 5, 1890, in ibid., 1:470-71. The sun dance, writes historian Arrell Gibson, was "the most important Teton Sioux ritual. . . . It was a time for giving thanks, for renewing national solidarity, and for gaining personal strength and status," Gibson, *American Indian,* 70.

26. Gibson, *American Indian,* 439-40; Walter L. Williams, "American Imperialism and the Indians," in Hoxie, *Indians in American History,* 235-37; *U.S. Statutes at Large,* 33:385; *United States v. Kagama,* 118 U.S. 375 (1886).

27. *Elk v. Wilkins,* 112 U.S. 94 (1884).

28. Prucha, *Great Father,* 1:582.

29. ARCIA, 1876, iii-iv; Gibson, *American Indian,* 430; Prucha, *Great Father,* 1:586-89; Red Cloud quoted in Armstrong, *I Have Spoken,* 93.

30. Paul Stuart, *The Indian Office: Growth and Development of an American Institution, 1865-1900* (Ann Arbor, MI, 1979), 5, 13, 20; Weeks, *Farewell,* 156, 197-204; Prucha, *Great Father,* 1:523.

31. Gibson, *American Indian,* 443, 451-55. Gibson noted, too, that by 1890 "the Indian population of the United States had been reduced from an estimated original 1,500,000 to less than 250,000."

32. David Rich Lewis, "Reservation Leadership and the Progressive-Traditional Dichotomy: William Wash and the Northern Utes, 1865-1928," in Albert L. Hurtado and Peter Iverson, eds., *Major Problems in American Indian History* (Lexington, MA, 1994), 420-34.

33. Gibson, *American Indian,* 472; Weeks, *Farewell,* 231; Berthrong. "Bitter Years," 167; C. Matthew Snipp, "Economic Conditions," in Mary B. Davis, ed., *Native America in the Twentieth Century: An Encyclopedia* (New York, 1994). 176.

34. Donald L. Parman, *Indians and the American West in the Twentieth Century* (Bloomington, IN, 1994), 9-10; Snipp, "Economic Conditions," 176.

35. Gibson, *American Indian,* 470-71; Edmund J. Danziger, Jr., *The Chippewas of Lake Superior* (Norman, OK, 1978), 94-97.

36. Weeks, *Farewell,* 231-32.

37. Gibson, *American Indian,* 466-69.

38. Quoted in Armstrong, *I Have Spoken,* 98.

39. Linderman, *Pretty-Shield,* 251.

40. Quoted in Armstrong, *I Have Spoken,* 126.

41. Ibid., 472-82; Utley, "Indian-United States Military Situation," 183.

42. Robert W. Mardock, "Indian Rights Movement until 1887," in Washburn, *Handbook,* 303-4; Hazel Whitman Hertzberg, "Indian Rights Movement, 1887-1973," in ibid., 305-6; Gibson, *American Indian,* 457-59, 494.

43. "Report for December 3, 1888," in Washburn, *Documentary History,* 1:421.

44. Prucha, *Great Father,* 2:656; "Statement of Objectives" (1885) in Prucha, *Americanizing the American Indians,* 43-44.

45. Table 10, ARCIA, 1895, 16; "Report of Acting Commissioner of Indian Affairs E. M. Marble," November 1, 1880, in Washburn, *Documentary History,* 1:283.

46. "Report of Morgan," 1890, in Washburn, *Documentary History,* 1:445; "Report of Commissioner of Indian Affairs J. D. C. Atkins," September 28, 1886, in ibid., 1:396.

47. "Report of Price," 1882, in Washburn, *Documentary History,* 1:330-31; "Report of Morgan," 1890, in ibid., 1:444-45.

48. "Report of Marble," 1880, in Washburn, *Documentary History,* 1:284.

49. ARCIA, 1895, 5; "Report of Morgan," October 1, 1889, in Washburn, *Documentary History,* 1:429-31; "Report of Price," 1882, in ibid., 1:333-34.

50. ARCIA, 1895, 5.

51. "Report of Morgan," 1890, in Washburn, *Documentary History,* 1:445-46.

52. ARCIA, 1895, 3-16; Frederick E. Hoxie, *A Final Promise: The Campaign to Assimilate the Indians, 1880-1920* (Lincoln, NE, 1984), 65. The trend toward educating Indians in the public schools continued, and by 1930 over half the enrolled native students attended these institutions. Margaret Connell Szasz and Carmelita Ryan, "American Indian Education," in Washburn, *Handbook,* 293.

53. Berthrong, "Bitter Years," 161-64; quoted in McLuhan, *Touch the Earth,* 104.

54. Berthrong, "Bitter Years," 162-64; Prucha, *The Great Father,* 2:699-700; Adams, "Bullets to Boarding Schools," 236-37; Robert A. Trennert, "Educating Indian Girls and Women at Nonreservation Boarding Schools, 1878-1920," in Hurtado and Iverson, *Major Problems in American Indian History,* 389-91.

55. "Report of Price," 1882, in Washburn, *Documentary History,* 1:336; "Report of Hayt," November 1, 1878, in ibid., 1:225-29. Objections to severalty during the 1880s are reviewed in the House Committee on Indian Affairs, "Minority Report on Land in Severalty Bill" (1880) in Prucha, *Americanizing the American Indians,* 122-28; and Hertzberg, "Indian Rights Movement," 306.

56. *Report on Indians Taxed,* 7:67; Gibson, "Indian Land Transfers," in Washburn, *Handbook,* 226-27.

57. *U.S. Statutes at Large,* 24:388-91. For a discussion of those tribes initially exempted from the Dawes Act see Gibson, *American Indian,* 497-98.

58. Hoxie, *Final Promise,* 70.

59. Merrill E. Gates, "Addresses at the Lake Mohonk Conferences," in Prucha, *Americanizing the American Indian,* 337, 342.

60. Quoted in Armstrong, *I Have Spoken,* 127-28.

61. Weeks, *Farewell,* 221-22; Wilcomb E. Washburn, ed., *The Assault on Indian Tribalism: The General Allotment Law (Dawes Act) of 1887* (Philadelphia, 1975), 30-31; Leonard A. Carlson, "Allotment," in Davis, *Native America in the Twentieth Century,* 29; Parman, *Indians and the American West in the Twentieth Century,* 3, 9-10.

62. Schurz, "Present Aspects of the Indian Problem," in Prucha, *Americanizing the American Indian,* 25. For a detailed analysis of how the idealistic purpose of the Dawes Act was subverted see Janet A. McDonnell, *The Dispossession of the American Indian 1887-1934* (Bloomington, IN, 1991).

63. Gibson, *American Indian,* 502.

64. Quoted in Armstrong, *I Have Spoken,* 129.

65. Red Cloud quoted in Wayne Moquin and Charles Van Doren, eds., *Great Documents in American Indian History* (New York, 1973), 265-66. For a thorough account of Wounded Knee see Robert M. Utley, *The Last Days of the Sioux Nation* (New Haven, CT, 1963).

66. Berthrong, "Nineteenth-Century Government Agencies," 263.

67. Davis, *Native America in the Twentieth Century,* xi.

. . .

FURTHER READING

Criticism

Carter, Paul A. *The Spiritual Crisis of the Gilded Age.* DeKalb: Northern Illinois University Press, 1971, 295 p.

A historical and literary account of the increased skepticism and secularism of the Gilded Age.

Daufenbach, Claus. "'Corruptionville': Washington, D. C., and the Portrait of an Era in Mark Twain's *The Gilded Age.*" In *Washington, D. C.: Interdisciplinary Approaches,* edited by Lothar Hönnighausen and Andreas Falke, pp. 151-66. Tübingen: Francke Verlag, 1993.

A defense of the historical merit of *The Gilded Age* for representing the artifice and greed of the times.

Dietrichson, Jan W. *The Image of Money in the American Novel of the Gilded Age.* New York: Humanities Press, 1969, 417 p.

A study of attitudes toward money expressed in Gilded Age-fiction, with special attention paid to William Dean Howells and Henry James.

Rugoff, Milton. *America's Gilded Age: Intimate Portraits from an Era of Extravagance and Change, 1850-1890.* New York: Henry Holt and Company, 1989, 374 p.

Combines biographies of many notable people from the Gilded Age with a more generalizing "social history."

Sproat, John G. *"The Best Men": Liberal Reformers in the Gilded Age.* New York: Oxford University Press, 1968, 356 p.

Focuses on the hopeful, yet often ineffective, progressive leaders of the Gilded Age.

Vandersee, Charles. "The Great Literary Mystery of the Gilded Age." *American Literary Realism* 7, No. 3 (Summer 1974): 245-72.

Unravels the mystery surrounding a political novel

published anonymously in 1883-84 and later attributed to John Milton Hay.

Walker, Robert H. *The Poet and the Gilded Age: Social Themes in Nineteenth Century American Verse.* Philadelphia: University of Pennsylvania Press, 1963, 387 p.

A study of Gilded-Age verse in light of its historical context and important themes of the day.

Utilitarianism

INTRODUCTION

Utilitarianism began as a movement in ethics of the late eighteenth-century primarily associated with the English philosopher Jeremy Bentham. The basic principle of Utilitarianism involves a calculus of happiness, in which actions are deemed to be good if they tend to produce happiness in the form of pleasure and evil if they tend to promote pain. As such, the philosophy is said to derive from the classical concept of hedonism, which values the pursuit of pleasure and avoidance of pain. The sophisticated system proposed by Bentham and later expanded by John Stuart Mill and others regards not only the end product of happiness, or utility, in actions, but also considers the motives of actions and the extent to which happiness can be created not only for the individual, but also for the members of society as a whole.

Both Bentham and Mill forwarded a belief in the intrinsic nature of value; thus good or the lack thereof could be regarded as inherent in an act or thing—a concept that allowed for the mathematical calculation of utility. Beginning from this view, the Utilitarians created systems of moral behavior as standards for how an individual ought to act in society. Bentham's principle of utility is frequently regarded as the "greatest happiness principle," the simple idea behind which is that individuals should endeavor to maximize happiness for the greatest number of people. While Bentham modified this concept over time, critics acknowledge that its essence remains intact throughout his work. Bentham developed this principle throughout a number of writings, including his most significant work of moral philosophy, *An Introduction to the Principles of Morals and Legislation* (1789). Ostensibly a plan for a penal code, *An Introduction* contains Bentham's view that individuals in society should act for the benefit of the community as a whole, and analyzes the means by which legislation should enumerate the penalties for those who refuse to contribute to the overall benefit of society. In this work, Bentham also sought to specifically record the sources of pleasure and pain, as well as to create a scale upon which the relative effects of individual acts in producing happiness or misery could be examined.

Notable among the Utilitarians to follow Bentham, the philosopher and economist John Stuart Mill made considerable contributions to Utilitarian philosophy, beginning with his succinct *apologia* for the doctrine in *Utilitarianism* (1861). The essay displays Mill's emphasis on rational calculation as the means by which human beings strive toward personal happiness. Mill's remaining philosophical writings elucidate his Utilitarianism, especially in regard to a number of related practical issues, including women's suffrage, and legislative and educational reform. Following his death, Mill's system was later expanded by his disciple Henry Sidgwick, who in his *Methods of Ethics* (1874) discussed the means by which individuals may endeavor to achieve moral action through reasoned behavior.

Numerous other individuals contributed to the Utilitarian movement in the nineteenth century, including the British philosophers John Austin and James Mill (J. S. Mill's father). In theory and in practice, Utilitarianism has continued to be influential, with the work of Bentham and Mill proving to be of the greatest importance and interest. Commentators on the writings of both men have continued the process of analyzing and codifying their work in order to more clearly define the doctrine. Among the principal interpretations have been a bifurcation of the philosophy into so-called "rule" and "act" Utilitarianism, the former emphasizing the importance of unbending codes of moral behavior that may not be violated, and the latter allowing for a freer interpretation that permits the breaking of certain Utilitarian rules under individual circumstances. Further criticism of Bentham's and Mill's Utilitarianism has focused on the important concept of justice as it applies to the principles of liberty and utility advocated by both. Additionally, critics have suggested the significant limitations of an ethical system that attempts to reduce human behavior and action to simple rational calculations of pleasure versus pain, but at the same time they acknowledge its considerable impact on nineteenth- and twentieth-century normative ethics.

REPRESENTATIVE WORKS

Jeremy Bentham
An Introduction to the Principles of Morals and Legislation (philosophy) 1789
Leading Principles of the Constitutional Code (philosophy) 1830

John Stuart Mill
A System of Logic, Ratiocinative And Inductive: Being A Connected View of The Principles Of Evidence, and the Methods of Scientific Investigation (philosophy) 1843
On Liberty (philosophy) 1859
Utilitarianism (philosophy) 1861
The Subjection of Women (philosophy) 1869

Henry Sidgwick
Methods of Ethics (philosophy) 1874

J. S. MILL'S UTILITARIANISM: LIBERTY, EQUALITY, JUSTICE

Jan Narveson (essay date 1979)

SOURCE: "Rights and Utilitarianism," in *New Essays on John Stuart Mill and Utilitarianism,* edited by Wesley E. Cooper, Kai Nielson, and Steven C. Patten, Canadian Association for Publishing in Philosophy, 1979, pp. 137-60.

[*In the following essay, Narveson explores the conflict between justice and utility in the thought of J. S. Mill.*]

I. Introduction

Few questions about utilitarianism have been more vexed than that of its relation to rights (and its associated notion, justice). It is commonplace to hold that there are nonutilitarian rights, rights not founded on considerations of utility. And it is even thought that the very notion of rights is inherently incapable of being significantly employed within the utilitarian framework. In the present paper, I wish to consider both of these matters. I propose to give reasons—mostly not really new—for rejecting the stronger, conceptual claim; and on the former, substantial question, I want to argue that the utilitarian at least has a respectable way of handling the vocabulary of rights, even a useful one. Further, I shall argue that what the utilitarian—in particular, J. S. Mill—has to say about rights is quite plausible, though I shall conclude with a question about how illuminating it is.

Ideally, we would begin with a detailed and thorough analysis of the notion, or perhaps we should say the notions, of rights. But this is scarcely possible within the limits envisaged here, and something more skeletal will have to do for present purposes. I will confine myself to three points here: correlativity, enforceability, and the distinction between positive and negative rights, this last being especially crucial in relation to the important subject of liberty. The three points are these.

(1) The *normative content,* as I shall call it, of rights claims is always to be found in statements about the obligations or duties of *others:* to say that A has some right or other is to say that some person or persons other than A have obligations or duties to do something or other in relation to A. (It might be in relation to some further person who is, e.g., a beneficiary, but if so, it is by virtue of A's relation to that person.) To attribute a right to A is not, as such, to say anything about what A ought to do, but only about what he *may* do; but the word 'may' here has its meaning in relation to the others in relation to whom A has the right:

that A "may" means that these others must *let* him if he wants, or something further (cf. point (3) below).

(2) There is a connection between rights and enforcement or enforceability, which can as well be made stipulative for present purposes. Mill, as we know, claimed that morality in general was enforceable[1], but if that is true, it will only be so by allowing rather attenuated methods of "enforcement" to count as enforcement.[2] However, we can just say that what we are especially concerned with are rights which are genuinely enforceable, at least *prima facie.*

(3) We must be aware of the distinction between *negative* and *positive* rights, a distinction which is crucial to the whole subject, since ambiguities generated by talk of rights are largely due to failure to bring it out. The distinction is between (a) obligations not to interfere and (b) obligations to assist, help, or enable. This distinction is not the same as that between rights to liberty and rights to welfare or to property; rather, it cuts across that distinction. *Whatever p* may be, A's having the right that *p* can consist either in others being obligated not to bring it about that not-*p* (negative right) *or* in their being obligated to help (to some degree) bring it about that *p*. My right to a house may be my right that you not damage, destroy, or use a house which I already have, *or* it can be a right that you help build one which I don't have, or help buy it, etc. This significance of the distinction will emerge below, especially in sections 3 and 4 below.

II. A Right to Utility?

With these preliminaries in mind, we now move to the question of how rights-talk fits into the utilitarian view. There are two general lines we can take on this, one a good deal more useful than the other. First, one can maintain that everybody (animals too, perhaps) has one basic right, namely the right to have one's utility counted equally with all others'. Second, and much more usefully, one can produce a schedule of more concrete rights which is to be grounded on the utility of having those rights recognized and adhered to in practice. The second is where "the action" is, but the first also deserves notice. I discuss it in this section.

In a lengthy footnote to the concluding chapter of *Utilitarianism,* Mill discusses an objection by Herbert Spencer to the effect that "the principle of utility presupposes the anterior principle, that everybody has an equal right to happiness". He goes on to note that this idea "may be more correctly described as supposing that equal amounts of happiness are equally desirable, whether felt by the same or different persons", and this, as he points out, is "not a *pre*-supposition . . . but the very principle of utility itself . . .". He concludes that "If there is any anterior principle implied, it can be no other than this, that the truths of arithmetic are applicable to the valuation of happiness, as of all other measurable quantities."[3] (58) Now, Mill is surely correct on the two main points here. He is correct that everyone's having an equal right to happiness is not the most accurate way of expressing what the principle of utility either says or implies. Why? Because it seems to suggest that there is some *equal amount* of happiness to which everyone *has a right;* and this the principle neither says nor supports. Mill's correction of Spencer on this point may be taken to be definitive of utilitarianism as it is currently understood among professional philosophers: that equal amounts of happiness are equally desirable, no matter which sentient being experiences them. And he is correct in saying that this latter principle is not some further thing pre-supposed by utilitarianism, but rather "the very principle itself". But it is less clear (a) that what is presupposed is *only* that arithmetical truths apply to quantities of utility, and (b) just where the notion of a *right* to utility, in some sense or other, should be brought in, if at all. A word about each of these is in order.

(a) Is anything "presupposed" by the principle of utility? If that principle is simply stated as Mill has it above, that equal amounts of utility are equally desirable, then it is arguable that a further assumption is needed, namely that *desirability is all that counts,* i.e., that right actions are actions which maximise what is, all things taken into account, desirable. This I take it, is what makes utilitarianism a "teleological" theory in the usual classifications of philosophers. A deontological theory, by contrast, is supposed to be one which says that something *else* besides desirability counts—that there are other sources of moral rightness than desirability (or, if you like, read 'goodness' for 'desirability'). Now, if this is logically open to dispute, then on the face of it there are two claims made by utilitarianism, and not just one: (i) that desirability is all that counts, and (ii) that desirability is measured exclusively by utility. There is, of course, disagreement, or at least unclarity, about just what utility is, but those disagreements would issue in different versions of utilitarianism, rather than rejections of utilitarianism, whereas rejections of either (i) or (ii) would yield rejections of utilitarianism. And here again, those who argue against utilitarianism on the score of its handling of rights may take the line that rights are not essentially concerned with desirability at all; or they may (but less interestingly, in my view) argue that rights are resistant to utilitarianism on the second score, holding that they are responsive to values other than utility.

Why is the second score less interesting from the point of view of the status of rights in moral theory? Partly because when we consider putative candidates for values other than utility, it is too easy to reply that these, after all, are simply some sources of utility among others; but more importantly because any supposedly other values introduced will behave so much like utility. To take an example which is not entirely a caricature, suppose that one espouses, *à la* Nietzsche, a concern for what we might call "supermanhood". Now Nietzscheans, some of them anyway, seem to hold that supermen count for more than others, And they seem to think also that egoism has some-

thing to do with it; but unfortunately, what it seems to have to do with it is that supermen get to be egoistic, unlike sheeppeople, who do not. But what if one superman, S1, has it within his power to kill another superman, S2, or more generally to do something, *x,* which would cripple his superman potential? And suppose that this other budding superman would in fact become more of a superman than the first one if this crippling act *x* were not performed. Now, ought S1, as a good Nietzschean, to perform *x* or not? Well, if he thinks that supermanhood is an intrinsically good thing, whether or not he himself exemplifies it, then he may have to back off from *x*—to sacrifice a bit of his own superman-potential in the interests of greater supermanhood on the whole. Apart from the supposedly nonutilitarian *value* of supermanhood, its arithmetic may well be the same as the utilitarians'.

More likely, though, is that the theorist in question thinks he has an objection along the lines of (ii) when in fact he has one along the lines of (i). For he may introduce a supposedly evaluative notion, "human dignity" or "autonomy" or "personhood", say, which in fact is not another *evaluative* notion at all, but rather, a claim that values aren't all that count. What counts instead, he maintains, is *whose* values are relevant to a certain decision. People have, he will say, the right to make their *own* decisions, not because they will likely be better decisions if made by the agent rather than someone else, but just because they *are* the agents. There is, it will be maintained, a certain sphere belonging, so to speak, to each individual such that within that sphere he may do as he pleases without the intervention of anyone else, and this *not* because any values of any kind will be promoted by having it so, but simply because that sphere is that agent's. If it's my arm, e.g., then I get to decide what is to be done with it, and this is so whether I use it stupidly or intelligently, whether I promote one value, another value, or none by my use of it. Clearly this is to introduce a purely deontic element into the picture: it is to say that *whose* values (if any) may properly be brought to bear on a given decision is to be determined by factors quite other than how much of any sort of value is thereby promoted. To this kind of view we shall return later in this paper.

(b) Meanwhile, what about a "right to have one's utility counted"? Is this something the utilitarian can countenance, or should? There are two aspects of this which we should distinguish. One is whether framing the principle of utility in such terms suggests considerations which go beyond the moral ambit of this theory. The other concerns what we might call the arithmetic of the theory. Both call for comment.

(1) Regarding the first, there is a continuance, in brackets, of the footnote by Mill which has occasioned this discussion, addressing itself to the question whether utilitarians, in addition to invoking "empirical generalisations from the observed rules of conduct", may also avail themselves of "the laws of life and the conditions of existence", thereby coming up with kinds of action which "necessarily tend to

promote happiness". And Mill agrees that they certainly may, taking exception, as a good empiricist, only to the term 'necessarily'. Now, if there are fundamental "laws" of human nature relating certain kinds of conduct to happiness, those might be the foundation for specific concrete rights—a possibility we will advert to later in this essay. But what Mill does not do here is to address himself to the rather different question whether the principle of utility is basically empirical *at all.* The point is this. If we ask *why* an individual would or should be inclined to embrace considerations of pure utility, counting the utility of others equal in its impact on his own conduct to the utility of himself, then what answers might be produced? Mill's answer to this, insofar as he addresses himself to the matter at all, is that we have, or at least are capable of coming to have, a "feeling of unity with all the rest" (Ev. 30), stemming from a "deeply rooted conception which every individual even now has of himself as a social being" (31). But apart from the question whether we really do have this degree of fellow-feeling, and whether the kind of fellow-feeling we have really works in utilitarian fashion, there seems to be a further question: *viz., why* we should inculcate this feeling (which Mill does not argue is innate in us but only acquired, though "natural" (28-30)) rather than some other? The situation is especially acute in view of Mill's apparent embracing of what seems to amount to psychological egoism. In his notorious discussion of the proof of utility, as so many writers have pointed out, Mill's major premise is that "desiring a thing and finding it pleasant, aversion to it and thinking of it as painful, are phenomena entirely inseparable . . ." (36). But, although Mill does not come right out and acknowledge the matter, his terminology being apparently neutral on the score of whose pleasure can be in question in this premise, it would surely be extraordinarily implausible for Mill to be maintaining that for any given person, A, the thought that just *any* other given person, B, is experiencing some pleasure is equivalent to *A's desiring* B to have that experience. Yet it is just that proposition which is required if we are to try to make the principle of utility fall out of the proof. Links seem to be required in order to connect the pleasure of an agent, which is what apparently motivates his actions on Mill's view (as it certainly was on Bentham's), with the pleasures of all others. Well, what can provide such a link? One candidate would be an *a priori* idea that one ought to regard the pleasures of any person equally with those of any others. This in fact was the option embraced by Sidgwick, who arrives at "the self-evident principle that the good of any one individual is of no more importance, from the point of view of (if I may say so) the Universe, than the good of any other . . . And it is evident to me that as a rational being I am bound to aim at good generally . . . not merely at a particular part of it."[4] And one way of expressing this claim would be by saying that each person has a *right* that his utility be counted equally with that of all others.

What is of interest about this option is that it utilizes one of the ideas which has often been associated with the idea of rights, namely, that they are basic, *a priori,* and/or prior

to considerations of the utility *of others.* The utilitarian cannot easily hold that the reason *why* we ought to account the utility of others as equal in value to that of our own is simply that the utility of others naturally and inherently must promote our *own* utility; both because that is implausible in itself and because it seems to make him a kind of egoist. It seems best for him to say that there is no further *reason* why the utility of others counts equally with our own—that it just *does.* But obviously this is more than the recognition that the "laws of arithmetic" also apply to quantities of utility. Some have, of course, denied that they do, in the sense that they deny the commensurability of interpersonal utility, the cardinalizability of measures of any utility, or both. But even if we grant both of those disputed points, there is still evidently a gap between my agreeing (a) that if I perform action *x,* the total utility for all persons concerned is *n,* whereas if I perform *y,* the total will be less than *n, but* the amount realized for *me* will be greater, and my agreeing (b) that I ought, then, to do *x* rather than *y.* If it makes any sense at all to "close" or "bridge" such a gap, the notion of an *a priori* right might be one way to bridge it. And it of course still leaves us with utilitarianism. So there is no conceptual impossibility about employing rights-talk as a utilitarian in this way. All that doing so will yield is room for a division between intuitionistic utilitarians and others (if there are any others); and that would be a dispute about meta-ethics, not about whether utilitarianism was correct as the substantial principle of ethics.

(2) A quite different issue, however, is also raised by the idea of expressing the principle of utility in terms of a right to have one's utility counted equally. For suppose we accept the idea that if A has the right to do *x,* then B must allow A to do *x* (at very least) *and* this entails enforceability; or, if this is different, that it entails the need for a substantial, rather than merely a very small, weight in whatever contrary consideration might override the right. This aspect of the idea of rights can, as will be discussed below, be effectively employed with regard to certain sources of utility rather than others. But can it be employed in a supposed right to have one's utility counted at all?

What we would need, to do so, is a distinction between cases where the agent goes wrong by virtue of having *misestimated* relevant utilities, or where although he estimates them properly he fails to act on the results, and cases where he simply *doesn't count* some relevant people's utility at all. Now, perhaps there is such a distinction. But it is hard to see how it could be the basis for a major distinction in our response to such cases. After all, the difference in resulting utility might easily be just as great due to misestimation as to failures to estimate at all; and given the principle of utility, what must matter is just the size of the difference, rather than its source. What the source is will be relevant to the determination of just what kind of corrective action to take (if any), but it is not obvious that any major difference in the degree of severity (say) with which we should treat such agents could be correlated with that factor. Indeed, when we reflect on this, we can readily identify a disposition which would be worse, in utilitarian terms, than the disposition to fail to count some persons' utility: namely, a disposition to promote disutility rather than utility. What is wrong with the malevolent person is not that he fails to count some people's utility, but rather than he counts it in, so to say, the debit column rather than the credit column. Now, it's not entirely clear what *not* "counting" someone's utility consists in. When people are close at hand, it must be a little difficult to ignore them entirely; and even if they aren't, provided that one is aware that they are in the picture at all, it's surely not too easy to pay no attention whatever to the question of how they might be affected by actions which do affect them. But one would still suppose that we could expect worse from someone who delights in the sufferings of others than from someone who doesn't go out of his way to determine how others will be affected. And if we want to say that the "right to have one's utility counted" is really the right to have it positively counted, i.e. positively evaluated on an equal basis, then the difference between that and simply reasserting the principle of utility is evidently zero.

In this second aspect of rights-talk, then, it seems at least misleading, at best pointless, and at worst incoherent to talk of a right to have one's utility counted.

III. UTILITARIAN RIGHTS

We turn, then, to the second and, I have said, "more useful" way of bringing rights into utilitarianism. This consists in identifying various types of actions, or dispositions, and signalling them out for special protection, or in identifying various sources of wellbeing which are thought to be more essential or more important than others, and granting positive rights to those who might readily fail to come in for enough of those goods otherwise. Both call for comment. (Indeed, both, but especially the former, could generate—have generated—books.); so too does the general idea. I shall discuss these in reverse order, first considering the general idea, then each category of rights within the utilitarian framework, following through with a case study of a putative nonutilitarian theorist who, I believe, turns out to be utilitarian despite himself.

(1) The general plan for utilitarian-based specific rights is implicit in Mill's treatment. To grant a right to someone is to grant protection to him in that respect: that is to say, to legitimize the use of some degree of coercion in preventing interferences with what he has the right to do or have. But these coercions have a cost: for those upon whom they fall are either injured or damaged in some degree, or at least deprived of some liberty, since they are either disenabled from doing certain things they want to do, or at least obstacles are put in their way. We are, in short, visiting some actual or potential disutility on violators or potential violators of the right. This is the cost of rights. In order for society to be justified in erecting them, therefore, the various actions which qualify for righthood must have at least enough utility (i.e., interference with them must

have enough disutility to the subjects of them and to others) to offset the cost. It is for this reason that it would be a crude error to imagine that any action, however trivial the difference in net utility between doing it and not doing it, will automatically qualify for righthood on utilitarian theory, and partly for this reason that it is an equally crude error to imagine that actions which do qualify for rights on this theory may be interfered with, and hence the right in question infringed or violated, for any slight gain in net utility supposed possible by comparing simply that action, taken in the abstract, with some other and incompatible configuration of acts. For if the expected utility from a certain type of act as compared with some incompatible configuration of acts were so nearly the same, it could not have qualified for righthood in the first place.

There is another, more problematic reason for the latter. Once you institutionalize a particular right, you of course also alter people's expectations in regard to that kind of activity, and so you increase the loss in utility from that right's being violated. One can no longer simply turn around and say that the incompatible configuration of actions has more utility, viewed abstractly. For we can no longer view it so: now we have to take into account the disruptive effects of doing things differently from what has been expected. Even so, of course, the right *can* be outweighed sometimes. But that may be an advantage for the theory, not a disadvantage. Few theorists seriously maintain that no concrete right may ever be justifiably contravened. The question is only whether utilitarianism makes this too "easy"; which remains to be seen. It is obvious, though, that a right which can be routinely overridden is no right at all, practically speaking. So if utilitarianism were to lead to the implication that any right can be routinely overridden, then it would be correct to claim that utilitarianism should dispense with the notion altogether.

(2) Positive rights are conceptually more comfortable on the utilitarian theory than any other (plausible) one. To have a positive right is for it to be the case that others must, if needed, *assist* one in doing or having the thing in question. It is sometimes wondered just who are the subjects of the duties which positive rights impose. The answer is not far to seek, given utilitarianism: in general they fall on everybody, more or less in proportion to ability to help out and thus equally on those equally able. But of course it will be the case that division of labor is called for: some will help out directly, others by paying salaries (for instance) to those who do so, and by being ready to contact the right people when needed, and so on. In addition there is a specific answer, for those who are in the best position to help will, of course, have the duty to do so; though this could be onerous for certain persons, and for those persons, other people will have the duty to organize a system for relieving them or compensating them. The puzzles which some have alleged to find probably stem from failure to distinguish three relevant kinds of actions: (a) organizational and stimulative actions, that is, actions designed to get others into action as opposed to actions directly responsive to the needs in question; (b) those

direct actions themselves, such as the application of artificial respiration or the supplying of food or shelter; and (c) *supporting* actions, such as the paying of money to professionals in the (a) and (b) departments. The duty of each and every individual will be to address himself to these rights and do what he can best and most easily do.

But when will there be positive rights? Again in form, the answer is simple enough. A will have a positive right against B if the amount which A gains by being enabled to do the action or be in the condition in question, less the amount which B loses by not only doing the enabling deed but also by being *required* to do it, gives more overall utility than would stem from *not* requiring B to do it. Well and good, but when is that? It must not be assumed that it is quite so easy for all those conditions to be realized as is often supposed by critics of utilitarianism. For to begin with, consider the prospect of spending one's entire life tending the sick, feeding the hungry, and so on, rather than the other things you could be doing with your time. The potential cost in quality of life may surely be enormous here. Of course, it *may* not. But suppose on the contrary that some people are attracted to these activities, would enjoy them and find their lives highly rewarding if devoted to them; and suppose that many others are so sympathetic with these activities that they will voluntarily give money and other kinds of help to make them possible. In that case, it may well be that the needs in question are pretty well catered to *without* imposing a duty on everyone to help out. Possibly it will be sufficient simply to inculcate a general disposition to approve and encourage those who do get more involved. It is never, of course, self-evident that any particular concretely specified action is right on utilitarian principles, and here is a case in point.

(3) It is fundamental in these matters that we realize that positive rights are incompatible with absolute negative rights. If you *must* do certain things, then you do not have the right not to do them if you don't want to. This will therefore militate against positive rights to the extent that there is a case for negative rights. Our utilitarian case for positive rights, in particular, is constrained by the utilitarian case for negative ones. The more utility we suppose there is to be got from granting negative rights, the less there can be from granting positive ones.

It is true, of course, that any granting of rights at all deprives people of some liberty, namely the liberty to interfere with what the right is a right to. Still, if it is possible to make a clear formulation of there being rights to liberty, so that the liberty we are deprived of by granting these rights is only the liberty to interfere with others' liberty, then it can be coherently argued that pure negative rights maximize liberty insofar as it is possible to do this for more than one person.

But *is* it possible to do this coherently? J. S. Mill, as we know, attempted to formulate a principle of liberty which looks at first sight to be purely Libertarian, in the contemporary sense of that term: i.e., it seems to grant only negative rights. "That principle is, that the sole end for which mankind are warranted, individually or collectively, in interfering with the liberty of action of any of their number, is self-protection. That the only purpose for which power can be rightly exercised over any member of a civilized community, against his will, is to prevent harm to others . . ." (Ev. 73). Though not devoid of unclarities, the force of this principle *looks* to be Libertarian, for it not only declares that the good of an individual, A, is not sufficient reason to prevent A from doing as A wishes, but it also implies that the good of any other individual or set of them is likewise not such reason; for it allows only the prospect of *harm* to others, rather than the prospect of *less promotion of their good* than otherwise, as reason to interfere. As D. G. Brown points out in his superb analysis of Mill's view on liberty and utility,[5] Mill can only salvage certain things which amount to positive rights on his principle by fudging the distinction between harming and not helping. If we unfudge that, the Principle of Liberty appears to yield no duty to help others, even others in dire need and at trifling cost to oneself.[6]

There is another aspect of the Libertarian idea in Mill, however, which urgently requires attention if we are to get as far as the conclusion just noted. This has to do, in effect, with private property. That this is relevant to ideas of liberty may seem at first sight astonishing, but it surely is so, as can be seen by reflecting briefly on, for instance, the principle of free speech and discussion. For it will surely be agreed to by anyone, even the most determined socialist, that whether a given person, A, may hold forth with a given speech, S, depends on whether, for instance, he is proposing to do it in your bedroom at 2:00 A.M. A theorist may want to hold that it is the duty of society to provide places in which A may deliver his speech, either when he pleases or at least at some specified times; another theorist may even want to hold that it is the duty of society to provide an audience to hear him out, however puerile his tirade. But those theorists are not, any longer, defending free speech as a negative right. They are instead holding it to be, to some degree at least, a *positive* right. In its pure negative form, which I believe is equivalent to asserting the right of free speech strictly as a *liberty* and not anything else, we must surely hold that it consists in being allowed to say what one pleases to whomever is willing to have you do so at the places and times in question. And *that* depends on whether those so willing are the ones whose will properly determines the disposition of those places and times. Is it my living room, and am I the audience? If so, then if I have permitted you to produce speech S there at time *t,* with me and others I am willing to have there who are willing to hear you utter S, *then* perhaps, your liberty to utter S is assured and absolute given the Libertarian principle. But in order for it to be so, it must be the case that the living room in question is genuinely mine. If it is not, then others have, in principle, some voice in the matter of whether you are to be allowed to give your speech there; and to that extent, you will not be entirely free to do so, even in the circumstances just specified.

This other aspect of the libertarian idea emerges in Mill when he discusses the bearing of social interests on various of our actions, allowing that when our actions essentially affect these interests, we may then be held responsible for our inactions as well as our actions. But, says Mill in a notorious passage, "there is a sphere of action in which society, as distinguished from the individual, has, if any, only an indirect interest; comprehending all that portion of a person's life and conduct which affects only himself, or as it also affects others, only with their free, voluntary, and undeceived consent and participation . . . This, then, is the appropriate region of human liberty". (75) Various critics have pointed out that it is not plausible to claim that there is any "region of action" which is *inherently* incapable of affecting others, and if allowing genuine liberty is contingent on there being any such region, then libertarianism is surely an ill-fated idea. But we should be clear that what Mill is in effect doing is arguing that the "inward domain of consciousness" is the *private property* of the person whose consciousness it is: that person, and no one else, may properly determine what goes on in that "sphere". The region of "tastes and pursuits", another on Mill's list, obviously can get us out into the public arena where these pursuits can bump up against the pursuits of others, and Mill's argument can only be construed to defend 'absolute' liberty in those actions up to the point where they do so; appropriately, he deduces a right of association next, for if I do *x* in your presence and you do *y* in mine, then this will be consistent with liberty only if we both agree to this—and only if our "presences" are *ours.* But what if the ground on which we stand belongs to someone else? To say that it does is to say that that someone, call him A, may declare us out of bounds and require us to move on, and no principle of freedom of tastes and pursuits can be invoked against this unless the property in question is *not* entirely that person's.

Now, *any* action requires the use of something or other by the actor: perhaps only a mind, as in the case of thinking, perhaps also an arm and a head, as in scratching one's head, and so on. In every case, to assert that one may do *as one pleases,* i.e. that one's own decision is a sufficient condition for the action decided upon to be legitimate, is *ipso facto* to assert that the things involved in the action, at least during the time when the liberty in question is a right for the person in question, do *belong* to that person. And if for any reason one thinks they do not, then to that extent one cannot coherently hold that the person in question is fully at liberty, has an unqualified right, to do the thing in question.

If the doctrine that literally *nothing but* harms to others licence interference with liberty, i.e. Libertarianism, is to get off the ground, then what seems to be required is that everything which can figure in any human action be divided up and assigned to distinct individuals. In form, the doctrine will get off the ground if this is done in an arbitrary manner, but certainly the doctrine will lack credibility unless it is done in a *non*-arbitrary manner. Mill does not go into this, nor does Brown in his analysis. In part, of course, Mill doesn't because he isn't really a Libertarian, being instead a utilitarian bent on championing *some* liberty as being in the interest of mankind. The interesting question is whether he could still have been arguing plausibly if he had gone farther, sticking to the evident meaning of the principle of liberty as he states it and swallowing the implication that we do not have the sort of duties which he supposed it obvious that we had, such as "to give evidence in a court of justice; to bear his fair share in the common defence, or in any other joint work necessary to the interest of the society of which he enjoys the protection; and to perform certain acts of individual beneficence, such as saving a fellow-creature's life . . ." (74). Or at any rate, the implication is that these are not rock-bottom duties, but instead, people would have them only insofar as they have voluntarily taken them, for instance as members of some organization which assumes these responsibilities. To do all that, I think, would require completing the doctrine about private property. And to argue that Libertarianism is actually supported by utilitarianism, one must in effect argue that *it is in the public interest to have everything private:* that the sum of human happiness (or whatever one takes utility to be) will be maximized if with respect to every particular thing there is some particular person or voluntarily acting group of persons such that what is done with that thing, within the limits of the rights of others, is determined entirely by the will of *that* person or group.

I certainly have no intention here of arguing for that conclusion, but I do want to point out that it is not logically impossible, at any rate, to proceed in that fashion. It is not, for example, incoherent to argue from public morality to private property just because the former is public and the latter is private. All morality, I take it, is public, as a matter of form: for something to be morally wrong is for it to be a sort of thing which there is a publicly-considered reason for condemning. But this does not logically imply anything about how much, if any, of the domain of humanly usable objects should be reckoned as in the private sphere. Its being in the private sphere *means* that we all ought to respect the will of the person who is the thing's owner, and the reason, if there is one, why we all ought to do so will itself be a publicly-considered one. Further, that publicly-considered reason *could* be that it is in the public interest to run things that way rather than some other. This, indeed, was the sort of argument given by Adam Smith on behalf of noninterventionism in the economic realm; and whether the argument was correct or not is open to question, but if it is wrong, it is not so on purely logical grounds.

But how might such an argument go? There are two general lines available. First, one can argue on extrinsic grounds, for example by pointing out that when usable entities are "public", then the determination of what is to happen to them is evidently going to have to be political, that politics is invariably messy, inefficient, even downright incompetent, that it involves enormous demands on the time and energy of the body politic which could well be better spent in other ways, and that it is fraught with dangers, including especially the dangers of harassment of innocent people and misuse of the overwhelming powers of government which is virtually necessitated by their being powers of that kind. One can argue that when activities are run as businesses, there are people who have a genuine and personal interest in the flourishing of those businesses, an interest, moreover, which compels them to cater to the people they serve rather than high-handedly telling those people what they ought to want and to remove their caps and stand humbly while waiting in line to get it. But even those arguments are not purely "extrinsic", looked at at all closely. They edge up toward the second sort of arguments, those on intrinsic grounds. These are arguments to the effect that to be at liberty, to have a sphere in which others cannot tell you what to do (but can only suggest), a sphere in which you do what you please, in short, is a good thing; as did Mill. But there are two versions of this argument the difference between which we need to take careful note of. One way is also exemplified by Mill, perhaps, for Mill, having stated that he has no brief with "abstract right as a thing independent of utility" and regards utility as "the ultimate appeal on all ethical questions", goes on to say "but it must be utility in the largest sense, grounded on the permanent interests of man as a progressive being" (74). But what about the interests of *un*progressive beings, beings who would rather sit and drink beer and watch television than participate in the higher activities of progressive mankind? Mill's official doctrine, actually, quite plainly defends the right of the unprogressive to be so as well; but then we may have our doubts about the amount of weight we should want to put on considerations of man as a "progressive being" in the ultimate doctrine by which we want to defend that right. It would be better, I think, to leave 'progressiveness' out of the picture at that level, and instead merely talk of the actual preferences and satisfactions of people—their interests as seen by *them,* rather than their "true interests" as seen by some high-brow social theorist.

And if we take this second option—the "lower" as opposed to the "higher" way, as we might call it—then it seems to me that the defense of liberty on intrinsic grounds is likely to be easier rather than harder. People want to do what they want to do, and not (necessarily) what anybody else wants them to do; and *prima facie,* then, they shall have more of what they want if their wanting to do it is taken to be a sufficient reason for others not to interfere. Obviously, there will be cases in which a person's long-run wants conflict with his short-run wants, and cases where his ignorance of relevant information creates a problem, since it may be that what he would want given that information and what he now claims to want also conflict. Here, notoriously, we get into the manifold problems of aggregating utility even at the individual level. Nevertheless, we do not clearly need to defend liberty "as an abstract right independent of utility". That there is a straightforward if *prima facie* argument at the ordinary level of what I have called "low-brow utility" is surely not to be ignored.

But it is, certainly, a good way from there to the defense on utilitarian grounds of liberty as a *right.* Granted that each person, A, seems *prima facie* to be in for more utility if A does what he wants rather than what others do, it does not follow that A wouldn't be in for still more utility if *other* people also did what A wants rather than what *they* want to do; nor is it self-evident that what each person gains from accepting the liberty principle generally will out-weigh what he loses from doing so.

Not self-evident, agreed. But a couple of reminders will push things along in that direction some considerable distance. For there is, remember, freedom of association, which follows straight off from the general idea of liberty. Now if a whole lot of people should think that they would be better off subscribing to certain positive rights and duties, then why wouldn't those people join together in a community, conditions of entrance into which involved likewise subscribing to those principles? And if those people did do that, while others who disagreed with the wisdom of those principles remained nonsubscribers in their Lockean state of nature, doesn't that look like going in the direction of each sort of party being happier? Doesn't that seem more plausible than cramming the duty down the throats of all?

IV. A CASE STUDY

Within the confines of this essay, it is, of course, not possible to flesh out arguments of the kind I have just been briefly sketching. Instead, I hope to advance our appreciation of the situation regarding rights and utility by examining with some care a recent contribution on the subject—in fact, a contribution to a recent volume in this series: "Rights, Utilities, and Contracts", by Alan Goldman.[7] This essay is intended to show "how rights are related to utilities by showing how they arise from interests", the thesis being that the "first purpose of recognizing rights is to protect certain interests of individuals against utility maximizing or additive calculations regarding (other) interests of others". (123)[8] ". . . we consider certain interests qualitatively more important than others, e.g. our interest in being able to say what we please more valuable in its satisfaction than our interest in not being offended. This ranking holds even though utility may lie occasionally on the side of silencing someone when many others take offense at what he intends to say . . . Part of the rationale.. is to protect these important interests against being overridden by additions of those less important." (123)

So it seems that what determines whether a given interest is also a right is *how important* it is. If so, of course, the next question would be what measures "importance". *Prima facie,* it would mean something like "more valuable"—which in turn usually means that it has more of what utilitarians call utility. Which in turn, of course, would usually mean that the point of recognizing rights is that there is more utility in doing so than in not doing so. But then, how is utility going to "occasionally lie on the side of silencing" the rightholder, for instance?

Or is this the view? Well, "It seems then that we recognize a *qualitative* two-fold distinction between types of interests, some generating rights and others remaining mere interests or utilities (when satisfied)". (123, my underlining) Perhaps what we have here is an espousal of turn-of-the-century G. E. Moore-type intuitionism, with some interests being not only more substantial but uniquely (and inexplicably) more "valuable" than others? Thus we have mentions of satisfactions of some interests being "intrinsically more valuable than the satisfaction of others", and of "intrinsic differences among interests" (127). But I don't believe Goldman really means this, and if he does, then he has some explaining to do to the agents who participate in the "contractarian framework" which, at the close of the article, he invokes to shore up these needed distinctions; for these agents, as usual, are first, *a la* Rawls, put into a condition of equality and then told to negotiate schedules of rights in the interests of what would be "prudent", (133), i.e., rational, i.e., most in the interests of the agent. Which suggests that the appeal to special "intrinsic values" is really, as one would expect, a fancy way of saying that they are very sizable interests. But wait a minute. Mightn't there be "trivial rights" which it would be silly to claim ought never to be overridden by mere utility? Take, for instance, my right to water my roses. Mightn't that be overridden by, say, the greater need of others for the water? Trouble is, if it's a really sizable need—e.g., if others would die of thirst if I exercised this right—then it will turn out that my right is overridden by a greater right, the right to life, say: find sizable enough utilities, and of course Goldman will discern a right hiding under them. However, he has two other gambits. One is to distinguish between one's *having* a right and its *being right to exercise it* on a particular occasion. But the example he chooses to illustrate this is rather infelicitous: Goldman's "right to eat dinner when I like" which, if exercised at four o'clock, say, might "greatly disrupt the activities of the rest of my family. . . . Must my right be honored at their expense?" No, because "I can have a right to eat dinner when I like and yet be wrong in choosing to exercise it at certain times when that would inconvenience others." (128) But what kind of right is this? Is it a positive right against the other members? If so, we might have our suspicions about how Goldman runs his family life, since its being a positive right against them would mean that if he wants to eat at 4:00, then they must scurry off, at his bidding, to round up the dinner—greatly to their inconvenience, indeed! Presumably, however, he doesn't intend that. He probably means only to assert a negative right. These, we will recall, entail only a duty on others not to prevent him from having dinner at 4:00; and this, it seems reasonable enough, they *do* have. But it also means that if he wants his dinner at 4:00, he's going to have to cook it himself, and maybe clean up afterward too! Even that might inconvenience others somewhat, of course, and so we might still agree that Goldman probably ought not to exercise this right. But this could reasonably be phrased in terms of a right on their part not to be inconvenienced, something which Goldman says would make "talk of rights lose all meaning here". But why would it? His right to have din-

ner when he pleases is surely exactly on all fours with their right not to be inconvenienced, if we are going to talk about rights in this family context at all. The one is as trivial as the other, and after all, Goldman is supposed to be producing an example of trivial rights at work. I conclude that Goldman still doesn't have an example of a nonutilitarian right somehow grounded on interests. What he has, if a right at all, is two utilitarian rights, both grounded in the general interest.

Goldman's other argument concerning "trivial" rights also has its problems. The argument is that "although these rights may not seem important in themselves, as parts of the general right to do whatever we please that is not morally forbidden, or that does not interfere with the rights of others, they represent an extremely important interest. This is our interest in being free from tyrannical interference with the everyday course of our lives, one which is more important than the satisfaction of our occasional desires to interfere in the course of others' lives." (128) This, unfortunately, is either to compound muddle or to play into Mill's hands. To say that a "trivial" right of his own may not be overridden by a (merely) greater utility of someone else's when he has a "trivial" right to do something "which is not morally forbidden, or that does not interfere with the rights of others", is question-begging, since what we want to know is whether others *do* have the right to override a trivial liberty of his on account of some urgent need on their part. And on the other hand, to say that we have a nontrivial interest in "being free from tyrannical interference with the everyday course of our lives" is simply to assert that what looks trivial is not so, on closer examination. For it is a *case* of something nontrivial (according to Goldman), namely our liberty to do as we please. If that is nontrivial, though, it means that it will take a substantial utility of someone else's to justify his interference: but if it's a substantial utility, it will then be important and he will have a right to do it, and mine will thus be overridden, and so we are back in the utilitarian ballpark.

What has happened here is, I fear, that Goldman has fallen into the error discussed in section III above, *viz.*, of supposing that on the utilitarian theory, the question whether something or other is a right, is identical with the question whether it, taken by itself, has more utility than something else which might interfere with it. But this, as we saw, is not the question. Rather, we are asking whether the utility we would get *from forcing the person to do something else instead* would exceed the utility of that other thing. *That* is why rights look unassimilable to utilitarian analysis, because it looks as though to recognize a right is to recognize that somebody may do something even if something else would have more utility. That is why we might be tempted to say that the very purpose of rights talk is to disallow "mere" utilitarian calculations. But it is a temptation we needn't succumb to, for we would simply have omitted a vital element in the calculation. Your need to do Y, which would require my assistance and thus collides with my doing X, which is what I want to do and can do without your assistance, does not override my right to do x *just* because it is more of a need; for what it must outweigh is not simply the utility of my doing X—which it might well—but the utility of someone's, or your, or everyone's, forcing me to help, this having a substantial amount of disutility, which must be *subtracted* from the utility you get from doing your act Y. And it will take a sizable difference to make up for that, especially when the forcing is done by means of the elaborate and expensive machinery of the law.

This may also be the place to make a point about contractarianism, and about lexically ordered interests and summed lesser interests of others. Goldman, like many other critics, is worried about the possibility, which seems to loom large on a utilitarian format, that the lesser utilities of many people will add up to something which overwhelms the individually greater utility of one or a few. And he evidently thinks, though it is not entirely clear from the text, that rights talk is designed to prevent this, in particular by looking at the interests involved only on a pairwise comparative basis and then granting a right to the higher rank-ordered interest, regardless of the relative incidence of the two. (. . ."we cannot allow [rights] to be overridden by interests in the lower category" (126), as well as the frequently reiterated claim that sums of smaller interests can't outweigh more important ones.) Further, a contractarian base is invoked to help this out, as it is in Rawls, who hopes to achieve the same sort of thing (e.g., "no one has a reason to acquiesce in an enduring loss for himself in order to bring about a greater net balance of satisfaction" (*TJ,* 14)). But it won't work. For what a rational individual will do, according to the standard view (accepted by Rawls and, one assumes, Goldman), is calculate the probability of his being the gainer in an arrangement whereby the larger individual utilities of one or a few can be overridden by the summed lesser utilities of many, times the amount of benefit in question; then subtract the amount one would stand to lose by being the one overridden times the probability of being that one; and then compare the resulting figure with the utilities of the alternatives. And of course it will sometimes be rational to accept membership in such an arrangement. It all depends on what the probabilities are, given your position—and of course, if you are behind something like a Veil of Ignorance, thus being required to choose a position where you don't yet know what your place in the system will be, then you'll end up always opting for general utility, with its implication that the summed utilities of many can outweigh the individually greater utilities of few. Naturally, one must include in one's calculation the fear of being the one overridden, for security may be (normally is, with most people and with respect to some things) an extra consideration, over and above the disutility incurred on a given occasion of being the one outweighed. Even so, nothing like a lexical priority rule will emerge. Nor is this unintuitive, carefully applied. The enormous convenience of being able to use automobiles is certainly fairly small by comparison with the interest in not being violently killed; but we grant the right to drive to virtually all and sundry though we know that a few thousand people will be violently killed annually. (It helps that we can, with care, reduce the probability of being killed quite a lot: but not to zero, or even a vanishingly small figure.) Invoking veil-of-ignorance contractarianism will therefore do no good: the utilitarian camel's nose crops up behind the veil, and soon it is apparent that the whole camel is grinning away at us!

The general conclusion is: once admit impartially considered interests as the basis of rights, and from there on in it's a losing battle against the pressure of utilitarianism. Whether we should admit that starting point at all is, of course, another matter: but Goldman has made his bed, and I suggest that a clearheaded look at the matter may yield the conclusion that lying in it would actually be rather nice.

V. A Concluding Reflection

This survey has been both rather long and yet, as I hope will be agreed, quite sketchy and nondefinitive. I wish to conclude it with a reflection which may go some way to explain the power of the utilitarian idea—and, perhaps, its futility.

The power of it is not far to seek. Consider some theorist who claims that justice ought to be done though the heavens fall, and that there are "abstract rights distinct from utility"; and let us ask this theorist which scenario for the future of mankind he would prefer as between S^1, in which all of his favorite rights were carefully respected but somehow nearly everyone was really quite miserable, and S^2, in which they were pretty generally violated but somehow nearly everyone was very happy indeed—a pair of scenarios which ought in principle to be possible (shouldn't they?) if indeed justice and utility are distinct or even, as such theorists tend to think, opposed. I think it unlikely that any serious philosopher, however enthusiastic for rights, will actually pick S^1. Why is this? I suspect that it is because it really would be absurd to say that not only are justice and *utility* opposed, but so too are justice and *goodness*. A theorist urging us to embrace strong schemes of rights could hardly be understood if he did not also imply that a world in which those schemes were respected would be a *better* world. But if he does say that, then he will be hard put to resist the plausibility of utility as the measure of betterness. Is it really possible that a human world should be better than another, but more miserable?

The catch is that the rights theorist may hold that the reason *why* people would be happier if their rights were respected is precisely that rights are so important to them. This, indeed, seems to be what nearly all theorists in the past few years do say. When they are busy "refuting" utilitarianism, their favorite gambit is to envisage some serious violation of what we generally allow to be rights *because of* the "general good". Yet if rights are so important as they suppose, how *can* serious violations of them be consistent with the general good? Anybody can see that if citizens are routinely able to be hauled off to concentration camps in the middle of the night on account of some supposed failure to regard the "public interest" which amounts to a lot less than a similar violation of the rights of still others by the victim himself, then their rights are not respected. And any reasonable person *would* be shocked and frightened by this. How, then, is a "general good" to be got off the launching pad which is great enough to offset this manifest disutility—as it quite obviously is? No theorist seems, after all, to have tried out *this* argument: "See here, utilitarianism implies that people would be allowed to cut right across your front yard, right after you've freshly replanted it too, and this merely in order to keep the other half of town from being flattened by a gas-main explosion!" Nor, curiously enough, have they tried out *this* one: Suppose there's a move to have a big parade, which lots of people and their children will enjoy; and the only feasible route is such that they'll have to block Jones' access to his own driveway for a couple of hours. Jones is against it—he doesn't like parades, and he finds the driveway-blockage a nuisance—but although he minds, he *doesn't mind very much.* There will be a violation of his rights, but it'll be a violation which doesn't *bother* him seriously—just a little. Will the theorist now say that it would genuinely be *wrong* to have the parade anyway, despite this unfortunate but unavoidable (without cancelling the parade) violation? (Or if they would, would they also regard its being wrong as any real *reason not to have the parade* in this case?) If so, we should like to know about it! But in fact, the sort of violations of rights "owing to the calculus of advantages" which these theorists seem to have in mind aren't quite like that. They are, instead, serious ones, where a great deal *is* at stake. But of course, the more is at stake, the more difficult it is to work up a plausible amount of "public utility" to outweigh it. And so, the stronger this argument *sounds,* the less plausible must it actually *be* as an argument against utilitarianism.

Nevertheless, it is possible that utilitarians have the cart before the horse. Perhaps the reason *why* people would be so unhappy if their rights were violated is that they really do have those rights, "naturally" and antecedently to any considerations of utility from any *other* course; but it's just that they are highly concerned about those rights, and so rights are the source of the utility, rather than the other way around as the utilitarian supposes. Well, suppose this is true. What follows? Why, it will then follow that the utilitarian will be enthusiastic about respecting those rights! His *reason* for being enthusiastic, of course, will be that those rights are the source of so much utility; but so long as they *are,* he can hardly *ignore* them. The effect, in short, is that the utilitarian can readily agree with the most telling things his opponent thought he was marshalling against him, leaving the opponent with arguments of the "let justice be done, though the heavens fall" form—arguments to which the deontologist is quite welcome, thank you!

But this same argument will also explain, perhaps, the futility of utilitarianism in these matters. In order to see this, we must note a further point about the notion of rights, not brought out in the introductory Section I of this paper.

This point is that there is a tendency to claim that talk of rights is not simply synonymous with talk of the obligations of others toward the right-holder. Some suppose that when Jones says, "Hey, you can't take that—it's mine!", the 'it's mine' part of his statement does more than just repeat the injunction not to take it. It is even thought that it does more than make some kind of reference to such things as how it came to be Jones' rather than someone else's, or that it is Jones' rather than someone else's rights which are in question. Some think that the claim that something belongs to Jones, that Jones has a right to it, actually *explains why* others have the obligation not to use it without his permission. Others think that that is a mystification and an indulgence in obscurantist metaphysics. Whether or not it is that, though, it does bring up the point that when someone has a right, there has to be something about him or her in virtue of which that someone has the right in question. And in the case of utilitarianism in particular, we should be clear that this something cannot *just* be the fact that more utility on the whole would be expected by having people generally let Jones use or decide who uses the thing in question. For obviously there has to be some reason for supposing that there will be such greater utility, and this reason will have to be something about Jones. Now these facts about Jones, or whoever's rights are in question, these properties giving rise to rights within utilitarianism, cannot be "founded on" utility. On the contrary, utility must be "founded" on *them.* It is surely clear that we can have no utilitarian considerations unless there is a background of human psychological facts which are their basis: *that* X gives pleasure to A must, if true at all, be simply true, or due to some basic fact about our natures, and we can get results from a principle of utility only if we have intervening premises of that kind. Is it possible that premises about rights are also in that category? Not, if the above argument is correct, premises about rights which can genuinely override considerations of utility. But yes, if we mean premises about rights which identify, in effect, important sources of utility. If so, it is unclear whether the victory of utilitarians is hollow. Perhaps, instead, it would show merely that much of the argumentation about the alleged conflict of justice and utility is misplaced. And in any case, what Mill said would still be quite true—and worth quoting as the conclusion of this essay:

> "It appears from what has been said, that justice is a name for certain moral requirements, which, regarded collectively, stand higher in the scale of social utility, and are therefore of more paramount obligation, than any others . . . Justice remains the appropriate name for certain social utilities which are vastly more important, and therefore more absolute and imperative, than any others are as a class . . . and which, therefore, ought to be, as well as naturally are, guided by a sentiment not only differing in degree, but in kind; distinguished from the milder feeling which attaches to the mere idea of promoting human pleasure or convenience, at once by the more definite nature of its commands, and by the sterner character of its sanctions." (60)[9]

Notes

1. Cf. Mill, *Utilitarianism,* Ch. 5: "We do not call anything wrong, unless we mean to imply that a

person ought to be punished in some way or other for doing it; . . ." (Everyman edition of *Utilitarianism, Liberty and Representative Government,* p. 45.)

2. Thus, continuation of the same sentence quoted in note 1: ". . . if not by law, by the opinion of his fellow-creatures; if not by opinion, by the reproaches of his own conscience."

3. Bracketed numbers attached to quotations from Mill all refer to pages in the Everyman edition cited above.

4. Henry Sidgwick, *The Methods of Ethics,* 7th edn., (Macmillan, London, 1907), p. 382.

5. D. G. Brown, "Mill on Liberty and Mortality", *Philosophical Review,* 81 (1972), 133-58.

6. *Op. cit.,* pp. 142-6.

7. In *New Essays on Contract Theory,* ed. Kai Nielsen and Roger A. Shiner, *Canadian Journal of Philosophy,* Suppl. Vol. III (1977), 121-35.

8. Bracketed numbers in this Section refer to pages in the volume cited in the text.

9. The ideas in this paper may be compared with some developed in my book, *Morality and Utility* (Johns Hopkins Press, Baltimore, 1967), especially Chs. VI-VIII, and in "Utilitarianism, Group Action, and Coordination", *Nous,* 10 (1976), 173-94.

John Stuart Mill (1806–1873)

D. A. Lloyd Thomas (essay date 1983)

SOURCE: "Rights, Consequences, and Mill on Liberty," in *Of Liberty,* edited by A. Phillips Griffiths, Cambridge University Press, 1983, pp. 167-80.

[*In the following essay, Thomas offers philosophical and moral justifications for Mill's liberty principle as contained in his essay,* On Liberty.]

Mill says that the object of his essay *On Liberty* is to defend a certain principle, which I will call the 'liberty principle', and will take to say the following[1]: 'It is permissible, in principle, for the state (through law) or society (through social pressure) to control the actions of individuals "only in respect to those actions of each, which concern the interest of other people" '.[2] The liberty principle is a prescription of intermediate generality. Mill intends it to support more specific political prescriptions, such as liberty of conscience, of expressing and publishing opinions, of framing a plan of life to suit our own character, and of combination for any purpose not involving harm to others (p. 75). The liberty principle is more general than these prescriptions but less general than its possible moral foundations, such as utilitarianism. My concern will be with attempts to defend the liberty principle by showing it to be supported by an acceptable moral position.

It is not my intention to offer a defence of a reading of the liberty principle in terms of 'interests', although I believe this is the most plausible construal of the text taking into account all of the formulations Mill offers. However, such a reading does call for an account of the term 'interests'. A distinction will be made between 'desire-based' interests and 'right-based' interests. It will be argued that Mill must have intended 'interests' to be taken as 'rights-based interests'.

To explain the notion of desire-based interests, let us suppose that each person has some set of non-instrumental desires: things desired not, or not only, as a means to something else. Let us further suppose that each can say which of his own set seem to him to be of greater significance. The most significant sets of non-instrumental desires may be expected to cluster around a person's more important activities, such as work (if not regarded merely as a means to other things) and various kinds of association with others. Such clusters of desires may be called a person's non-instrumental interests. Though based on desires, this account of interests allows for a distinction between a person's interests and his 'mere' likings, such as the desire to eat chocolate mousse, which may not be part of a cluster of non-instrumental desires a person regards as significant. And some of the things one is interested in (the career of Kiri te Kanawa) may not be part of one's interests, or something one has an interest (i.e. a stake) in. An account of desire-based interests must also include the notion of 'instrumental' interests: those things which, though they may not be desired as such, or even at all, are needed to secure a person's non-instrumental interests. Perhaps some instrumental interests are common to all people, such as health, while others vary from person to person according to what happen to be a person's non-instrumental interests. It is doubtful whether a person can be mistaken about his non-instrumental interests, but he can be mistaken about his instrumental interests: about what is in his interests.

Desire-based interests do not serve well for a reading of Mill's liberty principle. On this account actions concerning the interests of others would be those which impinge on another, either by way of affecting the pursuit of his non-instrumental goals, or by way of affecting his instrumental interests. Now whereas it is perhaps an exaggeration to say that any action would concern the interests of (some) others, some liberties Mill insists upon certainly would not be justified if we accepted this reading of 'interests'. Many exercises of the liberty to express and publish opinions (e.g. those by Ralph Nader) concern the desire-based interests of others. As this reading of 'interests' leaves little of significance that may not be controlled by the state or society it is to be rejected, for it is clear that Mill intends his liberty principle to leave much of significance.

An alternative conception of interests is based, not on desires, but on rights. We think of persons as having rights to control themselves and (if we believe in private property) segments of the material world external to their bodies. A person has the right to decide who has access to his body, and no one else has this right, except with his consent. On the rights-based conception of interests, a person's interests are all those things over which he has rights of control. On this view every person has a sphere protected by rights in which choices about how things are to be in that sphere are reserved for that person.

The question 'Does this action concern your interests?' may receive different answers depending upon which conception of interests is being used. Whether your rich aunt will strike you out of her will is a matter that concerns your desire-based interests (unless you are already wealthy enough). But her decision does not concern your rights-based interests, for it is your aunt, not you, who has rights of control over her assets. In striking you out of her will she does nothing that concerns your rights-based interests, for by so doing she does not invade your protected sphere. If you steal a trifle from your aunt you do something that concerns her rights-based interests, but stealing so little may have no effect on her desire-based interests.

Reading 'interests' as 'rights-based interests', i.e. as those things over which one has rights of control, makes better sense of the liberty principle, because then it will rule out, in principle, external control of many significant actions. It is also a reading that fits several passages in the essay.

> there is no parity between the feeling of a person for his own opinion, and the feeling of another who is offended at his holding it; no more than between the desire of a thief to take a purse, and the desire of the right owner to keep it (p. 140).

Holding an opinion is like owning something: you have rights of control over your opinions. That their existence is an annoyance (or worse) to me, and hence, possibly, in conflict with my desire-based interests, is of no more significance, so far as the rights of the situation go, than the fact that your owning a Gaugin I want has deshed one of my ambitions as a collector. One of a number of other passages which fit this construal of 'interests' is the following.

> The only part of the conduct of anyone, for which he is amenable to society, is that which concerns others. In the part which merely concerns himself, his independence is, *of right,* absolute. Over himself, over his own body and mind, the individual is sovereign.[3]

If the term 'interests' in the liberty principle is to be read as 'rights-based interests' the next question is 'What is the source of this account of rights?' In at least one passage Mill appears to draw his account of rights from what are recognized as such in a particular society:

> This conduct consists . . . in not injuring the interests of one another; or rather certain interests, which, either by express legal provision or by tacit understanding, ought to be considered as rights (p. 132).

But it is not clear that this passage *must* be read as having relativistic implications. For there are two ways in which it may be taken:

> (i) Express legal provision or tacit understanding is what *makes* certain considerations into rights-based interests for the purposes of the liberty principle.

> (ii) Certain considerations *are* interests, and their being so is not dependent on express legal provision or tacit understanding. These interests ought to be recognized for what they are—people's rights—either through legal recognition or tacit understanding.

The second way of taking the passage does not have relativistic implications.[4]

In any case, it is difficult to believe that Mill's considered position could be a relativistic one. For if it were it would follow that the significance of the liberty principle, in its applications, would vary from one jurisdiction (and set of social customs) to another. But Mill's stated objective is precisely to find a principle avoiding such variations.

> . . . the practical question, where to place the limit— how to make the fitting adjustment between individual independence and social control—is a subject on which nearly everything remains to be done . . . Some rules of conduct . . . must be imposed . . . What these rules should be is the principal question in human affairs; but if we except a few of the most obvious cases, it is one of those which least progress has been made in resolving. No two ages, and scarcely any two countries, have decided it alike; and the decision of one age or country is a wonder to another (pp. 68-69).

There follows an attack on deciding the matter by reference to the influence of custom. Further, those rights-based interests recognized in some jurisdictions (even in England) would not allow Mill to draw from the liberty principle the more specific liberties he wants, for example, the liberty to utter words offensive to Christianity (p. 90). But clearly Mill thinks that his liberty principle requires liberty of expressing and publishing opinions under any jurisdiction, anyway under any in a society not in a 'backward state' (p. 73).

Rights drawn from law or convention traditionally have been contrasted with natural rights. It would appear, however, that natural rights cannot be Mill's basis for an account of rights-based interests, for he says:

> I forgo any advantage which could be derived to my argument from the idea of abstract right, as a thing independent of utility (p. 74).

This passage is, I believe, incompatible with *one* account of natural rights. That account is to be found in places in Locke (though it is not his only account of natural rights), and also, more recently, in Nozick. On one Lockean view there is some characteristic(s) of each person such that possession of that characteristic implies each person's having a certain natural right. For example, that someone exists implies that he has a property in his own person. For this view of natural rights the label 'perceived' may be used, as it is thought that any rational person will be able to 'see' the connection between possession of the characteristic(s) and possession of the right.

This view of natural rights cannot be reconciled with the passage just quoted from Mill, nor with the more general consideration that Mill's ethical theory is consequentialist. A 'perceived' natural right requires no appeal to the consequences of its recognition as part of its justification, and therefore must be 'a thing independent of utility'. But there is another conception of rights, with a good claim to the title 'natural' (in that it too may be contrasted with rights conceived as deriving from positive law or convention) which is compatible with Mill's position. Natural rights may be seen as related to justifiable practices. The requirements of a practice supply the connection between the characteristic(s) possessed by a person, and the claim that he has a certain right. The justification of the practice requires a comparison of the consequences there would be if that practice existed with the consequences if alternative practices existed, the comparison to be made in terms of some end(s), such as aggregate utility. (This way of justifying rights will be referred to as 'practice consequentialism'.) On this view the connection between characteristics possessed by persons and rights must be made through a practice consequentially justified, whereas the justification of perceived natural rights does not require any reference to practices and their consequences.

We can use the term 'assigned' for natural rights justified in the practice consequentialist way. Persons are thought

of as in an initial condition of 'rightslessness', and are then assigned rights on the basis of justified practices. A reluctance to allow that assigned natural rights really are natural rights is due perhaps to the belief that natural rights must be 'natural' in both of two ways. They should be 'natural' rather than 'artificial' where 'artificial' indicates a construction of positive law or social convention. They also must be 'natural' rather than 'artificial' where 'artificial' indicates that no 'contrived' processes of reasoning are necessary for their attribution: they are simply properties people have. Assigned natural rights are 'natural' in the first way, but not in the second.

As Mill does not forgo making use of the notion of abstract right, but only of abstract right 'as a thing independent of utility', he could make use of a conception of natural rights assigned on the basis of the consequences of practices assessed in terms of utility. The rights-based interests made use of in the liberty principle therefore may be those things over which a person ought to have rights of control by reference to the best assignment of rights from the point of view of the principle of utility. We may call such interests 'utilitarian rights-based interests'. It should be noticed that there need be no connection between prescriptions justified by reference to utilitarian rights-based interests and prescriptions justified by the direct application of the principle of utility to desire-based interests. If the rule 'Whenever one person's desire-based interests are in conflict with another's, decide what is due to each by reference to what would maximize utility', then no one would have any rights and, ergo, no utilitarian rights-based interests. Direct applications of the principle of utility to desire-based interests would leave few, if any, classes of action not in principle controllable by the state or society.

Should the term 'interests' in Mill's liberty principle be understood as 'utilitarian rights-based interests'? Not if by 'utilitarian' is meant 'desire-satisfaction utilitarian', i.e. the view that a certain psychological state, satisfied desire, is the only intrinsically good thing, and that the goodness of anything other than satisfied desire is wholly dependent upon its relationship to satisfied desire, either by way of 'producing' it, being a precondition for it, etc.[5]

The reason why a conception of rights-based interests for use in the liberty principle cannot be grounded in desire-satisfaction utilitarianism is apparent if we consider, as an example, Mill's claim that we ought to have the liberty of 'framing the plan of our life to suit our own character' (p. 75). It follows from the formulation of desire-satisfaction utilitarianism that the consequential justification of a practice securing this liberty must be based solely on how granting or withholding it would affect the satisfaction of the desires of all concerned. The position over-all of granting or withholding that liberty may be regarded as the sum of how granting or withholding it would impinge upon each of the individuals concerned. So let us consider the case of one person, P, in isolation.

P's desires may be divided into two categories. Firstly, there is P's desire (or lack of it) to enjoy this liberty for its own sake, apart from the effect its possession may have on the satisfaction of P's other desires. Secondly, there is the incidence this liberty will have on the rest of P's desires (i.e. those other than the desire to enjoy this liberty as such). If it is likely that P's choice of a plan of life will be better (from the point of view of maximizing the satisfaction of P's desires) than someone else's choice on P's behalf, then there is a *prima facie* utilitarian case for P having this liberty. Thus a utilitarian defence of P's having this liberty will depend upon (a) how much P desires to frame her own plan of life, and (b) how well P can be expected to frame her own plan of life from the point of view of satisfying the rest of her desires.

Now clearly people differ in how much they desire this liberty and, if they have it, in how likely they are to frame a plan of life that will maximize the satisfaction of their desires. For some it is plausible that possession of this liberty will be for their utilitarian good, for they have a significant desire to enjoy it and can be expected to plan their lives better (from the point of view of satisfying desires) than anybody else could do it for them. Others, however, appear to have no strong desire to enjoy this liberty, nor much capacity to frame a plan suitable for maximizing desire-satisfaction. (They may prefer life in some clear institutional structure.) From a utilitarian point of view it would seem reasonable, therefore, to say that this liberty should be enjoyed by some but withheld from, or granted in only a qualified form to, others. But Mill believes that the liberty principle requires that this particular liberty should be enjoyed by all, at least in societies no longer in a backward state.

It may be objected to this argument that we think not only in terms of matching people's liberties to the desires they already have, but also of instituting a liberty in order to encourage a desire for it which does not as yet exist. If everyone is assigned the liberty to frame her own plan of life, then even if at present such an assignment is best only for some (perhaps a minority) it may encourage a desire for the liberty in many who do not as yet have it.

This objection fails, however, because the fact that a desire for such a liberty may be encouraged in this way can be of no significance for a desire-satisfaction utilitarian. To suppose that there is reason to encourage a desire that does not already exist is to assume that some objective value is placed on having that desire: a value not itself wholly desire-dependent.

To this it may be replied that there are cases where a utilitarian could advocate the encouragement of a desire in those who do not already have it, without assuming that some objective value is to be placed on having that desire. One example is the encouragement of a desire of a kind reasonably supposed to hold out particularly good possibilities of intense desire-satisfaction. This consideration does not, however, affect the present argument. While those deprived of liberty can desire it intensely, in general it would be implausible to encourage the desire for liberty

as such on the ground that it held out particularly good possibilities of intense desire-satisfaction.

There is another case where a desire-satisfaction utilitarian can justify a policy not in keeping with the existing distribution of desires, but do this without assuming that an objective value is to be placed on the satisfaction of some desires. Suppose most people desire to be dependent upon an addictive and debilitating drug. In the short run a policy of discouraging dependence is not optimal in utilitarian terms, as it does not provide people with what they want. However, a utilitarian may argue that if the dependence persists future aggregates of satisfied desire will diminish, and hence that there is a utilitarian case for the policy.

This objection also fails. The example of drug dependence differs from encouraging a desire to frame one's own plan of life in that the former calls for no discrimination between the objective value of satisfying various desires: if most are drug dependent the satisfaction of desires of whatever character can be expected to reduce to zero, including desires related to drug dependence. No similar consideration applies in the case of fostering a desire for liberty to frame one's own plan of life: the reason for encouraging that desire is a non-desire-dependent preference for it over more passive inclinations.

Mill recognizes that the value of framing one's own plan of life is not wholly desire dependent:

> He who lets the world . . . choose his plan of life for him, has no need of any other faculty than the ape-like one of imitation. He who chooses his plan for himself, employs all his faculties . . . And these qualities he requires and exercises exactly in proportion as the part of his conduct which he determines according to his own judgment and feelings is a large one. It is possible that he might be guided in some good path, and kept out of harm's way, without any of these things. But what will be his comparative worth as a human being? (p. 117).

Mill's utilitarianism is not, or not only, desire-satisfaction utilitarianism, and later it will be argued that the most interesting support Mill lends to his liberty principle does not derive from that form of utilitarianism. But it must be allowed that Mill sometimes places more emphasis on his Benthamite origins, as in this passage:

> Such are the differences among human beings in their sources of pleasure, their susceptibilities of pain, and the operation on them of different physical and moral agencies, that unless there is a corresponding diversity in their modes of life, they neither obtain their fair share of happiness, nor grow up to the mental, moral, and aesthetic stature of which their nature is capable (p. 125).

Such a justification of the liberty to frame one's own plan of life is weak. At best it is only a *prima facie* case, and over-all the case against allowing persons the liberty to lead new or unusual ways of life may be stronger. The gain for a few in being able to better match their particular desires and dispositions to an appropriate way of life easily could be outweighed by the distaste felt by many at people living lives like that. Such gains also might be out-weighed by the anxiety produced in many about the worth of their own more conventional ways of life.

An account of rights-based interests suitable for Mill's liberty principle is not to be found in desire-satisfaction utilitarianism. But it may be suggested that a more satisfactory account is to be found in a more complicated form of practice consequentialism. The consequences of the practices on which certain rights are based could be assessed by reference to certain supposed objective and intrinsic goods, such as individual autonomy, as well as by their tendency to maximize desire satisfaction. (To regard individual autonomy, say, as an objective good is to take account of it when estimating consequences in a way not wholly determined by its relationship to satisfying desire.) This amendment may repair the faults revealed in a justification based on desire satisfaction alone. For example, if individual autonomy is an objective and intrinsic good, it may be reasonable to assign a right to everyone to frame her own plan of life, not just those for whom it would be best in desire satisfaction terms.

But if this approach is taken some reason needs to be given why individual autonomy (say) should be regarded as an objective good—a reason not requiring Mill to seek support outside a consequentialist ethic. It will be argued that a suitable form of consequentialism ('experimental consequentialism') is to be found in Mill alongside the more familiar elements of desire-satisfaction utilitarianism. Experimental consequentialism does not give us precisely the conclusion that individual autonomy is an objective good, but it does provide reason for taking account of autonomy in a way not wholly dependent upon its effect on satisfying desires.

Experimental consequentialism may be introduced by way of noting an objection to desire-satisfaction utilitarianism. The claim that things other than desire satisfaction are of value only in so far as they are related to satisfied desire is plausible in some cases. The nicotine addict may allow that there is nothing good about his smoking other than that it satisfies one of his desires. If the desire to smoke were to cease he may then see nothing good about smoking. This is not, however, the way we view all objects of desire. With many we would not suppose that they ceased to be of value if our desires for them happened to cease. We separate the desirability of an object from its capacity to satisfy our desires. In some cases the occurrence of desire may be taken as a discovery of the value of the object of desire.

Experimental consequentialism is based on regarding the significance of some desires in this light. There well may be things other than the experience of satisfied desire which are intrinsically good. We come to believe that some things are intrinsically good by way of their capacity to arouse and to satisfy desire. The capacity to do this for some particular person is not, however, conclusive evidence that the object of desire is intrinsically good. Some-times we revise our beliefs about the value of the object of desire, at first thinking that the object itself is of value, but later finding that its value lies only in its capacity to satisfy our desires. The extent to which people who have experienced the object of desire regard it as intrinsically good is an indication, though no conclusive indication, that it is so.

Experimental consequentialism differs from desire-satisfaction utilitarianism in its attitude towards certainty and evaluative knowledge. The latter assumes that we know what is intrinsically good. Such room as there is for new evaluative knowledge will be about the kind of thing which can give rise to satisfied desire. We may come to desire new kinds of thing, or come to recognize new sources of satisfaction of the desires we already have, but in all this we make no discovery about that which is intrinsically good. By contrast, experimental consequentialism, though an objectivist position, makes no claims to certain evaluative knowledge: the attitude towards whether this or that has intrinsic value is provisional.

Experimental consequentialism contrasts with desire-satisfaction utilitarianism in one further way. If desiring something is a possible indication of the intrinsic goodness of that which is desired, then although it is through your desires that you come to realize this, its goodness is not dependent on its happening to be your desires, in particular, that are aroused or satisfied. There are objects of possible desire desirable as such, though we may remain uncertain about what they are. For a desire-satisfaction utilitarian, however, all statements about the desirability of things (other than desire-satisfaction itself) are implicitly person-relative.

Mill appears to adopt experimental consequentialism in some places in his ethical writings. J. L. Mackie bases his account of the 'proof' of the principle of utility on a similar interpretation of Mill.[6] There is further evidence that Mill took this view in the first two chapters of *Utilitarianism* and, especially, in the last chapter of *A System of Logic*. It is inappropriate to attempt to argue the case for attribution here. It is not claimed that this is Mill's only ethical position: frequently he appears to be defending desire-satisfaction utilitarianism.

The connection between experimental consequentialism and Mill's liberalism may be traced through these steps:

1. Possible objects of human desire may be divided into those whose existence is not dependent on human activity, and those created, partly or wholly, by human activity. Obviously most objects of human desire fall within the latter group, including what Mill calls 'a pattern of human existence' or a 'mode of life' (p. 125).

2. From experimental consequentialism we have the claim that the only way of recognizing that which is objectively good is through its becoming for us an object of desire. Though preferences may be expressed between 'modes of

life' known to us only through abstract characterizations or hearsay, such preferences are of little significance for a determination of their desirability.

3. The best indication, though still a fallible one, that a 'mode of existence' is intrinsically good (or contains elements that are so) is that many who are well acquainted with it come to desire it.

4. The foregoing considerations indicate two political desiderata:

(a) People should be free to participate in the creation of as great a variety of 'modes of existence' as possible.

> There is no reason that all human existence should be constructed on some one or some small number of patterns (p. 125).

(b) People should be free to experience as many 'modes of existence' as possible.

> As it is useful that while mankind are imperfect there should be different opinions, so it is that there should be different experiments of living; that free scope should be given to varieties of character, short of injury to others, and that the worth of different modes of life should be proved practically, when anyone thinks fit to try them (p. 115).

5. Thus, if a state or a society takes a constricted view of desirable 'modes of existence', making it difficult for anyone to live in other than one of a few acceptable ways, members of that society will be prevented from experiencing new 'modes of existence'; ones which may have contained something of worth. This could be a reason why Mill is, if anything, more concerned about freedom from social pressure than from illegality: a 'mode of existence can survive illegality in a tolerant social environment, but it is difficult for it to last in a hostile one, even if it is not threatened by illegality.

Two further assumptions must be added to arrive at Mill's political position: his commitment to specifically *individual* liberty, and his belief in progress.

The reason for Mill's preoccupation with the liberty of individuals becomes clearer in the light of the ethical theory attributed to him. In the chapter 'Of Individuality', Mill several times affirms that initiatives for experiments in new 'modes of existence' come from individuals. For example:

> . . . there are but few persons, in comparison with the whole of mankind, whose experiments, if adopted by others, would be likely to be any improvement on established practice. But these few are the salt of the earth; without them, human life would become a stagnant pool (p. 122; see also pp. 124 and 128).

Belief in progress is the remaining component in the relation between Mill's experimental consequentialism and his liberalism. For a desire-satisfaction utilitarian progress would *be* a process of reforming social and political insti-

tutions so as to make possible ever larger aggregates of desire satisfaction. His *belief* in progress would be a matter of supposing that scope for such improvement exists and is likely to be realized. But his commitment to maximizing desire satisfaction remains viable even with pessimism: his principle provides a basis for social choice even if it is believed that the best option available now is worse than the best option available in the past, and that future prospects will become worse still. By contrast, belief in progress is essential to Mill's position. He supposes that a process of individuals creating and choosing between new modes of existence under circumstances of freedom will have a direction. It will tend to throw up a wider variety of more significant modes of existence, and they will become available to a greater proportion of the population.

Belief that such progress *will* occur under circumstances of freedom is indispensable to Mill's position. If it were thought that choice under such circumstances would lead to the adoption of ever more insignificant modes of existence, this case for individual liberty would collapse: it then would be more reasonable to preserve such significant modes of life as already existed. A belief in progress *given* circumstances of freedom is essential to Mill's position, but a belief that there will be progress *towards* those circumstances is not, as is evidenced by his remarks on Chinese civilization (p. 129).

This defence of liberalism meets two conditions indicated earlier. It *is* consequentialist: persons ought to be free from control by the state and society because this is necessary for progress towards more significant modes of existence. Mill is not represented as regarding individual freedom as an end in itself. But although the defence is consequentialist, the importance of individual autonomy is not dependent on the consequences of protecting it in terms of desire satisfaction. Indeed the argument given for individual autonomy does not depend upon adherence to any particular conception of what is good, but on a view of the method by which we discover what is good.

There is a problem, however, about using this approach to defend Mill's liberty principle. What has been justified is a presumption favourable to experimentation with new modes of existence. The liberty principle is both more general and more specific than that. It is more general in that it allows liberty to persons and groups even if it is unlikely that they will participate in any experimentation. The liberty principle is also more specific. It says that people should be free from constraint in any activity not concerning the rights-based interests of others: it proposes specific freedoms and absences of freedom, thus indicating what experiments in modes of existence are permissible. Any particular system of rights-based interests defines and protects certain modes of existence and the values exemplified in them. The cost of this protection is that people may not pursue modes of existence incompatible with that system. For example, the conception of rights-based interests currently accepted in the West is incompatible with the pursuit of most private ways of life involving violence and its associated values. Mill recognizes that any given mode of existence requires restraint as well as freedom.

> All that makes existence valuable to any one, depends on the enforcement of restraints upon the actions of other people. Some rules of conduct, therefore, must be imposed, by law in the first place, and by opinion on many things which are not fit subjects for the operation of law (p. 69).

The assignment of any specific set of rights-based interests presupposes a definite view of what modes of existence are more, and what are less, worthwhile. It is implausible that all of those modes of existence made difficult or impossible to pursue because of our current conception of rights-based interests are ones in which there is simply nothing of value to be discerned. The attempt to formulate a liberty principle, however, supposes that there is a fixed framework of rights-based interests and that people should be free to choose their own plans of life provided they respect that framework. This supposition is consistent with a Lockean natural rights view, and it perhaps also could be justified by a form of consequentialism which assumed that we know that certain ends, other than desire satisfaction, have value. But if our consequentialism takes an experimental attitude towards what is intrinsically good, the supposed fixed framework of rights-based interests dissolves. There is no definitive knowledge of values by reference to which a fixed conception of rights-based interests can be assigned.

If experimental consequentialism is incompatible with a determinate conception of rights-based interests, and hence with even the project of formulating a liberty principle of the kind Mill sought to defend, what can liberalism amount to? One option would be to take as a starting point the set of rights-based interests implicit in the law and morality of a particular society. To be a liberal would be to take a certain attitude to that received conception: an awareness not only of the modes of existence protected by the existing assignment of rights, but also of the cost of that protection: the difficulties the present assignment of rights puts in the way of experiments in some new modes of existence. This way of formulating liberalism gives it one feature in common with conservatism: both are attitudes towards an existing social and legal structure rather than a definitive body of principles.

This characterization of liberalism cannot be formulated in 'one very simple principle' allowing us to read off stances on practical issues. Any modification to the existing conception of rights-based interests probably will involve costs for some modes of existence as well as possible gains for others. Nevertheless, one concession to the wish for principles can be made, though it is principle quite distinct from, and less ambitious than, Mill's liberty principle. Sometimes the existing conception of rights-based interests is unnecessarily restrictive, in that a more permissive one would protect present modes of existence just as well, while allowing people to follow new ones if they wished. Perhaps a conception of rights-based interests per-

mitting only heterosexual forms of sexual activity would be an instance. If it is possible to change current conceptions of rights-based interests so that the position for the present modes of existence is not significantly worsened, and experiments in new ones are made possible, such a change is warranted. That these changes may result in new modes of existence offensive to others (though they do not threaten their modes of existence) would be no reason against the change. But admittedly this is a limited outcome, and much more has to be done to explain the permanent significance of the traditional liberal freedoms from the approach of an experimental ethic.

Notes

1. This is a revised version of a lecture given in the Royal Institute of Philosophy series, February 1981, and at the Political Thought Conference, New College, Oxford, January 1981, under the title 'Mill's Kantian Liberalism'. My thanks are due to those present on both occasions, and to Jerry Cohen, John Gray, John Halliday, John Kelly and Anne Lloyd Thomas for their helpful and encouraging comments.

2. J. S. Mill, *On Liberty* (Everyman Edition), *Utilitarianism, Liberty and Representative Government,* 74. All page references in the text are to this edition of *On Liberty.* For a similar reading of Mill's principle, see J. Rees, 'A Re-reading of Mill on Liberty', in *Limits of Liberty,* Peter Radcliff (ed.) (California: Wadsworth, 1966), 100.

3. p. 73, emphasis added. Other passages favouring an interpretation in terms of rights-based interests are to be found on pp. 120, 121, 132, 136 and 137.

4. On the other hand Mill says at p. 132 that the conduct each is bound to observe includes 'bearing his share (to be fixed on some equitable principle) of the labours and sacrifices incurred for defending the society or its members from injury and molestation'. This suggests that there is a choice of acceptable 'equitable principles'. So perhaps Mill's view is that some of the interests he refers to in his formulations of the liberty principle are constant for any of its applications, while others are partly a matter of which of a permissible set of options a particular society chooses to take up.

5. The argument to follow would not be affected if we adopted the more plausible position that 'satisfied desire' covers a set of distinguishable psychological states. 'Desire-satisfaction utilitarianism' also could be adopted as a label for the different view that what is intrinsically good is the world coming to conform to how we desire it to be, whether or not this gives us 'satisfaction'.

6. J. L. Mackie, *Ethics—Inventing Right and Wrong* (Harmondsworth: Penguin Books, 1977), 142.

Mark Strasser (essay date 1991)

SOURCE: "Mill's Moral View," in *The Moral Philosophy*

of John Stuart Mill: Toward Modifications of Contemporary Utilitarianism, Longwood Academic, 1991, pp. 23-53.

[In the following essay, Strasser evaluates Mill's moral stance and characterizes Mill primarily as an "act-utilitarian."]

Both the quantity and the quality of pleasures must be considered in utility calculations. However, Mill's theory needs further explication, since we must discuss *whose* happiness should be promoted. For example, Mill might claim that an individual acts rightly if her action promotes her own happiness. Or, he might claim that an individual acts rightly if her action promotes the happiness of the society in which she lives. Mill chooses neither of these, instead suggesting that the promotion of humankind's utility is paramount.

To make matters more complicated, Mill writes ambiguously when he says that actions are morally right insofar as they promote happiness. He might mean that an agent acts rightly if she performs an *action* which will promote utility. Or, he might mean that an agent acts rightly if she performs an action which is in accord with a *rule,* the general acceptance and following of which will promote utility. Most of the time, this distinction is unimportant. An action which will promote utility will also be an action which is in accord with a rule, the general following of which will promote utility. Sometimes, however, the action which will promote utility is not in accord with a rule, the general following of which will promote utility. At these times, a choice must be made.

MILL AS UTILITARIAN: ACT OR RULE?

Whether one is an act-utilitarian or a rule-utilitarian, one believes that the principle of utility has a special status. It cannot be viewed as on a par with other moral rules because it is the principle upon which the whole moral system is based. The act-utilitarian believes that the principle of utility has a special status in that it is the principle by which all actions should be judged—if there is ever a conflict between the dictates of the principle of utility and any other principle or rule, the dictates of the principle of utility must be followed.

The rule-utilitarian believes that the principle of utility has a special status in that it should never be directly applied to actions. Instead, it should only be used to determine which rules people should accept and follow, i.e., those rules the general acceptance and following of which would promote the most good.[1] Once these rules are ascertained, people should always act in accord with them.

Some writers insist that Mill is an act-utilitarian (someone who believes that the rightness or wrongness of an action depends solely upon the consequences of performing that action). Act-utilitarians claim, for example, that the "rightness or wrongness of keeping a promise on a particular occasion depends only on the consequences of keeping or breaking the promise on that particular occasion."[2] If keeping the promise would maximize utility, then the promise should be kept. If breaking the promise would maximize utility, then the promise should be broken.

Others argue that Mill is a rule-utilitarian (someone who believes that a particular action is right if it is in accord with a moral rule, wrong if it is against a moral rule). A moral rule is a rule which, if generally followed, maximizes utility.

There seems to be evidence to support both sides. Yet, most of the statements which allegedly support Mill's rule-utilitarian position either give outright support to or are consistent with an act-utilitarian position. Ultimately, this debate will be seen to have been given undue importance in the recent literature. Mill would not have ascribed to either act-utilitarianism or rule-utilitarianism as they are currently understood. Act-utilitarians are too willing to break moral rules in their quest to maximize utility.[3] Rule-utilitarians are too rigid either in not building in enough exceptions into their rules or in insisting on following those rules when doing so would clearly be disutility-producing. Mill does not want secondary rules broken readily and hence does not want to characterize them as merely 'guides' or 'rules of thumb'. He also does not want secondary rules followed if doing so would clearly be disutility-producing, which is why he is more appropriately labeled an act-utilitarian than a rule-utilitarian.

There is an even more important reason why Mill is not accurately labeled as a standard act-utilitarian, much less a standard rule-utilitarian. While he believes that the act which maximizes utility is right, *he does not believe that an action must be utility-maximizing in order to be right.* That point will be explained . . . [elsewhere]. In this [essay], there will be an examination of Mill's view of the relations among acts, rules, and the principle of utility.

MILL AS ACT-UTILITARIAN

In *A System of Logic,* Mill denies that we can construct a perfect moral system. Basically, he offers two points:

> 1. Moral rules are extremely difficult to formulate because we cannot anticipate all of the circumstances which might obtain in future situations. If we cannot thus anticipate, then we will be unable to devise rules to cover all cases and our rules will be imperfect.
>
> 2. Even if we could formulate rules to include all of the appropriate exceptions, these rules would be so complicated that most people would not be able to learn and remember them.[4]

For example, generally, one should not steal. However, stealing is sometimes permissible; indeed, "to save a life, it may not only be allowable, but a duty, to steal, or take by force, the necessary food or medicine."[5] Doubtless, there are other extenuating circumstances in which stealing would also be permissible. Thus, because of the difficulties involved (a) in formulating perfect rules, and (b) in learning and remembering them, we must view moral rules as very good guides, as very useful rules of thumb. Moral rules are not principles which must always be obeyed, they are rules which should be obeyed most of the time. However, it is the act-utilitarian rather than the rule-utilitarian who uses moral rules as (even very useful) rules of thumb.[6]

One must "know what are the practical contingencies which require a modification of the rule, or *which are altogether exceptions to it* [my italics]." Mill argues that "rules of conduct point out the manner in which it will be least perilous to act, where time or means do not exist for analyzing the actual circumstances of the case, or where we cannot trust our judgment in estimating them."[7]

When we are considering whether to follow a rule, we must consider that:

> 1. Rules are imperfect. There are times at which we should disobey rules in favor of following courses of action which will produce much better results.

> 2. Our present rules have stood the test of time—they have been proven to be effective through the ages. We must think twice (and, perhaps, twice again) before disregarding a rule.

Mill argues that rules should occasionally be disobeyed and thus he cannot be accurately labeled a rule-utilitarian. However, he gives some very helpful advice: rules can be wrong but usually are not.

When one, as an unbiased, knowledgeable, careful deliberator, is *certain* that following the appropriate rule would produce bad results, one should definitely disobey the rule. Mill criticizes those who would insist upon following a rule despite their knowing that a different action would yield much better results. The person "who goes by rules rather than by their reasons, like the old-fashioned German tacticians who were vanquished by Napoleon, or the physician who preferred that his patients should die by rule rather than recover contrary to it, is rightly judged to be a mere pedant, and the slave of his formulas."[8]

Mill is not merely arguing that improper rules should not be used; he is suggesting that the world is such a complicated place that we will be unable to devise rules which will cover all of the situations which a doctor might face. So, too, we will be unable to devise rules to cover all of the situations which a moral agent will have to face.[9] Our complicated world sometimes warrants ignoring the rules and judging the particular case according to the principle of utility. Rules of thumb are good for most cases most of the time. In those cases in which one knows that the application of the 'appropriate' rule would not promote utility, one should ignore the rule and promote utility instead.

Mill clearly favors the act-utilitarian view. In "Bentham," he writes, "Insofar as Bentham's adoption of the principle of utility induced him to fix his attention upon the consequences of actions as the consideration determining their morality, he was indisputably in the right path."[10] In a re-

view of Taylor's *Statesman,* Mill comments, "To admit the balance of consequences as a test of right and wrong, necessarily implies the possibility of exceptions to any derivative rule of morality which may be adduced from the test."[11]

These passages explicitly show Mill's commitment to a type of act-utilitarianism. Further, when we consider that Mill is accepting the "creed which accepts as the foundation of morals, Utility, or the *Greatest Happiness Principle* [my italics],"[12] we have reason to believe that Mill's principle involves the *maximization* rather than merely the *promotion* of utility, i.e., Mill believes that action morally best which maximizes rather than merely promotes utility. He argues that the utilitarian standard involves the "*greatest* [my italics] amount of happiness altogether,"[13] and that "[a]ccording to the Greatest Happiness Principle, . . . the ultimate end . . . is an existence exempt *as far as possible* from pain and *as rich as possible* in enjoyments [my italics]."[14] Here, too, Mill is offering a maximizing condition. However, Mill does not believe that *only* those actions which maximize utility are morally right.[15]

MILL'S APPARENT RULE-UTILITARIANISM

Some critics interpret Mill to be claiming that an act is right if it is in accord with a rule the general acceptance and following of which will maximize utility, i.e., they claim that Mill is a rule-utilitarian.[16] They support their interpretation by citing Mill's claim that one can accept the principle of utility as the ultimate principle and yet still accept secondary rules as the rules by which one should live.[17]

Mill offers an often-cited analogy. "To inform a traveler respecting the place of his ultimate destination is not to forbid the use of landmarks and direction-posts on the way. The proposition that happiness is the end and aim of morality does not mean that no road ought to be laid down to that goal, or that persons going thither should not be advised to take one direction than another."[18] Just as a traveler can use landmarks to reach his final destination point, one can use secondary rules to help one maximize happiness.

Yet, Mill's example is somewhat misleading, since one's always using landmarks or secondary rules might be counter-productive.[19] From a special vantage point, one might see a much better route than is indicated by the direction-post. So, too, for example, although lying is usually immoral and we are 'directed' to speak truthfully, we might realize that, because of certain extenuating circumstances, lying would be morally permissible. Our special vantage point, i.e., our knowledge of the extenuating circumstances, would allow us to ignore the rule and instead to maximize utility.

We should not 'forbid the use of landmarks and direction-posts'. However, act- and rule-utilitarians agree that such aids should not be forbidden; they disagree about whether their use should be required. Quite simply, if the traveler knows of a much better route, the act-utilitarian will suggest that he take that route, while the rule-utilitarian will suggest that the traveler follow the direction-posts.

Individuals should not "test each individual action directly by the first principle [i.e., the principle of utility]," both because such a process would be too time-consuming and because such a process would sometimes result in the individuals' acting wrongly, e.g., because they miscalculated the utilities involved. Generally, secondary rules are the ones by which individuals should live.[20] However, if there is a conflict between a secondary rule and the principle of utility, one must follow the dictates of the principle of utility.

In a different passage, Mill seems to explicitly support a rule-utilitarian position. "In the case of abstinences indeed—of things which people forbear to do from moral considerations, though the consequences in the particular case might be beneficial—it would be unworthy of an intelligent agent not to be consciously aware that the action is of a class which, if practiced generally, would be generally injurious, and that this is the ground of the obligation to abstain from it."[21]

Mill seems to be saying that an action is wrong if the class of actions to which the action belongs should not be performed. A class of actions should not be performed if, were the actions generally performed, bad consequences would result. Mill's looking at whether an action is "of a class which, if practiced generally, would be generally injurious" as "the ground of the obligation to abstain from it," is similar to one's looking at an action to see whether it is in accord with some rule and then looking at the rule to see whether its generally being followed would be harmful.[22]

This reasoning seems rather confused. He acknowledges that the ultimate goal is to promote utility and that the action in question would be beneficial. Then, he objects that the action is of a class which, if practiced generally, would be harmful. However, the agent is not wondering whether she, generally, should perform this action; she is wondering whether she should perform it this particular time. Thus, as soon as Mill raises his objection, the agent will rightly respond, "But I don't want to do it all of the time. I want to do it just once."

Mill might then explain that the agent's performing this action would increase the probability that other people would also perform it. Others might see her performing the action or they might see the results of the action. In either case, they, too, would want to perform the action in question. Mill would then point out that many people's performing the action would be harmful. Thus, for fear of promoting the performance of the action at non-beneficial times, the agent should refrain from performing the action this time. In order for anyone to be justified in performing the action this time, the benefits must outweigh the harms produced by the agent's promoting others to perform the action at non-beneficial times.

The above analysis renders Mill's reasoning more understandable. Mill is not saying that the action is forbidden merely because it belongs to a class of actions which, if generally practiced, would be harmful. Such a claim is not very convincing. If an action were acceptable only if its general performance would produce good consequences, then many noble and praiseworthy activities, e.g., dying for one's family, country, religion, etc., would not be acceptable. Indeed, the uniqueness of an action can be part of its utility. For example, in military maneuvers or card play, a ploy may be successful in part because it is so unexpected.

Mill is pointing out that actions have various subtle effects which individuals often overlook when trying to ascertain the effects of a particular action. For example, someone might not consider that:

1. Other people will see that he has broken the rule. Their respect for the rule will be lessened and they will become more likely to break the rule at non-optimal times.

2. Seeing that the rule has been broken, other people will feel less secure that the rule will be followed when it should be. Even if these people realize that the rule was broken to promote greater utility and thus they will not be tempted to break the rule when such an infraction would cause disutility, they might not be so confident in their neighbors' perspicacity. Even though they understand why this particular rule-breaking was proper and thus would not be more likely to break the rules improperly, they could not be sure that others would so understand. Insecurity would result—an obvious disutility.[23]

3. Seeing that this rule has been broken, people will be more likely to break *other* rules at inappropriate times.

Mill is not as clear about the act/rule distinction as one might like. He argues that there is a "necessity that some rule, of a nature simple enough to be easily understood and remembered, should not only be laid down for guidance, but necessarily observed, in order that the various persons concerned may know what they have to expect." Mill believes that "the inconvenience of uncertainty [which results when rules are viewed as merely providing guidance] . . . [is] a greater evil than that which may possibly arise, in a minority of cases, from the imperfect adaptation of the rule to those cases."[24]

Mill seems to be offering a rule-utilitarian account in that the rules should be "necessarily observed." However, the reason that rules should necessarily be observed is that their non-observance will cause insecurity. If Mill is afraid that a particular act of rule-breaking will cause net disutility, then he should not claim that rules must be observed, but that rules should be broken only when the various disutilities (including the increased insecurity) would be outweighed by the utility of the rule-breaking. Indeed, in the next paragraph he amends the claim that rules should necessarily be observed by arguing that "the license of deviating from [the rules], if such be ever permitted, should be confined to definite classes of cases, and of a very peculiar and extreme nature."[25]

In a different work, Mill argues that the "admission of exceptions to rules is a necessity equally felt in all ethical systems of morality. To take an obvious instance, the rule against homicide [and] the rule against deceiving . . . are suspended against enemies in the field, and partially against malefactors in private life." The particular circumstances may *require* one to do something which is normally *forbidden*. "That the moralities arising from the special circumstances of the action may be so important as to overrule those arising from the class of acts to which it belongs, perhaps to take it out of the category of virtues into that of crimes, or *vice versa,* is a liability common to all ethical systems."[26] Here, Mill seems quite clearly to be advocating an act-utilitarian line. However, on the next page, he claims, "The essential is, that the exception should be itself a general rule; so that, being of definite extent, and not leaving the expediencies to the partial judgment of the agent in the individual case, it may not shake the stability of the wider rule in the cases to which the reason of the exception does not extend."[27]

Again, Mill is afraid that the stability of the rule will be undermined and that people will disobey the rule at inappropriate times. "No one who does not thoroughly know the modes of action which common experience has sanctioned is capable of judging of the circumstances which require a departure from those ordinary modes of action."[28] Agents must not haphazardly ignore rules, especially considering that their judgment might be biassed.[29] Were secondary moral rules *simply* rules of thumb, people adopting this theory would break rules too often.

Nonetheless, Mill ultimately holds that utility must be promoted. He believes that "where time or means do . . . exist for analyzing the actual circumstances of the cases, [and] where we [can] trust our judgment in estimating them,"[30] we must ignore the rule and promote utility. We should never perform an action which we (reliably) know to be disutility-producing. A man who does so "cannot discharge himself from moral responsibility by pleading that he had the general rule in his favor."[31]

Mill explains his position in a letter. "I agree with you that the right way of testing actions by their consequences, is to test them by the natural consequences of the particular action, and not by those which would follow if everyone did the same. But, for the most part, the consideration of what would happen if every one did the same, is the only means we have of discovering the tendency of the act in the particular case."[32] In order to look at the effects of a particular action, "[w]e must look at [the action] multiplied, and in large masses."[33] Thus, the insecurity which Mill fears would be produced by rule-breakings must be attributed to particular *acts* of rule-breaking. The destabilizing of rules, i.e., the increasing of the likelihood that rules will be broken at improper times, is an effect of particular *acts* of rule-breaking. These effects must be considered whenever one proposes to break a secondary rule.

When Mill considers consequences, he *includes* the often under-appreciated considerations of character. He criticizes Bentham for not having considered whether "the act or habit in question, though not in itself necessarily pernicious, may not form part of a *character* essentially pernicious, or at least essentially deficient in some quality eminently conducive to the 'greatest happiness',"[34] and Sedgwick for not having recognized that utilitarians also believe that "an essential part of the morality or immorality of an action or a rule of action consists in its influence upon the agent's own mind: upon his susceptibilities of pleasure or pain, upon the general direction of his thoughts, feelings, and imagination, or upon some particular association."[35]

Secondary rules are important because their generally being accepted and followed will tend to promote good character. They will also promote security, which is quite important. A "change, which has always hitherto characterized, and will assuredly continue to characterize, the progress of civilized society, is a continual increase of the security of person and property."[36] Mill writes, "Security of person and property and equal justice between individuals are the first needs of society and the primary ends of government."[37]

Another important feature of secondary rules is that they give specific dictates about how to act, which is necessary because "utility, or happiness, [is] much too complex and indefinite an end to be sought except through the medium of various secondary ends."[38] Individuals "who adopt utility as a standard seldom apply it truly except through the secondary principles."[39]

Yet, one would be wrong to think that it is obvious what the secondary rules should be, *even given a particular end* (e.g., the promotion of general utility). "The grand consideration is, not what any person regards as the ultimate end of human conduct, but through what intermediate ends he holds his ultimate end is attainable, and should be pursued; and in these there is a nearer agreement between some who differ, than between some who agree in their conception of the ultimate end."[40]

Once the secondary principles have been formulated, Mill *claims* that one can pretty readily decide which principle is appropriate in any particular case. "There is no case of moral obligation in which some secondary principle is not involved; and if only one, there can seldom be any real doubt which one it is, in the mind of any person by whom the principle itself is recognized." Indeed, he somewhat surprisingly further argues that "only in these cases of conflict between secondary principles is it requisite that first principles should be appealed to."[41]

Yet, one's having the ability to pick out the appropriate secondary rule does not imply that one has the ability to apply it correctly. The "common error of men [is] of sticking to their rules in a case whose specialties either take it out of the class to which the rules are applicable, or require a special adaptation of them."[42] Thus, it "is one thing to be master of general principles, and to be able to reason from them under assumed hypothetical circumstances: it is another thing to possess the talent of justly appreciating actual circumstances, so as to regulate the application of principles to any given case."[43]

Mill is a little misleading when he claims that the principle of utility should be appealed to only in cases involving conflicts between secondary rules, since such conflicts are easy to generate. We consider the case of lying. One secondary rule is 'Never lie'. Another secondary rule is 'Never lie unless doing so would promote utility and telling the truth would promote disutility'. In a case in which lying would promote utility and telling the truth would promote disutility, we have a conflict between rules and must appeal to the principle of utility.

"If evil will arise in any specific case from our telling truth, we are forbidden by a law of morality from doing that evil: we are forbidden by another law of morality from telling falsehood. Here then are two laws of morality in conflict, and we cannot satisfy both of them." When there is a conflict between two rules, we must "resort to the primary test of all right and wrong, and . . . make a specific calculation of the good or evil consequences, as fully and impartially as we can."[44]

Basically, Mill is suggesting that whenever one would produce net disutility by following one secondary rule, *one's act would not be in accord with a different secondary rule, viz.,* 'Do not produce evil' ('Do not produce net disutility'). Whenever there are conflicts between secondary rules, one must appeal to the principle of utility. Thus, rule-utilitarians are not representing Mill's position when they argue that one may morally permissibly produce net disutility as long as one's act is in accord with a rule the general following of which would maximize utility. Mill would argue that in such a case one's act would not be in accord with the secondary rule 'Do not produce net disutility'. He would then claim that one would have to appeal to the principle of utility to settle the conflict, and that the principle of utility would not allow the individual to perform a (net) disutility-producing act.

In general, a few principles emerge from Mill's writings with respect to the issue(s) at hand:

> 1. We should use secondary principles in our moral decision-making. Further, we should not be willing to break these secondary principles as readily as we would, were they merely guides to action.
>
> 2. These secondary principles should be simple enough so that they can be readily remembered and applied.
>
> 3. If, after including all of the relevant disutilities, we, as unbiased, knowledgeable, careful deliberators, are certain that following the rule would promote disutility and ignoring the rule would promote utility, then we must *disobey* the rule.[45]

CO-OPERATIVE UTILITARIANISM

Some critics believe that maximizing act-utilitarianism is untenable,[46] since agents who seek to maximize utility may be unable to do so because they lack information about what other people will do. This can easily be illustrated.

Suppose that Whiff and Poof each have to decide whether to push the buttons in front of them. The utilities can be summed up in the following diagram.[47]

		Poof	
		Push	Not-push
Whiff	Push	10	0
	Not-push	0	6

The optimal situation would involve both Whiff's and Poof's pushing the buttons. However, if one of them is not going to push a button, then neither of them should.

Suppose that neither knows what the other will do. What should Whiff do? If he pushes and Poof not-pushes, then no utiles will be produced.

As long as Whiff knows that Poof knows the possible outcomes and Poof knows that Whiff knows the possible outcomes, they will both push, since they are both seeking to maximize utility and their both pushing would produce optimal results. However, Whiff and Poof would not be helped by this solution if their situation were a little different. Suppose that as long as they both pushed or not-pushed, they each would produce ten utiles; otherwise, they each would produce minus five utiles. If neither has any idea what the other will do, neither can say what he himself ought to do.

Obviously, Whiff and Poof should talk to each other, if possible. If they cannot, then they are in a difficult position and each will simply have to make a guess about what the other will do.[48]

In discussing these issues, we must be careful to distinguish among several issues:

> 1. Did the agent act rightly?
>
> 2. Should the agent be blamed?
>
> 3. How much blame should he receive?

In the problem posed above, the agent does not know what to do. Should Whiff push the button? Yes, if Poof is going to push, and no, otherwise. If Whiff does not know what Poof is going to do, Whiff will have to guess, taking into account all that he knows about Proof. If Whiff guesses correctly, he will have acted rightly; otherwise, he will have acted wrongly.[49] Co-ordination problems do not prevent agents from acting rightly. They merely prevent agents from knowing what to do.

Should we blame Whiff for guessing wrongly? This is a separate issue. Whiff's lack of knowledge may affect whether or how much he should be blamed for his bad guess. It does not at all affect whether he in fact performed the right action.

Current theorists are correct that co-ordination problems may affect act-utilitarian analyses of the proper courses of action. Mill would welcome the suggestion that agents should try to be well-informed before making their decisions. However, the co-ordination utilitarians are in no better position than the act-utilitarians. Both should find out all they can about the situation at hand, *including* what other people are planning on doing, and then act accordingly.

WHICH CONSEQUENCES ARE THE EFFECTS OF PARTICULAR ACTIONS?

When Mill talks about the effects of an action, he includes many of the consequences which one might not (at first) attribute to the performance of a particular action. For example, Mill believes that one should be truthful because "the cultivation in ourselves of a sensitive feeling on the subject of veracity is one of the most useful, and the enfeeblement of that feeling one of the most hurtful, things to which our conduct can be instrumental." Thus, one's lying has a negative effect on one's character. Also, one's lying will help to "deprive mankind of the good, and inflict upon them the evil, involved in the greater or less reliance which they can place in each other's word."[50] People will feel less secure if I lie to them, both because they will trust me less and because they will tend to trust others less as well.

When Mill is trying to decide whether a particular lie would be justified, he does not merely look at the immediate effects of the lie, e.g., my being very pleased versus someone else's being slightly displeased. My lying will hurt my character, will make the other person less likely to believe people, and will make me less likely to believe people.

Mill argues that the consequences which rule-utilitarians claim should be traced back to rules can in fact be traced back to *actions*. By taking a rather broad view of which effects are correctly deemed the effects of particular actions, Mill can account for the considerations which a rule-utilitarian might cite, e.g., effects on character, security, etc., *and* Mill is able to secure an additional benefit. He can claim that lying is sometimes morally permissible,[51] for example, at those times when calamities might be averted by a little 'judicious' lying.

THE BENEFIT OF HUMANKIND

As a type of act-utilitarian, Mill believes that an action which maximizes utility is morally right. However, his view is somewhat unusual with respect to *whose* utility should be promoted.

Mill is quite concerned about promoting the happiness of the individual. He believes that one of the reasons that individuals should pursue the higher pleasures is that, by so doing, they will be both better and happier people.[52] Mill is also quite concerned about promoting the happiness of society, arguing that even if an individual, himself, is not

happier as a result of his becoming nobler, other people will thereby be happier.[53] Yet, neither the promotion of individual happiness nor the promotion of societal happiness is Mill's ultimate concern. Mill's ultimate concern is to promote the utility of humankind.

In *On Liberty*, Mill says, "I regard utility as the ultimate appeal on all ethical questions, but it must be utility in the largest sense, grounded on the permanent interests of man as a progressive being."[54] Mill's talking about "man as a progressive being" does not make each individual's interests of primary importance. Rather, the permanent interests of humankind are important. Each individual's utility is promoted as a fortunate by-product of the promotion of humankind's utility.

When talking about 'man', Mill might seem to be referring to the interests of society. Such an interpretation is incorrect.

The permanent interests of man are not simply the permanent interests of a particular society, e.g., Greek, Roman, or British. Rather, they are the interests of the Society of Man, i.e., Humankind. When Mill talks about Humankind, he is not merely talking about all of the people who happen to be living at a particular time. He is talking about "the Human Race, conceived as a continuous whole, including the past, the present and the future."[55]

Mill agrees with Comte that "reflection, guided by history, has taught us the intimacy of the connection of every age of humanity with every other."[56] We are narrow-minded if we think that we should promote the good of a particular society of a particular time period at the expense of the good of humankind. It is "the good of the human race [which] is the ultimate standard of right and wrong."[57]

Mill complains that Bentham's doctrine, which emphasizes individuals' acting out of self-interest, is very destructive of "all natural hope for good for the *human species* [my italics]." Bentham undermines "our hopes of happiness or moral perfection to the *species* [my italics]."[58]

In *A System of Logic*, Mill says that the ultimate standard is "conduciveness to the happiness of mankind."[59] In *Utilitarianism*, Mill also speaks about promoting the happiness of all humankind.[60]

Mill believes that we are able to predict what will promote the happiness of humankind, because "social phenomena conform to invariable laws."[61] We merely need to figure out what would be the ideal setting, e.g., which attitudes people should have and which actions people should perform, for happiness to be promoted. We can examine the history of humankind to see which rules and actions further that goal.[62]

When Mill talks about promoting the happiness of humankind, he does not specify whether he is talking about the average happiness or the (net) total happiness. The difference may be illustrated in the following way.

Suppose that there are four individuals in World W, each of whom is fairly happy. For the sake of illustration, we shall assign each of them a "happiness level" of 25. The question at hand is whether the world would be a better place were there an additional person, Jones, who over her lifetime would enjoy a happiness level of 10.

Were Jones to live in W, the (net) total level of happiness would be raised to 110 happiness units. However, the average happiness level would be lowered from 25 to 22. Thus, on the (net) total happiness account, W would be a better place were Jones also to live there. On the average happiness account, W would be a worse place were Jones to live there.

Family planning practices might differ, depending upon whether one adopted the former or latter account. Mill was clearly interested in promoting a decline in the population rate. "It appears to me impossible but that the increase of intelligence, of education, and of the love of independence among the working classes, must be attended with a corresponding growth of the good sense which manifests itself in provident habits of conduct, and that population, therefore, will bear a gradually diminishing ratio to capital and employment."[63] Here, he might be inferred to be promoting the average happiness. However, Mill would not be in favor of destroying all but two people (who happened to be very happy and to require no one else but themselves), even though the average happiness might thereby be increased.

Clearly, Mill wants future generations to be considered in calculations of utility. However, he does not specifically address some of the issues raised if one is indeed to consider future generations, e.g., whether one has a duty to procreate, whether future generations' interests should be discounted, if so, by how much, etc.[64]

An additional complicating factor which must be considered is that Mill does not believe that only rules and actions should be judged by the principle of utility. Attitudes should also promote utility. Mill criticizes Whewell for assuming that people's moral attitudes are above reproach. "The point in dispute is, what acts are the proper objects of those [moral] feelings; whether we ought to take the feelings as we find them, as accident or design has made them, or whether the tendency of actions to promote happiness affords a test to which the feelings of morality should conform."[65] Indeed, "intellectual progress [is] in no other way so beneficial as by creating a standard to guide the moral sentiments of mankind, and a mode of bringing those sentiments effectively to bear on conduct."[66] Thus, when Mill talks about promoting utility, he is talking about the utility of humankind. He is interested in changing both attitudes and actions in order to bring about his goal.

Merely because Mill is primarily interested in promoting the interests of humankind *does not mean* that Mill is un-

interested in protecting the individual. The protection of individual liberties is extremely important, because protecting them is the best way to promote the interests of humankind. *On Liberty* is written to demonstrate *on empirical grounds* that the protection of individual liberties will ultimately be the best way of promoting the interests of humankind.[67]

THE IMPORTANCE OF MILL'S BEING A TYPE OF ACT-UTILITARIAN

It might seem unimportant to ascertain whether Mill was an act-utilitarian, since even if this controversy could be resolved the result would seem to have little bearing on any contemporary philosophical discussions. Such a view is mistaken. In understanding Mill's act-utilitarianism, we shall see how contemporary act-utilitarians can refute some of their severest critics.

Act-utilitarians are often charged with being unable to show that justice will be preserved or that promises will be kept. Mill deflects these charges by talking about the hidden disutilities caused by the performance of such actions. If justice is not preserved, insecurity will result.[68] Insecurity will also result if people habitually lie. Mill is including these results as part of the total consequences of *particular* actions.

Mill is an act-utilitarian who looks at immediate *and* eventual consequences of actions in light of how these actions will affect the utility of humankind. He thus disagrees with act-utilitarians who only look at the immediate consequences of actions or who only look at consequences in light of how they will affect a particular society or even the world at a particular time.

When theorists talk about the *remote* effects of actions, e.g., "possible effects on the agent's character, and effects on the public at large,"[69] they are talking about effects which, according to Mill, are effects of particular actions. While even Mill admits that it is difficult to determine exactly how much disutility is promoted by a particular lie, he still believes that the disutility is produced *by the action*. We may have to look at many actions of a similar type in order to ascertain all of the effects, but it is the effects of the action that concern Mill.

Mill would be confused by a critic who claimed that effects on character or on public feelings of security are reasons not to support act-utilitarianism. For Mill, these would be reasons to support *his type* of act-utilitarianism.

Since Mill's act-utilitarianism takes into account many of the factors that are taken into account by various forms of rule-utilitarianism, it might seem unimportant to make the distinction. Such a claim is false *because of the way that rule-utilitarianism tends to be formulated.*

Suppose that even after one has taken all of the hidden disutilities of a particular action into account, one still sees that one should perform what is normally called an unjust action. The act-utilitarian will claim that the unjust action should be performed. She will explain her position in one of two ways:

> 1. She will claim that the performance of justice is not always morally correct, opting for a rather paradoxical view of both justice and morality.
>
> 2. She will adopt Mill's view and claim that because the dictates of justice cannot be disutility-producing, what is normally just (i.e., what the secondary rules of justice dictate to be just) is not just in this particular case.

The rule-utilitarian would say that even if the dictates of justice do not promote utility in this particular case, the dictates generally promote utility and thus must always be followed. There is a major difference between the act- and rule-utilitarian. In a situation in which the dictates of justice do not promote utility, the act-utilitarian claims that the dictates must be ignored, while the rule-utilitarian claims that the dictates of justice must be followed.

Mill argues, "In such cases [i.e., where justice and utility conflict], as we do not call anything justice which is not a virtue [e.g., which is disutility-producing], we usually say, not that justice must give way to some other moral principle, but that what is just in ordinary cases is, by reason of that other principle, not just in this particular case." By doing this, we will avoid conceptual difficulties. "By this useful accommodation of language, the character of indefeasibility attributed to justice is kept up, and we are saved from the necessity of maintaining that there can be laudable injustice."[70]

Mill is not merely making a semantic point here. He is claiming that since justice is founded on utility, justice cannot dictate that we perform disutility-producing actions. In cases in which the apparent rule of justice dictates that we do something which is obviously disutility-producing, we must either amend the rule or ignore it altogether.

Mill has little patience for those who would claim that not following the normal dictates of justice to promote utility would involve doing an 'evil'. He agrees with Whately's analysis of such a case. "[W]hen in a discussion, one party vindicates, on the ground of general expediency, a particular instance of resistance to government in a case of intolerable oppression, the opponent may gravely maintain that 'we ought not to do evil that good may come;' a proposition which of course has never been denied, the point in dispute being, 'whether resistance in this particular case *were* doing evil or not'."[71]

If truth-telling would be disutility-producing and lying would be utility-producing in a particular case, then lying would be morally required. Lying and acting 'unjustly', i.e., not following the normal dictates of justice, may not have (net) negative effects on one's character, on public security, or on others' lying or breaking other moral rules at inappropriate times. Lying has a bad effect on one's

character only when the lie would promote one's acting in disutility-producing ways. By the same token, acting unjustly would have a bad effect on one's character only when the 'injustice' would promote one's acting in disutility-producing ways. If I lie or act unjustly because doing so would slightly benefit me and would greatly hurt others, then my so acting would be wrong—I have counted my own interests too heavily. My character will suffer in that I am promoting my own tendency to act selfishly and in that I am promoting my own and others' tendency to lie or act unjustly at inappropriate times. However, if I lie to promote utility, then my character may not suffer. I should lie when doing so would promote utility, and my character is helped rather than harmed insofar as my tendency to lie at utility-producing times is promoted. True. If I lie to promote utility, then my character might suffer in that the tendency to lie in general rather than at only utility-promoting times might be strengthened. Further, my character might suffer in that the disposition to break other moral rules might also be strengthened. Nonetheless, the disutility produced might not be sufficient to outweigh the utility of telling the lie.[72]

Suppose that Ann and I agree to meet somewhere. I go there but she fails to keep the appointment. She has broken her promise. Much disutility can result from promise-breaking, e.g., I may grow to distrust her and others.

Suppose, however, that she has very good reasons for her promise-breaking. Once I have been apprised of the facts, I might have two very different reactions:

> 1. I might grow to trust her as much as or more than I did before. I would realize that she has exercised good judgment. Her action would *promote* feelings of security, both in myself because I know that she has acted as she should have, and in others, especially those who directly benefited from her good use of her judgment.
>
> 2. I might still be angry and resentful, despite my knowing that her action promoted utility. Mill would condemn my resentment rather than Ann's action. He would say that "just persons [resent] a hurt to society, though not otherwise a hurt to themselves, and [do] not [resent] a hurt to themselves, however painful, unless it be of the kind which society has a common interest with them in the repression of."[73]

Mill argues persuasively for the protection of liberty and the preservation of justice on *utilitarian* grounds. We learn from him, *not* (as some rule-utilitarians and deontologists seem to imply) that the preservation of justice is usually but not always utility-producing, but that the preservation of justice is *necessarily* utility-producing. When one, as an unbiased, knowledgeable, deliberate calculator, takes into consideration the effects of following the standard rules of justice and morality and one sees that following those rules will be disutility-producing, one will understand that those rules must be amended or ignored entirely.

It is important to understand Mill's act-utilitarianism because we can then see that some of the arguments (e.g., that insecurity and the formation of bad characters will result from performing certain actions) used by rule-utilitarians and deontologists to support their own theories, are used cogently and convincingly to support an act-utilitarian position. However, there is an important respect in which act-utilitarianism and rule-utilitarianism are not so far apart after all.

We should not conform our acts to socially useful rules when doing so would promote disutility. However, when making the appropriate calculations, we must include the remote effects of rule-breakings, e.g., effects on character, effects on general security, etc.

If we really know of a case in which following the rule would promote disutility and breaking the rule would promote utility (including all of the considerations above), then the rule-utilitarian will want to modify his rule to account for the exception, since the rule-utilitarian cannot justify a rule when the adoption of a different rule in its stead would produce more utility.[74] If we know that following a rule would be disutility-producing, then an act-utilitarian will claim that we should not *follow* that rule, i.e., he will say that we should disobey it. By the same token, if we know that our following a rule would be disutility-producing, then the rule-utilitarian will claim that we should not *have* that rule—she will say that we should instead have a different rule to follow.

Usually, agents *suspect* rather than *know* that following a particular rule would be disutility-producing. In such situations, the rule-utilitarian and the act-utilitarian face similar problems. The act-utilitarian must decide whether he should disobey the rule of thumb which is usually effective to follow. The rule-utilitarian must decide whether this rule is in need of an (or another) exception.

The claim here is *not* that act-utilitarianism and rule-utilitarianism are co-extensive. A rule-utilitarian might argue that we have to keep moral rules fairly simple if people are going to be able to accept and follow them correctly. Mill and act-utilitarians in general whole-heartedly agree with such a claim. The rule-utilitarian might further argue that these rules must be obeyed, even if on a particular occasion the rule's being obeyed would produce net disutility. At this point, Mill and act-utilitarians in general would disagree. They would argue that one must promote utility, even if one must break a secondary rule to do so.

It is important to understand Mill's act-utilitarianism because it is important to understand that he really is committed to the promotion of the utility of humankind above everything else. However, precisely because he is committed to the promotion of utility, he is justifiably worried that his calling secondary moral principles mere guides or mere rules of thumb would result in too many disutility-producing rule-breakings. As to whether Mill is better interpreted as claiming that the promotion of humankind's utility can best be achieved by ignoring disutility-producing rules or by simply amending them, this is a question which is, perhaps, neither answerable nor important to answer.

Notes

1. Another form of indirect utilitarianism would involve motivations rather than rules. Brandt writes, "An optimific indirect theory is a *normative* theory which *roughly* holds that any *other-person-involving* act is morally permissible if it would be *best* for the moral motivations of (roughly) all agents to *permit* acts of that type in its circumstances, and that an other-person-involving act is an agent's moral duty if it would be best for the moral motivations of (roughly) all agents to *require* acts of that type in those circumstances." He explains that he means "by a person's *moral motivations* a complex consisting of a desire/aversion for some kind of action for itself, in certain circumstances, a disposition to feel guilty if one does (does not) perform an act of this sort, and a disposition to disapprove or be indignant if someone else does (does not) perform an act of that type, in those circumstances." R. B. Brandt, "Fairness to Indirect Optimific Theories in Ethics," *Ethics* 98 (1988), pp. 342-343.

2. J. J. C. Smart, "Extreme and restricted utilitarianism" in *Mill: Utilitarianism with Critical Essays,* ed. Samuel Gorovitz (Indianapolis: Bobbs-Merrill Co., Inc, 1971), p. 195.

3. Alexander believes that act-utilitarianism's mandating that one break rules if doing so will be utility-maximizing may produce so many unwarranted rule-breakings (because agents would sometimes miscalculate and would thus break rules at inappropriate times) that one's adopting act-utilitarianism might produce less utility than would one's adopting rule-utilitarianism. See Larry Alexander, "Pursuing the Good—Indirectly," *Ethics* 95 (1985), p. 324. For an illustration of how these miscalculations might occur, see F. H. Bradley, "Pleasure for Pleasure's Sake" in *Ethical Studies* (first published 1876), Introduction by Ralph Ross (Indianapolis: Bobbs-Merrill Educational Publishing, 1951), p. 49.

4. John Stuart Mill, *A System of Logic,* Book 6, Ch. 12, Sec. 3, *CW* Vol. 8, p. 945.

5. *Utilitarianism,* Ch. 5, Par. 37, p. 259.

6. See Smart, "Extreme and restricted utilitarianism," p. 199.

7. *A System of Logic,* Book 6, Ch. 12, Sec. 3, pp. 945-946. For a similar point, see John Stuart Mill, *The Subjection of Women,* Ch. 3, Par. 10, *CW* 21, p. 307.

8. *A System of Logic,* Book 6, Ch. 12, Sec. 2, p. 944.

9. A number of theorists talk about the importance of rules' being fairly simple. See R. M. Hare, *Moral Thinking* (Oxford: University Press, 1981), p. 33; and John Rawls, "The Independence of Moral Theory," *American Philosophical Association Proceedings and Addresses* 48 (1974-1975), p. 14.

10. John Stuart Mill, "Bentham," *CW* Vol. 10, p. 111.

11. John Stuart Mill, "Taylor's Statesman," *CW* Vol. 19, p. 638.

12. *Utilitarianism,* Ch. 2, Par. 2, p. 210.

13. *Ibid.,* Ch. 2, Par. 9, p. 213.

14. *Ibid.,* Ch. 2, Par. 10, p. 214.

15. Rem Edwards claims that Mill was "neither a maximizing act nor rule utilitarian." See his "The Principle of Utility and Mill's Minimizing Utilitarianism," *Journal of Value Inquiry* 20 (1986), p. 132. See also his "J. S. Mill and Robert Veatch's Critique of Utilitarianism," *Southern Journal of Philosophy* 23 (1985), pp. 181-200. Here, it is argued that Mill agrees with standard act-utilitarians that those actions which maximize utility are right. However, he disagrees insofar as they claim that an action must be utility-maximizing in order to be right. For a related point, see Marcus Singer's "Actual Consequence Utilitarianism," *Mind* 86 (1977), p. 69.

16. See J. O. Urmson, "The Interpretation of the Moral Philosophy of J. S. Mill," *Mill: Utilitarianism with Critical Essays,* p. 170; and H. J. McCloskey, *John Stuart Mill: A Critical Study* (London: Macmillan and Co., Ltd., 1971), p. 58.

17. *Utilitarianism,* Ch. 2, Par. 24, p. 224.

18. *Ibid.,* pp. 224-225.

19. This is Mabbott's example. See J. D. Mabbott, "Interpretations of Mill's Utilitarianism" in *Mill: A Collection of Critical Essays,* ed. J. B. Schneewind (Garden City: Anchor Books, 1968), p. 194.

20. *Utilitarianism,* Ch. 2, Par. 24, p. 224.

21. *Ibid.,* Ch. 2, Par. 19, p. 220.

22. A class of actions is merely a set of actions, all of which meet one or more criteria. Or, to use a different description, a class of actions is a set of actions, all of which correspond to some rule(s). To be concerned with the consequences of performing actions of a certain class is to be concerned with the consequences of performing actions of a particular set, all of which correspond to the same rule(s). Thus, Mill seems to be espousing a rule-utilitarian position—one should not perform an action unless the rule with which it is in accord would promote the general good. The consequences which result from not following the rule seem to be of concern, not the consequences of performing the action.

23. For a similar argument, see Bernard Semmel, *John Stuart Mill and the Pursuit of Virtue* (New Haven: Yale University Press, 1984), p. 87. For related comments of Mill's, see "Whewell on Moral Philosophy," p. 182; and *On Liberty,* Ch. 4, Par. 8, *CW* Vol. 18, p. 280.

24. *A System of Logic, CW* Vol. 8, Book 6, Ch. 11, Sec. 6, Par. 3, pp. 1154-55.

25. *Ibid.,* Par. 4, p. 1155. These two passages were deleted after the 1846 edition. Mill may have deleted these passages because he simply changed his mind and wanted to espouse a much more act-utilitarian line. However, passages in other works would not support this explanation. I suspect that he deleted these passages, not because his position had changed but rather because they sounded too rule-oriented and thus did not represent his position. One can easily understand Mill's difficulty. He does not want to advocate blind rule-following, but also does not want to advocate a position which would result in frequent and inappropriate violations of secondary rules. Of course, it may be that the passages were deleted because of printing costs. However, even were that true, other passages in Mill's writings support the position offered here.

26. "Whewell on Moral Philosophy," p. 182.

27. *Ibid.,* p. 183.

28. *Considerations on Representative Government,* Ch. 5, Par. 8, p. 425.

29. "Whewell on Moral Philosophy," p. 183.

30. *A System of Logic,* Book 6, Ch. 12, Sec. 3, p. 946.

31. "Taylor's Statesman," p. 640. In Chapters 4-7, there will be a discussion of how much net utility one has a duty to promote.

32. *CW* Vol. 17, p. 1881. Brown points out this letter. See D. G. Brown, "Mill's Act-utilitarianism," *Philosophical Quarterly* 27 (1974), p. 68.

33. "Whewell on Moral Philosophy," p. 181.

34. "Remarks on Bentham's Philosophy," *CW* Vol. 10, p. 8.

35. "Sedgwick's Discourse," p. 56.

36. *Principles of Political Economy,* Book 4, Ch. 1, Sec. 2, Par. 2, Vol. 3, p. 706.

37. *Considerations on Representative Government,* Ch. 15, Par. 11, p. 541. See also "De Toqueville" (1), *CW* Vol. 18, p. 80.

38. "Bentham," p. 110.

39. *Ibid.,* p. 111.

40. "Blakey's History of Moral Science," *CW* Vol. 10, p. 29.

41. *Utilitarianism,* Ch. 2, Par. 25, p. 226.

42. *The Subjection of Women,* Ch. 3, Par. 10, p. 307. Mill seems to believe that the moral judgment of individuals improves as they become more 'civilized'. See "Civilization," *CW* Vol. 18, p. 132.

43. "Taylor's Stateman," pp. 622-623.

44. *Ibid.,* pp. 638-639. See also *Utilitarianism,* Ch. 2, Par. 23, p. 223 in which Mill writes that even the rule of truth-telling, "sacred as it is, admits of possible exceptions."

45. The position described here is quite compatible with Berger's "strategy" conception of moral rules. See

Berger, *Happiness, Justice and Freedom,* pp. 72 ff. The position here is also compatible with Henry West's. See his "Mill's Moral Conservatism," *Midwest Studies in Philosophy* 1 (1976), pp. 71-80.

46. See Lars Bergstrom, "Utilitarianism and Future Mistakes," *Theoria* 43 (1977), pp. 84-102; Jordan Sobel, "Utilitarianism and Past and Future Mistakes," *Nous* 10 (1976), pp. 195-219; Brian Ellis, "Retrospective and Prospective Utilitarianism," *Nous* 15 (1981), pp. 325-339; Hector-Neri Castaneda, "On the Problem of Formulating a Coherent Act-Utilitarianism," *Analysis* 32 (1972), pp. 118-124. For related comments, see Fred Feldman, *Doing the Best We Can* (Dordrecht: D. Reidel Publishing Co., 1986), Ch. 1.

These theorists make interesting and important points which will not be addressed here both because these points do not directly address Mill's system and because insofar as they do indirectly address his system, they (analogously, if not directly) might be made against many, if not all, moral systems. For example, there are serious problems raised by the notion of group actions *for moral theorists in general,* at least in part, because such a notion may force theorists to reassess the basic unit of moral evaluation. There are also serious problems raised insofar as one should consider others' and one's own probable future immoral actions.

Sympathizing with some of these criticisms directed at act-utilitarianism, Holbrook argues that "an action is right if and only if it is part of that series of actions that has the greatest overall pleasure as its result." See Daniel Holbrook, *Qualitative Utilitarianism* (Lanham: Press of America, 1988), p. 42. He does not seem to appreciate that on this account an agent may be held morally accountable for *others'* moral misdeeds. While we should try to anticipate and consider our own and others' future actions when we deliberate about what to do currently, a theory like Holbrook's demands much more than that and seems to destroy the notions both of individual agency and of (individual) moral responsibility. In any case, the kind of analysis required to handle these problems would have to be too extensive and too foundational to be appropriately handled here.

47. This is Regan's example. See Donald Regan, *Utilitarianism and Co-operation* (Oxford: Oxford University Press, 1980), p. 18

48. Information constraints create difficulties for a variety of theories. Suppose that we adopt Regan's position and say, "What each agent ought to do is co-operate, with whoever else is co-operating in the production of the best consequences possible given the behaviors of the non-co-operators." Regan, *Utilitarianism and Co-operation,* p. 124. Or, we can adopt the proposal suggested by Postow and say, "In

any given situation, any group of one or more agents ought to follow a course of action by means of which the group would produce the most good that it can produce in that situation." B. C. Postow, "Generalized Act Utilitarianism," *Analysis* 37 (1977), p. 51. (For a discussion of how agents who lack perfect knowledge should act if they wish to be rational, see David Gauthier, *Morals By Agreement* (Oxford: Oxford University Press, 1986), especially Ch. 3.) If there is no available information about what others are doing, the agent may have to flip a coin. Whether one is an act-utilitarian or a co-operative utilitarian, one will simply have to hope for the best.

49. In the next chapter, we shall see that Mill is sometimes thought to evaluate actions in terms of their foreseeable consequences. If Whiff has no reason to believe that Poof will act one way rather than the other, then neither of Whiff's alternatives is foreseeably better and he acts rightly no matter which of the two options he chooses, regardless of Poof's choice.

50. *Utilitarianism,* Ch. 2, Par. 23, p. 223.

51. *Ibid.*

52. *Ibid.,* Ch. 2, Par. 6, p. 212.

53. *Ibid.,* Ch. 2, Par. 9, p. 213.

54. John Stuart Mill, *On Liberty,* Ch. 1, Par. 11, p. 224.

55. "Auguste Comte and Positivism," p. 333.

56. *Ibid.,* p. 334.

57. *Ibid.,* p. 335. Levi argues that 'the permanent interests of man as a progressive being' are related to the actualization of certain human potentials. See Albert William Levi, "The Value of Freedom: Mill's Liberty (1859-1959)," *Ethics* 70 (1959), p. 40. That interpretation is quite compatible with this one, as long as the actualization of those potentials would indeed promote the general happiness of humankind.

By the same token, theorists are correct that Mill argues for the great importance of the promotion of autonomy and individuality, as long as they keep in mind that Mill so argues because he believes that the promotion of these qualities is necessary for the progress and well-being of humankind. See *On Liberty,* Ch. 3, Par. 1 ff, pp. 260 ff.

58. John Stuart Mill, "Remarks on Bentham's Philosophy," *CW* Vol. 10, p. 15. For related comments, see Richard Arneson, "Mill Versus Paternalism," *Ethics* 90 (1980), pp. 470-489.

59. *A System of Logic,* Book 6, Ch. 12, Sec. 7, p. 951.

60. *Utilitarianism,* Ch. 2, Par. 10, p. 214.

In the passages above, Mill is clearly interested in promoting humankind's utility. Sometimes, Mill writes as if he is interested in promoting the happiness of all sentient beings. It is not clear how the happiness of each sentient creature should be weighed, e.g., whether each counts for one and no one for more than one. See "Whewell on Moral Philosophy," pp. 186 ff. Mill writes that the maximization of the happiness of all sentient creatures would be best, "as far as the nature of things admits." *Utilitarianism,* Ch. 5, Par. 10, p. 214. It is not clear how this qualification should be treated.

In this work, it will be assumed that Mill believes that the act which maximizes humankind's (foreseeable) utility is morally best. The account can be suitably modified, depending upon how animals' interests should be weighed.

61. "Auguste Comte and Positivism," p. 290.

62. *Utilitarianism,* Ch. 2, Par. 24, p. 224.

63. *Principles of Political Economy,* Book 4, Ch. 7, Sec. 3, Par. 1, *CW* Vol. 3, p. 765. See also "Chapters on Socialism," *CW* 5, p. 729. For a brief, related (historical) discussion of Mill's views on the dissemination of birth control information, see Michael Packe, *The Life of John Stuart Mill* (London: Secker and Warburg, 1954), pp. 56 ff. See also Gertrude Himmelfarb, *On Liberty and Liberalism* (New York: Alfred A. Knopf, Inc., 1974), p. 121.

64. A vast literature has been devoted to the topic of our obligations to future generations. See, e.g., R. I. Sikora and Brian Barry (eds.), *Obligations to Future Generations* (Philadelphia: Temple University Press, 1978).

65. "Whewell on Moral Philosophy," p. 172. Brandt seems to want to attribute his theory of indirect utility to Mill. See Brandt's "Fairness to Indirect Optimific Theories in Ethics," p. 342. As will be explained more fully in later chapters, Mill evaluates an action's rightness according to the principle of utility and he evaluates a motivation's goodness according to the principle of utility, but *not* the moral goodness of an action in terms of the goodness of the motivation which, itself, is evaluated according to the principle of utility—Mill argues that the rightness of an action and the goodness of a motivation are each *directly* evaluated according to the principle of utility. The theory which Brandt describes is more appropriately attributed to Hutcheson. See my *Francis Hutcheson's Moral Theory: Its Form and Utility.*

66. "Auguste Comte and Positivism," pp. 322 ff.

67. See my "Mill and the Utility of Liberty," *Philosophical Quarterly* 34 (1984), pp. 63-68. See also Ted Honderich's "The Worth of J. S. Mill *On Liberty,*" *Political Studies* 22 (1974), pp. 463-470 and his "'On Liberty' and Morality-Dependent Harms," *Political Studies* 30 (1982), pp. 504-514.

68. *Utilitarianism,* Ch. 5, Par. 25, pp. 250-251.

69. See Williams's claim in J. J. C. Smart and Bernard Williams, *Utilitarianism For and Against* (Cambridge: Cambridge University Press, 1973), p. 100.

70. *Utilitarianism,* Ch. 5, Par. 37, p. 259. Narveson criticizes rule-utilitarianism because it might morally require that one perform what one knows to be a non-utility-maximizing action. See his *Morality and Utility* (Baltimore: Johns Hopkins Press, 1967), p. 128.

71. *A System of Logic,* Book 5, Ch. 7, Sec. 3, Par. 4, p. 829.

72. For a related discussions, see Copp on "generic effects." David Copp, "The Iterated-Utilitarianism of J. S. Mill," *New Essays on John Stuart Mill and Utilitarianism,* p. 94.

73. *Utilitarianism,* Ch. 5, Par. 21, p. 249.

74. Goldman points out that there is insufficient appreciation of the difficulty of providing the relevant description of the appropriate moral rule within certain forms of rule-utilitarianism. See Holly Goldman, "David Lyons on Utilitarian Generalization," *Philosophical Studies* 26 (1974), pp. 78 ff. Feldman claims that Lyons uses the wrong criterion for relevance. See Fred Feldman, "On the Extensional Equivalence of Simple and General Utilitarianism," *Nous* 8 (1974), pp. 191 ff. See also Gertrude Ezorsky, "A Defense of Rule-Utilitarianism Against David Lyons Who Insists on Tieing it to Act-Utilitarianism, Plus a Brand New Way of Checking Out General Utilitarian Properties," *Journal of Philosophy* 65 (1968). For an informative discussion on this and related matters, see Gerald Gaus, "Mill's Theory of Moral Rules," *Australasian Journal of Philosophy* 58 (1980), pp. 265-279.

Roger Crisp (essay date 1997)

SOURCE: "Utilitarianism and Equality: *The Subjection of Women,*" in *Mill on Utilitarianism,* Routledge, 1997, pp. 201-15.

[In the following essay, Crisp considers the implications of Mill's utilitarianism with regard to the equality of women.]

UNMASKING THE MORALITY OF MARITAL SLAVERY

. . . [The] cornerstone of Mill's practical view is the principle of utility. According to this principle, the right act is that which maximizes overall welfare. Some of our acts involve our taking part in the practices of everyday, or 'customary', morality. Because my child is less likely to attack others if I encourage her to feel proud at her self-control and kindness, and shame and guilt at her cruelty, it makes utilitarian sense to bring her up to feel these emotions at the proper times, and thus to guide her conduct in a utilitarian direction.

. . . Mill accepts that some parts of customary morality may well be grounded on the promotion of human welfare (The Subjection of Women: *SW* 1.5; cf. *SW* 1.4). These include certain 'secondary principles', such as principles of justice, which have been initiated and continued reflectively, and tested against alternatives. Other parts of customary morality, however, such as what he saw as the common readiness to permit interference with individuals for their own good, he finds abhorrent, and wishes to see replaced. In other words, the mere fact that a certain moral principle is widely accepted does not justify it. Custom itself has no authority.

Another area in which Mill thinks the customary morality of his day is in need of radical reform concerns the relations between the sexes. Here Mill recognized that he had a great battle on his hands, and it was one he fought throughout his life, from the time he was arrested at the age of 17 for handing out leaflets on contraception until the final period of his life, in which he attempted in Parliament to extend suffrage to women. The battle, as he sees it, is against custom, and the intense and irrational feelings which protect it (*SW* 1.2). One of Mill's primary tasks in *The Subjection of Women* is to reveal the reality of oppression behind the genteel appearance of Victorian chivalry:

> It was inevitable that this one case of a social relation grounded on force, would survive through generations of institutions grounded on equal justice, an almost solitary exception to the general character of their laws and customs; but which, so long as it does not proclaim its own origin, and as discussion has not brought out its true character, is not felt to jar with modern civilization, any more than domestic slavery among the Greeks jarred with their notion of themselves as a free people.
>
> (*SW* 1.6)

What, then, was the origin of the relative positions of men and women? According to Mill, fully to understand this requires one to grasp the history of morality itself, so that one can see how those relations are still governed by a morality which has in other areas of life become obsolete.

Mill suggests that in the very earliest human societies each woman, because of her physical weakness and sexual attractiveness, would be enslaved to a man. Out of this primitive Hobbesian state of nature developed legal systems which merely legitimized these ownership relations:

> Slavery, from being a mere affair of force between the master and the slave, became regularized and a matter of compact among the masters, who, binding themselves to one another for common protection, guaranteed by their collective strength the private possessions of each, including his slaves.
>
> (*SW* 1.5)

Primitive slavery, then, is the source of the inequality of women. And in the legitimation of this primitive relation is to be found the origin of social or legal obligation: those who disobeyed the 'law of force' were thought guilty of the most serious crime, and duly punished with great cruelty (*SW* 1. 7). Here we must not forget Mill's brief but important account of morality's origin in the desire to punish in *Utilitarianism* 5.14.

Gradually, a certain sense of obligation developed in some superiors towards some inferiors (though not slaves), as the result of the development of consciences which motivated the keeping, from a sense of duty, of promises originally made for convenience. This evolution out of the pure law of force was the beginning of what we might recognize as a morality:

> [T]he banishment of that primitive law even from so narrow a field, commenced the regeneration of human nature, by giving birth to sentiments of which experience soon demonstrated the immense value even for material interests, and which thenceforward only required to be enlarged, not created.
>
> (*SW* 1.7)

Then the view arose among the Stoics, and was taken up in Christianity, that there are obligations to slaves (*SW* 1.7; cf. *SW* 2.12). Though not widely adopted, this was the clearest example of a new stage in morality—the morality of chivalry, in which the strong would be praised for refraining from oppressing the weak (*SW* 2.12).

CHIVALRY AND JUSTICE

Women, in fact, had from very early times played a rôle in creating the conditions for the morality of chivalry (*SW* 4.8). Because of women's vulnerability, they encouraged men not to be violent, and because of female weakness, to settle disputes by non-violent means. Women did not, however, wish their men to be cowards, because, after all, they themselves needed protection. So courage was always encouraged in sons by their mothers, and in young men by their female lovers. A possessor of military virtue would also be admired by other men, and such admiration would provide another opportunity of entry into the affections of women. The morality of chivalry, then, consists in an apparently odd mix of militarism and gentleness, especially towards women, who used their sexual power to their best advantage.

The morality of chivalry, however, is a thing of the past (*SW* 4.9). The individualism of the warrior has been replaced by cooperation in business and industry: 'The main foundations of the moral life of modern times must be justice and prudence; the respect of each for the rights of every other, and the ability of each to take care of himself' (*SW* 4.9).

Chivalry was not entirely successful. It depended on praise rather than blame and punishment, and for that reason left untouched the behaviour of the majority, unimpressed by the rewards of honour. With the morality of justice, society has the collective means to enforce decency on the part of the strong without relying on their higher feelings, and indeed it has done so—except as regards the relation of women and men. The behaviour of most men towards most women is governed not by the morality of justice, nor even the morality of chivalry, but the morality of submission—the law of force.

The morality of justice is grounded on the equality of human beings. One's birth does not determine rigidly the course one's life must take; rather one is free to employ the talents one has in whatever career one wishes (*SW* 1.13; *SW* 4.5). And this freedom . . . protects autonomy, one of the most important sources of welfare. It is recognized both as an injustice to the individuals concerned, and as damaging to the interests of society as a whole, to place needless obstacles in the way of individual advancement: 'Nobody thinks it necessary to make a law that only a strong-armed man shall be a blacksmith.'

There is clearly some hyperbole in Mill's claims about the morality of justice, and indeed he does become more sanguine when reflecting upon the constraints placed on its development in society by the present relations of the sexes. But it is no doubt true that Mill is writing at a time in which sexual inequality is not widely recognized as a serious injustice. What is Mill's explanation?

One main cause is the continuing physical weakness of women (*SW* 1.6). Men have nothing to fear from women, and so have seen no good reason to concede ground to them. Mill notes that less than forty years before the publication of *The Subjection of Women,* British citizens could own other human beings, and that absolute monarchy or military despotism as systems of government had only recently begun to decline in Europe. 'Such is the power of an established system' (*SW* 1.8). Since every man has the advantage of despotism over those closest to him, is it any wonder that he has not resigned his power?

More support for the customary morality of sexism, Mill believes, is provided by the sentiments and feelings (*SW* 1.2). Given that men have inculcated in women duties of submission and self-abnegation (*SW* 1.11), it is no surprise that many women do not desire any reform.

But Mill realizes that many women have not been taken in (*SW* 1.10). Many women complain of sexism in their writings, and are petitioning vociferously for the vote and for education. In addition, even more women, though they do not complain of men as a whole, resent the tyranny of their own husband. Yet more would complain if the hold of husbands over wives were not so tight.

Mill believes that wives are in a position of slavery (*SW* 2.1). His hope is that once this is recognized, radical changes will follow. What those changes will be, and how they are to come about, we must now begin to consider.

Marriage, equal opportunity and the liberation of women

Mill is appalled by the position of women in his society. He is particularly concerned by the nature of marriage, which he sees women as being coerced into by the lack of

any serious alternative (*SW* 1.25). The history of marriage as he describes it is part of the history of morality. It has its origin, as did ordinary slavery, in the law of force, and women are owned either by their husbands or by their fathers (*SW* 2.1). A woman has no legal rights against her husband, who has literal sovereignty over her; under 'the old laws of England', murder of a husband had been considered high treason, the penalty being death by burning. Even now, Mill notes, a woman's avowal of obedience at the altar is upheld by the law, her property passing to her husband (but not *vice versa*). A woman has no time of her own; she is constantly at her husband's beck and call. Nor does she have any rights over her body; there is no crime of rape within marriage in the law of England. The husband has legal rights over the children, and most women have no real opportunity of escaping the tyranny of their husbands.

Sexism, of course, is not confined to the private sphere. Here Mill finds it unnecessary to go into detail (*SW* 3.1), since it is an undeniable fact that women are prohibited from applying for places at university, and from the 'greater number of lucrative occupations, and from almost all high social functions'. In particular, of course, women can neither vote nor stand for parliament (*SW* 3.2).

What is to be done? Mill says that the object of *The Subjection of Women* is to advocate 'a principle of perfect equality, admitting no power or privilege on the one side, nor disability on the other' (*SW* 1.1). Marriage should be on equal conditions (*SW* 1.25). As a voluntary association, it should be governed jointly, with a division of powers between wife and husband analogous to that between partners in a business (*SW* 2.7). Women should of course be given the vote, and be allowed admittance to the same positions in government, business and so on as men.

Mill's views, especially those on marriage, were considered dangerously radical even by most of those otherwise sympathetic to him. James Fitzjames Stephen, one of Mill's ablest critics, thought his position on female equality to be verging on the indecent (Stephen 1874: 134-5). It is no surprise, therefore, that Mill delayed the publication of the book, and strove to avoid particularly delicate issues such as divorce (*SW* 2.1).[1]

Nevertheless, a common criticism of Mill by modern writers is that he does not go far enough. Mill can be seen at best as a proponent of the rights of women, not their liberation (see e.g. Goldstein 1980). He advocates mere equality of opportunity for women, not seeing that the social conditioning of women, of which he was so aware, would prevent the majority's taking up any opportunities made available to them.

This criticism might be thought a little unfair to Mill. We know that he considers both law and customary morality to be important social tools for the maximizing of welfare, so it is to be expected that he will concentrate on reform within these institutions as a means to progress. He is quite aware of the indoctrination in women by society of exaggerated views about the moral and sexual importance of female meekness and submissiveness (*SW* 1.11). He believes, however, that equality in law and customary morality will result in important changes in the nature of the family and the relationships within it, and indeed in the character of society at large:

> The family, justly constituted, would be the real school of the virtues of freedom . . . What is needed is, that it should be a school of sympathy in equality, of living together in love, without power on the side or obedience on the other. This it ought to be between the parents. It would then be an exercise of those virtues which each requires to fit them for all other association, and a model to the children of the feelings and conduct which their temporary training by means of obedience is designed to render habitual.
>
> (*SW* 2.12)

Removing sexual discrimination would also allow women 'a life of rational freedom' (*SW* 4.19). Here Mill speaks of the 'liberation' of women, and he is clearly to be understood as speaking of women's being not only uncoerced by men, but positively free to make for themselves important decisions about the shape of their lives.

So Mill is concerned with the liberation of women, and with enabling them to exercise equal rights, not merely to possess them. And there is much in what he says. Were most in society, whether female or male, to begin to see women as the legal and moral equals of men in both private and public spheres, and not to view sex as relevant where it clearly is not, then the position of women would be greatly advanced. Nevertheless, as I shall show in the next section, the modern objection to Mill I have been discussing is not completely off target.

Mill's empiricism and the power of ideology

Mill recognizes the authority of custom. His error, perhaps, is not to see how entrenched are the views of women in modern society. In an early essay, Mill had claimed that there was no natural inequality between the sexes, except perhaps in physical strength (*O* 21.42). In *The Subjection of Women,* Mill is more circumspect. The debates about the nature of women raged during his day as they do in ours, and he was concerned to sidestep them. As a strict empiricist, ready only to accept the evidence of experience, Mill says that we can know nothing of the nature of women, other than, presumably because we are aware of the forces of distortion at work, that their present state is not the natural one (*SW* 1.18). History teaches us of the great openness of human beings to external influence (*SW* 1.19). Domination has always appeared natural, and indeed the unnatural is little more to most people than what is unusual (*SW* 1.9). Views of what is natural vary wildly (*SW* 1.9; *SW* 3.14). Women themselves have been permitted to say little of their own experience, and frankness is anyway hardly a common quality in unequal relationships (*SW* 1.21). But, Mill says, from the moral point of view this is all by the by: 'For, according to all the principles

involved in modern society, the question rests with women themselves—to be decided by their own experience, and by the use of their own faculties' (*SW* 1.23).

Unfortunately, however, in speaking of women as they are at present, Mill is less careful. While attempting to explain why women should be permitted to enter business and public life, Mill offers a set of generalizations about women's capacities which are unsupported in just the way he elsewhere criticizes (*SW* 3.8-13). Women are said to be more practical than men, and to possess 'intuition' and a sensitivity to particular facts instead of the male capacity to reason abstractly. They tend to be more nervous, their minds more mobile than men's, but less able to concentrate.

Admittedly Mill takes pains to stress that he is not making claims about the universal nature of women, but only women as they are. Nevertheless, his 'mere empirical generalizations, framed, without philosophy or analysis' (*SW* 3.14) not only make Mill the first to enter the quagmire of the sameness/difference debate which concerns many contemporary feminists, but suggest that it was perhaps fortunate that time did not permit him to carry out the programme of 'ethology' he describes at the end of the *System of Logic.* Whether Mill's claims be true or false, they are both irrelevant to the practicalities of his argument and based on no more evidence than claims about the nature of women as, say, instinctively maternal or sexually insatiable.

Even worse, Mill allows himself to express opinions about which choices women should make once liberated, and they are somewhat conservative:

> In an otherwise just state of things, it is not . . . a desirable custom, that the wife should contribute by her labour to the income of the family . . . Like a man when he chooses a profession, so, when a woman marries, it may in general be understood that she makes choice of the management of a household, and the bringing up of a family, as the first call upon her exertions.
>
> (*SW* 2.16)

One might think Mill says these things merely to ingratiate himself with his sexist audience, and so perhaps win them over to a more liberal position (compare his comments on Muslims and on common decency in *On Liberty*). But this is probably not the case. Mill believed that mothers were closer to children than their fathers ('Letter to Hooker' (1869) 17.1640), and does not raise the possibility that men could be involved in the raising of children (*SW* 3.1).

Mill's mistake is not just to generalize about women without good evidence when he has explicitly warned against so doing. He makes two further errors analogous to some I [have elsewhere] outlined in *On Liberty*. . . . [Concerning that] discussion of our attitude to self-regarding faults in *On Liberty,* Mill failed to see that social despotism might be based on the criticism of others which he permitted.

Here, he fails to note that, if it is widely believed that women should raise children and not work, this will create an atmosphere in which it is difficult for women to make a free choice. Other options may just not occur to them, and there may be social pressure to conform. Further, in the passage of *On Liberty* on self-regarding faults, Mill seems temporarily unaware not only of the authority of custom, but also of the authority of his own text. The same is true in *The Subjection of Women*. By advocating a domestic rôle for women, Mill was playing into the hands of those sexists who wished to prevent women from competing on equal terms with men by any means available.

The tension in Mill's writing on women demonstrates the power of the very ideology he attempted to reveal. On the one hand, he sees very clearly the intricate methods of subjection employed by men against women over the ages. On the other, he fails to recognize that he himself has been taken in by the myth that the rôle of the vast majority of women is to raise children, along with other myths, such as that the age of a husband, or the fact that he earns money, entitles him to a greater say in marriage (*SW* 2.9).

These blemishes, however, should not blind us to the force and eloquence of Mill's case for the equality of women. He does anyway allow that 'the utmost latitude ought to exist for the adaptation of general rules to individual suitabilities' (*SW* 2.16). And we find in his spelling out of the morality of justice a position which not only provides a resource for modifying his own position on child-rearing but is still important in debates about sexual equality:

> [I]t is felt to be an overstepping of the proper bounds of authority to fix beforehand, on some general presumption, that certain persons are not fit to do certain things. It is now thoroughly known and admitted that if some such presumptions exist, no such presumption is infallible. Even if it be well grounded in a majority of cases, which it is very likely not to be, there will be a minority of exceptional cases in which it does not hold: and in those it is both an injustice to the individuals, and a detriment to society, to place barriers in the way of their using their faculties for their own benefit and for that of others. In the cases, on the other hand, in which the unfitness is real, the ordinary motives of human conduct will on the whole suffice to prevent the incompetent person from making, or from persisting in, the attempt.

> (*SW* 1.13; cf. *SW* 3.1)

In 1869, Elizabeth Cady Stanton, a pioneer of women's liberation in America, wrote to Mill concerning his book:

> I lay the book down with a peace and joy I never felt before, for it is the first response from any man to show he is capable of seeing and feeling all the nice shades and degrees of women's wrongs and the central point of her weakness and degradation.

> (Lutz 1940: 171-2; cited in Rossi 1970: 62)

In the final section of this essay, let me show how Mill employed the theory he had developed in *Utilitarianism* and *On Liberty* to argue for women's equality.

THE BENEFITS OF REFORM

Mill advocates that, rather than allow the question of women's position in society to be decided by prevailing custom, one should think of it

> as a question of justice and expediency: the decision on this, as on any of the other social arrangements of mankind, depending on what an enlightened estimate of tendencies and consequences may show to be the most advantageous to humanity in general, without distinction of sex.

> (*SW* 1.17)

The morality of justice, then, is the customary morality which Mill believes suits modernity. In the circumstances in which we find ourselves, equality is to govern our relations with one another, because in this way human welfare will be best promoted.

In his discussion of justice in *Utilitarianism*, Mill suggests that there is more disagreement about equality than about any other component of justice (5.10). It is clear, however, what he means by equality between the sexes: a substantive equality of rights, allied with an attitude of equality of respect by each citizen towards every other, male or female. Equality for Mill is closely tied to desert: 'We should treat all equally well (when no higher duty forbids) who have deserved equally well of us' (5.36). And he is acutely aware, as we shall see below, of the distress caused to women who saw that the arrangements in their society prevented their exercising their talents as they wished.

What, then, would be the consequences of equality? The most important, of course, would be for women. First, they would be relieved from the terrible suffering inflicted by many husbands upon their wives (*SW* 2.1; *SW* 4.2). Mill, a husband himself, is of course aware that not all husbands are tyrants; but he is equally, and painfully, aware of the level of violence against women in the home and the lack of protection offered them by society and the law. Nor is it any surprise that women love their husbands whether they batter them or not: similar attachments were forged between slave and master in Greece and Rome.

Secondly, women might find a positive benefit in a marriage based on equality (*SW* 4.15-18). There might be far greater similarity in interests, tastes, wishes and inclinations, and a consequent decrease in painful disagreement. Mill compares the ideal marriage to friendship, in which association and sympathy enable each partner to enrich himself or herself through insight into the other's view of the world. There is little doubt that Mill is speaking here from the experience of his relationship with Harriet Taylor, and, given his view of sexual intercourse as an 'animal function' (*SW* 2.1), it is to be expected that he emphasize the non-sexual aspect of the marriage relationship.

Thirdly, and no less importantly, Mill's reforms would allow women a life of rational freedom in place of one of subjection to the will of men (*SW* 4.19-20). Here we see that Mill's case depends not only on *Utilitarianism,* and the conceptions of justice and human welfare there developed, but on the understanding of liberty and individuality worked out in *On Liberty.* Mill argues that, after food and clothing, freedom is the most important want of any human being. Mill asks his reader not to concentrate on how much freedom matters to others, but on how much it matters to the reader themselves—and then to base their conclusions about others on their own case:

> Whatever has been said or written, from the time of Herodotus to the present, of the ennobling influence of free government—the nerve and spring which it gives to all the faculties, the larger and higher objects which it presents to the intellect and feelings, the more unselfish public spirit, and calmer and broader views of duty, that it engenders, and the generally loftier platform on which it elevates the individual as a moral, spiritual, and social being—is every particle as true of women as of men. Are these things no important part of individual happiness?
>
> (*SW* 4.20)

The experience of freely running one's own life, then, is a central component of human welfare. Mill stresses two further elements which women will be able to incorporate in their lives through exercising this freedom: achievement, and the enjoyment of contemplating it (*SW* 4.21-2). As we have seen, Mill believes women should remain in the home, so his proposals as he conceives them concern mainly women who have brought up a family. He suggests that the only active outlet available to such women at present is charity, in which the effect is merely to remove the capacity for autonomy from those who are helped (*SW* 4.11). Not only could women achieve in the spheres in which men currently achieve, but they could enjoy their achievement, something again 'vitally important to the happiness of human beings', and be spared the undeserved disappointment and dissatisfaction of a wasted life.

Mill realizes that he cannot rest his case on the advantages of equality to women alone. Some benefits, he argues, will accrue to men. Like women, they will be able to enjoy a marriage of friendship with an equal. And there will be less obvious improvements to their position. For example, a man who wishes to live his life according to his own conscience and in accordance with the truth as he sees it will be able to do so, even if his opinions are at odds with those of the masses (*SW* 4.13-14; cf. *S* 2.5). At present, he would probably not attempt it, because of the social sacrifice he would be imposing on his family: 'Whoever has a wife and children has given hostages to Mrs Grundy.'² Mill was quite aware of the effects of social ostracism after the way he and Mrs Taylor were treated by society at large.

But the main advantages for men will come from those to society as a whole. Society will benefit from the constructive, as opposed to the mischievous, influence of women (*SW* 4.8-12, 20). At present, women denied liberty seek whatever power they can, without regard for its wider social implications. Sheer power depraves, whether it be held by a woman or a man. With equality, not only will women's interests move beyond the sphere of Mrs Grundy, but they will extend to combine the virtues of gentleness with a disinterested concern for society at large.

Discrimination is inefficient, resulting in the failure to realize or use the potential of those discriminated against (*SW* 1.13-14, 24; *SW* 3.1; *SW* 4.6-7). The equal education of women and their entry into professions previously prohibited to them would make available huge mental resources, as well as spur men to great competition.

Equal education would also affect the characters of both men and women: women would become more assertive, men more self-sacrificial (*SW* 2.10). And, as we saw above, there would be other effects on the morality of society, emerging from the family as a 'school of sympathy in equality' (*SW* 2.12). Present institutions result in men's becoming 'depraved' (*SW* 2.13; cf. *SW* 2.4). Mill is quite adamant about this: 'All the selfish propensities, the self-worship, the unjust self-preference, which exist among mankind, have their source and root in, and derive their principal nourishment from, the present constitution of the relation between men and women' (*SW* 4.4).

It might be thought that Mill is exaggerating. Certainly he is again sticking his neck out further than his empiricism might allow. But it is not implausible to suggest that were sexism to be rooted out, for the right reasons, from the family at all levels, many of those brought up within the institution would live up to the morality of justice elsewhere: 'Though the truth may not be felt or generally acknowledged for generations to come, the only school of genuine moral sentiment is society between equals' (*SW* 2.12).

The vision of a society in which all are granted the rights and respect they deserve is at the heart of the liberalism and egalitarianism which Mill's act utilitarianism supported. That vision is as important now as it ever was, and modern utilitarians have stressed that the boundaries of such a society should extend to include not only women, but human beings in all countries, and indeed non-human animals. Because of the depressing fact that Mill's ideal remains in many respects as distant as it did in his time, his moral and political writings, all of which must be read in the light of *Utilitarianism,* will rightly remain at the centre of moral and political debate for many years to come.

Notes

1. A tricky subject for him anyway, given his relationship with Mrs Taylor: see ch. 1.

2. Mrs Grundy, in Thomas Morton's *Speed the Plough* (1798), represents a narrow-minded sense of propriety.

Henry R. West (essay date 1997)

SOURCE: "Mill's 'Proof' of the Principle of Utility," in *Mill's Utilitarianism,* edited by David Lyons, Rowman & Littlefield Publishers, Inc., 1997, pp. 85-98.

[In the following essay, West asserts the logical plausibility of Mill's proof of his utility principle.]

Utilitarianism, in every one of its forms or formulations, requires a theory for the evaluation of consequences. Whether the units of behavior being judged are acts, rules, practices, attitudes, or institutions, to judge them by their utility, that is, by their contribution to good or bad ends, requires a theory of what count as good or bad ends. In the philosophies of the classical utilitarians, Jeremy Bentham and John Stuart Mill, some variety of hedonism served this purpose. Mill calls this

> the theory of life on which this theory of morality is grounded—namely that pleasure, and freedom from pain, are the only things desirable as ends; and that all desirable things (which are as numerous in the utilitarian as in any other scheme) are desirable either for the pleasure inherent in themselves, or as means to the promotion of pleasure and the prevention of pain.[1]

In Chapter IV of his essay entitled *Utilitarianism,* Mill addresses himself to the question of what sort of proof this principle is susceptible. The twelve paragraphs of the chapter present an argument which, if successful, is one of the most important arguments in all of moral philosophy, for, although Mill says questions of ultimate ends are not amenable to "direct proof," he believes that considerations may be presented capable of determining the intellect to give its assent to the doctrine.[2]

Unfortunately, few commentators on Mill have had their intellects convinced, and perhaps even fewer have agreed on the correct interpretation of the argument. J. B. Schneewind says of it:

> A greater mare's nest has seldom been constructed. It is now generally agreed that Mill is not, in this chapter, betraying his own belief that proof of a first moral principle is impossible, but there is not a general agreement as to what he is doing. In the last fifteen years there have been more essays dealing with the topic of "Mill's Proof" than with any other single topic in the history of ethical thought.[3]

Mill does say of the Utilitarian formula of ultimate ends that it is impossible to give a proof in the "ordinary or popular meaning of the term," but he continues,

> We are not, however, to infer that its acceptance or rejection must depend on blind impulse or arbitrary choice. . . . The subject is within the cognizance of the rational faculty, and neither does that faculty deal with it solely in the way of intuition. Considerations may be presented capable of determining the intellect either to give or withhold its assent to the doctrine, and this is the equivalent of proof.[4]

Furthermore, at the end of Chapter IV, he says that if the doctrine he has argued for is true, "the principle of utility *is proved.*"[5]

Given the claim, that he has proved his principle or presented something equivalent to proof, I think it is worthwhile to lay out the structure of the argument in deductive form. In that way we can determine the nature of the premises he introduces, locate the gaps that prevent it from being a valid deduction, and see if plausible assumptions can be formulated or interpretations offered that will support the premises and bridge the gaps. I shall present what I believe to be a reasonable interpretation of what Mill had in mind, and I shall claim that the assumptions necessary to make the argument sound are—though controversial—at least plausible.

The conclusion he is seeking is stated in Paragraph 2: "The utilitarian doctrine is that happiness is desirable, and the only thing desirable, as an end, all other things being only desirable as a means to that end." The connection between this idea and morality is mentioned at the end of Paragraph 9, where he says that the promotion of happiness is the test by which to judge all human conduct, "from whence it necessarily follows that it must be the criterion of morality, since a part is included in the whole." Mill has a complex view of the way the ultimate standard of the promotion of happiness is to be applied in morality, and morality is only one of the "three departments" of what he calls the "Art of Life." These general teleological views on testing conduct, and the place of morality within this teleological framework, are found elsewhere in the essay and in the *Logic.*[6] They are not part of this "proof," and I shall not be discussing them in this paper. I shall be examining only how he gets to the conclusion that happiness is desirable and the only thing desirable as an end.

The structure of the argument is very simple. In Paragraph 3 he argues that happiness is desirable. In the remainder of the chapter he argues that happiness is the only thing desirable. The outline of the argument can be given in Mill's own words:

> (1) "The sole evidence it is possible to produce that anything is desirable is that people do actually desire it." (Paragraph 3)
>
> (2) "Each person, so far as he believes it to be attainable, desires his own happiness." (Paragraph 3)
>
> (Therefore,)
>
> (3) "Happiness is a good." (Paragraph 3)

He substitutes the expression "is a good" for the expression "is desirable," but I presume that this is only for stylistic reasons. I think he would regard his use of these two as interchangeable in this context.[7]

The argument to show that happiness is the only thing desirable is likewise based on the evidence of actual desire:

> (4) "Human nature is so constituted as to desire nothing which is not either a part of happiness or a means of happiness." (Paragraph 9, but argued throughout Paragraphs 5-10)
>
> (Therefore,)
>
> (5) "Nothing is a good to human beings but insofar as it is either pleasurable or a means of attaining pleasure or averting pain." (Paragraph 11)

Here his use of "pleasure" and "pleasurable" instead of "happiness" is merely stylistic. Throughout the essay he says that by happiness he means pleasure and freedom from pain.

This is the simple outline of the argument. It is complicated by the fact that each individual's desire is for *his own* happiness, whereas the utilitarian doctrine that Mill is seeking to establish is that the *general* happiness is the foundation of morality.[8] In Paragraph 3, this distinction is explicit. Having said that each person desires his own happiness, Mill says we have all the proof it is possible to require

> that happiness is a good, that each person's happiness is a good to that person, and the general happiness, therefore, a good to the aggregate of all persons.

These propositions we may state as separate these:

> (3A) "Each person's happiness is a good to that person."

(Therefore,)

> (3B) "The general happiness [is] a good to the aggregate of all persons."

The distinction also can be introduced into the second part of the argument. Without doubt the psychological premise (4) means:

> (4) Each person desires nothing which is not either a part of his happiness or a means of his happiness.[9]

And parallel to (3A) and (3B) the distinction between each person and the aggregate of all persons can be introduced. This would give:

> (5A) Nothing is a good to each person but insofar as it is either a part of his happiness or a means of his happiness.

(Therefore,)

> (5B) Nothing is a good to the aggregate of all persons but insofar as it is either a part of the general happiness or a means of the general happiness.

From (3B) and (5B), we can then deduce an interpretation of the "utilitarian doctrine," as follows:

> (6) "[The general] happiness [or a part of the general happiness] is desirable, and the only thing desirable, as an end, all other things being only desirable as means to that end." (Paragraph 2)

Examining the argument, it can be seen that (1) is a methodological premise; (2) and (4) are factual psychological premises; (3) or (3A) and (5) or (5A) are supported by (2) and (4), respectively. (3B) and (5B) putatively follow from (3A) and (5A), respectively. The premise (2) is probably non-controversial. The controversial premises are (1) and (4), and the controversial steps are from the fact of happiness being desired to its being normatively desirable, and

from each person's happiness being desirable to that person to the conclusion that the general happiness is desirable to the aggregate of all people. There seem, then, to be three central issues: (A) Mill's methodology, which is to argue for what is desirable on the evidence of what is in fact desired; (B) his psychological hedonism, that each person desires his own happiness as an end and nothing as an end which is not a part of his happiness; and (C) the argument that if each person's happiness is a good and inclusive of the only good for him, as an end, the general happiness is a good, and encompasses the only good, as an end, to the aggregate of all persons. I shall take these issues up in turn.

A. DESIRE AS EVIDENCE OF DESIRABLE

I think it is hardly necessary to point out that Mill did not say that "desirable" or "the good" *means* "desired," as Moore says he does.[10] He is not committing a naturalistic or definist fallacy.[11] Mill is quite explicit in demarcating factual and normative propositions.[12]

I also think it is not likely he was misled by the similarity of the verbal endings of "visible" and "audible" into thinking that "desirable" means "able to be desired."[13] The significance of the analogy with visible and audible is announced in the first paragraph of the chapter. The first premises of our knowledge do not admit of proof by reasoning, but are subject to a direct appeal to the senses; he suggests that the first premises of conduct are subject to a direct appeal to our desiring faculty. It does not follow that he regards what is desirable as a "permanent possibility of desire." That would be to regard it as a matter of fact. The analogy is that as judgments of existence are based on the evidence of the senses and corrected by further evidence of the senses, so judgments of what is desirable are based on what is desired and corrected by further evidence of what is desired. The only evidence on which a recommendation of an end of conduct can be based is what is found appealing to the desiring faculty.

Mill also supports his appeal to desire by what is a pragmatic argument:

> If the end which the utilitarian doctrine proposes to itself were not, in theory and in practice, acknowledged to be an end, nothing could ever convince any person that it was so.[14]

Nothing about the logic of recommending an end of conduct prevents any end whatsoever from being recommended, but only one based on actual desires will be convincing. This is one respect in which the "proof" is not a proof in the ordinary sense. There is no necessity about accepting desire as the sole evidence for desirability. It is logically possible that ends of conduct that are not in fact desired be recommended without contradiction. The force of the appeal to what is desired is only to convince, not logically to rule out all other possibilities.

The import of premise (1), however, is primarily negative. It denies the existence of an intellectual intuition of the normative ends of conduct. The faculty to which Mill appeals is one that takes "cognizance" of practical ends, but by way of feeling or "sensibility" rather than intellect or moral sense. He is denying that we intuit what is intrinsically a good in some directly cognitive way.

The only way to argue a negative claim such as this conclusively would be to take each putative intuition and examine it critically to try to show that it can be reduced to desire or else to absurdity. I can obviously not do this to defend Mill's proof. I can only state that I find unconvincing all claims to intuit values, independent of desires (or likes and dislikes); so I find his skeptical starting point a plausible one. However, the desires we do have provide practical ends that will be pursued unless frustrated by the pursuit of the ends of other desires. This provides an arena in which practical reason can seek to bring order out of disorder by analyzing desires to determine which, if any, are illusory; which, if any, are fundamental; what, if anything, is the common object of them all. It is this last question that Mill's psychological hedonism claims to answer.

B. Psychological Hedonism

Mill's argument for (4) has two parts. One is in Paragraph 11, which classifies as mere habit those ends of conduct that are sought neither as means to happiness nor as a part of happiness. He claims that they have become ends of conduct:

> Will is the child of desire, and passes out of the domination of its parent only to come under that of habit. That which is the result of habit affords no presumption of being intrinsically good.[15]

That argument leaves him with everything that affords any presumption of being intrinsically good an object of conscious desire. I think it is unnecessary to accept Mill's Associationist accounts of all habitual conduct or his account of all nondeliberative nondesiring willed behavior as habit. It is enough if actions that are not the result of deliberation and conscious desire afford no presumption that their ends help to identify for us what is desirable. Evolutionary ethicists, natural law theorists, and many others would perhaps deny this, but I find it a plausible skepticism.

The other part of his argument is to claim that every object of conscious desire is associated with pleasure or the absence of pain, either as a means or an end. Many desires are acquired, such as the desire for virtue or for the possession of money, and have come to be desired through the mechanism of their association with pleasure or the absence of pain. Whether acquired or not, the ultimate ends of the desires can be regarded as experiences or states of affairs with a pleasure component: They are pleasures or "parts of happiness." Although they may fall under various other descriptions, it is the fact that they are ingredients of happiness that provides a common denominator and a unified account of desire.

If Mill is correct that there is a pleasure component to the ultimate end of every desire, and if no other common de-

nominator provides a unified account of desire, then Mill has a persuasive claim that it is the pleasure component (i.e., being part of happiness) that is the element in all objects of desire that makes them desirable as ends, which recommends them to the intellect as the basis for action and which can provide for critical assessment in case of conflict between desires.

It is tempting to read into Mill the claim that it is the agreeable quality of the state of consciousness desired that is the real object of desire. Just as the sense-data theorist claims that one sees only sense data, although it is palpable that he sees things that, in common languages, are decidedly distinguished from sense data (i.e., from whatever common language words are sense data words—"sights," "sounds," "appearances," or whatever), so Mill might be thought to hold that one desires only the pleasure component of desired experiences, although it is palpable that people "do desire things, which, in common language, are decidedly distinguished from happiness."[16] I think this is impossible to reconcile with Mill's talk of the objects of desire as being "music," "health," "virtue," "power," "fame," "possession of money," not just the agreeable feeling attending these. Furthermore, he does not need to make such a strong claim. He only needs to claim that, as a psychological fact, music, health, etc., would not be desired if no pleasure or freedom from pain or past association with these were connected with music, health, etc. Desire is evidence of desirability, but it does not confer desirability. This is obvious in the case of things desired as means. On reflection, it is obvious in the case of things desired as ends. The possession of money is desired by the miser. This desire does not make the possession of money a normative object of action for a reasonable person. The evidence furnished by desire must be analyzed; it is only by analysis of the fact that the miser desires the possession of money as part of his happiness—that he would be made happy by its possession—that the evidence of desire fits into a comprehensive theory. It is this comprehensive theory that identifies the pleasure inherent in desirable things as what makes them desirable. The pleasure inherent in them does not itself have to be discriminated as the *object* of desire.

Some commentators also have thought that Mill reduces the relation between desire and pleasures to a trivial one in the passage where he says that:

> desiring a thing and finding it pleasant, aversion to it and thinking of it as painful, are phenomena entirely inseparable, or rather two parts of the same phenomenon—in strictness of language, two different modes of naming the same psychological fact; that to think of an object as desirable (unless for the sake of its consequences), and to think of it as pleasant, are one and the same thing; and that to desire anything, except in proportion as the idea of it is pleasant, is a physical and metaphysical impossibility.[17]

This statement is certainly puzzling to the twentieth-century reader, but in context Mill is asking the reader to engage in "practiced self-consciousness and self-observation." If the terms were reducible to one another independent of observation, it is hard to see why he would invite one to attempt what appears to be an empirical discovery. A clue to interpretation is that "metaphysical" means approximately "psychological" for him.[18] In his notes on his father's *Analysis of the Phenomena of the Human Mind,* Mill takes issue with his father's statement, "The term 'Idea of a pleasure' expresses precisely the same thing as the term Desire. It does so by the very import of the words."[19] J. S. Mill says that desire:

> is more than the idea of pleasure desired, being, in truth, the initiatory state of Will. In what we call Desire there is, I think, always included a positive stimulation to action.[20]

According to J. S. Mill, then, a distinction is to be made between desiring a thing and thinking of it as pleasant. Desire is psychologically more complex and conceivably could have an object not thought of as pleasurable. It is obvious that it may have a more inclusive object, as is the case in desiring the means to an end when the means are unpleasant. In any case the question is a psychological, not a linguistic one.

Mill's substantive claim is that desire and pleasure (or the avoidance of pain) are psychologically inseparable. If this is true, two things follow: First, (4) is established—each person desires nothing that is not either a part of his happiness or a means of his happiness; second, since attainment of pleasure and avoidance of pain are the common denominators of desire, the evidence of desire supports the theory that it is the pleasure and pain aspects of the objects of desire and aversion that make them desirable and undesirable and that should serve as the criteria of good and bad consequences in a normative theory of conduct.

An adequate defense of Mill's position would require a more thorough analysis of desire and of pleasure and pain, happiness and unhappiness. I believe, however, that the interpretation given above shows that the position does not completely lack plausibility and that it might be supported by such a refined analysis.

C. From Each Person's Happiness to the General Happiness

If the intellect is convinced that the person's happiness is a good and the sole good to that person, does it follow that it will be convinced that the general happiness is a good and the sole good to the aggregate of all persons? Mill presumably thinks this is obvious, simply asserting it without argument. He apparently thinks he has practically established (3B) when he has established (3A), and (5B) when he has established (5A). I think Mill has been misinterpreted in this argument because commentators have thought his conclusion to be a much stronger claim than it is. He is making a very weak claim, which is seen when we notice what he means by "the general happiness."

According to Mill "the general happiness" is a mere sum of instances of individual happiness. Just as personal hap-

piness is not a "collective something" but simply a sum of pleasures,[21] so we can take Mill as holding that the general happiness is simply a sum of individual pleasures. There are still two ways of understanding the argument. One is that "to that person" represents the point of view of the agent when he is making prudential decisions; "to the aggregate" represents the point of view of the benevolent man when he is acting morally. Some things can be said in support of this interpretation, but I do not think that it is the correct one. I think rather that he believes that his analysis of desire shows that happiness is the *kind* of thing that constitutes intrinsic welfare, wherever it occurs. All instances of happiness will be parts of the personal welfare of someone, that is, "a good *to someone,*" but being instances of happiness, they have a common denominator that makes them the same kind of thing wherever they occur—whether in different experiences of a given individual or in the experiences of different individuals. Moreover, Mill assumes that the value of different instances of happiness can be thought of as summed up to generate a larger good. These assumptions are explicit in a letter Mill wrote regarding the move from (3A) to (3B):

> As to the sentence you quote from my *Utilitarianism,* when I said the general happiness is a good to the aggregate of all persons I did not mean that every human being's happiness is a good to every other human being, though I think in a good state of society and education it would be so. I merely meant in this particular sentence to argue that since A's happiness is a good, B's a good, C's a good, etc., the sum of all these goods must be a good.[22]

His assumptions are even more explicit in a footnote to Chapter V of *Utilitarianism.* There, answering the objection that the principle of utility presupposes the anterior principle that everybody has an equal right to happiness, Mill says:

> It may be more correctly described as supposing that equal amounts of happiness are equally desirable, whether felt by the same or by different persons. This, however, is not a presupposition, not a premise needful to support the principle of utility, but the very principle itself; . . . If there is an anterior principle implied, it can be no other than this—that the truths of arithmetic are applicable to the valuation of happiness, as of all other measurable quantities.[23]

It seems clear, then, that the "to each person" in (3A) and (5A) does not represent a "point of view," but simply the location or embodiment of welfare that cannot exist without location or embodiment, and the "to the aggregate of all persons" in (3B) and (5B) refers to the location or embodiment of welfare in a group of individuals, not a point of view. A good to the aggregate of A, B, C, etc., is interpreted by Mill to be a sum of goods to A, plus goods to B, plus goods to C, etc. He assumes both that happiness is arithmetical, capable of being summed up to find a total, "general" happiness, and that goods to different people are arithmetical, capable of being summed up to find a total good "to the aggregate of all persons."

With these assumptions, (3B) does follow from (3A), for to say that the general happiness is a good to the aggregate of all persons is merely to say that A's happiness, plus B's happiness, plus C's happiness, etc., constitutes a good to A, plus a good to B, plus a good to C, etc. And (5B) follows from (5A). If nothing is a good to each person but insofar as it is a part of his happiness (or a means to it), then nothing will be part of the sum of goods to A, plus goods to B, plus goods to C, etc., but insofar as it is a part of the happiness of A or part of the happiness of B, etc., or a means to these. This interpretation explains why Mill did not bother to state (5A) and (5B) explicitly and why he passed from (3A) to (3B) in one sentence. The evidence of desire shows that happiness is the *kind* of thing desirable as an end. It is not a different kind of thing when it is located in A's experience from what it is when it is located in B's experience. Thus, whether or not any single individual desires the general happiness, if each of its parts is shown to be desirable by the evidence of desire, because of the kind of thing each part is, then the sum of these parts will be desirable because it is simply a summation of instances of the same kind of thing.[24] Given this interpretation the "utilitarian doctrine" represented by (6), is perhaps better stated by making clear that Mill believes happiness, wherever it occurs, is what is desirable as an end. This could be restated with the following reinterpretation:

> (6) Happiness is [the kind of thing which is] desirable, and the only [kind of] thing desirable, as an end, all other things being desirable only as means to that end.

From this, the connection with morality is said to follow:

> (7) The promotion of [happiness] is the test by which to judge of all conduct from whence it necessarily follows that it must be the criterion of morality, since a part is included in the whole.[25]

If my earlier elucidation of Mill's argument for happiness as the kind of thing that makes the objects of desires desirable was convincing, then the argument has some plausibility. Desire does not confer desirability; it is evidence for what kind of thing constitutes welfare. Thus, that one desires only his own happiness does not restrict the desirability of happiness to one's own happiness. If the desirability of happiness *as such* is identified (and not created) by one's own desire for it in one's own experience, its desirability—wherever it is located—can be admitted by the intellect.

That the value of different instances of happiness is arithmetical is certainly controversial, but not, I think, indefensible. Without an operational definition for measurement, it is difficult to know how happy two different individuals are, but it seems plausible that if two people do happen to be equally happy, then twice as much happiness exists. Mill recognizes the difficulty in determining how happy a person is. He thinks Bentham's measures of intensity and duration are inadequate to capture the complex hedonic dimensions of experience, asserting that the only test of the comparative pleasure of two experiences is the unbiased preference of those who have experienced both. This is not a direct measurement of felt experience, since the ex-

periences are seldom if ever simultaneous. It is a judgment based on memory. In making interpersonal comparisons, it is even less reliable, since one can assume only a rough equality of sensibility between persons or make a rough estimate of difference in case evidence based on behavior or physiology shows a basis for difference. Thus summations of instances of happiness will be imprecise, but we do make judgments that one course of action will make oneself or another person more or less happy. These are not meaningless judgments; even if only rough estimates, they assume (and, I think, justifiably) that different instances of happiness are commensurable.

That the general happiness is simply the sum of the happiness of all individuals and that the good to the aggregate of all is simply the sum of the goods to each is, like Mill's methodological principle, primarily negative in its import. He is denying that there is any happiness or any value that cannot be analyzed without remainder as the happiness or the good of some individual or individuals. To prove this would require refutation of every claim to such an irreducible social good. So, again, I simply assert that I find his skepticism plausible.

If Mill's proof is plausible, as I have suggested, it does not follow that anyone will act on it. The intellect may be convinced that it is plausible or even that it is correct, without one thereby being moved to conduct his life in such a way as to maximize his own happiness or thereby being moved to identify the general happiness with his own and become a practicing utilitarian. That, according to Mill, requires a good state of society and education. But convincing the intellect may be a first step.

Notes

1. John Stuart Mill, *Utilitarianism,* Chapter II, Paragraph 2. *Utilitarianism,* published in 1861, is reprinted in *Collected Works of John Stuart Mill,* Volume X: *Essays on Ethics, Religion and Society,* ed. J. W. Robson (Toronto: University of Toronto Press, 1969), pp. 203-259, and in various other editions. References will be to chapter and paragraph. Unless otherwise noted, references will be to paragraphs of Chapter IV.

2. Chapter I, Paragraph 5.

3. "Introduction" to *Mill's Ethical Writings,* edited with an introduction by J. B. Schneewind (London: Collier-Macmillan Ltd., New York: Collier Books, 1965), p. 31. In the years following 1965 when Schneewind wrote this, the frequency of essays on the topic even increased.

4. Chapter I, Paragraph 5.

5. Paragraph 11. (Emphasis added).

6. Book VI, Chapter XII. For an analysis of these complex views, see D. P. Dryer, "Mill's Utilitarianism," in *Collected Works of John Stuart Mill,* Volume X: *Essays on Ethics, Religion and Society,* pp. lxiii-cxiii, especially xcv-cxiii, and

David Lyons, "Mill's Theory of Morality," *Nous* 10 (1976): 101-120.

7. In her essay, "Mill's Theory of Value," *Theoria* 36 (1970): 100-115, Dorothy Mitchell makes a distinction between "desirable" and "good" based on an analysis of the use of "desirable" in contexts of ordinary language. I think she is correct that they are not synonyms in English, but I think, nevertheless, that Mill is using them as such in this essay.

8. For a discussion of this point, see H. R. West, "Reconstructing Mill's 'Proof' of the Principle of Utility," *Mind* 81 (1972): 256-257.

9. This part of Mill's psychological doctrine is stated explicitly in his essay on "Whewell's Moral Philosophy." He quotes Whewell as saying that "we cannot desire anything else unless by identifying it with our happiness." To this Mill says he should have nothing to object, "if by identification was meant that what we desire unselfishly must first, by a mental process, become an actual part of what we seek as our own happiness; that the good of others becomes our pleasure because we have learnt to find pleasure in it; this is, we think, the true philosophical account of the matter." ("Whewell's Moral Philosophy," *Collected Works*, Volume X: *Essays on Ethics, Religion and Society*, p. 184 note; Schneewind, ed., *Mill's Ethical Writings*, p. 192 note.)

10. George Edward Moore, *Principia Ethics* (Cambridge: Cambridge University Press, 1948 [first edition 1903]), p. 66.

11. Moore's interpretation of Mill as committing the "naturalistic fallacy" is analyzed and refuted by E. W. Hall in "The 'Proof' of Utility in Bentham and Mill," *Ethics* 61 (1950-51): 66-68. R. F. Atkinson in "J. S. Mill's 'Proof' of the Principle of Utility," *Philosophy* 32 (1957): 158-167, calls attention to the continuing difficulty presented by a footnote in Chapter V where Mill says ". . . for what is the principle of utility, if it be not that 'happiness' and 'desirable' are synonymous terms." This is a puzzling use of "synonymous" but I do not think that it has to be interpreted (absurdly) as claiming that "Happiness is desirable" is a tautology. He may simply mean that the two terms are applicable to the same phenomena, one descriptively, the other normatively.

12. This is found in Book VI, Chapter XII, Section VI of the *Logic* where he says that a first principle of an Art (including the Art of Life, which embodies the first principles of all conduct) enunciates the object aimed at and affirms it to be a desirable object. It does not assert that anything is, but enjoins that something should be. "A proposition of which the predicate is expressed by the words *ought* or *should be*, is generically different from one which is expressed by *is*, or *will be*."

13. Another of Moore's charges, in *Principia*, p. 67.

14. Paragraph 3.

15. Paragraph 11.

16. Paragraph 4, J. S. Mill's father, James Mill, apparently did hold such a view: ". . . we have a desire for water to drink, for fire to warm us, and so on." But, ". . . it is not the water we desire, but the pleasure of drinking; not the fire we desire, but the pleasure of warmth." (James Mill, *Analysis of the Phenomena of the Human Mind*, 2nd edition, ed. John Stuart Mill, Chapter XIX.)

17. Paragraph 10.

18. For example, he says that "the peculiar character of what we term *moral* feelings is not a question of ethics but of metaphysics." ("Whewell's Moral Philosophy," p. 185.) This interpretation of the term "metaphysical" is argued forcefully in M. Mandelbaum, "On Interpreting Mill's *Utilitarianism*," *Journal of the History of Philosophy* 6 (1968): 39.

19. James Mill, *Analysis of the Phenomena of the Human Mind*, 2nd edition, Chapter XIX. The passage continues: "The idea of a pleasure, is the idea of something good to have. But what is desire, other than the idea of something good to have; good to have, being really nothing but desirable to have? The term, therefore, 'idea of pleasure,' and 'desire,' are but two names; the thing named, the state of consciousness, is one and the same."

20. James Mill, *Analysis of the Phenomena of the Human Mind*, 2nd edition, Volume II, Note 36.

21. Paragraph 5 and Paragraph 6.

22. *The Letters of John Stuart Mill*, 2 volumes, ed. H. S. R. Elliot (London: Longmans, Green, and Co., 1910), Vol. 2, p. 116; *Collected Works of John Stuart Mill*, Vol. XVI: *The Later Letters of John Stuart Mill 1819-1873*, edited by Francis E. Mineka and Dwight N. Lindley (Toronto: University of Toronto Press, 1972), p. 1414. Quoted in Schneewind (ed.), *Mill's Ethical Writings*, p. 339.

23. Chapter V, the second from the last paragraph of the chapter.

24. John Marshall, in "The Proof of Utility and Equity in Mill's Utilitarianism," *Canadian Journal of Philosophy* 3 (1973-74): 13-26, especially p. 16, points out the ambiguity in the question, "What is desirable as an end?" It can be taken to ask "What kind of thing?" or "What specific thing?" He interprets Mill as thinking more in terms of the first question in arguing that each person's happiness is desirable. I am claiming that Mill's proof is concerned only with the first question and believe that Marshall is reading in too much in finding a proof of equity as well. For a further statement of Marshall's position, see "Egalitarianism and the General Happiness" in *The Limits of Utilitarianism*,

ed. by Harlan B. Miller and William H. Williams (Minneapolis: University of Minnesota Press, 1982).

25. Paragraph 9.

JEREMY BENTHAM'S UTILITARIANISM: THE SCIENCE OF HAPPINESS

David Lyons (essay date 1973)

SOURCE: "Bentham's Utilitarianism: A Differential Interpretation" in *In the Interest of the Governed: A Study in Bentham's Philosophy of Utility and Law*, Clarendon Press, 1973, pp. 19-34.

[*In the following excerpt, Lyons explores Bentham's basic principle of utility and its relationship to morality, ethics, and government.*]

1. A SKETCH OF BENTHAM'S PRINCIPLE

The principle of utility, Bentham says, is the foundation of his work on morals and legislation. This is so, and in a variety of ways. The criterion of utility shapes his attitudes and judgements in every area of life. No philosopher has embraced a doctrine more consistently; none has ever attempted to apply a theory as extensively or systematically as Bentham has done. His principle determines his attitudes towards legislation, the use of punishment and reward, legal reform and codification. Its repercussions are felt even where one might think that utility had little to say. His analysis of human action and motivation and his theory of law, for example, seem to be arrived at by one who self-consciously assumes the standpoint of a legislator committed to the standard of utility. Even in the 'purest' philosophical investigations, Bentham never adopts a morally neutral attitude. This seems no accident; it is the deliberate approach of a thoroughly committed utilitarian.

But what, exactly, does Bentham's principle say? In most respects the answers have seemed certain. Rarely have commentators expressed any doubts or indicated any evidence that might not harmonize with a certain view of that principle. For our purposes, the most important assumption makes it 'universalistic', requiring that the interests of all persons (perhaps all sentient creatures, including other animals) be taken into account, on an equal basis, when action is evaluated. But I shall argue that this generally accepted view is unsatisfactory, for it ignores what Bentham actually *says*. His principle is not 'universalistic'. The beneficence it requires extends only to the borders of one's community. More precisely, Bentham embraces a dual standard, with community interest as the test within the public or political sphere, while self-interest is to rule in 'private' matters. But these standards are also conceived by him as resting on a more fundamental principle of utility—one which says (very roughly speaking) that government should serve the interests of the governed.

This aspect of Bentham's utilitarianism is not the only one that could profitably be explored, but is the one upon which we shall concentrate. We shall therefore ignore difficulties that may accrue to other features of his position unless they bear upon the main interpretive issue before us—the relations between community interest and self-interest and his principle of utility. This means that we shall take certain supposed elements of his position for granted, for we shall not examine them in close detail. Some of the assumptions that we shall make will be indicated by the following sketch of Bentham's principle.

Bentham's principle of utility is a standard for appraising actions—for determining which are right and which wrong, what ought to be done and what ought not. The principle is comprehensive, covering all acts, including 'measures of government' (*An Introduction to the Principles of Morals and Legislation: IPML*, I, 7). It is meant to be complete in that appeal to a supplementary principle is never required. Utility is also the ultimate criterion; it presupposes no other. It is therefore what some would call Bentham's 'first principle'. But the principle of utility alone does not suffice to tell us which specific acts are right or wrong. In order to discover that, one must apply the principle, and then one must be willing to predict an action's consequences. For it is the *effects* that acts have (or that they are likely to have), and nothing else, which determine what one should do. Acts are approved to the degree that they seem likely to promote happiness in particular. This is, roughly, what Bentham means by 'utility'.

The principle is supposed to have implications for the law and political affairs, and these are clearly Bentham's main concerns. But what has such a principle to say about the law? How can a principle that applies to human action have anything at all to say about legal rules and institutions? This is a theoretical question, affecting at least the formulation of the principle, about which utilitarians have had remarkably little to say. Bentham himself is not entirely clear about the answer (although he is clear about its covering the law), but he does suggest some possible answers. There are at least two different ways in which such a principle might be thought to apply to the law. It could be formulated so that it directly applies not only to acts as such but also to legal rules or other objects to be evaluated. As acts are to be judged by their effects on human happiness, so laws could be judged according to effects that are assignable to them. An alternative approach would be to limit direct applications of the principle to actions, and then take in law (and anything else that needs to be included) indirectly. For the making or changing of a law (or the playing a part in a legislative process) is conduct of a kind, and it can be judged on the basis of its own utility. These two ways of applying the standard of utility to the law are not equivalent, as can be seen from the fact that the most useful *legislative behaviour* does not necessarily yield what would otherwise be judged as the most useful *legal rules*. In applying the test of utility directly to the law itself, we neglect the costs and benefits of changing or maintaining the law. For many purposes, however, these differences can be ignored, and Bentham does so when he discusses legislation in most general terms, without taking into account the special circumstances of the legislators. But the differences between these two approaches will not affect the substance of our main argument.

When Bentham explains what he means by 'utility', one is struck by his failing to differentiate between benefit, advantage, pleasure, good, and happiness, on the one hand, or between mischief, pain, evil, and unhappiness on the other (*IPML*, I, 3). This appearance is partly superficial, but perhaps not entirely so. By defining happiness as 'enjoyment of pleasures, security from pains', he makes one such differentiation (*IPML*, VII, 1). And other items on the list might well be defined by him, in somewhat different ways, in terms of pain and pleasure, which seem to be the basic items. A special complication is introduced by his including good and evil in these lists, for this may seem to commit him to what G. E. Moore later called 'the naturalistic fallacy'.[1] But it is not implausible to understand Bentham not as defining good as pleasure and evil as pain, but as expressing fundamental value judgements (*IPML*, X, 10). At the same time, however, Bentham could be charged with using the various terms too loosely. Because his use of 'pleasure' and 'pain' is somewhat vague, his overall position is uncertain and sometimes seems inconstant. He seems to vacillate between the idea that pleasure and pain are felt sensations and the idea that they are the necessary consequents of getting or failing to get something that one wants or has wanted. Now, it can be argued that 'want-satisfaction' and 'want-frustration' in the latter sense are *not necessarily* accompanied or followed by any particular type of sensation of phenomenological condition, and thus that these two ideas should not be confused. But Bentham seems to confuse them (although he may simply think that there *is* such a relation). His position is therefore open to criticisms along these lines. But this is an aspect of his views that will not concern us any further. We shall be content to say that Bentham values happiness or human welfare most highly. And thus we are entitled to say, in accordance with the usual jargon, that he is an 'ethical hedonist'.

Now, utilitarians like Bentham are often singled out for valuing happiness so highly. But they are, in fact, far from alone. Many moralists seem to value happiness as much. This is shown, for example, by those who hold that happiness is the only fit reward for the truly virtuous. Such a view can be ascribed to Kant. He seems to say that everyone naturally, and rationally, seeks happiness for himself. But Kant believes that justice should apportion it, joining happiness with virtue and keeping it from the company of moral vice. Happiness must be earned, and any claim one has to it can be forfeited.[2]

Bentham would not agree. Each person should always get the best treatment that is possible. It may sometimes be right to make a person suffer, but that should always be regretted, never welcomed. Even the claim that someone deliberately causes unhappiness to others is *by itself* no justification for making him suffer. For pain is an evil, and punishment essentially involves pain, so its use must always be justified. The only justification possible is that greater pain can be prevented or that greater happiness can be purchased. The pain imposed by way of punishment always counts against imposing it; no type of pain or suffering may be discounted. Likewise, no pleasure may be discounted—not even the sadistic pleasure that one may secure by deliberately hurting another. This is Bentham's view, and it is entirely consistent with, even demanded by, a throughgoing utilitarianism. It is a view that few are brave enough—or, as Bentham might say, unprejudiced enough—to take. But it should be observed that Bentham makes some reassuring assumptions. He reasons, for example, that sadistic pleasures necessarily involve someone's pain, and then assumes (without justification) that the pains due to malevolence always far exceed the pleasures. This enables him to conclude that malevolent action could never be justified on the ground of its utility (by bringing more pleasure to the sadist, say, than pain to his victim). (See Bowring, I, 81, and *IPML*, Preface, note a; XIII, 2, note a.)

Whose happiness counts? Bentham will not allow us to neglect the interests of a man because he does wrong or has a malicious disposition. Does he mean, then, that it is always necessary (at least in principle) to considers everyone's interests? This might seem to follow, and its plausibility is enhanced by a few occasional comments, such as the suggestion that only the 'most extensive' benevolence coincides with the requirements of his principle (*IPML*, X, 36-7). He also seems to say that animals should receive the same consideration, for they too can suffer (*IPML*, XVII, 4, note b).

This suggests a universalistic utilitarianism—the kind embraced by J. S. Mill and most (if not all) other utilitarians after Bentham, and the one we are most familiar with today. We tend in fact to think of utilitarianism as essentially universalistic. No wonder, then, that the standard view of Bentham's principle has it say that each of us ought always to be aiming at the happiness of everyone. Whoever is likely to be affected by an action (or by its alternatives, since an action is to be compared with its alternatives) must be given due consideration. One may want to qualify this requirement, however, on the ground that it can sometimes be impossible actually to promote or protect the happiness of everyone affected because the interests of some might conflict with the interests of others and these conflicts can be beyond our immediate control. For this reason, it is sometimes said that the most generally applicable formulation of the utilitarian criterion is 'the greatest happiness of the greatest number'. Bentham uses the phrase himself, for just such reasons, and it can be found in many of his writings. It may come as a surprise, however, to learn that the phrase never once occurs in the book where he elaborates his principle most fully, the *Introduction*. It does not occur there because it does not represent his views about conflicts of interest when he wrote that book. And any universalistic connotations that the phrase may have are also foreign to that work. Let us see why this is so.

2. BENTHAM'S PAROCHIALISM

Let us begin by taking a timeless view of Bentham's works, considering them as a whole. This will suggest a second way of construing his principle of utility—a way that is far better supported by the evidence than the standard universalistic account. Bentham could be thought to have a (let us say) *parochial* principle, which requires not that everyone be taken into account, but only those within one's community. (We can speak either of the interest of the community or of its several members, for Bentham believes that these are the same; see *IPML*, I, 4.) I shall argue later that this interpretation would be mistaken, for it fails to account for very striking evidence. But that Bentham's view is (so to speak) more parochial than universalistic may be shown as follows.

If we consider the whole of Bentham's works, we find that in the majority of cases, when he gives a prominent statement of his standard he imposes the parochial restriction. When he states what end ought to be promoted he usually employs some 'greatest happiness' or 'greatest interest' formula, to which he sometimes adds 'of the greatest number'. But in the majority of all these cases combined, throughout his published works, Bentham explicitly limits the interests to be considered to those of the community in question.[3] Now, there is no other kind of evidence to suggest that Bentham vacillated between universalism and parochialism. It is therefore possible to regard the majority of cases, in which the parochial restriction is imposed, as fuller statements of the appropriate standard and the minority of cases, in which it is left out, as elliptical. After all, Bentham states his full position so often, at the start of so many of his works, that he may well assume it amply clear and not in need of complete elaboration every time. It should also be emphasized that this restriction is imposed throughout the *Introduction* (with a few crucial exceptions): in the first chapter, as we shall see, and in the first paragraphs of Chapters III, VII, XIII, and XVI— wherever occasion arises to state the appropriate general standard. This evidence makes it extremely difficult to regard Bentham as a universalist.

One might of course try to explain such evidence away. An argument like the following would be necessary. Since the restriction is sometimes added but sometimes omitted, perhaps Bentham adds it when (and only when) he thinks that the interests within the agent's community are the only ones that are likely to be affected by the actions under consideration. This would not explain why Bentham saw the need to impose such a qualification when he made general statements of principle; but some explanation is

needed for a defence of the standard, universalistic account, this one seems as good as any, and it is perfectly intelligible. But I believe that there is not a shred of evidence to support it. If we look at the various works (cited in the notes), we shall find no relevant feature linking those in which the restriction is omitted that is absent when it is imposed, or vice versa. Someone who wishes to stand by the traditional, universalistic interpretation may find reassurance in a few isolated passages, such as Bentham's ambivalent suggestion that animals' interests should be taken into account, or the passage suggesting that utility demands the most extensive benevolence (which can be understood, in context, as expressing opposition only to that 'partial' kind of goodwill that does not extend to all the members of one's community and that therefore fails to harmonize with the parochial standard). But a defender of the universalistic interpretation must also ignore a mass of evidence (only some of which has yet been cited) and turn his back upon the question why Bentham saw fit to add the parochial restriction.

Why does Bentham limit the interests to be considered to those within the community? If one considered only the evidence that is most readily available, such as the evidence I have already cited, from the *Introduction* and elsewhere, one might reasonably conclude that the basic principle is simply parochial. Whatever Bentham's reasons might be, and whether or not the result is a defensible position, no other conclusion would seem possible.

And this is striking, for a parochial principle has potentially significant implications. The interests of a powerful nation might tragically conflict with the interests of mankind at large, and one committed to testing acts by the interests of the agent's community could therefore find himself endorsing conduct detrimental to the welfare of mankind as a whole. A parochial political philosophy would have frightening possibilities in the realm of international relations.

But I shall argue that parochialism neither exhausts the whole of Bentham's position nor represents a basic principle for him. Bentham also seems to have come to more palatable conclusions about international affairs than his political standard of community interest might lead us to expect.

To the extent that Bentham is a parochialist, it is a most important fact about his doctrines. But the evidence which leads us to entertain this possibility should also force us to look at his writings with a fresh eye. We must not assume that his utilitarianism is a simple prototype of the view that later philosophers have considered.

3. THE 'EXPLICIT AND DETERMINATE ACCOUNT'

It is time to consider what Bentham actually says when he gives his most elaborate presentation of his principle of utility, in the *Introduction*:

> By the principle of utility is meant that principle which approves or disapproves of every action whatsoever,

according to the tendency which it appears to have to augment or diminish the happiness of the party whose interest is in question: or, what is the same thing in other words, to promote or to oppose that happiness. (*IPML*, I, 2)[4]

But whose interest is 'in question'? If Bentham were a universalist he would mean everyone's—at least everyone who might be affected by an act or its alternatives. But Bentham does not say that. Nor does he say what a parochial principle would require—that the interest of the community, or the interests of its several members, must always be considered. And the reason seems to be that neither of these is what he means. For he continues his account by explaining what he means by 'utility' (which presumably tells us more about what he means by the *principle of* utility). His concern is to emphasize that he does not mean by 'utility' conduciveness to just any end whatever, regardless of its connections with human happiness. He means specifically what promotes the welfare of persons. And in making this point he does seem to tell us more about his principle:

> By utility is meant that property in any object, whereby it tends to produce benefit, advantage, pleasure, good, or happiness (all this in the present case comes to the same thing) or (what comes again to the same thing) to prevent the happening of mischief, pain, evil, or unhappiness to the party whose interest is considered: if that party be the community in general, then the happiness of the community: if a particular individual, then the happiness of that individual. (*IPML*, I, 3)

This passage argues strongly against the universalistic interpretation, and the parochial account fares no better. For it seems quite reasonable to suppose that 'the party whose interest is in question', to whom Bentham refers in one paragraph when he states his principle, is the same as 'the party whose interest is considered', to whom he refers in the very next paragraph when he elaborates his notion of utility. And Bentham says that this party can be *either* the community (or, in other words, for Bentham, its several members) *or* some particular individual. So, the principle as given *never* seems to require that everyone's interests be considered—which rules out universalism; nor does it require that the interests of the entire community *always* be considered—which means that Bentham's principle is not simply parochial. The community must be considered in some cases, but only a particular individual need be considered in the others.

It must be admitted that the universalistic and parochial accounts are not conclusively defeated. Apart from other evidence that may encourage one or the other of them (evidence we shall look into later), one might try to explain away the apparent implications of this central and definitive passage. As before, one could hypothesize that Bentham speaks in these narrower terms when (but only when) he believes that in the relevant cases only the smaller class of interests would be affected. We have seen how such an argument might run, in favour of the universalistic interpretation, in the face of Bentham's frequent parochialistic statements. On behalf of a parochial interpretation (which we can now assume is more plausible than the universalistic account), the argument would run as follows. Bentham basically wants one to consider the interests of all the members of one's community, but he believes that sometimes only the interests of a particular individual can be affected by one's actions, and then of course one need only consider the interests of that person. The trouble with this suggestion is similar to before: no evidence can be found to support it, and there would be no reason for Bentham to qualify his most general statement of a parochial principle in such a way.

In fact, we can say much more. The rationale such an argument gives for Bentham's formulation is radically different from the one that Bentham himself seems to give. For he does indicate his reasons, though in a place where few, perhaps, have looked.

4. THE DIVISION OF ETHICS

Our question is why Bentham says that the interest of the community must be considered in some cases, while the interest of an individual is all that need be considered in the others. An answer can be found in the final chapter of the same book, the *Introduction*. We should note that the first section of this chapter marks a return to his discussion of morals and legislation at the most general level, which he had suspended some chapters earlier. Bentham devotes the first two chapters to explaining and defending his principle of utility and the next fourteen chapters chiefly to matters concerning its application, which requires his analysis of action and motivation, for example, and the development of guidelines for apportioning punishments to offences. In Chapter XVII Bentham returns to certain more general theoretical questions, for this was originally meant as a transition to the proposed penal code. He wishes first to explain 'the limits of the penal branch of jurisprudence', but he approaches this by discussing the 'Limits between private ethics and the art of legislation' (in XVII, i).

After an introductory paragraph, he proceeds by defining 'ethics' (which is done, as soon becomes clear, from a utilitarian point of view). What immediately interests us is his language, which is striking:

> Ethics at large may be defined, the art of directing men's actions to the production of the greatest possible quantity of happiness, on the part of those whose interest is in view. (*IPML*, XVII, 2)

That sort of phrase again: 'whose interest is in view'. Bentham defines ethics in the same kind of terms he uses in his 'explicit and determinate account' of the principle of utility. As we might expect from a general discussion of ethics from a utilitarian point of view, it looks as if further light may be thrown on the principle of utility.

We should also observe that Bentham defines ethics in terms of 'directing men's actions' towards a certain end—the maximum happiness 'of those whose interest is in view'. Who are these persons? We find out from his partition of ethics, which is done by reference to the person or persons whose actions are 'directed'. This seems important, for he neither defines nor divides ethics in terms of those whose interests are *affected,* as the traditional view would lead us to expect.

The main partition of ethics is presented as follows:

> What then are the actions which it can be in a man's power to direct? They must be either his own actions, or those of other agents. Ethics, in as far as it is the art of directing a man's own actions, may be styled the *art of self-government,* or *private ethics.*
>
> What other agents then are there, which at the same time that they are under the influence of man's direction, are susceptible of happiness? They are of two sorts: 1. Other human beings who are styled persons. 2. Other animals, which on account of their interests having been neglected by the insensibility of the ancient jurists, stand degraded into the class of *things.*[5] As to other human beings, the art of directing their actions to the above end [this means, apparently, towards their own happiness] is what we mean, or at least the only thing which, upon the principle of utility, we *ought* to mean, by the art of government: which, in as far as the measures it displays itself in are of a permanent nature, is generally distinguished by the name of *legislation:* as it is by that of *administration,* when they are of a temporary nature, determined by the occurrences of the day. (*IPML,* XVII, 3-4)

Thus, Bentham divides ethics into 'the art of self-government', or 'private ethics', on the one hand, and 'the art of government' (which, from its parts 'legislation' and 'administration', seems to be government in the ordinary, political sense), on the other. (As Bentham elsewhere suggests, we might balance this terminology by calling the latter 'public ethics'. See *IPML,* IV, 2, note a., and Bowring, I, 195.) Ethics—at least from a utilitarian standpoint—has a dual character. But so does utility itself (and, presumably, the principle of utility), for it concerns the happiness of either an individual or a community.

It seems reasonable to suppose that the respective parts of the two accounts correspond, and it is easy to reconstruct the most likely correspondence. We are virtually told that the art of government is the art of 'directing' persons towards their own happiness. And government (in the ordinary sense) may be thought to 'direct' all the members of a community. This correlates the public half of ethics with the kind of utility that concerns the happiness of the community—that is, of its several members. The other correlation is then obvious: it comes by identifying the 'particular individual' that the other kind of utility concerns as the self-directing or self-governing agent of private ethics. Under the art of government, or government according to the dictates of utility, the interests of the entire community (or all its members) are promoted. The principle of utility applies directly to the government as a whole, which can be regarded as doing the relevant 'directing', and which is called upon to serve the agents that are governed, by way of 'directing' them towards their own happiness. Under the art of self-government, however, only the interests of the single, *self*-directing agent who is concerned are to be promoted, by himself.

5. A PRELIMINARY ACCOUNT OF BENTHAM'S POSITION

We have now seen Bentham's most elaborate, 'explicit and determinate' account of the principle of utility and also his explicit and definitive discussion of ethics from a utilitarian point of view. Since both are found in the same early work, written entirely by Bentham himself, it is reasonable to assume that the discussion of ethics faithfully reflects Bentham's own current conception of his utilitarianism. This leads us to a tentative reconstruction of Bentham's basic utilitarian doctrines as follows. . . .

The basic principle of utility may be understood as saying, roughly, that one ought to promote the happiness of those under one's 'direction', that is, those subject to one's direction, influence, or control. All free or voluntary human action may be regarded as constituting the 'direction' of one or more human persons (either the agent himself, alone, or others as well), and the fundamental normative idea is that government should serve the interests of those being governed. We may call this a 'differential' principle because the range of relevant interests to be promoted is not fixed in the usual way; they are neither everyone's nor all those within the agent's community. The interests to be promoted are the interests of those being 'directed' rather than those who may be affected. The relevant interest for the purpose of applying the basic principle—the interest 'in question', 'to be considered', or 'in view'—the interest to be served—is always that of the person or persons who are under one's governance, whose behaviour is subject to one's direction, influence, or control.

Furthermore, Bentham seems to conceive of this basic principle as if it applied in only two contexts—public and private. Ethics is *private* when a man 'directs' his own behaviour and no one else is subject to his control. He decides what he himself shall do; he does not direct others. ('Private' does not mean that others are not *affected,* but that others are not under one's 'direction'.) The standard that accordingly applies (by application of the differential principle) is that of self-interest. Ethics is *public* in the context of government in the ordinary sense. Here, too, we may speak of behaviour being directed, influenced, or controlled, and it should be emphasized that government, for Bentham, is concerned not merely with determining what people ought to do, but also with controlling or at least influencing behaviour—with *getting* them to do it. The government as a whole (as personified for example in Bentham's 'legislator' or his 'sovereign') may be thought of as 'directing' all the members of the community.

All 'measures of government' must therefore serve the interests of the entire community, that is, the interests of all its members. Bentham accordingly embraces two distinct standards,[6] one for each branch of ethics. In political affairs the happiness of all members of the community

Jeremy Bentham (1748–1832)

should be served, while in private matters one should serve his own best interests.

I should emphasize that this is a preliminary account. . . . But the evidence for a reconstruction along such lines is much stronger than one might at first expect, given the widespread unquestioning acceptance of the universalistic interpretation. The evidence is not uniformly strong; parts of the account are determined by explicit textual evidence, while other parts result from an attempt to forge a coherent whole that fits the tenor of Bentham's thought as well as the texts. The initial evidence is extremely strong. That Bentham embraces a dual standard—at least in the *Introduction*—is made clear not just in the prominent passages which we have already examined but also by his summary at the end of that first section of Chapter XVII, where the definition and division of ethics have been given:

> To conclude this section, let us recapitulate and bring to a point the difference between private ethics, considered as an art or science, on the one hand, and that branch of jurisprudence which contains the art or science of legislation, on the other. Private ethics teaches how each man may dispose himself to pursue the course most conducive to his own happiness, by means of such motives as offer of themselves: the art of legislation (which may be considered as one branch of the science of jurisprudence) teaches how a multitude of men, composing a community, may be disposed to pursue that course which upon the whole is the most con-

ducive to the happiness of the whole community, by means of motives to be applied by the legislator. (*IPML,* XVII, 20)

Evidence like this is not, of course, absolutely conclusive, but it weighs quite strongly in favour of the account proposed, and it cannot be ignored. (See also *IPML,* XVI, 46, and Bowring, X, 560.)

The differential interpretation also enables us to account for Bentham's parochial restriction. In accordance with my earlier suggestion, let us assume that he has a parochial standard not only in the majority of cases throughout his works, where he explicitly imposes it, but also in the fewer cases, when he does not state it. We shall suppose that, while his parochialism is generally explicit, it is otherwise implicit and always there. Then we can note an interesting fact. Whenever Bentham says or (as we are assuming) implies that his principle requires us to promote the happiness of the community, he is concerned with what he would classify as political or public issues. The topics with which he deals in those places vary widely, from the character of law, through government structure and legal codification, to legal punishments and rewards, judicial procedure and evidence, political economy and tactics. But each subject falls under the public application of his principle, the part that coincides with the art of government. The parochial restriction is therefore not only consistent with but even required by the sort of reconstruction I am proposing. For, when the subject is political, his principle is taken by him to require that the interests of everyone in the community be taken into account. And thus we see that Bentham's parochialism, while undeniable, is nevertheless neither basic nor his entire view. It is drawn from a principle that requires us to promote the interests of those under our governance, the same principle that is taken to yield a different standard in private matters. It should be added that, whenever Bentham formulates his general position in the *Introduction* (outside the passages that we have considered closely), it has the parochial qualification added, and in each case it is clear (except for one case, to be considered, where it is arguable) that he conceives his main concern to be with matters of legislation or other public affairs. There is considerable evidence, then, that Bentham employs the standard of community interest in the appropriate places. This is true throughout his works (if we regard the small number of cases in which the parochial restriction is omitted as elliptical) and particularly in the *Introduction* (where no such added conjectures are needed).

Although we have so far considered only a few passages very closely, the ones upon which the proposed reconstruction is based are all prominent, explicitly general, and claimed to be definitive by Bentham himself. . . . [It] is the most defensible account of Bentham's utilitarianism.

Notes

1. *Principia Ethica,* ch. I, esp. pp. 17-19. But in view of Bentham's 'imperational' conception of moral

and legal discourse, it does not seem as if he could have been a 'naturalist' in Moore's special sense. See below, ch. 6.

2. See, e.g., *Foundations of the Metaphysics of Morals,* ch. I, pars. 1, 12.

3. I have found the following examples in prominent passages of works ascribed to Bentham (volumes and pages in the Bowring edn. are indicated in parentheses):

The parochial restriction is explicit in *An Essay on Political Tactics,* ch. I, sec. 2, par. 1 (II, 302); *Principles of International Law,* Essay I, par. 7 (II, 537); *A Manual of Political Economy,* ch. I, par. 2 (III, 33); *Pannomial Fragments,* ch. I, par. 2 (III, 211); *Codification Proposal,* full title (IV, 535); *Official Aptitude Maximised, Expense Minimised,* Paper I, Preface, par. 2 (V, 265); *Introductory View of the Rationale of Evidence,* ch. I, sec. 2, par. 3 (VI, 6); *Securities Against Misrule,* ch. I, sec. 2, par. 1 (VIII, 558); *Constitutional Code,* bk. I, Introduction (IX, 4-5).

The parochial restriction is omitted in *Principles of Judicial Procedure,* ch. I, par. 1 (II, 8); *The Rationale of Reward;* Preliminary Observations, par. 1 (II, 192); *Leading Principles of a Constitutional Code.* sec. 1, par. 1 (II, 269); *Letters to Count Toreno* (VIII, 491).

4. In a note added to the second edition of the *Introduction* Bentham formulates it as '*that principle* which states the greatest happiness of all those whose interest is in question, being the right and proper, and only right and proper and universally desirable, end of human action; of human action in every situation, and in particular in that of a functionary or set of functionaries exercising the powers of Government' (I, 1, note a).

5. Here Bentham appends a long note opposing cruelty to animals. This may suggest that the principle of utility requires that their interests be considered and thus that it is 'universalistic', comprehending all sentient beings. However, the point is made precisely where Bentham is regarding animals as 'agents', and this suggests that it can just as well be accommodated to the interpretation of his principle presented below.

6. I shall call these two derivative principles 'standards' and their conjunction 'the dual standard' simply to differentiate them from Bentham's basic principle.

Frederick Rosen (essay date 1983)

SOURCE: "The Greatest Happiness Principle," in *Jeremy Bentham and Representative Democracy: A Study of the 'Constitutional Code,'* Clarendon Press, 1983, pp. 200-20.

[*In the following essay, Rosen analyzes Jeremy Bentham's greatest happiness principle, focusing particularly on the related ideal of equality.*]

There is no necessary connection between utilitarianism and democracy. Many democrats have not been utilitarians and many utilitarians (including Bentham himself during a considerable portion of his life) have not been democrats. Nevertheless, the democratic principles of the *Constitutional Code* rest on a utilitarian foundation, and this study of Bentham's theory of democracy would be incomplete without an examination of it. In this [essay] we shall be concerned with the meaning and significance of the greatest happiness principle as it appears in the *Code* and in related writings.

Bentham formulates the greatest happiness principle in chapter II of the *Code* as follows:

Of this constitution, the all-comprehensive object, or end in view, is, from first to last, the greatest happiness of the greatest number; namely, of the individuals, of whom the political community, or state, of which it is the constitution, is composed; strict regard being all along had to what is due to every other—as to which, see Ch. vii, *Legislator's Inaugural Declaration.*

Correspondent fundamental principle: the *greatest happiness principle.*

Correspondent all-comprehensive and all-directing rule—*Maximize happiness.*[1]

It will be useful to compare this formulation with the second major statement of the principle which appears in chapter VII as part of the Legislator's Inaugural Declaration:

I recognize, as the *all-comprehensive,* and only right and proper end of Government, the greatest happiness of the greatest number of the members of the community: of all without exception, in so far as possible: of the greatest number, on every occasion on which the nature of the case renders it impossible by rendering it matter of necessity, to make sacrifice of a portion of the happiness of a few, to the greater happiness of the rest.[2]

In both of these accounts, Bentham states that the end of government is the greatest happiness of the greatest number. This is confirmed when he summarizes his principle in the same section of the Legislator's Inaugural Declaration as '*greatest happiness of greatest number maximized*'.[3] In his later years, however he became increasingly dissatisfied with the phrase, 'the greatest happiness of the greatest number'. Although he believed that the phrase was an improvement over the vague and somewhat general 'utility', he was troubled by several difficulties with it. He could not formulate it as the greatest happiness of all because (a) the happiness of all was often an impractical achievement and (b) the happiness of some might only be achieved at the expense of others.[4] For example, the notion of the greatest happiness of all could not incorporate deterrent punishments.[5] There is some evidence that he found the phrase cumbersome and the last part somewhat superfluous.[6] More importantly, Bentham realized that the phrase implied a disregard for the welfare of the minority in society so long as the happiness of the majority was maximized. In an unpublished manuscript, dated 3 June 1828, he expresses this fear:

> So long as the greatest number—the 1001—were in the enjoyment of the greatest degree of comfort, the greatest degree of torment might be the lot of the smallest of the two numbers—the 1000! and still the principal status or the proper object of endeavour of the greatest happiness of the greatest number be actually conformed to—not contravened.[7]

The date when Bentham abandoned the use of the phrase 'the greatest happiness of the greatest number' can now be roughly ascertained.[8] The two passages quoted from chapters II and VII above were most likely drafted in a final version at some time between 1824 and 1827. Although the *Code* was not published until 1830, these passages were in print by 1827.[9] Thus, 1827 can be the latest date of their composition and a slightly earlier one is more probable. Shackleton has noted a manuscript dated 8 June 1829 where Bentham states difficulties in the standard formulation of the greatest happiness principle; the *Westminster Review* article on the 'Greatest Happiness Principle' of July 1829, attributed to Bentham but subsequently denied, contains the revision of the 'greatest happiness of the greatest number' to more simply 'the greatest happiness'.[10] Since the *Code* passages quoted above retain the formula, 'the greatest happiness of the greatest number', at some point between 1827 and 1829 Bentham must have decided on the revision. Furthermore, in 1831 Bentham published a revised version of the Legislator's Inaugural Declaration (chapter VII of the *Code*) as a pamphlet and incorporated his new conception of the greatest happiness principle:

> I recognize, as the *all-comprehensive,* and only right and proper end of Government, the greatest happiness of the members of the community in question: the greatest happiness—of all of them, without exception, in so far as possible: the greatest happiness of the greatest number of them, on every occasion on which the nature of the case renders the provision of an equal quantity of happiness for every one of them impossible: it being rendered so, by its being matter of necessity, to make sacrifice of a portion of the happiness of a few, to the greater happiness of the rest.[11]

In the summary of the statement he replaced '*greatest happiness of the greatest number maximized*' with the new formulation, '*greatest happiness maximized*'.[12] By comparing this material with the earlier statement in chapter VII of the *Code,* we have direct proof from texts Bentham himself wrote, revised, and published of his determination to reduce the 'all-comprehensive end' of the 'greatest happiness of the greatest number' to 'the greatest happiness'. Nevertheless, the change does not seem to have been a substantive one, but rather an attempt by Bentham to remove some of the ambiguity from the way the main principle had been formulated. As Bahmueller has noted, the phrase 'greatest happiness of the greatest number' is retained to play a secondary role in explaining how the greatest happiness principle should be implemented.[13]

II

Having clarified this historical problem, we shall now examine several aspects of his conception of the greatest happiness principle. Returning to the initial formulation in chapter II, it is clear that the principle is initially restricted in application to the individual members of the political community to which the constitution is applied. This restricted application of the principle seems at first to confirm David Lyons's thesis that the principle is intended by Bentham to be 'parochial' rather than universal.[14] That is to say, the calculation of the greatest happiness requires that only members of the political community be taken into consideration and not everyone affected by an action or practice. Nevertheless, it is doubtful that Lyons's argument can survive much scrutiny. For the parochial limitation seems to follow rather than precede the context in which the greatest happiness principle is applied. In the passage in question Bentham is concerned not with the 'end in view' of mankind, but with the 'end in view' of the constitution. Those subject to the constitution are the members of the political community. If the context of Bentham's discussion were universal legislation, the greatest happiness principle might very well apply universally. Thus, it is arguable that the parochial limitation follows from the fact that Bentham is directing the constitution to limited political communities. The limitation may rest on a general or universal premiss that the practice in question should aim to maximize the greatest happiness of those affected by it. In the *Code* those affected by the laws simply happen to be members of distinct political communities.

After stating in the passage in chapter II that the object of the constitution is the greatest happiness of individuals making up the political community, Bentham adds the proviso: 'strict regard being all along had to what is due to every other—as to which, see ch. vii. Legislator's Inaugural Declaration.'[15] The phrase contains more than a cross-reference to chapter VII. It refers to duties to other states, duties which should accompany the direction of the greatest happiness principle to the more limited political society. In the statement of the greatest happiness principle in chapter VII (quoted above) the limitation of the principle to the political community is also repeated, but the qualification about duties to other states is not included, most probably because the Legislator's Inaugural Declaration itself contains a section dealing with relations between states.[16] The reference in chapter II to 'what is due to every other' presumably refers to this section, the only major section in the *Code* dealing with general principles of international relations. We might be able to determine from this material how Bentham conceives the greatest happiness principle operating beyond the confines of the political community.

Most of the principles set forth are concerned with the legislator's duties to other states. He promises to observe the same standards of justice and impartiality in dealing with other states as he does with his own constituents and other citizens. He agrees to add to the power and wealth of his state only through friendly competition, where other states do not lose from his gain. This precludes conquest of other states, the acquisition of dominions, and war except where fought to defend his country. He also favours the free movement of persons from state to state.[17] Lyons's argument about the relationship between Bentham's 'parochial' standard and relations between states, i.e. that Bentham never adopts a universal orientation but believes that 'internationalism is really in each nation's best interest', seems at first glance to be confirmed in the *Code*.[18] None of the provisions goes beyond the 'parochial' limit. Nevertheless, in one important passage the legislator comes closest to possessing duties to all people. Bentham writes:

> On every favourable occasion,—my endeavours shall be employed to the rendering, to the subjects, and for their sake to the constituted Authorities, of every foreign State, all such positive good offices, as can be rendered thereto, without its being at the expense of some other State or States, or against the rightly presumable inclination, as well as at the expense, of the majority of my fellow-countrymen, in this our State.[19]

It is true that the 'endeavours' of the legislator to the subjects of 'every foreign state' are restricted by the proviso that these are not done at the expense of the citizens of his own state. But Bentham also writes that these endeavours should not be at the expense of any other state. Although the former statement may support Lyons's 'parochial' standard and the principle on which it is based ('one ought to promote the happiness of those who are *subject to* one's direction, influence, or control—in other words, those under one's governance'),[20] the latter supports a universal outlook, that subject to the constraints imposed by one's constitution, one ought to promote as well the greatest happiness of the members of every foreign state. Bentham also constrains the legislator from acting in a way that causes expense to other states. None of these people is subject to his direct governance. Nor can they be said to be, except in the vaguest way, under his influence and control. Although the context of the constitution necessarily limits the perspective of the legislator to a primary concern for the members of his own political society, the universalistic character of the greatest happiness principle impels him to look beyond this in his calculations. His interests may still remain constrained by the perspective of seeing not 'mankind' but a number of foreign states and members therein. Nevertheless, Bentham is saying more than, as Lyons claims, that 'internationalism is really in each nation's best interest'. Bentham's position amounts to a universalism qualified by the conditions of political existence. This position hardly amounts to a 'parochial' standard in international relations. In spite of the initial limitation of the *Code* to the members of the political community, Lyons's conception of a 'parochial' standard for Bentham's greatest happiness principle is not established.

III

Another aspect of Bentham's formulation of the greatest happiness principle concerns the status and significance of what has been called 'psychological egoism'. In his first major discussion of securities in the *Code*, Bentham provides an important (and generally overlooked) statement of his principles as a series of assumptions on which his conception of securities is based.[21] He first grants that in all human minds there are 'propensities' towards both self-regard and sympathy for others.[22] These may exist in different proportions in different people, and presumably some people would exhibit stronger sympathetic motives for action than others. Bentham then argues that self-regard is a more fundamental characteristic than sympathy.[23] Without basic self-regard he believes that sympathy cannot exist, because self-regard ensures the physical survival of the species. If Adam thought only of Eve and never of himself and Eve thought similarly of Adam, sooner or later (but not as long as twelve months) the two, Bentham contends, would have perished.[24]

Having stated these assumptions Bentham then defines the role of the utilitarian legislator:

> To give increase to the influence of sympathy at the expense of that of self-regard, and of sympathy for the greater number at the expense of sympathy for the lesser number,—is the constant and arduous task, as of every moralist, so of every legislator who deserves to be so.[25]

Bentham's conception of the task of the moralist and legislator may seem self-defeating. If he succeeds in his duty of replacing self-regard with sympathy as the sole motive and influence on conduct, his subjects will perish. Bentham himself does not reach this conclusion, largely because he feels that it is physically impossible to replace self-regard completely with sympathy, and, furthermore, it would be imprudent to attempt to do so. But why then should he be concerned with increasing sympathy? Part of the difficulty with answering this question stems from an ambiguity in his argument. At one level he postulates self-regard to ensure physical survival. Each person must satisfy his physical desires at a certain basic level or perish. If he ignores them and devotes his whole attention to the welfare of others (ceases to eat, drink, etc.) he will die. Obviously, at this level sympathy is dependent on physical survival. But the struggle in which the legislator is called upon to engage, to maximize sympathy at the expense of self-regard, is not at this level. On a different plane Bentham seems to be conceiving self-regard in terms of selfishness and self-aggrandizement. Here he is concerned more with morality than with what might be called the physical conditions for morality. At this level, sympathy does not appear to be based on self-regard; it forms an opposing term. To advance the greatest happiness, the legislator's 'constant and arduous task' is to increase 'the influence of sympathy at the expense of self-regard'. Bentham does not distinguish between self-regard and sympathy on each of these levels, and the result renders his argument somewhat incoherent. As it stands, however, the argument uses the ambiguity to provide the further assumption that sympathy will never prevail over self-regard.[26] Otherwise, beyond physical survival, it would seem that sympathetic motives would be as strong as self-regarding ones. At times Bentham seems to suggest that this is so, but he also argues the primacy of self-regard on the basis of physical survival, and then uses the latter to establish the primacy of self-regard over sympathy. He succeeds in his overall argument only through his exploitation of the ambiguity.[27]

Bentham postulates this rule to guide the legislator:

> whatsoever evil it is possible for man to do for the advancement of his own private and personal interest . . . at the expense of the public interest,—that evil, sooner or later, he will do, unless by some means or other, intentional or otherwise, prevented from doing it.[28]

To be successful the legislator will on the one hand assume that sympathy plays a small role in human action and on the other hand use arrangements based on the primacy of self-regard to generate actions contributing to the greatest happiness. And while a few individuals in every society will be distinguished by their sympathy and regard for the greatest happiness, the legislator must proceed on the assumption that the individuals for whom he legislates are not.

Bentham's *Constitutional Code* is not a scheme for enabling the most sympathetic and benevolent actions to be performed. He does not, as Aristotle does, see the public sphere as one where all of the virtues can be cultivated and brought to perfection.[29] Throughout his writings, including the *Code,* Bentham endeavours to distinguish between two kinds of sympathetic action. The first is positive and is based on motives to enhance the happiness of others. The second is more negative and is manifest in forbearing to diminish the happiness of others.[30] Bentham's remarks on sympathy, which appear somewhat incoherent, may become more intelligible if this distinction is borne in mind. After he states that the legislator should act to increase sympathy as much as possible (see the quotation above), he adds the following:

> But, in regard to sympathy, the less the proportion of it is, the natural and actual existence of which he assumes as and for the basis of his arrangements, the greater will be the success of whatever endeavours he uses to give increase to it.[31]

Bentham seems to be saying that if we assume that people will act without much sympathy and build on this assumption the various entities of the state, the institutions, having been built on solid foundations, will actually increase sympathy. At the minimum they will increase the negative form of sympathy. But if this is his argument, he does not need to discuss sympathy at all in relation to the work of the legislator. By creating institutions which appeal to self-interested men, and preventing them from harming one another he is (like Hobbes) creating a successful and stable state. Nevertheless, Bentham does not want to deny that men act from sympathetic motives, because empirically they claim that they do. But he also does not wish to claim that a constitutional system will induce men to act with

positive benevolence towards one another. To aim at this sort of society is, for Bentham, to court disaster with one's constitutional arrangements. He does not jettison his concern with sympathy; he concentrates instead on enhancing negative benevolence which is manifest in the desire not to harm others. The institutions of his *Code* are designed so that power cannot be abused. Rulers are not trusted to behave wisely and benevolently; nor are they allowed to serve only themselves. They are induced to act benevolently in a limited sense by the threat of punishment or dismissal if they harm those they rule in order to serve themselves. The task of the legislator in designing securities is to enhance the limited, negative benevolence of rulers. In this way, Bentham feels that the legislator will be successful.

Bentham reflects this negative attitude towards benevolence in the way he formulates his 'moral code' for legislators, the Legislator's Inaugural Declaration. He states many of the principles in negative terms, so that the promises of the legislator amount to his agreeing not to harm others. The legislator, for example, is placed on his guard:

> against the power of all those appetites, to the sinister influence of which, the inalterable nature of my situation keeps me so constantly and perilously exposed: appetite for power, appetite for money, appetite for factitious honor and dignity, appetite for vengeance at the expense of opponents, appetite for ease at the expense of duty.[32]

Similarly, when the legislator promises to act with impartiality, which, as a positive principle, is difficult to reconcile with utility, Bentham again formulates the promise in a negative fashion:

> On every occasion . . . sincere and anxious shall be my endeavour, to keep my mind as clear as may be, of undue partiality in every sense: of partiality in favour of any class or individual, to the injury of any other: of partiality, through self-regarding interest: of partiality, through interest inspired by sympathy: of partiality, through interest inspired by antipathy.[33]

In Bentham's formulation, impartiality is conceived as not harming others with partiality. It lacks the positive notions of reason and equality which are usually associated with impartiality.[34]

It is clear that in the *Code* Bentham's psychological egoism has an important effect on the way in which the greatest happiness principle is to be realized in terms of constitutional arrangements. The legislator is not encouraged to establish any scheme which will promote happiness; it must be conceived in terms which will allow for human selfishness and will control aggressiveness. This limits the scope of the legislator in one sense, but it also makes his work more demanding. The legal system must create motives in self-regarding people to prevent them from oppressing others. The primacy of self-regard is compatible with this limited benevolence and Bentham sees here the key to successful legislation.

IV

A third aspect of Bentham's conception of the greatest happiness principle concerns the place of equality in its formulation. This is a complex and much debated problem, and most commentators accept A. J. Ayer's assertion that Bentham 'held, as he must have held to be at all consistent, that the right action was that which produced the greatest measure of happiness, no matter how it was distributed'.[35] Although the concept of equality can enter into utilitarian theory on a number of planes, we shall look first at the extent to which equality of distribution is part of Bentham's conception of the greatest happiness principle. To do this we shall examine again the three examples quoted above where Bentham sets forth his principle. In the first of these (chapter II of the *Code*) Bentham simply states that the object of the constitution is the greatest happiness of the greatest number of the individuals of the state in question. No reference to equality appears here, though in referring to the object of the constitution Bentham may have held implicitly that laws apply to all members of the state equally. Nevertheless, he does not develop this point.

In the second formulation of the greatest happiness principle (chapter VII), he adds the proviso that, where possible, the legislator should seek to maximize the greatest happiness of all, and, where not possible, that of the greatest number. This is a familiar contrast in Bentham, but it does not indicate whether or not he favours an equal distribution. One might be able to argue that in so far as he makes the contrast in the first place he favours the widest possible distribution. But this would depend on what he means when he says that the happiness of the greatest number is to be preferred to the greatest happiness of all 'on every occasion on which the nature of the case renders it impossible, by rendering it matter of necessity to make sacrifice of a portion of the happiness of a few, to the greater happiness of the rest'. If Bentham simply means that the greatest happiness of the greatest number should be preferred to the happiness of all where a greater sum of happiness can be produced by greater inequality or by the sacrifice of pleasures of a few for the sake of very much greater pleasures of the rest, his interest in equality is minimal. Nevertheless, on this interpretation it is not clear why Bentham would use such words as 'impossible' and 'necessity'. What would be at stake is simply a calculation of the greater amount of happiness. However, one point is certain: the greatest happiness of the greatest number seems to be a second-best criterion for distribution to which the legislator resorts when it is not possible to distribute according to the greatest happiness of all. On this interpretation, the best distribution would be the one which most closely approximates the greatest happiness of all. But we have still not determined how the greatest happiness of all is linked to equality.[36]

In the third formulation of the greatest happiness principle in the revised form of chapter VII which appeared in 1831 Bentham uses the notion of equality to explain what is meant by the greatest happiness of all in relation to the greatest happiness of the greatest number. Government is to maximize the greatest happiness: 'of all of them, without exception, in so far as possible: the greatest happiness of the greatest number of them, on every occasion on which the nature of the case renders the provision of *an equal quantity of happiness for every one of them* impossible.'[37] Clearly, Bentham means here by a policy, which serves the greatest happiness of all, one which does so equally to all. And if the greatest happiness of the greatest number is to approximate as closely as possible the greatest happiness of all, it must maximize the greatest quantity of happiness to as many as possible on an equal basis.

Bentham's formulation of his principle in this third example thus contains an explicit and conscious attempt to link the greatest happiness of all with equal distribution. The equality which he favours seems more than a formal equality, i.e. equal things for equal people depending on other principles, for example, need, desert, or ability, for the determination of how goods should be distributed. Nor is he referring to notions of 'equal respect' or 'equal rights' which are commonly invoked in discussions of equality but which may or may not entail a commitment to substantive equality in the distribution of goods.[38]

Bentham's overall position with regard to equal distribution as a substantive goal of legislation may be seen in the following passage:

> on the supposition of a new constitution coming to be established, with the greatest happiness of the greatest number for its end in view, sufficient reason would have place for taking the matter of wealth from the richest and transferring it to the less rich, till the fortunes of all were reduced to an equality, or a system of inequality, so little different from perfect equality that the difference would not be worth calculating.[39]

This position is in turn reflected in his conception of the place of equality in the greatest happiness principle. Nevertheless, Bentham's conception of equality needs further elaboration to see how he deals with equal distribution. His various discussions of equality rest on several assumptions to which more critical scrutiny would be given today. He assumes firstly that what will make one man happy will by and large do the same for another. He also assumes that to increase wealth and power (as instruments of felicity) leads to an increase in happiness, and a decrease in wealth and power leads to a decrease in happiness.[40] He is not naïve in his use of these assumptions. The character of each individual, he admits, is unique and inscrutable and the circumstances of two men are never the same. Nevertheless, if assumptions like these are not made, he argues that no general propositions about equality can be advanced. It is sufficient, he believes, that they are closer to the truth than another set of propositions and that they can be of use to the legislator with less inconvenience than any other set of assumptions.[41] He thus does not try to avoid the problem of equality by saying that human variability and subjectivity make all discussion fruitless.

Bentham relies most on various conceptions of diminishing marginal utility in his arguments regarding equality. In the early 'Principles of the Civil Code', a translation of part of Dumont's *Traités* of 1802,[42] he considers three cases of the effect of wealth on happiness, and in each case he argues that there is greater happiness as wealth is more equally distributed in society.[43] The first is concerned with the possession of wealth. Here he starts with the argument that a portion of wealth corresponds to a portion of happiness, and he who possesses the greatest wealth will possess the greatest happiness. He rejects the view that there is a point beyond which the possession of wealth will no longer bring happiness and that people will be satisfied with a determinable amount of wealth. Nevertheless, the happiness of a very rich man is not exactly proportionable to his wealth. A king with the wealth of a thousand labourers with sufficient earnings for their needs 'and a trifle to spare' will not be a thousand times happier than the labourers; he is unlikely to be even five or ten times as happy. A man born to wealth, he argues, is not aware of the value of his fortune. 'It is the pleasure of acquiring, and not the satisfaction of possessing, which is productive of the greatest enjoyment.'[44] This sharper pleasure belongs to the artisan more than it does to the king who already possesses so much. Bentham uses this argument to assert that as fortunes approach more closely to equality, there will be a greater mass of happiness, because more will approach the condition of the artisan and fewer that of the king. As to the second case, the acquisition of wealth, Bentham argues that where fortunes are equal, it is best that an equal distribution is made, and where fortunes are unequal, the distribution should aim to increase equality. In both of these instances the production of greater equality means the production of a greater total amount of happiness. Because of diminishing marginal utility, a movement towards increased inequality would not lead to a corresponding increase in happiness. Thus a condition of equality is preferable.

The third case is concerned with loss. Bentham begins by asserting that the loss of a given amount of wealth will produce a loss of happiness in proportion to the amount retained, so that a man who loses a fourth of his wealth will lose a fourth of his happiness. But he then qualifies this assertion by noting that loss beyond a certain stage becomes disproportionate to loss of happiness. If loss means the loss of the means of physical existence a slight loss at this level will produce a catastrophic loss of happiness. Bentham then advocates the equalization of loss or the distribution of loss so that the fortunes of those who suffer loss become more equal. He speaks favourably of schemes of insurance and compensation which distribute losses widely rather than have them fall heavily on a few. The argument for equality of outcome is presumably similar to those made earlier.

Bentham develops his argument further by examining some cases where one person profits at the expense of another. He presents a number of arguments to the effect that the person losing will suffer more pain than the person gaining will obtain pleasure. For example, if two men each have £1000 and one receives £500 from the other, the person who gains will gain a third more wealth, but the person who loses will lose half of his wealth. A redistribution according to the greatest happiness principle would favour a return to equality. Furthermore, the move back to equality would be favoured by weighing up the pain of disappointed expectations involved in the first loss against the pain of not having gained following the redistribution. Bentham feels that the former is much stronger than the latter; otherwise, 'every man would experience this evil with regard to every thing which he did not obtain'.[45] Finally, the pain of loss is stronger, Bentham believes, than the pleasure of gain. 'Mankind in general', he writes, 'appear to be more sensible of grief than pleasure from an equal cause.'[46] Where the person losing is poor and the gainer is rich, there are even stronger reasons for a return of the loss, as, in addition to the arguments above, the poor man may suffer greater pain from his loss in so far as it may affect his possession of the necessities of life. If a rich man suffers loss, he will also suffer the pains associated with a shock to his security, although Bentham admits that there will be some compensation in good arising from the movement towards equality.

Bentham does not depart very much from this early view of equality in his later writings. In *Leading Principles of the Constitutional Code,* he writes: 'In proportion as equality is departed from, inequality has place: and in proportion as inequality has place, evil has place.'[47] He also compares the happiness of the monarch with that of the artisan. Here, he reflects his later political radicalism in stating 'that the quantity of felicity habitually experienced by a gloomy, or ill-tempered or gouty, or otherwise habitually diseased monarch, is not so great as that habitually experienced by an habitually cheerful, and good tempered, and healthy, labourer' even though the monarch possesses the wealth of between 10,000 and 100,000 labourers.[48] In a body of late manuscript which was published posthumously in the Bowring edition under the title of 'Pannomial Fragments' he returns to the sort of arguments or 'axioms' he advances in the 'Principles of the Civil Code'.[49] To each particle of wealth, he begins, belongs a particle of happiness. The person with the most wealth must be regarded by the legislator as possessing the most happiness. But, as he argues earlier, happiness does not increase in the same proportion as wealth, and from this premiss (and others employed earlier) he reaches the same conclusion that with the greater equalization of wealth, a greater quantity of happiness will be produced. Furthermore, in *Leading Principles,* he speaks of an equal distribution of power as well as wealth.[50] The greater the concentration of power in society (and hence the greater the inequality of power) the greater will be the tendency to abuse it. Hence, with a movement towards greater equality of power (presumably in the replacement of monarchy with representative democracy based on universal suffrage) there will be less opportunity for the abuse of power and consequently more happiness. There should be no doubt now that Bentham regards substantive equality in the distribution of wealth and power as producing the greatest happiness. From the point of view of equality, therefore, the greatest happiness requires equal distribution or a distribution that moves people towards a condition of equality.

It is true that Bentham places limits on equality, but these do not diminish his view of the desirability of equality as an end for legislation. He recognizes, however, that there are other ends, namely, security, subsistence, and abundance (as future security) which have a higher status. Although he believes, as we have seen, that under a new constitution a redistribution of wealth which would correspond as closely as possible to equality would be desirable in the first instance, he immediately qualifies his argument to bring in evils of a second and third order which would limit such an action. The evil of the second order is the threat to security caused by such a proposed redistribution. The evil of the third order is the threat to subsistence by the extinction of any inducement to labour produced by compulsory equalization of property. Related to this is the possibility that with equal distribution there will be no accumulations of abundance to provide security against famine, calamity, etc. in future years. With greater inequality the wealthier members of society would possess this superfluity.[51]

Throughout his writings it is security (and recall the connection between security and liberty) which Bentham places over all other ends of legislation. Equality as a coordinate end comes into conflict most often with security. In the 'Principles of the Civil Code' Bentham sees equality mostly in opposition to security. Security, 'under the name of justice', requires that the legislator 'maintain the distribution [of property] which is actually established', though it is fair to say that security is extended equally to all members of society.[52] But where security is threatened, Bentham argues, so is subsistence and abundance; society without security 'would relapse into the savage state from which it has arisen'.[53] What threatens security most is a sudden movement towards equality. Bentham then argues that to an extent security and equality can be reconciled.[54] Limitations can be placed on inheritance to prevent too great an accumulation of property, but most important is a gradual progress towards equality which will take place in a society which values security and free trade. This will allow the development of industry and trade and consequently a movement towards equality of wealth as opposed to the polarization of wealth and power found under feudalism.

Bentham also argues that security in some senses must give way to achieve security in others. He notes that taxation to pay for a standing army reduces security in one sense by taking the citizen's property but increases the means by which he can enhance his security in another sense by ensuring security against foreign enemies.[55] Thus, he can envisage a considerable redistribution of property for the sake of security. But he is strongly opposed to a general shock to security which would follow a sudden move to introduce equality of property.

With Bentham's emphasis on security and especially security of property, one might well wonder how he reconciles this with his political opposition to monarchy and aristocracy and the inequalities inherent in these regimes. Does his later political radicalism founder on the principle of security? Bentham's main insight which enables him to be radical in politics, a committed egalitarian, but not to abandon the primacy of security is his belief, which appears only in his later writings, that equality can be an important means to achieve security. Only through equality of power (approached in universal suffrage) is it possible to gain security from arbitrary and tyrannical government. Universal suffrage and representative democracy have additional advantages in enabling security and equality to be advanced without disturbing security of property. This is the great achievement of democracy in America to which Bentham never tires of pointing.[56] The system of representative democracy also allows for reform which moves towards equality of property so long as there is no shock to security. The greatest happiness, as the 'end in view' means, as we have seen, equal happiness. In his later writings Bentham does not emphasize the maintenance of the existing distributions of property. The 'disappointment-prevention' principle allows for reform to take place towards equality so long as full compensation is paid for violations of 'fixed' expectations.[57] Although it is arguable that full compensation merely maintains the original distribution, in major projects of reform there are numerous consequences flowing from alterations of established states of affairs. Where the object is the production of the greatest happiness, the new arrangements may lead to a greater equality generally than existed before. Furthermore, we have seen in chapter VI that Bentham believes that government policies which require general taxation can be more readily justified if the benefits are distributed widely in society. He is highly critical of policies which tax the many and benefit the few.

Finally, one wonders whether Bentham would authorize the redistribution of property in circumstances where civil strife is prevalent and security can be re-established only with radical redistribution. In his early writings he notes that the overthrow of property by revolution, though of great importance, is transitory and leads usually to another system of property. It is far less dangerous than the direct attempt to establish permanently a system of equal property.[58] The former may provide only a temporary shock to security followed by enhanced security due to the benefits of the redistribution. The latter may constitute a permanent shock to security.

From this discussion, we might distinguish between the goal of equality of wealth and power in a substantive sense to which Bentham clearly subscribes and the means to achieve this end which are more limited. He recognizes, of course, that the goal can never be fully realized. The more egalitarian 'greatest happiness of all' must often give way to the 'greatest happiness of the greatest number'. The goal of equality must give way to security which has a higher status. Nevertheless, Bentham seems more apprehensive about the means to equality than the end. If a condition of equal wealth evolves in a stable representative democracy, he would see this condition as itself augmenting happiness. His great fear is the shock to security which any sudden move towards equality may cause. However, this fear about the means does not diminish the extent to which Bentham values the end of equality.

Having now seen the emphasis Bentham places on equality in his conception of the greatest happiness principle and generally in his thought, we must consider a remark, such as Parekh's, that 'in Bentham's view there is no prima-facie case for equality and fairness in the distribution of benefits or burdens', as mistaken.[59] There is indeed a prima-facie case made for equality, but not an absolute one. Similarly, John Rawls's comment that 'the striking feature of the utilitarian view of justice is that it does not matter, except indirectly, how this sum of satisfactions is distributed among individuals's a comment that leads him to the conclusion that 'utilitarianism does not take seriously the distinction between persons' will have to be revised.[60] In Bentham, at least, the principle of equality guides the distribution of benefits and burdens, providing a substantive goal within the framework of the greatest happiness principle.

Notes

1. Ch. II, Art. 1 (*CW*), pp. 18-19. The major discussions of the greatest happiness principle appear in chs. II, VII, and IX, § 25, Art. 1 (*CW*), pp. 18-25, 133-46, 419-20. Other references to 'ends in view' appear at ch. IX, § 1, Arts. 1-2; § 7, Bi§ 1, Arts. 2-5; § 15, Art. 1 (*CW*), pp. 170, 218-20, 297. Most commentators, including David Lyons, *In the Interest of the Governed,* Oxford, 1973, whose work is discussed here at length, rely on the compilation of manuscripts in Doane's 'Book I' (Bowring, ix. 1-145) some of which were not written for the *Code* or were subsequently excluded from it. This chapter is based primarily on that part of the *Code* Bentham himself published. Thus, Lyons's brief attempt to extend his discussion from the *Introduction to the Principles of Morals and Legislation* to the *Constitutional Code* suffers, because he does not use the important discussions in Bentham's own text.

2. Ch. VII, § 2 (*CW*), p. 136.

3. Ibid., (*CW*), p. 137.

4. See Bowring, ix. 6.

5. See UC xxxvii, 106 (15 June 1823).

6. See R. Shackleton, 'The Greatest Happiness of the Greatest Number: the History of Bentham's Phrase', *Studies on Voltaire and the Eighteenth Century,* xc (1972), 1480-1.

7. UC cxii, 154 (3 June 1828). The MS contains the notation 'not for 1830'. See also *Bentham's Political Thought,* ed. Parekh, pp. 309-10.

8. The development of Bentham's principle has been discussed recently by L. Werner, 'A Note about Bentham on Equality and about the Greatest Happiness Principle', *Journal of the History of Philosophy,* xi (1973), 237-51, which elaborates the earlier discussion of A. Goldworth, 'The Meaning of Bentham's Greatest Happiness Principle', *Journal of the History of Philosophy,* vii (1969), 315-21. Beginning with the view that 'despite the popularity of these convictions about Bentham's later opinion, the basis for holding them is pretty shaky', Werner (pp. 243-7) proceeds to show a firmer basis in the manuscripts used by Bowring for the *Deontology.* However, the account offered here will establish from texts written, published, revised, and published again by Bentham himself a clear account of the new formulation of the greatest happiness principle.

9. See the note by Doane to the Bowring edition, ix. p. iii.

10. Shackleton, op. cit., pp. 1480-1; see Werner, op. cit., pp. 245-7 where he provides substantiation for the claim of Perronet Thompson, the real author of the *Westminster Review* article, that Bentham did in fact revise the form of his principle. See also BL Add. MS 33,551, fo. 326. For the passage in the article which announces the change, see J. Lively and J. Rees, *Utilitarian Logic and Politics,* p. 149.

11. *Parliamentary Candidate's proposed Declaration of Principles: or say, A Test proposed for Parliamentary Candidates,* London, 1831, p. 7.

12. Ibid., p. 8. See also the copy of the *Constitutional Code,* vol. i, London, 1830 in the Library of University College London (shelf mark: Bentham Collection, 2 c. 19) where Bentham has crossed out the reference in ch. VII (see above, note 3) to the '*greatest happiness of greatest number maximized*' to leave '*greatest happiness maximized*'.

13. See Bahmueller, *The National Charity Company,* pp. 240-1 (note 121).

14. See Lyons, op. cit., pp. 24 ff. On Lyons's overall argument see also J. B. Stearns, 'Bentham on Public and Private Ethics', *Canadian Journal of Philosophy,* v (1975), 583-94; J. R. Dinwiddy, 'Bentham on Private Ethics and the Principle of Utility' (unpublished paper).

15. Ch. II, Art. 1 (*CW*), pp. 18-19.

16. Ch. VII, § 8 (*CW*), pp. 142-4.

17. Ibid.

18. Lyons, op. cit., p. 103.

19. Ch. VII, § 8 (*CW*), p. 144.

20. Lyons, op. cit., p. 85.

21. Ch. VI, § 31, Arts. 6 ff. (*CW*), pp. 118 ff.

22. Ibid., Art. 7 (*CW*), p. 119.

23. Ibid., Art. 8.

24. Ibid., Art. 9.

25. Ibid., Art. 10.

26. Cf. W. Godwin, *Enquiry concerning Political Justice,* London, 1793, Bk IV, ch. X, where this assumption is not made.

27. To clarify Bentham's argument we might distinguish between a physical egoism and a moral egoism. In each of these, Bentham assumes the primacy of self-regard, but he fails to make clear the status of sympathy. In relation to physical egoism a person's sympathy would be self-destructive; in relation to moral egoism, it would enhance his character and contribute to the greatest happiness of society. One might give up moral egoism while adhering to physical egoism in the sense of cultivating a benevolent disposition without jeopardizing physical existence. Nevertheless, Bentham's egoism (in either form) should not be conceived too narrowly. See S. R. Letwin, *The Pursuit of Certainty,* Cambridge, 1965, p. 141: 'the self-preference principle expressed, in an unusual, technical form, Bentham's awareness of an ultimate mystery and privacy about every man's view of life.'

28. Ch. VI, § 31, Art. 11 (*CW*), p. 119.

29. See Aristotle, *Nicomachean Ethics,* V, 1129b25 ff.

30. See ch. IX, § 21, Art. 26 (*CW*), p. 397; cf. *An Introduction to the Principles of Morals and Legislation,* XVII. 6-7 in *CW,* pp. 283-5.

31. Ch. VI, § 31, Art. 10 (*CW*), p. 119.

32. Ch. VII, § 3 (*CW*), pp. 137-8.

33. Ch. VII, § 9 (*CW*), p. 144.

34. See, for example, D. D. Raphael, *Problems of Political Philosophy,* London, 1970, pp. 175 ff. Bentham's conception of negative benevolence reflects his conception of liberty as non-interference. See chapter IV above.

35. A. J. Ayer, 'The Principle of Utility' *Jeremy Bentham and the Law,* eds. G. W. Keeton and G. Schwarzenberger, London, 1948, p. 250. Goldworth, p. 317n confirms Ayer's argument.

36. In the passage under consideration Bentham does not directly speak of equality. Curiously, in his summary of principles he includes the maxim, 'equality maximized' even though equality is not discussed in the text he summarizes.

37. *Parliamentary Candidate's Declaration,* p. 7 (my italics).

38. Bentham includes some of these notions in his concept of security and in other concepts, including equality, but these need not concern us here.

39. 'Pannomial Fragments' (Bowring, iii. 230).

40. 'Principles of the Civil Code' (Bowring, i. 304-5).

41. Ibid., p. 305.

42. It is arguable that this work, though based on Bentham's manuscripts, is Dumont's rather than Bentham's. I have treated it as a work of Bentham, especially as the material discussed here does not conflict with similar arguments made directly by Bentham himself.

43. Ibid., pp. 304-7.

44. Ibid., p. 305.

45. Ibid., p. 307.

46. Ibid.

47. Bowring, ii. 271.

48. Ibid.

49. Bowring, iii. 228-30. Some commentators dwell on Bentham's early 'Essay on Representation' of 1788 (UC clxx, 114-16, 89-92) for remarks relevant to equality and democracy. See Halévy, *La Formation du radicalisme philosophique,* i, pp. 424-39; Mary Mack, op. cit., pp. 448-53. The essay contains the argument about diminishing marginal utility and the assumption that people have a roughly equal capacity for happiness. Although Bentham gives the impression (see Werner, op. cit., p. 239) that he is indifferent to the distribution of happiness, he does qualify his remarks in the next paragraph with observations about diminishing marginal utility. However, the essay does not contain an account of equality in relation to the greatest happiness principle.

50. Bowring, ii. 271.

51. 'Pannomial Fragments' (Bowring, iii. 230).

52. Bowring, i. 311.

53. Ibid., pp. 312-13.

54. Ibid., p. 312.

55. See Ibid., p. 313.

56. See, for example, *Radical Reform Bill* (Bowring, iii. 560).

57. See ch. VI above.

58. See 'Principles of the Civil Code' (Bowring, i. 311-12).

59. B. Parekh, 'Bentham's Theory of Equality', *Political Studies,* xviii (1970), 494.

60. John Rawls, *A Theory of Justice,* pp. 26, 27.

James E. Crimmins (essay date 1990)

SOURCE: "Ethics and the Science of Legislation," in *Secular Utilitarianism: Social Science and the Critique of Religion in the Thought of Jeremy Bentham,* Clarendon Press, 1990, pp. 66-98.

[*In the following excerpt, Crimmins views the scientific basis of Bentham's utility principle and its hostility toward religious ethics.*]

Weak reasoners in morals, by a kind of instinct, take shelter behind the altar. Yet not even this shall save [them]. Mankind is too deeply interested in the display of those truths which [they] would keep concealed . . . to make it pardonable to desist from the pursuit. The Sanctuary is in its own nature common ground, unless where fenced about by Intolerance which it can never be but by the help of Usurpation . . . No foreign arguments are needed to set against [their] doctrines: to expound is to expose them: to *confront* them is *to confute.*

'Preparatory Principles', headed 'Divine Law', UC
69/107

Bentham's religious radicalism was not confined to the pages of unread manuscripts for over forty years, only to surface as an ingredient in the radical political attack of the second decade of the nineteenth century. A careful reading of the early celebrated writings on ethics and legislation (notably the *Introduction,* i.e. *IPML*) reveals in no uncertain terms the nature of Bentham's secularizing intentions. The *Introduction,* it should be said, was published long before his association with Bowring began in 1820; hence it was impossible for the latter to expunge its offending statements (a tactic employed with disastrous results in Bowring's 1834 edited version of the *Deontology*).[1] Bentham's animosity toward fundamental articles of Christian belief was clearly indicated here and in other writings of the period. Indeed, the critique of religion he supplied in the early works on ethics and legislation was typically of a radical nature and there is no question that he was there mapping out an entirely secular science of society.

Bentham set out to establish that as an agent of moral welfare religion is inadequate, not to say pernicious, and that we should look to legislation to replace it as the principal means of harmonizing interests in society in order to produce the greatest happiness. In the process he consciously contrasted his rational legislative version of the utilitarian doctrine with the religious brand of utilitarian thought that dominated English ethics at that time. It will assist our understanding of the relationship between religion, ethics, and legislation in Bentham's thought, therefore, if we know precisely what it was that he rejected. The intellectual context of his thought is incomplete if we fail to take notice of the writings of the eighteenth century 'theological' exponents of utility,[2] for the moral theory to which they gave voice was integral to the social and political fabric of the age against which secularists, like Bentham, rebelled.

1. THE RELIGIOUS TRADITION OF UTILITARIAN ETHICS

Bentham's attentions were focused on religious affairs primarily in two periods or phases of his life—from 1773 to 1782, and from 1809 to 1823. In the early period he wrote *A Comment on the Commentaries* (largely completed 1774-5, with additions 1776-7, but not published until 1928),[3] *A Fragment on Government* (1776), and the *Introduction* (printed 1780, published 1789).[4] In these works and in other manuscripts which date from this time, especially those headed 'Crit[ical] Jur[isprudence] Crim[inal]'—part of the proposed *magnum opus*—Bentham struggled to confine his thoughts on religion to a critical, but generally restrained (when compared with the later works) appraisal of the traditional relationships between religion, ethics, and legislation. For the most part religion is here viewed apart from ecclesiastical establishments, though there is some trace of the anticlericalism which pervades the later religious publications. With the notable exception of his preface to *Le Taureau blanc* and the unpublished fragments on subscription, Bentham at this time refrained from overt criticism of the Established Church. Even so, his basic denial of the truth of religion is evident from the beginning, and it is this which lies at the heart of his religious radicalism.

The second and later phase is the period in which Bentham's views on the Church and on the nature of religion generally reached a final form and were published at great, not to say excruciating, length. In these works Bentham launched a massive strike at all the various manifestations of Church influence, both spiritual and temporal. No longer content to confine himself to the particular theoretical deficiencies of religion as an agency of moral welfare, his critique now encompassed Church institutions and practices as well as fundamental Christian beliefs. The test of utility was applied to both and the results were overwhelmingly negative.

What this pattern of development in Bentham's thoughts on religion indicates is the striking transformation that 'utilitarianism' as a social philosophy underwent in his hands. For it has rarely been acknowledged that, in the age before he wrote, the doctrine of utility was nurtured at the breast of the same Church that he came so much to revile.

A few years before Bentham published his now famous *Introduction* another advocate of utility had made a reputation in the field of ethics in England. In 1785 the Revd William Paley (1743-1805) published his *Principles of Moral and Political Philosophy.*[5] His account of a utilitarian God promoting the happiness of his basically self-interested human creatures was similar to that expounded by his near contemporary and admirer Edmund Law, Bishop of Carlisle (1703-87); had been set out a generation before by the Revd John Brown (1715-66) and Abraham Tucker (1705-74); and, a generation before these, though in much less detail, by the Revd John Gay (1699-1745), while a little earlier than Gay one can find similar ideas set out in unsystematic form in the work of George Berkeley, Bishop of Cloyne (1685-1753).[6] *Contra* Hume, throughout the century these Church moralists expounded a doctrine of utility which depended as much on orthodox Christian teaching as Bentham was to depend on empiricism, reason, and an abhorrence for traditional metaphysics. The religious tenets of their ethics demanded belief in a benevolent God whose will is to be obeyed, in the immortal nature of the soul, and in a future day of reckoning when virtue will be rewarded and evil punished. But the persuasive power of the theory had its source not in these beliefs alone, but in their succinct combination with a hedonistic psychology as a prerequisite to understanding and directing human nature. Preaching spiritual perfection and happiness as the indispensible criteria of the good life, both in this world and in the world to come, the principle of utility nestled comfortably in the proselytizing arms of the Church, and added substance to the claim that for the sake of the well-being of the community the privileged position of the clergy as the guardian of the nation's morals should be protected by the state.

All these religious moralists employed the utilitarian language of happiness and its component parts. From Locke they learnt that it is considerations of pleasure and pain that supply individuals with the impulse to action, and to this they added that the criterion of virtue is the standard of universal happiness.[7] But what specifically distinguishes them is the endeavour to reintroduce, against the current trend, religion into ethics. The problem they addressed was to what extent the obligation to pursue personal happiness could in practical terms influence individuals to pursue the great end of virtue, the maximization of the happiness of all. The solution lay not in postulating a 'moral sense', in unsupported reason, or in the mere observance of human laws, but in the adherence to the will of God and in the Christian belief that at some time after death he will dispense to each his just deserts.[8]

John Brown (who was to earn high praise from no less than J. S. Mill for the ability with which he set out the doctrine of utility),[9] reasoned that legislation was inadequate to the task of motivating individuals to practise virtue, that is, to the pursuit of general happiness. He did not say that laws were entirely ineffectual, but pointed out their limitations as the foundation for a progressive system of ethics. In the *Essays on the Characteristics of the Earl of Shaftesbury* (1751) Brown recognized that laws endeavour 'by the infliction of Punishment on Offenders, to establish the general happiness of Society, by making the *acknowledged Interest* of every *Individual* to coincide and unite with the *public* Welfare'.[10] Nevertheless, laws, by their very nature, are fundamentally limited in what they can effect in the way of motivation. They can only govern external actions, invariably leaving inner thoughts untouched. As the impetus for benevolence must come from within, so virtue cannot depend on laws alone; a 'natural' or 'internal' motive is required, and this only religion can supply. Religion, the law of God, and not human law, therefore, is the chief and essential support of morality; it supplies universally the ethical imperative to be good which legislation provides imperfectly. People can only be uniformly convinced of their duty to pursue universal happiness by 'the lively and active Belief of an all-seeing and all-powerful God, who will hereafter make them happy or miserable, according as they designedly promote or violate the Happiness of their Fellow Creatures'.[11] The harmony between the private interests of the individual and those of the public at large is here firmly based on the necessity that each person, according to the teachings of Christ, take into account in all their thoughts and deeds their own eternal happiness. As William Paley was to remark:

A man who is in earnest in his endeavours after the happiness of a future state, has in this respect, an advantage over all the world: for, he had constantly before his eyes an object of supreme importance, productive of perpetual engagement and activity, and of which the pursuit (which can be said of no pursuit besides) lasts him to his life's end.[12]

The communal rewards of this doctrine are manifest. Each individual is responsible not only for his own spiritual well-being, but (towards this end) for the temporal well-being of everyone else with whom he has an association. To 'be good' means that we actively pursue the happiness of others whenever it is within our power, for only by so doing can we secure our own happiness in the most encompassing sense of this term—eternal happiness.

To divorce morality from religion, therefore, was a sophistication (if that it be) which it did not occur to the religious utilitarians to entertain. On the contrary, the threats posed to religion by, on the one hand, the theological divisions of the day, and on the other, the apparent indifference of the laity to (and even disdain for) its established norms and practices, made the defence of Christian beliefs of paramount interest to moralists, like Brown and Paley, who found in religion the means by which the desired end of morality could be achieved. Mounting public enthusiasm for a more worldly approach to ethics not only lent a sense of urgency to this defence, but also required that it take a practical as well as a theoretical form.

When Ernest Albee came to trace the history of utilitarianism at the beginning of the twentieth century he represented its secular and theological exponents as each in turn contributing to the stockpile of utilitarian thought as it expanded and was handed down from one generation of moralists to the next. If John Gay influenced Brown and Paley, so this argument goes, then indirectly he also influenced Bentham.[13] But did Gay really have an influence on Bentham? Gay's 'Dissertation' is indeed a seminal work and shares certain features with Bentham's *Introduction*. We should not, however, read too much into this. For example, it suits Albee's argument to draw our attention to the similarity between the list of sanctions that each set out—physical (or natural), moral (or virtuous), political (or civil), and religious[14]—but the supposed connection may well be spurious since it is likely that both were borrowing from Locke.[15] A more telling point of comparison (though one less supportive of Albee's thesis) centres upon the degree of importance each attributed to the authority or will of God. As we have seen, as a source of pleasures and pains Bentham thought this a 'fiction'. Nowhere did he acknowledge any necessity for the intercession of religion in the practical moral life. 'The principle of utility', he wrote, 'neither requires nor admits of any other regulator than itself' (*IPML* 33).[16] Gay, on the other hand, reduced all forms of obligation to the religious—'the will of God is the immediate criterion of Virtue, and the happiness of mankind the criterion of the will of God'.[17] The language of happiness is common to both, but the spiritual part of human nature, fundamental to the thought of the religious exponents of utility, is not considered a factor by Bentham.

Indeed, it was principally as a consequence of the efforts of Bentham that utility came to be identified with a social philosophy opposed to the teachings of Christianity. A feature of this development, closely connected in the mind of Bentham with the application of the methods of natural science to social analysis, is the substitution of legislation for religion as the paramount agency for resolving conflict between the personal interests of private individuals and the general needs of society. This feature is central to my analysis of the relationship between religion, ethics, and legislation in utilitarian thought.

Bentham described the difference between the object of his own ethical system and that of the 'religionists' in his Commonplace Book of the years 1781-5: 'The laws of perfection derived from religion, have more for their object the goodness of the man who observes them, than that of the society in which they are observed. Civil laws on the contrary have more for their object the moral goodness of men in general than that of individuals' (*Works*, x. 143). There is a curious tension here between Bentham's nominalism with its regard for discrete entities and the emphasis he places on the abstract and collective, but the shift in focus indicated clearly distinguishes the central aim of his work from that of his Christian precursors. Moreover, it heralded the approaching demise of the religious version of the doctrine of utility as the basis of a persuasive theory of morals.[18] For in the course of the attempt to prove the worth to society of a rational system of jurisprudence, founded on empiricism and nominalist logic, Bentham took great pains to discredit religion as a necessary motivational factor in effecting the occurrence of actions conducive to general happiness. In later life he articulated the essence of this intellectual appraisal of the role of religion in society thus: 'How did I improve and fortify my mind? I got hold of the greatest happiness principle: I asked myself how this or that institution contributed to the greatest happiness—*Did* it contribute?—If not, what institution *would* contribute to it?' (*Works*, x. 581). The probing of the deficiencies of religion as an agency of social welfare in the work on ethics and legislation was eventually to be complemented by the explicit political attack on the Church in the later works, but the connection between the interests of society and the legislative means to advancing these was present and prevalent from the first.[19]

2. SECULAR INFLUENCES

Bentham's disdain for religion and emphasis on legislation had its source not only in his scientific method but also in two distinct areas of his early life: his personal experiences with religion and the influence of writers to whose thought he found himself most receptive. As noted above, Mary Mack has claimed that Bentham's early brushes with religion at Oxford lay at the bottom of his utilitarianism, and Bentham himself late in life lent this view some credence (*CE*, pp. xiii-xxvii). As an explanatory factor, however, it is limited. While it indicates his early disaffection with religion, it does not sufficiently explain the peculiar scientific nature of his utilitarianism with its all-pervasive

emphasis on the role of legislation. Attention is better directed to the intellectual influences and exemplars to which he was exposed as a youth, for it was these who gave form and direction to his immature thoughts and grievances.

Throughout his life Bentham claimed that in developing the key practical ideas of his moral and legal philosophy he was indebted above all others to Helvétius and Beccaria—that is, to theorists sympathetic to utility but of a very different cast of mind from the religious exponents of the doctrine. In the previous chapter I tried to show that it was in the work of these continental *philosophes,* among others, that he found principles of natural science employed as the foundation of social philosophy. Here I am more particularly concerned with the priority they gave to legislation as the principal means to achieving social felicity at the expense of the claims of theology. Before discussing the nature of these influences on the moral and legal thought of the young Bentham, however, we should perhaps say something of David Hume, whose major works Bentham had read and who was an undeniable presence in the history of secular thought during this period.[20] Bentham could not help but note Hume's deliberate and concerted efforts to introduce the 'experimental method' into moral reasoning. None the less, there is an understandable ambivalence in his references to Hume's moral thought which, since Hume is frequently cited as of integral significance in the development of eighteenth-century utilitarian thought, deserve our attention.

It was in Hume's *Treatise*—which declared that all social inquiry should be based on the 'experimental Method of Reasoning'—that Bentham tells us he found virtue equated with utility:

> That the foundations of all *virtue* are laid in *utility,* is there demonstrated, after a few exceptions made, with the strongest force of evidence: . . .

> For my own part, I well remember, no sooner had I read that part of the work which touches on this subject, than I felt as if scales had fallen from my eyes. I then, for the first time, learnt to call the cause of the people the cause of Virtue. (*FG* 440 n.).[21]

Bentham goes on to say that he could not see any more than Helvétius the reason for Hume's exceptions to this rule, but this is understandable when Bentham's dogmatic utilitarianism is compared with the more sensitive handling of the logic of moral judgement set out by Hume. The 'exceptions' are indicative of Hume's commitment to a 'moral sense' account of obligations. Later on Bentham's disappointment with Hume became explicit. 'Added Observations' on the *Table of the Springs of Action* include the following remarks:

> 611. Of ERROR, inconsistency is a natural accompaniment—not so of TRUTH.

> 612. Hume acknowledges the dominion of utility, but so he does of the moral sense: . . .

> 614. Here then is a compromise of incompatible contradictions—necessary result inconsistency (*Deon.* 57).

The 'inconsistency' consists in the exempting of some cases from the governance of utility—some actions can be assumed to be self-interested, but not all; social analysis is based on the calculation of consequences, but this is not always the case. Such disregard for uniformity in first principles seemed guaranteed to undermine the effort to place ethics upon a scientific footing. On another occasion, reflecting on his intellectual influences in the 'Article on Utilitarianism', Bentham states that the idea attached to utility by Hume was 'altogether vague' and consequently of little practical use (*Deon.* 290).[22] Fully cognizant of the differences between his own speculations in the realm of morals and those of the Scotsman, in later life Bentham even went so far as to state that he gained little from his reading of Hume. Having forgotten, it seems, his generous if qualified praise of the *Treatise* in *A Fragment on Government,* in the *Chrestomathia* he was only prepared to single out the lesson taught by Hume's distinction between 'is' and 'ought' (*Works,* viii. 128 n.). As important a discovery as this was to the young Bentham in his subsequent career as critic and inventor, it is difficult to believe that Hume's influence can be reduced to this. Even if only in terms of a general awareness of Hume's reputation as a critic of things established and as an unbeliever—and this is the very least one can surmise since Bentham had read the *Treatise* and, by his own admission, profited from it—we can assume an influence greater than Bentham was willing to allow in later life.

It was disingenuous of Hume to suggest that his essay 'On Miracles' alone was, of all his writings, offensive to Christians.[23] Not only had he produced other writings critical of Christianity, but the omission of the essays 'Of Suicide' and 'Of the Immortality of the Soul' (under threat of a law suit) from the *Dissertations* (1757) is an indication that he knew that he had.[24] Equally likely to give the impression that Hume was an unbeliever are such writings as the *Natural History of Religion* (1757), the essays 'Of Superstition' and 'Of Enthusiasm', the posthumously published *Dialogues concerning Natural Religion* (1779), those parts of the *Enquiries* where religion is indicated as the corrupter of true philosophy, and occasional passages in *The History of England* (1754-62), at least parts of which Bentham had read.[25] It is possible that Hume was not an atheist in the modern sense (that is, one who is certain that God does not exist), but he openly if cautiously undertook to show that belief in the existence of God could not be based on empirical grounds. He was an equally open and scathing critic of organized religion, entirely happy to trace the origins of religion to natural causes, to reduce the allegedly supernatural to the natural.

Admittedly, there is no evidence that Bentham had absorbed Hume's far-reaching philosophical critique of the basic tenets of Christianity contained in these various works. But, at the same time, the secular direction of Hume's thought could not be missed by so perceptive a mind as the young Bentham possessed—he could not help, for example, but be impressed that in the *Treatise* Hume ignored God and religion altogether. The first assumption of

Hume's science of politics is that human nature is uniform; everyone is governed in the public realm, whether acting alone or in combination, by self-interest. It is, he claimed, 'a just *political* maxim, *that every man must be supposed a knave*'.[26] Given this assumption of motivation, it is the task of the legislator to draw up plans to balance the interests that are advanced among the nation's citizens for the general good of the community. This being the case the nation's capacity to survive in an orderly and virtuous condition depends upon its institutions. Just as the 'tumultuous governments' of classical Athens were due to 'defects in the original constitution', so the stability of modern Venice is firmly grounded on the orderly form of its government.[27] Constitutions, government institutions, and legislation are for Hume the primary determining factors of the moral and political welfare of the State. It is these structural arrangements which give it order and upon which the comfort and well-being of its citizens depend. Religion, therefore, will only be of incidental interest for the inquirer anxious to provide a scientific study of political life. What the legislator will learn from this science is that, on the basis that there exists a certain regularity between causes and effects, 'wise regulations in any commonwealth, are the most valuable legacy that can be left to future ages'.[28]

The 'science of man', then, for Hume underlay all moral reasoning. Theology was no longer to be enlisted to explain natural phenomena where common sense could supply cogent explanations based on other principles, and the criterion for assessing the moral worth of actions was to be not God's will but the happiness of people and usefulness to the community. Critical judgement based on observation and experience was to be substituted for blind faith and superstitious fancies. The rewards and punishments of futurity play no part in Hume's scheme of ethics; social morality is utilitarian and secular.

Helvétius wrote in the same spirit of secularized positivism. In his Commonplace Book of the 1770s Bentham noted that 'From Locke [the law] must receive the ruling principles of its form—from Helvétius of its matter' (*Works,* x. 71), and there are many other references to Helvétius in the manuscript material of this period. After reading Helvétius's *De l'esprit* (1758) in 1769 Bentham was inspired to ask himself 'Have I a *genius* for anything?' and more specifically, since Helvétius had pointed to legislation as the most important of earthly pursuits, 'have I indeed a genius for legislation?'. To which he replied 'fearfully and tremblingly—Yes?!' (*Works,* x. 27).[29] There can be no doubt that the influence of *De l'esprit* upon Bentham was considerable. If he vacillated in the case of Hume, his praise for *De l'esprit* was rarely qualified. In an 'Article on Utilitarianism', written in later life, he maintained the same enthusiasm he had for the work sixty years before:

> Important is the service for which morals and legislation stand indebted to this work: . . . The light it spreads, on the field of this branch of art and science, is to that steady light which would be diffused over it by a regular institute or say didactic treatise, like what

the meridian sun sheds over a place when bursting forth one moment from behind a cloud it hides itself the next moment behind another, is to that comparatively pale but regular and steady system of illumination afforded to a street by two constantly lighted rows of lamps. (*Deon.* 325)

It was not merely for the idea of the relationship between genius and legislation that Bentham was grateful to Helvétius. In a manner infinitely more determinate than that shown by Hume, Helvétius gave form to the project of maximizing public utility. In *De l'esprit,* announced Bentham, 'a commencement was made of the application of the principle of utility to practical uses' (*Deon.* 290). Helvétius's contribution in this respect was twofold. First, he established the connection 'between the idea attached to the word "happiness", and the ideas respectively attached to the words "pleasure" and "pain" . . . [A]ttached to the words "utility" and "principle of utility" were now ideas in abundance, ideas which could not be but continually present and familiar to the most inattentive, unobservant and scantily-instructed minds' (*Deon.* 290). Secondly, he suggested the implicit relationship that *ought* to exist between the principle of utility and legislation. Near the beginning of *De l'esprit* Helvétius announced that it was upon the Newtonian principle of physical motion that he sought to found moral science: 'If the physical universe be subject to the laws of motion, the moral universe is equally so to those of interest.' Interest is 'the mighty magician' of action and a principle 'so agreeable to experience' that it is, therefore, 'the only and universal estimator of the merit of human actions'.[30] Just as gravitation is the great causal principle which explains the behaviour of the heavenly bodies, so interest or personal happiness is the causal principle which explains human behaviour. Utility, therefore, understood as general happiness, 'ought to inspire the legislator with the resolution to force the people to submit to his laws; to this principle, in short, he ought to sacrifice all his sentiments, and even those of humanity itself'.[31] The combination of these two features of Helvétius's thought gave Bentham the rough outline of his legislative project to fashion a society based on utilitarian principles. Helvétius had written that 'morality is evidently no more than a frivolous science, unless blended with policy and legislation. . . . if philosophers would be of use to the world, they should survey objects from the same point of view as the legislator.'[32] It was from this that Bentham took his lead: utility can only be maximized by designing a system in which each person by following his own interest will contribute to the general happiness. It is the task of the legislator so to arrange matters, employing coercion where necessary, so that self-interest and general interest coincide. As Helvétius put it: 'All the art therefore of the legislator consists in forcing [us] by self-love to be always just to each other.'[33]

Bentham was always loud in his praise of Helvétius's refusal to compromise his scientific principles by making concessions to theology. 'What Bacon was to the physical world, Helvétius was to the moral', is a typical pronouncement from the enthusiastic Bentham (UC 32/158). But if

Bacon was a philosopher dedicated to understanding the intricacies of a world divinely ordered by the hand of God, Helvétius was just as keen to keep theological considerations out of the matter. He not only dispensed with religion but condemned it bitterly. Even in the face of Jesuitical persecution, he was virulently critical of the role hitherto played by religion in moral life.[34] Those 'of more piety than knowledge', he declared in the later *De l'homme* (1777), who argue that the virtue of a nation, its humanity, and refinement of manners depend on the purity of its religious worship are 'hypocrites', and sadly 'the common part of mankind' have believed them 'without examination'. All experience and history show that the prosperity and virtue of a nation depends on the excellence of its legislation and little else. Religion is not merely ineffectual in the pursuit of happiness, it is an obstacle to it. 'What does the history of religions teach us? That they have every where lighted up the torch of intolerance, strewed the plains with carcasses, embued the fields with blood, burned cities, and laid waste empires; but they have never made men better.' The 'true doctors of morality' are not the priests but the magistrates, since only 'sagacious laws' can produce 'universal felicity'.[35]

If in Helvétius Bentham found the essential connections between the idea of happiness and the ideas of pleasure and pain and between these and the role of legislation, to Cesare Beccaria he gave the laurel for inspiring him to introduce 'the precision and clearness and incontestableness of mathematical calculation' into the field of jurisprudence (*Works,* iii. 286). This was Beccaria's unique addition to the project initiated by Helvétius. With the idea that it was possible for legislators to calculate the precise amounts of punishment required to deter persons from criminal acts, in *Dei delitti e delle pene* (1764) Beccaria wrote that 'If geometry were applicable to the infinite and obscure combinations of human actions, there ought to be a corresponding scale of punishments, descending from the greatest to the least.'[36] By thus measuring utility, with 'geometrical precision', appropriate punishments could be devised in order to effect deterrence. The end in view is to harmonize self-interest with social well-being by constructing a system of laws and punishments 'upon the foundation of self-love', making 'the general interest . . . the result of the interests of each'.[37]

In the pantheon of the young Bentham's exemplars Beccaria stands as 'the father of *Censorial Jurisprudence*' (*FG* 403), a philosopher not afraid to tackle the established legal systems of the day. Bentham was later moved to address the following eulogy to the Italian *philosophe:* 'Oh, my master, the first evangelist of Reason . . . you who have made so many useful excursions into the path of utility, what is there left for us to do?—Never to turn aside from that path.'[38] Concerned in the first place to offer a critical challenge to the legal systems of the age, but perhaps mindful too of the persecution that was the reward of unbelievers who dared to publish their heresy, Beccaria cautiously refrained from considering religion. He mentioned it in passing as one of the three sources, together with 'natural law' and the 'established conventions of society', of the moral and political principles that govern our lives.[39] However, by concentrating upon the 'established conventions' Beccara's aim was to apply systematically the principles enunciated by Helvétius, specifically those regarding the nature of motivation and the role of legislation. In the course of doing so he made much of, and expressed almost word for word, the utilitarian formula 'the greatest happiness of the greatest number', later popularized by Bentham, as the criterion for evaluating the measures of the legislator.[40] Beccaria, more than anyone else of the day, made jurisprudence a secular science.

It was in 1769 that the works of Hume, Helvétius, and Beccaria had first come to Bentham's attention. The next few years were spent elucidating the insights they provided principally within the context of his study of the law. From the first, however, criticisms of religion were intimately connected in his mind with the belief that the role of the legislator should be paramount in all matters of social felicity. By the early 1770s, as he himself testified in the early correspondence and in the later memoirs, Bentham had before him the basic principles of his system.[41] In an unpublished manuscript of this time he writes that the fewer the principles to which a science can be reduced the nearer it is to perfection, and that before Helvétius and Beccaria the principles of morality and censorial jurisprudence were many:

> Happily this is the case no longer. Beccaria has with an applause that in this country seems to be universal, Beccaria has established . . . for . . . censorial Jurisprudence, as Helvétius for morality in general as an all commanding principle the principle of utility. To this then all other . . . principles that . . . can be proposed, if legitimate . . . stand in subordination: . . . any one . . . which cannot is to be . . . cast out as spurious. (UC 69/17)

And cast out as spurious religion was to be. Drawing freely upon the work of Helvétius and Beccaria, Bentham began to map out the details of his secular view of social life and in the process trained a critical eye upon the claims of religion.

In the manuscript pages of 'Crit[ical] Jur[isprudence] Crim[inal]'—a surprising number of which are devoted to an analysis of the religious sanction, he intimated distaste for the practice of mixing religion with law. 'Religion', he writes, 'is a source from whence the Legisl'or hitherto at least has drawn & continues to draw more mischief than he . . . has benefit.' To the objection that divine justice serves a higher end than human justice he replies that 'The only merit of Human Justice is its subserviency to Human Happiness. If Divine Justice has not that merit, what *has* it?' (UC 69/13). And again, this time concerning the uncertainty of the supposed rewards and punishments of the afterlife, he remarks:

> I protest against the embarrassing this or any other political question with theological considerations. I . . . lay myself at the feet of one of the most illustrious fathers of our Church [William Warburton], for I aver

with him that the happiness of this life is the only proper object of the Legislator . . . Unlike God man's knowledge is confined to experience, hence he has knowledge only of what has been and what is, and nothing of what will be. (UC 69/140)

Another reason why religion should not be mixed with jurisprudence was because it lent the latter a sanctimonious air which frequently posed an obstacle to its reform. Bentham took up this theme in his work on Blackstone's *Commentaries:* 'nurtured in the Sanctuary of religion [Oxford]', Blackstone could not see his way to criticizing the legal system he purported to analyse; he saw only what is and nothing of what might or should be. The *Commentaries* was a work of exposition merely and, therefore, unavoidably fraught with the fictions and fallacies that attend its subject-matter (*Comm.*, ch. 1, sec. 3). For example, according to Blackstone the Law of Revelation is included in the general concept of the law of nature, and 'no human laws are of any validity, if contrary to this; and such of them as are valid derive all their force, and all their authority, mediately or immediately, from this original'.[42] The law of nature is the will of God, and we are to discover this law by virtue of our reason. But if this is so, quips Bentham, 'it is in the regions of non-entity [reason] is to discover them' (*Comm.* 14). Such philosophizing is a confusion of discredited theories. To say that human laws which conflict with Divine Law are not binding, that is to say, are not laws, is to talk nonsense, and the concept of Natural Law is itself 'nothing but a phrase', a 'formidable non-entity' (*Comm.* 20). Nor could Revelation be of service in solving these apparent contradictions, for it is a thousand times easier to say even what the Common Law might be than it is to determine Divine Law from the Scriptures. Blackstone's propositions are repugnant to 'real fact'. Anyone 'who had been at all accustomed to examine into the import of words' could have seen this. 'The wonder is the greater', writes Bentham, 'as the fictitiousness of the "precept", the "command" in one case, and the reality of it in the other, is all that he could have, according to the amount he gives us of the Law of Revelation, to distinguish that from this' (*Comm.* 13 n.). In a manuscript of *c.*1773 Bentham's position is clearly conveyed by the margin heading 'The Idea of God useless in Jurisprudence' (UC 96/139).

3. SECULAR VERSUS RELIGIOUS UTILITARIANISM

By the time Bentham printed the *Introduction* in 1780 his views on the obstacles posed by religion to a rational system of jurisprudence were complete in all important details, and they stayed with him for the rest of his days. True to the spirit of Helvétius and Beccaria, he announced that the principle of utility is the foundation of his system. Its object 'is to rear the fabric of felicity by the hands of reason and law' (*IPML* 11), and the principal means to achieve this is through government, whose business it is 'to promote the happiness of the society by punishing and rewarding' (*IPML* 74). As nearly as legislation conforms to the calculations demanded by utility 'so near will such process approach the character of an exact one' (*IPML* 40).

On these terms the science of legislation is viewed as a means to a practical end, that is, to the beneficial reform of society. As surely as the prevailing legal system favoured special privileges for the few at the expense of the happiness of the many, by changing the laws the evils of social life can be alleviated. The science of legislation must, therefore, be a study both of what the law is and of what the law ought to be. The first Bentham called 'expositional jurisprudence'; the second he referred to as 'censorial jurisprudence'. The 'expositor' is principally occupied in stating or in enquiring after facts; the 'censor' in discussing reasons: 'To the *Expositor* it belongs to shew what the *Legislator* and his underworkman the *Judge* have done *already:* to the *Censor* it belongs to suggest what the *Legislator ought* to do *in future*' (*FG* 397-8). To augment knowledge is the function of the 'expositor'; refining knowledge is the task of the 'censor'.

These two aspects of the science of legislation, however, are not clearly distinct: the process of enlightenment began for Bentham with the criticism of established ideas but, as Douglas Long has pointed out, the Censor in defending his own censorial stance becomes his own Expositor. Hence Bentham's endeavour to perfect knowledge was to be achieved by a synthesis of the expository and censorial functions.[43] It is the special aim of the latter to provide an objective standard capable of evaluating the law as it is and spelling out what the law ought to be in order to conform to human nature. Accordingly, in the *Introduction* Bentham recognized that religion was of some influence in the field of morals, but there can be little doubt that he believed that its influence should be entirely obliterated. In the relative safety of the unpublished 'Crit[ical] Jur[isprudence] Crim[inal]' he had already stated as much:

> A great source and subject of diversity, will be those whimsies, or those weaknesses or those prejudices, or those oppressions, or those impostures, which under the several national establishments come under the title Religion. With this title I shall have . . . no other concern else than to shew that reason which every lover of . . . mankind has to wish . . . to see it . . . greatly narrow'd at least if not . . . totally expunged. (UC 69/14)

In the rational society, a society organized and governed according to the dictates of utility, religion is superfluous to ethics and need not be a consideration for the legislator. But Bentham does not confuse the censorial and expositional functions of his study; in the knowledge that conditions are not yet ripe for its eradication he includes religion in his list of sanctions (together with the physical, moral, and legal) at the disposal of the legislator (*IPML* 37). While it exists and has influence, while it is yet a factor in moral motivation, the legislator can and should make use of it. Where social evils are beyond the curative power of other sanctions the legislator might on occasion have recourse to the religious sanction. Such occasions are those of drunkenness (not then restricted by legislation), and any evil act where there are not witnesses, such as smuggling. Here supernatural fears and threats might be of some use. Like the moral sanction the religious sanction can be con-

sidered an 'auxiliary' sanction which the legislator can employ to supplement the work of the legal or political sanction (*LG* 196). The pleasures and pains of piety, those 'that accompany the belief of man's being in the . . . possession of the good-will or favour of the Supreme Being' (*IPML* 44), or his 'being obnoxious to the displeasure of the Supreme Being', are useful weapons in the legislator's armoury (*IPML* 48). If only as a game of bluff, then, religion has its uses. But Bentham is not concerned for its supposed impact in the afterlife, since 'this is a matter which comes not within the cognizance of the legislator' (*IPML* 202n.). In this respect the religious sanction is an empty formula. Unlike the other sanctions which operate immediately in this world, the religious sanction holds out only an uncertain threat. The pleasures and pains of futurity are not intelligible to us. Not being experienced in this life they cannot be observed, and as they are not observable it cannot be said that we can truly know any thing of them (*IPML* 36).[44]

Bentham well understood that the clergy employ the religious sanction to some effect. No doubt the inculcation of the belief in the power of a supreme invisible being is useful in that it supplies the deficiencies in point of efficacy of the religious powers of this world, who cannot see all the acts which require punishment, nor be sure that the punishment they administer will always reach an offender (*IPML* 201). But where the motives supplied by religion are efficacious they are at best 'semi-social' in the sense that their consequences reach only to the sect or society governed by the particular religion from which they emanate. On the whole, however, religion ranks last in the list of sources of efficacious motives because it is the least likely to coincide with utility. Despite the ingenuity of the attempt, William Warburton (1698-1779), the erstwhile Bishop of Gloucester, had failed to substantiate the claim of the first book of the *Divine Legation of Moses* (1738), that the religious sanction has always been inculcated by legislators because of its utility. And, unless it can be shown that the actions enjoined or condemned by that sanction are useful to society, the mere inculcation of the belief in the afterlife is useless and may even be pernicious (UC 140/2). Only if God were universally supposed to be as benevolent as he is wise and powerful would the dictates of religion coincide in all cases with those of utility (*IPML* 119). In plain terms, and quite apart from his epistemological difficulties regarding the existence of God, Bentham's position was that unless God aimed at increasing worldly happiness he could not be described as benevolent. In a manuscript of the period he notes: 'God is not good, if he prohibits our possessing the least atom of clear happiness which he has given us the physical capacity of attaining' (UC 70a/25). In other words, if God does not support utility this proves not that utility is not good, but that God is not good. Too often, it is God's malevolence that is brought to view by the teachers of Christianity:

> They call him benevolent in words, but they do not mean that he is so in reality. . . . For if they did, they would recognise that the dictates of religion could be

neither more nor less than the dictates of utility: not a
title different: not a title less nor more. But the case is,
that on a thousand occasions, they turn their backs on
the principle of utility. (*IPML* 120)

Acts induced by the religious sanction which do not tend
to the advantage of society are to be restricted by law, for
religion itself is only a good in so far as it is the auxiliary
of virtue. In short, its tendency ought to be in conformity
with the plan of utility. Though he was ready to make use
of religion in the existing social system, then, Bentham's
reasons were not of a spiritual nature.

What of acts offensive to religion which are not prevented
by human laws? Bentham derisively suggests that such actions do not need the punishment of mere mortals, because
God will punish all sinfulness by his wrath—only the im-
pious claim the right of punishment in such instances. The
misery occasioned by penal laws meant to maintain the religious beliefs of official or established religion for ever
raised his ire. 'When, when, alas!', he asks in the manuscript pages of 'Crit[ical] Jur[isprudence] Crim[inal]',
'will men cure themselves of the fond pretension of assisting the all-wise with their counsel, the almighty with their
power?' Is it not written 'Vengeance is mine, saith the
Lord'? (UC 140/13).

As an admirer of Voltaire, Bentham would not tolerate the
clergy playing the role of 'middleman' in order to reveal
God's will. Religious texts require interpretation, no doubt,
but we are all fallible. In a more critical vein, Bentham
charged that the clergy could not be trusted to live up to
the otherwise meritorious features of their faith. Too often
they have applied the title 'Divine Justice' to dictates
'which could have no other origin than the worst sort of
human caprice' (*IPML* 110n.). Too often they invoke the
name of God to achieve ends wholly contrary to his supposed benevolent will and pernicious to society. In language reminiscent of Helvétius, Bentham chides the zealous advocates of Christianity with causing the 'sufferings
of uncalled martyrs, the calamities of holy wars and religious persecutions, the mischiefs of intolerant laws' (*IPML*
121).

As a principle of ethics in the hands of its official professors, then, religion is found to be vague, theoretically deficient, and open to manipulation. In a direct attack on the
religious exponents of utility, Bentham even argues that to
unite this principle with religion is to apply it in a
'perverse' manner—in two respects. It is perverse in the
first place because it lends credence to religious asceticism
as a bona fide moral life. In a sense, asceticism can be
said to have been a target for Bentham from the beginning, and in religion he found its primary vehicle. Having
briefly touched on the subject in 1774 in connection with
'Sexual Nonconformity' (UC 73/90-100; 74a/1-25) he returned to it in the *Introduction* to give it a definitely religious context. His exhaustive analysis of the role of the
religious sanction in morals and legislation during the
1770s brought him to this stand against religious asceticism, and he once again pondered the subject in 1780 in

connection with his writings on 'indirect legislation' (UC
87/17-41). Religious asceticism repressed the quest for
pleasure on the premiss that the pleasures and pains of this
life are nothing in comparison with those of the future
state (UC 69/12). 'The greater the . . . pleasures of a future life, the less ratio do the greatest possible pleasures or
. . . pains of the present bear to them' (UC 140/2). Motivated by the prospect of pain which is 'the offspring of superstitious fancy', the religious ascetic is led by fear to approve of actions which diminish happiness and to
disapprove of those that tend to augment it (*IPML* 17-18).
Where the ascetic is not a 'fanatic' attempting to influence
the happiness of others, religious asceticism is strictly a
principle of private ethics and not therefore a subject for
legislation (*IPML* 19). But if this principle should ever become general, were the world peopled by religious ascet-
ics, they would turn it into a temporal hell (*IPML* 20). For
the motive supplied by religion produces worse secondary
mischief than even the worst in Bentham's category of
motives—ill-will. Because it is a more constant motive
than ill-will (vengeance and antipathy) it is all the more
dangerous. Wherever it gives birth to mischievous acts
and becomes fanaticism, it will normally be more pernicious than even the most dissocial of motives (*IPML* 156).
Moreover, religious asceticism seems to be accompanied
by a special intellectual blindness. The religious fanatic is
not able to see that he is fighting against adversaries who
'think, or perhaps only speak, differently upon a subject
which neither party understands' (*IPML* 156n.); he does
not realize that there would be even more heretics if there
were more thinkers (*IPML* 133). Fanaticism, particularly
religious fanaticism, 'never sleeps: it is never glutted: it is
never stopped by philanthropy: it is never stopped by conscience: for it has pressed conscience into its service. Avarice, lust, and vengeance, have piety, benevolence, honour:
fanaticism has nothing to oppose it' (*IPML* 156n.).

Secondly, the union of utility and religion is perverse because it deflects the science of morals from its true focus
of study—the observation and calculation of pleasures and
pains. In the preface to the *Introduction* Bentham writes
that, 'There is, or rather there ought to be, a *logic of the
will,* as well as of the understanding' (*IPML* 8). Philosophers from Aristotle down have neglected the former and
directed their attentions to the study of the latter. Yet the
science of law is absolutely dependent upon a logic of the
will. As John Hill Burton observed, for Bentham sanctions
are 'the chains . . . which bind a man from following his
own wild will'.[45] The science of legislation is, therefore,
founded on this logic, on the study of the connection between pleasures and pains and actions. In essence this constitutes Bentham's advance from the work of Helvétius.
As Long again has observed, 'his "logic of the will" was
meant to be the social and moral equivalent of Newton's
physical laws of motion: the core of a science of human
nature upon which an entire catalogue of social sciences
might be based'.[46]

For the 'theological' exponents of utility, the operations of
the will were not understood in the way just outlined. It is

not how wisely legislation binds the will to its purpose, but how nearly the will conforms to God's laws that is important. In the truly Christian commonwealth the will would be neither wild nor aimless, but would naturally be directed to the fulfillment of God's purpose. In short, the human will would become one with the Divine will. In the less perfect commonwealth the moral and legal sanctions serve their purpose, but more weight attaches to the wrath of God, which is reserved for those who openly and deliberately flaunt his laws. For these laws, unlike those of society, are perfect, eternal, and immutably directed to the enduring happiness of all. Hence, the religious exponents of utility reduced all forms of obligation to the religious. As John Gay expressed it, 'the will of God is the immediate criterion of Virtue and the happiness of mankind the criterion of the will of God'.[47]

John Brown's explanation of the dimensions of the motivation supplied by religion was perhaps the subtlest of those set out by the religious utilitarians. What Brown, in language peculiar to the day, termed 'the religious principle', has two branches, the first of which is fear. His defence of religion in terms of this is of little interest. Fear, and specifically the fear of divine punishment, being a passion which we all have the capacity to feel, constitutes the lowest base from which we could become virtuous. Even so, says Brown, there is nothing slavish in this; rather it 'implies a lively and habitual Belief, that we shall be hereafter miserable, if we disobey [God's] Laws', and this does no more than induce 'a *rational Sense*' of evil and the determination to avoid it.[48] Of more interest is Brown's elucidation of the second branch of the religious principle, since it is here that the positive character of the motive to virtuous action which Christianity supplies is to be found. This branch of the principle is 'the Hope and Prospect of higher Degrees of future Happiness and perfection'.[49] To understand fully what Brown meant by this his theological position as a defender of orthodox beliefs must be borne in mind. Among the faithful of the day the spiritual dimension of the perfection of the soul was commonly held to be integral to the idea of personal happiness in its most encompassing sense. In Brown's Christian version of the doctrine of utility it could be no less so: here temporal happiness joins hands with the eternal happiness of the soul in pursuit of the ideal, the perfect harmony of virtue and happiness. For Brown,

> 'Man is never so sincerely or heartily *benevolent,* as when he is truly *happy* in himself'. Thus the high Consciousness of his being numbered among the Children of GOD, and that his Lot is among the Saints; that he is destined to an endless Progression of Happiness, and to rise from high to higher Degrees of Perfection, must needs inspire him with that Tranquility and Joy, which will naturally diffuse itself in Acts of sincere Benevolence to all his Fellow-Creatures.[50]

Only when a man 'is truly *happy* in himself' can he be expected to progress in ever greater degrees towards perfection, and it is religious consciousness which provides this happy disposition, making his own perfection and his contribution to human happiness possible. Neither happiness

nor perfection on this view can be said to be the primary consideration for the true Christian, but each is essential for the possibility of the other. As Brown put it elsewhere,

> the whole *Weight* and *Energy* of the *Gospel* is employed in enforcing the Idea of *moral Perfection,* of our *nobler* SELF, of Self-Interest in the *higher* Sense, of the Necessity of extirpating every meaner Passion, and cherishing the great one of *unbounded Love,* as the necessary and only Discipline that can qualify us for future Happiness.[51]

Hence it is not that religion merely promises an extension or rectification of human justice, nor that the rewards and punishments of futurity are simply an addition to the imperfect rewards and punishments established by civil society. There is a specific aspect of religion which cannot be accounted for in such terms, something over and above the religious sanction which imparts to the doctrines of Christianity an undeniable efficacy. It is a spiritual quality which has nothing to do with visions or ecstasies, but everything to do with the will to be and to do good. This will is most appropriately characterized as love, and it is a love which causes each person to be loved in return, such that ever increasing numbers open their souls to benevolence. The notion of posthumous rewards and punishments provides an aid to this moral endeavour, but it is in religion in its positive role—that which prompts individuals not merely to refrain from evil but actually to do good, to love their friends and neighbours and thus progress on the path to perfection—that the Christian finds himself most fully in accord with God's benevolent will.

It was on these grounds that the religious exponents of utility held that the religious principle gave the fullest scope to human development. Its reality does not rest on simple *post facto* evidence, but is derived from the theological consideration that human nature has a spiritual as well as a physiological side. Despite their emphasis on the importance of the appeal to the concern for future happiness, Paley, Brown, and the others recognized that the moral efficacy of religion is not constituted by this alone. Virtuous effort demands that we form an ideal of the highest good towards which this effort tends. That ideal is the harmony of virtue and happiness according to the laws and purpose of God, a harmony which is approachable in the present life but which is only truly realizable in the life to come. The virtuous person constantly reaches forth in a seemingly endless effort to reach perfection, but such endeavour, though fundamentally spiritual, is of great temporal significance in ordinary social and political life. It manifests itself in love, the love of God, and through him the love of all with whom one comes into contact; its consequence is a peaceful and ordered society and, in the best of all possible worlds, extensive benevolence leading to universal happiness.

Bentham's argument against this form of reasoning is founded upon his metaphysics and reveals how little he could empathize with or enter into the language of religion. The will of God, having no existence in reality that can be observed, is a fictitious entity. As he wrote in 1816, that 'such or such a thing is a cause of pain or pleasure is a matter of fact and experience: that the use of it has been prohibited by the Deity, is a matter of inference and conjecture' (UC 58/210).[52] In the *Introduction* he was equally clear that when moralists refer us to the 'will of God' their meaning is frequently confused, and this is not only a source of error but of positive evil. The revealed will of the Scriptures is too vague and subject to too great a range of interpretation to provide a general standard of ethics. What moralists usually settle for is 'the *presumptive* will: (that is to say, that which is presumably to be his will on account of the conformity of its dictates to those of some other principle' (*IPML* 31). But if this principle is not general happiness in this life then it is nothing more than either the principle of 'sympathy' or 'antipathy' in some other shape (*IPML* 31). The potential for evil lies in the fact that these principles—sympathy and antipathy—approve and disapprove of actions, not on account of their augmenting or diminishing happiness, 'but merely because a man finds himself disposed to approve or disapprove of them'. They provide no external criterion or 'extrinsic ground' for judgement; therefore, all is uncertain and unpredictable (*IPML* 25).

Bentham was later to expose this evil in terms of the influence on the will of the citizen exerted by illegitimate, as opposed to legitimate, sources of authority in society. The influence of a Church, which relies on interpretations of the 'will of God' and not on utility to determine what is or is not admissable, is just such an illegitimate use of authority, and where an ecclesiastical establishment has an influence in government the dangers to the comfort and well-being of the citizen are multiplied. However, Bentham's arguments concerning the redundancies of religious doctrines and their pernicious consequences when propagated by an unscrupulous clergy were clearly stated in his writings on ethics and jurisprudence during the early period of his career. Entirely cynical concerning the value of religion to society he demanded that it be replaced as the central agency of moral control and social regulation. Hence, we find that his critique of religion is closely associated with his emphasis on legislation and the logic of the will as the only sure means for promoting human happiness. At the heart of this vision of a secular society stands the principle of utility, and Bentham never doubted that it was an appropriate standard by which to measure the worth of religion. In the manuscript pages of 'Crit[ical] Jur[isprudence] Crim[inal]' he commended those writers who had gone before him in this:

> A numerous tribe of anonymous writers in whom the acrimony they have shown in their attacks against religion in general, has been more conspicuous than any strength or regularity which they have display'd in the manner of conducting them, have mostly however had this merit in common, that they have professed to take this principle (utility) for their standard. (UC 159/270)

To advocate the principle of utility as the ultimate standard of all policies is to advocate the eradication of the influence of religion over the mind and the demotion of offi-cial religion from its privileged position as the protected ally of government. Legislation is to hold centre stage. Its aim is to achieve the greatest happiness by bringing about the concurrence of private and public interests. Government must induce individuals to follow the optimal path by holding out the prospect of rewards and punishments for the adherence to, or infringement of, laws prescribed in order to create the conditions in which the greatest happiness can be achieved.

Notes

1. See the editorial introduction to *Deon.*, p. xxxii.

2. The term 'theological utilitarianism' was coined by W. H. Lecky and later used by Ernest Albee to describe the moral thought of those 18th-cent. moralists who, while giving prominence to the principle of utility as the standard for assessing the worth of an action, found in the Christian religion the essential motive to virtue. Neither Lecky nor Albee, however, saw any need to present these moralists as exponents of a distinctive doctrine. They appear to have assumed that before Bentham utilitarianism as a school of thought in England was a loose and somewhat diffuse one, encompassing writers of different temperaments and purposes. Theological utilitarianism, though significant, represented merely a transitory stage prior to the final, secularized, maturity of utilitarian moral theory. See W. E. H. Lecky, *History of European Morals from Augustine to Charlemagne,* 2 vols. (London, 1869); E. Albee, *A History of English Utilitarianism* (London, 1901); and for a discussion see my 'John Brown and the Theological Tradition of Utilitarian Ethics', *History of Political Thought,* 4:3 (1983), 523-50.

3. J. Bentham, *A Comment on the Commentaries,* ed. C. W. Everett (1928; repr. Darmstadt, 1976).

4. *LG* also belongs to this early period: a continuation of *IPML* substantially completed by 1782, the manuscripts were discovered at University College Library by C. W. Everett in 1939 and subsequently edited and published by him as *The Limits of Jurisprudence Defined* (New York, 1945).

5. *IPML* had been completed and printed as early as 1780 but not published until 1789. George Wilson wrote to Bentham (24 Sept. 1786) during his sojourn in Russia informing him of Paley's success, in reply to which (19-30 Dec. 1786) Bentham affected indifference (*Corr.* iii. 490-1 and 513-14).

6. G. Berkeley, 'Passive Obedience' (1712) and 'An Essay towards preventing the ruin of Great Britain' (1721), in *The Works of George Berkeley Bishop of Cloyne,* ed. A. A. Luce and T. E. Jessop, 9 vols. (London, 1948-57), vi; J. Gay, 'Preliminary Dissertation concerning the Fundamental Principle of Virtue or Morality', prefixed to W. King, *Essay on the Origin of Evil* (London, 1732); [A. Tucker], *The Light of Nature Pursued* by 'Edward Search', 7

vols. (London, 1768-78); J. Brown, *Essays on the Characteristics of the Earl of Shaftesbury* (1751; 3rd edn. London, 1752); E. Law, 'On Morality and Religion' and 'The Nature of Obligation of Man, as a sensible and rational Being', in W. King, *Essay on the Origin of Evil,* trans. E. Law (1732; 5th edn. London, 1781).

7. See A. P. Brogan, 'John Locke and Utilitarianism', *Ethics,* 69:2 (1959), where he argues that Locke formulated the basic theses of 18th-cent. utilitarianism. Brogan, however, seems to assume that utilitarian ethics in the century after Locke was all of a kind, and that John Gay and others simply 'took Locke's theses and organized them into a systematic presentation'.

8. It is true that the rudiments of a similar view of the motivation supplied by the afterlife are to be found in Locke, but it is hardly developed by him. See *Essay concerning Human Understanding,* in *Works,* ii, Bk. II, ch. 21, secs. 38, 70. For Locke, Christian ethics are 'natural': the reason for doing what Christ said is not simply that Christ had said it, but that in conforming to his will one promotes one's own happiness, and to this end all men are impelled by their natural self-love. Even so, it is a fact of some interest that Locke ultimately failed to live up to the promise of his maxim that 'reason must be our last judge in everything' (ibid., Bk. IV, ch. 19, sec. 14) and instead recommended a morality based on faith and revelation.

9. 'We never saw an abler defence of utility than in a book written in refutation of Shaftesbury, and now little read—Brown's "Essays on the Characteristics" ' (Mill, 'Bentham', in *Collected Works,* x. 86-7).

10. Brown, *Essays on the Characteristics,* p. 209.

11. Ibid. 210.

12. W. Paley, *Principles of Moral and Political Philosophy,* Bk. I, ch. 6, in *The Complete Works of William Paley,* 4 vols. (London, 1825), i. 34.

13. See Albee, *A History of English Utilitarianism,* ch. 9.

14. See ibid. 182; L. A. Selby-Bigge (ed.), *British Moralists: Being Selections from Writers Principally of the Eighteenth Century,* 2 vols. (Oxford, 1897), ii, sec. 863; *IPML* 34.

15. Locke, *Essay concerning Human Understanding,* in *Works,* ii, Bk. II, ch. 28, sec. 7. The 3 sanctions set out by Bentham in *FG* correspond precisely to those of Locke (both omit the physical; added by Bentham in *IPML*).

16. In the earlier *Comm.* Bentham put it thus: 'The principle of utility once adopted as the governing principle, admits of no rival, admits not even of an associate' (*Comm.* 27). Another variation occurs in the marginals for the *Table of the Spring of Action:* 'Principle of Utility allows no rival. Whatever is not under is opposite to it' (*Deon.* 31).

17. Selby-Bigge, *British Moralists,* ii, sec. 864.

18. It does not alter this assessment that John Austin set out a version of the religious doctrine of utility in the lectures he gave at UCL, published under the title *The Province of Jurisprudence Determined* (1832; London, 1971). It was Bentham's secular version of the doctrine that came to dominate in 19th-cent. England.

19. Yet it was well into the 19th-cent. before the radical nature of Bentham's utilitarianism was appreciated outside the band of philosophical radicals that gathered about him. As J. B. Schneewind has so rightly said, it was only from the middle of the 1830s that Paley was no longer considered the central figure in philosophical discussions of utilitarianism, *Sidgwick's Ethics and Victorian Moral Philosophy* (Oxford, 1977), 151. It should also be noted that though Dr Southwood Smith, W. J. Fox, and John Bowring were closely associated in practical affairs with Bentham, other Unitarian philosophers saw Paley as the fountain-head of the utilitarian doctrine. For instance Bentham is mentioned only in passing by T. Belsham in *Elements of Philosophy of the Human Mind and of Moral Philosophy* (London, 1801); and by W. Jevons in *Systematic Morality,* 2 vols. (London, 1827).

20. For the influence of Hume, Helvétius, and Beccaria on Bentham see Mack, *Jeremy Bentham,* ch. 3; N. Rosenblum, *Bentham's Theory of the Modern State* (Cambridge, Mass., 1978), ch. 2; H. L. A. Hart, 'Bentham and Beccaria', in *Essays on Bentham: Studies on Jurisprudence and Political Theory* (Oxford, 1982); Harrison, *Bentham,* esp. ch. 5.

21. It is likely that Bentham was mistaken and that he had in mind Hume's *Enquiry Concerning the Principles of Morals* (1751), in *Enquiries concerning Human Understanding and concerning the Principles of Morals,* ed. L. A. Selby-Bigge (3rd edn. rev. P. H. Hidditch, 1748, 1751; Oxford, 1975), sec. 5, 'Why utility pleases'.

22. There is little to substantiate and, if this were the place, much to say against the claim of John Plamenatz that Hume 'is rightly regarded as the founder of utilitarianism'. Plamenatz appears to base this on the fact that Hume provided his successors with the concept of 'utility'. Hume's employment of the term and his tendency to equate it with 'virtue' are not in question, but his connection with the 'moral sense' school of moral thought is no less important. With this in mind Plamenatz's statement that Hume 'is a utilitarian but . . . not a complete one' does not do justice to the richness of Hume's ethics; J. Plamenatz, *The English Utilitarians* (Oxford, 1958), 22, 28.

23. Hume to Hugh Blair (1761), *The Letters of David Hume,* ed. J. Y. T. Greig, 2 vols. (Oxford, 1932), i. 351.

24. E. C. Mossner, *The Life of David Hume* (Edinburgh, 1954), 319-35.

25. For these references and an analysis of Hume's religious scepticism in the *Enquiry concerning Human Understanding* I am indebted to D. F. Norton, *David Hume: Commonsense Moralist, Sceptical Metaphysician* (Princeton, 1982), 279-90.

26. D. Hume, 'Of the Independency of Parliament', in *Essays Literary, Moral, and Political* (London, n.d. [1870?]), 29.

27. Hume, 'That Politics may be reduced to a Science', ibid. 19. See also Hume, *An Enquiry concerning Human Understanding* (1748), in *Enquiries*, sec. 8, pt. 1, p. 90.

28. Hume, 'That Politics may be reduced to a Science', in *Essays Literary, Moral, and Political*, p. 19. See also the essay 'Of National Characters' in the same volume.

29. There are several sections of *De l'esprit* devoted to a discussion of 'genius', by which Helvétius meant the ability of men to discover or invent objects of importance to the well-being of mankind. In this respect Helvétius mentions the effect on human progress of the work of a wide variety of literary and philosophical figures including, naturally, Newton and Locke. For Helvétius's discussion of 'genius' see esp. *De l'esprit*, Essay III, ch. 1.

30. Ibid., Essay II, ch. 2, pp. 42-3.

31. Ibid., ch. 6, p. 63.

32. Ibid., ch. 15, pp. 124-5.

33. Ibid., ch. 24, p. 185.

34. That the Jesuits posed a formidable personal threat to Helvétius after the publication of *De l'esprit* in 1758 is part of the story of D. W. Smith's *Helvétius: A Study in Persecution* (Oxford, 1965).

35. C. A. Helvétius, *A Treatise on Man: His Intellectual Faculties and his Education* [*De l'homme*, 1777], trans. W. Hooper, 2 vols. (London, 1810), i. 144, 148, 196.

36. C. Beccaria, *An Essay on Crimes and Punishments* [*Dei delitti e delle pene*, 1764; first Eng. trans. 1767], trans. H. Paolucci (Indianapolis, 1975), ch. 3, p. 64.

37. Ibid. 10, 59.

38. UC 32, a fragment headed 'Introduction, Principes Project Matiere', (*c.*1785-90), trans. from Bentham's French by Halévy, *The Growth of Philosophic Radicalism*, p. 21. The reference to the evangelical nature of Beccaria's work is consistent with Bentham's habit of borrowing the terminology of religion to dramatize the efforts of the secularists, including his own. This is discussed below in the Conclusion.

39. Beccaria, *An Essay on Crimes and Punishments*, p. 5.

40. How this formula travelled from Francis Hutcheson via several hands to Beccaria, later to be taken up by Bentham, is the subject of Robert Shackleton's informative essay 'The Greatest Happiness of the Greatest Number: The History of Bentham's Phrase', *Studies on Voltaire and the Eighteenth Century*, 90 (1972), 1461-82.

41. See *Corr.* i, Letter 192; ii, Letters 248, 250, and 251; and *Works*, x. 70, 79, 142. Bentham was always happy to indicate his pleasure whenever he found these basic principles enunciated. Hence, despite the concessions to Christianity it contained, he could still commend the Marquis de Chastellux's *An Essay on Public Happiness* [*De la félicité publique, ou considérations sur le sort des hommes dans les différentes époques de l'histoire*, 1772], 2 vols. (London, 1774; repr. New York, 1969). See UC 142/211-13.

42. Blackstone, *Commentaries*, i. 41.

43. Long, *Bentham on Liberty*, p. 13.

44. Elsewhere Bentham was not so circumspect: 'under the guidance of religion men have made to themselves an almighty being, whose delight is in human misery, and who, to prevent a man's escaping from whatsoever misery he may be threatened with in the present life, has without having denounced it formed a determination, in the event of any such escape, to plunge him into infinitely greater misery in a life to come' (*Deon.* 131).

45. Burton, *Benthamiana*, p. 358.

46. D. G. Long, 'Physical Sciences and Social Sciences: The Case of Jeremy Bentham' (unpublished), *Proceedings of the Canadian Political Science Association Annual Convention 1975*, 3.

47. Gay, 'Preliminary Dissertation concerning the Fundamental Principle of Virtue or Morality', in Selby-Bigge, *British Moralists*, ii, sec. 864.

48. Brown, *Essays on the Characteristics*, p. 214.

49. Ibid. 215.

50. Brown, *Essays on the Characteristics*, p. 221.

51. Ibid. 329.

52. Among MSS used by Bowring for the 1st vol. of *Deon.* published in 1834. Written in the hand of Bowring, it is likely that this is a rephrasing by him of Bentham's original, probably dating from 1816.

FURTHER READING

Criticism

Johnson, Edgar. "*A Christmas Carol* Criticizes England's Economic System." In *Readings on Charles Dickens*, edited by Clarice Swisher, pp. 86-93. San Diego, Calif.: Greenhaven Press, 1998.

Views Charles Dickens's *A Christmas Carol* as "an attack upon both the economic behavior of the nineteenth-century businessman and the supporting theory of doctrinaire utilitarianism."

Kelly, P. J. *Utilitarianism and Distributive Justice: Jeremy Bentham and the Civil Law*. Oxford: Clarendon Press, 1990, 240 p.

Begins a revisionist assessment of Bentham's moral theory that takes into account the philosopher's concern with the equal distribution of justice and other liberal values.

Kim, Ki Su. "John Stuart Mill's Concepts of Quality and Pedagogical Norms." *The Journal of General Education* 38, No. 2 (1986): 120-33.

Explores Mill's thought as it applies to the problem of quality and equality in education, and considers his influence on liberal educational theories.

Manning, D. J. *The Mind of Jeremy Bentham*. London: Longmans, Green and Co. Ltd., 1968, 118 p.

An elucidation, rather than a critique, of key concepts in Bentham's thought, including his principle of utility.

Mulvihill, James. "The Poetics of Utility: Benthamite Literary Reviewing, 1824-1836." *English Studies in Canada* XV, No. 2 (June 1989): 149-61.

Investigates the application of the principles of utilitarianism to the criticism of literature in the *Westminster Review*.

Rosen, F. *Bentham, Byron, and Greece: Constitutionalism, Nationalism, and Early Liberal Political Thought*. Oxford: Clarendon Press, 1992, 332 p.

Examines Bentham's intellectual involvement in the Greek fight for independence during the 1820s.

Schultz, Bart, ed. *Essays on Henry Sidgwick*. Cambridge: Cambridge University Press, 1992, 421 p.

Collection of essays by various contributors concerning Sidgwick's ethical theory and its effect on the program of utilitarianism.

How to Use This Index

The main references

> **Calvino, Italo**
> 1923-1985 .... CLC **5, 8, 11, 22, 33, 39,**
> **73; SSC 3**

list all author entries in the following Gale Literary Criticism series:

BLC = *Black Literature Criticism*
CLC = *Contemporary Literary Criticism*
CLR = *Children's Literature Review*
CMLC = *Classical and Medieval Literature Criticism*
DA = *DISCovering Authors*
DAB = *DISCovering Authors: British*
DAC = *DISCovering Authors: Canadian*
DAM = *DISCovering Authors: Modules*
　　　DRAM: Dramatists Module; *MST: Most-Studied Authors Module;*
　　　MULT: Multicultural Authors Module; *NOV: Novelists Module;*
　　　POET: Poets Module; *POP: Popular Fiction and Genre Authors Module*
DC = *Drama Criticism*
HLC = *Hispanic Literature Criticism*
LC = *Literature Criticism from 1400 to 1800*
NCLC = *Nineteenth-Century Literature Criticism*
NNAL = *Native North American Literature*
PC = *Poetry Criticism*
SSC = *Short Story Criticism*
TCLC = *Twentieth-Century Literary Criticism*
WLC = *World Literature Criticism, 1500 to the Present*

The cross-references

> See also CANR 23; CA 85-88;
> obituary CA116

list all author entries in the following Gale biographical and literary sources:

AAYA = *Authors & Artists for Young Adults*
AITN = *Authors in the News*
BEST = *Bestsellers*
BW = *Black Writers*
CA = *Contemporary Authors*
CAAS = *Contemporary Authors Autobiography Series*
CABS = *Contemporary Authors Bibliographical Series*
CANR = *Contemporary Authors New Revision Series*
CAP = *Contemporary Authors Permanent Series*
CDALB = *Concise Dictionary of American Literary Biography*
CDBLB = *Concise Dictionary of British Literary Biography*
DLB = *Dictionary of Literary Biography*
DLBD = *Dictionary of Literary Biography Documentary Series*
DLBY = *Dictionary of Literary Biography Yearbook*
HW = *Hispanic Writers*
JRDA = *Junior DISCovering Authors*
MAICYA = *Major Authors and Illustrators for Children and Young Adults*
MTCW = *Major 20th-Century Writers*
SAAS = *Something about the Author Autobiography Series*
SATA = *Something about the Author*
YABC = *Yesterday's Authors of Books for Children*

Literary Criticism Series
Cumulative Author Index

Ainsworth, William Harrison 1805-1882
NCLC **13**
See also DLB 21; SATA 24

Aitmatov, Chingiz (Torekulovich)
1928- .... CLC **71**
See also CA 103; CANR 38; MTCW 1;
SATA 56

Akers, Floyd
See Baum, L(yman) Frank

Akhmadulina, Bella Akhatovna
1937- .... CLC **53; DAM POET**
See also CA 65-68

Akhmatova, Anna 1888-1966 ..... CLC **11, 25,**
64, 126; DAM POET; PC 2
See also CA 19-20; 25-28R; CANR 35;
CAP 1; DA3; MTCW 1, 2

Aksakov, Sergei Timofeyvich 1791-1859
NCLC **2**
See also DLB 198

Aksenov, Vassily
See Aksyonov, Vassily (Pavlovich)

Akst, Daniel 1956- .... CLC **109**
See also CA 161

Aksyonov, Vassily (Pavlovich)
1932- .... CLC **22, 37, 101**
See also CA 53-56; CANR 12, 48, 77

Akutagawa, Ryunosuke
1892-1927 .... TCLC **16**
See also CA 117; 154

Alain 1868-1951 .... TCLC **41**
See also CA 163

Alain-Fournier .... TCLC **6**
See also Fournier, Henri Alban DLB 65

Alarcon, Pedro Antonio de
1833-1891 .... NCLC **1**

Alas (y Urena), Leopoldo (Enrique Garcia)
1852-1901 .... TCLC **29**
See also CA 113; 131; HW 1

Albee, Edward (Franklin III) 1928- . CLC **1,**
2, 3, 5, 9, 11, 13, 25, 53, 86, 113; DA;
DAB; DAC; DAM DRAM, MST; DC
11; WLC
See also AITN 1; CA 5-8R; CABS 3;
CANR 8, 54, 74; CDALB 1941-1968;
DA3; DLB 7; INT CANR-8; MTCW 1, 2

Alberti, Rafael 1902- .... CLC **7**
See also CA 85-88; CANR 81; DLB 108;
HW 2

Albert the Great 1200(?)-1280 ...... CMLC **16**
See also DLB 115

Alcala-Galiano, Juan Valera y
See Valera y Alcala-Galiano, Juan

Alcott, Amos Bronson 1799-1888 .... NCLC **1**
See also DLB 1

Alcott, Louisa May 1832-1888 . NCLC **6, 58,**
83; DA; DAB; DAC; DAM MST, NOV;
SSC 27; WLC
See also AAYA 20; CDALB 1865-1917;
CLR 1, 38; DA3; DLB 1, 42, 79; DLBD
14; JRDA; MAICYA; SATA 100; YABC
1

Aldanov, M. A.
See Aldanov, Mark (Alexandrovich)

Aldanov, Mark (Alexandrovich)
1886(?)-1957 .... TCLC **23**
See also CA 118; 181

Aldington, Richard 1892-1962 .... CLC **49**
See also CA 85-88; CANR 45; DLB 20, 36,
100, 149

Aldiss, Brian W(ilson) 1925- . CLC **5, 14, 40;**
DAM NOV; SSC 36
See also CA 5-8R; CAAS 2; CANR 5, 28,
64; DLB 14; MTCW 1, 2; SATA 34

Alegria, Claribel 1924- .... CLC **75; DAM**
MULT; HLCS 1; PC 26
See also CA 131; CAAS 15; CANR 66;
DLB 145; HW 1; MTCW 1

Alegria, Fernando 1918- .... CLC **57**
See also CA 9-12R; CANR 5, 32, 72; HW
1, 2

Aleichem, Sholom .... TCLC **1, 35; SSC 33**
See also Rabinovitch, Sholem

Aleixandre, Vicente 1898-1984
See also CANR 81; HLCS 1; HW 2

Alepoudelis, Odysseus
See Elytis, Odysseus

Aleshkovsky, Joseph 1929-
See Aleshkovsky, Yuz
See also CA 121; 128

Aleshkovsky, Yuz .... CLC **44**
See also Aleshkovsky, Joseph

Alexander, Lloyd (Chudley) 1924- ... CLC **35**
See also AAYA 1, 27; CA 1-4R; CANR 1,
24, 38, 55; CLR 1, 5, 48; DLB 52; JRDA;
MAICYA; MTCW 1; SAAS 19; SATA 3,
49, 81

Alexander, Meena 1951- .... CLC **121**
See also CA 115; CANR 38, 70

Alexander, Samuel 1859-1938 .... TCLC **77**

Alexie, Sherman (Joseph, Jr.)
1966- .... CLC **96; DAM MULT**
See also AAYA 28; CA 138; CANR 65;
DA3; DLB 175, 206; MTCW 1; NNAL

Alfau, Felipe 1902- .... CLC **66**
See also CA 137

Alfred, Jean Gaston
See Ponge, Francis

Alger, Horatio Jr., Jr. 1832-1899 .... NCLC **8,**
83
See also DLB 42; SATA 16

Algren, Nelson 1909-1981 ..... CLC **4, 10, 33;**
SSC 33
See also CA 13-16R; 103; CANR 20, 61;
CDALB 1941-1968; DLB 9; DLBY 81,
82; MTCW 1, 2

Ali, Ahmed 1910- .... CLC **69**
See also CA 25-28R; CANR 15, 34

Alighieri, Dante
See Dante

Allan, John B.
See Westlake, Donald E(dwin)

Allan, Sidney
See Hartmann, Sadakichi

Allan, Sydney
See Hartmann, Sadakichi

Allen, Edward 1948- .... CLC **59**

Allen, Fred 1894-1956 .... TCLC **87**

Allen, Paula Gunn 1939- .... CLC **84; DAM**
MULT
See also CA 112; 143; CANR 63; DA3;
DLB 175; MTCW 1; NNAL

Allen, Roland
See Ayckbourn, Alan

Allen, Sarah A.
See Hopkins, Pauline Elizabeth

Allen, Sidney H.
See Hartmann, Sadakichi

Allen, Woody 1935- .... CLC **16, 52; DAM**
POP
See also AAYA 10; CA 33-36R; CANR 27,
38, 63; DLB 44; MTCW 1

Allende, Isabel 1942- . CLC **39, 57, 97; DAM**
MULT, NOV; HLC 1; WLCS
See also AAYA 18; CA 125; 130; CANR
51, 74; DA3; DLB 145; HW 1, 2; INT
130; MTCW 1, 2

Alleyn, Ellen
See Rossetti, Christina (Georgina)

Allingham, Margery (Louise)
1904-1966 .... CLC **19**
See also CA 5-8R; 25-28R; CANR 4, 58;
DLB 77; MTCW 1, 2

Allingham, William 1824-1889 ...... NCLC **25**
See also DLB 35

Allison, Dorothy E. 1949- .... CLC **78**
See also CA 140; CANR 66; DA3; MTCW
1

Allston, Washington 1779-1843 .... NCLC **2**
See also DLB 1

Almedingen, E. M. .... CLC **12**
See also Almedingen, Martha Edith von
SATA 3

Almedingen, Martha Edith von 1898-1971
See Almedingen, E. M.
See also CA 1-4R; CANR 1

Almodovar, Pedro 1949(?)- .... CLC **114;**
HLCS 1
See also CA 133; CANR 72; HW 2

Almqvist, Carl Jonas Love
1793-1866 .... NCLC **42**

Alonso, Damaso 1898-1990 .... CLC **14**
See also CA 110; 131; 130; CANR 72; DLB
108; HW 1, 2

Alov
See Gogol, Nikolai (Vasilyevich)

Alta 1942- .... CLC **19**
See also CA 57-60

Alter, Robert B(ernard) 1935- .... CLC **34**
See also CA 49-52; CANR 1, 47

Alther, Lisa 1944- .... CLC **7, 41**
See also CA 65-68; CAAS 30; CANR 12,
30, 51; MTCW 1

Althusser, L.
See Althusser, Louis

Althusser, Louis 1918-1990 .... CLC **106**
See also CA 131; 132

Altman, Robert 1925- .... CLC **16, 116**
See also CA 73-76; CANR 43

Alurista 1949-
See Urista, Alberto H.
See also DLB 82; HLCS 1

Alvarez, A(lfred) 1929- .... CLC **5, 13**
See also CA 1-4R; CANR 3, 33, 63; DLB
14, 40

Alvarez, Alejandro Rodriguez 1903-1965
See Casona, Alejandro
See also CA 131; 93-96; HW 1

Alvarez, Julia 1950- .... CLC **93; HLCS 1**
See also AAYA 25; CA 147; CANR 69;
DA3; MTCW 1

Alvaro, Corrado 1896-1956 .... TCLC **60**
See also CA 163

Amado, Jorge 1912- .... CLC **13, 40, 106;**
DAM MULT, NOV; HLC 1
See also CA 77-80; CANR 35, 74; DLB
113; HW 2; MTCW 1, 2

Ambler, Eric 1909-1998 .... **CLC 4, 6, 9**
See also CA 9-12R; 171; CANR 7, 38, 74; DLB 77; MTCW 1, 2

Amichai, Yehuda 1924- ... **CLC 9, 22, 57, 116**
See also CA 85-88; CANR 46, 60; MTCW 1

Amichai, Yehudah
See Amichai, Yehuda

Amiel, Henri Frederic 1821-1881 .... **NCLC 4**

Amis, Kingsley (William)
1922-1995 ...... **CLC 1, 2, 3, 5, 8, 13, 40, 44; DA; DAB; DAC; DAM MST, NOV**
See also AITN 2; CA 9-12R; 150; CANR 8, 28, 54; CDBLB 1945-1960; DA3; DLB 15, 27, 100, 139; DLBY 96; INT CANR-8; MTCW 1, 2

Amis, Martin (Louis) 1949- .... **CLC 4, 9, 38, 62, 101**
See also BEST 90:3; CA 65-68; CANR 8, 27, 54, 73; DA3; DLB 14, 194; INT CANR-27; MTCW 1

Ammons, A(rchie) R(andolph)
1926- ...... **CLC 2, 3, 5, 8, 9, 25, 57, 108; DAM POET; PC 16**
See also AITN 1; CA 9-12R; CANR 6, 36, 51, 73; DLB 5, 165; MTCW 1, 2

Amo, Tauraatua i
See Adams, Henry (Brooks)

Amory, Thomas 1691(?)-1788 .... **LC 48**

Anand, Mulk Raj 1905- .. **CLC 23, 93; DAM NOV**
See also CA 65-68; CANR 32, 64; MTCW 1, 2

Anatol
See Schnitzler, Arthur

Anaximander c. 610B.C.-c.
546B.C. .... **CMLC 22**

Anaya, Rudolfo A(lfonso) 1937- ...... **CLC 23; DAM MULT, NOV; HLC 1**
See also AAYA 20; CA 45-48; CAAS 4; CANR 1, 32, 51; DLB 82, 206; HW 1; MTCW 1, 2

Andersen, Hans Christian
1805-1875 .... **NCLC 7, 79; DA; DAB; DAC; DAM MST, POP; SSC 6; WLC**
See also CLR 6; DA3; MAICYA; SATA 100; YABC 1

Anderson, C. Farley
See Mencken, H(enry) L(ouis); Nathan, George Jean

Anderson, Jessica (Margaret) Queale 1916-
CLC 37
See also CA 9-12R; CANR 4, 62

Anderson, Jon (Victor) 1940- . **CLC 9; DAM POET**
See also CA 25-28R; CANR 20

Anderson, Lindsay (Gordon)
1923-1994 .... **CLC 20**
See also CA 125; 128; 146; CANR 77

Anderson, Maxwell 1888-1959 .... **TCLC 2; DAM DRAM**
See also CA 105; 152; DLB 7; MTCW 2

Anderson, Poul (William) 1926- .... **CLC 15**
See also AAYA 5; CA 1-4R, 181; CAAE 181; CAAS 2; CANR 2, 15, 34, 64; CLR 58; DLB 8; INT CANR-15; MTCW 1, 2; SATA 90; SATA-Brief 39; SATA-Essay 106

Anderson, Robert (Woodruff)
1917- .... **CLC 23; DAM DRAM**
See also AITN 1; CA 21-24R; CANR 32; DLB 7

Anderson, Sherwood 1876-1941 ..... **TCLC 1, 10, 24; DA; DAB; DAC; DAM MST, NOV; SSC 1; WLC**
See also AAYA 30; CA 104; 121; CANR 61; CDALB 1917-1929; DA3; DLB 4, 9, 86; DLBD 1; MTCW 1, 2

Andier, Pierre
See Desnos, Robert

Andouard
See Giraudoux, (Hippolyte) Jean

Andrade, Carlos Drummond de ...... **CLC 18**
See also Drummond de Andrade, Carlos

Andrade, Mario de 1893-1945 .... **TCLC 43**

Andreae, Johann V(alentin)
1586-1654 .... **LC 32**
See also DLB 164

Andreas-Salome, Lou 1861-1937 ... **TCLC 56**
See also CA 178; DLB 66

Andress, Lesley
See Sanders, Lawrence

Andrewes, Lancelot 1555-1626 .... **LC 5**
See also DLB 151, 172

Andrews, Cicily Fairfield
See West, Rebecca

Andrews, Elton V.
See Pohl, Frederik

Andreyev, Leonid (Nikolaevich) 1871-1919
TCLC 3
See also CA 104

Andric, Ivo 1892-1975 .... **CLC 8; SSC 36**
See also CA 81-84; 57-60; CANR 43, 60; DLB 147; MTCW 1

Androvar
See Prado (Calvo), Pedro

Angelique, Pierre
See Bataille, Georges

Angell, Roger 1920- .... **CLC 26**
See also CA 57-60; CANR 13, 44, 70; DLB 171, 185

Angelou, Maya 1928- .... **CLC 12, 35, 64, 77; BLC 1; DA; DAB; DAC; DAM MST, MULT, POET, POP; WLCS**
See also AAYA 7, 20; BW 2, 3; CA 65-68; CANR 19, 42, 65; CDALBS; CLR 53; DA3; DLB 38; MTCW 1, 2; SATA 49

Anna Comnena 1083-1153 .... **CMLC 25**

Annensky, Innokenty (Fyodorovich)
1856-1909 .... **TCLC 14**
See also CA 110; 155

Annunzio, Gabriele d'
See D'Annunzio, Gabriele

Anodos
See Coleridge, Mary E(lizabeth)

Anon, Charles Robert
See Pessoa, Fernando (Antonio Nogueira)

Anouilh, Jean (Marie Lucien Pierre)
1910-1987 .... **CLC 1, 3, 8, 13, 40, 50; DAM DRAM; DC 8**
See also CA 17-20R; 123; CANR 32; MTCW 1, 2

Anthony, Florence
See Ai

Anthony, John
See Ciardi, John (Anthony)

Anthony, Peter
See Shaffer, Anthony (Joshua); Shaffer, Peter (Levin)

Anthony, Piers 1934- .... **CLC 35; DAM POP**
See also AAYA 11; CA 21-24R; CANR 28, 56, 73; DLB 8; MTCW 1, 2; SAAS 22; SATA 84

Anthony, Susan B(rownell)
1916-1991 .... **TCLC 84**
See also CA 89-92; 134

Antoine, Marc
See Proust, (Valentin-Louis-George-Eugene-) Marcel

Antoninus, Brother
See Everson, William (Oliver)

Antonioni, Michelangelo 1912- .... **CLC 20**
See also CA 73-76; CANR 45, 77

Antschel, Paul 1920-1970
See Celan, Paul
See also CA 85-88; CANR 33, 61; MTCW 1

Anwar, Chairil 1922-1949 .... **TCLC 22**
See also CA 121

Anzaldua, Gloria 1942-
See also CA 175; DLB 122; HLCS 1

Apess, William 1798-1839(?) .... **NCLC 73; DAM MULT**
See also DLB 175; NNAL

Apollinaire, Guillaume 1880-1918 .. **TCLC 3, 8, 51; DAM POET; PC 7**
See also Kostrowitzki, Wilhelm Apollinaris de CA 152; MTCW 1

Appelfeld, Aharon 1932- .... **CLC 23, 47**
See also CA 112; 133; CANR 86

Apple, Max (Isaac) 1941- .... **CLC 9, 33**
See also CA 81-84; CANR 19, 54; DLB 130

Appleman, Philip (Dean) 1926- .... **CLC 51**
See also CA 13-16R; CAAS 18; CANR 6, 29, 56

Appleton, Lawrence
See Lovecraft, H(oward) P(hillips)

Apteryx
See Eliot, T(homas) S(tearns)

Apuleius, (Lucius Madaurensis)
125(?)-175(?) .... **CMLC 1**
See also DLB 211

Aquin, Hubert 1929-1977 .... **CLC 15**
See also CA 105; DLB 53

Aquinas, Thomas 1224(?)-1274 ..... **CMLC 33**
See also DLB 115

Aragon, Louis 1897-1982 .. **CLC 3, 22; DAM NOV, POET**
See also CA 69-72; 108; CANR 28, 71; DLB 72; MTCW 1, 2

Arany, Janos 1817-1882 .... **NCLC 34**

Aranyos, Kakay
See Mikszath, Kalman

Arbuthnot, John 1667-1735 .... **LC 1**
See also DLB 101

Archer, Herbert Winslow
See Mencken, H(enry) L(ouis)

Archer, Jeffrey (Howard) 1940- ...... **CLC 28; DAM POP**
See also AAYA 16; BEST 89:3; CA 77-80; CANR 22, 52; DA3; INT CANR-22

Archer, Jules 1915- .... **CLC 12**
See also CA 9-12R; CANR 6, 69; SAAS 5; SATA 4, 85

Beecher, John 1904-1980 .... **CLC 6**
See also AITN 1; CA 5-8R; 105; CANR 8

Beer, Johann 1655-1700 .... **LC 5**
See also DLB 168

Beer, Patricia 1924-1999 .... **CLC 58**
See also CA 61-64; 183; CANR 13, 46;
DLB 40

Beerbohm, Max
See Beerbohm, (Henry) Max(imilian)

Beerbohm, (Henry) Max(imilian) 1872-1956
TCLC 1, 24
See also CA 104; 154; CANR 79; DLB 34,
100

Beer-Hofmann, Richard
1866-1945 .... **TCLC 60**
See also CA 160; DLB 81

Begiebing, Robert J(ohn) 1946- .... **CLC 70**
See also CA 122; CANR 40

Behan, Brendan 1923-1964 ...... **CLC 1, 8, 11,
15, 79; DAM DRAM**
See also CA 73-76; CANR 33; CDBLB
1945-1960; DLB 13; MTCW 1, 2

Behn, Aphra 1640(?)-1689 .... **LC 1, 30, 42;
DA; DAB; DAC; DAM DRAM, MST,
NOV, POET; DC 4; PC 13; WLC**
See also DA3; DLB 39, 80, 131

Behrman, S(amuel) N(athaniel) 1893-1973
CLC 40
See also CA 13-16; 45-48; CAP 1; DLB 7,
44

Belasco, David 1853-1931 .... **TCLC 3**
See also CA 104; 168; DLB 7

Belcheva, Elisaveta 1893- .... **CLC 10**
See also Bagryana, Elisaveta

Beldone, Phil "Cheech"
See Ellison, Harlan (Jay)

Beleno
See Azuela, Mariano

Belinski, Vissarion Grigoryevich 1811-1848
NCLC 5
See also DLB 198

Belitt, Ben 1911- .... **CLC 22**
See also CA 13-16R; CAAS 4; CANR 7,
77; DLB 5

Bell, Gertrude (Margaret Lowthian)
1868-1926 .... **TCLC 67**
See also CA 167; DLB 174

Bell, J. Freeman
See Zangwill, Israel

Bell, James Madison 1826-1902 ... **TCLC 43;
BLC 1; DAM MULT**
See also BW 1; CA 122; 124; DLB 50

Bell, Madison Smartt 1957- ...... **CLC 41, 102**
See also CA 111, 183; CAAE 183; CANR
28, 54, 73; MTCW 1

Bell, Marvin (Hartley) 1937- ...... **CLC 8, 31;
DAM POET**
See also CA 21-24R; CAAS 14; CANR 59;
DLB 5; MTCW 1

Bell, W. L. D.
See Mencken, H(enry) L(ouis)

Bellamy, Atwood C.
See Mencken, H(enry) L(ouis)

Bellamy, Edward 1850-1898 .... **NCLC 4**
See also DLB 12

Belli, Gioconda 1949-
See also CA 152; HLCS 1

Bellin, Edward J.
See Kuttner, Henry

**Belloc, (Joseph) Hilaire (Pierre Sebastien
Rene Swanton)** 1870- .... **TCLC 7, 18;
DAM POET; PC 24**
See also CA 106; 152; DLB 19, 100, 141,
174; MTCW 1; SATA 112; YABC 1

Belloc, Joseph Peter Rene Hilaire
See Belloc, (Joseph) Hilaire (Pierre Sebastien Rene Swanton)

Belloc, Joseph Pierre Hilaire
See Belloc, (Joseph) Hilaire (Pierre Sebastien Rene Swanton)

Belloc, M. A.
See Lowndes, Marie Adelaide (Belloc)

Bellow, Saul 1915- . **CLC 1, 2, 3, 6, 8, 10, 13,
15, 25, 33, 34, 63, 79; DA; DAB; DAC;
DAM MST, NOV, POP; SSC 14; WLC**
See also AITN 2; BEST 89:3; CA 5-8R;
CABS 1; CANR 29, 53; CDALB 1941-
1968; DA3; DLB 2, 28; DLBD 3; DLBY
82; MTCW 1, 2

Belser, Reimond Karel Maria de 1929-
See Ruyslinck, Ward
See also CA 152

Bely, Andrey .... **TCLC 7; PC 11**
See also Bugayev, Boris Nikolayevich
MTCW 1

Belyi, Andrei
See Bugayev, Boris Nikolayevich

Benary, Margot
See Benary-Isbert, Margot

Benary-Isbert, Margot 1889-1979 .... **CLC 12**
See also CA 5-8R; 89-92; CANR 4, 72;
CLR 12; MAICYA; SATA 2; SATA-Obit
21

Benavente (y Martinez), Jacinto 1866-1954
**TCLC 3; DAM DRAM, MULT; HLCS
1**
See also CA 106; 131; CANR 81; HW 1, 2;
MTCW 1, 2

Benchley, Peter (Bradford) 1940- . **CLC 4, 8;
DAM NOV, POP**
See also AAYA 14; AITN 2; CA 17-20R;
CANR 12, 35, 66; MTCW 1, 2; SATA 3,
89

Benchley, Robert (Charles)
1889-1945 .... **TCLC 1, 55**
See also CA 105; 153; DLB 11

Benda, Julien 1867-1956 .... **TCLC 60**
See also CA 120; 154

Benedict, Ruth (Fulton)
1887-1948 .... **TCLC 60**
See also CA 158

Benedict, Saint c. 480-c. 547 .... **CMLC 29**

Benedikt, Michael 1935- .... **CLC 4, 14**
See also CA 13-16R; CANR 7; DLB 5

Benet, Juan 1927- .... **CLC 28**
See also CA 143

Benet, Stephen Vincent 1898-1943 . **TCLC 7;
DAM POET; SSC 10**
See also CA 104; 152; DA3; DLB 4, 48,
102; DLBY 97; MTCW 1; YABC 1

Benet, William Rose 1886-1950 .... **TCLC 28;
DAM POET**
See also CA 118; 152; DLB 45

Benford, Gregory (Albert) 1941- ..... **CLC 52**
See also CA 69-72, 175; CAAE 175; CAAS
27; CANR 12, 24, 49; DLBY 82

Bengtsson, Frans (Gunnar)
1894-1954 .... **TCLC 48**
See also CA 170

Benjamin, David
See Slavitt, David R(ytman)

Benjamin, Lois
See Gould, Lois

Benjamin, Walter 1892-1940 .... **TCLC 39**
See also CA 164

Benn, Gottfried 1886-1956 .... **TCLC 3**
See also CA 106; 153; DLB 56

Bennett, Alan 1934- .... **CLC 45, 77; DAB;
DAM MST**
See also CA 103; CANR 35, 55; MTCW 1,
2

Bennett, (Enoch) Arnold
1867-1931 .... **TCLC 5, 20**
See also CA 106; 155; CDBLB 1890-1914;
DLB 10, 34, 98, 135; MTCW 2

Bennett, Elizabeth
See Mitchell, Margaret (Munnerlyn)

Bennett, George Harold 1930-
See Bennett, Hal
See also BW 1; CA 97-100; CANR 87

Bennett, Hal .... **CLC 5**
See also Bennett, George Harold DLB 33

Bennett, Jay 1912- .... **CLC 35**
See also AAYA 10; CA 69-72; CANR 11,
42, 79; JRDA; SAAS 4; SATA 41, 87;
SATA-Brief 27

Bennett, Louise (Simone) 1919- ...... **CLC 28;
BLC 1; DAM MULT**
See also BW 2, 3; CA 151; DLB 117

Benson, E(dward) F(rederic) 1867-1940
TCLC 27
See also CA 114; 157; DLB 135, 153

Benson, Jackson J. 1930- .... **CLC 34**
See also CA 25-28R; DLB 111

Benson, Sally 1900-1972 .... **CLC 17**
See also CA 19-20; 37-40R; CAP 1; SATA
1, 35; SATA-Obit 27

Benson, Stella 1892-1933 .... **TCLC 17**
See also CA 117; 155; DLB 36, 162

Bentham, Jeremy 1748-1832 .... **NCLC 38**
See also DLB 107, 158

Bentley, E(dmund) C(lerihew) 1875-1956
TCLC 12
See also CA 108; DLB 70

Bentley, Eric (Russell) 1916- .... **CLC 24**
See also CA 5-8R; CANR 6, 67; INT
CANR-6

Beranger, Pierre Jean de
1780-1857 .... **NCLC 34**

Berdyaev, Nicolas
See Berdyaev, Nikolai (Aleksandrovich)

Berdyaev, Nikolai (Aleksandrovich)
1874-1948 .... **TCLC 67**
See also CA 120; 157

Berdyayev, Nikolai (Aleksandrovich)
See Berdyaev, Nikolai (Aleksandrovich)

Berendt, John (Lawrence) 1939- ...... **CLC 86**
See also CA 146; CANR 75; DA3; MTCW
1

Beresford, J(ohn) D(avys)
1873-1947 .... **TCLC 81**
See also CA 112; 155; DLB 162, 178, 197

Bergelson, David 1884-1952 .... **TCLC 81**

Berger, Colonel
See Malraux, (Georges-)Andre

Berger, John (Peter) 1926- .... **CLC 2, 19**
See also CA 81-84; CANR 51, 78; DLB 14,
207

Berger, Melvin H. 1927- .... **CLC 12**
See also CA 5-8R; CANR 4; CLR 32;
SAAS 2; SATA 5, 88
Berger, Thomas (Louis) 1924- .. **CLC 3, 5, 8, 11, 18, 38; DAM NOV**
See also CA 1-4R; CANR 5, 28, 51; DLB
2; DLBY 80; INT CANR-28; MTCW 1, 2
Bergman, (Ernst) Ingmar 1918- ...... **CLC 16, 72**
See also CA 81-84; CANR 33, 70; MTCW 2
Bergson, Henri(-Louis) 1859-1941 . **TCLC 32**
See also CA 164
Bergstein, Eleanor 1938- .... **CLC 4**
See also CA 53-56; CANR 5
Berkoff, Steven 1937- .... **CLC 56**
See also CA 104; CANR 72
Bermant, Chaim (Icyk) 1929- .... **CLC 40**
See also CA 57-60; CANR 6, 31, 57
Bern, Victoria
See Fisher, M(ary) F(rances) K(ennedy)
Bernanos, (Paul Louis) Georges 1888-1948
TCLC 3
See also CA 104; 130; DLB 72
Bernard, April 1956- .... **CLC 59**
See also CA 131
Berne, Victoria
See Fisher, M(ary) F(rances) K(ennedy)
Bernhard, Thomas 1931-1989 ..... **CLC 3, 32, 61**
See also CA 85-88; 127; CANR 32, 57;
DLB 85, 124; MTCW 1
Bernhardt, Sarah (Henriette Rosine)
1844-1923 .... **TCLC 75**
See also CA 157
Berriault, Gina 1926- . **CLC 54, 109; SSC 30**
See also CA 116; 129; CANR 66; DLB 130
Berrigan, Daniel 1921- .... **CLC 4**
See also CA 33-36R; CAAS 1; CANR 11,
43, 78; DLB 5
Berrigan, Edmund Joseph Michael, Jr.
1934-1983
See Berrigan, Ted
See also CA 61-64; 110; CANR 14
Berrigan, Ted .... **CLC 37**
See also Berrigan, Edmund Joseph Michael,
Jr. DLB 5, 169
Berry, Charles Edward Anderson 1931-
See Berry, Chuck
See also CA 115
Berry, Chuck .... **CLC 17**
See also Berry, Charles Edward Anderson
Berry, Jonas
See Ashbery, John (Lawrence)
Berry, Wendell (Erdman) 1934- ... **CLC 4, 6, 8, 27, 46; DAM POET; PC 28**
See also AITN 1; CA 73-76; CANR 50, 73;
DLB 5, 6; MTCW 1
Berryman, John 1914-1972 ... **CLC 1, 2, 3, 4, 6, 8, 10, 13, 25, 62; DAM POET**
See also CA 13-16; 33-36R; CABS 2;
CANR 35; CAP 1; CDALB 1941-1968;
DLB 48; MTCW 1, 2
Bertolucci, Bernardo 1940- .... **CLC 16**
See also CA 106
Berton, Pierre (Francis Demarigny) 1920-
CLC 104
See also CA 1-4R; CANR 2, 56; DLB 68;
SATA 99

Bertrand, Aloysius 1807-1841 .... **NCLC 31**
Bertran de Born c. 1140-1215 .... **CMLC 5**
Besant, Annie (Wood) 1847-1933 ..... **TCLC 9**
See also CA 105
Bessie, Alvah 1904-1985 .... **CLC 23**
See also CA 5-8R; 116; CANR 2, 80; DLB
26
Bethlen, T. D.
See Silverberg, Robert
Beti, Mongo . **CLC 27; BLC 1; DAM MULT**
See also Biyidi, Alexandre CANR 79
Betjeman, John 1906-1984 ...... **CLC 2, 6, 10, 34, 43; DAB; DAM MST, POET**
See also CA 9-12R; 112; CANR 33, 56;
CDBLB 1945-1960; DA3; DLB 20;
DLBY 84; MTCW 1, 2
Bettelheim, Bruno 1903-1990 .... **CLC 79**
See also CA 81-84; 131; CANR 23, 61;
DA3; MTCW 1, 2
Betti, Ugo 1892-1953 .... **TCLC 5**
See also CA 104; 155
Betts, Doris (Waugh) 1932- ...... **CLC 3, 6, 28**
See also CA 13-16R; CANR 9, 66, 77;
DLBY 82; INT CANR-9
Bevan, Alistair
See Roberts, Keith (John Kingston)
Bey, Pilaff
See Douglas, (George) Norman
Bialik, Chaim Nachman
1873-1934 .... **TCLC 25**
See also CA 170
Bickerstaff, Isaac
See Swift, Jonathan
Bidart, Frank 1939- .... **CLC 33**
See also CA 140
Bienek, Horst 1930- .... **CLC 7, 11**
See also CA 73-76; DLB 75
Bierce, Ambrose (Gwinett) 1842-1914(?)
**TCLC 1, 7, 44; DA; DAC; DAM MST;
SSC 9; WLC**
See also CA 104; 139; CANR 78; CDALB
1865-1917; DA3; DLB 11, 12, 23, 71, 74,
186
Biggers, Earl Derr 1884-1933 .... **TCLC 65**
See also CA 108; 153
Billings, Josh
See Shaw, Henry Wheeler
Billington, (Lady) Rachel (Mary)
1942- .... **CLC 43**
See also AITN 2; CA 33-36R; CANR 44
Binyon, T(imothy) J(ohn) 1936- .... **CLC 34**
See also CA 111; CANR 28
Bioy Casares, Adolfo 1914-1999 ... **CLC 4, 8, 13, 88; DAM MULT; HLC 1; SSC 17**
See also CA 29-32R; 177; CANR 19, 43,
66; DLB 113; HW 1, 2; MTCW 1, 2
Bird, Cordwainer
See Ellison, Harlan (Jay)
Bird, Robert Montgomery
1806-1854 .... **NCLC 1**
See also DLB 202
Birkerts, Sven 1951- .... **CLC 116**
See also CA 128; 133; 176; CAAE 176;
CAAS 29; INT 133
Birney, (Alfred) Earle 1904-1995 .. **CLC 1, 4, 6, 11; DAC; DAM MST, POET**
See also CA 1-4R; CANR 5, 20; DLB 88;
MTCW 1

Biruni, al 973-1048(?) .... **CMLC 28**
Bishop, Elizabeth 1911-1979 ..... **CLC 1, 4, 9, 13, 15, 32; DA; DAC; DAM MST, POET; PC 3**
See also CA 5-8R; 89-92; CABS 2; CANR
26, 61; CDALB 1968-1988; DA3; DLB
5, 169; MTCW 1, 2; SATA-Obit 24
Bishop, John 1935- .... **CLC 10**
See also CA 105
Bissett, Bill 1939- .... **CLC 18; PC 14**
See also CA 69-72; CAAS 19; CANR 15;
DLB 53; MTCW 1
Bissoondath, Neil (Devindra)
1955- .... **CLC 120; DAC**
See also CA 136
Bitov, Andrei (Georgievich) 1937- ... **CLC 57**
See also CA 142
Biyidi, Alexandre 1932-
See Beti, Mongo
See also BW 1, 3; CA 114; 124; CANR 81;
DA3; MTCW 1, 2
Bjarme, Brynjolf
See Ibsen, Henrik (Johan)
Bjoernson, Bjoernstjerne (Martinius)
1832-1910 .... **TCLC 7, 37**
See also CA 104
Black, Robert
See Holdstock, Robert P.
Blackburn, Paul 1926-1971 .... **CLC 9, 43**
See also CA 81-84; 33-36R; CANR 34;
DLB 16; DLBY 81
Black Elk 1863-1950 .... **TCLC 33; DAM MULT**
See also CA 144; MTCW 1; NNAL
Black Hobart
See Sanders, (James) Ed(ward)
Blacklin, Malcolm
See Chambers, Aidan
Blackmore, R(ichard) D(oddridge)
1825-1900 .... **TCLC 27**
See also CA 120; DLB 18
Blackmur, R(ichard) P(almer) 1904-1965
CLC 2, 24
See also CA 11-12; 25-28R; CANR 71;
CAP 1; DLB 63
Black Tarantula
See Acker, Kathy
Blackwood, Algernon (Henry) 1869-1951
TCLC 5
See also CA 105; 150; DLB 153, 156, 178
Blackwood, Caroline 1931-1996 .... **CLC 6, 9, 100**
See also CA 85-88; 151; CANR 32, 61, 65;
DLB 14, 207; MTCW 1
Blade, Alexander
See Hamilton, Edmond; Silverberg, Robert
Blaga, Lucian 1895-1961 .... **CLC 75**
See also CA 157
Blair, Eric (Arthur) 1903-1950
See Orwell, George
See also CA 104; 132; DA; DAB; DAC;
DAM MST, NOV; DA3; MTCW 1, 2;
SATA 29
Blair, Hugh 1718-1800 .... **NCLC 75**
Blais, Marie-Claire 1939- .... **CLC 2, 4, 6, 13, 22; DAC; DAM MST**
See also CA 21-24R; CAAS 4; CANR 38,
75; DLB 53; MTCW 1, 2

Blaise, Clark 1940- .... **CLC 29**
  See also AITN 2; CA 53-56; CAAS 3;
  CANR 5, 66; DLB 53
Blake, Fairley
  See De Voto, Bernard (Augustine)
Blake, Nicholas
  See Day Lewis, C(ecil)
  See also DLB 77
Blake, William 1757-1827 .... **NCLC 13, 37,**
  57; DA; DAB; DAC; DAM MST,
  POET; PC 12; WLC
  See also CDBLB 1789-1832; CLR 52;
  DA3; DLB 93, 163; MAICYA; SATA 30
Blasco Ibanez, Vicente
  1867-1928 .... **TCLC 12; DAM NOV**
  See also CA 110; 131; CANR 81; DA3; HW
  1, 2; MTCW 1
Blatty, William Peter 1928- .... **CLC 2; DAM**
  POP
  See also CA 5-8R; CANR 9
Bleeck, Oliver
  See Thomas, Ross (Elmore)
Blessing, Lee 1949- .... **CLC 54**
Blish, James (Benjamin) 1921-1975 . **CLC 14**
  See also CA 1-4R; 57-60; CANR 3; DLB
  8; MTCW 1; SATA 66
Bliss, Reginald
  See Wells, H(erbert) G(eorge)
Blixen, Karen (Christentze Dinesen)
  1885-1962
  See Dinesen, Isak
  See also CA 25-28; CANR 22, 50; CAP 2;
  DA3; MTCW 1, 2; SATA 44
Bloch, Robert (Albert) 1917-1994 .... **CLC 33**
  See also AAYA 29; CA 5-8R, 179; 146;
  CAAE 179; CAAS 20; CANR 5, 78;
  DA3; DLB 44; INT CANR-5; MTCW 1;
  SATA 12; SATA-Obit 82
Blok, Alexander (Alexandrovich) 1880-1921
  TCLC 5; PC 21
  See also CA 104; 183
Blom, Jan
  See Breytenbach, Breyten
Bloom, Harold 1930- .... **CLC 24, 103**
  See also CA 13-16R; CANR 39, 75; DLB
  67; MTCW 1
Bloomfield, Aurelius
  See Bourne, Randolph S(illiman)
Blount, Roy (Alton), Jr. 1941- .... **CLC 38**
  See also CA 53-56; CANR 10, 28, 61; INT
  CANR-28; MTCW 1, 2
Bloy, Leon 1846-1917 .... **TCLC 22**
  See also CA 121; 183; DLB 123
Blume, Judy (Sussman) 1938- .. **CLC 12, 30;**
  DAM NOV, POP
  See also AAYA 3, 26; CA 29-32R; CANR
  13, 37, 66; CLR 2, 15; DA3; DLB 52;
  JRDA; MAICYA; MTCW 1, 2; SATA 2,
  31, 79
Blunden, Edmund (Charles)
  1896-1974 .... **CLC 2, 56**
  See also CA 17-18; 45-48; CANR 54; CAP
  2; DLB 20, 100, 155; MTCW 1
Bly, Robert (Elwood) 1926- .... **CLC 1, 2, 5,**
  10, 15, 38, 128; DAM POET
  See also CA 5-8R; CANR 41, 73; DA3;
  DLB 5; MTCW 1, 2
Boas, Franz 1858-1942 .... **TCLC 56**
  See also CA 115; 181
Bobette
  See Simenon, Georges (Jacques Christian)

Boccaccio, Giovanni 1313-1375 ... **CMLC 13;**
  SSC 10
Bochco, Steven 1943- .... **CLC 35**
  See also AAYA 11; CA 124; 138
Bodel, Jean 1167(?)-1210 .... **CMLC 28**
Bodenheim, Maxwell 1892-1954 .... **TCLC 44**
  See also CA 110; DLB 9, 45
Bodker, Cecil 1927- .... **CLC 21**
  See also CA 73-76; CANR 13, 44; CLR 23;
  MAICYA; SATA 14
Boell, Heinrich (Theodor)
  1917-1985 ..... **CLC 2, 3, 6, 9, 11, 15, 27,**
  32, 72; DA; DAB; DAC; DAM MST,
  NOV; SSC 23; WLC
  See also CA 21-24R; 116; CANR 24; DA3;
  DLB 69; DLBY 85; MTCW 1, 2
Boerne, Alfred
  See Doeblin, Alfred
Boethius 480(?)-524(?) .... **CMLC 15**
  See also DLB 115
Boff, Leonardo (Genezio Darci) 1938-
  See also CA 150; DAM MULT; HLC 1;
  HW 2
Bogan, Louise 1897-1970 .... **CLC 4, 39, 46,**
  93; DAM POET; PC 12
  See also CA 73-76; 25-28R; CANR 33, 82;
  DLB 45, 169; MTCW 1, 2
Bogarde, Dirk 1921-1999 .... **CLC 19**
  See also Van Den Bogarde, Derek Jules
  Gaspard Ulric Niven CA 179; DLB 14
Bogosian, Eric 1953- .... **CLC 45**
  See also CA 138
Bograd, Larry 1953- .... **CLC 35**
  See also CA 93-96; CANR 57; SAAS 21;
  SATA 33, 89
Boiardo, Matteo Maria 1441-1494 .... **LC 6**
Boileau-Despreaux, Nicolas 1636-1711 . **LC 3**
Bojer, Johan 1872-1959 .... **TCLC 64**
Boland, Eavan (Aisling) 1944- .. **CLC 40, 67,**
  113; DAM POET
  See also CA 143; CANR 61; DLB 40;
  MTCW 2
Boll, Heinrich
  See Boell, Heinrich (Theodor)
Bolt, Lee
  See Faust, Frederick (Schiller)
Bolt, Robert (Oxton) 1924-1995 ...... **CLC 14;**
  DAM DRAM
  See also CA 17-20R; 147; CANR 35, 67;
  DLB 13; MTCW 1
Bombal, Maria Luisa 1910-1980 ...... **SSC 37;**
  HLCS 1
  See also CA 127; CANR 72; HW 1
Bombet, Louis-Alexandre-Cesar
  See Stendhal
Bomkauf
  See Kaufman, Bob (Garnell)
Bonaventura .... **NCLC 35**
  See also DLB 90
Bond, Edward 1934- .... **CLC 4, 6, 13, 23;**
  DAM DRAM
  See also CA 25-28R; CANR 38, 67; DLB
  13; MTCW 1
Bonham, Frank 1914-1989 .... **CLC 12**
  See also AAYA 1; CA 9-12R; CANR 4, 36;
  JRDA; MAICYA; SAAS 3; SATA 1, 49;
  SATA-Obit 62

Bonnefoy, Yves 1923- .. **CLC 9, 15, 58; DAM**
  MST, POET
  See also CA 85-88; CANR 33, 75; MTCW
  1, 2
Bontemps, Arna(ud Wendell)
  1902-1973 ..... **CLC 1, 18; BLC 1; DAM**
  MULT, NOV, POET
  See also BW 1; CA 1-4R; 41-44R; CANR
  4, 35; CLR 6; DA3; DLB 48, 51; JRDA;
  MAICYA; MTCW 1, 2; SATA 2, 44;
  SATA-Obit 24
Booth, Martin 1944- .... **CLC 13**
  See also CA 93-96; CAAS 2
Booth, Philip 1925- .... **CLC 23**
  See also CA 5-8R; CANR 5; DLBY 82
Booth, Wayne C(layson) 1921- .... **CLC 24**
  See also CA 1-4R; CAAS 5; CANR 3, 43;
  DLB 67
Borchert, Wolfgang 1921-1947 .... **TCLC 5**
  See also CA 104; DLB 69, 124
Borel, Petrus 1809-1859 .... **NCLC 41**
Borges, Jorge Luis 1899-1986 ... **CLC 1, 2, 3,**
  4, 6, 8, 9, 10, 13, 19, 44, 48, 83; DA;
  DAB; DAC; DAM MST, MULT; HLC
  1; PC 22; SSC 4; WLC
  See also AAYA 26; CA 21-24R; CANR 19,
  33, 75; DA3; DLB 113; DLBY 86; HW 1,
  2; MTCW 1, 2
Borowski, Tadeusz 1922-1951 .... **TCLC 9**
  See also CA 106; 154
Borrow, George (Henry)
  1803-1881 .... **NCLC 9**
  See also DLB 21, 55, 166
Bosch (Gavino), Juan 1909-
  See also CA 151; DAM MST, MULT; DLB
  145; HLCS 1; HW 1, 2
Bosman, Herman Charles
  1905-1951 .... **TCLC 49**
  See also Malan, Herman CA 160
Bosschere, Jean de 1878(?)-1953 ... **TCLC 19**
  See also CA 115
Boswell, James 1740-1795 ...... **LC 4, 50; DA;**
  DAB; DAC; DAM MST; WLC
  See also CDBLB 1660-1789; DLB 104, 142
Bottoms, David 1949- .... **CLC 53**
  See also CA 105; CANR 22; DLB 120;
  DLBY 83
Boucicault, Dion 1820-1890 .... **NCLC 41**
Boucolon, Maryse 1937(?)-
  See Conde, Maryse
  See also BW 3; CA 110; CANR 30, 53, 76
Bourget, Paul (Charles Joseph) 1852-1935
  TCLC 12
  See also CA 107; DLB 123
Bourjaily, Vance (Nye) 1922- .... **CLC 8, 62**
  See also CA 1-4R; CAAS 1; CANR 2, 72;
  DLB 2, 143
Bourne, Randolph S(illiman) 1886-1918
  TCLC 16
  See also CA 117; 155; DLB 63
Bova, Ben(jamin William) 1932- ...... **CLC 45**
  See also AAYA 16; CA 5-8R; CAAS 18;
  CANR 11, 56; CLR 3; DLBY 81; INT
  CANR-11; MAICYA; MTCW 1; SATA 6,
  68
Bowen, Elizabeth (Dorothea Cole) 1899-1973
  CLC 1, 3, 6, 11, 15, 22, 118; DAM NOV;
  SSC 3, 28
  See also CA 17-18; 41-44R; CANR 35;
  CAP 2; CDBLB 1945-1960; DA3; DLB
  15, 162; MTCW 1, 2

Bowering, George 1935- .... **CLC 15, 47**
See also CA 21-24R; CAAS 16; CANR 10;
DLB 53

Bowering, Marilyn R(uthe) 1949- .... **CLC 32**
See also CA 101; CANR 49

Bowers, Edgar 1924- .... **CLC 9**
See also CA 5-8R; CANR 24; DLB 5

Bowie, David .... **CLC 17**
See also Jones, David Robert

Bowles, Jane (Sydney) 1917-1973 ..... **CLC 3, 68**
See also CA 19-20; 41-44R; CAP 2

Bowles, Paul (Frederick) 1910- ..... **CLC 1, 2, 19, 53; SSC 3**
See also CA 1-4R; CAAS 1; CANR 1, 19, 50, 75; DA3; DLB 5, 6; MTCW 1, 2

Box, Edgar
See Vidal, Gore

Boyd, Nancy
See Millay, Edna St. Vincent

Boyd, William 1952- .... **CLC 28, 53, 70**
See also CA 114; 120; CANR 51, 71

Boyle, Kay 1902-1992 .... **CLC 1, 5, 19, 58, 121; SSC 5**
See also CA 13-16R; 140; CAAS 1; CANR 29, 61; DLB 4, 9, 48, 86; DLBY 93; MTCW 1, 2

Boyle, Mark
See Kienzle, William X(avier)

Boyle, Patrick 1905-1982 .... **CLC 19**
See also CA 127

Boyle, T. C. 1948-
See Boyle, T(homas) Coraghessan

Boyle, T(homas) Coraghessan 1948- .... **CLC 36, 55, 90; DAM POP; SSC 16**
See also BEST 90:4; CA 120; CANR 44, 76; DA3; DLBY 86; MTCW 2

Boz
See Dickens, Charles (John Huffam)

Brackenridge, Hugh Henry 1748-1816 .... **NCLC 7**
See also DLB 11, 37

Bradbury, Edward P.
See Moorcock, Michael (John)
See also MTCW 2

Bradbury, Malcolm (Stanley) 1932- .... **CLC 32, 61; DAM NOV**
See also CA 1-4R; CANR 1, 33; DA3; DLB 14, 207; MTCW 1, 2

Bradbury, Ray (Douglas) 1920- .... **CLC 1, 3, 10, 15, 42, 98; DA; DAB; DAC; DAM MST, NOV, POP; SSC 29; WLC**
See also AAYA 15; AITN 1, 2; CA 1-4R; CANR 2, 30, 75; CDALB 1968-1988; DA3; DLB 2, 8; MTCW 1, 2; SATA 11, 64

Bradford, Gamaliel 1863-1932 .... **TCLC 36**
See also CA 160; DLB 17

Bradley, David (Henry), Jr. 1950- ... **CLC 23, 118; BLC 1; DAM MULT**
See also BW 1, 3; CA 104; CANR 26, 81; DLB 33

Bradley, John Ed(mund, Jr.) 1958- . **CLC 55**
See also CA 139

Bradley, Marion Zimmer 1930- ...... **CLC 30; DAM POP**
See also AAYA 9; CA 57-60; CAAS 10; CANR 7, 31, 51, 75; DA3; DLB 8; MTCW 1, 2; SATA 90

Bradstreet, Anne 1612(?)-1672 ...... **LC 4, 30; DA; DAC; DAM MST, POET; PC 10**
See also CDALB 1640-1865; DA3; DLB 24

Brady, Joan 1939- .... **CLC 86**
See also CA 141

Bragg, Melvyn 1939- .... **CLC 10**
See also BEST 89:3; CA 57-60; CANR 10, 48; DLB 14

Brahe, Tycho 1546-1601 .... **LC 45**

Braine, John (Gerard) 1922-1986 . **CLC 1, 3, 41**
See also CA 1-4R; 120; CANR 1, 33; CD-BLB 1945-1960; DLB 15; DLBY 86; MTCW 1

Bramah, Ernest 1868-1942 .... **TCLC 72**
See also CA 156; DLB 70

Brammer, William 1930(?)-1978 ...... **CLC 31**
See also CA 77-80

Brancati, Vitaliano 1907-1954 .... **TCLC 12**
See also CA 109

Brancato, Robin F(idler) 1936- .... **CLC 35**
See also AAYA 9; CA 69-72; CANR 11, 45; CLR 32; JRDA; SAAS 9; SATA 97

Brand, Max
See Faust, Frederick (Schiller)

Brand, Millen 1906-1980 .... **CLC 7**
See also CA 21-24R; 97-100; CANR 72

Branden, Barbara .... **CLC 44**
See also CA 148

Brandes, Georg (Morris Cohen) 1842-1927 **TCLC 10**
See also CA 105

Brandys, Kazimierz 1916- .... **CLC 62**

Branley, Franklyn M(ansfield) 1915- .... **CLC 21**
See also CA 33-36R; CANR 14, 39; CLR 13; MAICYA; SAAS 16; SATA 4, 68

Brathwaite, Edward (Kamau) 1930- ...... **CLC 11; BLCS; DAM POET**
See also BW 2, 3; CA 25-28R; CANR 11, 26, 47; DLB 125

Brautigan, Richard (Gary) 1935-1984 .... **CLC 1, 3, 5, 9, 12, 34, 42; DAM NOV**
See also CA 53-56; 113; CANR 34; DA3; DLB 2, 5, 206; DLBY 80, 84; MTCW 1; SATA 56

Brave Bird, Mary 1953-
See Crow Dog, Mary (Ellen)
See also NNAL

Braverman, Kate 1950- .... **CLC 67**
See also CA 89-92

Brecht, (Eugen) Bertolt (Friedrich) 1898-1956 .... **TCLC 1, 6, 13, 35; DA; DAB; DAC; DAM DRAM, MST; DC 3; WLC**
See also CA 104; 133; CANR 62; DA3; DLB 56, 124; MTCW 1, 2

Brecht, Eugen Berthold Friedrich
See Brecht, (Eugen) Bertolt (Friedrich)

Bremer, Fredrika 1801-1865 .... **NCLC 11**

Brennan, Christopher John 1870-1932 .... **TCLC 17**
See also CA 117

Brennan, Maeve 1917-1993 .... **CLC 5**
See also CA 81-84; CANR 72

Brent, Linda
See Jacobs, Harriet A(nn)

Brentano, Clemens (Maria) 1778-1842 .... **NCLC 1**
See also DLB 90

Brent of Bin Bin
See Franklin, (Stella Maria Sarah) Miles (Lampe)

Brenton, Howard 1942- .... **CLC 31**
See also CA 69-72; CANR 33, 67; DLB 13; MTCW 1

Breslin, James 1930-1996
See Breslin, Jimmy
See also CA 73-76; CANR 31, 75; DAM NOV; MTCW 1, 2

Breslin, Jimmy .... **CLC 4, 43**
See also Breslin, James AITN 1; DLB 185; MTCW 2

Bresson, Robert 1901- .... **CLC 16**
See also CA 110; CANR 49

Breton, Andre 1896-1966 .. **CLC 2, 9, 15, 54; PC 15**
See also CA 19-20; 25-28R; CANR 40, 60; CAP 2; DLB 65; MTCW 1, 2

Breytenbach, Breyten 1939(?)- .. **CLC 23, 37, 126; DAM POET**
See also CA 113; 129; CANR 61

Bridgers, Sue Ellen 1942- .... **CLC 26**
See also AAYA 8; CA 65-68; CANR 11, 36; CLR 18; DLB 52; JRDA; MAICYA; SAAS 1; SATA 22, 90; SATA-Essay 109

Bridges, Robert (Seymour) 1844-1930 ... **TCLC 1; DAM POET; PC 28**
See also CA 104; 152; CDBLB 1890-1914; DLB 19, 98

Bridie, James .... **TCLC 3**
See also Mavor, Osborne Henry DLB 10

Brin, David 1950- .... **CLC 34**
See also AAYA 21; CA 102; CANR 24, 70; INT CANR-24; SATA 65

Brink, Andre (Philippus) 1935- . **CLC 18, 36, 106**
See also CA 104; CANR 39, 62; INT 103; MTCW 1, 2

Brinsmead, H(esba) F(ay) 1922- ...... **CLC 21**
See also CA 21-24R; CANR 10; CLR 47; MAICYA; SAAS 5; SATA 18, 78

Brittain, Vera (Mary) 1893(?)-1970 . **CLC 23**
See also CA 13-16; 25-28R; CANR 58; CAP 1; DLB 191; MTCW 1, 2

Broch, Hermann 1886-1951 .... **TCLC 20**
See also CA 117; DLB 85, 124

Brock, Rose
See Hansen, Joseph

Brodkey, Harold (Roy) 1930-1996 ... **CLC 56**
See also CA 111; 151; CANR 71; DLB 130

Brodskii, Iosif
See Brodsky, Joseph

Brodsky, Iosif Alexandrovich 1940-1996
See Brodsky, Joseph
See also AITN 1; CA 41-44R; 151; CANR 37; DAM POET; DA3; MTCW 1, 2

Brodsky, Joseph 1940-1996 ..... **CLC 4, 6, 13, 36, 100; PC 9**
See also Brodskii, Iosif; Brodsky, Iosif Alexandrovich MTCW 1

Brodsky, Michael (Mark) 1948- .... **CLC 19**
See also CA 102; CANR 18, 41, 58

Bromell, Henry 1947- .... **CLC 5**
See also CA 53-56; CANR 9

Bromfield, Louis (Brucker)
    1896-1956 .... **TCLC 11**
    See also CA 107; 155; DLB 4, 9, 86
Broner, E(sther) M(asserman)
    1930- .... **CLC 19**
    See also CA 17-20R; CANR 8, 25, 72; DLB
    28
Bronk, William (M.) 1918-1999 .... **CLC 10**
    See also CA 89-92; 177; CANR 23; DLB
    165
Bronstein, Lev Davidovich
    See Trotsky, Leon
Bronte, Anne 1820-1849 .... **NCLC 4, 71**
    See also DA3; DLB 21, 199
Bronte, Charlotte 1816-1855 ...... **NCLC 3, 8,
    33, 58; DA; DAB; DAC; DAM MST,
    NOV; WLC**
    See also AAYA 17; CDBLB 1832-1890;
    DA3; DLB 21, 159, 199
Bronte, Emily (Jane) 1818-1848 ... **NCLC 16,
    35; DA; DAB; DAC; DAM MST, NOV,
    POET; PC 8; WLC**
    See also AAYA 17; CDBLB 1832-1890;
    DA3; DLB 21, 32, 199
Brooke, Frances 1724-1789 .... **LC 6, 48**
    See also DLB 39, 99
Brooke, Henry 1703(?)-1783 .... **LC 1**
    See also DLB 39
Brooke, Rupert (Chawner)
    1887-1915 .... **TCLC 2, 7; DA; DAB;
    DAC; DAM MST, POET; PC 24; WLC**
    See also CA 104; 132; CANR 61; CDBLB
    1914-1945; DLB 19; MTCW 1, 2
Brooke-Haven, P.
    See Wodehouse, P(elham) G(renville)
Brooke-Rose, Christine 1926(?)- ...... **CLC 40**
    See also CA 13-16R; CANR 58; DLB 14
Brookner, Anita 1928- .... **CLC 32, 34, 51;
    DAB; DAM POP**
    See also CA 114; 120; CANR 37, 56, 87;
    DA3; DLB 194; DLBY 87; MTCW 1, 2
Brooks, Cleanth 1906-1994 . **CLC 24, 86, 110**
    See also CA 17-20R; 145; CANR 33, 35;
    DLB 63; DLBY 94; INT CANR-35;
    MTCW 1, 2
Brooks, George
    See Baum, L(yman) Frank
Brooks, Gwendolyn 1917- ..... **CLC 1, 2, 4, 5,
    15, 49, 125; BLC 1; DA; DAC; DAM
    MST, MULT, POET; PC 7; WLC**
    See also AAYA 20; AITN 1; BW 2, 3; CA
    1-4R; CANR 1, 27, 52, 75; CDALB 1941-
    1968; CLR 27; DA3; DLB 5, 76, 165;
    MTCW 1, 2; SATA 6
Brooks, Mel .... **CLC 12**
    See also Kaminsky, Melvin AAYA 13; DLB
    26
Brooks, Peter 1938- .... **CLC 34**
    See also CA 45-48; CANR 1
Brooks, Van Wyck 1886-1963 .... **CLC 29**
    See also CA 1-4R; CANR 6; DLB 45, 63,
    103
Brophy, Brigid (Antonia)
    1929-1995 .... **CLC 6, 11, 29, 105**
    See also CA 5-8R; 149; CAAS 4; CANR
    25, 53; DA3; DLB 14; MTCW 1, 2
Brosman, Catharine Savage 1934- ..... **CLC 9**
    See also CA 61-64; CANR 21, 46
Brossard, Nicole 1943- .... **CLC 115**
    See also CA 122; CAAS 16; DLB 53

Brother Antoninus
    See Everson, William (Oliver)
The Brothers Quay
    See Quay, Stephen; Quay, Timothy
Broughton, T(homas) Alan 1936- ..... **CLC 19**
    See also CA 45-48; CANR 2, 23, 48
Broumas, Olga 1949- .... **CLC 10, 73**
    See also CA 85-88; CANR 20, 69
Brown, Alan 1950- .... **CLC 99**
    See also CA 156
Brown, Charles Brockden
    1771-1810 .... **NCLC 22, 74**
    See also CDALB 1640-1865; DLB 37, 59,
    73
Brown, Christy 1932-1981 .... **CLC 63**
    See also CA 105; 104; CANR 72; DLB 14
Brown, Claude 1937- .... **CLC 30; BLC 1;
    DAM MULT**
    See also AAYA 7; BW 1, 3; CA 73-76;
    CANR 81
Brown, Dee (Alexander) 1908- . **CLC 18, 47;
    DAM POP**
    See also AAYA 30; CA 13-16R; CAAS 6;
    CANR 11, 45, 60; DA3; DLBY 80;
    MTCW 1, 2; SATA 5, 110
Brown, George
    See Wertmueller, Lina
Brown, George Douglas
    1869-1902 .... **TCLC 28**
    See also CA 162
Brown, George Mackay 1921-1996 ... **CLC 5,
    48, 100**
    See also CA 21-24R; 151; CAAS 6; CANR
    12, 37, 67; DLB 14, 27, 139; MTCW 1;
    SATA 35
Brown, (William) Larry 1951- .... **CLC 73**
    See also CA 130; 134; INT 133
Brown, Moses
    See Barrett, William (Christopher)
Brown, Rita Mae 1944- .... **CLC 18, 43, 79;
    DAM NOV, POP**
    See also CA 45-48; CANR 2, 11, 35, 62;
    DA3; INT CANR-11; MTCW 1, 2
Brown, Roderick (Langmere) Haig-
    See Haig-Brown, Roderick (Langmere)
Brown, Rosellen 1939- .... **CLC 32**
    See also CA 77-80; CAAS 10; CANR 14,
    44
Brown, Sterling Allen 1901-1989 ...... **CLC 1,
    23, 59; BLC 1; DAM MULT, POET**
    See also BW 1, 3; CA 85-88; 127; CANR
    26; DA3; DLB 48, 51, 63; MTCW 1, 2
Brown, Will
    See Ainsworth, William Harrison
Brown, William Wells 1813-1884 ... **NCLC 2;
    BLC 1; DAM MULT; DC 1**
    See also DLB 3, 50
Browne, (Clyde) Jackson 1948(?)- ... **CLC 21**
    See also CA 120
Browning, Elizabeth Barrett 1806-1861
    **NCLC 1, 16, 61, 66; DA; DAB; DAC;
    DAM MST, POET; PC 6; WLC**
    See also CDBLB 1832-1890; DA3; DLB
    32, 199
Browning, Robert 1812-1889 . **NCLC 19, 79;
    DA; DAB; DAC; DAM MST, POET;
    PC 2; WLCS**
    See also CDBLB 1832-1890; DA3; DLB
    32, 163; YABC 1

Browning, Tod 1882-1962 .... **CLC 16**
    See also CA 141; 117
Brownson, Orestes Augustus 1803-1876
    NCLC 50
    See also DLB 1, 59, 73
Bruccoli, Matthew J(oseph) 1931- ... **CLC 34**
    See also CA 9-12R; CANR 7, 87; DLB 103
Bruce, Lenny .... **CLC 21**
    See also Schneider, Leonard Alfred
Bruin, John
    See Brutus, Dennis
Brulard, Henri
    See Stendhal
Brulls, Christian
    See Simenon, Georges (Jacques Christian)
Brunner, John (Kilian Houston) 1934-1995
    CLC 8, 10; DAM POP
    See also CA 1-4R; 149; CAAS 8; CANR 2,
    37; MTCW 1, 2
Bruno, Giordano 1548-1600 .... **LC 27**
Brutus, Dennis 1924- .... **CLC 43; BLC 1;
    DAM MULT, POET; PC 24**
    See also BW 2, 3; CA 49-52; CAAS 14;
    CANR 2, 27, 42, 81; DLB 117
Bryan, C(ourtlandt) D(ixon) B(arnes) 1936-
    CLC 29
    See also CA 73-76; CANR 13, 68; DLB
    185; INT CANR-13
Bryan, Michael
    See Moore, Brian
Bryan, William Jennings
    1860-1925 .... **TCLC 99**
Bryant, William Cullen 1794-1878 . **NCLC 6,
    46; DA; DAB; DAC; DAM MST,
    POET; PC 20**
    See also CDALB 1640-1865; DLB 3, 43,
    59, 189
Bryusov, Valery Yakovlevich 1873-1924
    TCLC 10
    See also CA 107; 155
Buchan, John 1875-1940 .... **TCLC 41; DAB;
    DAM POP**
    See also CA 108; 145; DLB 34, 70, 156;
    MTCW 1; YABC 2
Buchanan, George 1506-1582 .... **LC 4**
    See also DLB 152
Buchheim, Lothar-Guenther 1918- .... **CLC 6**
    See also CA 85-88
Buchner, (Karl) Georg 1813-1837 . **NCLC 26**
Buchwald, Art(hur) 1925- .... **CLC 33**
    See also AITN 1; CA 5-8R; CANR 21, 67;
    MTCW 1, 2; SATA 10
Buck, Pearl S(ydenstricker)
    1892-1973 .... **CLC 7, 11, 18, 127; DA;
    DAB; DAC; DAM MST, NOV**
    See also AITN 1; CA 1-4R; 41-44R; CANR
    1, 34; CDALBS; DA3; DLB 9, 102;
    MTCW 1, 2; SATA 1, 25
Buckler, Ernest 1908-1984 .... **CLC 13; DAC;
    DAM MST**
    See also CA 11-12; 114; CAP 1; DLB 68;
    SATA 47
Buckley, Vincent (Thomas)
    1925-1988 .... **CLC 57**
    See also CA 101
Buckley, William F(rank), Jr. 1925- . **CLC 7,
    18, 37; DAM POP**
    See also AITN 1; CA 1-4R; CANR 1, 24,
    53; DA3; DLB 137; DLBY 80; INT
    CANR-24; MTCW 1, 2

Buechner, (Carl) Frederick 1926- . CLC 2, 4,
6, 9; DAM NOV
See also CA 13-16R; CANR 11, 39, 64;
DLBY 80; INT CANR-11; MTCW 1, 2
Buell, John (Edward) 1927- .... CLC 10
See also CA 1-4R; CANR 71; DLB 53
Buero Vallejo, Antonio 1916- ..... CLC 15, 46
See also CA 106; CANR 24, 49, 75; HW 1;
MTCW 1, 2
Bufalino, Gesualdo 1920(?)- .... CLC 74
See also DLB 196
Bugayev, Boris Nikolayevich 1880-1934
TCLC 7; PC 11
See also Bely, Andrey CA 104; 165; MTCW
1
Bukowski, Charles 1920-1994 ... CLC 2, 5, 9,
41, 82, 108; DAM NOV, POET; PC 18
See also CA 17-20R; 144; CANR 40, 62;
DA3; DLB 5, 130, 169; MTCW 1, 2
Bulgakov, Mikhail (Afanas'evich) 1891-1940
TCLC 2, 16; DAM DRAM, NOV; SSC
18
See also CA 105; 152
Bulgya, Alexander Alexandrovich 1901-1956
TCLC 53
See also Fadeyev, Alexander CA 117; 181
Bullins, Ed 1935- .... CLC 1, 5, 7; BLC 1;
DAM DRAM, MULT; DC 6
See also BW 2, 3; CA 49-52; CAAS 16;
CANR 24, 46, 73; DLB 7, 38; MTCW 1,
2
Bulwer-Lytton, Edward (George Earle
Lytton) 1803-1873 .... NCLC 1, 45
See also DLB 21
Bunin, Ivan Alexeyevich
1870-1953 .... TCLC 6; SSC 5
See also CA 104
Bunting, Basil 1900-1985 ..... CLC 10, 39, 47;
DAM POET
See also CA 53-56; 115; CANR 7; DLB 20
Bunuel, Luis 1900-1983 .. CLC 16, 80; DAM
MULT; HLC 1
See also CA 101; 110; CANR 32, 77; HW
1
Bunyan, John 1628-1688 ... LC 4; DA; DAB;
DAC; DAM MST; WLC
See also CDBLB 1660-1789; DLB 39
Burckhardt, Jacob (Christoph) 1818-1897
NCLC 49
Burford, Eleanor
See Hibbert, Eleanor Alice Burford
Burgess, Anthony .. CLC 1, 2, 4, 5, 8, 10, 13,
15, 22, 40, 62, 81, 94; DAB
See also Wilson, John (Anthony) Burgess
AAYA 25; AITN 1; CDBLB 1960 to
Present; DLB 14, 194; DLBY 98; MTCW
1
Burke, Edmund 1729(?)-1797 .... LC 7, 36;
DA; DAB; DAC; DAM MST; WLC
See also DA3; DLB 104
Burke, Kenneth (Duva) 1897-1993 ... CLC 2,
24
See also CA 5-8R; 143; CANR 39, 74; DLB
45, 63; MTCW 1, 2
Burke, Leda
See Garnett, David
Burke, Ralph
See Silverberg, Robert
Burke, Thomas 1886-1945 .... TCLC 63
See also CA 113; 155; DLB 197

Burney, Fanny 1752-1840 .. NCLC 12, 54, 81
See also DLB 39
Burns, Robert 1759-1796 . LC 3, 29, 40; DA;
DAB; DAC; DAM MST, POET; PC 6;
WLC
See also CDBLB 1789-1832; DA3; DLB
109
Burns, Tex
See L'Amour, Louis (Dearborn)
Burnshaw, Stanley 1906- .... CLC 3, 13, 44
See also CA 9-12R; DLB 48; DLBY 97
Burr, Anne 1937- .... CLC 6
See also CA 25-28R
Burroughs, Edgar Rice 1875-1950 . TCLC 2,
32; DAM NOV
See also AAYA 11; CA 104; 132; DA3;
DLB 8; MTCW 1, 2; SATA 41
Burroughs, William S(eward) 1914-1997
CLC 1, 2, 5, 15, 22, 42, 75, 109; DA;
DAB; DAC; DAM MST, NOV, POP;
WLC
See also AITN 2; CA 9-12R; 160; CANR
20, 52; DA3; DLB 2, 8, 16, 152; DLBY
81, 97; MTCW 1, 2
Burton, SirRichard F(rancis) 1821-1890
NCLC 42
See also DLB 55, 166, 184
Busch, Frederick 1941- .... CLC 7, 10, 18, 47
See also CA 33-36R; CAAS 1; CANR 45,
73; DLB 6
Bush, Ronald 1946- .... CLC 34
See also CA 136
Bustos, F(rancisco)
See Borges, Jorge Luis
Bustos Domecq, H(onorio)
See Bioy Casares, Adolfo; Borges, Jorge
Luis
Butler, Octavia E(stelle) 1947- .... CLC 38,
121; BLCS; DAM MULT, POP
See also AAYA 18; BW 2, 3; CA 73-76;
CANR 12, 24, 38, 73; DA3; DLB 33;
MTCW 1, 2; SATA 84
Butler, Robert Olen (Jr.) 1945- .... CLC 81;
DAM POP
See also CA 112; CANR 66; DLB 173; INT
112; MTCW 1
Butler, Samuel 1612-1680 .... LC 16, 43
See also DLB 101, 126
Butler, Samuel 1835-1902 . TCLC 1, 33; DA;
DAB; DAC; DAM MST, NOV; WLC
See also CA 143; CDBLB 1890-1914; DA3;
DLB 18, 57, 174
Butler, Walter C.
See Faust, Frederick (Schiller)
Butor, Michel (Marie Francois)
1926- .... CLC 1, 3, 8, 11, 15
See also CA 9-12R; CANR 33, 66; DLB
83; MTCW 1, 2
Butts, Mary 1892(?)-1937 .... TCLC 77
See also CA 148
Buzo, Alexander (John) 1944- .... CLC 61
See also CA 97-100; CANR 17, 39, 69
Buzzati, Dino 1906-1972 .... CLC 36
See also CA 160; 33-36R; DLB 177
Byars, Betsy (Cromer) 1928- .... CLC 35
See also AAYA 19; CA 33-36R, 183; CAAE
183; CANR 18, 36, 57; CLR 1, 16; DLB
52; INT CANR-18; JRDA; MAICYA;
MTCW 1; SAAS 1; SATA 4, 46, 80;
SATA-Essay 108

Byatt, A(ntonia) S(usan Drabble)
1936- ..... CLC 19, 65; DAM NOV, POP
See also CA 13-16R; CANR 13, 33, 50, 75;
DA3; DLB 14, 194; MTCW 1, 2
Byrne, David 1952- .... CLC 26
See also CA 127
Byrne, John Keyes 1926-
See Leonard, Hugh
See also CA 102; CANR 78; INT 102
Byron, George Gordon (Noel) 1788-1824
NCLC 2, 12; DA; DAB; DAC; DAM
MST, POET; PC 16; WLC
See also CDBLB 1789-1832; DA3; DLB
96, 110
Byron, Robert 1905-1941 .... TCLC 67
See also CA 160; DLB 195
C. 3. 3.
See Wilde, Oscar
Caballero, Fernan 1796-1877 .... NCLC 10
Cabell, Branch
See Cabell, James Branch
Cabell, James Branch 1879-1958 .... TCLC 6
See also CA 105; 152; DLB 9, 78; MTCW
1
Cable, George Washington
1844-1925 .... TCLC 4; SSC 4
See also CA 104; 155; DLB 12, 74; DLBD
13
Cabral de Melo Neto, Joao 1920- ... CLC 76;
DAM MULT
See also CA 151
Cabrera Infante, G(uillermo) 1929- . CLC 5,
25, 45, 120; DAM MULT; HLC 1
See also CA 85-88; CANR 29, 65; DA3;
DLB 113; HW 1, 2; MTCW 1, 2
Cade, Toni
See Bambara, Toni Cade
Cadmus and Harmonia
See Buchan, John
Caedmon fl. 658-680 .... CMLC 7
See also DLB 146
Caeiro, Alberto
See Pessoa, Fernando (Antonio Nogueira)
Cage, John (Milton, Jr.) 1912-1992 . CLC 41
See also CA 13-16R; 169; CANR 9, 78;
DLB 193; INT CANR-9
Cahan, Abraham 1860-1951 .... TCLC 71
See also CA 108; 154; DLB 9, 25, 28
Cain, G.
See Cabrera Infante, G(uillermo)
Cain, Guillermo
See Cabrera Infante, G(uillermo)
Cain, James M(allahan) 1892-1977 .. CLC 3,
11, 28
See also AITN 1; CA 17-20R; 73-76;
CANR 8, 34, 61; MTCW 1
Caine, Hall 1853-1931 .... TCLC 99
Caine, Mark
See Raphael, Frederic (Michael)
Calasso, Roberto 1941- .... CLC 81
See also CA 143
Calderon de la Barca, Pedro
1600-1681 .... LC 23; DC 3; HLCS 1
Caldwell, Erskine (Preston)
1903-1987 .. CLC 1, 8, 14, 50, 60; DAM
NOV; SSC 19
See also AITN 1; CA 1-4R; 121; CAAS 1;
CANR 2, 33; DA3; DLB 9, 86; MTCW
1, 2

Caldwell, (Janet Miriam) Taylor (Holland)
1900-1985 .. **CLC 2, 28, 39; DAM NOV, POP**
See also CA 5-8R; 116; CANR 5; DA3; DLBD 17

Calhoun, John Caldwell
1782-1850 .... **NCLC 15**
See also DLB 3

Calisher, Hortense 1911- ..... **CLC 2, 4, 8, 38; DAM NOV; SSC 15**
See also CA 1-4R; CANR 1, 22, 67; DA3; DLB 2; INT CANR-22; MTCW 1, 2

Callaghan, Morley Edward
1903-1990 ...... **CLC 3, 14, 41, 65; DAC; DAM MST**
See also CA 9-12R; 132; CANR 33, 73; DLB 68; MTCW 1, 2

Callimachus c. 305B.C.-c.
240B.C. .... **CMLC 18**
See also DLB 176

Calvin, John 1509-1564 .... **LC 37**

Calvino, Italo 1923-1985 .... **CLC 5, 8, 11, 22, 33, 39, 73; DAM NOV; SSC 3**
See also CA 85-88; 116; CANR 23, 61; DLB 196; MTCW 1, 2

Cameron, Carey 1952- .... **CLC 59**
See also CA 135

Cameron, Peter 1959- .... **CLC 44**
See also CA 125; CANR 50

Camoens, Luis Vaz de 1524(?)-1580
See also HLCS 1

Camoes, Luis de 1524(?)-1580
See also HLCS 1

Campana, Dino 1885-1932 .... **TCLC 20**
See also CA 117; DLB 114

Campanella, Tommaso 1568-1639 .... **LC 32**

Campbell, John W(ood, Jr.)
1910-1971 .... **CLC 32**
See also CA 21-22; 29-32R; CANR 34; CAP 2; DLB 8; MTCW 1

Campbell, Joseph 1904-1987 .... **CLC 69**
See also AAYA 3; BEST 89:2; CA 1-4R; 124; CANR 3, 28, 61; DA3; MTCW 1, 2

Campbell, Maria 1940- .... **CLC 85; DAC**
See also CA 102; CANR 54; NNAL

Campbell, (John) Ramsey 1946- ..... **CLC 42; SSC 19**
See also CA 57-60; CANR 7; INT CANR-7

Campbell, (Ignatius) Roy (Dunnachie)
1901-1957 .... **TCLC 5**
See also CA 104; 155; DLB 20; MTCW 2

Campbell, Thomas 1777-1844 .... **NCLC 19**
See also DLB 93; 144

Campbell, Wilfred .... **TCLC 9**
See also Campbell, William

Campbell, William 1858(?)-1918
See Campbell, Wilfred
See also CA 106; DLB 92

Campion, Jane .... **CLC 95**
See also CA 138; CANR 87

Camus, Albert 1913-1960 ...... **CLC 1, 2, 4, 9, 11, 14, 32, 63, 69, 124; DA; DAB; DAC; DAM DRAM, MST, NOV; DC 2; SSC 9; WLC**
See also CA 89-92; DA3; DLB 72; MTCW 1, 2

Canby, Vincent 1924- .... **CLC 13**
See also CA 81-84

Cancale
See Desnos, Robert

Canetti, Elias 1905-1994 .. **CLC 3, 14, 25, 75, 86**
See also CA 21-24R; 146; CANR 23, 61; 79; DA3; DLB 85, 124; MTCW 1, 2

Canfield, Dorothea F.
See Fisher, Dorothy (Frances) Canfield

Canfield, Dorothea Frances
See Fisher, Dorothy (Frances) Canfield

Canfield, Dorothy
See Fisher, Dorothy (Frances) Canfield

Canin, Ethan 1960- .... **CLC 55**
See also CA 131; 135

Cannon, Curt
See Hunter, Evan

Cao, Lan 1961- .... **CLC 109**
See also CA 165

Cape, Judith
See Page, P(atricia) K(athleen)

Capek, Karel 1890-1938 ... **TCLC 6, 37; DA; DAB; DAC; DAM DRAM, MST, NOV; DC 1; SSC 36; WLC**
See also CA 104; 140; DA3; MTCW 1

Capote, Truman 1924-1984 . **CLC 1, 3, 8, 13, 19, 34, 38, 58; DA; DAB; DAC; DAM MST, NOV, POP; SSC 2; WLC**
See also CA 5-8R; 113; CANR 18, 62; CDALB 1941-1968; DA3; DLB 2, 185; DLBY 80, 84; MTCW 1, 2; SATA 91

Capra, Frank 1897-1991 .... **CLC 16**
See also CA 61-64; 135

Caputo, Philip 1941- .... **CLC 32**
See also CA 73-76; CANR 40

Caragiale, Ion Luca 1852-1912 ...... **TCLC 76**
See also CA 157

Card, Orson Scott 1951- ..... **CLC 44, 47, 50; DAM POP**
See also AAYA 11; CA 102; CANR 27, 47, 73; DA3; INT CANR-27; MTCW 1, 2; SATA 83

Cardenal, Ernesto 1925- .... **CLC 31; DAM MULT, POET; HLC 1; PC 22**
See also CA 49-52; CANR 2, 32, 66; HW 1, 2; MTCW 1, 2

Cardozo, Benjamin N(athan) 1870-1938
TCLC 65
See also CA 117; 164

Carducci, Giosue (Alessandro Giuseppe)
1835-1907 .... **TCLC 32**
See also CA 163

Carew, Thomas 1595(?)-1640 . **LC 13; PC 29**
See also DLB 126

Carey, Ernestine Gilbreth 1908- ...... **CLC 17**
See also CA 5-8R; CANR 71; SATA 2

Carey, Peter 1943- .... **CLC 40, 55, 96**
See also CA 123; 127; CANR 53, 76; INT 127; MTCW 1, 2; SATA 94

Carleton, William 1794-1869 .... **NCLC 3**
See also DLB 159

Carlisle, Henry (Coffin) 1926- .... **CLC 33**
See also CA 13-16R; CANR 15, 85

Carlsen, Chris
See Holdstock, Robert P.

Carlson, Ron(ald F.) 1947- .... **CLC 54**
See also CA 105; CANR 27

Carlyle, Thomas 1795-1881 .. **NCLC 70; DA; DAB; DAC; DAM MST**
See also CDBLB 1789-1832; DLB 55; 144

Carman, (William) Bliss
1861-1929 .... **TCLC 7; DAC**
See also CA 104; 152; DLB 92

Carnegie, Dale 1888-1955 .... **TCLC 53**

Carossa, Hans 1878-1956 .... **TCLC 48**
See also CA 170; DLB 66

Carpenter, Don(ald Richard)
1931-1995 .... **CLC 41**
See also CA 45-48; 149; CANR 1, 71

Carpenter, Edward 1844-1929 .... **TCLC 88**
See also CA 163

Carpentier (y Valmont), Alejo 1904-1980
CLC 8, 11, 38, 110; DAM MULT; HLC 1; SSC 35
See also CA 65-68; 97-100; CANR 11, 70; DLB 113; HW 1, 2

Carr, Caleb 1955(?)- .... **CLC 86**
See also CA 147; CANR 73; DA3

Carr, Emily 1871-1945 .... **TCLC 32**
See also CA 159; DLB 68

Carr, John Dickson 1906-1977 .... **CLC 3**
See also Fairbairn, Roger CA 49-52; 69-72; CANR 3, 33, 60; MTCW 1, 2

Carr, Philippa
See Hibbert, Eleanor Alice Burford

Carr, Virginia Spencer 1929- .... **CLC 34**
See also CA 61-64; DLB 111

Carrere, Emmanuel 1957- .... **CLC 89**

Carrier, Roch 1937- .... **CLC 13, 78; DAC; DAM MST**
See also CA 130; CANR 61; DLB 53; SATA 105

Carroll, James P. 1943(?)- .... **CLC 38**
See also CA 81-84; CANR 73; MTCW 1

Carroll, Jim 1951- .... **CLC 35**
See also AAYA 17; CA 45-48; CANR 42

Carroll, Lewis .... **NCLC 2, 53; PC 18; WLC**
See also Dodgson, Charles Lutwidge CDBLB 1832-1890; CLR 2, 18; DLB 18, 163, 178; DLBY 98; JRDA

Carroll, Paul Vincent 1900-1968 ...... **CLC 10**
See also CA 9-12R; 25-28R; DLB 10

Carruth, Hayden 1921- ..... **CLC 4, 7, 10, 18, 84; PC 10**
See also CA 9-12R; CANR 4, 38, 59; DLB 5, 165; INT CANR-4; MTCW 1, 2; SATA 47

Carson, Rachel Louise 1907-1964 ... **CLC 71; DAM POP**
See also CA 77-80; CANR 35; DA3; MTCW 1, 2; SATA 23

Carter, Angela (Olive) 1940-1992 ...... **CLC 5, 41, 76; SSC 13**
See also CA 53-56; 136; CANR 12, 36, 61; DA3; DLB 14, 207; MTCW 1, 2; SATA 66; SATA-Obit 70

Carter, Nick
See Smith, Martin Cruz

Carver, Raymond 1938-1988 ..... **CLC 22, 36, 53, 55, 126; DAM NOV; SSC 8**
See also CA 33-36R; 126; CANR 17, 34, 61; DA3; DLB 130; DLBY 84, 88; MTCW 1, 2

Cary, Elizabeth, Lady Falkland 1585-1639
LC 30

Cary, (Arthur) Joyce (Lunel) 1888-1957
TCLC 1, 29
See also CA 104; 164; CDBLB 1914-1945; DLB 15, 100; MTCW 2

Casanova de Seingalt, Giovanni Jacopo
1725-1798 .... **LC 13**

Casares, Adolfo Bioy
See Bioy Casares, Adolfo

Casely-Hayford, J(oseph) E(phraim)
1866-1930 ...... **TCLC 24; BLC 1; DAM MULT**
See also BW 2; CA 123; 152

Casey, John (Dudley) 1939- .... **CLC 59**
See also BEST 90:2; CA 69-72; CANR 23

Casey, Michael 1947- .... **CLC 2**
See also CA 65-68; DLB 5

Casey, Patrick
See Thurman, Wallace (Henry)

Casey, Warren (Peter) 1935-1988 .... **CLC 12**
See also CA 101; 127; INT 101

Casona, Alejandro .... **CLC 49**
See also Alvarez, Alejandro Rodriguez

Cassavetes, John 1929-1989 .... **CLC 20**
See also CA 85-88; 127; CANR 82

Cassian, Nina 1924- .... **PC 17**

Cassill, R(onald) V(erlin) 1919- ... **CLC 4, 23**
See also CA 9-12R; CAAS 1; CANR 7, 45; DLB 6

Cassirer, Ernst 1874-1945 .... **TCLC 61**
See also CA 157

Cassity, (Allen) Turner 1929- .... **CLC 6, 42**
See also CA 17-20R; CAAS 8; CANR 11; DLB 105

Castaneda, Carlos (Cesar Aranha)
1931(?)-1998 .... **CLC 12, 119**
See also CA 25-28R; CANR 32, 66; HW 1; MTCW 1

Castedo, Elena 1937- .... **CLC 65**
See also CA 132

Castedo-Ellerman, Elena
See Castedo, Elena

Castellanos, Rosario 1925-1974 .... **CLC 66; DAM MULT; HLC 1**
See also CA 131; 53-56; CANR 58; DLB 113; HW 1; MTCW 1

Castelvetro, Lodovico 1505-1571 .... **LC 12**

Castiglione, Baldassare 1478-1529 ...... **LC 12**

Castle, Robert
See Hamilton, Edmond

Castro (Ruz), Fidel 1926(?)-
See also CA 110; 129; CANR 81; DAM MULT; HLC 1; HW 2

Castro, Guillen de 1569-1631 .... **LC 19**

Castro, Rosalia de 1837-1885 ... **NCLC 3, 78; DAM MULT**

Cather, Willa
See Cather, Willa Sibert

Cather, Willa Sibert 1873-1947 ...... **TCLC 1, 11, 31, 99; DA; DAB; DAC; DAM MST, NOV; SSC 2; WLC**
See also AAYA 24; CA 104; 128; CDALB 1865-1917; DA3; DLB 9, 54, 78; DLBD 1; MTCW 1, 2; SATA 30

Catherine, Saint 1347-1380 .... **CMLC 27**

Cato, Marcus Porcius 234B.C.-149B.C. **CMLC 21**
See also DLB 211

Catton, (Charles) Bruce 1899-1978 . **CLC 35**
See also AITN 1; CA 5-8R; 81-84; CANR 7, 74; DLB 17; SATA 2; SATA-Obit 24

Catullus c. 84B.C.-c. 54B.C. .... **CMLC 18**
See also DLB 211

Cauldwell, Frank
See King, Francis (Henry)

Caunitz, William J. 1933-1996 .... **CLC 34**
See also BEST 89:3; CA 125; 130; 152; CANR 73; INT 130

Causley, Charles (Stanley) 1917- .... **CLC 7**
See also CA 9-12R; CANR 5, 35; CLR 30; DLB 27; MTCW 1; SATA 3, 66

Caute, (John) David 1936- .... **CLC 29; DAM NOV**
See also CA 1-4R; CAAS 4; CANR 1, 33, 64; DLB 14

Cavafy, C(onstantine) P(eter) 1863-1933 **TCLC 2, 7; DAM POET**
See also Kavafis, Konstantinos Petrou CA 148; DA3; MTCW 1

Cavallo, Evelyn
See Spark, Muriel (Sarah)

Cavanna, Betty .... **CLC 12**
See also Harrison, Elizabeth Cavanna JRDA; MAICYA; SAAS 4; SATA 1, 30

Cavendish, Margaret Lucas
1623-1673 .... **LC 30**
See also DLB 131

Caxton, William 1421(?)-1491(?) .... **LC 17**
See also DLB 170

Cayer, D. M.
See Duffy, Maureen

Cayrol, Jean 1911- .... **CLC 11**
See also CA 89-92; DLB 83

Cela, Camilo Jose 1916- .... **CLC 4, 13, 59, 122; DAM MULT; HLC 1**
See also BEST 90:2; CA 21-24R; CAAS 10; CANR 21, 32, 76; DLBY 89; HW 1; MTCW 1, 2

Celan, Paul .... **CLC 10, 19, 53, 82; PC 10**
See also Antschel, Paul DLB 69

Celine, Louis-Ferdinand ... **CLC 1, 3, 4, 7, 9, 15, 47, 124**
See also Destouches, Louis-Ferdinand DLB 72

Cellini, Benvenuto 1500-1571 .... **LC 7**

Cendrars, Blaise 1887-1961 ...... **CLC 18, 106**
See also Sauser-Hall, Frederic

Cernuda (y Bidon), Luis
1902-1963 .... **CLC 54; DAM POET**
See also CA 131; 89-92; DLB 134; HW 1

Cervantes, Lorna Dee 1954-
See also CA 131; CANR 80; DLB 82; HLCS 1; HW 1

Cervantes (Saavedra), Miguel de 1547-1616
LC 6, 23; DA; DAB; DAC; DAM MST, NOV; SSC 12; WLC

Cesaire, Aime (Fernand) 1913- . **CLC 19, 32, 112; BLC 1; DAM MULT, POET; PC 25**
See also BW 2, 3; CA 65-68; CANR 24, 43, 81; DA3; MTCW 1, 2

Chabon, Michael 1963- .... **CLC 55**
See also CA 139; CANR 57

Chabrol, Claude 1930- .... **CLC 16**
See also CA 110

Challans, Mary 1905-1983
See Renault, Mary
See also CA 81-84; 111; CANR 74; DA3; MTCW 2; SATA 23; SATA-Obit 36

Challis, George
See Faust, Frederick (Schiller)

Chambers, Aidan 1934- .... **CLC 35**
See also AAYA 27; CA 25-28R; CANR 12, 31, 58; JRDA; MAICYA; SAAS 12; SATA 1, 69, 108

Chambers, James 1948-
See Cliff, Jimmy
See also CA 124

Chambers, Jessie
See Lawrence, D(avid) H(erbert Richards)

Chambers, Robert W(illiam) 1865-1933 **TCLC 41**
See also CA 165; DLB 202; SATA 107

Chamisso, Adelbert von
1781-1838 .... **NCLC 82**
See also DLB 90

Chandler, Raymond (Thornton) 1888-1959 **TCLC 1, 7; SSC 23**
See also AAYA 25; CA 104; 129; CANR 60; CDALB 1929-1941; DA3; DLBD 6; MTCW 1, 2

Chang, Eileen 1920-1995 .... **SSC 28**
See also CA 166

Chang, Jung 1952- .... **CLC 71**
See also CA 142

Chang Ai-Ling
See Chang, Eileen

Channing, William Ellery
1780-1842 .... **NCLC 17**
See also DLB 1, 59

Chao, Patricia 1955- .... **CLC 119**
See also CA 163

Chaplin, Charles Spencer
1889-1977 .... **CLC 16**
See also Chaplin, Charlie CA 81-84; 73-76

Chaplin, Charlie
See Chaplin, Charles Spencer
See also DLB 44

Chapman, George 1559(?)-1634 .... **LC 22; DAM DRAM**
See also DLB 62, 121

Chapman, Graham 1941-1989 .... **CLC 21**
See also Monty Python CA 116; 129; CANR 35

Chapman, John Jay 1862-1933 .... **TCLC 7**
See also CA 104

Chapman, Lee
See Bradley, Marion Zimmer

Chapman, Walker
See Silverberg, Robert

Chappell, Fred (Davis) 1936- ..... **CLC 40, 78**
See also CA 5-8R; CAAS 4; CANR 8, 33, 67; DLB 6, 105

Char, Rene(-Emile) 1907-1988 .... **CLC 9, 11, 14, 55; DAM POET**
See also CA 13-16R; 124; CANR 32; MTCW 1, 2

Charby, Jay
See Ellison, Harlan (Jay)

Chardin, Pierre Teilhard de
See Teilhard de Chardin, (Marie Joseph) Pierre

Charlemagne 742-814 .... **CMLC 37**

Charles I 1600-1649 .... **LC 13**

Charriere, Isabelle de 1740-1805 .. **NCLC 66**

Charyn, Jerome 1937- .... **CLC 5, 8, 18**
See also CA 5-8R; CAAS 1; CANR 7, 61; DLBY 83; MTCW 1

Chase, Mary (Coyle) 1907-1981 .... **DC 1**
See also CA 77-80; 105; SATA 17; SATA-Obit 29

Chase, Mary Ellen 1887-1973 .... **CLC 2**
See also CA 13-16; 41-44R; CAP 1; SATA 10

Chase, Nicholas
See Hyde, Anthony

Chateaubriand, Francois Rene de 1768-1848 **NCLC 3**

See also DLB 119

Chatterje, Sarat Chandra 1876-1936(?)
See Chatterji, Saratchandra
See also CA 109

Chatterji, Bankim Chandra 1838-1894
NCLC 19

Chatterji, Saratchandra .... **TCLC 13**
See also Chatterji, Sarat Chandra

Chatterton, Thomas 1752-1770 ..... **LC 3, 54;**
DAM POET
See also DLB 109

Chatwin, (Charles) Bruce
1940-1989 . **CLC 28, 57, 59; DAM POP**
See also AAYA 4; BEST 90:1; CA 85-88;
127; DLB 194, 204

Chaucer, Daniel
See Ford, Ford Madox

Chaucer, Geoffrey 1340(?)-1400 .... **LC 17;**
DA; DAB; DAC; DAM MST, POET;
PC 19; WLCS
See also CDBLB Before 1660; DA3; DLB
146

Chavez, Denise (Elia) 1948-
See also CA 131; CANR 56, 81; DAM
MULT; DLB 122; HLC 1; HW 1, 2;
MTCW 2

Chaviaras, Strates 1935-
See Haviaras, Stratis
See also CA 105

Chayefsky, Paddy .... **CLC 23**
See also Chayefsky, Sidney DLB 7, 44;
DLBY 81

Chayefsky, Sidney 1923-1981
See Chayefsky, Paddy
See also CA 9-12R; 104; CANR 18; DAM
DRAM

Chedid, Andree 1920- .... **CLC 47**
See also CA 145

Cheever, John 1912-1982 ..... **CLC 3, 7, 8, 11,**
15, 25, 64; DA; DAB; DAC; DAM
MST, NOV, POP; SSC 1, 38; WLC
See also CA 5-8R; 106; CABS 1; CANR 5,
27, 76; CDALB 1941-1968; DA3; DLB
2, 102; DLBY 80, 82; INT CANR-5;
MTCW 1, 2

Cheever, Susan 1943- .... **CLC 18, 48**
See also CA 103; CANR 27, 51; DLBY 82;
INT CANR-27

Chekhonte, Antosha
See Chekhov, Anton (Pavlovich)

Chekhov, Anton (Pavlovich) 1860-1904
TCLC 3, 10, 31, 55, 96; DA; DAB;
DAC; DAM DRAM, MST; DC 9; SSC
2, 28; WLC
See also CA 104; 124; DA3; SATA 90

Chernyshevsky, Nikolay Gavrilovich
1828-1889 .... **NCLC 1**

Cherry, Carolyn Janice 1942-
See Cherryh, C. J.
See also CA 65-68; CANR 10

Cherryh, C. J. .... **CLC 35**
See also Cherry, Carolyn Janice AAYA 24;
DLBY 80; SATA 93

Chesnutt, Charles W(addell) 1858-1932
TCLC 5, 39; BLC 1; DAM MULT; SSC
7
See also BW 1, 3; CA 106; 125; CANR 76;
DLB 12, 50, 78; MTCW 1, 2

Chester, Alfred 1929(?)-1971 .... **CLC 49**
See also CA 33-36R; DLB 130

Chesterton, G(ilbert) K(eith) 1874-1936
TCLC 1, 6, 64; DAM NOV, POET; PC
28; SSC 1
See also CA 104; 132; CANR 73; CDBLB
1914-1945; DLB 10, 19, 34, 70, 98, 149,
178; MTCW 1, 2; SATA 27

Chiang, Pin-chin 1904-1986
See Ding Ling
See also CA 118

Ch'ien Chung-shu 1910- .... **CLC 22**
See also CA 130; CANR 73; MTCW 1, 2

Child, L. Maria
See Child, Lydia Maria

Child, Lydia Maria 1802-1880 .. **NCLC 6, 73**
See also DLB 1, 74; SATA 67

Child, Mrs.
See Child, Lydia Maria

Child, Philip 1898-1978 .... **CLC 19, 68**
See also CA 13-14; CAP 1; SATA 47

Childers, (Robert) Erskine
1870-1922 .... **TCLC 65**
See also CA 113; 153; DLB 70

Childress, Alice 1920-1994 .. **CLC 12, 15, 86,**
96; BLC 1; DAM DRAM, MULT,
NOV; DC 4
See also AAYA 8; BW 2, 3; CA 45-48; 146;
CANR 3, 27, 50, 74; CLR 14; DA3; DLB
7, 38; JRDA; MAICYA; MTCW 1, 2;
SATA 7, 48, 81

Chin, Frank (Chew, Jr.) 1940- .... **DC 7**
See also CA 33-36R; CANR 71; DAM
MULT; DLB 206

Chislett, (Margaret) Anne 1943- ...... **CLC 34**
See also CA 151

Chitty, Thomas Willes 1926- .... **CLC 11**
See also Hinde, Thomas CA 5-8R

Chivers, Thomas Holley
1809-1858 .... **NCLC 49**
See also DLB 3

Choi, Susan .... **CLC 119**

Chomette, Rene Lucien 1898-1981
See Clair, Rene
See also CA 103

Chopin, Kate .. **TCLC 5, 14; DA; DAB; SSC**
8; WLCS
See also Chopin, Katherine CDALB 1865-
1917; DLB 12, 78

Chopin, Katherine 1851-1904
See Chopin, Kate
See also CA 104; 122; DAC; DAM MST,
NOV; DA3

Chretien de Troyes c. 12th cent. - . **CMLC 10**
See also DLB 208

Christie
See Ichikawa, Kon

Christie, Agatha (Mary Clarissa) 1890-1976
CLC 1, 6, 8, 12, 39, 48, 110; DAB; DAC;
DAM NOV
See also AAYA 9; AITN 1, 2; CA 17-20R;
61-64; CANR 10, 37; CDBLB 1914-1945;
DA3; DLB 13, 77; MTCW 1, 2; SATA 36

Christie, (Ann) Philippa
See Pearce, Philippa
See also CA 5-8R; CANR 4

Christine de Pizan 1365(?)-1431(?) .... **LC 9**
See also DLB 208

Chubb, Elmer
See Masters, Edgar Lee

Chulkov, Mikhail Dmitrievich
1743-1792 .... **LC 2**
See also DLB 150

Churchill, Caryl 1938- .... **CLC 31, 55; DC 5**
See also CA 102; CANR 22, 46; DLB 13;
MTCW 1

Churchill, Charles 1731-1764 .... **LC 3**
See also DLB 109

Chute, Carolyn 1947- .... **CLC 39**
See also CA 123

Ciardi, John (Anthony) 1916-1986 . **CLC 10,**
40, 44; DAM POET
See also CA 5-8R; 118; CAAS 2; CANR 5,
33; CLR 19; DLB 5; DLBY 86; INT
CANR-5; MAICYA; MTCW 1, 2; SAAS
26; SATA 1, 65; SATA-Obit 46

Cicero, Marcus Tullius 106B.C.-43B.C.
CMLC 3
See also DLB 211

Cimino, Michael 1943- .... **CLC 16**
See also CA 105

Cioran, E(mil) M. 1911-1995 .... **CLC 64**
See also CA 25-28R; 149

Cisneros, Sandra 1954- . **CLC 69, 118; DAM**
MULT; HLC 1; SSC 32
See also AAYA 9; CA 131; CANR 64; DA3;
DLB 122, 152; HW 1, 2; MTCW 2

Cixous, Helene 1937- .... **CLC 92**
See also CA 126; CANR 55; DLB 83;
MTCW 1, 2

Clair, Rene .... **CLC 20**
See also Chomette, Rene Lucien

Clampitt, Amy 1920-1994 .... **CLC 32; PC 19**
See also CA 110; 146; CANR 29, 79; DLB
105

Clancy, Thomas L., Jr. 1947-
See Clancy, Tom
See also CA 125; 131; CANR 62; DA3;
INT 131; MTCW 1, 2

Clancy, Tom .... **CLC 45, 112; DAM NOV,**
POP
See also Clancy, Thomas L., Jr. AAYA 9;
BEST 89:1, 90:1; MTCW 2

Clare, John 1793-1864 .... **NCLC 9; DAB;**
DAM POET; PC 23
See also DLB 55, 96

Clarin
See Alas (y Urena), Leopoldo (Enrique
Garcia)

Clark, Al C.
See Goines, Donald

Clark, (Robert) Brian 1932- .... **CLC 29**
See also CA 41-44R; CANR 67

Clark, Curt
See Westlake, Donald E(dwin)

Clark, Eleanor 1913-1996 .... **CLC 5, 19**
See also CA 9-12R; 151; CANR 41; DLB 6

Clark, J. P.
See Clark, John Pepper
See also DLB 117

Clark, John Pepper 1935- . **CLC 38; BLC 1;**
DAM DRAM, MULT; DC 5
See also Clark, J. P. BW 1; CA 65-68;
CANR 16, 72; MTCW 1

Clark, M. R.
See Clark, Mavis Thorpe

Clark, Mavis Thorpe 1909- .... **CLC 12**
See also CA 57-60; CANR 8, 37; CLR 30;
MAICYA; SAAS 5; SATA 8, 74

Clark, Walter Van Tilburg
    1909-1971 .... CLC 28
    See also CA 9-12R; 33-36R; CANR 63;
    DLB 9, 206; SATA 8

Clark Bekederemo, J(ohnson) P(epper)
    See Clark, John Pepper

Clarke, Arthur C(harles) 1917- .... CLC 1, 4,
    13, 18, 35; DAM POP; SSC 3
    See also AAYA 4; CA 1-4R; CANR 2, 28,
    55, 74; DA3; JRDA; MAICYA; MTCW
    1, 2; SATA 13, 70

Clarke, Austin 1896-1974 ... CLC 6, 9; DAM
    POET
    See also CA 29-32; 49-52; CAP 2; DLB 10,
    20

Clarke, Austin C(hesterfield) 1934- .. CLC 8,
    53; BLC 1; DAC; DAM MULT
    See also BW 1; CA 25-28R; CAAS 16;
    CANR 14, 32, 68; DLB 53, 125

Clarke, Gillian 1937- .... CLC 61
    See also CA 106; DLB 40

Clarke, Marcus (Andrew Hislop) 1846-1881
    NCLC 19

Clarke, Shirley 1925- .... CLC 16

Clash, The
    See Headon, (Nicky) Topper; Jones, Mick;
    Simonon, Paul; Strummer, Joe

Claudel, Paul (Louis Charles Marie)
    1868-1955 .... TCLC 2, 10
    See also CA 104; 165; DLB 192

Claudius, Matthias 1740-1815 .... NCLC 75
    See also DLB 97

Clavell, James (duMaresq)
    1925-1994 .. CLC 6, 25, 87; DAM NOV,
    POP
    See also CA 25-28R; 146; CANR 26, 48;
    DA3; MTCW 1, 2

Cleaver, (Leroy) Eldridge
    1935-1998 . CLC 30, 119; BLC 1; DAM
    MULT
    See also BW 1, 3; CA 21-24R; 167; CANR
    16, 75; DA3; MTCW 2

Cleese, John (Marwood) 1939- .... CLC 21
    See also Monty Python CA 112; 116;
    CANR 35; MTCW 1

Cleishbotham, Jebediah
    See Scott, Walter

Cleland, John 1710-1789 .... LC 2, 48
    See also DLB 39

Clemens, Samuel Langhorne 1835-1910
    See Twain, Mark
    See also CA 104; 135; CDALB 1865-1917;
    DA; DAB; DAC; DAM MST, NOV; DA3;
    DLB 11, 12, 23, 64, 74, 186, 189; JRDA;
    MAICYA; SATA 100; YABC 2

Cleophil
    See Congreve, William

Clerihew, E.
    See Bentley, E(dmund) C(lerihew)

Clerk, N. W.
    See Lewis, C(live) S(taples)

Cliff, Jimmy .... CLC 21
    See also Chambers, James

Cliff, Michelle 1946- .... CLC 120; BLCS
    See also BW 2; CA 116; CANR 39, 72;
    DLB 157

Clifton, (Thelma) Lucille 1936- .... CLC 19,
    66; BLC 1; DAM MULT, POET; PC
    17
    See also BW 2, 3; CA 49-52; CANR 2, 24,
    42, 76; CLR 5; DA3; DLB 5, 41; MAI-
    CYA; MTCW 1, 2; SATA 20, 69

Clinton, Dirk
    See Silverberg, Robert

Clough, Arthur Hugh 1819-1861 ... NCLC 27
    See also DLB 32

Clutha, Janet Paterson Frame 1924-
    See Frame, Janet
    See also CA 1-4R; CANR 2, 36, 76; MTCW
    1, 2

Clyne, Terence
    See Blatty, William Peter

Cobalt, Martin
    See Mayne, William (James Carter)

Cobb, Irvin S(hrewsbury)
    1876-1944 .... TCLC 77
    See also CA 175; DLB 11, 25, 86

Cobbett, William 1763-1835 .... NCLC 49
    See also DLB 43, 107, 158

Coburn, D(onald) L(ee) 1938- .... CLC 10
    See also CA 89-92

Cocteau, Jean (Maurice Eugene Clement)
    1889-1963 .... CLC 1, 8, 15, 16, 43; DA;
    DAB; DAC; DAM DRAM, MST, NOV;
    WLC
    See also CA 25-28; CANR 40; CAP 2;
    DA3; DLB 65; MTCW 1, 2

Codrescu, Andrei 1946- .... CLC 46, 121;
    DAM POET
    See also CA 33-36R; CAAS 19; CANR 13,
    34, 53, 76; DA3; MTCW 2

Coe, Max
    See Bourne, Randolph S(illiman)

Coe, Tucker
    See Westlake, Donald E(dwin)

Coen, Ethan 1958- .... CLC 108
    See also CA 126; CANR 85

Coen, Joel 1955- .... CLC 108
    See also CA 126

The Coen Brothers
    See Coen, Ethan; Coen, Joel

Coetzee, J(ohn) M(ichael) 1940- ...... CLC 23,
    33, 66, 117; DAM NOV
    See also CA 77-80; CANR 41, 54, 74; DA3;
    MTCW 1, 2

Coffey, Brian
    See Koontz, Dean R(ay)

Coffin, Robert P(eter) Tristram 1892-1955
    TCLC 95
    See also CA 123; 169; DLB 45

Cohan, George M(ichael)
    1878-1942 .... TCLC 60
    See also CA 157

Cohen, Arthur A(llen) 1928-1986 ...... CLC 7,
    31
    See also CA 1-4R; 120; CANR 1, 17, 42;
    DLB 28

Cohen, Leonard (Norman) 1934- ...... CLC 3,
    38; DAC; DAM MST
    See also CA 21-24R; CANR 14, 69; DLB
    53; MTCW 1

Cohen, Matt 1942- .... CLC 19; DAC
    See also CA 61-64; CAAS 18; CANR 40;
    DLB 53

Cohen-Solal, Annie 19(?)- .... CLC 50

Colegate, Isabel 1931- .... CLC 36
    See also CA 17-20R; CANR 8, 22, 74; DLB
    14; INT CANR-22; MTCW 1

Coleman, Emmett
    See Reed, Ishmael

Coleridge, M. E.
    See Coleridge, Mary E(lizabeth)

Coleridge, Mary E(lizabeth) 1861-1907
    TCLC 73
    See also CA 116; 166; DLB 19, 98

Coleridge, Samuel Taylor
    1772-1834 .... NCLC 9, 54; DA; DAB;
    DAC; DAM MST, POET; PC 11; WLC
    See also CDBLB 1789-1832; DA3; DLB
    93, 107

Coleridge, Sara 1802-1852 .... NCLC 31
    See also DLB 199

Coles, Don 1928- .... CLC 46
    See also CA 115; CANR 38

Coles, Robert (Martin) 1929- .... CLC 108
    See also CA 45-48; CANR 3, 32, 66, 70;
    INT CANR-32; SATA 23

Colette, (Sidonie-Gabrielle)
    1873-1954 . TCLC 1, 5, 16; DAM NOV;
    SSC 10
    See also CA 104; 131; DA3; DLB 65;
    MTCW 1, 2

Collett, (Jacobine) Camilla (Wergeland)
    1813-1895 .... NCLC 22

Collier, Christopher 1930- .... CLC 30
    See also AAYA 13; CA 33-36R; CANR 13,
    33; JRDA; MAICYA; SATA 16, 70

Collier, James L(incoln) 1928- .... CLC 30;
    DAM POP
    See also AAYA 13; CA 9-12R; CANR 4,
    33, 60; CLR 3; JRDA; MAICYA; SAAS
    21; SATA 8, 70

Collier, Jeremy 1650-1726 .... LC 6

Collier, John 1901-1980 .... SSC 19
    See also CA 65-68; 97-100; CANR 10;
    DLB 77

Collingwood, R(obin) G(eorge) 1889(?)-1943
    TCLC 67
    See also CA 117; 155

Collins, Hunt
    See Hunter, Evan

Collins, Linda 1931- .... CLC 44
    See also CA 125

Collins, (William) Wilkie
    1824-1889 .... NCLC 1, 18
    See also CDBLB 1832-1890; DLB 18, 70,
    159

Collins, William 1721-1759 . LC 4, 40; DAM
    POET
    See also DLB 109

Collodi, Carlo 1826-1890 .... NCLC 54
    See also Lorenzini, Carlo CLR 5

Colman, George 1732-1794
    See Glassco, John

Colt, Winchester Remington
    See Hubbard, L(afayette) Ron(ald)

Colter, Cyrus 1910- .... CLC 58
    See also BW 1; CA 65-68; CANR 10, 66;
    DLB 33

Colton, James
    See Hansen, Joseph

Colum, Padraic 1881-1972 .... CLC 28
    See also CA 73-76; 33-36R; CANR 35;
    CLR 36; MAICYA; MTCW 1; SATA 15

Colvin, James
    See Moorcock, Michael (John)

Colwin, Laurie (E.) 1944-1992 .... CLC 5, 13,
    23, 84
    See also CA 89-92; 139; CANR 20, 46;
    DLBY 80; MTCW 1

Comfort, Alex(ander) 1920- .... **CLC 7; DAM POP**
See also CA 1-4R; CANR 1, 45; MTCW 1

Comfort, Montgomery
See Campbell, (John) Ramsey

Compton-Burnett, I(vy)
1884(?)-1969 .... **CLC 1, 3, 10, 15, 34; DAM NOV**
See also CA 1-4R; 25-28R; CANR 4; DLB 36; MTCW 1

Comstock, Anthony 1844-1915 ...... **TCLC 13**
See also CA 110; 169

Comte, Auguste 1798-1857 .... **NCLC 54**

Conan Doyle, Arthur
See Doyle, Arthur Conan

Conde (Abellan), Carmen 1901-
See also CA 177; DLB 108; HLCS 1; HW 2

Conde, Maryse 1937- .... **CLC 52, 92; BLCS; DAM MULT**
See also Boucolon, Maryse BW 2; MTCW 1

Condillac, Etienne Bonnot de
1714-1780 .... **LC 26**

Condon, Richard (Thomas)
1915-1996 ...... **CLC 4, 6, 8, 10, 45, 100; DAM NOV**
See also BEST 90:3; CA 1-4R; 151; CAAS 1; CANR 2, 23; INT CANR-23; MTCW 1, 2

Confucius 551B.C.-479B.C. .. **CMLC 19; DA; DAB; DAC; DAM MST; WLCS**
See also DA3

Congreve, William 1670-1729 .... **LC 5, 21; DA; DAB; DAC; DAM DRAM, MST, POET; DC 2; WLC**
See also CDBLB 1660-1789; DLB 39, 84

Connell, Evan S(helby), Jr. 1924- . **CLC 4, 6, 45; DAM NOV**
See also AAYA 7; CA 1-4R; CAAS 2; CANR 2, 39, 76; DLB 2; DLBY 81; MTCW 1, 2

Connelly, Marc(us Cook) 1890-1980 . **CLC 7**
See also CA 85-88; 102; CANR 30; DLB 7; DLBY 80; SATA-Obit 25

Connor, Ralph .... **TCLC 31**
See also Gordon, Charles William DLB 92

Conrad, Joseph 1857-1924 .... **TCLC 1, 6, 13, 25, 43, 57; DA; DAB; DAC; DAM MST, NOV; SSC 9; WLC**
See also AAYA 26; CA 104; 131; CANR 60; CDBLB 1890-1914; DA3; DLB 10, 34, 98, 156; MTCW 1, 2; SATA 27

Conrad, Robert Arnold
See Hart, Moss

Conroy, Pat
See Conroy, (Donald) Pat(rick)
See also MTCW 2

Conroy, (Donald) Pat(rick) 1945- ... **CLC 30, 74; DAM NOV, POP**
See also Conroy, Pat AAYA 8; AITN 1; CA 85-88; CANR 24, 53; DA3; DLB 6; MTCW 1

Constant (de Rebecque), (Henri) Benjamin
1767-1830 .... **NCLC 6**
See also DLB 119

Conybeare, Charles Augustus
See Eliot, T(homas) S(tearns)

Cook, Michael 1933- .... **CLC 58**
See also CA 93-96; CANR 68; DLB 53

Cook, Robin 1940- .... **CLC 14; DAM POP**
See also AAYA 32; BEST 90:2; CA 108; 111; CANR 41; DA3; INT 111

Cook, Roy
See Silverberg, Robert

Cooke, Elizabeth 1948- .... **CLC 55**
See also CA 129

Cooke, John Esten 1830-1886 .... **NCLC 5**
See also DLB 3

Cooke, John Estes
See Baum, L(yman) Frank

Cooke, M. E.
See Creasey, John

Cooke, Margaret
See Creasey, John

Cook-Lynn, Elizabeth 1930- . **CLC 93; DAM MULT**
See also CA 133; DLB 175; NNAL

Cooney, Ray .... **CLC 62**

Cooper, Douglas 1960- .... **CLC 86**

Cooper, Henry St. John
See Creasey, John

Cooper, J(oan) California (?)- .... **CLC 56; DAM MULT**
See also AAYA 12; BW 1; CA 125; CANR 55; DLB 212

Cooper, James Fenimore
1789-1851 .... **NCLC 1, 27, 54**
See also AAYA 22; CDALB 1640-1865; DA3; DLB 3; SATA 19

Coover, Robert (Lowell) 1932- ...... **CLC 3, 7, 15, 32, 46, 87; DAM NOV; SSC 15**
See also CA 45-48; CANR 3, 37, 58; DLB 2; DLBY 81; MTCW 1, 2

Copeland, Stewart (Armstrong)
1952- .... **CLC 26**

Copernicus, Nicolaus 1473-1543 .... **LC 45**

Coppard, A(lfred) E(dgar)
1878-1957 .... **TCLC 5; SSC 21**
See also CA 114; 167; DLB 162; YABC 1

Coppee, Francois 1842-1908 .... **TCLC 25**
See also CA 170

Coppola, Francis Ford 1939- ... **CLC 16, 126**
See also CA 77-80; CANR 40, 78; DLB 44

Corbiere, Tristan 1845-1875 .... **NCLC 43**

Corcoran, Barbara 1911- .... **CLC 17**
See also AAYA 14; CA 21-24R; CAAS 2; CANR 11, 28, 48; CLR 50; DLB 52; JRDA; SAAS 20; SATA 3, 77

Cordelier, Maurice
See Giraudoux, (Hippolyte) Jean

Corelli, Marie 1855-1924 .... **TCLC 51**
See also Mackay, Mary DLB 34, 156

Corman, Cid 1924- .... **CLC 9**
See also Corman, Sidney CAAS 2; DLB 5, 193

Corman, Sidney 1924-
See Corman, Cid
See also CA 85-88; CANR 44; DAM POET

Cormier, Robert (Edmund) 1925- ... **CLC 12, 30; DA; DAB; DAC; DAM MST, NOV**
See also AAYA 3, 19; CA 1-4R; CANR 5, 23, 76; CDALB 1968-1988; CLR 12, 55; DLB 52; INT CANR-23; JRDA; MAI-CYA; MTCW 1, 2; SATA 10, 45, 83

Corn, Alfred (DeWitt III) 1943- .... **CLC 33**
See also CA 179; CAAE 179; CAAS 25; CANR 44; DLB 120; DLBY 80

Corneille, Pierre 1606-1684 ..... **LC 28; DAB; DAM MST**

Cornwell, David (John Moore)
1931- .... **CLC 9, 15; DAM POP**
See also le Carre, John CA 5-8R; CANR 13, 33, 59; DA3; MTCW 1, 2

Corso, (Nunzio) Gregory 1930- .... **CLC 1, 11**
See also CA 5-8R; CANR 41, 76; DA3; DLB 5, 16; MTCW 1, 2

Cortazar, Julio 1914-1984 ... **CLC 2, 3, 5, 10, 13, 15, 33, 34, 92; DAM MULT, NOV; HLC 1; SSC 7**
See also CA 21-24R; CANR 12, 32, 81; DA3; DLB 113; HW 1, 2; MTCW 1, 2

CORTES, HERNAN 1484-1547 .... **LC 31**

Corvinus, Jakob
See Raabe, Wilhelm (Karl)

Corwin, Cecil
See Kornbluth, C(yril) M.

Cosic, Dobrica 1921- .... **CLC 14**
See also CA 122; 138; DLB 181

Costain, Thomas B(ertram)
1885-1965 .... **CLC 30**
See also CA 5-8R; 25-28R; DLB 9

Costantini, Humberto 1924(?)-1987 . **CLC 49**
See also CA 131; 122; HW 1

Costello, Elvis 1955- .... **CLC 21**

Costenoble, Philostene
See Ghelderode, Michel de

Cotes, Cecil V.
See Duncan, Sara Jeannette

Cotter, Joseph Seamon Sr.
1861-1949 ...... **TCLC 28; BLC 1; DAM MULT**
See also BW 1; CA 124; DLB 50

Couch, Arthur Thomas Quiller
See Quiller-Couch, SirArthur (Thomas)

Coulton, James
See Hansen, Joseph

Couperus, Louis (Marie Anne) 1863-1923
TCLC 15
See also CA 115

Coupland, Douglas 1961- ..... **CLC 85; DAC; DAM POP**
See also CA 142; CANR 57

Court, Wesli
See Turco, Lewis (Putnam)

Courtenay, Bryce 1933- .... **CLC 59**
See also CA 138

Courtney, Robert
See Ellison, Harlan (Jay)

Cousteau, Jacques-Yves 1910-1997 .. **CLC 30**
See also CA 65-68; 159; CANR 15, 67; MTCW 1; SATA 38, 98

Coventry, Francis 1725-1754 .... **LC 46**

Cowan, Peter (Walkinshaw) 1914- .... **SSC 28**
See also CA 21-24R; CANR 9, 25, 50, 83

Coward, Noel (Peirce) 1899-1973 . **CLC 1, 9, 29, 51; DAM DRAM**
See also AITN 1; CA 17-18; 41-44R; CANR 35; CAP 2; CDBLB 1914-1945; DA3; DLB 10; MTCW 1, 2

Cowley, Abraham 1618-1667 .... **LC 43**
See also DLB 131, 151

Cowley, Malcolm 1898-1989 .... **CLC 39**
See also CA 5-8R; 128; CANR 3, 55; DLB 4, 48; DLBY 81, 89; MTCW 1, 2

Cowper, William 1731-1800 . **NCLC 8; DAM POET**
See also DA3; DLB 104, 109

Dahl, Roald 1916-1990 ...... **CLC 1, 6, 18, 79; DAB; DAC; DAM MST, NOV, POP**
See also AAYA 15; CA 1-4R; 133; CANR 6, 32, 37, 62; CLR 1, 7, 41; DA3; DLB 139; JRDA; MAICYA; MTCW 1, 2; SATA 1, 26, 73; SATA-Obit 65

Dahlberg, Edward 1900-1977 .. **CLC 1, 7, 14**
See also CA 9-12R; 69-72; CANR 31, 62; DLB 48; MTCW 1

Daitch, Susan 1954- .... **CLC 103**
See also CA 161

Dale, Colin .... **TCLC 18**
See also Lawrence, T(homas) E(dward)

Dale, George E.
See Asimov, Isaac

Dalton, Roque 1935-1975
See also HLCS 1; HW 2

Daly, Elizabeth 1878-1967 .... **CLC 52**
See also CA 23-24; 25-28R; CANR 60; CAP 2

Daly, Maureen 1921- .... **CLC 17**
See also AAYA 5; CANR 37, 83; JRDA; MAICYA; SAAS 1; SATA 2

Damas, Leon-Gontran 1912-1978 .... **CLC 84**
See also BW 1; CA 125; 73-76

Dana, Richard Henry Sr.
1787-1879 .... **NCLC 53**

Daniel, Samuel 1562(?)-1619 .... **LC 24**
See also DLB 62

Daniels, Brett
See Adler, Renata

Dannay, Frederic 1905-1982 . **CLC 11; DAM POP**
See also Queen, Ellery CA 1-4R; 107; CANR 1, 39; DLB 137; MTCW 1

D'Annunzio, Gabriele 1863-1938 ... **TCLC 6, 40**
See also CA 104; 155

Danois, N. le
See Gourmont, Remy (-Marie-Charles) de

Dante 1265-1321 .... **CMLC 3, 18; DA; DAB; DAC; DAM MST, POET; PC 21; WLCS**
See also DA3

d'Antibes, Germain
See Simenon, Georges (Jacques Christian)

Danticat, Edwidge 1969- .... **CLC 94**
See also AAYA 29; CA 152; CANR 73; MTCW 1

Danvers, Dennis 1947- .... **CLC 70**

Danziger, Paula 1944- .... **CLC 21**
See also AAYA 4; CA 112; 115; CANR 37; CLR 20; JRDA; MAICYA; SATA 36, 63, 102; SATA-Brief 30

Da Ponte, Lorenzo 1749-1838 .... **NCLC 50**

Dario, Ruben 1867-1916 .... **TCLC 4; DAM MULT; HLC 1; PC 15**
See also CA 131; CANR 81; HW 1, 2; MTCW 1, 2

Darley, George 1795-1846 .... **NCLC 2**
See also DLB 96

Darrow, Clarence (Seward)
1857-1938 .... **TCLC 81**
See also CA 164

Darwin, Charles 1809-1882 .... **NCLC 57**
See also DLB 57, 166

Daryush, Elizabeth 1887-1977 ...... **CLC 6, 19**
See also CA 49-52; CANR 3, 81; DLB 20

Dasgupta, Surendranath
1887-1952 .... **TCLC 81**
See also CA 157

Dashwood, Edmee Elizabeth Monica de la Pasture 1890-1943
See Delafield, E. M.
See also CA 119; 154

Daudet, (Louis Marie) Alphonse 1840-1897 **NCLC 1**
See also DLB 123

Daumal, Rene 1908-1944 .... **TCLC 14**
See also CA 114

Davenant, William 1606-1668 .... **LC 13**
See also DLB 58, 126

Davenport, Guy (Mattison, Jr.)
1927- .... **CLC 6, 14, 38; SSC 16**
See also CA 33-36R; CANR 23, 73; DLB 130

Davidson, Avram (James) 1923-1993
See Queen, Ellery
See also CA 101; 171; CANR 26; DLB 8

Davidson, Donald (Grady)
1893-1968 .... **CLC 2, 13, 19**
See also CA 5-8R; 25-28R; CANR 4, 84; DLB 45

Davidson, Hugh
See Hamilton, Edmond

Davidson, John 1857-1909 .... **TCLC 24**
See also CA 118; DLB 19

Davidson, Sara 1943- .... **CLC 9**
See also CA 81-84; CANR 44, 68; DLB 185

Davie, Donald (Alfred) 1922-1995 .... **CLC 5, 8, 10, 31; PC 29**
See also CA 1-4R; 149; CAAS 3; CANR 1, 44; DLB 27; MTCW 1

Davies, Ray(mond Douglas) 1944- ... **CLC 21**
See also CA 116; 146

Davies, Rhys 1901-1978 .... **CLC 23**
See also CA 9-12R; 81-84; CANR 4; DLB 139, 191

Davies, (William) Robertson
1913-1995 .... **CLC 2, 7, 13, 25, 42, 75, 91; DA; DAB; DAC; DAM MST, NOV, POP; WLC**
See also BEST 89:2; CA 33-36R; 150; CANR 17, 42; DA3; DLB 68; INT CANR-17; MTCW 1, 2

Davies, Walter C.
See Kornbluth, C(yril) M.

Davies, William Henry 1871-1940 ... **TCLC 5**
See also CA 104; 179; DLB 19, 174

Davis, Angela (Yvonne) 1944- .... **CLC 77; DAM MULT**
See also BW 2, 3; CA 57-60; CANR 10, 81; DA3

Davis, B. Lynch
See Bioy Casares, Adolfo; Borges, Jorge Luis

Davis, B. Lynch
See Bioy Casares, Adolfo

Davis, H(arold) L(enoir) 1894-1960 . **CLC 49**
See also CA 178; 89-92; DLB 9, 206

Davis, Rebecca (Blaine) Harding 1831-1910 **TCLC 6; SSC 38**
See also CA 104; 179; DLB 74

Davis, Richard Harding
1864-1916 .... **TCLC 24**
See also CA 114; 179; DLB 12, 23, 78, 79, 189; DLBD 13

Davison, Frank Dalby 1893-1970 ..... **CLC 15**
See also CA 116

Davison, Lawrence H.
See Lawrence, D(avid) H(erbert Richards)

Davison, Peter (Hubert) 1928- .... **CLC 28**
See also CA 9-12R; CAAS 4; CANR 3, 43, 84; DLB 5

Davys, Mary 1674-1732 .... **LC 1, 46**
See also DLB 39

Dawson, Fielding 1930- .... **CLC 6**
See also CA 85-88; DLB 130

Dawson, Peter
See Faust, Frederick (Schiller)

Day, Clarence (Shepard, Jr.) 1874-1935 **TCLC 25**
See also CA 108; DLB 11

Day, Thomas 1748-1789 .... **LC 1**
See also DLB 39; YABC 1

Day Lewis, C(ecil) 1904-1972 . **CLC 1, 6, 10; DAM POET; PC 11**
See also Blake, Nicholas CA 13-16; 33-36R; CANR 34; CAP 1; DLB 15, 20; MTCW 1, 2

Dazai Osamu 1909-1948 .... **TCLC 11**
See also Tsushima, Shuji CA 164; DLB 182

de Andrade, Carlos Drummond 1892-1945
See Drummond de Andrade, Carlos

Deane, Norman
See Creasey, John

Deane, Seamus (Francis) 1940- ...... **CLC 122**
See also CA 118; CANR 42

de Beauvoir, Simone (Lucie Ernestine Marie Bertrand)
See Beauvoir, Simone (Lucie Ernestine Marie Bertrand) de

de Beer, P.
See Bosman, Herman Charles

de Brissac, Malcolm
See Dickinson, Peter (Malcolm)

de Campos, Alvaro
See Pessoa, Fernando (Antonio Nogueira)

de Chardin, Pierre Teilhard
See Teilhard de Chardin, (Marie Joseph) Pierre

Dee, John 1527-1608 .... **LC 20**

Deer, Sandra 1940- .... **CLC 45**

De Ferrari, Gabriella 1941- .... **CLC 65**
See also CA 146

Defoe, Daniel 1660(?)-1731 .... **LC 1, 42; DA; DAB; DAC; DAM MST, NOV; WLC**
See also AAYA 27; CDBLB 1660-1789; CLR 61; DA3; DLB 39, 95, 101; JRDA; MAICYA; SATA 22

de Gourmont, Remy(-Marie-Charles)
See Gourmont, Remy (-Marie-Charles) de

de Hartog, Jan 1914- .... **CLC 19**
See also CA 1-4R; CANR 1

de Hostos, E. M.
See Hostos (y Bonilla), Eugenio Maria de

de Hostos, Eugenio M.
See Hostos (y Bonilla), Eugenio Maria de

Deighton, Len .... **CLC 4, 7, 22, 46**
See also Deighton, Leonard Cyril AAYA 6; BEST 89:2; CDBLB 1960 to Present; DLB 87

Deighton, Leonard Cyril 1929-
See Deighton, Len
See also CA 9-12R; CANR 19, 33, 68; DAM NOV, POP; DA3; MTCW 1, 2

Dickinson, Peter (Malcolm) 1927- .. **CLC 12, 35**

See also AAYA 9; CA 41-44R; CANR 31, 58; CLR 29; DLB 87, 161; JRDA; MAICYA; SATA 5, 62, 95

Dickson, Carr

See Carr, John Dickson

Dickson, Carter

See Carr, John Dickson

Diderot, Denis 1713-1784 .... **LC 26**

Didion, Joan 1934- .... **CLC 1, 3, 8, 14, 32; DAM NOV**

See also AITN 1; CA 5-8R; CANR 14, 52, 76; CDALB 1968-1988; DA3; DLB 2, 173, 185; DLBY 81, 86; MTCW 1, 2

Dietrich, Robert

See Hunt, E(verette) Howard, (Jr.)

Difusa, Pati

See Almodovar, Pedro

Dillard, Annie 1945- .. **CLC 9, 60, 115; DAM NOV**

See also AAYA 6; CA 49-52; CANR 3, 43, 62; DA3; DLBY 80; MTCW 1, 2; SATA 10

Dillard, R(ichard) H(enry) W(ilde) 1937- **CLC 5**

See also CA 21-24R; CAAS 7; CANR 10; DLB 5

Dillon, Eilis 1920-1994 .... **CLC 17**

See also CA 9-12R, 182; 147; CAAE 182; CAAS 3; CANR 4, 38, 78; CLR 26; MAICYA; SATA 2, 74; SATA-Essay 105; SATA-Obit 83

Dimont, Penelope

See Mortimer, Penelope (Ruth)

Dinesen, Isak .... **CLC 10, 29, 95; SSC 7**

See also Blixen, Karen (Christentze Dinesen) MTCW 1

Ding Ling .... **CLC 68**

See also Chiang, Pin-chin

Diphusa, Patty

See Almodovar, Pedro

Disch, Thomas M(ichael) 1940- ... **CLC 7, 36**

See also AAYA 17; CA 21-24R; CAAS 4; CANR 17, 36, 54; CLR 18; DA3; DLB 8; MAICYA; MTCW 1, 2; SAAS 15; SATA 92

Disch, Tom

See Disch, Thomas M(ichael)

d'Isly, Georges

See Simenon, Georges (Jacques Christian)

Disraeli, Benjamin 1804-1881 ... **NCLC 2, 39, 79**

See also DLB 21, 55

Ditcum, Steve

See Crumb, R(obert)

Dixon, Paige

See Corcoran, Barbara

Dixon, Stephen 1936- .... **CLC 52; SSC 16**

See also CA 89-92; CANR 17, 40, 54; DLB 130

Doak, Annie

See Dillard, Annie

Dobell, Sydney Thompson
1824-1874 .... **NCLC 43**

See also DLB 32

Doblin, Alfred .... **TCLC 13**

See also Doeblin, Alfred

Dobrolyubov, Nikolai Alexandrovich
1836-1861 .... **NCLC 5**

Dobson, Austin 1840-1921 .... **TCLC 79**

See also DLB 35; 144

Dobyns, Stephen 1941- .... **CLC 37**

See also CA 45-48; CANR 2, 18

Doctorow, E(dgar) L(aurence)
1931- .... **CLC 6, 11, 15, 18, 37, 44, 65, 113; DAM NOV, POP**

See also AAYA 22; AITN 2; BEST 89:3; CA 45-48; CANR 2, 33, 51, 76; CDALB 1968-1988; DA3; DLB 2, 28, 173; DLBY 80; MTCW 1, 2

Dodgson, Charles Lutwidge 1832-1898

See Carroll, Lewis

See also CLR 2; DA; DAB; DAC; DAM MST, NOV, POET; DA3; MAICYA; SATA 100; YABC 2

Dodson, Owen (Vincent)
1914-1983 .... **CLC 79; BLC 1; DAM MULT**

See also BW 1; CA 65-68; 110; CANR 24; DLB 76

Doeblin, Alfred 1878-1957 .... **TCLC 13**

See also Doblin, Alfred CA 110; 141; DLB 66

Doerr, Harriet 1910- .... **CLC 34**

See also CA 117; 122; CANR 47; INT 122

Domecq, H(onorio Bustos)

See Bioy Casares, Adolfo

Domecq, H(onorio) Bustos

See Bioy Casares, Adolfo; Borges, Jorge Luis

Domini, Rey

See Lorde, Audre (Geraldine)

Dominique

See Proust, (Valentin-Louis-George-Eugene-) Marcel

Don, A

See Stephen, SirLeslie

Donaldson, Stephen R. 1947- .... **CLC 46; DAM POP**

See also CA 89-92; CANR 13, 55; INT CANR-13

Donleavy, J(ames) P(atrick) 1926- .... **CLC 1, 4, 6, 10, 45**

See also AITN 2; CA 9-12R; CANR 24, 49, 62, 80; DLB 6, 173; INT CANR-24; MTCW 1, 2

Donne, John 1572-1631 .... **LC 10, 24; DA; DAB; DAC; DAM MST, POET; PC 1; WLC**

See also CDBLB Before 1660; DLB 121, 151

Donnell, David 1939(?)- .... **CLC 34**

Donoghue, P. S.

See Hunt, E(verette) Howard, (Jr.)

Donoso (Yanez), Jose 1924-1996 ... **CLC 4, 8, 11, 32, 99; DAM MULT; HLC 1; SSC 34**

See also CA 81-84; 155; CANR 32, 73; DLB 113; HW 1, 2; MTCW 1, 2

Donovan, John 1928-1992 .... **CLC 35**

See also AAYA 20; CA 97-100; 137; CLR 3; MAICYA; SATA 72; SATA-Brief 29

Don Roberto

See Cunninghame Graham, R(obert) B(ontine)

Doolittle, Hilda 1886-1961 . **CLC 3, 8, 14, 31, 34, 73; DA; DAC; DAM MST, POET; PC 5; WLC**

See also H. D. CA 97-100; CANR 35; DLB 4, 45; MTCW 1, 2

Dorfman, Ariel 1942- ...... **CLC 48, 77; DAM MULT; HLC 1**

See also CA 124; 130; CANR 67, 70; HW 1, 2; INT 130

Dorn, Edward (Merton) 1929- ... **CLC 10, 18**

See also CA 93-96; CANR 42, 79; DLB 5; INT 93-96

Dorris, Michael (Anthony)
1945-1997 .... **CLC 109; DAM MULT, NOV**

See also AAYA 20; BEST 90:1; CA 102; 157; CANR 19, 46, 75; CLR 58; DA3; DLB 175; MTCW 2; NNAL; SATA 75; SATA-Obit 94

Dorris, Michael A.

See Dorris, Michael (Anthony)

Dorsan, Luc

See Simenon, Georges (Jacques Christian)

Dorsange, Jean

See Simenon, Georges (Jacques Christian)

Dos Passos, John (Roderigo)
1896-1970 ... **CLC 1, 4, 8, 11, 15, 25, 34, 82; DA; DAB; DAC; DAM MST, NOV; WLC**

See also CA 1-4R; 29-32R; CANR 3; CDALB 1929-1941; DA3; DLB 4, 9; DLBD 1, 15; DLBY 96; MTCW 1, 2

Dossage, Jean

See Simenon, Georges (Jacques Christian)

Dostoevsky, Fedor Mikhailovich 1821-1881 **NCLC 2, 7, 21, 33, 43; DA; DAB; DAC; DAM MST, NOV; SSC 2, 33; WLC**

See also DA3

Doughty, Charles M(ontagu) 1843-1926 **TCLC 27**

See also CA 115; 178; DLB 19, 57, 174

Douglas, Ellen .... **CLC 73**

See also Haxton, Josephine Ayres; Williamson, Ellen Douglas

Douglas, Gavin 1475(?)-1522 .... **LC 20**

See also DLB 132

Douglas, George

See Brown, George Douglas

Douglas, Keith (Castellain)
1920-1944 .... **TCLC 40**

See also CA 160; DLB 27

Douglas, Leonard

See Bradbury, Ray (Douglas)

Douglas, Michael

See Crichton, (John) Michael

Douglas, (George) Norman
1868-1952 .... **TCLC 68**

See also CA 119; 157; DLB 34, 195

Douglas, William

See Brown, George Douglas

Douglass, Frederick 1817(?)-1895 .. **NCLC 7, 55; BLC 1; DA; DAC; DAM MST, MULT; WLC**

See also CDALB 1640-1865; DA3; DLB 1, 43, 50, 79; SATA 29

Dourado, (Waldomiro Freitas) Autran 1926- **CLC 23, 60**

See also CA 25-28R; 179; CANR 34, 81; DLB 145; HW 2

Duras, Marguerite 1914-1996 . **CLC 3, 6, 11, 20, 34, 40, 68, 100**
   See also CA 25-28R; 151; CANR 50; DLB 83; MTCW 1, 2

Durban, (Rosa) Pam 1947- .... **CLC 39**
   See also CA 123

Durcan, Paul 1944- .... **CLC 43, 70; DAM POET**
   See also CA 134

Durkheim, Emile 1858-1917 .... **TCLC 55**

Durrell, Lawrence (George) 1912-1990 .... **CLC 1, 4, 6, 8, 13, 27, 41; DAM NOV**
   See also CA 9-12R; 132; CANR 40, 77; CDBLB 1945-1960; DLB 15, 27, 204; DLBY 90; MTCW 1, 2

Durrenmatt, Friedrich
   See Duerrenmatt, Friedrich

Dutt, Toru 1856-1877 .... **NCLC 29**

Dwight, Timothy 1752-1817 .... **NCLC 13**
   See also DLB 37

Dworkin, Andrea 1946- .... **CLC 43**
   See also CA 77-80; CAAS 21; CANR 16, 39, 76; INT CANR-16; MTCW 1, 2

Dwyer, Deanna
   See Koontz, Dean R(ay)

Dwyer, K. R.
   See Koontz, Dean R(ay)

Dwyer, Thomas A. 1923- .... **CLC 114**
   See also CA 115

Dye, Richard
   See De Voto, Bernard (Augustine)

Dylan, Bob 1941- .... **CLC 3, 4, 6, 12, 77**
   See also CA 41-44R; DLB 16

E. V. L.
   See Lucas, E(dward) V(errall)

Eagleton, Terence (Francis) 1943-
   See Eagleton, Terry
   See also CA 57-60; CANR 7, 23, 68; MTCW 1, 2

Eagleton, Terry .... **CLC 63**
   See also Eagleton, Terence (Francis) MTCW 1

Early, Jack
   See Scoppettone, Sandra

East, Michael
   See West, Morris L(anglo)

Eastaway, Edward
   See Thomas, (Philip) Edward

Eastlake, William (Derry) 1917-1997 .... **CLC 8**
   See also CA 5-8R; 158; CAAS 1; CANR 5, 63; DLB 6, 206; INT CANR-5

Eastman, Charles A(lexander) 1858-1939 **TCLC 55; DAM MULT**
   See also CA 179; DLB 175; NNAL; YABC 1

Eberhart, Richard (Ghormley) 1904- .. **CLC 3, 11, 19, 56; DAM POET**
   See also CA 1-4R; CANR 2; CDALB 1941-1968; DLB 48; MTCW 1

Eberstadt, Fernanda 1960- .... **CLC 39**
   See also CA 136; CANR 69

Echegaray (y Eizaguirre), Jose (Maria Waldo) 1832-1916 .... **TCLC 4; HLCS 1**
   See also CA 104; CANR 32; HW 1; MTCW 1

Echeverria, (Jose) Esteban (Antonino) 1805-1851 .... **NCLC 18**

Echo
   See Proust, (Valentin-Louis-George-Eugene-) Marcel

Eckert, Allan W. 1931- .... **CLC 17**
   See also AAYA 18; CA 13-16R; CANR 14, 45; INT CANR-14; SAAS 21; SATA 29, 91; SATA-Brief 27

Eckhart, Meister 1260(?)-1328(?) ... **CMLC 9**
   See also DLB 115

Eckmar, F. R.
   See de Hartog, Jan

Eco, Umberto 1932- .... **CLC 28, 60; DAM NOV, POP**
   See also BEST 90:1; CA 77-80; CANR 12, 33, 55; DA3; DLB 196; MTCW 1, 2

Eddison, E(ric) R(ucker) 1882-1945 .... **TCLC 15**
   See also CA 109; 156

Eddy, Mary (Ann Morse) Baker 1821-1910 **TCLC 71**
   See also CA 113; 174

Edel, (Joseph) Leon 1907-1997 .. **CLC 29, 34**
   See also CA 1-4R; 161; CANR 1, 22; DLB 103; INT CANR-22

Eden, Emily 1797-1869 .... **NCLC 10**

Edgar, David 1948- .. **CLC 42; DAM DRAM**
   See also CA 57-60; CANR 12, 61; DLB 13; MTCW 1

Edgerton, Clyde (Carlyle) 1944- ...... **CLC 39**
   See also AAYA 17; CA 118; 134; CANR 64; INT 134

Edgeworth, Maria 1768-1849 .... **NCLC 1, 51**
   See also DLB 116, 159, 163; SATA 21

Edison, Thomas 1847-1931 .... **TCLC 96**

Edmonds, Paul
   See Kuttner, Henry

Edmonds, Walter D(umaux) 1903-1998 .... **CLC 35**
   See also CA 5-8R; CANR 2; DLB 9; MAI-CYA; SAAS 4; SATA 1, 27; SATA-Obit 99

Edmondson, Wallace
   See Ellison, Harlan (Jay)

Edson, Russell .... **CLC 13**
   See also CA 33-36R

Edwards, Bronwen Elizabeth
   See Rose, Wendy

Edwards, G(erald) B(asil) 1899-1976 .... **CLC 25**
   See also CA 110

Edwards, Gus 1939- .... **CLC 43**
   See also CA 108; INT 108

Edwards, Jonathan 1703-1758 .... **LC 7, 54; DA; DAC; DAM MST**
   See also DLB 24

Efron, Marina Ivanovna Tsvetaeva
   See Tsvetaeva (Efron), Marina (Ivanovna)

Ehle, John (Marsden, Jr.) 1925- ...... **CLC 27**
   See also CA 9-12R

Ehrenbourg, Ilya (Grigoryevich)
   See Ehrenburg, Ilya (Grigoryevich)

Ehrenburg, Ilya (Grigoryevich) 1891-1967 **CLC 18, 34, 62**
   See also CA 102; 25-28R

Ehrenburg, Ilyo (Grigoryevich)
   See Ehrenburg, Ilya (Grigoryevich)

Ehrenreich, Barbara 1941- .... **CLC 110**
   See also BEST 90:4; CA 73-76; CANR 16, 37, 62; MTCW 1, 2

Eich, Guenter 1907-1972 .... **CLC 15**
   See also CA 111; 93-96; DLB 69, 124

Eichendorff, Joseph Freiherr von 1788-1857 **NCLC 8**
   See also DLB 90

Eigner, Larry .... **CLC 9**
   See also Eigner, Laurence (Joel) CAAS 23; DLB 5

Eigner, Laurence (Joel) 1927-1996
   See Eigner, Larry
   See also CA 9-12R; 151; CANR 6, 84; DLB 193

Einstein, Albert 1879-1955 .... **TCLC 65**
   See also CA 121; 133; MTCW 1, 2

Eiseley, Loren Corey 1907-1977 .... **CLC 7**
   See also AAYA 5; CA 1-4R; 73-76; CANR 6; DLBD 17

Eisenstadt, Jill 1963- .... **CLC 50**
   See also CA 140

Eisenstein, Sergei (Mikhailovich) 1898-1948 **TCLC 57**
   See also CA 114; 149

Eisner, Simon
   See Kornbluth, C(yril) M.

Ekeloef, (Bengt) Gunnar 1907-1968 ... **CLC 27; DAM POET; PC 23**
   See also CA 123; 25-28R

Ekelof, (Bengt) Gunnar
   See Ekeloef, (Bengt) Gunnar

Ekelund, Vilhelm 1880-1949 .... **TCLC 75**

Ekwensi, C. O. D.
   See Ekwensi, Cyprian (Odiatu Duaka)

Ekwensi, Cyprian (Odiatu Duaka) 1921- **CLC 4; BLC 1; DAM MULT**
   See also BW 2, 3; CA 29-32R; CANR 18, 42, 74; DLB 117; MTCW 1, 2; SATA 66

Elaine .... **TCLC 18**
   See also Leverson, Ada

El Crummo
   See Crumb, R(obert)

Elder, Lonne III 1931-1996 .... **DC 8**
   See also BLC 1; BW 1, 3; CA 81-84; 152; CANR 25; DAM MULT; DLB 7, 38, 44

Elia
   See Lamb, Charles

Eliade, Mircea 1907-1986 .... **CLC 19**
   See also CA 65-68; 119; CANR 30, 62; MTCW 1

Eliot, A. D.
   See Jewett, (Theodora) Sarah Orne

Eliot, Alice
   See Jewett, (Theodora) Sarah Orne

Eliot, Dan
   See Silverberg, Robert

Eliot, George 1819-1880 ...... **NCLC 4, 13, 23, 41, 49; DA; DAB; DAC; DAM MST, NOV; PC 20; WLC**
   See also CDBLB 1832-1890; DA3; DLB 21, 35, 55

Eliot, John 1604-1690 .... **LC 5**
   See also DLB 24

Eliot, T(homas) S(tearns) 1888-1965 ...... **CLC 1, 2, 3, 6, 9, 10, 13, 15, 24, 34, 41, 55, 57, 113; DA; DAB; DAC; DAM DRAM, MST, POET; PC 5; WLC**
   See also AAYA 28; CA 5-8R; 25-28R;

CANR 41; CDALB 1929-1941; DA3; DLB 7, 10, 45, 63; DLBY 88; MTCW 1, 2

Elizabeth 1866-1941 .... **TCLC 41**

Elkin, Stanley L(awrence)
  1930-1995 .. **CLC 4, 6, 9, 14, 27, 51, 91; DAM NOV, POP; SSC 12**
  See also CA 9-12R; 148; CANR 8, 46; DLB 2, 28; DLBY 80; INT CANR-8; MTCW 1, 2

Elledge, Scott .... **CLC 34**

Elliot, Don
  See Silverberg, Robert

Elliott, Don
  See Silverberg, Robert

Elliott, George P(aul) 1918-1980 .... **CLC 2**
  See also CA 1-4R; 97-100; CANR 2

Elliott, Janice 1931- .... **CLC 47**
  See also CA 13-16R; CANR 8, 29, 84; DLB 14

Elliott, Sumner Locke 1917-1991 ..... **CLC 38**
  See also CA 5-8R; 134; CANR 2, 21

Elliott, William
  See Bradbury, Ray (Douglas)

Ellis, A. E. .... **CLC 7**

Ellis, Alice Thomas .... **CLC 40**
  See also Haycraft, Anna DLB 194; MTCW 1

Ellis, Bret Easton 1964- ..... **CLC 39, 71, 117; DAM POP**
  See also AAYA 2; CA 118; 123; CANR 51, 74; DA3; INT 123; MTCW 1

Ellis, (Henry) Havelock
  1859-1939 .... **TCLC 14**
  See also CA 109; 169; DLB 190

Ellis, Landon
  See Ellison, Harlan (Jay)

Ellis, Trey 1962- .... **CLC 55**
  See also CA 146

Ellison, Harlan (Jay) 1934- ... **CLC 1, 13, 42; DAM POP; SSC 14**
  See also AAYA 29; CA 5-8R; CANR 5, 46; DLB 8; INT CANR-5; MTCW 1, 2

Ellison, Ralph (Waldo) 1914-1994 .... **CLC 1, 3, 11, 54, 86, 114; BLC 1; DA; DAB; DAC; DAM MST, MULT, NOV; SSC 26; WLC**
  See also AAYA 19; BW 1, 3; CA 9-12R; 145; CANR 24, 53; CDALB 1941-1968; DA3; DLB 2, 76; DLBY 94; MTCW 1, 2

Ellmann, Lucy (Elizabeth) 1956- ..... **CLC 61**
  See also CA 128

Ellmann, Richard (David)
  1918-1987 .... **CLC 50**
  See also BEST 89:2; CA 1-4R; 122; CANR 2, 28, 61; DLB 103; DLBY 87; MTCW 1, 2

Elman, Richard (Martin)
  1934-1997 .... **CLC 19**
  See also CA 17-20R; 163; CAAS 3; CANR 47

Elron
  See Hubbard, L(afayette) Ron(ald)

Eluard, Paul .... **TCLC 7, 41**
  See also Grindel, Eugene

Elyot, Sir Thomas 1490(?)-1546 .... **LC 11**

Elytis, Odysseus 1911-1996 .... **CLC 15, 49, 100; DAM POET; PC 21**
  See also CA 102; 151; MTCW 1, 2

Emecheta, (Florence Onye) Buchi
  1944- .. **CLC 14, 48, 128; BLC 2; DAM MULT**
  See also BW 2, 3; CA 81-84; CANR 27, 81; DA3; DLB 117; MTCW 1, 2; SATA 66

Emerson, Mary Moody
  1774-1863 .... **NCLC 66**

Emerson, Ralph Waldo 1803-1882 . **NCLC 1, 38; DA; DAB; DAC; DAM MST, POET; PC 18; WLC**
  See also CDALB 1640-1865; DA3; DLB 1, 59, 73

Eminescu, Mihail 1850-1889 .... **NCLC 33**

Empson, William 1906-1984 ... **CLC 3, 8, 19, 33, 34**
  See also CA 17-20R; 112; CANR 31, 61; DLB 20; MTCW 1, 2

Enchi, Fumiko (Ueda) 1905-1986 ..... **CLC 31**
  See also CA 129; 121; DLB 182

Ende, Michael (Andreas Helmuth)
  1929-1995 .... **CLC 31**
  See also CA 118; 124; 149; CANR 36; CLR 14; DLB 75; MAICYA; SATA 61; SATA-Brief 42; SATA-Obit 86

Endo, Shusaku 1923-1996 ..... **CLC 7, 14, 19, 54, 99; DAM NOV**
  See also CA 29-32R; 153; CANR 21, 54; DA3; DLB 182; MTCW 1, 2

Engel, Marian 1933-1985 .... **CLC 36**
  See also CA 25-28R; CANR 12; DLB 53; INT CANR-12

Engelhardt, Frederick
  See Hubbard, L(afayette) Ron(ald)

Enright, D(ennis) J(oseph) 1920- .. **CLC 4, 8, 31**
  See also CA 1-4R; CANR 1, 42, 83; DLB 27; SATA 25

Enzensberger, Hans Magnus
  1929- .... **CLC 43; PC 28**
  See also CA 116; 119

Ephron, Nora 1941- .... **CLC 17, 31**
  See also AITN 2; CA 65-68; CANR 12, 39, 83

Epicurus 341B.C.-270B.C. .... **CMLC 21**
  See also DLB 176

Epsilon
  See Betjeman, John

Epstein, Daniel Mark 1948- .... **CLC 7**
  See also CA 49-52; CANR 2, 53

Epstein, Jacob 1956- .... **CLC 19**
  See also CA 114

Epstein, Jean 1897-1953 .... **TCLC 92**

Epstein, Joseph 1937- .... **CLC 39**
  See also CA 112; 119; CANR 50, 65

Epstein, Leslie 1938- .... **CLC 27**
  See also CA 73-76; CAAS 12; CANR 23, 69

Equiano, Olaudah 1745(?)-1797 .... **LC 16; BLC 2; DAM MULT**
  See also DLB 37, 50

ER .... **TCLC 33**
  See also CA 160; DLB 85

Erasmus, Desiderius 1469(?)-1536 ...... **LC 16**

Erdman, Paul E(mil) 1932- .... **CLC 25**
  See also AITN 1; CA 61-64; CANR 13, 43, 84

Erdrich, Louise 1954- .... **CLC 39, 54, 120; DAM MULT, NOV, POP**
  See also AAYA 10; BEST 89:1; CA 114; CANR 41, 62; CDALBS; DA3; DLB 152, 175, 206; MTCW 1; NNAL; SATA 94

Erenburg, Ilya (Grigoryevich)
  See Ehrenburg, Ilya (Grigoryevich)

Erickson, Stephen Michael 1950-
  See Erickson, Steve
  See also CA 129

Erickson, Steve 1950- .... **CLC 64**
  See also Erickson, Stephen Michael CANR 60, 68

Ericson, Walter
  See Fast, Howard (Melvin)

Eriksson, Buntel
  See Bergman, (Ernst) Ingmar

Ernaux, Annie 1940- .... **CLC 88**
  See also CA 147

Erskine, John 1879-1951 .... **TCLC 84**
  See also CA 112; 159; DLB 9, 102

Eschenbach, Wolfram von
  See Wolfram von Eschenbach

Eseki, Bruno
  See Mphahlele, Ezekiel

Esenin, Sergei (Alexandrovich) 1895-1925
  TCLC 4
  See also CA 104

Eshleman, Clayton 1935- .... **CLC 7**
  See also CA 33-36R; CAAS 6; DLB 5

Espriella, Don Manuel Alvarez
  See Southey, Robert

Espriu, Salvador 1913-1985 .... **CLC 9**
  See also CA 154; 115; DLB 134

Espronceda, Jose de 1808-1842 ..... **NCLC 39**

Esquivel, Laura 1951(?)-
  See also AAYA 29; CA 143; CANR 68; DA3; HLCS 1; MTCW 1

Esse, James
  See Stephens, James

Esterbrook, Tom
  See Hubbard, L(afayette) Ron(ald)

Estleman, Loren D. 1952- ..... **CLC 48; DAM NOV, POP**
  See also AAYA 27; CA 85-88; CANR 27, 74; DA3; INT CANR-27; MTCW 1, 2

Euclid 306B.C.-283B.C. .... **CMLC 25**

Eugenides, Jeffrey 1960(?)- .... **CLC 81**
  See also CA 144

Euripides c. 485B.C.-406B.C. .... **CMLC 23; DA; DAB; DAC; DAM DRAM, MST; DC 4; WLCS**
  See also DA3; DLB 176

Evan, Evin
  See Faust, Frederick (Schiller)

Evans, Caradoc 1878-1945 .... **TCLC 85**

Evans, Evan
  See Faust, Frederick (Schiller)

Evans, Marian
  See Eliot, George

Evans, Mary Ann
  See Eliot, George

Evarts, Esther
  See Benson, Sally

Everett, Percival L. 1956- .... **CLC 57**
  See also BW 2; CA 129

Everson, R(onald) G(ilmour) 1903- . **CLC 27**
  See also CA 17-20R; DLB 88

Everson, William (Oliver)
1912-1994 .... **CLC 1, 5, 14**
See also CA 9-12R; 145; CANR 20; DLB
212; MTCW 1

Evtushenko, Evgenii Aleksandrovich
See Yevtushenko, Yevgeny (Alexandrovich)

Ewart, Gavin (Buchanan)
1916-1995 .... **CLC 13, 46**
See also CA 89-92; 150; CANR 17, 46;
DLB 40; MTCW 1

Ewers, Hanns Heinz 1871-1943 ..... **TCLC 12**
See also CA 109; 149

Ewing, Frederick R.
See Sturgeon, Theodore (Hamilton)

Exley, Frederick (Earl) 1929-1992 .... **CLC 6, 11**
See also AITN 2; CA 81-84; 138; DLB 143;
DLBY 81

Eynhardt, Guillermo
See Quiroga, Horacio (Sylvestre)

Ezekiel, Nissim 1924- .... **CLC 61**
See also CA 61-64

Ezekiel, Tish O'Dowd 1943- .... **CLC 34**
See also CA 129

Fadeyev, A.
See Bulgya, Alexander Alexandrovich

Fadeyev, Alexander .... **TCLC 53**
See also Bulgya, Alexander Alexandrovich

Fagen, Donald 1948- .... **CLC 26**

Fainzilberg, Ilya Arnoldovich 1897-1937
See Ilf, Ilya
See also CA 120; 165

Fair, Ronald L. 1932- .... **CLC 18**
See also BW 1; CA 69-72; CANR 25; DLB
33

Fairbairn, Roger
See Carr, John Dickson

Fairbairns, Zoe (Ann) 1948- .... **CLC 32**
See also CA 103; CANR 21, 85

Falco, Gian
See Papini, Giovanni

Falconer, James
See Kirkup, James

Falconer, Kenneth
See Kornbluth, C(yril) M.

Falkland, Samuel
See Heijermans, Herman

Fallaci, Oriana 1930- .... **CLC 11, 110**
See also CA 77-80; CANR 15, 58; MTCW
1

Faludy, George 1913- .... **CLC 42**
See also CA 21-24R

Faludy, Gyoergy
See Faludy, George

Fanon, Frantz 1925-1961 ... **CLC 74; BLC 2; DAM MULT**
See also BW 1; CA 116; 89-92

Fanshawe, Ann 1625-1680 .... **LC 11**

Fante, John (Thomas) 1911-1983 ..... **CLC 60**
See also CA 69-72; 109; CANR 23; DLB
130; DLBY 83

Farah, Nuruddin 1945- ...... **CLC 53; BLC 2; DAM MULT**
See also BW 2, 3; CA 106; CANR 81; DLB
125

Fargue, Leon-Paul 1876(?)-1947 .... **TCLC 11**
See also CA 109

Farigoule, Louis
See Romains, Jules

Farina, Richard 1936(?)-1966 .... **CLC 9**
See also CA 81-84; 25-28R

Farley, Walter (Lorimer)
1915-1989 .... **CLC 17**
See also CA 17-20R; CANR 8, 29, 84; DLB
22; JRDA; MAICYA; SATA 2, 43

Farmer, Philip Jose 1918- .... **CLC 1, 19**
See also AAYA 28; CA 1-4R; CANR 4, 35;
DLB 8; MTCW 1; SATA 93

Farquhar, George 1677-1707 ... **LC 21; DAM DRAM**
See also DLB 84

Farrell, J(ames) G(ordon)
1935-1979 .... **CLC 6**
See also CA 73-76; 89-92; CANR 36; DLB
14; MTCW 1

Farrell, James T(homas) 1904-1979 . **CLC 1, 4, 8, 11, 66; SSC 28**
See also CA 5-8R; 89-92; CANR 9, 61;
DLB 4, 9, 86; DLBD 2; MTCW 1, 2

Farren, Richard J.
See Betjeman, John

Farren, Richard M.
See Betjeman, John

Fassbinder, Rainer Werner
1946-1982 .... **CLC 20**
See also CA 93-96; 106; CANR 31

Fast, Howard (Melvin) 1914- .... **CLC 23; DAM NOV**
See also AAYA 16; CA 1-4R, 181; CAAE
181; CAAS 18; CANR 1, 33, 54, 75; DLB
9; INT CANR-33; MTCW 1; SATA 7;
SATA-Essay 107

Faulcon, Robert
See Holdstock, Robert P.

Faulkner, William (Cuthbert) 1897-1962
**CLC 1, 3, 6, 8, 9, 11, 14, 18, 28, 52, 68;
DA; DAB; DAC; DAM MST, NOV;
SSC 1, 35; WLC**
See also AAYA 7; CA 81-84; CANR 33;
CDALB 1929-1941; DA3; DLB 9, 11, 44,
102; DLBD 2; DLBY 86, 97; MTCW 1, 2

Fauset, Jessie Redmon
1884(?)-1961 .... **CLC 19, 54; BLC 2; DAM MULT**
See also BW 1; CA 109; CANR 83; DLB
51

Faust, Frederick (Schiller) 1892-1944(?)
TCLC 49; DAM POP
See also CA 108; 152

Faust, Irvin 1924- .... **CLC 8**
See also CA 33-36R; CANR 28, 67; DLB
2, 28; DLBY 80

Fawkes, Guy
See Benchley, Robert (Charles)

Fearing, Kenneth (Flexner)
1902-1961 .... **CLC 51**
See also CA 93-96; CANR 59; DLB 9

Fecamps, Elise
See Creasey, John

Federman, Raymond 1928- .... **CLC 6, 47**
See also CA 17-20R; CAAS 8; CANR 10,
43, 83; DLBY 80

Federspiel, J(uerg) F. 1931- .... **CLC 42**
See also CA 146

Feiffer, Jules (Ralph) 1929- ..... **CLC 2, 8, 64; DAM DRAM**
See also AAYA 3; CA 17-20R; CANR 30,
59; DLB 7, 44; INT CANR-30; MTCW
1; SATA 8, 61, 111

Feige, Hermann Albert Otto Maximilian
See Traven, B.

Feinberg, David B. 1956-1994 .... **CLC 59**
See also CA 135; 147

Feinstein, Elaine 1930- .... **CLC 36**
See also CA 69-72; CAAS 1; CANR 31,
68; DLB 14, 40; MTCW 1

Feldman, Irving (Mordecai) 1928- ..... **CLC 7**
See also CA 1-4R; CANR 1; DLB 169

Felix-Tchicaya, Gerald
See Tchicaya, Gerald Felix

Fellini, Federico 1920-1993 .... **CLC 16, 85**
See also CA 65-68; 143; CANR 33

Felsen, Henry Gregor 1916-1995 ..... **CLC 17**
See also CA 1-4R; 180; CANR 1; SAAS 2;
SATA 1

Fenno, Jack
See Calisher, Hortense

Fenollosa, Ernest (Francisco) 1853-1908
TCLC 91

Fenton, James Martin 1949- .... **CLC 32**
See also CA 102; DLB 40

Ferber, Edna 1887-1968 .... **CLC 18, 93**
See also AITN 1; CA 5-8R; 25-28R; CANR
68; DLB 9, 28, 86; MTCW 1, 2; SATA 7

Ferguson, Helen
See Kavan, Anna

Ferguson, Samuel 1810-1886 .... **NCLC 33**
See also DLB 32

Fergusson, Robert 1750-1774 .... **LC 29**
See also DLB 109

Ferling, Lawrence
See Ferlinghetti, Lawrence (Monsanto)

Ferlinghetti, Lawrence (Monsanto) 1919(?)-
**CLC 2, 6, 10, 27, 111; DAM POET; PC
1**
See also CA 5-8R; CANR 3, 41, 73;
CDALB 1941-1968; DA3; DLB 5, 16;
MTCW 1, 2

Fernandez, Vicente Garcia Huidobro
See Huidobro Fernandez, Vicente Garcia

Ferre, Rosario 1942- .... **SSC 36; HLCS 1**
See also CA 131; CANR 55, 81; DLB 145;
HW 1, 2; MTCW 1

Ferrer, Gabriel (Francisco Victor) Miro
See Miro (Ferrer), Gabriel (Francisco
Victor)

Ferrier, Susan (Edmonstone) 1782-1854
NCLC 8
See also DLB 116

Ferrigno, Robert 1948(?)- .... **CLC 65**
See also CA 140

Ferron, Jacques 1921-1985 .... **CLC 94; DAC**
See also CA 117; 129; DLB 60

Feuchtwanger, Lion 1884-1958 .... **TCLC 3**
See also CA 104; DLB 66

Feuillet, Octave 1821-1890 .... **NCLC 45**
See also DLB 192

Feydeau, Georges (Leon Jules Marie)
1862-1921 .... **TCLC 22; DAM DRAM**
See also CA 113; 152; CANR 84; DLB 192

Fichte, Johann Gottlieb
1762-1814 .... **NCLC 62**
See also DLB 90

Ficino, Marsilio 1433-1499 .... **LC 12**

Fiedeler, Hans
See Doeblin, Alfred

Fiedler, Leslie A(aron) 1917- .. **CLC 4, 13, 24**
See also CA 9-12R; CANR 7, 63; DLB 28,
67; MTCW 1, 2

Field, Andrew 1938- .... **CLC 44**
See also CA 97-100; CANR 25

Field, Eugene 1850-1895 .... **NCLC 3**
See also DLB 23, 42, 140; DLBD 13; MAI-CYA; SATA 16

Field, Gans T.
See Wellman, Manly Wade

Field, Michael 1915-1971 .... **TCLC 43**
See also CA 29-32R

Field, Peter
See Hobson, Laura Z(ametkin)

Fielding, Henry 1707-1754 ..... **LC 1, 46; DA; DAB; DAC; DAM DRAM, MST, NOV; WLC**
See also CDBLB 1660-1789; DA3; DLB 39, 84, 101

Fielding, Sarah 1710-1768 .... **LC 1, 44**
See also DLB 39

Fields, W. C. 1880-1946 .... **TCLC 80**
See also DLB 44

Fierstein, Harvey (Forbes) 1954- .... **CLC 33; DAM DRAM, POP**
See also CA 123; 129; DA3

Figes, Eva 1932- .... **CLC 31**
See also CA 53-56; CANR 4, 44, 83; DLB 14

Finch, Anne 1661-1720 .... **LC 3; PC 21**
See also DLB 95

Finch, Robert (Duer Claydon)
1900- .... **CLC 18**
See also CA 57-60; CANR 9, 24, 49; DLB 88

Findley, Timothy 1930- . **CLC 27, 102; DAC; DAM MST**
See also CA 25-28R; CANR 12, 42, 69; DLB 53

Fink, William
See Mencken, H(enry) L(ouis)

Firbank, Louis 1942-
See Reed, Lou
See also CA 117

Firbank, (Arthur Annesley) Ronald
1886-1926 .... **TCLC 1**
See also CA 104; 177; DLB 36

Fisher, Dorothy (Frances) Canfield
1879-1958 .... **TCLC 87**
See also CA 114; 136; CANR 80; DLB 9, 102; MAICYA; YABC 1

Fisher, M(ary) F(rances) K(ennedy)
1908-1992 .... **CLC 76, 87**
See also CA 77-80; 138; CANR 44; MTCW 1

Fisher, Roy 1930- .... **CLC 25**
See also CA 81-84; CAAS 10; CANR 16; DLB 40

Fisher, Rudolph 1897-1934 .. **TCLC 11; BLC 2; DAM MULT; SSC 25**
See also BW 1, 3; CA 107; 124; CANR 80; DLB 51, 102

Fisher, Vardis (Alvero) 1895-1968 ...... **CLC 7**
See also CA 5-8R; 25-28R; CANR 68; DLB 9, 206

Fiske, Tarleton
See Bloch, Robert (Albert)

Fitch, Clarke
See Sinclair, Upton (Beall)

Fitch, John IV
See Cormier, Robert (Edmund)

Fitzgerald, Captain Hugh
See Baum, L(yman) Frank

FitzGerald, Edward 1809-1883 .... **NCLC 9**
See also DLB 32

Fitzgerald, F(rancis) Scott (Key) 1896-1940 **TCLC 1, 6, 14, 28, 55; DA; DAB; DAC; DAM MST, NOV; SSC 6, 31; WLC**
See also AAYA 24; AITN 1; CA 110; 123; CDALB 1917-1929; DA3; DLB 4, 9, 86; DLBD 1, 15, 16; DLBY 81, 96; MTCW 1, 2

Fitzgerald, Penelope 1916- ... **CLC 19, 51, 61**
See also CA 85-88; CAAS 10; CANR 56, 86; DLB 14, 194; MTCW 2

Fitzgerald, Robert (Stuart)
1910-1985 .... **CLC 39**
See also CA 1-4R; 114; CANR 1; DLBY 80

FitzGerald, Robert D(avid)
1902-1987 .... **CLC 19**
See also CA 17-20R

Fitzgerald, Zelda (Sayre)
1900-1948 .... **TCLC 52**
See also CA 117; 126; DLBY 84

Flanagan, Thomas (James Bonner) 1923- **CLC 25, 52**
See also CA 108; CANR 55; DLBY 80; INT 108; MTCW 1

Flaubert, Gustave 1821-1880 .... **NCLC 2, 10, 19, 62, 66; DA; DAB; DAC; DAM MST, NOV; SSC 11; WLC**
See also DA3; DLB 119

Flecker, Herman Elroy
See Flecker, (Herman) James Elroy

Flecker, (Herman) James Elroy 1884-1915 **TCLC 43**
See also CA 109; 150; DLB 10, 19

Fleming, Ian (Lancaster) 1908-1964 . **CLC 3, 30; DAM POP**
See also AAYA 26; CA 5-8R; CANR 59; CDBLB 1945-1960; DA3; DLB 87, 201; MTCW 1, 2; SATA 9

Fleming, Thomas (James) 1927- ...... **CLC 37**
See also CA 5-8R; CANR 10; INT CANR-10; SATA 8

Fletcher, John 1579-1625 .... **LC 33; DC 6**
See also CDBLB Before 1660; DLB 58

Fletcher, John Gould 1886-1950 .... **TCLC 35**
See also CA 107; 167; DLB 4, 45

Fleur, Paul
See Pohl, Frederik

Flooglebuckle, Al
See Spiegelman, Art

Flying Officer X
See Bates, H(erbert) E(rnest)

Fo, Dario 1926- .... **CLC 32, 109; DAM DRAM; DC 10**
See also CA 116; 128; CANR 68; DA3; DLBY 97; MTCW 1, 2

Fogarty, Jonathan Titulescu Esq.
See Farrell, James T(homas)

Follett, Ken(neth Martin) 1949- ..... **CLC 18; DAM NOV, POP**
See also AAYA 6; BEST 89:4; CA 81-84; CANR 13, 33, 54; DA3; DLB 87; DLBY 81; INT CANR-33; MTCW 1

Fontane, Theodor 1819-1898 .... **NCLC 26**
See also DLB 129

Foote, Horton 1916- .... **CLC 51, 91; DAM DRAM**
See also CA 73-76; CANR 34, 51; DA3; DLB 26; INT CANR-34

Foote, Shelby 1916- ..... **CLC 75; DAM NOV, POP**
See also CA 5-8R; CANR 3, 45, 74; DA3; DLB 2, 17; MTCW 2

Forbes, Esther 1891-1967 .... **CLC 12**
See also AAYA 17; CA 13-14; 25-28R; CAP 1; CLR 27; DLB 22; JRDA; MAICYA; SATA 2, 100

Forche, Carolyn (Louise) 1950- .... **CLC 25, 83, 86; DAM POET; PC 10**
See also CA 109; 117; CANR 50, 74; DA3; DLB 5, 193; INT 117; MTCW 1

Ford, Elbur
See Hibbert, Eleanor Alice Burford

Ford, Ford Madox 1873-1939 ... **TCLC 1, 15, 39, 57; DAM NOV**
See also CA 104; 132; CANR 74; CDBLB 1914-1945; DA3; DLB 162; MTCW 1, 2

Ford, Henry 1863-1947 .... **TCLC 73**
See also CA 115; 148

Ford, John 1586-(?) .... **DC 8**
See also CDBLB Before 1660; DAM DRAM; DA3; DLB 58

Ford, John 1895-1973 .... **CLC 16**
See also CA 45-48

Ford, Richard 1944- .... **CLC 46, 99**
See also CA 69-72; CANR 11, 47, 86; MTCW 1

Ford, Webster
See Masters, Edgar Lee

Foreman, Richard 1937- .... **CLC 50**
See also CA 65-68; CANR 32, 63

Forester, C(ecil) S(cott) 1899-1966 ... **CLC 35**
See also CA 73-76; 25-28R; CANR 83; DLB 191; SATA 13

Forez
See Mauriac, Francois (Charles)

Forman, James Douglas 1932- .... **CLC 21**
See also AAYA 17; CA 9-12R; CANR 4, 19, 42; JRDA; MAICYA; SATA 8, 70

Fornes, Maria Irene 1930- . **CLC 39, 61; DC 10; HLCS 1**
See also CA 25-28R; CANR 28, 81; DLB 7; HW 1, 2; INT CANR-28; MTCW 1

Forrest, Leon (Richard) 1937-1997 .. **CLC 4; BLCS**
See also BW 2; CA 89-92; 162; CAAS 7; CANR 25, 52, 87; DLB 33

Forster, E(dward) M(organ)
1879-1970 ...... **CLC 1, 2, 3, 4, 9, 10, 13, 15, 22, 45, 77; DA; DAB; DAC; DAM MST, NOV; SSC 27; WLC**
See also AAYA 2; CA 13-14; 25-28R; CANR 45; CAP 1; CDBLB 1914-1945; DA3; DLB 34, 98, 162, 178, 195; DLBD 10; MTCW 1, 2; SATA 57

Forster, John 1812-1876 .... **NCLC 11**
See also DLB 144, 184

Forsyth, Frederick 1938- .... **CLC 2, 5, 36; DAM NOV, POP**
See also BEST 89:4; CA 85-88; CANR 38, 62; DLB 87; MTCW 1, 2

Forten, Charlotte L. .... **TCLC 16; BLC 2**
See also Grimke, Charlotte L(ottie) Forten
DLB 50

Foscolo, Ugo 1778-1827 .... **NCLC 8**

Fosse, Bob .... **CLC 20**
See also Fosse, Robert Louis

Fosse, Robert Louis 1927-1987
See Fosse, Bob
See also CA 110; 123

Foster, Stephen Collins
1826-1864 .... **NCLC 26**

Foucault, Michel 1926-1984 . **CLC 31, 34, 69**
See also CA 105; 113; CANR 34; MTCW
1, 2

Fouque, Friedrich (Heinrich Karl) de la
Motte 1777-1843 .... **NCLC 2**
See also DLB 90

Fourier, Charles 1772-1837 .... **NCLC 51**

Fournier, Pierre 1916- .... **CLC 11**
See also Gascar, Pierre CA 89-92; CANR
16, 40

Fowles, John (Philip) 1926- .. **CLC 1, 2, 3, 4,**
6, 9, 10, 15, 33, 87; DAB; DAC; DAM
MST; SSC 33
See also CA 5-8R; CANR 25, 71; CDBLB
1960 to Present; DA3; DLB 14, 139, 207;
MTCW 1, 2; SATA 22

Fox, Paula 1923- .... **CLC 2, 8, 121**
See also AAYA 3; CA 73-76; CANR 20,
36, 62; CLR 1, 44; DLB 52; JRDA; MAI-
CYA; MTCW 1; SATA 17, 60

Fox, William Price (Jr.) 1926- .... **CLC 22**
See also CA 17-20R; CAAS 19; CANR 11;
DLB 2; DLBY 81

Foxe, John 1516(?)-1587 .... **LC 14**
See also DLB 132

Frame, Janet 1924- . **CLC 2, 3, 6, 22, 66, 96;**
SSC 29
See also Clutha, Janet Paterson Frame

France, Anatole .... **TCLC 9**
See also Thibault, Jacques Anatole Francois
DLB 123; MTCW 1

Francis, Claude 19(?)- .... **CLC 50**

Francis, Dick 1920- .... **CLC 2, 22, 42, 102;**
DAM POP
See also AAYA 5, 21; BEST 89:3; CA 5-8R;
CANR 9, 42, 68; CDBLB 1960 to Present;
DA3; DLB 87; INT CANR-9; MTCW 1,
2

Francis, Robert (Churchill)
1901-1987 .... **CLC 15**
See also CA 1-4R; 123; CANR 1

Frank, Anne(lies Marie)
1929-1945 . **TCLC 17; DA; DAB; DAC;**
DAM MST; WLC
See also AAYA 12; CA 113; 133; CANR
68; DA3; MTCW 1, 2; SATA 87; SATA-
Brief 42

Frank, Bruno 1887-1945 .... **TCLC 81**
See also DLB 118

Frank, Elizabeth 1945- .... **CLC 39**
See also CA 121; 126; CANR 78; INT 126

Frankl, Viktor E(mil) 1905-1997 ...... **CLC 93**
See also CA 65-68; 161

Franklin, Benjamin
See Hasek, Jaroslav (Matej Frantisek)

Franklin, Benjamin 1706-1790 .. **LC 25; DA;**
DAB; DAC; DAM MST; WLCS
See also CDALB 1640-1865; DA3; DLB
24, 43, 73

Franklin, (Stella Maria Sarah) Miles
(Lampe) 1879-1954 .... **TCLC 7**
See also CA 104; 164

Fraser, (Lady) Antonia (Pakenham) 1932-
CLC 32, 107
See also CA 85-88; CANR 44, 65; MTCW
1, 2; SATA-Brief 32

Fraser, George MacDonald 1925- ...... **CLC 7**
See also CA 45-48, 180; CAAE 180; CANR
2, 48, 74; MTCW 1

Fraser, Sylvia 1935- .... **CLC 64**
See also CA 45-48; CANR 1, 16, 60

Frayn, Michael 1933- .... **CLC 3, 7, 31, 47;**
DAM DRAM, NOV
See also CA 5-8R; CANR 30, 69; DLB 13,
14, 194; MTCW 1, 2

Fraze, Candida (Merrill) 1945- .... **CLC 50**
See also CA 126

Frazer, J(ames) G(eorge)
1854-1941 .... **TCLC 32**
See also CA 118

Frazer, Robert Caine
See Creasey, John

Frazer, Sir James George
See Frazer, J(ames) G(eorge)

Frazier, Charles 1950- .... **CLC 109**
See also CA 161

Frazier, Ian 1951- .... **CLC 46**
See also CA 130; CANR 54

Frederic, Harold 1856-1898 .... **NCLC 10**
See also DLB 12, 23; DLBD 13

Frederick, John
See Faust, Frederick (Schiller)

Frederick the Great 1712-1786 .... **LC 14**

Fredro, Aleksander 1793-1876 .... **NCLC 8**

Freeling, Nicolas 1927- .... **CLC 38**
See also CA 49-52; CAAS 12; CANR 1,
17, 50, 84; DLB 87

Freeman, Douglas Southall
1886-1953 .... **TCLC 11**
See also CA 109; DLB 17; DLBD 17

Freeman, Judith 1946- .... **CLC 55**
See also CA 148

Freeman, Mary E(leanor) Wilkins 1852-1930
TCLC 9; SSC 1
See also CA 106; 177; DLB 12, 78

Freeman, R(ichard) Austin
1862-1943 .... **TCLC 21**
See also CA 113; CANR 84; DLB 70

French, Albert 1943- .... **CLC 86**
See also BW 3; CA 167

French, Marilyn 1929- .... **CLC 10, 18, 60;**
DAM DRAM, NOV, POP
See also CA 69-72; CANR 3, 31; INT
CANR-31; MTCW 1, 2

French, Paul
See Asimov, Isaac

Freneau, Philip Morin 1752-1832 ... **NCLC 1**
See also DLB 37, 43

Freud, Sigmund 1856-1939 .... **TCLC 52**
See also CA 115; 133; CANR 69; MTCW
1, 2

Friedan, Betty (Naomi) 1921- .... **CLC 74**
See also CA 65-68; CANR 18, 45, 74;
MTCW 1, 2

Friedlander, Saul 1932- .... **CLC 90**
See also CA 117; 130; CANR 72

Friedman, B(ernard) H(arper)
1926- .... **CLC 7**
See also CA 1-4R; CANR 3, 48

Friedman, Bruce Jay 1930- ...... **CLC 3, 5, 56**
See also CA 9-12R; CANR 25, 52; DLB 2,
28; INT CANR-25

Friel, Brian 1929- .... **CLC 5, 42, 59, 115; DC**
8
See also CA 21-24R; CANR 33, 69; DLB
13; MTCW 1

Friis-Baastad, Babbis Ellinor
1921-1970 .... **CLC 12**
See also CA 17-20R; 134; SATA 7

Frisch, Max (Rudolf) 1911-1991 ... **CLC 3, 9,**
14, 18, 32, 44; DAM DRAM, NOV
See also CA 85-88; 134; CANR 32, 74;
DLB 69, 124; MTCW 1, 2

Fromentin, Eugene (Samuel Auguste)
1820-1876 .... **NCLC 10**
See also DLB 123

Frost, Frederick
See Faust, Frederick (Schiller)

Frost, Robert (Lee) 1874-1963 .. **CLC 1, 3, 4,**
9, 10, 13, 15, 26, 34, 44; DA; DAB;
DAC; DAM MST, POET; PC 1; WLC
See also AAYA 21; CA 89-92; CANR 33;
CDALB 1917-1929; DA3; DLB 54;
DLBD 7; MTCW 1, 2; SATA 14

Froude, James Anthony
1818-1894 .... **NCLC 43**
See also DLB 18, 57, 144

Froy, Herald
See Waterhouse, Keith (Spencer)

Fry, Christopher 1907- .... **CLC 2, 10, 14;**
DAM DRAM
See also CA 17-20R; CAAS 23; CANR 9,
30, 74; DLB 13; MTCW 1, 2; SATA 66

Frye, (Herman) Northrop
1912-1991 .... **CLC 24, 70**
See also CA 5-8R; 133; CANR 8, 37; DLB
67, 68; MTCW 1, 2

Fuchs, Daniel 1909-1993 .... **CLC 8, 22**
See also CA 81-84; 142; CAAS 5; CANR
40; DLB 9, 26, 28; DLBY 93

Fuchs, Daniel 1934- .... **CLC 34**
See also CA 37-40R; CANR 14, 48

Fuentes, Carlos 1928- .. **CLC 3, 8, 10, 13, 22,**
41, 60, 113; DA; DAB; DAC; DAM
MST, NOV, MULT; HLC 1; SSC 24;
WLC
See also AAYA 4; AITN 2; CA 69-72;
CANR 10, 32, 68; DA3; DLB 113; HW
1, 2; MTCW 1, 2

Fuentes, Gregorio Lopez y
See Lopez y Fuentes, Gregorio

Fuertes, Gloria 1918- .... **PC 27**
See also CA 178, 180; DLB 108; HW 2

Fugard, (Harold) Athol 1932- . **CLC 5, 9, 14,**
25, 40, 80; DAM DRAM; DC 3
See also AAYA 17; CA 85-88; CANR 32,
54; MTCW 1

Fugard, Sheila 1932- .... **CLC 48**
See also CA 125

Fuller, Charles (H., Jr.) 1939- .... **CLC 25;**
BLC 2; DAM DRAM, MULT; DC 1
See also BW 2; CA 108; 112; CANR 87;
DLB 38; INT 112; MTCW 1

Fuller, John (Leopold) 1937- .... **CLC 62**
See also CA 21-24R; CANR 9, 44; DLB 40

Fuller, Margaret .... **NCLC 5, 50**
See also Fuller, Sarah Margaret

Fuller, Roy (Broadbent) 1912-1991 ... **CLC 4,**
28
See also CA 5-8R; 135; CAAS 10; CANR
53, 83; DLB 15, 20; SATA 87

Fuller, Sarah Margaret 1810-1850
See Fuller, Margaret
See also CDALB 1640-1865; DLB 1, 59,
73, 83

Fulton, Alice 1952- .... **CLC 52**
See also CA 116; CANR 57; DLB 193

Furphy, Joseph 1843-1912 .... **TCLC 25**
See also CA 163

Fussell, Paul 1924- .... **CLC 74**
    See also BEST 90:1; CA 17-20R; CANR 8,
    21, 35, 69; INT CANR-21; MTCW 1, 2

Futabatei, Shimei 1864-1909 .... **TCLC 44**
    See also CA 162; DLB 180

Futrelle, Jacques 1875-1912 .... **TCLC 19**
    See also CA 113; 155

Gaboriau, Emile 1835-1873 .... **NCLC 14**

Gadda, Carlo Emilio 1893-1973 .... **CLC 11**
    See also CA 89-92; DLB 177

Gaddis, William 1922-1998 ... **CLC 1, 3, 6, 8,**
    10, 19, 43, 86
    See also CA 17-20R; 172; CANR 21, 48;
    DLB 2; MTCW 1, 2

Gage, Walter
    See Inge, William (Motter)

Gaines, Ernest J(ames) 1933- ...... **CLC 3, 11,**
    18, 86; BLC 2; DAM MULT
    See also AAYA 18; AITN 1; BW 2, 3; CA
    9-12R; CANR 6, 24, 42, 75; CDALB
    1968-1988; CLR 62; DA3; DLB 2, 33,
    152; DLBY 80; MTCW 1, 2; SATA 86

Gaitskill, Mary 1954- .... **CLC 69**
    See also CA 128; CANR 61

Galdos, Benito Perez
    See Perez Galdos, Benito

Gale, Zona 1874-1938 .... **TCLC 7; DAM**
    DRAM
    See also CA 105; 153; CANR 84; DLB 9,
    78

Galeano, Eduardo (Hughes) 1940- . **CLC 72;**
    HLCS 1
    See also CA 29-32R; CANR 13, 32; HW 1

Galiano, Juan Valera y Alcala
    See Valera y Alcala-Galiano, Juan

Galilei, Galileo 1546-1642 .... **LC 45**

Gallagher, Tess 1943- ...... **CLC 18, 63; DAM**
    POET; PC 9
    See also CA 106; DLB 212

Gallant, Mavis 1922- .. **CLC 7, 18, 38; DAC;**
    DAM MST; SSC 5
    See also CA 69-72; CANR 29, 69; DLB 53;
    MTCW 1, 2

Gallant, Roy A(rthur) 1924- .... **CLC 17**
    See also CA 5-8R; CANR 4, 29, 54; CLR
    30; MAICYA; SATA 4, 68, 110

Gallico, Paul (William) 1897-1976 ..... **CLC 2**
    See also AITN 1; CA 5-8R; 69-72; CANR
    23; DLB 9, 171; MAICYA; SATA 13

Gallo, Max Louis 1932- .... **CLC 95**
    See also CA 85-88

Gallois, Lucien
    See Desnos, Robert

Gallup, Ralph
    See Whitemore, Hugh (John)

Galsworthy, John 1867-1933 .... **TCLC 1, 45;**
    DA; DAB; DAC; DAM DRAM, MST,
    NOV; SSC 22; WLC
    See also CA 104; 141; CANR 75; CDBLB
    1890-1914; DA3; DLB 10, 34, 98, 162;
    DLBD 16; MTCW 1

Galt, John 1779-1839 .... **NCLC 1**
    See also DLB 99, 116, 159

Galvin, James 1951- .... **CLC 38**
    See also CA 108; CANR 26

Gamboa, Federico 1864-1939 .... **TCLC 36**
    See also CA 167; HW 2

Gandhi, M. K.
    See Gandhi, Mohandas Karamchand

Gandhi, Mahatma
    See Gandhi, Mohandas Karamchand

Gandhi, Mohandas Karamchand 1869-1948
    TCLC 59; DAM MULT
    See also CA 121; 132; DA3; MTCW 1, 2

Gann, Ernest Kellogg 1910-1991 ..... **CLC 23**
    See also AITN 1; CA 1-4R; 136; CANR 1,
    83

Garcia, Cristina 1958- .... **CLC 76**
    See also CA 141; CANR 73; HW 2

Garcia Lorca, Federico 1898-1936 . **TCLC 1,**
    7, 49; DA; DAB; DAC; DAM DRAM,
    MST, MULT, POET; DC 2; HLC 2;
    PC 3; WLC
    See also CA 104; 131; CANR 81; DA3;
    DLB 108; HW 1, 2; MTCW 1, 2

Garcia Marquez, Gabriel (Jose)
    1928- .... **CLC 2, 3, 8, 10, 15, 27, 47, 55,**
    68; DA; DAB; DAC; DAM MST,
    MULT, NOV, POP; HLC 1; SSC 8;
    WLC
    See also AAYA 3; BEST 89:1, 90:4; CA 33-
    36R; CANR 10, 28, 50, 75, 82; DA3;
    DLB 113; HW 1, 2; MTCW 1, 2

Garcilaso de la Vega, El Inca 1503-1536
    See also HLCS 1

Gard, Janice
    See Latham, Jean Lee

Gard, Roger Martin du
    See Martin du Gard, Roger

Gardam, Jane 1928- .... **CLC 43**
    See also CA 49-52; CANR 2, 18, 33, 54;
    CLR 12; DLB 14, 161; MAICYA; MTCW
    1; SAAS 9; SATA 39, 76; SATA-Brief 28

Gardner, Herb(ert) 1934- .... **CLC 44**
    See also CA 149

Gardner, John (Champlin), Jr. 1933-1982
    CLC 2, 3, 5, 7, 8, 10, 18, 28, 34; DAM
    NOV, POP; SSC 7
    See also AITN 1; CA 65-68; 107; CANR
    33, 73; CDALBS; DA3; DLB 2; DLBY
    82; MTCW 1; SATA 40; SATA-Obit 31

Gardner, John (Edmund) 1926- ...... **CLC 30;**
    DAM POP
    See also CA 103; CANR 15, 69; MTCW 1

Gardner, Miriam
    See Bradley, Marion Zimmer

Gardner, Noel
    See Kuttner, Henry

Gardons, S. S.
    See Snodgrass, W(illiam) D(e Witt)

Garfield, Leon 1921-1996 .... **CLC 12**
    See also AAYA 8; CA 17-20R; 152; CANR
    38, 41, 78; CLR 21; DLB 161; JRDA;
    MAICYA; SATA 1, 32, 76; SATA-Obit 90

Garland, (Hannibal) Hamlin 1860-1940
    TCLC 3; SSC 18
    See also CA 104; DLB 12, 71, 78, 186

Garneau, (Hector de) Saint-Denys 1912-1943
    TCLC 13
    See also CA 111; DLB 88

Garner, Alan 1934- ..... **CLC 17; DAB; DAM**
    POP
    See also AAYA 18; CA 73-76, 178; CAAE
    178; CANR 15, 64; CLR 20; DLB 161;
    MAICYA; MTCW 1, 2; SATA 18, 69;
    SATA-Essay 108

Garner, Hugh 1913-1979 .... **CLC 13**
    See also CA 69-72; CANR 31; DLB 68

Garnett, David 1892-1981 .... **CLC 3**
    See also CA 5-8R; 103; CANR 17, 79; DLB
    34; MTCW 2

Garos, Stephanie
    See Katz, Steve

Garrett, George (Palmer) 1929- .. **CLC 3, 11,**
    51; SSC 30
    See also CA 1-4R; CAAS 5; CANR 1, 42,
    67; DLB 2, 5, 130, 152; DLBY 83

Garrick, David 1717-1779 .... **LC 15; DAM**
    DRAM
    See also DLB 84

Garrigue, Jean 1914-1972 .... **CLC 2, 8**
    See also CA 5-8R; 37-40R; CANR 20

Garrison, Frederick
    See Sinclair, Upton (Beall)

Garro, Elena 1920(?)-1998
    See also CA 131; 169; DLB 145; HLCS 1;
    HW 1

Garth, Will
    See Hamilton, Edmond; Kuttner, Henry

Garvey, Marcus (Moziah, Jr.) 1887-1940
    TCLC 41; BLC 2; DAM MULT
    See also BW 1; CA 120; 124; CANR 79

Gary, Romain .... **CLC 25**
    See also Kacew, Romain DLB 83

Gascar, Pierre .... **CLC 11**
    See also Fournier, Pierre

Gascoyne, David (Emery) 1916- .... **CLC 45**
    See also CA 65-68; CANR 10, 28, 54; DLB
    20; MTCW 1

Gaskell, Elizabeth Cleghorn 1810-1865
    NCLC 70; DAB; DAM MST; SSC 25
    See also CDBLB 1832-1890; DLB 21, 144,
    159

Gass, William H(oward) 1924- . **CLC 1, 2, 8,**
    11, 15, 39; SSC 12
    See also CA 17-20R; CANR 30, 71; DLB
    2; MTCW 1, 2

Gassendi, Pierre 1592-1655 .... **LC 54**

Gasset, Jose Ortega y
    See Ortega y Gasset, Jose

Gates, Henry Louis, Jr. 1950- .... **CLC 65;**
    BLCS; DAM MULT
    See also BW 2, 3; CA 109; CANR 25, 53,
    75; DA3; DLB 67; MTCW 1

Gautier, Theophile 1811-1872 .. **NCLC 1, 59;**
    DAM POET; PC 18; SSC 20
    See also DLB 119

Gawsworth, John
    See Bates, H(erbert) E(rnest)

Gay, John 1685-1732 .. **LC 49; DAM DRAM**
    See also DLB 84, 95

Gay, Oliver
    See Gogarty, Oliver St. John

Gaye, Marvin (Penze) 1939-1984 ..... **CLC 26**
    See also CA 112

Gebler, Carlo (Ernest) 1954- .... **CLC 39**
    See also CA 119; 133

Gee, Maggie (Mary) 1948- .... **CLC 57**
    See also CA 130; DLB 207

Gee, Maurice (Gough) 1931- .... **CLC 29**
    See also CA 97-100; CANR 67; CLR 56;
    SATA 46, 101

Gelbart, Larry (Simon) 1923- .... **CLC 21, 61**
    See also CA 73-76; CANR 45

Gelber, Jack 1932- .... **CLC 1, 6, 14, 79**
    See also CA 1-4R; CANR 2; DLB 7

Gellhorn, Martha (Ellis)
1908-1998 .... **CLC 14, 60**
See also CA 77-80; 164; CANR 44; DLBY 82, 98

Genet, Jean 1910-1986 .. **CLC 1, 2, 5, 10, 14, 44, 46; DAM DRAM**
See also CA 13-16R; CANR 18; DA3; DLB 72; DLBY 86; MTCW 1, 2

Gent, Peter 1942- .... **CLC 29**
See also AITN 1; CA 89-92; DLBY 82

Gentile, Giovanni 1875-1944 .... **TCLC 96**
See also CA 119

Gentlewoman in New England, A
See Bradstreet, Anne

Gentlewoman in Those Parts, A
See Bradstreet, Anne

George, Jean Craighead 1919- .... **CLC 35**
See also AAYA 8; CA 5-8R; CANR 25; CLR 1; DLB 52; JRDA; MAICYA; SATA 2, 68

George, Stefan (Anton) 1868-1933 . **TCLC 2, 14**
See also CA 104

Georges, Georges Martin
See Simenon, Georges (Jacques Christian)

Gerhardi, William Alexander
See Gerhardie, William Alexander

Gerhardie, William Alexander 1895-1977 **CLC 5**
See also CA 25-28R; 73-76; CANR 18; DLB 36

Gerstler, Amy 1956- .... **CLC 70**
See also CA 146

Gertler, T. .... **CLC 34**
See also CA 116; 121; INT 121

Ghalib .... **NCLC 39, 78**
See also Ghalib, Hsadullah Khan

Ghalib, Hsadullah Khan 1797-1869
See Ghalib
See also DAM POET

Ghelderode, Michel de 1898-1962 ..... **CLC 6, 11; DAM DRAM**
See also CA 85-88; CANR 40, 77

Ghiselin, Brewster 1903- .... **CLC 23**
See also CA 13-16R; CAAS 10; CANR 13

Ghose, Aurabinda 1872-1950 .... **TCLC 63**
See also CA 163

Ghose, Zulfikar 1935- .... **CLC 42**
See also CA 65-68; CANR 67

Ghosh, Amitav 1956- .... **CLC 44**
See also CA 147; CANR 80

Giacosa, Giuseppe 1847-1906 .... **TCLC 7**
See also CA 104

Gibb, Lee
See Waterhouse, Keith (Spencer)

Gibbon, Lewis Grassic .... **TCLC 4**
See also Mitchell, James Leslie

Gibbons, Kaye 1960- .... **CLC 50, 88; DAM POP**
See also CA 151; CANR 75; DA3; MTCW 1

Gibran, Kahlil 1883-1931 .... **TCLC 1, 9; DAM POET, POP; PC 9**
See also CA 104; 150; DA3; MTCW 2

Gibran, Khalil
See Gibran, Kahlil

Gibson, William 1914- .. **CLC 23; DA; DAB; DAC; DAM DRAM, MST**
See also CA 9-12R; CANR 9, 42, 75; DLB 7; MTCW 1; SATA 66

Gibson, William (Ford) 1948- ... **CLC 39, 63; DAM POP**
See also AAYA 12; CA 126; 133; CANR 52; DA3; MTCW 1

Gide, Andre (Paul Guillaume) 1869-1951 **TCLC 5, 12, 36; DA; DAB; DAC; DAM MST, NOV; SSC 13; WLC**
See also CA 104; 124; DA3; DLB 65; MTCW 1, 2

Gifford, Barry (Colby) 1946- .... **CLC 34**
See also CA 65-68; CANR 9, 30, 40

Gilbert, Frank
See De Voto, Bernard (Augustine)

Gilbert, W(illiam) S(chwenck) 1836-1911 **TCLC 3; DAM DRAM, POET**
See also CA 104; 173; SATA 36

Gilbreth, Frank B., Jr. 1911- .... **CLC 17**
See also CA 9-12R; SATA 2

Gilchrist, Ellen 1935- ...... **CLC 34, 48; DAM POP; SSC 14**
See also CA 113; 116; CANR 41, 61; DLB 130; MTCW 1, 2

Giles, Molly 1942- .... **CLC 39**
See also CA 126

Gill, Eric 1882-1940 .... **TCLC 85**

Gill, Patrick
See Creasey, John

Gilliam, Terry (Vance) 1940- .... **CLC 21**
See also Monty Python AAYA 19; CA 108; 113; CANR 35; INT 113

Gillian, Jerry
See Gilliam, Terry (Vance)

Gilliatt, Penelope (Ann Douglass) 1932-1993 **CLC 2, 10, 13, 53**
See also AITN 2; CA 13-16R; 141; CANR 49; DLB 14

Gilman, Charlotte (Anna) Perkins (Stetson)
1860-1935 .... **TCLC 9, 37; SSC 13**
See also CA 106; 150; MTCW 1

Gilmour, David 1949- .... **CLC 35**
See also CA 138, 147

Gilpin, William 1724-1804 .... **NCLC 30**

Gilray, J. D.
See Mencken, H(enry) L(ouis)

Gilroy, Frank D(aniel) 1925- .... **CLC 2**
See also CA 81-84; CANR 32, 64, 86; DLB 7

Gilstrap, John 1957(?)- .... **CLC 99**
See also CA 160

Ginsberg, Allen 1926-1997 .... **CLC 1, 2, 3, 4, 6, 13, 36, 69, 109; DA; DAB; DAC; DAM MST, POET; PC 4; WLC**
See also AITN 1; CA 1-4R; 157; CANR 2, 41, 63; CDALB 1941-1968; DA3; DLB 5, 16, 169; MTCW 1, 2

Ginzburg, Natalia 1916-1991 .... **CLC 5, 11, 54, 70**
See also CA 85-88; 135; CANR 33; DLB 177; MTCW 1, 2

Giono, Jean 1895-1970 .... **CLC 4, 11**
See also CA 45-48; 29-32R; CANR 2, 35; DLB 72; MTCW 1

Giovanni, Nikki 1943- .... **CLC 2, 4, 19, 64, 117; BLC 2; DA; DAB; DAC; DAM MST, MULT, POET; PC 19; WLCS**
See also AAYA 22; AITN 1; BW 2, 3; CA 29-32R; CAAS 6; CANR 18, 41, 60; CDALBS; CLR 6; DA3; DLB 5, 41; INT CANR-18; MAICYA; MTCW 1, 2; SATA 24, 107

Giovene, Andrea 1904- .... **CLC 7**
See also CA 85-88

Gippius, Zinaida (Nikolayevna) 1869-1945
See Hippius, Zinaida
See also CA 106

Giraudoux, (Hippolyte) Jean 1882-1944 **TCLC 2, 7; DAM DRAM**
See also CA 104; DLB 65

Gironella, Jose Maria 1917- .... **CLC 11**
See also CA 101

Gissing, George (Robert)
1857-1903 .... **TCLC 3, 24, 47; SSC 37**
See also CA 105; 167; DLB 18, 135, 184

Giurlani, Aldo
See Palazzeschi, Aldo

Gladkov, Fyodor (Vasilyevich) 1883-1958 **TCLC 27**
See also CA 170

Glanville, Brian (Lester) 1931- .... **CLC 6**
See also CA 5-8R; CAAS 9; CANR 3, 70; DLB 15, 139; SATA 42

Glasgow, Ellen (Anderson Gholson)
1873-1945 .... **TCLC 2, 7; SSC 34**
See also CA 104; 164; DLB 9, 12; MTCW 2

Glaspell, Susan 1882(?)-1948 . **TCLC 55; DC 10**
See also CA 110; 154; DLB 7, 9, 78; YABC 2

Glassco, John 1909-1981 .... **CLC 9**
See also CA 13-16R; 102; CANR 15; DLB 68

Glasscock, Amnesia
See Steinbeck, John (Ernst)

Glasser, Ronald J. 1940(?)- .... **CLC 37**

Glassman, Joyce
See Johnson, Joyce

Glendinning, Victoria 1937- .... **CLC 50**
See also CA 120; 127; CANR 59; DLB 155

Glissant, Edouard 1928- . **CLC 10, 68; DAM MULT**
See also CA 153

Gloag, Julian 1930- .... **CLC 40**
See also AITN 1; CA 65-68; CANR 10, 70

Glowacki, Aleksander
See Prus, Boleslaw

Gluck, Louise (Elisabeth) 1943- .. **CLC 7, 22, 44, 81; DAM POET; PC 16**
See also CA 33-36R; CANR 40, 69; DA3; DLB 5; MTCW 2

Glyn, Elinor 1864-1943 .... **TCLC 72**
See also DLB 153

Gobineau, Joseph Arthur (Comte) de
1816-1882 .... **NCLC 17**
See also DLB 123

Godard, Jean-Luc 1930- .... **CLC 20**
See also CA 93-96

Godden, (Margaret) Rumer
1907-1998 .... **CLC 53**
See also AAYA 6; CA 5-8R; 172; CANR 4, 27, 36, 55, 80; CLR 20; DLB 161; MAICYA; SAAS 12; SATA 3, 36; SATA-Obit 109

Godoy Alcayaga, Lucila 1889-1957
See Mistral, Gabriela
See also BW 2; CA 104; 131; CANR 81; DAM MULT; HW 1, 2; MTCW 1, 2

Grau, Shirley Ann 1929- . CLC 4, 9; SSC 15
    See also CA 89-92; CANR 22, 69; DLB 2;
    INT CANR-22; MTCW 1
Gravel, Fern
    See Hall, James Norman
Graver, Elizabeth 1964- .... CLC 70
    See also CA 135; CANR 71
Graves, Richard Perceval 1945- .... CLC 44
    See also CA 65-68; CANR 9, 26, 51
Graves, Robert (von Ranke)
    1895-1985 .. CLC 1, 2, 6, 11, 39, 44, 45;
    DAB; DAC; DAM MST, POET; PC 6
    See also CA 5-8R; 117; CANR 5, 36; CD-
    BLB 1914-1945; DA3; DLB 20, 100, 191;
    DLBD 18; DLBY 85; MTCW 1, 2; SATA
    45
Graves, Valerie
    See Bradley, Marion Zimmer
Gray, Alasdair (James) 1934- .... CLC 41
    See also CA 126; CANR 47, 69; DLB 194;
    INT 126; MTCW 1, 2
Gray, Amlin 1946- .... CLC 29
    See also CA 138
Gray, Francine du Plessix 1930- ..... CLC 22;
    DAM NOV
    See also BEST 90:3; CA 61-64; CAAS 2;
    CANR 11, 33, 75, 81; INT CANR-11;
    MTCW 1, 2
Gray, John (Henry) 1866-1934 ...... TCLC 19
    See also CA 119; 162
Gray, Simon (James Holliday)
    1936- .... CLC 9, 14, 36
    See also AITN 1; CA 21-24R; CAAS 3;
    CANR 32, 69; DLB 13; MTCW 1
Gray, Spalding 1941- ..... CLC 49, 112; DAM
    POP; DC 7
    See also CA 128; CANR 74; MTCW 2
Gray, Thomas 1716-1771 .... LC 4, 40; DA;
    DAB; DAC; DAM MST; PC 2; WLC
    See also CDBLB 1660-1789; DA3; DLB
    109
Grayson, David
    See Baker, Ray Stannard
Grayson, Richard (A.) 1951- .... CLC 38
    See also CA 85-88; CANR 14, 31, 57
Greeley, Andrew M(oran) 1928- ..... CLC 28;
    DAM POP
    See also CA 5-8R; CAAS 7; CANR 7, 43,
    69; DA3; MTCW 1, 2
Green, Anna Katharine
    1846-1935 .... TCLC 63
    See also CA 112; 159; DLB 202
Green, Brian
    See Card, Orson Scott
Green, Hannah
    See Greenberg, Joanne (Goldenberg)
Green, Hannah 1927(?)-1996 .... CLC 3
    See also CA 73-76; CANR 59
Green, Henry 1905-1973 .... CLC 2, 13, 97
    See also Yorke, Henry Vincent CA 175;
    DLB 15
Green, Julian (Hartridge) 1900-1998
    See Green, Julien
    See also CA 21-24R; 169; CANR 33, 87;
    DLB 4, 72; MTCW 1
Green, Julien .... CLC 3, 11, 77
    See also Green, Julian (Hartridge) MTCW
    2

Green, Paul (Eliot) 1894-1981 .... CLC 25;
    DAM DRAM
    See also AITN 1; CA 5-8R; 103; CANR 3;
    DLB 7, 9; DLBY 81
Greenberg, Ivan 1908-1973
    See Rahv, Philip
    See also CA 85-88
Greenberg, Joanne (Goldenberg)
    1932- .... CLC 7, 30
    See also AAYA 12; CA 5-8R; CANR 14,
    32, 69; SATA 25
Greenberg, Richard 1959(?)- .... CLC 57
    See also CA 138
Greene, Bette 1934- .... CLC 30
    See also AAYA 7; CA 53-56; CANR 4; CLR
    2; JRDA; MAICYA; SAAS 16; SATA 8,
    102
Greene, Gael .... CLC 8
    See also CA 13-16R; CANR 10
Greene, Graham (Henry)
    1904-1991 .... CLC 1, 3, 6, 9, 14, 18, 27,
    37, 70, 72, 125; DA; DAB; DAC; DAM
    MST, NOV; SSC 29; WLC
    See also AITN 2; CA 13-16R; 133; CANR
    35, 61; CDBLB 1945-1960; DA3; DLB
    13, 15, 77, 100, 162, 201, 204; DLBY 91;
    MTCW 1, 2; SATA 20
Greene, Robert 1558-1592 .... LC 41
    See also DLB 62, 167
Greer, Richard
    See Silverberg, Robert
Gregor, Arthur 1923- .... CLC 9
    See also CA 25-28R; CAAS 10; CANR 11;
    SATA 36
Gregor, Lee
    See Pohl, Frederik
Gregory, Isabella Augusta (Persse)
    1852-1932 .... TCLC 1
    See also CA 104; DLB 10
Gregory, J. Dennis
    See Williams, John A(lfred)
Grendon, Stephen
    See Derleth, August (William)
Grenville, Kate 1950- .... CLC 61
    See also CA 118; CANR 53
Grenville, Pelham
    See Wodehouse, P(elham) G(renville)
Greve, Felix Paul (Berthold Friedrich)
    1879-1948
    See Grove, Frederick Philip
    See also CA 104; 141; 175; CANR 79;
    DAC; DAM MST
Grey, Zane 1872-1939 . TCLC 6; DAM POP
    See also CA 104; 132; DA3; DLB 212;
    MTCW 1, 2
Grieg, (Johan) Nordahl (Brun) 1902-1943
    TCLC 10
    See also CA 107
Grieve, C(hristopher) M(urray) 1892-1978
    CLC 11, 19; DAM POET
    See also MacDiarmid, Hugh; Pteleon CA
    5-8R; 85-88; CANR 33; MTCW 1
Griffin, Gerald 1803-1840 .... NCLC 7
    See also DLB 159
Griffin, John Howard 1920-1980 ..... CLC 68
    See also AITN 1; CA 1-4R; 101; CANR 2
Griffin, Peter 1942- .... CLC 39
    See also CA 136

Griffith, D(avid Lewelyn) W(ark)
    1875(?)-1948 .... TCLC 68
    See also CA 119; 150; CANR 80
Griffith, Lawrence
    See Griffith, D(avid Lewelyn) W(ark)
Griffiths, Trevor 1935- .... CLC 13, 52
    See also CA 97-100; CANR 45; DLB 13
Griggs, Sutton Elbert
    1872-1930(?) .... TCLC 77
    See also CA 123; DLB 50
Grigson, Geoffrey (Edward Harvey)
    1905-1985 .... CLC 7, 39
    See also CA 25-28R; 118; CANR 20, 33;
    DLB 27; MTCW 1, 2
Grillparzer, Franz 1791-1872 .... NCLC 1;
    SSC 37
    See also DLB 133
Grimble, Reverend Charles James
    See Eliot, T(homas) S(tearns)
Grimke, Charlotte L(ottie) Forten
    1837(?)-1914
    See Forten, Charlotte L.
    See also BW 1; CA 117; 124; DAM MULT,
    POET
Grimm, Jacob Ludwig Karl 1785-1863
    NCLC 3, 77; SSC 36
    See also DLB 90; MAICYA; SATA 22
Grimm, Wilhelm Karl 1786-1859 .. NCLC 3,
    77; SSC 36
    See also DLB 90; MAICYA; SATA 22
Grimmelshausen, Johann Jakob Christoffel
    von 1621-1676 .... LC 6
    See also DLB 168
Grindel, Eugene 1895-1952
    See Eluard, Paul
    See also CA 104
Grisham, John 1955- .... CLC 84; DAM POP
    See also AAYA 14; CA 138; CANR 47, 69;
    DA3; MTCW 2
Grossman, David 1954- .... CLC 67
    See also CA 138
Grossman, Vasily (Semenovich) 1905-1964
    CLC 41
    See also CA 124; 130; MTCW 1
Grove, Frederick Philip .... TCLC 4
    See also Greve, Felix Paul (Berthold
    Friedrich) DLB 92
Grubb
    See Crumb, R(obert)
Grumbach, Doris (Isaac) 1918- . CLC 13, 22,
    64
    See also CA 5-8R; CAAS 2; CANR 9, 42,
    70; INT CANR-9; MTCW 2
Grundtvig, Nicolai Frederik Severin
    1783-1872 .... NCLC 1
Grunge
    See Crumb, R(obert)
Grunwald, Lisa 1959- .... CLC 44
    See also CA 120
Guare, John 1938- .... CLC 8, 14, 29, 67;
    DAM DRAM
    See also CA 73-76; CANR 21, 69; DLB 7;
    MTCW 1, 2
Gudjonsson, Halldor Kiljan 1902-1998
    See Laxness, Halldor
    See also CA 103; 164
Guenter, Erich
    See Eich, Guenter

Herbert, Frank (Patrick)
1920-1986 .... **CLC 12, 23, 35, 44, 85;
DAM POP**
See also AAYA 21; CA 53-56; 118; CANR
5, 43; CDALBS; DLB 8; INT CANR-5;
MTCW 1, 2; SATA 9, 37; SATA-Obit 47

Herbert, George 1593-1633 ..... **LC 24; DAB;
DAM POET; PC 4**
See also CDBLB Before 1660; DLB 126

Herbert, Zbigniew 1924-1998 ..... **CLC 9, 43;
DAM POET**
See also CA 89-92; 169; CANR 36, 74;
MTCW 1

Herbst, Josephine (Frey)
1897-1969 .... **CLC 34**
See also CA 5-8R; 25-28R; DLB 9

Heredia, Jose Maria 1803-1839
See also HLCS 2

Hergesheimer, Joseph 1880-1954 ... **TCLC 11**
See also CA 109; DLB 102, 9

Herlihy, James Leo 1927-1993 .... **CLC 6**
See also CA 1-4R; 143; CANR 2

Hermogenes fl. c. 175- .... **CMLC 6**

Hernandez, Jose 1834-1886 .... **NCLC 17**

Herodotus c. 484B.C.-429B.C. .... **CMLC 17**
See also DLB 176

Herrick, Robert 1591-1674 .... **LC 13; DA;
DAB; DAC; DAM MST, POP; PC 9**
See also DLB 126

Herring, Guilles
See Somerville, Edith

Herriot, James 1916-1995 ..... **CLC 12; DAM
POP**
See also Wight, James Alfred AAYA 1; CA
148; CANR 40; MTCW 2; SATA 86

Herrmann, Dorothy 1941- .... **CLC 44**
See also CA 107

Herrmann, Taffy
See Herrmann, Dorothy

Hersey, John (Richard) 1914-1993 .... **CLC 1,
2, 7, 9, 40, 81, 97; DAM POP**
See also CA 17-20R; 140; CANR
33; CDALBS; DLB 6, 185; MTCW 1, 2;
SATA 25; SATA-Obit 76

Herzen, Aleksandr Ivanovich 1812-1870
NCLC 10, 61

Herzl, Theodor 1860-1904 .... **TCLC 36**
See also CA 168

Herzog, Werner 1942- .... **CLC 16**
See also CA 89-92

Hesiod c. 8th cent. B.C.- .... **CMLC 5**
See also DLB 176

Hesse, Hermann 1877-1962 ... **CLC 1, 2, 3, 6,
11, 17, 25, 69; DA; DAB; DAC; DAM
MST, NOV; SSC 9; WLC**
See also CA 17-18; CAP 2; DA3; DLB 66;
MTCW 1, 2; SATA 50

Hewes, Cady
See De Voto, Bernard (Augustine)

Heyen, William 1940- .... **CLC 13, 18**
See also CA 33-36R; CAAS 9; DLB 5

Heyerdahl, Thor 1914- .... **CLC 26**
See also CA 5-8R; CANR 5, 22, 66, 73;
MTCW 1, 2; SATA 2, 52

Heym, Georg (Theodor Franz Arthur)
1887-1912 .... **TCLC 9**
See also CA 106; 181

Heym, Stefan 1913- .... **CLC 41**
See also CA 9-12R; CANR 4; DLB 69

Heyse, Paul (Johann Ludwig von) 1830-1914
TCLC 8
See also CA 104; DLB 129

Heyward, (Edwin) DuBose
1885-1940 .... **TCLC 59**
See also CA 108; 157; DLB 7, 9, 45; SATA
21

Hibbert, Eleanor Alice Burford 1906-1993
CLC 7; DAM POP
See also BEST 90:4; CA 17-20R; 140;
CANR 9, 28, 59; MTCW 2; SATA 2;
SATA-Obit 74

Hichens, Robert (Smythe)
1864-1950 .... **TCLC 64**
See also CA 162; DLB 153

Higgins, George V(incent) 1939-... **CLC 4, 7,
10, 18**
See also CA 77-80; CAAS 5; CANR 17,
51; DLB 2; DLBY 81, 98; INT CANR-
17; MTCW 1

Higginson, Thomas Wentworth 1823-1911
TCLC 36
See also CA 162; DLB 1, 64

Highet, Helen
See MacInnes, Helen (Clark)

Highsmith, (Mary) Patricia
1921-1995 .... **CLC 2, 4, 14, 42, 102;
DAM NOV, POP**
See also CA 1-4R; 147; CANR 1, 20, 48,
62; DA3; MTCW 1, 2

Highwater, Jamake (Mamake)
1942(?)- .... **CLC 12**
See also AAYA 7; CA 65-68; CAAS 7;
CANR 10, 34, 84; CLR 17; DLB 52;
DLBY 85; JRDA; MAICYA; SATA 32,
69; SATA-Brief 30

Highway, Tomson 1951- .... **CLC 92; DAC;
DAM MULT**
See also CA 151; CANR 75; MTCW 2;
NNAL

Higuchi, Ichiyo 1872-1896 .... **NCLC 49**

Hijuelos, Oscar 1951- .... **CLC 65; DAM
MULT, POP; HLC 1**
See also AAYA 25; BEST 90:1; CA 123;
CANR 50, 75; DA3; DLB 145; HW 1, 2;
MTCW 2

Hikmet, Nazim 1902(?)-1963 .... **CLC 40**
See also CA 141; 93-96

Hildegard von Bingen 1098-1179 . **CMLC 20**
See also DLB 148

Hildesheimer, Wolfgang 1916-1991 .. **CLC 49**
See also CA 101; 135; DLB 69, 124

Hill, Geoffrey (William) 1932- ...... **CLC 5, 8,
18, 45; DAM POET**
See also CA 81-84; CANR 21; CDBLB
1960 to Present; DLB 40; MTCW 1

Hill, George Roy 1921- .... **CLC 26**
See also CA 110; 122

Hill, John
See Koontz, Dean R(ay)

Hill, Susan (Elizabeth) 1942- ... **CLC 4, 113;
DAB; DAM MST, NOV**
See also CA 33-36R; CANR 29, 69; DLB
14, 139; MTCW 1

Hillerman, Tony 1925- . **CLC 62; DAM POP**
See also AAYA 6; BEST 89:1; CA 29-32R;
CANR 21, 42, 65; DA3; DLB 206; SATA
6

Hillesum, Etty 1914-1943 .... **TCLC 49**
See also CA 137

Hilliard, Noel (Harvey) 1929- .... **CLC 15**
See also CA 9-12R; CANR 7, 69

Hillis, Rick 1956- .... **CLC 66**
See also CA 134

Hilton, James 1900-1954 .... **TCLC 21**
See also CA 108; 169; DLB 34, 77; SATA
34

Himes, Chester (Bomar) 1909-1984 .. **CLC 2,
4, 7, 18, 58, 108; BLC 2; DAM MULT**
See also BW 2; CA 25-28R; 114; CANR
22; DLB 2, 76, 143; MTCW 1, 2

Hinde, Thomas .... **CLC 6, 11**
See also Chitty, Thomas Willes

Hine, (William) Daryl 1936- .... **CLC 15**
See also CA 1-4R; CAAS 15; CANR 1, 20;
DLB 60

Hinkson, Katharine Tynan
See Tynan, Katharine

Hinojosa(-Smith), Rolando (R.) 1929-
See Hinojosa-Smith, Rolando
See also CA 131; CAAS 16; CANR 62;
DAM MULT; DLB 82; HLC 1; HW 1, 2;
MTCW 2

Hinojosa-Smith, Rolando 1929-
See Hinojosa(-Smith), Rolando (R.)
See also CAAS 16; HLC 1; MTCW 2

Hinton, S(usan) E(loise) 1950- .... **CLC 30,
111; DA; DAB; DAC; DAM MST,
NOV**
See also AAYA 2; CA 81-84; CANR 32,
62; CDALBS; CLR 3, 23; DA3; JRDA;
MAICYA; MTCW 1, 2; SATA 19, 58

Hippius, Zinaida .... **TCLC 9**
See also Gippius, Zinaida (Nikolayevna)

Hiraoka, Kimitake 1925-1970
See Mishima, Yukio
See also CA 97-100; 29-32R; DAM DRAM;
DA3; MTCW 1, 2

Hirsch, E(ric) D(onald), Jr. 1928- .... **CLC 79**
See also CA 25-28R; CANR 27, 51; DLB
67; INT CANR-27; MTCW 1

Hirsch, Edward 1950- .... **CLC 31, 50**
See also CA 104; CANR 20, 42; DLB 120

Hitchcock, Alfred (Joseph)
1899-1980 .... **CLC 16**
See also AAYA 22; CA 159; 97-100; SATA
27; SATA-Obit 24

Hitler, Adolf 1889-1945 .... **TCLC 53**
See also CA 117; 147

Hoagland, Edward 1932- .... **CLC 28**
See also CA 1-4R; CANR 2, 31, 57; DLB
6; SATA 51

Hoban, Russell (Conwell) 1925- . **CLC 7, 25;
DAM NOV**
See also CA 5-8R; CANR 23, 37, 66; CLR
3; DLB 52; MAICYA; MTCW 1, 2; SATA
1, 40, 78

Hobbes, Thomas 1588-1679 .... **LC 36**
See also DLB 151

Hobbs, Perry
See Blackmur, R(ichard) P(almer)

Hobson, Laura Z(ametkin)
1900-1986 .... **CLC 7, 25**
See also CA 17-20R; 118; CANR 55; DLB
28; SATA 52

Hochhuth, Rolf 1931- .. **CLC 4, 11, 18; DAM
DRAM**
See also CA 5-8R; CANR 33, 75; DLB 124;
MTCW 1, 2

Hochman, Sandra 1936- .... **CLC 3, 8**
See also CA 5-8R; DLB 5

Hochwaelder, Fritz 1911-1986 .... **CLC 36;**
DAM DRAM
See also CA 29-32R; 120; CANR 42;
MTCW 1

Hochwalder, Fritz
See Hochwaelder, Fritz

Hocking, Mary (Eunice) 1921- .... **CLC 13**
See also CA 101; CANR 18, 40

Hodgins, Jack 1938- .... **CLC 23**
See also CA 93-96; DLB 60

Hodgson, William Hope
1877(?)-1918 .... **TCLC 13**
See also CA 111; 164; DLB 70, 153, 156,
178; MTCW 2

Hoeg, Peter 1957- .... **CLC 95**
See also CA 151; CANR 75; DA3; MTCW
2

Hoffman, Alice 1952- ... **CLC 51; DAM NOV**
See also CA 77-80; CANR 34, 66; MTCW
1, 2

Hoffman, Daniel (Gerard) 1923- . **CLC 6, 13,**
23
See also CA 1-4R; CANR 4; DLB 5

Hoffman, Stanley 1944- .... **CLC 5**
See also CA 77-80

Hoffman, William M(oses) 1939- ..... **CLC 40**
See also CA 57-60; CANR 11, 71

Hoffmann, E(rnst) T(heodor) A(madeus)
1776-1822 .... **NCLC 2; SSC 13**
See also DLB 90; SATA 27

Hofmann, Gert 1931- .... **CLC 54**
See also CA 128

Hofmannsthal, Hugo von
1874-1929 ...... **TCLC 11; DAM DRAM;**
DC 4
See also CA 106; 153; DLB 81, 118

Hogan, Linda 1947- .. **CLC 73; DAM MULT**
See also CA 120; CANR 45, 73; DLB 175;
NNAL

Hogarth, Charles
See Creasey, John

Hogarth, Emmett
See Polonsky, Abraham (Lincoln)

Hogg, James 1770-1835 .... **NCLC 4**
See also DLB 93, 116, 159

Holbach, Paul Henri Thiry Baron 1723-1789
LC 14

Holberg, Ludvig 1684-1754 .... **LC 6**

Holden, Ursula 1921- .... **CLC 18**
See also CA 101; CAAS 8; CANR 22

Holderlin, (Johann Christian) Friedrich
1770-1843 .... **NCLC 16; PC 4**

Holdstock, Robert
See Holdstock, Robert P.

Holdstock, Robert P. 1948- .... **CLC 39**
See also CA 131; CANR 81

Holland, Isabelle 1920- .... **CLC 21**
See also AAYA 11; CA 21-24R, 181; CAAE
181; CANR 10, 25, 47; CLR 57; JRDA;
MAICYA; SATA 8, 70; SATA-Essay 103

Holland, Marcus
See Caldwell, (Janet Miriam) Taylor
(Holland)

Hollander, John 1929- .... **CLC 2, 5, 8, 14**
See also CA 1-4R; CANR 1, 52; DLB 5;
SATA 13

Hollander, Paul
See Silverberg, Robert

Holleran, Andrew 1943(?)- .... **CLC 38**
See also CA 144

Holley, Marietta 1836(?)-1926 ...... **TCLC 100**
See also CA 118; DLB 11

Hollinghurst, Alan 1954- .... **CLC 55, 91**
See also CA 114; DLB 207

Hollis, Jim
See Summers, Hollis (Spurgeon, Jr.)

Holly, Buddy 1936-1959 .... **TCLC 65**

Holmes, Gordon
See Shiel, M(atthew) P(hipps)

Holmes, John
See Souster, (Holmes) Raymond

Holmes, John Clellon 1926-1988 ...... **CLC 56**
See also CA 9-12R; 125; CANR 4; DLB 16

Holmes, Oliver Wendell, Jr.
1841-1935 .... **TCLC 77**
See also CA 114

Holmes, Oliver Wendell
1809-1894 .... **NCLC 14, 81**
See also CDALB 1640-1865; DLB 1, 189;
SATA 34

Holmes, Raymond
See Souster, (Holmes) Raymond

Holt, Victoria
See Hibbert, Eleanor Alice Burford

Holub, Miroslav 1923-1998 .... **CLC 4**
See also CA 21-24R; 169; CANR 10

Homer c. 8th cent. B.C.- .. **CMLC 1, 16; DA;**
DAB; DAC; DAM MST, POET; PC
23; WLCS
See also DA3; DLB 176

Hongo, Garrett Kaoru 1951- .... **PC 23**
See also CA 133; CAAS 22; DLB 120

Honig, Edwin 1919- .... **CLC 33**
See also CA 5-8R; CAAS 8; CANR 4, 45;
DLB 5

Hood, Hugh (John Blagdon) 1928- . **CLC 15,**
28
See also CA 49-52; CAAS 17; CANR 1,
33, 87; DLB 53

Hood, Thomas 1799-1845 .... **NCLC 16**
See also DLB 96

Hooker, (Peter) Jeremy 1941- .... **CLC 43**
See also CA 77-80; CANR 22; DLB 40

hooks, bell .... **CLC 94; BLCS**
See also Watkins, Gloria Jean MTCW 2

Hope, A(lec) D(erwent) 1907- ...... **CLC 3, 51**
See also CA 21-24R; CANR 33, 74; MTCW
1, 2

Hope, Anthony 1863-1933 .... **TCLC 83**
See also CA 157; DLB 153, 156

Hope, Brian
See Creasey, John

Hope, Christopher (David Tully)
1944- .... **CLC 52**
See also CA 106; CANR 47; SATA 62

Hopkins, Gerard Manley
1844-1889 .... **NCLC 17; DA; DAB;**
DAC; DAM MST, POET; PC 15; WLC
See also CDBLB 1890-1914; DA3; DLB
35, 57

Hopkins, John (Richard) 1931-1998 .. **CLC 4**
See also CA 85-88; 169

Hopkins, Pauline Elizabeth
1859-1930 ...... **TCLC 28; BLC 2; DAM**
MULT
See also BW 2, 3; CA 141; CANR 82; DLB
50

Hopkinson, Francis 1737-1791 .... **LC 25**
See also DLB 31

Hopley-Woolrich, Cornell George 1903-1968
See Woolrich, Cornell
See also CA 13-14; CANR 58; CAP 1;
MTCW 2

Horatio
See Proust, (Valentin-Louis-George-
Eugene-) Marcel

Horgan, Paul (George Vincent
O'Shaughnessy) 1903-1995 . **CLC 9, 53;**
DAM NOV
See also CA 13-16R; 147; CANR 9, 35;
DLB 212; DLBY 85; INT CANR-9;
MTCW 1, 2; SATA 13; SATA-Obit 84

Horn, Peter
See Kuttner, Henry

Hornem, Horace Esq.
See Byron, George Gordon (Noel)

Horney, Karen (Clementine Theodore
Danielsen) 1885-1952 .... **TCLC 71**
See also CA 114; 165

Hornung, E(rnest) W(illiam) 1866-1921
TCLC 59
See also CA 108; 160; DLB 70

Horovitz, Israel (Arthur) 1939- ...... **CLC 56;**
DAM DRAM
See also CA 33-36R; CANR 46, 59; DLB 7

Horvath, Odon von
See Horvath, Oedoen von
See also DLB 85, 124

Horvath, Oedoen von 1901-1938 ... **TCLC 45**
See also Horvath, Odon von CA 118

Horwitz, Julius 1920-1986 .... **CLC 14**
See also CA 9-12R; 119; CANR 12

Hospital, Janette Turner 1942- .... **CLC 42**
See also CA 108; CANR 48

Hostos, E. M. de
See Hostos (y Bonilla), Eugenio Maria de

Hostos, Eugenio M. de
See Hostos (y Bonilla), Eugenio Maria de

Hostos, Eugenio Maria
See Hostos (y Bonilla), Eugenio Maria de

Hostos (y Bonilla), Eugenio Maria de
1839-1903 .... **TCLC 24**
See also CA 123; 131; HW 1

Houdini
See Lovecraft, H(oward) P(hillips)

Hougan, Carolyn 1943- .... **CLC 34**
See also CA 139

Household, Geoffrey (Edward West)
1900-1988 .... **CLC 11**
See also CA 77-80; 126; CANR 58; DLB
87; SATA 14; SATA-Obit 59

Housman, A(lfred) E(dward) 1859-1936
TCLC 1, 10; DA; DAB; DAC; DAM
MST, POET; PC 2; WLCS
See also CA 104; 125; DA3; DLB 19;
MTCW 1, 2

Housman, Laurence 1865-1959 .... **TCLC 7**
See also CA 106; 155; DLB 10; SATA 25

Howard, Elizabeth Jane 1923- ..... **CLC 7, 29**
See also CA 5-8R; CANR 8, 62

Howard, Maureen 1930- .... **CLC 5, 14, 46**
See also CA 53-56; CANR 31, 75; DLBY
83; INT CANR-31; MTCW 1, 2

Howard, Richard 1929- .... **CLC 7, 10, 47**
See also AITN 1; CA 85-88; CANR 25, 80;
DLB 5; INT CANR-25

Howard, Robert E(rvin)
1906-1936 .... **TCLC 8**
See also CA 105; 157

Howard, Warren F.
See Pohl, Frederik

Howe, Fanny (Quincy) 1940- .... **CLC 47**
See also CA 117; CAAS 27; CANR 70;
SATA-Brief 52

Howe, Irving 1920-1993 .... **CLC 85**
See also CA 9-12R; 141; CANR 21, 50;
DLB 67; MTCW 1, 2

Howe, Julia Ward 1819-1910 .... **TCLC 21**
See also CA 117; DLB 1, 189

Howe, Susan 1937- .... **CLC 72**
See also CA 160; DLB 120

Howe, Tina 1937- .... **CLC 48**
See also CA 109

Howell, James 1594(?)-1666 .... **LC 13**
See also DLB 151

Howells, W. D.
See Howells, William Dean

Howells, William D.
See Howells, William Dean

Howells, William Dean 1837-1920 .. **TCLC 7,
17, 41; SSC 36**
See also CA 104; 134; CDALB 1865-1917;
DLB 12, 64, 74, 79, 189; MTCW 2

Howes, Barbara 1914-1996 .... **CLC 15**
See also CA 9-12R; 151; CAAS 3; CANR
53; SATA 5

Hrabal, Bohumil 1914-1997 .... **CLC 13, 67**
See also CA 106; 156; CAAS 12; CANR
57

Hroswitha of Gandersheim c. 935-c. 1002
CMLC 29
See also DLB 148

Hsun, Lu
See Lu Hsun

Hubbard, L(afayette) Ron(ald) 1911-1986
CLC 43; DAM POP
See also CA 77-80; 118; CANR 52; DA3;
MTCW 2

Huch, Ricarda (Octavia)
1864-1947 .... **TCLC 13**
See also CA 111; DLB 66

Huddle, David 1942- .... **CLC 49**
See also CA 57-60; CAAS 20; DLB 130

Hudson, Jeffrey
See Crichton, (John) Michael

Hudson, W(illiam) H(enry)
1841-1922 .... **TCLC 29**
See also CA 115; DLB 98, 153, 174; SATA
35

Hueffer, Ford Madox
See Ford, Ford Madox

Hughart, Barry 1934- .... **CLC 39**
See also CA 137

Hughes, Colin
See Creasey, John

Hughes, David (John) 1930- .... **CLC 48**
See also CA 116; 129; DLB 14

Hughes, Edward James
See Hughes, Ted
See also DAM MST, POET; DA3

Hughes, (James) Langston
1902-1967 .... **CLC 1, 5, 10, 15, 35, 44,
108; BLC 2; DA; DAB; DAC; DAM
DRAM, MST, MULT, POET; DC 3;
PC 1; SSC 6; WLC**
See also AAYA 12; BW 1, 3; CA 1-4R; 25-
28R; CANR 1, 34, 82; CDALB 1929-

1941; CLR 17; DA3; DLB 4, 7, 48, 51,
86; JRDA; MAICYA; MTCW 1, 2; SATA
4, 33

Hughes, Richard (Arthur Warren)
1900-1976 .... **CLC 1, 11; DAM NOV**
See also CA 5-8R; 65-68; CANR 4; DLB
15, 161; MTCW 1; SATA 8; SATA-Obit
25

Hughes, Ted 1930-1998 . **CLC 2, 4, 9, 14, 37,
119; DAB; DAC; PC 7**
See also Hughes, Edward James CA 1-4R;
171; CANR 1, 33, 66; CLR 3; DLB 40,
161; MAICYA; MTCW 1, 2; SATA 49;
SATA-Brief 27; SATA-Obit 107

Hugo, Richard F(ranklin)
1923-1982 .... **CLC 6, 18, 32; DAM
POET**
See also CA 49-52; 108; CANR 3; DLB 5,
206

Hugo, Victor (Marie) 1802-1885 .... **NCLC 3,
10, 21; DA; DAB; DAM DRAM,
MST, NOV, POET; PC 17; WLC**
See also AAYA 28; DA3; DLB 119, 192;
SATA 47

Huidobro, Vicente
See Huidobro Fernandez, Vicente Garcia

Huidobro Fernandez, Vicente Garcia
1893-1948 .... **TCLC 31**
See also CA 131; HW 1

Hulme, Keri 1947- .... **CLC 39**
See also CA 125; CANR 69; INT 125

Hulme, T(homas) E(rnest)
1883-1917 .... **TCLC 21**
See also CA 117; DLB 19

Hume, David 1711-1776 .... **LC 7**
See also DLB 104

Humphrey, William 1924-1997 .... **CLC 45**
See also CA 77-80; 160; CANR 68; DLB
212

Humphreys, Emyr Owen 1919- .... **CLC 47**
See also CA 5-8R; CANR 3, 24; DLB 15

Humphreys, Josephine 1945- ..... **CLC 34, 57**
See also CA 121; 127; INT 127

Huneker, James Gibbons
1857-1921 .... **TCLC 65**
See also DLB 71

Hungerford, Pixie
See Brinsmead, H(esba) F(ay)

Hunt, E(verette) Howard, (Jr.)
1918- .... **CLC 3**
See also AITN 1; CA 45-48; CANR 2, 47

Hunt, Francesca
See Holland, Isabelle

Hunt, Kyle
See Creasey, John

Hunt, (James Henry) Leigh
1784-1859 .... **NCLC 1, 70; DAM POET**
See also DLB 96, 110, 144

Hunt, Marsha 1946- .... **CLC 70**
See also BW 2, 3; CA 143; CANR 79

Hunt, Violet 1866(?)-1942 .... **TCLC 53**
See also DLB 162, 197

Hunter, E. Waldo
See Sturgeon, Theodore (Hamilton)

Hunter, Evan 1926- .... **CLC 11, 31; DAM
POP**
See also CA 5-8R; CANR 5, 38, 62; DLBY
82; INT CANR-5; MTCW 1; SATA 25

Hunter, Kristin (Eggleston) 1931- .... **CLC 35**
See also AITN 1; BW 1; CA 13-16R;
CANR 13; CLR 3; DLB 33; INT CANR-
13; MAICYA; SAAS 10; SATA 12

Hunter, Mary
See Austin, Mary (Hunter)

Hunter, Mollie 1922- .... **CLC 21**
See also McIlwraith, Maureen Mollie
Hunter AAYA 13; CANR 37, 78; CLR 25;
DLB 161; JRDA; MAICYA; SAAS 7;
SATA 54, 106

Hunter, Robert (?)-1734 .... **LC 7**

Hurston, Zora Neale 1903-1960 .. **CLC 7, 30,
61; BLC 2; DA; DAC; DAM MST,
MULT, NOV; SSC 4; WLCS**
See also AAYA 15; BW 1, 3; CA 85-88;
CANR 61; CDALBS; DA3; DLB 51, 86;
MTCW 1, 2

Husserl, E. G.
See Husserl, Edmund (Gustav Albrecht)

Husserl, Edmund (Gustav Albrecht)
1859-1938 .... **TCLC 100**
See also CA 116; 133

Huston, John (Marcellus)
1906-1987 .... **CLC 20**
See also CA 73-76; 123; CANR 34; DLB
26

Hustvedt, Siri 1955- .... **CLC 76**
See also CA 137

Hutten, Ulrich von 1488-1523 .... **LC 16**
See also DLB 179

Huxley, Aldous (Leonard)
1894-1963 .... **CLC 1, 3, 4, 5, 8, 11, 18,
35, 79; DA; DAB; DAC; DAM MST,
NOV; WLC**
See also AAYA 11; CA 85-88; CANR 44;
CDBLB 1914-1945; DA3; DLB 36, 100,
162, 195; MTCW 1, 2; SATA 63

Huxley, T(homas) H(enry)
1825-1895 .... **NCLC 67**
See also DLB 57

Huysmans, Joris-Karl 1848-1907 ... **TCLC 7,
69**
See also CA 104; 165; DLB 123

Hwang, David Henry 1957- .. **CLC 55; DAM
DRAM; DC 4**
See also CA 127; 132; CANR 76; DA3;
DLB 212; INT 132; MTCW 2

Hyde, Anthony 1946- .... **CLC 42**
See also CA 136

Hyde, Margaret O(ldroyd) 1917- ..... **CLC 21**
See also CA 1-4R; CANR 1, 36; CLR 23;
JRDA; MAICYA; SAAS 8; SATA 1, 42,
76

Hynes, James 1956(?)- .... **CLC 65**
See also CA 164

Hypatia c. 370-415 .... **CMLC 35**

Ian, Janis 1951- .... **CLC 21**
See also CA 105

Ibanez, Vicente Blasco
See Blasco Ibanez, Vicente

Ibarbourou, Juana de 1895-1979
See also HLCS 2; HW 1

Ibarguengoitia, Jorge 1928-1983 ...... **CLC 37**
See also CA 124; 113; HW 1

Ibsen, Henrik (Johan) 1828-1906 ... **TCLC 2,
8, 16, 37, 52; DA; DAB; DAC; DAM
DRAM, MST; DC 2; WLC**
See also CA 104; 141; DA3

Kinsey, Alfred C(harles)
1894-1956 .... **TCLC 91**
See also CA 115; 170; MTCW 2

Kipling, (Joseph) Rudyard
1865-1936 .... **TCLC 8, 17; DA; DAB;**
DAC; DAM MST, POET; PC 3; SSC
5; WLC
See also AAYA 32; CA 105; 120; CANR
33; CDBLB 1890-1914; CLR 39; DA3;
DLB 19, 34, 141, 156; MAICYA; MTCW
1, 2; SATA 100; YABC 2

Kirkup, James 1918- .... **CLC 1**
See also CA 1-4R; CAAS 4; CANR 2; DLB
27; SATA 12

Kirkwood, James 1930(?)-1989 .... **CLC 9**
See also AITN 2; CA 1-4R; 128; CANR 6,
40

Kirshner, Sidney
See Kingsley, Sidney

Kis, Danilo 1935-1989 .... **CLC 57**
See also CA 109; 118; 129; CANR 61; DLB
181; MTCW 1

Kivi, Aleksis 1834-1872 .... **NCLC 30**

Kizer, Carolyn (Ashley) 1925- ... **CLC 15, 39,**
80; DAM POET
See also CA 65-68; CAAS 5; CANR 24,
70; DLB 5, 169; MTCW 2

Klabund 1890-1928 .... **TCLC 44**
See also CA 162; DLB 66

Klappert, Peter 1942- .... **CLC 57**
See also CA 33-36R; DLB 5

Klein, A(braham) M(oses)
1909-1972 . **CLC 19; DAB; DAC; DAM**
MST
See also CA 101; 37-40R; DLB 68

Klein, Norma 1938-1989 .... **CLC 30**
See also AAYA 2; CA 41-44R; 128; CANR
15, 37; CLR 2, 19; INT CANR-15; JRDA;
MAICYA; SAAS 1; SATA 7, 57

Klein, T(heodore) E(ibon) D(onald) 1947-
CLC 34
See also CA 119; CANR 44, 75

Kleist, Heinrich von 1777-1811 ...... **NCLC 2,**
37; DAM DRAM; SSC 22
See also DLB 90

Klima, Ivan 1931- .... **CLC 56; DAM NOV**
See also CA 25-28R; CANR 17, 50

Klimentov, Andrei Platonovich 1899-1951
See Platonov, Andrei
See also CA 108

Klinger, Friedrich Maximilian von
1752-1831 .... **NCLC 1**
See also DLB 94

Klingsor the Magician
See Hartmann, Sadakichi

Klopstock, Friedrich Gottlieb 1724-1803
NCLC 11
See also DLB 97

Knapp, Caroline 1959- .... **CLC 99**
See also CA 154

Knebel, Fletcher 1911-1993 .... **CLC 14**
See also AITN 1; CA 1-4R; 140; CAAS 3;
CANR 1, 36; SATA 36; SATA-Obit 75

Knickerbocker, Diedrich
See Irving, Washington

Knight, Etheridge 1931-1991 . **CLC 40; BLC**
2; DAM POET; PC 14
See also BW 1, 3; CA 21-24R; 133; CANR
23, 82; DLB 41; MTCW 2

Knight, Sarah Kemble 1666-1727 .... **LC 7**
See also DLB 24, 200

Knister, Raymond 1899-1932 .... **TCLC 56**
See also DLB 68

Knowles, John 1926- . **CLC 1, 4, 10, 26; DA;**
DAC; DAM MST, NOV
See also AAYA 10; CA 17-20R; CANR 40,
74, 76; CDALB 1968-1988; DLB 6;
MTCW 1, 2; SATA 8, 89

Knox, Calvin M.
See Silverberg, Robert

Knox, John c. 1505-1572 .... **LC 37**
See also DLB 132

Knye, Cassandra
See Disch, Thomas M(ichael)

Koch, C(hristopher) J(ohn) 1932- .... **CLC 42**
See also CA 127; CANR 84

Koch, Christopher
See Koch, C(hristopher) J(ohn)

Koch, Kenneth 1925- .... **CLC 5, 8, 44; DAM**
POET
See also CA 1-4R; CANR 6, 36, 57; DLB
5; INT CANR-36; MTCW 2; SATA 65

Kochanowski, Jan 1530-1584 .... **LC 10**

Kock, Charles Paul de 1794-1871 . **NCLC 16**

Koda Shigeyuki 1867-1947
See Rohan, Koda
See also CA 121; 183

Koestler, Arthur 1905-1983 ... **CLC 1, 3, 6, 8,**
15, 33
See also CA 1-4R; 109; CANR 1, 33; CD-
BLB 1945-1960; DLBY 83; MTCW 1, 2

Kogawa, Joy Nozomi 1935- .. **CLC 78; DAC;**
DAM MST, MULT
See also CA 101; CANR 19, 62; MTCW 2;
SATA 99

Kohout, Pavel 1928- .... **CLC 13**
See also CA 45-48; CANR 3

Koizumi, Yakumo
See Hearn, (Patricio) Lafcadio (Tessima
Carlos)

Kolmar, Gertrud 1894-1943 .... **TCLC 40**
See also CA 167

Komunyakaa, Yusef 1947- .... **CLC 86, 94;**
BLCS
See also CA 147; CANR 83; DLB 120

Konrad, George
See Konrad, Gyoergy

Konrad, Gyoergy 1933- .... **CLC 4, 10, 73**
See also CA 85-88

Konwicki, Tadeusz 1926- .... **CLC 8, 28, 54,**
117
See also CA 101; CAAS 9; CANR 39, 59;
MTCW 1

Koontz, Dean R(ay) 1945- .... **CLC 78; DAM**
NOV, POP
See also AAYA 9, 31; BEST 89:3, 90:2; CA
108; CANR 19, 36, 52; DA3; MTCW 1;
SATA 92

Kopernik, Mikolaj
See Copernicus, Nicolaus

Kopit, Arthur (Lee) 1937- ..... **CLC 1, 18, 33;**
DAM DRAM
See also AITN 1; CA 81-84; CABS 3; DLB
7; MTCW 1

Kops, Bernard 1926- .... **CLC 4**
See also CA 5-8R; CANR 84; DLB 13

Kornbluth, C(yril) M. 1923-1958 .... **TCLC 8**
See also CA 105; 160; DLB 8

Korolenko, V. G.
See Korolenko, Vladimir Galaktionovich

Korolenko, Vladimir
See Korolenko, Vladimir Galaktionovich

Korolenko, Vladimir G.
See Korolenko, Vladimir Galaktionovich

Korolenko, Vladimir Galaktionovich
1853-1921 .... **TCLC 22**
See also CA 121

Korzybski, Alfred (Habdank Skarbek)
1879-1950 .... **TCLC 61**
See also CA 123; 160

Kosinski, Jerzy (Nikodem)
1933-1991 .... **CLC 1, 2, 3, 6, 10, 15, 53,**
70; DAM NOV
See also CA 17-20R; 134; CANR 9, 46;
DA3; DLB 2; DLBY 82; MTCW 1, 2

Kostelanetz, Richard (Cory) 1940- .. **CLC 28**
See also CA 13-16R; CAAS 8; CANR 38,
77

Kostrowitzki, Wilhelm Apollinaris de
1880-1918
See Apollinaire, Guillaume
See also CA 104

Kotlowitz, Robert 1924- .... **CLC 4**
See also CA 33-36R; CANR 36

Kotzebue, August (Friedrich Ferdinand) von
1761-1819 .... **NCLC 25**
See also DLB 94

Kotzwinkle, William 1938- ..... **CLC 5, 14, 35**
See also CA 45-48; CANR 3, 44, 84; CLR
6; DLB 173; MAICYA; SATA 24, 70

Kowna, Stancy
See Szymborska, Wislawa

Kozol, Jonathan 1936- .... **CLC 17**
See also CA 61-64; CANR 16, 45

Kozoll, Michael 1940(?)- .... **CLC 35**

Kramer, Kathryn 19(?)- .... **CLC 34**

Kramer, Larry 1935- .. **CLC 42; DAM POP;**
DC 8
See also CA 124; 126; CANR 60

Krasicki, Ignacy 1735-1801 .... **NCLC 8**

Krasinski, Zygmunt 1812-1859 .... **NCLC 4**

Kraus, Karl 1874-1936 .... **TCLC 5**
See also CA 104; DLB 118

Kreve (Mickevicius), Vincas 1882-1954
TCLC 27
See also CA 170

Kristeva, Julia 1941- .... **CLC 77**
See also CA 154

Kristofferson, Kris 1936- .... **CLC 26**
See also CA 104

Krizanc, John 1956- .... **CLC 57**

Krleza, Miroslav 1893-1981 .... **CLC 8, 114**
See also CA 97-100; 105; CANR 50; DLB
147

Kroetsch, Robert 1927- .... **CLC 5, 23, 57;**
DAC; DAM POET
See also CA 17-20R; CANR 8, 38; DLB
53; MTCW 1

Kroetz, Franz
See Kroetz, Franz Xaver

Kroetz, Franz Xaver 1946- .... **CLC 41**
See also CA 130

Kroker, Arthur (W.) 1945- .... **CLC 77**
See also CA 161

Kropotkin, Peter (Aleksieevich) 1842-1921
TCLC 36
See also CA 119

Author Index

Mano, D. Keith 1942- .... **CLC 2, 10**
    See also CA 25-28R; CAAS 6; CANR 26, 57; DLB 6

Mansfield, Katherine . **TCLC 2, 8, 39; DAB; SSC 9, 23, 38; WLC**
    See also Beauchamp, Kathleen Mansfield
    DLB 162

Manso, Peter 1940- .... **CLC 39**
    See also CA 29-32R; CANR 44

Mantecon, Juan Jimenez
    See Jimenez (Mantecon), Juan Ramon

Manton, Peter
    See Creasey, John

Man Without a Spleen, A
    See Chekhov, Anton (Pavlovich)

Manzoni, Alessandro 1785-1873 .... **NCLC 29**

Map, Walter 1140-1209 .... **CMLC 32**

Mapu, Abraham (ben Jekutiel) 1808-1867
    NCLC 18

Mara, Sally
    See Queneau, Raymond

Marat, Jean Paul 1743-1793 .... **LC 10**

Marcel, Gabriel Honore 1889-1973 . **CLC 15**
    See also CA 102; 45-48; MTCW 1, 2

March, William 1893-1954 .... **TCLC 96**

Marchbanks, Samuel
    See Davies, (William) Robertson

Marchi, Giacomo
    See Bassani, Giorgio

Margulies, Donald .... **CLC 76**

Marie de France c. 12th cent. - ..... **CMLC 8; PC 22**
    See also DLB 208

Marie de l'Incarnation 1599-1672 ...... **LC 10**

Marier, Captain Victor
    See Griffith, D(avid Lewelyn) W(ark)

Mariner, Scott
    See Pohl, Frederik

Marinetti, Filippo Tommaso 1876-1944
    TCLC 10
    See also CA 107; DLB 114

Marivaux, Pierre Carlet de Chamblain de
    1688-1763 .... **LC 4; DC 7**

Markandaya, Kamala .... **CLC 8, 38**
    See also Taylor, Kamala (Purnaiya)

Markfield, Wallace 1926- .... **CLC 8**
    See also CA 69-72; CAAS 3; DLB 2, 28

Markham, Edwin 1852-1940 .... **TCLC 47**
    See also CA 160; DLB 54, 186

Markham, Robert
    See Amis, Kingsley (William)

Marks, J
    See Highwater, Jamake (Mamake)

Marks-Highwater, J
    See Highwater, Jamake (Mamake)

Markson, David M(errill) 1927- .... **CLC 67**
    See also CA 49-52; CANR 1

Marley, Bob .... **CLC 17**
    See also Marley, Robert Nesta

Marley, Robert Nesta 1945-1981
    See Marley, Bob
    See also CA 107; 103

Marlowe, Christopher 1564-1593 ...... **LC 22, 47; DA; DAB; DAC; DAM DRAM, MST; DC 1; WLC**
    See also CDBLB Before 1660; DA3; DLB 62

Marlowe, Stephen 1928-
    See Queen, Ellery
    See also CA 13-16R; CANR 6, 55

Marmontel, Jean-Francois 1723-1799 .. **LC 2**

Marquand, John P(hillips)
    1893-1960 .... **CLC 2, 10**
    See also CA 85-88; CANR 73; DLB 9, 102; MTCW 2

Marques, Rene 1919-1979 ..... **CLC 96; DAM MULT; HLC 2**
    See also CA 97-100; 85-88; CANR 78; DLB 113; HW 1, 2

Marquez, Gabriel (Jose) Garcia
    See Garcia Marquez, Gabriel (Jose)

Marquis, Don(ald Robert Perry) 1878-1937
    TCLC 7
    See also CA 104; 166; DLB 11, 25

Marric, J. J.
    See Creasey, John

Marryat, Frederick 1792-1848 .... **NCLC 3**
    See also DLB 21, 163

Marsden, James
    See Creasey, John

Marsh, Edward 1872-1953 .... **TCLC 99**

Marsh, (Edith) Ngaio 1899-1982 .... **CLC 7, 53; DAM POP**
    See also CA 9-12R; CANR 6, 58; DLB 77; MTCW 1, 2

Marshall, Garry 1934- .... **CLC 17**
    See also AAYA 3; CA 111; SATA 60

Marshall, Paule 1929- .. **CLC 27, 72; BLC 3; DAM MULT; SSC 3**
    See also BW 2, 3; CA 77-80; CANR 25, 73; DA3; DLB 157; MTCW 1, 2

Marshallik
    See Zangwill, Israel

Marsten, Richard
    See Hunter, Evan

Marston, John 1576-1634 .... **LC 33; DAM DRAM**
    See also DLB 58, 172

Martha, Henry
    See Harris, Mark

Marti (y Perez), Jose (Julian) 1853-1895
    NCLC 63; DAM MULT; HLC 2
    See also HW 2

Martial c. 40-c. 104 .... **CMLC 35; PC 10**
    See also DLB 211

Martin, Ken
    See Hubbard, L(afayette) Ron(ald)

Martin, Richard
    See Creasey, John

Martin, Steve 1945- .... **CLC 30**
    See also CA 97-100; CANR 30; MTCW 1

Martin, Valerie 1948- .... **CLC 89**
    See also BEST 90:2; CA 85-88; CANR 49

Martin, Violet Florence
    1862-1915 .... **TCLC 51**

Martin, Webber
    See Silverberg, Robert

Martindale, Patrick Victor
    See White, Patrick (Victor Martindale)

Martin du Gard, Roger
    1881-1958 .... **TCLC 24**
    See also CA 118; DLB 65

Martineau, Harriet 1802-1876 .... **NCLC 26**
    See also DLB 21, 55, 159, 163, 166, 190; YABC 2

Martines, Julia
    See O'Faolain, Julia

Martinez, Enrique Gonzalez
    See Gonzalez Martinez, Enrique

Martinez, Jacinto Benavente y
    See Benavente (y Martinez), Jacinto

Martinez Ruiz, Jose 1873-1967
    See Azorin; Ruiz, Jose Martinez
    See also CA 93-96; HW 1

Martinez Sierra, Gregorio
    1881-1947 .... **TCLC 6**
    See also CA 115

Martinez Sierra, Maria (de la O'LeJarraga)
    1874-1974 .... **TCLC 6**
    See also CA 115

Martinsen, Martin
    See Follett, Ken(neth Martin)

Martinson, Harry (Edmund)
    1904-1978 .... **CLC 14**
    See also CA 77-80; CANR 34

Marut, Ret
    See Traven, B.

Marut, Robert
    See Traven, B.

Marvell, Andrew 1621-1678 .. **LC 4, 43; DA; DAB; DAC; DAM MST, POET; PC 10; WLC**
    See also CDBLB 1660-1789; DLB 131

Marx, Karl (Heinrich) 1818-1883 . **NCLC 17**
    See also DLB 129

Masaoka Shiki .... **TCLC 18**
    See also Masaoka Tsunenori

Masaoka Tsunenori 1867-1902
    See Masaoka Shiki
    See also CA 117

Masefield, John (Edward)
    1878-1967 ..... **CLC 11, 47; DAM POET**
    See also CA 19-20; 25-28R; CANR 33; CAP 2; CDBLB 1890-1914; DLB 10, 19, 153, 160; MTCW 1, 2; SATA 19

Maso, Carole 19(?)- .... **CLC 44**
    See also CA 170

Mason, Bobbie Ann 1940- ... **CLC 28, 43, 82; SSC 4**
    See also AAYA 5; CA 53-56; CANR 11, 31, 58, 83; CDALBS; DA3; DLB 173; DLBY 87; INT CANR-31; MTCW 1, 2

Mason, Ernst
    See Pohl, Frederik

Mason, Lee W.
    See Malzberg, Barry N(athaniel)

Mason, Nick 1945- .... **CLC 35**

Mason, Tally
    See Derleth, August (William)

Mass, William
    See Gibson, William

Master Lao
    See Lao Tzu

Masters, Edgar Lee 1868-1950 .... **TCLC 2, 25; DA; DAC; DAM MST, POET; PC 1; WLCS**
    See also CA 104; 133; CDALB 1865-1917; DLB 54; MTCW 1, 2

Masters, Hilary 1928- .... **CLC 48**
    See also CA 25-28R; CANR 13, 47

Mastrosimone, William 19(?)- .... **CLC 36**

Mathe, Albert
    See Camus, Albert

Mather, Cotton 1663-1728 .... **LC 38**
    See also CDALB 1640-1865; DLB 24, 30, 140

Mather, Increase 1639-1723 .... **LC 38**
See also DLB 24

Matheson, Richard Burton 1926- .... **CLC 37**
See also AAYA 31; CA 97-100; DLB 8, 44;
INT 97-100

Mathews, Harry 1930- .... **CLC 6, 52**
See also CA 21-24R; CAAS 6; CANR 18,
40

Mathews, John Joseph 1894-1979 .. **CLC 84;**
DAM MULT
See also CA 19-20; 142; CANR 45; CAP 2;
DLB 175; NNAL

Mathias, Roland (Glyn) 1915- .... **CLC 45**
See also CA 97-100; CANR 19, 41; DLB
27

Matsuo Basho 1644-1694 .... **PC 3**
See also DAM POET

Mattheson, Rodney
See Creasey, John

Matthews, (James) Brander
1852-1929 .... **TCLC 95**
See also DLB 71, 78; DLBD 13

Matthews, Greg 1949- .... **CLC 45**
See also CA 135

Matthews, William (Procter, III) 1942-1997
CLC 40
See also CA 29-32R; 162; CAAS 18; CANR
12, 57; DLB 5

Matthias, John (Edward) 1941- .... **CLC 9**
See also CA 33-36R; CANR 56

Matthiessen, F. O. 1902-1950 .... **TCLC 100**
See also DLB 63

Matthiessen, Peter 1927- ... **CLC 5, 7, 11, 32,**
64; DAM NOV
See also AAYA 6; BEST 90:4; CA 9-12R;
CANR 21, 50, 73; DA3; DLB 6, 173;
MTCW 1, 2; SATA 27

Maturin, Charles Robert
1780(?)-1824 .... **NCLC 6**
See also DLB 178

Matute (Ausejo), Ana Maria 1925- .. **CLC 11**
See also CA 89-92; MTCW 1

Maugham, W. S.
See Maugham, W(illiam) Somerset

Maugham, W(illiam) Somerset 1874-1965
CLC 1, 11, 15, 67, 93; DA; DAB; DAC;
DAM DRAM, MST, NOV; SSC 8; WLC
See also CA 5-8R; 25-28R; CANR 40; CD-
BLB 1914-1945; DA3; DLB 10, 36, 77,
100, 162, 195; MTCW 1, 2; SATA 54

Maugham, William Somerset
See Maugham, W(illiam) Somerset

Maupassant, (Henri Rene Albert) Guy de
1850-1893 . **NCLC 1, 42, 83; DA; DAB;**
DAC; DAM MST; SSC 1; WLC
See also DA3; DLB 123

Maupin, Armistead 1944- ..... **CLC 95; DAM**
POP
See also CA 125; 130; CANR 58; DA3;
INT 130; MTCW 2

Maurhut, Richard
See Traven, B.

Mauriac, Claude 1914-1996 .... **CLC 9**
See also CA 89-92; 152; DLB 83

Mauriac, Francois (Charles)
1885-1970 .... **CLC 4, 9, 56; SSC 24**
See also CA 25-28; CAP 2; DLB 65;
MTCW 1, 2

Mavor, Osborne Henry 1888-1951
See Bridie, James
See also CA 104

Maxwell, William (Keepers, Jr.)
1908- .... **CLC 19**
See also CA 93-96; CANR 54; DLBY 80;
INT 93-96

May, Elaine 1932- .... **CLC 16**
See also CA 124; 142; DLB 44

Mayakovski, Vladimir (Vladimirovich)
1893-1930 .... **TCLC 4, 18**
See also CA 104; 158; MTCW 2

Mayhew, Henry 1812-1887 .... **NCLC 31**
See also DLB 18, 55, 190

Mayle, Peter 1939(?)- .... **CLC 89**
See also CA 139; CANR 64

Maynard, Joyce 1953- .... **CLC 23**
See also CA 111; 129; CANR 64

Mayne, William (James Carter)
1928- .... **CLC 12**
See also AAYA 20; CA 9-12R; CANR 37,
80; CLR 25; JRDA; MAICYA; SAAS 11;
SATA 6, 68

Mayo, Jim
See L'Amour, Louis (Dearborn)

Maysles, Albert 1926- .... **CLC 16**
See also CA 29-32R

Maysles, David 1932- .... **CLC 16**

Mazer, Norma Fox 1931- .... **CLC 26**
See also AAYA 5; CA 69-72; CANR 12,
32, 66; CLR 23; JRDA; MAICYA; SAAS
1; SATA 24, 67, 105

Mazzini, Guiseppe 1805-1872 .... **NCLC 34**

McAlmon, Robert (Menzies) 1895-1956
TCLC 97
See also CA 107; 168; DLB 4, 45; DLBD
15

McAuley, James Phillip 1917-1976 .. **CLC 45**
See also CA 97-100

McBain, Ed
See Hunter, Evan

McBrien, William Augustine 1930- .. **CLC 44**
See also CA 107

McCaffrey, Anne (Inez) 1926- .... **CLC 17;**
DAM NOV, POP
See also AAYA 6; AITN 2; BEST 89:2; CA
25-28R; CANR 15, 35, 55; CLR 49; DA3;
DLB 8; JRDA; MAICYA; MTCW 1, 2;
SAAS 11; SATA 8, 70

McCall, Nathan 1955(?)- .... **CLC 86**
See also BW 3; CA 146

McCann, Arthur
See Campbell, John W(ood, Jr.)

McCann, Edson
See Pohl, Frederik

McCarthy, Charles, Jr. 1933-
See McCarthy, Cormac
See also CANR 42, 69; DAM POP; DA3;
MTCW 2

McCarthy, Cormac 1933- ...... **CLC 4, 57, 59,**
101
See also McCarthy, Charles, Jr. DLB 6, 143;
MTCW 2

McCarthy, Mary (Therese)
1912-1989 .. **CLC 1, 3, 5, 14, 24, 39, 59;**
SSC 24
See also CA 5-8R; 129; CANR 16, 50, 64;
DA3; DLB 2; DLBY 81; INT CANR-16;
MTCW 1, 2

McCartney, (James) Paul 1942- . **CLC 12, 35**
See also CA 146

McCauley, Stephen (D.) 1955- .... **CLC 50**
See also CA 141

McClure, Michael (Thomas) 1932- ... **CLC 6,**
10
See also CA 21-24R; CANR 17, 46, 77;
DLB 16

McCorkle, Jill (Collins) 1958- .... **CLC 51**
See also CA 121; DLBY 87

McCourt, Frank 1930- .... **CLC 109**
See also CA 157

McCourt, James 1941- .... **CLC 5**
See also CA 57-60

McCourt, Malachy 1932- .... **CLC 119**

McCoy, Horace (Stanley)
1897-1955 .... **TCLC 28**
See also CA 108; 155; DLB 9

McCrae, John 1872-1918 .... **TCLC 12**
See also CA 109; DLB 92

McCreigh, James
See Pohl, Frederik

McCullers, (Lula) Carson (Smith) 1917-1967
CLC 1, 4, 10, 12, 48, 100; DA; DAB;
DAC; DAM MST, NOV; SSC 9, 24;
WLC
See also AAYA 21; CA 5-8R; 25-28R;
CABS 1, 3; CANR 18; CDALB 1941-
1968; DA3; DLB 2, 7, 173; MTCW 1, 2;
SATA 27

McCulloch, John Tyler
See Burroughs, Edgar Rice

McCullough, Colleen 1938(?)- .... **CLC 27,**
107; DAM NOV, POP
See also CA 81-84; CANR 17, 46, 67; DA3;
MTCW 1, 2

McDermott, Alice 1953- .... **CLC 90**
See also CA 109; CANR 40

McElroy, Joseph 1930- .... **CLC 5, 47**
See also CA 17-20R

McEwan, Ian (Russell) 1948- .... **CLC 13, 66;**
DAM NOV
See also BEST 90:4; CA 61-64; CANR 14,
41, 69, 87; DLB 14, 194; MTCW 1, 2

McFadden, David 1940- .... **CLC 48**
See also CA 104; DLB 60; INT 104

McFarland, Dennis 1950- .... **CLC 65**
See also CA 165

McGahern, John 1934- ... **CLC 5, 9, 48; SSC**
17
See also CA 17-20R; CANR 29, 68; DLB
14; MTCW 1

McGinley, Patrick (Anthony) 1937- . **CLC 41**
See also CA 120; 127; CANR 56; INT 127

McGinley, Phyllis 1905-1978 .... **CLC 14**
See also CA 9-12R; 77-80; CANR 19; DLB
11, 48; SATA 2, 44; SATA-Obit 24

McGinniss, Joe 1942- .... **CLC 32**
See also AITN 2; BEST 89:2; CA 25-28R;
CANR 26, 70; DLB 185; INT CANR-26

McGivern, Maureen Daly
See Daly, Maureen

McGrath, Patrick 1950- .... **CLC 55**
See also CA 136; CANR 65

McGrath, Thomas (Matthew) 1916-1990
CLC 28, 59; DAM POET
See also CA 9-12R; 132; CANR 6, 33;
MTCW 1; SATA 41; SATA-Obit 66

McGuane, Thomas (Francis III)
1939- .... **CLC 3, 7, 18, 45, 127**
See also AITN 2; CA 49-52; CANR 5, 24, 49; DLB 2, 212; DLBY 80; INT CANR-24; MTCW 1

McGuckian, Medbh 1950- .... **CLC 48; DAM POET; PC 27**
See also CA 143; DLB 40

McHale, Tom 1942(?)-1982 .... **CLC 3, 5**
See also AITN 1; CA 77-80; 106

McIlvanney, William 1936- .... **CLC 42**
See also CA 25-28R; CANR 61; DLB 14, 207

McIlwraith, Maureen Mollie Hunter
See Hunter, Mollie
See also SATA 2

McInerney, Jay 1955- .... **CLC 34, 112; DAM POP**
See also AAYA 18; CA 116; 123; CANR 45, 68; DA3; INT 123; MTCW 2

McIntyre, Vonda N(eel) 1948- .... **CLC 18**
See also CA 81-84; CANR 17, 34, 69; MTCW 1

McKay, Claude . **TCLC 7, 41; BLC 3; DAB; PC 2**
See also McKay, Festus Claudius DLB 4, 45, 51, 117

McKay, Festus Claudius 1889-1948
See McKay, Claude
See also BW 1, 3; CA 104; 124; CANR 73; DA; DAC; DAM MST, MULT, NOV, POET; MTCW 1, 2; WLC

McKuen, Rod 1933- .... **CLC 1, 3**
See also AITN 1; CA 41-44R; CANR 40

McLoughlin, R. B.
See Mencken, H(enry) L(ouis)

McLuhan, (Herbert) Marshall 1911-1980
CLC 37, 83
See also CA 9-12R; 102; CANR 12, 34, 61; DLB 88; INT CANR-12; MTCW 1, 2

McMillan, Terry (L.) 1951- .... **CLC 50, 61, 112; BLCS; DAM MULT, NOV, POP**
See also AAYA 21; BW 2, 3; CA 140; CANR 60; DA3; MTCW 2

McMurtry, Larry (Jeff) 1936- .. **CLC 2, 3, 7, 11, 27, 44, 127; DAM NOV, POP**
See also AAYA 15; AITN 2; BEST 89:2; CA 5-8R; CANR 19, 43, 64; CDALB 1968-1988; DA3; DLB 2, 143; DLBY 80, 87; MTCW 1, 2

McNally, T. M. 1961- .... **CLC 82**

McNally, Terrence 1939- ... **CLC 4, 7, 41, 91; DAM DRAM**
See also CA 45-48; CANR 2, 56; DA3; DLB 7; MTCW 2

McNamer, Deirdre 1950- .... **CLC 70**

McNeal, Tom .... **CLC 119**

McNeile, Herman Cyril 1888-1937
See Sapper
See also DLB 77

McNickle, (William) D'Arcy
1904-1977 .... **CLC 89; DAM MULT**
See also CA 9-12R; 85-88; CANR 5, 45; DLB 175, 212; NNAL; SATA-Obit 22

McPhee, John (Angus) 1931- .... **CLC 36**
See also BEST 90:1; CA 65-68; CANR 20, 46, 64, 69; DLB 185; MTCW 1, 2

McPherson, James Alan 1943- .. **CLC 19, 77; BLCS**
See also BW 1, 3; CA 25-28R; CAAS 17; CANR 24, 74; DLB 38; MTCW 1, 2

McPherson, William (Alexander)
1933- .... **CLC 34**
See also CA 69-72; CANR 28; INT CANR-28

Mead, George Herbert 1873-1958 . **TCLC 89**

Mead, Margaret 1901-1978 .... **CLC 37**
See also AITN 1; CA 1-4R; 81-84; CANR 4; DA3; MTCW 1, 2; SATA-Obit 20

Meaker, Marijane (Agnes) 1927-
See Kerr, M. E.
See also CA 107; CANR 37, 63; INT 107; JRDA; MAICYA; MTCW 1; SATA 20, 61, 99; SATA-Essay 111

Medoff, Mark (Howard) 1940- ... **CLC 6, 23; DAM DRAM**
See also AITN 1; CA 53-56; CANR 5; DLB 7; INT CANR-5

Medvedev, P. N.
See Bakhtin, Mikhail Mikhailovich

Meged, Aharon
See Megged, Aharon

Meged, Aron
See Megged, Aharon

Megged, Aharon 1920- .... **CLC 9**
See also CA 49-52; CAAS 13; CANR 1

Mehta, Ved (Parkash) 1934- .... **CLC 37**
See also CA 1-4R; CANR 2, 23, 69; MTCW 1

Melanter
See Blackmore, R(ichard) D(oddridge)

Melies, Georges 1861-1938 .... **TCLC 81**

Melikow, Loris
See Hofmannsthal, Hugo von

Melmoth, Sebastian
See Wilde, Oscar

Meltzer, Milton 1915- .... **CLC 26**
See also AAYA 8; CA 13-16R; CANR 38; CLR 13; DLB 61; JRDA; MAICYA; SAAS 1; SATA 1, 50, 80

Melville, Herman 1819-1891 ..... **NCLC 3, 12, 29, 45, 49; DA; DAB; DAC; DAM MST, NOV; SSC 1, 17; WLC**
See also AAYA 25; CDALB 1640-1865; DA3; DLB 3, 74; SATA 59

Menander c. 342B.C.-c. 292B.C. ... **CMLC 9; DAM DRAM; DC 3**
See also DLB 176

Menchu, Rigoberta 1959-
See also HLCS 2

Menchu, Rigoberta 1959-
See also CA 175; HLCS 2

Mencken, H(enry) L(ouis)
1880-1956 .... **TCLC 13**
See also CA 105; 125; CDALB 1917-1929; DLB 11, 29, 63, 137; MTCW 1, 2

Mendelsohn, Jane 1965(?)- .... **CLC 99**
See also CA 154

Mercer, David 1928-1980 .... **CLC 5; DAM DRAM**
See also CA 9-12R; 102; CANR 23; DLB 13; MTCW 1

Merchant, Paul
See Ellison, Harlan (Jay)

Meredith, George 1828-1909 .. **TCLC 17, 43; DAM POET**
See also CA 117; 153; CANR 80; CDBLB 1832-1890; DLB 18, 35, 57, 159

Meredith, William (Morris) 1919- .... **CLC 4, 13, 22, 55; DAM POET; PC 28**
See also CA 9-12R; CAAS 14; CANR 6, 40; DLB 5

Merezhkovsky, Dmitry Sergeyevich
1865-1941 .... **TCLC 29**
See also CA 169

Merimee, Prosper 1803-1870 ... **NCLC 6, 65; SSC 7**
See also DLB 119, 192

Merkin, Daphne 1954- .... **CLC 44**
See also CA 123

Merlin, Arthur
See Blish, James (Benjamin)

Merrill, James (Ingram) 1926-1995 .. **CLC 2, 3, 6, 8, 13, 18, 34, 91; DAM POET; PC 28**
See also CA 13-16R; 147; CANR 10, 49, 63; DA3; DLB 5, 165; DLBY 85; INT CANR-10; MTCW 1, 2

Merriman, Alex
See Silverberg, Robert

Merriman, Brian 1747-1805 .... **NCLC 70**

Merritt, E. B.
See Waddington, Miriam

Merton, Thomas 1915-1968 ..... **CLC 1, 3, 11, 34, 83; PC 10**
See also CA 5-8R; 25-28R; CANR 22, 53; DA3; DLB 48; DLBY 81; MTCW 1, 2

Merwin, W(illiam) S(tanley) 1927- ... **CLC 1, 2, 3, 5, 8, 13, 18, 45, 88; DAM POET**
See also CA 13-16R; CANR 15, 51; DA3; DLB 5, 169; INT CANR-15; MTCW 1, 2

Metcalf, John 1938- .... **CLC 37**
See also CA 113; DLB 60

Metcalf, Suzanne
See Baum, L(yman) Frank

Mew, Charlotte (Mary) 1870-1928 .. **TCLC 8**
See also CA 105; DLB 19, 135

Mewshaw, Michael 1943- .... **CLC 9**
See also CA 53-56; CANR 7, 47; DLBY 80

Meyer, Conrad Ferdinand
1825-1905 .... **NCLC 81**
See also DLB 129

Meyer, June
See Jordan, June

Meyer, Lynn
See Slavitt, David R(ytman)

Meyer-Meyrink, Gustav 1868-1932
See Meyrink, Gustav
See also CA 117

Meyers, Jeffrey 1939- .... **CLC 39**
See also CA 73-76; CANR 54; DLB 111

Meynell, Alice (Christina Gertrude Thompson) 1847-1922 .... **TCLC 6**
See also CA 104; 177; DLB 19, 98

Meyrink, Gustav .... **TCLC 21**
See also Meyer-Meyrink, Gustav DLB 81

Michaels, Leonard 1933- .... **CLC 6, 25; SSC 16**
See also CA 61-64; CANR 21, 62; DLB 130; MTCW 1

Michaux, Henri 1899-1984 .... **CLC 8, 19**
See also CA 85-88; 114

Micheaux, Oscar (Devereaux) 1884-1951
TCLC 76
See also BW 3; CA 174; DLB 50

Montagu, Elizabeth 1720-1800 .... **NCLC 7**
Montagu, Elizabeth 1917- .... **NCLC 7**
    See also CA 9-12R
Montagu, Mary (Pierrepont) Wortley
    1689-1762 .... **LC 9; PC 16**
    See also DLB 95, 101
Montagu, W. H.
    See Coleridge, Samuel Taylor
Montague, John (Patrick) 1929- ..... **CLC 13,
46**
    See also CA 9-12R; CANR 9, 69; DLB 40;
    MTCW 1
Montaigne, Michel (Eyquem) de 1533-1592
    **LC 8; DA; DAB; DAC; DAM MST;
    WLC**
Montale, Eugenio 1896-1981 ... **CLC 7, 9, 18;
PC 13**
    See also CA 17-20R; 104; CANR 30; DLB
    114; MTCW 1
Montesquieu, Charles-Louis de Secondat
    1689-1755 .... **LC 7**
Montgomery, (Robert) Bruce 1921(?)-1978
    See Crispin, Edmund
    See also CA 179; 104
Montgomery, L(ucy) M(aud) 1874-1942
    TCLC 51; DAC; DAM MST
    See also AAYA 12; CA 108; 137; CLR 8;
    DA3; DLB 92; DLBD 14; JRDA; MAI-
    CYA; MTCW 2; SATA 100; YABC 1
Montgomery, Marion H., Jr. 1925- .... **CLC 7**
    See also AITN 1; CA 1-4R; CANR 3, 48;
    DLB 6
Montgomery, Max
    See Davenport, Guy (Mattison, Jr.)
Montherlant, Henry (Milon) de 1896-1972
    CLC 8, 19; DAM DRAM
    See also CA 85-88; 37-40R; DLB 72;
    MTCW 1
Monty Python
    See Chapman, Graham; Cleese, John
    (Marwood); Gilliam, Terry (Vance); Idle,
    Eric; Jones, Terence Graham Parry; Palin,
    Michael (Edward)
    See also AAYA 7
Moodie, Susanna (Strickland) 1803-1885
    NCLC 14
    See also DLB 99
Mooney, Edward 1951-
    See Mooney, Ted
    See also CA 130
Mooney, Ted .... **CLC 25**
    See also Mooney, Edward
Moorcock, Michael (John) 1939- ...... **CLC 5,
27, 58**
    See also Bradbury, Edward P. AAYA 26;
    CA 45-48; CAAS 5; CANR 2, 17, 38, 64;
    DLB 14; MTCW 1, 2; SATA 93
Moore, Brian 1921-1999 ... **CLC 1, 3, 5, 7, 8,
19, 32, 90; DAB; DAC; DAM MST**
    See also CA 1-4R; 174; CANR 1, 25, 42,
    63; MTCW 1, 2
Moore, Edward
    See Muir, Edwin
Moore, G. E. 1873-1958 .... **TCLC 89**
Moore, George Augustus
    1852-1933 .... **TCLC 7; SSC 19**
    See also CA 104; 177; DLB 10, 18, 57, 135
Moore, Lorrie .... **CLC 39, 45, 68**
    See also Moore, Marie Lorena

Moore, Marianne (Craig)
    1887-1972 .... **CLC 1, 2, 4, 8, 10, 13, 19,
    47; DA; DAB; DAC; DAM MST,
    POET; PC 4; WLCS**
    See also CA 1-4R; 33-36R; CANR 3, 61;
    CDALB 1929-1941; DA3; DLB 45;
    DLBD 7; MTCW 1, 2; SATA 20
Moore, Marie Lorena 1957-
    See Moore, Lorrie
    See also CA 116; CANR 39, 83
Moore, Thomas 1779-1852 .... **NCLC 6**
    See also DLB 96, 144
Mora, Pat(ricia) 1942-
    See also CA 129; CANR 57, 81; CLR 58;
    DAM MULT; DLB 209; HLC 2; HW 1,
    2; SATA 92
Moraga, Cherrie 1952- .... **CLC 126; DAM
MULT**
    See also CA 131; CANR 66; DLB 82; HW
    1, 2
Morand, Paul 1888-1976 .... **CLC 41; SSC 22**
    See also CA 69-72; DLB 65
Morante, Elsa 1918-1985 .... **CLC 8, 47**
    See also CA 85-88; 117; CANR 35; DLB
    177; MTCW 1, 2
Moravia, Alberto 1907-1990 .... **CLC 2, 7, 11,
27, 46; SSC 26**
    See also Pincherle, Alberto DLB 177;
    MTCW 2
More, Hannah 1745-1833 .... **NCLC 27**
    See also DLB 107, 109, 116, 158
More, Henry 1614-1687 .... **LC 9**
    See also DLB 126
More, Sir Thomas 1478-1535 .... **LC 10, 32**
Moreas, Jean .... **TCLC 18**
    See also Papadiamantopoulos, Johannes
Morgan, Berry 1919- .... **CLC 6**
    See also CA 49-52; DLB 6
Morgan, Claire
    See Highsmith, (Mary) Patricia
Morgan, Edwin (George) 1920- .... **CLC 31**
    See also CA 5-8R; CANR 3, 43; DLB 27
Morgan, (George) Frederick 1922- .. **CLC 23**
    See also CA 17-20R; CANR 21
Morgan, Harriet
    See Mencken, H(enry) L(ouis)
Morgan, Jane
    See Cooper, James Fenimore
Morgan, Janet 1945- .... **CLC 39**
    See also CA 65-68
Morgan, Lady 1776(?)-1859 .... **NCLC 29**
    See also DLB 116, 158
Morgan, Robin (Evonne) 1941- .... **CLC 2**
    See also CA 69-72; CANR 29, 68; MTCW
    1; SATA 80
Morgan, Scott
    See Kuttner, Henry
Morgan, Seth 1949(?)-1990 .... **CLC 65**
    See also CA 132
Morgenstern, Christian 1871-1914 .. **TCLC 8**
    See also CA 105
Morgenstern, S.
    See Goldman, William (W.)
Moricz, Zsigmond 1879-1942 .... **TCLC 33**
    See also CA 165
Morike, Eduard (Friedrich) 1804-1875
    NCLC 10
    See also DLB 133
Moritz, Karl Philipp 1756-1793 .... **LC 2**
    See also DLB 94

Morland, Peter Henry
    See Faust, Frederick (Schiller)
Morley, Christopher (Darlington) 1890-1957
    TCLC 87
    See also CA 112; DLB 9
Morren, Theophil
    See Hofmannsthal, Hugo von
Morris, Bill 1952- .... **CLC 76**
Morris, Julian
    See West, Morris L(anglo)
Morris, Steveland Judkins 1950(?)-
    See Wonder, Stevie
    See also CA 111
Morris, William 1834-1896 .... **NCLC 4**
    See also CDBLB 1832-1890; DLB 18, 35,
    57, 156, 178, 184
Morris, Wright 1910-1998 .. **CLC 1, 3, 7, 18,
37**
    See also CA 9-12R; 167; CANR 21, 81;
    DLB 2, 206; DLBY 81; MTCW 1, 2
Morrison, Arthur 1863-1945 .... **TCLC 72**
    See also CA 120; 157; DLB 70, 135, 197
Morrison, Chloe Anthony Wofford
    See Morrison, Toni
Morrison, James Douglas 1943-1971
    See Morrison, Jim
    See also CA 73-76; CANR 40
Morrison, Jim .... **CLC 17**
    See also Morrison, James Douglas
Morrison, Toni 1931- . **CLC 4, 10, 22, 55, 81,
87; BLC 3; DA; DAB; DAC; DAM
MST, MULT, NOV, POP**
    See also AAYA 1, 22; BW 2, 3; CA 29-32R;
    CANR 27, 42, 67; CDALB 1968-1988;
    DA3; DLB 6, 33, 143; DLBY 81; MTCW
    1, 2; SATA 57
Morrison, Van 1945- .... **CLC 21**
    See also CA 116; 168
Morrissy, Mary 1958- .... **CLC 99**
Mortimer, John (Clifford) 1923- ..... **CLC 28,
43; DAM DRAM, POP**
    See also CA 13-16R; CANR 21, 69; CD-
    BLB 1960 to Present; DA3; DLB 13; INT
    CANR-21; MTCW 1, 2
Mortimer, Penelope (Ruth) 1918- ...... **CLC 5**
    See also CA 57-60; CANR 45
Morton, Anthony
    See Creasey, John
Mosca, Gaetano 1858-1941 .... **TCLC 75**
Mosher, Howard Frank 1943- .... **CLC 62**
    See also CA 139; CANR 65
Mosley, Nicholas 1923- .... **CLC 43, 70**
    See also CA 69-72; CANR 41, 60; DLB 14,
    207
Mosley, Walter 1952- .... **CLC 97; BLCS;
DAM MULT, POP**
    See also AAYA 17; BW 2; CA 142; CANR
    57; DA3; MTCW 2
Moss, Howard 1922-1987 ...... **CLC 7, 14, 45,
50; DAM POET**
    See also CA 1-4R; 123; CANR 1, 44; DLB
    5
Mossgiel, Rab
    See Burns, Robert
Motion, Andrew (Peter) 1952- .... **CLC 47**
    See also CA 146; DLB 40
Motley, Willard (Francis)
    1909-1965 .... **CLC 18**
    See also BW 1; CA 117; 106; DLB 76, 143

Osborne, Lawrence 1958- .... **CLC 50**

Osbourne, Lloyd 1868-1947 .... **TCLC 93**

Oshima, Nagisa 1932- .... **CLC 20**
    See also CA 116; 121; CANR 78

Oskison, John Milton 1874-1947 .. **TCLC 35;**
    DAM MULT
       See also CA 144; CANR 84; DLB 175;
       NNAL

Ossian c. 3rd cent. - .... **CMLC 28**
    See also Macpherson, James

Ostrovsky, Alexander 1823-1886 .. **NCLC 30,**
    57

Otero, Blas de 1916-1979 .... **CLC 11**
    See also CA 89-92; DLB 134

Otto, Rudolf 1869-1937 .... **TCLC 85**

Otto, Whitney 1955- .... **CLC 70**
    See also CA 140

Ouida .... **TCLC 43**
    See also De La Ramee, (Marie) Louise DLB
    18, 156

Ousmane, Sembene 1923- ... **CLC 66; BLC 3**
    See also BW 1, 3; CA 117; 125; CANR 81;
    MTCW 1

Ovid 43B.C.-17 . **CMLC 7; DAM POET; PC**
    2
    See also DA3; DLB 211

Owen, Hugh
    See Faust, Frederick (Schiller)

Owen, Wilfred (Edward Salter) 1893-1918
    TCLC 5, 27; DA; DAB; DAC; DAM
    MST, POET; PC 19; WLC
       See also CA 104; 141; CDBLB 1914-1945;
       DLB 20; MTCW 2

Owens, Rochelle 1936- .... **CLC 8**
    See also CA 17-20R; CAAS 2; CANR 39

Oz, Amos 1939- ...... **CLC 5, 8, 11, 27, 33, 54;**
    DAM NOV
       See also CA 53-56; CANR 27, 47, 65;
       MTCW 1, 2

Ozick, Cynthia 1928- .... **CLC 3, 7, 28, 62;**
    DAM NOV, POP; SSC 15
       See also BEST 90:1; CA 17-20R; CANR
       23, 58; DA3; DLB 28, 152; DLBY 82;
       INT CANR-23; MTCW 1, 2

Ozu, Yasujiro 1903-1963 .... **CLC 16**
    See also CA 112

Pacheco, C.
    See Pessoa, Fernando (Antonio Nogueira)

Pacheco, Jose Emilio 1939-
    See also CA 111; 131; CANR 65; DAM
    MULT; HLC 2; HW 1, 2

Pa Chin .... **CLC 18**
    See also Li Fei-kan

Pack, Robert 1929- .... **CLC 13**
    See also CA 1-4R; CANR 3, 44, 82; DLB 5

Padgett, Lewis
    See Kuttner, Henry

Padilla (Lorenzo), Heberto 1932- ..... **CLC 38**
    See also AITN 1; CA 123; 131; HW 1

Page, Jimmy 1944- .... **CLC 12**

Page, Louise 1955- .... **CLC 40**
    See also CA 140; CANR 76

Page, P(atricia) K(athleen) 1916- ...... **CLC 7,**
    18; DAC; DAM MST; PC 12
       See also CA 53-56; CANR 4, 22, 65; DLB
       68; MTCW 1

Page, Thomas Nelson 1853-1922 .... **SSC 23**
    See also CA 118; 177; DLB 12, 78; DLBD
    13

Pagels, Elaine Hiesey 1943- .... **CLC 104**
    See also CA 45-48; CANR 2, 24, 51

Paget, Violet 1856-1935
    See Lee, Vernon
    See also CA 104; 166

Paget-Lowe, Henry
    See Lovecraft, H(oward) P(hillips)

Paglia, Camille (Anna) 1947- .... **CLC 68**
    See also CA 140; CANR 72; MTCW 2

Paige, Richard
    See Koontz, Dean R(ay)

Paine, Thomas 1737-1809 .... **NCLC 62**
    See also CDALB 1640-1865; DLB 31, 43,
    73, 158

Pakenham, Antonia
    See Fraser, (Lady) Antonia (Pakenham)

Palamas, Kostes 1859-1943 .... **TCLC 5**
    See also CA 105

Palazzeschi, Aldo 1885-1974 .... **CLC 11**
    See also CA 89-92; 53-56; DLB 114

Pales Matos, Luis 1898-1959
    See also HLCS 2; HW 1

Paley, Grace 1922- .... **CLC 4, 6, 37; DAM**
    POP; SSC 8
       See also CA 25-28R; CANR 13, 46, 74;
       DA3; DLB 28; INT CANR-13; MTCW 1,
       2

Palin, Michael (Edward) 1943- .... **CLC 21**
    See also Monty Python CA 107; CANR 35;
    SATA 67

Palliser, Charles 1947- .... **CLC 65**
    See also CA 136; CANR 76

Palma, Ricardo 1833-1919 .... **TCLC 29**
    See also CA 168

Pancake, Breece Dexter 1952-1979
    See Pancake, Breece D'J
    See also CA 123; 109

Pancake, Breece D'J .... **CLC 29**
    See also Pancake, Breece Dexter DLB 130

Panko, Rudy
    See Gogol, Nikolai (Vasilyevich)

Papadiamantis, Alexandros
    1851-1911 .... **TCLC 29**
    See also CA 168

Papadiamantopoulos, Johannes 1856-1910
    See Moreas, Jean
    See also CA 117

Papini, Giovanni 1881-1956 .... **TCLC 22**
    See also CA 121; 180

Paracelsus 1493-1541 .... **LC 14**
    See also DLB 179

Parasol, Peter
    See Stevens, Wallace

Pardo Bazan, Emilia 1851-1921 .... **SSC 30**

Pareto, Vilfredo 1848-1923 .... **TCLC 69**
    See also CA 175

Parfenie, Maria
    See Codrescu, Andrei

Parini, Jay (Lee) 1948- .... **CLC 54**
    See also CA 97-100; CAAS 16; CANR 32,
    87

Park, Jordan
    See Kornbluth, C(yril) M.; Pohl, Frederik

Park, Robert E(zra) 1864-1944 ..... **TCLC 73**
    See also CA 122; 165

Parker, Bert
    See Ellison, Harlan (Jay)

Parker, Dorothy (Rothschild)
    1893-1967 .... **CLC 15, 68; DAM POET;**
    PC 28; SSC 2
       See also CA 19-20; 25-28R; CAP 2; DA3;
       DLB 11, 45, 86; MTCW 1, 2

Parker, Robert B(rown) 1932- .... **CLC 27;**
    DAM NOV, POP
       See also AAYA 28; BEST 89:4; CA 49-52;
       CANR 1, 26, 52; INT CANR-26; MTCW
       1

Parkin, Frank 1940- .... **CLC 43**
    See also CA 147

Parkman, Francis Jr., Jr.
    1823-1893 .... **NCLC 12**
    See also DLB 1, 30, 186

Parks, Gordon (Alexander Buchanan) 1912-
    CLC 1, 16; BLC 3; DAM MULT
       See also AITN 2; BW 2, 3; CA 41-44R;
       CANR 26, 66; DA3; DLB 33; MTCW 2;
       SATA 8, 108

Parmenides c. 515B.C.-c.
    450B.C. .... **CMLC 22**
    See also DLB 176

Parnell, Thomas 1679-1718 .... **LC 3**
    See also DLB 94

Parra, Nicanor 1914- ...... **CLC 2, 102; DAM**
    MULT; HLC 2
       See also CA 85-88; CANR 32; HW 1;
       MTCW 1

Parra Sanojo, Ana Teresa de la 1890-1936
    See also HLCS 2

Parrish, Mary Frances
    See Fisher, M(ary) F(rances) K(ennedy)

Parson
    See Coleridge, Samuel Taylor

Parson Lot
    See Kingsley, Charles

Partridge, Anthony
    See Oppenheim, E(dward) Phillips

Pascal, Blaise 1623-1662 .... **LC 35**

Pascoli, Giovanni 1855-1912 .... **TCLC 45**
    See also CA 170

Pasolini, Pier Paolo 1922-1975 .. **CLC 20, 37,**
    106; PC 17
       See also CA 93-96; 61-64; CANR 63; DLB
       128, 177; MTCW 1

Pasquini
    See Silone, Ignazio

Pastan, Linda (Olenik) 1932- .... **CLC 27;**
    DAM POET
       See also CA 61-64; CANR 18, 40, 61; DLB
       5

Pasternak, Boris (Leonidovich) 1890-1960
    CLC 7, 10, 18, 63; DA; DAB; DAC;
    DAM MST, NOV, POET; PC 6; SSC 31;
    WLC
       See also CA 127; 116; DA3; MTCW 1, 2

Patchen, Kenneth 1911-1972 .. **CLC 1, 2, 18;**
    DAM POET
       See also CA 1-4R; 33-36R; CANR 3, 35;
       DLB 16, 48; MTCW 1

Pater, Walter (Horatio) 1839-1894 .. **NCLC 7**
    See also CDBLB 1832-1890; DLB 57, 156

Paterson, A(ndrew) B(arton) 1864-1941
    TCLC 32
    See also CA 155; SATA 97

Paterson, Katherine (Womeldorf)
    1932- .... **CLC 12, 30**
       See also AAYA 1, 31; CA 21-24R; CANR
       28, 59; CLR 7, 50; DLB 52; JRDA; MAI-
       CYA; MTCW 1; SATA 13, 53, 92

Phillips, Richard
See Dick, Philip K(indred)

Phillips, Robert (Schaeffer) 1938- .... **CLC 28**
See also CA 17-20R; CAAS 13; CANR 8; DLB 105

Phillips, Ward
See Lovecraft, H(oward) P(hillips)

Piccolo, Lucio 1901-1969 .... **CLC 13**
See also CA 97-100; DLB 114

Pickthall, Marjorie L(owry) C(hristie)
1883-1922 .... **TCLC 21**
See also CA 107; DLB 92

Pico della Mirandola, Giovanni 1463-1494
LC 15

Piercy, Marge 1936- .... **CLC 3, 6, 14, 18, 27, 62, 128; PC 29**
See also CA 21-24R; CAAS 1; CANR 13, 43, 66; DLB 120; MTCW 1, 2

Piers, Robert
See Anthony, Piers

Pieyre de Mandiargues, Andre 1909-1991
See Mandiargues, Andre Pieyre de
See also CA 103; 136; CANR 22, 82

Pilnyak, Boris .... **TCLC 23**
See also Vogau, Boris Andreyevich

Pincherle, Alberto 1907-1990 .... **CLC 11, 18; DAM NOV**
See also Moravia, Alberto CA 25-28R; 132; CANR 33, 63; MTCW 1

Pinckney, Darryl 1953- .... **CLC 76**
See also BW 2, 3; CA 143; CANR 79

Pindar 518B.C.-446B.C. .... **CMLC 12; PC 19**
See also DLB 176

Pineda, Cecile 1942- .... **CLC 39**
See also CA 118

Pinero, Arthur Wing 1855-1934 ... **TCLC 32; DAM DRAM**
See also CA 110; 153; DLB 10

Pinero, Miguel (Antonio Gomez) 1946-1988
CLC 4, 55
See also CA 61-64; 125; CANR 29; HW 1

Pinget, Robert 1919-1997 .... **CLC 7, 13, 37**
See also CA 85-88; 160; DLB 83

Pink Floyd
See Barrett, (Roger) Syd; Gilmour, David; Mason, Nick; Waters, Roger; Wright, Rick

Pinkney, Edward 1802-1828 .... **NCLC 31**

Pinkwater, Daniel Manus 1941- .... **CLC 35**
See also Pinkwater, Manus AAYA 1; CA 29-32R; CANR 12, 38; CLR 4; JRDA; MAICYA; SAAS 3; SATA 46, 76

Pinkwater, Manus
See Pinkwater, Daniel Manus
See also SATA 8

Pinsky, Robert 1940- .... **CLC 9, 19, 38, 94, 121; DAM POET; PC 27**
See also CA 29-32R; CAAS 4; CANR 58; DA3; DLBY 82, 98; MTCW 2

Pinta, Harold
See Pinter, Harold

Pinter, Harold 1930- .. **CLC 1, 3, 6, 9, 11, 15, 27, 58, 73; DA; DAB; DAC; DAM DRAM, MST; WLC**
See also CA 5-8R; CANR 33, 65; CDBLB 1960 to Present; DA3; DLB 13; MTCW 1, 2

Piozzi, Hester Lynch (Thrale) 1741-1821
NCLC 57
See also DLB 104, 142

Pirandello, Luigi 1867-1936 ...... **TCLC 4, 29; DA; DAB; DAC; DAM DRAM, MST; DC 5; SSC 22; WLC**
See also CA 104; 153; DA3; MTCW 2

Pirsig, Robert M(aynard) 1928- ... **CLC 4, 6, 73; DAM POP**
See also CA 53-56; CANR 42, 74; DA3; MTCW 1, 2; SATA 39

Pisarev, Dmitry Ivanovich
1840-1868 .... **NCLC 25**

Pix, Mary (Griffith) 1666-1709 .... **LC 8**
See also DLB 80

Pixerecourt, (Rene Charles) Guilbert de
1773-1844 .... **NCLC 39**
See also DLB 192

Plaidy, Jean
See Hibbert, Eleanor Alice Burford

Planche, James Robinson
1796-1880 .... **NCLC 42**

Plant, Robert 1948- .... **CLC 12**

Plante, David (Robert) 1940- ...... **CLC 7, 23, 38; DAM NOV**
See also CA 37-40R; CANR 12, 36, 58, 82; DLBY 83; INT CANR-12; MTCW 1

Plath, Sylvia 1932-1963 ..... **CLC 1, 2, 3, 5, 9, 11, 14, 17, 50, 51, 62, 111; DA; DAB; DAC; DAM MST, POET; PC 1; WLC**
See also AAYA 13; CA 19-20; CANR 34; CAP 2; CDALB 1941-1968; DA3; DLB 5, 6, 152; MTCW 1, 2; SATA 96

Plato 428(?)B.C.-348(?)B.C. ... **CMLC 8; DA; DAB; DAC; DAM MST; WLCS**
See also DA3; DLB 176

Platonov, Andrei .... **TCLC 14; SSC 38**
See also Klimentov, Andrei Platonovich

Platt, Kin 1911- .... **CLC 26**
See also AAYA 11; CA 17-20R; CANR 11; JRDA; SAAS 17; SATA 21, 86

Plautus c. 251B.C.-184B.C. ... **CMLC 24; DC 6**
See also DLB 211

Plick et Plock
See Simenon, Georges (Jacques Christian)

Plimpton, George (Ames) 1927- .... **CLC 36**
See also AITN 1; CA 21-24R; CANR 32, 70; DLB 185; MTCW 1, 2; SATA 10

Pliny the Elder c. 23-79 .... **CMLC 23**
See also DLB 211

Plomer, William Charles Franklin 1903-1973
CLC 4, 8
See also CA 21-22; CANR 34; CAP 2; DLB 20, 162, 191; MTCW 1; SATA 24

Plowman, Piers
See Kavanagh, Patrick (Joseph)

Plum, J.
See Wodehouse, P(elham) G(renville)

Plumly, Stanley (Ross) 1939- .... **CLC 33**
See also CA 108; 110; DLB 5, 193; INT 110

Plumpe, Friedrich Wilhelm
1888-1931 .... **TCLC 53**
See also CA 112

Po Chu-i 772-846 .... **CMLC 24**

Poe, Edgar Allan 1809-1849 ..... **NCLC 1, 16, 55, 78; DA; DAB; DAC; DAM MST, POET; PC 1; SSC 34; WLC**
See also AAYA 14; CDALB 1640-1865; DA3; DLB 3, 59, 73, 74; SATA 23

Poet of Titchfield Street, The
See Pound, Ezra (Weston Loomis)

Pohl, Frederik 1919- .... **CLC 18; SSC 25**
See also AAYA 24; CA 61-64; CAAS 1; CANR 11, 37, 81; DLB 8; INT CANR-11; MTCW 1, 2; SATA 24

Poirier, Louis 1910-
See Gracq, Julien
See also CA 122; 126

Poitier, Sidney 1927- .... **CLC 26**
See also BW 1; CA 117

Polanski, Roman 1933- .... **CLC 16**
See also CA 77-80

Poliakoff, Stephen 1952- .... **CLC 38**
See also CA 106; DLB 13

Police, The
See Copeland, Stewart (Armstrong); Summers, Andrew James; Sumner, Gordon Matthew

Polidori, John William 1795-1821 . **NCLC 51**
See also DLB 116

Pollitt, Katha 1949- .... **CLC 28, 122**
See also CA 120; 122; CANR 66; MTCW 1, 2

Pollock, (Mary) Sharon 1936- .... **CLC 50; DAC; DAM DRAM, MST**
See also CA 141; DLB 60

Polo, Marco 1254-1324 .... **CMLC 15**

Polonsky, Abraham (Lincoln)
1910- .... **CLC 92**
See also CA 104; DLB 26; INT 104

Polybius c. 200B.C.-c. 118B.C. ...... **CMLC 17**
See also DLB 176

Pomerance, Bernard 1940- ... **CLC 13; DAM DRAM**
See also CA 101; CANR 49

Ponge, Francis 1899-1988 . **CLC 6, 18; DAM POET**
See also CA 85-88; 126; CANR 40, 86

Poniatowska, Elena 1933-
See also CA 101; CANR 32, 66; DAM MULT; DLB 113; HLC 2; HW 1, 2

Pontoppidan, Henrik 1857-1943 .... **TCLC 29**
See also CA 170

Poole, Josephine .... **CLC 17**
See also Helyar, Jane Penelope Josephine SAAS 2; SATA 5

Popa, Vasko 1922-1991 .... **CLC 19**
See also CA 112; 148; DLB 181

Pope, Alexander 1688-1744 .... **LC 3; DA; DAB; DAC; DAM MST, POET; PC 26; WLC**
See also CDBLB 1660-1789; DA3; DLB 95, 101

Porter, Connie (Rose) 1959(?)- .... **CLC 70**
See also BW 2, 3; CA 142; SATA 81

Porter, Gene(va Grace) Stratton
1863(?)-1924 .... **TCLC 21**
See also CA 112

Porter, Katherine Anne 1890-1980 ... **CLC 1, 3, 7, 10, 13, 15, 27, 101; DA; DAB; DAC; DAM MST, NOV; SSC 4, 31**
See also AITN 2; CA 1-4R; 101; CANR 1, 65; CDALBS; DA3; DLB 4, 9, 102; DLBD 12; DLBY 80; MTCW 1, 2; SATA 39; SATA-Obit 23

Porter, Peter (Neville Frederick)
1929- .... **CLC 5, 13, 33**
See also CA 85-88; DLB 40

Reed, Eliot
　See Ambler, Eric
Reed, Ishmael 1938- .. **CLC 2, 3, 5, 6, 13, 32, 60; BLC 3; DAM MULT**
　See also BW 2, 3; CA 21-24R; CANR 25, 48, 74; DA3; DLB 2, 5, 33, 169; DLBD 8; MTCW 1, 2
Reed, John (Silas) 1887-1920 .... **TCLC 9**
　See also CA 106
Reed, Lou .... **CLC 21**
　See also Firbank, Louis
Reese, Lizette Woodworth 1856-1935 . **PC 29**
　See also CA 180; DLB 54
Reeve, Clara 1729-1807 .... **NCLC 19**
　See also DLB 39
Reich, Wilhelm 1897-1957 .... **TCLC 57**
Reid, Christopher (John) 1949- ...... **CLC 33**
　See also CA 140; DLB 40
Reid, Desmond
　See Moorcock, Michael (John)
Reid Banks, Lynne 1929-
　See Banks, Lynne Reid
　See also CA 1-4R; CANR 6, 22, 38, 87; CLR 24; JRDA; MAICYA; SATA 22, 75, 111
Reilly, William K.
　See Creasey, John
Reiner, Max
　See Caldwell, (Janet Miriam) Taylor (Holland)
Reis, Ricardo
　See Pessoa, Fernando (Antonio Nogueira)
Remarque, Erich Maria
　1898-1970 ... **CLC 21; DA; DAB; DAC; DAM MST, NOV**
　See also AAYA 27; CA 77-80; 29-32R; DA3; DLB 56; MTCW 1, 2
Remington, Frederic 1861-1909 ..... **TCLC 89**
　See also CA 108; 169; DLB 12, 186, 188; SATA 41
Remizov, A.
　See Remizov, Aleksei (Mikhailovich)
Remizov, A. M.
　See Remizov, Aleksei (Mikhailovich)
Remizov, Aleksei (Mikhailovich) 1877-1957
　TCLC 27
　See also CA 125; 133
Renan, Joseph Ernest 1823-1892 .. **NCLC 26**
Renard, Jules 1864-1910 .... **TCLC 17**
　See also CA 117
Renault, Mary .... **CLC 3, 11, 17**
　See also Challans, Mary DLBY 83; MTCW 2
Rendell, Ruth (Barbara) 1930- . **CLC 28, 48; DAM POP**
　See also Vine, Barbara CA 109; CANR 32, 52, 74; DLB 87; INT CANR-32; MTCW 1, 2
Renoir, Jean 1894-1979 .... **CLC 20**
　See also CA 129; 85-88
Resnais, Alain 1922- .... **CLC 16**
Reverdy, Pierre 1889-1960 .... **CLC 53**
　See also CA 97-100; 89-92
Rexroth, Kenneth 1905-1982 .... **CLC 1, 2, 6, 11, 22, 49, 112; DAM POET; PC 20**
　See also CA 5-8R; 107; CANR 14, 34, 63; CDALB 1941-1968; DLB 16, 48, 165, 212; DLBY 82; INT CANR-14; MTCW 1, 2

Reyes, Alfonso 1889-1959 .. **TCLC 33; HLCS 2**
　See also CA 131; HW 1
Reyes y Basoalto, Ricardo Eliecer Neftali
　See Neruda, Pablo
Reymont, Wladyslaw (Stanislaw)
　1868(?)-1925 .... **TCLC 5**
　See also CA 104
Reynolds, Jonathan 1942- .... **CLC 6, 38**
　See also CA 65-68; CANR 28
Reynolds, Joshua 1723-1792 .... **LC 15**
　See also DLB 104
Reynolds, Michael Shane 1937- .... **CLC 44**
　See also CA 65-68; CANR 9
Reznikoff, Charles 1894-1976 .... **CLC 9**
　See also CA 33-36; 61-64; CAP 2; DLB 28, 45
Rezzori (d'Arezzo), Gregor von 1914-1998
　CLC 25
　See also CA 122; 136; 167
Rhine, Richard
　See Silverstein, Alvin
Rhodes, Eugene Manlove
　1869-1934 .... **TCLC 53**
Rhodius, Apollonius c. 3rd cent.
　B.C.- .... **CMLC 28**
　See also DLB 176
R'hoone
　See Balzac, Honore de
Rhys, Jean 1890(?)-1979 ...... **CLC 2, 4, 6, 14, 19, 51, 124; DAM NOV; SSC 21**
　See also CA 25-28R; 85-88; CANR 35, 62; CDBLB 1945-1960; DA3; DLB 36, 117, 162; MTCW 1, 2
Ribeiro, Darcy 1922-1997 .... **CLC 34**
　See also CA 33-36R; 156
Ribeiro, Joao Ubaldo (Osorio Pimentel)
　1941- .... **CLC 10, 67**
　See also CA 81-84
Ribman, Ronald (Burt) 1932- .... **CLC 7**
　See also CA 21-24R; CANR 46, 80
Ricci, Nino 1959- .... **CLC 70**
　See also CA 137
Rice, Anne 1941- .. **CLC 41, 128; DAM POP**
　See also AAYA 9; BEST 89:2; CA 65-68; CANR 12, 36, 53, 74; DA3; MTCW 2
Rice, Elmer (Leopold) 1892-1967 ...... **CLC 7, 49; DAM DRAM**
　See also CA 21-22; 25-28R; CAP 2; DLB 4, 7; MTCW 1, 2
Rice, Tim(othy Miles Bindon)
　1944- .... **CLC 21**
　See also CA 103; CANR 46
Rich, Adrienne (Cecile) 1929- ... **CLC 3, 6, 7, 11, 18, 36, 73, 76, 125; DAM POET; PC 5**
　See also CA 9-12R; CANR 20, 53, 74; CDALBS; DA3; DLB 5, 67; MTCW 1, 2
Rich, Barbara
　See Graves, Robert (von Ranke)
Rich, Robert
　See Trumbo, Dalton
Richard, Keith .... **CLC 17**
　See also Richards, Keith
Richards, David Adams 1950- .... **CLC 59; DAC**
　See also CA 93-96; CANR 60; DLB 53

Richards, I(vor) A(rmstrong)
　1893-1979 .... **CLC 14, 24**
　See also CA 41-44R; 89-92; CANR 34, 74; DLB 27; MTCW 2
Richards, Keith 1943-
　See Richard, Keith
　See also CA 107; CANR 77
Richardson, Anne
　See Roiphe, Anne (Richardson)
Richardson, Dorothy Miller
　1873-1957 .... **TCLC 3**
　See also CA 104; DLB 36
Richardson, Ethel Florence (Lindesay)
　1870-1946
　See Richardson, Henry Handel
　See also CA 105
Richardson, Henry Handel .... **TCLC 4**
　See also Richardson, Ethel Florence (Lindesay) DLB 197
Richardson, John 1796-1852 .... **NCLC 55; DAC**
　See also DLB 99
Richardson, Samuel 1689-1761 ...... **LC 1, 44; DA; DAB; DAC; DAM MST, NOV; WLC**
　See also CDBLB 1660-1789; DLB 39
Richler, Mordecai 1931- ...... **CLC 3, 5, 9, 13, 18, 46, 70; DAC; DAM MST, NOV**
　See also AITN 1; CA 65-68; CANR 31, 62; CLR 17; DLB 53; MAICYA; MTCW 1, 2; SATA 44, 98; SATA-Brief 27
Richter, Conrad (Michael)
　1890-1968 .... **CLC 30**
　See also AAYA 21; CA 5-8R; 25-28R; CANR 23; DLB 9, 212; MTCW 1, 2; SATA 3
Ricostranza, Tom
　See Ellis, Trey
Riddell, Charlotte 1832-1906 .... **TCLC 40**
　See also CA 165; DLB 156
Ridge, John Rollin 1827-1867 ...... **NCLC 82; DAM MULT**
　See also CA 144; DLB 175; NNAL
Ridgway, Keith 1965- .... **CLC 119**
　See also CA 172
Riding, Laura .... **CLC 3, 7**
　See also Jackson, Laura (Riding)
Riefenstahl, Berta Helene Amalia 1902-
　See Riefenstahl, Leni
　See also CA 108
Riefenstahl, Leni .... **CLC 16**
　See also Riefenstahl, Berta Helene Amalia
Riffe, Ernest
　See Bergman, (Ernst) Ingmar
Riggs, (Rolla) Lynn 1899-1954 ..... **TCLC 56; DAM MULT**
　See also CA 144; DLB 175; NNAL
Riis, Jacob A(ugust) 1849-1914 ..... **TCLC 80**
　See also CA 113; 168; DLB 23
Riley, James Whitcomb
　1849-1916 .... **TCLC 51; DAM POET**
　See also CA 118; 137; MAICYA; SATA 17
Riley, Tex
　See Creasey, John
Rilke, Rainer Maria 1875-1926 .. **TCLC 1, 6, 19; DAM POET; PC 2**
　See also CA 104; 132; CANR 62; DA3; DLB 81; MTCW 1, 2
Rimbaud, (Jean Nicolas) Arthur 1854-1891
　NCLC 4, 35, 82; DA; DAB; DAC; DAM

MST, POET; PC 3; WLC
See also DA3

Rinehart, Mary Roberts
1876-1958 .... **TCLC 52**
See also CA 108; 166

Ringmaster, The
See Mencken, H(enry) L(ouis)

Ringwood, Gwen(dolyn Margaret) Pharis
1910-1984 .... **CLC 48**
See also CA 148; 112; DLB 88

Rio, Michel 19(?)- .... **CLC 43**

Ritsos, Giannes
See Ritsos, Yannis

Ritsos, Yannis 1909-1990 .... **CLC 6, 13, 31**
See also CA 77-80; 133; CANR 39, 61;
MTCW 1

Ritter, Erika 1948(?)- .... **CLC 52**

Rivera, Jose Eustasio 1889-1928 ... **TCLC 35**
See also CA 162; HW 1, 2

Rivera, Tomas 1935-1984
See also CA 49-52; CANR 32; DLB 82;
HLCS 2; HW 1

Rivers, Conrad Kent 1933-1968 .... **CLC 1**
See also BW 1; CA 85-88; DLB 41

Rivers, Elfrida
See Bradley, Marion Zimmer

Riverside, John
See Heinlein, Robert A(nson)

Rizal, Jose 1861-1896 .... **NCLC 27**

Roa Bastos, Augusto (Antonio)
1917- .... **CLC 45; DAM MULT; HLC 2**
See also CA 131; DLB 113; HW 1

Robbe-Grillet, Alain 1922- .... **CLC 1, 2, 4, 6,**
8, 10, 14, 43, 128
See also CA 9-12R; CANR 33, 65; DLB
83; MTCW 1, 2

Robbins, Harold 1916-1997 .... **CLC 5; DAM**
NOV
See also CA 73-76; 162; CANR 26, 54;
DA3; MTCW 1, 2

Robbins, Thomas Eugene 1936-
See Robbins, Tom
See also CA 81-84; CANR 29, 59; DAM
NOV, POP; DA3; MTCW 1, 2

Robbins, Tom .... **CLC 9, 32, 64**
See also Robbins, Thomas Eugene AAYA
32; BEST 90:3; DLBY 80; MTCW 2

Robbins, Trina 1938- .... **CLC 21**
See also CA 128

Roberts, Charles G(eorge) D(ouglas)
1860-1943 .... **TCLC 8**
See also CA 105; CLR 33; DLB 92; SATA
88; SATA-Brief 29

Roberts, Elizabeth Madox
1886-1941 .... **TCLC 68**
See also CA 111; 166; DLB 9, 54, 102;
SATA 33; SATA-Brief 27

Roberts, Kate 1891-1985 .... **CLC 15**
See also CA 107; 116

Roberts, Keith (John Kingston)
1935- .... **CLC 14**
See also CA 25-28R; CANR 46

Roberts, Kenneth (Lewis)
1885-1957 .... **TCLC 23**
See also CA 109; DLB 9

Roberts, Michele (B.) 1949- .... **CLC 48**
See also CA 115; CANR 58

Robertson, Ellis
See Ellison, Harlan (Jay); Silverberg, Robert

Robertson, Thomas William 1829-1871
NCLC 35; DAM DRAM

Robeson, Kenneth
See Dent, Lester

Robinson, Edwin Arlington
1869-1935 ... **TCLC 5; DA; DAC; DAM**
MST, POET; PC 1
See also CA 104; 133; CDALB 1865-1917;
DLB 54; MTCW 1, 2

Robinson, Henry Crabb
1775-1867 .... **NCLC 15**
See also DLB 107

Robinson, Jill 1936- .... **CLC 10**
See also CA 102; INT 102

Robinson, Kim Stanley 1952- .... **CLC 34**
See also AAYA 26; CA 126; SATA 109

Robinson, Lloyd
See Silverberg, Robert

Robinson, Marilynne 1944- .... **CLC 25**
See also CA 116; CANR 80; DLB 206

Robinson, Smokey .... **CLC 21**
See also Robinson, William, Jr.

Robinson, William, Jr. 1940-
See Robinson, Smokey
See also CA 116

Robison, Mary 1949- .... **CLC 42, 98**
See also CA 113; 116; CANR 87; DLB 130;
INT 116

Rod, Edouard 1857-1910 .... **TCLC 52**

Roddenberry, Eugene Wesley 1921-1991
See Roddenberry, Gene
See also CA 110; 135; CANR 37; SATA 45;
SATA-Obit 69

Roddenberry, Gene .... **CLC 17**
See also Roddenberry, Eugene Wesley
AAYA 5; SATA-Obit 69

Rodgers, Mary 1931- .... **CLC 12**
See also CA 49-52; CANR 8, 55; CLR 20;
INT CANR-8; JRDA; MAICYA; SATA 8

Rodgers, W(illiam) R(obert)
1909-1969 .... **CLC 7**
See also CA 85-88; DLB 20

Rodman, Eric
See Silverberg, Robert

Rodman, Howard 1920(?)-1985 .... **CLC 65**
See also CA 118

Rodman, Maia
See Wojciechowska, Maia (Teresa)

Rodo, Jose Enrique 1872(?)-1917
See also CA 178; HLCS 2; HW 2

Rodriguez, Claudio 1934- .... **CLC 10**
See also DLB 134

Rodriguez, Richard 1944-
See also CA 110; CANR 66; DAM MULT;
DLB 82; HLC 2; HW 1, 2

Roelvaag, O(le) E(dvart)
1876-1931 .... **TCLC 17**
See also CA 117; 171; DLB 9

Roethke, Theodore (Huebner) 1908-1963
CLC 1, 3, 8, 11, 19, 46, 101; DAM
POET; PC 15
See also CA 81-84; CABS 2; CDALB 1941-
1968; DA3; DLB 5, 206; MTCW 1, 2

Rogers, Samuel 1763-1855 .... **NCLC 69**
See also DLB 93

Rogers, Thomas Hunton 1927- .... **CLC 57**
See also CA 89-92; INT 89-92

Rogers, Will(iam Penn Adair) 1879-1935
TCLC 8, 71; DAM MULT

See also CA 105; 144; DA3; DLB 11;
MTCW 2; NNAL

Rogin, Gilbert 1929- .... **CLC 18**
See also CA 65-68; CANR 15

Rohan, Koda .... **TCLC 22**
See also Koda Shigeyuki

Rohlfs, Anna Katharine Green
See Green, Anna Katharine

Rohmer, Eric .... **CLC 16**
See also Scherer, Jean-Marie Maurice

Rohmer, Sax .... **TCLC 28**
See also Ward, Arthur Henry Sarsfield DLB
70

Roiphe, Anne (Richardson) 1935- .. **CLC 3, 9**
See also CA 89-92; CANR 45, 73; DLBY
80; INT 89-92

Rojas, Fernando de 1465-1541 .... **LC 23;**
HLCS 1

Rojas, Gonzalo 1917-
See also HLCS 2; HW 2

Rojas, Gonzalo 1917-
See also CA 178; HLCS 2

Rolfe, Frederick (William Serafino Austin
Lewis Mary) 1860-1913 .... **TCLC 12**
See also CA 107; DLB 34, 156

Rolland, Romain 1866-1944 .... **TCLC 23**
See also CA 118; DLB 65

Rolle, Richard c. 1300-c. 1349 ...... **CMLC 21**
See also DLB 146

Rolvaag, O(le) E(dvart)
See Roelvaag, O(le) E(dvart)

Romain Arnaud, Saint
See Aragon, Louis

Romains, Jules 1885-1972 .... **CLC 7**
See also CA 85-88; CANR 34; DLB 65;
MTCW 1

Romero, Jose Ruben 1890-1952 .... **TCLC 14**
See also CA 114; 131; HW 1

Ronsard, Pierre de 1524-1585 . **LC 6, 54; PC**
11

Rooke, Leon 1934- . **CLC 25, 34; DAM POP**
See also CA 25-28R; CANR 23, 53

Roosevelt, Franklin Delano
1882-1945 .... **TCLC 93**
See also CA 116; 173

Roosevelt, Theodore 1858-1919 ..... **TCLC 69**
See also CA 115; 170; DLB 47, 186

Roper, William 1498-1578 .... **LC 10**

Roquelaure, A. N.
See Rice, Anne

Rosa, Joao Guimaraes 1908-1967 ... **CLC 23;**
HLCS 1
See also CA 89-92; DLB 113

Rose, Wendy 1948- .. **CLC 85; DAM MULT;**
PC 13
See also CA 53-56; CANR 5, 51; DLB 175;
NNAL; SATA 12

Rosen, R. D.
See Rosen, Richard (Dean)

Rosen, Richard (Dean) 1949- .... **CLC 39**
See also CA 77-80; CANR 62; INT
CANR-30

Rosenberg, Isaac 1890-1918 .... **TCLC 12**
See also CA 107; DLB 20

Rosenblatt, Joe .... **CLC 15**
See also Rosenblatt, Joseph

Rosenblatt, Joseph 1933-
See Rosenblatt, Joe
See also CA 89-92; INT 89-92

Rosenfeld, Samuel
See Tzara, Tristan

Rosenstock, Sami
See Tzara, Tristan

Rosenstock, Samuel
See Tzara, Tristan

Rosenthal, M(acha) L(ouis)
1917-1996 .... **CLC 28**
See also CA 1-4R; 152; CAAS 6; CANR 4,
51; DLB 5; SATA 59

Ross, Barnaby
See Dannay, Frederic

Ross, Bernard L.
See Follett, Ken(neth Martin)

Ross, J. H.
See Lawrence, T(homas) E(dward)

Ross, John Hume
See Lawrence, T(homas) E(dward)

Ross, Martin
See Martin, Violet Florence
See also DLB 135

Ross, (James) Sinclair 1908-1996 ... **CLC 13;
DAC; DAM MST; SSC 24**
See also CA 73-76; CANR 81; DLB 88

Rossetti, Christina (Georgina) 1830-1894
**NCLC 2, 50, 66; DA; DAB; DAC; DAM
MST, POET; PC 7; WLC**
See also DA3; DLB 35, 163; MAICYA;
SATA 20

Rossetti, Dante Gabriel 1828-1882 . **NCLC 4,
77; DA; DAB; DAC; DAM MST,
POET; WLC**
See also CDBLB 1832-1890; DLB 35

Rossner, Judith (Perelman) 1935- . **CLC 6, 9,
29**
See also AITN 2; BEST 90:3; CA 17-20R;
CANR 18, 51, 73; DLB 6; INT CANR-
18; MTCW 1, 2

Rostand, Edmond (Eugene Alexis)
1868-1918 .... **TCLC 6, 37; DA; DAB;
DAC; DAM DRAM, MST; DC 10**
See also CA 104; 126; DA3; DLB 192;
MTCW 1

Roth, Henry 1906-1995 ..... **CLC 2, 6, 11, 104**
See also CA 11-12; 149; CANR 38, 63;
CAP 1; DA3; DLB 28; MTCW 1, 2

Roth, Philip (Milton) 1933- ... **CLC 1, 2, 3, 4,
6, 9, 15, 22, 31, 47, 66, 86, 119; DA;
DAB; DAC; DAM MST, NOV, POP;
SSC 26; WLC**
See also BEST 90:3; CA 1-4R; CANR 1,
22, 36, 55; CDALB 1968-1988; DA3;
DLB 2, 28, 173; DLBY 82; MTCW 1, 2

Rothenberg, Jerome 1931- .... **CLC 6, 57**
See also CA 45-48; CANR 1; DLB 5, 193

Roumain, Jacques (Jean Baptiste) 1907-1944
TCLC 19; BLC 3; DAM MULT
See also BW 1; CA 117; 125

Rourke, Constance (Mayfield) 1885-1941
TCLC 12
See also CA 107; YABC 1

Rousseau, Jean-Baptiste 1671-1741 ...... **LC 9**

Rousseau, Jean-Jacques 1712-1778 .... **LC 14,
36; DA; DAB; DAC; DAM MST; WLC**
See also DA3

Roussel, Raymond 1877-1933 .... **TCLC 20**
See also CA 117

Rovit, Earl (Herbert) 1927- .... **CLC 7**
See also CA 5-8R; CANR 12

Rowe, Elizabeth Singer 1674-1737 ..... **LC 44**
See also DLB 39, 95

Rowe, Nicholas 1674-1718 .... **LC 8**
See also DLB 84

Rowley, Ames Dorrance
See Lovecraft, H(oward) P(hillips)

Rowson, Susanna Haswell 1762(?)-1824
NCLC 5, 69
See also DLB 37, 200

Roy, Arundhati 1960(?)- .... **CLC 109**
See also CA 163; DLBY 97

Roy, Gabrielle 1909-1983 .... **CLC 10, 14;
DAB; DAC; DAM MST**
See also CA 53-56; 110; CANR 5, 61; DLB
68; MTCW 1; SATA 104

Royko, Mike 1932-1997 .... **CLC 109**
See also CA 89-92; 157; CANR 26

Rozewicz, Tadeusz 1921- .. **CLC 9, 23; DAM
POET**
See also CA 108; CANR 36, 66; DA3;
MTCW 1, 2

Ruark, Gibbons 1941- .... **CLC 3**
See also CA 33-36R; CAAS 23; CANR 14,
31, 57; DLB 120

Rubens, Bernice (Ruth) 1923- .... **CLC 19, 31**
See also CA 25-28R; CANR 33, 65; DLB
14, 207; MTCW 1

Rubin, Harold
See Robbins, Harold

Rudkin, (James) David 1936- .... **CLC 14**
See also CA 89-92; DLB 13

Rudnik, Raphael 1933- .... **CLC 7**
See also CA 29-32R

Ruffian, M.
See Hasek, Jaroslav (Matej Frantisek)

Ruiz, Jose Martinez .... **CLC 11**
See also Martinez Ruiz, Jose

Rukeyser, Muriel 1913-1980 . **CLC 6, 10, 15,
27; DAM POET; PC 12**
See also CA 5-8R; 93-96; CANR 26, 60;
DA3; DLB 48; MTCW 1, 2; SATA-Obit
22

Rule, Jane (Vance) 1931- .... **CLC 27**
See also CA 25-28R; CAAS 18; CANR 12,
87; DLB 60

Rulfo, Juan 1918-1986 ...... **CLC 8, 80; DAM
MULT; HLC 2; SSC 25**
See also CA 85-88; 118; CANR 26; DLB
113; HW 1, 2; MTCW 1, 2

Rumi, Jalal al-Din 1297-1373 .... **CMLC 20**

Runeberg, Johan 1804-1877 .... **NCLC 41**

Runyon, (Alfred) Damon
1884(?)-1946 .... **TCLC 10**
See also CA 107; 165; DLB 11, 86, 171;
MTCW 2

Rush, Norman 1933- .... **CLC 44**
See also CA 121; 126; INT 126

Rushdie, (Ahmed) Salman 1947- .... **CLC 23,
31, 55, 100; DAB; DAC; DAM MST,
NOV, POP; WLCS**
See also BEST 89:3; CA 108; 111; CANR
33, 56; DA3; DLB 194; INT 111; MTCW
1, 2

Rushforth, Peter (Scott) 1945- .... **CLC 19**
See also CA 101

Ruskin, John 1819-1900 .... **TCLC 63**
See also CA 114; 129; CDBLB 1832-1890;
DLB 55, 163, 190; SATA 24

Russ, Joanna 1937- .... **CLC 15**
See also CANR 11, 31, 65; DLB 8; MTCW
1

Russell, George William 1867-1935
See Baker, Jean H.
See also CA 104; 153; CDBLB 1890-1914;
DAM POET

Russell, (Henry) Ken(neth Alfred)
1927- .... **CLC 16**
See also CA 105

Russell, William Martin 1947- .... **CLC 60**
See also CA 164

Rutherford, Mark .... **TCLC 25**
See also White, William Hale DLB 18

Ruyslinck, Ward 1929- .... **CLC 14**
See also Belser, Reimond Karel Maria de

Ryan, Cornelius (John) 1920-1974 ..... **CLC 7**
See also CA 69-72; 53-56; CANR 38

Ryan, Michael 1946- .... **CLC 65**
See also CA 49-52; DLBY 82

Ryan, Tim
See Dent, Lester

Rybakov, Anatoli (Naumovich) 1911-1998
CLC 23, 53
See also CA 126; 135; 172; SATA 79;
SATA-Obit 108

Ryder, Jonathan
See Ludlum, Robert

Ryga, George 1932-1987 .... **CLC 14; DAC;
DAM MST**
See also CA 101; 124; CANR 43; DLB 60

S. H.
See Hartmann, Sadakichi

S. S.
See Sassoon, Siegfried (Lorraine)

Saba, Umberto 1883-1957 .... **TCLC 33**
See also CA 144; CANR 79; DLB 114

Sabatini, Rafael 1875-1950 .... **TCLC 47**
See also CA 162

Sabato, Ernesto (R.) 1911- .... **CLC 10, 23;
DAM MULT; HLC 2**
See also CA 97-100; CANR 32, 65; DLB
145; HW 1, 2; MTCW 1, 2

Sa-Carniero, Mario de 1890-1916 . **TCLC 83**

Sacastru, Martin
See Bioy Casares, Adolfo

Sacastru, Martin
See Bioy Casares, Adolfo

Sacher-Masoch, Leopold von 1836(?)-1895
NCLC 31

Sachs, Marilyn (Stickle) 1927- .... **CLC 35**
See also AAYA 2; CA 17-20R; CANR 13,
47; CLR 2; JRDA; MAICYA; SAAS 2;
SATA 3, 68; SATA-Essay 110

Sachs, Nelly 1891-1970 .... **CLC 14, 98**
See also CA 17-18; 25-28R; CANR 87;
CAP 2; MTCW 2

Sackler, Howard (Oliver)
1929-1982 .... **CLC 14**
See also CA 61-64; 108; CANR 30; DLB 7

Sacks, Oliver (Wolf) 1933- .... **CLC 67**
See also CA 53-56; CANR 28, 50, 76; DA3;
INT CANR-28; MTCW 1, 2

Sadakichi
See Hartmann, Sadakichi

**Sade, Donatien Alphonse Francois, Comte
de** 1740-1814 .... **NCLC 47**

Sadoff, Ira 1945- .... **CLC 9**
See also CA 53-56; CANR 5, 21; DLB 120

Saetone
See Camus, Albert

Safire, William 1929- .... **CLC 10**
See also CA 17-20R; CANR 31, 54

Sagan, Carl (Edward) 1934-1996 .... **CLC 30, 112**
See also AAYA 2; CA 25-28R; 155; CANR 11, 36, 74; DA3; MTCW 1, 2; SATA 58; SATA-Obit 94

Sagan, Francoise .... **CLC 3, 6, 9, 17, 36**
See also Quoirez, Francoise DLB 83; MTCW 2

Sahgal, Nayantara (Pandit) 1927- .... **CLC 41**
See also CA 9-12R; CANR 11

Saint, H(arry) F. 1941- .... **CLC 50**
See also CA 127

St. Aubin de Teran, Lisa 1953-
See Teran, Lisa St. Aubin de
See also CA 118; 126; INT 126

Saint Birgitta of Sweden c.
1303-1373 .... **CMLC 24**

Sainte-Beuve, Charles Augustin 1804-1869
NCLC 5

Saint-Exupery, Antoine (Jean Baptiste Marie Roger) de 1900-1944 .... **TCLC 2, 56; DAM NOV; WLC**
See also CA 108; 132; CLR 10; DA3; DLB 72; MAICYA; MTCW 1, 2; SATA 20

St. John, David
See Hunt, E(verette) Howard, (Jr.)

Saint-John Perse
See Leger, (Marie-Rene Auguste) Alexis Saint-Leger

Saintsbury, George (Edward Bateman)
1845-1933 .... **TCLC 31**
See also CA 160; DLB 57, 149

Sait Faik .... **TCLC 23**
See also Abasiyanik, Sait Faik

Saki .... **TCLC 3; SSC 12**
See also Munro, H(ector) H(ugh) MTCW 2

Sala, George Augustus .... **NCLC 46**

Saladin 1138-1193 .... **CMLC 38**

Salama, Hannu 1936- .... **CLC 18**

Salamanca, J(ack) R(ichard) 1922- .. **CLC 4, 15**
See also CA 25-28R

Salas, Floyd Francis 1931-
See also CA 119; CAAS 27; CANR 44, 75; DAM MULT; DLB 82; HLC 2; HW 1, 2; MTCW 2

Sale, J. Kirkpatrick
See Sale, Kirkpatrick

Sale, Kirkpatrick 1937- .... **CLC 68**
See also CA 13-16R; CANR 10

Salinas, Luis Omar 1937- ..... **CLC 90; DAM MULT; HLC 2**
See also CA 131; CANR 81; DLB 82; HW 1, 2

Salinas (y Serrano), Pedro 1891(?)-1951
TCLC 17
See also CA 117; DLB 134

Salinger, J(erome) D(avid) 1919- .. **CLC 1, 3, 8, 12, 55, 56; DA; DAB; DAC; DAM MST, NOV, POP; SSC 2, 28; WLC**
See also AAYA 2; CA 5-8R; CANR 39; CDALB 1941-1968; CLR 18; DA3; DLB 2, 102, 173; MAICYA; MTCW 1, 2; SATA 67

Salisbury, John
See Caute, (John) David

Salter, James 1925- .... **CLC 7, 52, 59**
See also CA 73-76; DLB 130

Saltus, Edgar (Everton) 1855-1921 . **TCLC 8**
See also CA 105; DLB 202

Saltykov, Mikhail Evgrafovich 1826-1889
NCLC 16

Samarakis, Antonis 1919- .... **CLC 5**
See also CA 25-28R; CAAS 16; CANR 36

Sanchez, Florencio 1875-1910 .... **TCLC 37**
See also CA 153; HW 1

Sanchez, Luis Rafael 1936- .... **CLC 23**
See also CA 128; DLB 145; HW 1

Sanchez, Sonia 1934- .... **CLC 5, 116; BLC 3; DAM MULT; PC 9**
See also BW 2, 3; CA 33-36R; CANR 24, 49, 74; CLR 18; DA3; DLB 41; DLBD 8; MAICYA; MTCW 1, 2; SATA 22

Sand, George 1804-1876 ..... **NCLC 2, 42, 57; DA; DAB; DAC; DAM MST, NOV; WLC**
See also DA3; DLB 119, 192

Sandburg, Carl (August) 1878-1967 . **CLC 1, 4, 10, 15, 35; DA; DAB; DAC; DAM MST, POET; PC 2; WLC**
See also AAYA 24; CA 5-8R; 25-28R; CANR 35; CDALB 1865-1917; DA3; DLB 17, 54; MAICYA; MTCW 1, 2; SATA 8

Sandburg, Charles
See Sandburg, Carl (August)

Sandburg, Charles A.
See Sandburg, Carl (August)

Sanders, (James) Ed(ward) 1939- ... **CLC 53; DAM POET**
See also CA 13-16R; CAAS 21; CANR 13, 44, 78; DLB 16

Sanders, Lawrence 1920-1998 .... **CLC 41; DAM POP**
See also BEST 89:4; CA 81-84; 165; CANR 33, 62; DA3; MTCW 1

Sanders, Noah
See Blount, Roy (Alton), Jr.

Sanders, Winston P.
See Anderson, Poul (William)

Sandoz, Mari(e Susette) 1896-1966 .. **CLC 28**
See also CA 1-4R; 25-28R; CANR 17, 64; DLB 9, 212; MTCW 1, 2; SATA 5

Saner, Reg(inald Anthony) 1931- .... **CLC 9**
See also CA 65-68

Sankara 788-820 .... **CMLC 32**

Sannazaro, Jacopo 1456(?)-1530 .... **LC 8**

Sansom, William 1912-1976 .... **CLC 2, 6; DAM NOV; SSC 21**
See also CA 5-8R; 65-68; CANR 42; DLB 139; MTCW 1

Santayana, George 1863-1952 .... **TCLC 40**
See also CA 115; DLB 54, 71; DLBD 13

Santiago, Danny .... **CLC 33**
See also James, Daniel (Lewis) DLB 122

Santmyer, Helen Hoover 1895-1986 . **CLC 33**
See also CA 1-4R; 118; CANR 15, 33; DLBY 84; MTCW 1

Santoka, Taneda 1882-1940 .... **TCLC 72**

Santos, Bienvenido N(uqui)
1911-1996 .... **CLC 22; DAM MULT**
See also CA 101; 151; CANR 19, 46

Sapper .... **TCLC 44**
See also McNeile, Herman Cyril

Sapphire
See Sapphire, Brenda

Sapphire, Brenda 1950- .... **CLC 99**

Sappho fl. 6th cent. B.C.- ..... **CMLC 3; DAM POET; PC 5**
See also DA3; DLB 176

Saramago, Jose 1922- ..... **CLC 119; HLCS 1**
See also CA 153

Sarduy, Severo 1937-1993 .... **CLC 6, 97; HLCS 1**
See also CA 89-92; 142; CANR 58, 81; DLB 113; HW 1, 2

Sargeson, Frank 1903-1982 .... **CLC 31**
See also CA 25-28R; 106; CANR 38, 79

Sarmiento, Domingo Faustino 1811-1888
See also HLCS 2

Sarmiento, Felix Ruben Garcia
See Dario, Ruben

Saro-Wiwa, Ken(ule Beeson)
1941-1995 .... **CLC 114**
See also BW 2; CA 142; 150; CANR 60; DLB 157

Saroyan, William 1908-1981 ... **CLC 1, 8, 10, 29, 34, 56; DA; DAB; DAC; DAM DRAM, MST, NOV; SSC 21; WLC**
See also CA 5-8R; 103; CANR 30; CDALBS; DA3; DLB 7, 9, 86; DLBY 81; MTCW 1, 2; SATA 23; SATA-Obit 24

Sarraute, Nathalie 1900- . **CLC 1, 2, 4, 8, 10, 31, 80**
See also CA 9-12R; CANR 23, 66; DLB 83; MTCW 1, 2

Sarton, (Eleanor) May 1912-1995 ..... **CLC 4, 14, 49, 91; DAM POET**
See also CA 1-4R; 149; CANR 1, 34, 55; DLB 48; DLBY 81; INT CANR-34; MTCW 1, 2; SATA 36; SATA-Obit 86

Sartre, Jean-Paul 1905-1980 . **CLC 1, 4, 7, 9, 13, 18, 24, 44, 50, 52; DA; DAB; DAC; DAM DRAM, MST, NOV; DC 3; SSC 32; WLC**
See also CA 9-12R; 97-100; CANR 21; DA3; DLB 72; MTCW 1, 2

Sassoon, Siegfried (Lorraine)
1886-1967 . **CLC 36; DAB; DAM MST, NOV, POET; PC 12**
See also CA 104; 25-28R; CANR 36; DLB 20, 191; DLBD 18; MTCW 1, 2

Satterfield, Charles
See Pohl, Frederik

Saul, John (W. III) 1942- ...... **CLC 46; DAM NOV, POP**
See also AAYA 10; BEST 90:4; CA 81-84; CANR 16, 40, 81; SATA 98

Saunders, Caleb
See Heinlein, Robert A(nson)

Saura (Atares), Carlos 1932- .... **CLC 20**
See also CA 114; 131; CANR 79; HW 1

Sauser-Hall, Frederic 1887-1961 ...... **CLC 18**
See also Cendrars, Blaise CA 102; 93-96; CANR 36, 62; MTCW 1

Saussure, Ferdinand de
1857-1913 .... **TCLC 49**

Savage, Catharine
See Brosman, Catharine Savage

Savage, Thomas 1915- .... **CLC 40**
See also CA 126; 132; CAAS 15; INT 132

Savan, Glenn 19(?)- .... **CLC 50**

Sayers, Dorothy L(eigh)
1893-1957 .... **TCLC 2, 15; DAM POP**
See also CA 104; 119; CANR 60; CDBLB 1914-1945; DLB 10, 36, 77, 100; MTCW 1, 2

Selby, Hubert, Jr. 1928- .... **CLC 1, 2, 4, 8; SSC 20**
See also CA 13-16R; CANR 33, 85; DLB 2

Selzer, Richard 1928- .... **CLC 74**
See also CA 65-68; CANR 14

Sembene, Ousmane
See Ousmane, Sembene

Senancour, Etienne Pivert de 1770-1846 **NCLC 16**
See also DLB 119

Sender, Ramon (Jose) 1902-1982 ...... **CLC 8; DAM MULT; HLC 2**
See also CA 5-8R; 105; CANR 8; HW 1; MTCW 1

Seneca, Lucius Annaeus c. 1-c. 65 .... **CMLC 6; DAM DRAM; DC 5**
See also DLB 211

Senghor, Leopold Sedar 1906- .... **CLC 54; BLC 3; DAM MULT, POET; PC 25**
See also BW 2; CA 116; 125; CANR 47, 74; MTCW 1, 2

Senna, Danzy 1970- .... **CLC 119**
See also CA 169

Serling, (Edward) Rod(man) 1924-1975 .... **CLC 30**
See also AAYA 14; AITN 1; CA 162; 57-60; DLB 26

Serna, Ramon Gomez de la
See Gomez de la Serna, Ramon

Serpieres
See Guillevic, (Eugene)

Service, Robert
See Service, Robert W(illiam)
See also DAB; DLB 92

Service, Robert W(illiam) 1874(?)-1958 **TCLC 15; DA; DAC; DAM MST, POET; WLC**
See also Service, Robert CA 115; 140; CANR 84; SATA 20

Seth, Vikram 1952- .... **CLC 43, 90; DAM MULT**
See also CA 121; 127; CANR 50, 74; DA3; DLB 120; INT 127; MTCW 2

Seton, Cynthia Propper 1926-1982 .. **CLC 27**
See also CA 5-8R; 108; CANR 7

Seton, Ernest (Evan) Thompson 1860-1946 **TCLC 31**
See also CA 109; CLR 59; DLB 92; DLBD 13; JRDA; SATA 18

Seton-Thompson, Ernest
See Seton, Ernest (Evan) Thompson

Settle, Mary Lee 1918- .... **CLC 19, 61**
See also CA 89-92; CAAS 1; CANR 44, 87; DLB 6; INT 89-92

Seuphor, Michel
See Arp, Jean

Sevigne, Marie (de Rabutin-Chantal) Marquise de 1626-1696 .... **LC 11**

Sewall, Samuel 1652-1730 .... **LC 38**
See also DLB 24

Sexton, Anne (Harvey) 1928-1974 ..... **CLC 2, 4, 6, 8, 10, 15, 53; DA; DAB; DAC; DAM MST, POET; PC 2; WLC**
See also CA 1-4R; 53-56; CABS 2; CANR 3, 36; CDALB 1941-1968; DA3; DLB 5, 169; MTCW 1, 2; SATA 10

Shaara, Jeff 1952- .... **CLC 119**
See also CA 163

Shaara, Michael (Joseph, Jr.) 1929-1988 .... **CLC 15; DAM POP**
See also AITN 1; CA 102; 125; CANR 52, 85; DLBY 83

Shackleton, C. C.
See Aldiss, Brian W(ilson)

Shacochis, Bob .... **CLC 39**
See also Shacochis, Robert G.

Shacochis, Robert G. 1951-
See Shacochis, Bob
See also CA 119; 124; INT 124

Shaffer, Anthony (Joshua) 1926- ..... **CLC 19; DAM DRAM**
See also CA 110; 116; DLB 13

Shaffer, Peter (Levin) 1926- .. **CLC 5, 14, 18, 37, 60; DAB; DAM DRAM, MST; DC 7**
See also CA 25-28R; CANR 25, 47, 74; CDBLB 1960 to Present; DA3; DLB 13; MTCW 1, 2

Shakey, Bernard
See Young, Neil

Shalamov, Varlam (Tikhonovich) 1907(?)-1982 .... **CLC 18**
See also CA 129; 105

Shamlu, Ahmad 1925- .... **CLC 10**

Shammas, Anton 1951- .... **CLC 55**

Shange, Ntozake 1948- .... **CLC 8, 25, 38, 74, 126; BLC 3; DAM DRAM, MULT; DC 3**
See also AAYA 9; BW 2; CA 85-88; CABS 3; CANR 27, 48, 74; DA3; DLB 38; MTCW 1, 2

Shanley, John Patrick 1950- .... **CLC 75**
See also CA 128; 133; CANR 83

Shapcott, Thomas W(illiam) 1935- .. **CLC 38**
See also CA 69-72; CANR 49, 83

Shapiro, Jane .... **CLC 76**

Shapiro, Karl (Jay) 1913- . **CLC 4, 8, 15, 53; PC 25**
See also CA 1-4R; CAAS 6; CANR 1, 36, 66; DLB 48; MTCW 1, 2

Sharp, William 1855-1905 .... **TCLC 39**
See also CA 160; DLB 156

Sharpe, Thomas Ridley 1928-
See Sharpe, Tom
See also CA 114; 122; CANR 85; INT 122

Sharpe, Tom .... **CLC 36**
See also Sharpe, Thomas Ridley DLB 14

Shaw, Bernard .... **TCLC 45**
See also Shaw, George Bernard BW 1; MTCW 2

Shaw, G. Bernard
See Shaw, George Bernard

Shaw, George Bernard 1856-1950 .. **TCLC 3, 9, 21; DA; DAB; DAC; DAM DRAM, MST; WLC**
See also Shaw, Bernard CA 104; 128; CDBLB 1914-1945; DA3; DLB 10, 57, 190; MTCW 1, 2

Shaw, Henry Wheeler 1818-1885 .. **NCLC 15**
See also DLB 11

Shaw, Irwin 1913-1984 .... **CLC 7, 23, 34; DAM DRAM, POP**
See also AITN 1; CA 13-16R; 112; CANR 21; CDALB 1941-1968; DLB 6, 102; DLBY 84; MTCW 1, 21

Shaw, Robert 1927-1978 .... **CLC 5**
See also AITN 1; CA 1-4R; 81-84; CANR 4; DLB 13, 14

Shaw, T. E.
See Lawrence, T(homas) E(dward)

Shawn, Wallace 1943- .... **CLC 41**
See also CA 112

Shea, Lisa 1953- .... **CLC 86**
See also CA 147

Sheed, Wilfrid (John Joseph) 1930- . **CLC 2, 4, 10, 53**
See also CA 65-68; CANR 30, 66; DLB 6; MTCW 1, 2

Sheldon, Alice Hastings Bradley 1915(?)-1987
See Tiptree, James, Jr.
See also CA 108; 122; CANR 34; INT 108; MTCW 1

Sheldon, John
See Bloch, Robert (Albert)

Shelley, Mary Wollstonecraft (Godwin) 1797-1851 ..... **NCLC 14, 59; DA; DAB; DAC; DAM MST, NOV; WLC**
See also AAYA 20; CDBLB 1789-1832; DA3; DLB 110, 116, 159, 178; SATA 29

Shelley, Percy Bysshe 1792-1822 .. **NCLC 18; DA; DAB; DAC; DAM MST, POET; PC 14; WLC**
See also CDBLB 1789-1832; DA3; DLB 96, 110, 158

Shepard, Jim 1956- .... **CLC 36**
See also CA 137; CANR 59; SATA 90

Shepard, Lucius 1947- .... **CLC 34**
See also CA 128; 141; CANR 81

Shepard, Sam 1943- .... **CLC 4, 6, 17, 34, 41, 44; DAM DRAM; DC 5**
See also AAYA 1; CA 69-72; CABS 3; CANR 22; DA3; DLB 7, 212; MTCW 1, 2

Shepherd, Michael
See Ludlum, Robert

Sherburne, Zoa (Lillian Morin) 1912-1995 **CLC 30**
See also AAYA 13; CA 1-4R; 176; CANR 3, 37; MAICYA; SAAS 18; SATA 3

Sheridan, Frances 1724-1766 .... **LC 7**
See also DLB 39, 84

Sheridan, Richard Brinsley 1751-1816 .. **NCLC 5; DA; DAB; DAC; DAM DRAM, MST; DC 1; WLC**
See also CDBLB 1660-1789; DLB 89

Sherman, Jonathan Marc .... **CLC 55**

Sherman, Martin 1941(?)- .... **CLC 19**
See also CA 116; 123; CANR 86

Sherwin, Judith Johnson 1936-
See Johnson, Judith (Emlyn)
See also CANR 85

Sherwood, Frances 1940- .... **CLC 81**
See also CA 146

Sherwood, Robert E(mmet) 1896-1955 .... **TCLC 3; DAM DRAM**
See also CA 104; 153; CANR 86; DLB 7, 26

Shestov, Lev 1866-1938 .... **TCLC 56**

Shevchenko, Taras 1814-1861 .... **NCLC 54**

Shiel, M(atthew) P(hipps) 1865-1947 .... **TCLC 8**
See also Holmes, Gordon CA 106; 160; DLB 153; MTCW 2

Shields, Carol 1935- .... **CLC 91, 113; DAC**
See also CA 81-84; CANR 51, 74; DA3; MTCW 2

Shields, David 1956- .... **CLC 97**
See also CA 124; CANR 48

Shiga, Naoya 1883-1971 ..... **CLC 33; SSC 23**
See also CA 101; 33-36R; DLB 180

Shikibu, Murasaki c. 978-c. 1014 ... **CMLC 1**

Shilts, Randy 1951-1994 .... **CLC 85**
See also AAYA 19; CA 115; 127; 144;
CANR 45; DA3; INT 127; MTCW 2

Shimazaki, Haruki 1872-1943
See Shimazaki Toson
See also CA 105; 134; CANR 84

Shimazaki Toson 1872-1943 .... **TCLC 5**
See also Shimazaki, Haruki DLB 180

Sholokhov, Mikhail (Aleksandrovich)
1905-1984 .... **CLC 7, 15**
See also CA 101; 112; MTCW 1, 2; SATA-
Obit 36

Shone, Patric
See Hanley, James

Shreve, Susan Richards 1939- .... **CLC 23**
See also CA 49-52; CAAS 5; CANR 5, 38,
69; MAICYA; SATA 46, 95; SATA-Brief
41

Shue, Larry 1946-1985 .... **CLC 52; DAM
DRAM**
See also CA 145; 117

Shu-Jen, Chou 1881-1936
See Lu Hsun
See also CA 104

Shulman, Alix Kates 1932- .... **CLC 2, 10**
See also CA 29-32R; CANR 43; SATA 7

Shuster, Joe 1914- .... **CLC 21**

Shute, Nevil .... **CLC 30**
See also Norway, Nevil Shute MTCW 2

Shuttle, Penelope (Diane) 1947- .... **CLC 7**
See also CA 93-96; CANR 39, 84; DLB 14,
40

Sidney, Mary 1561-1621 .... **LC 19, 39**

Sidney, Sir Philip 1554-1586 .... **LC 19, 39;
DA; DAB; DAC; DAM MST, POET**
See also CDBLB Before 1660; DA3; DLB
167

Siegel, Jerome 1914-1996 .... **CLC 21**
See also CA 116; 169; 151

Siegel, Jerry
See Siegel, Jerome

Sienkiewicz, Henryk (Adam Alexander Pius)
1846-1916 .... **TCLC 3**
See also CA 104; 134; CANR 84

Sierra, Gregorio Martinez
See Martinez Sierra, Gregorio

Sierra, Maria (de la O'LeJarraga) Martinez
See Martinez Sierra, Maria (de la
O'LeJarraga)

Sigal, Clancy 1926- .... **CLC 7**
See also CA 1-4R; CANR 85

Sigourney, Lydia Howard (Huntley)
1791-1865 .... **NCLC 21**
See also DLB 1, 42, 73

Siguenza y Gongora, Carlos de 1645-1700
LC 8; HLCS 2

Sigurjonsson, Johann 1880-1919 ... **TCLC 27**
See also CA 170

Sikelianos, Angelos 1884-1951 ...... **TCLC 39;
PC 29**

Silkin, Jon 1930- .... **CLC 2, 6, 43**
See also CA 5-8R; CAAS 5; DLB 27

Silko, Leslie (Marmon) 1948- .... **CLC 23, 74,
114; DA; DAC; DAM MST, MULT,
POP; SSC 37; WLCS**
See also AAYA 14; CA 115; 122; CANR
45, 65; DA3; DLB 143, 175; MTCW 2;
NNAL

Sillanpaa, Frans Eemil 1888-1964 ... **CLC 19**
See also CA 129; 93-96; MTCW 1

Sillitoe, Alan 1928- ... **CLC 1, 3, 6, 10, 19, 57**
See also AITN 1; CA 9-12R; CAAS 2;
CANR 8, 26, 55; CDBLB 1960 to Present;
DLB 14, 139; MTCW 1, 2; SATA 61

Silone, Ignazio 1900-1978 .... **CLC 4**
See also CA 25-28; 81-84; CANR 34; CAP
2; MTCW 1

Silver, Joan Micklin 1935- .... **CLC 20**
See also CA 114; 121; INT 121

Silver, Nicholas
See Faust, Frederick (Schiller)

Silverberg, Robert 1935- .... **CLC 7; DAM
POP**
See also AAYA 24; CA 1-4R; CAAS 3;
CANR 1, 20, 36, 85; CLR 59; DLB 8;
INT CANR-20; MAICYA; MTCW 1, 2;
SATA 13, 91; SATA-Essay 104

Silverstein, Alvin 1933- .... **CLC 17**
See also CA 49-52; CANR 2; CLR 25;
JRDA; MAICYA; SATA 8, 69

Silverstein, Virginia B(arbara Opshelor)
1937- .... **CLC 17**
See also CA 49-52; CANR 2; CLR 25;
JRDA; MAICYA; SATA 8, 69

Sim, Georges
See Simenon, Georges (Jacques Christian)

Simak, Clifford D(onald) 1904-1988 . **CLC 1,
55**
See also CA 1-4R; 125; CANR 1, 35; DLB
8; MTCW 1; SATA-Obit 56

Simenon, Georges (Jacques Christian)
1903-1989 .... **CLC 1, 2, 3, 8, 18, 47;
DAM POP**
See also CA 85-88; 129; CANR 35; DA3;
DLB 72; DLBY 89; MTCW 1, 2

Simic, Charles 1938- ... **CLC 6, 9, 22, 49, 68;
DAM POET**
See also CA 29-32R; CAAS 4; CANR 12,
33, 52, 61; DA3; DLB 105; MTCW 2

Simmel, Georg 1858-1918 .... **TCLC 64**
See also CA 157

Simmons, Charles (Paul) 1924- .... **CLC 57**
See also CA 89-92; INT 89-92

Simmons, Dan 1948- .... **CLC 44; DAM POP**
See also AAYA 16; CA 138; CANR 53, 81

Simmons, James (Stewart Alexander) 1933-
CLC 43
See also CA 105; CAAS 21; DLB 40

Simms, William Gilmore
1806-1870 .... **NCLC 3**
See also DLB 3, 30, 59, 73

Simon, Carly 1945- .... **CLC 26**
See also CA 105

Simon, Claude 1913-1984 . **CLC 4, 9, 15, 39;
DAM NOV**
See also CA 89-92; CANR 33; DLB 83;
MTCW 1

Simon, (Marvin) Neil 1927- ... **CLC 6, 11, 31,
39, 70; DAM DRAM**
See also AAYA 32; AITN 1; CA 21-24R;
CANR 26, 54, 87; DA3; DLB 7; MTCW
1, 2

Simon, Paul (Frederick) 1941(?)- ..... **CLC 17**
See also CA 116; 153

Simonon, Paul 1956(?)- .... **CLC 30**

Simpson, Harriette
See Arnow, Harriette (Louisa) Simpson

Simpson, Louis (Aston Marantz)
1923- ...... **CLC 4, 7, 9, 32; DAM POET**
See also CA 1-4R; CAAS 4; CANR 1, 61;
DLB 5; MTCW 1, 2

Simpson, Mona (Elizabeth) 1957- .... **CLC 44**
See also CA 122; 135; CANR 68

Simpson, N(orman) F(rederick)
1919- .... **CLC 29**
See also CA 13-16R; DLB 13

Sinclair, Andrew (Annandale) 1935- . **CLC 2,
14**
See also CA 9-12R; CAAS 5; CANR 14,
38; DLB 14; MTCW 1

Sinclair, Emil
See Hesse, Hermann

Sinclair, Iain 1943- .... **CLC 76**
See also CA 132; CANR 81

Sinclair, Iain MacGregor
See Sinclair, Iain

Sinclair, Irene
See Griffith, D(avid Lewelyn) W(ark)

Sinclair, Mary Amelia St. Clair 1865(?)-1946
See Sinclair, May
See also CA 104

Sinclair, May 1863-1946 .... **TCLC 3, 11**
See also Sinclair, Mary Amelia St. Clair CA
166; DLB 36, 135

Sinclair, Roy
See Griffith, D(avid Lewelyn) W(ark)

Sinclair, Upton (Beall) 1878-1968 ..... **CLC 1,
11, 15, 63; DA; DAB; DAC; DAM
MST, NOV; WLC**
See also CA 5-8R; 25-28R; CANR 7;
CDALB 1929-1941; DA3; DLB 9; INT
CANR-7; MTCW 1, 2; SATA 9

Singer, Isaac
See Singer, Isaac Bashevis

Singer, Isaac Bashevis 1904-1991 .. **CLC 1, 3,
6, 9, 11, 15, 23, 38, 69, 111; DA; DAB;
DAC; DAM MST, NOV; SSC 3; WLC**
See also AAYA 32; AITN 1, 2; CA 1-4R;
134; CANR 1, 39; CDALB 1941-1968;
CLR 1; DA3; DLB 6, 28, 52; DLBY 91;
JRDA; MAICYA; MTCW 1, 2; SATA 3,
27; SATA-Obit 68

Singer, Israel Joshua 1893-1944 .... **TCLC 33**
See also CA 169

Singh, Khushwant 1915- .... **CLC 11**
See also CA 9-12R; CAAS 9; CANR 6, 84

Singleton, Ann
See Benedict, Ruth (Fulton)

Sinjohn, John
See Galsworthy, John

Sinyavsky, Andrei (Donatevich) 1925-1997
CLC 8
See also CA 85-88; 159

Sirin, V.
See Nabokov, Vladimir (Vladimirovich)

Sissman, L(ouis) E(dward)
1928-1976 .... **CLC 9, 18**
See also CA 21-24R; 65-68; CANR 13;
DLB 5

Sisson, C(harles) H(ubert) 1914- .... **CLC 8**
See also CA 1-4R; CAAS 3; CANR 3, 48,
84; DLB 27

Taylor, Peter (Hillsman) 1917-1994 .. **CLC 1, 4, 18, 37, 44, 50, 71; SSC 10**
See also CA 13-16R; 147; CANR 9, 50; DLBY 81, 94; INT CANR-9; MTCW 1, 2

Taylor, Robert Lewis 1912-1998 .... **CLC 14**
See also CA 1-4R; 170; CANR 3, 64; SATA 10

Tchekhov, Anton
See Chekhov, Anton (Pavlovich)

Tchicaya, Gerald Felix 1931-1988 .. **CLC 101**
See also CA 129; 125; CANR 81

Tchicaya U Tam'si
See Tchicaya, Gerald Felix

Teasdale, Sara 1884-1933 .... **TCLC 4**
See also CA 104; 163; DLB 45; SATA 32

Tegner, Esaias 1782-1846 .... **NCLC 2**

Teilhard de Chardin, (Marie Joseph) Pierre 1881-1955 .... **TCLC 9**
See also CA 105

Temple, Ann
See Mortimer, Penelope (Ruth)

Tennant, Emma (Christina) 1937- .. **CLC 13, 52**
See also CA 65-68; CAAS 9; CANR 10, 38, 59; DLB 14

Tenneshaw, S. M.
See Silverberg, Robert

Tennyson, Alfred 1809-1892 ... **NCLC 30, 65; DA; DAB; DAC; DAM MST, POET; PC 6; WLC**
See also CDBLB 1832-1890; DA3; DLB 32

Teran, Lisa St. Aubin de .... **CLC 36**
See also St. Aubin de Teran, Lisa

Terence c. 184B.C.-c. 159B.C. ...... **CMLC 14; DC 7**
See also DLB 211

Teresa de Jesus, St. 1515-1582 .... **LC 18**

Terkel, Louis 1912-
See Terkel, Studs
See also CA 57-60; CANR 18, 45, 67; DA3; MTCW 1, 2

Terkel, Studs .... **CLC 38**
See also Terkel, Louis AAYA 32; AITN 1; MTCW 2

Terry, C. V.
See Slaughter, Frank G(ill)

Terry, Megan 1932- .... **CLC 19**
See also CA 77-80; CABS 3; CANR 43; DLB 7

Tertullian c. 155-c. 245 .... **CMLC 29**

Tertz, Abram
See Sinyavsky, Andrei (Donatevich)

Tesich, Steve 1943(?)-1996 .... **CLC 40, 69**
See also CA 105; 152; DLBY 83

Tesla, Nikola 1856-1943 .... **TCLC 88**

Teternikov, Fyodor Kuzmich 1863-1927
See Sologub, Fyodor
See also CA 104

Tevis, Walter 1928-1984 .... **CLC 42**
See also CA 113

Tey, Josephine .... **TCLC 14**
See also Mackintosh, Elizabeth DLB 77

Thackeray, William Makepeace 1811-1863 **NCLC 5, 14, 22, 43; DA; DAB; DAC; DAM MST, NOV; WLC**
See also CDBLB 1832-1890; DA3; DLB 21, 55, 159, 163; SATA 23

Thakura, Ravindranatha
See Tagore, Rabindranath

Tharoor, Shashi 1956- .... **CLC 70**
See also CA 141

Thelwell, Michael Miles 1939- .... **CLC 22**
See also BW 2; CA 101

Theobald, Lewis, Jr.
See Lovecraft, H(oward) P(hillips)

Theodorescu, Ion N. 1880-1967
See Arghezi, Tudor
See also CA 116

Theriault, Yves 1915-1983 .... **CLC 79; DAC; DAM MST**
See also CA 102; DLB 88

Theroux, Alexander (Louis) 1939- .... **CLC 2, 25**
See also CA 85-88; CANR 20, 63

Theroux, Paul (Edward) 1941- ..... **CLC 5, 8, 11, 15, 28, 46; DAM POP**
See also AAYA 28; BEST 89:4; CA 33-36R; CANR 20, 45, 74; CDALBS; DA3; DLB 2; MTCW 1, 2; SATA 44, 109

Thesen, Sharon 1946- .... **CLC 56**
See also CA 163

Thevenin, Denis
See Duhamel, Georges

Thibault, Jacques Anatole Francois 1844-1924
See France, Anatole
See also CA 106; 127; DAM NOV; DA3; MTCW 1, 2

Thiele, Colin (Milton) 1920- .... **CLC 17**
See also CA 29-32R; CANR 12, 28, 53; CLR 27; MAICYA; SAAS 2; SATA 14, 72

Thomas, Audrey (Callahan) 1935- .... **CLC 7, 13, 37, 107; SSC 20**
See also AITN 2; CA 21-24R; CAAS 19; CANR 36, 58; DLB 60; MTCW 1

Thomas, Augustus 1857-1934 .... **TCLC 97**

Thomas, D(onald) M(ichael) 1935- . **CLC 13, 22, 31**
See also CA 61-64; CAAS 11; CANR 17, 45, 75; CDBLB 1960 to Present; DA3; DLB 40, 207; INT CANR-17; MTCW 1, 2

Thomas, Dylan (Marlais) 1914-1953 ... **TCLC 1, 8, 45; DA; DAB; DAC; DAM DRAM, MST, POET; PC 2; SSC 3; WLC**
See also CA 104; 120; CANR 65; CDBLB 1945-1960; DA3; DLB 13, 20, 139; MTCW 1, 2; SATA 60

Thomas, (Philip) Edward 1878-1917 .... **TCLC 10; DAM POET**
See also CA 106; 153; DLB 98

Thomas, Joyce Carol 1938- .... **CLC 35**
See also AAYA 12; BW 2, 3; CA 113; 116; CANR 48; CLR 19; DLB 33; INT 116; JRDA; MAICYA; MTCW 1, 2; SAAS 7; SATA 40, 78

Thomas, Lewis 1913-1993 .... **CLC 35**
See also CA 85-88; 143; CANR 38, 60; MTCW 1, 2

Thomas, M. Carey 1857-1935 .... **TCLC 89**

Thomas, Paul
See Mann, (Paul) Thomas

Thomas, Piri 1928- .... **CLC 17; HLCS 2**
See also CA 73-76; HW 1

Thomas, R(onald) S(tuart) 1913- ...... **CLC 6, 13, 48; DAB; DAM POET**
See also CA 89-92; CAAS 4; CANR 30; CDBLB 1960 to Present; DLB 27; MTCW 1

Thomas, Ross (Elmore) 1926-1995 .. **CLC 39**
See also CA 33-36R; 150; CANR 22, 63

Thompson, Francis Clegg
See Mencken, H(enry) L(ouis)

Thompson, Francis Joseph 1859-1907 .... **TCLC 4**
See also CA 104; CDBLB 1890-1914; DLB 19

Thompson, Hunter S(tockton) 1939- ... **CLC 9, 17, 40, 104; DAM POP**
See also BEST 89:1; CA 17-20R; CANR 23, 46, 74, 77; DA3; DLB 185; MTCW 1, 2

Thompson, James Myers
See Thompson, Jim (Myers)

Thompson, Jim (Myers) 1906-1977(?) .... **CLC 69**
See also CA 140

Thompson, Judith .... **CLC 39**

Thomson, James 1700-1748 ... **LC 16, 29, 40; DAM POET**
See also DLB 95

Thomson, James 1834-1882 .... **NCLC 18; DAM POET**
See also DLB 35

Thoreau, Henry David 1817-1862 .. **NCLC 7, 21, 61; DA; DAB; DAC; DAM MST; WLC**
See also CDALB 1640-1865; DA3; DLB 1

Thornton, Hall
See Silverberg, Robert

Thucydides c. 455B.C.-399B.C. ..... **CMLC 17**
See also DLB 176

Thumboo, Edwin 1933- .... **PC 29**

Thurber, James (Grover) 1894-1961 .... **CLC 5, 11, 25, 125; DA; DAB; DAC; DAM DRAM, MST, NOV; SSC 1**
See also CA 73-76; CANR 17, 39; CDALB 1929-1941; DA3; DLB 4, 11, 22, 102; MAICYA; MTCW 1, 2; SATA 13

Thurman, Wallace (Henry) 1902-1934 .... **TCLC 6; BLC 3; DAM MULT**
See also BW 1, 3; CA 104; 124; CANR 81; DLB 51

Tibullus, Albius c. 54B.C.-c. 19B.C. .... **CMLC 36**
See also DLB 211

Ticheburn, Cheviot
See Ainsworth, William Harrison

Tieck, (Johann) Ludwig 1773-1853 .... **NCLC 5, 46; SSC 31**
See also DLB 90

Tiger, Derry
See Ellison, Harlan (Jay)

Tilghman, Christopher 1948(?)- .... **CLC 65**
See also CA 159

Tillinghast, Richard (Williford) 1940- .... **CLC 29**
See also CA 29-32R; CAAS 23; CANR 26, 51

Timrod, Henry 1828-1867 .... **NCLC 25**
See also DLB 3

Wagner-Martin, Linda (C.) 1936- .... **CLC 50**
See also CA 159

Wagoner, David (Russell) 1926- .... **CLC 3, 5, 15**
See also CA 1-4R; CAAS 3; CANR 2, 71; DLB 5; SATA 14

Wah, Fred(erick James) 1939- .... **CLC 44**
See also CA 107; 141; DLB 60

Wahloo, Per 1926-1975 .... **CLC 7**
See also CA 61-64; CANR 73

Wahloo, Peter
See Wahloo, Per

Wain, John (Barrington) 1925-1994 . **CLC 2, 11, 15, 46**
See also CA 5-8R; 145; CAAS 4; CANR 23, 54; CDBLB 1960 to Present; DLB 15, 27, 139, 155; MTCW 1, 2

Wajda, Andrzej 1926- .... **CLC 16**
See also CA 102

Wakefield, Dan 1932- .... **CLC 7**
See also CA 21-24R; CAAS 7

Wakoski, Diane 1937- ...... **CLC 2, 4, 7, 9, 11, 40; DAM POET; PC 15**
See also CA 13-16R; CAAS 1; CANR 9, 60; DLB 5; INT CANR-9; MTCW 2

Wakoski-Sherbell, Diane
See Wakoski, Diane

Walcott, Derek (Alton) 1930- .... **CLC 2, 4, 9, 14, 25, 42, 67, 76; BLC 3; DAB; DAC; DAM MST, MULT, POET; DC 7**
See also BW 2; CA 89-92; CANR 26, 47, 75, 80; DA3; DLB 117; DLBY 81; MTCW 1, 2

Waldman, Anne (Lesley) 1945- .... **CLC 7**
See also CA 37-40R; CAAS 17; CANR 34, 69; DLB 16

Waldo, E. Hunter
See Sturgeon, Theodore (Hamilton)

Waldo, Edward Hamilton
See Sturgeon, Theodore (Hamilton)

Walker, Alice (Malsenior) 1944- ... **CLC 5, 6, 9, 19, 27, 46, 58, 103; BLC 3; DA; DAB; DAC; DAM MST, MULT, NOV, POET, POP; SSC 5; WLCS**
See also AAYA 3; BEST 89:4; BW 2, 3; CA 37-40R; CANR 9, 27, 49, 66, 82; CDALB 1968-1988; DA3; DLB 6, 33, 143; INT CANR-27; MTCW 1, 2; SATA 31

Walker, David Harry 1911-1992 ...... **CLC 14**
See also CA 1-4R; 137; CANR 1; SATA 8; SATA-Obit 71

Walker, Edward Joseph 1934-
See Walker, Ted
See also CA 21-24R; CANR 12, 28, 53

Walker, George F. 1947- . **CLC 44, 61; DAB; DAC; DAM MST**
See also CA 103; CANR 21, 43, 59; DLB 60

Walker, Joseph A. 1935- .... **CLC 19; DAM DRAM, MST**
See also BW 1, 3; CA 89-92; CANR 26; DLB 38

Walker, Margaret (Abigail) 1915-1998 .... **CLC 1, 6; BLC; DAM MULT; PC 20**
See also BW 2, 3; CA 73-76; 172; CANR 26, 54, 76; DLB 76, 152; MTCW 1, 2

Walker, Ted .... **CLC 13**
See also Walker, Edward Joseph DLB 40

Wallace, David Foster 1962- ..... **CLC 50, 114**
See also CA 132; CANR 59; DA3; MTCW 2

Wallace, Dexter
See Masters, Edgar Lee

Wallace, (Richard Horatio) Edgar 1875-1932 **TCLC 57**
See also CA 115; DLB 70

Wallace, Irving 1916-1990 .... **CLC 7, 13; DAM NOV, POP**
See also AITN 1; CA 1-4R; 132; CAAS 1; CANR 1, 27; INT CANR-27; MTCW 1, 2

Wallant, Edward Lewis 1926-1962 ... **CLC 5, 10**
See also CA 1-4R; CANR 22; DLB 2, 28, 143; MTCW 1, 2

Wallas, Graham 1858-1932 .... **TCLC 91**

Walley, Byron
See Card, Orson Scott

Walpole, Horace 1717-1797 .... **LC 49**
See also DLB 39, 104

Walpole, Hugh (Seymour) 1884-1941 .... **TCLC 5**
See also CA 104; 165; DLB 34; MTCW 2

Walser, Martin 1927- .... **CLC 27**
See also CA 57-60; CANR 8, 46; DLB 75, 124

Walser, Robert 1878-1956 .... **TCLC 18; SSC 20**
See also CA 118; 165; DLB 66

Walsh, Jill Paton .... **CLC 35**
See also Paton Walsh, Gillian CLR 2

Walter, Villiam Christian
See Andersen, Hans Christian

Wambaugh, Joseph (Aloysius, Jr.) 1937- .... **CLC 3, 18; DAM NOV, POP**
See also AITN 1; BEST 89:3; CA 33-36R; CANR 42, 65; DA3; DLB 6; DLBY 83; MTCW 1, 2

Wang Wei 699(?)-761(?) .... **PC 18**

Ward, Arthur Henry Sarsfield 1883-1959
See Rohmer, Sax
See also CA 108; 173

Ward, Douglas Turner 1930- .... **CLC 19**
See also BW 1; CA 81-84; CANR 27; DLB 7, 38

Ward, E. D.
See Lucas, E(dward) V(errall)

Ward, Mary Augusta
See Ward, Mrs. Humphry

Ward, Mrs. Humphry 1851-1920 .. **TCLC 55**
See also DLB 18

Ward, Peter
See Faust, Frederick (Schiller)

Warhol, Andy 1928(?)-1987 .... **CLC 20**
See also AAYA 12; BEST 89:4; CA 89-92; 121; CANR 34

Warner, Francis (Robert le Plastrier) 1937- **CLC 14**
See also CA 53-56; CANR 11

Warner, Marina 1946- .... **CLC 59**
See also CA 65-68; CANR 21, 55; DLB 194

Warner, Rex (Ernest) 1905-1986 ...... **CLC 45**
See also CA 89-92; 119; DLB 15

Warner, Susan (Bogert) 1819-1885 .... **NCLC 31**
See also DLB 3, 42

Warner, Sylvia (Constance) Ashton
See Ashton-Warner, Sylvia (Constance)

Warner, Sylvia Townsend 1893-1978 .... **CLC 7, 19; SSC 23**
See also CA 61-64; 77-80; CANR 16, 60; DLB 34, 139; MTCW 1, 2

Warren, Mercy Otis 1728-1814 ..... **NCLC 13**
See also DLB 31, 200

Warren, Robert Penn 1905-1989 .. **CLC 1, 4, 6, 8, 10, 13, 18, 39, 53, 59; DA; DAB; DAC; DAM MST, NOV, POET; SSC 4; WLC**
See also AITN 1; CA 13-16R; 129; CANR 10, 47; CDALB 1968-1988; DA3; DLB 2, 48, 152; DLBY 80, 89; INT CANR-10; MTCW 1, 2; SATA 46; SATA-Obit 63

Warshofsky, Isaac
See Singer, Isaac Bashevis

Warton, Thomas 1728-1790 ..... **LC 15; DAM POET**
See also DLB 104, 109

Waruk, Kona
See Harris, (Theodore) Wilson

Warung, Price 1855-1911 .... **TCLC 45**

Warwick, Jarvis
See Garner, Hugh

Washington, Alex
See Harris, Mark

Washington, Booker T(aliaferro) 1856-1915 **TCLC 10; BLC 3; DAM MULT**
See also BW 1; CA 114; 125; DA3; SATA 28

Washington, George 1732-1799 .... **LC 25**
See also DLB 31

Wassermann, (Karl) Jakob 1873-1934 .... **TCLC 6**
See also CA 104; 163; DLB 66

Wasserstein, Wendy 1950- .. **CLC 32, 59, 90; DAM DRAM; DC 4**
See also CA 121; 129; CABS 3; CANR 53, 75; DA3; INT 129; MTCW 2; SATA 94

Waterhouse, Keith (Spencer) 1929- . **CLC 47**
See also CA 5-8R; CANR 38, 67; DLB 13, 15; MTCW 1, 2

Waters, Frank (Joseph) 1902-1995 .. **CLC 88**
See also CA 5-8R; 149; CAAS 13; CANR 3, 18, 63; DLB 212; DLBY 86

Waters, Roger 1944- .... **CLC 35**

Watkins, Frances Ellen
See Harper, Frances Ellen Watkins

Watkins, Gerrold
See Malzberg, Barry N(athaniel)

Watkins, Gloria Jean 1952(?)-
See hooks, bell
See also BW 2; CA 143; CANR 87; MTCW 2

Watkins, Paul 1964- .... **CLC 55**
See also CA 132; CANR 62

Watkins, Vernon Phillips 1906-1967 .... **CLC 43**
See also CA 9-10; 25-28R; CAP 1; DLB 20

Watson, Irving S.
See Mencken, H(enry) L(ouis)

Watson, John H.
See Farmer, Philip Jose

Watson, Richard F.
See Silverberg, Robert

Waugh, Auberon (Alexander) 1939- .. **CLC 7**
See also CA 45-48; CANR 6, 22; DLB 14, 194

Wouk, Herman 1915- ... **CLC 1, 9, 38; DAM NOV, POP**
See also CA 5-8R; CANR 6, 33, 67; CDALBS; DA3; DLBY 82; INT CANR-6; MTCW 1, 2

Wright, Charles (Penzel, Jr.) 1935- .. **CLC 6, 13, 28, 119**
See also CA 29-32R; CAAS 7; CANR 23, 36, 62; DLB 165; DLBY 82; MTCW 1, 2

Wright, Charles Stevenson 1932- ... **CLC 49; BLC 3; DAM MULT, POET**
See also BW 1; CA 9-12R; CANR 26; DLB 33

Wright, Frances 1795-1852 .... **NCLC 74**
See also DLB 73

Wright, Frank Lloyd 1867-1959 .... **TCLC 95**
See also CA 174

Wright, Jack R.
See Harris, Mark

Wright, James (Arlington)
1927-1980 .... **CLC 3, 5, 10, 28; DAM POET**
See also AITN 2; CA 49-52; 97-100; CANR 4, 34, 64; CDALBS; DLB 5, 169; MTCW 1, 2

Wright, Judith (Arandell) 1915- ..... **CLC 11, 53; PC 14**
See also CA 13-16R; CANR 31, 76; MTCW 1, 2; SATA 14

Wright, L(aurali) R. 1939- .... **CLC 44**
See also CA 138

Wright, Richard (Nathaniel)
1908-1960 .... **CLC 1, 3, 4, 9, 14, 21, 48, 74; BLC 3; DA; DAB; DAC; DAM MST, MULT, NOV; SSC 2; WLC**
See also AAYA 5; BW 1; CA 108; CANR 64; CDALB 1929-1941; DA3; DLB 76, 102; DLBD 2; MTCW 1, 2

Wright, Richard B(ruce) 1937- .... **CLC 6**
See also CA 85-88; DLB 53

Wright, Rick 1945- .... **CLC 35**

Wright, Rowland
See Wells, Carolyn

Wright, Stephen 1946- .... **CLC 33**

Wright, Willard Huntington 1888-1939
See Van Dine, S. S.
See also CA 115; DLBD 16

Wright, William 1930- .... **CLC 44**
See also CA 53-56; CANR 7, 23

Wroth, LadyMary 1587-1653(?) .... **LC 30**
See also DLB 121

Wu Ch'eng-en 1500(?)-1582(?) .... **LC 7**

Wu Ching-tzu 1701-1754 .... **LC 2**

Wurlitzer, Rudolph 1938(?)- ... **CLC 2, 4, 15**
See also CA 85-88; DLB 173

Wyatt, Thomas c. 1503-1542 .... **PC 27**
See also DLB 132

Wycherley, William 1641-1715 ...... **LC 8, 21; DAM DRAM**
See also CDBLB 1660-1789; DLB 80

Wylie, Elinor (Morton Hoyt) 1885-1928
TCLC 8; PC 23
See also CA 105; 162; DLB 9, 45

Wylie, Philip (Gordon) 1902-1971 ... **CLC 43**
See also CA 21-22; 33-36R; CAP 2; DLB 9

Wyndham, John .... **CLC 19**
See also Harris, John (Wyndham Parkes Lucas) Beynon

Wyss, Johann David Von
1743-1818 .... **NCLC 10**
See also JRDA; MAICYA; SATA 29; SATA-Brief 27

Xenophon c. 430B.C.-c. 354B.C. ... **CMLC 17**
See also DLB 176

Yakumo Koizumi
See Hearn, (Patricio) Lafcadio (Tessima Carlos)

Yamamoto, Hisaye 1921- .... **SSC 34; DAM MULT**

Yanez, Jose Donoso
See Donoso (Yanez), Jose

Yanovsky, Basile S.
See Yanovsky, V(assily) S(emenovich)

Yanovsky, V(assily) S(emenovich) 1906-1989
CLC 2, 18
See also CA 97-100; 129

Yates, Richard 1926-1992 .... **CLC 7, 8, 23**
See also CA 5-8R; 139; CANR 10, 43; DLB 2; DLBY 81, 92; INT CANR-10

Yeats, W. B.
See Yeats, William Butler

Yeats, William Butler 1865-1939 .... **TCLC 1, 11, 18, 31, 93; DA; DAB; DAC; DAM DRAM, MST, POET; PC 20; WLC**
See also CA 104; 127; CANR 45; CDBLB 1890-1914; DA3; DLB 10, 19, 98, 156; MTCW 1, 2

Yehoshua, A(braham) B. 1936- .. **CLC 13, 31**
See also CA 33-36R; CANR 43

Yellow Bird
See Ridge, John Rollin

Yep, Laurence Michael 1948- .... **CLC 35**
See also AAYA 5, 31; CA 49-52; CANR 1, 46; CLR 3, 17, 54; DLB 52; JRDA; MAICYA; SATA 7, 69

Yerby, Frank G(arvin) 1916-1991 . **CLC 1, 7, 22; BLC 3; DAM MULT**
See also BW 1, 3; CA 9-12R; 136; CANR 16, 52; DLB 76; INT CANR-16; MTCW 1

Yesenin, Sergei Alexandrovich
See Esenin, Sergei (Alexandrovich)

Yevtushenko, Yevgeny (Alexandrovich) 1933-
CLC 1, 3, 13, 26, 51, 126; DAM POET
See also CA 81-84; CANR 33, 54; MTCW 1

Yezierska, Anzia 1885(?)-1970 .... **CLC 46**
See also CA 126; 89-92; DLB 28; MTCW 1

Yglesias, Helen 1915- .... **CLC 7, 22**
See also CA 37-40R; CAAS 20; CANR 15, 65; INT CANR-15; MTCW 1

Yokomitsu Riichi 1898-1947 .... **TCLC 47**
See also CA 170

Yonge, Charlotte (Mary)
1823-1901 .... **TCLC 48**
See also CA 109; 163; DLB 18, 163; SATA 17

York, Jeremy
See Creasey, John

York, Simon
See Heinlein, Robert A(nson)

Yorke, Henry Vincent 1905-1974 ..... **CLC 13**
See also Green, Henry CA 85-88; 49-52

Yosano Akiko 1878-1942 .... **TCLC 59; PC 11**
See also CA 161

Yoshimoto, Banana .... **CLC 84**
See also Yoshimoto, Mahoko

Yoshimoto, Mahoko 1964-
See Yoshimoto, Banana
See also CA 144

Young, Al(bert James) 1939- . **CLC 19; BLC 3; DAM MULT**
See also BW 2, 3; CA 29-32R; CANR 26, 65; DLB 33

Young, Andrew (John) 1885-1971 ...... **CLC 5**
See also CA 5-8R; CANR 7, 29

Young, Collier
See Bloch, Robert (Albert)

Young, Edward 1683-1765 .... **LC 3, 40**
See also DLB 95

Young, Marguerite (Vivian)
1909-1995 .... **CLC 82**
See also CA 13-16; 150; CAP 1

Young, Neil 1945- .... **CLC 17**
See also CA 110

Young Bear, Ray A. 1950- ..... **CLC 94; DAM MULT**
See also CA 146; DLB 175; NNAL

Yourcenar, Marguerite 1903-1987 ... **CLC 19, 38, 50, 87; DAM NOV**
See also CA 69-72; CANR 23, 60; DLB 72; DLBY 88; MTCW 1, 2

Yuan, Chu 340(?)B.C.-278(?)B.C. . **CMLC 36**

Yurick, Sol 1925- .... **CLC 6**
See also CA 13-16R; CANR 25

Zabolotsky, Nikolai Alekseevich 1903-1958
TCLC 52
See also CA 116; 164

Zagajewski, Adam .... **PC 27**

Zamiatin, Yevgenii
See Zamyatin, Evgeny Ivanovich

Zamora, Bernice (B. Ortiz) 1938- .. **CLC 89; DAM MULT; HLC 2**
See also CA 151; CANR 80; DLB 82; HW 1, 2

Zamyatin, Evgeny Ivanovich 1884-1937
TCLC 8, 37
See also CA 105; 166

Zangwill, Israel 1864-1926 .... **TCLC 16**
See also CA 109; 167; DLB 10, 135, 197

Zappa, Francis Vincent, Jr. 1940-1993
See Zappa, Frank
See also CA 108; 143; CANR 57

Zappa, Frank .... **CLC 17**
See also Zappa, Francis Vincent, Jr.

Zaturenska, Marya 1902-1982 ..... **CLC 6, 11**
See also CA 13-16R; 105; CANR 22

Zeami 1363-1443 .... **DC 7**

Zelazny, Roger (Joseph) 1937-1995 . **CLC 21**
See also AAYA 7; CA 21-24R; 148; CANR 26, 60; DLB 8; MTCW 1, 2; SATA 57; SATA-Brief 39

Zhdanov, Andrei Alexandrovich 1896-1948
TCLC 18
See also CA 117; 167

Zhukovsky, Vasily (Andreevich) 1783-1852
NCLC 35
See also DLB 205

Ziegenhagen, Eric .... **CLC 55**

Zimmer, Jill Schary
See Robinson, Jill

Zimmerman, Robert
See Dylan, Bob

Zindel, Paul 1936- ..... **CLC 6, 26; DA; DAB; DAC; DAM DRAM, MST, NOV; DC 5**
See also AAYA 2; CA 73-76; CANR 31, 65; CDALBS; CLR 3, 45; DA3; DLB 7, 52; JRDA; MAICYA; MTCW 1, 2; SATA 16, 58, 102

Zinov'Ev, A. A.
See Zinoviev, Alexander (Aleksandrovich)

Zinoviev, Alexander (Aleksandrovich) 1922- **CLC 19**
See also CA 116; 133; CAAS 10

Zoilus
See Lovecraft, H(oward) P(hillips)

Zola, Emile (Edouard Charles Antoine) 1840-1902 .... **TCLC 1, 6, 21, 41; DA; DAB; DAC; DAM MST, NOV; WLC**
See also CA 104; 138; DA3; DLB 123

Zoline, Pamela 1941- .... **CLC 62**
See also CA 161

Zorrilla y Moral, Jose 1817-1893 .... **NCLC 6**

Zoshchenko, Mikhail (Mikhailovich) 1895-1958 .... **TCLC 15; SSC 15**
See also CA 115; 160

Zuckmayer, Carl 1896-1977 .... **CLC 18**
See also CA 69-72; DLB 56, 124

Zuk, Georges
See Skelton, Robin

Zukofsky, Louis 1904-1978 ... **CLC 1, 2, 4, 7, 11, 18; DAM POET; PC 11**
See also CA 9-12R; 77-80; CANR 39; DLB 5, 165; MTCW 1

Zweig, Paul 1935-1984 .... **CLC 34, 42**
See also CA 85-88; 113

Zweig, Stefan 1881-1942 .... **TCLC 17**
See also CA 112; 170; DLB 81, 118

Zwingli, Huldreich 1484-1531 .... **LC 37**
See also DLB 179

Literary Criticism Series
Cumulative Topic Index

This index lists all topic entries in Gale's *Classical and Medieval Literature Criticism, Contemporary Literary Criticism, Literature Criticism from 1400 to 1800, Nineteenth-Century Literature Criticism,* and *Twentieth-Century Literary Criticism.*

Topic Index

Topic Index

NCLC Cumulative Nationality Index

Carleton, William 3
Croker, John Wilson 10
Darley, George 2
Edgeworth, Maria 1, 51
Ferguson, Samuel 33
Griffin, Gerald 7
Jameson, Anna 43
Le Fanu, Joseph Sheridan 9, 58
Lever, Charles (James) 23
Maginn, William 8
Mangan, James Clarence 27
Maturin, Charles Robert 6
Merriman, Brian 70
Moore, Thomas 6
Morgan, Lady 29
O'Brien, Fitz-James 21

ITALIAN

Collodi, Carlo 54
Foscolo, Ugo 8
Gozzi, (Conte) Carlo 23
Leopardi, (Conte) Giacomo 22
Manzoni, Alessandro 29
Mazzini, Guiseppe 34
Nievo, Ippolito 22

JAPANESE

Higuchi, Ichiyo 49
Motoori, Norinaga 45

LITHUANIAN

Mapu, Abraham (ben Jekutiel) 18

MEXICAN

Lizardi, Jose Joaquin Fernandez de 30

NORWEGIAN

Collett, (Jacobine) Camilla (Wergeland) 22
Wergeland, Henrik Arnold 5

POLISH

Fredro, Aleksander 8
Krasicki, Ignacy 8

Krasinski, Zygmunt 4
Mickiewicz, Adam 3
Norwid, Cyprian Kamil 17
Slowacki, Juliusz 15

ROMANIAN

Eminescu, Mihail 33

RUSSIAN

Aksakov, Sergei Timofeyvich 2
Bakunin, Mikhail (Alexandrovich) 25, 58
Bashkirtseff, Marie 27
Belinski, Vissarion Grigoryevich 5
Chernyshevsky, Nikolay Gavrilovich 1
Dobrolyubov, Nikolai Alexandrovich 5
Dostoevsky, Fedor Mikhailovich 2, 7, 21, 33, 43
Gogol, Nikolai (Vasilyevich) 5, 15, 31
Goncharov, Ivan Alexandrovich 1, 63
Granovsky, Timofei Nikolaevich 75
Herzen, Aleksandr Ivanovich 10, 61
Karamzin, Nikolai Mikhailovich 3
Krylov, Ivan Andreevich 1
Lermontov, Mikhail Yuryevich 5
Leskov, Nikolai (Semyonovich) 25
Nekrasov, Nikolai Alekseevich 11
Ostrovsky, Alexander 30, 57
Pisarev, Dmitry Ivanovich 25
Pushkin, Alexander (Sergeyevich) 3, 27, 83
Saltykov, Mikhail Evgrafovich 16
Smolenskin, Peretz 30
Turgenev, Ivan 21
Tyutchev, Fyodor 34
Zhukovsky, Vasily (Andreevich) 35

SCOTTISH

Baillie, Joanna 2
Beattie, James 25
Blair, Hugh 75
Campbell, Thomas 19
Carlyle, Thomas 22
Ferrier, Susan (Edmonstone) 8
Galt, John 1

Hogg, James 4
Jeffrey, Francis 33
Lockhart, John Gibson 6
Mackenzie, Henry 41
Oliphant, Margaret (Oliphant Wilson) 11, 61
Scott, Walter 15, 69
Stevenson, Robert Louis (Balfour) 5, 14, 63
Thomson, James 18
Wilson, John 5
Wright, Frances 74

SPANISH

Alarcon, Pedro Antonio de 1
Caballero, Fernan 10
Castro, Rosalia de 3, 78
Espronceda, Jose de 39
Larra (y Sanchez de Castro), Mariano Jose de 17
Tamayo y Baus, Manuel 1
Zorrilla y Moral, Jose 6

SWEDISH

Almqvist, Carl Jonas Love 42
Bremer, Fredrika 11
Stagnelius, Eric Johan 61
Tegner, Esaias 2

SWISS

Amiel, Henri Frederic 4
Burckhardt, Jacob (Christoph) 49
Charriere, Isabelle de 66
Keller, Gottfried 2
Meyer, Conrad Ferdinand 81
Wyss, Johann David Von 10

UKRAINIAN

Shevchenko, Taras 54

Nationality Index

ISBN 0-7876-3260-0

90000

9 780787 632601